Collins Discovery World Atlas

Collins
An imprint of HarperCollinsPublishers
77–85 Fulham Palace Road
London
w6 8jb

First Published 2004
Originally published as Collins World Atlas Illustrated
Edition 2003

Printed in Thailand

British Library Cataloguing in Publication Data.
A catalogue record for this book is available from
the British Library.

ISBN-10: 0 06 081883-2
ISBN-13: 978 0 06 081883-8

RH11820 Imp 001

All mapping in this atlas is generated from Collins
Bartholomew digital databases. Collins Bartholomew,
the UK's leading independent geographical information
supplier, can provide a digital, custom, and premium
mapping service to a variety of markets.
For further information:
Tel: +44 (0) 141 306 3752
e-mail: collinsbartholomew@harpercollins.co.uk

We also offer a choice of books, atlases and maps that
can be customized to suit a customer's own
requirements. For further information:
Tel: +44 (0) 141 306 3209
e-mail: business.gifts@harpercollins.co.uk

or visit our website at: www.collinsbartholomew.com

www.collins.co.uk

Collins

Collins Discovery World Atlas

Collins

An Imprint of HarperCollinsPublishers

Contents

Map Symbols

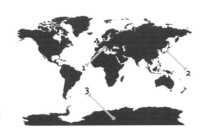

Southern Europe   1

Japan   2

Antarctica   3

Settlements

Population	National capital	Administrative capital	Other city or town
over 10 million	**BEIJING** ✪	**Karachi** ◉	**New York** ◉
5 million to 10 million	**JAKARTA** ✪	**Tianjin** ◉	**Nova Iguaçu** ◉
1 million to 5 million	**KĀBUL** ✪	**Sydney** ◉	**Kaohsiung** ◉
500 000 to 1 million	BANGUI ✿	Trujillo ◎	Jeddah ◎
100 000 to 500 000	WELLINGTON ✿	Mansa ◎	Apucarana ◎
50 000 to 100 000	PORT OF SPAIN ✿	Potenza ◎	Arecibo ○
10 000 to 50 000	MALABO ✿	Chinhoyi ○	Ceres ○
under 10 000	VALLETTA ✿	Ati ○	Venta ○

🗺 Built-up area

Boundaries

▬▬▬▬	International boundary
▪▪▪▪	Disputed international boundary or alignment unconfirmed
———	Administrative boundary
•••••	Ceasefire line

Miscellaneous

---------	National park
··········	Reserve or Regional park
✿	Site of specific interest
▭▭▭▭	Wall

Land and sea features

	Desert
◡	Oasis
	Lava field
1234 △	Volcano height in metres
	Marsh
	Ice cap or Glacier
	Escarpment
	Coral reef
⌇1234	Pass height in metres

Lakes and rivers

	Lake
	Impermanent lake
	Salt lake or lagoon
	Impermanent salt lake
	Dry salt lake or salt pan
123	Lake height surface height above sea level, in metres
———	River
	Impermanent river or watercourse
	Waterfall
—	Dam
	Barrage

Relief

Contour intervals and layer colours

Height
metres
6000
5000
4000
3000
2000
1000
500
200
0
below sea level
0
200
2000
4000
6000

Depth

1234 △	Summit height in metres
-123	Spot height height in metres
123	Ocean deep depth in metres

Transport

▬▬▷▬ ┈┈┈	Motorway (tunnel; under construction)
——▷— -----	Main road (tunnel; under construction)
——▷— -----	Secondary road (tunnel; under construction)
··········	Track
▬▬▷▬ ▬▬▬	Main railway (tunnel; under construction)
——▷— -----	Secondary railway (tunnel; under construction)
——▷— -----	Other railway (tunnel; under construction)
———	Canal
✈	Main airport
✈	Regional airport

SPOT

Space Shuttle

IKONOS

Satellite imagery - The thematic pages in the atlas contain a wide variety of photographs and images. These are a mixture of terrestrial and aerial photographs and satellite imagery. All are used to illustrate specific themes and to give an indication of the variety of imagery available today. The main types of imagery used in the atlas are described in the table below. The sensor for each satellite image is detailed on the acknowledgements page.

Main satellites/sensors

Satellite/sensor name	Launch dates	Owner	Aims and applications	Internet links	Additional internet links
Landsat 4, 5, 7	July 1972–April 1999	National Aeronautics and Space Administration (NASA), USA	The first satellite to be designed specifically for observing the Earth's surface. Originally set up to produce images of use for agriculture and geology. Today is of use for numerous environmental and scientific applications.	geo.arc.nasa.gov landsat.gsfc.nasa.gov	asterweb.jpl.nasa.gov earth.jsc.nasa.gov earthnet.esrin.esa.it
SPOT 1, 2, 3, 4, 5 (Satellite Pour l'Observation de la Terre)	February 1986–March 1998	Centre National d'Etudes Spatiales (CNES) and Spot Image, France	Particularly useful for monitoring land use, water resources research, coastal studies and cartography.	www.cnes.fr www.spotimage.fr	earthobservatory.nasa.gov eol.jsc.nasa.gov modis.gsfc.nasa.gov
Space Shuttle	Regular launches from 1981	NASA, USA	Each shuttle mission has separate aims. Astronauts take photographs with high specification hand held cameras. The Shuttle Radar Topography Mission (SRTM) in 2000 obtained the most complete near-global high-resolution database of the earth's topography.	science.ksc.nasa.gov/shuttle/countdown www.jpl.nasa.gov/srtm	seawifs.gsfc.nasa.gov topex-www.jpl.nasa.gov visibleearth.nasa.gov www.rsi.ca
IKONOS	September 1999	Space Imaging	First commercial high-resolution satellite. Useful for a variety of applications mainly Cartography, Defence, Urban Planning, Agriculture, Forestry and Insurance.	www.spaceimaging.com	www.usgs.gov

| The Alps | 1 | Amsterdam, Netherlands | 2 | Italy | 3 |

Europe		Area sq km	Area sq miles	Population	Capital	Languages	Religions	Currency
ALBANIA		28 748	11 100	3 166 000	Tirana	Albanian, Greek	Sunni Muslim, Albanian Orthodox, Roman Catholic	Lek
ANDORRA		465	180	71 000	Andorra la Vella	Spanish, Catalan, French	Roman Catholic	Euro
AUSTRIA		83 855	32 377	8 116 000	Vienna	German, Croatian, Turkish	Roman Catholic, Protestant	Euro
BELARUS		207 600	80 155	9 895 000	Minsk	Belorussian, Russian	Belorussian Orthodox, Roman Catholic	Belarus rouble
BELGIUM		30 520	11 784	10 318 000	Brussels	Dutch (Flemish), French (Walloon), German	Roman Catholic, Protestant	Euro
BOSNIA-HERZEGOVINA		51 130	19 741	4 161 000	Sarajevo	Bosnian, Serbian, Croatian	Sunni Muslim, Serbian Orthodox, Roman Catholic, Protestant	Marka
BULGARIA		110 994	42 855	7 897 000	Sofia	Bulgarian, Turkish, Romany, Macedonian	Bulgarian Orthodox, Sunni Muslim	Lev
CROATIA		56 538	21 829	4 428 000	Zagreb	Croatian, Serbian	Roman Catholic, Serbian Orthodox, Sunni Muslim	Kuna
CZECH REPUBLIC		78 864	30 450	10 236 000	Prague	Czech, Moravian, Slovak	Roman Catholic, Protestant	Czech koruna
DENMARK		43 075	16 631	5 364 000	Copenhagen	Danish	Protestant	Danish krone
ESTONIA		45 200	17 452	1 332 000	Tallinn	Estonian, Russian	Protestant, Estonian and Russian Orthodox	Kroon
FINLAND		338 145	130 559	5 207 000	Helsinki	Finnish, Swedish	Protestant, Greek Orthodox	Euro
FRANCE		543 965	210 026	60 144 000	Paris	French, Arabic	Roman Catholic, Protestant, Sunni Muslim	Euro
GERMANY		357 022	137 849	82 476 000	Berlin	German, Turkish	Protestant, Roman Catholic	Euro
GREECE		131 957	50 949	10 976 000	Athens	Greek	Greek Orthodox, Sunni Muslim	Euro
HUNGARY		93 030	35 919	9 877 000	Budapest	Hungarian	Roman Catholic, Protestant	Forint
ICELAND		102 820	39 699	290 000	Reykjavík	Icelandic	Protestant	Icelandic króna
IRELAND, REPUBLIC OF		70 282	27 136	3 956 000	Dublin	English, Irish	Roman Catholic, Protestant	Euro
ITALY		301 245	116 311	57 423 000	Rome	Italian	Roman Catholic	Euro
LATVIA		63 700	24 595	2 307 000	Rīga	Latvian, Russian	Protestant, Roman Catholic, Russian Orthodox	Lats
LIECHTENSTEIN		160	62	34 000	Vaduz	German	Roman Catholic, Protestant	Swiss franc
LITHUANIA		65 200	25 174	3 444 000	Vilnius	Lithuanian, Russian, Polish	Roman Catholic, Protestant, Russian Orthodox	Litas
LUXEMBOURG		2 586	998	453 000	Luxembourg	Letzeburgish, German, French	Roman Catholic	Euro
MACEDONIA (F.Y.R.O.M.)		25 713	9 928	2 056 000	Skopje	Macedonian, Albanian, Turkish	Macedonian Orthodox, Sunni Muslim	Macedonian denar
MALTA		316	122	394 000	Valletta	Maltese, English	Roman Catholic	Maltese lira
MOLDOVA		33 700	13 012	4 267 000	Chişinău	Romanian, Ukrainian, Gagauz, Russian	Romanian Orthodox, Russian Orthodox	Moldovan leu
MONACO		2	1	34 000	Monaco-Ville	French, Monegasque, Italian	Roman Catholic	Euro
NETHERLANDS		41 526	16 033	16 149 000	Amsterdam/The Hague	Dutch, Frisian	Roman Catholic, Protestant, Sunni Muslim	Euro
NORWAY		323 878	125 050	4 533 000	Oslo	Norwegian	Protestant, Roman Catholic	Norwegian krone
POLAND		312 683	120 728	38 587 000	Warsaw	Polish, German	Roman Catholic, Polish Orthodox	Złoty
PORTUGAL		88 940	34 340	10 062 000	Lisbon	Portuguese	Roman Catholic, Protestant	Euro
ROMANIA		237 500	91 699	22 334 000	Bucharest	Romanian, Hungarian	Romanian Orthodox, Protestant, Roman Catholic	Romanian leu
RUSSIAN FEDERATION		17 075 400	6 592 849	143 246 000	Moscow	Russian, Tatar, Ukrainian, local languages	Russian Orthodox, Sunni Muslim, Protestant	Russian rouble
SAN MARINO		61	24	28 000	San Marino	Italian	Roman Catholic	Euro
SERBIA AND MONTENEGRO		102 173	39 449	10 527 000	Belgrade	Serbian, Albanian, Hungarian	Serbian Orthodox, Montenegrin Orthodox, Sunni Muslim	Serbian dinar, Euro
SLOVAKIA		49 035	18 933	5 402 000	Bratislava	Slovak, Hungarian, Czech	Roman Catholic, Protestant, Orthodox	Slovakian koruna
SLOVENIA		20 251	7 819	1 984 000	Ljubljana	Slovene, Croatian, Serbian	Roman Catholic, Protestant	Tólar
SPAIN		504 782	194 897	41 060 000	Madrid	Castilian, Catalan, Galician, Basque	Roman Catholic	Euro
SWEDEN		449 964	173 732	8 876 000	Stockholm	Swedish	Protestant, Roman Catholic	Swedish krona
SWITZERLAND		41 293	15 943	7 169 000	Bern	German, French, Italian, Romansch	Roman Catholic, Protestant	Swiss franc
UKRAINE		603 700	233 090	48 523 000	Kiev	Ukrainian, Russian	Ukrainian Orthodox, Ukrainian Catholic, Roman Catholic	Hryvnia
UNITED KINGDOM		243 609	94 058	58 789 194	London	English, Welsh, Gaelic	Protestant, Roman Catholic, Muslim	Pound sterling
VATICAN CITY		0.5	0.2	472	Vatican City	Italian	Roman Catholic	Euro

Dependent territories		Territorial status		Area sq km	Area sq miles	Population	Capital	Languages	Religions	Currency
Azores		Autonomous Region of Portugal		2 300	888	242 073	Ponta Delgada	Portuguese	Roman Catholic, Protestant	Euro
Faroe Islands		Self-governing Danish Territory		1 399	540	47 000	Tórshavn	Faroese, Danish	Protestant	Danish krone
Gibraltar		United Kingdom Overseas Territory		7	3	27 000	Gibraltar	Engllish, Spanish	Roman Catholic, Protestant, Sunni Muslim	Gibraltar pound
Guernsey		United Kingdom Crown Dependency		78	30	62 701	St Peter Port	English, French	Protestant, Roman Catholic	Pound sterling
Isle of Man		United Kingdom Crown Dependency		572	221	75 000	Douglas	English	Protestant, Roman Catholic	Pound sterling
Jersey		United Kingdom Crown Dependency		116	45	87 186	St Helier	English, French	Protestant, Roman Catholic	Pound sterling

Ganges Delta, India   **1**

Cyprus, eastern Mediterranean   **2**

Indian subcontinent   **3**

Asia		Area sq km	Area sq miles	Population	Capital	Languages	Religions	Currency
AFGHANISTAN		652 225	251 825	23 897 000	Kābul	Dari, Pushtu, Uzbek, Turkmen	Sunni Muslim, Shi'a Muslim	Afghani
ARMENIA		29 800	11 506	3 061 000	Yerevan	Armenian, Azeri	Armenian Orthodox	Dram
AZERBAIJAN		86 600	33 436	8 370 000	Baku	Azeri, Armenian, Russian, Lezgian	Shi'a Muslim, Sunni Muslim, Russian and Armenian Orthodox	Azerbaijani manat
BAHRAIN		691	267	724 000	Manama	Arabic, English	Shi'a Muslim, Sunni Muslim, Christian	Bahrain dinar
BANGLADESH		143 998	55 598	146 736 000	Dhaka	Bengali, English	Sunni Muslim, Hindu	Taka
BHUTAN		46 620	18 000	2 257 000	Thimphu	Dzongkha, Nepali, Assamese	Buddhist, Hindu	Ngultrum, Indian rupee
BRUNEI		5 765	2 226	358 000	Bandar Seri Begawan	Malay, English, Chinese	Sunni Muslim, Buddhist, Christian	Brunei dollar
CAMBODIA		181 035	69 884	14 144 000	Phnom Penh	Khmer, Vietnamese	Buddhist, Roman Catholic, Sunni Muslim	Riel
CHINA		9 584 492	3 700 593	1 289 161 000	Beijing	Mandarin, Wu, Cantonese, Hsiang, regional languages	Confucian, Taoist, Buddhist, Christian, Sunni Muslim	Yuan, HK dollar*, Macau pataca
CYPRUS		9 251	3 572	802 000	Nicosia	Greek, Turkish, English	Greek Orthodox, Sunni Muslim	Cyprus pound
EAST TIMOR		14 874	5 743	778 000	Dili	Portuguese, Tetun, English	Roman Catholic	United States dollar
GEORGIA		69 700	26 911	5 126 000	T'bilisi	Georgian, Russian, Armenian, Azeri, Ossetian, Abkhaz	Georgian Orthodox, Russian Orthodox, Sunni Muslim	Lari
INDIA		3 064 898	1 183 364	1 065 462 000	New Delhi	Hindi, English, many regional languages	Hindu, Sunni Muslim, Shi'a Muslim, Sikh, Christian	Indian rupee
INDONESIA		1 919 445	741 102	219 883 000	Jakarta	Indonesian, local languages	Sunni Muslim, Protestant, Roman Catholic, Hindu, Buddhist	Rupiah
IRAN		1 648 000	636 296	68 920 000	Tehrān	Farsi, Azeri, Kurdish, regional languages	Shi'a Muslim, Sunni Muslim	Iranian rial
IRAQ		438 317	169 235	25 175 000	Baghdād	Arabic, Kurdish, Turkmen	Shi'a Muslim, Sunni Muslim, Christian	Iraqi dinar
ISRAEL		20 770	8 019	6 433 000	Jerusalem *(De facto capital. Disputed.)*	Hebrew, Arabic	Jewish, Sunni Muslim, Christian, Druze	Shekel
JAPAN		377 727	145 841	127 654 000	Tōkyō	Japanese	Shintoist, Buddhist, Christian	Yen
JORDAN		89 206	34 443	5 473 000	'Ammān	Arabic	Sunni Muslim, Christian	Jordanian dinar
KAZAKHSTAN		2 717 300	1 049 155	15 433 000	Astana	Kazakh, Russian, Ukrainian, German, Uzbek, Tatar	Sunni Muslim, Russian Orthodox, Protestant	Tenge
KUWAIT		17 818	6 880	2 521 000	Kuwait	Arabic	Sunni Muslim, Shi'a Muslim, Christian, Hindu	Kuwaiti dinar
KYRGYZSTAN		198 500	76 641	5 138 000	Bishkek	Kyrgyz, Russian, Uzbek	Sunni Muslim, Russian Orthodox	Kyrgyz som
LAOS		236 800	91 429	5 657 000	Vientiane	Lao, local languages	Buddhist, traditional beliefs	Kip
LEBANON		10 452	4 036	3 653 000	Beirut	Arabic, Armenian, French	Shi'a Muslim, Sunni Muslim, Christian	Lebanese pound
MALAYSIA		332 965	128 559	24 425 000	Kuala Lumpur/Putrajaya	Malay, English, Chinese, Tamil, local languages	Sunni Muslim, Buddhist, Hindu, Christian, traditional beliefs	Ringgit
MALDIVES		298	115	318 000	Male	Divehi (Maldivian)	Sunni Muslim	Rufiyaa
MONGOLIA		1 565 000	604 250	2 594 000	Ulan Bator	Khalka (Mongolian), Kazakh, local languages	Buddhist, Sunni Muslim	Tugrik (tögrög)
MYANMAR		676 577	261 228	49 485 000	Rangoon	Burmese, Shan, Karen, local languages	Buddhist, Christian, Sunni Muslim	Kyat
NEPAL		147 181	56 827	25 164 000	Kathmandu	Nepali, Maithili, Bhojpuri, English, local languages	Hindu, Buddhist, Sunni Muslim	Nepalese rupee
NORTH KOREA		120 538	46 540	22 664 000	P'yŏngyang	Korean	Traditional beliefs, Chondoist, Buddhist	North Korean won
OMAN		309 500	119 499	2 851 000	Muscat	Arabic, Baluchi, Indian languages	Ibadhi Muslim, Sunni Muslim	Omani riyal
PAKISTAN		803 940	310 403	153 578 000	Islamabad	Urdu, Punjabi, Sindhi, Pushtu, English	Sunni Muslim, Shi'a Muslim, Christian, Hindu	Pakistani rupee
PALAU		497	192	20 000	Koror	Palauan, English	Roman Catholic, Protestant, traditional beliefs	United States dollar
PHILIPPINES		300 000	115 831	79 999 000	Manila	English, Pilipino, Cebuano, local languages	Roman Catholic, Protestant, Sunni Muslim, Aglipayan	Philippine peso
QATAR		11 437	4 416	610 000	Doha	Arabic	Sunni Muslim	Qatari riyal
RUSSIAN FEDERATION		17 075 400	6 592 849	143 246 000	Moscow	Russian, Tatar, Ukrainian, local languages	Russian Orthodox, Sunni Muslim, Protestant	Russian rouble
SAUDI ARABIA		2 200 000	849 425	24 217 000	Riyadh	Arabic	Sunni Muslim, Shi'a Muslim	Saudi Arabian riyal
SINGAPORE		639	247	4 253 000	Singapore	Chinese, English, Malay, Tamil	Buddhist, Taoist, Sunni Muslim, Christian, Hindu	Singapore dollar
SOUTH KOREA		99 274	38 330	47 700 000	Seoul	Korean	Buddhist, Protestant, Roman Catholic	South Korean won
SRI LANKA		65 610	25 332	19 065 000	Sri Jayewardenepura Kotte	Sinhalese, Tamil, English	Buddhist, Hindu, Sunni Muslim, Roman Catholic	Sri Lankan rupee
SYRIA		185 180	71 498	17 800 000	Damascus	Arabic, Kurdish, Armenian	Sunni Muslim, Shi'a Muslim, Christian	Syrian pound
TAIWAN		36 179	13 969	22 548 000	T'aipei	Mandarin, Min, Hakka, local languages	Buddhist, Taoist, Confucian, Christian	Taiwan dollar
TAJIKISTAN		143 100	55 251	6 245 000	Dushanbe	Tajik, Uzbek, Russian	Sunni Muslim	Somoni
THAILAND		513 115	198 115	62 833 000	Bangkok	Thai, Lao, Chinese, Malay, Mon-Khmer languages	Buddhist, Sunni Muslim	Baht
TURKEY		779 452	300 948	71 325 000	Ankara	Turkish, Kurdish	Sunni Muslim, Shi'a Muslim	Turkish lira
TURKMENISTAN		488 100	188 456	4 867 000	Ashgabat	Turkmen, Uzbek, Russian	Sunni Muslim, Russian Orthodox	Turkmen manat
UNITED ARAB EMIRATES		77 700	30 000	2 995 000	Abu Dhabi	Arabic, English	Sunni Muslim, Shi'a Muslim	United Arab Emirates dirham
UZBEKISTAN		447 400	172 742	26 093 000	Tashkent	Uzbek, Russian, Tajik, Kazakh	Sunni Muslim, Russian Orthodox	Uzbek som
VIETNAM		329 565	127 246	81 377 000	Ha Nôi	Vietnamese, Thai, Khmer, Chinese, local languages	Buddhist, Taoist, Roman Catholic, Cao Dai, Hoa Hao	Dong
YEMEN		527 968	203 850	20 010 000	Şan'ā'	Arabic	Sunni Muslim, Shi'a Muslim	Yemeni rial

Dependent and disputed territories		Territorial status	Area sq km	Area sq miles	Population	Capital	Languages	Religions	Currency
Christmas Island		Australian External Territory	135	52	1 560	The Settlement	English	Buddhist, Sunni Muslim, Protestant, Roman Catholic	Australian dollar
Cocos Islands		Australian External Territory	14	5	632	West Island	English	Sunni Muslim, Christian	Australian dollar
Gaza		Semi-autonomous region	363	140	1 203 591	Gaza	Arabic	Sunni Muslim, Shi'a Muslim	Israeli shekel
Jammu and Kashmir		Disputed territory (India/Pakistan)	222 236	85 806	13 000 000	Srinagar			
West Bank		Disputed territory	5 860	2 263	2 303 660		Arabic, Hebrew	Sunni Muslim, Jewish, Shi'a Muslim, Christian	Jordanian dinar, Israeli shekel

*Hong Kong dollar

Victoria Falls   1

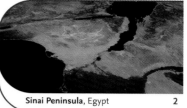
Sinai Peninsula, Egypt   2

Africa		Area sq km	Area sq miles	Population	Capital	Languages	Religions	Currency
ALGERIA		2 381 741	919 595	31 800 000	Algiers	Arabic, French, Berber	Sunni Muslim	Algerian dinar
ANGOLA		1 246 700	481 354	13 625 000	Luanda	Portuguese, Bantu, local languages	Roman Catholic, Protestant, traditional beliefs	Kwanza
BENIN		112 620	43 483	6 736 000	Porto-Novo	French, Fon, Yoruba, Adja, local languages	Traditional beliefs, Roman Catholic, Sunni Muslim	CFA franc*
BOTSWANA		581 370	224 468	1 785 000	Gaborone	English, Setswana, Shona, local languages	Traditional beliefs, Protestant, Roman Catholic	Pula
BURKINA		274 200	105 869	13 002 000	Ouagadougou	French, Moore (Mossi), Fulani, local languages	Sunni Muslim, traditional beliefs, Roman Catholic	CFA franc*
BURUNDI		27 835	10 747	6 825 000	Bujumbura	Kirundi (Hutu, Tutsi), French	Roman Catholic, traditional beliefs, Protestant	Burundian franc
CAMEROON		475 442	183 569	16 018 000	Yaoundé	French, English, Fang, Bamileke, local languages	Roman Catholic, traditional beliefs, Sunni Muslim, Protestant	CFA franc*
CAPE VERDE		4 033	1 557	463 000	Praia	Portuguese, creole	Roman Catholic, Protestant	Cape Verde escudo
CENTRAL AFRICAN REPUBLIC		622 436	240 324	3 865 000	Bangui	French, Sango, Banda, Baya, local languages	Protestant, Roman Catholic, traditional beliefs, Sunni Muslim	CFA franc*
CHAD		1 284 000	495 755	8 598 000	Ndjamena	Arabic, French, Sara, local languages	Sunni Muslim, Roman Catholic, Protestant, traditional beliefs	CFA franc*
COMOROS		1 862	719	768 000	Moroni	Comorian, French, Arabic	Sunni Muslim, Roman Catholic	Comoros franc
CONGO		342 000	132 047	3 724 000	Brazzaville	French, Kongo, Monokutuba, local languages	Roman Catholic, Protestant, traditional beliefs, Sunni Muslim	CFA franc*
CONGO, DEMOCRATIC REP. OF		2 345 410	905 568	52 771 000	Kinshasa	French, Lingala, Swahili, Kongo, local languages	Christian, Sunni Muslim	Congolese franc
CÔTE D'IVOIRE		322 463	124 504	16 631 000	Yamoussoukro	French, creole, Akan, local languages	Sunni Muslim, Roman Catholic, traditional beliefs, Protestant	CFA franc*
DJIBOUTI		23 200	8 958	703 000	Djibouti	Somali, Afar, French, Arabic	Sunni Muslim, Christian	Djibouti franc
EGYPT		1 000 250	386 199	71 931 000	Cairo	Arabic	Sunni Muslim, Coptic Christian	Egyptian pound
EQUATORIAL GUINEA		28 051	10 831	494 000	Malabo	Spanish, French, Fang	Roman Catholic, traditional beliefs	CFA franc*
ERITREA		117 400	45 328	4 141 000	Asmara	Tigrinya, Tigre	Sunni Muslim, Coptic Christian	Nakfa
ETHIOPIA		1 133 880	437 794	70 678 000	Addis Ababa	Oromo, Amharic, Tigrinya, local languages	Ethiopian Orthodox, Sunni Muslim, traditional beliefs	Birr
GABON		267 667	103 347	1 329 000	Libreville	French, Fang, local languages	Roman Catholic, Protestant, traditional beliefs	CFA franc*
THE GAMBIA		11 295	4 361	1 426 000	Banjul	English, Malinke, Fulani, Wolof	Sunni Muslim, Protestant	Dalasi
GHANA		238 537	92 100	20 922 000	Accra	English, Hausa, Akan, local languages	Christian, Sunni Muslim, traditional beliefs	Cedi
GUINEA		245 857	94 926	8 480 000	Conakry	French, Fulani, Malinke, local languages	Sunni Muslim, traditional beliefs, Christian	Guinea franc
GUINEA-BISSAU		36 125	13 948	1 493 000	Bissau	Portuguese, crioulo, local languages	Traditional beliefs, Sunni Muslim, Christian	CFA franc*
KENYA		582 646	224 961	31 987 000	Nairobi	Swahili, English, local languages	Christian, traditional beliefs	Kenyan shilling
LESOTHO		30 355	11 720	1 802 000	Maseru	Sesotho, English, Zulu	Christian, traditional beliefs	Loti, S. African rand
LIBERIA		111 369	43 000	3 367 000	Monrovia	English, creole, local languages	Traditional beliefs, Christian, Sunni Muslim	Liberian dollar
LIBYA		1 759 540	679 362	5 551 000	Tripoli	Arabic, Berber	Sunni Muslim	Libyan dinar
MADAGASCAR		587 041	226 658	17 404 000	Antananarivo	Malagasy, French	Traditional beliefs, Christian, Sunni Muslim	Malagasy franc
MALAWI		118 484	45 747	12 105 000	Lilongwe	Chichewa, English, local languages	Christian, traditional beliefs, Sunni Muslim	Malawian kwacha
MALI		1 240 140	478 821	13 007 000	Bamako	French, Bambara, local languages	Sunni Muslim, traditional beliefs, Christian	CFA franc*
MAURITANIA		1 030 700	397 955	2 893 000	Nouakchott	Arabic, French, local languages	Sunni Muslim	Ouguiya
MAURITIUS		2 040	788	1 221 000	Port Louis	English, creole, Hindi, Bhojpurī, French	Hindu, Roman Catholic, Sunni Muslim	Mauritius rupee
MOROCCO		446 550	172 414	30 566 000	Rabat	Arabic, Berber, French	Sunni Muslim	Moroccan dirham
MOZAMBIQUE		799 380	308 642	18 863 000	Maputo	Portuguese, Makua, Tsonga, local languages	Traditional beliefs, Roman Catholic, Sunni Muslim	Metical
NAMIBIA		824 292	318 261	1 987 000	Windhoek	English, Afrikaans, German, Ovambo, local languages	Protestant, Roman Catholic	Namibian dollar
NIGER		1 267 000	489 191	11 972 000	Niamey	French, Hausa, Fulani, local languages	Sunni Muslim, traditional beliefs	CFA franc*
NIGERIA		923 768	356 669	124 009 000	Abuja	English, Hausa, Yoruba, Ibo, Fulani, local languages	Sunni Muslim, Christian, traditional beliefs	Naira
RWANDA		26 338	10 169	8 387 000	Kigali	Kinyarwanda, French, English	Roman Catholic, traditional beliefs, Protestant	Rwandan franc
SÃO TOMÉ AND PRÍNCIPE		964	372	161 000	São Tomé	Portuguese, creole	Roman Catholic, Protestant	Dobra
SENEGAL		196 720	75 954	10 095 000	Dakar	French, Wolof, Fulani, local languages	Sunni Muslim, Roman Catholic, traditional beliefs	CFA franc*
SEYCHELLES		455	176	81 000	Victoria	English, French, creole	Roman Catholic, Protestant	Seychelles rupee
SIERRA LEONE		71 740	27 699	4 971 000	Freetown	English, creole, Mende, Temne, local languages	Sunni Muslim, traditional beliefs	Leone
SOMALIA		637 657	246 201	9 890 000	Mogadishu	Somali, Arabic	Sunni Muslim	Somali shilling
SOUTH AFRICA, REPUBLIC OF		1 219 090	470 693	45 026 000	Pretoria/Cape Town	Afrikaans, English, nine official local languages	Protestant, Roman Catholic, Sunni Muslim, Hindu	Rand
SUDAN		2 505 813	967 500	33 610 000	Khartoum	Arabic, Dinka, Nubian, Beja, Nuer, local languages	Sunni Muslim, traditional beliefs, Christian	Sudanese dinar
SWAZILAND		17 364	6 704	1 077 000	Mbabane	Swazi, English	Christian, traditional beliefs	Emalangeni, South African rand
TANZANIA		945 087	364 900	36 977 000	Dodoma	Swahili, English, Nyamwezi, local languages	Shi'a Muslim, Sunni Muslim, traditional beliefs, Christian	Tanzanian shilling
TOGO		56 785	21 925	4 909 000	Lomé	French, Ewe, Kabre, local languages	Traditional beliefs, Christian, Sunni Muslim	CFA franc*
TUNISIA		164 150	63 379	9 832 000	Tunis	Arabic, French	Sunni Muslim	Tunisian dinar
UGANDA		241 038	93 065	25 827 000	Kampala	English, Swahili, Luganda, local languages	Roman Catholic, Protestant, Sunni Muslim, traditional beliefs	Ugandan shilling
ZAMBIA		752 614	290 586	10 812 000	Lusaka	English, Bemba, Nyanja, Tonga, local languages	Christian, traditional beliefs	Zambian kwacha
ZIMBABWE		390 759	150 873	12 891 000	Harare	English, Shona, Ndebele	Christian, traditional beliefs	Zimbabwean dollar

Dependent and disputed territories		Territorial status	Area sq km	Area sq km	Population	Capital	Languages	Religions	Currency
Canary Islands		Autonomous Community of Spain	7 447	2 875	1 694 477	Santa Cruz de Tenerife, Las Palmas	Spanish	Roman Catholic	Euro
Madeira		Autonomous Region of Portugal	779	301	242 603	Funchal	Portuguese	Roman Catholic, Protestant	Euro
Mayotte		French Territorial Collectivity	373	144	171 000	Dzaoudzi	French, Mahorian	Sunni Muslim, Christian	Euro
Réunion		French Overseas Department	2 551	985	756 000	St-Denis	French, creole	Roman Catholic	Euro
St Helena and Dependencies		United Kingdom Overseas Territory	121	47	5 644	Jamestown	English	Protestant, Roman Catholic	St Helena pound
Western Sahara		Disputed territory (Morocco)	266 000	102 703	308 000	Laâyoune	Arabic	Sunni Muslim	Moroccan dirham

*Communauté Financière Africaine franc

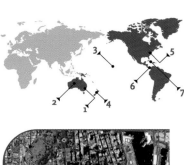

Sydney, Australia   1

Uluṟu (Ayers Rock), Australia   2

Oceania		Area sq km	Area sq miles	Population	Capital	Languages	Religions	Currency
AUSTRALIA		7 692 024	2 969 907	19 731 000	Canberra	English, Italian, Greek	Protestant, Roman Catholic, Orthodox	Australian dollar
FIJI		18 330	7 077	839 000	Suva	English, Fijian, Hindi	Christian, Hindu, Sunni Muslim	Fiji dollar
KIRIBATI		717	277	88 000	Bairiki	Gilbertese, English	Roman Catholic, Protestant	Australian dollar
MARSHALL ISLANDS		181	70	53 000	Delap-Uliga-Djarrit	English, Marshallese	Protestant, Roman Catholic	United States dollar
MICRONESIA, FEDERATED STATES OF		701	271	109 000	Palikir	English, Chuukese, Pohnpeian, local languages	Roman Catholic, Protestant	United States dollar
NAURU		21	8	13 000	Yaren	Nauruan, English	Protestant, Roman Catholic	Australian dollar
NEW ZEALAND		270 534	104 454	3 875 000	Wellington	English, Maori	Protestant, Roman Catholic	New Zealand dollar
PAPUA NEW GUINEA		462 840	178 704	5 711 000	Port Moresby	English, Tok Pisin (creole), local languages	Protestant, Roman Catholic, traditional beliefs	Kina
SAMOA		2 831	1 093	178 000	Apia	Samoan, English	Protestant, Roman Catholic	Tala
SOLOMON ISLANDS		28 370	10 954	477 000	Honiara	English, creole, local languages	Protestant, Roman Catholic	Solomon Islands dollar
TONGA		748	289	104 000	Nuku'alofa	Tongan, English	Protestant, Roman Catholic	Pa'anga
TUVALU		25	10	11 000	Vaiaku	Tuvaluan, English	Protestant	Australian dollar
VANUATU		12 190	4 707	212 000	Port Vila	English, Bislama (creole), French	Protestant, Roman Catholic, traditional beliefs	Vatu

Dependent territories		Territorial status	Area sq km	Area sq miles	Population	Capital	Languages	Religions	Currency
American Samoa		United States Unincorporated Territory	197	76	67 000	Fagatoga	Samoan, English	Protestant, Roman Catholic	United States dollar
Cook Islands		Self-governing New Zealand Territory	293	113	18 000	Avarua	English, Maori	Protestant, Roman Catholic	New Zealand dollar
French Polynesia		French Overseas Territory	3 265	1 261	244 000	Papeete	French, Tahitian, Polynesian languages	Protestant, Roman Catholic	CFP franc*
Guam		United States Unincorporated Territory	541	209	163 000	Hagåtña	Chamorro, English, Tapalog	Roman Catholic	United States dollar
New Caledonia		French Overseas Territory	19 058	7 358	228 000	Nouméa	French, local languages	Roman Catholic, Protestant, Sunni Muslim	CFP franc*
Niue		Self-governing New Zealand Territory	258	100	2 000	Alofi	English, Polynesian	Christian	New Zealand dollar
Norfolk Island		Australian External Territory	35	14	2 037	Kingston	English	Protestant, Roman Catholic	Australian Dollar
Northern Mariana Islands		United States Commonwealth	477	184	79 000	Capitol Hill	English, Chamorro, local languages	Roman Catholic	United States dollar
Pitcairn Islands		United Kingdom Overseas Territory	45	17	51	Adamstown	English	Protestant	New Zealand dollar
Tokelau		New Zealand Overseas Territory	10	4	2 000		English, Tokelauan	Christian	New Zealand dollar
Wallis and Futuna Islands		French Overseas Territory	274	106	15 000	Matā'utu	French, Wallisian, Futunian	Roman Catholic	CFP franc*

*Franc des Comptoirs Français du Pacifique

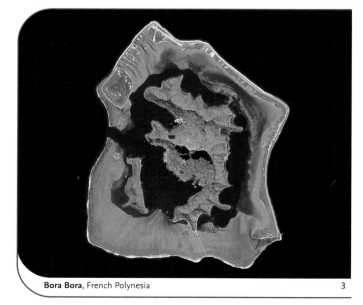

Bora Bora, French Polynesia   3

Mount Cook, New Zealand   4

The Pentagon, Washington DC, USA 5

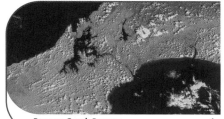

Panama Canal, Panama 6

Cuba, Caribbean Sea 7

North America

North America		Area sq km	Area sq miles	Population	Capital	Languages	Religions	Currency
ANTIGUA AND BARBUDA		442	171	73 000	St John's	English, creole	Protestant, Roman Catholic	East Caribbean dollar
THE BAHAMAS		13 939	5 382	314 000	Nassau	English, creole	Protestant, Roman Catholic	Bahamian dollar
BARBADOS		430	166	270 000	Bridgetown	English, creole	Protestant, Roman Catholic	Barbados dollar
BELIZE		22 965	8 867	256 000	Belmopan	English, Spanish, Mayan, creole	Roman Catholic, Protestant	Belize dollar
CANADA		9 984 670	3 855 103	31 510 000	Ottawa	English, French	Roman Catholic, Protestant, Eastern Orthodox, Jewish	Canadian dollar
COSTA RICA		51 100	19 730	4 173 000	San José	Spanish	Roman Catholic, Protestant	Costa Rican colón
CUBA		110 860	42 803	11 300 000	Havana	Spanish	Roman Catholic, Protestant	Cuban peso
DOMINICA		750	290	79 000	Roseau	English, creole	Roman Catholic, Protestant	East Caribbean dollar
DOMINICAN REPUBLIC		48 442	18 704	8 745 000	Santo Domingo	Spanish, creole	Roman Catholic, Protestant	Dominican peso
EL SALVADOR		21 041	8 124	6 515 000	San Salvador	Spanish	Roman Catholic, Protestant	El Salvador colón, United States dollar
GRENADA		378	146	80 000	St George's	English, creole	Roman Catholic, Protestant	East Caribbean dollar
GUATEMALA		108 890	42 043	12 347 000	Guatemala City	Spanish, Mayan languages	Roman Catholic, Protestant	Quetzal, United States dollar
HAITI		27 750	10 714	8 326 000	Port-au-Prince	French, creole	Roman Catholic, Protestant, Voodoo	Gourde
HONDURAS		112 088	43 277	6 941 000	Tegucigalpa	Spanish, Amerindian languages	Roman Catholic, Protestant	Lempira
JAMAICA		10 991	4 244	2 651 000	Kingston	English, creole	Protestant, Roman Catholic	Jamaican dollar
MEXICO		1 972 545	761 604	103 457 000	Mexico City	Spanish, Amerindian languages	Roman Catholic, Protestant	Mexican peso
NICARAGUA		130 000	50 193	5 466 000	Managua	Spanish, Amerindian languages	Roman Catholic, Protestant	Córdoba
PANAMA		77 082	29 762	3 120 000	Panama City	Spanish, English, Amerindian languages	Roman Catholic, Protestant, Sunni Muslim	Balboa
ST KITTS AND NEVIS		261	101	42 000	Basseterre	English, creole	Protestant, Roman Catholic	East Caribbean dollar
ST LUCIA		616	238	149 000	Castries	English, creole	Roman Catholic, Protestant	East Caribbean dollar
ST VINCENT AND THE GRENADINES		389	150	120 000	Kingstown	English, creole	Protestant, Roman Catholic	East Caribbean dollar
TRINIDAD AND TOBAGO		5 130	1 981	1 303 000	Port of Spain	English, creole, Hindi	Roman Catholic, Hindu, Protestant, Sunni Muslim	Trinidad and Tobago dollar
UNITED STATES OF AMERICA		9 826 635	3 794 085	294 043 000	Washington, D.C.	English, Spanish	Protestant, Roman Catholic, Sunni Muslim, Jewish	United States dollar

Dependent territories		Territorial status	Area sq km	Area sq miles	Population	Capital	Languages	Religions	Currency
Anguilla		United Kingdom Overseas Territory	155	60	12 000	The Valley	English	Protestant, Roman Catholic	East Caribbean dollar
Aruba		Self-governing Netherlands Territory	193	75	100 000	Oranjestad	Papiamento, Dutch, English	Roman Catholic, Protestant	Arubian florin
Bermuda		United Kingdom Overseas Territory	54	21	82 000	Hamilton	English	Protestant, Roman Catholic	Bermuda dollar
Cayman Islands		United Kingdom Overseas Territory	259	100	40 000	George Town	English	Protestant, Roman Catholic	Cayman Islands dollar
Greenland		Self-governing Danish Territory	2 175 600	840 004	57 000	Nuuk	Greenlandic, Danish	Protestant	Danish krone
Guadeloupe		French Overseas Department	1 780	687	440 000	Basse-Terre	French, creole	Roman Catholic	Euro
Martinique		French Overseas Department	1 079	417	393 000	Fort-de-France	French, creole	Roman Catholic, traditional beliefs	Euro
Montserrat		United Kingdom Overseas Territory	100	39	4 000	Plymouth	English	Protestant, Roman Catholic	East Caribbean dollar
Netherlands Antilles		Self-governing Netherlands Territory	800	309	221 000	Willemstad	Dutch, Papiamento, English	Roman Catholic, Protestant	Netherlands guilder
Puerto Rico		United States Commonwealth	9 104	3 515	3 879 000	San Juan	Spanish, English	Roman Catholic, Protestant	United States dollar
St Pierre and Miquelon		French Territorial Collectivity	242	93	6 000	St-Pierre	French	Roman Catholic	Euro
Turks and Caicos Islands		United Kingdom Overseas Territory	430	166	21 000	Grand Turk	English	Protestant	United States dollar
Virgin Islands (U.K.)		United Kingdom Overseas Territory	153	59	21 000	Road Town	English	Protestant, Roman Catholic	United States dollar
Virgin Islands (U.S.A.)		United States Unincorporated Territory	352	136	111 000	Charlotte Amalie	English, Spanish	Protestant, Roman Catholic	United States dollar

South America

South America		Area sq km	Area sq miles	Population	Capital	Languages	Religions	Currency
ARGENTINA		2 766 889	1 068 302	38 428 000	Buenos Aires	Spanish, Italian, Amerindian languages	Roman Catholic, Protestant	Argentinian peso
BOLIVIA		1 098 581	424 164	8 808 000	La Paz/Sucre	Spanish, Quechua, Aymara	Roman Catholic, Protestant, Baha'i	Boliviano
BRAZIL		8 514 879	3 287 613	178 470 000	Brasília	Portuguese	Roman Catholic, Protestant	Real
CHILE		756 945	292 258	15 805 000	Santiago	Spanish, Amerindian languages	Roman Catholic, Protestant	Chilean peso
COLOMBIA		1 141 748	440 831	44 222 000	Bogotá	Spanish, Amerindian languages	Roman Catholic, Protestant	Colombian peso
ECUADOR		272 045	105 037	13 003 000	Quito	Spanish, Quechua, other Amerindian languages	Roman Catholic	US dollar
GUYANA		214 969	83 000	765 000	Georgetown	English, creole, Amerindian languages	Protestant, Hindu, Roman Catholic, Sunni Muslim	Guyana dollar
PARAGUAY		406 752	157 048	5 878 000	Asunción	Spanish, Guaraní	Roman Catholic, Protestant	Guaraní
PERU		1 285 216	496 225	27 167 000	Lima	Spanish, Quechua, Aymara	Roman Catholic, Protestant	Sol
SURINAME		163 820	63 251	436 000	Paramaribo	Dutch, Surinamese, English, Hindi	Hindu, Roman Catholic, Protestant, Sunni Muslim	Suriname guilder
URUGUAY		176 215	68 037	3 415 000	Montevideo	Spanish	Roman Catholic, Protestant, Jewish	Uruguayan peso
VENEZUELA		912 050	352 144	25 699 000	Caracas	Spanish, Amerindian languages	Roman Catholic, Protestant	Bolívar

Dependent territories		Territorial status	Area sq km	Area sq miles	Population	Capital	Languages	Religions	Currency
Falkland Islands		United Kingdom Overseas Territory	12 170	4 699	3 000	Stanley	English	Protestant, Roman Catholic	Falkland Islands pound
French Guiana		French Overseas Department	90 000	34 749	178 000	Cayenne	French, creole	Roman Catholic	Euro

The current pattern of the world's countries and territories is a result of a long history of exploration, colonialism, conflict and politics. The fact that there are currently 193 independent countries in the world – the most recent, East Timor, only being created in May 2002 – illustrates the significant political changes which have occurred since 1950 when there were only eighty two. There has been a steady progression away from colonial influences over the last fifty years, although many dependent overseas territories remain.

The shapes of countries and the pattern of international boundaries reflect both physical and political processes. Some borders follow natural features – rivers, mountain ranges, etc – others are defined according to political agreement or as a result of war. Some are still subject to dispute between two or more countries, and many remain undefined on the ground.

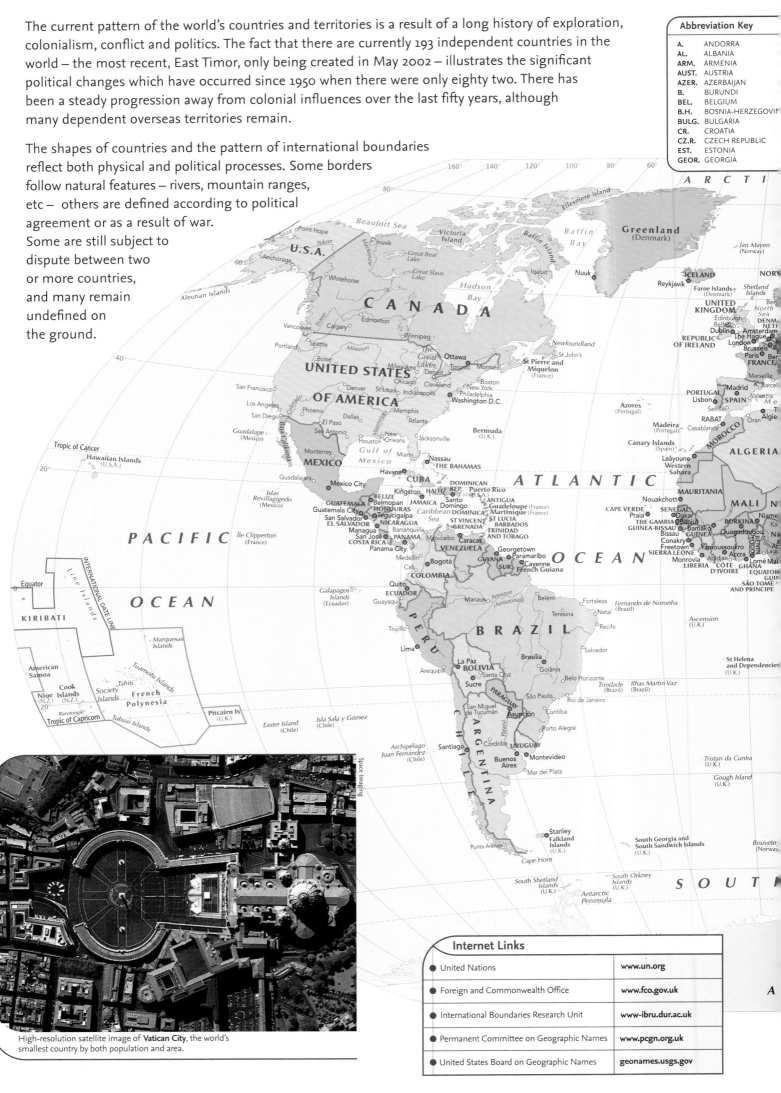

Abbreviation Key	
A.	ANDORRA
AL.	ALBANIA
ARM.	ARMENIA
AUST.	AUSTRIA
AZER.	AZERBAIJAN
B.	BURUNDI
BEL.	BELGIUM
B.H.	BOSNIA-HERZEGOVIN
BULG.	BULGARIA
CR.	CROATIA
CZ.R.	CZECH REPUBLIC
EST.	ESTONIA
GEOR.	GEORGIA

High-resolution satellite image of **Vatican City**, the world's smallest country by both population and area.

Internet Links	
United Nations	www.un.org
Foreign and Commonwealth Office	www.fco.gov.uk
International Boundaries Research Unit	www-ibru.dur.ac.uk
Permanent Committee on Geographic Names	www.pcgn.org.uk
United States Board on Geographic Names	geonames.usgs.gov

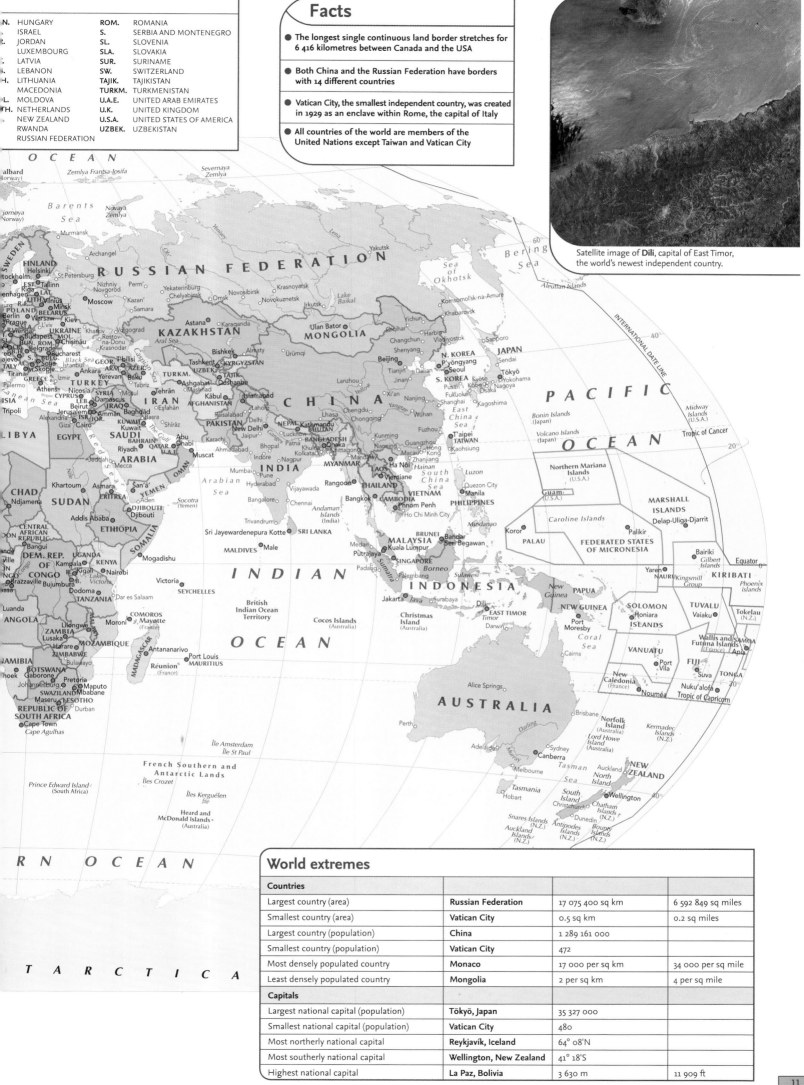

N.	HUNGARY	ROM.	ROMANIA
	ISRAEL	S.	SERBIA AND MONTENEGRO
R.	JORDAN	SL.	SLOVENIA
	LUXEMBOURG	SLA.	SLOVAKIA
	LATVIA	SUR.	SURINAME
	LEBANON	SW.	SWITZERLAND
H.	LITHUANIA	TAJIK.	TAJIKISTAN
	MACEDONIA	TURKM.	TURKMENISTAN
L.	MOLDOVA	U.A.E.	UNITED ARAB EMIRATES
TH.	NETHERLANDS	U.K.	UNITED KINGDOM
	NEW ZEALAND	U.S.A.	UNITED STATES OF AMERICA
	RWANDA	UZBEK.	UZBEKISTAN
	RUSSIAN FEDERATION		

Facts

● The longest single continuous land border stretches for 6 416 kilometres between Canada and the USA

● Both China and the Russian Federation have borders with 14 different countries

● Vatican City, the smallest independent country, was created in 1929 as an enclave within Rome, the capital of Italy

● All countries of the world are members of the United Nations except Taiwan and Vatican City

Satellite image of **Dili**, capital of East Timor, the world's newest independent country.

World extremes

Countries			
Largest country (area)	**Russian Federation**	17 075 400 sq km	6 592 849 sq miles
Smallest country (area)	**Vatican City**	0.5 sq km	0.2 sq miles
Largest country (population)	**China**	1 289 161 000	
Smallest country (population)	**Vatican City**	472	
Most densely populated country	**Monaco**	17 000 per sq km	34 000 per sq mile
Least densely populated country	**Mongolia**	2 per sq km	4 per sq mile
Capitals			
Largest national capital (population)	**Tōkyō, Japan**	35 327 000	
Smallest national capital (population)	**Vatican City**	480	
Most northerly national capital	**Reykjavík, Iceland**	64° 08'N	
Most southerly national capital	**Wellington, New Zealand**	41° 18'S	
Highest national capital	**La Paz, Bolivia**	3 630 m	11 909 ft

The earth's physical features, both on land and on the sea bed, closely reflect its geological structure. The current shapes of the continents and oceans have evolved over millions of years. Movements of the tectonic plates which make up the earth's crust have created some of the best-known and most spectacular features. The processes which have shaped the earth continue today with earthquakes, volcanoes, erosion, climatic variations and man's activities all affecting the earth's landscapes.

The total topographic range of the earth's surface is nearly 20 000 metres, from the highest point Mount Everest, to the lowest point in the Mariana Trench. Major mountain ranges include the Himalaya, the Andes and the Rocky Mountains, each of which give rise to some of the world's greatest rivers. In contrast, the deserts of the Sahara, Australia, the Arabian Peninsula and the Gobi cover vast areas and each provide unique landscapes.

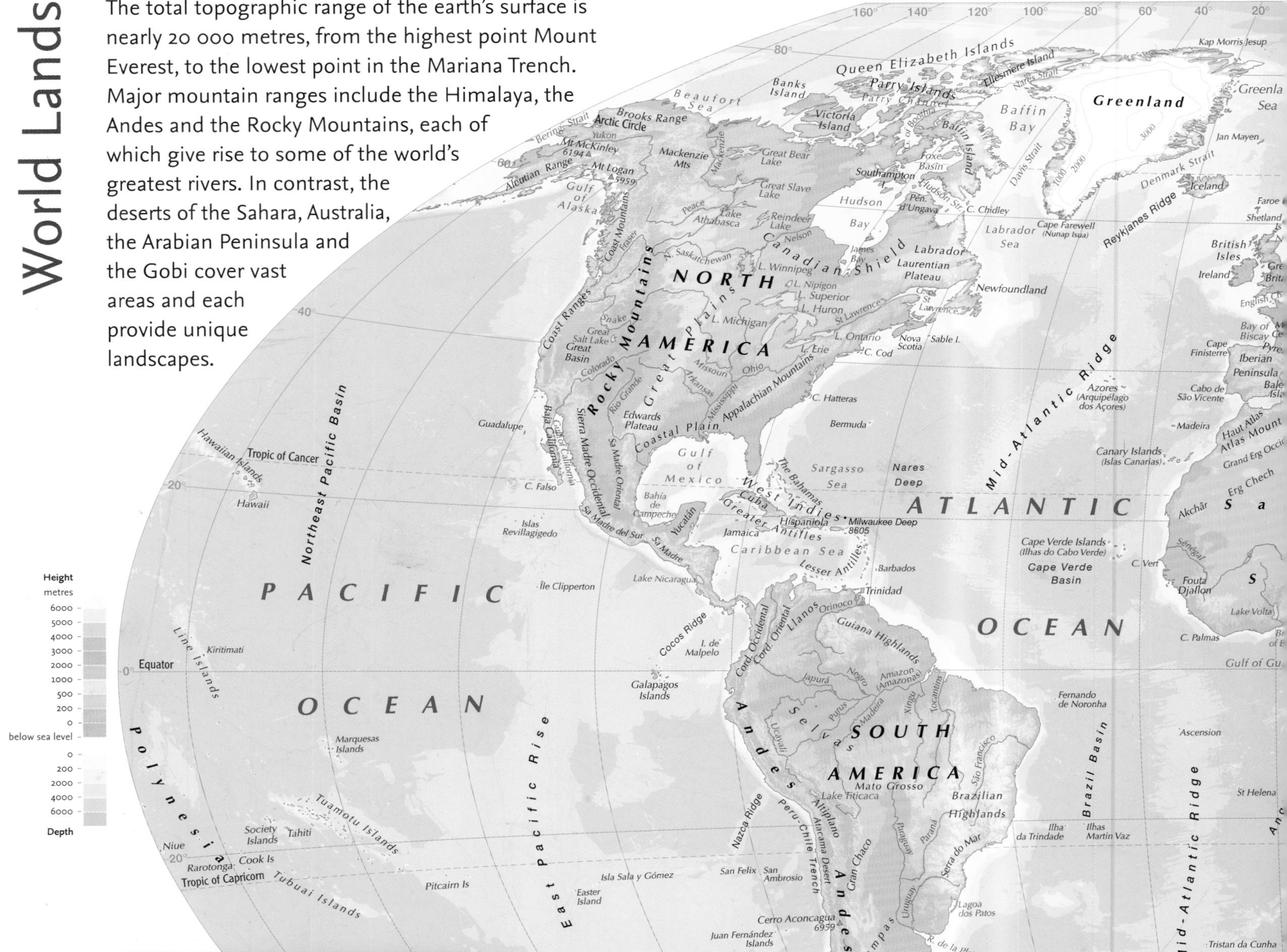

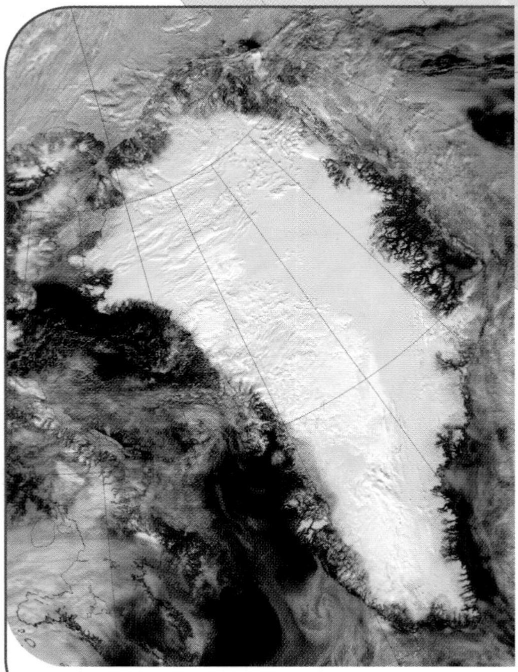

Height
metres
6000
5000
4000
3000
2000
1000
500
200
0
below sea level
0
200
2000
4000
6000
Depth

Greenland, the world's largest island, located almost entirely within the Arctic Circle.

Facts

- Approximately 10% of the earth's land surface is permanently covered by ice
- The Pacific Ocean is larger than all the continents' land areas combined
- The world's highest waterfall, 980 metres high, is Angel Falls, Venezuela
- 52% of the earth's land surface is below 500 metres
- The mean elevation of the earth's land surface is 840 metres
- Lake Baikal is the world's deepest lake with a maximum depth of 1 637 metres

Internet Links

- United Nations Environment Programme
- International Union for Conservation of Nature
- NASA Visible Earth
- NASA Earth Observatory
- Earth Resources Observation Systems

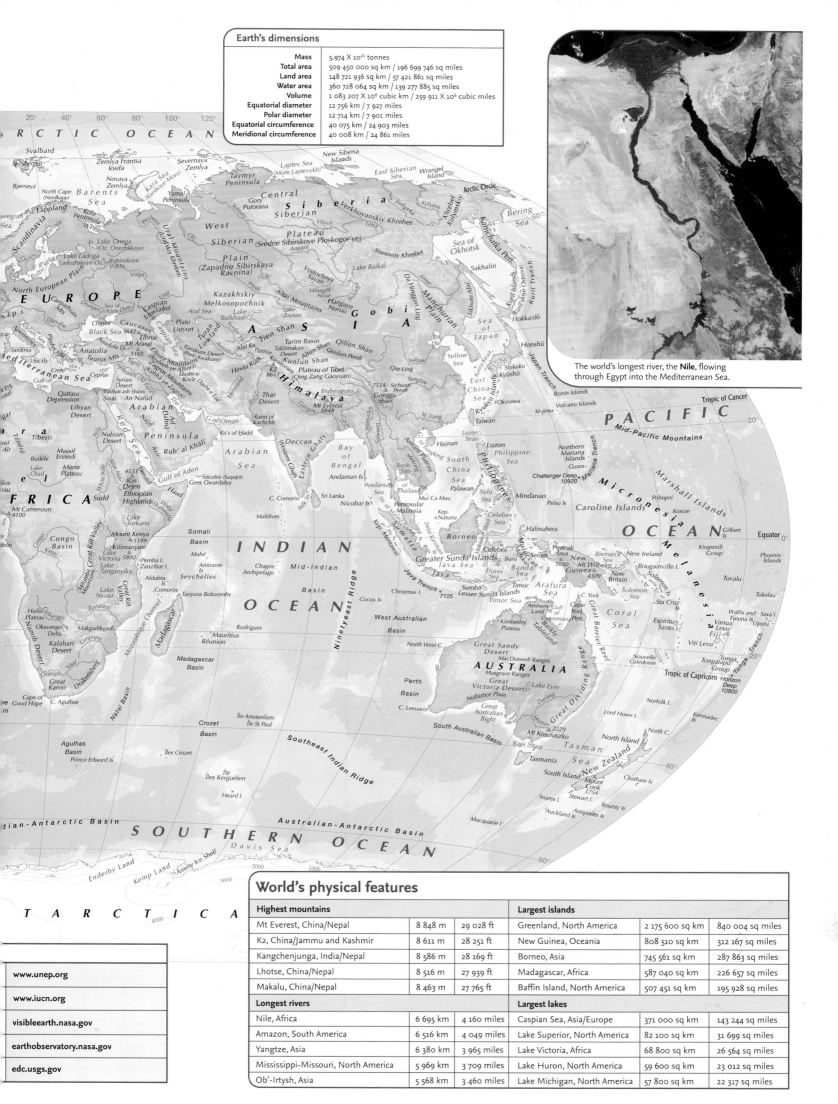

Earth's dimensions

Mass	5.974 X 10²¹ tonnes
Total area	509 450 000 sq km / 196 699 746 sq miles
Land area	148 721 936 sq km / 57 421 861 sq miles
Water area	360 728 064 sq km / 139 277 885 sq miles
Volume	1 083 207 X 10⁶ cubic km / 259 911 X 10⁶ cubic miles
Equatorial diameter	12 756 km / 7 927 miles
Polar diameter	12 714 km / 7 901 miles
Equatorial circumference	40 075 km / 24 903 miles
Meridional circumference	40 008 km / 24 861 miles

The world's longest river, the **Nile**, flowing through Egypt into the Mediterranean Sea.

World's physical features

Highest mountains			Largest islands		
Mt Everest, China/Nepal	8 848 m	29 028 ft	Greenland, North America	2 175 600 sq km	840 004 sq miles
K2, China/Jammu and Kashmir	8 611 m	28 251 ft	New Guinea, Oceania	808 510 sq km	312 167 sq miles
Kangchenjunga, India/Nepal	8 586 m	28 169 ft	Borneo, Asia	745 561 sq km	287 863 sq miles
Lhotse, China/Nepal	8 516 m	27 939 ft	Madagascar, Africa	587 040 sq km	226 657 sq miles
Makalu, China/Nepal	8 463 m	27 765 ft	Baffin Island, North America	507 451 sq km	195 928 sq miles
Longest rivers			**Largest lakes**		
Nile, Africa	6 695 km	4 160 miles	Caspian Sea, Asia/Europe	371 000 sq km	143 244 sq miles
Amazon, South America	6 516 km	4 049 miles	Lake Superior, North America	82 100 sq km	31 699 sq miles
Yangtze, Asia	6 380 km	3 965 miles	Lake Victoria, Africa	68 800 sq km	26 564 sq miles
Mississippi-Missouri, North America	5 969 km	3 709 miles	Lake Huron, North America	59 600 sq km	23 012 sq miles
Ob'-Irtysh, Asia	5 568 km	3 460 miles	Lake Michigan, North America	57 800 sq km	22 317 sq miles

World Earthquakes and Volcanoes

Earthquakes and volcanoes hold a constant fascination because of their power, their beauty, and the fact that they cannot be controlled or accurately predicted. Our understanding of these phenomena relies mainly on the theory of plate tectonics. This defines the earth's surface as a series of 'plates' which are constantly moving relative to each other, at rates of a few centimetres per year. As plates move against each other enormous pressure builds up and when the rocks can no longer bear this pressure they fracture, and energy is released as an earthquake. The pressures involved can also melt the rock to form magma which then rises to the earth's surface to form a volcano.

The distribution of earthquakes and volcanoes therefore relates closely to plate boundaries. In particular, most active volcanoes and much of the earth's seismic activity are centred on the 'Ring of Fire' around the Pacific Ocean.

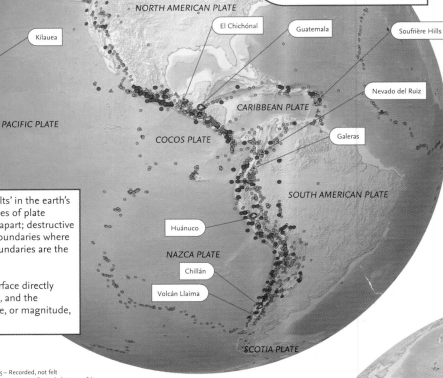

Earthquakes

Earthquakes are caused by movement along fractures or 'faults' in the earth's crust, particularly along plate boundaries. There are three types of plate boundary: constructive boundaries where plates are moving apart; destructive boundaries where two or more plates collide; conservative boundaries where plates slide past each other. Destructive and conservative boundaries are the main sources of earthquake activity.

The epicentre of an earthquake is the point on the earth's surface directly above its source. If this is near to large centres of population, and the earthquake is powerful, major devastation can result. The size, or magnitude, of an earthquake is generally measured on the Richter Scale.

Deadliest earthquakes, 1900–2003

Year	Location	Deaths
1905	**Kangra**, India	19 000
1907	west of **Dushanbe**, Tajikistan	12 000
1908	**Messina**, Italy	110 000
1915	**Abruzzo**, Italy	35 000
1917	**Bali**, Indonesia	15 000
1920	**Ningxia Province**, China	200 000
1923	**Tōkyō**, Japan	142 807
1927	**Qinghai Province**, China	200 000
1932	**Gansu Province**, China	70 000
1933	**Sichuan Province**, China	10 000
1934	**Nepal/India**	10 700
1935	**Quetta**, Pakistan	30 000
1939	**Chillán**, Chile	28 000
1939	**Erzincan**, Turkey	32 700
1948	**Ashgabat**, Turkmenistan	19 800
1962	**Northwest Iran**	12 225
1970	**Huánuco Province**, Peru	66 794
1974	**Yunnan** and **Sichuan Provinces**, China	20 000
1975	**Liaoning Province**, China	10 000
1976	central **Guatemala**	22 778
1976	**Hebei Province**, China	255 000
1978	**Khorāsan Province**, Iran	20 000
1980	**Ech Chélif**, Algeria	11 000
1988	**Spitak**, Armenia	25 000
1990	**Manjil**, Iran	50 000
1999	**Kocaeli (İzmit)**, Turkey	17 000
2001	**Gujarat**, India	20 000
2003	**Bam**, Iran	26 271

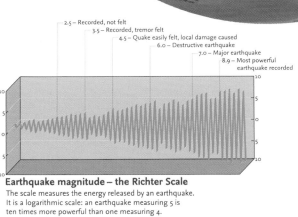

2.5 – Recorded, not felt
3.5 – Recorded, tremor felt
4.5 – Quake easily felt, local damage caused
6.0 – Destructive earthquake
7.0 – Major earthquake
8.9 – Most powerful earthquake recorded

Earthquake magnitude – the Richter Scale

The scale measures the energy released by an earthquake. It is a logarithmic scale: an earthquake measuring 5 is ten times more powerful than one measuring 4.

Extensive damage caused by major earthquake centred on **Bam, Iran** in December 2003.

Deadliest earthquake

Earthquake of magnitude 7.5 or greater

Earthquake of magnitude 5.5 – 7.4

Major volcano

Other volcano

Volcanoes

The majority of volcanoes occur along destructive plate boundaries in the 'subduction zone' where one plate passes under another. The friction and pressure causes the rock to melt and to form magma which is forced upwards to the earth's surface where it erupts as molten rock (lava) or as particles of ash or cinder. This process created the numerous volcanoes in the Andes, where the Nazca Plate is passing under the South American Plate. Volcanoes can be defined by the nature of the material they emit. 'Shield' volcanoes have extensive, gentle slopes formed from free-flowing lava, while steep-sided 'continental' volcanoes are created from thicker, slow-flowing lava and ash.

Lava flow from **Mt Etna, Sicily, Italy** threatens the town of Zafferana Etnea.

Major volcanic eruptions, 1980–2002

Volcano	Country	Date
Mt St Helens	USA	1980
El Chichónal	Mexico	1982
Gunung Galunggung	Indonesia	1982
Kilauea	Hawaii	1983
Ō-yama	Japan	1983
Nevado del Ruiz	Colombia	1985
Mt Pinatubo	Philippines	1991
Unzen-dake	Japan	1991
Mayon	Philippines	1993
Galeras	Colombia	1993
Volcán Llaima	Chile	1994
Rabaul	Papua New Guinea	1994
Soufrière Hills	Montserrat	1997
Hekla	Iceland	2000
Mt Etna	Italy	2001
Nyiragongo	Democratic Republic of Congo	2002

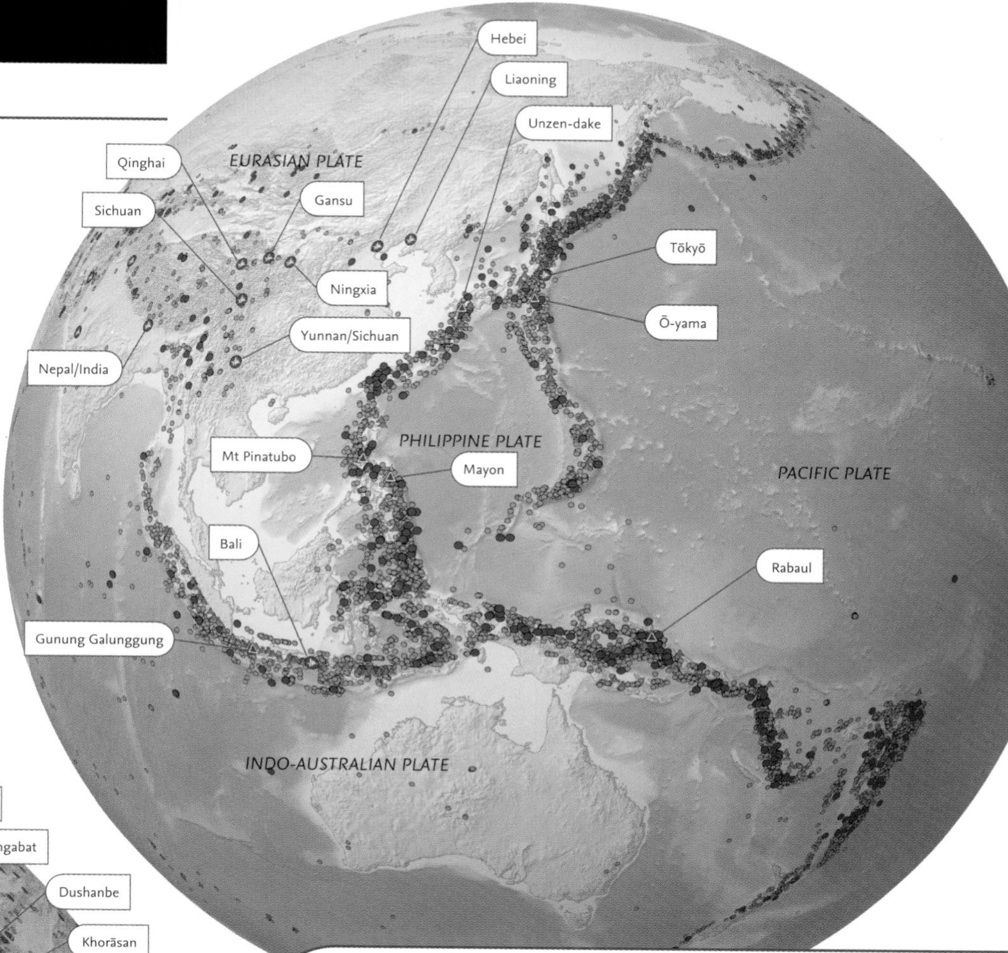

EURASIAN PLATE

Hebei
Liaoning
Unzen-dake
Qinghai
Sichuan
Gansu
Tōkyō
Ningxia
Ō-yama
Yunnan/Sichuan
Nepal/India
PHILIPPINE PLATE
PACIFIC PLATE
Mt Pinatubo
Mayon
Bali
Rabaul
Gunung Galunggung
INDO-AUSTRALIAN PLATE

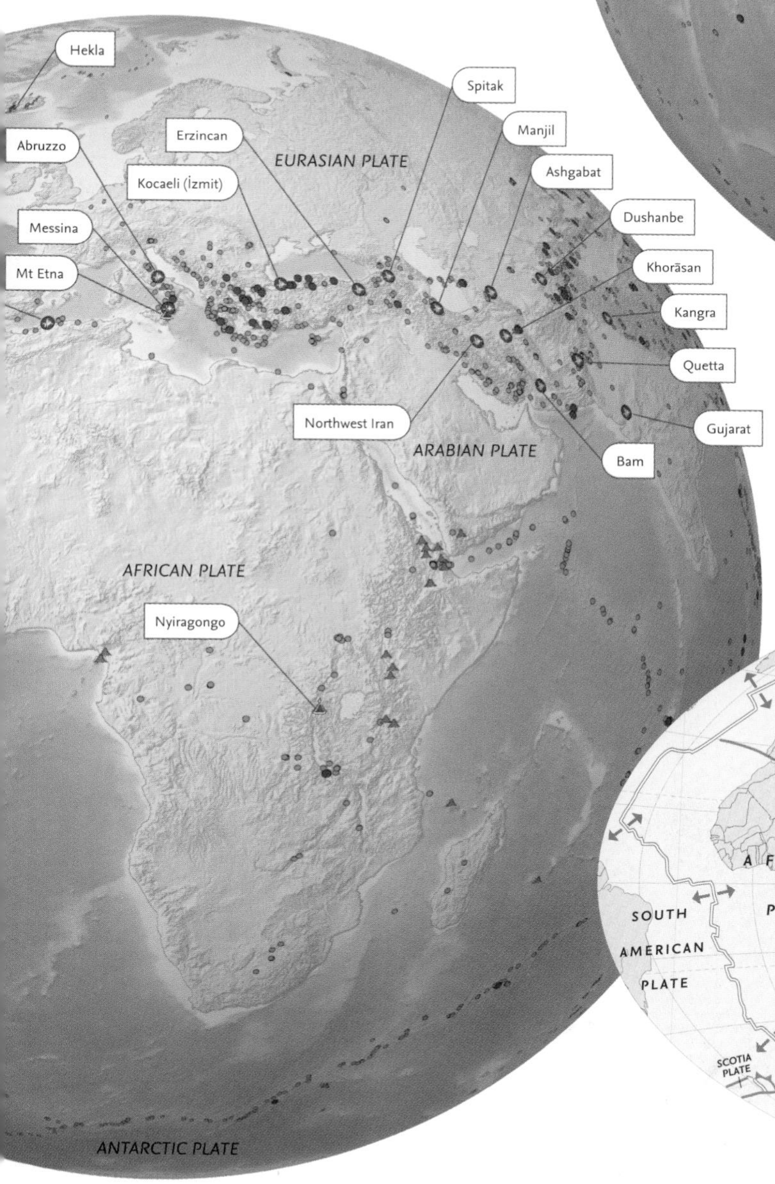

Hekla
Spitak
Abruzzo
Erzincan
Manjil
EURASIAN PLATE
Ashgabat
Kocaeli (İzmit)
Dushanbe
Messina
Khorāsan
Mt Etna
Kangra
Quetta
Northwest Iran
Gujarat
ARABIAN PLATE
Bam

AFRICAN PLATE
Nyiragongo

ANTARCTIC PLATE

Internet Links

USGS National Earthquake Information Center	neic.usgs.gov
USGS Volcano Information	volcanoes.usgs.gov
British Geological Survey	www.bgs.ac.uk
NASA Natural Hazards	earthobservatory.nasa.gov/NaturalHazards
Volcano World	volcano.und.nodak.edu

Constructive boundary
Destructive boundary
Conservative boundary

Plate boundaries

EURASIAN PLATE
NORTH AMERICAN PLATE
ARABIAN PLATE
PHILIPPINE PLATE
PACIFIC PLATE
CARIBBEAN PLATE
COCOS PLATE
AFRICAN PLATE
SOUTH AMERICAN PLATE
INDO-AUSTRALIAN PLATE
NAZCA PLATE
SOUTH AMERICAN PLATE
SCOTIA PLATE
SCOTIA PLATE
ANTARCTIC PLATE

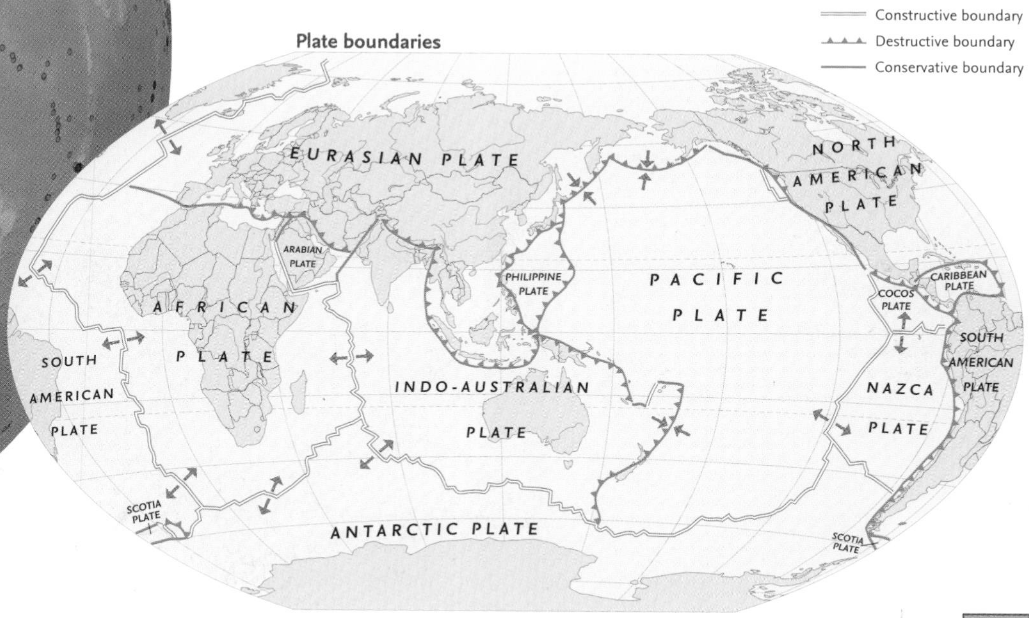

The climate of a region is defined by its long-term prevailing weather conditions. Classification of Climate Types is based on the relationship between temperature and humidity and how these factors are affected by latitude, altitude, ocean currents and winds. Weather is the specific short term condition which occurs locally and consists of events such as thunderstorms, hurricanes, blizzards and heat waves. Temperature and rainfall data recorded at weather stations can be plotted graphically and the graphs shown here, typical of each climate region, illustrate the various combinations of temperature and rainfall which exist worldwide for each month of the year. Data used for climate graphs are based on average monthly figures recorded over a minimum period of thirty years.

World Statistics: see pages 154–160

Tropical storm Dina, January 2002, northeast of Mauritius and Réunion, Indian Ocean.

Weather extremes

Highest recorded temperature	**57.8°C/136°F** Al'Azīzīyah, Libya (September 1922)
Hottest place - annual mean	**34.4°C/93.6°F** Dalol, Ethiopia
Driest place - annual mean	**0.1mm/0.004 inches** Atacama Desert, Chile
Most sunshine - annual mean	**90%** Yuma, Arizona, USA (over 4000 hours)
Lowest recorded temperature	**-89.2°C/-128.6°F** Vostok Station, Antarctica (July 1983)
Coldest place - annual mean	**-56.6°C/-69.9°F** Plateau Station, Antarctica
Wettest place annual mean	**11 873 mm/467.4 inches** Meghalaya, India
Greatest snowfall	**31 102 mm/1 224.5 inches** Mount Rainier, Washington, USA (February 1971 – February 1972)
Windiest place	**322 km per hour/200 miles per hour** (in gales) Commonwealth Bay, Antarctica

Facts

- Arctic Sea ice thickness has declined 4% in the last 40 years

- 2001 marked the end of the La Niña episode

- Sea levels are rising by one centimetre per decade

- Precipitation in the northern hemisphere is increasing

- Droughts have increased in frequency and intensity in parts of Asia and Africa

Climate change

In 2001 the global mean temperature was 0.63°C higher than that at the end of the nineteenth century. Most of this warming is caused by human activities which result in a build-up of greenhouse gases, mainly carbon dioxide, allowing heat to be trapped within the atmosphere. Carbon dioxide emissions have increased since the beginning of the industrial revolution due to burning of fossil fuels, increased urbanization, population growth, deforestation and industrial pollution. Annual climate indicators such as number of frost-free days, length of growing season, heat wave frequency, number of wet days, length of dry spells and frequency of weather extremes are used to monitor climate change. The map highlights some events of 2001 which indicate climate change. Until carbon dioxide emissions are reduced it is likely that this trend will continue.

1. Warmest winter recorded in **Alaska and Yukon**.
2. Third warmest year on record in **Canada**.
3. Severe rainfall deficit in **northwest USA**.
4. Costliest storm in US history was tropical storm **Alison**.
5. Extreme summer drought in **Central America**.
6. Strongest hurricane to hit Cuba since 1952 was **Michelle**.

14. Continued drought in area around **Horn of Africa**.
15. Widespread minimum winter temperatures near -60°C in **Siberia and Mongolia**.
16. 1998 drought continues in **Southern Asia**.
17. Severe drought and water shortages in **Northern China, Korean Peninsula and Japan**.
18. Extensive flooding in September caused by Typhoon **Nari**.
19. Severe flooding August to October in **Vietnam and Cambodia**.

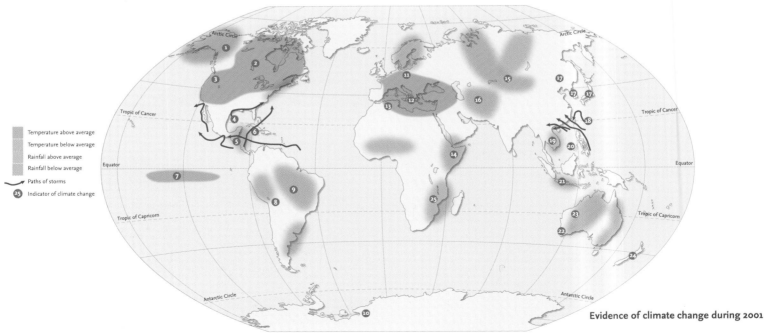

Evidence of climate change during 2001

Temperature above average
Temperature below average
Rainfall above average
Rainfall below average
Paths of storms
25 Indicator of climate change

7. End of **La Niña** episode.
8. Severe flooding in **Bolivia**.
9. Normal rainy season hit by drought in **Brazil**.
10. Longer lasting ozone hole than previous years in **Antarctica**.
11. Worst flooding since 1997 in **southwest Poland and Czech Republic**.
12. Temperatures 1°–2°C above average for 2001 in **Europe and Middle East**.
13. Severe November flooding in **Algeria**.

20. Severe flooding causes more than 400 deaths when four tropical cyclones, **Durian, Yutu, Ulor and Toraji** made landfall in July.
21. Major flooding in February on **Java**.
22. Driest summer on record in **Perth**.
23. Cooler and wetter than normal in **Western Australia**.
24. One of the driest summers recorded in **New Zealand**.
25. Severe flooding February to April in **Mozambique, Zambia, Malawi and Zimbabwe**.

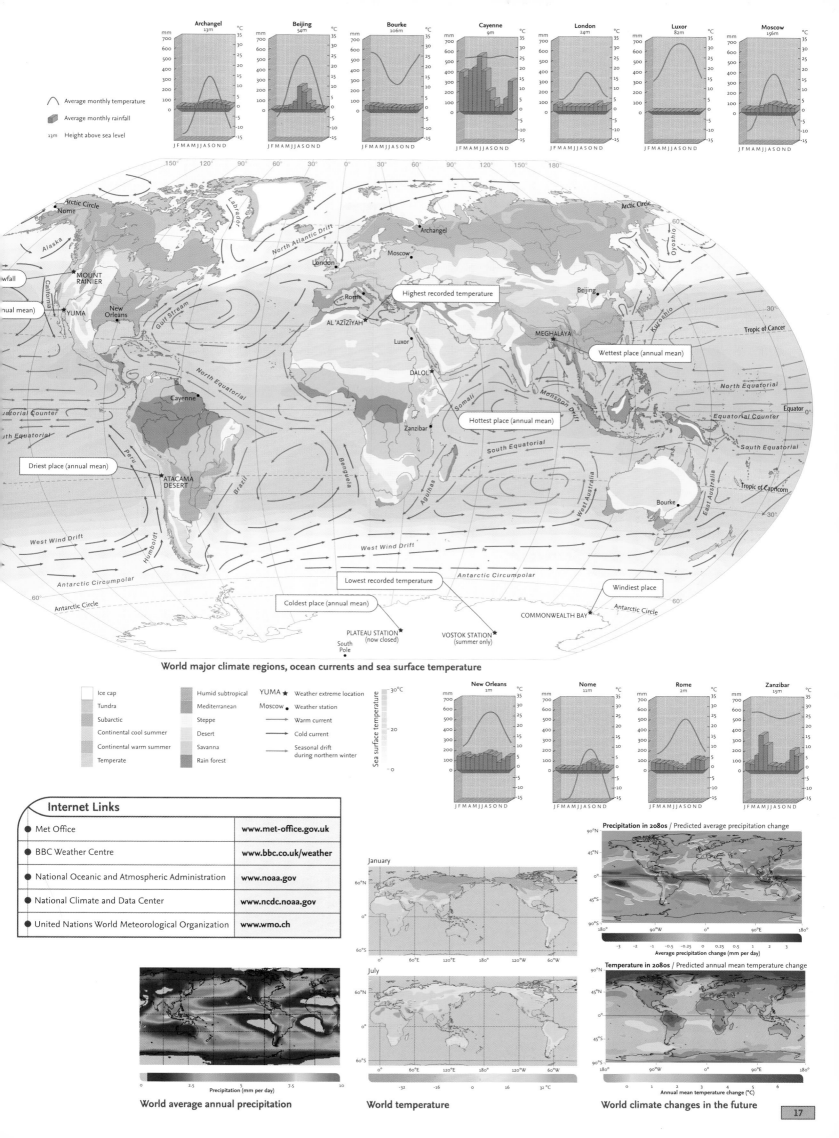

Climate graphs (top row)

Archangel 13m

Beijing 54m

Bourke 106m

Cayenne 9m

London 24m

Luxor 82m

Moscow 156m

Legend:
- Average monthly temperature
- Average monthly rainfall
- 13m Height above sea level

World major climate regions, ocean currents and sea surface temperature

Map labels include:
Nome, Alaska, MOUNT RAINIER, YUMA, New Orleans, California, Gulf Stream, North Equatorial, Equatorial Counter, South Equatorial, Peru, Humboldt, Brazil, West Wind Drift, Antarctic Circumpolar, Antarctic Circle, ATACAMA DESERT, Cayenne

Arctic Circle, Labrador, North Atlantic Drift, London, Rome, Archangel, Moscow, AL 'AZĪZĪYAH, Luxor, DALOL, Benguela, Agulhas, Somali, Zanzibar

Oyashio, Beijing, Kuroshio, Tropic of Cancer, MEGHALAYA, Monsoon Drift, North Equatorial, Equatorial Counter, Equator, South Equatorial, East Australia, West Australia, Tropic of Capricorn, Bourke

COMMONWEALTH BAY, Antarctic Circumpolar, Antarctic Circle, West Wind Drift

Annotation boxes:
- Highest recorded temperature
- Wettest place (annual mean)
- Hottest place (annual mean)
- Driest place (annual mean)
- Lowest recorded temperature
- Coldest place (annual mean)
- Windiest place
- PLATEAU STATION (now closed)
- VOSTOK STATION (summer only)
- South Pole

Legend

Ice cap		Humid subtropical	YUMA ★ Weather extreme location		
Tundra		Mediterranean	Moscow ● Weather station		
Subarctic		Steppe	→ Warm current		
Continental cool summer		Desert	→ Cold current		
Continental warm summer		Savanna	→ Seasonal drift during northern winter		
Temperate		Rain forest			

Sea surface temperature: 30°C / 20 / 0

Climate graphs (bottom row)

New Orleans 1m

Nome 11m

Rome 2m

Zanzibar 15m

Internet Links

Met Office	www.met-office.gov.uk
BBC Weather Centre	www.bbc.co.uk/weather
National Oceanic and Atmospheric Administration	www.noaa.gov
National Climate and Data Center	www.ncdc.noaa.gov
United Nations World Meteorological Organization	www.wmo.ch

World temperature

January

July

-32 -16 0 16 32 °C

World average annual precipitation

0 2.5 5 7.5 10
Precipitation (mm per day)

World climate changes in the future

Precipitation in 2080s / Predicted average precipitation change

-3 -2 -1 -0.5 -0.25 0 0.25 0.5 1 2 3
Average precipitation change (mm per day)

Temperature in 2080s / Predicted annual mean temperature change

0 1 2 3 4 5 6
Annual mean temperature change (°C)

The oxygen- and water- rich environment of the earth has helped create a wide range of habitats. Forest and woodland ecosystems form the predominant natural land cover over most of the earth's surface. Tropical rainforests are part of an intricate land-atmosphere relationship that is disturbed by land cover changes. Forests in the tropics are believed to hold most of the world's bird, animal, and plant species. Grassland, shrubland and deserts collectively cover most of the unwooded land surface, with tundra on frozen subsoil at high northern latitudes. These areas tend to have lower species diversity than most forests, with the notable exception of Mediterranean shrublands, which support some of the most diverse floras on the earth. Humans have extensively altered most grassland and shrubland areas, usually through conversion to agriculture, burning and introduction of domestic livestock. They have had less immediate impact on tundra and true desert regions, although these remain vulnerable to global climate change.

Land cover legend
Evergreen needleleaf forest
Evergreen broadleaf forest
Deciduous needleleaf forest
Deciduous broadleaf forest
Mixed forest
Closed shrubland
Open shrubland
Woody savanna
Savanna
Grassland
Permanent wetland
Cropland
Urban and built-up
Cropland/Natural vegetation mosaic
Snow and Ice
Barren or sparsely vegetated
Water bodies

Snow and ice, Spitsbergen, Svalbard, inside the Arctic Circle.

World land cover
Map courtesy of IGBP, JRC and USGS

Internet Links

World Resources Institute	www.wri.org
World Conservation Monitoring Centre	www.unep-wcmc.org
United Nations Environment Programme (UNEP)	www.unep.org
IUCN The World Conservation Union	www.iucn.org
Land Cover at Boston University	geography.bu.edu/landcover/index.html

Top 20 protected areas by size

Rank	Protected area	Country	Size (sq km)	Designation
1	Greenland	Greenland	972 000	National Park
2	Rub' al Khālī	Saudi Arabia	640 000	Wildlife Management Area
3	Great Barrier Reef Marine Park	Australia	344 360	Marine Park
4	Northwestern Hawaiian Islands	United States	341 362	Coral Reef Ecosystem Reserve
5	Amazonia	Colombia	326 329	Forest Reserve
6	Qiangtang	China	298 000	Nature Reserve
7	Macquarie Island	Australia	162 060	Marine Park
8	Sanjiangyuan	China	152 300	Nature Reserve
9	Cape Churchill	Canada	137 072	Wildlife Management Area
10	Galapagos Islands	Ecuador	133 000	Marine Reserve
11	Northern Wildlife Management Zone	Saudi Arabia	100 875	Wildlife Management Area
12	Ngaanyatjarra Lands	Australia	98 129	Indigenous Protected Area
13	Alto Orinoco-Casiquiare	Venezuela	84 000	Biosphere Reserve
14	Vale do Javari	Brazil	83 380	Indigenous Area
15	Ouadi Rimé-Ouadi Achim	Chad	80 000	Faunal Reserve
16	Arctic	United States	78 049	National Wildlife Refuge
17	Yanomami	Brazil	77 519	Indigenous Park
18	Yukon Delta	United States	77 425	National Wildlife Refuge
19	Aïr and Ténéré	Niger	77 360	National Nature Reserve
20	Pacifico	Colombia	73 981	Forest Reserve

Urban, La Paz, Bolivia.

Land cover

The land cover map shown here was derived from data aquired by the Advanced Very High Resolution Radiometer sensor on board the polar orbiting satellites of the US National Oceanic and Atmospheric Administration. The high resolution (ground resolution of 1km) of the imagery used to compile the data set and map allows detailed interpretation of land cover patterns across the world. Important uses include managing forest resources, improving estimates of the earth's water and energy cycles, and modelling climate change.

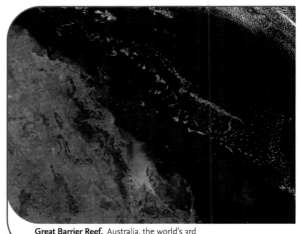

Great Barrier Reef, Australia, the world's 3rd largest protected area.

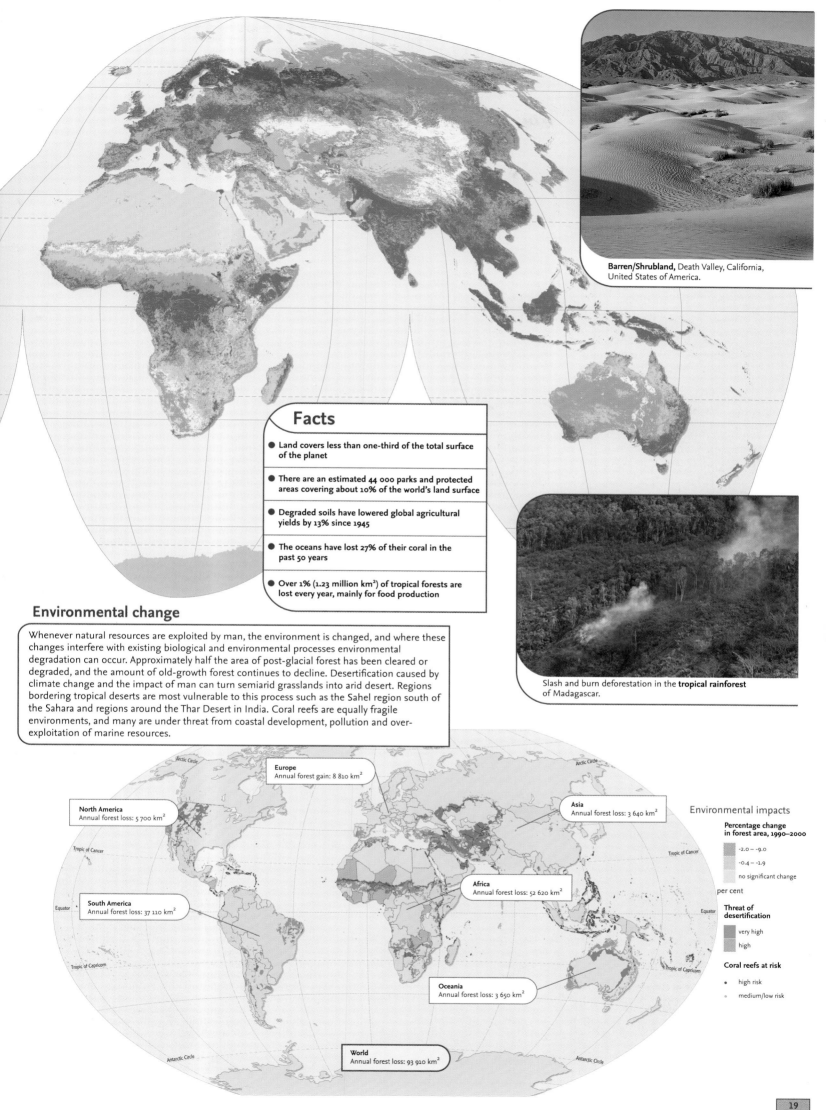

Barren/Shrubland, Death Valley, California, United States of America.

Facts

- Land covers less than one-third of the total surface of the planet

- There are an estimated 44 000 parks and protected areas covering about 10% of the world's land surface

- Degraded soils have lowered global agricultural yields by 13% since 1945

- The oceans have lost 27% of their coral in the past 50 years

- Over 1% (1.23 million km²) of tropical forests are lost every year, mainly for food production

Environmental change

Whenever natural resources are exploited by man, the environment is changed, and where these changes interfere with existing biological and environmental processes environmental degradation can occur. Approximately half the area of post-glacial forest has been cleared or degraded, and the amount of old-growth forest continues to decline. Desertification caused by climate change and the impact of man can turn semiarid grasslands into arid desert. Regions bordering tropical deserts are most vulnerable to this process such as the Sahel region south of the Sahara and regions around the Thar Desert in India. Coral reefs are equally fragile environments, and many are under threat from coastal development, pollution and over-exploitation of marine resources.

Slash and burn deforestation in the **tropical rainforest** of Madagascar.

Europe
Annual forest gain: 8 810 km²

North America
Annual forest loss: 5 700 km²

Asia
Annual forest loss: 3 640 km²

South America
Annual forest loss: 37 110 km²

Africa
Annual forest loss: 52 620 km²

Oceania
Annual forest loss: 3 650 km²

World
Annual forest loss: 93 910 km²

Environmental impacts

Percentage change in forest area, 1990–2000

- -2.0 – -9.0
- -0.4 – -1.9
- no significant change

per cent

Threat of desertification

- very high
- high

Coral reefs at risk

- high risk
- medium/low risk

World Population

After increasing very slowly for most of human history, world population more than doubled in the last half century. Whereas world population did not pass the one billion mark until 1804 and took another 123 years to reach two billion in 1927, it then added the third billion in 33 years, the fourth in 14 years and the fifth in 13 years. Just twelve years later on October 12, 1999 the United Nations announced that the global population had reached the six billion mark. It is expected that another three billion people will have been added to the world's population by 2050.

world statistics: see pages 154–160

Facts

- The world's population is growing at an annual rate of 76 million people per year

- Today's population is only 5.7% of the total number of people who ever lived on the earth

- It is expected that in 2050 there will be more people aged over 60 than children aged less than 14

- More than 90% of the 70 million inhabitants of Egypt are located around the River Nile

- India's population reached 1 billion in August 1999

Top 20 countries by population density, 2003
(persons per square kilometre)

Rank	Country	Population density
1	Monaco	17 000
2	Singapore	6 656
3	Malta	1 247
4	Maldives	1 067
5	Bahrain	1 048
6	Bangladesh	1 019
7	Vatican City	944
8	Barbados	628
9	Taiwan	623
10	Nauru	619
11	Mauritius	599
12	South Korea	480
13	San Marino	459
14	Tuvalu	440
15	Comoros	412
16	Netherlands	389
17	Lebanon	350
18	India	348
19	Belgium	338
20	Japan	338

Top 20 countries by population, 2003

Rank	Country	Population
1	China	1 289 161 000
2	India	1 065 462 000
3	United States of America	294 043 000
4	Indonesia	219 883 000
5	Brazil	178 470 000
6	Pakistan	153 578 000
7	Bangladesh	146 736 000
8	Russian Federation	143 246 000
9	Japan	127 654 000
10	Nigeria	124 009 000
11	Mexico	103 457 000
12	Germany	82 476 000
13	Vietnam	81 377 000
14	Philippines	79 999 000
15	Egypt	71 931 000
16	Turkey	71 325 000
17	Ethiopia	70 678 000
18	Iran	68 920 000
19	Thailand	62 833 000
20	France	60 144 000

Population distribution

The world's population in mid-2003 had reached 6 301 million, over half of which live in six countries: China, India, USA, Indonesia, Brazil and Pakistan. Over 80% (5 098 million) of the total population live in less developed regions. As shown on the population distribution map, over a quarter of the land area is uninhabited or has extremely low population density. Barely a quarter of the land area is occupied at densities of 25 or more persons per square km, with the three largest concentrations in east Asia, the Indian subcontinent and Europe accounting for over half the world total.

World population distribution
Population density, continental populations (2002) and continental population change (2000–2005)

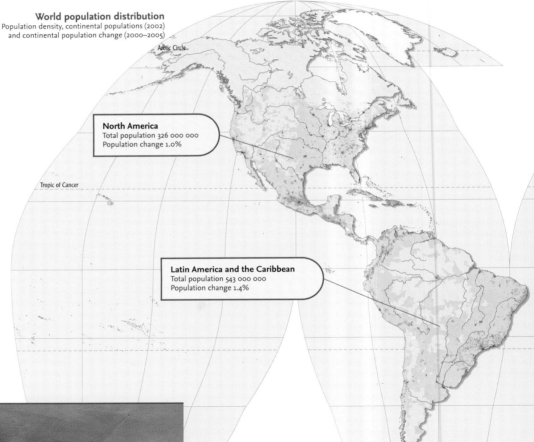

North America
Total population 326 000 000
Population change 1.0%

Latin America and the Caribbean
Total population 543 000 000
Population change 1.4%

over 2 500	over 1 000
1 250 – 2 500	500 – 1 000
625 – 1 250	250 – 500
250 – 625	100 – 250
125 – 250	50 – 100
62.5 – 125	25 – 50
12.5 – 62.5	5 – 25
2.5 – 12.5	1 – 5
0 – 2.5	0 – 1
Uninhabited	Uninhabited

Inhabitants (per sq mile) | Inhabitants (per sq km)

Kuna Indians inhabit this congested island off the north coast of Panama.

Population change by country, 2000–2005

Average annual rate of population change
(per cent) and the top ten contributors to
world population growth (net annual addition)

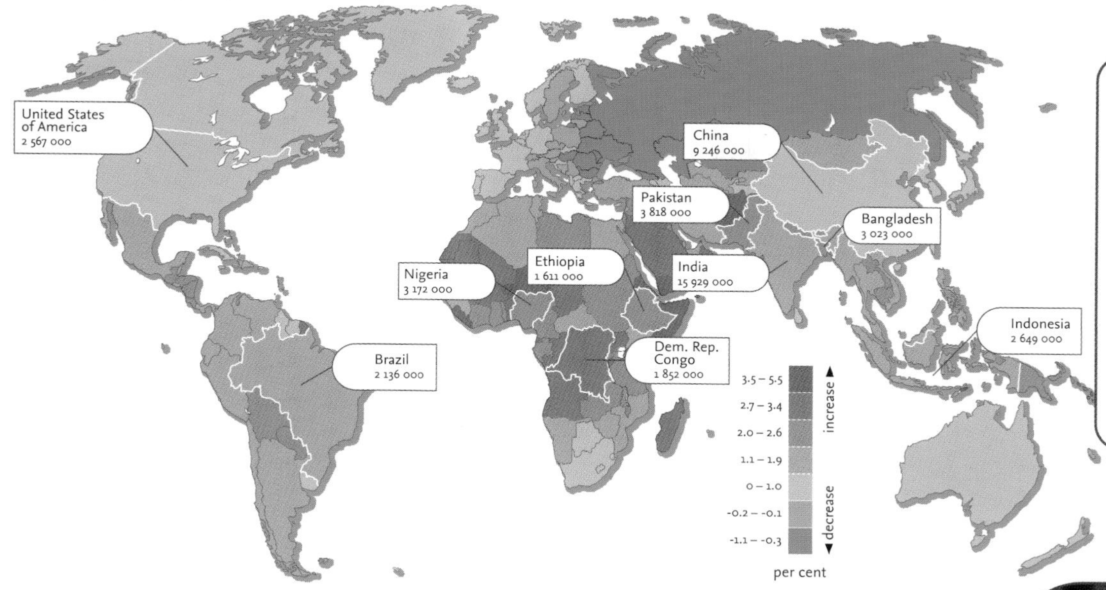

United States
of America
2 567 000

China
9 246 000

Pakistan
3 818 000

Bangladesh
3 023 000

Nigeria
3 172 000

Ethiopia
1 611 000

India
15 929 000

Brazil
2 136 000

Dem. Rep.
Congo
1 852 000

Indonesia
2 649 000

	per cent
3.5 – 5.5	increase
2.7 – 3.4	
2.0 – 2.6	
1.1 – 1.9	
0 – 1.0	
-0.2 – -0.1	decrease
-1.1 – -0.3	

World population change

Population growth since 1950 has been spread very
unevenly between the continents. While overall numbers
have been growing rapidly since 1950, a massive 89 per
cent increase has taken place in the less developed
regions, especially southern and eastern Asia. In contrast,
Europe's population level has been almost stationary and
is expected to decrease in the future. India and China
alone are responsible for over one-third of current
growth. But most of the highest rates of growth are to be
found in Sub-Saharan Africa with Liberia and Sierra Leone
experiencing the highest percentage increases in
population between 2000 and 2005. Until population
growth is brought under tighter control, the developing
world in particular will continue to face enormous
problems of supporting a rising population.

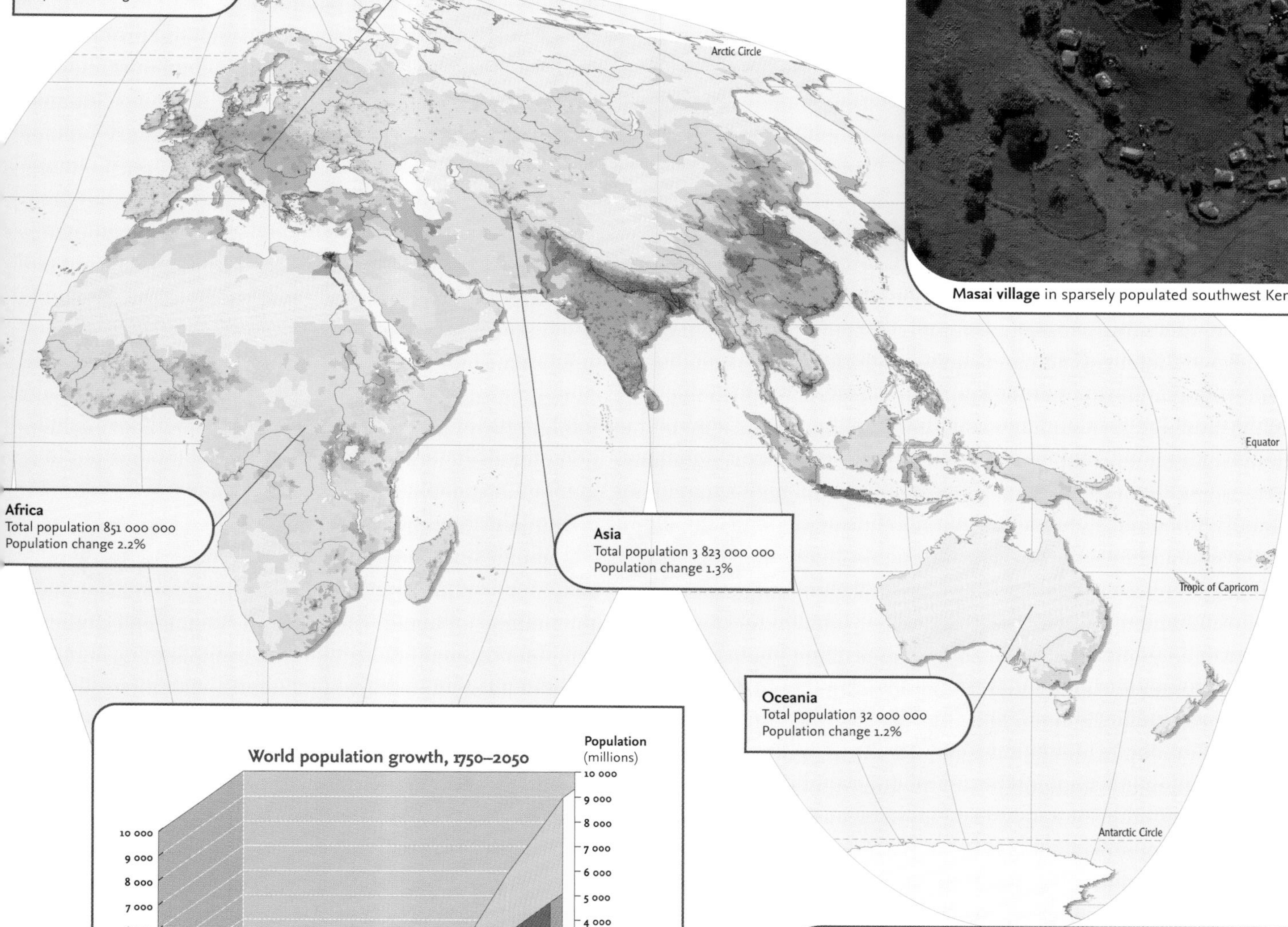

World
Total population 6 301 000 000
Population change 1.2%

Europe
Total population 726 000 000
Population change -0.1%

Arctic Circle

Africa
Total population 851 000 000
Population change 2.2%

Asia
Total population 3 823 000 000
Population change 1.3%

Equator

Tropic of Capricorn

Oceania
Total population 32 000 000
Population change 1.2%

Antarctic Circle

Masai village in sparsely populated southwest Kenya.

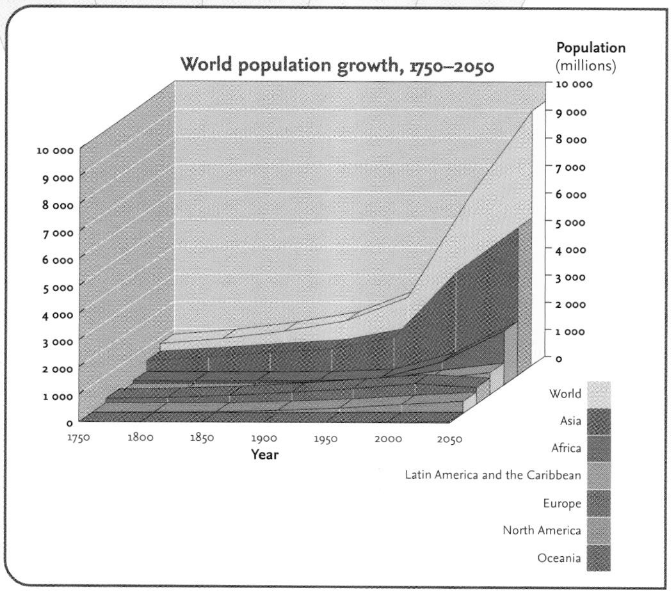

World population growth, 1750–2050

Population
(millions)

Year	
1750	
1800	
1850	
1900	
1950	
2000	
2050	

World
Asia
Africa
Latin America and the Caribbean
Europe
North America
Oceania

Internet Links

● United Nations Population Information Network	**www.un.org/popin**
● US Census Bureau	**www.census.gov**
● UK Census	**www.statistics.gov.uk/census2001**
● Population Reference Bureau Pop Net	**www.popnet.org**
● Socioeconomic Data and Applications Center	**sedac.ciesin.columbia.edu**

World Urbanization and Cities

The world is becoming increasingly urban but the level of urbanization varies greatly between and within continents. At the beginning of the twentieth century only fourteen per cent of the world's population was urban and by 1950 this had increased to thirty per cent. In the more developed regions and in Latin America and the Caribbean seventy per cent of the population is urban while in Africa and Asia the figure is less than one third. In recent decades urban growth has increased rapidly to nearly fifty per cent and there are now 387 cities with over 1 000 000 inhabitants. It is in the developing regions that the most rapid increases are taking place and it is expected that by 2030 over half of urban dwellers worldwide will live in Asia. Migration from the countryside to the city in the search for better job opportunities is the main factor in urban growth.

World Statistics: see pages 154–160

Facts

- Cities occupy less than 2% of the earth's land surface but house almost half of the human population

- Urban growth rates in Africa are the highest in the world

- Antarctica is uninhabited and most settlements in the Arctic regions have less than 5 000 inhabitants

- India has 32 cities with over one million inhabitants; by 2015 there will be 50

- London was the first city to reach a population of over 5 million

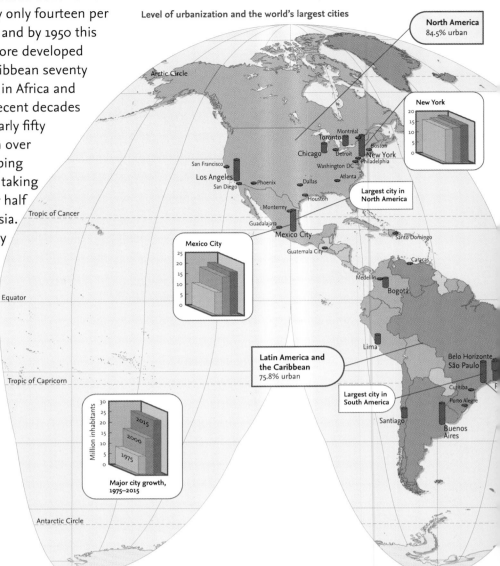

Level of urbanization and the world's largest cities

North America 84.5% urban

New York

Largest city in North America

Mexico City

Latin America and the Caribbean 75.8% urban

Largest city in South America

Major city growth, 1975–2015

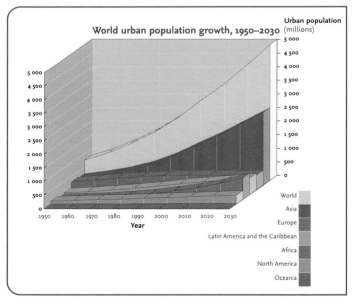

World urban population growth, 1950–2030

Urban population (millions)

World
Asia
Europe
Latin America and the Caribbean
Africa
North America
Oceania

Characteristic high-rise development and densely packed low-rise buildings in Tōkyō, the world's largest city.

Internet Links

United Nations Population Division	www.un.org/esa/population/unpop.htm
United Nations World Urbanization Prospects	www.un.org/esa/population/publications/wup2003/2003WUP.htm
United Nations Population Information Network	www.un.org/popin
The World Bank - Urban Development	www.worldbank.org/urban/
City Populations	www.citypopulation.de

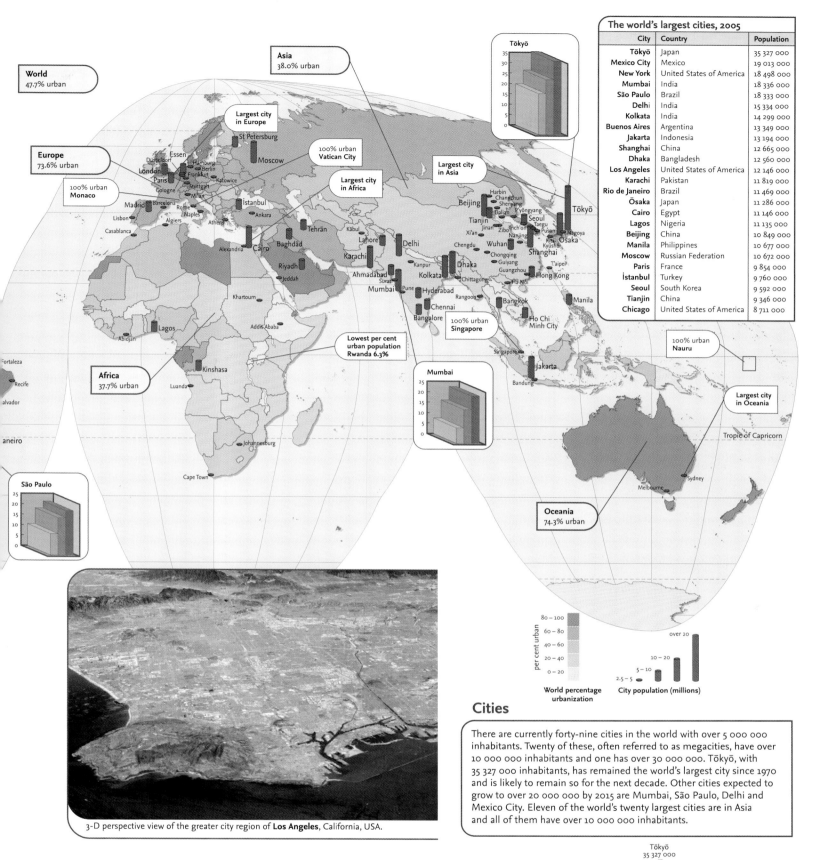

World
47.7% urban

Europe
73.6% urban

100% urban
Monaco

Africa
37.7% urban

Asia
38.0% urban

Largest city
in Europe

100% urban
Vatican City

Largest city
in Asia

Largest city
in Africa

Lowest per cent
urban population
Rwanda 6.3%

100% urban
Singapore

100% urban
Nauru

Largest city
in Oceania

Oceania
74.3% urban

Tōkyō

Mumbai

São Paulo

Tropic of Capricorn

The world's largest cities, 2005

City	Country	Population
Tōkyō	Japan	35 327 000
Mexico City	Mexico	19 013 000
New York	United States of America	18 498 000
Mumbai	India	18 336 000
São Paulo	Brazil	18 333 000
Delhi	India	15 334 000
Kolkata	India	14 299 000
Buenos Aires	Argentina	13 349 000
Jakarta	Indonesia	13 194 000
Shanghai	China	12 665 000
Dhaka	Bangladesh	12 560 000
Los Angeles	United States of America	12 146 000
Karachi	Pakistan	11 819 000
Rio de Janeiro	Brazil	11 469 000
Ōsaka	Japan	11 286 000
Cairo	Egypt	11 146 000
Lagos	Nigeria	11 135 000
Beijing	China	10 849 000
Manila	Philippines	10 677 000
Moscow	Russian Federation	10 672 000
Paris	France	9 854 000
İstanbul	Turkey	9 760 000
Seoul	South Korea	9 592 000
Tianjin	China	9 346 000
Chicago	United States of America	8 711 000

per cent urban

80 – 100	
60 – 80	
40 – 60	
20 – 40	
0 – 20	

**World percentage
urbanization**

City population (millions)

over 20
10 – 20
5 – 10
2.5 – 5

3-D perspective view of the greater city region of **Los Angeles**, California, USA.

Cities

There are currently forty-nine cities in the world with over 5 000 000
inhabitants. Twenty of these, often referred to as megacities, have over
10 000 000 inhabitants and one has over 30 000 000. Tōkyō, with
35 327 000 inhabitants, has remained the world's largest city since 1970
and is likely to remain so for the next decade. Other cities expected to
grow to over 20 000 000 by 2015 are Mumbai, São Paulo, Delhi and
Mexico City. Eleven of the world's twenty largest cities are in Asia
and all of them have over 10 000 000 inhabitants.

Major cities by continent

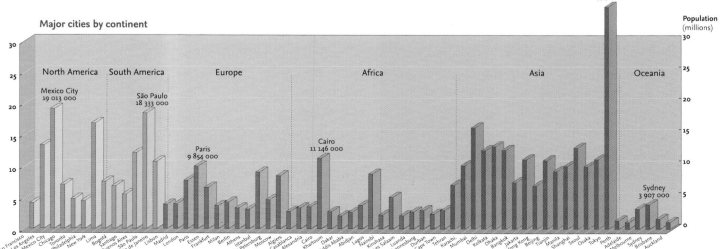

North America   South America   Europe   Africa   Asia   Oceania

Tōkyō
35 327 000

Population
(millions)

Mexico City
19 013 000

São Paulo
18 333 000

Paris
9 854 000

Cairo
11 146 000

Sydney
3 907 000

Increased availability and ownership of telecommunications equipment since the beginning of the 1970s has aided the globalization of the world economy. Over half of the world's fixed telephone lines have been installed since the mid-1980s and the majority of the world's internet hosts have come on line since 1997. There are now over one billion fixed telephone lines in the world. The number of mobile cellular subscribers has grown dramatically from sixteen million in 1991 to well over one billion today.

The internet is the fastest growing communications network of all time. It is relatively cheap and now links over 140 million host computers globally. Its growth has resulted in the emergence of hundreds of Internet Service Providers (ISPs) and internet traffic is now doubling every six months. In 1993 the number of internet users was estimated to be just under ten million, there are now over half a billion.

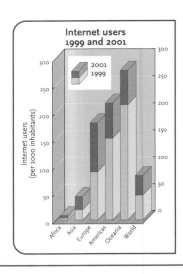

Internet users 1999 and 2001

Internet Links	
● OECD Information and Communication Technologies	**www.oecd.org**
● Telegeography Inc.	**www.telegeography.com**
● International Telecommunication Union	**www.itu.int**

Internet users per 1 000 inhabitants

- over 200
- 150 – 200
- 100 – 149
- 10 – 99
- 0 – 9
- no data

Major interregional internet routes

- 0.0 – 0.9
- 1.0 – 4.9
- 5.0 – 24.9
- 25.0 – 125.0

○ London

Internet hub cities, 2001

Internet users and major Internet routes

A visualization of **global internet traffic**. Each line represents the path of a data probe sent to specific internet locations.

The Internet

The Internet is a global network of millions of computers around the world, all capable of being connected to each other. Internet Service Providers (ISPs) provide access via 'host' computers, of which there are now over 140 million. It has become a vital means of communication and data transfer for businesses, governments and financial and academic institutions, with a steadily increasing proportion of business transactions being carried out on-line.

Top 20 Internet Service Providers (ISPs)

Internet Service	Web Address	Subscribers (000s)
AOL (USA)	www.aol.com	20 500
T-Online (Germany)	www.t-online.de	4 151
Nifty-Serve (Japan)	www.nifty.com	3 500
EarthLink (USA)	www.earthlink.com	3 122
Biglobe (Japan)	www.biglobe.ne.jp	2 720
MSN (USA)	www.msn.com	2 700
Chollian (South Korea)	www.chollian.net	2 000
Tin.it (Italy)	www.tin.it	1 990
Freeserve (UK)	www.freeserve.com	1 575
AT&T WorldNet (USA)	www.att.net	1 500
Prodigy (USA)	www.prodigy.com	1 502
NetZero (USA)	www.netzero.com	1 450
Terra Networks (Spain)	www.terra.es	1 317
HiNet (Taiwan-China)	www.hinet.net	1 200
Wanadoo (France)	www.wanadoo.fr	1 124
AltaVista	www.microav.com	750
Freei (USA)	www.freei.com	750
SBC Internet Services	www.sbc.com	720
Telia Internet (Sweden)	www.telia.se	613
Netvigator (Hongkong SAR)	www.netvigator.com	561

Satellite communications

International telecommunications use either fibre-optic cables or satellites as transmission media. Although cables carry the vast majority of traffic around the world, communications satellites are important for person-to-person communication, including cellular telephones, and for broadcasting. The positions of communications satellites are critical to their use, and reflect the demand for such communications in each part of the world. Such satellites are placed in 'geostationary' orbit 36 000 km above the equator. This means that they move at the same speed as the earth and remain fixed above a single point on the earth's surface.

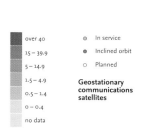

Geostationary communications satellites

- over 40
- 15 – 39.9
- 5 – 14.9
- 1.5 – 4.9
- 0.5 – 1.4
- 0 – 0.4
- no data

⊙ In service
● Inclined orbit
○ Planned

Cellular mobile subscribers per 100 inhabitants

Facts

- Luxembourg has the world's highest density of telephone lines per person with more telephones than Bangladesh – a country with more than 300 times as many people.

- Fibre-optic cables can now carry approximately 20 million simultaneous telephone calls

- The first transatlantic telegraph cable came into operation in 1858

- The internet is the fastest growing communications network of all time and now has over 140 million host computers

- Sputnik, the world's first artificial satellite, was launched in 1957

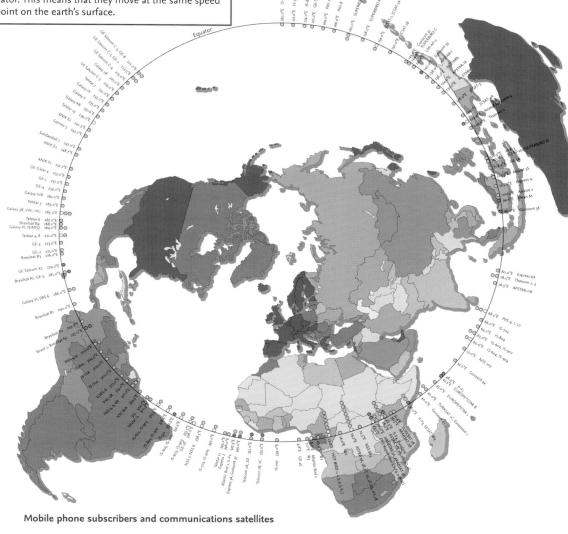

Mobile phone subscribers and communications satellites

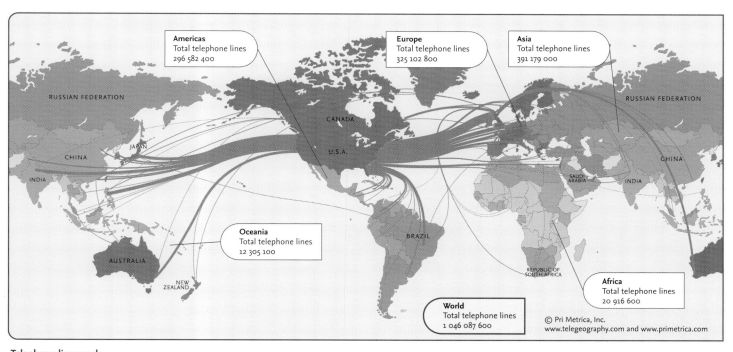

Americas
Total telephone lines
296 582 400

Europe
Total telephone lines
325 102 800

Asia
Total telephone lines
391 179 000

Oceania
Total telephone lines
12 305 100

Africa
Total telephone lines
20 916 600

World
Total telephone lines
1 046 087 600

© Pri Metrica, Inc.
www.telegeography.com and www.primetrica.com

Telephone lines and telecommunications traffic

- over 50.0
- 35.0 – 50.0
- 15.0 – 34.9
- 10.0 – 14.9
- 5.0 – 9.9
- 1.0 – 4.9
- 0 – 0.9
- no data

Telephone lines per 100 inhabitants

5 000   2 500   1 000   100

Million minutes of telecommunications traffic (mMiTTs)

Traffic flows

Countries are often judged on their level of economic development, but national and personal wealth are not the only measures of a country's status. Numerous other indicators can give a better picture of the overall level of development and standard of living achieved by a country. The availability and standard of health services, levels of educational provision and attainment, levels of nutrition, water supply, life expectancy and mortality rates are just some of the factors which can be measured to assess and compare countries.

While nations strive to improve their economies, and hopefully also to improve the standard of living of their citizens, the measurement of such indicators often exposes great discrepancies between the countries of the 'developed' world and those of the 'less developed' world. They also show great variations within continents and regions and at the same time can hide great inequalities within countries.

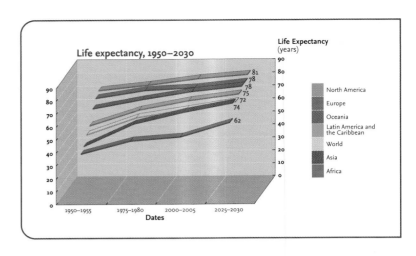

Life expectancy, 1950–2030

Life Expectancy (years)

North America
Europe
Oceania
Latin America and the Caribbean
World
Asia
Africa

World Statistics: see pages 154–160

Internet Links

● United Nation Development Programme	**www.undp.org**
● World Health Organization	**www.who.int**
● United Nations Statistics Division	**unstats.un.org**
● United Nations Millennium Development Goals	**millenniumindicators.un.org**

UN Millennium Development Goals
From the Millennium Declaration, 2000

Goal 1	Eradicate extreme poverty and hunger
Goal 2	Achieve universal primary education
Goal 3	Promote gender equality and empower women
Goal 4	Reduce child mortality
Goal 5	Improve maternal health
Goal 6	Combat HIV/AIDS, malaria and other diseases
Goal 7	Ensure environmental sustainability
Goal 8	Develop a global partnership for development

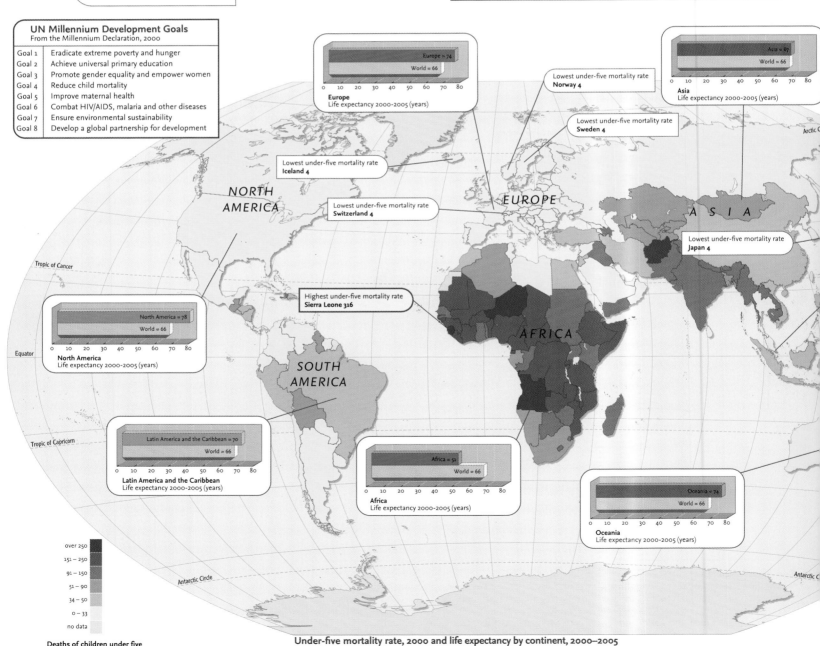

Europe = 74
World = 66

Europe
Life expectancy 2000-2005 (years)

Asia = 67
World = 66

Asia
Life expectancy 2000-2005 (years)

Lowest under-five mortality rate
Norway 4

Lowest under-five mortality rate
Sweden 4

Lowest under-five mortality rate
Iceland 4

Lowest under-five mortality rate
Switzerland 4

Lowest under-five mortality rate
Japan 4

NORTH AMERICA

EUROPE

ASIA

Highest under-five mortality rate
Sierra Leone 316

AFRICA

North America = 78
World = 66

North America
Life expectancy 2000-2005 (years)

SOUTH AMERICA

Latin America and the Caribbean = 70
World = 66

Latin America and the Caribbean
Life expectancy 2000-2005 (years)

Africa = 51
World = 66

Africa
Life expectancy 2000-2005 (years)

Oceania = 74
World = 66

Oceania
Life expectancy 2000-2005 (years)

over 250
151 – 250
91 – 150
51 – 90
34 – 50
0 – 33
no data

Deaths of children under five per 1 000 live births

Under-five mortality rate, 2000 and life expectancy by continent, 2000–2005

Outdoor education at a school in Bahia state, northeast Brazil.

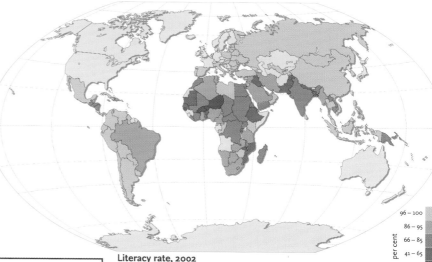
Literacy rate, 2002
Percentage of population aged 15–24 with
at least a basic ability to read and write

per cent
96 – 100
86 – 95
66 – 85
41 – 65
0 – 40
no data

Measuring development

Measuring the extent to which a country is 'developed' is difficult, and although there have been many attempts to standardize techniques there is no universally accepted method. One commonly used measure is the Human Development Index (HDI), which is based on a combination of statistics relating to life expectancy, education (literacy and school enrolment) and wealth (Gross Domestic Product – GDP).

At the Millennium Summit in September 2000, the United Nations identified eight Millennium Development Goals (MDGs) which aim to combat poverty, hunger, disease, illiteracy, environmental degradation and discrimination against women. Forty eight indicators have been identified which will measure the progress each country is making towards achieving these goals.

Doctors per 100 000 people
Number of trained doctors per 100 000 people

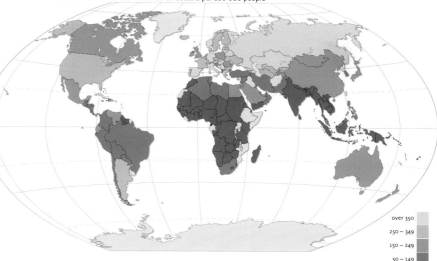

	over 350
	250 – 349
	150 – 249
	50 – 149
	0 – 49
	no data

Facts

● Of the 10 countries with under-5 mortality rates of more than 200, 9 are in Africa

● Many western countries believe they have achieved satisfactory levels of education and no longer closely monitor levels of literacy

● Children born in Nepal have only a 12% chance of their birth being attended by trained health personnel, for most European countries the figure is 100%

● The illiteracy rate among young women in the Middle East and north Africa is almost twice the rate for young men.

Lowest under-five mortality rate
Singapore 4

Tropic of Cancer

Equator

Tropic of Capricorn

OCEANIA

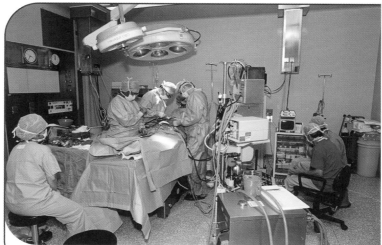
High class **health care facilities** such as these are not available in many parts of the world.

Health and education

Perhaps the most important indicators used for measuring the level of national development are those relating to health and education. Both of these key areas are vital to the future development of a country, and if there are concerns in standards attained in either (or worse, in both) of these, then they may indicate fundamental problems within the country concerned. The ability to read and write (literacy) is seen as vital in educating people and encouraging development, while easy access to appropriate health services and specialists is an important requirement in maintaining satisfactory levels of basic health.

Human Development Index (HDI), 2002	
Top 10	
Rank	**Country**
1	Norway
2	Sweden
3	Canada
4	Belgium
5	Australia
6	USA
7	Iceland
8	Netherlands
9	Japan
10	Finland
Bottom 10	
Rank	**Country**
164	Mali
165	Central African Republic
166	Chad
167	Guinea-Bissau
168	Ethiopia
169	Burkina
170	Mozambique
171	Burundi
172	Niger
173	Sierra Leone

The globalization of the economy is making the world appear a smaller place. However, this shrinkage is an uneven process. Countries are being included in and excluded from the global economy to differing degrees. The wealthy countries of the developed world, with their market-led economies, access to productive new technologies and international markets, dominate the world economic system. Great inequalities exist between and also within countries. There may also be discrepancies between social groups within countries due to gender and ethnic divisions. Differences between countries are evident by looking at overall wealth on a national and individual level.

World Statistics: see pages 154–160

The City, London, the world's largest financial centre.

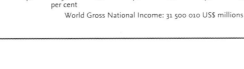

Regional distribution of wealth

- High-income economies
- Latin America and the Caribbean
- East Asia and Pacific
- Europe and Central Asia
- South Asia
- Middle East and North Africa
- Sub-Saharan Africa

per cent

World Gross National Income: 31 500 010 US$ millions

Facts

- The City, one of 33 London boroughs, is the world's largest financial centre and contains Europe's biggest stock market

- Half the world's population earns only 5% of the world's wealth

- During the second half of the 20th century rich countries gave over US$1 trillion in aid

- For every £1 in grant aid to developing countries, more than £13 comes back in debt repayments

- On average, The World Bank distributes US$30 billion each year between 100 countries

Personal wealth

A poverty line set at $1 a day has been accepted as the working definition of extreme poverty in low-income countries. It is estimated that a total of 1.2 billion people live below that poverty line. This indicator has also been adopted by the United Nations in relation to their Millennium Development Goals. The United Nations goal is to halve the proportion of people living on less than $1 a day in 1990 to 14.5 per cent by 2015. Today, over 80 per cent of the total population of Ethiopia, Uganda and Nicaragua live on less than this amount.

Percentage of population living on less than $1 a day

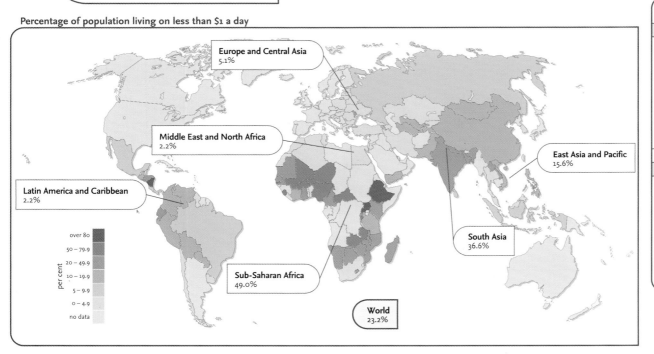

Europe and Central Asia
5.1%

Middle East and North Africa
2.2%

East Asia and Pacific
15.6%

Latin America and Caribbean
2.2%

South Asia
36.6%

Sub-Saharan Africa
49.0%

World
23.2%

per cent
- over 80
- 50 – 79.9
- 20 – 49.9
- 10 – 19.9
- 5 – 9.9
- 0 – 4.9
- no data

Gross National Income per capita

Highest

Rank	Country	US$ 2001
1	Luxembourg	41 770
2	Switzerland	36 970
3	Japan	35 990
4	Norway	35 530
5	United States	34 870
6	Denmark	31 090
7	Iceland	28 880
8	Sweden	25 400
9	United Kingdom	24 230
10	Netherlands	24 040

Lowest

Rank	Country	US$ 2001
150	Mozambique	210
151	Chad	200
152	Eritrea	190
153	Tajikistan	170
154	Malawi	170
155	Niger	170
156	Guinea-Bissau	160
157	Sierra Leone	140
158	Burundi	100
159	Ethiopia	100

Key economic indicators by region

	World	High-income economies	East Asia and Pacific	Europe and Central Asia	Latin America and The Caribbean	Middle East and North Africa	South Asia	Sub-Saharan Africa
Gross National Income (US$ millions)	31 500 010	25 506 410	1 649 435	930 455	1 861 820	601 270	615 596	317 045
Gross National Income per capita (US$)	5 170	27 680	1 060	2 010	3 670	2 090	440	470
Gross Domestic Product (US$ millions)	31 283 840	25 103 680	1 664 211	986 652	1 943 350	no data	615 307	315 269
Gross Domestic Product growth (annual %, US$ millions)	1.41	1.07	5.49	2.50	0.42	no data	4.39	3.00
Aid per capita received (US$)	9.64	1.99	4.68	22.91	9.67	15.63	3.13	20.42
External debt, total (US$ millions)	no data	no data	632 953	499 344	774 418	203 785	164 375	215 794
Official development assistance and official aid received (US$ millions)	58 369	1 887	8 463	10 867	4 987	4 609	4 241	13 453
Total debt service (US$ millions)	no data	no data	92 730	74 902	179 221	24 921	14 517	12 342

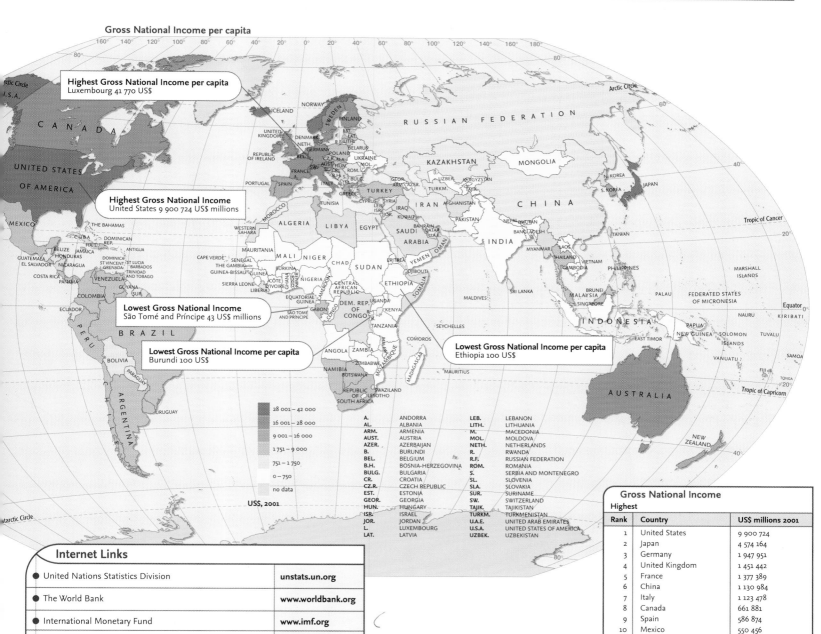

Gross National Income per capita

Highest Gross National Income per capita
Luxembourg 41 770 US$

Highest Gross National Income
United States 9 900 724 US$ millions

Lowest Gross National Income
São Tomé and Príncipe 43 US$ millions

Lowest Gross National Income per capita
Burundi 100 US$

Lowest Gross National Income per capita
Ethiopia 100 US$

28 001 – 42 000
16 001 – 28 000
9 001 – 16 000
1 751 – 9 000
751 – 1 750
0 – 750
no data

US$, 2001

A.	ANDORRA	LEB.	LEBANON
AL.	ALBANIA	LITH.	LITHUANIA
ARM.	ARMENIA	M.	MACEDONIA
AUST.	AUSTRIA	MOL.	MOLDOVA
AZER.	AZERBAIJAN	NETH.	NETHERLANDS
B.	BURUNDI	R.	RWANDA
BEL.	BELGIUM	R.F.	RUSSIAN FEDERATION
B.H.	BOSNIA-HERZEGOVINA	ROM.	ROMANIA
BULG.	BULGARIA	S.	SERBIA AND MONTENEGRO
CR.	CROATIA	SL.	SLOVENIA
CZ.R.	CZECH REPUBLIC	SLA.	SLOVAKIA
EST.	ESTONIA	SUR.	SURINAME
GEOR.	GEORGIA	SW.	SWITZERLAND
HUN.	HUNGARY	TAJIK.	TAJIKISTAN
ISR.	ISRAEL	TURKM.	TURKMENISTAN
JOR.	JORDAN	U.A.E.	UNITED ARAB EMIRATES
L.	LUXEMBOURG	U.S.A.	UNITED STATES OF AMERICA
LAT.	LATVIA	UZBEK.	UZBEKISTAN

Internet Links

●	United Nations Statistics Division	unstats.un.org
●	The World Bank	www.worldbank.org
●	International Monetary Fund	www.imf.org
●	Organisation for Economic Co-operation and Development	www.oecd.org

Gross National Income

Highest

Rank	Country	US$ millions 2001
1	United States	9 900 724
2	Japan	4 574 164
3	Germany	1 947 951
4	United Kingdom	1 451 442
5	France	1 377 389
6	China	1 130 984
7	Italy	1 123 478
8	Canada	661 881
9	Spain	586 874
10	Mexico	550 456

Lowest

Rank	Country	US$ millions 2001
150	Solomon Islands	253
151	Dominica	224
152	Comoros	217
153	Vanuatu	212
154	Guinea-bissau	202
155	Tonga	154
156	Palau	132
157	Marshall Islands	115
158	Kiribati	77
159	São Tomé and Príncipe	43

The world's biggest companies

Rank	Name	Sales (US$ millions)
1	Wal-Mart Stores	256 330
2	BP	232 570
3	ExxonMobil	222 880
4	General Motors	185 520
5	Ford Motor	164 200
6	DaimlerChrysler	157 130
7	Toyota Motor	135 820
8	General Electric	134 190
9	Royal Dutch/Shell Group	133 500
10	Total	131 640

Measuring wealth

One of the indicators used to determine a country's wealth is its Gross National Income (GNI). This gives a broad measure of an economy's performance. This is the value of the final output of goods and services produced by a country plus net income from non-resident sources. The total GNI is divided by the country's population to give an average figure of the GNI per capita. From this it is evident that the developed countries dominate the world economy with the United States having the highest GNI. China is a growing world economic player with the sixth highest GNI figure and a relatively high GNI per capita (US$890) in proportion to its huge population.

Rural homesteads, **Sudan** – most of the world's poorest countries are in Africa.

Geo-political issues shape the countries of the world and the current political situation in many parts of the world reflects a long history of armed conflict. Since the Second World War conflicts have been fairly localized, but there are numerous 'flash points' where factors such as territorial claims, ideology, religion, ethnicity and access to resources can cause friction between two or more countries. Such factors also lie behind the recent growth in global terrorism.

Military expenditure can take up a disproportionate amount of a country's wealth – Eritrea, with a Gross National Income (GNI) per capita of only US$190 spends over twenty seven per cent of its total GNI on military activity. There is an encouraging trend towards wider international cooperation, mainly through the United Nations (UN) and the North Atlantic Treaty Organization (NATO), to prevent escalation of conflicts and on peacekeeping missions.

Facts

- There have been nearly 70 civil or internal wars throughout the world since 1945
- The Iran-Iraq war in the 1980s is estimated to have cost half a million lives
- The UN are currently involved in 15 peacekeeping operations
- It is estimated that there are nearly 20 million refugees throughout the world
- Over 1 600 UN peacekeepers have been killed since 1948

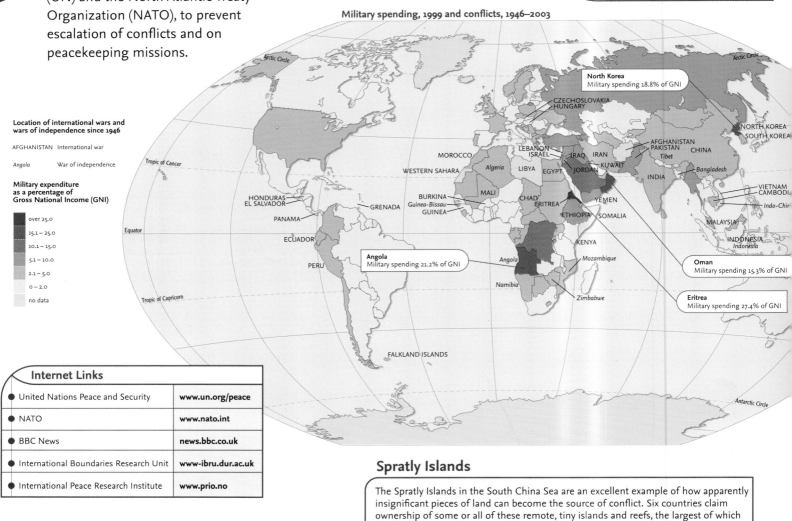

Military spending, 1999 and conflicts, 1946–2003

Location of international wars and wars of independence since 1946

AFGHANISTAN   International war

Angola   War of independence

Military expenditure as a percentage of Gross National Income (GNI)

- over 25.0
- 15.1 – 25.0
- 10.1 – 15.0
- 5.1 – 10.0
- 2.1 – 5.0
- 0 – 2.0
- no data

North Korea Military spending 18.8% of GNI

Angola Military spending 21.2% of GNI

Oman Military spending 15.3% of GNI

Eritrea Military spending 27.4% of GNI

Internet Links

United Nations Peace and Security	www.un.org/peace
NATO	www.nato.int
BBC News	news.bbc.co.uk
International Boundaries Research Unit	www-ibru.dur.ac.uk
International Peace Research Institute	www.prio.no

Spratly Islands

The Spratly Islands in the South China Sea are an excellent example of how apparently insignificant pieces of land can become the source of conflict. Six countries claim ownership of some or all of these remote, tiny islands and reefs, the largest of which covers less than half a square kilometre. The islands are strategically important – approximately a quarter of all the world's shipping trade passes through the area – and ownership of the group would mean access to 250 000 square kilometres of valuable fishing grounds and sea bed believed to be rich in oil and gas reserves. Five of the claimant countries have occupied individual islands to endorse their claims, although there appears little prospect of international agreement on ownership.

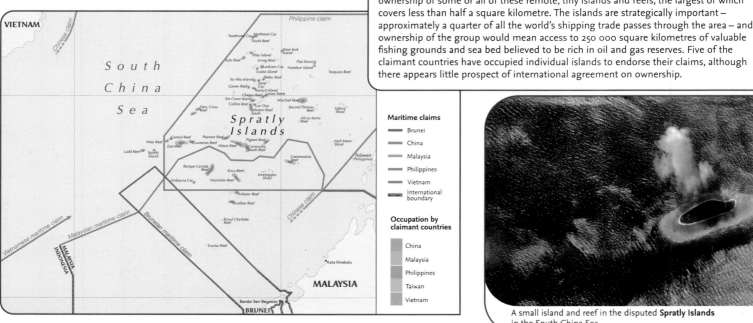

Maritime claims
- Brunei
- China
- Malaysia
- Philippines
- Vietnam
- International boundary

Occupation by claimant countries
- China
- Malaysia
- Philippines
- Taiwan
- Vietnam

A small island and reef in the disputed **Spratly Islands** in the South China Sea.

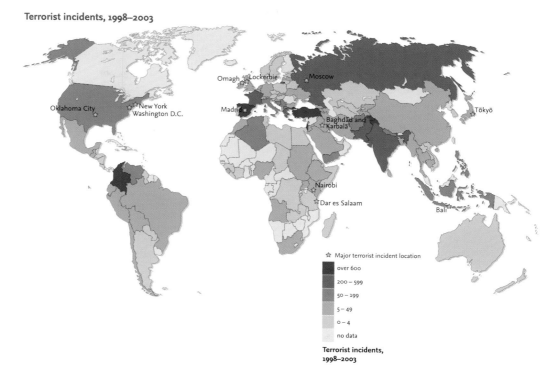

Terrorist incidents, 1998–2003

☆ Major terrorist incident location

■	over 600
■	200 – 599
■	50 – 199
■	5 – 49
■	0 – 4
☐	no data

Terrorist incidents, 1998–2003

Investigators inspect wreckage outside the Neve Shalom synagogue, **Istanbul, Turkey** after car bombs killed 20 people and injured more than 250.

Global terrorism

Terrorism is defined by the United Nations as "All criminal acts directed against a State and intended or calculated to create a state of terror in the minds of particular persons or a group of persons or the general public". The world has become increasingly concerned about terrorism and the possibility that terrorists could acquire and use nuclear, chemical and biological weapons. One common form of terrorist attack is suicide bombing. Pioneered by Tamil secessionists in Sri Lanka, it has been widely used by Palestinian groups fighting against Israeli occupation of the West Bank and Gaza. In recent years it has also been used by the Al Qaida network in its attacks on the western world.

Major terrorist incidents

Date	Location	Summary	Killed	Injured
December 1988	Lockerbie, Scotland	Airline bombing	270	5
March 1995	Tōkyō, Japan	Sarin gas attack on subway	12	5700
April 1995	Oklahoma City, USA	Bomb in the Federal building	168	over 500
August 1998	Nairobi, Kenya and Dar es Salaam, Tanzania	US Embassy bombings	257	over 4000
August 1998	Omagh, Northern Ireland	Town centre bombing	29	330
September 2001	New York and Washington D.C., USA	Airline hijacking and crashing	2752	4300
October 2002	Bali, Indonesia	Car bomb outside nightclub	202	300
October 2002	Moscow, Russian Federation	Theatre siege	170	over 600
March 2004	Bāghdad and Karbalā', Iraq	Suicide bombing of pilgrims	181	over 400
March 2004	Madrid, Spain	Train bombings	191	1800

Middle East politics

Changing boundaries in Israel/Palestine, 1922–2003

West Bank
Population
97% Palestinian Arab
610 000 refugees

West Bank
Security
18% of land under Palestinian control
23% of land under Palestinian civil control and joint security control
59% of land under Israeli control

Gaza
Population
98% Palestinian Arab
865 000 refugees

Gaza
Security
60% of land under Palestinian control
40% of land under Israeli control or settlement

Security fence along the **Egypt/Gaza** border near Rafiah.

The Middle East

The on-going Israeli/Palestinian conflict reflects decades of unrest in the region of Palestine which, after the First World War, was placed under British control. In 1947 the United Nations (UN) proposed a partitioning into separate Jewish and Arab states – a plan which was rejected by the Palestinians and by the Arab states in the region. When Britain withdrew in 1948, Israel declared its independence. This led to an Arab-Israeli war which left Israel with more land than originally proposed under the UN plan. Hundreds of thousands of Palestinians were forced out of their homeland and became refugees, mainly in Jordan and Lebanon. The 6-Day War in 1967 resulted in Israel taking possession of Sinai and Gaza from Egypt, West Bank from Jordan, and the Golan Heights from Syria. These territories (except Sinai which was subsequently returned to Egypt) remain occupied by Israel – the main reason for the Palestinian uprising or 'Intifada' against Israel. The situation remains complex, with poor prospects for peace and for mutually acceptable independent states being established.

—·—·—	International boundary
—×—×—	Disputed International boundary
··········	Ceasefire line
———	British Mandate Boundary 1922–1948
———	Israel Boundary 1948
▨	Land occupied by Israel 1967
Jenin ☐	Main Palestinian towns

With the process of globalization has come an increased awareness of, and direct interest in, issues which have global implications. Social issues can now affect large parts of the world and can impact on large sections of society. Perhaps the current issues of greatest concern are those of national security, including the problem of international terrorism (see World Conflict pages 30–31), health, crime and natural resources. The three issues highlighted here reflect this and are of immediate concern.

The international drugs trade, and the crimes commonly associated with it, can impact society and individuals in devastating ways; scarcity of water resources and lack of access to safe drinking water can have major economic implications and causes severe health problems; and the AIDS epidemic is having disastrous consequences in large parts of the world, particularly in sub-Saharan Africa.

Internet Links	
● UNESCO	**www.unesco.org**
● UNAIDS	**www.unaids.org**
● WaterAid	**www.wateraid.org.uk**
● World Health Organization	**www.who.int**
● United Nations Office on Drugs and Crime	**www.unodc.org**

The drugs trade

The international trade in illegal drugs is estimated to be worth over US$400 billion. While it may be a lucrative business for the criminals involved, the effects of the drugs on individual users and on society in general can be devastating. Patterns of drug production and abuse vary, but there are clear centres for the production of the most harmful drugs – the opiates (opium, morphine and heroin) and cocaine. The 'Golden Triangle' of Laos, Myanmar and Thailand, and western South America respectively are the main producing areas for these drugs. Significant efforts are expended to counter the drugs trade, and there have been signs recently of downward trends in the production of heroin and cocaine.

Soldiers in **Colombia**, a major producer of cocaine, destroy an illegal drug processing laboratory.

The international drugs trade
Main producers and trafficking routes for
opiates (opium, morphine, heroin) and cocaine

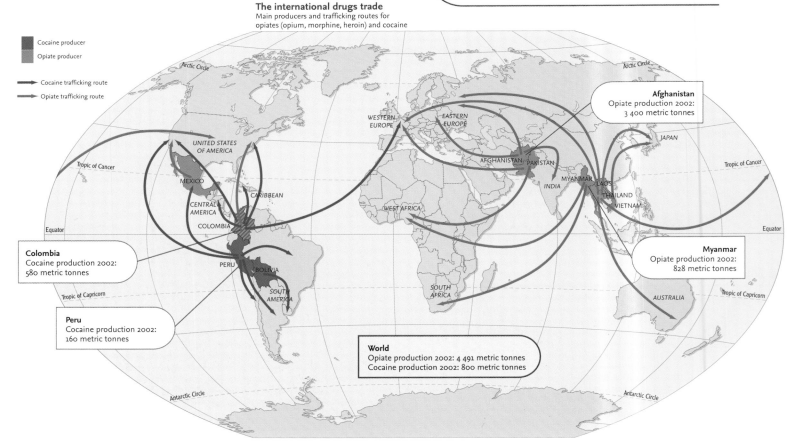

Cocaine producer
Opiate producer

→ Cocaine trafficking route
→ Opiate trafficking route

Afghanistan
Opiate production 2002:
3 400 metric tonnes

Colombia
Cocaine production 2002:
580 metric tonnes

Peru
Cocaine production 2002:
160 metric tonnes

Myanmar
Opiate production 2002:
828 metric tonnes

World
Opiate production 2002: 4 491 metric tonnes
Cocaine production 2002: 800 metric tonnes

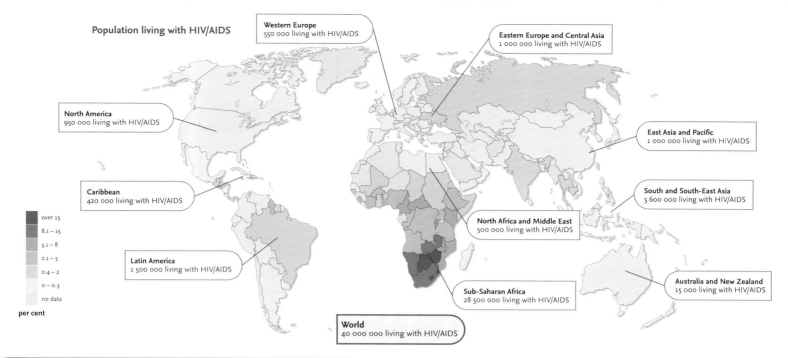

Population living with HIV/AIDS

Western Europe
550 000 living with HIV/AIDS

Eastern Europe and Central Asia
1 000 000 living with HIV/AIDS

North America
950 000 living with HIV/AIDS

East Asia and Pacific
1 000 000 living with HIV/AIDS

Caribbean
420 000 living with HIV/AIDS

South and South-East Asia
5 600 000 living with HIV/AIDS

North Africa and Middle East
500 000 living with HIV/AIDS

Latin America
1 500 000 living with HIV/AIDS

Sub-Saharan Africa
28 500 000 living with HIV/AIDS

Australia and New Zealand
15 000 living with HIV/AIDS

World
40 000 000 living with HIV/AIDS

over 15
8.1 – 15
5.1 – 8
2.1 – 5
0.4 – 2
0 – 0.3
no data

per cent

AIDS poster in **Zambia**, one of the countries worst affected by the AIDS epidemic.

Aids epidemic

With over 40 million people living with HIV/AIDS (Human Immunodeficiency Virus/Acquired Immune Deficiency Syndrome) and more than 20 million deaths from the disease, the AIDS epidemic poses one of the biggest threats to public health. The UNAIDS project estimated that 5 million people were newly infected in 2003 and that 3 million AIDS sufferers died. Estimates into the future look bleak, especially for poorer developing countries where an additional 45 million people are likely to become infected by 2010. The human cost is huge. As well as the death count itself, more than 11 million African children, half of whom are between the ages of 10 and 14, have been orphaned as a result of the disease.

Access to safe water, 2000
Percentage of population with access to improved drinking water

91 – 100
66 – 90
51 – 65
31 – 50
0 – 30
no data

per cent

Facts

- The majority of people infected with **HIV**, if not treated, develop signs of AIDS within 8 to 10 years

- One in five developing countries will face water shortages by 2030

- Over 5 million people die each year from water-related diseases such as cholera and dysentery

- Estimates suggest that 200 million people consume illegal drugs around the world

Water resources

Water is one of the fundamental requirements of life, and yet in some countries it is becoming more scarce due to increasing population and climate change. Safe drinking water, basic hygiene, health education and sanitation facilities are often virtually nonexistent for impoverished people in developing countries throughout the world. WHO/UNICEF estimate that the combination of these conditions results in 6 000 deaths every day, most of these being children. Currently over 1.2 billion people drink unclean water and expose themselves to serious health risks, while political struggles over diminishing water resources are increasingly likely to be the cause of international conflict.

Domestic use of **untreated water** in Kathmandu, Nepal.

Many parts of the world are undergoing significant changes which can have widespread and long-lasting effects. The principal causes of change are environmental – particularly climatic – factors and the influence of man. However, it is often difficult to separate these causes because man's activities can influence and exaggerate environmental change. Changes, whatever their cause, can have significant effects on the local population, on the wider region and even on a global scale. Major social, economic and environmental impacts can result from often irreversible changes – land reclamation can destroy fragile marine ecosystems, major dams and drainage schemes can affect whole drainage basins, and local communities can be changed beyond recognition through such projects.

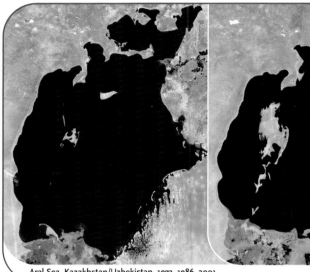

Aral Sea, Kazakhstan/Uzbekistan, 1973, 1986, 2001.

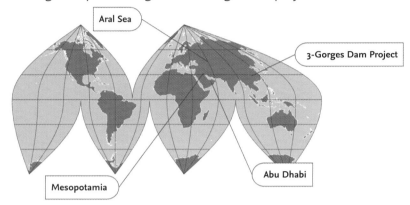

Aral Sea

3-Gorges Dam Project

Mesopotamia

Abu Dhabi

Internet Links	
● NASA Visible Earth	visibleearth.nasa.gov
● NASA Earth Observatory	earthobservatory.nasa.gov
● USGS Earthshots	earthshots.usgs.gov

Man-made change

Human activity has irreversibly changed the environment in many parts of the world. Major engineering projects and the expansion of towns and cities create completely new environments and have major social and economic impacts. The 3-Gorges Dam project in China will control the flow of the Yangtze river and generate enormous amounts of hydro-electric power. During its construction, millions of people were relocated as over 100 towns and villages were inundated by the new reservoir.

The city of Abu Dhabi, capital of the United Arab Emirates, has been built largely on land reclaimed from The Gulf. From a small fishing village it has grown, through a dramatic re-modelling of the coastline, into a major city.

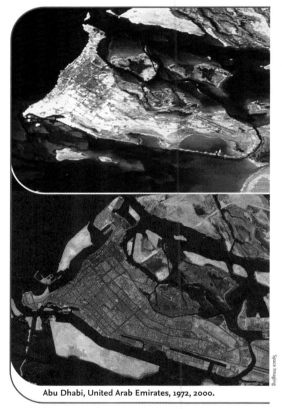

Abu Dhabi, United Arab Emirates, 1972, 2000.

Part of the **Yangtze** river, China, in the region of the 3-Gorges, before construction of the new reservoir.

The **3-Gorges Dam** under construction.

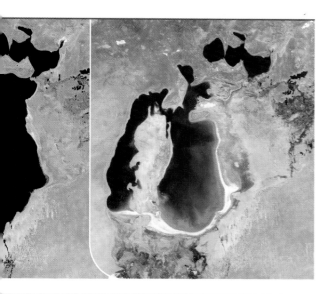

Environmental change

Water resources in certain parts of the world are becoming increasingly scarce. The Aral Sea in central Asia was once the world's fourth largest lake but it now ranks only tenth after shrinking by almost 40 000 square kilometres. This shrinkage has been due to climatic change and to the diversion, for farming purposes, of the major rivers which feed the lake. The change has had a devastating effect on the local fishing industry and has caused health problems for the local population.

The marshlands of Mesopotamia in Iraq have also undergone significant change. It is estimated that only 7 per cent of these ecologically valuable wetlands now remain after systematic drainage of the area and upstream diversion of the Tigris and Euphrates rivers.

Facts

- Earth-observing satellites can now detect land detail, and therefore changes in land cover, of less than 1 metre extent

- Over 90 000 square kilometres of precious tropical forest and wetland habitats are lost each year

- The surface level of the Dead Sea has fallen by 16 metres over the last 30 years

- Hong Kong International Airport, opened in 1998 and covering an area of over 12 square kilometres, was built almost entirely on reclaimed land

Mesopotamian marshlands, Iraq, 1973. Large areas of dense marsh vegetation show as dark red.

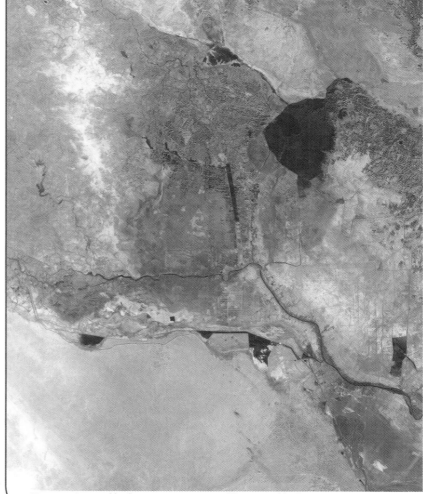

Mesopotamian marshlands, Iraq, 2000. Vast areas of former marshland now appear as grey-green areas of sparse vegetation or bare ground.

Europe, the westward extension of the Asian continent and the second smallest of the world's continents, has a remarkable variety of physical features and landscapes. The continent is bounded by mountain ranges of varying character – the highlands of Scandinavia and northwest Britain, the Pyrenees, the Alps, the Carpathian Mountains, the Caucasus and the Ural Mountains. Two of these, the Caucasus and Ural Mountains define the eastern limits of Europe, with the Black Sea and the Bosporus defining its southeastern boundary with Asia.

Across the centre of the continent stretches the North European Plain, broken by some of Europe's greatest rivers, including the Volga and the Dnieper and containing some of its largest lakes. To the south, the Mediterranean Sea divides Europe from Africa. The Mediterranean region itself has a very distinct climate and landscape.

Iceland in winter, one of Europe's largest islands.

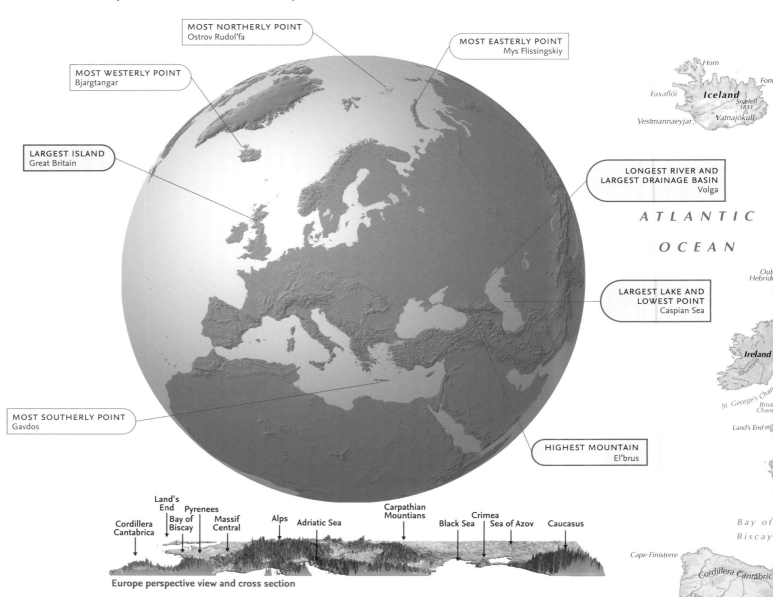

MOST NORTHERLY POINT
Ostrov Rudol'fa

MOST EASTERLY POINT
Mys Flissingskiy

MOST WESTERLY POINT
Bjargtangar

LARGEST ISLAND
Great Britain

LONGEST RIVER AND
LARGEST DRAINAGE BASIN
Volga

LARGEST LAKE AND
LOWEST POINT
Caspian Sea

MOST SOUTHERLY POINT
Gavdos

HIGHEST MOUNTAIN
El'brus

Europe perspective view and cross section

Cordillera Cantabrica · Land's End · Bay of Biscay · Pyrenees · Massif Central · Alps · Adriatic Sea · Carpathian Mountians · Black Sea · Crimea · Sea of Azov · Caucasus

Europe's greatest physical features

Highest mountain	El'brus, Russian Federation	5 642 metres	18 510 feet
Longest river	Volga, Russian Federation	3 688 km	2 292 miles
Largest lake	Caspian Sea	371 000 sq km	143 243 sq miles
Largest island	Great Britain, United Kingdom	218 476 sq km	84 354 sq miles
Largest drainage basin	Volga, Russian Federation	1 380 000 sq km	532 818 sq miles

Europe's extent

Total Land Area	9 908 599 sq km / 3 825 710 sq miles
Most northerly point	Ostrov Rudol'fa, Russian Federation
Most southerly point	Gavdos, Crete, Greece
Most westerly point	Bjargtangar, Iceland
Most easterly point	Mys Flissingskiy, Russian Federation

ATLANTIC

OCEAN

Horn
Font
Faxaflói
Iceland
Snæfell 1833
Vestmannaeyjar
Vatnajökull

Oute Hebride

Ireland
Shannon

St George's Chan
Briste Chann

Land's End

Bay of Biscay

Cape Finisterre

Cordillera Cantabric

Douro

Tagus

Iberian

Peninsula

Sierra Morena
Guadalquivir

Cabo de São Vicente

Mulhacén 3482
Sierra Nevada

Strait of Gibraltar

A F F

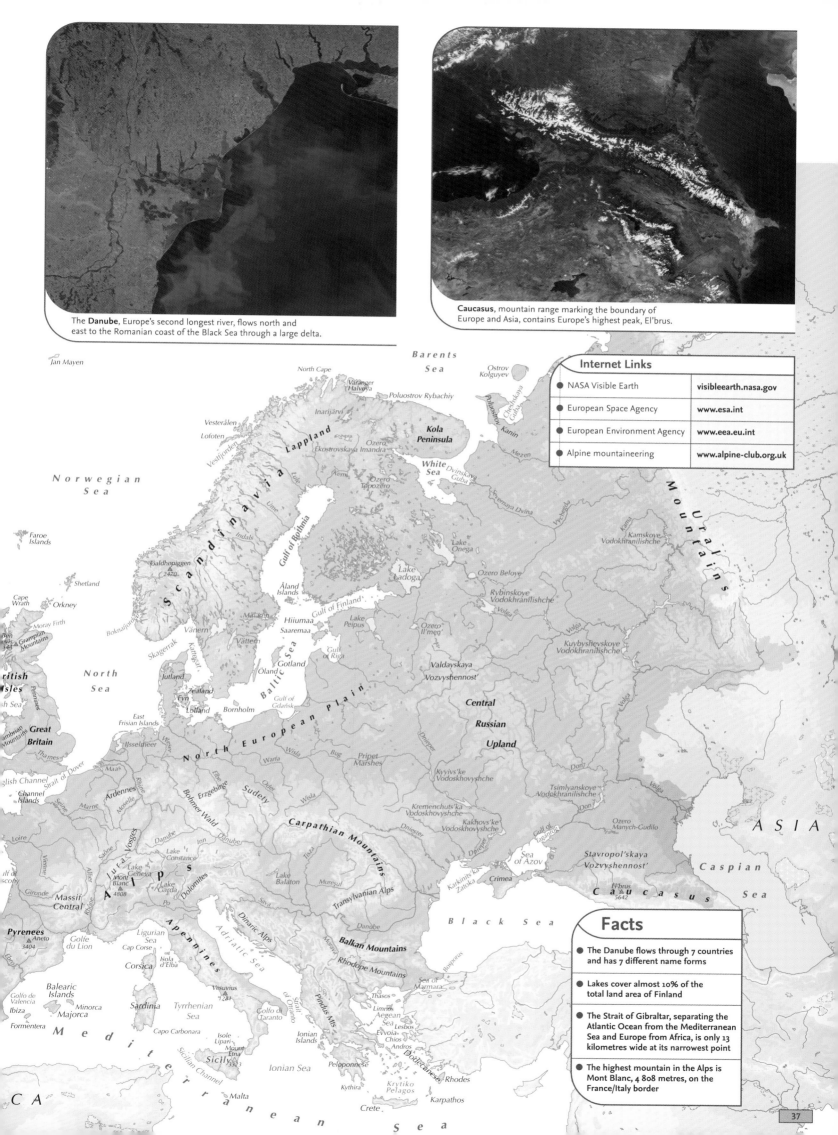

The **Danube**, Europe's second longest river, flows north and east to the Romanian coast of the Black Sea through a large delta.

Caucasus, mountain range marking the boundary of Europe and Asia, contains Europe's highest peak, El'brus.

Internet Links

● NASA Visible Earth	**visibleearth.nasa.gov**
● European Space Agency	**www.esa.int**
● European Environment Agency	**www.eea.eu.int**
● Alpine mountaineering	**www.alpine-club.org.uk**

Facts

● The Danube flows through 7 countries and has 7 different name forms

● Lakes cover almost 10% of the total land area of Finland

● The Strait of Gibraltar, separating the Atlantic Ocean from the Mediterranean Sea and Europe from Africa, is only 13 kilometres wide at its narrowest point

● The highest mountain in the Alps is Mont Blanc, 4 808 metres, on the France/Italy border

Jan Mayen

Barents Sea

North Cape

Varanger Halvoya

Poluostrov Rybachiy

Ostrov Kolguyev

Poluostrov Kanin

Chenskaya Guba

Inarijärvi

Vesterålen

Lappland

Kola Peninsula

Lofoten

Vestfjorden

Ozero Ekostrovskaya Imandra

White Sea

Dvinskaya Guba

Norwegian Sea

Ozero Topozero

Mezen

Severnaya Dvina

Vychegda

Mountains

Kama

Ural

Luleå

Kemi

Ume

Lake Onega

Kamskoye Vodokhranilishche

Faroe Islands

Galdhøpiggen 2470

Gulf of Bothnia

Lake Ladoga

Ozero Beloye

Rybinskoye Vodokhranilishche

Volga

Shetland

Åland Islands

Mälaren

Lake Onega

Kuybyshevskoye Vodokhranilishche

Cape Wrath

Orkney

Moray Firth

Indals

Gulf of Finland

Hiiumaa

Saaremaa

Lake Peipus

Ozero Il'men'

Volga

Ben Nevis 344

Grampian Mountains

Vänern

Vättern

Öland

Gulf of Riga

Valdayskaya Vozvyshennost'

Boknafjorden

Skagerrak

Kattegat

Gotland

Central

Russian

Upland

North Sea

Jutland

Fyn

Zealand

Lolland

Bornholm

Gulf of Gdańsk

Great Britain

ritish sles

Cambrian Mountains

Pennines

Thames

East Frisian Islands

Ijsselmeer

North European Plain

Wisla

Warta

Bug

Pripet Marshes

Kyyivs'ke Vodoskhovyshche

Dnieper

Don

English Channel

Strait of Dover

Channel Islands

Maas

Rhine

Ardennes

Moselle

Elbe

Oder

Wisla

Warta

Sudety

Erzgebirge

Böhmer Wald

Dniester

Kremenchuts'ka Vodoskhovyshche

Kakhovs'ke Vodoskhovyshche

Tsimlyanskoye Vodokhranilishche

Don

Volga

Loire

Seine

Marne

Vosges

Jura

Danube

Inn

Lake Constance

Carpathian Mountains

Tisza

Dniester

Ozero Manych-Gudilo

ASIA

ulf of scony

Vienne

Saône

Rhône

Mont Blanc 4808

Lake Geneva

A l p s

Dolomites

Lake Garda

Lake Balaton

Mureșul

Transylvanian Alps

Dnieper

Sea of Azov

Stavropol'skaya Vozvyshennost'

Caspian Sea

Gironde

Massif Central

Po

Sava

Karkinits'ka Zatoka

Crimea

Gulf of Taganrog

El'brus 5642

C a u c a s u s

Pyrenees

Aneto 3404

Golfe du Lion

Ligurian Sea

Cap Corse

Dinaric Alps

Adriatic Sea

Danube

Balkan Mountains

Black Sea

Corsica

Isola d'Elba

Apennines

Rhodope Mountains

Bosporus

Balearic Islands

Golfo de Valencia

Minorca

Majorca

Sardinia

Vesuvius 728

Tyrrhenian Sea

Golfo di Taranto

Pindus Mts

Thasos

Limnos

Sea of Marmara

Ibiza

Formentera

Isole Lipari

Mount Etna 3323

Capo Carbonara

Isola d'Elba

Golfo di Taranto

Ionian Islands

Aegean Sea

Lesbos

Evvoia

Chios

Andros

Dodecanese

Rhodes

CA

Sicilian Channel

Sicily

Ionian Sea

Peloponnese

Kythira

Krytiko Pelagos

Karpathos

M e d i t e r r a n e a n   S e a

Malta

Crete

Europe Countries

The predominantly temperate climate of Europe has led to it becoming the most densely populated of the continents. It is highly industrialized, and has exploited its great wealth of natural resources and agricultural land to become one of the most powerful economic regions in the world.

The current pattern of countries within Europe is a result of numerous and complicated changes throughout its history. Ethnic, religious and linguistic differences have often been the cause of conflict, particularly in the Balkan region which has a very complex ethnic pattern. Current boundaries reflect, to some extent, these divisions which continue to be a source of tension. The historic distinction between 'Eastern' and 'Western' Europe is no longer made, following the collapse of Communism and the break up of the Soviet Union in 1991.

Paris, the capital of France and Europe's largest capital city with 9 630 000 residents.

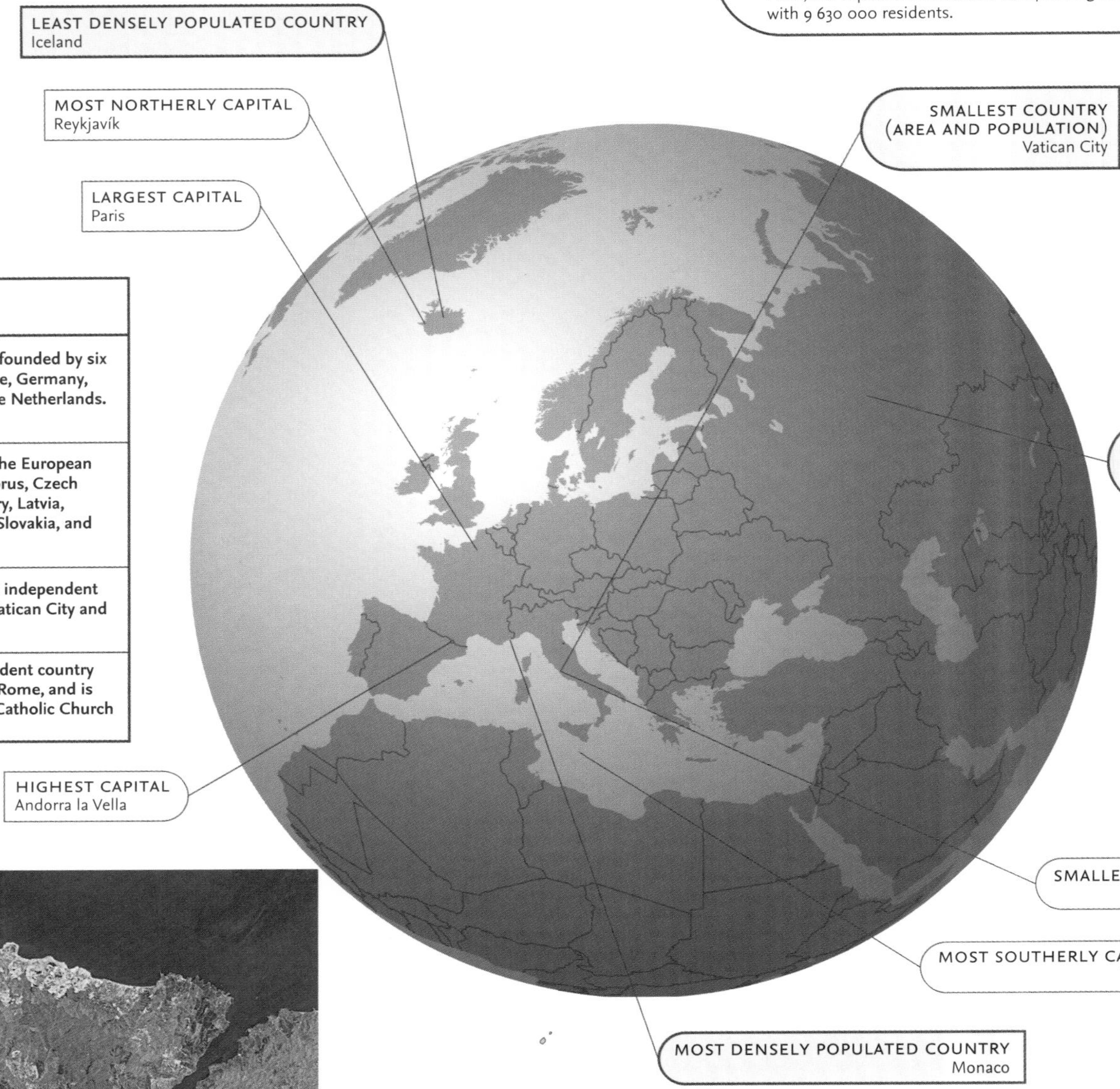

LEAST DENSELY POPULATED COUNTRY
Iceland

MOST NORTHERLY CAPITAL
Reykjavík

LARGEST CAPITAL
Paris

SMALLEST COUNTRY (AREA AND POPULATION)
Vatican City

Facts

- The European Union was founded by six countries: Belgium, France, Germany, Italy, Luxembourg, and the Netherlands. It now has 25 members

- The newest members of the European Union joined in 2004: Cyprus, Czech Republic, Estonia, Hungary, Latvia, Lithuania, Malta, Poland, Slovakia, and Slovenia

- Europe has the 2 smallest independent countries in the world – Vatican City and Monaco

- Vatican City is an independent country entirely within the city of Rome, and is the centre of the Roman Catholic Church

LARGEST COUNTRY (AREA AND POPULATION)
Russian Federation

ATLANTIC OCEAN

HIGHEST CAPITAL
Andorra la Vella

SMALLEST CAPITAL
Vatican City

MOST SOUTHERLY CAPITAL
Valletta

MOST DENSELY POPULATED COUNTRY
Monaco

Reykjavík **ICELAND**

REPUBLIC OF IRELAND Dublin

Brest

Bay of Biscay

Azores (Portugal)

Cape Finisterre · A Coruña · Bilbao

Oporto · **PORTUGAL** · Salamanca · Madrid

Lisbon · **SPAIN**

Cabo de São Vicente · Seville · Córdoba · Cartage

Cádiz · Málaga · Gibraltar

Str. of Gibraltar · Gibraltar

A F

Europe's capitals

Largest capital (population)	Paris, France	9 854 000
Smallest capital (population)	Vatican City	480
Most northerly capital	Reykjavík, Iceland	64° 39'N
Most southerly capital	Valletta, Malta	35° 54'N
Highest capital	Andorra la Vella, Andorra	1 029 metres 3 376 feet

Bosporus, Turkey, a narrow strait of water which separates Europe from Asia.

Europe (excluding Russian Federation) percentage of total population and land area

per cent

Population
Land area

Ukraine France Spain Sweden Germany Finland Norway Poland Italy UK Romania Belarus Greece Bulgaria Iceland Serb. and Mont. Hungary Portugal Austria Czech Rep. Rep. of Ireland Lithuania Latvia Croatia Bosnia-Herz. Slovakia Estonia Denmark Netherlands Switzerland Moldova Belgium Albania Macedonia Slovenia Luxembourg Andorra Malta Liechtenstein San Marino Monaco Vatican City

Europe's countries

Largest country (area)	Russian Federation	17 075 400 sq km	6 592 812 sq miles
Smallest country (area)	Vatican City	0.5 sq km	0.2 sq miles
Largest country (population)	Russian Federation	143 246 000	
Smallest country (population)	Vatican City	472	
Most densely populated country	Monaco	17 000 per sq km	34 000 per sq mile
Least densely populated country	Iceland	3 per sq km	7 per sq mile

Belgrade, the capital of Serbia and Montenegro, stands at the junction of the Danube, Europe's second longest river, and the Sava river.

Internet Links	
● European Union	**europa.eu.int**
● UK Foreign and Commonwealth Office	**www.fco.gov.uk**
● CIA World Factbook	**www.cia.gov/cia/publications/factbook**

Conic Equidistant Projection

1:10 000 000

0   100   200   300   400 miles

0   100 200 300 400 500 600 km

Europe
Western Russian Federation

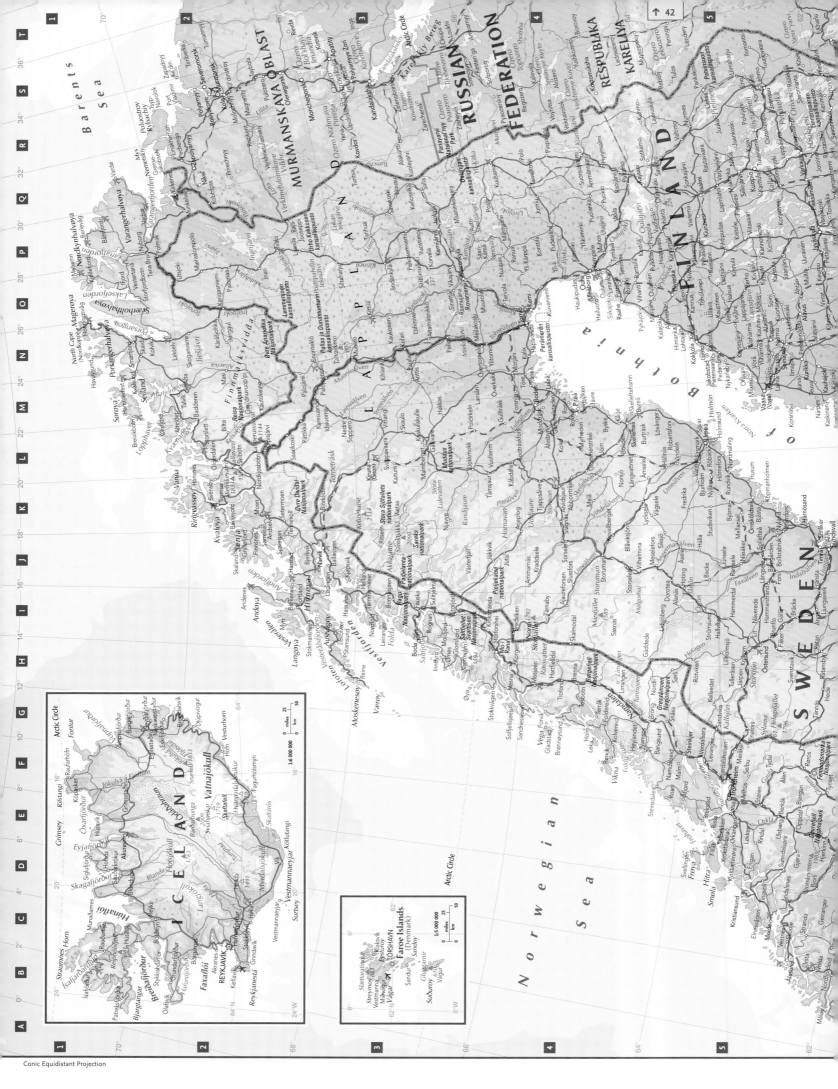

47 →

Europe
Scandinavia and the Baltic States

Conic Equidistant Projection

1:5 000 000

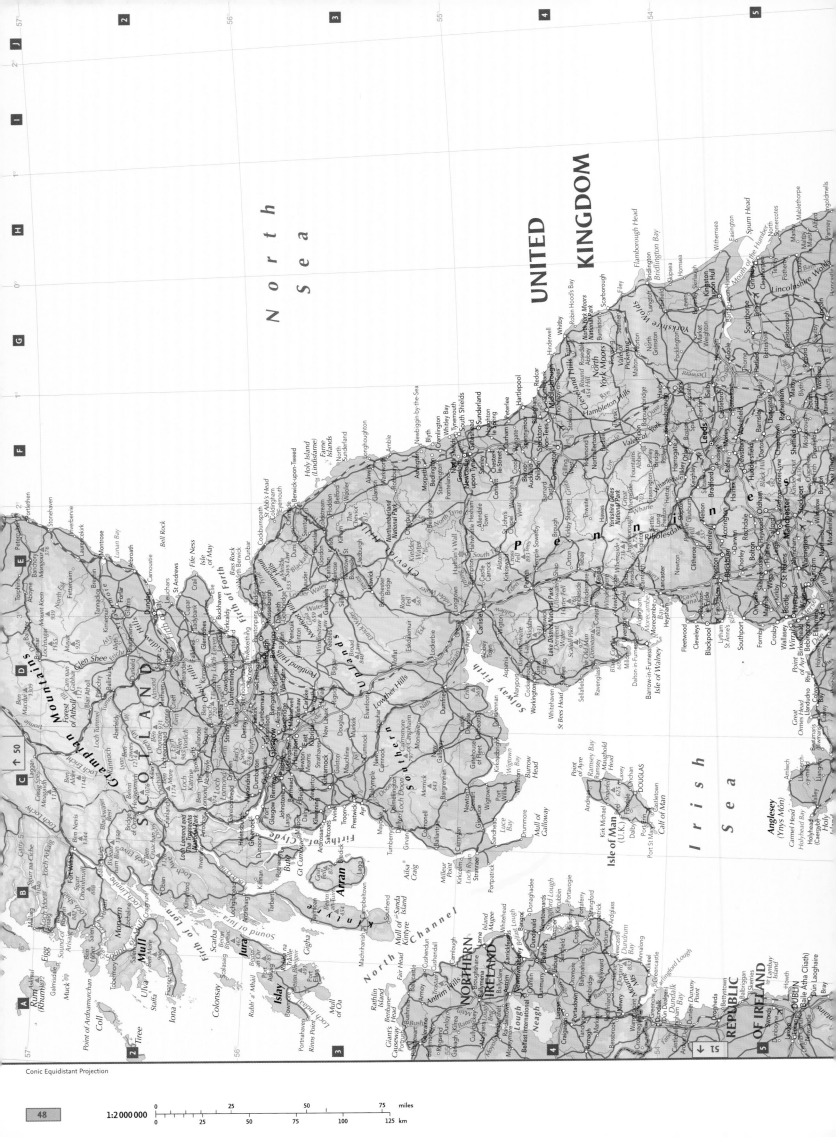

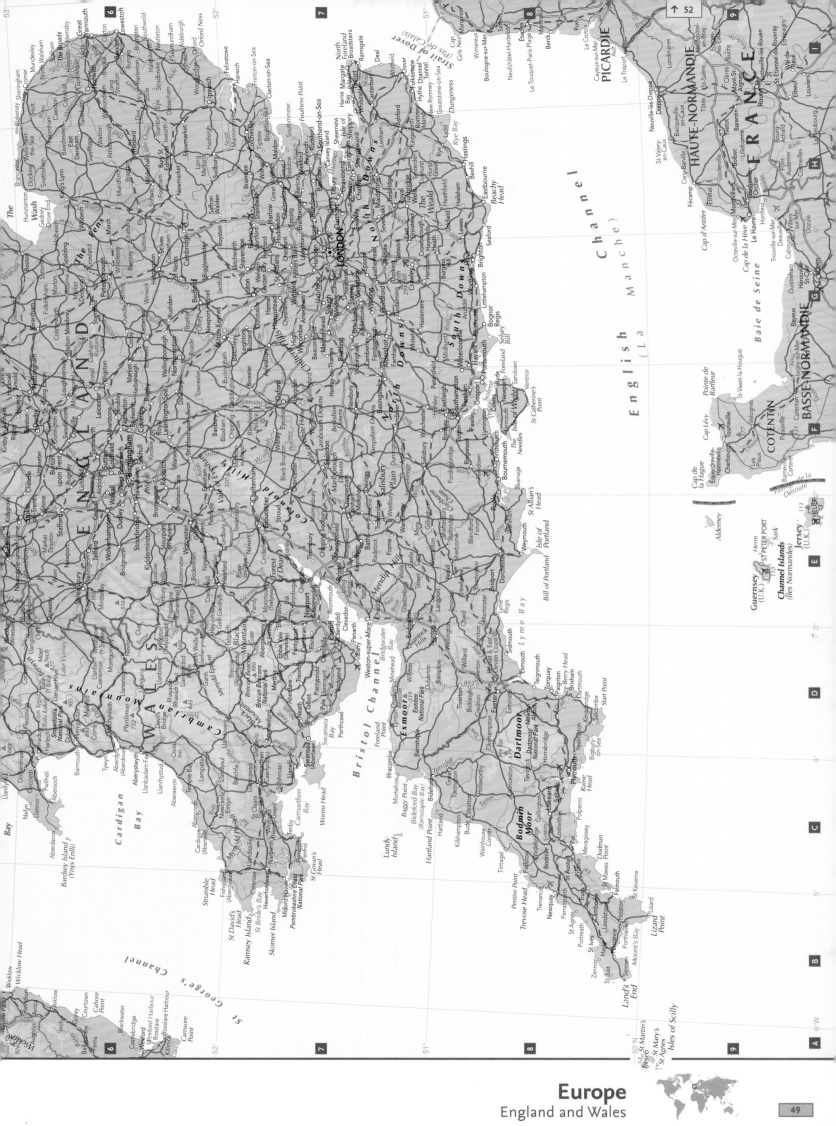

Europe
England and Wales

Europe
Scotland

Conic Equidistant Projection

1:2 000 000

Conic Equidistant Projection

1:2 000 000

0   25   50   75   miles

0   25   50   75   100   125 km

Europe
Ireland

51

N o r t h

S e a

UNITED
KINGDOM

ENGLAND

NETHERLANDS

AMSTERDAM

THE HAGUE
('s-Gravenhage)

Rotterdam

FLANDRE

BELGIUM

BRUSSELS
Bruxelles

NORD—PAS-DE-CALAIS

ARTOIS

HAINAUT

CONDROZ

LUXEMBOURG

LUXEMBOURG

PICARDY

PICARDIE

Ardennes

GAUME

FRANCE

CHAMPAGNE-
ARDENNE

LORRAINE

HAUTE-
NORMANDIE

VEXIN

NORMAND

LORRAINE

MULTIEN

PARIS

ÎLE DE FRANCE

SAULNOIS

THYMERAIS

Conic Equidistant Projection

1:2 000 000

0   25   50   75   miles

0   25   50   75   100   125 km

Europe

Southern Europe and the Mediterranean

55

Conic Equidistant Projection

Europe
France

1:5 000 000

Europe
Spain and Portugal

1:5 000 000

Conic Equidistant Projection

1:5 000 000

0   50   100   150   miles

0   50   100   150   200   250   km

Asia is the world's largest continent and occupies almost one-third of the world's total land area. Stretching across approximately 165° of longitude from the Mediterranean Sea to the easternmost point of the Russian Federation on the Bering Strait, it contains the world's highest and lowest points and some of the world's greatest physical features. Its mountain ranges include the Himalaya, Hindu Kush, Karakoram and the Ural Mountains and its major rivers – including the Yangtze, Tigris-Euphrates, Indus, Ganges and Mekong – are equally well-known and evocative.

Asia's deserts include the Gobi, the Taklimakan, and those on the Arabian Peninsula, and significant areas of volcanic and tectonic activity are present on the Kamchatka Peninsula, in Japan, and on Indonesia's numerous islands. The continent's landscapes are greatly influenced by climatic variations, with great contrasts between the islands of the Arctic Ocean and the vast Siberian plains in the north, and the tropical islands of Indonesia.

Ice and snow covered peaks of the volcanic mountains on the **Kamchatka Peninsula**, northeast Russian Federation.

Facts

- 90 of the world's 100 highest mountains are in Asia

- The Indonesian archipelago is made up of over 13 500 islands

- The height of the land in Nepal ranges from 60 metres to 8 848 metres

- The deepest lake in the world is Lake Baikal, Russian Federation, which is over 1 600 metres deep

Asia's physical features

Highest mountain	Mt Everest, China/Nepal	8 848 metres	29 028 feet
Longest river	Yangtze, China	6 380 km	3 965 miles
Largest lake	Caspian Sea	371 000 sq km	143 243 sq miles
Largest island	Borneo	745 561 sq km	287 861 sq miles
Largest drainage basin	Ob'-Irtysh, Kazakhstan/Russian Federation	2 990 000 sq km	1 154 439 sq miles
Lowest point	Dead Sea	-398 metres	-1 306 feet

Internet Links

● NASA Visible Earth	visibleearth.nasa.gov
● NASA Earth Observatory	earthobservatory.nasa.gov
● Peakware World Mountain Encyclopedia	www.peakware.com
● The Himalaya	himalaya.alpine-club.org.uk

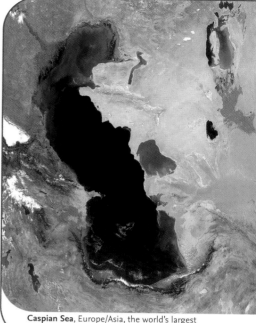

Caspian Sea, Europe/Asia, the world's largest expanse of inland water.

MOST EASTERLY POINT
Mys Dezhneva

MOST NORTHERLY POINT
Mys Arkticheskiy

LARGEST DRAINAGE BASIN
Ob'-Irtysh

LARGEST LAKE
Caspian Sea

HIGHEST MOUNTAIN
Mt Everest

MOST WESTERLY POINT
Bozcaada

LONGEST RIVER
Yangtze

LOWEST POINT
Dead Sea

LARGEST ISLAND
Borneo

MOST SOUTHERLY POINT
Pamana

Mediterranean Sea · Cyprus · Caucasus · Caspian Sea · Turan Lowlands · Tien Shan · Tarim Basin · Plateau of Tibet · Gobi · Yellow Sea · Sea of Japan · Honshu

Asia perspective view and cross section

Asia's extent

TOTAL LAND AREA	45 036 492 sq km / 17 388 686 sq miles
Most northerly point	Mys Arkticheskiy, Russian Federation
Most southerly point	Pamana, Indonesia
Most westerly point	Bozcaada, Turkey
Most easterly point	Mys Dezhneva, Russian Federation

Hahajima-rettō
Bonin Islands
cano lands

PACIFIC OCEAN

Palau lands

Irah eran
Puncak Jaya 5030
New Guinea

Kepulauan Aru
pulauan imbar
fura Sea

The **Yangtze**, China, Asia's longest river, flowing into the East China Sea near Shanghai.

Asia Countries

With approximately sixty per cent of the world's population, Asia is home to numerous cultures, people groups and lifestyles. Several of the world's earliest civilizations were established in Asia, including those of Sumeria, Babylonia and Assyria. Cultural and historical differences have led to a complex political pattern, and the continent has been, and continues to be, subject to numerous territorial and political conflicts – including the current disputes in the Middle East and in Jammu and Kashmir.

Separate regions within Asia can be defined by the cultural, economic and political systems they support. The major regions are: the arid, oil-rich, mainly Islamic southwest; southern Asia with its distinct cultures, isolated from the rest of Asia by major mountain ranges; the Indian- and Chinese-influenced monsoon region of southeast Asia; the mainly Chinese-influenced industrialized areas of eastern Asia; and Soviet Asia, made up of most of the former Soviet Union.

Timor island in southeast Asia, on which East Timor, the world's newest independent state, is located.

Facts

- Over 60% of the world's population live in Asia
- Asia has 11 of the world's 20 largest cities
- East Timor is Asia's newest independent country – founded in May 2002
- The Korean peninsula was divided into North Korea and South Korea in 1948 approximately along the 38th parallel

Asia's countries

Largest country (area)	Russian Federation	17 075 400 sq km	6 592 812 sq miles
Smallest country (area)	Maldives	298 sq km	115 sq miles
Largest country (population)	China	1 289 161 000	
Smallest country (population)	Palau	20 000	
Most densely populated country	Singapore	6 656 per sq km	17 219 per sq mile
Least densely populated country	Mongolia	2 per sq km	4 per sq mile

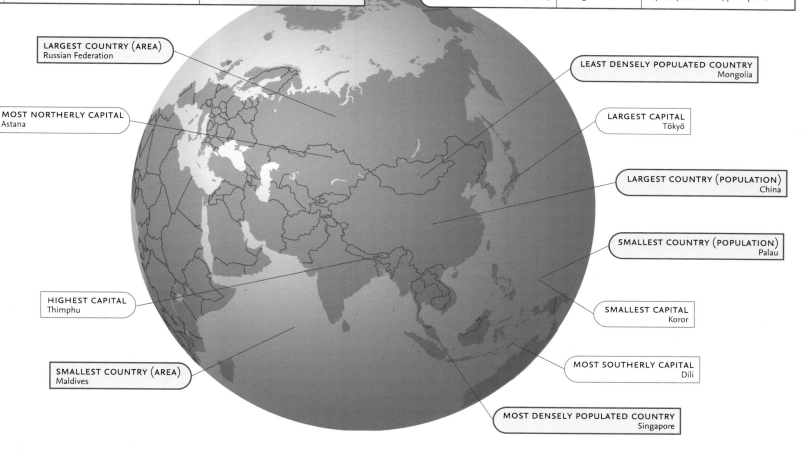

LARGEST COUNTRY (AREA)
Russian Federation

MOST NORTHERLY CAPITAL
Astana

HIGHEST CAPITAL
Thimphu

SMALLEST COUNTRY (AREA)
Maldives

LEAST DENSELY POPULATED COUNTRY
Mongolia

LARGEST CAPITAL
Tōkyō

LARGEST COUNTRY (POPULATION)
China

SMALLEST COUNTRY (POPULATION)
Palau

SMALLEST CAPITAL
Koror

MOST SOUTHERLY CAPITAL
Dili

MOST DENSELY POPULATED COUNTRY
Singapore

Different land use patterns help identify the borders between **Egypt**, **Israel** and **Gaza** in this space shuttle photograph.

Asia (excluding Russian Federation) percentage of total population and land area

per cent

■ Population
■ Land area

China · India · Kazakhstan · Saudi Arabia · Indonesia · Iran · Mongolia · Pakistan · Turkey · Myanmar · Afghanistan · Yemen · Thailand · Turkmenistan · Uzbekistan · Iraq · Japan · Malaysia · Vietnam · Oman · Philippines · Laos · Kyrgyzstan · Syria · Cambodia · Nepal · Tajikistan · Bangladesh · North Korea · South Korea · Jordan · Azerbaijan · UAE · Georgia · Sri Lanka · Bhutan · Taiwan · Armenia · Israel · Kuwait · East Timor · Qatar · Lebanon · Cyprus · Brunei · Bahrain · Singapore · Palau · Maldives

Koror
PALAU

Jayapura

New Guinea

Asia's capitals

Largest capital (population)	Tōkyō, Japan	35 327 000
Smallest capital (population)	Koror, Palau	14 000
Most northerly capital	Astana, Kazakhstan	51° 10'N
Most southerly capital	Dili, East Timor	8° 35'S
Highest capital	Thimphu, Bhutan	2 423 metres 7 949 feet

Beijing, capital of China, the most populous country in the world.

Conic Equidistant Projection

1:20 000 000

Asia
Northern Asia

Albers Conic Equal Area Projection

1:20 000 000

| 0 | 200 | 400 | 600 | miles |
| 0 | 200 | 400 | 600 | 800 | 1000 | km |

Asia

Eastern and Southeast Asia

Mercator Projection

1:15 000 000

PACIFIC

OCEAN

TAIWAN

PHILIPPINES

MANILA

Philippine
Sea

Luzon

Northern
Mariana
Islands
(U.S.A.)

CAPITOL HILL
Saipan
Tinian
Aguijan
Rota

HAGÅTÑA
Guam
(U.S.A.)

FEDERATED STATES

OF MICRONESIA

PALAU

Palau Islands
Eil Malk   KOROR
Angaur

Caroline
Islands

Celebes
Sea

Laut Maluku
(Molucca Sea)

Halmahera

Moluccas
(Maluku)

Laut Banda
(Banda Sea)

Laut Flores
(Flores Sea)

EAST TIMOR

EAST TIMOR

DILI

Timor

Timor
Sea

Laut Sawu
(Savu Sea)

Arafura

Sea

New

Guinea

PAPUA

NEW GUINEA

Bismarck

Archipelago

Bismarck
Sea

New
Britain

Gulf
of
Papua

PORT MORESBY

AUSTRALIA

Mercator Projection

1:7 000 000

Asia

Myanmar, Thailand, Peninsular Malaysia and Indo-China

Albers Conic Equal Area Projection

1:15 000 000

0   200   400   miles

0   200   400   600   800 km

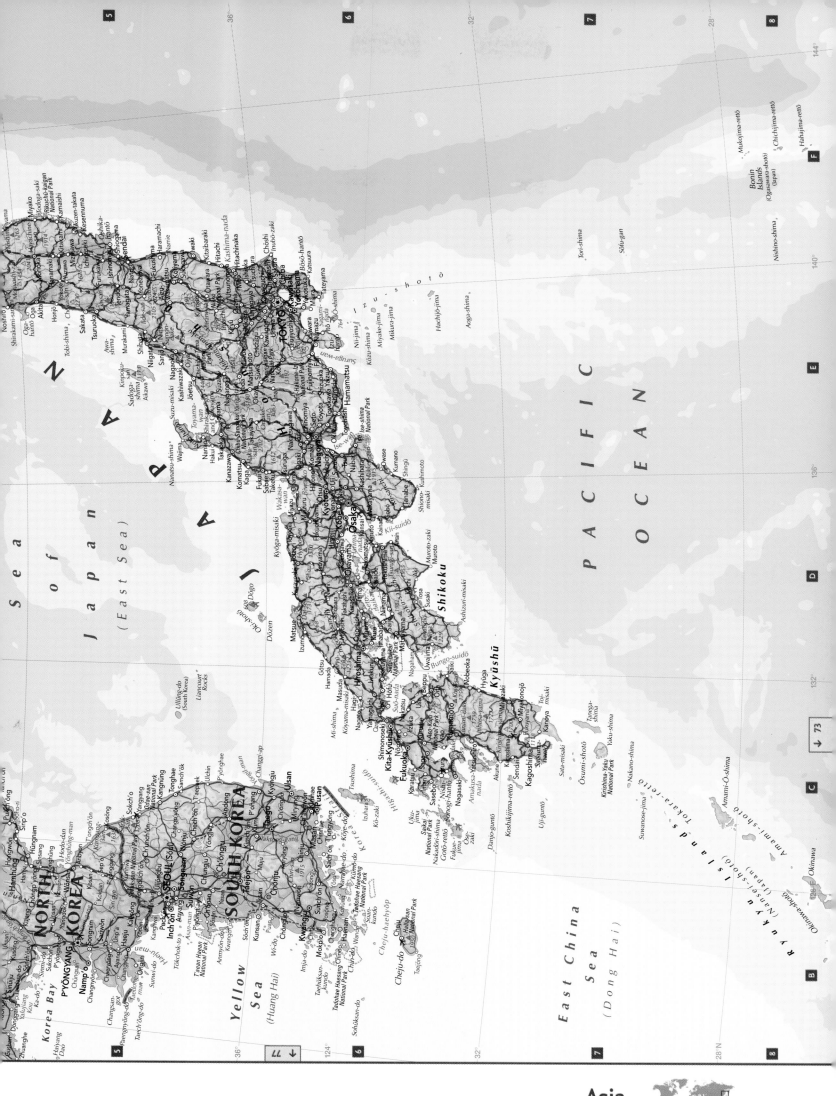

Asia

Japan, North Korea and South Korea

Conic Equidistant Projection

1:7 000 000

| | 0 | | 100 | | 200 | | miles |
| 0 | 100 | 200 | 300 | 400 km |

Albers Conic Equal Area Projection

1:20 000 000

| 0 | 200 | 400 | 600 miles |

| 0 | 200 | 400 | 600 | 800 | 1000 km |

Albers Equal Area Conic Projection

1:13 000 000

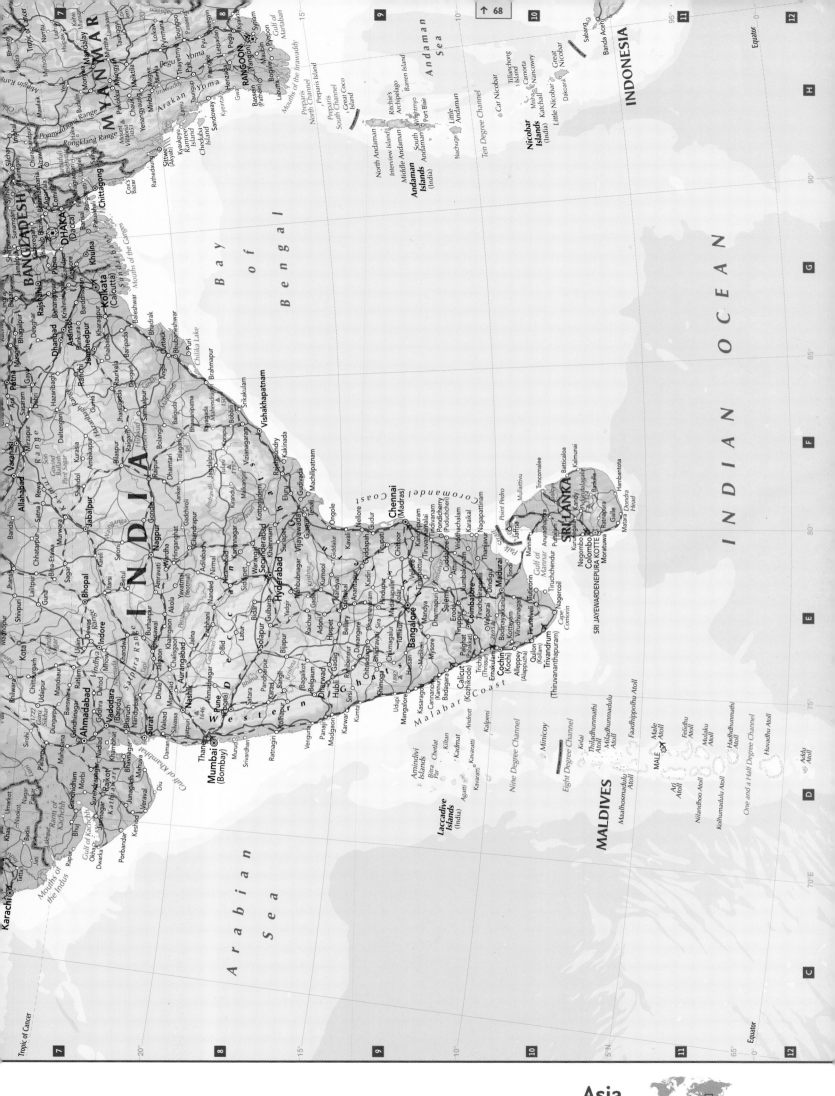

Asia
Southern Asia

Conic Equidistant Projection

1:7 000 000

Arabian
Sea

Bay
of
Bengal

GUJARAT
RAJASTHAN
MADHYA PRADESH
CHHATTISGARH
ORISSA
JHARKHAND
DHALBHUM
MAHARASHTRA
INDIA
Deccan
ANDHRA PRADESH
Eastern Ghats
Nallamalai Hills
Velikonda Range
Coromandel Coast
GOA
KARNATAKA
Ghats
Palkonda Range
Seshachalam Hills
TAMIL
NADU
KERALA
Palni Hills
Nilgiri Hills
Anaimalai Hills
Malabar Coast
Gulf of Mannar
Palk Strait
Palk Bay
SRI LANKA
Ruhuna National Park
Wilpattu National Park

Laccadive
Islands
Amindivi
Islands
LAKSHADWEEP
(India)
Cannanore
Islands
Nine Degree Channel
Eight Degree Channel
MALDIVES

Ahmadabad
Vadodara (Baroda)
Surat
Nashik
Mumbai (Bombay)
Pune (Poona)
Indore
Bhopal
Jabalpur
Nagpur
CHHATTISGARH
Bhilai
Raipur
Durg
Aurangabad
Solapur
Hyderabad
Secunderabad
Vishakhapatnam
Rajahmundry
Kakinada
Vijayawada
Guntur
Machilipatnam
Nellore
Dharwad
Hubli
Bangalore
Chennai (Madras)
Mangalore
Mysore
Salem
Coimbatore
Calicut (Kozhikode)
Cochin (Kochi)
Alleppey (Alappuzha)
Madurai
Tuticorin
Trivandrum (Thiruvananthapuram)
Nagercoil
Cape Comorin
Jaffna
Trincomalee
Anuradhapura
Kandy
Colombo
SRI JAYEWARDENEPURA KOTTE
Moratuwa
Galle

Conic Equidistant Projection

Asia
Southern India and Sri Lanka

1:7 000 000

84

Administrative divisions in India
numbered on the map:

1. DADRA AND NAGAR HAVELI (B1)
2. DAMAN AND DIU (A1, B1)
3. PONDICHERRY (C4)

Conic Equidistant Projection

Asia
Middle East

1:3 000 000

| 0 | 25 | 50 | 75 | 100 | miles |
| 0 | 25 | 50 | 75 | 100 | 125 | 150 | 175 | km |

85

Albers Conic Equal Area Projection

1:13 000 000

Asia
Southwest Asia

Conic Equidistant Projection

88   1:7 000 000

Administrative divisions in Russian Federation
numbered on the map:

1. RESPUBLIKA KALMYKIYA – KHALM'G-TANGCH (G1)
2. RESPUBLIKA DAGESTAN (G2)
3. CHECHENSKAYA RESPUBLIKA (G2)
4. RESPUBLIKA INGUSHETIYA (G2)
5. RESPUBLIKA SEVERNAYA OSETIYA – ALANIYA (G2)
6. KABARDINO-BALKARSKAYA RESPUBLIKA (F2)
7. KARACHAYEVO-CHERKESSKAYA RESPUBLIKA (F2)
8. RESPUBLIKA ADYGEYA (F1)

Conic Equidistant Projection

90

1:7 000 000

	miles
0	100	200
0	100	200	300	400 km

Some of the world's greatest physical features are in Africa, the world's second largest continent. Variations in climate and elevation give rise to the continent's great variety of landscapes. The Sahara, the world's largest desert, extends across the whole continent from west to east, and covers an area of over nine million square kilometres. Other significant African deserts are the Kalahari and the Namib. In contrast, some of the world's greatest rivers flow in Africa, including the Nile, the world's longest, and the Congo.

The Great Rift Valley is perhaps Africa's most notable geological feature. It stretches for nearly 3 000 kilometres from Jordan, through the Red Sea and south to Mozambique, and contains many of Africa's largest lakes. Significant mountain ranges on the continent are the Atlas Mountains and the Ethiopian Highlands in the north, the Ruwenzori in east central Africa, and the Drakensberg in the far southeast.

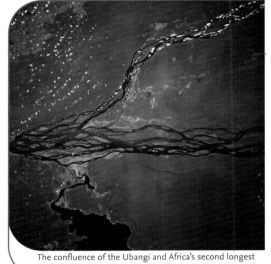

The confluence of the Ubangi and Africa's second longest river, the **Congo**.

Africa's extent

TOTAL LAND AREA	30 343 578 sq km / 11 715 655 sq miles
Most northerly point	La Galite, Tunisia
Most southerly point	Cape Agulhas, South Africa
Most westerly point	Santo Antão, Cape Verde
Most easterly point	Raas Xaafuun, Somalia

Internet Links

● NASA Visible Earth	visibleearth.nasa.gov
● NASA Astronaut Photography	eol.jsc.nasa.gov
● Peace Parks Foundation	www.peaceparks.org

Madeira

Canary Islands
Tenerife
Gran
Canaria

Akchâr

Aou

Cape Verde Santo
Antão
Boa
Ilhas dos Vista
Cabo Verde
Fogo Santiago Cap Vert

Sénégal

Gambia

Fouta
Djallon

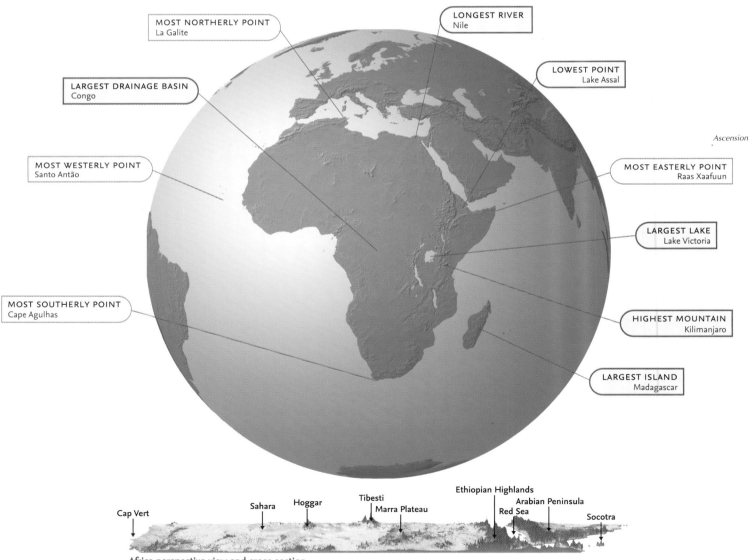

MOST NORTHERLY POINT
La Galite

LONGEST RIVER
Nile

LOWEST POINT
Lake Assal

LARGEST DRAINAGE BASIN
Congo

MOST WESTERLY POINT
Santo Antão

Ascension

MOST EASTERLY POINT
Raas Xaafuun

LARGEST LAKE
Lake Victoria

MOST SOUTHERLY POINT
Cape Agulhas

HIGHEST MOUNTAIN
Kilimanjaro

LARGEST ISLAND
Madagascar

Cap Vert
Sahara
Hoggar
Tibesti
Marra Plateau
Ethiopian Highlands
Arabian Peninsula
Red Sea
Socotra

Africa perspective view and cross section

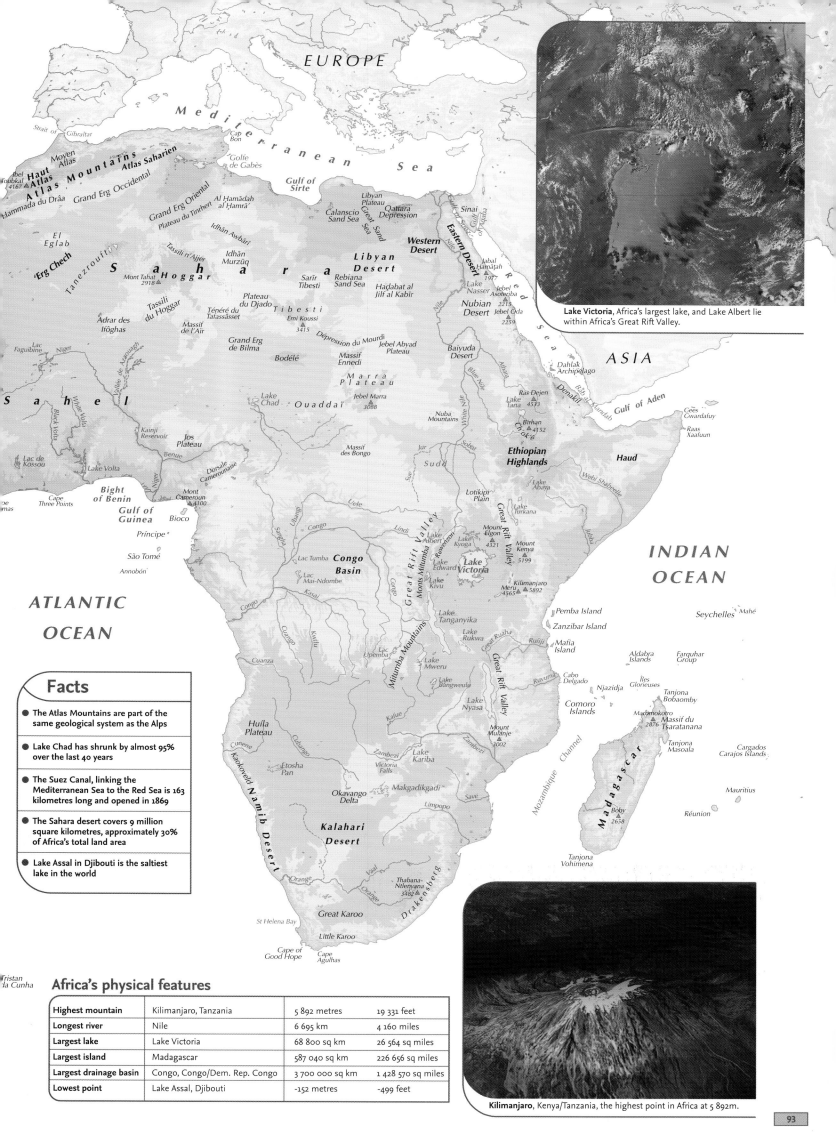

EUROPE

Strait of Gibraltar
Cape Bon

Mediterranean Sea

Moyen Atlas
Jebel Toubkal 4167
Haut Atlas
Atlas Mountains
Atlas Saharien
Hammada du Drâa
Grand Erg Occidental

Golfe de Gabès
Gulf of Sirte

El Eglab
'Erg Chech
Tanezrouft
Sahara
Mont Tahat 2918
Hoggar

Grand Erg Oriental
Plateau du Tinrhert
Al Ḥamādah al Ḥamrāʾ
Idhān Awbārī
Tassili n'Ajjer
Idhān Murzūq
Sarīr Tibesti
Rebiana Sand Sea

Calanscio Sand Sea
Libyan Plateau
Great Sand Sea
Qattara Depression

Sinai
Gulf of Suez
Gulf of Aqaba

Western Desert
Eastern Desert

Libyan Desert

Ḥaḍabat al Jilf al Kabīr

Lake Nasser
Jabal Ḥamāṭah 1977

Nubian Desert
Jebel Oda 2259
Jebel Asoteriba 2215

Tassili du Hoggar
Adrar des Ifôghas
Ténéré du Tafassâsset
Massif de l'Aïr

Plateau du Djado
Tibesti
Emi Koussi 3415
Grand Erg de Bilma
Bodélé
Massif Ennedi
Dépression du Mourdi
Jebel Abyad Plateau

Marra Plateau
Jebel Marra 3088

Baiyuda Desert

Red Sea

Lac Faguibine
Niger
Vallée de Azaouagh
Lake Chad
Ouaddaï

Nuba Mountains
Nuba Mountains

Atbara
Lake Tana 4533
Ras Dejen

Dahlak Archipelago

ASIA

Gulf of Aden
Cees Gwardafuy
Raas Xaafuun

Sahel
White Volta
Black Volta
Kainji Reservoir
Jos Plateau
Benue

Massif des Bongo

Jur
Sue
Sudd
Sobat
Blue Nile
White Nile

Birhan 4152
Chok'e

Ethiopian Highlands

Lake Abaya

Haud

Webi Shabeelle

Lac de Kossou
Lake Volta

Dorsale Camerounaise
Mont Cameroun 4100
Bioco

Cape Three Points
Bight of Benin
Gulf of Guinea

Uele
Ubangi

Lotikipi Plain
Lake Turkana

Jubba

Príncipe
São Tomé
Annobón

Lac Tumba
Congo
Congo Basin
Lac Mai-Ndombe

Sangha
Congo
Lindi

Great Rift Valley
Monts Mitumba
Lake Albert
Ruwenzori
Mount Elgon 4321
Lake Kyoga
Lake Edward
Lake Kivu
Lake Victoria
Meru 4565
Mount Kenya 5199
Kilimanjaro 5892

ATLANTIC

OCEAN

Cuanza
Kwilu
Kasai
Cuango

Lac Upemba
Lake Tanganyika
Lake Rukwa

INDIAN

OCEAN

Pemba Island
Zanzibar Island
Mafia Island
Great Ruaha
Rufiji

Seychelles Mahé

Facts

• The Atlas Mountains are part of the same geological system as the Alps

• Lake Chad has shrunk by almost 95% over the last 40 years

• The Suez Canal, linking the Mediterranean Sea to the Red Sea is 163 kilometres long and opened in 1869

• The Sahara desert covers 9 million square kilometres, approximately 30% of Africa's total land area

• Lake Assal in Djibouti is the saltiest lake in the world

Huíla Plateau

Kafue
Cunene
Cubango

Lake Mweru
Lake Bangweulu
Lake Nyasa
Mount Mulanje 3002

Mitumba Mountains

Ruvuma
Cabo Delgado
Njazidja

Comoro Islands

Aldabra Islands
Îles Glorieuses
Farquhar Group

Tanjona Bobaomby
Maromokotro 2876
Massif du Tsaratanana

Great Rift Valley
Mozambique Channel

Madagascar

Tanjona Masoala

Cargados Carajos Islands

Kaokoveld
Namib Desert
Etosha Pan
Okavango Delta
Kalahari Desert
Makgadikgadi

Zambezi
Victoria Falls
Lake Kariba
Zambezi
Limpopo
Save

Mauritius
Réunion

Boby 2658

Tanjona Vohimena

Orange
Vaal
Orange
Great Karoo
Little Karoo
St Helena Bay
Cape of Good Hope
Cape Agulhas

Thabana-Ntlenyana 3482
Drakensberg

Tristan da Cunha

Africa's physical features

Highest mountain	Kilimanjaro, Tanzania	5 892 metres	19 331 feet
Longest river	Nile	6 695 km	4 160 miles
Largest lake	Lake Victoria	68 800 sq km	26 564 sq miles
Largest island	Madagascar	587 040 sq km	226 656 sq miles
Largest drainage basin	Congo, Congo/Dem. Rep. Congo	3 700 000 sq km	1 428 570 sq miles
Lowest point	Lake Assal, Djibouti	-152 metres	-499 feet

Lake Victoria, Africa's largest lake, and Lake Albert lie within Africa's Great Rift Valley.

Kilimanjaro, Kenya/Tanzania, the highest point in Africa at 5 892m.

Africa is a complex continent, with over fifty independent countries and a long history of political change. It supports a great variety of ethnic groups, with the Sahara creating the major divide between Arab and Berber groups in the north and a diverse range of groups, including the Yoruba and Masai, in the south.

The current pattern of countries in Africa is a product of a long and complex history, including the colonial period, which saw European control of the vast majority of the continent from the fifteenth century until widespread moves to independence began in the 1950s. Despite its great wealth of natural resources, Africa is by far the world's poorest continent. Many of its countries are heavily dependent upon foreign aid and many are also subject to serious political instability.

Cape Verde, North Atlantic Ocean, a small group of islands lying 500 kilometres off the coast of west Africa.

Madeira
(Portugal)

Canary Islands
(Spain)

Laâyoune

WESTERN SAHARA

Nouâdhibou

MAURITANIA
Nouakchott

St-Louis

CAPE VERDE
Praia

Dakar · SENEGAL · Kayes
Kaolack
Banjul · THE GAMBIA
Bissau
GUINEA-BISSAU · GUINEA
Conakry · Kank
Freetown
SIERRA LEONE
Monrovia
LIBERI

MOST NORTHERLY CAPITAL
Tunis

LARGEST CAPITAL
Cairo

LARGEST COUNTRY (AREA)
Sudan

LARGEST COUNTRY (POPULATION)
Nigeria

HIGHEST CAPITAL
Addis Ababa

SMALLEST CAPITAL
Victoria

Ascension
(U.K.)

SMALLEST COUNTRY
(AREA AND POPULATION)
Seychelles

LEAST DENSELY POPULATED COUNTRY
Namibia

MOST DENSELY POPULATED COUNTRY
Mauritius

MOST SOUTHERLY CAPITAL
Cape Town

Internet Links	
● UK Foreign and Commonwealth Office	www.fco.gov.uk
● CIA World Factbook	www.odci.gov/cia/publications/factbook
● Southern African Development Community	www.sadc.int
● Satellite imagery	www.spaceimaging.com

Facts

● Africa has over 1 000 linguistic and cultural groups

● Only Liberia and Ethiopia have remained free from colonial rule throughout their history

● Over 30% of the world's minerals, and over 50% of the world's diamonds, come from Africa

● 9 of the 10 poorest countries in the world are in Africa

Africa percentage of total population and land area

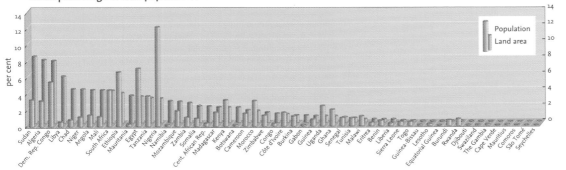

EUROPE

Mediterranean Sea

ASIA

Cairo, capital of Egypt and the largest city in Africa with 11 146 000 inhabitants.

Cape Town, legislative capital of the Republic of South Africa and the most southerly African capital city.

Africa's countries

Largest country (area)	Sudan	2 505 813 sq km	967 494 sq miles
Smallest country (area)	Seychelles	455 sq km	176 sq miles
Largest country (population)	Nigeria	124 009 000	
Smallest country (population)	Seychelles	81 000	
Most densely populated country	Mauritius	599 per sq km	1 549 per sq mile
Least densely populated country	Namibia	2 per sq km	6 per sq mile

Africa's capitals

Largest capital (population)	Cairo, Egypt	11 146 000	
Smallest capital (population)	Victoria, Seychelles	30 000	
Most northerly capital	Tunis, Tunisia	36° 46'N	
Most southerly capital	Cape Town, Republic of South Africa	33° 57'S	
Highest capital	Addis Ababa, Ethiopia	2 408 metres	7 900 feet

1:16 000 000

Lambert Azimuthal Equal Area Projection

Africa
Northern Africa

Lambert Azimuthal Equal Area Projection

1:16 000 000

Africa

Central and Southern Africa

BOTSWANA

GHANZI

Central Kalahari Game Reserve

KWENENG

KGALAGADI

K a l a h a r i

D e s e r t

SOUTHERN

NAMIBIA

ERONGO

KHOMAS

OMAHEKE

WINDHOEK

Tropic of Capricorn

HARDAP

Namib-
Nauktuft
Game
Park

N a m i b   D e s e r t

GREAT NAMAQUALAND

KARAS

Gemsbok
National Park

Kalahari
Gemsbok
National
Park

NORTH

GRIQUALAND WEST

REPUBLIC

OF

NORTHERN

CAPE

SOUTH AFR

NAMAQUALAND

Richtersveld
National Park

Ai-Ais Hot Springs
and Fish River
Canyon Park

Great   Karoo

ATLANTIC

OCEAN

WESTERN CAPE

Little Karoo

CAPE TOWN

False
Bay

Cape of Good Hope
Nature Reserve
Cape of Good Hope

Oceania comprises Australia, New Zealand, New Guinea and the islands of the Pacific Ocean. It is the smallest of the world's continents by land area. Its dominating feature is Australia, which is mainly flat and very dry. Australia's western half consists of a low plateau, broken in places by higher mountain ranges, which has very few permanent rivers or lakes. The narrow, fertile coastal plain of the east coast is separated from the interior by the Great Dividing Range, which includes the highest mountain in Australia.

The numerous Pacific islands of Oceania are generally either volcanic in origin or consist of coral. They can be divided into three main regions of Micronesia, north of the equator between Palau and the Gilbert islands; Melanesia, stretching from mountainous New Guinea to Fiji; and Polynesia, covering a vast area of the eastern and central Pacific Ocean.

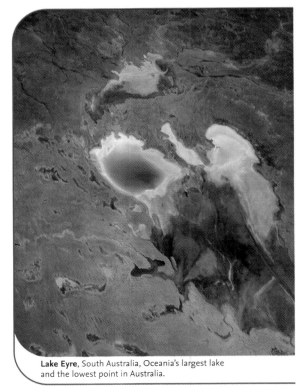

Lake Eyre, South Australia, Oceania's largest lake and the lowest point in Australia.

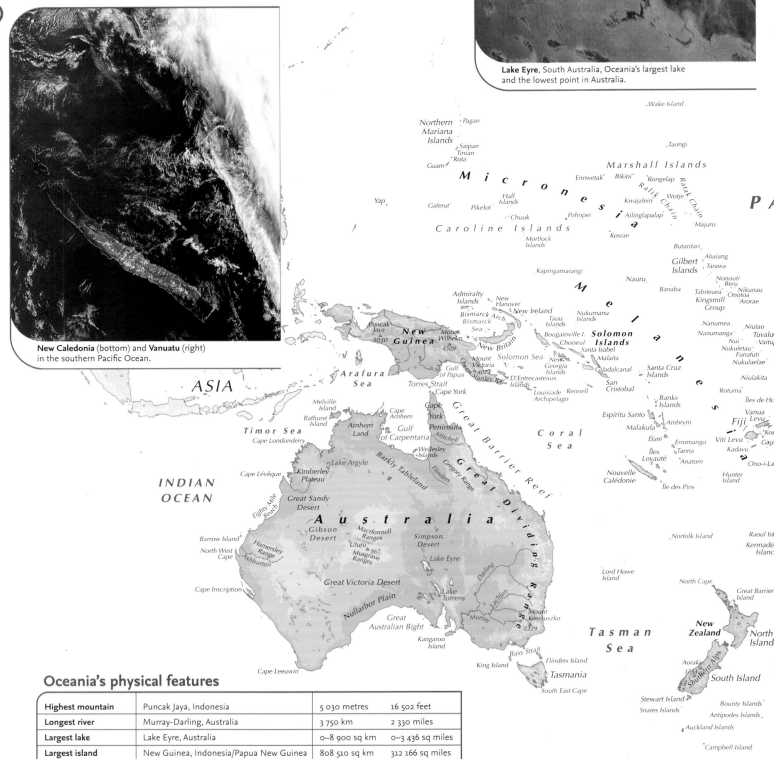

New Caledonia (bottom) and **Vanuatu** (right) in the southern Pacific Ocean.

Oceania's physical features

Highest mountain	Puncak Jaya, Indonesia	5 030 metres	16 502 feet
Longest river	Murray–Darling, Australia	3 750 km	2 330 miles
Largest lake	Lake Eyre, Australia	0–8 900 sq km	0–3 436 sq miles
Largest island	New Guinea, Indonesia/Papua New Guinea	808 510 sq km	312 166 sq miles
Largest drainage basin	Murray–Darling, Australia	1 058 000 sq km	408 494 sq miles
Lowest point	Lake Eyre, Australia	-16 metres	-53 feet

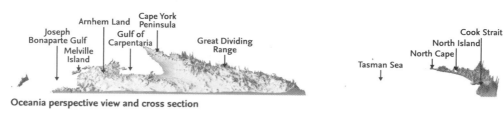

Oceania perspective view and cross section

Cape York
Peninsula
Arnhem Land
Gulf of
Carpentaria
Great Dividing
Range
Joseph
Bonaparte Gulf
Melville
Island

Cook Strait
North Island
North Cape
Tasman Sea

Internet Links

● NASA Visible Earth	visibleearth.nasa.gov
● NASA Astronaut Photography	eol.jsc.nasa.gov
● Great Barrier Reef Marine Park Authority	www.gbrmpa.gov.au

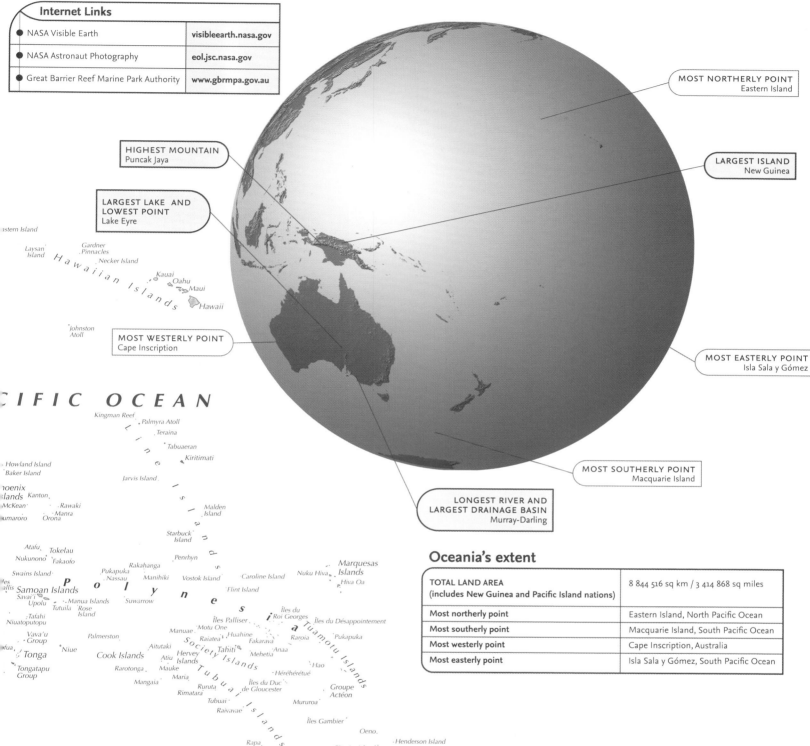

MOST NORTHERLY POINT
Eastern Island

HIGHEST MOUNTAIN
Puncak Jaya

LARGEST ISLAND
New Guinea

**LARGEST LAKE AND
LOWEST POINT**
Lake Eyre

MOST WESTERLY POINT
Cape Inscription

MOST EASTERLY POINT
Isla Sala y Gómez

MOST SOUTHERLY POINT
Macquarie Island

**LONGEST RIVER AND
LARGEST DRAINAGE BASIN**
Murray-Darling

eastern Island

Laysan
Island

Gardner
Pinnacles
Necker Island

Kauai
Oahu
Maui

Hawaiian Islands

Hawaii

Johnston
Atoll

CIFIC OCEAN

Kingman Reef
Palmyra Atoll
Teraina
Tabuaeran
Kiritimati

Line Islands

Howland Island
Baker Island
Jarvis Island

hoenix
lands
Kanton
McKean
Rawaki
Manra
umaroro
Orona

Malden
Island

Starbuck
Island

Atafu
Tokelau
Nukunono
Fakaofo
Swains Island

Penrhyn

**Marquesas
Islands**
Nuku Hiva
Hiva Oa

allis
P o l y n e
Samoan Islands
Savai'i
Upolu
Manua Islands
Tutuila
Rose
Island

Pukapuka
Rakahanga
Nassau
Manihiki

Caroline Island

Vostok Island

Flint Island

s i

Tafahi
Niuatoputapu

Suwarrow

i a

Îles du
Roi Georges
Îles du Désappointement

Vava'u
Group
Niue
Palmerston

Manuae
Motu One
Raiatea
Huahine
Pukapuka
Fakarava
Raroia

ufua
Tonga
Cook Islands
Aitutaki
Atiu
Tahiti
Hervey
Islands
Mauke
Mehetia
Anaa
Hao

Tuamotu Islands

Tongatapu
Group
Rarotonga
Maria

Society Islands

Hérehérétué

Mangaia
Ruruta
Rimatara
Îles du Duc
de Gloucester

Groupe
Actéon

Tubuai Islands

Tubuai
Raivavae
Mururoa

Rapa
Marotiri

Îles Gambier

Oeno

Henderson Island
Pitcairn Island
Ducie Island

Oceania's extent

TOTAL LAND AREA (includes New Guinea and Pacific Island nations)	8 844 516 sq km / 3 414 868 sq miles
Most northerly point	Eastern Island, North Pacific Ocean
Most southerly point	Macquarie Island, South Pacific Ocean
Most westerly point	Cape Inscription, Australia
Most easterly point	Isla Sala y Gómez, South Pacific Ocean

Facts

● Australia's Great Barrier Reef is the world's largest coral reef and stretches for over 2 000 kilometres

● The highest point of Tuvalu is only 5 metres above sea level

● New Zealand lies directly on the boundary between the Pacific and Indo-Australian tectonic plates

● The Mariana Trench in the Pacific Ocean contains the earth's deepest point – Challenger Deep, 10 920 metres below sea level

hatham Islands
t Island

The spectacular **Banks Peninsula**, South Island, New Zealand, formed by two overlapping volcanic centres.

HERN OCEAN

Stretching across almost the whole width of the Pacific Ocean, Oceania has a great variety of cultures and an enormously diverse range of countries and territories. Australia, by far the largest and most industrialized country in the continent, contrasts with the numerous tiny Pacific island nations which have smaller, and more fragile economies based largely on agriculture, fishing and the exploitation of natural resources.

The division of the Pacific island groups into the main regions of Micronesia, Melanesia and Polynesia – often referred to as the South Sea islands – broadly reflects the ethnological differences across the continent. There is a long history of colonial influence in the region, which still contains dependent territories belonging to Australia, France, New Zealand, the UK and the USA.

Wellington, capital of New Zealand and the most southerly national capital in the world.

Tasmania, a small Australian island state, separated from the mainland by the Bass Strait.

Facts

- Over 91% of Australia's population live in urban areas
- The Maori name for New Zealand is Aotearoa, meaning 'land of the long white cloud'
- Auckland, New Zealand, has the largest Polynesian population of any city in Oceania
- Over 800 different languages are spoken in Papua New Guinea

Internet Links

UK Foreign and Commonwealth Office	www.fco.gov.uk
CIA World Factbook	www.odci.gov/cia/publications/factbook
Geoscience Australia	www.ga.gov.au

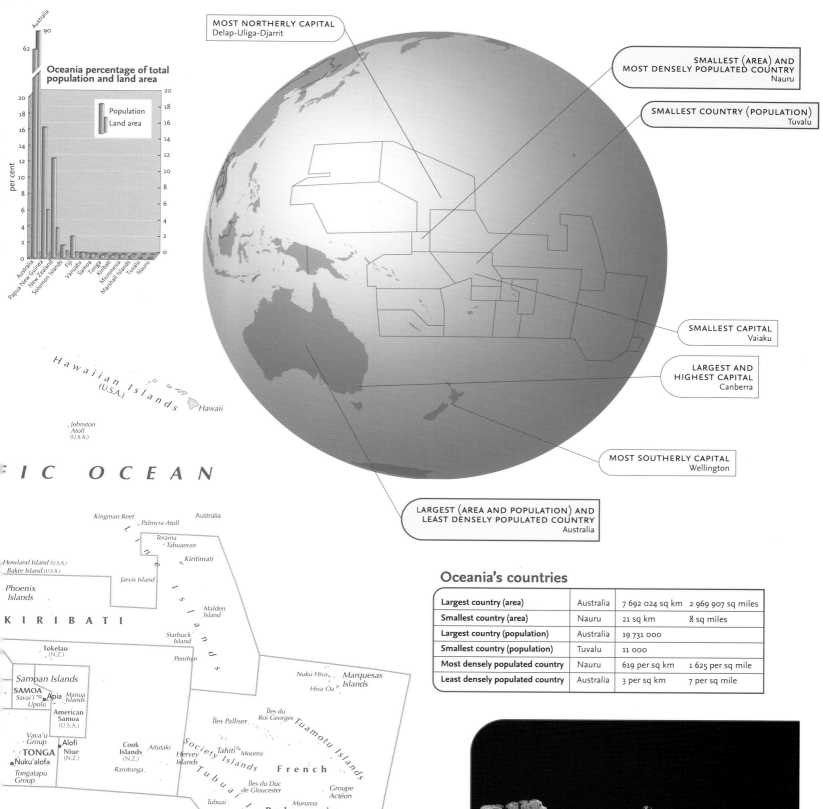

Oceania percentage of total population and land area

per cent

Population
Land area

Australia
Papua New Guinea
New Zealand
Solomon Islands
Fiji
Vanuatu
Samoa
Tonga
Kiribati
Micronesia
Marshall Islands
Tuvalu
Nauru

MOST NORTHERLY CAPITAL
Delap-Uliga-Djarrit

SMALLEST (AREA) AND MOST DENSELY POPULATED COUNTRY
Nauru

SMALLEST COUNTRY (POPULATION)
Tuvalu

SMALLEST CAPITAL
Vaiaku

LARGEST AND HIGHEST CAPITAL
Canberra

MOST SOUTHERLY CAPITAL
Wellington

LARGEST (AREA AND POPULATION) AND LEAST DENSELY POPULATED COUNTRY
Australia

F I C   O C E A N

Hawaiian Islands (U.S.A.)

Hawaii

Johnston Atoll (U.S.A.)

Kingman Reef
Palmyra Atoll
Australia
Teraina
Tabuaeran
Kiritimati
Howland Island (U.S.A.)
Baker Island (U.S.A.)
Jarvis Island
Phoenix Islands
Malden Island
K I R I B A T I
Starbuck Island
Tokelau (N.Z.)
Penrhyn
Line Islands
Nuku Hiva
Marquesas Islands
Hiva Oa
Samoan Islands
SAMOA
Savai'i
Apia Manua Islands
Upolu
American Samoa (U.S.A.)
Îles du Roi Georges
Îles Palliser
Tuamotu Islands
Vava'u Group
Alofi
Niue (N.Z.)
Cook Islands (N.Z.)
Aitutaki
Society Islands
Tahiti Moorea
TONGA
Hervey Islands
Nuku'alofa
Rarotonga
French
Tongatapu Group
Tubuai Islands
Îles du Duc de Gloucester
Groupe Actéon
Tubuai
Mururoa
Polynesia
Îles Gambier
Pitcairn Is (U.K.)
Henderson Island
Rapa
Pitcairn Island

Chatham Islands (N.Z.)

Oceania's countries

Largest country (area)	Australia	7 692 024 sq km	2 969 907 sq miles
Smallest country (area)	Nauru	21 sq km	8 sq miles
Largest country (population)	Australia	19 731 000	
Smallest country (population)	Tuvalu	11 000	
Most densely populated country	Nauru	619 per sq km	1 625 per sq mile
Least densely populated country	Australia	3 per sq km	7 per sq mile

Oceania's capitals

Largest capital (population)	Canberra, Australia	387 000	
Smallest capital (population)	Vaiaku, Tuvalu	5 100	
Most northerly capital	Delap-Uliga-Djarrit, Marshall Islands	7° 7'N	
Most southerly capital	Wellington, New Zealand	41° 18'S	
Highest capital	Canberra, Australia	581 metres	1 906 feet

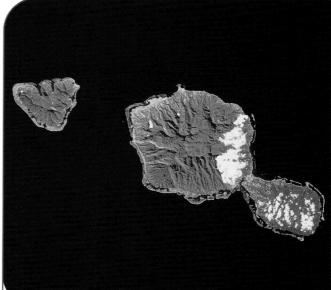

Tahiti and **Moorea**, islands in the Society Islands group which form part of the dependent territory of French Polynesia.

O C E A N

Aranuka
Howland Island (U.S.A.)
Baker Island (U.S.A.)
Nauru
YAREN
Banaba (Ocean Island)
Nonouti
NAURU
Beru
Nikunau
Tabiteuea
K I R I B A T I
Onotoa
Kingsmill Group
Tamana
Arorae
Phoenix Islands
Kanton
McKean
Rawaki
Tauu Islands
Nukumanu Islands
Nanumea
Orona
Manra
SOLOMON ISLANDS
Ontong Java Atoll
Nanumanga
Choiseul
Niutao
Roncador Reef
Santa Isabel
Nui
2
New Georgia Sound
Iombangara
Buala
Vaitupu
New Georgia
Malu'u
Stewart Islands
TUVALU
Funafuti
VAIAKU
Tokelau (New Zealand)
Atafu
Nukunono
Florida Islands
Malaita
Maramasike
Nukufetau
Guadalcanal
Ulawa Island
Nukulaelae
Fakaofo
Santa Ana
Kirakira
Nupani
Swallow Islands
Niulakita
Swains Island
San Cristobal (Makira)
Ndeni
Santa Cruz Islands (Solomon Islands)
Pukapuka (Danger Islands)
Rennell
Indispensable Reefs
Utupua
Cherry Island
Rotuma (Fiji)
Wallis and Futuna Islands (France)
Îles Wallis
SAMOA
Nassau
Vanikoro Islands
Tikopia
MATĀ'UTU
American Samoa (U.S.A.)
Suwarrow
al Sea
Torres Islands
Uréparapara
Mitre Island
Îles de Hoorn
Savai'i
Manua Islands
Vanua Lava
Banks Islands
Santa María Island
Upolu
APIA
Tutuila
FAGATOGO
Rose Island
Espíritu Santo
Aoba
Maéwo
Tabwémasana
Mount
1879
Pentecost Island
Great Sea Reef
Vanua Levu
Niuafo'ou
Tafahi
VANUATU
Norsup
Ambrym
Yasawa Group
Bligh Water
Labasa (Lambasa)
210
Niuatoputapu
Malakula
1270
Epi
Lautoka
Tomanivi (Mt. Victoria)
Taveuni
Northern Lau Group
Cook Islands (New Zealand)
Émae
Shepherd Islands
Koro
3
Récifs d'Entrecasteaux
PORT VILA
Éfaté
Viti Levu
Koro Sea
Koro
Gau
Lakeba
Grand Passage
Erromango
SUVA
Kadavu Passage
Vava'u Group
Grand Récif de Cook
Kadavu
Moala
Kabara
Southern Lau Group
Îles Chesterfield (France)
Tanna
361
Futuna
FIJI
Kadavu
Matuku
Vatoa
ALOFI
Niue (New Zealand)
Palmerston
Récif des Français
Îles Belep
Nouvelle Calédonie
Îles loyauté (France)
Anatom (Aneityum)
Ceva-i-Ra (Conway Reef)
Doi
Ono-i-Lau
Tofua
500
Ha'apai Group
Koumac
Lifou
Ouvéa
Tofua
New Caledonia (France)
Bourail
Tadin
Maré
Hunter Island
100
TONGA
Yaté
Ata
NUKU'ALOFA
Tongatapu Group
NOUMÉA
Île des Pins
Grand Récif du Sud
Minerva Reefs
20°
P A C I F I C   O C E A N
Tropic of Capricorn
160°
Norfolk Island (Australia)
KINGSTON
4
Lord Howe Island (Australia)
Raoul Island
Kermadec Islands (New Zealand)
Macauley Island
Curtis Island
Havre Rock
L'Espérance Rock
Three Kings Islands
North Cape
30°
Cape Maria van Diemen
Awanui
Whangarei
North Island
Great Barrier Island
NEW ZEALAND
Takapuna
Auckland
Manukau
Hamilton
Tauranga
East Cape
man Sea
Te Kuiti
Tokoroa
Whakatane
Gisborne
New Plymouth
Taupo
Wairoa
Mount Taranaki (Mount Egmont)
Mount Ruapehu
2518
Mahia Peninsula
Hawera
Napier
Wanganui
Hastings
Cape Farewell
Palmerston North
5
Westport
Nelson
Tasman Bay
Levin
Masterton
South Island
Picton
Lower Hutt
Hokitika
Blenheim
WELLINGTON
Greymouth
Cook Strait
Chatham Islands (New Zealand)
Aoraki (Mount Cook) 3724
Southern Alps
Ashburton
Christchurch
Banks Peninsula
Chatham Island
Waitangi
Mount Aspiring 3030
Timaru
Mount Christina 2502
Queenstown
Oamaru
Pitt Island
Cape Providence
Gore
Dunedin
Foveaux Strait
Invercargill
Stewart Island
South West Cape
Bounty Islands (New Zealand)
Snares Islands
6
Auckland Islands (New Zealand)
Antipodes Islands (New Zealand)

Oceania
Australia, New Zealand and Southwest Pacific

Lambert Azimuthal Equal Area Projection

1:8 000 000

Oceania
Western Australia

Louisiade Archipelago
Rossel Island
Tagula Island
The Calvados Chain
Misima Island
Conflict Group
Bonvouloir Islands
Normanby Island
Dobu
Daloloia Group
Normanby Island
Esa'ala
Numanuma
ala
1758
Mount Suckling 3676
Amau
Abau
Suau
Tutubu
Hood Point

PAPUA NEW GUINEA

Yedau
Mount 3676 Suckling
Magarida
Gadaisu

Coral Sea

C o r a l   S e a

Coral Sea Islands Territory (Australia)

Eastern Fields
Ashmore Reefs

Lihou Reef and Cays
Carola Cay
Marion Reef
Diamantina Bank
Diane Bank
Willis Group
Magdelaine Cays
Coringa Islands
Diamond Islets
Paget Cay
Swain Reefs
Holmes Reef
Flinders Reefs
Herald Cays
Malay Reef
Abington Reef
Tregosse Islets and Reefs
Moore Reef
Osprey Reef
Shark Reef
Bougainville Reef

Frederick Reef
Kenn Reef
Wreck Reef
Cato Island and Bank
Saumarez Reef
Hinson Cay
Bell Cay
Tropic of Capricorn

Gulf of Carpentaria

G u l f   o f   C a r p e n t a r i a

Arafura Sea

A r a f u r a   S e a

Arnhem Land

NORTHERN TERRITORY

QUEENSLAND

Q U E E N S L A N D

Cape York Peninsula

Great Dividing Range

Gregory Range

Great Barrier Reef

G   r   e   a   t   B   a   r   r   i   e   r   R   e   e   f

Barkly Tableland

Simpson

Gulf of Carpentaria

Great Barrier Reef Marine Park (Far North Section)
Great Barrier Reef Marine Park (Cairns Section)
Great Barrier Reef Marine Park (Central Section)
Great Barrier Reef Marine Park (Capricorn Section)

Lambert Azimuthal Equal Area Projection

1:8 000 000

0   100   200   300   miles
0   100   200   300   400   500   km

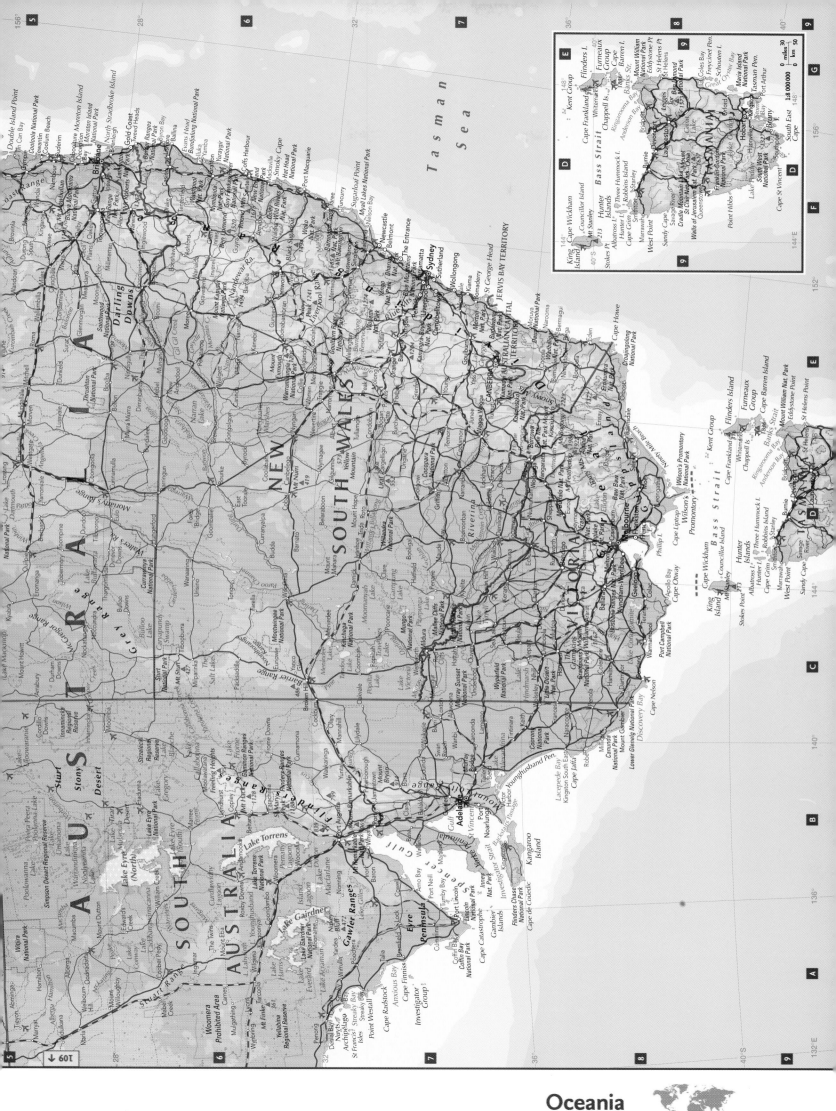

Oceania
Eastern Australia

Oceania
Southeast Australia

Lambert Azimuthal Equal Area Projection

1:5 000 000

New Zealand

NEW ZEALAND

Tasman Sea

North Island

South Island

PACIFIC OCEAN

Conic Equidistant Projection

1:5 250 000

North America Landscapes

North America, the world's third largest continent, supports a wide range of landscapes from the Arctic north to sub-tropical Central America. The main physiographic regions of the continent are the mountains of the west coast, stretching from Alaska in the north to Mexico and Central America in the south; the vast, relatively flat Canadian Shield; the Great Plains which make up the majority of the interior; the Appalachian Mountains in the east; and the Atlantic coastal plain.

These regions contain some significant physical features, including the Rocky Mountains, the Great Lakes – three of which are amongst the five largest lakes in the world – and the Mississippi-Missouri river system which is the world's fourth longest river. The Caribbean Sea contains a complex pattern of islands, many volcanic in origin, and the continent is joined to South America by the narrow Isthmus of Panama.

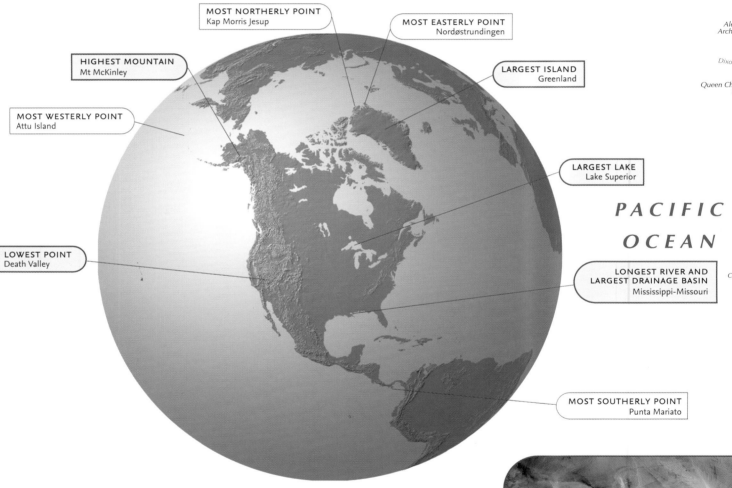

MOST NORTHERLY POINT
Kap Morris Jesup

MOST EASTERLY POINT
Nordøstrundingen

HIGHEST MOUNTAIN
Mt McKinley

LARGEST ISLAND
Greenland

MOST WESTERLY POINT
Attu Island

LARGEST LAKE
Lake Superior

LOWEST POINT
Death Valley

LONGEST RIVER AND LARGEST DRAINAGE BASIN
Mississippi-Missouri

MOST SOUTHERLY POINT
Punta Mariato

PACIFIC OCEAN

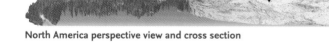

Coast Ranges — Rocky Mountains — Great Plains — Lake Michigan — Lake Huron — Lake Erie — Chesapeake Bay — Appalachian Mountains — Long Island — Cape Cod — Nova Scotia

North America perspective view and cross section

North America's physical features

Highest mountain	Mt McKinley, USA	6 194 metres	20 321 feet
Longest river	Mississippi-Missouri, USA	5 969 km	3 709 miles
Largest lake	Lake Superior, Canada/USA	82 100 sq km	31 699 sq miles
Largest island	Greenland	2 175 600 sq km	839 999 sq miles
Largest drainage basin	Mississippi-Missouri, USA	3 250 000 sq km	1 254 825 sq miles
Lowest point	Death Valley, USA	-86 metres	-282 feet

North America's longest river system, the Mississippi-Missouri, flows into the Gulf of Mexico through the **Mississippi Delta**.

North America's extent

TOTAL LAND AREA (including Hawaiian Islands)	24 680 331 sq km / 9 529 076 sq miles
Most northerly point	Kap Morris Jesup, Greenland
Most southerly point	Punta Mariato, Panama
Most westerly point	Attu Island, USA
Most easterly point	Nordostrundingen, Greenland

The **Grand Canyon**, Arizona, USA, the world's largest and most spectacular land canyon.

Facts

- Devon Island, Canada, is the world's largest uninhabited island
- Canada has the longest coastline of any country in the world
- Lake Superior is the world's largest freshwater lake
- Over 320 000 square kilometres of the USA is protected for conservation purposes

The **Yucatán peninsula**, Mexico, divides the Gulf of Mexico from the Caribbean Sea.

ARCTIC OCEAN

ATLANTIC OCEAN

SOUTH AMERICA

Greenland Sea

Greenland

Baffin Bay

Hudson Bay

Labrador Sea

Gulf of Mexico

Caribbean Sea

West Indies

Greater Antilles

Lesser Antilles

115

North America has been dominated economically and politically by the USA since the nineteenth century. Before that, the continent was subject to colonial influences, particularly of Spain in the south and of Britain and France in the east. The nineteenth century saw the steady development of the western half of the continent. The wealth of natural resources and the generally temperate climate were an excellent basis for settlement, agriculture and industrial development which has led to the USA being the richest nation in the world today.

Although there are twenty three independent countries and fourteen dependent territories in North America, Canada, Mexico and the USA have approximately eighty five per cent of the continent's population and eighty eight per cent of its land area. Large parts of the north remain sparsely populated, while the most densely populated areas are in the northeast USA, and the Caribbean.

Washington DC, a leading international political centre and capital city of the United States.

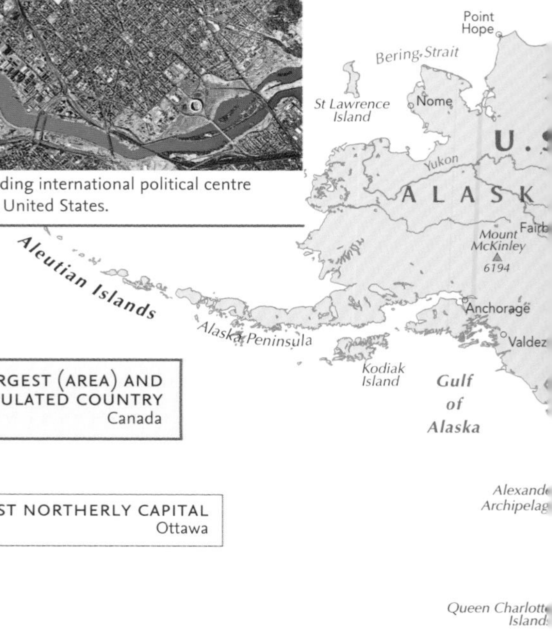

LARGEST COUNTRY (POPULATION)
United States of America

LARGEST (AREA) AND
LEAST DENSELY POPULATED COUNTRY
Canada

MOST NORTHERLY CAPITAL
Ottawa

LARGEST AND
HIGHEST CAPITAL
Mexico City

SMALLEST COUNTRY
(AREA AND POPULATION)
St Kitts and Nevis

MOST DENSELY POPULATED COUNTRY
Barbados

SMALLEST CAPITAL
Belmopan

MOST SOUTHERLY CAPITAL
Panama City

North America's capitals

Largest capital (population)	Mexico City, Mexico	19 013 000	
Smallest capital (population)	Belmopan, Belize	9 000	
Most northerly capital	Ottawa, Canada	45° 25'N	
Most southerly capital	Panama City, Panama	8° 56'N	
Highest capital	Mexico City, Mexico	2 300 metres	7 546 feet

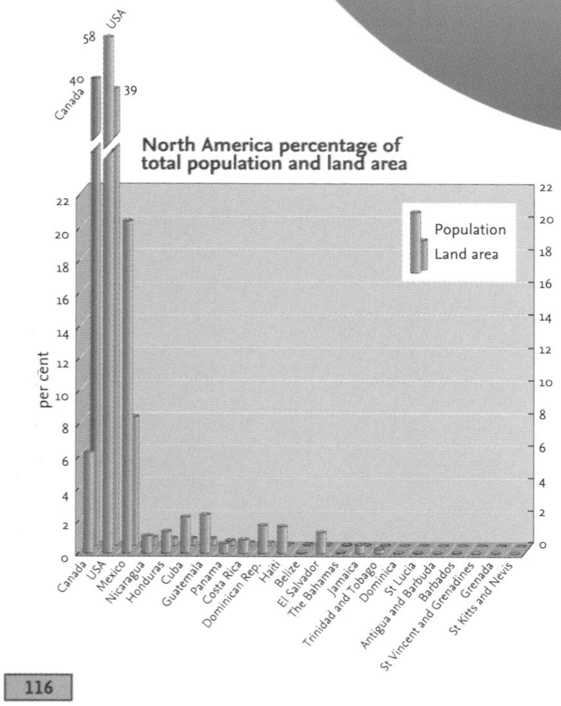

North America percentage of total population and land area

per cent

Population
Land area

Canada 40
USA 58
39

Canada, USA, Mexico, Nicaragua, Honduras, Cuba, Guatemala, Panama, Costa Rica, Dominican Rep., Haiti, Belize, The Bahamas, El Salvador, Jamaica, Trinidad and Tobago, Dominica, Antigua and Barbuda, St Lucia, Barbados, St. Vincent and Grenadines, Grenada, St Kitts and Nevis

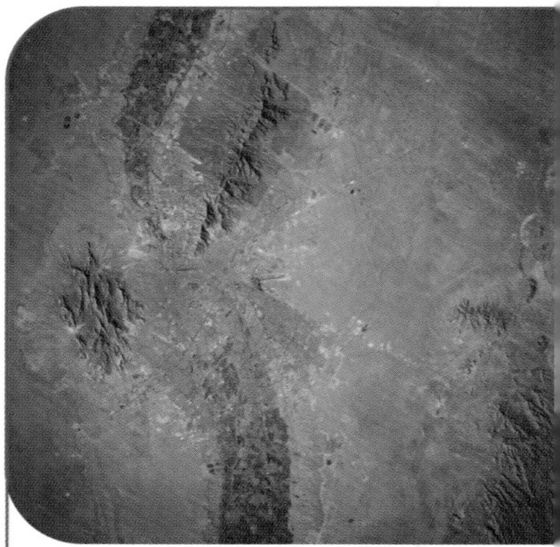

The cities of **El Paso**, USA, and **Ciudad Juarez**, Mexico, are located on the Rio Grande which forms part of the USA/Mexico border.

North America's countries

Largest country (area)	Canada	9 984 670 sq km	3 855 103 sq miles
Smallest country (area)	St Kitts and Nevis	261 sq km	101 sq miles
Largest country (population)	United States of America	294 043 000	
Smallest country (population)	St Kitts and Nevis	42 000	
Most densely populated country	Barbados	628 per sq km	1 627 per sq mile
Least densely populated country	Canada	3 per sq km	8 per sq mile

Point Hope
Bering Strait
St Lawrence Island
Nome
U.S
Yukon
A L A S K A
Mount McKinley 6194
Fairb
Anchorage
Valdez
Aleutian Islands
Alaska Peninsula
Kodiak Island
Gulf of Alaska
Alexander Archipelag
Queen Charlotte Island

The Bahamas, a chain of islands in the North Atlantic Ocean, lying southeast of Florida, USA.

Facts

- The Panama Canal, opened in 1914, cut the journey between the Atlantic and the Pacific by over 14 000 km

- Mexico City is the highest city in North America and houses approximately 18% of Mexico's population

- The state of Alaska was bought by the USA from Russia in 1867

- The territory of Nunavut is Canada's newest administrative division, created in 1999 from the eastern part of Northwest Territories

117

Lambert Conformal Conic Projection

1:16 000 000

| 0 | | 200 | | 400 | miles |
| 0 | 200 | 400 | 600 | 800 | km |

North America
Canada

Conic Equidistant Projection

1:7 000 000

I J K L M N O P

NUNAVUT

Hudson
Bay

ITORIES

ADA

SASKATCHEWAN

MANITOBA

ONTARIO

U. MONTANA S. A.

NORTH
DAKOTA

MINNESOTA

North America
Western Canada

Conic Equidistant Projection

1:7 000 000

| 0 | 100 | 200 | miles |

| 0 | 100 | 200 | 300 | 400 | km |

Clutterbuck Head Island William Smith 2
Vachon Kangirsuk North Aulatsivik Island

Ungava Bay Seven Islands Bay

Labrador
Sea

L a b r a d o r

NEWFOUNDLAND
AND LABRADOR

NEWFOUNDLAND
AND LABRADOR

QUÉBEC

Gulf of
St Lawrence

St Pierre
and Miquelon
(France)

Péninsule
de Gaspé

MAINE

NEW
BRUNSWICK

PRINCE EDWARD
ISLAND

NOVA SCOTIA

Bay of Fundy

Gulf of
Maine

A T L A N T I C

O C E A N

Lambert Conformal Conic Projection

1:12 000 000

| 0 | 100 | 200 | 300 | 400 | miles |

| 0 | 100 | 200 | 300 | 400 | 500 | 600 | 700 | km |

North America
United States of America

Lambert Conformal Conic Projection

1:7 000 000

miles

km

→ 136

North America
Western United States

PACIFIC

OCEAN

NEVADA

CALIFORNIA

UNIT

Channel
Islands

Gulf of
Santa
Catalina

BAJA C

Lambert Conformal Conic Projection

1:3 500 000

| 0 | 50 | 100 | miles |

| 0 | 50 | 100 | 150 | 200 | km |

North America
Southwest United States

Lambert Conformal Conic Projection

1:7 000 000

miles
0   100   200
0   100   200   300   400 km

North America
Central United States

Lambert Conformal Conic Projection

1:7 000 000

| 0 | 100 | 200 | miles |

| 0 | 100 | 200 | 300 | 400 | km |

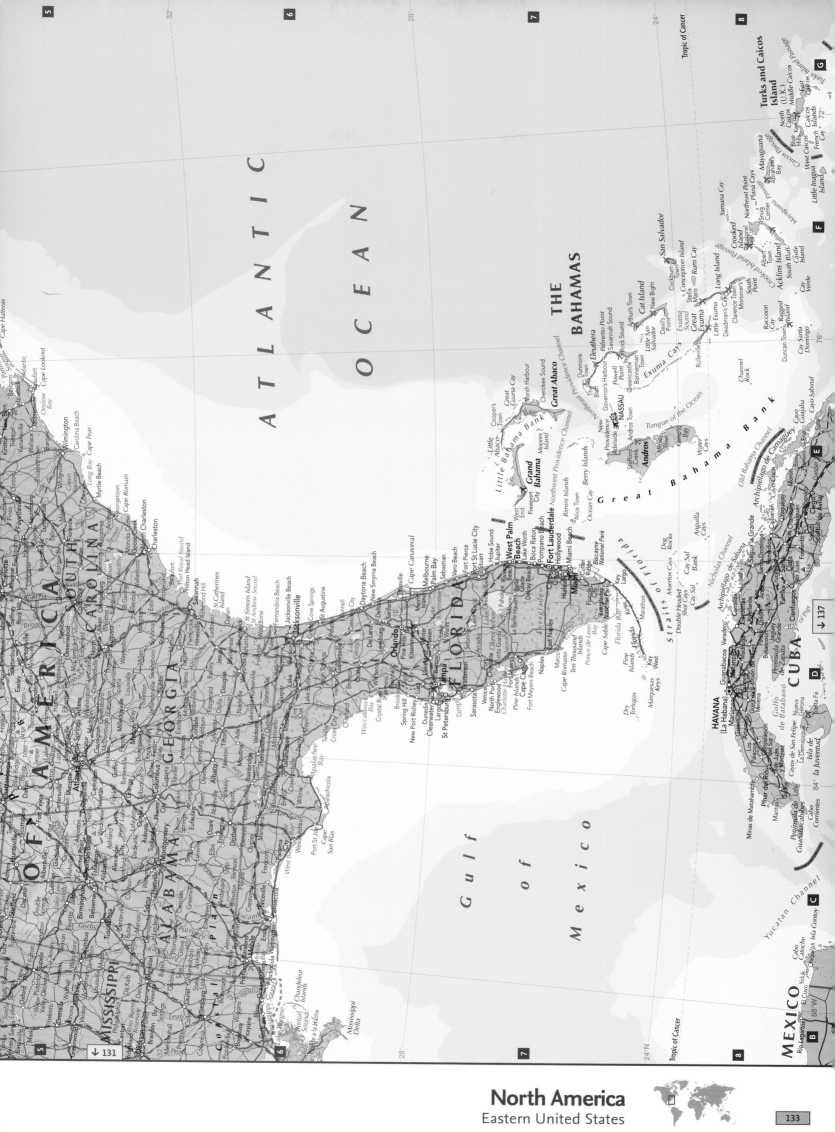

ATLANTIC OCEAN

THE BAHAMAS

Gulf of Mexico

CUBA

MEXICO

North America
Eastern United States

Lambert Conformal Conic Projection

1:3 500 000

miles
0   50   100

km
0   50   100   150   200

Lambert Conformal Conic Projection

1:14 000 000

0   200   400   miles

0   200   400   600   800   km

KENTUCKY
Bowling Green Beckley WEST Charlottesville Richmond 75°
Somerset London VIRGINIA Lynchburg Petersburg
Nashville Morristown Roanoke Newport News Virginia Beach
Gallatin Knoxville Mt Mitchell Danville Norfolk Chesapeake 55° 1

ATLANTIC
Atlanta
GEORGIA
NORTH CAROLINA
SOUTH CAROLINA
Cape Hatteras 2

OCEAN

HAMILTON • Bermuda
(U.K.) 3

Tropic of Cancer

THE BAHAMAS

NASSAU

West Indies

CUBA
HAVANA
(La Habana)

HAITI
PORT-AU-PRINCE
DOMINICAN
REPUBLIC
SANTO
DOMINGO

Puerto Rico
(U.S.A.)
SAN JUAN

Virgin
Islands

Leeward Islands

ANTIGUA
AND BARBUDA

DOMINICA

Lesser Antilles

MARTINIQUE
(France)

ST LUCIA

ST VINCENT
AND
THE GRENADINES BARBADOS

GRENADA

Caribbean Sea

JAMAICA
KINGSTON

NICARAGUA
MANAGUA

COSTA RICA
SAN
JOSE

PANAMA
PANAMA
CITY

VENEZUELA
CARACAS

COLOMBIA
BOGOTÁ

GUYANA

BRAZIL

↓ 142

North America
Central America and the Caribbean

137

South America is a continent of great contrasts, with landscapes varying from the tropical rainforests of the Amazon Basin, to the Atacama Desert, the driest place on earth, and the sub-Antarctic regions of southern Chile and Argentina. The dominant physical features are the Andes, stretching along the entire west coast of the continent and containing numerous mountains over 6 000 metres high, and the Amazon, which is the second longest river in the world and has the world's largest drainage basin.

The Altiplano is a high plateau lying between two of the Andes ranges. It contains Lake Titicaca, the world's highest navigable lake. By contrast, large lowland areas dominate the centre of the continent, lying between the Andes and the Guiana and Brazilian Highlands. These vast grasslands stretch from the Llanos of the north through the Selvas and the Gran Chaco to the Pampas of Argentina.

South America's largest lake, **Lake Titicaca**, high in the Andes on the border between Bolivia and Peru.

South America perspective view and cross section

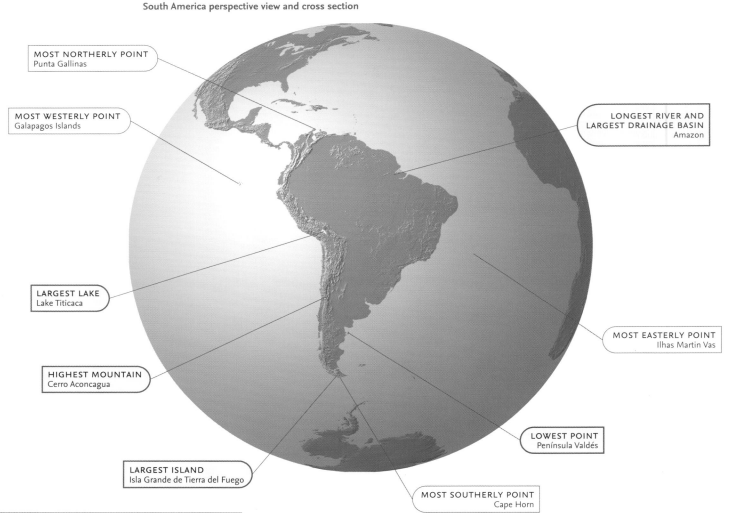

MOST NORTHERLY POINT
Punta Gallinas

MOST WESTERLY POINT
Galapagos Islands

LONGEST RIVER AND LARGEST DRAINAGE BASIN
Amazon

LARGEST LAKE
Lake Titicaca

MOST EASTERLY POINT
Ilhas Martin Vas

HIGHEST MOUNTAIN
Cerro Aconcagua

LOWEST POINT
Península Valdés

LARGEST ISLAND
Isla Grande de Tierra del Fuego

MOST SOUTHERLY POINT
Cape Horn

Internet Links

South America's physical features

Highest mountain	Cerro Aconcagua, Argentina	6 959 metres	22 831 feet
Longest river	Amazon	6 516 km	4 049 miles
Largest lake	Lake Titicaca, Bolivia/Peru	8 340 sq km	3 220 sq miles
Largest island	Isla Grande de Tierra del Fuego, Argentina/Chile	47 000 sq km	18 147 sq miles
Largest drainage basin	Amazon	7 050 000 sq km	2 722 005 sq miles
Lowest point	Península Valdés, Argentina	-40 metres	-131 feet

NORTH AMERICA

Caribbean Sea

Punta Gallinas
Golfo del Darién
Gulf of Panama
Cabo Corrientes
Isla de Malpelo

Lake Maracaibo
Golfo de Venezuela
Isla de Margarita
Orinoco
Orinoco Delta
Waini Point

Cordillera Occidental
Cordillera Central
Cordillera Oriental
Llanos
Meta
Cerro Yavi 2285 ▲
Guiana Highlands
La Gran Sabana
Pakaraima Mountains
Point Isère
Cabo Orange
Ilha de Maracá

Guaviare
Orinoco
Branco
Maroni

Volcán Cotopaxi 5896 ▲
6310 ▲ Chimborazo
Punta Santa Elena
Golfo de Guayaquil

Caquetá
Japurá
Amazon Basin
Negro
Represa de Balbina
Mouths of the Amazon
Amazon
Ilha de Marajó
Baía de São Marcos

Galapagos Islands

Putumayo
Amazon
Marañón
Juruá
Purus
Selvas
Madeira
Tapajós
Xingu
Tocantins
Represa Tucuruí
Cabo de São Roque

Punta Negra
A n d e s
Nevado de Huascarán 6768 ▲
Ucayali
Madeira
Teles Pires
Iriri
Paraíba

Cordillera Central
Cordillera Oriental
Juruena
Arinos
Xingu
Araguaia
Tocantins
Barragem de Sobradinho
São Francisco

Cordillera Occidental
Beni
Guaporé
Jiparaná
Planalto do Mato Grosso
Chapada Diamantina

Lago de San Luis
Mamoré
Yungas
São Francisco
Velhas
Cabo Santo Antonio

Lake Titicaca
Altiplano
San Miguel
Paraguay
Pantanal
Brazilian Highlands

Punta de Coles
Lago de Poopó
Bañados del Izozog
Grande
Ponta da Baleia

A t a c a m a   D e s e r t
Salar de Uyuni
Paraguaná
Paranaíba
São Francisco
Cabo de São Tomé

Punta Tetas
Gran Chaco
Pilcomayo
Teuco
Paraguay
Paraná
Paranapanema

Punta Ballena
Nevado Ojos del Salado 6908 ▲
Cerro Bonete 6872 ▲
Salado
Iguaçu
Iguaçu Falls
Ilha de São Sebastião

Islas de los Desventurados

Salinas Grandes
Uruguay
Paraná

Cerro Aconcagua 6959 ▲
Desaguadero
Sierras de Córdoba
Salado
P a m p a s
Paraná
Rio de la Plata
Punta Norte
Punta Sur

Punta Lavapié
Colorado
Negro
Bahía Blanca
Lagoa dos Patos
Lagoa Mirim
Serra do Mar

Punta Galera
A n d e s
Negro
Golfo San Matías
Península Valdés

Isla de Chiloé
Chubut
P a t a g o n i a
Golfo de San Jorge
Cabo Tres Puntas

Archipiélago de los Chonos
Golfo de Penas

Lago San Martín
Lago Argentino
Bahía Grande
Falkland Islands
West Falkland
East Falkland

Strait of Magellan
Isla Grande de Tierra del Fuego
Isla de los Estados

South Georgia

Cape Horn
Drake Passage
Scotia Sea

PACIFIC OCEAN

ATLANTIC OCEAN

South America's extent

TOTAL LAND AREA	17 815 420 sq km / 6 878 534 sq miles
Most northerly point	Punta Gallinas, Colombia
Most southerly point	Cape Horn, Chile
Most westerly point	Galapagos Islands, Ecuador
Most easterly point	Ilhas Martin Vas, Atlantic Ocean

Isla Grande de Tierra del Fuego, South America's largest island, situated at the southernmost tip of the continent.

Confluence of the **Amazon** and **Negro** rivers at Manaus, northern Brazil.

Facts

- Water flow along the Amazon is over 1 500 times that of the River Thames

- Cerro Aconcagua, 6 959 metres, is the highest point in the western hemisphere

- The Amazon rainforest supports approximately half of all the world's living species

- The Pantanal in Brazil is the largest area of wetland in the world

- The world's driest desert is the Atacama, where only 1mm of rain may fall as infrequently as once every 5–20 years

South America Countries

French Guiana, a French Department, is the only remaining territory under overseas control on a continent which has seen a long colonial history. Much of South America was colonized by Spain in the sixteenth century, with Britain, Portugal and the Netherlands each claiming territory in the northeast of the continent. This colonization led to the conquering of ancient civilizations, including the Incas in Peru. Most countries became independent from Spain and Portugal in the early nineteenth century.

The population of the continent reflects its history, being composed primarily of indigenous Indian peoples and mestizos – reflecting the long Hispanic influence. There has been a steady process of urbanization within the continent, with major movements of the population from rural to urban areas. The majority of the population now live in the major cities and within 300 kilometres of the coast.

Rio de Janeiro, third largest city in Brazil and the capital until 1960 when the status of capital was transferred to Brasília.

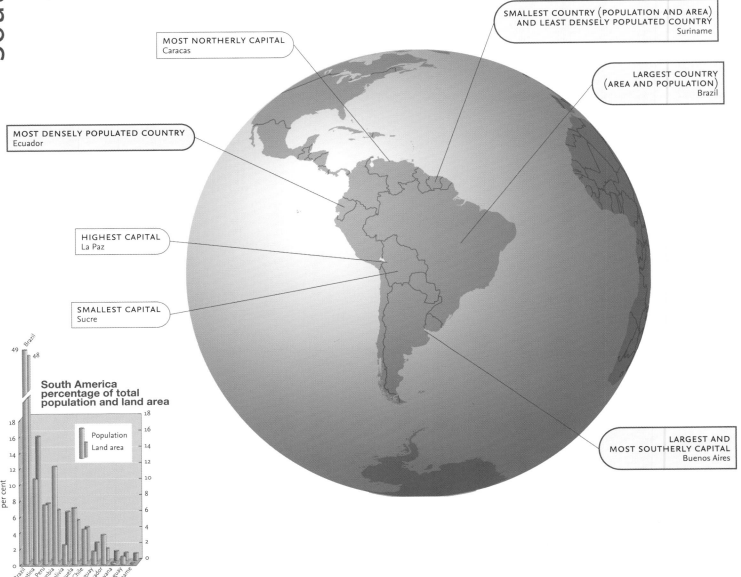

MOST NORTHERLY CAPITAL
Caracas

SMALLEST COUNTRY (POPULATION AND AREA) AND LEAST DENSELY POPULATED COUNTRY
Suriname

LARGEST COUNTRY (AREA AND POPULATION)
Brazil

MOST DENSELY POPULATED COUNTRY
Ecuador

HIGHEST CAPITAL
La Paz

SMALLEST CAPITAL
Sucre

LARGEST AND MOST SOUTHERLY CAPITAL
Buenos Aires

South America percentage of total population and land area

Population
Land area

per cent

Brazil, Argentina, Peru, Colombia, Bolivia, Venezuela, Chile, Paraguay, Ecuador, Guyana, Uruguay, Suriname

South America's countries

Largest country (area)	Brazil	8 514 879 sq km	3 287 613 sq miles
Smallest country (area)	Suriname	163 820 sq km	63 251 sq miles
Largest country (population)	Brazil	178 470 000	
Smallest country (population)	Suriname	436 000	
Most densely populated country	Ecuador	48 per sq km	124 per sq mile
Least densely populated country	Suriname	3 per sq km	7 per sq mile

Internet Links	
● UK Foreign and Commonwealth Office	www.fco.gov.uk
● CIA World Factbook	www.odci.gov/cia/publications/factbook
● Caribbean Community (Caricom)	www.caricom.org
● Latin American Network Information Center	lanic.utexas.edu

South America's capitals

Largest capital (population)	Buenos Aires, Argentina	13 349 000
Smallest capital (population)	Sucre, Bolivia	183 000
Most northerly capital	Caracas, Venezuela	10° 28'N
Most southerly capital	Buenos Aires, Argentina	34° 36'S
Highest capital	La Paz, Bolivia	3 630 metres 11 909 feet

Caribbean Sea

NORTH AMERICA

PACIFIC OCEAN

ATLANTIC OCEAN

Punta Gallinas

Barranquilla
Cartagena
Maracaibo
Cabimas
Maracay
Caracas
Cumaná

Montería
Barquisimeto
Valencia
Ciudad Bolívar
San Cristóbal
VENEZUELA
Georgetown
Paramaribo

Medellín
Tunja
Puerto Ayacucho
GUYANA
Cayenne

Ibagué
Bogotá
SURINAME
French Guiana

Cali
COLOMBIA
Boa Vista

Neiva
Orinoco

Isla de Malpelo (Colombia)

Pasto
Caquetá
Orinoco

Esmeraldas
Mouths of the Amazon

Quito
ECUADOR
Represa de Balbina
Belém

Manta
Guayaquil
Cuenca
Amazon
Manaus
Santarém
São Luís
Parnaíba

Galapagos Islands (Ecuador)

Iquitos
Marañón
Fortaleza

Sullana
Tonantins
Represa Tucuruí
Maraba
Teresina
Natal

Chiclayo
Tarapoto
Carauari
BRAZIL

Trujillo
Cruzeiro do Sul
Porto Velho
Madeira
João Pessoa
Floresta
Recife

Pucallpa
Rio Branco
Juàzeiro
Maceió

PERU
Huancayo
Puerto Maldonado
Aracaju

Callao
Lima
Rio Branco
Cuiabá
Salvador

Cusco
Ica
Trinidad
Brasília
Ilhéus

Juliaca
Lago de San Luis
Goiânia

Arequipa
Lake Titicaca
La Paz
BOLIVIA
Teófilo Otôni
Patos de Minas

Arica
Cochabamba
Santa Cruz
Uberaba
Belo Horizonte
Vitória

Iquique
Sucre
Campo Grande
Araçatuba
Ribeirão Preto
Nova Iguaçu

Potosí
PARAGUAY
Maringá
Campinas
Rio de Janeiro

Antofagasta
Tarija
Pedro Juan Caballero
São Paulo
Curitiba

Copiapó
San Salvador de Jujuy
Asunción
Foz do Iguaçu

San Miguel de Tucumán
Formosa
Encarnación
Florianópolis

Catamarca
Resistencia
Corrientes
Posadas
Santa Maria
Porto Alegre

La Rioja
Paraná
Uruguay
Concordia
Lagoa dos Patos

San Juan
Córdoba
Santa Fé
Paysandú
Rio Grande

Cerro Aconcagua 6959
Valparaíso
Santiago
Mendoza
San Luis
Rosario
URUGUAY
Montevideo

Talca
San Rafael
Buenos Aires
La Plata
Río de la Plata

Concepción
Chillán
ARGENTINA
Santa Rosa
Bahía Blanca
Mar del Plata

Valdivia
Neuquén
Negro

Puerto Montt
Colorado

Isla de Chiloé
Viedma

Patagonia
Trelew

Archipiélago de los Chonos
Comodoro Rivadavia
Golfo de San Jorge

Punta Medanosa

Falkland Islands (U.K.)

Puerto Natales
Rio Gallegos
Bahía Grande
Stanley

Punta Arenas
Isla Grande de Tierra del Fuego

Ushuaia

Cape Horn

South Georgia (U.K.)

Galapagos Islands, an island territory of Ecuador which lies on the equator in the eastern Pacific Ocean over 900 kilometres west of the coast of Ecuador.

Falkland Islands, an overseas UK territory in the South Atlantic Ocean.

Facts

- South America is often referred to as 'Latin America', reflecting the historic influences of Spain and Portugal

- The largest city in each South American country is the capital, except in Brazil and Ecuador

- South America has only 2 landlocked countries – Bolivia and Paraguay

- Chile is over 4 000 kilometres long but has an average width of only 177 kilometres

ni Point
Anna Regina
GEORGETOWN
Bartica
Linden
New Amsterdam
GUYANA
Itúni
Mahdia
s
PARAMARIBO
Nieuw
Nickerie
Onverwacht
Apoera
Albina
St-Laurent-
du-Maroni
Pointe Isère
Organabo
Sinnamary
Kourou
CAYENNE
Pointe Béhague

SURINAME
Wilhelmina
Gebergte
1250
Juliana Top
Brokopondo
Professor van
Blommestein Meer
Petit Saut
Dam
Régina
**French
Guiana**
Cabo Orange
Cabo Caciporé

A T L A N T I C

O C E A N

Parque Nacional
de Cabo Orange
Calçoene
Ilha de Maracá

Biloku
Serra Acaraí
Serra Tumucumaque
Serra Lombarda
Tacalé
Amapá

**Mouths of the
Amazon**

Maloca
Ferreira-
Gomes
Araguari
Terezinha
Porto Grande
Macapá
Ilha Caviana
Ilha Mexiana
Afuá
Baía de Marajó
Salinópolis

resa
Balbina
Santa
Maria
Oriximiná
Óbidos
Alenquer
Prainha
Morro
Grande
Lago
do Erepecu
629
Monte Dourado
Ilha Grande
de Gurupá
Boca do Jari
Gurupá
Breves
Ilha
de Marajó
Souré
Cachoeira
do Arari
Anajás
Vigia
Bragança
Viseu

Urucara
Faro
Juruti
Santarém
Boim
Pacoval
Almeirim
Porto
de Moz
Portel
Cametá
Abaetetuba
Belém
Castanhal
Capanema
Santa
Helena
Ilhas de São João

Parintins
Barreirinha
Monte Alegre
Belo Monte
Altamira
Pombal
Acará
Irituia
Gurupi
Guimarães
São Luís
Icatu
Rosário
Araioses
Parnaíba

BRAZIL
Parque Nacional
Amazônia
Itaituba
São Luís
Represa
Tucuruí
Jacundá
Tucuruí
Paragominas
Santa
Inês
Viana
Santa
Pinheiro
Araiosos
Itapicuru Mirim
Camocim
Acaraú
Fortaleza
(Ceará)

ATLANTIC

OCEAN

South America
Southern South America

Lambert Azimuthal Equal Area Projection

1:14 000 000

MATO GROSSO

GOIÁS

DISTRITO FEDERAL
BRASÍLIA

BRAZIL

BAHIA

Chapada

MINAS GERAIS

Serra do Espinhaço

ESPÍRITO SANTO

SÃO PAULO

São Paulo

Santos

Serra da Mantiqueira

RIO DE JANEIRO

Rio de Janeiro
Niterói

PARANÁ

Curitiba

SANTA CATARINA

Florianópolis

RIO GRANDE DO SUL

ATLANTIC OCEAN

Tropic of Capricorn

Lambert Azimuthal Equal Area Projection

1:7 000 000

100   200   miles
100   200   300   400   km

South America
Southeast Brazil

Between them, the world's oceans and polar regions cover approximately seventy per cent of the earth's surface. The oceans contain ninety six per cent of the earth's water and a vast range of flora and fauna. They are a major influence on the world's climate, particularly through ocean currents. The Arctic and Antarctica are the coldest and most inhospitable places on the earth. They both have vast amounts of ice which, if global warming continues, could have a major influence on sea level across the globe.

Our understanding of the oceans and polar regions has increased enormously over the last twenty years through the development of new technologies, particularly that of satellite remote sensing, which can generate vast amounts of data relating to, for example, topography (both on land and the seafloor), land cover and sea surface temperature.

The Oceans

The world's major oceans are the Pacific, the Atlantic and the Indian Oceans. The Arctic Ocean is generally considered as part of the Atlantic, and the Southern Ocean, which stretches around the whole of Antarctica is usually treated as an extension of each of the three major oceans.

One of the most important factors affecting the earth's climate is the circulation of water within and between the oceans. Differences in temperature and surface winds create ocean currents which move enormous quantities of water around the globe. These currents re-distribute heat which the oceans have absorbed from the sun, and so have a major effect on the world's climate system. El Niño is one climatic phenomenon directly influenced by these ocean processes.

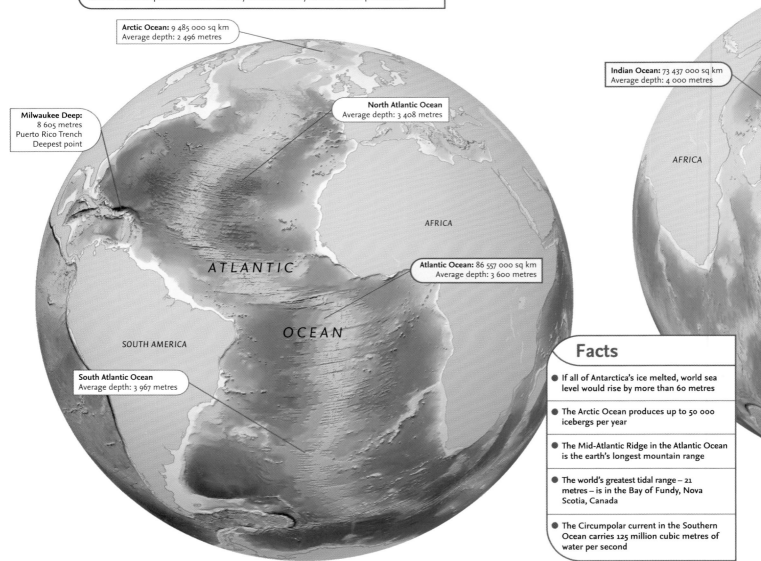

Pacific Ocean
World's largest ocean: 166 241 000 sq km
Average depth: 4 200m

North Pacific Ocean
Average depth: 4 573 metres

NORTH AMERICA

PACIFIC

OCEAN

AUSTRALIA

Challenger Deep: 10 920 metres
Mariana Trench
Deepest point

South Pacific Ocean
Average depth: 3 935 metres

Arctic Ocean: 9 485 000 sq km
Average depth: 2 496 metres

Milwaukee Deep:
8 605 metres
Puerto Rico Trench
Deepest point

North Atlantic Ocean
Average depth: 3 408 metres

Indian Ocean: 73 437 000 sq km
Average depth: 4 000 metres

AFRICA

AFRICA

ATLANTIC

Atlantic Ocean: 86 557 000 sq km
Average depth: 3 600 metres

OCEAN

SOUTH AMERICA

South Atlantic Ocean
Average depth: 3 967 metres

Facts

● If all of Antarctica's ice melted, world sea level would rise by more than 60 metres

● The Arctic Ocean produces up to 50 000 icebergs per year

● The Mid-Atlantic Ridge in the Atlantic Ocean is the earth's longest mountain range

● The world's greatest tidal range – 21 metres – is in the Bay of Fundy, Nova Scotia, Canada

● The Circumpolar current in the Southern Ocean carries 125 million cubic metres of water per second

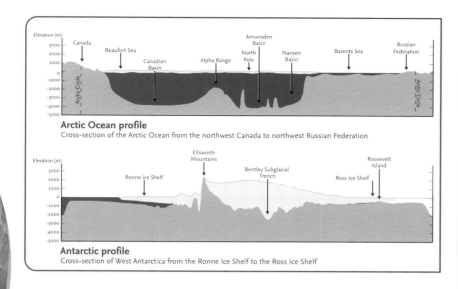

Arctic Ocean profile
Cross-section of the Arctic Ocean from the northwest Canada to northwest Russian Federation

Antarctic profile
Cross-section of West Antarctica from the Ronne Ice Shelf to the Ross Ice Shelf

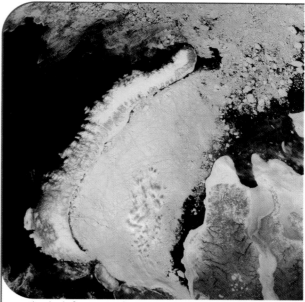

The island of **Novaya Zemlya**, Russian Federation, prevents the Kara Sea (right) from being affected by the warming influence of the Gulf Stream in the Atlantic Ocean and the Barents Sea (left).

Internet Links

● National Oceanic and Atmospheric Administration	**www.noaa.gov**
● Southampton Oceanography Centre	**www.soc.soton.ac.uk**
● British Antarctic Survey	**www.bas.ac.uk**
● Scott Polar Research Institute (SPRI)	**www.spri.cam.ac.uk**
● The National Snow and Ice Data Center (NSIDC)	**nsidc.org**

Polar Regions

Although a harsh climate is common to the two polar regions, there are major differences between the Arctic and Antarctica. The North Pole is surrounded by the Arctic Ocean, much of which is permanently covered by sea ice, while the South Pole lies on the huge land mass of Antarctica. This is covered by a permanent ice cap which reaches a maximum thickness of over four kilometres. Antarctica has no permanent population, but Europe, Asia and North America all stretch into the Arctic region which is populated by numerous ethnic groups. Antarctica is subject to the Antarctic Treaty of 1959 which does not recognize individual land claims and protects the continent in the interests of international scientific cooperation.

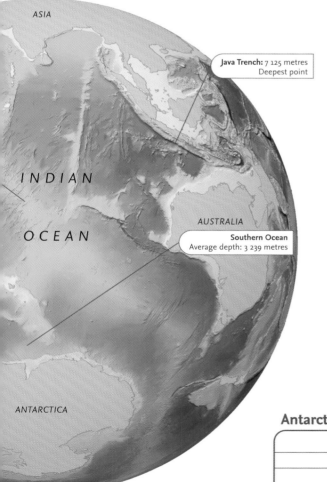

Java Trench: 7 125 metres
Deepest point

Southern Ocean
Average depth: 3 239 metres

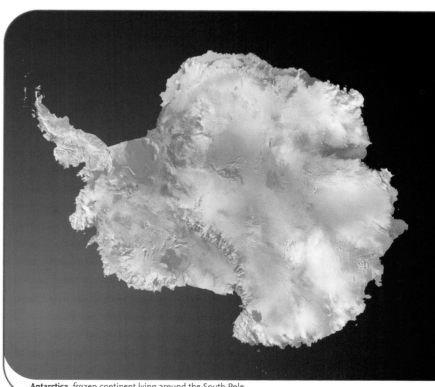

Antarctica, frozen continent lying around the South Pole.

Antarctica's physical features

Highest mountain: Vinson Massif	4 897 m	16 066 ft
Total land area (excluding ice shelves)	12 093 000 sq km	4 669 292 sq miles
Ice shelves	1 559 000 sq km	601 954 sq miles
Exposed rock	49 000 sq km	18 920 sq miles
Lowest bedrock elevation (Bentley Subglacial Trench)	2 496 m below sea level	8 189 ft below sea level
Maximum ice thickness (Astrolabe Subglacial Basin)	4 776 m	15 669 ft
Mean ice thickness (including ice shelves)	1 859 m	6 099 ft
Volume of ice sheet (including ice shelves)	25 400 000 cubic km	10 160 000 cubic miles

Atlantic Ocean
Indian Ocean

149

Lambert Azimuthal Equal Area Projection

150

1:50 000 000

| 0 | 500 | 1000 | 1500 miles |
| 0 | 500 | 1000 | 1500 | 2000 | 2500 km |

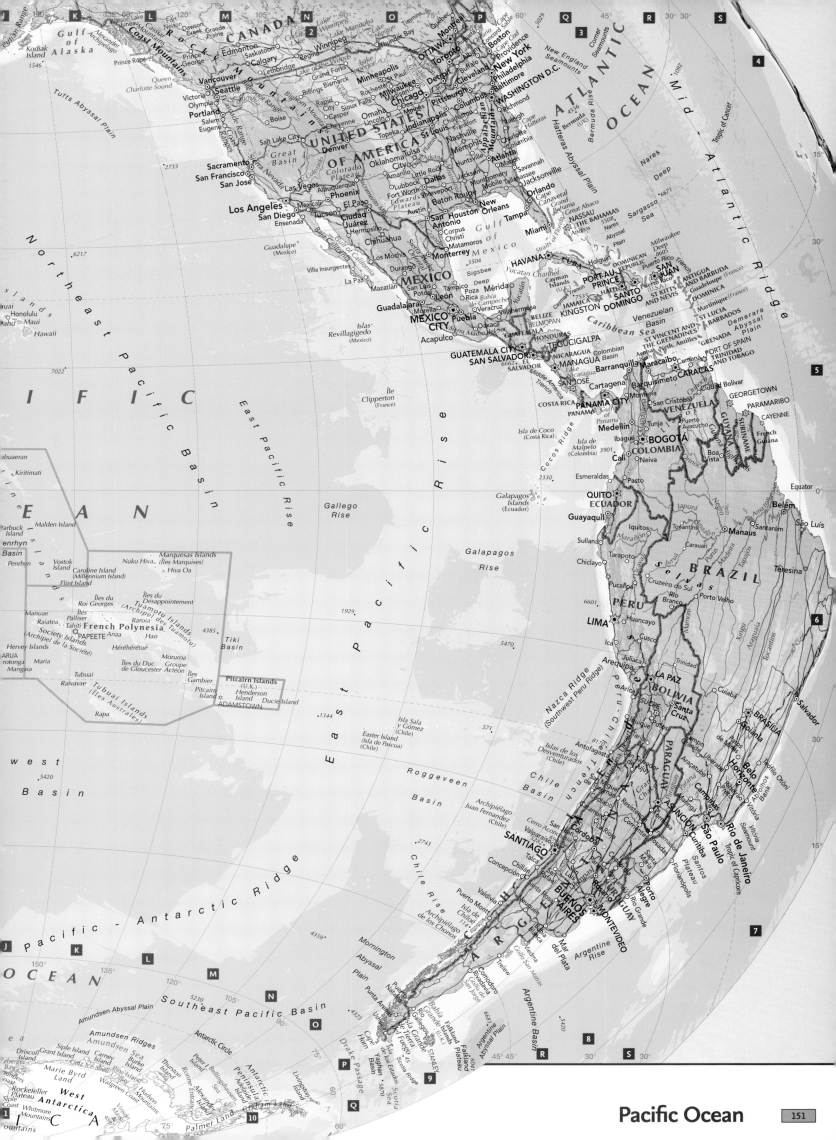

Pacific Ocean

151

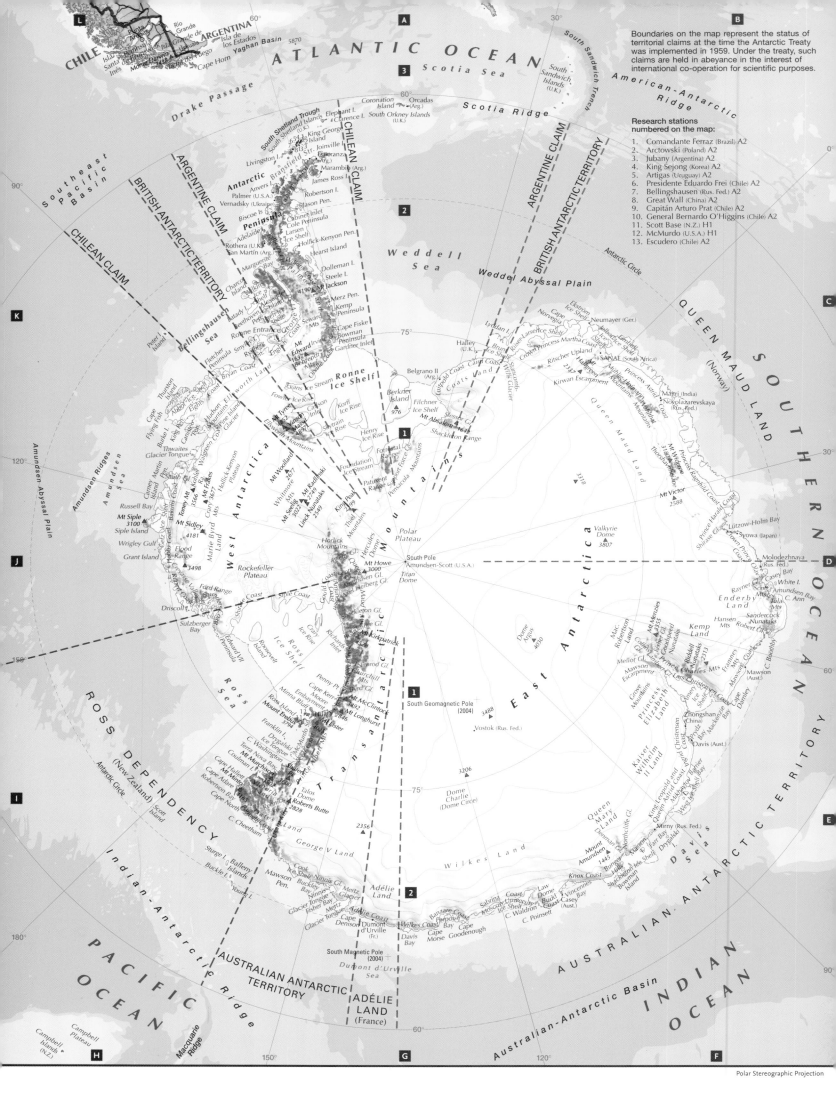

CHILE ARGENTINA

Rio Grande
Punta Arenas
Isla de los Estados
Tierra del Fuego
Cape Horn
Santa Inés
Monte Darwin

Yaghan Basin 5870

ATLANTIC OCEAN

Scotia Sea

South Sandwich Islands (U.K.)

Boundaries on the map represent the status of territorial claims at the time the Antarctic Treaty was implemented in 1959. Under the treaty, such claims are held in abeyance in the interest of international co-operation for scientific purposes.

Scotia Ridge

American-Antarctic Ridge

Drake Passage

Coronation Island   Orcadas (Arg.)
South Orkney Islands (U.K.)

Elephant I.
South Shetland Trough
South Shetland Islands (U.K.)
King George Island
Livingston I.
Clarence I.
Esperanza (Arg.)
Marambio (Arg.)
James Ross I.
Robertson I.
Gibson Inlet

Antarctic
Anvers I.
Palmer (U.S.A.)
Vernadsky (Ukraine)
Biscoe Is.
Cabinet Inlet
Cole Peninsula
Larsen Ice Shelf
Adelaide I.
Rothera (U.K.)
San Martín (Arg.)
Hollick-Kenyon Pen.
Hearst Island

Research stations numbered on the map:

1. Comandante Ferraz (Brazil) A2
2. Arctowski (Poland) A2
3. Jubany (Argentina) A2
4. King Sejong (Korea) A2
5. Artigas (Uruguay) A2
6. Presidente Eduardo Frei (Chile) A2
7. Bellingshausen (Rus. Fed.) A2
8. Great Wall (China) A2
9. Capitán Arturo Prat (Chile) A2
10. General Bernardo O'Higgins (Chile) A2
11. Scott Base (N.Z.) H1
12. McMurdo (U.S.A.) H1
13. Escudero (Chile) A2

ARGENTINE CLAIM

BRITISH ANTARCTIC TERRITORY

CHILEAN CLAIM

CHILEAN CLAIM

ARGENTINE CLAIM

BRITISH ANTARCTIC TERRITORY

Antarctic Circle

Peter I Island

Bellingshausen Sea

Weddell Sea

Weddel Abyssal Plain

QUEEN MAUD LAND (Norway)

SOUTHERN OCEAN

Fletcher Peninsula
Bryan Coast
Cape Flying Fish
Thurston Island
Abbot Ice Shelf
Eights Coast

Ronne Entrance
Charcot Island
Alexander I.

Edward
Marguerite Bay
Ronne Ice Shelf

Steele I.
Dolleman I.
Merz Pen.
Kemp Peninsula
Seward Mts.
Bowman Peninsula
Cape Fiske
Gardner Inlet

Belgrano II (Arg.)

Berkner Island 976

Filchner Ice Shelf

Neumayer (Ger.)

Cape Norvegia
Ekström Ice Shelf
Riiser-Larsen Ice Shelf
Brunt Ice Shelf
Halley (U.K.)
Princess Martha Coast
Crown Princess Martha Coast
Ritscher Upland
SANAE (South Africa)
Kirwan Escarpment

Maitri (India)
Novolazarevskaya (Rus. Fed.)

Queen Maud Mountains

3318

Mt Victor 2588

Lützow-Holm Bay
Syowa (Japan)

Molodezhnaya (Rus. Fed.)

West Antarctica

Hudson Mountains
Pine Island Glacier
Ellsworth Mountains
Henry Ice Rise
Korff Ice Rise

Mt Absalom 1648
Shackleton Range

Forrestal Range

Pensacola Mountains

Patuxent Range

Ellsworth Land
Walgreen Coast

Amundsen Ridges
Amundsen Sea

Russell Bay

Mt Siple 3100
Siple Island
Wrigley Gulf
Grant Island

Mt Sidley
4181

Marie Byrd Land

3498

Flood Range

Carney Island
Getz Ice Shelf
Smith Coast

Bakutis Coast

Mt Woollard 2057
Whitmore Mts.
Mt Seelig 3022
Mt Radlinski 2749
Linck Nunataks 2549
Thiel Mountains
King Peak

Horlick Mountains

Rockefeller Plateau

Ford Range

Ross Ice Shelf
Roosevelt Island
Edward VII Peninsula

Sulzberger Bay
Driscoll I.

Amundsen Abyssal Plain

Dome Argus 4010

Valkyrie Dome 3807

East Antarctica

Mac. Robertson Land
Mawson Escarpment
Mt Menzies 3355
Goodspeed Nunataks
Prince Charles Mts.
2313

Grove Mountains
Mellor Gl.
Lambert Gl.
Fisher Gl.

Enderby Land
Hansen Mts.
Kemp Land
Casey Bay
White I.
Amundsen Bay
Mt Tula
C. Ann
Sandercock Nunataks
Robert Gl.
Mawson
Mawson (Aust.)
C. Boothby

Transantarctic Mountains

Polar Plateau

South Pole
Amundsen-Scott (U.S.A.)

Titan Dome

Mt Howe 3000

Horlick Mountains
Hercules Dome

Queen Maud Mountains

Shackleton Ice Shelf

Siple Coast

South Geomagnetic Pole (2004)

Vostok (Rus. Fed.)

3488

3206

Dome Charlie (Dome Circe)

Queen Mary Land

Princess Elizabeth Land
Kaiser Wilhelm II Land

Kemp Land
Zhongshan (China)
Davis (Aust.)
Prydz Bay
Mac Robertson Coast

ROSS DEPENDENCY (New Zealand)

Ross Sea

Richardson Inlet

Mt Kirkpatrick
Shackleton Gl.
Nimrod Gl.
Churchill Mts.
Mt McClintock 3492
Mt Longhurst

Penny Pt.
Cape Kerr
Minna Bluff
Ross Island
Mount Erebus 3794
Franklin I.
Drygalski Ice Tongue
Terra Nova Bay
C. Washington
Mt Murchison
Coulman I.

Cape Hallett
Mt Minto
Robertson Bay
Cape Adare
Cape North
C. Cheetham

Mt McLintock

Mt Howe

George V Land

Mertz Glacier
Ninnis Gl.
Mertz Gl.

Adélie Land

Talos Dome
Roberts Butte 2828

2356

South Magnetic Pole (2004)

Wilkes Land

2356

Dumont d'Urville Sea

Wilkes Coast
Cape Denison
Dumont d'Urville (Fr.)
Davis Bay
Cape Morse
Cape Goodenough

Banzare Coast
Porpoise Bay
Sabrina Coast
Moscow University Ice Shelf
C. Waldron
Vincennes Bay
Law Dome
Budd Coast
Casey (Aust.)
C. Poinsett

Queen Mary Land
Denman Gl.
Northcliffe Gl.

Mount Amundsen 1445
Knox Coast

Mirny (Rus. Fed.)
Farr Bay
Mawson
Bunger Hills
Drygalski
Shackleton Ice Shelf
Bowman Island

Davis Sea

AUSTRALIAN ANTARCTIC TERRITORY

PACIFIC OCEAN

Macquarie Ridge

Campbell Islands (N.Z.)
Campbell Plateau

Indian-Antarctic Ridge

Balleny Islands
Sturge I.
Buckle I.
Young I.
Cook I.

Mawson Pen.
Ninnis Gl.
Buckley
Ninnis Bay
Glacier Tongue

AUSTRALIAN ANTARCTIC TERRITORY

ADÉLIE LAND (France)

Australian-Antarctic Basin

INDIAN OCEAN

Antarctic Circle

Scott Island

ROSS DEPENDENCY (New Zealand)

Southeast Pacific Basin

Polar Stereographic Projection

Antarctica

1:26 000 000

| 0 | 200 | 400 | 600 | 800 | 1000 miles |

| 0 | 200 | 400 | 600 | 800 | 1000 | 1200 | 1400 | 1600 km |

The Arctic

Polar Stereographic Projection

1:26 000 000

| 0 | 200 | 400 | 600 | 800 | 1000 miles |
| 0 | 200 | 400 | 600 | 800 | 1000 | 1200 | 1400 | 1600 km |

See page 160 for explanatory table and sources

World Statistics

	Population				Population by age (000s)		2050 projected population	Economy					
	Total population	Population change (%)	% urban	Total fertility	0–14	65 or over		Total Gross National Income (GNI) (US$M)	GNI per capita (US$)	Total debt service (US$)	Debt service ratio (% GNI)	Aid receipts (% GNI)	Military spending (% GNI)
WORLD	6 301 000 000	1.2	47.7	2.7	1 814 525	418 420	9 322 251 000	31 500 010	5 170	...	...	...	2.3
AFGHANISTAN	23 897 000	3.7	22.3	6.8	9 466	619	72 267 000	...	...	...	...	...	...
ALBANIA	3 166 000	0.6	42.9	2.3	939	184	3 905 000	4 236	1 230	27 000 000	0.7	8.5	1.3
ALGERIA	31 800 000	1.8	57.5	2.8	10 554	1 248	51 180 000	50 355	1 630	4 466 500 096	8.8	0.3	4.0
ANDORRA	71 000	4.1	92.2	...	...	...	193 000						...
ANGOLA	13 625 000	3.0	34.9	7.2	6 326	373	53 328 000	6 707	500	1 204 499 968	25.4	8.1	21.2
ANTIGUA AND BARBUDA	73 000	0.3	37.1	...	...	...	73 000	621	9 070			1.5	...
ARGENTINA	38 428 000	1.2	88.3	2.4	10 265	3 592	54 522 000	260 994	6 960	27 345 100 800	9.9	...	1.6
ARMENIA	3 061 000	0.1	67.2	1.1	898	327	3 150 000	2 127	560	43 000 000	2.2	11.2	5.8
AUSTRALIA	19 731 000	1.0	91.2	1.8	3 927	2 346	26 502 000	383 291	19 770				1.8
AUSTRIA	8 116 000	-0.1	67.4	1.2	1 343	1 256	6 452 000	194 463	23 940				0.8
AZERBAIJAN	8 370 000	0.6	51.8	1.5	2 330	546	8 897 000	5 283	650	180 900 000	3.7	2.9	6.6
THE BAHAMAS	314 000	1.2	88.9	2.3	90	16	449 000	...	...			0.1	...
BAHRAIN	724 000	1.7	92.5	2.3	180	19	1 008 000	...	...				8.1
BANGLADESH	146 736 000	2.1	25.6	3.6	53 190	4 291	265 432 000	49 882	370	789 699 968	1.7	2.4	1.3
BARBADOS	270 000	0.4	50.5	1.5	55	28	263 000	...	...				0.5
BELARUS	9 895 000	-0.4	69.6	1.2	1 904	1 357	8 305 000	11 892	1 190	232 200 000	0.8	0.1	1.3
BELGIUM	10 318 000	0.1	97.4	1.5	1 771	1 744	9 583 000	239 779	23 340				1.4
BELIZE	256 000	1.9	48.1	2.9	87	10	392 000	718	2 910	66 100 000	8.6	1.9	1.6
BENIN	6 736 000	2.8	43.0	5.7	2 907	172	18 070 000	2 349	360	76 700 000	3.6	10.6	1.4
BHUTAN	2 257 000	2.6	7.4	5.1	891	88	5 569 000	529	640	6 600 000	1.3	11.6	...
BOLIVIA	8 808 000	2.2	62.9	3.9	3 300	334	16 966 000	8 044	940	661 600 000	8.2	5.8	1.8
BOSNIA-HERZEGOVINA	4 161 000	1.1	43.4	1.3	753	393	3 458 000	5 037	1 240	334 000 000	7.2	16.2	4.5
BOTSWANA	1 785 000	0.5	49.4	3.9	649	44	2 109 000	5 863	3 630	68 000 000	1.3	0.6	4.7
BRAZIL	178 470 000	1.2	81.7	2.2	49 077	8 760	247 244 000	528 503	3 060	62 787 600 384	11.0	0.1	1.9
BRUNEI	358 000	1.8	72.8	2.5	105	11	565 000	...	...				4.0
BULGARIA	7 897 000	-1.0	67.4	1.1	1 252	1 282	4 531 000	12 644	1 560	1 189 200 000	10.2	2.7	3.0
BURKINA	13 002 000	3.0	16.9	6.8	5 617	375	46 304 000	2 395	210	54 700 000	2.5	14.0	1.6
BURUNDI	6 825 000	3.0	9.3	6.8	3 023	182	20 219 000	692	100	21 400 000	3.2	13.8	7.0
CAMBODIA	14 144 000	2.4	17.5	4.8	5 749	367	29 883 000	3 329	270	31 400 000	1.0	12.6	4.0
CAMEROON	16 018 000	2.1	49.7	4.7	6 411	545	32 284 000	8 723	570	561 900 032	6.8	4.7	1.8
CANADA	31 510 000	0.8	78.9	1.6	5 882	3 875	40 407 000	661 881	21 340				1.4
CAPE VERDE	463 000	2.1	63.5	3.2	168	20	807 000	596	1 310	16 100 000	2.9	17.0	0.9
CENTRAL AFRICAN REPUBLIC	3 865 000	1.6	41.7	4.9	1 599	150	8 195 000	1 006	270	14 100 000	1.5	7.9	2.8
CHAD	8 598 000	3.1	24.1	6.7	3 663	247	27 732 000	1 597	200	26 300 000	1.9	9.6	2.4
CHILE	15 805 000	1.2	86.1	2.4	4 328	1 090	22 215 000	66 915	4 350	6 162 599 936	9.0	0.1	3.0
CHINA	1 289 161 000	0.7	36.7	1.8	316 838	87 428	1 462 058 000	1 130 984	890	21 728 299 008	2.0	0.2	2.3
COLOMBIA	44 222 000	1.6	75.5	2.6	13 806	1 993	70 862 000	82 017	1 910	5 170 599 936	6.6	0.2	3.2
COMOROS	768 000	2.9	33.8	5.0	304	19	1 900 000	217	380	2 700 000	1.3	9.3	...
CONGO	3 724 000	3.0	66.1	6.3	1 396	101	10 744 000	2 171	700	42 800 000	1.9	1.5	3.5
CONGO, DEMOCRATIC REPUBLIC OF	52 771 000	3.3	30.7	6.7	24 846	1 465	203 527 000	...	...	24 800 000	...	...	14.4
COSTA RICA	4 173 000	2.0	59.5	2.7	1 302	205	7 195 000	15 332	3 950	649 900 032	4.4	0.1	0.5
CÔTE D'IVOIRE	16 631 000	2.1	44.0	4.6	6 745	495	32 185 000	10 259	630	1 020 300 032	11.8	3.7	0.8
CROATIA	4 428 000	0.0	58.1	1.7	840	658	4 180 000	20 366	4 550	2 437 400 064	13.0	0.3	3.3
CUBA	11 300 000	0.3	75.5	1.6	2 377	1 072	10 764 000	...	...				1.9
CYPRUS	802 000	0.8	70.2	1.9	181	90	910 000	...	...				3.4
CZECH REPUBLIC	10 236 000	-0.1	74.5	1.2	1 686	1 421	8 429 000	54 108	5 270	4 773 499 904	9.5	0.9	2.3
DENMARK	5 364 000	0.2	85.1	1.7	971	798	5 080 000	166 345	31 090				1.6
DJIBOUTI	703 000	1.0	84.2	5.8	273	20	1 068 000	572	890	13 500 000	2.4	12.5	4.3
DOMINICA	79 000	-0.1	71.4	...	...	...	72 000	224	3 060	10 200 000	4.3	6.4	...
DOMINICAN REPUBLIC	8 745 000	1.5	66.0	2.7	2 805	359	11 960 000	18 955	2 230	520 800 000	2.8	0.3	0.7
EAST TIMOR	778 000	3.9	7.5	3.9	317	20	1 410 000	...	...				...
ECUADOR	13 003 000	1.7	63.4	2.8	4 278	594	21 190 000	15 952	1 240	1 276 099 968	10.3	1.2	3.7
EGYPT	71 931 000	1.7	42.7	2.9	24 004	2 808	113 840 000	99 406	1 530	1 813 400 064	1.8	1.3	2.7
EL SALVADOR	6 515 000	1.8	61.5	2.9	2 235	312	10 855 000	13 088	2 050	373 700 000	2.9	1.4	0.9
EQUATORIAL GUINEA	494 000	2.8	49.3	5.9	200	18	1 378 000	327	700	5 300 000	1.1	...	3.2
ERITREA	4 141 000	4.2	19.1	5.3	1 608	106	10 028 000	792	190	3 300 000	0.5	25.3	27.4
ESTONIA	1 323 000	-1.1	69.4	1.2	247	200	752 000	5 255	3 810	427 600 000	9.3	1.4	1.5
ETHIOPIA	70 678 000	2.4	15.9	6.8	28 414	1 859	186 452 000	6 767	100	139 400 000	2.2	11.1	8.8
FIJI	839 000	1.1	50.2	3.0	271	28	916 000	1 755	2 130	30 100 000	2.1	2.0	2.0
FINLAND	5 207 000	0.1	58.5	1.6	933	773	4 693 000	124 171	23 940				1.4
FRANCE	60 144 000	0.4	75.5	1.8	11 098	9 462	61 833 000	1 377 389	22 690				2.7
GABON	1 329 000	2.5	82.3	5.4	494	72	3 164 000	3 990	3 160	467 900 000	11.0	0.3	2.4
THE GAMBIA	1 426 000	2.4	31.3	4.8	525	40	2 605 000	440	330	18 600 000	4.5	12.4	1.3
GEORGIA	5 126 000	-0.5	56.5	1.4	1 077	680	3 219 000	3 097	620	116 900 000	3.8	5.3	1.2

	Social Indicators					Environment				Communications				
Infant mortality rate	Life expectancy M	Life expectancy F	Literacy rate (%)	Access to safe water (%)	Doctors per 100 000 people	Forest area (%)	Annual change in forest area (%)	Protected land area (%)	CO_2 emissions	Telephone lines per 100 people	Cellular phones per 100 people	Internet connections per 1 000 people	International dialling code	Time zone
83	**63.9**	**68.1**	**...**	**82**	**...**	**29.6**	**-0.2**	**6.4**	**...**	**17.2**	**15.6**	**82.3**	**...**	**...**
257	43.0	43.5	...	13	...	2.1	...	0.3	0.0	...	...	...	...	+4.5
31	70.9	76.7	98.2	97	129	36.2	-0.8	2.9	0.5	5.0	8.8	2.5	355	+1
65	69.9	73.3	90.4	89	85	0.9	1.3	2.5	3.6	6.0	0.3	1.9	213	+1
7	...	...	...	100	...	...	...	...	...	43.8	30.2	89.7	376	+1
295	44.5	47.1	...	38	8	56.0	-0.2	6.6	0.5	0.6	0.6	4.4	244	+1
15	...	...	...	91	114	20.5	...	...	5.0	47.4	31.8	65.2	1 268	-4
21	70.6	77.7	98.6	...	268	12.7	-0.8	1.8	3.8	21.6	18.6	80.0	54	-3
30	70.3	76.2	99.8	...	316	12.4	1.3	7.6	0.9	14.0	0.7	142.1	374	+4
6	76.4	82.0	...	100	240	20.1	-0.2	7.0	17.7	52.0	57.8	372.3	61	+8 to +10.5
5	75.4	81.5	...	100	302	47.0	0.2	29.2	7.9	46.8	80.7	319.4	43	+1
105	68.7	75.5	...	78	360	13.1	1.3	5.5	4.9	11.1	8.0	3.2	994	+4
18	65.2	73.9	97.4	97	152	84.1	...	...	6.1	40.0	19.7	55.0	1 242	-5
16	72.1	76.3	98.6	...	100	...	14.9	...	29.1	24.7	42.5	198.9	973	+3
82	60.6	60.8	52.1	97	20	10.2	1.3	0.7	0.2	0.4	0.4	1.1	880	+6
14	74.5	79.5	...	100	125	4.7	...	...	5.9	46.3	10.6	37.4	1 246	-4
20	62.8	74.4	99.8	100	443	45.3	3.2	6.3	6.0	27.9	1.4	41.2	375	+2
6	75.7	81.9	...	...	395	22.2	-0.2	2.8	9.9	49.3	74.7	280.0	32	+1
41	73.0	75.9	98.2	92	55	59.1	-2.3	20.9	1.8	14.4	11.6	73.8	501	-6
154	52.5	55.7	55.5	63	6	24.0	-2.3	6.9	0.1	0.9	1.9	3.9	229	+1
100	62.0	64.5	...	62	16	64.2	...	21.2	0.5	2.0	...	3.6	975	+6
80	61.9	65.3	96.3	83	130	48.9	-0.3	14.2	1.5	6.2	9.0	14.6	591	-4
18	71.3	76.7	...	...	...	44.6	...	0.5	1.2	11.1	5.7	11.1	387	+2
101	38.7	37.4	89.1	95	24	21.9	-0.9	18.0	2.4	9.3	16.7	15.4	267	+2
38	64.7	72.6	93.0	87	127	64.3	-0.4	4.4	1.8	21.8	16.7	46.6	55	-2 to -5
7	74.2	78.9	99.5	...	85	83.9	-0.2	...	17.1	24.5	28.9	104.5	673	+8
16	67.1	74.8	99.7	100	345	33.4	0.6	4.5	5.7	35.9	19.1	74.6	359	+2
198	47.0	49.0	36.9	42	3	25.9	-0.2	10.4	0.1	0.5	0.6	1.7	226	GMT
190	39.8	41.4	66.1	78	...	3.7	-9.0	5.3	0.0	0.3	0.3	0.9	257	+2
135	53.6	58.6	80.1	30	30	52.9	-0.6	15.8	0.1	0.3	1.7	0.7	855	+7
154	49.3	50.6	94.4	58	7	51.3	-0.9	4.4	0.1	0.7	2.0	3.0	237	+1
6	76.2	81.8	...	100	229	26.5	...	9.1	15.5	65.5	32.0	435.3	1	-3.5 to -8
40	67.0	72.8	89.2	74	17	21.1	9.3	...	0.3	14.3	7.2	27.5	238	-1
180	42.7	46.0	69.9	70	4	36.8	-0.1	8.2	0.1	0.3	0.3	0.5	236	+1
198	45.1	47.5	69.9	27	3	10.1	-0.6	9.0	0.0	0.1	0.3	0.5	235	+1
12	73.0	79.0	99.0	93	110	20.7	-0.1	18.7	4.1	23.9	34.0	200.2	56	-4
40	69.1	73.5	98.2	75	162	17.5	1.2	6.2	2.5	13.8	11.2	26.0	86	+8
30	69.2	75.3	97.2	91	116	47.8	-0.4	8.2	1.7	17.1	7.6	27.0	57	-5
82	59.4	62.2	59.0	96	7	4.3	-4.3	...	0.1	1.2	...	3.4	269	+3
108	49.6	53.7	97.8	51	25	64.6	-0.1	4.5	0.6	0.7	4.8	0.2	242	+1
207	51.0	53.3	83.7	45	7	59.6	-0.4	4.3	0.1	0.0	0.3	0.1	243	+1 to +2
12	75.0	79.7	98.4	95	141	38.5	-0.8	14.2	1.4	23.0	7.6	93.4	506	-6
173	47.7	48.1	67.6	81	9	22.4	-3.1	5.2	0.9	1.8	4.5	4.3	225	GMT
9	70.3	78.1	99.8	...	229	31.9	0.1	7.4	4.5	36.5	37.7	55.9	385	+1
9	74.8	78.7	99.8	91	530	21.4	1.3	17.2	2.2	5.1	0.1	10.7	53	-5
7	76.0	80.5	99.8	100	255	18.6	3.7	...	7.9	64.3	46.4	221.6	357	+2
5	72.1	78.7	...	...	303	34.1	...	15.8	11.5	37.4	65.9	136.3	420	+1
5	74.2	79.1	...	100	290	10.7	0.2	32.0	10.1	72.3	73.7	447.2	45	+1
146	...	...	85.7	100	14	0.3	...	...	0.6	1.5	0.5	5.1	253	+3
16	...	...	...	97	49	61.3	-0.7	...	...	29.1	1.6	77.8	1 767	-4
48	64.4	70.1	91.7	86	216	28.4	...	31.3	2.5	11.0	14.7	21.5	1 809	-4
...	49.2	50.9	...	...	...	34.3	-0.6	...	...	...	...	...	670	+9
32	68.3	73.5	97.5	85	170	38.1	-1.2	42.6	2.2	10.4	6.7	25.4	593	-5
43	68.2	71.9	71.3	97	202	0.1	3.3	0.8	1.7	10.3	4.3	9.3	20	+2
40	67.7	73.7	89.0	77	107	5.8	-4.6	0.2	1.0	9.3	12.5	8.0	503	-6
156	52.4	55.6	97.4	44	25	62.5	-0.6	0.0	0.6	1.5	3.2	1.9	240	+1
114	51.1	53.7	72.0	46	3	13.5	-0.3	4.3	...	0.8	...	2.6	291	+3
21	65.8	76.4	99.8	...	297	48.7	0.6	11.1	12.1	35.2	45.5	300.5	372	+2
174	42.8	43.8	57.2	24	...	4.2	-0.8	5.0	0.0	0.5	0.0	0.4	251	+3
22	68.1	71.5	99.2	47	48	44.6	-0.2	1.1	0.9	11.0	9.3	18.3	679	+12
5	74.4	81.5	...	100	299	72.0	...	5.5	10.4	54.8	77.8	430.3	358	+2
5	75.2	82.8	...	...	303	27.9	0.4	13.5	6.3	57.4	60.5	263.8	33	+1
90	53.1	55.1	...	86	...	84.7	...	2.7	2.4	3.0	20.5	13.5	241	+1
128	45.7	48.5	60.0	62	4	48.1	1.0	2.0	0.2	2.6	3.2	13.5	220	GMT
29	69.5	77.6	...	79	436	43.7	...	2.8	1.0	15.9	5.4	4.6	995	+4

World Statistics

	Population							Economy					
	Total population	Population change (%)	% urban	Total fertility	Population by age (000s)		2050 projected population	Total Gross National Income (GNI) (US$M)	GNI per capita (US$)	Total debt service (US$)	Debt service ratio (% GNI)	Aid receipts (% GNI)	Military spending (% GNI)
					0 – 14	65 or over							
GERMANY	82 476 000	0.0	87.7	1.3	12 739	13 453	70 805 000	1 947 951	23 700	...	...	...	1.6
GHANA	20 922 000	2.2	36.4	4.2	7 901	627	40 056 000	5 731	290	471 800 000	9.4	11.5	0.8
GREECE	10 976 000	0.0	60.3	1.2	1 598	1 862	8 983 000	124 553	11 780	...	...	...	4.7
GRENADA	80 000	0.3	38.4	...	...	...	105 000	368	3 720	12 000 000	3.2	4.7	...
GUATEMALA	12 347 000	2.6	39.9	4.4	4 965	404	26 551 000	19 559	1 670	438 000 000	2.3	1.4	0.7
GUINEA	8 480 000	1.5	27.9	5.8	3 592	226	20 711 000	3 043	400	133 000 000	4.5	5.0	1.6
GUINEA-BISSAU	1 493 000	2.4	32.3	6.0	521	43	3 276 000	202	160	6 200 000	3.1	37.7	2.7
GUYANA	765 000	0.2	36.7	2.3	233	38	504 000	641	840	115 600 000	17.5	16.3	0.8
HAITI	8 326 000	1.6	36.3	4.0	3 305	302	13 982 000	3 887	480	41 700 000	1.0	5.4	...
HONDURAS	6 941 000	2.3	53.7	3.7	2 682	216	12 845 000	5 922	900	578 099 968	10.0	7.8	0.7
HUNGARY	9 877 000	-0.5	64.8	1.2	1 689	1 460	7 486 000	48 924	4 800	7 945 900 032	18.0	0.6	1.7
ICELAND	290 000	0.7	92.7	1.9	65	33	333 000	8 201	28 880	...	...	...	...
INDIA	1 065 462 000	1.5	27.9	3.0	337 921	50 096	1 572 055 000	474 323	460	9 694 000 128	2.1	0.3	2.5
INDONESIA	219 883 000	1.2	42.1	2.3	65 232	10 221	311 335 000	144 731	680	18 771 900 416	13.2	1.2	1.1
IRAN	68 920 000	1.4	64.7	2.8	26 302	2 364	121 424 000	112 855	1 750	3 438 200 064	3.3	0.1	2.9
IRAQ	25 175 000	2.7	67.4	4.8	9 554	659	53 574 000	...	...	...	...	...	5.5
IRELAND, REPUBLIC OF	3 956 000	1.0	59.3	2.0	820	431	5 366 000	88 385	23 060	...	...	...	1.0
ISRAEL	6 433 000	2.0	91.8	2.7	1 706	596	10 065 000	...	...	...	...	...	8.8
ITALY	57 423 000	-0.1	67.1	1.2	8 216	10 396	42 962 000	1 123 478	19 470	...	...	...	2.0
JAMAICA	2 651 000	0.9	56.6	2.4	810	186	3 816 000	7 264	2 720	643 400 000	9.2	0.2	0.8
JAPAN	127 654 000	0.1	78.9	1.3	18 694	21 826	109 220 000	4 574 164	35 990	...	...	...	1.0
JORDAN	5 473 000	2.8	78.7	4.3	1 968	137	11 709 000	8 786	1 750	669 200 000	8.0	6.8	9.2
KAZAKHSTAN	15 433 000	-0.4	55.8	2.0	4 364	1 109	15 302 000	20 146	1 360	1 839 500 032	10.8	1.2	0.9
KENYA	31 987 000	1.9	34.4	4.2	13 331	869	55 368 000	10 309	340	481 000 000	4.7	5.0	1.9
KIRIBATI	88 000	1.3	38.6	...	...	...	138 000	77	830	...	...	21.8	...
KUWAIT	2 521 000	2.6	96.1	2.7	599	42	4 001 000	...	...	...	...	...	7.7
KYRGYZSTAN	5 138 000	1.2	34.3	2.3	1 670	297	7 538 000	1 386	280	173 200 000	14.2	17.8	2.4
LAOS	5 657 000	2.3	19.7	4.8	2 256	184	11 438 000	1 650	310	41 900 000	2.5	17.1	2.0
LATVIA	2 307 000	-0.6	59.8	1.1	421	357	1 744 000	7 719	3 260	561 600 000	7.8	1.3	0.9
LEBANON	3 653 000	1.6	90.1	2.2	1 089	212	5 018 000	17 585	4 010	1 821 200 000	10.5	1.2	4.0
LESOTHO	1 802 000	0.7	28.8	4.5	799	85	2 478 000	1 127	550	65 800 000	5.7	3.7	2.6
LIBERIA	3 367 000	5.5	45.5	6.8	1 244	83	14 370 000	...	...	700 000	...	...	1.2
LIBYA	5 551 000	2.2	88.0	3.3	1 795	179	9 969 000	...	...	...	...	...	...
LIECHTENSTEIN	34 000	1.1	21.5	...	...	...	39 000	...	...	...	...	...	...
LITHUANIA	3 444 000	-0.2	68.6	1.2	719	494	2 989 000	11 401	3 270	906 000 000	8.1	0.9	1.3
LUXEMBOURG	453 000	1.2	91.9	1.8	81	63	715 000	18 550	41 770	...	...	...	0.8
MACEDONIA (F.Y.R.O.M.)	2 056 000	0.3	59.4	1.5	460	203	1 894 000	3 445	1 690	161 300 000	4.6	7.7	2.5
MADAGASCAR	17 404 000	2.8	30.1	5.7	7 143	481	47 030 000	4 170	260	92 700 000	2.4	8.1	1.2
MALAWI	12 105 000	2.2	15.1	6.3	5 239	332	31 114 000	1 778	170	58 700 000	3.5	24.9	0.6
MALAYSIA	24 425 000	1.7	58.1	2.9	7 575	918	37 850 000	86 510	3 640	5 967 200 256	7.2	0.1	2.3
MALDIVES	318 000	3.0	28.0	5.4	127	10	868 000	578	2 040	19 900 000	3.8	4.7	...
MALI	13 007 000	2.9	30.9	7.0	5 235	454	41 724 000	2 280	210	97 200 000	4.3	15.6	2.3
MALTA	394 000	0.4	91.2	1.8	79	48	400 000	...	...	...	...	...	0.8
MARSHALL ISLANDS	53 000	...	66.0	...	...	...	85 000	115	2 190	...	...	56.6	...
MAURITANIA	2 893 000	3.0	59.1	6.0	1 176	84	8 452 000	974	350	100 300 000	11.0	23.3	4.0
MAURITIUS	1 221 000	0.8	41.6	1.9	298	72	1 426 000	4 592	3 830	553 299 968	12.7	0.5	0.2
MEXICO	103 457 000	1.4	74.6	2.5	32 770	4 671	146 652 000	550 456	5 540	58 258 698 240	10.4	...	0.6
MICRONESIA, FEDERATED STATES OF	109 000	2.4	28.6	...	...	...	269 000	258	2 150	...	...	39.5	...
MOLDOVA	4 267 000	-0.3	41.4	1.4	993	400	3 577 000	1 399	380	135 400 000	10.0	9.1	0.5
MONACO	34 000	0.9	100.0	...	...	...	38 000	...	...	...	...	...	...
MONGOLIA	2 594 000	1.1	56.5	2.3	892	96	4 146 000	962	400	29 200 000	3.1	23.7	2.1
MOROCCO	30 566 000	1.8	56.1	3.0	10 355	1 238	50 361 000	34 555	1 180	3 332 699 904	10.3	1.3	4.3
MOZAMBIQUE	18 863 000	1.8	33.3	5.9	8 037	591	38 837 000	3 747	210	87 500 000	2.5	24.8	2.5
MYANMAR	49 485 000	1.2	28.1	2.8	15 806	2 193	68 546 000	...	...	87 000 000	...	...	7.8
NAMIBIA	1 987 000	1.7	31.4	4.9	768	66	3 663 000	3 520	1 960	...	...	4.4	2.9
NAURU	13 000	2.3	100.0	...	...	...	26 000	...	...	...	...	...	...
NEPAL	25 164 000	2.3	12.2	4.5	9 455	859	52 415 000	5 879	250	99 700 000	1.8	7.2	0.8
NETHERLANDS	16 149 000	0.3	89.6	1.5	2 902	2 165	15 845 000	385 401	24 040	...	...	...	1.8
NEW ZEALAND	3 875 000	0.7	85.9	2.0	867	441	4 439 000	47 632	12 380	...	...	...	1.2
NICARAGUA	5 466 000	2.6	56.5	3.8	2 162	155	11 477 000	...	...	300 200 000	14.2	25.7	1.2
NIGER	11 972 000	3.6	21.1	8.0	5 401	218	51 872 000	1 953	170	28 300 000	1.6	11.5	1.2
NIGERIA	124 009 000	2.6	44.9	5.4	51 300	3 471	278 788 000	37 116	290	1 009 299 968	2.7	0.5	1.6
NORTH KOREA	22 664 000	0.7	60.5	2.1	5 902	1 315	28 038 000	...	...	...	...	...	18.8
NORWAY	4 533 000	0.4	75.0	1.7	883	687	4 880 000	160 577	35 530	...	...	...	2.2
OMAN	2 851 000	3.3	76.5	5.5	1 119	63	8 751 000	...	...	864 099 968	...	...	15.3

Social Indicators						Environment				Communications				
Infant mortality rate	Life expectancy		Literacy rate (%)	Access to safe water (%)	Doctors per 100 000 people	Forest area (%)	Annual change in forest area (%)	Protected land area (%)	CO$_2$ emissions	Telephone lines per 100 people	Cellular phones per 100 people	Internet connections per 1 000 people	International dialling code	Time zone
	M	F												
5	75.0	81.1	...	...	350	30.7	...	26.9	10.1	63.5	68.3	364.3	49	+1
102	56.0	58.5	92.1	73	6	27.8	-1.7	4.6	0.2	1.2	0.9	1.9	233	GMT
6	75.9	81.2	99.8	...	392	27.9	0.9	3.6	8.1	52.9	75.1	132.1	30	+2
26	...	...	...	95	50	14.7	0.9	...	1.9	32.8	6.4	52.0	1 473	-4
59	63.0	68.9	80.3	92	93	26.3	-1.7	16.8	0.9	6.5	9.7	17.1	502	-6
175	48.0	49.0	...	48	13	28.2	-0.5	0.7	0.2	0.3	0.7	1.9	224	GMT
215	44.0	46.9	60.9	56	17	60.5	-0.9	0.0	...	1.0	...	3.3	245	GMT
74	58.0	66.9	99.8	94	18	78.5	-0.3	0.3	2.2	9.2	8.7	109.2	592	-4
125	50.2	56.5	66.2	46	8	3.2	-5.7	0.3	0.2	1.0	1.1	3.6	509	-5
40	63.2	69.1	84.2	88	83	48.1	-1.0	6.0	0.8	4.7	3.6	6.2	504	-6
9	67.8	76.1	99.8	99	357	19.9	0.4	7.0	5.8	37.4	49.8	148.4	36	+1
4	77.1	81.8	...	...	326	0.3	2.2	9.5	7.6	66.4	82.0	679.4	354	GMT
96	63.6	64.9	74.1	84	48	21.6	0.1	4.4	1.1	3.4	0.6	6.8	91	+5.5
48	65.3	69.3	98.0	78	16	58.0	-1.2	10.1	1.2	3.7	2.5	18.6	62	+7 to +9
44	68.8	70.8	94.8	92	85	4.5	...	5.1	4.7	16.0	2.7	6.2	98	+3.5
130	63.5	66.5	45.3	85	...	1.8	...	<0.1	3.7	...	...	...	964	+3
6	74.4	79.6	...	...	219	9.6	3.0	0.9	10.3	48.5	72.9	233.1	353	GMT
6	77.1	81.0	99.5	...	385	6.4	4.9	15.5	10.1	47.6	80.8	230.5	972	+2
6	75.5	81.9	99.8	...	554	34.0	0.3	7.3	7.2	47.1	83.9	275.8	39	+1
20	73.7	77.8	94.5	92	140	30.0	-1.5	0.1	4.3	19.7	26.9	38.5	1 876	-5
4	77.8	85.0	...	...	193	64.0	...	6.8	9.0	59.7	58.8	454.7	81	+9
34	69.7	72.5	99.5	96	166	1.0	...	3.3	3.0	12.7	14.4	40.9	962	+2
75	59.6	70.7	...	91	353	4.5	2.2	2.7	8.2	11.3	3.6	6.2	7	+4 to +6
120	48.7	49.9	95.8	57	13	30.0	-0.5	6.0	0.3	1.0	1.6	16.0	254	+3
70	...	...	...	48	...	38.4	...	...	0.3	4.0	0.5	25.0	686	+12 to +14
10	74.9	79.0	93.1	...	189	0.3	3.5	1.5	26.3	24.0	24.8	101.5	965	+3
63	64.8	72.3	...	77	301	5.2	2.6	3.5	1.3	7.7	0.5	10.6	996	+5
105	53.3	55.8	73.3	37	24	54.4	-0.4	0.0	0.1	0.9	0.5	1.8	856	+7
21	65.7	76.2	99.8	...	282	47.1	0.4	12.5	3.2	30.8	27.9	72.3	371	+2
32	71.9	75.1	95.6	100	210	3.5	-0.4	0.5	3.9	19.5	21.3	85.8	961	+2
133	37.5	35.1	91.1	78	5	0.5	...	0.2	...	1.0	1.5	2.3	266	+2
235	54.6	56.7	71.7	...	...	31.3	-2.0	1.2	0.1	...	...	...	231	GMT
20	70.7	74.8	97.0	72	128	0.2	1.4	0.1	7.2	10.9	0.9	3.6	218	+2
11	...	...	...	...	...	46.7	1.2	...	...	...	...	...	423	+1
21	67.6	77.7	99.8	...	395	31.9	0.2	9.9	4.2	31.3	25.3	67.9	370	+2
5	74.6	80.9	...	...	272	...	...	...	18.0	78.3	96.7	226.6	352	+1
26	71.4	75.8	...	...	204	35.6	...	7.1	6.1	26.4	10.9	34.3	389	+1
139	52.5	54.8	81.5	47	11	20.2	-0.9	1.9	0.1	0.4	0.9	2.1	261	+3
188	39.6	39.0	72.5	57	...	27.2	-2.4	8.9	0.1	0.5	0.5	1.7	265	+2
9	70.6	75.5	97.9	...	66	58.7	-1.2	4.6	5.4	19.9	30.0	239.5	60	+8
80	68.3	67.0	99.2	100	40	3.3	...	...	1.3	10.1	6.8	37.0	960	+5
233	51.1	53.0	69.9	65	5	10.8	-0.7	3.7	0.1	0.4	0.4	2.6	223	GMT
6	75.9	81.0	98.7	100	261	n.s.	...	...	4.7	53.0	35.4	252.6	356	+1
68	...	...	...	...	...	...	...	...	...	6.0	0.1	12.9	692	+12
183	50.9	54.1	49.6	37	14	43.9	...	1.7	1.2	0.7	0.3	2.6	222	GMT
20	68.4	75.8	94.3	100	85	7.9	-0.6	...	1.5	25.6	25.0	131.7	230	+4
30	70.4	76.4	97.2	88	186	28.9	-1.1	3.4	3.9	13.7	21.7	36.2	52	-6 to -8
24	...	...	...	...	...	21.7	-4.5	...	...	8.3	...	33.8	691	+10 to +11
33	62.8	70.3	99.8	92	350	9.9	0.2	1.4	2.3	15.4	4.8	13.7	373	+2
5	...	...	...	100	...	...	...	...	...	...	...	...	377	+1
78	61.9	65.9	99.6	60	243	6.8	-0.5	11.5	3.3	4.8	7.6	15.6	976	+8
46	68.3	72.0	69.6	80	46	6.8	...	0.7	1.2	3.9	15.7	13.2	212	GMT
200	37.3	38.6	62.8	57	...	39.0	-0.2	6.0	0.1	0.4	0.8	0.7	258	+2
110	53.8	58.8	91.4	72	30	52.3	-1.4	0.3	0.2	0.6	0.0	0.2	95	+6.5
69	48.9	49.0	92.3	77	30	9.8	-0.9	12.9	0.0	6.6	5.6	25.2	264	+2
30	...	...	...	...	...	...	...	...	...	...	...	...	674	+12
100	60.1	59.6	62.8	88	4	27.3	-1.8	7.6	0.1	1.3	0.1	2.5	977	+5.75
5	75.6	81.0	98.3	100	251	11.1	0.3	5.7	10.4	62.1	73.9	329.2	31	+1
6	75.3	80.7	...	...	218	29.7	0.5	23.4	7.9	47.1	62.1	280.7	64	+12
45	67.2	71.9	72.3	77	86	27.0	-3.0	7.0	0.7	3.1	3.0	9.9	505	-6
270	45.9	46.5	24.4	59	4	1.0	-3.7	7.7	0.1	0.2	0.0	1.1	227	+1
184	52.0	52.2	88.5	62	18	14.8	-2.6	3.3	0.7	0.4	0.3	1.8	234	+1
30	62.5	68.0	...	100	...	68.2	...	2.6	10.3	...	...	...	850	+9
4	76.0	81.9	...	100	413	28.9	0.4	6.5	7.6	72.0	82.5	596.3	47	+1
14	70.2	73.2	98.5	39	133	0.0	5.3	16.1	8.8	9.0	12.4	45.8	968	+4

	Population						Economy					
	Total population	Population change (%)	% urban	Total fertility	Population by age (000s)		2050 projected population	Total Gross National Income (GNI) (US$M)	GNI per capita (US$)	Total debt service (US$)	Debt service ratio (% GNI)	Aid receipts (% GNI)	Military spending (% GNI)
					0 – 14	65 or over							
PAKISTAN	153 578 000	2.5	33.4	5.1	59 021	5 195	344 170 000	59 637	420	2 856 600 064	4.8	1.1	5.9
PALAU	20 000	2.1	69.3	...			39 000	131	6 730	...			...
PANAMA	3 120 000	1.4	56.5	2.4	...	...	4 262 000	9 532	3 290	928 400 000	9.9	0.2	1.4
PAPUA NEW GUINEA	5 711 000	2.2	17.6	4.3	1 929	117	10 980 000	3 026	580	304 500 000	8.3	7.2	1.1
PARAGUAY	5 878 000	2.5	56.7	3.8	2 173	191	12 565 000	7 345	1 300	330 000 000	4.4	1.1	1.1
PERU	27 167 000	1.6	73.1	2.6	8 567	1 238	42 122 000	52 147	2 000	4 305 299 968	8.3	0.8	2.4
PHILIPPINES	79 999 000	1.9	59.4	3.2	28 395	2 670	128 383 000	80 845	1 050	6 736 699 904	8.5	0.7	1.4
POLAND	38 587 000	-0.1	62.5	1.3	7 395	4 685	33 370 000	163 907	4 240	10 290 299 904	6.6	0.9	2.1
PORTUGAL	10 062 000	0.1	65.8	1.5	1 672	1 563	9 006 000	109 156	10 670	...			2.1
QATAR	610 000	1.5	92.9	3.3	151	9	831 000	...	...	...			10.0
ROMANIA	22 334 000	-0.3	55.2	1.3	4 095	2 986	18 150 000	38 388	1 710	2 340 800 000	6.4	1.2	1.6
RUSSIAN FEDERATION	143 246 000	-0.6	72.9	1.1	26 123	18 170	104 259 000	253 413	1 750	11 670 700 032	4.9	0.7	5.6
RWANDA	8 387 000	2.1	6.3	5.8	3 370	200	18 523 000	1 884	220	35 000 000	2.0	18.3	4.5
SAMOA	178 000	0.3	22.3	4.2	65	7	223 000	260	1 520	8 500 000	3.6	11.6	...
SAN MARINO	28 000	1.1	90.4	...			30 000	...	...	...			...
SÃO TOMÉ AND PRÍNCIPE	161 000	1.8	47.7	...			294 000	43	280	4 400 000	10.1	79.5	1.0
SAUDI ARABIA	24 217 000	3.1	86.7	5.5	8 735	602	59 683 000	...	...	...			14.9
SENEGAL	10 095 000	2.5	48.2	5.1	4 176	236	22 711 000	4 726	480	228 000 000	5.3	9.8	1.7
SERBIA AND MONTENEGRO	10 527 000	-0.1	51.7	1.6	2 113	1 381	9 030 000	...	...	177 400 000	2.1		5.0
SEYCHELLES	81 000	1.3	64.6	...			145 000	...	...	17 400 000	3.0	3.0	...
SIERRA LEONE	4 971 000	4.5	37.3	6.5	1 949	128	14 351 000	726	140	42 600 000	6.9	29.0	3.0
SINGAPORE	4 253 000	1.7	100.0	1.5	878	291	4 620 000	...	...	...			4.8
SLOVAKIA	5 402 000	0.1	57.6	1.3	1 054	615	4 674 000	20 028	3 700	2 590 000 128	13.8	0.6	1.8
SLOVENIA	1 984 000	-0.1	49.1	1.1	316	277	1 527 000	19 447	9 780	...		0.3	1.4
SOLOMON ISLANDS	477 000	3.3	20.2	5.3	200	12	1 458 000	253	580	9 100 000	3.2	24.0	...
SOMALIA	9 890 000	4.2	27.9	7.3	4 209	211	40 936 000	...	...	...			...
SOUTH AFRICA, REPUBLIC OF	45 026 000	0.8	57.7	2.9	14 734	1 545	47 301 000	125 486	2 900	3 859 599 872	3.1	0.4	1.5
SOUTH KOREA	47 700 000	0.7	82.5	1.5	9 740	3 305	51 561 000	447 698	9 400	23 204 999 168	5.1		2.9
SPAIN	41 060 000	0.0	77.8	1.1	5 874	6 767	31 282 000	586 874	14 860	...			1.3
SRI LANKA	19 065 000	0.9	23.1	2.1	4 976	1 186	23 066 000	16 294	830	737 500 032	4.6	1.7	4.7
ST KITTS AND NEVIS	42 000	-0.7	34.2	...			34 000	283	6 880	19 600 000	7.1	1.4	...
ST LUCIA	149 000	1.1	38.0	2.5	47	8	189 000	628	3 970	40 300 000	6.0	1.6	...
ST VINCENT AND THE GRENADINES	120 000	0.6	56.0	...			138 000	312	2 690	15 400 000	4.9	2.0	...
SUDAN	33 610 000	2.3	37.1	4.5	12 474	1 071	63 530 000	10 346	330	61 000 000	0.6	2.3	4.8
SURINAME	436 000	0.4	74.8	2.1	127	23	418 000	709	1 690	...			1.8
SWAZILAND	1 077 000	0.9	26.7	4.4	385	32	1 391 000	1 388	1 300	23 600 000	1.6	1.0	1.5
SWEDEN	8 876 000	-0.1	83.3	1.3	1 609	1 541	7 777 000	225 894	25 400	...			2.3
SWITZERLAND	7 169 000	-0.1	67.3	1.4	1 194	1 147	5 607 000	266 503	36 970	...			1.2
SYRIA	17 800 000	2.5	51.8	3.7	6 612	507	36 345 000	16 608	1 000	343 600 000	2.2	1.0	7.0
TAIWAN	22 548 000	0.7	36.7	...			...	...	...	...			...
TAJIKISTAN	6 245 000	0.7	27.7	2.9	2 397	279	9 763 000	1 051	170	87 500 000	9.3	15.3	1.3
TANZANIA	36 977 000	2.3	33.3	5.0	15 800	857	82 740 000	9 198	270	216 700 000	2.4	11.2	1.4
THAILAND	62 833 000	1.1	20.0	2.0	16 742	3 282	82 491 000	120 872	1 970	14 016 499 712	11.6	0.5	1.7
TOGO	4 909 000	2.6	33.9	5.4	2 004	142	11 832 000	1 279	270	29 600 000	2.5	5.5	1.8
TONGA	104 000	0.4	33.0	...			125 000	154	1 530	4 100 000	2.6	12.1	...
TRINIDAD AND TOBAGO	1 303 000	0.5	74.5	1.5	323	86	1 378 000	7 249	5 540	500 200 000	7.5		1.4
TUNISIA	9 832 000	1.1	66.2	2.1	2 809	554	14 076 000	20 051	2 070	1 900 000 000	10.2	1.2	1.8
TURKEY	71 325 000	1.3	66.2	2.3	20 021	3 847	98 818 000	168 335	2 540	21 135 800 320	10.5	0.2	5.3
TURKMENISTAN	4 867 000	1.9	44.9	3.2	1 783	202	8 401 000	5 236	950	...		0.7	3.4
TUVALU	11 000	1.3	53.2	...			16 000	...	...	...			...
UGANDA	25 827 000	3.2	14.5	7.1	11 466	586	101 524 000	6 286	280	159 300 000	2.6	13.1	2.3
UKRAINE	48 523 000	-0.9	68.0	1.1	8 840	6 849	29 959 000	35 185	720	3 660 699 904	11.9	1.7	3.0
UNITED ARAB EMIRATES	2 995 000	1.7	87.2	2.9	678	71	3 709 000	...	...	...			4.1
UNITED KINGDOM	58 789 194	0.2	89.5	1.6	11 272	9 359	58 933 000	1 451 442	24 230	...			2.5
UNITED STATES OF AMERICA	294 043 000	0.9	77.4	1.9	61 507	34 831	397 063 000	9 900 724	34 870	...			3.0
URUGUAY	3 415 000	0.7	92.1	2.3	827	430	4 249 000	19 036	5 670	1 313 100 032	6.8	0.1	1.3
UZBEKISTAN	26 093 000	1.4	36.6	2.3	9 022	1 163	40 513 000	13 780	550	898 700 032	12.1	1.4	1.7
VANUATU	212 000	2.5	22.1	4.3	83	6	462 000	212	1 050	2 200 000	1.0	20.4	...
VATICAN CITY	472	...	100.0	...			1 000	...	...	...			...
VENEZUELA	25 699 000	1.8	87.2	2.7	8 227	1 075	42 152 000	117 169	4 760	5 846 099 968	4.9	0.1	1.4
VIETNAM	81 377 000	1.3	24.5	2.3	26 070	4 178	123 782 000	32 578	410	1 303 200 000	4.2	5.4	...
YEMEN	20 010 000	4.1	25.0	7.6	9 188	423	102 379 000	8 304	460	221 400 000	3.0	3.5	6.1
ZAMBIA	10 812 000	2.1	39.8	5.7	4 850	307	29 262 000	3 336	320	185 600 000	6.7	28.7	1.0
ZIMBABWE	12 891 000	1.7	36.0	4.5	5 709	403	23 546 000	6 164	480	471 400 000	6.6	2.6	5.0

	Socal Indicators					Environment				Communications				
Infant mortality rate	Life expectancy		Literacy rate (%)	Access to safe water (%)	Doctors per 100 000 people	Forest area (%)	Annual change in forest area (%)	Protected land area (%)	CO₂ emissions	Telephone lines per 100 people	Cellular phones per 100 people	Internet connections per 1 000 people	International dialling code	Time zone
	M	F												
110	61.2	60.9	58.7	90	57	3.1	-1.5	4.7	0.7	2.4	0.6	3.5	92	+5
29	...	...	...	79	...	76.1	...	...	...	...	...	...	680	+9
26	...	...	97.0	90	167	38.6	-1.6	18.8	2.1	14.8	20.7	31.7	507	-5
112	56.8	58.7	76.9	42	7	67.6	-0.4	<0.1	0.5	1.4	0.2	28.1	675	+10
31	68.6	73.1	97.3	78	110	58.8	-0.5	3.4	0.9	5.1	20.4	10.6	595	-4
50	67.3	72.4	97.1	80	93	50.9	-0.4	2.7	1.1	7.8	5.9	115.0	51	-5
40	68.0	72.0	98.8	86	123	19.4	-1.4	4.8	1.0	4.0	13.7	25.9	63	+8
10	69.8	78.0	99.8	...	236	29.7	0.2	9.1	8.3	29.5	26.0	98.4	48	+1
6	72.6	79.6	99.8	...	312	40.1	1.7	6.6	5.5	42.7	77.4	349.4	351	GMT
16	69.4	72.1	95.3	...	126	0.1	9.6	...	85.7	27.5	29.3	65.6	974	+3
22	66.5	73.3	99.7	58	184	28.0	0.2	4.6	4.1	18.3	17.2	44.7	40	+2
22	60.0	72.5	99.8	99	421	50.4	...	3.1	9.8	24.3	3.8	29.3	7	+2 to +12
187	40.2	41.7	84.9	41	...	12.4	-3.9	13.8	0.1	0.3	0.8	2.5	250	+2
26	66.9	73.5	99.8	99	34	37.2	-2.1	...	0.8	5.6	1.7	16.7	685	-11
6	...	...	...	...	...	...	...	...	...	...	...	...	378	+1
75	...	...	...	...	47	28.3	...	...	0.5	3.6	...	60.0	239	GMT
29	71.1	73.7	93.6	95	166	0.7	...	2.3	14.4	14.5	11.3	13.4	966	+3
139	52.5	56.2	52.9	78	8	32.2	-0.7	11.1	0.4	2.5	4.0	10.4	221	GMT
20	70.9	75.6	...	98	...	28.3	-0.1	3.3	...	22.9	18.7	56.2	381	+1
17	...	...	...	...	132	66.7	...	...	2.5	26.7	55.2	112.5	248	+4
316	39.2	41.8	...	57	7	14.7	-2.9	1.1	0.1	0.5	0.6	1.4	232	GMT
4	75.9	80.3	99.8	100	163	3.3	...	4.7	21.0	47.1	72.4	605.2	65	+8
9	69.8	77.6	...	100	353	45.3	0.9	22.1	7.1	28.8	39.7	120.3	421	+1
5	72.3	79.6	99.8	100	228	55.0	0.2	5.9	7.4	40.1	76.0	300.8	386	+1
25	67.9	70.7	...	71	14	88.8	-0.2	0.0	0.4	1.6	0.2	4.3	677	+11
225	47.4	50.5	...	...	...	12.0	-1.0	0.3	0.0	...	...	...	252	+3
70	42.5	42.3	91.8	86	56	7.3	-0.1	5.4	8.3	11.4	21.0	70.1	27	+2
5	71.8	79.1	99.8	92	136	63.3	-0.1	6.9	7.8	47.6	60.8	510.7	82	+9
5	75.4	82.3	99.8	...	424	28.8	0.6	8.4	6.3	43.1	65.5	182.8	34	+1
19	69.9	75.9	97.1	77	36	30.0	-1.6	13.3	0.4	4.3	3.8	7.9	94	+6
25	...	...	...	98	117	11.1	-0.6	...	2.5	56.9	3.1	51.6	1 869	-4
19	71.1	76.4	...	98	47	14.8	-4.9	...	1.3	...	...	...	1 758	-4
25	...	...	...	93	88	15.4	-1.4	...	1.4	22.0	2.1	30.9	1 784	-4
108	57.6	60.6	79.1	75	9	25.9	-1.4	3.4	0.1	1.4	0.3	1.8	249	+3
33	68.5	73.7	...	82	25	90.5	...	4.5	5.2	17.6	19.1	33.0	597	-3
142	35.8	34.8	91.2	...	15	30.3	1.2	...	0.4	3.1	6.5	13.7	268	+2
4	77.6	82.6	...	100	311	65.9	...	8.1	5.5	73.9	79.0	516.3	46	+1
4	75.9	82.3	...	100	323	30.3	0.4	25.7	5.9	71.8	72.4	404.0	41	+1
29	70.6	73.1	88.3	80	144	2.5	...	0.0	3.3	10.9	1.2	3.6	963	+2
...	...	...	...	...	...	...	...	...	...	57.3	96.6	349.0	886	+8
73	65.2	70.8	99.8	60	201	2.8	0.5	4.1	0.8	3.6	0.0	0.5	992	+5
165	50.1	52.0	91.6	68	4	43.9	-0.2	14.6	0.1	0.4	1.2	8.3	255	+3
29	67.9	73.8	99.0	84	24	28.9	-0.7	13.8	3.2	9.4	11.9	55.6	66	+7
142	51.1	53.3	77.4	54	8	9.4	-3.4	7.6	0.2	1.0	2.0	10.7	228	GMT
21	...	...	...	100	...	5.5	...	...	1.2	9.9	0.1	10.2	676	+13
20	72.5	77.2	99.8	90	79	50.5	-0.8	6.0	17.4	24.0	17.3	92.3	1 868	-4
28	70.8	73.7	94.3	80	70	3.1	0.2	0.3	2.4	10.9	4.0	41.2	216	+1
45	68.0	73.2	96.9	82	121	13.3	0.2	1.3	3.2	28.5	30.2	37.7	90	+2
70	63.9	70.4	...	...	300	8.0	...	4.1	5.7	8.0	0.2	1.7	993	+5
53	...	...	...	...	...	...	...	...	...	...	...	...	688	+12
127	45.3	46.8	80.3	52	...	21.0	-2.0	7.9	0.1	0.3	1.4	2.7	256	+3
21	62.7	73.5	99.9	98	299	16.5	0.3	1.6	7.0	21.2	4.4	11.9	380	+2
9	74.1	78.4	91.5	...	181	3.8	2.8	...	32.4	39.7	72.0	339.2	971	+4
6	75.7	80.7	...	100	164	11.6	0.6	20.4	9.2	58.8	78.3	399.5	44	GMT
8	74.6	80.4	...	100	279	24.7	0.2	13.1	19.8	66.5	44.4	499.5	1	-5 to -10
17	71.6	78.9	99.3	98	370	7.4	5.0	0.3	1.8	28.3	15.5	119.0	598	-3
67	66.8	72.5	99.7	85	309	4.8	0.2	1.8	4.5	6.6	0.3	5.9	998	+5
44	67.5	70.5	...	88	12	36.7	0.1	...	0.3	3.4	0.2	27.4	678	+11
...	...	...	...	...	...	...	...	...	...	...	...	...	39	+1
23	70.9	76.7	98.2	83	236	56.1	-0.4	35.4	6.7	11.2	26.4	52.8	58	-4
39	66.9	71.6	97.3	77	48	30.2	0.5	3.0	0.6	3.8	1.5	4.9	84	+7
117	60.7	62.9	67.8	69	23	0.9	-1.9	0.0	0.9	2.2	0.8	0.9	967	+3
202	42.6	41.7	89.1	64	7	42.0	-2.4	8.5	0.2	0.8	0.9	2.4	260	+2
117	43.3	42.4	97.6	83	14	49.2	-1.5	7.9	1.2	1.9	2.4	7.3	263	+2

Definitions

Indicator	Definition
Population	
Total population	Interpolated mid-year population, 2003.
Population change	Percentage annual rate of change, 2000–2005.
% urban	Urban population as a percentage of the total population, 2001.
Total fertility	Average number of children a women will have during her child-bearing years, 2000–2005.
Population by age	Population in age groups 0–14 and 65 or over, in thousands, 2000.
2050 projected population	Projected total population for the year 2050.
Economy	
Total Gross National Income (GNI)	The sum of value added to the economy by all resident producers plus taxes, less subsidies, plus net receipts of primary income from abroad. Data are in U.S. dollars (millions), 2001. Formerly known as Gross National Product (GNP).
GNI per capita	Gross National Income per person in U.S. dollars using the World Bank Atlas method, 2001.
Total debt service	Sum of principal repayments and interest paid on long-term debt, interest paid on short-term debt and repayments to the International Monetary Fund (IMF), 2000.
Debt service ratio	Debt service as a percentage of GNI, 2000.
Aid receipts	Aid received as a percentage of GNI from the Development Assistance Committee (DAC) of the Organization for Economic Co-operation and Development (OECD), 2000.
Military spending	Military-related spending, including recruiting, training, construction, and the purchase of military supplies and equipment, as a percentage of Gross National Income, 1999.
Social Indicators	
Infant mortality rate	Number of deaths of children aged under 5 per 1 000 live births, 2000.
Life expectancy	Average life expectancy, at birth in years, male and female, 2000–2005.
Literacy rate	Percentage of population aged 15–24 with at least a basic ability to read and write, 2002.
Access to safe water	Percentage of the population with sustainable access to sources of improved drinking water, 2000.
Doctors	Number of trained doctors per 100 000 people, most recent year figures obtained.
Environment	
Forest area	Percentage of total land area covered by forest.
Change in forest area	Average annual percentage change in forest area, 1990–2000.
Protected land area	Percentage of total land area designated as protected land.
CO_2 emissions	Emissions of carbon dioxide from the burning of fossil fuels and the manufacture of cement, divided by the population, expressed in metric tons, 1998.
Communications	
Telephone lines	Main telephone lines per 100 inhabitants, 2001.
Cellular phones	Cellular mobile subscribers per 100 inhabitants, 2001.
Internet connections	Internet users per 1 000 inhabitants, 2001.
International dialling code	The country code prefix to be used when dialling from another country.
Time zone	Time difference in hours between local standard time and Greenwich Mean Time.

Main Statistical Sources	Internet Links
United Nations Statistics Division	unstats.un.org/unsd
World Population Prospects: The 2002 Revision and World Urbanization Prospects: The 2001 Revision, United Nations Population Division	www.un.org/esa/population/unpop
United Nations Population Information Network	www.un.org/popin
United Nations Development Programme	www.undp.org
Organisation for Economic Cooperation and Development	www.oecd.org
State of the World's Forests 2001, Food and Agriculture Organization of the United Nations	www.fao.org
World Development Indicators 2002, World Bank	www.worldbank.org/data
World Resources 2000–2001, World Resources Institute	www.wri.org
International Telecommunication Union	www.itu.int

Introduction to the index

The index includes all names shown on the reference maps in the atlas. Each entry includes the country or geographical area in which the feature is located, a page number and an alphanumeric reference. Additional entry details and aspects of the index are explained below.

Name forms
The names policy in this atlas is generally to use local name forms which are officially recognized by the governments of the countries concerned. Rules established by the Permanent Committee on Geographical Names for British Official Use (PCGN) are applied to the conversion of non-roman alphabet names, for example in the Russian Federation, into the roman alphabet used in English.

However, English conventional name forms are used for the most well-known places for which such a form is in common use. In these cases, the local form is included in brackets on the map and appears as a cross-reference in the index. Other alternative names, such as well-known historical names or those in other languages, may also be included in brackets on the map and as cross-references in the index. All country names and those for international physical features appear in their English forms. Names appear in full in the index, although they may appear in abbreviated form on the maps.

Referencing
Names are referenced by page number and by grid reference. The grid reference relates to the alphanumeric values which appear on the edges of each map. These reflect the graticule on the map – the letter relates to longitude divisions, the number to latitude divisions. Names are generally referenced to the largest scale map page on which they appear. For large geographical features, including countries, the reference is to the largest scale map on which the feature appears in its entirety, or on which the majority of it appears.

Rivers are referenced to their lowest downstream point – either their mouth or their confluence with another river. The river name will generally be positioned as close to this point as possible.

Alternative names
Alternative names appear as cross-references and refer the user to the index entry for the form of the name used on the map.

For rivers with multiple names - for example those which flow through several countries - all alternative name forms are included within the main index entries, with details of the countries in which each form applies.

Administrative qualifiers
Administrative divisions are included in entries to differentiate duplicate names - entries of exactly the same name and feature type within the one country - where these division names are shown on the maps. In such cases, duplicate names are alphabetized in the order of the administrative division names.

Additional qualifiers are included for names within selected geographical areas, to indicate more clearly their location.

Descriptors
Entries, other than those for towns and cities, include a descriptor indicating the type of geographical feature. Descriptors are not included where the type of feature is implicit in the name itself, unless there is a town or city of exactly the same name.

Insets
Where relevant, the index clearly indicates [inset] if a feature appears on an inset map.

Alphabetical order
The Icelandic characters Þ and þ are transliterated and alphabetized as 'Th' and 'th'. The German character ß is alphabetized as 'ss'. Names beginning with Mac or Mc are alphabetized exactly as they appear. The terms Saint, Sainte, etc, are abbreviated to St, Ste, etc, but alphabetized as if in the full form.

Numerical entries
Entries beginning with numerals appear at the beginning of the index, in numerical order. Elsewhere, numerals are alphabetized before 'a'.

Permuted terms
Names beginning with generic geographical terms are permuted - the descriptive term is placed after, and the index alphabetized by, the main part of the name. For example, Mount Everest is indexed as Everest, Mount; Lake Superior as Superior, Lake. This policy is applied to all languages. Permuting has not been applied to names of towns, cities or administrative divisions beginning with such geographical terms. These remain in their full form, for example, Lake Isabella, USA.

Gazetteer entries and connections
Selected entries have been extended to include gazetteer-style information. Important geographical facts which relate specifically to the entry are included within the entry in coloured type.

Entries for features which also appear on, or which have a topical link to, the thematic pages of the atlas include a reference to those pages.

Abbreviations

admin. dist.	administrative district	IL	Illinois	plat.	plateau
admin. div.	administrative division	imp. l.	impermanent lake	P.N.G.	Papua New Guinea
admin. reg.	administrative region	IN	Indiana	Port.	Portugal
Afgh.	Afghanistan	Indon.	Indonesia	pref.	prefecture
AK	Alaska	Kazakh.	Kazakhstan	prov.	province
AL	Alabama	KS	Kansas	pt	point
Alg.	Algeria	KY	Kentucky	Qld	Queensland
AR	Arkansas	Kyrg.	Kyrgyzstan	Que.	Québec
Arg.	Argentina	l.	lake	r.	river
aut. comm.	autonomous community	LA	Louisiana	reg.	region
aut. reg.	autonomous region	lag.	lagoon	res.	reserve
aut. rep.	autonomous republic	Lith.	Lithuania	resr	reservoir
AZ	Arizona	Lux.	Luxembourg	RI	Rhode Island
Azer.	Azerbaijan	MA	Massachusetts	Rus. Fed.	Russian Federation
b.	bay	Madag.	Madagascar	S.	South, Southern
Bangl.	Bangladesh	Man.	Manitoba	S.A.	South Australia
B.C.	British Columbia	MD	Maryland	salt l.	salt lake
Bol.	Bolivia	ME	Maine	Sask.	Saskatchewan
Bos.-Herz.	Bosnia-Herzegovina	Mex.	Mexico	SC	South Carolina
Bulg.	Bulgaria	MI	Michigan	SD	South Dakota
c.	cape	MN	Minnesota	sea chan.	sea channel
CA	California	MO	Missouri	Serb. and Mont.	Serbia and Montenegro
Cent. Afr. Rep.	Central African Republic	Moz.	Mozambique	Sing.	Singapore
CO	Colorado	MS	Mississippi	Switz.	Switzerland
Col.	Colombia	MT	Montana	Tajik.	Tajikistan
CT	Connecticut	mt.	mountain	Tanz.	Tanzania
Czech Rep.	Czech Republic	mts	mountains	Tas.	Tasmania
DC	District of Columbia	N.	North, Northern	terr.	territory
DE	Delaware	nat. park	national park	Thai.	Thailand
Dem. Rep. Congo	Democratic Republic of Congo	N.B.	New Brunswick	TN	Tennessee
depr.	depression	NC	North Carolina	Trin. and Tob.	Trinidad and Tobago
des.	desert	ND	North Dakota	Turkm.	Turkmenistan
Dom. Rep.	Dominican Republic	NE	Nebraska	TX	Texas
E.	East, Eastern	Neth.	Netherlands	U.A.E.	United Arab Emirates
Equat. Guinea	Equatorial Guinea	NH	New Hampshire	U.K.	United Kingdom
esc.	escarpment	NJ	New Jersey	Ukr.	Ukraine
est.	estuary	NM	New Mexico	U.S.A.	United States of America
Eth.	Ethiopia	N.S.	Nova Scotia	UT	Utah
Fin.	Finland	N.S.W.	New South Wales	Uzbek.	Uzbekistan
FL	Florida	N.T.	Northern Territory	VA	Virginia
for.	forest	NV	Nevada	Venez.	Venezuela
Fr. Guiana	French Guiana	N.W.T.	Northwest Territories	Vic.	Victoria
F.Y.R.O.M.	Former Yugoslav Republic of Macedonia	NY	New York	vol.	volcano
g.	gulf	N.Z.	New Zealand	vol. crater	volcanic crater
GA	Georgia	OH	Ohio	VT	Vermont
Guat.	Guatemala	OK	Oklahoma	W.	West, Western
HI	Hawaii	OR	Oregon	WA	Washington
H.K.	Hong Kong	PA	Pennsylvania	W.A.	Western Australia
Hond.	Honduras	Para.	Paraguay	WI	Wisconsin
i.	island	P.E.I.	Prince Edward Island	WV	West Virginia
IA	Iowa	pen.	peninsula	WY	Wyoming
ID	Idaho	Phil.	Philippines	Y.T.	Yukon Territory

1

3-y Severnyy Rus. Fed. 41 S3
5 de Outubro Angola see Xá-Muteba
9 de Julio Arg. 144 D5
25 de Mayo Buenos Aires Arg. 144 D5
25 de Mayo La Pampa Arg. 140 C5
26 Bakı Komissarı Azer. 91 H3
70 Mile House Canada 120 F5
100 Mile House Canada 120 F5
150 Mile House Canada 120 F4

A

Aabenraa Denmark see Åbenrå
Aachen Germany 52 G4
Aalborg Denmark see Ålborg
Aalborg Bugt b. Denmark see Ålborg Bugt
Aalen Germany 53 K6
Aalesund Norway see Ålesund
Aaley Lebanon see Aley
Aalst Belgium 52 E4
Aanaar Fin. see Inari
Aarhus Denmark see Århus
Aarlen Belgium see Arlon
Aars Denmark see Års
Aarschot Belgium 52 E4
Aasiaat Greenland 119 M3
Aath Belgium see Ath
Aba China 76 D1
Aba Dem. Rep. Congo 98 D3
Aba Nigeria 96 D4
Abacaxis r. Brazil 143 G4
Ābādān Iran 88 C4
Ābādeh Iran 88 D4
Ābādeh Ţashk Iran 88 D4
Abadla Alg. 54 D5
Abaeté Brazil 145 B2
Abaetetuba Brazil 143 I4
Abagnar Qi China see Xilinhot
Abaiang atoll Kiribati 150 H5
Abajo Peak U.S.A. 129 I3
Abakaliki Nigeria 96 D4
Abakan Rus. Fed. 72 G2
Abakanskiy Khrebet mts Rus. Fed. 72 F2
Abalak Niger 96 D3
Abana Turkey 90 D2
Abancay Peru 142 D6
Abariringa atoll Kiribati see Kanton
Abarkūh, Kavīr-e des. Iran 88 D4
Abarqū Iran 88 D4
Abarshahr Iran see Neyshābūr
Abashiri Japan 74 G3
Abashiri-wan b. Japan 74 G3
Abasolo Mex. 131 D7
Abau P.N.G. 110 E1
Abaya, Lake Eth. 98 D3
Ābaya Hāyk' l. Eth. see Abaya, Lake
Ābay Wenz r. Eth. 98 D2 see Blue Nile
Abaza Rus. Fed. 72 G2
Abba Cent. Afr. Rep. 98 B3
Abbasabad Iran 88 D3
'Abbāsābad Iran 88 E2
Abbasanta Sardinia Italy 58 C4
Abbatis Villa France see Abbeville
Abbe, Lake Djibouti/Eth. 86 F7
Abbeville France 52 B4
Abbeville AL U.S.A. 133 C6
Abbeville GA U.S.A. 133 D6
Abbeville LA U.S.A. 131 E6
Abbeville SC U.S.A. 133 D5
Abbey Canada 121 I5
Abbeyfeale Rep. of Ireland 51 C5
Abbey Town U.K. 48 D4
Abborrträsk Sweden 44 K4
Abbot, Mount Australia 110 D4
Abbot Ice Shelf Antarctica 148 K2
Abbotsford Canada 120 F5
Abbott NM U.S.A. 127 G5
Abbott VA U.S.A. 134 E5
Abbottabad Pak. 89 I3
'Abd al 'Azīz, Jabal hill Syria 87 F3
'Abd al Kūrī i. Yemen 86 H7
'Abd Allah, Khawr sea chan. Iraq/Kuwait 88 C4
Abd al Ma'asīr well Saudi Arabia 85 D4
Ābdānān Iran 88 B3
Abdollāhābād Iran 88 D3
Abdulino Rus. Fed. 41 Q5
Abéché Chad 97 F3
Abellinum Italy see Avellino
Abel Tasman National Park N.Z. 113 D5
Abengourou Côte d'Ivoire 96 C4
Åbenrå Denmark 45 F9
Abensberg Germany 53 L6
Abeokuta Nigeria 96 D4
Aberaeron U.K. 49 C6
Aberchirder U.K. 50 G3
Abercorn Zambia see Mbala
Abercrombie r. Australia 112 D4
Aberdare U.K. 49 D7
Aberdaron U.K. 49 C6
Aberdaugleddau U.K. see Milford Haven
Aberdeen Australia 112 E4
Aberdeen Hong Kong China 77 [inset]
Aberdeen S. Africa 100 G7
Aberdeen U.K. 50 G3
Aberdeen U.S.A. 130 D2
Aberdeen Lake Canada 121 L1
Aberdovey U.K. see Aberdyfi
Aberdyfi U.K. 49 C6
Aberfeldy U.K. 50 F4
Aberford U.K. 48 F5
Aberfoyle U.K. 50 E4
Abergavenny U.K. 49 D7
Abergwaun U.K. see Fishguard
Aberhonddu U.K. see Brecon
Abermaw U.K. see Barmouth
Abernathy U.S.A. 131 C5
Aberporth U.K. 49 C6
Abersoch U.K. 49 C6
Abertawe U.K. see Swansea
Aberteifi U.K. see Cardigan
Aberystwyth U.K. 49 C6
Abeshr Chad see Abéché
Abez' Rus. Fed. 41 S2
Āb Gāh Iran 89 E5
Abhā Saudi Arabia 86 F6
Abhar Iran 88 C2
Abiad, Bahr el r. Sudan/Uganda 86 D6 see White Nile

▶Abidjan Côte d'Ivoire 96 C4
Former capital of Côte d'Ivoire. 4th most populous city in Africa.

Abijatta-Shalla National Park Eth. 98 D3
Ab-i-Kavīr salt flat Iran 88 E3
Abilene KS U.S.A. 130 D4
Abilene TX U.S.A. 131 D5
Abingdon U.K. 49 F7
Abingdon U.S.A. 134 D5
Abington Reef Australia 110 E3
Abinsk Rus. Fed. 90 E1
Abiseo, Parque Nacional nat. park Peru 142 C5
Abitau Lake Canada 121 J2
Abitibi, Lake Canada 122 E4
Ab Khūr Iran 88 E3
Abminga Australia 109 F6
Abnūb Egypt 90 C6
Åbo Fin. see Turku
Abohar India 82 C3
Aboisso Côte d'Ivoire 96 C4
Aboite U.S.A. 134 C3
Abomey Benin 96 D4
Abongabong, Gunung mt. Indon. 71 B6
Abong Mbang Cameroon 96 E4
Abou Déia Chad 97 E3
Abovyan Armenia 91 G2
Aboyne U.K. 50 G3
Abqaiq Saudi Arabia 88 C5
Abraham's Bay Bahamas 133 F8
Abramov, Mys pt Rus. Fed. 42 I2
Abrantes Port. 57 B4
Abra Pampa Arg. 144 C2
Abreojos, Punta pt Mex. 127 E8
'Abri Sudan 86 D5
Abrolhos Bank sea feature S. Atlantic Ocean 148 F7
Abruzzo, Parco Nazionale d' nat. park Italy 58 E4
Absalom, Mount Antarctica 152 B1
Absaroka Range mts U.S.A. 126 F3
Abtar, Jabal al hills Syria 85 C2
Abtsgmünd Germany 53 J6
Abū aḍ Ḍuhūr Syria 85 C2
Abū al Ḥusayn, Qā' imp. l. Jordan 85 D3
Abū 'Alī i. Saudi Arabia 88 C5
Abū al Jirāb i. U.A.E. 88 D5
Abū 'Āmūd, Wādī watercourse Jordan 85 C4
Abū 'Arīsh Saudi Arabia 86 F6
Abu 'Aweigīla well Egypt see Abū 'Uwayqilah
Abu Deleiq Sudan 86 D6

▶Abu Dhabi U.A.E. 88 D5
Capital of the United Arab Emirates.

Abū Du'ān Syria 85 D1
Abu Gubeiha Sudan 86 D7
Abū Ḥafnah, Wādī watercourse Jordan 85 D3
Abu Haggag Egypt see Ra's al Ḥikmah
Abū Ḥallūfah, Jabal hill Jordan 85 C4
Abu Hamed Sudan 86 D6

▶Abuja Nigeria 96 D4
Capital of Nigeria.

Abū Jifān well Saudi Arabia 88 B5
Abū Jurdhān Jordan 85 B4
Abū Kamāl Syria 91 F4
Abu Matariq Sudan 97 F3
Abumombazi Dem. Rep. Congo 98 C3
Abu Musa i. The Gulf 88 D5
Abū Mūsā, Jazīreh-ye i. The Gulf see Abu Musa
Abunã r. Bol. 142 E5
Abunã Brazil 142 E5
Ābune Yosēf mt. Eth. 86 E7
Abū Nujaym Libya 97 E1
Abū Qa'ṭūr Syria 85 C2
Abū Rawthah, Jabal mt. Egypt 85 B5
Aburo mt. Dem. Rep. Congo 98 D3
Abu Road India 79 G4
Abū Rujmayn, Jabal mts Syria 85 D2
Abu Rûtha, Gebel mt. Egypt see Abū Rawthah, Jabal
Abū Sawādah well Saudi Arabia 88 C5
Abu Simbil Egypt see Abū Sunbul
Abū Sunbul Egypt 86 D5
Abū Ṭarfā', Wādī watercourse Egypt 85 A5
Abut Head hd N.Z. 113 C6
Abū 'Uwayqilah well Egypt 85 B4
Abu Zabad Sudan 86 C7
Abū Ẓabī U.A.E. see Abu Dhabi
Abūzam Iran 88 C4
Abū Zanīmah Egypt 90 D5
Abu Zenîma Egypt see Abū Zanīmah
Abyad Sudan 86 C7
Abyaḍ, Jabal al mts Syria 85 C2
Abyār al Ḥakīm well Libya 90 A5
Abydos Australia 108 B5
Abyei Sudan 86 C8
Abyssinia country Africa see Ethiopia
Academician Vernadskiy research station Antarctica see Vernadsky
Academy Bay Rus. Fed. see Akademii, Zaliv
Acadia prov. Canada see Nova Scotia
Acadia National Park U.S.A. 132 G2
Açailândia Brazil 143 I5
Acamarachi mt. Chile see Pili, Cerro
Acampamento de Caça do Mucusso Angola 99 C5
Acandí Col. 142 C2
A Cañiza Spain 57 B2
Acaponeta Mex. 136 C4
Acapulco Mex. 136 E5
Acapulco de Juárez Mex. see Acapulco
Acará Brazil 143 I4
Acaraú Brazil 143 J4
Acaray, Represa de resr Para. 144 E3
Acari, Serra hills Brazil/Guyana 143 G3
Acarigua Venez. 142 E2
Acatlan Mex. 136 E5
Accho Israel see 'Akko
Accomac U.S.A. 135 H5
Accomack U.S.A. see Accomac

▶Accra Ghana 96 C4
Capital of Ghana.

Accrington U.K. 48 E5
Ach r. Germany 53 L6
Achacachi Bol. 142 E7
Achaguas Venez. 142 E2
Achalpur India 82 D5
Achampet India 84 C2
Achan Rus. Fed. 74 E2
Achayvayam Rus. Fed. 65 S3
Acheng China 74 B3
Achhota India 84 D1
Achicourt France 52 C4
Achill Rep. of Ireland 51 C4
Achillbeg Island Rep. of Ireland 51 C4
Achill Island Rep. of Ireland 51 B4
Achiltibuie U.K. 50 D2
Achim Germany 53 J1
Achinsk Rus. Fed. 64 K4
Achit Rus. Fed. 41 R4
Achit Nuur l. Mongolia 80 H2
Achkhoy-Martan Rus. Fed. 91 G2
Achna Cyprus 85 A2
Achnasheen U.K. 50 D3
Acıgöl l. Turkey 59 M6
Acıpayam Turkey 59 M6
Acireale Sicily Italy 58 F6
Ackerman U.S.A. 131 F5
Ackley U.S.A. 130 E3
Acklins Island Bahamas 133 F8
Acle U.K. 49 I6

▶Aconcagua, Cerro mt. Arg. 144 B4
Highest mountain in South America.
South America 138–139

Acopiara Brazil 143 K5
A Coruña Spain 57 B2
Acqui Terme Italy 58 C2
Acra U.S.A. 135 H2
Acragas Sicily Italy see Agrigento
Acraman, Lake salt flat Australia 111 A7
Acre r. Brazil 142 E6
Acre Israel see 'Akko
Acre, Bay of Israel see Haifa, Bay of
Acri Italy 58 G5
Ács Hungary 47 Q7
Actaeon Group is Fr. Polynesia see Actéon, Groupe
Actéon, Groupe is Fr. Polynesia 151 K7
Acton Canada 134 E2
Acton U.S.A. 128 D4
Acungui Brazil 145 A4
Acunum Acusio France see Montélimar
Ada MN U.S.A. 130 D2
Ada OH U.S.A. 134 D3
Ada OK U.S.A. 131 D5
Ada WI U.S.A. 134 B2
Adabazar Turkey see Sakarya
Adaja r. Spain 57 D3
Adalia Turkey see Antalya
Adam Oman 87 I5
Adam, Mount hill Falkland Is 144 E8
Adamantina Brazil 145 A3
Adams IN U.S.A. 134 C4
Adams KY U.S.A. 134 D4
Adams MA U.S.A. 135 I2
Adams NY U.S.A. 135 G2
Adams, Mount U.S.A. 126 C3
Adams Center U.S.A. 135 G2
Adams Lake Canada 120 G5
Adams Mountain U.S.A. 120 D4
Adam's Peak Sri Lanka 84 D5
Adams Peak U.S.A. 128 C2

▶Adamstown Pitcairn Is 151 L7
Capital of the Pitcairn Islands.

'Adan Yemen see Aden
Adana Turkey 85 B1
Adana prov. Turkey 85 B1
Adana Yemen see Aden
Adapazarı Turkey see Sakarya
Adare Rep. of Ireland 51 D5
Adare, Cape Antarctica 152 H2
Adavale Australia 111 D5
Adban Afgh. 89 H2
Ad Dabbah Sudan see Ed Debba
Aḍ Ḍabbīyah well Saudi Arabia 88 C5
Ad Dafinah Saudi Arabia 86 F5
Ad Dahnā' des. Saudi Arabia 86 G5
Ad Dakhla W. Sahara 96 B2
Ad Damir Sudan see Ed Damer
Ad Dammām Saudi Arabia see Dammam
Addanki India 84 C3
Ad Dār al Ḥamrā' Saudi Arabia 86 E4
Ad Darb Saudi Arabia 86 F6
Ad Dawādimī Saudi Arabia 86 F5
Ad Dawḥah Qatar see Doha
Ad Dawr Iraq 91 F4
Ad Daww plain Syria 85 C2
Ad Dayr Iraq 91 G5
Ad Dibdibah plain Saudi Arabia 88 B5
Aḍ Ḍiffah plat. Egypt see Libyan Plateau

▶Addis Ababa Eth. 98 D3
Capital of Ethiopia.

Addison U.S.A. 135 G2
Ad Dīwānīyah Iraq 91 G5
Addlestone U.K. 49 G7
Addo Elephant National Park S. Africa 101 G7
Addoo Atoll Maldives see Addu Atoll
Addu Atoll Maldives 81 D12
Ad Duwayd well Saudi Arabia 91 F5
Ad Duwaym Sudan see Ed Dueim
Ad Duwayris well Saudi Arabia 88 C6
Adegaon India 82 D5
Adel GA U.S.A. 133 D6
Adel IA U.S.A. 130 E3

▶Adelaide Australia 111 B7
State capital of South Australia.

Adelaide r. Australia 108 E3
Adelaide Bahamas 133 E7
Adelaide Island Antarctica 152 L2
Adelaide River Australia 108 E3
Adele Island Australia 108 C3
Adélie Coast Antarctica 152 G2
Adélie Land reg. Antarctica 152 G2
Adelong Australia 112 D5
Aden Yemen 86 F7
Aden, Gulf of Somalia/Yemen 86 G7
Adena U.S.A. 134 E3
Adenau Germany 52 G4
Adendorf Germany 53 K1
Aderbissinat Niger 96 D3
Aderno Sicily Italy see Adrano
Adesar India 82 B5
Adhan, Jabal mt. U.A.E. 88 E5
Adh Dhāyūf well Saudi Arabia 91 G6
'Adhfā' well Saudi Arabia 91 F5
'Ādhirīyāt, Jibāl al mts Jordan 85 C4
Adi i. Indon. 69 I7
Ādī Ārk'ay Eth. 86 E7
Adige r. Italy 58 E2
Ādīgrat Eth. 98 D2
Adilabad India 84 C2
Adilcevaz Turkey 91 F3
Adin U.S.A. 126 C4
Adīrī Libya 97 E2
Adirondack Mountains U.S.A. 135 H1
Ādīs Ābeba Eth. see Addis Ababa
Adi Ugri Eritrea see Mendefera
Adıyaman Turkey 90 E3
Adjud Romania 59 L1
Adlavik Islands Canada 123 K3
Admiralty Island Canada 119 H3
Admiralty Island U.S.A. 120 C3
Admiralty Island National Monument - Kootznoowoo Wilderness nat. park U.S.A. 120 C3
Admiralty Islands P.N.G. 69 L7
Ado-Ekiti Nigeria 96 D4
Adok Sudan 86 D8
Adolfo L. Mateos Mex. 127 E8
Adolphus U.S.A. 134 B5
Adonara i. Indon. 108 C2
Adoni India 84 C3
Adorf Germany 53 M4
Adorf (Diemelsee) Germany 53 I3
Ado-Tymovo Rus. Fed. 74 F2
Adour r. France 56 D5
Adra Spain 57 E5
Adramyttium Turkey see Edremit
Adramyttium, Gulf of Turkey see Edremit Körfezi
Adrano Sicily Italy 58 F6
Adrar Alg. 96 C2
Adrar hills Mali see Ifôghas, Adrar des
Adraskand r. Afgh. 89 F3
Adré Chad 97 F3
Adrian MI U.S.A. 134 C3
Adrian TX U.S.A. 131 C5
Adrianople Turkey see Edirne
Adrianopolis Turkey see Edirne
Adriatic Sea Europe 58 E2
Adua Eth. see Ādwa
Adunara i. Indon. see Adonara
Adusa Dem. Rep. Congo 98 C3
Aduwa Eth. see Ādwa
Adverse Well Australia 108 C5
Ādwa Eth. 98 D2
Adycha r. Rus. Fed. 65 O3
Adyk Rus. Fed. 43 J7
Adzhiyan Turkm. 88 D2
Adzopé Côte d'Ivoire 96 C4
Aegean Sea Greece/Turkey 59 K5
Aegina i. Greece see Aigina
Aegyptus country Africa see Egypt
Aela Jordan see Al 'Aqabah
Aelana Jordan see Al 'Aqabah
Aelia Capitolina Israel/West Bank see Jerusalem
Aelönlaplap atoll Marshall Is see Ailinglaplap
Aenus Turkey see Enez
Aerzen Germany 53 J2
Aesernia Italy see Isernia
A Estrada Spain 57 B2
Afabet Eritrea 86 E6
Afanas'yevo Rus. Fed. 42 L4
Affreville Alg. see Khemis Miliana
Afghānestān country Asia see Afghanistan
▶Afghanistan country Asia 89 G3
Asia 6, 62–63
Afgooye Somalia 98 E3
'Afīf Saudi Arabia 86 F5
Afiun Karahissar Turkey see Afyon
Åfjord Norway 44 G5
Aflou Alg. 54 E5
Afmadow Somalia 98 E3
Afogados da Ingazeira Brazil 143 K5
A Fonsagrada Spain 57 C2
Afonso Cláudio Brazil 145 C3
Āfrēra Terara vol. Eth. 86 F7
Africa Nova country Africa see Tunisia
'Afrīn Syria 85 C1
'Afrīn, Nahr r. Syria/Turkey 85 C1
Afşin Turkey 90 E3
Afsluitdijk barrage Neth. 52 F2
Afton U.S.A. 126 F4
Afuá Brazil 143 H4
'Afula Israel 85 B3
Afyon Turkey 59 N5
Afyonkarahisar Turkey see Afyon
Aga Germany 53 M4
Agadès Niger see Agadez
Agadez Niger 96 D3
Agadir Morocco 96 C1
Agadyr' Kazakh. 80 D2
Agalega Islands Mauritius 149 L6
Agana Guam see Hagåtña
Agara Georgia 91 F2
Agartala India 83 G5
Agashi India 84 B2
Agate Canada 122 E4
Agathe France see Agde
Agathonisi i. Greece 59 L6
Agats Indon. 69 J8
Agatti i. India 84 B4
Agboville Côte d'Ivoire 96 C4
Ağcabädi Azer. 91 G2
Ağdam Azer. 91 G3
Ağdaş Azer. 91 G2
Agdash Azer. see Ağdaş
Agde France 56 F5
Agdzhabedi Azer. see Ağcabädi
Agedabia Libya see Ajdābiyā
Agen France 56 E4
Aggeneys S. Africa 100 D5
Aggteleki nat. park Hungary 47 R6
Aghil Pass China/Jammu and Kashmir 82 D1
Agiabampo Mex. 127 F8
Agiguan i. N. Mariana Is see Aguijan
Ağın Turkey 90 E3
Aginskoye Rus. Fed. 72 G1
Aginum France see Agen
Agios Dimitrios Greece 59 J6
Agios Efstratios i. Greece 59 K5
Agios Georgios i. Greece 59 J6
Agios Nikolaos Greece 59 K7
Agios Theodoros Cyprus 85 B2
Agiou Orous, Kolpos b. Greece 59 J4
Agirwat Hills Sudan 86 E6
Agisanang S. Africa 101 G4
Agnes, Mount hill Australia 109 E6
Agnew Australia 109 C6
Agnibilékrou Côte d'Ivoire 96 C4
Agnita Romania 59 K2
Agniye-Afanas'yevsk Rus. Fed. 74 E2
Agra India 82 D4
Agrakhanskiy Poluostrov pen. Rus. Fed. 91 G2
Agram Croatia see Zagreb
Ağrı Turkey 91 F3
Agria Gramvousa i. Greece 59 J7
Agrigan i. N. Mariana Is see Agrihan
Agrigento Sicily Italy 58 E6
Agrigentum Sicily Italy see Agrigento
Agrihan i. N. Mariana Is 69 L3
Agrinio Greece 59 I5
Agropoli Italy 58 F4
Agryz Rus. Fed. 41 Q4
Ağsu Azer. 91 H2
Agua, Volcán de vol. Guat. 136 F6
Água Clara Brazil 144 F2
Aguadilla Puerto Rico 137 K5
Agua Escondida Arg. 144 C5
Agua Fria r. U.S.A. 129 G5
Agua Fria National Monument nat. park U.S.A. 129 G4
Aguanaval r. Mex. 131 C7
Aguanga U.S.A. 128 E5
Aguanus r. Canada 123 J4
Aguapeí r. Brazil 145 A3
Agua Prieta Mex. 127 F7
Aguaro-Guariquito, Parque Nacional nat. park Venez. 142 E2
Aguascalientes Mex. 136 D4
Agudos Brazil 145 A3
Águeda Port. 57 B3
Aguemour reg. Alg. 96 D2
Aguié Niger 96 D3
Aguijan i. N. Mariana Is 69 L4
Aguilar U.S.A. 127 G5
Aguilar de Campóo Spain 57 D2
Águilas Spain 57 F5

▶Agulhas, Cape S. Africa 100 E8
Most southerly point of Africa.

Agulhas Basin sea feature Southern Ocean 149 J9
Agulhas Negras mt. Brazil 145 B3
Agulhas Plateau sea feature Southern Ocean 149 J8
Agulhas Ridge sea feature S. Atlantic Ocean 148 I8
Ağva Turkey 59 M4
Agvali Rus. Fed. 91 G2
Ahaggar plat. Alg. see Hoggar
Āhangarān Iran 89 F3
Ahar Iran 88 B2
Ahaura N.Z. 113 C6
Ahaus Germany 52 H2
Ahipara Bay N.Z. 113 D2
Ahiri India 84 D2
Ahklun Mountains U.S.A. 118 B4
Ahlen Germany 53 H3
Ahmadabad India 82 C5
Aḥmadābād Iran 89 E3
Aḥmad al Bāqir, Jabal mt. Jordan 85 B5
Ahmadī Iran 88 E5
Ahmadnagar India 84 B2
Ahmadpur East Pak. 89 H4
Ahmar mts Eth. 98 E3
Ahmar Mountains Eth. see Ahmar
Ahmedabad India see Ahmadabad
Ahmednagar India see Ahmadnagar
Ahorn Germany 53 K4
Ahr r. Germany 52 H4
Ahram Iran 88 C4
Ahrensburg Germany 53 K1
Āhtäri Fin. 44 N5
Ahtme Estonia 45 O7
Ahu China 77 H1
Āhū Iran 88 C4
Ahun France 56 F3
Ahuzhen China see Ahu
Ahvāz Iran 88 C4
Ahwa India 84 B1
Ahwāz Iran see Ahvāz
Ai-Ais Namibia 100 C4
Ai-Ais Hot Springs and Fish River Canyon Park nature res. Namibia 100 C4
Aichwara India 82 D4
Aid U.S.A. 134 D4
Aidin Turkm. 88 D2
Aigialousa Cyprus 85 B2
Aigina i. Greece 59 J6
Aigio Greece 59 J5
Aigle de Chambeyron mt. France 56 H4
Aigües Tortes i Estany de Sant Maurici, Parc Nacional d' nat. park Spain 57 G2
Ai He r. China 74 B4
Aihua China see Yunxian
Aihui China see Heihe
Aijal India see Aizawl
Aikawa Japan 75 E5
Aiken U.S.A. 133 D5
Ailao Shan mts China 76 D3
Aileron Australia 108 F5
Ailinglabelab atoll Marshall Is see Ailinglaplap
Ailinglaplap atoll Marshall Is 150 H5
Ailly-sur-Noye France 52 C5
Ailsa Craig Canada 134 E2
Ailsa Craig i. U.K. 50 D5
Aimangala India 84 C3
Aimorés, Serra dos hills Brazil 145 C2
Aïn Beïda Alg. 58 B7
'Aïn Ben Tili Mauritania 96 C2
'Ain Dâlla spring Egypt see 'Ayn Dāllah
Aïn Defla Alg. 57 H5
Aïn Deheb Alg. 57 G6
Aïn el Hadjel Alg. 57 H6
'Ain el Maqfi spring Egypt see 'Ayn al Maqfī
Aïn el Melh Alg. 57 I6
Aïn Mdila well Alg. 58 B7
Aïn-M'Lila Alg. 54 F4
Aïn Oussera Alg. 57 H6
Aïn Salah Alg. see In Salah
Aïn Sefra Alg. 54 D5
Ainsworth U.S.A. 130 D3
Aintab Turkey see Gaziantep
Aïn Taya Alg. 57 H5
Aïn Tédélès Alg. 57 G6
Aïn Temouchent Alg. 57 F6
'Ain Tibaghbagh spring Egypt see 'Ayn Tabaghbugh
'Ain Timeira spring Egypt see 'Ayn Tumayrah
'Ain Zeitûn Egypt see 'Ayn Zaytūn
Aiquile Bol. 142 E7
Air i. Indon. 71 D7
Airaines France 52 B5
Airdrie Canada 120 H5
Airdrie U.K. 50 F5
Aire r. France 52 E5
Aire, Canal d' France 52 C4
Aire-sur-l'Adour France 56 D5
Air Force Island Canada 119 K3
Airpanas Indon. 108 D1
Aisatung Mountain Myanmar 70 A2
Aisch r. Germany 53 L5
Aishihik Canada 120 B2
Aishihik Lake Canada 120 B2
Aisne r. France 52 C5
Aïssa, Djebel mt. Alg. 54 D5
Aitamännikkö Fin. 44 N3
Aitana mt. Spain 57 F4
Aït Benhaddou tourist site Morocco 54 C5
Aiterach r. Germany 53 M6
Aitkin U.S.A. 130 E2
Aiud Romania 59 J1
Aix France see Aix-en-Provence
Aix-en-Provence France 56 G5
Aix-la-Chapelle Germany see Aachen
Aix-les-Bains France 56 G4
Aíyina i. Greece see Aigina
Aíyion Greece see Aigio
Aizawl India 83 H5
Aizkraukle Latvia 45 N8
Aizpute Latvia 45 L8
Aizu-wakamatsu Japan 75 E5
Ajaccio Corsica France 56 I6
Ajanta India 84 B1
Ajanta Range hills India see Sahyadriparvat Range
Ajaureforsen Sweden 44 I4
Ajax Canada 134 F2
Ajayameru India see Ajmer
Ajban U.A.E. 88 D5
Aj Bogd Uul mt. Mongolia 80 I3
Ajdābiyā Libya 97 F1
a-Jiddét des. Oman see Ḥarāsīs, Jiddat al
'Ajlūn Jordan 85 B3
'Ajman U.A.E. 88 D5
Ajmer India 82 C4
Ajmer-Merwara India see Ajmer
Ajnala India 82 C3
Ajo U.S.A. 129 G5
Ajo, Mount U.S.A. 129 G5
Ajrestan Afgh. 89 G3
Akademii, Zaliv b. Rus. Fed. 74 E1
Akademii Nauk, Khrebet mt. Tajik. see Akademiyai Fanho, Qatorkŭhi
Akademiyai Fanho, Qatorkŭhi mt. Tajik. 89 H2
Akagera National Park Rwanda 98 D4
Akalkot India 84 C2
Akama, Akra c. Cyprus see Arnauti, Cape
Akamagaseki Japan see Shimonoseki
Akan National Park Japan 74 G4
Akaroa N.Z. 113 D6
Akas reg. India 76 B3
Akāshat Iraq 91 E4
Akbarābād Iran 91 I5
Akbarpur Uttar Pradesh India 82 E4
Akbarpur Uttar Pradesh India 83 E4
Akbaytal, Pereval pass Tajik. 89 I2
Akbaytal Pass Tajik. see Akbaytal, Pereval
Akbez Turkey 85 C1
Akçadağ Turkey 90 E3
Akçakale Turkey 85 D1
Akçakoca Turkey 59 N4
Akçakoca Dağları mts Turkey 55 N4
Akçakoyunlu Turkey 85 C1
Akçalı Dağları mts Turkey 85 A1
Akchâr reg. Mauritania 96 B3
Akchi Kazakh. see Akshiy
Akdağlar mts Turkey 59 M6
Akdağmadeni Turkey 90 D3
Akdere Turkey 85 A1
Akelamo Indon. 69 H6
Åkersberga Sweden 45 K7
Akersloot Neth. 52 E2
Aketi Dem. Rep. Congo 98 C3
Akgyr Erezi hills Turkm. see Akkyr, Gory
Akhali-Afoni Georgia see Akhali Ap'oni
Akhali Ap'oni Georgia 91 F2
Akhḍar, Al Jabal al mts Libya 97 F1
Akhḍar, Jabal mts Oman 88 E6
Akhisar Turkey 59 L5
Akhnoor Jammu and Kashmir 82 C2
Akhsu Azer. see Ağsu
Akhta Armenia see Hrazdan
Akhtarīn Syria 85 C1
Akhtubinsk Rus. Fed. 43 J6
Akhty Rus. Fed. 91 G2
Akhtyrka Ukr. see Okhtyrka
Aki Japan 75 D6
Akiéni Gabon 98 B4
Akimiski Island Canada 122 E3
Akishma r. Rus. Fed. 74 D1

Alon Myanmar 70 A2
Along India 83 H3
Alongshan China 74 A2
Alonnisos *i.* Greece 59 J5
Alor *i.* Indon. 108 D2
Alor, Kepulauan *is* Indon. 108 D2
Alor Setar Malaysia 71 C6
Alor Star Malaysia *see* **Alor Setar**
Alost Belgium *see* **Aalst**
Aloysius, Mount Australia 109 E6
Alozero Rus. Fed. 44 Q4
Alpen Germany 52 G3
Alpena U.S.A. 134 D1
Alpercatas, Serra das *hills* Brazil 143 J5
Alpha Australia 110 D4
Alpha Ridge *sea feature* Arctic Ocean 153 A1
Alpine *AZ* U.S.A. 129 I5
Alpine *NY* U.S.A. 135 G2
Alpine *TX* U.S.A. 131 C6
Alpine *WY* U.S.A. 126 F4
Alpine National Park Australia 112 C6
Alps *mts* Europe 56 H4
Al Qa'āmīyāt *reg.* Saudi Arabia 86 G6
Al Qaddāḩīyah Libya 97 E1
Al Qadmūs Syria 85 C2
Al Qaffāy *i.* U.A.E. 88 D5
Al Qāhirah Egypt *see* **Cairo**
Al Qā'īyah Saudi Arabia 86 F5
Al Qā'īyah *well* Saudi Arabia 88 B5
Al Qalībah Saudi Arabia 90 E5
Al Qāmishlī Syria 91 F3
Al Qar'ah Libya 90 B5
Al Qar'ah *well* Saudi Arabia 88 B5
Al Qar'ah *lava field* Syria 85 C3
Al Qardāḩah Syria 85 C2
Al Qarqar Saudi Arabia 85 C4
Al Qaryatayn Syria 85 C2
Al Qaşab *Ar Riyāḑ* Saudi Arabia 88 B5
Al Qaşab *Ash Sharqīyah* Saudi Arabia 88 C6
Al Qaţīf Saudi Arabia 88 C5
Al Qaţn Yemen 86 G6
Al Qaţrānah Jordan 85 C4
Al Qaţrūn Libya 97 E2
Al Qāyşūmah *well* Saudi Arabia 91 F5
Al Qumur *country* Africa *see* **Comoros**
Al Qunayţirah Syria 85 B3
Al Qunfidhah Saudi Arabia 86 F6
Al Qurayyāt Saudi Arabia 85 C4
Al Qurnah Iraq 91 G5
Al Quşaymah Egypt 85 B4
Al Quşayr Egypt 86 D4
Al Quşayr Syria 85 C2
Al Qūşīyah Egypt 90 C6
Al Qūşūrīyah Saudi Arabia 88 B6
Al Quţayfah Syria 85 C3
Al Quwayī' Saudi Arabia 88 B6
Al Quwayīyah Saudi Arabia 86 G5
Al Quwayrah Jordan 85 B5
Al Rabbād *reg.* U.A.E. 88 D6
Alroy Downs Australia 110 B3
Alsace *admin. reg.* France 53 H6
Alsace *reg.* France 56 H2
Alsager U.K. 49 E5
Al Samīt *well* Iraq 91 F5
Alsask Canada 121 I5
Alsatia *reg.* France *see* **Alsace**
Alsek *r.* U.S.A. 120 B3
Alsfeld Germany 53 J4
Alsleben (Saale) Germany 53 L3
Alston U.K. 48 E4
Alstonville Australia 112 F2
Alsunga Latvia 45 L8
Alta Norway 44 M2
Alta, Mount N.Z. 113 B7
Altaelva *r.* Norway 44 M2
Altafjorden *sea chan.* Norway 44 M1
Alta Floresta Brazil 143 G5
Altai Mountains Asia 72 F3
Altamaha *r.* U.S.A. 133 D6
Altamira Brazil 143 H4
Altamura Italy 58 G4
Altan Shiret China 73 J5
Altan Xiret China *see* **Altan Shiret**
Alta Paraiso de Goiás Brazil 145 B1
Altar *r.* Mex. 127 F7
Altar, Desierto de *des.* Mex. 125 F6
Altavista U.S.A. 134 F5
Altay China 80 G2
Altay Mongolia 80 I2
Altayskiy Rus. Fed. 80 G1
Altayskiy Khrebet *mts* Asia *see* **Altai Mountains**
Altdorf Switz. 56 I3
Altea Spain 57 F4
Alteidet Norway 44 M1
Altenahr Germany 52 G4
Altenberge Germany 53 H2
Altenburg Germany 53 M4
Altenkirchen (Westerwald) Germany 53 H4
Altenqoke China 83 H1
Altin Köprü Iraq 91 G4
Altınoluk Turkey 59 L5
Altınözü Turkey 85 C1
Altıntaş Turkey 59 N5
Altiplano *plain* Bol. 142 E7
Altmark *reg.* Germany 53 L2
Altmühl *r.* Germany 53 L6
Alto, Monte *hill* Italy 58 D2
Alto Chicapa Angola 99 B5
Alto del Moncayo *mt.* Spain 57 F3
Alto de Pencoso *hills* Arg. 144 C4
Alto Garças Brazil 143 H7
Alto Madidi, Parque Nacional *nat. park* Bol. 142 E6
Alton *CA* U.S.A. 128 A1
Alton *IL* U.S.A. 130 F4
Alton *MO* U.S.A. 131 F4
Alton *NH* U.S.A. 135 J2
Altona Canada 120 F3
Altoona U.S.A. 135 F3
Alto Parnaíba Brazil 143 I5
Altötting Germany 47 N6
Altrincham U.K. 48 E5
Alt Schwerin Germany 53 M1
Altūn Kūbrī Iraq *see* **Altin Köprü**
Altun Shan *mts* China 80 G4
Alturas U.S.A. 126 C4
Altus U.S.A. 131 D5
Al Ubaylah Saudi Arabia 98 F1
Alucra Turkey 90 E2
Alūksne Latvia 45 O8
Alūm Iran 88 C3
Alum Bridge U.S.A. 134 E4
Al 'Uqaylah Libya 97 E1
Al 'Uqaylah Saudi Arabia *see* **An Nabk**
Al Uqşur Egypt *see* **Luxor**
Alur India 84 C3
Al Urayq *des.* Saudi Arabia 90 E5
Al 'Urdun *country* Asia *see* **Jordan**
Alur Setar Malaysia *see* **Alor Setar**
'Alūt Iran 88 B3
Aluva India *see* **Alwaye**
Al 'Uwayjā' *well* Saudi Arabia 88 C6
Al 'Uwaynāt Libya 86 B5
Al 'Uwayqīlah Saudi Arabia 91 F5
Al 'Uzayr Iraq 91 G5
Alva U.S.A. 131 D4
Alvand, Kūh-e *mt.* Iran 88 C3
Alvarães Brazil 142 F4
Alvaton U.S.A. 134 B5
Alvdal Norway 44 G5
Älvdalen Sweden 45 I6
Alvesta Sweden 45 I8
Ålvik Norway 45 E6
Alvik Sweden 44 J5
Alvin U.S.A. 131 E6
Alvorada do Norte Brazil 145 B1
Älvsbyn Sweden 44 L4
Al Wafrah Kuwait 88 B4
Al Wajh Saudi Arabia 86 E4
Al Wakrah Qatar 88 C5
Al Waqbá *well* Saudi Arabia 88 B4
Alwar India 82 D4
Al Warī'ah Saudi Arabia 86 G4
Al Wāţīyah *well* Egypt 90 B5
Alwaye India 84 C4
Al Widyān *plat.* Iraq/Saudi Arabia 91 F4
Al Wusayţ *well* Saudi Arabia 88 B4
Alxa Youqi China *see* **Ehen Hudag**
Alxa Zuoqi China *see* **Bayan Hot**
Al Yamāmah Saudi Arabia 88 B5
Al Yaman *country* Asia *see* **Yemen**
Alyangula Australia 110 B2
Al Yāsāt *i.* U.A.E. 88 C5
Alyth U.K. 50 F4
Alytus Lith. 45 N9
Alzette *r.* Lux. 52 G5
Alzey Germany 53 I5
Amacayacu, Parque Nacional *nat. park* Col. 142 D4
Amadeus, Lake *salt flat* Australia 109 E6
Amadjuak Lake Canada 119 K3
Amadora Port. 57 B4
Amakusa-nada *b.* Japan 75 C6
Åmål Sweden 45 H7
Amalia S. Africa 101 G4
Amaliada Greece 59 I6
Amalner India 82 C5
Amamapare Indon. 69 J7
Amambaí Brazil 144 E2
Amambaí, Serra de *hills* Brazil/Para. 144 E2
Amami-Ō-shima *i.* Japan 75 C7
Amami-shotō *is* Japan 75 B8
Amamula Dem. Rep. Congo 98 C4
Amanab P.N.G. 69 K7
Amangel'dy Kazakh. 80 C1
Amankeldi Kazakh. *see* **Amangel'dy**
Amantea Italy 58 G5
Amanzimtoti S. Africa 101 J6
Amapá Brazil 143 H3
Amarante Brazil 143 J5
Amarapura Myanmar 70 B2
Amareleja Port. 57 C4
Amargosa Brazil 145 D1
Amargosa *watercourse* U.S.A. 128 E3
Amargosa Desert U.S.A. 128 E3
Amargosa Range *mts* U.S.A. 128 E3
Amargosa Valley U.S.A. 128 E3
Amarillo U.S.A. 131 C5
Amarillo, Cerro *mt.* Arg. 144 C4
Amarkantak India 83 E5
Amasia Turkey *see* **Amasya**
Amasine W. Sahara 96 B2
Amasra Turkey 90 D2
Amasya Turkey 90 D2
Amata Australia 109 E6
Amatulla India 83 H4
Amau P.N.G. 110 E1
Amay Belgium 52 F4
Amazar Rus. Fed. 74 A1
Amazar *r.* Rus. Fed. 74 A1

▶**Amazon** *r.* S. America 142 F4
Longest river and largest drainage basin in South America and 2nd longest river in the world.
Also known as Amazonas or Solimões.
South America 138–139
World 12–13

Amazon, Mouths of the Brazil 143 I3
Amazonas *r.* S. America 142 F4 *see* **Amazon**
Amazon Cone *sea feature* S. Atlantic Ocean 148 E5
Amazônia, Parque Nacional *nat. park* Brazil 143 G4
Ambajogai India 84 C2
Ambala India 82 D3
Ambalangoda Sri Lanka 84 D5
Ambalavao Madag. 99 E6
Ambam Cameroon 98 B3
Ambar Iran 88 E4
Ambarchik Rus. Fed. 65 R3
Ambarnyy Rus. Fed. 44 R4
Ambasa India *see* **Ambassa**
Ambasamudram India 84 C4
Ambassa India 83 G5
Ambathala Australia 111 D5
Ambato Ecuador 142 C4
Ambato Boeny Madag. 99 E5
Ambato Finandrahana Madag. 99 E6
Ambatolampy Madag. 99 E5
Ambatomainty Madag. 99 E5
Ambatondrazaka Madag. 99 E5
Ambejogai India *see* **Ambajogai**
Ambelau *i.* Indon. 69 H7
Ambeno *enclave* East Timor *see* **Ocussi**
Amberg Germany 53 L5
Ambergris Cay *i.* Belize 136 G5
Ambérieu-en-Bugey France 56 G4
Amberley Canada 134 E1
Ambgaon India 84 D1
Ambianum France *see* **Amiens**
Ambikapur India 83 E5
Ambilobe Madag. 99 E5
Ambition, Mount Canada 120 D3
Amble U.K. 48 F3
Ambler U.S.A. 118 C3
Ambleside U.K. 48 E4
Amblève *r.* Belgium 52 F4
Ambo India 83 F5
Amboasary Madag. 99 E6
Ambodifotatra Madag. 99 E5
Ambohimahasoa Madag. 99 E6
Ambohitra *mt.* Madag. 99 E5
Amboina Indon. *see* **Ambon**
Ambon Indon. 69 H7
Ambon *i.* Indon. 69 H7
Amboró, Parque Nacional *nat. park* Bol. 142 F7
Ambositra Madag. 99 E6
Ambovombe Madag. 99 E6
Amboy U.S.A. 129 F4
Ambre, Cap d' *c.* Madag. *see* **Bobaomby, Tanjona**
Ambrim *i.* Vanuatu *see* **Ambrym**
Ambriz Angola 99 B4
Ambrizete Angola *see* **N'zeto**
Ambrosia Lake U.S.A. 129 J4
Ambrym *i.* Vanuatu 107 G3
Ambunti P.N.G. 69 K7
Ambur India 84 C3
Am-Dam Chad 97 F3
Amded, Oued *watercourse* Alg. 96 D2
Amdo China 83 G2
Ameland *i.* Neth. 52 F1
Amelia Court House U.S.A. 135 G5
Amenia U.S.A. 135 I3
Amer, Erg d' *des.* Alg. 98 A1
Amereli India *see* **Amreli**
American, North Fork *r.* U.S.A. 128 C2
Americana Brazil 145 B3
American-Antarctic Ridge *sea feature* S. Atlantic Ocean 148 G9
American Falls U.S.A. 126 E4
American Falls Reservoir U.S.A. 126 E4
American Fork U.S.A. 129 H1

▶**American Samoa** *terr.* S. Pacific Ocean 107 J3
United States Unincorporated Territory.
Oceania 8, 104–105

Americus U.S.A. 133 C5
Amersfoort Neth. 52 F2
Amersfoort S. Africa 101 I4
Amersham U.K. 49 G7
Amery Canada 121 M3
Amery Ice Shelf Antarctica 152 E2
Ames U.S.A. 130 E3
Amesbury U.K. 49 F7
Amesbury U.S.A. 135 J2
Amet India 82 C4
Amethi India 83 E4
Amfissa Greece 59 J5
Amga Rus. Fed. 65 O3
Amgalang China 73 L3
Amgu Rus. Fed. 74 E3
Amguid Alg. 96 D2
Amgun' *r.* Rus. Fed. 74 E1
Amherst Canada 123 I5
Amherst Myanmar *see* **Kyaikkami**
Amherst *MA* U.S.A. 135 I2
Amherst *OH* U.S.A. 134 D3
Amherst *VA* U.S.A. 134 F5
Amherstburg Canada 134 D2
Amherst Island Canada 135 G1
Amiata, Monte *mt.* Italy 58 D3
Amida Turkey *see* **Diyarbakır**
Amidon U.S.A. 130 C2
Amiens France 52 C5
'Amīj, Wādī *watercourse* Iraq 91 F4
Amik Ovası *marsh* Turkey 85 C1
'Amīnābād Iran 88 D4
Amindivi *atoll* India *see* **Amini**
Amindivi Islands India 84 B4
Amini *atoll* India 84 B4
Amino Eth. 98 E3
Aminuis Namibia 100 D2
Amīrābād Iran 88 B3
Amirante Islands Seychelles 149 L6
Amirante Trench *sea feature* Indian Ocean 149 L6
Amisk Lake Canada 121 K4
Amistad, Represa de *resr* Mex./U.S.A. *see* **Amistad Reservoir**
Amistad Reservoir Mex./U.S.A. 131 C6
Amisus Turkey *see* **Samsun**
Amite U.S.A. 131 F6
Amity Point Australia 112 F1
Amla India 82 D5
Amlapura Indon. *see* **Karangasem**
Amlash Iran 88 C2
Amlekhganj Nepal 83 F4
Åmli Norway 45 F7
Amlia Island U.S.A. 118 A4
Amlwch U.K. 48 C5

▶**'Ammān** Jordan 85 B4
Capital of Jordan.

Ammanazar Turkm. 88 D2
Ammanford U.K. 49 D7
Ämmänsaari Fin. 44 P4
'Ammār, Tall *hill* Syria 85 C3
Ammarnäs Sweden 44 J4
Ammaroo Australia 110 A4
Ammassalik Greenland 153 J2
Ammerland *reg.* Germany 53 H1
Ammern Germany 53 K3
Ammochostos Cyprus *see* **Famagusta**
Ammochostos Bay Cyprus 85 B2
Am Nābiyah Yemen 86 F7
Amne Machin Range *mts* China *see* **A'nyêmaqên Shan**
Amnok-kang *r.* China/N. Korea *see* **Yalu Jiang**
Amo Jiang *r.* China 76 D4
Amol Iran 88 D2
Amorbach Germany 53 J5
Amorgos *i.* Greece 59 K6
Amory U.S.A. 131 F5
Amos Canada 122 F4
Amourj Mauritania 96 C3
Amoy China *see* **Xiamen**
Ampani India 84 D2
Ampanihy Madag. 99 E6
Amparai Sri Lanka 84 D5
Amparo Brazil 145 B3
Ampasimanolotra Madag. 99 E5
Amphitheatre Australia 112 A6
Amphitrite Group *is* Paracel Is 68 E3
Ampoa Indon. 69 G7
Amraoti India *see* **Amravati**
Amravati India 84 C1
Amrawad India 82 D5
Amreli India 82 B5
Amri Pak. 89 H5
Amring India 83 H4
'Amrīt Syria 85 B2
Amritsar India 82 C3
Amroha India 82 D3
Amsden U.S.A. 134 D3
Åmsele Sweden 44 K4
Amstelveen Neth. 52 E2

▶**Amsterdam** Neth. 52 E2
Official capital of the Netherlands.

Amsterdam S. Africa 101 J4
Amsterdam U.S.A. 135 H2
Amsterdam, Île *i.* Indian Ocean 149 N8
Amstetten Austria 47 O6
Am Timan Chad 97 F3
Amudar'ya *r.* Asia 89 F2
Amudaryo *r.* Asia *see* **Amudar'ya**
Amund Ringnes Island Canada 119 I2
Amundsen, Mount Antarctica 152 F2
Amundsen Abyssal Plain *sea feature* Southern Ocean 152 J2
Amundsen Basin *sea feature* Arctic Ocean 153 H1
Amundsen Bay Antarctica 152 D2
Amundsen Coast Antarctica 152 J1
Amundsen Glacier Antarctica 152 I1
Amundsen Gulf Canada 118 F2
Amundsen Ridges *sea feature* Southern Ocean 152 J2
Amundsen-Scott *research station* Antarctica 152 C1
Amundsen Sea Antarctica 152 K2
Amuntai Indon. 68 F7
Amur *r.* China 74 D2
also known as Heilong Jiang (China)
Amur *r.* Rus. Fed. 74 F1
'Amur, Wadi *watercourse* Sudan 86 D6
Amur Oblast *admin. div.* Rus. Fed. *see* **Amurskaya Oblast'**
Amursk Rus. Fed. 74 E2
Amurskaya Oblast' *admin. div.* Rus. Fed. 74 C1
Amurskiy liman *strait* Rus. Fed. 74 F1
Amurzet Rus. Fed. 74 C3
Amvrosiyivka Ukr. 43 H7
Amyderya *r.* Asia *see* **Amudar'ya**
Am-Zoer Chad 97 F3
An Myanmar 70 A3
Anaa *atoll* Fr. Polynesia 151 K7
Anabanua Indon. 69 G7
Anabar *r.* Rus. Fed. 65 M2
Anacapa Islands U.S.A. 128 D4
Anaconda U.S.A. 126 E3
Anacortes U.S.A. 126 C2
Anadarko U.S.A. 131 D5
Anadolu Dağları *mts* Turkey 90 E2
Anadyr' Rus. Fed. 65 S3
Anadyr, Gulf of Rus. Fed. *see* **Anadyrskiy Zaliv**
Anadyrskiy Zaliv *b.* Rus. Fed. 65 T3
Anafi *i.* Greece 59 K6
Anagé Brazil 145 C1
'Ānah Iraq 91 F4
Anaheim U.S.A. 128 E5
Anahim Lake Canada 120 E4
Anáhuac Mex. 131 C7
Anahuac U.S.A. 131 E6
Anaimalai Hills India 84 C4
Anaiteum *i.* Vanuatu *see* **Anatom**
Anajás Brazil 143 I4
Anakie Australia 110 D4
Analalava Madag. 99 E5
Anamã Brazil 142 F4
Anambas, Kepulauan *is* Indon. 71 D7
Anamosa U.S.A. 130 F3
Anamur Turkey 85 A1
Anan Japan 75 D6
Anand India 82 C5
Anandapur India 83 F5
Anantapur India 84 C3
Ananthapur India *see* **Anantapur**
Anantnag India 82 C2
Anant Peth India 82 D4
Anantpur India *see* **Anantapur**
Ananyev Ukr. *see* **Anan'yiv**
Anan'yiv Ukr. 43 F7
Anapa Rus. Fed. 90 E1
Anápolis Brazil 145 A2
Anār Fin. *see* **Inari**
Anār Iran 88 D4
Anardara Afgh. 89 F3
Anatahan *i.* N. Mariana Is 69 L3
Anatajan *i.* N. Mariana Is *see* **Anatahan**
Anatolia *reg.* Turkey 90 D3
Anatom *i.* Vanuatu 107 G4
Añatuya Arg. 144 D3
Anaypazari Turkey *see* **Gülnar**
An Biên Vietnam 71 D5
Anbūr-e Kālārī Iran 88 D5
Anbyon N. Korea 75 B5
Ancenis France 56 D3
Anchorage U.S.A. 118 D3
Anchorage Island *atoll* Cook Is *see* **Suwarrow**
Anchor Bay U.S.A. 134 D2
Anchuthengu India *see* **Anjengo**
Anci China *see* **Langfang**
An Cóbh Rep. of Ireland *see* **Cóbh**
Ancona Italy 58 E3
Ancud, Golfo de *g.* Chile 144 B6
Ancyra Turkey *see* **Ankara**
Anda *Heilong.* China 74 B3
Anda *Heilong.* China *see* **Daqing**
Andacollo Chile 144 B4
Andado Australia 110 A5
Andahuaylas Peru 142 D6
Andal India 83 F5
Åndalsnes Norway 44 E5
Andalucía *aut. comm.* Spain 53 D5
Andalusia *aut. comm.* Spain *see* **Andalucía**
Andalusia U.S.A. 133 C6
Andaman Basin *sea feature* Indian Ocean 149 O5
Andaman Islands India 71 A4
Andaman Sea Indian Ocean 71 A5
Andaman Strait India 71 A4
Andamooka Australia 111 B6
Andapa Madag. 99 E5
Andarāb *reg.* Afgh. 89 H3
Ande China 76 E4
Andegavum France *see* **Angers**
Andelle *r.* France 52 B5
Andenes Norway 44 J2
Andenne Belgium 52 F4
Andéramboukane Mali 96 D3
Anderlecht Belgium 52 E4
Andermatt Switz. 56 I3
Andernos-les-Bains France 56 D4
Anderson *r.* Canada 118 F3
Anderson *AK* U.S.A. 118 D3
Anderson *IN* U.S.A. 134 C3
Anderson *SC* U.S.A. 133 D5
Anderson *TX* U.S.A. 131 E6
Anderson Bay Australia 111 [inset]
Anderson Lake Canada 120 F5
Andes *mts* S. America 144 C4
Andfjorden *sea chan.* Norway 40 J2
Andhíparos *i.* Greece *see* **Antiparos**
Andhra Lake India 84 B2
Andhra Pradesh *state* India 84 C2
Andijon Uzbek. *see* **Andizhan**
Andikithira *i.* Greece *see* **Antikythira**
Andilamena Madag. 99 E5
Andilanatoby Madag. 99 E5
Andīmeshk Iran 88 C3
Andímilos *i.* Greece *see* **Antimilos**
Andípsara *i.* Greece *see* **Antipsara**
Andırın Turkey 90 E3
Andirlangar China 83 E1
Andizhan Uzbek. 80 D3
Andkhvoy Afgh. 89 G2
Andoany Madag. 99 E5
Andoas Peru 142 C4
Andogskaya Gryada *hills* Rus. Fed. 42 H4
Andol India 84 C2
Andong China *see* **Dandong**
Andong S. Korea 75 C5
Andongwei China 77 H1
Andoom Australia 110 C2
▶**Andorra** *country* Europe 57 G2
Europe 5, 38–39

▶**Andorra la Vella** Andorra 57 G2
Capital of Andorra.

Andorra la Vieja Andorra *see* **Andorra la Vella**
Andover U.K. 49 F7
Andover *NY* U.S.A. 135 G2
Andover *OH* U.S.A. 134 E3
Andøya *i.* Norway 44 I2
Andrade U.S.A. 129 F5
Andradina Brazil 145 A3
Andranomavo Madag. 99 E5
Andranopasy Madag. 99 E6
Andreanof Islands U.S.A. 150 I2
Andreapol' Rus. Fed. 42 G4
Andreas Isle of Man 48 C4
André Félix, Parc National de *nat. park* Cent. Afr. Rep. 98 C3
Andrelândia Brazil 145 B3
Andrew Canada 121 H4
Andrew Bay Myanmar 70 A3
Andrews *SC* U.S.A. 133 E5
Andrews *TX* U.S.A. 131 C5
Andreyevka Kazakh. 80 F2
Andria Italy 58 G4
Androka Madag. 99 E6
Andropov Rus. Fed. *see* **Rybinsk**
Andros *i.* Bahamas 133 E7
Andros *i.* Greece 59 K6
Androscoggin *r.* U.S.A. 135 K2
Andros Town Bahamas 133 E7
Androtti *i.* India 84 B4
Andselv Norway 44 K2
Andújar Spain 57 D4
Andulo Angola 99 B5
Anec, Lake *salt flat* Australia 105 E5
Āneen-Kio *terr.* N. Pacific Ocean *see* **Wake Island**
Anéfis Mali 96 D3
Anegada, Bahía *b.* Arg. 144 D6
Anegada Passage Virgin Is (U.K.) 137 L5
Anécho Togo 96 D4
Aneityum *i.* Vanuatu *see* **Anatom**
'Aneiza, Jabal *hill* Iraq *see* **'Unayzah, Jabal**
Anemourion *tourist site* Turkey 85 A1
Anepmete P.N.G. 69 L8
Anet France 52 B6
Anetchom, Île *i.* Vanuatu *see* **Anatom**
Aneto *mt.* Spain 57 G2
Ānewetak *atoll* Marshall Is *see* **Enewetak**
Aney Niger 96 E3
Aneytioum, Île *i.* Vanuatu *see* **Anatom**
Anfu China 77 G3
Angalarri *r.* Australia 108 E3
Angamos, Punta *pt* Chile 144 B2
Ang'angxi China 74 A3

▶**Angara** *r.* Rus. Fed. 72 G1
Part of the Yenisey-Angara-Selenga, 3rd longest river in Asia.

Angarsk Rus. Fed. 72 I2
Angas Downs Australia 109 F6
Angatuba Brazil 145 A3
Angaur *i.* Palau 69 I5
Ånge Sweden 44 I5
Angel, Salto *waterfall* Venez. *see* **Angel Falls**
Ángel de la Guarda, Isla *i.* Mex. 127 E7

▶**Angel Falls** *waterfall* Venez. 142 F2
Highest waterfall in the world.

Ängelholm Sweden 45 H8
Angellala Creek *r.* Australia 112 C1
Angels Camp U.S.A. 128 C2
Ångermanälven *r.* Sweden 44 J5
Angers France 56 D3
Angikuni Lake Canada 121 L2
Angiola U.S.A. 128 D4
Angkor *tourist site* Cambodia 71 C4
Anglesea Australia 112 B7
Anglesey *i.* U.K. 48 C5
Angleton U.S.A. 131 E6
Anglo-Egyptian Sudan *country* Africa *see* **Sudan**
Angmagssalik Greenland *see* **Ammassalik**
Ang Mo Kio Sing. 71 [inset]
Ango Dem. Rep. Congo 98 C3
Angoche Moz. 99 D5
Angohrān Iran 88 E5
Angol Chile 144 B5
▶**Angola** *country* Africa 99 B5
Africa 7, 94–95
Angola *IN* U.S.A. 134 C3
Angola *NY* U.S.A. 134 F2
Angola Basin *sea feature* S. Atlantic Ocean 148 H7
Angora Turkey *see* **Ankara**
Angostura Mex. 127 F8
Angoulême France 56 E4
Angra dos Reis Brazil 145 B3
Angren Uzbek. 80 D3
Ang Thong Thai. 71 C4
Anguang China 74 A3

▶**Anguilla** *terr.* West Indies 137 L5
United Kingdom Overseas Territory.
North America 9, 116–117

Anguilla Cays *is* Bahamas 133 E8
Anguille, Cape Canada 123 K5
Angul India 84 E1
Angus Canada 134 F1
Angutia Char *i.* Bangl. 83 G5
Anholt *i.* Denmark 45 G8
Anhua China 77 F2
Anhui *prov.* China 77 H1
Anhumas Brazil 143 H7
Anhwei *prov.* China *see* **Anhui**
Aniak U.S.A. 118 C3
Aniakchak National Monument and Preserve *nat. park* U.S.A. 118 C4
Anin Myanmar 70 B4
Anitápolis Brazil 145 A4
Anıtlı Turkey 85 A1
Aniva Rus. Fed. 74 F3
Aniva, Mys *c.* Rus. Fed. 74 F3
Aniva, Zaliv *b.* Rus. Fed. 74 F3
Anizy-le-Château France 52 D5
Anjadip *i.* India 84 B3
Anjalankoski Fin. 45 O6
Anjar *tourist site* Lebanon 85 B3
Anjengo India 84 C4
Anji China 77 H2
Anjir Avand Iran 88 D3
Anjoman Iran 88 E3
Anjou *reg.* France 56 D3
Anjouan *i.* Comoros *see* **Nzwani**
Anjozorobe Madag. 99 E5
Anjuman *reg.* Afgh. 89 H3
Anjuthengu India *see* **Anjengo**
Ankang China 77 F1

▶**Ankara** Turkey 90 D3
Capital of Turkey.

Ankaratra *mt.* Madag. 99 E5
Ankazoabo Madag. 99 E6
Ankeny U.S.A. 130 E3
An Khê Vietnam 71 E4
Ankleshwar India 82 C5
Anklesvar India *see* **Ankleshwar**
Ankola India 84 B3
Ankouzhen China 76 E1
Anlong China 76 E3
Anlu China 77 G2
Anmoore U.S.A. 134 E4
An Muileann gCearr Rep. of Ireland *see* **Mullingar**
Anmyŏn-do *i.* S. Korea 75 B5
Ann, Cape Antarctica 152 D2
Ann, Cape U.S.A. 135 J2
Anna Rus. Fed. 43 I6
Anna, Lake U.S.A. 135 G4
Annaba Alg. 58 B6
Annaberg-Buchholtz Germany 53 N4
An Nabk Saudi Arabia 85 C4
An Nabk Syria 85 C2
An Nafūd *des.* Saudi Arabia 91 F5
An Najaf Iraq 91 G5
Annalee *r.* Rep. of Ireland 51 E3
Annalong U.K. 51 G3
Annam *reg.* Vietnam 68 D3
Annam Highlands *mts* Laos/Vietnam 70 D3
Annan U.K. 50 F6
Annan *r.* U.K. 50 F6
'Annān, Wādī al *watercourse* Syria 85 D2
Annandale U.S.A. 135 G4
Anna Plains Australia 108 C4

▶**Annapolis** U.S.A. 135 G4
State capital of Maryland.

Annapurna Conservation Area *nature res.* Nepal 83 F3
Annapurna I *mt.* Nepal 83 E3
Ann Arbor U.S.A. 134 D2
Anna Regina Guyana 143 G2
An Nás Rep. of Ireland *see* **Naas**
An Nāşirīyah Iraq 91 G5
An Naşrānī, Jabal *mts* Syria 81 C3
Annean, Lake *salt flat* Australia 109 B6
Anne Arundel Town U.S.A. *see* **Annapolis**
Annecy France 56 H4
Anne Marie Lake Canada 123 J3
Annen Neth. 52 G1
Annette Island U.S.A. 120 D4
An Nimārah Syria 85 C3
An Nimāş Saudi Arabia 86 F6
Anning China 76 D3
Anniston U.S.A. 133 C5
Annobón *i.* Equat. Guinea 96 D5
Annonay France 56 G4
An Nu'mānīyah Iraq 91 G4

An Nuşayrīyah, Jabal mts Syria 85 C2
Anonima atoll Micronesia see Namonuito
Anoón de Sardinas, Bahía de b. Col. 142 C3
Anorontany, Tanjona hd Madag. 99 E5
Ano Viannos Greece 59 K7
Anpu Gang b. China 77 F4
Anqing China 77 H2
Anren China 77 G3
Ans Belgium 52 F4
Ansbach Germany 53 K5
Anser Group is Australia 112 C7
Anshan China 74 A4
Anshun China 76 E3
Anshunchang China 76 D2
An Sirḩān, Wādī watercourse Saudi Arabia 90 E5
Ansley U.S.A. 130 D3
Anson U.S.A. 131 D5
Anson Bay Australia 108 E3
Ansongo Mali 96 D3
Ansonville Canada 122 E4
Ansted U.S.A. 134 E4
Ansudu Indon. 69 J7
Antabamba Peru 142 D6
Antakya Turkey 85 C1
Antalaha Madag. 99 F5
Antalya Turkey 59 N6
Antalya prov. Turkey 85 A1
Antalya Körfezi g. Turkey 59 N6

▶Antananarivo Madag. 99 E5
Capital of Madagascar.

An tAonach Rep. of Ireland see Nenagh

▶Antarctica 152
Most southerly and coldest continent, and the continent with the highest average elevation.
Poles 146–147

Antarctic Peninsula Antarctica 152 L2
Antas r. Brazil 145 A5
An Teallach mt. U.K. 50 D3
Antelope Island U.S.A. 129 G1
Antelope Range mts U.S.A. 128 E2
Antequera Spain 57 D5
Anthony Lagoon Australia 110 A3
Anti Atlas mts Morocco 54 C6
Antibes France 56 H5
Anticosti, Île d' i. Canada 123 J4
Anticosti Island Canada see Anticosti, Île d'
Antifer, Cap d' c. France 49 H9
Antigo U.S.A. 130 F2
Antigonish Canada 123 J5
Antigua i. Antigua and Barbuda 137 L5
Antigua country West Indies see Antigua and Barbuda
▶Antigua and Barbuda country West Indies 137 L5
North America 9, 116–117
Antikythira i. Greece 59 J7
Antikythiro, Steno sea chan. Greece 59 J7
Anti Lebanon mts Lebanon/Syria see Sharqī, Jabal ash
Antimilos i. Greece 59 K6
Antimony U.S.A. 129 H2
An tInbhear Mór Rep. of Ireland see Arklow
Antioch Turkey see Antakya
Antioch U.S.A. 128 C2
Antiocheia ad Cragum tourist site Turkey 85 A1
Antiochia Turkey see Antakya
Antiparos i. Greece 59 K6
Antipodes Islands N.Z. 107 H6
Antipsara i. Greece 59 K5
Antium Italy see Anzio
Antlers U.S.A. 131 E5
Antofagasta Chile 144 B2
Antofagasta de la Sierra Arg. 144 C3
Antofalla, Volcán vol. Arg. 144 C3
Antoing Belgium 52 D4
António Enes Moz. see Angoche
Antri India 82 D4
Antrim U.K. 51 F3
Antrim Hills U.K. 51 F2
Antrim Plateau Australia 108 E4
Antropovo Rus. Fed. 42 I4
Antsalova Madag. 99 E5
Antseranana Madag. see Antsirañana
Antsirabe Madag. 99 E5
Antsirañana Madag. 99 E5
Antsla Estonia 45 O8
Antsohihy Madag. 99 E5
Anttis Sweden 44 M3
Anttola Fin. 45 O6
An Tuc Vietnam see An Khê
Antwerp Belgium 52 E3
Antwerp U.S.A. 135 H1
Antwerpen Belgium see Antwerp
An Uaimh Rep. of Ireland see Navan
Anuc, Lac l. Canada 122 G2
Anuchino Rus. Fed. 74 D4
Anugul India see Angul
Anupgarh India 82 C3
Anuradhapura Sri Lanka 84 D4
Anveh Iran 88 D5
Anvers Island Antarctica 152 L2
Anvik U.S.A. 118 B3
Anvil Range mts Canada 120 C2
Anxi Fujian China 77 H3
Anxi Gansu China 80 I3
Anxiang China 77 G2
Anxious Bay Australia 109 F8
Anyang Guangxi China see Du'an
Anyang Henan China 73 K5
Anyang S. Korea 75 B5
A'nyêmaqên Shan mts China 76 C1
Anyuan Jiangxi China 77 G3
Anyuan Jiangxi China 77 G3
Anyue China 76 E2
Anyuy r. Rus. Fed. 74 E2
Anyuysk Rus. Fed. 65 R3
Anzac Alta Canada 121 I3
Anzac B.C. Canada 120 F4
Anzhero-Sudzhensk Rus. Fed. 64 J4
Anzi Dem. Rep. Congo 98 C4
Anzio Italy 58 E4
Aoba i. Vanuatu 107 G3
Aoga-shima i. Japan 75 E6
Aokal Afgh. 89 F3
Ao Kham, Laem pt Thai. 71 B5
Aomen China see Macau
Aomen Tebie Xingzhengqu aut. reg. China see Macau
Aomori Japan 74 F4
Ao Phang Nga National Park Thai. 71 B5

▶Aoraki mt. N.Z. 113 C6
Highest mountain in New Zealand.

Aôral, Phnum mt. Cambodia 71 D4
Aorangi mt. N.Z. see Aoraki
Aosta Italy 58 B2
Aotearoa country Oceania see New Zealand
Aouk, Bahr r. Cent. Afr. Rep./Chad 97 E4
Aoukâr reg. Mali/Mauritania 96 C2
Aoulef Alg. 96 D2
Aozou Chad 97 E2
Apa r. Brazil 144 E2
Apache Creek U.S.A. 129 I5
Apache Junction U.S.A. 129 H5
Apaiang atoll Kiribati see Abaiang
Apalachee Bay U.S.A. 133 C6
Apalachicola U.S.A. 133 C6
Apalachicola r. U.S.A. 133 C6
Apalachin U.S.A. 135 G2
Apamea Turkey see Dinar
Apaporis r. Col. 142 E4
Aparecida do Tabuado Brazil 145 A3
Aparima N.Z. see Riverton
Aparri Phil. 150 E4
Apatity Rus. Fed. 44 R3
Apatzingán Mex. 136 D5
Ape Latvia 45 O8
Apeldoorn Neth. 52 F2
Apelern Germany 53 J2
Apennines mts Italy 58 C2
Apensen Germany 53 J1
Apex Mountain Canada 120 B2
Api mt. Nepal 82 E3
Api i. Vanuatu see Epi
Apia atoll Kiribati see Abaiang

▶Apia Samoa 107 I3
Capital of Samoa.

Apiacas, Serra dos hills Brazil 143 G6
Apiaí Brazil 145 A4
Apishapa r. U.S.A. 130 C4
Apiti N.Z. 113 E4
Apizolaya Mex. 131 C7
Aplao Peru 142 D7
Apo, Mount vol. Phil. 69 H5
Apoera Suriname 143 G2
Apolda Germany 53 L3
Apollo Bay Australia 112 A7
Apollonia Bulg. see Sozopol
Apolo Bol. 142 E6
Aporé Brazil 145 A2
Aporé r. Brazil 145 A2
Apostle Islands U.S.A. 130 F2
Apostolens Tommelfinger mt. Greenland 119 N3
Apostolos Andreas, Cape Cyprus 85 B2
Apoteri Guyana 143 G3
Apozai Pak. 89 H4
Appalachian Mountains U.S.A. 134 D5
Appalla i. Fiji see Kabara
Appennino mts Italy see Apennines
Appennino Abruzzese mts Italy 58 E3
Appennino Tosco-Emiliano mts Italy 58 D3
Appennino Umbro-Marchigiano mts Italy 58 E3
Appingedam Neth. 52 G1
Applecross U.K. 50 D3
Appleton MN U.S.A. 130 D2
Appleton WI U.S.A. 134 A1
Apple Valley U.S.A. 128 E4
Appomattox U.S.A. 135 F5
Aprilia Italy 58 E4
Aprunyi India 76 B2
Apsheronsk Rus. Fed. 91 E1
Apsheronskaya Rus. Fed. see Apsheronsk
Apsley Canada 135 F1
Apt France 56 G5
Apucarana Brazil 145 A3
Apucarana, Serra da hills Brazil 145 A3
Apulum Romania see Alba Iulia
Aq"a Georgia see Sokhumi
'Aqaba Jordan see Al 'Aqabah
Aqaba, Gulf of Asia 90 D5
'Aqaba, Wâdi el watercourse Egypt see 'Aqabah, Wādī al
'Aqabah, Birkat al well Iraq 88 A4
'Aqabah, Wādī al watercourse Egypt 85 A4
Aqadyr Kazakh. see Agadyr'
Aqdoghmish r. Iran 88 B2
Aqköl Akmolinskaya Oblast' Kazakh. see Akkol'
Aqköl Atyrauskaya Oblast' Kazakh. see Akkol'
Aqmola Kazakh. see Astana
Aqqan China 83 F1
Aqqikkol Hu salt l. China 83 G1
Aqra', Jabal al mt. Syria/Turkey 85 B2
'Aqran hill Saudi Arabia 85 D4
Aqsay Kazakh. see Aksay
Aqsayqin Hit terr. Asia see Aksai Chin
Aqshī Kazakh. see Akshiy
Aqshuqyr Kazakh. see Akshukur
Aqsū Kazakh. see Aksu
Aqsūat Kazakh. see Aksuat
Aqsū-Ayuly Kazakh. see Aksu-Ayuly
Aqtaū Kazakh. see Aktau
Aqtōbe Kazakh. see Aktobe
Aqtoghay Kazakh. see Aktogay
Aquae Grani Germany see Aachen
Aquae Gratianae France see Aix-les-Bains
Aquae Sextiae France see Aix-en-Provence
Aquae Statiellae Italy see Acqui Terme
Aquarius Mountains U.S.A. 129 G4
Aquarius Plateau U.S.A. 129 H3
Aquaviva delle Fonti Italy 58 G4
Aquidauana Brazil 144 E2
Aquiles Mex. 127 G7
Aquincum Hungary see Budapest
Aquiry r. Brazil see Acre
Aquisgranum Germany see Aachen
Aquitaine reg. France 56 D5
Aquitania reg. France see Aquitaine
Aqzhayqyn Köli salt l. Kazakh. see Akzhaykyn, Ozero
Ara India 83 F4
Āra Ārba Eth. 98 E3
Arab Afgh. 89 G4
Arab, Bahr el watercourse Sudan 97 F4
'Arab, Khalîg el b. Egypt see 'Arab, Khalīj al
'Arab, Khalīj al b. Egypt 90 C5
'Arabah, Wādī al watercourse Israel/Jordan 85 B5
Arabian Basin sea feature Indian Ocean 149 M5
Arabian Gulf Asia see The Gulf
Arabian Peninsula Asia 86 G5
Arabian Sea Indian Ocean 87 K6
Araç Turkey 90 D2
Araça r. Brazil 142 F4
Aracaju Brazil 143 K6
Aracati Brazil 143 K4
Aracatu Brazil 145 C1
Araçatuba Brazil 145 A3
Aracena Spain 57 C5
Aracruz Brazil 145 C2
Araçuaí Brazil 145 C2
Araçuaí r. Brazil 145 C2
'Arad Israel 85 B4
Arad Romania 59 I1
'Arādah U.A.E. 88 D6
Arafura Sea Australia/Indon. 106 D2
Arafura Shelf sea feature Australia/Indon. 150 E6
Aragarças Brazil 143 H7
Aragón r. Spain 57 F2
Araguaçu Brazil 145 A1
Araguaia r. Brazil 145 A1
Araguaia, Parque Nacional de nat. park Brazil 143 H6
Araguaiana Brazil 145 A1
Araguaína Brazil 143 I5
Araguari Brazil 145 A2
Araguari r. Brazil 143 H3
Araguatins Brazil 143 I5
Arai Brazil 145 B1
'Arâif el Naga, Gebel hill Egypt see 'Urayf an Nāqah, Jabal
Araiosos Brazil 143 J4
Arak Alg. 96 D2
Arāk Iran 88 C3
Arak Syria 85 D2
Arakan reg. Myanmar 70 A2
Arakan Yoma mts Myanmar 70 A2
Arakkonam India 84 C3
Araks r. Armenia see Araz
Araku India 84 D2
Aral China 80 F3
Aral Kazakh. see Aral'sk
Aral Tajik. see Vose

▶Aral Sea salt l. Kazakh./Uzbek. 80 B2
3rd largest lake in Asia.

Aral'sk Kazakh. 80 B2
Aral'skoye More salt l. Kazakh./Uzbek. see Aral Sea
Aralsor, Ozero l. Kazakh. 43 K6
Aral Tengizi salt l. Kazakh./Uzbek. see Aral Sea
Aramac Australia 110 D4
Aramac Creek watercourse Australia 110 D4
Aramah plat. Saudi Arabia 88 B5
Aramberri Mex. 131 D7
Aramia r. P.N.G. 69 K8
Aran r. India 84 C2
Aranda de Duero Spain 57 E3
Arandai Indon. 69 I7
Aranđelovac Serb. and Mont. 59 I2
Arandis Namibia 100 B2
Arang India 83 E5
Arani India 84 C3
Aran Island Rep. of Ireland 51 D3
Aran Islands Rep. of Ireland 51 C4
Aranjuez Spain 57 E3
Aranos Namibia 100 D3
Aransas Pass U.S.A. 131 D7
Arantangi India 84 C4
Aranuka atoll Kiribati 107 H1
Aranyaprathet Thai. 71 C4
Arao Japan 75 C6
Araouane Mali 96 C3
Arapaho U.S.A. 131 D5
Arapgir Turkey 90 E3
Arapiraca Brazil 143 K5
Arapis, Akra pt Greece 59 K4
Arapkir Turkey see Arapgir
Arapongas Brazil 145 A3
Araquari Brazil 145 A4
'Ar'ar Saudi Arabia 91 F5
Araracuara Col. 142 D4
Araranguá Brazil 145 A5
Araraquara Brazil 145 A3
Araras Brazil 143 H5
Ararat Armenia 91 G3
Ararat Australia 112 A6
Ararat, Mount Turkey 91 G3
Araria India 83 F4
Araripina Brazil 143 J5
Aras Turkey 91 F3
Aras r. Turkey see Araz
Arataca Brazil 145 D1
Arauca Col. 142 D2
Arauca r. Venez. 142 E2
Aravalli Range mts India 82 C4
Aravete Estonia 45 N7
Arawa P.N.G. 106 F2
Araxá Brazil 145 B2
Araxes r. Asia see Araz
Arayıt Dağı mt. Turkey 59 N5
Araz r. Azer. 91 H2
also spelt Araks (Armenia), Aras (Turkey), formerly known as Araxes
Arbailu Iraq see Arbīl
Arbat Iraq 91 G4
Arbela Iraq see Arbīl
Arberth U.K. see Narberth
Arbīl Iraq 91 G3
Arboga Sweden 45 I7
Arborfield Canada 121 K4
Arborg Canada 121 L5
Arbroath U.K. 50 G4
Arbuckle U.S.A. 128 B2
Arbu Lut, Dasht-e des. Afgh. 89 F4
Arcachon France 56 D4
Arcade U.S.A. 135 F2
Arcadia FL U.S.A. 133 D7
Arcadia LA U.S.A. 131 E5
Arcadia MI U.S.A. 134 B1
Arcanum U.S.A. 134 C4
Arcata U.S.A. 126 B4
Arc Dome mt. U.S.A. 128 E2
Arcelia Mex. 136 D5
Archangel Rus. Fed. 42 I2
Archer r. Australia 67 G9
Archer Bend National Park Australia 110 C2
Archer City U.S.A. 131 D5
Arches National Park U.S.A. 129 I2
Archipiélago Los Roques nat. park Venez. 142 E1
Ärçivan Azer. 91 H3
Arckaringa watercourse Australia 111 A6
Arco U.S.A. 126 E4
Arcos Brazil 145 B3
Arcos de la Frontera Spain 57 D5
Arctic Bay Canada 119 J2
Arctic Institute Islands Rus. Fed. see Arkticheskogo Instituta, Ostrova
Arctic Mid-Ocean Ridge sea feature Arctic Ocean 153 H1
▶Arctic Ocean 153 B1
Poles 146–147
Arctic Red r. Canada 118 E3
Arctowski research station Antarctica 152 A2
Arda r. Bulg. 59 L4
also known as Ardas (Greece)
Ardabīl Iran 88 C2
Ardahan Turkey 91 F2
Ardakān Iran 88 D3
Årdalstangen Norway 45 E6
Ardara Rep. of Ireland 51 D3
Ardas r. Bulg. see Arda
Ard aş Şawwān plain Jordan 85 C4
Ardatov Nizhegorodskaya Oblast' Rus. Fed. 43 I5
Ardatov Respublika Mordoviya Rus. Fed. 43 J5
Ardee Rep. of Ireland 51 F4
Ardennes plat. Belgium 52 E5
Ardennes, Canal des France 52 E5
Arden Town U.S.A. 128 C2
Arderin hill Rep. of Ireland 51 E4
Ardestān Iran 88 D3
Ardglass U.K. 51 G3
Ardila r. Port. 57 C4
Ardlethan Australia 112 C5
Ardmore U.S.A. 131 D5
Ardnamurchan, Point of U.K. 50 C4
Ardon Rus. Fed. 91 G2
Ardrishaig U.K. 50 D4
Ardrossan U.K. 50 E5
Ardvasar U.K. 50 D3
Areia Branca Brazil 143 K4
Arel Belgium see Arlon
Arelas France see Arles
Arelate France see Arles
Aremberg hill Germany 52 G4
Arena, Point U.S.A. 128 B2
Arenas de San Pedro Spain 57 D3
Arendal Norway 45 F7
Arendsee (Altmark) Germany 53 L2
Areopoli Greece 59 J6
Arequipa Peru 142 D7
Arere Brazil 143 H4
Arévalo Spain 57 D3
Arezzo Italy 58 D3
'Arfajah well Saudi Arabia 85 D4
Argadargada Australia 110 B4
Arganda Spain 57 E3
Argel Alg. see Algiers
Argentan France 56 D2
Argentario, Monte hill Italy 58 D3
Argentera, Cima dell' mt. Italy 58 B2
Argenthal Germany 53 H5

▶Argentina country S. America 144 C5
2nd largest country in South America. 3rd most populous country in South America.
South America 9, 140–141

Argentine Abyssal Plain sea feature S. Atlantic Ocean 148 E9
Argentine Basin sea feature S. Atlantic Ocean 148 F8
Argentine Republic country S. America see Argentina
Argentine Rise sea feature S. Atlantic Ocean 148 E8
Argentino, Lago l. Arg. 144 B8
Argenton-sur-Creuse France 56 E3
Argentoratum France see Strasbourg
Argeș r. Romania 59 L2
Arghandab r. Afgh. 89 G4
Argi r. Rus. Fed. 74 C1
Argolikos Kolpos b. Greece 59 J6
Argos Greece 59 J6
Argos U.S.A. 134 B3
Argostoli Greece 59 I5
Arguís Spain 57 F2
Argun' r. China/Rus. Fed. 73 M2
Argun Rus. Fed. 91 G2
Argungu Nigeria 96 D3
Argus Range mts U.S.A. 128 E4
Argyle Canada 123 I6
Argyle, Lake Australia 108 E4
Argyrokastron Albania see Gjirokastër
Ar Horqin Qi China see Tianshan
Århus Denmark 45 G8
Ariah Park Australia 112 C5
Ariamsvlei Namibia 100 D5
Ariana Tunisia see L'Ariana
Ariano Irpino Italy 58 F4
Ari Atoll Maldives 81 D11
Aribinda Burkina 96 C3
Arica Chile 142 D7
Arid, Cape Australia 109 C8
Arigza China 76 C1
Arīḩā Syria 85 C2
Arīḩā West Bank see Jericho
Arikaree r. U.S.A. 130 C3
Arima Trin. and Tob. 137 L6
Ariminum Italy see Rimini
Arinos Brazil 145 B1
Aripuanã Brazil 143 G6
Aripuanã r. Brazil 142 F5
Ariquemes Brazil 142 F5
Aris Namibia 100 C2
Arisaig U.K. 50 D4
Arisaig, Sound of sea chan. U.K. 50 D4
'Arīsh, Wādī al watercourse Egypt 85 A4
Aristazabal Island Canada 120 D4
Arixang China see Wenquan
Ariyalur India 84 C4
Arizaro, Salar de salt flat Arg. 144 C2
Arizona Arg. 144 C5
Arizona state U.S.A. 127 F6
Arizpe Mex. 127 F7
'Arjah Saudi Arabia 86 F5
Arjasa Indon. 68 F8
Arjeplog Sweden 44 J3
Arjuni India 82 E5
Arkadak Rus. Fed. 43 I6
Arkadelphia U.S.A. 131 E5
Arkaig, Loch l. U.K. 50 D4
Arkalyk Kazakh. 80 C1
Arkansas r. U.S.A. 131 F5
Arkansas state U.S.A. 131 E5
Arkansas City AR U.S.A. 131 F5
Arkansas City KS U.S.A. 131 D4
Arkatag Shan mts China 83 G1
Arkell, Mount Canada 120 C2
Arkenu, Jabal mt. Libya 86 B5
Arkhangel'sk Rus. Fed. see Archangel
Arkhara Rus. Fed. 74 C2
Arkhipovka Rus. Fed. 74 D4
Árki i. Greece see Arkoi
Arklow Rep. of Ireland 51 F5
Arkoi i. Greece 59 L6
Arkona Canada 134 E2
Arkona, Kap c. Germany 47 N3
Arkonam India see Arakkonam
Arkport U.S.A. 135 G2
Arkticheskogo Instituta, Ostrova is Rus. Fed. 64 J2
Arkul' Rus. Fed. 42 K4
Arlang, Gora mt. Turkm. 88 D2
Arles France 56 G5
Arlington S. Africa 101 H5
Arlington NY U.S.A. 135 I3
Arlington OH U.S.A. 134 D3
Arlington SD U.S.A. 130 D2
Arlington VA U.S.A. 135 G4
Arlington Heights U.S.A. 134 A2
Arlit Niger 96 D3
Arlon Belgium 52 F5
Arm r. Canada 121 J5
Armadale Australia 109 A8
Armagh U.K. 51 F3
Armant Egypt 86 D4
Armavir Rus. Fed. 91 F1
▶Armenia country Asia 91 G2
Asia 6, 62–63
Armenia Col. 142 C3
Armenopolis Romania see Gherla
Armeria Mex. 136 D5
Armidale Australia 112 E3
Armington U.S.A. 126 F3
Armit Lake Canada 121 N1
Armori India 84 D1
Armour U.S.A. 130 D3
Armoy U.K. 51 F2
Armstrong r. Australia 108 E4
Armstrong Canada 122 C4
Armstrong, Mount Canada 120 C2
Armstrong Island Cook Is see Rarotonga
Armu r. Rus. Fed. 74 E3
Armur India 84 C2
Armutçuk Dağı mts Turkey 59 L5
Armyanskaya S.S.R. country Asia see Armenia
Arnaoutis, Cape Cyprus see Arnauti, Cape
Arnaud r. Canada 123 H2
Arnauti, Cape Cyprus 85 A2
Årnes Norway 45 G6
Arnett U.S.A. 131 D4
Arnhem Neth. 52 F3
Arnhem, Cape Australia 110 B2
Arnhem Land reg. Australia 108 F3
Arno r. Italy 58 D3
Arno Bay Australia 111 B7
Arnold U.K. 49 F5
Arnold's Cove Canada 123 L5
Arnon r. Jordan see Mawjib, Wādī al
Arnprior Canada 135 G1
Arnsberg Germany 53 I3
Arnstadt Germany 53 K4
Arnstein Germany 53 J5
Arnstorf Germany 53 M6
Aroab Namibia 100 D4
Aroland Canada 122 D4
Arolsen Germany 53 J3
Aroma Sudan 86 E6
Arona Italy 58 C2
Arorae i. Kiribati 107 H2
Arore i. Kiribati see Arorae
Aros r. Mex. 127 F7
Arossi i. Solomon Is see San Cristobal
Arqalyq Kazakh. see Arkalyk
Arquipélago da Madeira aut. reg. Port. 96 B1
Arrabury Australia 111 C5
Arrah India see Ara
Arraias Brazil 145 B1
Arraias, Serra de hills Brazil 145 B1
Ar Ramādī Iraq 91 F4
Ar Ramlah Jordan 85 B5
Ar Ramthā Jordan 85 C3
Arran i. U.K. 50 D5
Ar Raqqah Syria 85 D2
Arras France 52 C4
Ar Rass Saudi Arabia 86 F4
Ar Rastān Syria 85 C2
Ar Rayyān Qatar 88 C5
Arrecife Canary Is 96 B2
Arretium Italy see Arezzo
Arriagá Mex. 136 F5
Ar Rifā'ī Iraq 91 G5
Ar Rihāb salt flat Iraq 91 G5
Ar Rimāl reg. Saudi Arabia 98 F1
Arrington U.S.A. 135 F5
Ar Riyāḑ Saudi Arabia see Riyadh
Arrochar U.K. 50 E4
Arrojado r. Brazil 145 B1
Arrow, Lough l. Rep. of Ireland 51 D3
Arrowsmith, Mount N.Z. 113 C6
Arroyo Grande U.S.A. 128 C4
Ar Rubay'iyah Saudi Arabia 88 B5
Ar Rummān Jordan 85 B3
Ar Ruq'ī well Saudi Arabia 88 B4
Ar Ruşāfah Syria 85 D2
Ar Ruşayfah Jordan 85 C3
Ar Rustāq Oman 88 E6
Ar Ruţbah Iraq 91 F4
Ar Ruwaydah Saudi Arabia 88 B5
Ar Ruwayḑah Saudi Arabia 88 B6
Ar Ruwayḑah Syria 85 C2
Års Denmark 45 F8
Ars Iran 88 B2
Arseno Lake Canada 120 H1
Arsen'yev Rus. Fed. 74 D3
Arsk Rus. Fed. 42 K4
Arta Greece 59 I5
Artem Rus. Fed. 74 D4
Artemisa Cuba 133 D8
Artemivs'k Ukr. 43 H6
Artemovsk Ukr. see Artemivs'k
Artenay France 56 E2
Artesia AZ U.S.A. 129 I5
Artesia NM U.S.A. 127 G6
Arthur Canada 134 E2
Arthur NE U.S.A. 130 C3
Arthur TN U.S.A. 134 D5
Arthur, Lake U.S.A. 134 E3
Arthur's Pass National Park N.Z. 113 C6
Arthur's Town Bahamas 133 F7
Arti Rus. Fed. 41 R4
Artigas research station Antarctica 152 A2
Artigas Uruguay 144 E4
Art'ik Armenia 91 F2
Artillery Lake Canada 121 I2
Artisia Botswana 101 H3
Artois reg. France 52 B4
Artois, Collines d' hills France 52 B4
Artos Dağı mt. Turkey 91 F3
Artova Turkey 90 E2
Artsakh aut. reg. Azer. see Dağlıq Qarabağ
Artsiz Ukr. see Artsyz
Artsyz Ukr. 59 M2
Artur de Paiva Angola see Kuvango
Artux China 80 E4
Artvin Turkey 91 F2
Artyk Turkm. 88 E2
Aru, Kepulauan is Indon. 108 F1
Arua Uganda 98 D3
Aruanã Brazil 145 A1

▶Aruba terr. West Indies 137 K6
Self-governing Netherlands Territory.
North America 9, 116–117

Arumã Brazil 142 F4
Arunachal Pradesh state India 83 H4
Arundel U.K. 49 G8
Arun Gol r. China 74 B3
Arun He r. China see Arun Gol
Arun Qi China see Naji
Aruppukkottai India 84 C4
Arusha Tanz. 98 D4
Aruwimi r. Dem. Rep. Congo 98 C3
Arvada U.S.A. 126 G5
Arvagh Rep. of Ireland 51 E4
Arvayheer Mongolia 80 J2
Arviat Canada 121 M2
Arvidsjaur Sweden 44 K4
Arvika Sweden 45 H7
Arvonia U.S.A. 135 F5
Arwā' Saudi Arabia 88 B6
Arwād i. Syria 85 B2
Arwala Indon. 108 D1
Arxan China 73 L3
Aryanah Tunisia see L'Ariana
Arys' Kazakh. 80 C3
Arzamas Rus. Fed. 43 I5
Arzanah i. U.A.E. 88 D5
Arzberg Germany 53 M4
Arzew Alg. 57 F6
Arzgir Rus. Fed. 91 G1
Arzila Morocco see Asilah
Aš Czech Rep. 53 M4
Asaba Nigeria 96 D4
Asad, Buḩayrat al resr Syria 85 D1
Asadābād Afgh. 89 H3
Asadābād Iran 88 C3
Asahi-dake vol. Japan 74 F4
Asahikawa Japan 74 F4
'Asal Egypt 85 A5
Āsalē l. Eth. 98 E2
Asālem Iran 88 C2
'Asalūyeh Iran 88 D5
Asan-man b. S. Korea 75 B5
Asansol India 83 F5
Āsayita Eth. 98 E2
Asbach Germany 53 H4
Asbestos Mountains S. Africa 100 F5
Asbury Park U.S.A. 135 H3
Ascalon Israel see Ashqelon
Ascea Italy 58 F4
Ascensión Bol. 142 F7
Ascensión Mex. 127 G7
Ascension atoll Micronesia see Pohnpei

▶Ascension i. S. Atlantic Ocean 148 H6
Dependency of St Helena.

Aschaffenburg Germany 53 J5
Ascheberg Germany 53 H3
Aschersleben Germany 53 L3
Ascoli Piceno Italy 58 E3
Asculum Italy see Ascoli Piceno
Asculum Picenum Italy see Ascoli Piceno
Ascutney U.S.A. 135 I2
Āseb Eritrea see Assab
Åseda Sweden 45 I8
Åsele Sweden 44 J4
Asenovgrad Bulg. 59 K3
Aşfar, Jabal al mt. Jordan 85 C3
Aşfar, Tall al hill Syria 85 C3
Aşgabat Turkm. see Ashgabat
Asha Rus. Fed. 41 R5
Ashburn U.S.A. 133 D6
Ashburton watercourse Australia 108 A5
Ashburton N.Z. 113 C6
Ashburton Range hills Australia 108 F4
Ashdod Israel 85 B4
Ashdown U.S.A. 131 E5

Bābol Iran 88 D2
Bābol Sar Iran 88 D2
Babongo Cameroon 97 E4
Baboon Point S. Africa 100 D7
Baboua Cent. Afr. Rep. 98 B3
Babruysk Belarus 43 F5
Babstovo Rus. Fed. 74 D2
Babu China *see* **Hezhou**
Babuhri India 82 B4
Babusar Pass Pak. 89 I3
Babuyan *i.* Phil. 69 G3
Babuyan Channel Phil. 69 G3
Babuyan Islands Phil. 69 G3
Bacaadweyn Somalia 98 E3
Bacabal Brazil 143 J4
Bacan *i.* Indon. 69 H7
Bacanora Mex. 127 F7
Bacău Romania 59 L1
Baccaro Point Canada 123 I6
Bắc Giang Vietnam 70 D2
Bacha China 74 D2
Bach Ice Shelf Antarctica 152 L2
Bach Long Vi, Đao *i.* Vietnam 70 D2
Bachu China 80 E4
Bachuan China *see* **Tongliang**
Back *r.* Australia 110 C3
Back *r.* Canada 121 M1
Bačka Palanka Serb. and Mont. 59 H2
Backbone Mountain U.S.A. 134 F4
Backbone Ranges *mts* Canada 120 D2
Backe Sweden 44 J5
Backstairs Passage Australia 111 B7
Bac Lac Vietnam 70 D2
Bac Liêu Vietnam 71 D5
Bắc Ninh Vietnam 70 D2
Bacoachi Mex. 127 F7
Bacoachi *watercourse* Mex. 127 F7
Bacobampo Mex. 127 F8
Bacolod Phil. 69 G4
Bắc Quang Vietnam 70 D2
Bacqueville, Lac *l.* Canada 122 G2
Bacqueville-en-Caux France 49 H9
Bacubirito Mex. 127 G8
Bād Iran 88 D3
Bada China *see* **Xilin**
Bada *mt.* Eth. 98 D3
Bada *i.* Myanmar 71 B5
Bad Abbach Germany 53 M6
Badagara India 84 B4
Badain Jaran Shamo *des.* China 80 J3
Badajoz Spain 57 C4
Badami India 84 B3
Badampaharh India 83 F5
Badanah Saudi Arabia 91 F5
Badanjilin Shamo *des.* China *see* **Badain Jaran Shamo**
Badaojiang China *see* **Baishan**
Badarpur India 83 H4
Badaun India *see* **Budaun**
Bad Axe U.S.A. 134 D2
Bad Bergzabern Germany 53 H5
Bad Berleburg Germany 53 I3
Bad Bevensen Germany 53 K1
Bad Blankenburg Germany 53 L4
Bad Camberg Germany 53 I4
Badderen Norway 44 M2
Bad Driburg Germany 53 J3
Bad Düben Germany 53 M3
Bad Dürkheim Germany 53 I5
Bad Dürrenberg Germany 53 M3
Bademli Turkey *see* **Aladağ**
Bademli Geçidi *pass* Turkey 90 C3
Bad Ems Germany 53 H4
Baden Austria 47 P6
Baden Switz. 56 I3
Baden-Baden Germany 53 I6
Baden-Württemberg *land* Germany 53 I6
Bad Essen Germany 53 I2
Bad Grund (Harz) Germany 53 K3
Bad Harzburg Germany 53 K3
Bad Hersfeld Germany 53 J4
Bad Hofgastein Austria 47 N7
Bad Homburg vor der Höhe Germany 53 I4
Badia Polesine Italy 58 D2
Badin Pak. 89 H5
Bad Ischl Austria 47 N7
Bādiyat ash Shām *des.* Asia *see* **Syrian Desert**
Badkhyzskiy Zapovednik *nature res.* Turkm. 89 F3
Bad Kissingen Germany 53 K4
Bad Königsdorff Poland *see* **Jastrzębie-Zdrój**
Bad Kösen Germany 53 L3
Bad Kreuznach Germany 53 H5
Bad Laasphe Germany 53 I4
Badlands *reg. ND* U.S.A. 130 C2
Badlands *reg. SD* U.S.A. 130 C3
Badlands National Park U.S.A. 130 C3
Bad Langensalza Germany 53 K3
Bad Lauterberg im Harz Germany 53 K3
Bad Liebenwerda Germany 53 N3
Bad Lippspringe Germany 53 I3
Bad Marienberg (Westerwald) Germany 53 H4
Bad Mergentheim Germany 53 J5
Bad Nauheim Germany 53 I4
Badnawar India 82 C5
Badnera India 84 C1
Bad Neuenahr-Ahrweiler Germany 52 H4
Bad Neustadt an der Saale Germany 53 K4
Badnor India 82 C4
Badong China 77 F2
Ba Đông Vietnam 71 D5
Badou Togo 96 D4
Bad Pyrmont Germany 53 J3
Badrah Iraq 91 G4
Bad Reichenhall Germany 47 N7
Badr Ḥunayn Saudi Arabia 86 E5
Bad Sachsa Germany 53 K3
Bad Salzdetfurth Germany 53 K2
Bad Salzuflen Germany 53 I2
Bad Salzungen Germany 53 K4
Bad Schwalbach Germany 53 I4
Bad Schwartau Germany 47 M4
Bad Segeberg Germany 47 M4
Badu Island Australia 110 C1
Badulla Sri Lanka 84 D5
Bad Vilbel Germany 53 I4
Bad Wilsnack Germany 53 L2
Bad Windsheim Germany 53 K5
Badzhal Rus. Fed. 74 D2
Badzhal'skiy Khrebet *mts* Rus. Fed. 74 D2
Bad Zwischenahn Germany 53 I1
Bae Colwyn U.K. *see* **Colwyn Bay**
Baesweiler Germany 52 G4
Baeza Spain 57 E5
Bafatá Guinea-Bissau 96 B3
Baffa Pak. 89 I3
Baffin Bay *sea* Canada/Greenland 119 L2

▶**Baffin Island** Canada 119 L3
2nd largest island in North America and 5th in the world.
World 12–13

Bafia Cameroon 96 E4
Bafilo Togo 96 D4
Bafing *r.* Africa 96 B3
Bafoulabé Mali 96 B3
Bafoussam Cameroon 96 E4
Bāfq Iran 88 D4
Bafra Turkey 90 D2
Bafra Burnu *pt* Turkey 90 D2
Bāft Iran 88 E4
Bafwaboli Dem. Rep. Congo 98 C3
Bafwasende Dem. Rep. Congo 98 C3
Bagaha India 83 F4
Bagalkot India 84 B2
Bagalkote India *see* **Bagalkot**
Bagamoyo Tanz. 99 D4
Bagan China 76 C1
Bagan Datoh Malaysia *see* **Bagan Datuk**
Bagan Datuk Malaysia 71 C7
Bagansiapiapi Indon. 71 C7
Bagata Dem. Rep. Congo 98 B4
Bagdad U.S.A. 129 G4
Bagdarin Rus. Fed. 73 K2
Bagé Brazil 144 F4
Bagerhat Bangl. 83 G5
Bageshwar India 82 D3
Baggs U.S.A. 126 G4
Baggy Point U.K. 49 C7
Bagh India 82 C5
Bàgh a' Chaisteil U.K. *see* **Castlebay**
Baghak Pak. 89 G4
Baghbaghū Iran 89 F2

▶**Baghdād** Iraq 91 G4
Capital of Iraq.

Bāgh-e Malek Iran 88 C4
Bagherhat Bangl. *see* **Bagerhat**
Bāghīn Iran 88 E4
Baghlān Afgh. 89 H2
Baghrān Afgh. 89 G3
Bağırsak *r.* Turkey 85 C1
Bağırsak Deresi *r.* Syria/Turkey *see* **Sājūr, Nahr**
Bagley U.S.A. 130 E2
Baglung Nepal 83 E3
Bagnères-de-Luchon France 56 E5
Bago Myanmar *see* **Pegu**
Bago Phil. 69 G4
Bagong China *see* **Sansui**
Bagor India 89 I5
Bagrationovsk Rus. Fed. 45 L9
Bagrax China *see* **Bohu**
Bagrax Hu *l.* China *see* **Bosten Hu**
Baguio Phil. 69 G3
Bagur, Cabo *c.* Spain *see* **Begur, Cap de**
Bagzane, Monts *mts* Niger 96 D3
Bahādorābād-e Bālā Iran 88 E4
Bahalda India 83 F5
Bahāmabād Iran *see* **Rafsanjān**
▶**Bahamas, The** *country* West Indies 133 E7
North America 9, 116–117
Bahara Pak. 89 G5
Baharampur India 83 G4
Bahardipur Pak. 89 H5
Bahariya Oasis *oasis* Egypt *see* **Bahrīyah, Wāḥāt al**
Bahau Malaysia 71 C7
Bahawalnagar Pak. 89 I4
Bahawalpur Pak. 89 H4
Bahçe *Adana* Turkey 85 B1
Bahçe *Osmaniye* Turkey 90 E3
Baher Dar Eth. *see* **Bahir Dar**
Baheri India 82 D3
Bahia Brazil *see* **Salvador**
Bahia *state* Brazil 145 C1
Bahía Asunción Mex. 127 E8
Bahía Blanca Arg. 144 D5
Bahía Kino Mex. 127 F7
Bahía Laura Arg. 144 C7
Bahía Negra Para. 144 E2
Bahía Tortugas Mex. 127 E8
Bahir Dar Eth. 98 D2
Bahl India 82 C3
Bahlā Oman 88 E6
Bahomonte Indon. 69 G7
Bahraich India 83 E4
▶**Bahrain** *country* Asia 88 C5
Asia 6, 62–63
Bahrain, Gulf of Asia 88 C5
Bahrām Beyg Iran 88 C2
Bahrāmjerd Iran 88 E4
Bahrīyah, Wāḥāt al *oasis* Egypt 90 C6
Bahuaja-Sonene, Parque Nacional *nat. park* Peru 142 E6
Baia Mare Romania 59 J1
Baiazeh Iran 88 D3
Baicang China 83 G3
Bai Canh, Hon *i.* Vietnam 71 D5
Baicheng *Henan* China *see* **Xiping**
Baicheng *Jilin* China 74 A3
Baicheng *Xinjiang* China 80 F3
Baidoa Somalia *see* **Baydhabo**
Baidoi Co *l.* China 83 F2
Baidu China 77 H3
Baie-aux-Feuilles Canada *see* **Tasiujaq**
Baie-Comeau Canada 123 H4
Baie-du-Poste Canada *see* **Mistissini**
Baie-St-Paul Canada 123 H5
Baie-Trinite Canada 123 I4
Baie Verte Canada 123 K4
Baiguan China *see* **Shangyu**
Baiguo *Hubei* China 77 G2
Baiguo *Hunan* China 77 G3
Baihanchang China 76 C3
Baihar India 82 E5
Baihe *Jilin* China 74 C4
Baihe *Shaanxi* China 77 F1
Baiji Iraq *see* **Bayjī**

▶**Baikal, Lake** Rus. Fed. 72 J2
Deepest lake in the world and in Asia. 3rd largest lake in Asia.

Baikunthpur India 83 E5
Baile Átha Cliath Rep. of Ireland *see* **Dublin**
Baile Átha Luain Rep. of Ireland *see* **Athlone**
Baile Mhartainn U.K. 50 B3
Băileşti Romania 59 J2
Bailey Range *hills* Australia 109 C7
Bailianhe Shuiku *resr* China 77 G2
Bailieborough Rep. of Ireland 51 F4
Bailleul France 52 C4
Baillie *r.* Canada 121 J1
Bailong China *see* **Hadapu**
Bailong Jiang *r.* China 76 E1
Baima *Qinghai* China 76 D1
Baima *Xizang* China *see* **Baxoi**
Baima Jian *mt.* China 77 H2
Baimuru P.N.G. 69 K8
Bain *r.* U.K. 48 G5
Bainang China 83 G3
Bainbridge *GA* U.S.A. 133 C6
Bainbridge *IN* U.S.A. 134 B4
Bainbridge *NY* U.S.A. 135 H2
Bainduru India 84 B3
Baingoin China 83 G3
Baini China *see* **Yuqing**
Baiona Spain 57 B2
Baiqên China 76 D1
Baiquan China 74 B3
Bā'ir Jordan 85 C4
Bā'ir, Wādī *watercourse* Jordan/Saudi Arabia 85 C4
Bairab Co *l.* China 83 E2
Bairat India 82 D4
Baird U.S.A. 131 D5
Baird Mountains U.S.A. 118 C3

▶**Bairiki** Kiribati 150 H5
Capital of Kiribati, on Tarawa atoll.

Bairin Youqi China *see* **Daban**
Bairnsdale Australia 112 C6
Baisha *Chongqing* China 76 E2
Baisha *Hainan* China 77 F5
Baisha *Sichuan* China 77 F2
Baishan *Guangxi* China *see* **Mashan**
Baishan *Jilin* China 74 B4
Baishan *Jilin* China *see* **Baishanzhen**
Baishanzhen China 74 B4
Baishui *Shaanxi* China 77 F1
Baishui *Sichuan* China 76 E1
Baishui Jiang *r.* China 76 E1
Baisogala Lith. 45 M9
Baitadi Nepal 82 E3
Baitang China 76 C1
Bai Thương Vietnam 70 D3
Baixi China *see* **Yibin**
Baiyashi China *see* **Dong'an**
Baiyin China 72 I5
Baiyü China 76 C2
Baiyuda Desert Sudan 86 D6
Baja Hungary 58 H1
Baja, Punta *pt* Mex. 127 E7
Baja California *pen.* Mex. 127 E7
Baja California *state* Mex. 127 E7
Baja California Norte *state* Mex. *see* **Baja California**
Baja California Sur *state* Mex. 127 E8
Bajan Mex. 131 C7
Bajau *i.* Indon. 71 D7
Bajaur *reg.* Pak. 89 H3
Bajawa Indon. 108 C2
Baj Baj India 83 G5
Bājgīrān Iran 88 E2
Bājil Yemen 86 F7
Bajo Caracoles Arg. 144 B7
Bajoga Nigeria 96 E3
Bajoi China 76 D2
Bajrakot India 83 F5
Bakala Cent. Afr. Rep. 97 F4
Bakanas Kazakh. 80 E3
Bakar Pak. 89 H5
Bakel Senegal 96 B3
Baker *CA* U.S.A. 128 E4
Baker *ID* U.S.A. 126 E3
Baker *LA* U.S.A. 131 F6
Baker *MT* U.S.A. 126 G3
Baker *NV* U.S.A. 129 F2
Baker *OR* U.S.A. 126 D3
Baker *WV* U.S.A. 135 F4
Baker, Mount *vol.* U.S.A. 126 C2
Baker Butte *mt.* U.S.A. 129 H4

▶**Baker Island** *terr.* N. Pacific Ocean 107 I1
United States Unincorporated Territory.

Baker Island U.S.A. 120 C4
Baker Lake *salt flat* Australia 109 D6
Baker Lake Canada 121 M1
Baker Lake *l.* Canada 121 M1
Baker's Dozen Islands Canada 122 F2
Bakersfield U.S.A. 128 D4
Bakersville U.S.A. 132 D4
Bâ Kêv Cambodia 71 D4
Bakhardok Turkm. 88 E2
Bākharz *mts* Iran 89 F3
Bakhasar India 82 B4
Bakhirevo Rus. Fed. 74 C2
Bakhmach Ukr. 43 G6
Bakhma Dam Iraq *see* **Bēkma, Sadd**
Bakhmut Ukr. *see* **Artemivs'k**
Bākhtarān Iran *see* **Kermānshāh**
Bakhtegan, Daryācheh-ye *l.* Iran 88 D4
Bakhtiari Country *reg.* Iran 88 C3
Bakı Azer. *see* **Baku**
Bakırköy Turkey 59 M4
Bakkejord Norway 44 K2
Bakloh India 82 C2
Bako Eth. 98 D3
Bakongan Indon. 71 B7
Bakouma Cent. Afr. Rep. 98 C3
Baksan Rus. Fed. 91 F2

▶**Baku** Azer. 91 H2
Capital of Azerbaijan.

Baku Dem. Rep. Congo 98 D3
Bakutis Coast Antarctica 152 J2
Baky Azer. *see* **Baku**
Balâ Turkey 90 D3
Bala U.K. 49 D6
Bala, Cerros de *mts* Bol. 142 E6
Balabac *i.* Phil. 68 F5
Balabac Strait Malaysia/Phil. 68 F5
Baladeh *Māzandarān* Iran 88 C2
Baladeh *Māzandarān* Iran 88 C2
Baladek Rus. Fed. 74 D1
Balaghat India 82 E5
Balaghat Range *hills* India 84 B2
Bālā Ḥowz Iran 88 E4
Balaka Malawi 99 D5
Balakān Azer. 91 G2
Balakhna Rus. Fed. 42 I4
Balakhta Rus. Fed. 72 G1
Balaklava Australia 111 B7
Balaklava Ukr. 90 D1
Balakleya Ukr. *see* **Balakliya**
Balakliya Ukr. 43 H6
Balakovo Rus. Fed. 43 J5
Bala Lake U.K. *see* **Tegid, Llyn**
Balaman India 82 E4
Balan India 82 B4
Balanda Rus. Fed. *see* **Kalininsk**
Balanda *r.* Rus. Fed. 43 J6
Balan Dağı *hill* Turkey 59 M6
Balanga Phil. 69 G4
Balangir India *see* **Bolangir**
Balaözen *r.* Kazakh./Rus. Fed. *see* **Malyy Uzen'**
Balarampur India *see* **Balrampur**
Balashov Rus. Fed. 43 I6
Balasore India *see* **Baleshwar**
Balaton, Lake Hungary 58 G1
Balatonboglár Hungary 58 G1
Balatonfüred Hungary 58 G1
Balbina Brazil 143 G4
Balbina, Represa de *resr* Brazil 143 G4
Balbriggan Rep. of Ireland 51 F4
Balchik Bulg. 59 M3
Balclutha N.Z. 113 B8
Balcones Escarpment U.S.A. 131 C6
Bald Knob U.S.A. 134 E5
Bald Mountain U.S.A. 129 F3
Baldock Lake Canada 121 L3
Baldwin Canada 134 F1
Baldwin *FL* U.S.A. 133 D6
Baldwin *MI* U.S.A. 134 C2
Baldwin *PA* U.S.A. 134 F3
Baldy Mount Canada 126 D2
Baldy Mountain *hill* Canada 121 K5
Baldy Peak U.S.A. 129 I5
Bale Indon. 68 C7
Bâle Switz. *see* **Basel**
Baléa Mali 96 B3
Baleares *is* Spain *see* **Balearic Islands**
Baleares, Islas *is* Spain *see* **Balearic Islands**
Baleares Insulae *is* Spain *see* **Balearic Islands**
Balearic Islands *is* Spain 57 G4
Balears *is* Spain *see* **Balearic Islands**
Balears, Illes *is* Spain *see* **Balearic Islands**
Baleia, Ponta da *pt* Brazil 145 D2
Bale Mountains National Park Eth. 98 D3
Baler Phil. 69 G3
Baleshwar India 83 F5
Balestrand Norway 45 E6
Baléyara Niger 96 D3
Balezino Rus. Fed. 41 Q4
Balfe's Creek Australia 110 D4
Balfour Downs Australia 108 C5
Balgo Australia 108 D5
Balguntay China 80 G3
Bali India 82 C4
Bali *i.* Indon. 108 A2
Bali, Laut *sea* Indon. 108 A1
Balia India *see* **Ballia**
Baliapal India 83 F5
Balige Indon. 71 B7
Baliguda India 84 D1
Balıkesir Turkey 59 L5
Balīkh *r.* Syria/Turkey 85 D2
Balikpapan Indon. 68 F7
Balimila Reservoir India 84 D2
Balimo P.N.G. 69 K8
Balin China 74 A2
Baling Malaysia 71 C6
Balingen Germany 47 L6
Balintore U.K. 50 F3
Bali Sea Indon. *see* **Bali, Laut**
Balk Neth. 52 F2
Balkan Mountains Bulg./Serb. and Mont. 59 J3
Balkassar Pak. 89 I3
Balkhash Kazakh. 80 D2

▶**Balkhash, Lake** Kazakh. 80 D2
4th largest lake in Asia.

Balkhash, Ozero *l.* Kazakh. *see* **Balkhash, Lake**
Balkuduk Kazakh. 43 J7
Ballachulish U.K. 50 D4
Balladonia Australia 109 C8
Balladoran Australia 112 D3
Ballaghaderreen Rep. of Ireland 51 D4
Ballan Australia 112 B6
Ballangen Norway 44 J2
Ballantine U.S.A. 126 F3
Ballantrae U.K. 50 E5
Ballarat Australia 112 A6
Ballard, Lake *salt flat* Australia 105 C7
Ballarpur India 84 C2
Ballater U.K. 50 F3
Ballé Mali 96 C3
Ballena, Punta *pt* Chile 144 B3
Balleny Islands Antarctica 152 H2
Ballia India 83 F4
Ballina Australia 112 F2
Ballina Rep. of Ireland 51 C3
Ballinafad Rep. of Ireland 51 D3
Ballinalack Rep. of Ireland 51 E4
Ballinamore Rep. of Ireland 51 E3
Ballinasloe Rep. of Ireland 51 D4
Ballindine Rep. of Ireland 51 D4
Ballinger U.S.A. 131 D6
Ballinluig U.K. 50 F4
Ballinrobe Rep. of Ireland 51 C4
Ballon d'Alsace *mt.* France 47 K7
Ballston Spa U.S.A. 135 I2
Ballybay Rep. of Ireland 51 F3
Ballybrack Rep. of Ireland 51 B6
Ballybunnion Rep. of Ireland 51 C5
Ballycanew Rep. of Ireland 51 F5
Ballycastle Rep. of Ireland 51 C3
Ballycastle U.K. 51 F2
Ballyclare U.K. 51 G3
Ballyconnell Rep. of Ireland 51 E3
Ballygar Rep. of Ireland 51 D4
Ballygawley U.K. 51 E3
Ballygorman Rep. of Ireland 51 E2
Ballyhaunis Rep. of Ireland 51 D4
Ballyheigue Rep. of Ireland 51 C5
Ballykelly U.K. 51 E2
Ballylynan Rep. of Ireland 51 E5
Ballymacmague Rep. of Ireland 51 E5
Ballymahon Rep. of Ireland 51 E4
Ballymena U.K. 51 F3
Ballymoney U.K. 51 F2
Ballymote Rep. of Ireland 51 D3
Ballynahinch U.K. 51 G3
Ballyshannon Rep. of Ireland 51 D3
Ballyteige Bay Rep. of Ireland 51 F5
Ballyvaughan Rep. of Ireland 51 C4
Ballyward U.K. 51 F3
Balmartin U.K. *see* **Baile Mhartainn**
Balmer India *see* **Barmer**
Balmertown Canada 121 M5
Balmorhea U.S.A. 131 C6
Balochistan *prov.* Pak. 89 G4
Balombo Angola 99 B5
Balonne *r.* Australia 112 D2
Balotra India 82 C4
Balqash Kazakh. *see* **Balkhash**
Balqash Köli *l.* Kazakh. *see* **Balkhash, Lake**
Balrampur India 83 E4
Balranald Australia 112 A5
Balş Romania 59 K2
Balsam Lake Canada 135 F1
Balsas Brazil 143 I5
Balta Ukr. 43 F7
Baltasound U.K. 50 [inset]
Baltay Rus. Fed. 43 J5
Bălţi Moldova 43 E7
Baltic U.S.A. 134 E3
Baltic Sea *g.* Europe 45 J9
Balṭîm Egypt *see* **Balṭīm**
Balṭīm Egypt 90 C5
Baltimore S. Africa 101 I2
Baltimore *MD* U.S.A. 135 G4
Baltimore *OH* U.S.A. 134 D4
Baltinglass Rep. of Ireland 51 F5
Baltistan *reg.* Jammu and Kashmir 82 C2
Baltiysk Rus. Fed. 45 K9
Balu India 76 B3
Baluarte, Arroyo *watercourse* U.S.A. 131 D7
Baluch Ab *well* Iran 88 E4
Balumundam Indon. 71 B7
Balurghat India 83 G4
Balve Germany 53 H3
Balvi Latvia 45 O8
Balya Turkey 59 L5
Balykchy Kyrg. 80 E3
Balykshi Kazakh. 78 E2
Balyqshy Kazakh. *see* **Balykshi**
Bam Iran 88 E4
Bām Iran 88 E2
Bama China 76 E3

▶**Bamako** Mali 96 C3
Capital of Mali.

Bamba Mali 96 C3
Bambari Cent. Afr. Rep. 98 C3
Bambel Indon. 71 B7
Bamberg Germany 53 K5
Bamberg U.S.A. 133 D5
Bambili Dem. Rep. Congo 98 C3
Bambio Cent. Afr. Rep. 98 B3
Bamboesberg *mts* S. Africa 101 H6
Bamboo Creek Australia 108 C5
Bambouti Cent. Afr. Rep. 98 C3
Bambuí Brazil 145 B3
Bamda China 76 C2
Bamenda Cameroon 96 E4
Bāmīān Afgh. 89 G3
Bamiantong China *see* **Muling**
Bamingui Cent. Afr. Rep. 98 C3
Bamingui-Bangoran, Parc National du *nat. park* Cent. Afr. Rep. 98 B3
Bâmnak Cambodia 71 D4
Bamnet Narong Thai. 70 C4
Bamor India 82 D4
Bamori India 84 C1
Bam Posht *reg.* Iran 89 F5
Bam Posht, Kūh-e *mts* Iran 89 F5
Bampton U.K. 49 D8
Bampūr Iran 89 F5
Bampūr *watercourse* Iran 89 E5
Bamrūd Iran 89 F3
Bam Tso *l.* China 83 G3
Bamyili Australia 108 F3
Banaba *i.* Kiribati 107 G2
Banabuiu, Açude *resr* Brazil 139 K5
Bañados del Izozog *swamp* Bol. 142 F7
Banagher Rep. of Ireland 51 E4
Banalia Dem. Rep. Congo 98 C3
Banamana, Lagoa *l.* Moz. 101 K2
Banamba Mali 96 C3
Banámichi Mex. 127 F7
Banana Australia 110 E5
Bananal, Ilha do *i.* Brazil 143 H6
Bananga India 71 A6
Banapur India 84 E2
Banas *r.* India 82 D4
Banaz Turkey 59 M5
Ban Ban Laos 70 C3
Banbar China 76 B2
Ban Bo Laos 70 C3
Banbridge U.K. 51 F3
Ban Bua Chum Thai. 70 C4
Ban Bua Yai Thai. 70 C4
Ban Bungxai Laos 70 D4
Banbury U.K. 49 F6
Ban Cang Vietnam 70 C2
Banc d'Arguin, Parc National du *nat. park* Mauritania 96 B2
Ban Channabot Thai. 70 C3
Banchory U.K. 50 G3
Bancroft Canada 135 G1
Bancroft Zambia *see* **Chililabombwe**
Banda Dem. Rep. Congo 98 C3
Banda India 82 E4
Banda, Kepulauan *is* Indon. 69 H7
Banda, Laut *sea* Indon. 69 H8
Banda Aceh Indon. 71 A6
Banda Banda, Mount Australia 112 F3
Banda Daud Shah Pak. 89 H3
Bandahara, Gunung *mt.* Indon. 71 B7
Bandama *r.* Côte d'Ivoire 96 C4
Bandān Kūh *mts* Iran 89 F4
Bandar India *see* **Machilipatnam**
Bandar Moz. 99 D5
Bandar Abbas Iran *see* **Bandar-e 'Abbās**
Bandarban Bangl. 83 H5
Bandar-e 'Abbās Iran 88 E5
Bandar-e Anzalī Iran 88 C2
Bandar-e Deylam Iran 88 C4
Bandar-e Emām Khomeynī Iran 88 C4
Bandar-e Lengeh Iran 88 D5
Bandar-e Ma'shur Iran 88 C4
Bandar-e Nakhīlū Iran 88 D5
Bandar-e Pahlavī Iran *see* **Bandar-e Anzalī**
Bandar-e Shāh Iran *see* **Bandar-e Torkeman**
Bandar-e Shāhpūr Iran *see* **Bandar-e Emām Khomeynī**
Bandar-e Shīū' Iran 88 D5
Bandar-e Torkeman Iran 88 D2
Bandar Labuan Malaysia *see* **Labuan**
Bandar Lampung Indon. 68 D8
Bandarpunch *mt.* India 82 D3

▶**Bandar Seri Begawan** Brunei 68 E6
Capital of Brunei.

Banda Sea *sea* Indon. *see* **Banda, Laut**
Band-e Amīr *l.* Afgh. 89 G3
Band-e Amīr, Daryā-ye *r.* Afgh. 89 G2
Band-e Bābā *mts* Afgh. 89 F3
Bandeira Brazil 145 C1
Bandeirante Brazil 145 A1
Bandeiras, Pico de *mt.* Brazil 145 C3
Bandelierkop S. Africa 101 I2
Banderas Mex. 131 B6
Banderas, Bahía de *b.* Mex. 136 C4
Band-e Sar Qom Iran 88 D3
Band-e Torkestān *mts* Afgh. 89 F3
Bandhi Pak. 89 H5
Bandhogarh India 82 E5
Bandi *r.* India 82 C4
Bandiagara Mali 96 C3
Bandikui India 82 D4
Bandipur National Park India 84 C4
Bandırma Turkey 59 L4
Bandjarmasin Indon. *see* **Banjarmasin**
Bandon Rep. of Ireland 51 D6
Bandon *r.* Rep. of Ireland 51 D6
Ban Don Thai. *see* **Surat Thani**
Bandon U.S.A. 126 B4
Band Qīr Iran 88 C4
Bandra India 84 B2
Bandundu Dem. Rep. Congo 98 B4
Bandung Indon. 68 D8
Bandya Australia 109 C6
Bāneh Iran 88 B3
Banera India 82 C4
Banes Cuba 137 I4
Banff Canada 120 H5
Banff U.K. 50 G3
Banff National Park Canada 120 G5
Banfora Burkina 96 C3
Banga Dem. Rep. Congo 99 C4
Bangalore India 84 C3
Bangalow Australia 112 F2
Bangaon India 83 G5
Bangar Brunei 68 F6
Bangassou Cent. Afr. Rep. 98 C3
Bangdag Co *salt l.* China 83 E2
Banggai Indon. 69 G7
Banggai, Kepulauan *is* Indon. 69 G7
Banggi *i.* Malaysia 68 F5
Banghāzī Libya *see* **Benghazi**
Banghiang, Xé *r.* Laos 70 D3
Bangka *i.* Indon. 68 D7
Bangka, Selat *sea chan.* Indon. 68 D7
Bangkalan Indon. 68 E8
Bangkaru *i.* Indon. 71 B7
Bangko Indon. 68 C7

▶**Bangkok** Thai. 71 C4
Capital of Thailand.

Bangkok, Bight of *b.* Thai. 71 C4
Bangkor China 83 F3
Bangla *state* India *see* **West Bengal**
▶**Bangladesh** *country* Asia 83 G4
Asia 6, 62–63
Bangma Shan *mts* China 76 C4
Bang Mun Nak Thai. 70 C3
Bangolo Côte d'Ivoire 96 C4
Bangong Co *salt l.* China/Jammu and Kashmir 82 D2
Bangor *Northern Ireland* U.K. 51 G3
Bangor *Wales* U.K. 48 C5
Bangor *ME* U.S.A. 132 G2
Bangor *MI* U.S.A. 134 B2
Bangor *PA* U.S.A. 135 H3
Bangor Erris Rep. of Ireland 51 C3
Bangs, Mount U.S.A. 129 G3
Bang Saphan Yai Thai. 71 B5
Bangsund Norway 44 G4
Bangued Phil. 69 G3

▶**Bangui** Cent. Afr. Rep. 98 B3
Capital of Central African Republic.

Bangweulu, Lake Zambia 99 C5
Banhā Egypt 90 C5
Banhine, Parque Nacional de *nat. park* Moz. 101 K2
Ban Hin Heup Laos 70 C3
Ban Houayxay Laos 70 C2
Ban Houei Sai Laos *see* **Ban Houayxay**
Ban Huai Khon Thai. 70 C3
Ban Huai Yang Thai. 71 B5
Bani, Jbel *ridge* Morocco 54 C6
Bania Cent. Afr. Rep. 98 B3
Bani-Bangou Niger 96 D3
Banifing *r.* Mali 96 C3
Banī Forūr, Jazīreh-ye *i.* Iran 88 D5

Banihal Pass and Tunnel Jammu and Kashmir 82 C2
Banister r. U.S.A. 134 F5
Banī Suwayf Egypt 90 C5
Banī Walīd Libya 97 E1
Banī Wuṭayfān well Saudi Arabia 88 C5
Bāniyās Al Qunayṭirah Syria 85 B3
Bāniyās Ṭarṭūs Syria 85 B2
Bani Yas reg. U.A.E. 88 D6
Banja Luka Bos.-Herz. 58 G2
Banjarmasin Indon. 68 E7
Banjes, Liqeni i resr Albania 59 I4

▶Banjul Gambia 96 B3
Capital of The Gambia.

Banka India 83 F4
Banka Banka Australia 108 F4
Bankapur India 84 B3
Bankass Mali 96 C3
Ban Kengkabao Laos 70 D3
Ban Khao Yoi Thai. 71 B4
Ban Khok Kloi Thai. 71 B5
Bankilaré Niger 96 D3
Banks Island B.C. Canada 120 D4
Banks Island N.W.T. Canada 118 F2
Banks Islands Vanuatu 107 G3
Banks Lake Canada 121 M2
Banks Lake U.S.A. 126 D3
Banks Peninsula N.Z. 113 D6
Banks Strait Australia 111 [inset]
Bankura India 83 F5
Ban Lamduan Thai. 71 C4
Banlan China 77 F3
Ban Mae La Luang Thai. 70 B3
Banmaw Myanmar see Bhamo
Banmo Myanmar see Bhamo
Bann r. Rep. of Ireland 51 F5
Bann r. U.K. 51 F2
Ban Nakham Laos 70 D3
Bannerman Town Bahamas 133 E7
Banning U.S.A. 128 E5
Banningville Dem. Rep. Congo see Bandundu
Ban Noi Myanmar 70 B3
Ban Nong Kung Thai. 70 D3
Bannu Pak. 89 H3
Bano India 83 F5
Bañolas Spain see Banyoles
Ban Phai Thai. 70 C3
Ban Phôn Laos see Ban Phon
Ban Phon Laos 70 D4
Banqiao Yunnan China 76 C3
Banqiao Yunnan China 76 E3
Bansi Bihar India 83 F4
Bansi Rajasthan India 82 C4
Bansi Uttar Pradesh India 82 D4
Bansi Uttar Pradesh India 83 E4
Bansihari India 83 G4
Banská Bystrica Slovakia 47 Q6
Banspani India 83 F5
Bansur India 82 D4
Ban Sut Ta Thai. 70 B3
Ban Suwan Wari Thai. 70 D4
Banswara India 82 C5
Banteer Rep. of Ireland 51 D5
Ban Tha Song Yang Thai. 70 B3
Banthat mts Cambodia/Thai. see Cardamom Range
Ban Tha Tum Thai. 70 C4
Ban Tôp Laos 70 D3
Bantry Rep. of Ireland 51 C6
Bantry Bay Rep. of Ireland 51 C6
Bantval India 84 B3
Ban Wang Chao Thai. 70 B3
Ban Woen Laos 70 C3
Ban Xepian Laos 70 D4
Banyak, Pulau-pulau is Indon. 71 B7
Ban Yang Yong Thai. 71 B4
Banyo Cameroon 96 E4
Banyoles Spain 57 H2
Banyuwangi Indon. 108 A2
Banzare Coast Antarctica 152 G2
Banzare Seamount sea feature Indian Ocean 149 N9
Banzart Tunisia see Bizerte
Banzkow Germany 53 L1
Banzyville Dem. Rep. Congo see Mobayi-Mbongo
Bao'an China see Shenzhen
Baochang China 73 L4
Baocheng China 76 E1
Baoding China 73 L5
Baofeng China 77 G1
Bao Ha Vietnam 70 D2
Baohe China see Weixi
Baoji Shaanxi China 76 E1
Baoji Shaanxi China 76 E1
Baokang Hubei China 77 F2
Baokang Nei Mongol China 74 A3
Baolin China 74 C3
Bao Lôc Vietnam 71 D5
Baoqing China 74 D3
Baoro Cent. Afr. Rep. 98 B3
Baoshan China 76 C3
Baotou China 73 K4
Baotou Shan mt. China/N. Korea 74 C4
Baoulé r. Mali 96 C3
Baoxing China 76 D2
Baoying China 77 H1
Baoyou China see Ledong
Bap India 82 C4
Bapatla India 84 D3
Bapaume France 52 C4
Baptiste Lake Canada 135 F1
Bapu China see Meigu
Baq'a' oasis Saudi Arabia 91 F6
Baqbaq Egypt see Buqbuq
Baqên Xizang China 76 B1
Baqên Xizang China 76 B2
Baqiu China 77 G3
Ba'qūbah Iraq 91 G4
Bar Serb. and Mont. 59 H3
Bara Sudan 86 D7
Baraawe Somalia 98 E3
Bara Banki India see Barabanki
Barabanki India 82 E4
Baraboo U.S.A. 130 F3
Baracaju r. Brazil 145 A1
Baracaldo Spain see Barakaldo
Baracoa Cuba 137 J4
Baradá, Nahr r. Syria 85 C3
Baradine Australia 112 D3
Baradine r. Australia 112 D3
Baragarh India see Bargarh
Barahona Dom. Rep. 137 J5
Barail Range mts India 83 H4
Baraka watercourse Eritrea/Sudan 97 G3
Barakaldo Spain 57 E2
Barakī Barak Afgh. 89 H3
Baralaba Australia 110 E5
Bara Lacha Pass India 82 D2
Baralzon Lake Canada 121 L3
Baram India 83 F5
Baram r. Malaysia 68 E6
Baramati India 84 B2
Baramula India see Baramulla
Baramulla India 82 C2
Baran India 82 D4
Baran r. Pak. 89 H5
Bārān, Kūh-e mts Iran 89 F3
Baranavichy Belarus 45 O10
Barang, Dasht-i des. Afgh. 89 F3
Baranikha Rus. Fed. 65 R3
Baranīs Egypt 86 E5
Baranîs Egypt see Baranīs
Barannda India 82 E4
Baranof Island U.S.A. 120 C3
Baranovichi Belarus see Baranavichy
Baranowicze Belarus see Baranavichy
Baraouéli Mali 96 C3
Baraque de Fraiture hill Belgium 52 F4
Barasat India 83 G5
Barat Daya, Kepulauan is Indon. 108 D1
Baraut India 82 D3
Barbacena Brazil 145 C3
▶Barbados country West Indies 137 M6
North America 9, 116–117
Barbar, Gebel el mt. Egypt see Barbar, Jabal
Barbar, Jabal mt. Egypt 85 A5
Barbara Lake Canada 122 D4
Barbastro Spain 57 G2
Barbate de Franco Spain 57 D5
Barberton S. Africa 101 J3
Barberton U.S.A. 134 E3
Barbezieux-St-Hilaire France 56 D4
Barbour Bay Canada 121 M2
Barbourville U.S.A. 134 D5
Barboza Phil. 69 G4
Barbuda i. Antigua and Barbuda 137 L5
Barby (Elbe) Germany 53 L3
Barcaldine Australia 110 D4
Barce Libya see Al Marj
Barcelona Spain 57 H3
Barcelona Venez. 142 F1
Barcelonnette France 56 H4
Barcelos Brazil 142 F4
Barchfeld Germany 53 K4
Barcino Spain see Barcelona
Barclay de Tolly atoll Fr. Polynesia see Raroia
Barclayville Liberia 96 C4
Barcoo watercourse Australia 110 C5
Barcoo Creek watercourse Australia see Cooper Creek
Barcoo National Park Australia see Welford National Park
Barcs Hungary 58 G2
Bärdä Azer. 91 G2
Bárðarbunga mt. Iceland 44 [inset]
Bardaskan Iran 88 E3
Bardawil, Khabrat al salt pan Saudi Arabia 85 D4
Bardawīl, Sabkhat al lag. Egypt 85 A4
Barddhaman India 83 F5
Bardejov Slovakia 43 D6
Bardera Somalia see Baardheere
Bardhaman India see Barddhaman
Bar Đôn Vietnam 71 D4
Bardsey Island U.K. 49 C6
Bardsīr Iran 88 E4
Barðsneshorn pt Iceland 40 D2
Bardstown U.S.A. 134 C5
Barduli Italy see Barletta
Bardwell U.S.A. 131 F4
Bareilly India 82 D3
Barellan Australia 112 C5
Barentin France 49 H9
Barentsburg Svalbard 64 C2
Barents Sea Arctic Ocean 42 I1
Barentu Eritrea 86 E6
Barfleur, Pointe de pt France 49 F9
Bārgāh Iran 88 E5
Bargarh India 83 E5
Barghamad Iran 88 E2
Bargrennan U.K. 50 E5
Bargteheide Germany 53 K1
Barguna Bangl. 83 G5
Barhaj India 83 E4
Barham Australia 112 B5
Bari Italy 58 G4
Bari Doab lowland Pak. 89 I4
Barika Alg. 54 F4
Barinas Venez. 142 D2
Baripada India 83 F5
Bariri Brazil 145 A3
Bari Sadri India 82 C4
Barisal Bangl. 83 G5
Barisan, Pegunungan mts Indon. 68 C7
Barito r. Indon. 68 E7
Barium Italy see Bari
Barkal Bangl. 83 H5
Barkam China 76 D2
Barkan, Ra's-e pt Iran 88 C4
Barkava Latvia 45 O8
Bark Lake Canada 135 G1
Barkly East S. Africa 101 H6
Barkly Homestead Australia 110 A3
Barkly-Oos S. Africa see Barkly East
Barkly Tableland reg. Australia 110 A3
Barkly-Wes S. Africa see Barkly West
Barkly West S. Africa 100 G5
Barkol China 80 H3
Barla Turkey 59 N5
Bârlad Romania 59 L1
Bar-le-Duc France 52 F6
Barlee, Lake salt flat Australia 109 B7
Barlee Range hills Australia 109 A5
Barletta Italy 58 G4
Barlow Canada 120 B2
Barlow Lake Canada 121 K2
Barmah Forest Australia 112 B5
Barmedman Australia 112 C5
Barmen-Elberfeld Germany see Wuppertal
Barmer India 82 B4
Barm Fīrūz, Kūh-e mt. Iran 88 C4
Barmouth U.K. 49 C6
Barnala India 82 C3
Barnard Castle U.K. 48 F4
Barnato Australia 112 B3
Barnaul Rus. Fed. 72 E2
Barnegat Bay U.S.A. 135 H4
Barnes Icecap Canada 119 K2
Barnesville GA U.S.A. 133 D5
Barnesville MN U.S.A. 130 D2
Barneveld Neth. 52 F2
Barneville-Carteret France 49 F9
Barneys Lake imp. l. Australia 112 B4
Barney Top mt. U.S.A. 129 H3
Barnsley U.K. 48 F5
Barnstable U.S.A. 135 J3
Barnstaple U.K. 49 C7
Barnstaple Bay U.K. see Bideford Bay
Barnstorf Germany 53 I2
Baro Nigeria 96 D4
Baroda Gujarat India see Vadodara
Baroda Madhya Pradesh India 82 D4
Baroghil Pass Afgh. 89 I2
Barong China 76 C2
Barons Range hills Australia 109 D6
Barpathar India 76 B3
Barpeta India 83 G4
Bar Pla Soi Thai. see Chon Buri
Barques, Point Aux U.S.A. 134 D1
Barquisimeto Venez. 142 E1
Barra Brazil 143 J6
Barra i. U.K. 50 B4
Barra, Ponta da pt Moz. 101 L2
Barra, Sound of sea chan. U.K. 50 B3
Barraba Australia 112 E3
Barra Bonita Brazil 145 A3
Barracão do Barreto Brazil 143 G5
Barra do Bugres Brazil 143 G7
Barra do Corda Brazil 143 I5
Barra do Cuieté Brazil 145 C2
Barra do Garças Brazil 143 H7
Barra do Piraí Brazil 145 C3
Barra do São Manuel Brazil 143 G5
Barra do Turvo Brazil 145 A4
Barra Falsa, Ponta da pt Moz. 101 L2
Barraigh i. U.K. see Barra
Barra Mansa Brazil 145 B3
Barranca Pak. 89 I4
Barranca Peru 142 C4
Barranqueras Arg. 144 E3
Barranquilla Col. 142 D1
Barre MA U.S.A. 135 I2
Barre VT U.S.A. 135 I1
Barre des Ecrins mt. France 56 H4
Barreiras Brazil 143 J6
Barreirinha Brazil 143 G4
Barreirinhas Brazil 143 J4
Barreiro Port. 57 B4
Barreiros Brazil 143 K5
Barren Island India 71 A4
Barren Island Kiribati see Starbuck Island
Barren River Lake U.S.A. 134 B5
Barretos Brazil 145 A3
Barrett, Mount hill Australia 108 D4
Barrhead Canada 120 H4
Barrhead U.K. 50 E5
Barrie Canada 134 F1
Barrier Bay Antarctica 152 E2
Barrière Canada 120 F5
Barrier Range hills Australia 111 C6
Barrington Canada 123 I6
Barrington, Mount Australia 112 E4
Barrington Tops National Park Australia 112 E4
Barringun Australia 112 B2
Barro Alto Brazil 145 A1
Barrocão Brazil 145 C2
Barron U.S.A. 130 F2
Barrow r. Rep. of Ireland 51 F5
Barrow U.S.A. 118 C2
Barrow, Point U.S.A. 118 C2
Barrow Creek Australia 108 F5
Barrow-in-Furness U.K. 48 D4
Barrow Island Australia 108 A5
Barrow Range hills Australia 105 D6
Barrow Strait Canada 119 I2
Barr Smith Range hills Australia 109 C6
Barry U.K. 49 D7
Barrydale S. Africa 100 E7
Barry Mountains Australia 112 C6
Barrys Bay Canada 135 G1
Barryville U.S.A. 135 H3
Barsa-Kel'mes, Shor salt marsh Uzbek. 91 J2
Barsalpur India 82 C3
Barshatas Kazakh. 80 E2
Barshi India see Barsi
Barsi India 84 B2
Barsinghausen Germany 53 J2
Barstow U.S.A. 128 E4
Barsur India 84 D2
Bar-sur-Aube France 56 G2
Bartang Tajik. 89 H2
Barth Germany 47 N3
Bartica Guyana 143 G2
Bartın Turkey 90 D2
Bartle Frere, Mount Australia 110 D3
Bartlett U.S.A. 130 D3
Bartlett Reservoir U.S.A. 129 H5
Barton U.S.A. 135 I1
Barton-upon-Humber U.K. 48 G5
Bartoszyce Poland 47 R3
Bartow U.S.A. 133 D7
Barú, Volcán vol. Panama 137 H7
Barung i. Indon. 68 E8
Barunga Australia see Bamyili
Barun-Torey, Ozero l. Rus. Fed. 73 L2
Barus Indon. 71 B7
Baruunturuun Mongolia 80 H2
Baruun-Urt Mongolia 73 K3
Baruva India 84 E2
Barwani India 82 C5
Barwéli Mali see Baraouéli
Barwon r. Australia 112 C3
Barygaza India see Bharuch
Barysaw Belarus 45 P9
Barysh Rus. Fed. 43 J5
Basaga Turkm. 89 G2
Basăk, Tônlé r. Cambodia 71 D5
Basalt r. Australia 110 D3
Basalt Island Hong Kong China 77 [inset]
Basankusu Dem. Rep. Congo 98 B3
Basar India 84 C2
Basarabi Romania 59 M2
Basargechar Armenia see Vardenis
Bascuñán, Cabo c. Chile 144 B3
Basel Switz. 56 H3
Bashākerd, Kūhhā-ye mts Iran 88 E5
Bashanta Rus. Fed. see Gorodovikovsk
Bashaw Canada 120 H4
Bashee r. S. Africa 101 I7
Bāshī Iran 88 C4
Bashi Channel Phil./Taiwan 69 G2
Bashmakovo Rus. Fed. 43 I5
Bāsht Iran 88 C4
Bashtanka Ukr. 43 G7
Basi Punjab India 82 D3
Basi Rajasthan India 82 D4
Basia India 83 F5
Basilan i. Phil. 69 G5
Basildon U.K. 49 H7
Basile, Pico mt. Equat. Guinea 92 D4
Basin U.S.A. 126 F3
Basingstoke U.K. 49 F7
Basin Lake Canada 121 J4
Basirhat India 83 G5
Basīţ, Ra's al pt Syria 85 B2
Başkale Turkey 91 G3
Baskatong, Réservoir resr Canada 122 G5
Baskerville, Cape Australia 108 C4
Başkomutan Tarıhı Milli Parkı nat. park Turkey 59 N5
Başköy Turkey 85 A1
Baskunchak, Ozero l. Rus. Fed. 43 J6
Basle Switz. see Basel
Basmat India 84 C2
Basoko Dem. Rep. Congo 98 C3
Basra Iraq 91 G5
Bassano Canada 121 H5
Bassano del Grappa Italy 58 D2
Bassar Togo 96 D4
Bassas da India reef Indian Ocean 99 D6
Bassas de Pedro Padua Bank sea feature India 84 B3
Bassein Myanmar 70 A3
Bassein r. Myanmar 70 A3
Basse-Normandie admin. reg. France 49 F9
Bassenthwaite Lake U.K. 48 D4
Basse Santa Su Gambia 96 B3

▶Basse-Terre Guadeloupe 137 L5
Capital of Guadeloupe.

▶Basseterre St Kitts and Nevis 137 L5
Capital of St Kitts and Nevis.

Bassett NE U.S.A. 130 D3
Bassett VA U.S.A. 134 F5
Bassikounou Mauritania 96 C3
Bass Rock i. U.K. 50 G4
Bass Strait Australia 111 D8
Bassum Germany 53 I2
Basswood Lake Canada 122 C4
Båstad Sweden 45 H8
Bastānābād Iran 88 B2
Bastheim Germany 53 K4
Basti India 83 E4
Bastia Corsica France 56 I5
Bastioes r. Brazil 143 K5
Bastogne Belgium 52 F4
Bastrop LA U.S.A. 131 F5
Bastrop TX U.S.A. 131 D6
Basul r. Pak. 89 G5
Basuo China see Dongfang
Basutoland country Africa see Lesotho
Başyayla Turkey 85 A1
Bata Equat. Guinea 96 D4
Batabanó, Golfo de b. Cuba 133 H4
Batagay Rus. Fed. 65 O3
Batala India 82 C3
Batalha Port. 57 B4
Batam i. Indon. 71 D7
Batamay Rus. Fed. 65 N3
Batamshinskiy Kazakh. 80 A1
Batamshy Kazakh. see Batamshinskiy
Batan Jiangsu China 77 I1
Batan Qinghai China 76 D1
Batan i. Phil. 69 G2
Batang China 76 C2
Batangafo Cent. Afr. Rep. 98 B3
Batangas Phil. 69 G4
Batangtoru Indon. 71 B7
Batan Islands Phil. 69 G2
Batavia Indon. see Jakarta
Batavia NY U.S.A. 135 F2
Batavia OH U.S.A. 134 C4
Bataysk Rus. Fed. 43 H7
Batchawana Mountain hill Canada 122 D5
Bătdâmbâng Cambodia 71 C4
Bateemeucica, Gunung mt. Indon. 71 A6
Batéké, Plateaux Congo 98 B4
Batemans Bay Australia 112 E5
Bates Range hills Australia 109 C6
Batesville AR U.S.A. 131 F5
Batesville IN U.S.A. 134 C4
Batesville MS U.S.A. 131 F5
Batetskiy Rus. Fed. 42 F4
Bath N.B. Canada 123 I5
Bath Ont. Canada 135 G1
Bath U.K. 49 E7
Bath ME U.S.A. 135 K2
Bath NY U.S.A. 135 G2
Bath PA U.S.A. 135 H3
Batha watercourse Chad 97 E3
Bathgate U.K. 50 F5
Bathinda India 82 C3
Bathurst Australia 112 D4
Bathurst Canada 123 I5
Bathurst Gambia see Banjul
Bathurst S. Africa 101 H7
Bathurst, Cape Canada 118 F2
Bathurst, Lake Australia 112 D5
Bathurst Inlet Canada 118 H3
Bathurst Inlet inlet Canada 118 H3
Bathurst Island Australia 108 E2
Bathurst Island Canada 119 I2
Batié Burkina 96 C4
Batı Menteşe Dağları mts Turkey 59 L6
Batı Toroslar mts Turkey 59 N6
Batken Kyrg. 80 D4
Batkes Indon. 108 E1
Bāṭlāq-e Gavkhūnī marsh Iran 88 D3
Batley U.K. 48 F5
Batlow Australia 112 D5
Batman Turkey 91 F3
Batna Alg. 54 F4
Batok, Bukit hill Sing. 71 [inset]

▶Baton Rouge U.S.A. 131 F6
State capital of Louisiana.

Batopilas Mex. 127 G8
Batouri Cameroon 97 E4
Batrā' tourist site Jordan see Petra
Batrā', Jabal al mt. Jordan 85 B5
Batroûn Lebanon 85 B2
Båtsfjord Norway 44 P1
Battambang Cambodia see Bătdâmbâng
Batticaloa Sri Lanka 84 D5
Batti Malv i. India 71 A5
Battipaglia Italy 58 F4
Battle r. Canada 121 I4
Battle Creek U.S.A. 134 C2
Battleford Canada 121 I4
Battle Mountain U.S.A. 128 E1
Battle Mountain mt. U.S.A. 128 E1
Battura Glacier Jammu and Kashmir 82 C1
Batu mt. Eth. 98 D3
Batu, Pulau-pulau is Indon. 68 B7
Batudaka i. Indon. 69 G7
Batu Gajah Malaysia 71 C6
Batum Georgia see Bat'umi
Bat'umi Georgia 91 F2
Batu Pahat Malaysia 71 C7
Batu Putih, Gunung mt. Malaysia 71 C6
Baturaja Indon. 68 C7
Baturité Brazil 143 K4
Batyrevo Rus. Fed. 43 J5
Batys Qazaqstan admin. div. Kazakh. see Zapadnyy Kazakhstan
Bau Sarawak Malaysia 68 E6
Baubau Indon. 69 G8
Baucau East Timor 108 D2
Bauchi Nigeria 96 D3
Bauda India see Boudh
Baudette U.S.A. 130 E1
Baudh India see Boudh
Baugé France 56 D3
Bauhinia Australia 110 E5
Baukau East Timor see Baucau
Bauld, Cape Canada 123 L4
Baume-les-Dames France 56 H3
Baunach r. Germany 53 K5
Baundal India 82 C2
Baura Bangl. 83 G4
Bauru Brazil 145 A3
Bausendorf Germany 52 G4
Bauska Latvia 45 N8
Bautino Kazakh. 91 H1
Bautzen Germany 47 O5
Bavaria land Germany see Bayern
Bavaria reg. Germany 53 L6
Bavda India 84 B2
Baviaanskloofberge mts S. Africa 100 F7
Bavispe r. Mex. 127 F7
Bavla India 82 C5
Bavly Rus. Fed. 41 Q5
Baw Myanmar 70 A2
Bawal India 82 D3
Baw Baw National Park Australia 112 C6
Bawdeswell U.K. 49 I6
Bawdwin Myanmar 70 B2
Bawean i. Indon. 68 E8
Bawinkel Germany 53 H2
Bawlake Myanmar 70 B3
Bawolung China 76 D2
Baxi China 76 D1
Baxley U.S.A. 133 D6
Baxoi China 76 C2
Baxter Mountain U.S.A. 129 J2
Bay China see Baicheng
Bayamo Cuba 137 I4
Bayan Heilong. China 74 B3
Bayan Qinghai China 76 C1
Bayan Mongolia 73 K3
Bayana India 82 D4
Bayanaul Kazakh. 80 E1
Bayanbulag Mongolia 80 I2
Bayanbulak China 80 F3
Bayanday Rus. Fed. 72 J2
Bayan Gol China see Dengkou
Bayan Har Shan mts China 76 B1
Bayan Har Shankou pass China 76 C1
Bayanhongor Mongolia 80 J2
Bayan Hot China 72 J5
Bayan Mod China 72 I4
Bayan Obo China 73 J4
Bayan-Ovoo Mongolia 80 H3
Bayan Ul Hot China 73 L4
Bayard U.S.A. 129 I5
Bayasgalant Mongolia 73 K3
Bayat Turkey 59 N5
Bayāẓ Iran 88 E4
Baybay Phil. 69 G4
Bayboro U.S.A. 133 E5
Bayburt Turkey 91 F2
Bay City MI U.S.A. 134 D2
Bay City TX U.S.A. 131 D6
Baydaratskaya Guba Rus. Fed. 64 H3
Baydhabo Somalia 98 E3
Bayerischer Wald mts Germany 53 M5
Bayerischer Wald nat. park Germany 53 M5
Bayern land Germany 53 L6
Bayer Wald, Nationalpark nat. park Germany 47 N6
Bayeux France 49 G9
Bayfield Canada 134 E2
Bayındır Turkey 59 L5
Bay Islands is Hond. see La Bahía, Islas de
Bayizhen China 76 B2
Bayjī Iraq 91 F4
Baykal, Ozero l. Rus. Fed. see Baikal, Lake
Baykal-Amur Magistral Rus. Fed. 74 C1
Baykal Range mts Rus. Fed. see Baykal'skiy Khrebet
Baykal'skiy Khrebet mts Rus. Fed. 73 J2
Baykan Turkey 91 F3
Bay-Khaak Rus. Fed. 80 H1
Baykibashevo Rus. Fed. 41 R4
Baykonur Kazakh. see Baykonyr
Baykonyr Kazakh. 80 B2
Baymak Rus. Fed. 64 G4
Bay Minette U.S.A. 133 C6
Baynūna'h reg. U.A.E. 88 D6
Bayombong Phil. 69 G3
Bayona Spain see Baiona
Bayonne France 56 D5
Bayonne U.S.A. 135 H3
Bay Port U.S.A. 134 D2
Bayqongyr Kazakh. see Baykonyr
Bayram-Ali Turkm. see Bayramaly
Bayramaly Turkm. 89 F2
Bayramiç Turkey 59 L5
Bayreuth Germany 53 L5
Bayrūt Lebanon see Beirut
Bays, Lake of Canada 134 F1
Bayshore U.S.A. 134 C1
Bay Shore U.S.A. 135 I3
Bay Springs U.S.A. 131 F6
Bayston Hill U.K. 49 E6
Baysun Uzbek. 89 G2
Bayt Lahm West Bank see Bethlehem
Baytown U.S.A. 131 E6
Bay View N.Z. 113 F4
Bayy al Kabīr, Wādī watercourse Libya 97 E1
Baza Spain 57 E5
Baza, Sierra de mts Spain 57 E5
Bazardüzü Dağı mt. Azer./Rus. Fed. see Bazardyuzyu, Gora
Bazardyuzyu, Gora mt. Azer./Rus. Fed. 91 G2
Bāzār-e Māsāl Iran 88 C2
Bazarnyy Karabulak Rus. Fed. 43 J5
Bazaruto, Ilha do i. Moz. 99 D6
Bazdar Pak. 89 G5
Bazhong China 76 E2
Bazhou China see Bazhong
Bazin r. Canada 122 G5
Bazmān Iran 89 F5
Bazmān, Kūh-e mt. Iran 89 F4
Bcharré Lebanon 85 C2
Be r. Vietnam 71 D5
Beach U.S.A. 130 C2
Beachy Head hd U.K. 49 H8
Beacon U.S.A. 135 I3
Beacon Bay S. Africa 101 H7
Beaconsfield U.K. 49 G7
Beagle, Canal sea chan. Arg. 144 C8
Beagle Bank reef Australia 108 C3
Beagle Bay Australia 108 C4
Beagle Gulf Australia 108 E3
Bealanana Madag. 99 E5
Béal an Átha Rep. of Ireland see Ballina
Béal Átha na Sluaighe Rep. of Ireland see Ballinasloe
Beale, Lake India 84 B2
Beaminster U.K. 49 E8
Bear r. U.S.A. 126 E4
Bearalváhki Norway see Berlevåg
Bear Cove Point Canada 121 O2
Beardmore Canada 122 D4
Beardmore Glacier Antarctica 152 H1
Beardmore Reservoir Australia 112 D1
Bear Island Arctic Ocean see Bjørnøya
Bear Island Canada 122 E3
Bear Island Rep. of Ireland 51 C6
Bear Lake l. Canada 122 A3
Bear Lake U.S.A. 134 B1
Bear Lake l. U.S.A. 126 F4
Bearma r. India 82 D4
Bear Mountain U.S.A. 130 C3
Bearnaraigh i. U.K. see Berneray
Bear Paw Mountain U.S.A. 126 F2
Bearpaw Mountains U.S.A. 126 F2
Bearskin Lake Canada 121 N4
Beas Dam India 82 C3
Beata, Cabo c. Dom. Rep. 137 J5
Beatrice U.S.A. 130 D3
Beatrice, Cape Australia 110 B2
Beatton r. Canada 120 F3
Beatton River Canada 120 F3
Beatty U.S.A. 128 E3
Beattyville Canada 122 F4
Beattyville U.S.A. 134 D5
Beaucaire France 56 G5
Beauchene Island Falkland Is 144 E8
Beaufort Australia 112 A6
Beaufort NC U.S.A. 133 E5
Beaufort SC U.S.A. 133 D5
Beaufort Island Hong Kong China 77 [inset]
Beaufort Sea Canada/U.S.A. 118 D2
Beaufort West S. Africa 100 F7
Beaulieu r. Canada 121 H2
Beauly U.K. 50 E3
Beauly r. U.K. 50 E3
Beaumaris U.K. 48 C5
Beaumont Belgium 52 E4
Beaumont N.Z. 113 B7
Beaumont MS U.S.A. 131 F6
Beaumont TX U.S.A. 131 E6
Beaune France 56 G3
Beaupréau France 56 D3
Beauquesne France 52 C4
Beauraing Belgium 52 E4
Beauséjour Canada 121 L5
Beauvais France 52 C5
Beauval France 52 C4
Beaver r. Alberta/Saskatchewan Canada 121 J4
Beaver r. Ont. Canada 122 D3
Beaver r. Y.T. Canada 120 E3
Beaver OK U.S.A. 131 C4
Beaver PA U.S.A. 134 E3
Beaver UT U.S.A. 129 G2
Beaver r. U.S.A. 129 G2
Beaver Creek Canada 153 A2
Beavercreek U.S.A. 134 C4
Beaver Creek r. MT U.S.A. 130 B1
Beaver Creek r. ND U.S.A. 130 C2
Beaver Dam KY U.S.A. 134 B5
Beaver Dam WI U.S.A. 130 F3
Beaver Falls U.S.A. 134 E3
Beaverhead Mountains U.S.A. 126 E3
Beaverhill Lake Alta Canada 121 H4
Beaver Hill Lake Canada 121 M4
Beaverhill Lake N.W.T. Canada 121 J2
Beaver Island U.S.A. 132 C2
Beaverlodge Canada 120 G4

Beaverton Canada 134 F1
Beaverton MI U.S.A. 134 C2
Beaverton OR U.S.A. 126 C3
Beawar India 82 C4
Beazley Arg. 144 C4
Bebedouro Brazil 145 A3
Bebington U.K. 48 D5
Bebra Germany 53 J4
Bêca China 76 C2
Bécard, Lac l. Canada 123 G1
Beccles U.K. 49 I6
Bečej Serb. and Mont. 59 I2
Becerreá Spain 57 C2
Béchar Alg. 54 D5
Bechhofen Germany 53 K5
Bechuanaland country Africa see Botswana
Beckley U.S.A. 134 E5
Beckum Germany 53 I3
Becky Peak U.S.A. 129 F2
Bečov nad Teplou Czech Rep. 53 M4
Bedale U.K. 48 F4
Bedburg Germany 52 G4
Bedelē Eth. 98 D3
Bederkesa Germany 53 I1
Bedford N.S. Canada 123 J5
Bedford Que. Canada 135 I1
Bedford E. Cape S. Africa 101 H7
Bedford Kwazulu-Natal S. Africa 101 J5
Bedford U.K. 49 G6
Bedford IN U.S.A. 134 B4
Bedford KY U.S.A. 134 C4
Bedford PA U.S.A. 135 F3
Bedford VA U.S.A. 134 F5
Bedford, Cape Australia 110 D2
Bedford Downs Australia 108 D4
Bedgerebong Australia 112 C4
Bedi India 82 B5
Bedla India 82 C4
Bedlington U.K. 48 F3
Bedok Sing. 71 [inset]
Bedok Jetty Sing. 71 [inset]
Bedok Reservoir Sing. 71 [inset]
Bedou China 77 F3
Bedourie Australia 110 B5
Bedum Neth. 52 G1
Bedworth U.K. 49 F6
Beechworth Australia 112 C6
Beechy Canada 121 J5
Beecroft Peninsula Australia 112 E5
Beed India see Bid
Beelitz Germany 53 M2
Beenleigh Australia 112 F1
Beernem Belgium 52 D3
Beersheba Israel 85 B4
Be'ér Sheva' Israel see Beersheba
Be'ér Sheva' watercourse Israel 85 B4
Beervlei Dam S. Africa 100 F7
Beerwah Australia 112 F1
Beetaloo Australia 108 F4
Beethoven Peninsula Antarctica 152 L2
Beeville U.S.A. 131 D6
Befori Dem. Rep. Congo 98 C3
Beg, Lough l. U.K. 51 F3
Bega Australia 112 D6
Begari r. Pak. 89 H4
Begicheva, Ostrov i. Rus. Fed. see Bol'shoy Begichev, Ostrov
Begur, Cap de c. Spain 57 H3
Begusarai India 83 F4
Béhague, Pointe pt Fr. Guiana 143 H3
Behbehān Iran 88 C4
Behrendt Mountains Antarctica 152 L2
Behrūsī Iran 88 D4
Behshahr Iran 88 D2
Behsūd Afgh. 89 G3
Bei'an China 74 B2
Bei'ao China see Dongtou
Beibei China 76 E2
Beichuan China 76 E2
Beida Libya see Al Bayḍā'
Beigang Taiwan see Peikang
Beiguan China see Anyang
Beihai China 77 F4
Bei Hulsan Hu salt l. China 83 H1

▶Beijing China 73 L5
Capital of China.

Beijing municipality China 73 L4
Beik Myanmar see Mergui
Beilen Neth. 52 G2
Beiliu China 77 F4
Beilngries Germany 53 L5
Beiluheyan China 76 B1
Beinn an Oir hill U.K. 50 D5
Beinn an Tuirc hill U.K. 50 D5
Beinn Bheigeir hill U.K. 50 C5
Beinn Bhreac hill U.K. 50 D4
Beinn Dearg mt. U.K. 50 E3
Beinn Heasgarnich mt. U.K. 50 E4
Beinn Mholach hill U.K. 50 C2
Beinn Mhòr hill U.K. 50 B3
Beinn na Faoghlia i. U.K. see Benbecula
Beipan Jiang r. China 76 E3
Beipiao China 73 M4
Beira Moz. 99 D5

▶Beirut Lebanon 85 B3
Capital of Lebanon.

Bei Shan mts China 80 I3
Beitbridge Zimbabwe 99 C6
Beith U.K. 50 E5
Beit Jālā West Bank 85 B4
Beja Port. 57 C4
Béja Tunisia 58 C6
Bejaïa Alg. 57 I5
Béjar Spain 57 D3
Beji r. Pak. 80 C6
Bekaa valley Lebanon see El Béqaa
Bekdash Turkm. 91 I2
Békés Hungary 59 I1
Békéscsaba Hungary 59 I1
Bekily Madag. 99 E6
Bekkai Japan 74 G4
Bēkma, Sadd dam Iraq 91 G3
Bekovo Rus. Fed. 43 I5
Bekwai Ghana 96 C4
Bela India 83 E4
Bela Pak. 89 G5
Belab r. Pak. 89 H4
Bela-Bela S. Africa 101 I3
Bélabo Cameroon 96 E4
Bela Crkva Serb. and Mont. 59 I2
Bel Air U.S.A. 135 G4
Belalcázar Spain 57 D4
Bělá nad Radbuzou Czech Rep. 53 M5
Belapur India 84 B2
Belaraboon Australia 112 B4
▶Belarus country Europe 43 E5
Europe 5, 38–39
Belau country N. Pacific Ocean see Palau
Bela Vista Brazil 144 E2
Bela Vista Moz. 101 K4
Bela Vista de Goiás Brazil 145 A2
Belawan Indon. 71 B7
Belaya r. Rus. Fed. 65 S3
also known as Bila
Belaya Glina Rus. Fed. 43 I7
Belaya Kalitva Rus. Fed. 43 I6
Belaya Kholunitsa Rus. Fed. 42 K4
Belaya Tserkva Ukr. see Bila Tserkva
Belbédji Niger 96 D3
Bełchatów Poland 47 Q5
Belcher U.S.A. 134 D5
Belcher Islands Canada 122 F2
Belchiragh Afgh. 89 G3
Belcoo U.K. 51 E3
Belden U.S.A. 128 C1
Belding U.S.A. 134 C2
Beleapani reef India see Cherbaniani Reef
Belebey Rus. Fed. 41 Q5
Beledweyne Somalia 98 E3
Belém Brazil 143 I4
Belém Novo Brazil 145 A5
Belén Arg. 144 C3
Belen Antalya Turkey 85 A1
Belen Hatay Turkey 85 C1
Belen U.S.A. 127 G6
Belep, Îles is New Caledonia 107 G3
Belev Rus. Fed. 43 H5
Belfast S. Africa 101 J3

▶Belfast U.K. 51 G3
Capital of Northern Ireland.

Belfast U.S.A. 132 G2
Belfast Lough inlet U.K. 51 G3
Bēlfodiyo Eth. 98 D2
Belford U.K. 48 F3
Belfort France 56 H3
Belgaum India 84 B3
Belgern Germany 53 N3
Belgian Congo country Africa see Congo, Democratic Republic of
België country Europe see Belgium
Belgique country Europe see Belgium
▶Belgium country Europe 52 E4
Europe 5, 38–39
Belgorod Rus. Fed. 43 H6
Belgorod-Dnestrovskyy Ukr. see Bilhorod-Dnistrovs'kyy
Belgrade ME U.S.A. 135 K1
Belgrade MT U.S.A. 126 F3

▶Belgrade Serb. and Mont. 59 I2
Capital of Serbia and Montenegro.

Belgrano II research station Antarctica 152 A1
Belice r. Sicily Italy 58 E6
Belinskiy Rus. Fed. 43 I5
Belinyu Indon. 68 D7
Belitung i. Indon. 68 D7
Belize Angola 99 B4

▶Belize Belize 136 G5
Former capital of Belize.

▶Belize country Central America 136 G5
North America 9, 116–117
Beljak Austria see Villach
Belkina, Mys pt Rus. Fed. 74 E3
Bel'kovskiy, Ostrov i. Rus. Fed. 65 O2
Bell Australia 112 E1
Bell r. Australia 112 D4
Bell r. Canada 122 F4
Bella Bella Canada 120 D4
Bellac France 56 E3
Bella Coola Canada 120 E4
Bellaire U.S.A. 134 C1
Bellary India 84 C3
Bellata Australia 112 D2
Bella Unión Uruguay 144 E4
Bella Vista U.S.A. 128 B1
Bellbrook Australia 112 F3
Bell Cay reef Australia 110 E4
Belledonne mts France 56 G4
Bellefontaine U.S.A. 134 D3
Bellefonte U.S.A. 135 G3
Belle Fourche U.S.A. 130 C2
Belle Fourche r. U.S.A. 130 C2
Belle Glade U.S.A. 133 D7
Belle-Île i. France 56 C3
Belle Isle i. Canada 123 L4
Belle Isle, Strait of Canada 123 K4
Belleville Canada 135 G1
Belleville IL U.S.A. 130 F4
Belleville KS U.S.A. 130 D4
Bellevue IA U.S.A. 130 F3
Bellevue MI U.S.A. 134 C2
Bellevue OH U.S.A. 134 D3
Bellevue WA U.S.A. 126 C3
Bellin Canada see Kangirsuk
Bellingham U.K. 48 E3
Bellingham U.S.A. 126 C2
Bellingshausen research station Antarctica 152 A2
Bellingshausen Sea Antarctica 152 L2
Bellinzona Switz. 56 I3
Bellows Falls U.S.A. 135 I2
Bellpat Pak. 89 H4
Belluno Italy 58 E1
Belluru India 84 C3
Bell Ville Arg. 144 D4
Bellville S. Africa 100 D7
Belm Germany 53 I2
Belmont Australia 112 E4
Belmont U.K. 50 [inset]
Belmont U.S.A. 135 F2
Belmonte Brazil 145 D1

▶Belmopan Belize 136 G5
Capital of Belize.

Belmore, Mount hill Australia 112 F2
Belmullet Rep. of Ireland 51 C3
Belo Madag. 99 E6
Belo Campo Brazil 145 C1
Belœil Belgium 52 D4
Belogorsk Rus. Fed. 74 C2
Belogorsk Ukr. see Bilohirs'k
Beloha Madag. 99 E6
Belo Horizonte Brazil 145 C2
Beloit KS U.S.A. 130 D4
Beloit WI U.S.A. 130 F3
Belokurikha Rus. Fed. 80 F1
Belo Monte Brazil 143 H4
Belomorsk Rus. Fed. 42 G2
Belonia India 83 G5
Belorechensk Rus. Fed. 91 E1
Belorechenskaya Rus. Fed. see Belorechensk
Belören Turkey 90 D3
Beloretsk Rus. Fed. 64 G4
Belorussia country Europe see Belarus
Belorusskaya S.S.R. country Europe see Belarus
Belostok Poland see Białystok
Belot, Lac l. Canada 118 F3
Belo Tsiribihina Madag. 99 E5
Belovo Rus. Fed. 72 F2
Beloyarskiy Rus. Fed. 41 T3
Beloye, Ozero l. Rus. Fed. 42 H3
Beloye More sea Rus. Fed. see White Sea
Belozersk Rus. Fed. 42 H3
Belpre U.S.A. 134 E4
Beltana Australia 111 B6
Belted Range mts U.S.A. 128 E3
Belton U.S.A. 131 D6
Bel'ts' Moldova see Bălţi
Bel'tsy Moldova see Bălţi
Belukha, Gora mt. Kazakh./Rus. Fed. 80 G2
Belush'ye Rus. Fed. 42 J2
Belvidere IL U.S.A. 130 F3
Belvidere NJ U.S.A. 135 H3
Belyando r. Australia 110 D4
Belyayevka Ukr. see Bilyayivka
Belyy Rus. Fed. 42 G5
Belyy, Ostrov i. Rus. Fed. 64 I2
Belzig Germany 53 M2
Belzoni U.S.A. 131 F5
Bemaraha, Plateau du Madag. 99 E5
Bembe Angola 99 B4
Bemidji U.S.A. 130 E2
Béna Burkina 96 C3
Bena Dibele Dem. Rep. Congo 98 C4
Ben Alder mt. U.K. 50 E4
Benalla Australia 112 B6
Benares India see Varanasi
Ben Arous Tunisia 58 D6
Benavente Spain 57 D2
Ben Avon mt. U.K. 50 F3
Benbane Head hd U.K. 51 F2
Benbecula i. U.K. 50 B3
Ben Boyd National Park Australia 112 E6
Benburb U.K. 51 F3
Bên Cat Vietnam 71 D5
Bencha China 77 I1
Ben Chonzie hill U.K. 50 F4
Ben Cleuch hill U.K. 50 F4
Ben Cruachan mt. U.K. 50 D4
Bend U.S.A. 126 C3
Bendearg mt. S. Africa 101 H6
Bender Moldova see Tighina
Bender-Bayla Somalia 98 F3
Bendery Moldova see Tighina
Bendigo Australia 112 B6
Bendoc Australia 112 D6
Bene Moz. 99 D5
Benedict, Mount hill Canada 123 K3
Benenitra Madag. 99 E6
Benešov Czech Rep. 47 O6
Bénestroff France 52 G6
Benevento Italy 58 F4
Beneventum Italy see Benevento
Benezette U.S.A. 135 F3
Beng, Nam r. Laos 70 C3
Bengal, Bay of sea Indian Ocean 81 G8
Bengamisa Dem. Rep. Congo 98 C3
Bengbu China 77 H1
Benghazi Libya 97 F1
Bengkalis Indon. 71 C7
Bengkalis i. Indon. 71 C7
Bengkulu Indon. 68 C7
Bengtsfors Sweden 45 H7
Benguela Angola 99 B5
Benha Egypt see Banhā
Ben Hiant hill U.K. 50 C4
Ben Hope hill U.K. 50 E2
Ben Horn hill U.K. 50 E2
Beni r. Bol. 142 E6
Beni Dem. Rep. Congo 98 C3
Beni Nepal 83 E3
Beni-Abbès Alg. 54 D5
Beniah Lake Canada 121 H2
Benidorm Spain 57 F4
Beni Mellal Morocco 54 C5
▶Benin country Africa 96 D4
Africa 7, 94–95
Benin, Bight of g. Africa 96 D4
Benin City Nigeria 96 D4
Beni-Saf Alg. 57 F6
Beni Snassen, Monts des mts Morocco 57 E6
Beni Suef Egypt see Banī Suwayf
Benito, Islas is Mex. 127 E7
Benito Juárez Arg. 144 E5
Benito Juárez Mex. 129 F5
Benjamim Constant Brazil 142 E4
Benjamin U.S.A. 131 D5
Benjamín Hill Mex. 127 F7
Benjina Indon. 69 I8
Benkelman U.S.A. 130 C3
Ben Klibreck hill U.K. 50 E2
Ben Lavin Nature Reserve S. Africa 101 I2
Ben Lawers mt. U.K. 50 E4
Ben Lomond mt. Australia 112 E3
Ben Lomond hill U.K. 50 E4
Ben Lomond National Park Australia 111 [inset]
Ben Macdui mt. U.K. 50 F3
Benmara Australia 110 B3
Ben More hill U.K. 50 C4
Ben More mt. U.K. 50 E4
Benmore, Lake N.Z. 113 C7
Ben More Assynt hill U.K. 50 E2
Bennetta, Ostrov i. Rus. Fed. 65 P2
Bennett Island Rus. Fed. see Bennetta, Ostrov
Bennett Lake Canada 120 C3
Bennettsville U.S.A. 133 E5
Ben Nevis mt. U.K. 50 D4
Bennington NH U.S.A. 135 J2
Bennington VT U.S.A. 135 I2
Benoni S. Africa 101 I4
Ben Rinnes hill U.K. 50 F3
Bensheim Germany 53 I5
Benson AZ U.S.A. 129 H6
Benson MN U.S.A. 130 E2
Benta Seberang Malaysia 71 C6
Benteng Indon. 69 G8
Bentinck Island Myanmar 71 B5
Bentiu Sudan 86 C8
Bent Jbaïl Lebanon 85 B3
Bentley U.K. 48 F5
Bento Gonçalves Brazil 145 A5
Benton AR U.S.A. 131 E5
Benton CA U.S.A. 128 D3
Benton IL U.S.A. 130 F4
Benton KY U.S.A. 131 F4
Benton LA U.S.A. 131 E5
Benton MO U.S.A. 131 F4
Benton PA U.S.A. 135 G3
Bentong Malaysia see Bentung
Benton Harbor U.S.A. 134 B2
Bentonville U.S.A. 131 E4
Bên Tre Vietnam 71 D5
Bentuang Karimun National Park Indon. 68 E6
Bentung Malaysia 71 C7
Benue r. Nigeria 96 D4
Benum, Gunung mt. Malaysia 71 C7
Ben Vorlich hill U.K. 50 E4
Benwee Head hd Rep. of Ireland 51 C3
Benwood U.S.A. 134 E3
Ben Wyvis mt. U.K. 50 E3
Benxi Liaoning China 74 A4
Benxi Liaoning China 74 B4
Beograd Serb. and Mont. see Belgrade
Béoumi Côte d'Ivoire 96 C4
Beppu Japan 75 C6
Béqaa valley Lebanon see El Béqaa
Berach r. India 82 C4
Beraketa Madag. 99 E6
Bérard, Lac l. Canada 123 H2
Berasia India 82 D5
Berat Albania 59 H4
Beravina Madag. 99 E5
Berbak National Park Indon. 68 C7
Berber Sudan 86 D6
Berbera Somalia 98 E2
Berbérati Cent. Afr. Rep. 98 B3
Berchtesgaden, Nationalpark nat. park Germany 47 N7
Berck France 52 B4
Berdichev Ukr. see Berdychiv
Berdigestyakh Rus. Fed. 65 N3
Berdyans'k Ukr. 43 H7
Berdychiv Ukr. 43 F6
Berea KY U.S.A. 134 C5
Berea OH U.S.A. 134 E3
Beregovo Ukr. see Berehove
Beregovoy Rus. Fed. 74 B1
Berehove Ukr. 43 D6
Bereina P.N.G. 69 L8
Bereket Turkm. see Gazandzhyk
Berekum Ghana 96 C4
Berenice Egypt see Baranīs
Berenice Libya see Benghazi
Berens r. Canada 121 L4
Berens Island Canada 121 L4
Berens River Canada 121 L4
Beresford U.S.A. 130 D3
Bereza Belarus see Byaroza
Berezino Belarus see Byerazino
Berezivka Ukr. 43 F7
Berezne Ukr. 43 E6
Bereznik Rus. Fed. 42 I3
Berezniki Rus. Fed. 41 R4
Berezov Rus. Fed. see Berezovo
Berezovka Rus. Fed. 74 B2
Berezovka Ukr. see Berezivka
Berezovo Rus. Fed. 41 T3
Berezovyy Rus. Fed. 74 D2
Berga Germany 53 L3
Berga Spain 57 G2
Bergama Turkey 59 L5
Bergamo Italy 58 C2
Bergby Sweden 45 J6
Bergen Mecklenburg-Vorpommern Germany 47 N3
Bergen Niedersachsen Germany 49 J2
Bergen Norway 45 D6
Bergen U.S.A. 135 G2
Bergen op Zoom Neth. 52 E3
Bergerac France 56 E4
Bergères-lès-Vertus France 52 E6
Bergheim (Erft) Germany 52 G4
Bergisches Land reg. Germany 53 H4
Bergisch Gladbach Germany 52 H4
Bergland Namibia 100 C2
Bergomum Italy see Bergamo
Bergoo U.S.A. 134 E4
Bergsjö Sweden 45 J6
Bergsviken Sweden 44 L4
Bergtheim Germany 53 K5
Bergues France 52 C4
Bergum Neth. 52 G1
Bergville S. Africa 101 I5
Berhampur India see Baharampur
Beringa, Ostrov i. Rus. Fed. 65 R4
Beringen Belgium 52 F3
Beringovskiy Rus. Fed. 65 S3
Bering Sea N. Pacific Ocean 65 S4
Bering Strait Rus. Fed./U.S.A. 65 U3
Beris, Ra's pt Iran 89 F5
Berislav Ukr. see Beryslav
Berkåk Norway 44 G5
Berkane Morocco 57 E6
Berkel r. Neth. 52 G2
Berkeley U.S.A. 128 B3
Berkeley Springs U.S.A. 135 F4
Berkhout Neth. 52 F2
Berkner Island Antarctica 152 A1
Berkovitsa Bulg. 59 J3
Berkshire Downs hills U.K. 49 F7
Berkshire Hills U.S.A. 135 I2
Berland r. Canada 120 G4
Berlare Belgium 52 E3
Berlevåg Norway 44 P1

▶Berlin Germany 53 N2
Capital of Germany.

Berlin land Germany 53 N2
Berlin MD U.S.A. 135 H4
Berlin NH U.S.A. 135 J1
Berlin PA U.S.A. 135 F4
Berlin Lake U.S.A. 134 E3
Bermagui Australia 112 E6
Bermejo r. Arg./Bol. 144 E3
Bermejo Bol. 142 F8
Bermen, Lac l. Canada 123 H3

▶Bermuda terr. N. Atlantic Ocean 137 L2
United Kingdom Overseas Territory.
North America 9, 116–117

Bermuda Rise sea feature N. Atlantic Ocean 148 D4

▶Bern Switz. 56 H3
Capital of Switzerland.

Bernalillo U.S.A. 127 G6
Bernardino de Campos Brazil 145 A3
Bernardo O'Higgins, Parque Nacional nat. park Chile 144 B7
Bernasconi Arg. 144 D5
Bernau Germany 53 N2
Bernburg (Saale) Germany 53 L3
Berne Germany 53 I1
Berne Switz. see Bern
Berne U.S.A. 134 C3
Berner Alpen mts Switz. 56 H3
Berneray i. Scotland U.K. 50 B3
Berneray i. Scotland U.K. 50 B4
Bernier Island Australia 109 A6
Bernina Pass Switz. 56 J3
Bernkastel-Kues Germany 52 H5
Beroea Greece see Veroia
Beroea Syria see Aleppo
Beroroha Madag. 99 E6
Beroun Czech Rep. 47 O6
Berounka r. Czech Rep. 47 O6
Berovina Madag. see Beravina
Berri Australia 111 C7
Berriane Alg. 54 E5
Berridale Australia 112 D6
Berriedale U.K. 50 F2
Berrigan Australia 112 B5
Berrima Australia 112 E5
Berrouaghia Alg. 57 H5
Berry Australia 112 E5
Berry U.S.A. 134 C4
Berryessa, Lake U.S.A. 128 B2
Berry Head hd U.K. 49 D8
Berry Islands Bahamas 133 E7
Berryville U.S.A. 135 G4
Berseba Namibia 100 C4
Bersenbrück Germany 53 H2
Bertam Malaysia 71 C6
Berté, Lac l. Canada 123 H4
Berthoud Pass U.S.A. 126 G5
Bertolinía Brazil 143 J5
Bertoua Cameroon 96 E4
Bertraghboy Bay Rep. of Ireland 51 C4
Beru atoll Kiribati 107 H2
Beruri Brazil 142 F4
Beruwala Sri Lanka 84 C5
Berwick Australia 112 B7
Berwick U.S.A. 135 G3
Berwick-upon-Tweed U.K. 48 E3
Berwyn hills U.K. 49 D6
Beryslav Ukr. 59 O1
Berytus Lebanon see Beirut
Besalampy Madag. 99 E5
Besançon France 56 H3
Besar, Gunung mt. Malaysia 71 C7
Besbay Kazakh. 80 A2
Beserah Malaysia 71 C7
Beshkent Uzbek. 89 G2
Beshneh Iran 88 D4
Besikama Indon. 108 D2
Besitang Indon. 71 B6
Beskra Alg. see Biskra
Beslan Rus. Fed. 91 G2
Besnard Lake Canada 121 J4
Besni Turkey 90 E3
Besor watercourse Israel 85 B4
Beşparmak Dağları mts Cyprus see Pentadaktylos Range
Bessbrook U.K. 51 F3
Bessemer U.S.A. 133 C5
Besshoky, Gora hill Kazakh. 91 I1
Besskorbnaya Rus. Fed. 43 I7
Bessonovka Rus. Fed. 43 J5
Betanzos Spain 57 B2
Bethal S. Africa 101 I4
Bethanie Namibia 100 C4
Bethany U.S.A. 130 E3
Bethel U.S.A. 123 H5
Bethel Park U.S.A. 134 E3
Bethesda U.K. 48 C5
Bethesda MD U.S.A. 135 G4
Bethesda OH U.S.A. 134 E3
Bethlehem S. Africa 101 I5
Bethlehem U.S.A. 135 H3
Bethlehem West Bank 85 B4
Bethulie S. Africa 101 G6
Béthune France 52 C4
Beti Pak. 89 H4
Betim Brazil 145 B2
Bet Lehem West Bank see Bethlehem
Betma India 82 C5
Betong Thai. 71 C6
Betoota Australia 110 C5
Betpak-Dala plain Kazakh. 80 D2
Betroka Madag. 99 E6
Bet She'an Israel 85 B3
Betsiamites Canada 123 H4
Betsiamites r. Canada 123 H4
Bettiah India 83 F4
Bettyhill U.K. 50 E2
Bettystown Rep. of Ireland 51 F4
Betul India 82 D5
Betwa r. India 82 D4
Betws-y-coed U.K. 49 D5
Betzdorf Germany 53 H4
Beulah Australia 111 C7
Beulah MI U.S.A. 134 B1
Beulah ND U.S.A. 130 C2
Beult r. U.K. 49 H7
Beuthen Poland see Bytom
Bever r. Germany 53 H2
Beverley U.K. 48 G5
Beverly MA U.S.A. 135 J2
Beverly OH U.S.A. 134 E4
Beverly Hills U.S.A. 128 D4
Beverly Lake Canada 121 K1
Beverstedt Germany 53 I1
Beverungen Germany 53 J3
Beverwijk Neth. 52 E2
Bewani P.N.G. 69 K7
Bexbach Germany 53 H5
Bexhill U.K. 49 H8
Bexley, Cape Canada 118 G3
Beyānlū Iran 88 B3
Beyce Turkey see Orhaneli
Bey Dağları mts Turkey 59 N6
Beykoz Turkey 59 M4
Beyla Guinea 96 C4
Beylagan Azer. see Beyläqan
Beyläqan Azer. 91 G3
Beyneu Kazakh. 78 E2
Beypazarı Turkey 59 N4
Beypınarı Turkey 90 E3
Beypore India 84 B4
Beyrouth Lebanon see Beirut
Beyşehir Turkey 90 C3
Beyşehir Gölü l. Turkey 90 C3
Beytonovo Rus. Fed. 74 B1
Beytüşşebap Turkey 91 F3
Bezameh Iran 88 E3
Bezbozhnik Rus. Fed. 42 K4
Bezhanitsy Rus. Fed. 42 F4
Bezhetsk Rus. Fed. 42 H4
Béziers France 56 F5
Bezmein Turkm. see Byuzmeyin
Bezwada India see Vijayawada
Bhabha India see Bhabhua
Bhabhar India 82 B4
Bhabhua India 83 E4
Bhabua India see Bhabhua
Bhachau India 82 B5
Bhachbhar India 82 B4
Bhadgaon Nepal see Bhaktapur
Bhadohi India 83 E4
Bhadra India 82 C3
Bhadrachalam Road Station India see Kottagudem
Bhadrak India 83 F5
Bhadrakh India see Bhadrak
Bhadravati India 84 B3
Bhag Pak. 89 G4
Bhagalpur India 83 F4
Bhainsa India 84 C2
Bhainsdehi India 82 D5
Bhairab Bazar Bangl. 83 G4
Bhairi Hol mt. Pak. 89 G5
Bhaktapur Nepal 83 F4
Bhalki India 84 C2
Bhamo Myanmar 70 B1
Bhamragarh India 84 D2
Bhandara India 82 D5
Bhanjanagar India 84 E2
Bhanrer Range hills India 82 D5
Bhaptiahi India 83 F4
Bharat country Asia see India
Bharatpur India 82 D4
Bhareli r. India 83 H4
Bharuch India 82 C5
Bhatapara India 83 E5
Bhatarsaigh i. U.K. see Vatersay
Bhatghar Lake India 84 B2
Bhatinda India see Bathinda
Bhatnair India see Hanumangarh
Bhatpara India 83 G5
Bhaunagar India see Bhavnagar
Bhavani r. India 84 C4
Bhavani Sagar l. India 84 C4
Bhavnagar India 82 C5
Bhawana Pak. 89 I4
Bhawanipatna India 84 D2
Bhearnaraigh, Eilean i. U.K. see Berneray
Bheemavaram India see Bhimavaram
Bhekuzulu S. Africa 101 J4
Bhera Pak. 89 I3
Bhikhna Thori Nepal 83 F4
Bhilai India 82 E5
Bhildi India 82 C4
Bhilwara India 82 C4
Bhima r. India 84 C2
Bhimar India 82 B4
Bhimavaram India 84 D2
Bhimlath India 82 E5
Bhind India 82 D4
Bhinga India 83 E4
Bhiwandi India 84 B2
Bhiwani India 82 D3
Bhogaipur India 82 D4
Bhojpur Nepal 83 F4
Bhola Bangl. 83 G5
Bhongweni S. Africa 101 I6
Bhopal India 82 D5
Bhopalpatnam India 84 D2
Bhrigukaccha India see Bharuch
Bhuban India 84 E1
Bhubaneshwar India 84 E1
Bhubaneswar India see Bhubaneshwar
Bhuj India 82 B5
Bhumiphol Dam Thai. 70 B3
Bhusawal India 82 C5
▶Bhutan country Asia 83 G4
Asia 6, 62–63
Bhuttewala India 82 B4
Bia r. Ghana 96 C4
Bia, Phou mt. Laos 70 C3
Bīābān mts Iran 88 E5
Biafo Glacier Jammu and Kashmir 82 C2
Biafra, Bight of g. Africa see Benin, Bight of
Biak Indon. 69 J7
Biak i. Indon. 69 J7
Biała Podlaska Poland 43 D5
Białogard Poland 47 O4
Białystok Poland 43 D5

Bianco, Monte *mt.* France/Italy *see* **Blanc, Mont**
Biandangang Kou *r. mouth* China **77** I1
Bianzhao China **74** A3
Bianzhuang China *see* **Cangshan**
Biaora India **82** D5
Biarritz France **56** D5
Bi'ār Tabrāk *well* Saudi Arabia **88** B5
Bibai Japan **74** F4
Bibbenluke Australia **112** D6
Bibbiena Italy **58** D3
Bibby Island Canada **121** M2
Biberach an der Riß Germany **47** L6
Bibile Sri Lanka **84** D5
Biblis Germany **53** I5
Biblos Lebanon *see* **Jbail**
Bicas Brazil **145** C3
Biçer Turkey **59** N5
Bicester U.K. **49** F7
Bichabhera India **82** C4
Bicheng China *see* **Bishan**
Bichevaya Rus. Fed. **74** D3
Bichi *r.* Rus. Fed. **74** E1
Bickerton Island Australia **110** B2
Bickleigh U.K. **49** D8
Bicknell U.S.A. **134** B4
Bicuari, Parque Nacional do *nat. park* Angola **99** B5
Bid India **84** B2
Bida Nigeria **96** D4
Bidar India **84** C2
Biddeford U.S.A. **135** J2
Biddinghuizen Neth. **52** F2
Bidean nam Bian *mt.* U.K. **50** D4
Bideford U.K. **49** C7
Bideford Bay U.K. **49** C7
Bidokht Iran **88** E3
Bidzhan Rus. Fed. **74** C3
Bié Angola *see* **Kuito**
Biedenkopf Germany **53** I4
Biel Switz. **56** H3
Bielawa Poland **47** P5
Bielefeld Germany **53** I2
Bielitz Poland *see* **Bielsko-Biała**
Biella Italy **58** C2
Bielsko-Biała Poland **47** Q6
Bielstein *hill* Germany **53** J3
Bienenbüttel Germany **53** K1
Biên Hoa Vietnam **71** D5
Bienne Switz. *see* **Biel**
Bienville, Lac *l.* Canada **123** G3
Bié Plateau Angola **99** B5
Bierbank Australia **112** B1
Biesiesvlei S. Africa **101** G4
Bietigheim-Bissingen Germany **53** J6
Bièvre Belgium **52** F5
Bifoun Gabon **98** B4
Big *r.* Canada **123** K3
Biga Turkey **59** L4
Bigadiç Turkey **59** M5
Biga Yarımadası *pen.* Turkey **59** L5
Big Baldy Mountain U.S.A. **126** F3
Big Bar Creek Canada **120** F5
Big Bear Lake U.S.A. **128** E4
Big Belt Mountains U.S.A. **126** F3
Big Bend Swaziland **101** J4
Big Bend National Park U.S.A. **131** C6
Bigbury-on-Sea U.K. **49** D8
Big Canyon *watercourse* U.S.A. **131** C6
Biger Nuur *salt l.* Mongolia **80** I2
Big Falls U.S.A. **130** E1
Big Fork *r.* U.S.A. **130** E1
Biggar Canada **121** J4
Biggar U.K. **50** F5
Biggar, Lac *l.* Canada **122** G4
Biggenden Australia **111** F5
Bigger, Mount Canada **120** B3
Biggesee *l.* Germany **53** H3
Biggleswade U.K. **49** G6
Biggs *CA* U.S.A. **128** C2
Biggs *OR* U.S.A. **126** C3
Big Hole *r.* U.S.A. **126** E3
Bighorn *r.* U.S.A. **126** G3
Bighorn Mountains U.S.A. **126** G3
Big Island *Nunavut* Canada **119** K3
Big Island *N.W.T.* Canada **120** G2
Big Island *Ont.* Canada **121** M5
Big Kalzas Lake Canada **120** C2
Big Lake *l.* Canada **121** H1
Big Lake U.S.A. **131** C6
Bignona Senegal **96** B3
Big Pine U.S.A. **128** D3
Big Pine Peak U.S.A. **128** D4
Big Raccoon *r.* U.S.A. **134** B4
Big Rapids U.S.A. **134** C2
Big River Canada **121** J4
Big Sable Point U.S.A. **134** B1
Big Salmon *r.* Canada **120** C2
Big Sand Lake Canada **121** L3
Big Sandy *r.* U.S.A. **126** F4
Big Sandy Lake Canada **121** J4
Big Smokey Valley U.S.A. **128** E2
Big South Fork National River and Recreation Area *park* U.S.A. **134** C5
Big Spring U.S.A. **131** C5
Big Stone Canada **121** I5
Big Stone Gap U.S.A. **134** D5
Bigstone Lake Canada **121** M4
Big Timber U.S.A. **126** F3
Big Trout Lake Canada **121** N4
Big Trout Lake *l.* Canada **121** N4
Big Valley Canada **121** H4
Big Water U.S.A. **129** H3
Bihać Bos.-Herz. **58** F2
Bihar *state* India **83** F4
Bihariganj India **83** F4
Bihar Sharif India **83** F4
Bihor, Vârful *mt.* Romania **59** J1
Bihoro Japan **74** G4
Bijagós, Arquipélago dos *is* Guinea-Bissau **96** B3
Bijaipur India **82** D4
Bijapur India **84** B2
Bījār Iran **88** B3
Bijbehara Jammu and Kashmir **82** C2
Bijeljina Bos.-Herz. **59** H2
Bijelo Polje Serb. and Mont. **59** H3
Bijeraghogarh India **82** E5
Bijiang China *see* **Zhiziluo**
Bijie China **76** E3
Bijji India **84** D2
Bijnor India **82** D3
Bijnore India *see* **Bijnor**
Bijnot Pak. **89** H4
Bijrān *well* Saudi Arabia **88** C5
Bijrān, Khashm *hill* Saudi Arabia **88** C5
Bikampur India **82** C4
Bikaner India **82** C3
Bīkhūyeh Iran **88** D5
Bikin Rus. Fed. **74** D3
Bikin *r.* Rus. Fed. **74** D3
Bikini *atoll* Marshall Is **150** H5
Bikori Sudan **86** D7
Bikoro Dem. Rep. Congo **98** B4
Bikou China **76** E1
Bikramganj India **83** F4
Bilād Banī Bū 'Alī Oman **87** I5
Bilaigarh India **84** D1
Bilara India **82** C4
Bilaspur *Chhattisgarh* India **83** E5
Bilaspur *Himachal Pradesh* India **82** D3
Biläsuvar Azer. **91** H3
Bila Tserkva Ukr. **43** F6
Bilauktaung Range *mts* Myanmar/Thai. **71** B4
Bilbao Spain **57** E2
Bilbays Egypt **90** C5
Bilbeis Egypt *see* **Bilbays**
Bilbo Spain *see* **Bilbao**
Bilecik Turkey **59** M4
Biłgoraj Poland **43** D6
Bilharamulo Tanz. **98** D4
Bilhaur India **82** E4
Bilhorod-Dnistrovs'kyy Ukr. **59** N1
Bili Dem. Rep. Congo **98** C3
Bilibino Rus. Fed. **65** R3
Bilin Myanmar **70** B3
Bill U.S.A. **126** G4
Billabalong Australia **109** A6
Billabong Creek *r.* Australia *see* **Moulamein Creek**
Billericay U.K. **49** H7
Billiluna Australia **108** D4
Billingham U.K. **48** F4
Billings U.S.A. **126** F3
Billiton *i.* Indon. *see* **Belitung**
Bill of Portland *hd* U.K. **49** E8
Bill Williams *r.* U.S.A. **129** F4
Bill Williams Mountain U.S.A. **129** G4
Bilma Niger **96** E3
Bilo *r.* Rus. Fed. *see* **Belaya**
Biloela Australia **110** E5
Bilohirs'k Ukr. **90** D1
Bilohir"ya Ukr. **43** E6
Biloku Guyana **143** G3
Biloli India **84** C2
Bilovods'k Ukr. **43** H6
Biloxi U.S.A. **131** F6
Bilpa Morea Claypan *salt flat* Australia **110** B5
Bilston U.K. **50** F5
Biltine Chad **97** F3
Bilto Norway **44** L2
Bilugyun Island Myanmar **70** B3
Bilyayivka Ukr. **59** N1
Bilzen Belgium **52** F4
Bima Indon. **108** B2
Bimberi, Mount Australia **112** D5
Bimini Islands Bahamas **133** E7
Bimlipatam India **84** D2
Bīnāb Iran **88** C2
Bina-Etawa India **82** D4
Binaija, Gunung *mt.* Indon. **67** E8
Bīnālūd, Kūh-e *mts* Iran **88** E2
Binboğa Daği *mt.* Turkey **90** E3
Bincheng China *see* **Binzhou**
Binchuan China **76** D3
Bindebango Australia **112** C1
Bindle Australia **112** D1
Bindu Dem. Rep. Congo **99** B4
Bindura Zimbabwe **99** D5
Binefar Spain **57** G3
Binga Zimbabwe **99** C5
Binga, Monte *mt.* Moz. **99** D5
Bingara Australia **112** B2
Bingaram *i.* India **84** B4
Bing Bong Australia **110** B2
Bingen am Rhein Germany **53** H5
Bingham U.S.A. **135** K1
Binghamton U.S.A. **135** H2
Bingmei China *see* **Congjiang**
Bingöl Turkey **91** F3
Bingol Dağı *mt.* Turkey **91** F3
Bingxi China *see* **Yushan**
Bingzhongluo China **76** C2
Binh Gia Vietnam **70** D2
Binika India **83** E5
Binjai Indon. **71** B7
Bin Mürkhan *well* U.A.E. **88** D5
Binnaway Australia **112** D3
Binpur India **83** F5
Bintan *i.* Indon. **71** D7
Bint Jbeil Lebanon *see* **Bent Jbaïl**
Bintulu *Sarawak* Malaysia **68** E6
Binxian *Heilong.* China **74** B3
Binxian *Shaanxi* China **77** F1
Binya Australia **112** C5
Binyang China **77** F4
Bin-Yauri Nigeria **96** D3
Binzhou *Guangxi* China *see* **Binyang**
Binzhou *Heilong.* China *see* **Binxian**
Binzhou *Shandong* China **73** L5
Bioco *i.* Equat. Guinea **96** D4
Biograd na Moru Croatia **58** F3
Bioko *i.* Equat. Guinea *see* **Bioco**
Biokovo *mts* Croatia **58** G3
Biquinhas Brazil **145** B2
Bir India *see* **Bid**
Bira Rus. Fed. **74** D2
Bi'r Abū Jady *oasis* Syria **85** D1
Bīrag, Kūh-e *mts* Iran **89** F5
Birāk Libya **97** E2
Birakan Rus. Fed. **74** C2
Bi'r al 'Abd Egypt **85** A4
Bi'r al Halbā *well* Syria **85** D2
Bi'r al Jifjāfah *well* Egypt **85** A4
Bi'r al Khamsah *well* Egypt **90** B5
Bi'r al Māliḥah *well* Egypt **85** A5
Bi'r al Mulūsi Iraq **91** F4
Bi'r al Munbaṭiḥ *well* Syria **85** D2
Bi'r al Qaṭrānī *well* Egypt **90** B5
Bi'r al Ubbayiḍ *well* Egypt **90** B6
Birandozero Rus. Fed. **42** H3
Bi'r an Nuṣf *well* Egypt *see* **Bi'r an Nuṣṣ**
Bi'r an Nuṣṣ *well* Egypt **90** B5
Bir Anzarane W. Sahara **96** B2
Birao Cent. Afr. Rep. **98** C2
Bi'r ar Rābiyah *well* Egypt **90** B5
Biratnagar Nepal **83** F4
Bi'r aṭ Ṭarfāwī *well* Libya **90** B5
Bi'r Başīrī *well* Syria **85** C2
Bi'r Bayḍā' *well* Egypt **85** B4
Bi'r Baylī *well* Egypt **90** B5
Bîr Beiḍa *well* Egypt *see* **Bi'r Bayḍā'**
Bi'r Buṭaymān Syria **91** E3
Birch *r.* Canada **121** H3
Birch Hills Canada **121** J4
Birch Island Canada **120** G5
Birch Lake *N.W.T.* Canada **120** G2
Birch Lake *Ont.* Canada **121** M5
Birch Lake *Sask.* Canada **121** I4
Birch Mountains Canada **120** H3
Birch River U.S.A. **134** E4
Birch Run U.S.A. **134** D2
Bircot Eth. **98** E3
Birdaard Neth. **52** F1
Bîr Dignâsh *well* Egypt *see* **Bi'r Diqnāsh**
Bi'r Diqnāsh *well* Egypt **90** B5
Bird Island N. Mariana Is *see* **Farallon de Medinilla**
Birdseye U.S.A. **129** H2
Birdsville Australia **111** B5
Birecik Turkey **90** E3
Bîr el 'Abd Egypt *see* **Bi'r al 'Abd**
Bir el Arbi *well* Alg. **57** I6
Bîr el Istabl *well* Egypt *see* **Bi'r Iṣṭabl**
Bîr el Khamsa *well* Egypt *see* **Bi'r al Khamsah**
Bîr el Nuṣṣ *well* Egypt *see* **Bi'r an Nuṣṣ**
Bîr el Obeiyid *well* Egypt *see* **Bi'r al Ubbayiḍ**
Bîr el Qaṭrâni *well* Egypt *see* **Bi'r al Qaṭrānī**
Bîr el Râbia *well* Egypt *see* **Bi'r ar Rābiyah**
Birendranagar Nepal *see* **Surkhet**
Bir en Natrûn *well* Sudan **86** C6
Bireun Indon. **71** B6
Bi'r Fāḍil *well* Saudi Arabia **88** C6
Bi'r Fajr *well* Saudi Arabia **90** E5
Bi'r Fu'ād *well* Egypt **90** B5
Bîr Gifgâfa *well* Egypt *see* **Bi'r al Jifjāfah**
Bi'r Ḥajal *well* Syria **85** D2
Birhan *mt.* Eth. **98** D2
Bi'r Ḥasanah *well* Egypt **85** A4
Bi'r Ḥayzān *well* Saudi Arabia **90** E6
Bi'r Ibn Hirmās Saudi Arabia *see* **Al Bi'r**
Bir Ibn Juhayyim Saudi Arabia **88** C6
Birigüi Brazil **145** A3
Bīrīn Syria **85** C2
Bi'r Iṣṭabl *well* Egypt **90** B5
Birjand Iran **88** E3
Bi'r Jubnī *well* Libya **90** B5
Birkát Hamad *well* Iraq **91** G5
Birkenfeld Germany **53** H5
Birkenhead U.K. **48** D5
Birkirkara Malta **58** F7
Birksgate Range *hills* Australia **109** E6
Bîrlad Romania *see* **Bârlad**
Bi'r Lahfān *well* Egypt **85** A4
Birlik Kazakh. *see* **Brlik**
Birmal *reg.* Afgh. **89** H3
Birmingham U.K. **49** F6
Birmingham U.S.A. **133** C5
Bîr Mogreïn Mauritania **96** B2
Bi'r Muḥaymid al Wazwaz *well* Syria **85** D2
Bi'r Nāḥid *oasis* Egypt **90** C5
Birnin-Gwari Nigeria **96** D3
Birnin-Kebbi Nigeria **96** D3
Birnin Konni Niger **96** D3
Birobidzhan Rus. Fed. **74** D2
Bi'r Qaṣīr as Sirr *well* Egypt **90** B5
Birr Rep. of Ireland **51** E4
Bi'r Rawḍ Sālim *well* Egypt **85** A4
Birrie *r.* Australia **112** C2
Birrindudu Australia **108** E4
Bîr Rôd Sâlim *well* Egypt *see* **Bi'r Rawḍ Sālim**
Birsay U.K. **50** F1
Bi'r Shalatayn Egypt **86** E5
Bîr Shalatein Egypt *see* **Bi'r Shalatayn**
Birsk Rus. Fed. **41** R4
Birstall U.K. **49** F6
Birstein Germany **53** J4
Bir Ṭalḥah *well* Saudi Arabia **88** B6
Birthday Mountain *hill* Australia **110** C2
Birtle Canada **121** K5
Biru China **76** B2
Birur India **84** B3
Bi'r Usaylīlah *well* Saudi Arabia **88** B6
Biruxiong China *see* **Biru**
Biržai Lith. **45** N8
Bisa India **70** A1
Bisa *i.* Indon. **69** H7
Bisalpur India **82** D3
Bisau India **82** C3
Bisbee U.S.A. **127** F7
Biscay, Bay of *sea* France/Spain **56** B4
Biscay Abyssal Plain *sea feature* N. Atlantic Ocean **148** H3
Biscayne National Park U.S.A. **133** D7
Biscoe Islands Antarctica **152** L2
Biscotasi Lake Canada **122** E5
Biscotasing Canada **122** E5
Bisezhai China **76** D4
Bishan China **76** E2
Bishbek Kyrg. *see* **Bishkek**
Bishenpur India *see* **Bishnupur**

▶**Bishkek** Kyrg. **80** D3
Capital of Kyrgyzstan.

Bishnath India **76** B3
Bishnupur *Manipur* India **83** H4
Bishnupur *W. Bengal* India **83** F5
Bisho S. Africa **101** H7
Bishop U.S.A. **128** D3
Bishop Auckland U.K. **48** F4
Bishop Lake Canada **120** G1
Bishop's Stortford U.K. **49** H7
Bishopville U.S.A. **133** D5
Bishrī, Jabal *hills* Syria **85** D2
Bishui *Heilong.* China **74** A1
Bishui *Henan* China *see* **Biyang**
Biskra Alg. **54** F5
Bislig Phil. **69** H5

▶**Bismarck** U.S.A. **130** C2
State capital of North Dakota.

Bismarck Archipelago *is* P.N.G. **69** L7
Bismarck Range *mts* P.N.G. **69** K7
Bismarck Sea P.N.G. **69** L7
Bismark (Altmark) Germany **53** L2
Bismil Turkey **91** F3
Bismo Norway **44** F6
Bison U.S.A. **130** C2
Bispgården Sweden **44** J5
Bispingen Germany **53** K1
Bissa, Djebel *mt.* Alg. **57** G5
Bissamcuttak India **84** D2

▶**Bissau** Guinea-Bissau **96** B3
Capital of Guinea-Bissau.

Bissaula Nigeria **96** E4
Bissett Canada **121** M5
Bistcho Lake Canada **120** G3
Bistrița Romania **59** K1
Bistrița *r.* Romania **59** L1
Bitburg Germany **52** G5
Bitche France **53** H5
Bithur India **82** E4
Bithynia *reg.* Turkey **59** M4
Bitkine Chad **97** E3
Bitlis Turkey **91** F3
Bitola Macedonia **59** I4
Bitolj Macedonia *see* **Bitola**
Bitonto Italy **58** G4
Bitrān, Jabal *hill* Saudi Arabia **84** B6
Bitra Par *reef* India **84** B4
Bitter Creek *r.* U.S.A. **129** I2
Bitterfeld Germany **53** M3
Bitterfontein S. Africa **100** D6
Bitter Lakes Egypt **90** D5
Bitterroot *r.* U.S.A. **126** E3
Bitterroot Range *mts* U.S.A. **126** E3
Bitterwater U.S.A. **128** C3
Bittkau Germany **53** L2
Bitung Indon. **69** H6
Biu Nigeria **96** E3
Biwa-ko *l.* Japan **75** D6
Biwmaris U.K. *see* **Beaumaris**
Biyang China **77** G1
Bīye K'obē Eth. **98** E2
Biysk Rus. Fed. **72** F2
Bizana S. Africa **101** I6
Bizerta Tunisia *see* **Bizerte**
Bizerte Tunisia **58** C6
Bīzhanābād Iran **88** E5

▶**Bjargtangar** *hd* Iceland **44** [inset]
Most westerly point of Europe.

Bjästa Sweden **44** K5
Bjelovar Croatia **58** G2
Bjerkvik Norway **44** J2
Bjerringbro Denmark **45** F8
Bjørgan Norway **44** G5
Björkliden Sweden **44** K2
Björklinge Sweden **45** J6
Bjorli Norway **44** F5
Björna Sweden **44** K5
Björneborg Fin. *see* **Pori**

▶**Bjørnøya** *i.* Arctic Ocean **64** C2
Part of Norway.

Bjurholm Sweden **44** K5
Bla Mali **96** C3
Black *r. Man.* Canada **121** L5
Black *r. Ont.* Canada **122** E4
Black *r. AR* U.S.A. **131** F5
Black *r. AR* U.S.A. **131** F5
Black *r. AZ* U.S.A. **129** H5
Black *r.* Vietnam **70** D2
Blackadder Water *r.* U.K. **50** G5
Blackall Australia **110** D5
Blackbear *r.* Canada **121** N4
Black Birch Lake Canada **121** J3
Black Bourton U.K. **49** F7
Blackbull Australia **110** C3
Blackburn U.K. **48** E5
Blackbutt Australia **112** F1
Black Butte *mt.* U.S.A. **128** B2
Black Butte Lake U.S.A. **128** B2
Black Canyon *gorge* U.S.A. **129** F4
Black Canyon of the Gunnison National Park U.S.A. **129** J2
Black Combe *hill* U.K. **48** D4
Black Creek *watercourse* U.S.A. **129** I4
Black Donald Lake Canada **135** G1
Blackdown Tableland National Park Australia **110** E4
Blackduck U.S.A. **130** E2
Blackfalds Canada **120** H4
Blackfoot U.S.A. **126** E4
Black Foot *r.* U.S.A. **126** E3
Black Forest *mts* Germany **47** L7
Black Hill *hill* U.K. **48** F5
Black Hills *SD* U.S.A. **124** G3
Black Hills *SD* U.S.A. **126** G3
Black Island Canada **121** L5
Black Lake Canada **121** J3
Black Lake *l.* Canada **121** J3
Black Lake *l.* U.S.A. **134** C1
Black Mesa *mt.* U.S.A. **129** I5
Black Mesa *ridge* U.S.A. **129** H3
Black Mountain Pak. **89** I3
Black Mountain *hill* U.K. **49** D7
Black Mountain *AK* U.S.A. **118** B3
Black Mountain *CA* U.S.A. **128** E4
Black Mountain *KY* U.S.A. **134** D5
Black Mountain *NM* U.S.A. **129** I5
Black Mountains *hills* U.K. **49** D7
Black Mountains U.S.A. **129** F4
Black Nossob *watercourse* Namibia **100** D2
Black Pagoda India *see* **Konarka**
Blackpool U.K. **48** D5
Black Range *mts* U.S.A. **129** I5
Black River *MI* U.S.A. **134** D1
Black River *NY* U.S.A. **135** H1
Black River Falls U.S.A. **130** F2
Black Rock *hill* Jordan *see* **'Unāb, Jabal al**
Black Rock Desert U.S.A. **126** D4
Blacksburg U.S.A. **134** E5
Black Sea Asia/Europe **43** H8
Blacks Fork *r.* U.S.A. **126** F4
Blackshear U.S.A. **133** D6
Blacksod Bay Rep. of Ireland **51** B3
Black Springs U.S.A. **128** D2
Blackstairs Mountains *hills* Rep. of Ireland **51** F5
Blackstone U.S.A. **135** F5
Black Sugarloaf *mt.* Australia **112** E3
Black Tickle Canada **123** L3
Blackville Australia **112** E3
Blackwater Australia **110** E4
Blackwater Rep. of Ireland **51** F5
Blackwater *r.* Rep. of Ireland **51** E5
Blackwater *r.* Rep. of Ireland/U.K. **51** F3
Blackwater *watercourse* U.S.A. **131** C5
Blackwater Lake Canada **120** F2
Blackwater Reservoir U.K. **50** E4
Blackwood *r.* Australia **109** A8
Blackwood National Park Australia **110** D4
Bladensburg National Park Australia **110** C4
Blaenavon U.K. **49** D7
Blagodarnyy Rus. Fed. **91** F1
Blagoevgrad Bulg. **59** J3
Blagoveshchensk *Amurskaya Oblast'* Rus. Fed. **74** B2
Blagoveshchensk *Respublika Bashkortostan* Rus. Fed. **41** R4
Blaikiston, Mount Canada **120** H5
Blaine Lake Canada **121** J4
Blair U.S.A. **130** D3
Blair Athol Australia **110** D4
Blair Atholl U.K. **50** F4
Blairgowrie U.K. **50** F4
Blairsden U.S.A. **128** C2
Blairsville U.S.A. **133** D5
Blakang Mati, Pulau *i.* Sing. *see* **Sentosa**
Blakely U.S.A. **133** C6
Blakeney U.K. **49** I6

▶**Blanc, Mont** *mt.* France/Italy **56** H4
5th highest mountain in Europe.

Blanca, Bahía *b.* Arg. **144** D5
Blanca, Sierra *mt.* U.S.A. **127** G6
Blanca Peak U.S.A. **127** G5
Blanche, Lake *salt flat S.A.* Australia **111** B6
Blanche, Lake *salt flat W.A.* Australia **108** C5
Blanchester U.S.A. **134** D4
Blanc Nez, Cap *c.* France **52** B4
Blanco *r.* Bol. **142** F6
Blanco U.S.A. **129** J3
Blanco, Cape U.S.A. **126** B4
Blanc-Sablon Canada **123** K4
Bland *r.* Australia **112** C4
Bland U.S.A. **134** E5
Blanda *r.* Iceland **44** [inset]
Blandford Forum U.K. **49** E8
Blanding U.S.A. **129** I3
Blanes Spain **57** H3
Blangah, Telok Sing. **71** [inset]
Blangkejeren Indon. **71** B7
Blangpidie Indon. **71** B7
Blankenberge Belgium **52** D3
Blankenheim Germany **52** G4
Blanquilla, Isla *i.* Venez. **142** F1
Blansko Czech Rep. **47** P6
Blantyre Malawi **99** D5
Blarney Rep. of Ireland **51** D6
Blaufelden Germany **53** J5
Blåviksjön Sweden **44** K4
Blaye France **56** D4
Blayney Australia **112** D4
Blaze, Point Australia **108** E3
Bleckede Germany **53** K1
Bleilochtalsperre *resr* Germany **53** L4
Blenheim Canada **134** E2
Blenheim N.Z. **113** D5
Blenheim Palace *tourist site* U.K. **49** F7
Blerick Neth. **52** G3
Blessington Lakes Rep. of Ireland **51** F4
Bletchley U.K. **49** G6
Blida Alg. **57** H5
Blies *r.* Germany **53** H5
Bligh Water *b.* Fiji **107** H3
Blind River Canada **122** E5
Bliss U.S.A. **126** E4
Blissfield U.S.A. **134** D3
Blitta Togo **96** D4
Blocher U.S.A. **134** C4
Block Island U.S.A. **135** J3
Block Island Sound *sea chan.* U.S.A. **135** J3
Bloemfontein S. Africa **101** H5
Bloemhof S. Africa **101** G4
Bloemhof Dam S. Africa **101** G4
Bloemhof Dam Nature Reserve S. Africa **101** G4
Blomberg Germany **53** J3
Blönduós Iceland **44** [inset]
Blongas Indon. **108** B2
Bloods Range *mts* Australia **109** E6
Bloodsworth Island U.S.A. **135** G4
Bloodvein *r.* Canada **121** L5
Bloody Foreland *pt* Rep. of Ireland **51** D2
Bloomer U.S.A. **130** F2
Bloomfield Canada **135** G2
Bloomfield *IA* U.S.A. **130** E3
Bloomfield *IN* U.S.A. **134** B4
Bloomfield *MO* U.S.A. **131** F4
Bloomfield *NM* U.S.A. **129** J3
Blooming Prairie U.S.A. **130** E3
Bloomington *IL* U.S.A. **130** F3
Bloomington *IN* U.S.A. **134** B4
Bloomington *MN* U.S.A. **130** E2
Bloomsburg U.S.A. **135** G3
Blossburg U.S.A. **135** G3
Blosseville Kyst *coastal area* Greenland **119** P3
Blouberg S. Africa **101** I2
Blouberg Nature Reserve S. Africa **101** I2
Blountstown U.S.A. **133** C6
Blountville U.S.A. **134** D5
Bloxham U.K. **49** F6
Blue *r.* Canada **120** D3
Blue *watercourse* U.S.A. **129** I5
Blue Bell Knoll *mt.* U.S.A. **129** H2
Blueberry *r.* Canada **120** F3
Blue Diamond U.S.A. **129** F3
Blue Earth U.S.A. **130** E3
Bluefield *VA* U.S.A. **132** D4
Bluefield *WV* U.S.A. **134** E5
Bluefields Nicaragua **137** H6
Blue Hills Turks and Caicos Is **129** F8
Blue Knob *hill* U.S.A. **135** F3
Blue Mesa Reservoir U.S.A. **129** J2
Blue Mountain *hill* Canada **123** K4
Blue Mountain India **83** H5
Blue Mountain Lake U.S.A. **135** H2
Blue Mountain Pass Lesotho **101** H5
Blue Mountains Australia **112** D4
Blue Mountains U.S.A. **126** D3
Blue Mountains National Park Australia **112** E4
Blue Nile *r.* Eth./Sudan **86** D6
also known as Ābay Wenz (Ethiopia), Bahr el Azraq (Sudan)
Bluenose Lake Canada **118** G3
Blue Ridge *GA* U.S.A. **133** C5
Blue Ridge *VA* U.S.A. **134** F5
Blue Ridge *mts* U.S.A. **134** E5
Blue Stack *hill* Rep. of Ireland **51** D3
Blue Stack Mts *hills* Rep. of Ireland **51** D3
Bluestone Lake U.S.A. **134** E5
Bluewater U.S.A. **129** J4
Bluff N.Z. **113** B8
Bluff U.S.A. **129** I3
Bluffdale U.S.A. **129** H1
Bluff Island *Hong Kong* China **73** [inset]
Bluff Knoll *mt.* Australia **109** B8
Bluffton *IN* U.S.A. **134** C3
Bluffton *OH* U.S.A. **134** D3
Blumenau Brazil **145** A4
Blustry Mountain Canada **126** C2
Blyde River Canyon Nature Reserve S. Africa **101** J3
Blyth Canada **134** E2
Blyth *England* U.K. **48** F3
Blyth *England* U.K. **48** F5
Blythe U.S.A. **129** F5
Blytheville U.S.A. **131** F5
Bø Norway **45** F7
Bo Sierra Leone **96** B4
Boa Esperança Brazil **145** B3
Bo'ai *Henan* China **77** G1
Bo'ai *Yunnan* China **76** E4
Boali Cent. Afr. Rep. **98** B3
Boalsert Neth. *see* **Bolsward**
Boane Moz. **101** K4
Boa Nova Brazil **145** C1
Boardman U.S.A. **134** E3
Boatlaname Botswana **101** G2
Boa Viagem Brazil **143** K5
Boa Vista Brazil **142** F3
Boa Vista *i.* Cape Verde **96** [inset]
Bobadah Australia **112** C4
Bobai China **77** F4
Bobaomby, Tanjona *c.* Madag. **99** E5
Bobbili India **84** D2
Bobcaygeon Canada **135** F1
Bobo-Dioulasso Burkina **96** C3
Bobotov Kuk *mt.* Serb. and Mont. *see* **Durmitor**
Bobriki Rus. Fed. *see* **Novomoskovsk**
Bobrinets Ukr. *see* **Bobrynets'**
Bobrov Rus. Fed. **43** I6
Bobrovitsa Ukr. *see* **Bobrovytsya**
Bobrovytsya Ukr. **43** F6
Bobruysk Belarus *see* **Babruysk**
Bobrynets' Ukr. **43** G6
Bobs Lake Canada **135** G1
Bobuk Sudan **86** D7
Bobures Venez. **142** D2
Boby *mt.* Madag. **99** E6
Boca de Macareo Venez. **142** F2
Boca do Acre Brazil **142** E5
Boca do Jari Brazil **143** H4
Bocaiúva Brazil **145** C2
Bocaranga Cent. Afr. Rep. **98** B3
Boca Raton U.S.A. **133** D7
Bocas del Toro Panama **137** H7
Bochnia Poland **47** R6
Bocholt Germany **52** G3
Bochum Germany **53** H3
Bochum S. Africa **101** I2
Bockenem Germany **53** K2
Bocoio Angola **99** B5
Bocoyna Mex. **127** G8
Boda Cent. Afr. Rep. **98** B3
Bodalla Australia **112** E6
Bodallin Australia **109** B7
Bodaybo Rus. Fed. **65** M4
Boddam U.K. **50** H3
Bode *r.* Germany **53** L3
Bodega Head *hd* U.S.A. **128** B2
Bodélé *reg.* Chad **97** E3
Boden Sweden **44** L4
Bodenham U.K. **49** E6
Bodensee *l.* Germany/Switz. *see* **Constance, Lake**
Bodenteich Germany **53** K2
Bodenwerder Germany **53** J3
Bodie U.S.A. **128** D2
Bodinayakkanur India **84** C4
Bodmin U.K. **49** C8
Bodmin Moor *moorland* U.K. **49** C8
Bodø Norway **44** I3
Bodoquena Brazil **143** G7
Bodoquena, Serra da *hills* Brazil **144** E2
Bodrum Turkey **59** L6
Bodträskfors Sweden **44** L3
Boechout Belgium **52** E3
Boende Dem. Rep. Congo **97** F5
Boerne U.S.A. **131** D6
Boeuf *r.* U.S.A. **131** F6
Boffa Guinea **96** B3
Bogalay Myanmar *see* **Bogale**
Bogale Myanmar **70** A3
Bogale *r.* Myanmar **70** A4
Bogalusa U.S.A. **131** F6
Bogan *r.* Australia **112** C2
Bogandé Burkina **96** C3
Bogan Gate Australia **112** C4
Bogani Nani Wartabone National Park Indon. **69** G6
Boğazlıyan Turkey **90** D3
Bogcang Zangbo *r.* China **83** F3
Bogda Shan *mts* China **80** G3
Boggabilla Australia **112** E2
Boggabri Australia **112** E3
Boggeragh Mts *hills* Rep. of Ireland **51** C5
Boghar Alg. **57** H6
Boghari Alg. *see* **Ksar el Boukhari**

Bognor Regis U.K. 49 G8
Bogodukhov Ukr. see Bohodukhiv
Bog of Allen reg. Rep. of Ireland 51 E4
Bogong, Mount Australia 112 C6
Bogopol' Rus. Fed. 74 D3
Bogor Indon. 68 D8
Bogoroditsk Rus. Fed. 43 H5
Bogorodsk Rus. Fed. 42 I4
Bogorodskoye *Khabarovskiy Kray* Rus. Fed. 74 F1
Bogorodskoye *Kirovskaya Oblast'* Rus. Fed. 42 K4

▶Bogotá Col. 142 D3
Capital of Colombia and 5th most populous city in South America.

Bogotol Rus. Fed. 64 J4
Bogoyavlenskoye Rus. Fed. see Pervomayskiy
Bogra Bangl. 83 G4
Boguchany Rus. Fed. 65 K4
Boguchar Rus. Fed. 43 I6
Bogué Mauritania 96 B3
Bo Hai g. China 73 L5
Bohain-en-Vermandois France 52 D5
Bohai Wan b. China 66 D4
Bohemia reg. Czech Rep. 47 N6
Bohemian Forest mts Germany see Böhmer Wald
Böhlen Germany 53 M3
Bohlokong S. Africa 101 I5
Böhme r. Germany 53 J2
Böhmer Wald mts Germany 53 M5
Bohmte Germany 53 I2
Bohodukhiv Ukr. 43 G6
Bohol i. Phil. 69 G5
Bohol Sea Phil. 69 G5
Böhöt Mongolia 73 J3
Bohu China 80 G3
Boiaçu Brazil 142 F4
Boichoko S. Africa 100 F5
Boigu Island Australia 69 K8
Boikhutso S. Africa 101 H4
Boileau, Cape Australia 108 C4
Boim Brazil 143 G4
Boipeba, Ilha i. Brazil 145 D1
Bois r. Brazil 145 A2
Bois Blanc Island U.S.A. 132 C2

▶Boise U.S.A. 126 D4
State capital of Idaho.

Boise City U.S.A. 131 C4
Boissevain Canada 121 K5
Boitumelong S. Africa 101 G4
Boizenburg Germany 53 K1
Bojd Iran 88 E3
Bojnūrd Iran 88 E2
Bokaak atoll Marshall Is see Taongi
Bokajan India 83 H4
Bokaro India 83 F5
Bokaro Reservoir India 83 F5
Bokatola Dem. Rep. Congo 98 B4
Boké Guinea 96 B3
Bokele Dem. Rep. Congo 98 C4
Bokhara r. Australia 112 C2
Bo Kheo Cambodia see Bâ Kêv
Boknafjorden sea chan. Norway 45 D7
Bokoko Dem. Rep. Congo 98 C3
Bokoro Chad 97 E3
Bokovskaya Rus. Fed. 43 I6
Bokspits S. Africa 100 E4
Boktor Rus. Fed. 74 E2
Bokurdak Turkm. see Bakhardok
Bol Chad 97 E3
Bolaiti Dem. Rep. Congo 97 F5
Bolama Guinea-Bissau 96 B3
Bolangir India 84 D1
Bolan Pass Pak. 89 G4
Bolbec France 56 E2
Bole China 80 F3
Bole Ghana 96 C4
Boleko Dem. Rep. Congo 98 B4
Bolen Rus. Fed. 74 D2
Bolgar Rus. Fed. 43 K5
Bolgatanga Ghana 96 C3
Bolgrad Ukr. see Bolhrad
Bolhrad Ukr. 59 M2
Boli China 74 C3
Bolia Dem. Rep. Congo 98 B4
Boliden Sweden 44 L4
Bolingbrook U.S.A. 134 A3
Bolintin-Vale Romania 59 K2
Bolívar Peru 142 C5
Bolivar NY U.S.A. 135 F2
Bolivar TN U.S.A. 131 F5
Bolívar, Pico mt. Venez. 142 D2
Bolivia Cuba 133 E8

▶Bolivia country S. America 142 E7
5th largest country in South America.
South America 9, 140–141

Bolkhov Rus. Fed. 43 H5
Bollène France 56 G4
Bollnäs Sweden 45 J6
Bollon Australia 112 C2
Bollstabruk Sweden 44 J5
Bolmen l. Sweden 45 H8
Bolobo Dem. Rep. Congo 98 B4
Bologna Italy 58 D2
Bolognesi Peru 142 D5
Bologoye Rus. Fed. 42 G4
Bolokanang S. Africa 101 G5
Bolomba Dem. Rep. Congo 98 B3
Bolon' Rus. Fed. see Achan
Bolovens, Phouphieng plat. Laos 70 D4
Bolpur India 83 F5
Bolsena, Lago di l. Italy 58 D3
Bol'shakovo Rus. Fed. 45 L9
Bol'shaya Chernigovka Rus. Fed. 41 Q5
Bol'shaya Glushitsa Rus. Fed. 43 K5
Bol'shaya Imandra, Ozero l. Rus. Fed. 44 R3
Bol'shaya Martinovka Rus. Fed. 39 I7
Bol'shaya Tsarevshchina Rus. Fed. see Volzhskiy
Bol'shenarymskoye Kazakh. 80 F2
Bol'shevik, Ostrov i. Rus. Fed. 65 L2
Bol'shezemel'skaya Tundra lowland Rus. Fed. 42 L2
Bol'shiye Barsuki, Peski des. Kazakh. 80 A2
Bol'shiye Chirki Rus. Fed. 42 J3
Bol'shiye Kozly Rus. Fed. 42 H2
Bol'shoy Aluy r. Rus. Fed. 65 Q3
Bol'shoy Begichev, Ostrov i. Rus. Fed. 153 E2
Bol'shoye Murashkino Rus. Fed. 42 J5
Bol'shoy Irgiz r. Rus. Fed. 43 J6
Bol'shoy Kamen' Rus. Fed. 74 D4
Bol'shoy Kavkaz mts Asia/Europe see Caucasus
Bol'shoy Kundysh r. Rus. Fed. 42 J4
Bol'shoy Lyakhovskiy, Ostrov i. Rus. Fed. 65 P2
Bol'shoy Tokmak Kyrg. see Tokmok
Bol'shoy Tokmak Ukr. see Tokmak
Bolsward Neth. 52 F1
Bolton Canada 134 F2
Bolton U.K. 48 E5
Bolu Turkey 59 N4
Boluntay China 83 H1
Boluo China 77 G4
Bolus Head hd Rep. of Ireland 51 B6
Bolvadin Turkey 59 N5
Bolzano Italy 58 D1
Boma Dem. Rep. Congo 99 B4
Bomaderry Australia 112 E5
Bombala Australia 112 D6
Bombay India see Mumbai
Bombay Beach U.S.A. 129 F5
Bomberai, Semenanjung pen. Indon. 69 I7
Bomboma Dem. Rep. Congo 98 B3
Bom Comércio Brazil 142 E5
Bomdila India 83 H4
Bomi China 76 B2
Bomili Dem. Rep. Congo 98 C3
Bom Jardim Brazil 145 D1
Bom Jardim de Goiás Brazil 145 A2
Bom Jesus Brazil 145 A5
Bom Jesus da Gurgueia, Serra do hills Brazil 143 J5
Bom Jesus da Lapa Brazil 145 C1
Bom Jesus do Norte Brazil 145 C3
Bømlo i. Norway 45 D7
Bomokandi r. Dem. Rep. Congo 98 C3
Bom Retiro Brazil 145 A4
Bom Sucesso Brazil 145 B3
Bon, Cap c. Tunisia 58 D6
Bon, Ko i. Thai. 71 B5
Bona Alg. see Annaba
Bona, Mount U.S.A. 120 A2
Bonāb Iran 88 B2
Bon Air U.S.A. 135 G5
Bonaire i. Neth. Antilles 137 K6
Bonanza Peak U.S.A. 126 C2
Bonaparte Archipelago is Australia 108 D3
Bonaparte Lake Canada 120 F5
Bonar Bridge U.K. 50 E3
Bonavista Canada 123 L4
Bonavista Bay Canada 123 L4
Bonchester Bridge U.K. 50 G5
Bondo Dem. Rep. Congo 98 C3
Bondokodi Indon. 68 F8
Bondoukou Côte d'Ivoire 96 C4
Bonduel U.S.A. 134 A1
Bondyuzhskiy Rus. Fed. see Mendeleyevsk
Bône Alg. see Annaba
Bone, Teluk b. Indon. 69 G8
Bönen Germany 53 H3
Bonerate, Kepulauan is Indon. 108 C1
Bo'ness U.K. 50 F4

▶Bonete, Cerro mt. Arg. 144 C3
3rd highest mountain in South America.

Bonga Eth. 98 D3
Bongaigaon India 83 G4
Bongandanga Dem. Rep. Congo 98 C3
Bongani S. Africa 100 F5
Bongao Phil. 68 F5
Bongba China 82 E2
Bong Co l. China 83 G3
Bongo, Massif des mts Cent. Afr. Rep. 98 C3
Bongo, Serra do mts Angola 99 B4
Bongolava mts Madag. 99 E5
Bongor Chad 97 E3
Bông Sơn Vietnam 71 E4
Bonham U.S.A. 131 D5
Bonheiden Belgium 52 E3
Boni Mali 96 C3
Bonifacio Corsica France 56 I6
Bonifacio, Bocche di strait France/Italy see Bonifacio, Strait of
Bonifacio, Bouches de strait France/Italy see Bonifacio, Strait of
Bonifacio, Strait of France/Italy 56 I6

▶Bonin Islands Japan 75 F8
Part of Japan.

▶Bonn Germany 52 H4
Former capital of Germany.

Bonna Germany see Bonn
Bonnåsjøen Norway 44 I3
Bonners Ferry U.S.A. 126 D2
Bonnet, Lac du resr Canada 117 M5
Bonneville France 56 H3
Bonneville Salt Flats U.S.A. 129 G1
Bonnières-sur-Seine France 52 B5
Bonnie Rock Australia 109 B7
Bonnieville U.S.A. 134 C5
Bonnyrigg U.K. 50 F5
Bonnyville Canada 121 I4
Bonobono Phil. 68 F5
Bonom Mhai mt. Vietnam 71 D5
Bononia Italy see Bologna
Bonorva Sardinia Italy 58 C4
Bonshaw Australia 112 E2
Bontebok National Park S. Africa 100 E8
Bonthe Sierra Leone 96 B4
Bontoc Phil. 77 I5
Bontosunggu Indon. 68 F8
Bontrug S. Africa 101 G7
Bonvouloir Islands P.N.G. 110 E1
Bonwapitse Botswana 101 H2
Boo, Kepulauan is Indon. 69 H7
Book Cliffs ridge U.S.A. 129 I2
Booker U.S.A. 131 C4
Boolba Australia 112 D2
Booligal Australia 112 B4
Boomer U.S.A. 134 E4
Boomi Australia 112 D2
Boon U.S.A. 134 C1
Boonah Australia 112 F1
Boone CO U.S.A. 127 G5
Boone IA U.S.A. 130 E3
Boone NC U.S.A. 132 D4
Boone Lake U.S.A. 134 D5
Boones Mill U.S.A. 134 F5
Booneville AR U.S.A. 131 E5
Booneville KY U.S.A. 134 D5
Booneville MS U.S.A. 131 F5
Böön Tsagaan Nuur salt l. Mongolia 80 I2
Boonville CA U.S.A. 128 B2
Boonville IN U.S.A. 134 B4
Boonville MO U.S.A. 130 E4
Boonville NY U.S.A. 135 H2
Boorabin National Park Australia 109 C7
Boorama Somalia 98 E3
Booroorban Australia 112 B5
Boorowa Australia 112 D5
Boort Australia 112 A6
Boothby, Cape Antarctica 152 D2
Boothia, Gulf of Canada 119 J3
Boothia Peninsula Canada 119 I2
Bootle U.K. 48 E5
Booué Gabon 98 B4
Boppard Germany 53 H4
Boqê China 83 G3
Boqueirão, Serra do hills Brazil 143 J6
Bor Czech Rep. 53 M5
Bor Rus. Fed. 42 J4
Bor Sudan 97 G4
Bor Turkey 90 D3
Bor Serb. and Mont. 59 J2
Boraha, Nosy i. Madag. 99 F5
Borah Peak U.S.A. 126 E3
Borai India 84 D1
Borakalalo Nature Reserve S. Africa 101 H3
Boran Kazakh. see Buran
Boraphet, Bung l. Thai. 70 C4
Boraphet, Nong l. Thai. see Boraphet, Bung
Borås Sweden 45 H8
Borasambar India 84 D1
Borāzjān Iran 88 C4
Borba Brazil 143 G4
Borba China 76 C1
Borborema, Planalto da plat. Brazil 143 K5
Borchen Germany 53 I3
Borçka Turkey 91 F2
Bor Dağı mt. Turkey 59 M6
Bordeaux France 56 D4
Borden Island Canada 119 G2
Borden Peninsula Canada 119 J2
Border Ranges National Park Australia 112 F2
Borðeyri Iceland 44 [inset]
Bordj Bou Arréridj Alg. 57 I5
Bordj Bounaama Alg. 57 G6
Bordj Flye Ste-Marie Alg. 96 C2
Bordj Messaouda Alg. 54 F5
Bordj Mokhtar Alg. 96 D2
Bordj Omar Driss Alg. see Bordj Omer Driss
Bordj Omer Driss Alg. 96 D2
Boreas Abyssal Plain sea feature Arctic Ocean 153 H1
Borel r. Canada 123 H2
Borgå Fin. see Porvoo
Borgarfjörður Iceland 44 [inset]
Borgarnes Iceland 44 [inset]
Børgefjell Nasjonalpark nat. park Norway 44 H4
Borger U.S.A. 131 C5
Borgholm Sweden 45 J8
Borgne, Lake b. U.S.A. 131 F6
Borgo San Lorenzo Italy 58 D3
Bori India 84 C1
Bori r. India 82 C5
Borikhan Laos 70 C3
Borislav Ukr. see Boryslav
Borisoglebsk Rus. Fed. 43 I6
Borisov Belarus see Barysaw
Borisovka Rus. Fed. 43 H6
Borispol' Ukr. see Boryspil'
Bo River Post Sudan 97 F4
Borja Peru 142 C4
Borken Germany 52 G3
Borkenes Norway 44 J2
Borkovskaya Rus. Fed. 42 K2
Borkum Germany 52 G1
Borkum i. Germany 52 G1
Borlänge Sweden 45 I6
Borlaug Norway 45 E6
Borlu Turkey 59 M5
Borna Germany 53 M3
Born-Berge hill Germany 53 K3
Borndiep sea chan. Neth. 52 F1
Borne Neth. 52 G2

▶Borneo i. Asia 68 E6
Largest island in Asia and 3rd in the world.
Asia 60–61
World 12–13

Bornholm county Denmark 153 H3
Bornholm i. Denmark 45 I9
Bornova Turkey 59 L5
Borodino Rus. Fed. 64 J3
Borodinskoye Rus. Fed. 45 P6
Borogontsy Rus. Fed. 65 O3
Borohoro Shan mts China 80 F3
Borok-Sulezhskiy Rus. Fed. 42 H4
Boromo Burkina 96 C3
Boron U.S.A. 128 E4
Borondi India 84 D2
Boroughbridge U.K. 48 F4
Borovichi Rus. Fed. 42 G4
Borovoy *Kirovskaya Oblast'* Rus. Fed. 42 K4
Borovoy *Respublika Kareliya* Rus. Fed. 44 R4
Borovoy *Respublika Komi* Rus. Fed. 42 L3
Borpeta India see Barpeta
Borrisokane Rep. of Ireland 51 D5
Borroloola Australia 110 B3
Børsa Norway 44 G5
Borşa Romania 43 E7
Borshchiv Ukr. 43 E6
Borshchovochnyy Khrebet mts Rus. Fed. 73 J3
Bortala China see Bole
Borton U.S.A. 134 B4
Borūjen Iran 88 C4
Borūjerd Iran 88 C3
Borun Iran 88 E3
Borve U.K. 50 C3
Boryslav Ukr. 43 D6
Boryspil' Ukr. 43 F6
Borzna Ukr. 43 G6
Borzya Rus. Fed. 73 L2
Bosanska Dubica Bos.-Herz. 58 G2
Bosanska Gradiška Bos.-Herz. 58 G2
Bosanska Krupa Bos.-Herz. 58 G2
Bosanski Novi Bos.-Herz. 58 G2
Bosansko Grahovo Bos.-Herz. 58 G2
Boscawen Island Tonga see Niuatoputopu
Bose China 76 E4
Boshof S. Africa 101 G5
Boshruyeh Iran 88 E3
Bosna i Hercegovina country Europe see Bosnia-Herzegovina
Bosna Saray Bos.-Herz. see Sarajevo
▶Bosnia-Herzegovina country Europe 58 G2
Europe 5, 38–39
Bosobogolo Pan salt pan Botswana 100 F3
Bosobolo Dem. Rep. Congo 98 B3
Bōsō-hantō pen. Japan 75 F6
Bosporus strait Turkey 59 M4
Bossaga Turkm. see Basaga
Bossangoa Cent. Afr. Rep. 98 B3
Bossembélé Cent. Afr. Rep. 98 B3
Bossier City U.S.A. 131 E5
Bossiesvlei Namibia 100 C3
Bossut, Cape Australia 108 C4
Bostan China 83 F1
Bostān Iran 88 B4
Bostan Pak. 89 G4
Bostāneh, Ra's-e pt Iran 88 D5
Bosten Hu l. China 80 G3
Boston U.K. 49 G6

▶Boston U.S.A. 135 J2
State capital of Massachusetts.

Boston Mountains U.S.A. 131 E5
Boston Spa U.K. 48 F5
Boswell U.S.A. 134 B3
Botad India 82 B5
Botany Bay Australia 112 E4
Botev mt. Bulg. 59 K3
Botevgrad Bulg. 59 J3
Bothaville S. Africa 101 H4
Bothnia, Gulf of Fin./Sweden 45 K6
Bothwell Canada 134 E2
Botkins U.S.A. 134 C3
Botlikh Rus. Fed. 91 G2
Botoşani Romania 43 E7
Botou China 73 L5
Bô Trach Vietnam 70 D3
Botshabelo S. Africa 101 H5
▶Botswana country Africa 99 C6
Africa 7, 94–95
Botte Donato, Monte mt. Italy 58 G5
Bottenviken g. Fin./Sweden see Bothnia, Gulf of
Bottesford U.K. 48 G5
Bottrop Germany 52 G3
Botucatu Brazil 145 A3
Botuporã Brazil 145 C1
Botwood Canada 123 L4
Bouaflé Côte d'Ivoire 96 C4
Bouaké Côte d'Ivoire 96 C4
Bouar Cent. Afr. Rep. 98 B3
Bouârfa Morocco 54 D5
Bouba Ndjida, Parc National de nat. park Cameroon 97 E4
Bouca Cent. Afr. Rep. 98 B3
Boucaut Bay Australia 108 F3
Bouchain France 52 D4
Bouctouche Canada 123 I5
Boudh India 84 E1
Bougaa Alg. 57 I5
Bougainville, Cape Australia 104 D3
Bougainville Island P.N.G. 106 F2
Bougainville Reef Australia 110 D2
Boughessa Mali 96 D3
Bougie Alg. see Bejaïa
Bougouni Mali 96 C3
Bougtob Alg. 54 E5
Bouillon Belgium 52 F5
Bouira Alg. 57 H5
Bou Izakarn Morocco 96 C2
Boujdour W. Sahara 96 B2
Boulder Australia 109 C7
Boulder CO U.S.A. 126 G4
Boulder MT U.S.A. 126 E3
Boulder UT U.S.A. 129 H3
Boulder Canyon gorge U.S.A. 129 F3
Boulder City U.S.A. 129 F4
Boulevard U.S.A. 128 E5
Boulia Australia 110 B4
Boulogne France see Boulogne-sur-Mer
Boulogne-Billancourt France 52 C6
Boulogne-sur-Mer France 52 B4
Boumerdes Alg. 57 H5
Bouna Côte d'Ivoire 96 C4
Bou Naceur, Jbel mt. Morocco 54 D5
Boû Nâga Mauritania 96 B3
Boundary Mountains U.S.A. 135 J1
Boundary Peak U.S.A. 128 D3
Boundiali Côte d'Ivoire 96 C4
Boundji Congo 98 B4
Boun Nua Laos 70 C2
Bountiful U.S.A. 129 H1
Bounty Islands N.Z. 107 H6
Bounty Trough sea feature S. Pacific Ocean 150 H9
Bourail New Caledonia 107 G4
Bourbon reg. France see Bourbonnais
Bourbon terr. Indian Ocean see Réunion
Bourbon U.S.A. 134 B3
Bourbonnais reg. France 56 F3
Bourem Mali 96 C3
Bouressa Mali see Boughessa
Bourg-Achard France 49 H9
Bourganeuf France 56 E4
Bourg-en-Bresse France 56 G3
Bourges France 56 F3
Bourget Canada 135 H1
Bourgogne reg. France see Burgundy
Bourgogne, Canal de France 52 G3
Bourke Australia 112 B3
Bourne U.K. 49 G6
Bournemouth U.K. 49 F8
Bourtoutou Chad 97 F3
Bou Saâda Alg. 57 I6
Bou Salem Tunisia 58 C6
Bouse U.S.A. 129 F5
Bouse Wash watercourse U.S.A. 129 F4
Boussu Belgium 52 D4
Boutilimit Mauritania 96 B3
Bouvet Island terr. S. Atlantic Ocean see Bouvetøya

▶Bouvetøya terr. S. Atlantic Ocean 148 I9
Dependency of Norway.

Bouy France 52 E5
Bova Marina Italy 58 F6
Bovenden Germany 53 J3
Bow r. Alta Canada 121 I5
Bowa China see Muli
Bowbells U.S.A. 130 C1
Bowden U.S.A. 134 F4
Bowditch atoll Tokelau see Fakaofo
Bowen Australia 110 E4
Bowen, Mount Australia 112 D6
Bowenville Australia 112 E1
Bowers Ridge sea feature Bering Sea 150 H2
Bowie Australia 110 D4
Bowie AZ U.S.A. 129 I5
Bowie TX U.S.A. 131 D5
Bow Island Canada 121 I5
Bowkan Iran 88 B2
Bowling Green KY U.S.A. 134 B5
Bowling Green MO U.S.A. 130 F4
Bowling Green OH U.S.A. 134 D3
Bowling Green VA U.S.A. 135 G4
Bowling Green Bay National Park Australia 110 D3
Bowman U.S.A. 130 C2
Bowman, Mount Canada 126 C2
Bowman Island Antarctica 152 F2
Bowman Peninsula Antarctica 152 L2
Bowmore U.K. 50 C5
Bowo China see Bomi
Bowral Australia 112 E5
Bowser Lake Canada 120 D3
Boxberg Germany 53 J5
Box Elder U.S.A. 130 C2
Box Elder r. U.S.A. 130 C2
Boxtel Neth. 52 F3
Boyabat Turkey 90 D2
Boyana tourist site Bulg. 59 J3
Boyang China 77 H2
Boyd r. Australia 112 F2
Boyd Lagoon salt flat Australia 109 D6
Boyd Lake Canada 121 K2
Boydton U.S.A. 135 F5
Boyers U.S.A. 134 F3
Boykins U.S.A. 135 G5
Boyle Canada 121 H4
Boyle Rep. of Ireland 51 D4
Boyne r. Rep. of Ireland 51 F4
Boyne City U.S.A. 134 C1
Boysen Reservoir U.S.A. 126 F4
Boysun Uzbek. see Baysun
Boyuibe Bol. 142 F8
Böyük Qafqaz mts Asia/Europe see Caucasus

▶Bozcaada i. Turkey 59 L5
Most westerly point of Asia.

Bozdağ mt. Turkey 59 L5
Bozdağ mt. Turkey 85 C1
Boz Dağları mts Turkey 59 L5
Bozdoğan Turkey 59 M6
Bozeat U.K. 49 G6
Bozeman U.S.A. 126 F3
Bozen Italy see Bolzano
Bozhou China 77 G1
Bozoum Cent. Afr. Rep. 98 B3
Bozova Turkey 90 E3
Bozqūsh, Kūh-e mts Iran 88 B2
Bozüyük Turkey 59 N5
Bozyazı Turkey 85 A1
Bra Italy 58 B2
Brač i. Croatia 58 G3
Bracadale U.K. 50 C3
Bracadale, Loch b. U.K. 50 C3
Bracara Port. see Braga
Bracciano, Lago di l. Italy 58 E3
Bracebridge Canada 134 F1
Brachet, Lac au l. Canada 123 H4
Bräcke Sweden 44 I5
Brackenheim Germany 53 J5
Brackettville U.S.A. 131 C6
Bracknell U.K. 49 G7
Bradano r. Italy 58 G4
Bradenton U.S.A. 133 D7
Bradford Canada 134 F1
Bradford U.K. 48 F5
Bradford OH U.S.A. 134 C3
Bradford PA U.S.A. 135 F3
Bradley U.S.A. 134 B3
Brady U.S.A. 131 D6
Brady Glacier U.S.A. 120 B3
Brae U.K. 50 [inset]
Braemar U.K. 50 F3
Braga Port. 57 B3
Bragado Arg. 144 D5
Bragança Brazil 143 I4
Bragança Port. 57 C3
Bragança Paulista Brazil 145 B3
Brahin Belarus 43 F6
Brahlstorf Germany 53 K1
Brahmanbaria Bangl. 83 G5
Brahmapur India 84 E2
Brahmaputra r. Asia 83 H4
also known as Dihang (India) or Jamuna (Bangladesh) or Siang (India) or Yarlung Zangbo (China)
Brahmaur India 82 D2
Brăila Romania 59 L2
Braine France 52 D5
Braine-le-Comte Belgium 52 E4
Brainerd U.S.A. 130 E2
Braintree U.K. 49 H7
Braithwaite Point Australia 108 F2
Brak r. S. Africa 101 I2
Brake (Unterweser) Germany 53 I1
Brakel Belgium 52 D4
Brakel Germany 53 J3
Brakwater Namibia 100 C2
Bramfield Australia 109 F8
Bramming Denmark 45 F9
Brämön i. Sweden 44 J5
Brampton Canada 134 F2
Brampton *England* U.K. 48 E4
Brampton *England* U.K. 49 I6
Bramsche Germany 53 I2
Bramwell Australia 110 C2
Brancaster U.K. 49 H6
Branch Canada 123 L5
Branco r. Brazil 142 F4
Brandberg mt. Namibia 99 B6
Brandbu Norway 45 G6
Brande Denmark 45 F9
Brandenburg Germany 53 M2
Brandenburg land Germany 53 N2
Brandenburg U.S.A. 134 B5
Brandfort S. Africa 101 H5
Brandis Germany 53 N3
Brandon Canada 121 L5
Brandon U.K. 49 H6
Brandon MS U.S.A. 131 F5
Brandon VT U.S.A. 135 I2
Brandon Head hd Rep. of Ireland 51 B5
Brandon Mountain hill Rep. of Ireland 51 B5
Brandvlei S. Africa 100 E6
Braniewo Poland 47 Q3
Bransfield Strait Antarctica 152 L2
Branson U.S.A. 131 C4
Brantford Canada 134 E2
Branxton Australia 112 E4
Bras d'Or Lake Canada 123 J5
Brasil country S. America see Brazil
Brasil, Planalto do plat. Brazil 143 J7
Brasileia Brazil 142 E6

▶Brasília Brazil 145 B1
Capital of Brazil.

Brasília de Minas Brazil 145 B2
Braslav Belarus see Braslaw
Braslaw Belarus 45 O9
Braşov Romania 59 K2
Brassey, Mount Australia 109 F5
Brassey Range hills Australia 109 C6
Brasstown Bald mt. U.S.A. 133 D5

▶Bratislava Slovakia 47 P6
Capital of Slovakia.

Bratsk Rus. Fed. 72 I1
Bratskoye Vodokhranilishche resr Rus. Fed. 72 I1
Brattleboro U.S.A. 135 I2
Braunau am Inn Austria 47 N6
Braunfels Germany 53 I4
Braunlage Germany 53 K3
Braunsbedra Germany 53 L3
Braunschweig Germany 53 K2
Brava i. Cape Verde 96 [inset]
Brave U.S.A. 134 E4
Bråviken inlet Sweden 45 J7
Bravo, Cerro mt. Bol. 142 F7
Bravo del Norte, Río r. Mex./U.S.A. 127 G7 see Rio Grande
Brawley U.S.A. 129 F5
Bray Rep. of Ireland 51 F4
Bray Island Canada 119 K3
Brazeau r. Canada 120 H4
Brazeau, Mount Canada 120 G4

▶Brazil country S. America 143 G5
Largest country in South America and 5th in the world. Most populous country in South America and 5th in the world.
South America 9, 140–141

Brazil U.S.A. 134 B4
Brazil Basin sea feature S. Atlantic Ocean 148 G7
Brazos r. U.S.A. 131 E6

▶Brazzaville Congo 99 B4
Capital of Congo.

Brčko Bos.-Herz. 58 H2
Bré Rep. of Ireland see Bray
Breadalbane Australia 110 B4
Breaksea Sound inlet N.Z. 113 A7
Bream Bay N.Z. 113 E2
Brechfa U.K. 49 C7
Brechin U.K. 50 G4
Brecht Belgium 52 E3
Breckenridge MI U.S.A. 134 C2
Breckenridge MN U.S.A. 130 D2
Breckenridge TX U.S.A. 131 D5
Břeclav Czech Rep. 47 P6
Brecon U.K. 49 D7
Brecon Beacons reg. U.K. 49 D7
Brecon Beacons National Park U.K. 49 D7
Breda Neth. 52 E3
Bredasdorp S. Africa 100 E8
Bredbo Australia 112 D5
Breddin Germany 53 M2
Bredevoort Neth. 52 G3
Bredviken Sweden 44 I3
Bree Belgium 52 F3
Breed U.S.A. 134 A1
Bregenz Austria 47 L7
Breiðafjörður b. Iceland 44 [inset]
Breiðdalsvík Iceland 44 [inset]
Breidenbach Germany 53 I4
Breien U.S.A. 130 C2
Breitenfelde Germany 53 K1
Breitengüßbach Germany 53 K5
Breiter Luzinsee l. Germany 53 N1
Breivikbotn Norway 44 M1
Breizh reg. France see Brittany
Brejo Velho Brazil 145 C1
Brekstad Norway 44 F5
Bremen Germany 53 I1

Bremen land Germany 53 I1
Bremen IN U.S.A. 134 B3
Bremen OH U.S.A. 134 D4
Bremer Bay Australia 109 B8
Bremerhaven Germany 53 I1
Bremer Range hills Australia 105 C8
Bremersdorp Swaziland see Manzini
Bremervörde Germany 53 J1
Bremm Germany 52 H4
Brenham U.S.A. 131 D6
Brenna Norway 44 H3
Brennero, Passo di pass Austria/Italy see Brenner Pass
Brennerpaß pass Austria/Italy see Brenner Pass
Brenner Pass Austria/Italy 58 D1
Brentwood U.K. 49 H7
Brescia Italy 58 D2
Breslau Poland see Wrocław
Bresle r. France 52 B4
Brésolles, Lac l. Canada 123 H3
Bressanone Italy 58 D1
Bressay i. U.K. 50 [inset]
Bressuire France 56 D3
Brest Belarus 45 M10
Brest France 56 B2
Brest-Litovsk Belarus see Brest
Bretagne reg. France see Brittany
Breteuil France 52 C5
Brétigny-sur-Orge France 52 C6
Breton Canada 120 H4
Breton Sound b. U.S.A. 131 F6
Brett, Cape N.Z. 113 E2
Bretten Germany 53 I5
Bretton U.K. 48 E5
Breueh, Pulau i. Indon. 71 A6
Brevard U.S.A. 133 D5
Breves Brazil 143 H4
Brewarrina Australia 112 C2
Brewer U.S.A. 132 G2
Brewster NE U.S.A. 130 D3
Brewster OH U.S.A. 134 E3
Brewster, Kap c. Greenland see Kangikajik
Brewster, Lake imp. l. Australia 112 B4
Brewton U.S.A. 133 C6
Breyten S. Africa 101 I4
Breytovo Rus. Fed. 42 H4
Brezhnev Rus. Fed. see Naberezhnyye Chelny
Brezno Slovakia 47 Q6
Brezovo Bulg. 59 K3
Brezovo Polje hill Croatia 58 G2
Bria Cent. Afr. Rep. 98 C3
Briançon France 56 H4
Brian Head mt. U.S.A. 129 G3
Bribbaree Australia 112 C5
Bribie Island Australia 112 F1
Briceni Moldova 43 E6
Brichany Moldova see Briceni
Brichen' Moldova see Briceni
Bridgend U.K. 49 D7
Bridge of Orchy U.K. 50 E4
Bridgeport CA U.S.A. 128 D2
Bridgeport CT U.S.A. 135 I3
Bridgeport IL U.S.A. 134 B4
Bridgeport NE U.S.A. 130 C3
Bridger Peak U.S.A. 126 G4
Bridgeton U.S.A. 135 H4
Bridgetown Australia 109 B8

▶Bridgetown Barbados 137 M6
Capital of Barbados.

Bridgetown Canada 123 I5
Bridgeville U.S.A. 135 H4
Bridgewater Canada 123 I5
Bridgewater U.S.A. 135 H2
Bridgnorth U.K. 49 E6
Bridgton U.S.A. 135 J1
Bridgwater U.K. 49 D7
Bridgwater Bay U.K. 49 D7
Bridlington U.K. 48 G4
Bridlington Bay U.K. 48 G4
Bridport Australia 111 [inset]
Bridport U.K. 49 E8
Brie reg. France 56 F2
Brie-Comte-Robert France 52 C6
Brieg Poland see Brzeg
Briery Knob mt. U.S.A. 134 E4
Brig Switz. 56 H3
Brigg U.K. 48 G5
Brigham City U.S.A. 126 E4
Brightlingsea U.K. 49 I7
Brighton Canada 135 G1
Brighton U.K. 49 G8
Brighton CO U.S.A. 126 G5
Brighton MI U.S.A. 134 D2
Brighton NY U.S.A. 135 G2
Brighton WV U.S.A. 134 D4
Brignoles France 56 H5
Brikama Gambia 96 B3
Brillion U.S.A. 134 A1
Brilon Germany 53 I3
Brindisi Italy 58 G4
Brinkley U.S.A. 131 F5
Brion, Île i. Canada 123 J5
Brioude France 56 F4
Brisay Canada 123 H3

▶Brisbane Australia 112 F1
State capital of Queensland and 3rd most populous city in Oceania.

Brisbane Ranges National Park Australia 112 B6
Bristol U.K. 49 E7
Bristol CT U.S.A. 135 I3
Bristol FL U.S.A. 133 C6
Bristol NH U.S.A. 135 J2
Bristol RI U.S.A. 135 J3
Bristol TN U.S.A. 134 D5
Bristol VT U.S.A. 135 I1
Bristol Bay U.S.A. 118 B4
Bristol Channel est. U.K. 49 C7
Bristol Lake U.S.A. 129 F4
Britannia Island New Caledonia see Maré
British Antarctic Territory reg. Antarctica 152 L2
British Columbia prov. Canada 120 F5
British Empire Range mts Canada 119 J1
British Guiana country S. America see Guyana
British Honduras country Central America see Belize

▶British Indian Ocean Territory terr. Indian Ocean 149 M6
United Kingdom Overseas Territory.

British Solomon Islands country S. Pacific Ocean see Solomon Islands
Brito Godins Angola see Kiwaba N'zogi
Brits S. Africa 101 H3
Britstown S. Africa 100 F6
Brittany reg. France 56 C2
Britton U.S.A. 130 D2
Brive-la-Gaillarde France 56 E4
Briviesca Spain 57 E2
Brixham U.K. 49 D8
Brixia Italy see Brescia
Brlik Kazakh. 80 D3
Brno Czech Rep. 47 P6
Broach India see Bharuch
Broad r. U.S.A. 133 D5
Broadalbin U.S.A. 135 H2
Broad Arrow Australia 109 C7
Broadback r. Canada 122 F4
Broad Bay U.K. see Tuath, Loch a'
Broadford Australia 112 B6
Broadford Rep. of Ireland 51 D5
Broadford U.K. 50 D3
Broad Law hill U.K. 50 F5
Broadmere Australia 110 A3
Broad Peak China/Jammu and Kashmir 89 J3
Broad Sound sea chan. Australia 110 E4
Broadstairs U.K. 49 I7
Broadus U.S.A. 126 G3
Broadview Canada 121 K5
Broadway U.S.A. 135 F4
Broadwood N.Z. 113 D2
Brochet Canada 121 K3
Brochet, Lac l. Canada 121 K3
Brocken mt. Germany 53 K3
Brockman, Mount Australia 108 B5
Brockport NY U.S.A. 135 G2
Brockport PA U.S.A. 135 F3
Brockton U.S.A. 135 J2
Brockville Canada 135 H1
Brockway U.S.A. 135 F3
Brodeur Peninsula Canada 119 J2
Brodhead U.S.A. 134 C5
Brodick U.K. 50 D5
Brodnica Poland 47 Q4
Brody Ukr. 43 E6
Broken Arrow U.S.A. 131 E4
Broken Bay Australia 112 E4
Broken Bow NE U.S.A. 130 D3
Broken Bow OK U.S.A. 131 E5
Brokenhead r. Canada 121 L5
Broken Hill Australia 111 C6
Broken Hill Zambia see Kabwe
Broken Plateau sea feature Indian Ocean 149 O8
Brokopondo Suriname 143 G2
Brokopondo Stuwmeer resr Suriname see Professor van Blommestein Meer
Bromberg Poland see Bydgoszcz
Brome Germany 53 K2
Bromsgrove U.K. 49 E6
Brønderslev Denmark 45 F8
Brønnøysund Norway 44 H4
Bronson FL U.S.A. 133 D6
Bronson MI U.S.A. 134 C3
Brooke U.K. 49 I6
Brookfield U.S.A. 134 A2
Brookhaven U.S.A. 131 F6
Brookings OR U.S.A. 126 B4
Brookings SD U.S.A. 130 D2
Brookline U.S.A. 135 J2
Brooklyn U.S.A. 134 C2
Brooklyn Park U.S.A. 130 E2
Brookneal U.S.A. 135 F5
Brooks Canada 121 I5
Brooks Brook Canada 120 C2
Brooks Range mts U.S.A. 118 D3
Brookston U.S.A. 134 B3
Brooksville FL U.S.A. 133 D6
Brooksville KY U.S.A. 134 C4
Brookton Australia 109 B8
Brookville IN U.S.A. 134 C4
Brookville PA U.S.A. 134 F3
Brookville Lake U.S.A. 134 C4
Broom, Loch inlet U.K. 50 D3
Broome Australia 108 C4
Brora U.K. 50 F2
Brora r. U.K. 50 F2
Brösarp Sweden 45 I9
Brosna r. Rep. of Ireland 51 E4
Brosville U.S.A. 134 F5
Brothers is India 71 A5
Brough U.K. 48 E4
Brough Ness pt U.K. 50 G2
Broughshane U.K. 51 F3
Broughton Island Canada see Qikiqtarjuaq
Broughton Islands Australia 112 F4
Brovary Ukr. 43 F6
Brovinia Australia 111 E5
Brovst Denmark 45 F8
Brown City U.S.A. 134 D2
Brown Deer U.S.A. 134 B2
Browne Range hills Australia 109 D6
Brownfield U.S.A. 131 C5
Browning U.S.A. 126 E2
Brown Mountain U.S.A. 128 E4
Brownstown U.S.A. 134 B4
Brownsville KY U.S.A. 134 B5
Brownsville PA U.S.A. 134 F3
Brownsville TN U.S.A. 131 F5
Brownsville TX U.S.A. 131 D7
Brownwood U.S.A. 131 D6
Browse Island Australia 108 C3
Bruay-la-Bussière France 52 C4
Bruce Peninsula Canada 134 E1
Bruce Peninsula National Park Canada 134 E1
Bruce Rock Australia 109 B7
Bruchsal Germany 53 I5
Brück Germany 53 M2
Bruck an der Mur Austria 47 O7
Brue r. U.K. 49 E7
Bruges Belgium see Brugge
Brugge Belgium 52 D3
Brühl Baden-Württemberg Germany 53 I5
Brühl Nordrhein-Westfalen Germany 52 G4
Bruin KY U.S.A. 134 D4
Bruin PA U.S.A. 134 F3
Bruin Point mt. U.S.A. 129 H2
Bruint India 83 I3
Brûk, Wâdi el watercourse Egypt see Burūk, Wādī al
Brukkaros Namibia 100 D3
Brûlé Canada 120 G4
Brûlé, Lac l. Canada 123 J3
Brûly Belgium 52 E5
Brumado Brazil 145 C1
Brumath France 53 H6
Brumunddal Norway 45 G6
Brunau Germany 53 L2
Brundisium Italy see Brindisi
Bruneau U.S.A. 126 E4
▶Brunei country Asia 68 E6
Asia 6, 62–63
Brunei Brunei see Bandar Seri Begawan
Brunette Downs Australia 110 A3
Brunflo Sweden 44 I5
Brunico Italy 58 D1
Brünn Czech Rep. see Brno
Brunner, Lake N.Z. 113 C6
Bruno Canada 121 J4
Brunswick Germany see Braunschweig
Brunswick GA U.S.A. 133 D6
Brunswick MD U.S.A. 135 G4
Brunswick ME U.S.A. 135 K2
Brunswick, Península de pen. Chile 144 B8
Brunswick Bay Australia 108 D3
Brunswick Lake Canada 122 E4
Bruntál Czech Rep. 47 P6
Brunt Ice Shelf Antarctica 152 B2
Bruntville S. Africa 101 J5
Bruny Island Australia 111 [inset]
Brusa Turkey see Bursa
Brusenets Rus. Fed. 42 I3
Brushton U.S.A. 135 H1
Brusque Brazil 145 A4
Brussel Belgium see Brussels

▶Brussels Belgium 52 E4
Capital of Belgium.

Bruthen Australia 112 C6
Bruxelles Belgium see Brussels
Bruzual Venez. 142 E2
Bryan OH U.S.A. 134 C3
Bryan TX U.S.A. 131 D6
Bryan, Mount hill Australia 111 B7
Bryan Coast Antarctica 152 L2
Bryansk Rus. Fed. 43 G5
Bryanskoye Rus. Fed. 91 G1
Bryant Pond U.S.A. 135 J1
Bryantsburg U.S.A. 134 C4
Bryce Canyon National Park U.S.A. 129 G3
Bryce Mountain U.S.A. 129 I5
Brynbuga U.K. see Usk
Bryne Norway 45 D7
Bryukhovetskaya Rus. Fed. 43 H7
Brzeg Poland 47 P5
Brześć nad Bugiem Belarus see Brest
Bua r. Malawi 99 D5
Bu'aale Somalia 98 E3
Buala Solomon Is 107 F2
Bu'ayj well Saudi Arabia 88 C5
Būbīyān Island Kuwait 88 C4
Bucak Turkey 59 N6
Bucaramanga Col. 142 D2
Buccaneer Archipelago is Australia 108 C4
Buchanan Liberia 96 B4
Buchanan MI U.S.A. 134 B3
Buchanan VA U.S.A. 134 F5
Buchanan, Lake salt flat Australia 110 D4
Buchan Gulf Canada 119 K2

▶Bucharest Romania 59 L2
Capital of Romania.

Büchen Germany 53 K1
Buchen (Odenwald) Germany 53 J5
Buchholz Germany 53 M1
Bucholz in der Nordheide Germany 53 J1
Buchon, Point U.S.A. 128 C4
Buchy France 52 B5
Bucin, Pasul pass Romania 59 K1
Buckambool Mountain hill Australia 112 B3
Bückeburg Germany 53 J2
Bücken Germany 53 J2
Buckeye U.S.A. 129 G5
Buckhannon U.S.A. 134 E4
Buckhaven U.K. 50 F4
Buckhorn Lake Canada 135 F1
Buckie U.K. 50 G3
Buckingham U.K. 49 G6
Buckingham U.S.A. 135 F5
Buckingham Bay Australia 67 F9
Buckland Tableland reg. Australia 110 E5
Buckleboo Australia 109 G8
Buckle Island Antarctica 152 H2
Buckley watercourse Australia 110 B4
Buckley Bay Antarctica 152 G2
Bucklin U.S.A. 130 D4
Buckskin Mountains U.S.A. 129 G4
Bucks Mountain U.S.A. 128 C2
Bucksport U.S.A. 123 H5
Bückwitz Germany 53 M2
București Romania see Bucharest
Bucyrus U.S.A. 134 D3
Buda-Kashalyova Belarus 43 F5
Budalin Myanmar 70 A2

▶Budapest Hungary 59 H1
Capital of Hungary.

Budaun India 82 D3
Budawang National Park Australia 112 E5
Budda Australia 112 B3
Budd Coast Antarctica 152 F2
Buddusò Sardinia Italy 58 C4
Bude U.K. 49 C8
Bude U.S.A. 131 F6
Budennovsk Rus. Fed. 91 G1
Buderim Australia 112 F1
Būding Iran 88 E5
Büdingen Germany 53 J4
Budīyah, Jabal hills Egypt 85 A5
Budongquan China 83 H2
Budoni Sardinia Italy 58 C4
Budū', Sabkhat al salt pan Saudi Arabia 88 C6
Budweis Czech Rep. see České Budějovice
Buenaventura Col. 142 C3
Buena Vista i. N. Mariana Is see Tinian
Buena Vista CO U.S.A. 126 G5
Buena Vista VA U.S.A. 134 F5
Buendia, Embalse de resr Spain 57 E3

▶Buenos Aires Arg. 144 E4
Capital of Argentina. 2nd most populous city in South America.

Buenos Aires, Lago l. Arg./Chile 144 B7
Buerarema Brazil 145 D1
Buet r. Canada 123 H1
Búfalo Mex. 131 B7
Buffalo r. Canada 120 H2
Buffalo KY U.S.A. 134 C5
Buffalo MO U.S.A. 130 E4
Buffalo NY U.S.A. 135 F2
Buffalo OK U.S.A. 131 D4
Buffalo SD U.S.A. 130 C2
Buffalo TX U.S.A. 131 D6
Buffalo WY U.S.A. 126 G3
Buffalo Head Hills Canada 120 G3
Buffalo Head Prairie Canada 120 G3
Buffalo Hump mt. U.S.A. 126 E3
Buffalo Lake Alta Canada 121 H4
Buffalo Lake N.W.T. Canada 120 H2
Buffalo Narrows Canada 121 I4
Buffels watercourse S. Africa 100 C5
Buffels Drift S. Africa 101 H2
Buftea Romania 59 K2
Bug r. Poland 47 S5
Buga Col. 142 C3
Bugaldie Australia 112 D3
Bugdayli Turkm. 88 D2
Buggenhout Belgium 52 E3
Bugojno Bos.-Herz. 58 G2
Bugrino Rus. Fed. 42 K1
Bugsuk i. Phil. 68 F5
Bugt China 74 A2
Bugul'ma Rus. Fed. 41 Q5
Bugun' Kazakh. 80 B2
Bügür China see Luntai
Buguruslan Rus. Fed. 41 Q5
Būhābād Iran 88 D4
Buhera Zimbabwe 99 D5
Bühl Germany 53 I6
Buhuși Romania 59 L1
Buick Canada 120 F3
Builth Wells U.K. 49 D6
Bui National Park Ghana 96 C4
Buinsk Rus. Fed. 43 K5
Bu'in Zahrā Iran 88 C3
Buir Nur l. Mongolia 73 L3
Buitepos Namibia 100 D2
Bujanovac Serb. and Mont. 59 I3

▶Bujumbura Burundi 98 C4
Capital of Burundi.

Bukachacha Rus. Fed. 73 L2
Buka Daban mt. China 83 G1
Buka Island P.N.G. 106 F2
Būkand Iran 88 D4
Bukavu Dem. Rep. Congo 98 C4
Bukhara Uzbek. 89 G2
Bukhoro Uzbek. see Bukhara
Bukit Baka - Bukit Raya National Park Indon. 68 E7
Bukit Timah Sing. 71 [inset]
Bukittinggi Indon. 68 C7
Bukkapatnam India 84 C3
Bukoba Tanz. 98 D4
Bükreș Romania see Bucharest
Būl, Kūh-e mt. Iran 88 D4
Bula P.N.G. 69 K8
Bülach Switz. 56 I3
Bulan i. Indon. 71 C7
Bulancak Turkey 90 E2
Bulandshahr India 82 D3
Bulanık Turkey 91 F3
Bulava Rus. Fed. 74 F2
Bulawayo Zimbabwe 99 C6
Buldan Turkey 59 M5
Buldana India see Buldhana
Buldhana India 84 C1
Buleda reg. Pak. 89 F5
Bulembu Swaziland 101 J3
Bulgan Bulgan Mongolia 80 J2
Bulgan Hovd Mongolia see Bürenhayrhan
Bulgar Rus. Fed. see Bolgar
▶Bulgaria country Europe 59 K3
Europe 5, 38–39
Bŭlgariya country Europe see Bulgaria
Bulkley Ranges mts Canada 120 D4
Bullawarra, Lake salt flat Australia 112 A1
Bullen r. Canada 121 K1
Buller r. N.Z. 113 C5
Buller, Mount Australia 112 C6
Bulleringa National Park Australia 110 C3
Bullfinch Australia 109 B7
Bullhead City U.S.A. 129 F4
Bulli Australia 112 E5
Bullion Mountains U.S.A. 128 E4
Bullo r. Australia 108 E3
Bulloo Downs Australia 111 C6
Bulloo Lake salt flat Australia 111 C6
Büllsport Namibia 100 C3
Bully Choop Mountain U.S.A. 128 B1
Bulman Australia 108 F3
Bulman Gorge Australia 108 F3
Bulmer Lake Canada 120 F2
Buloh, Pulau i. Sing. 71 [inset]
Buloke, Lake dry lake Australia 112 A6
Bulolo P.N.G. 69 L8
Bulsar India see Valsad
Bultfontein S. Africa 101 H5
Bulukumba Indon. 69 G8
Bulun Rus. Fed. 65 N2
Bulungu Dem. Rep. Congo 99 C4
Bulungur Uzbek. 89 G2
Bumba Dem. Rep. Congo 98 C3
Būmbah Libya 90 A4
Bumbah, Khalīj b. Libya 90 A4
Bumhkang Myanmar 70 B1
Bumpha Bum mt. Myanmar 70 B1
Buna Dem. Rep. Congo 98 B4
Buna Kenya 98 D3
Bunayyān well Saudi Arabia 88 C6
Bunazi Tanz. 98 D4
Bunbeg Rep. of Ireland 51 D2
Bunbury Australia 109 A8
Bunclody Rep. of Ireland 51 F5
Buncrana Rep. of Ireland 51 E2
Bunda Tanz. 98 D4
Bundaberg Australia 110 F5
Bundaleer Australia 112 C2
Bundarra Australia 112 E3
Bundi India 82 C4
Bundjalung National Park Australia 112 F2
Bundoran Rep. of Ireland 51 D3
Bunduqiya Sudan 97 G4
Buner reg. Pak. 89 I3
Bungalaut, Selat sea chan. Indon. 68 B7
Bungay U.K. 49 I6
Bungendore Australia 112 D5
Bunger Hills Antarctica 152 F2
Bungle Bungle National Park Australia see Purnululu National Park
Bungo-suidō sea chan. Japan 71 D6
Bunguran, Kepulauan is Indon. see Natuna, Kepulauan
Bunguran, Pulau i. Indon. see Natuna Besar
Bunia Dem. Rep. Congo 98 D3
Buniangga Dem. Rep. Congo 98 C4
Buningonia well Australia 109 C7
Bunji Jammu and Kashmir 82 C2
Bunker Group atolls Australia 110 F4
Bunkeya Dem. Rep. Congo 99 C5
Bunnell U.S.A. 133 D6
Bünsum China 83 E3
Bunya Mountains National Park Australia 112 E1
Bünyan Turkey 90 D3
Bunyu i. Indon. 68 F6
Buôn Mê Thuôt Vietnam 71 E4
Buorkhaya, Guba b. Rus. Fed. 65 O2
Bup r. China 83 F3
Buqayq Saudi Arabia see Abqaiq
Buqbuq Egypt 90 B5
Bura Kenya 98 D4
Buraan Somalia 98 E2
Buram Sudan 97 F3
Buran Kazakh. 80 G2
Buranhaém Brazil 145 C2
Buranhaém r. Brazil 145 D2
Burao Somalia 98 E3
Burāq Syria 85 C3
Buray r. India 82 C5
Buraydah Saudi Arabia 86 F4
Burbach Germany 53 I4
Burbank U.S.A. 128 D4
Burcher Australia 112 C4
Burdaard Neth. see Birdaard
Burdalyk Turkm. 89 G2
Burdigala France see Bordeaux
Burdur Turkey 59 N6
Burdur Gölü l. Turkey 59 N6
Burdwan India see Barddhaman
Burē Eth. 98 D2
Bure r. U.K. 49 I6
Bureå Sweden 44 L4
Bureinskiy Khrebet mts Rus. Fed. 74 D2
Bürenhayrhan Mongolia 80 H2
Bureya r. Rus. Fed. 74 C2
Bureya Range mts Rus. Fed. see Bureinskiy Khrebet
Bureyinski Zapovednik nature res. Rus. Fed. 74 D2
Burford Canada 134 E2
Burgas Bulg. 59 L3
Burgaw U.S.A. 133 E5
Burg bei Magdeburg Germany 53 L2
Burgbernheim Germany 53 K5
Burgdorf Germany 53 K2
Burgeo Canada 123 K5
Burgersdorp S. Africa 101 H6
Burgersfort S. Africa 101 J3
Burges, Mount hill Australia 109 C7
Burgess Hill U.K. 49 G8
Burghaun Germany 53 J4
Burghausen Germany 47 N6
Burghead U.K. 50 F3
Burgh-Haamstede Neth. 52 D3
Burgio, Serra di hill Sicily Italy 58 F6
Burglengenfeld Germany 53 M5
Burgos Mex. 131 D7
Burgos Spain 57 E2
Burgstädt Germany 53 M4
Burgsvik Sweden 45 K8
Burgum Neth. see Bergum
Burgundy reg. France 56 G3
Burhan Budai Shan mts China 80 H4
Burhaniye Turkey 59 L5
Burhanpur India 82 D5
Burhar-Dhanpuri India 83 E5
Buri Brazil 145 A3
Burias i. Phil. 69 G4
Burin Canada 123 L5
Burin Peninsula Canada 123 L5
Buriram Thai. 70 C4
Buritama Brazil 145 A3
Buriti Alegre Brazil 145 A2
Buriti Bravo Brazil 143 J5
Buritirama Brazil 143 J6
Buritis Brazil 145 B1
Burj Pak. 89 G4
Burke U.S.A. 130 D3
Burke Island Antarctica 152 K2
Burke Pass N.Z. see Burkes Pass
Burkes Pass N.Z. 113 C7
Burkesville U.S.A. 134 C5
Burketown Australia 110 B3
Burkeville U.S.A. 135 F5
▶Burkina country Africa 96 C3
Africa 7, 94–95
Burkina Faso country Africa see Burkina
Burk's Falls Canada 122 F5
Burley U.S.A. 126 E4
Burlington Canada 134 F2
Burlington CO U.S.A. 130 C4
Burlington IA U.S.A. 130 F3
Burlington KS U.S.A. 130 E4
Burlington KY U.S.A. 134 C4
Burlington VT U.S.A. 135 I1
Burlington WI U.S.A. 134 A2
Burmantovo Rus. Fed. 41 S3
Burnaby Canada 120 F5
Burnet U.S.A. 131 D6
Burney U.S.A. 128 C1
Burney, Monte vol. Chile 144 B8
Burnham U.S.A. 135 G3
Burnie Australia 111 [inset]
Burniston U.K. 48 G4
Burnley U.K. 48 E5
Burns U.S.A. 126 D4
Burnside r. Canada 118 H3
Burnside U.S.A. 134 C5
Burnside, Lake salt flat Australia 109 C6
Burns Junction U.S.A. 126 D4
Burns Lake Canada 120 E4
Burntisland U.K. 50 F4
Burnt Lake Canada see Brûlé, Lac
Burntwood r. Canada 121 L4
Burog Co l. China 83 F2
Buron r. Canada 123 H2
Burovoy Uzbek. 89 F1
Burqin China 80 G2
Burqu' Jordan 85 D3
Burra Australia 111 B7
Burravoe U.K. 50 [inset]
Burrel Albania 59 I4
Burrel U.S.A. 128 D3
Burren reg. Rep. of Ireland 51 C4
Burrendong Reservoir Australia 112 D4
Burren Junction Australia 112 D3
Burrewarra Point Australia 112 E5
Burrinjuck Australia 112 D5
Burrinjuck Reservoir Australia 112 D5
Burro, Serranías del mts Mex. 131 C6
Burr Oak Reservoir U.S.A. 134 D4
Burro Creek watercourse U.S.A. 129 G4
Burro Peak U.S.A. 129 I5
Burrowa Pine Mountain National Park Australia 112 C6
Burrow Head hd U.K. 50 E6
Burrows U.S.A. 134 B3
Burrundie Australia 108 E3
Bursa Turkey 59 M4
Bûr Safâga Egypt see Būr Safājah
Būr Safājah Egypt 86 D4
Bûr Sa'îd Egypt see Port Said
Būr Sa'īd Egypt see Port Said
Bûr Sa'îd governorate Egypt see Būr Sa'īd
Būr Sa'īd governorate Egypt 85 A4
Bursinskoye Vodokhranilishche resr Rus. Fed. 74 C2
Bürstadt Germany 53 I5
Būr Sudan Sudan see Port Sudan
Burt Lake U.S.A. 132 C2
Burton U.S.A. 134 D2
Burton, Lac l. Canada 122 F3
Burtonport Rep. of Ireland 51 D3
Burton upon Trent U.K. 49 F6
Burträsk Sweden 44 L4
Burt Well Australia 109 F5
Buru i. Indon. 69 H7
Burūk, Wādī al watercourse Egypt 85 A4
Burullus, Baḥra el lag. Egypt see Burullus, Lake
Burullus, Buḥayrat al lag. Egypt see Burullus, Lake
Burullus, Lake lag. Egypt 90 C5
Burultokay China see Fuhai
Burūn, Ra's pt Egypt 85 A4
▶Burundi country Africa 98 C4
Africa 7, 94–95
Burunniy Rus. Fed. see Tsagan Aman
Bururi Burundi 98 C4
Burwash Landing Canada 120 B2
Burwick U.K. 50 G2
Buryn' Ukr. 43 G6
Bury St Edmunds U.K. 49 H6
Burzil Pass Jammu and Kashmir 82 C2
Busan S. Korea see Pusan
Busanga Dem. Rep. Congo 98 C4
Busby U.S.A. 126 G3
Buseire Syria see Al Buşayrah
Bush r. U.K. 51 F2
Būshehr Iran 88 C4
Bushêngcaka China 83 E2
Bushenyi Uganda 98 D4
Bushire Iran see Būshehr
Bushmills U.K. 51 F2
Bushnell U.S.A. 133 D6
Businga Dem. Rep. Congo 98 C3
Buşrá ash Shām Syria 85 C3
Busse Rus. Fed. 74 B2
Busselton Australia 109 A8
Bussum Neth. 52 F2
Bustillos, Lago l. Mex. 127 G7
Busto Arsizio Italy 58 C2
Buta Dem. Rep. Congo 98 C3
Butare Rwanda 98 C4
Butaritari atoll Kiribati 150 H5
Bute Australia 111 B7
Bute i. U.K. 50 D5
Butedale Canada 120 D4
Butha Buthe Lesotho 101 I5
Butha Qi China see Zalantun
Buthidaung Myanmar 70 A2
Butler AL U.S.A. 131 F5
Butler GA U.S.A. 133 C5
Butler IN U.S.A. 134 C3
Butler KY U.S.A. 134 C4
Butler MO U.S.A. 130 E4
Butler PA U.S.A. 134 F3
Butlers Bridge Rep. of Ireland 51 E3
Buton i. Indon. 69 G7
Bütow Germany 53 M1
Butte MT U.S.A. 126 E3
Butte NE U.S.A. 130 D3
Buttelstedt Germany 53 L3
Butterworth Malaysia 71 C6
Butterworth S. Africa 101 I7
Buttes, Sierra mt. U.S.A. 128 C2
Buttevant Rep. of Ireland 51 D5
Butt of Lewis hd U.K. 50 C2
Button Bay Canada 121 M3
Butuan Phil. 69 H5
Butuo China 76 D3
Buturlinovka Rus. Fed. 43 I6
Butwal Nepal 83 E4
Butzbach Germany 53 I4
Buulobarde Somalia 98 E3
Buur Gaabo Somalia 98 E4
Buurhabaka Somalia 98 E3
Buxar India 83 F4
Buxtehude Germany 53 J1
Buxton U.K. 48 F5

Buy Rus. Fed. 42 I4
Buyant Mongolia 80 I2
Buynaksk Rus. Fed. 91 G2
Büyükçekmece Turkey 90 C2
Büyük Egri Dağ mt. Turkey 85 A1
Büyükmenderes r. Turkey 59 L6
Buzancy France 52 E5
Buzău Romania 59 L2
Buzdyak Rus. Fed. 41 Q5
Búzi Moz. 99 D5
Büzmeýin Turkm. see Byuzmeyin
Buzuluk Rus. Fed. 41 Q5
Buzuluk r. Rus. Fed. 43 I6
Buzzards Bay U.S.A. 135 J3
Byakar Bhutan see Jakar
Byala Bulg. 59 K3
Byala Slatina Bulg. 59 J3
Byalynichy Belarus 43 F5
Byarezina r. Belarus 43 F5
Byaroza Belarus 45 N10
Byblos tourist site Lebanon 85 B2
Bydgoszcz Poland 47 Q4
Byelorussia country Europe see Belarus
Byerazino Belarus 43 F5
Byers U.S.A. 126 G5
Byeshankovichy Belarus 43 F5
Byesville U.S.A. 134 E4
Bygland Norway 45 E7
Bykhaw Belarus 43 F5
Bykhov Belarus see Bykhaw
Bykle Norway 45 E7
Bykovo Rus. Fed. 43 J6
Bylas U.S.A. 129 H5
Bylot Island Canada 119 K2
Byramgore Reef India 84 A4
Byrd Glacier Antarctica 152 H1
Byrdstown U.S.A. 134 C5
Byrkjelo Norway 45 E6
Byrock Australia 112 C3
Byron U.S.A. 135 J1
Byron, Cape Australia 112 F2
Byron Bay Australia 112 F2
Byron Island Kiribati see Nikunau
Byrranga, Gory mts Rus. Fed. 65 K2
Byske Sweden 44 L4
Byssa Rus. Fed. 74 C1
Byssa r. Rus. Fed. 74 C1
Bytom Poland 47 Q5
Bytów Poland 47 P3
Byurgyutli Turkm. 88 D2
Byuzmeyin Turkm. 88 E2
Byzantium Turkey see İstanbul

C

Ca, Sông r. Vietnam 70 D3
Caacupé Para. 144 E3
Caatinga Brazil 145 B2
Caazapá Para. 144 E3
Cabaiguán Cuba 133 E8
Caballas Peru 142 C6
Caballococha Peru 142 D4
Cabanaconde Peru 142 D7
Cabanatuan Phil. 69 G3
Cabano Canada 123 H5
Cabdul Qaadir Somalia 98 E2
Cabeceira Rio Manso Brazil 139 G7
Cabeceiras Brazil 145 B1
Cabeza del Buey Spain 57 D4
Cabezas Bol. 142 F7
Cabimas Venez. 142 D1
Cabinda Angola 99 B4
Cabinda prov. Angola 99 B5
Cabinet Inlet Antarctica 152 L2
Cabinet Mountains U.S.A. 126 E2
Cabistra Turkey see Ereğli
Cabo Frio Brazil 145 C3
Cabo Frio, Ilha do i. Brazil 145 C3
Cabonga, Réservoir resr Canada 122 F5
Cabool U.S.A. 131 E4
Caboolture Australia 112 F1
Cabo Orange, Parque Nacional de nat. park Brazil 143 H3
Cabo Pantoja Peru 142 C4
Cabora Bassa, Lake resr Moz. 99 D5
Cabo Raso Arg. 144 C6
Caborca Mex. 127 E7
Cabot Head hd Canada 134 E1
Cabot Strait Canada 123 J5
Cabourg France 49 G9
Cabo Verde country N. Atlantic Ocean see Cape Verde
Cabo Verde, Ilhas do is N. Atlantic Ocean 96 [inset]
Cabo Yubi Morocco see Tarfaya
Cabral, Serra do mts Brazil 145 B2
Cäbrayıl Azer. 91 G3
Cabrera i. Spain 57 H4
Cabri Canada 121 I5
Cabullona Mex. 127 F7
Caçador Brazil 145 A4
Çacagoin China see Qagca
Čačak Serb. and Mont. 59 I3
Caccia, Capo c. Sardinia Italy 58 C4
Cacequi Brazil 144 F3
Cáceres Brazil 143 G7
Cáceres Spain 57 C4
Cache Creek Canada 120 F5
Cache Peak U.S.A. 126 E4
Cacheu Guinea-Bissau 96 B3
Cachi, Nevados de mts Arg. 144 C2
Cachimbo, Serra do hills Brazil 143 H5
Cachoeira Brazil 145 D1
Cachoeira Alta Brazil 145 A2
Cachoeira de Goiás Brazil 145 A2
Cachoeira do Arari Brazil 143 I4
Cachoeiro de Itapemirim Brazil 145 C3
Cacine Guinea-Bissau 96 B3
Caciporé, Cabo c. Brazil 143 H3
Cacolo Angola 99 B5
Caconga Angola 99 B4
Cactus U.S.A. 131 C4
Caçu Brazil 145 A2
Caculé Brazil 145 C1
Čadca Slovakia 47 Q6
Cadereyta Mex. 131 C7
Cadibarrawirracanna, Lake salt flat Australia 111 A6
Cadillac Canada 121 J5
Cadillac U.S.A. 134 C1
Cadiz Phil. 69 G4
Cádiz Spain 57 C5
Cadiz IN U.S.A. 134 C4
Cadiz KY U.S.A. 132 C4
Cadiz OH U.S.A. 134 E3
Cádiz, Golfo de g. Spain 57 C5
Cadiz Lake U.S.A. 129 F4
Cadomin Canada 120 G4
Cadotte r. Canada 120 G3
Cadotte Lake Canada 120 G3
Caen France 56 D2
Caerdydd U.K. see Cardiff
Caerffili U.K. see Caerphilly
Caerfyrddin U.K. see Carmarthen
Caergybi U.K. see Holyhead
Caernarfon U.K. 49 C5
Caernarfon Bay U.K. 49 C5
Caernarvon U.K. see Caernarfon
Caerphilly U.K. 49 D7
Caesaraugusta Spain see Zaragoza
Caesarea Alg. see Cherchell
Caesarea Cappadociae Turkey see Kayseri
Caesarea Philippi Syria see Bāniyās
Caesarodunum France see Tours
Caesaromagus U.K. see Chelmsford
Caetité Brazil 145 C1
Cafayate Arg. 144 C3
Cafelândia Brazil 145 A3
Caffa Ukr. see Feodosiya
Cagayan de Oro Phil. 69 G5
Cagles Mill Lake U.S.A. 134 B4
Cagli Italy 58 E3
Cagliari Sardinia Italy 58 C5
Cagliari, Golfo di b. Sardinia Italy 58 C5
Cahama Angola 99 B5
Caha Mts hills Rep. of Ireland 51 C6
Cahermore Rep. of Ireland 51 B6
Cahersiveen Rep. of Ireland 51 B6
Cahir Rep. of Ireland 51 E5
Cahirciveen Rep. of Ireland see Cahersiveen
Cahora Bassa, Lago de resr Moz. see Cabora Bassa, Lake
Cahore Point Rep. of Ireland 51 F5
Cahors France 56 E4
Cahuapanas Peru 142 C5
Cahul Moldova 59 M2
Caia Moz. 99 D5
Caiabis, Serra dos hills Brazil 143 G6
Caianda Angola 99 C5
Caiapó r. Brazil 145 A1
Caiapó, Serra do mts Brazil 145 A2
Caiapônia Brazil 145 A2
Caibarién Cuba 133 E8
Cai Bâu, Đao i. Vietnam 70 D2
Caicara Venez. 142 E2
Caicos Islands Turks and Caicos Is 137 J4
Caicos Passage Bahamas/Turks and Caicos Is 133 F8
Caidian China 77 G2
Caiguna Australia 109 D8
Caimodorro mt. Spain 57 F3
Cainnyigoin China 76 D1
Cains Store U.S.A. 134 C5
Caipe Arg. 144 C2
Caird Coast Antarctica 152 B1
Cairngorm Mountains U.K. 50 F3
Cairnryan U.K. 50 D6
Cairns Australia 110 D3
Cairnsmore of Carsphairn hill U.K. 50 E5
▶Cairo Egypt 90 C5
Capital of Egypt and most populous city in Africa.
Cairo U.S.A. 133 C6
Caisleán an Bharraigh Rep. of Ireland see Castlebar
Caiundo Angola 99 B5
Caiwarro Australia 112 B2
Caiyuanzhen China see Shengsi
Caizi Hu l. China 77 H2
Cajamarca Peru 142 C5
Cajati Brazil 145 A4
Cajuru Brazil 145 B3
Caka'lho China see Yanjing
Čakovec Croatia 58 G1
Çal Denizli Turkey 59 M5
Çal Hakkâri Turkey see Çukurca
Cala S. Africa 101 H6
Calabar Nigeria 96 D4
Calabogie Canada 135 G1
Calabria, Parco Nazionale della nat. park Italy 58 G5
Calafat Romania 59 J3
Calagua Mex. 127 F8
Calagurris Spain see Calahorra
Calahorra Spain 57 F2
Calai Angola 99 B5
Calais France 52 B4
Calais U.S.A. 123 I5
Calalasteo, Sierra de mts Arg. 144 C3
Calama Brazil 142 F5
Calama Chile 144 C2
Calamajué Mex. 127 E7
Calamar Col. 142 D1
Calamian Group is Phil. 68 F4
Calamocha Spain 57 F3
Calandula Angola 99 B4
Calang Indon. 71 A6
Calanscio Sand Sea des. Libya 86 B3
Calapan Phil. 69 G4
Călărași Romania 59 L2
Calatayud Spain 57 F3
Calayan i. Phil. 69 G3
Calbayog Phil. 69 G4
Calbe (Saale) Germany 53 L3
Calçoene Brazil 143 H3
Calcutta India see Kolkata
Caldas da Rainha Port. 57 B4
Caldas Novas Brazil 143 I7
Calden Germany 53 J3
Calder r. Canada 120 G1
Caldera Chile 144 B3
Caldervale Australia 110 D5
Caldew r. U.K. 48 E4
Caldwell ID U.S.A. 126 D4
Caldwell KS U.S.A. 131 D4
Caldwell OH U.S.A. 134 E4
Caldwell TX U.S.A. 131 D6
Caledon r. Lesotho/S. Africa 101 H6
Caledon S. Africa 100 D8
Caledon Bay Australia 110 B2
Caledonia Canada 134 F2
Caledonia admin. div. U.K. see Scotland
Caledonia U.S.A. 135 G2
Caleta el Cobre Chile 144 B2
Calexico U.S.A. 129 F5
Calf of Man i. Isle of Man 48 C4
Calgary Canada 120 H5
Calhoun U.S.A. 134 B5
Cali Col. 142 C3
Calicut India 84 B4
Caliente U.S.A. 129 F3
California U.S.A. 134 F3
California state U.S.A. 127 C4
California, Golfo de g. Mex. see California, Gulf of
California, Gulf of Mex. 127 E7
California Aqueduct canal U.S.A. 128 C3
Cälilabad Azer. 91 H3
Calingasta Arg. 144 C4
Calipatria U.S.A. 129 F5
Calistoga U.S.A. 128 B2
Calkiní Mex. 136 F4
Callabonna, Lake salt flat Australia 111 C6
Callabonna Creek watercourse Australia 111 C6
Callaghan, Mount U.S.A. 128 E2
Callan Rep. of Ireland 51 E5
Callan r. U.K. 51 F3
Callander Canada 122 F5
Callander U.K. 50 E4
Callang Phil. 77 I5
Callao Peru 142 C6
Callao U.S.A. 129 G2
Callicoon U.S.A. 135 H3
Calling Lake Canada 120 H4
Callington U.K. 49 C8
Calliope Australia 110 E5
Callipolis Turkey see Gallipoli
Calmar U.S.A. 130 F3
Caloosahatchee r. U.S.A. 133 D7
Caloundra Australia 112 F1
Caltagirone Sicily Italy 58 F6
Caltanissetta Sicily Italy 58 F6
Calucinga Angola 99 B5
Calulo Angola 99 B4
Calunga Angola 99 B5
Caluquembe Angola 99 B5
Caluula Somalia 98 F2
Caluula, Raas pt Somalia 98 F2
Calvert Hills Australia 110 B3
Calvert Island Canada 120 D5
Calvi Corsica France 56 I5
Calvià Spain 57 H4
Calvinia S. Africa 100 D6
Calvo, Monte mt. Italy 58 F4
Cam r. U.K. 49 H6
Camaçari Brazil 145 D1
Camache Reservoir U.S.A. 128 C2
Camachigama r. Canada 122 F5
Camacho Mex. 131 C7
Camacuio Angola 99 B5
Camacupa Angola 99 B5
Camagüey Cuba 137 I4
Camagüey, Archipiélago de is Cuba 137 I4
Camah, Gunung mt. Malaysia 71 C6
Camamu Brazil 145 D1
Camana Peru 142 D7
Camanongue Angola 99 C5
Camapuã Brazil 143 H7
Camaquã Brazil 144 F4
Çamardı Turkey 90 D3
Camargo Bol. 142 E8
Camargue reg. France 56 G5
Camarillo U.S.A. 128 D4
Camarones Arg. 144 C6
Camarones, Bahía b. Arg. 144 C6
Camas r. U.S.A. 126 E4
Ca Mau Vietnam 71 D5
Cambay India see Khambhat
Cambay, Gulf of India see Khambhat, Gulf of
Camberley U.K. 49 G7
▶Cambodia country Asia 71 D4
Asia 6, 62–63
Camboriú Brazil 145 A4
Camborne U.K. 49 B8
Cambrai France 52 D4
Cambria admin. div. U.K. see Wales
Cambrian Mountains hills U.K. 49 D6
Cambridge Canada 134 E2
Cambridge N.Z. 113 E3
Cambridge U.K. 49 H6
Cambridge MA U.S.A. 135 J2
Cambridge MD U.S.A. 135 G4
Cambridge MN U.S.A. 130 E2
Cambridge NY U.S.A. 135 I2
Cambridge OH U.S.A. 134 E3
Cambridge Bay Canada 119 H3
Cambridge City U.S.A. 134 C4
Cambridge Springs U.S.A. 134 E3
Cambrien, Lac l. Canada 123 H2
Cambulo Angola 99 C4
Cambundi-Catembo Angola 99 B5
Cambuquira Brazil 145 B3
Cam Co l. China 83 E2
Camden AL U.S.A. 133 C5
Camden AR U.S.A. 131 E5
Camden NJ U.S.A. 135 H4
Camden NY U.S.A. 135 H2
Camden SC U.S.A. 133 D5
Camdenton U.S.A. 130 E4
Cameia Angola 99 C5
Cameia, Parque Nacional da nat. park Angola 99 C5
Cameron AZ U.S.A. 129 H4
Cameron LA U.S.A. 131 E6
Cameron MO U.S.A. 130 E4
Cameron TX U.S.A. 131 D6
Cameron Highlands mts Malaysia 71 C6
Cameron Hills Canada 120 G3
Cameron Island Canada 119 H2
Cameron Park U.S.A. 128 C2
▶Cameroon country Africa 96 E4
Africa 7, 94–95
Cameroon, Mount vol. Cameroon see Cameroun, Mont
Cameroun country Africa see Cameroon
Cameroun, Mont vol. Cameroon 96 D4
Cametá Brazil 143 I4
Camiña Chile 142 E7
Camiri Bol. 142 F8
Camisea Peru 142 D6
Camocim Brazil 143 J4
Camooweal Australia 110 B3
Camooweal Caves National Park Australia 110 B4
Camorta i. India 81 H10
Campana Mex. 131 C7
Campana, Isla i. Chile 144 A7
Campania Island Canada 120 D4
Campbell S. Africa 100 F5
Campbell, Cape N.Z. 113 E5
Campbell, Mount hill Australia 108 E5
Campbellford Canada 135 G1
Campbell Hill hill U.S.A. 134 D3
Campbell Island N.Z. 150 H9
Campbell Lake Canada 121 J2
Campbell Plateau sea feature S. Pacific Ocean 150 H9
Campbell Range hills Australia 108 D3
Campbell River Canada 120 E5
Campbellsville U.S.A. 134 C5
Campbellton Canada 123 I5
Campbelltown Australia 112 E5
Campbeltown U.K. 50 D5
Campeche Mex. 136 F5
Campeche, Bahía de g. Mex. 136 F5
Camperdown Australia 112 A7
Câmpina Romania 59 K2
Campina Grande Brazil 143 K5
Campinas Brazil 145 B3
Campina Verde Brazil 145 A2
Campo Cameroon 96 D4
Campobasso Italy 58 F4
Campo Belo Brazil 145 B3
Campo Belo do Sul Brazil 145 A4
Campo de Diauarum Brazil 143 H6
Campo Florido Brazil 145 A2
Campo Gallo Arg. 144 D3
Campo Grande Brazil 144 F2
Campo Largo Brazil 145 A4
Campo Maior Brazil 143 J4
Campo Maior Port. 57 C4
Campo Mourão Brazil 144 F2
Campos Brazil 145 C3
Campos Altos Brazil 145 B2
Campos Novos Brazil 145 A4
Campos Sales Brazil 143 J5
Campton U.S.A. 134 D5
Câmpulung Romania 59 K2
Câmpulung Moldovenesc Romania 59 K1
Camp Verde U.S.A. 129 H4
Cam Ranh Vietnam 71 E5
Camrose Canada 121 H4
Camrose U.K. 49 B7
Camsell Lake Canada 121 I2
Camsell Portage Canada 121 I3
Camsell Range mts Canada 120 F2
Camulodunum U.K. see Colchester
Çan Turkey 59 L4
Canaan r. Canada 123 I5
Canaan U.S.A. 135 I2
Canaan Peak U.S.A. 129 H3
Canabrava Brazil 145 B2
Canacona India 84 B3
▶Canada country N. America 118 H4
Largest country in North America and 2nd in the world. 3rd most populous country in North America.
North America 9, 116–117
Canada Basin sea feature Arctic Ocean 153 A1
Canadian U.S.A. 131 C5
Canadian r. U.S.A. 131 E5
Canadian Abyssal Plain sea feature Arctic Ocean 153 A1
Cañadon Grande, Sierra mts Arg. 144 C7
Canaima, Parque Nacional nat. park Venez. 142 F2
Çanakkale Turkey 59 L4
Çanakkale Boğazı strait Turkey see Dardanelles
Canalejas Arg. 144 C5
Cañamares Spain 57 E3
Canandaigua U.S.A. 135 G2
Cananea Mex. 127 F7
Cananéia Brazil 145 B4
Canápolis Brazil 145 A2
Cañar Ecuador 142 C4
Canarias terr. N. Atlantic Ocean see Canary Islands
Canárias, Ilha das i. Brazil 143 J4
Canarias, Islas terr. N. Atlantic Ocean see Canary Islands
▶Canary Islands terr. N. Atlantic Ocean 96 B2
Autonomous Community of Spain.
Africa 7, 94–95
Canaseraga U.S.A. 135 G2
Canastota U.S.A. 135 H2
Canastra, Serra da mts Brazil 145 B2
Canastra, Serra da mts Brazil 145 A1
Canatiba Brazil 145 C1
Canatlán Mex. 131 B7
Canaveral, Cape U.S.A. 133 D6
Cañaveras Spain 57 E3
Canavieiras Brazil 145 D1
Canbelego Australia 112 C3
▶Canberra Australia 112 D5
Capital of Australia.
Cancún Mex. 137 G4
Çandar Turkey see Kastamonu
Çandarlı Turkey 59 L5
Candela Mex. 131 C7
Candela r. Mex. 131 C7
Candelaria Mex. 127 G7
Candia Greece see Iraklion
Cândido de Abreu Brazil 145 A4
Çandır Turkey 90 D2
Candle Lake Canada 121 J4
Candlewood, Lake U.S.A. 135 I3
Cando U.S.A. 130 D1
Candon Phil. 77 I5
Cane r. Australia 108 A5
Canea Greece see Chania
Canela Brazil 145 A5
Canelones Uruguay 144 E4
Cane Valley U.S.A. 134 C5
Cangallo Peru 142 D6
Cangamba Angola 99 B5
Cangandala, Parque Nacional de nat. park Angola 99 B4
Cangbu r. China see Brahmaputra
Cango Caves S. Africa 100 F7
Cangola Angola 99 B4
Cangshan China 77 H1
Canguaretama Brazil 143 K5
Canguçu Brazil 144 F4
Canguçu, Serra do hills Brazil 144 F4
Cangwu China 77 F4
Cangzhou China 73 L5
Caniapiscau Canada 123 H3
Caniapiscau r. Canada 123 H2
Caniapiscau, Lac l. Canada 123 H3
Caniçado Moz. see Guija
Canicatti Sicily Italy 58 E6
Canim Lake Canada 120 F5
Canindé Brazil 143 K4
Canisteo U.S.A. 135 G2
Canisteo r. U.S.A. 135 G2
Canisteo Peninsula Antarctica 152 K2
Cañitas de Felipe Pescador Mex. 131 C8
Çankırı Turkey 90 D2
Canna Australia 109 A7
Canna i. U.K. 50 C3
Cannanore India 84 B4
Cannanore Islands India 84 B4
Cannelton U.S.A. 134 B5
Cannes France 56 H5
Cannock U.K. 49 E6
Cannon Beach U.S.A. 126 C3
Cann River Australia 112 D6
Canoas Brazil 145 A5
Canōas, Rio das r. Brazil 145 A4
Canoeiros Brazil 145 B2
Canoe Lake Canada 121 I4
Canoe Lake l. Canada 121 I4
Canoinhas Brazil 145 A4
Canon City U.S.A. 127 G5
Cañon Largo watercourse U.S.A. 129 J3
Canoona Australia 110 E4
Canora Canada 121 K5
Canowindra Australia 112 D4
Canso Canada 123 J5
Canso, Cape Canada 123 J5
Cantabrian Mountains Spain see Cantábrica, Cordillera
Cantábrica, Cordillera mts Spain 57 D2
Cantábrico, Mar sea Spain 57 C2
Canterbury U.K. 49 I7
Canterbury Bight b. N.Z. 113 C7
Canterbury Plains N.Z. 113 C6
Cần Thơ Vietnam 71 D5
Cantil U.S.A. 128 E4
Canton GA U.S.A. 133 C5
Canton IL U.S.A. 130 F3
Canton MO U.S.A. 130 F3
Canton MS U.S.A. 131 F5
Canton NY U.S.A. 135 H1
Canton OH U.S.A. 134 E3
Canton PA U.S.A. 135 G3
Canton SD U.S.A. 130 D3
Canton TX U.S.A. 131 E5
Canton Island atoll Kiribati see Kanton
Cantuaria U.K. see Canterbury
Canunda National Park Australia 111 C8
Canutama Brazil 142 F5
Canutillo Mex. 131 B7
Canvey Island U.K. 49 H7
Canwood Canada 121 J4
Cany-Barville France 49 H9
Canyon Canada 120 B2
Canyon U.S.A. 131 C5
Canyon City U.S.A. 126 D3
Canyondam U.S.A. 128 C1
Canyon de Chelly National Monument nat. park U.S.A. 129 I3
Canyon Ferry Lake U.S.A. 126 F3
Canyon Lake U.S.A. 129 H5
Canyonlands National Park U.S.A. 129 I2
Canyon Ranges mts Canada 120 E2
Canyons of the Ancients National Monument nat. park U.S.A. 129 I3
Canyonville U.S.A. 126 C4
Cao Băng Vietnam 70 D2
Caocheng China see Caoxian
Caohai China see Weining
Caohe China see Qichun
Caohu China 80 F3
Caojiahe China see Qichun
Caojian China 76 C3
Cao Nguyên Đắc Lắc plat. Vietnam 71 E4
Caoshi China 74 B4
Caoxian China 77 G1
Caozhou China see Heze
Capac U.S.A. 134 D2
Çapakçur Turkey see Bingöl
Capanaparo r. Venez. 142 E2
Capanema Brazil 143 I4
Capão Bonito Brazil 145 A4
Caparaó, Serra do mts Brazil 145 C3
Cap-aux-Meules Canada 123 J5
Cap-de-la-Madeleine Canada 123 G5
Cape r. Australia 110 D4
Cape Arid National Park Australia 109 C8
Cape Barren Island Australia 111 [inset]
Cape Basin sea feature S. Atlantic Ocean 148 I8
Cape Breton Highlands National Park Canada 123 J5
Cape Breton Island Canada 123 J5
Cape Charles Canada 123 L3
Cape Charles U.S.A. 135 G5
Cape Coast Ghana 96 C4
Cape Coast Castle Ghana see Cape Coast
Cape Cod Bay U.S.A. 135 J3
Cape Cod National Seashore nature res. U.S.A. 135 K3
Cape Coral U.S.A. 133 D7
Cape Crawford Australia 110 A3
Cape Dorset Canada 119 K3
Cape Fanshaw U.S.A. 120 C3
Cape Fear r. U.S.A. 133 E5
Cape George Canada 123 J5
Cape Girardeau U.S.A. 131 F4
Cape Johnson Depth sea feature N. Pacific Ocean 150 E5
Cape Juby Morocco see Tarfaya
Cape Krusenstern National Monument nat. park U.S.A. 118 B3
Capel Australia 109 A8
Cape Le Grand National Park Australia 109 C8
Capelinha Brazil 145 C2
Capella Australia 110 E4
Capelle aan de IJssel Neth. 52 E3
Capelongo Angola see Kuvango
Cape May U.S.A. 135 H4
Cape May Court House U.S.A. 135 H4
Cape May Point U.S.A. 135 H4
Cape Melville National Park Australia 110 D2
Capenda-Camulemba Angola 99 B4
Cape of Good Hope Nature Reserve S. Africa 100 D8
Cape Palmerston National Park Australia 110 E4
Cape Range National Park Australia 108 A5
Cape St George Canada 123 K4
▶Cape Town S. Africa 100 D7
Legislative capital of South Africa.
Cape Tribulation National Park Australia 110 D2
Cape Upstart National Park Australia 110 D3
▶Cape Verde country N. Atlantic Ocean 96 [inset]
Africa 7, 94–95
Cape Verde Basin sea feature N. Atlantic Ocean 148 F5
Cape Verde Plateau sea feature N. Atlantic Ocean 148 F4
Cape Vincent U.S.A. 135 G1
Cape York Peninsula Australia 110 C2
Cap-Haïtien Haiti 137 J5
Capim r. Brazil 143 I4
Capitán Arturo Prat research station Antarctica 152 A2
▶Capitol Hill N. Mariana Is 69 L3
Capital of the Northern Mariana Islands, on Saipan.
Capitol Reef National Park U.S.A. 129 H2
Capivara, Represa resr Brazil 145 A3
Čapljina Bos.-Herz. 58 G3
Cappoquin Rep. of Ireland 51 E5
Capraia, Isola di i. Italy 58 C3
Caprara, Punta pt Sardinia Italy 58 C4
Capri, Isola di i. Italy 58 F4
Capricorn Channel Australia 110 E4
Capricorn Group atolls Australia 110 F4
Caprivi Strip reg. Namibia 99 C5
Cap Rock Escarpment U.S.A. 131 C5
Capsa Tunisia see Gafsa
Captain Cook HI U.S.A. 127 [inset]
Captina r. U.S.A. 134 E4
Capuava Brazil 145 B4
Caquetá r. Col. 142 E4
Caracal Romania 59 K2
▶Caracas Venez. 142 E1
Capital of Venezuela.
Caraguatatuba Brazil 145 B3
Caraí Brazil 145 C2
Carajás Brazil 143 H5
Carajás, Serra dos hills Brazil 143 H5
Carales Sardinia Italy see Cagliari
Caralis Sardinia Italy see Cagliari
Carandaí Brazil 145 C3
Caransebeș Romania 59 J2
Caraquet Canada 123 I5
Caratasca, Laguna de lag. Hond. 137 H5
Caratinga Brazil 145 C2
Carauari Brazil 142 E4
Caravaca de la Cruz Spain 57 F4
Caravelas Brazil 145 D2
Carberry Canada 121 L5
Carbó Mex. 127 F7
Carbonara, Capo c. Sardinia Italy 58 C5
Carbondale CO U.S.A. 129 J2
Carbondale PA U.S.A. 135 H3
Carboneras Mex. 131 D7
Carbonia Sardinia Italy 58 C5
Carbonita Brazil 145 C2
Carcaixent Spain 57 F4
Carcajou Canada 120 G3
Carcajou r. Canada 120 D1
Carcar Phil. 69 G4
Carcassonne France 56 F5
Cardamomes, Chaîne des mts Cambodia/Thai. see Cardamom Range
Cardamom Hills India 84 C4
Cardamom Range mts Cambodia/Thai. 71 C4
Cárdenas Cuba 137 H4
Cárdenas Mex. 136 E4
Cardenyabba watercourse Australia 112 A2
Çardi Turkey see Harmancık
Cardiel, Lago l. Arg. 144 B7
▶Cardiff U.K. 49 D7
Capital of Wales.
Cardiff U.S.A. 135 G4
Cardigan U.K. 49 C6
Cardigan Bay U.K. 49 C6
Cardinal Lake Canada 120 G3
Cardington U.S.A. 134 D3
Cardón, Cerro hill Mex. 127 E8
Cardoso Brazil 145 A3
Cardoso, Ilha do i. Brazil 145 B4
Cardston Canada 120 H5
Careen Lake Canada 121 I3
Carei Romania 59 J1
Carentan France 56 D2
Carey U.S.A. 134 D3
Carey, Lake salt flat Australia 109 C7
Carey Lake Canada 121 K2
Cargados Carajos Islands Mauritius 149 L7
Carhaix-Plouguer France 56 C2
Cariacica Brazil 145 C3
Cariamanga Ecuador 142 C4
Caribbean Sea N. Atlantic Ocean 137 H5
Cariboo Mountains Canada 120 F4

Caribou *r.* Man. Canada 121 M3
Caribou *r.* N.W.T. Canada 120 E2
Caribou U.S.A. 132 G2
Caribou Lake Canada 119 J4
Caribou Mountains Canada 120 H3
Carichic Mex. 127 G8
Carignan France 52 F5
Carinda Australia 112 C3
Cariñena Spain 57 F3
Carinhanha *r.* Brazil 145 C1
Carlabhagh U.K. *see* **Carloway**
Carleton U.S.A. 134 D2
Carleton, Mount *hill* Canada 123 I5
Carletonville S. Africa 101 H4
Carlin U.S.A. 128 E1
Carlingford Lough *inlet* Rep. of Ireland/U.K. 51 F3
Carlinville U.S.A. 130 F4
Carlisle U.K. 48 E4
Carlisle *IN* U.S.A. 134 B4
Carlisle *KY* U.S.A. 134 C4
Carlisle *NY* U.S.A. 135 H2
Carlisle *PA* U.S.A. 135 G3
Carlisle Lakes *salt flat* Australia 109 D7
Carlit, Pic *mt.* France 56 E5
Carlos Chagas Brazil 145 C2
Carlow Rep. of Ireland 51 F5
Carloway U.K. 50 C2
Carlsbad Czech Rep. *see* **Karlovy Vary**
Carlsbad *CA* U.S.A. 128 E5
Carlsbad *NM* U.S.A. 127 G6
Carlsbad Caverns National Park U.S.A. 127 G6
Carlsberg Ridge *sea feature* Indian Ocean 149 L5
Carlson Inlet Antarctica 152 L1
Carlton U.S.A. 130 E2
Carlton Hill Australia 108 E3
Carluke U.K. 50 F5
Carlyle Canada 121 K5
Carmacks Canada 120 B2
Carmagnola Italy 58 B2
Carman Canada 121 L5
Carmana Iran *see* **Kermān**
Carmarthen U.K. 49 C7
Carmarthen Bay U.K. 49 C7
Carmaux France 56 F4
Carmel *IN* U.S.A. 134 B4
Carmel *NY* U.S.A. 135 I3
Carmel, Mount *hill* Israel 85 B3
Carmel Head *hd* U.K. 48 C5
Carmel Valley U.S.A. 128 C3
Carmen *r.* Mex. 131 B6
Carmen U.S.A. 127 F7
Carmen, Isla *i.* Mex. 127 F8
Carmen de Patagones Arg. 144 D6
Carmi U.S.A. 130 F4
Carmichael U.S.A. 128 C2
Carmo da Cachoeira Brazil 145 B3
Carmo do Paranaíba Brazil 145 B2
Carmona Angola *see* **Uíge**
Carmona Spain 57 D5
Carnac France 56 C3
Carnamah Australia 109 A7
Carnarvon Australia 109 A6
Carnarvon S. Africa 100 F6
Carnarvon National Park Australia 110 D5
Carnarvon Range *hills* Australia 109 C6
Carnarvon Range *mts* Australia 110 E5
Carn Dearg *hill* U.K. 50 E3
Carndonagh Rep. of Ireland 51 E2
Carnegie Australia 109 C6
Carnegie, Lake *salt flat* Australia 109 C6
Carn Eighe *mt.* U.K. 50 D3
Carnes Australia 109 F7
Carney Island Antarctica 152 J2
Carnforth U.K. 48 E4
Carn Glas-choire *hill* U.K. 50 F3
Car Nicobar *i.* India 71 A5
Carnlough U.K. 51 G3
Carn nan Gabhar *mt.* U.K. 50 F4
Carn Odhar *hill* U.K. 50 E3
Carnot Cent. Afr. Rep. 98 B3
Carnoustie U.K. 50 G4
Carnsore Point Rep. of Ireland 51 F5
Carnwath U.K. 50 F5
Caro U.S.A. 134 D2
Carola Cay *reef* Australia 110 F3
Carol City U.S.A. 133 D7
Carolina Brazil 143 I5
Carolina S. Africa 101 J4
Carolina Beach U.S.A. 133 E5
Caroline Canada 120 H4
Caroline Island *atoll* Kiribati 151 J6
Caroline Islands N. Pacific Ocean 69 K5
Caroline Peak N.Z. 113 A7
Caroline Range *hills* Australia 108 D4
Caroní *r.* Venez. 142 F2
Carp Canada 135 G1
Carpathian Mountains Europe 43 C6
Carpații *mts* Europe *see* **Carpathian Mountains**
Carpații Meridionali *mts* Romania *see* **Transylvanian Alps**
Carpații Occidentali *mts* Romania 59 J2
Carpentaria, Gulf of Australia 110 B2
Carpentras France 56 G4
Carpi Italy 58 D2
Carpinteria U.S.A. 128 D4
Carpio U.S.A. 130 C1
Carra, Lough *l.* Rep. of Ireland 51 C4
Carraig na Siuire Rep. of Ireland *see* **Carrick-on-Suir**
Carrantuohill *mt.* Rep. of Ireland 51 C6
Carrara Italy 58 D2
Carrasco, Parque Nacional *nat. park* Bol. 142 F7
Carrathool Australia 112 B5
Carrhae Turkey *see* **Harran**
Carrickfergus U.K. 51 G3
Carrickmacross Rep. of Ireland 51 F4
Carrick-on-Shannon Rep. of Ireland 51 D4
Carrick-on-Suir Rep. of Ireland 51 E5
Carrigallen Rep. of Ireland 51 E4
Carrigtwohill Rep. of Ireland 51 D6
Carrillo Mex. 131 C7
Carrington U.S.A. 130 D2
Carrizal Mex. 127 G7
Carrizal Bajo Chile 144 B3
Carrizo U.S.A. 129 H4
Carrizo Creek *r.* U.S.A. 131 C4
Carrizo Springs U.S.A. 131 D6
Carrizo Wash *watercourse* U.S.A. 129 I4
Carrizozo U.S.A. 127 G6
Carroll U.S.A. 130 E3
Carrollton *AL* U.S.A. 131 F5
Carrollton *GA* U.S.A. 133 C5
Carrollton *IL* U.S.A. 130 F4
Carrollton *KY* U.S.A. 134 C4
Carrollton *MO* U.S.A. 130 E4
Carrollton *OH* U.S.A. 134 E3
Carrolltown U.S.A. 135 F3
Carron *r.* U.K. 50 E3
Carrot *r.* Canada 121 K4
Carrothers U.S.A. 134 D3
Carrot River Canada 121 K4
Carrowmore Lake Rep. of Ireland 51 C3
Carrsville U.S.A. 135 G5
Carruthers Lake Canada 121 K2
Carruthersville U.S.A. 131 F4
Carry Falls Reservoir U.S.A. 135 H1
Çarşamba Turkey 90 E2
Carson *r.* U.S.A. 128 D2
Carson City *MI* U.S.A. 134 C2

▶**Carson City** *NV* U.S.A. 128 D2
State capital of Nevada.

Carson Escarpment Australia 108 D3
Carson Lake U.S.A. 128 D2
Carson Sink *l.* U.S.A. 128 D2
Carstensz Pyramid *mt.* Indon. *see* **Jaya, Puncak**
Carstensz-top *mt.* Indon. *see* **Jaya, Puncak**
Carswell Lake Canada 121 I3
Cartagena Col. 142 C1
Cartagena Spain 57 F5
Carteret Group *is* P.N.G. *see* **Kilinailau Islands**
Carteret Island Solomon Is *see* **Malaita**
Cartersville U.S.A. 133 C5
Carthage *tourist site* Tunisia 58 D6
Carthage *MO* U.S.A. 131 E4
Carthage *NC* U.S.A. 133 E5
Carthage *NY* U.S.A. 135 H2
Carthage *TX* U.S.A. 131 E5
Carthago *tourist site* Tunisia *see* **Carthage**
Carthago Nova Spain *see* **Cartagena**
Cartier Island Australia 108 C3
Cartmel U.K. 48 E4
Cartwright *Man.* Canada 121 L5
Cartwright *Nfld. and Lab.* Canada 123 K3
Caruarú Brazil 143 K5
Carúpano Venez. 142 F1
Carver U.S.A. 134 D5
Carvin France 52 C4
Cary U.S.A. 132 E5
Caryapundy Swamp Australia 111 C6
Casablanca Morocco 54 C5
Casa Branca Brazil 145 B3
Casa de Piedra, Embalse *resr* Arg. 144 C5
Casa Grande U.S.A. 129 H5
Casale Monferrato Italy 58 C2
Casalmaggiore Italy 58 D2
Casas Grandes Mex. 127 G7
Casca Brazil 145 A5
Cascada de Bassaseachic, Parque Nacional *nat. park* Mex. 127 F7
Cascade Australia 109 C8
Cascade *r.* N.Z. 113 B7
Cascade *ID* U.S.A. 126 D3
Cascade *MT* U.S.A. 126 F3
Cascade Point N.Z. 113 B7
Cascade Range *mts* Canada/U.S.A. 126 C4
Cascade Reservoir U.S.A. 126 D3
Cascais Port. 57 B4
Cascavel Brazil 144 F2
Casco Bay U.S.A. 135 K2
Caserta Italy 58 F4
Casey *research station* Antarctica 152 F2
Casey Bay Antarctica 152 D2
Caseyr, Raas *c.* Somalia *see* **Gwardafuy, Gees**
Cashel Rep. of Ireland 51 E5
Cashmere Australia 112 D1
Casino Australia 112 F2
Casiquiare, Canal *r.* Venez. 142 E3
Casita Mex. 127 F7
Casnewydd U.K. *see* **Newport**
Caspe Spain 57 F3
Casper U.S.A. 126 G4
Caspian Lowland Kazakh./Rus. Fed. 78 D2

▶**Caspian Sea** *l.* Asia/Europe 91 H1
Largest lake in the world and in Asia/Europe. Lowest point in Europe.
Asia 60–61
Europe 36–37
World 12–13

Cass U.S.A. 134 F4
Cass *r.* U.S.A. 134 D2
Cassacatiza Moz. 99 D5
Cassadaga U.S.A. 134 F2
Cassaigne Alg. *see* **Sidi Ali**
Cassamba Angola 99 C5
Cass City U.S.A. 134 D2
Cassel France 52 C4
Casselman Canada 135 H1
Cássia Brazil 145 B3
Cassiar Mountains Canada 120 D2
Cassilândia Brazil 145 A2
Cassilis Australia 112 D4
Cassino Italy 58 E4
Cassley *r.* U.K. 50 E3
Cassongue Angola 99 B5
Cassopolis U.S.A. 134 B3
Cassville U.S.A. 131 E4
Castanhal Brazil 143 I4
Castanho Brazil 142 F5
Castaños Mex. 131 C7
Castelfranco Veneto Italy 58 D2
Castell-nedd U.K. *see* **Neath**
Castell Newydd Emlyn U.K. *see* **Newcastle Emlyn**
Castelló de la Plana Spain 57 F4
Castellón Spain *see* **Castelló de la Plana**
Castellón de la Plana Spain *see* **Castelló de la Plana**
Castelo Branco Port. 57 C4
Castelo de Vide Port. 57 C4
Casteltermini *Sicily* Italy 58 E6
Castelvetrano *Sicily* Italy 58 E6
Castiglione della Pescaia Italy 58 D3
Castignon, Lac *l.* Canada 123 H2
Castilla y León *reg.* Spain 56 B6
Castlebar Rep. of Ireland 51 C4
Castlebay U.K. 50 B4
Castlebellingham Rep. of Ireland 51 F4
Castleblayney Rep. of Ireland 51 F3
Castlebridge Rep. of Ireland 51 F5
Castle Carrock U.K. 48 E4
Castle Cary U.K. 49 E7
Castle Dale U.S.A. 129 H2
Castlederg U.K. 51 E3
Castledermot Rep. of Ireland 51 F5
Castle Dome Mountains U.S.A. 129 F5
Castle Donington U.K. 49 F6
Castle Douglas U.K. 50 F6
Castleford U.K. 48 F5
Castlegar Canada 120 G5
Castlegregory Rep. of Ireland 51 B5
Castle Island Bahamas 133 F8
Castleisland Rep. of Ireland 51 C5
Castlemaine Australia 112 B6
Castlemaine Rep. of Ireland 51 C5
Castlemartyr Rep. of Ireland 51 D6
Castle Mountain *Alta* Canada 120 H5
Castle Mountain *Y.T.* Canada 120 C1
Castle Mountain U.S.A. 128 C4
Castle Peak *hill Hong Kong* China 77 [inset]
Castle Peak Bay *Hong Kong* China 77 [inset]
Castlepoint N.Z. 113 F5
Castlepollard Rep. of Ireland 51 E4
Castlerea Rep. of Ireland 51 D4
Castlereagh *r.* Australia 112 C3
Castle Rock U.S.A. 126 G5
Castletown Isle of Man 48 C4
Castletown Rep. of Ireland 51 E5
Castor Canada 121 I4
Castor *r.* U.S.A. 131 F4
Castor, Rivière du *r.* Canada 122 F3
Castra Regina Germany *see* **Regensburg**
Castres France 56 F5
Castricum Neth. 52 E2

▶**Castries** St Lucia 137 L6
Capital of St Lucia.

Castro Brazil 145 A4
Castro Chile 144 B6
Castro Alves Brazil 145 D1
Castro Verde Port. 57 B5
Castroville U.S.A. 128 C3
Çat Turkey 91 F3
Catacaos Peru 142 B5
Cataguases Brazil 145 C3
Catahoula Lake U.S.A. 131 E6
Çatak Turkey 91 F3
Catalão Brazil 145 B2
Çatalca Yarımadası *pen.* Turkey 59 M4
Catalina U.S.A. 129 H5
Catalonia *aut. comm.* Spain *see* **Cataluña**
Cataluña *aut. comm.* Spain 57 G3
Catalunya *aut. comm.* Spain *see* **Cataluña**
Catamarca Arg. 144 C3
Catana *Sicily* Italy *see* **Catania**
Catanduanes *i.* Phil. 69 G4
Catanduva Brazil 145 A3
Catania *Sicily* Italy 58 F6
Catanzaro Italy 58 G5
Cataract Creek *watercourse* U.S.A. 129 G3
Catarina U.S.A. 131 D6
Catarino Rodriguez Mex. 131 C7
Catarman Phil. 69 G4
Catastrophe, Cape Australia 111 A7
Catawba *r.* U.S.A. 133 D5
Cataxa Moz. 99 D5
Cat Ba, Đao *i.* Vietnam 70 D2
Catbalogan Phil. 69 G4
Catembe Moz. 101 K4
Catengue Angola 99 B5
Catete Angola 99 B4
Cathcart Australia 112 D6
Cathcart S. Africa 101 H7
Cathedral Peak S. Africa 101 I5
Cathedral Rock National Park Australia 112 F3
Catherdaniel Rep. of Ireland 51 B6
Catherine, Mount U.S.A. 129 G2
Catheys Valley U.S.A. 128 C3
Cathlamet U.S.A. 126 C3
Catió Guinea-Bissau 96 B3
Catisimiña Venez. 142 F3
Cat Island Bahamas 133 F7
Cat Lake Canada 121 N5
Catlettsburg U.S.A. 134 D4
Catoche, Cabo *c.* Mex. 133 C8
Cato Island and Bank *reef* Australia 110 F4
Catriló Arg. 144 D5
Cats, Mont des *hill* France 52 C4
Catskill U.S.A. 135 I2
Catskill Mountains U.S.A. 135 H2
Catuane Moz. 101 K4
Cauayan Phil. 69 G5
Caubvick, Mount Canada 123 J2
Cauca *r.* Col. 137 J7
Caucaia Brazil 143 K4
Caucasia Col. 142 C2
Caucasus *mts* Asia/Europe 91 F2
Cauchon Lake Canada 121 L4
Caudry France 52 D4
Caulonia Italy 58 G5
Caungula Angola 99 B4
Cauquenes Chile 144 B5
Causapscal Canada 123 I4
Cavaglià Italy 58 C2
Cavalcante, Serra do *hills* Brazil 145 B1
Cavalier U.S.A. 130 D1
Cavan Rep. of Ireland 51 E4
Çavdır Turkey 59 M6
Cave City U.S.A. 134 C5
Cave Creek U.S.A. 129 H5
Caveira *r.* Brazil 145 C1
Cavern Island Myanmar 71 B5
Cave Run Lake U.S.A. 134 D4
Caviana, Ilha *i.* Brazil 143 H3
Cawdor U.K. 50 F3
Cawnpore India *see* **Kanpur**
Cawston U.K. 49 I6
Caxias Brazil 143 J4
Caxias do Sul Brazil 145 A5
Caxito Angola 99 B4
Çay Turkey 59 N5
Cayambe, Volcán *vol.* Ecuador 142 C3
Çaybaşı Turkey *see* **Çayeli**
Çaycuma Turkey 59 O4
Çayeli Turkey 91 F2

▶**Cayenne** Fr. Guiana 143 H3
Capital of French Guiana.

Cayeux-sur-Mer France 52 B4
Çayırhan Turkey 59 N4
Cayman Brac *i.* Cayman Is 137 I5

▶**Cayman Islands** *terr.* West Indies 137 H5
United Kingdom Overseas Territory.
North America 9, 116–117

Cayman Trench *sea feature* Caribbean Sea 148 C4
Caynabo Somalia 98 E3
Cay Sal *i.* Bahamas 133 D8
Cay Sal Bank *sea feature* Bahamas 133 D8
Cay Santa Domingo *i.* Bahamas 133 F8
Cayucos U.S.A. 128 C4
Cayuga Canada 134 F2
Cayuga Lake U.S.A. 135 G2
Cay Verde *i.* Bahamas 133 F8
Cazê China 83 F3
Cazenovia U.S.A. 135 H2
Cazombo Angola 99 C5
Ceadâr-Lunga Moldova *see* **Ciadîr-Lunga**
Ceanannus Mór Rep. of Ireland *see* **Kells**
Ceann a Deas na Hearadh *pen.* U.K. *see* **South Harris**
Ceará Brazil *see* **Fortaleza**
Ceara Abyssal Plain *sea feature* S. Atlantic Ocean 148 F6
Ceatharlach Rep. of Ireland *see* **Carlow**
Ceballos Mex. 131 B7
Cebu Phil. 69 G4
Cebu *i.* Phil. 69 G4
Cecil Plains Australia 112 E1
Cecil Rhodes, Mount *hill* Australia 109 C6
Cecina Italy 58 D3
Cedar *r. ND* U.S.A. 130 C2
Cedar *r. NE* U.S.A. 130 D3
Cedar City U.S.A. 129 G3
Cedaredge U.S.A. 129 J2
Cedar Falls U.S.A. 130 E3
Cedar Grove U.S.A. 134 B2
Cedar Hill *NM* U.S.A. 129 J3
Cedar Hill *TN* U.S.A. 134 B5
Cedar Island U.S.A. 135 H5
Cedar Lake Canada 121 K4
Cedar Point U.S.A. 134 D3
Cedar Rapids U.S.A. 130 F3
Cedar Run U.S.A. 135 H4
Cedar Springs U.S.A. 134 C2
Cedartown U.S.A. 133 C5
Cedarville S. Africa 101 I6
Cedros Mex. 127 F8
Cedros, Cerro *mt.* Mex. 127 E7
Cedros, Isla *i.* Mex. 127 E7
Ceduna Australia 109 F8
Ceeldheere Somalia 98 E3
Ceerigaabo Somalia 98 E2
Cefalù *Sicily* Italy 58 F5
Cegléd Hungary 59 H1
Cêgnê China 76 B1
Ceheng China 76 E3
Çekerek Turkey 90 D2
Celaya Mex. 136 D4
Celbridge Rep. of Ireland 51 F4

▶**Celebes** *i.* Indon. 69 G7
4th largest island in Asia.

Celebes Basin *sea feature* Pacific Ocean 150 E5
Celebes Sea Indon./Phil. 69 G6
Celestún Mex. 136 F4
Celina *OH* U.S.A. 134 C3
Celina *TN* U.S.A. 134 C5
Celje Slovenia 58 F1
Celle Germany 53 K2
Celovec Austria *see* **Klagenfurt**
Celtic Sea Rep. of Ireland/U.K. 46 D5
Celtic Shelf *sea feature* N. Atlantic Ocean 148 H2
Cenderawasih, Teluk *b.* Indon. 69 J7
Centane S. Africa *see* **Kentani**
Centenary Zimbabwe 99 D5
Center *NE* U.S.A. 130 D3
Center *TX* U.S.A. 131 E6
Centereach U.S.A. 135 I3
Center Point U.S.A. 133 C5
Centerville *AL* U.S.A. 133 C5
Centerville *IA* U.S.A. 130 E3
Centerville *MO* U.S.A. 131 F4
Centerville *TX* U.S.A. 131 E6
Centerville *WV* U.S.A. 134 E4
Centrafricaine, République *country* Africa *see* **Central African Republic**
Central *admin. dist.* Botswana 101 H2
Central U.S.A. 129 I5
Central, Cordillera *mts* Col. 142 C3
Central, Cordillera *mts* Peru 142 C6
Central African Empire *country* Africa *see* **Central African Republic**
▶**Central African Republic** *country* Africa 98 B3
Africa 7, 94–95
Central Brahui Range *mts* Pak. 89 G4
Central Butte Canada 126 G2
Central City U.S.A. 130 D3
Centralia *IL* U.S.A. 130 F4
Centralia *WA* U.S.A. 126 C3
Central Kalahari Game Reserve *nature res.* Botswana 100 F2
Central Kara Rise *sea feature* Arctic Ocean 153 F1
Central Makran Range *mts* Pak. 89 G5
Central Mount Stuart *hill* Australia 108 F5
Central Pacific Basin *sea feature* Pacific Ocean 150 H5
Central Provinces *state* India *see* **Madhya Pradesh**
Central Range *mts* P.N.G. 69 K7
Central Russian Upland *hills* Rus. Fed. 43 H5
Central Siberian Plateau Rus. Fed. 65 M3
Central Square U.S.A. 135 G2
Centre U.S.A. 133 C5
Centreville U.S.A. 135 G4
Cenxi China 77 F4
Cenyang China *see* **Hengfeng**
Ceos *i.* Greece *see* **Kea**
Cephaloedium *Sicily* Italy *see* **Cefalù**
Cephalonia *i.* Greece 59 I5
Ceram *i.* Indon. *see* **Seram**
Ceram Sea Indon. *see* **Seram, Laut**
Cerbat Mountains U.S.A. 129 F4
Čerchov *mt.* Czech Rep. 53 M5
Ceres Arg. 144 D3
Ceres Brazil 145 A1
Ceres S. Africa 100 D7
Ceres U.S.A. 128 C3
Céret France 56 F5
Cerezo de Abajo Spain 57 E3
Cerignola Italy 58 F4
Cerigo *i.* Greece *see* **Kythira**
Cêringgolêb China *see* **Dongco**
Çerkeş Turkey 90 D2
Çerkeşli Turkey 59 M4
Çermik Turkey 91 E3
Cernăuți Ukr. *see* **Chernivtsi**
Cernavodă Romania 59 M2
Cerralvo, Isla *i.* Mex. 136 C4
Cërrik Albania 59 H4
Cerritos Mex. 136 D4
Cerro Azul Brazil 145 A4
Cerro de Pasco Peru 142 C6
Cerros Colorados, Embalse *resr* Arg. 144 C5
Cervantes, Cerro *mt.* Arg. 144 B8
Cervati, Monte *mt.* Italy 58 F4
Cervione *Corsica* France 56 I5
Cervo Spain 57 C2
Cesena Italy 58 E2
Cēsis Latvia 45 N8
Česká Republika *country* Europe *see* **Czech Republic**
České Budějovice Czech Rep. 47 O6
Českomoravská Vysočina *hills* Czech Rep. 47 O6
Český Krumlov Czech Rep. 47 O6
Český Les *mts* Czech Rep./Germany 53 M5
Çeşme Turkey 59 L5
Cessnock Australia 112 E4
Cetatea Albă Ukr. *see* **Bilhorod-Dnistrovs'kyy**
Cetinje Serb. and Mont. 58 H3
Cetraro Italy 58 F5

▶**Ceuta** N. Africa 57 D6
Spanish Territory.

Ceva-i-Ra *reef* Fiji 107 H4
Cévennes *mts* France 56 F5
Cévennes, Parc National des *nat. park* France 56 F4
Cevizli Turkey 85 C1
Cevizlik Turkey *see* **Maçka**
Ceyhan Turkey 90 D3
Ceyhan *r.* Turkey 85 B1
Ceyhan Boğazı *r. mouth* Turkey 85 B1
Ceylanpınar Turkey 91 F3
Ceylon *country* Asia *see* **Sri Lanka**
Chaacha Turkm. 89 F2
Chābahār Iran 89 F5
Chabrol *i.* New Caledonia *see* **Lifou**
Chabug China 83 E2
Chabyêr Caka *salt l.* China 83 F3
Chachapoyas Peru 142 C5
Chāche Turkm. *see* **Chaacha**
Chachoengsao Thai. 71 C4
Chachran Pak. 89 H4
Chachro Pak. 89 H5
Chaco *r.* U.S.A. 129 I3
Chaco Boreal *reg.* Para. 144 E2
Chaco Culture National Historical Park *nat. park* U.S.A. 129 J3
Chaco Mesa *plat.* U.S.A. 129 J4

▶**Chad** *country* Africa 97 E3
5th largest country in Africa.
Africa 7, 94–95

Chad, Lake Africa 97 E3
Chadaasan Mongolia 72 I3
Chadan Rus. Fed. 80 H1
Chadibe Botswana 101 H2
Chadileo *r.* Arg. 144 C5
Chadron U.S.A. 130 C3
Chadyr-Lunga Moldova *see* **Ciadîr-Lunga**
Chae Hom Thai. 70 B3
Chaeryŏng N. Korea 75 B5
Chae Son National Park Thai. 66 B3
Chagai Pak. 89 G4
Chagai Hills Afgh./Pak. 89 F4
Chagdo Kangri *mt.* China 83 F2
Chaghā Khūr *mt.* Iran 88 C4
Chaghcharān Afgh. 89 G3
Chagny France 56 G3
Chagoda Rus. Fed. 42 G4
Chagos Archipelago *is* B.I.O.T. 149 M6
Chagos-Laccadive Ridge *sea feature* Indian Ocean 149 M6
Chagos Trench *sea feature* Indian Ocean 149 M6
Chagoyan Rus. Fed. 74 C1
Chagrayskoye Plato *plat.* Kazakh. *see* **Shagyray, Plato**
Chagyl Turkm. 91 I2
Chāh Ākhvor Iran 89 E3
Chāh 'Ali Akbar Iran 88 E3
Chahbounia Alg. 57 H6
Chahchaheh Turkm. 89 F2
Chāh-e Āb Afgh. 89 H2
Chāh-e Bāgh *well* Iran 88 D4
Chāh-e Bāzargānī Iran 88 D4
Chāh-e Dow Chāhī Iran 88 D4
Chāh-e Gonbad *well* Iran 88 D3
Chāh-e Kavīr *well* Iran 88 E3
Chāh-e Khorāsān *well* Iran 88 D3
Chāh-e Khoshāb Iran 88 E3
Chāh-e Malek *well* Iran 88 D3
Chāh-e Malek Mīrzā *well* Iran 84 D4
Chāh-e Mūjān *well* Iran 88 D3
Chāh-e Qeyṣar *well* Iran 88 D4
Chāh-e Qobād *well* Iran 88 D3
Chāh-e Rāh Iran 88 D4
Chāh-e Raḥmān *well* Iran 89 E4
Chāh-e Shūr *well* Iran 88 D3
Chāh-e Tūnī *well* Iran 88 E3
Chāh Kūh Iran 88 D4
Chāh Lak Iran 88 E5
Chāh Pās *well* Iran 88 D3
Chah Sandan Pak. 89 F4
Chaibasa India 83 F5
Chaigneau, Lac *l.* Canada 123 I3
Chainat Thai. 70 C4
Chainjoin Co *l.* China 83 F2
Chai Prakan Thai. 70 B3
Chaitén Chile 144 B6
Chai Wan *Hong Kong* China 73 [inset]
Chaiya Thai. 71 B5
Chaiyaphum Thai. 70 C4
Chajarí Arg. 144 E4
Chakai India 83 F4
Chak Amru Pak. 89 I3
Chakar *r.* Pak. 89 H4
Chakaria Bangl. 83 H5
Chakdarra Pak. 89 I3
Chakku Pak. 89 G5
Chakmaktin Lake Afgh. 89 I2
Chakonipau, Lac *l.* Canada 123 H2
Chakoria Bangl. *see* **Chakaria**
Ch'ak'vi Georgia 91 F2
Chala Peru 142 D7
Chalap Dalan *mts* Afgh. 89 G3
Chalatenango El Salvador 136 G6
Chaláua Moz. 99 D5
Chalaxung China 76 C1
Chalcedon Turkey *see* **Kadıköy**
Chalengkou China 80 H4
Chaleur Bay *inlet* Canada 123 I4
Chaleurs, Baie des *inlet* Canada *see* **Chaleur Bay**
Chali China 76 C2
Chaling China 77 G3
Chalisgaon India 84 B1
Chalki *i.* Greece 59 L6
Chalkida Greece 59 J5
Challakere India 84 C3
Challans France 56 D3
Challapata Bol. 142 E7

▶**Challenger Deep** *sea feature* N. Pacific Ocean 150 F5
Deepest point in the world (Mariana Trench).

Challenger Fracture Zone *sea feature* S. Pacific Ocean 150 M8
Challis U.S.A. 126 E3
Chalmette U.S.A. 131 F6
Châlons-en-Champagne France 52 E6
Châlons-sur-Marne France *see* **Châlons-en-Champagne**
Chalon-sur-Saône France 56 G3
Chālūs Iran 88 C2
Cham Germany 53 M5
Cham, Kūh-e *hill* Iran 88 C3
Chamaico Arg. 144 D5
Chamais Bay Namibia 100 B4
Chaman Pak. 78 F3
Chaman Bid Iran 88 E2
Chamao, Khao *mt.* Thai. 71 C4
Chamba India 82 D2
Chamba Tanz. 99 D5
Chambal *r.* India 82 D4
Chambas Cuba 133 E8
Chambeaux, Lac *l.* Canada 123 H3
Chamberlain *r.* Australia 108 D4
Chamberlain Canada 121 J5
Chamberlain U.S.A. 130 D3
Chamberlain Lake U.S.A. 132 G2
Chambers U.S.A. 129 I4
Chambersburg U.S.A. 135 G4
Chambers Island U.S.A. 134 B1
Chambéry France 56 G4
Chambeshi *r.* Zambia 99 C5
Chambi, Jebel *mt.* Tunisia 58 C7
Chamdo China *see* **Qamdo**
Chamechaude *mt.* France 56 G4
Chamisš Bay Canada 120 E5
Chamoli India *see* **Gopeshwar**
Chamonix-Mont-Blanc France 56 H4
Champa India 83 E5
Champagne-Ardenne *admin. reg.* France 52 E6
Champagne Castle *mt.* S. Africa 101 I5
Champagne Humide *reg.* France 56 G2
Champagne Pouilleuse *reg.* France 56 F2
Champagnole France 56 G3
Champagny Islands Australia 108 D3
Champaign U.S.A. 130 F3
Champasak Laos 70 D4
Champdoré, Lac *l.* Canada 123 I3
Champhai India 83 H5
Champion Canada 120 H5
Champlain U.S.A. 135 G4
Champlain, Lake Canada/U.S.A. 135 I1
Champotón Mex. 136 F5
Chamrajnagar India 84 C4
Chamzinka Rus. Fed. 43 J5
Chana Thai. 71 C6
Chanak Turkey *see* **Çanakkale**
Chañaral Chile 144 B3
Chanārān Iran 88 E2
Chanda India *see* **Chandrapur**
Chandalar *r.* U.S.A. 118 D3
Chandausi India 82 D3
Chandbali India 83 F5
Chandeleur Islands U.S.A. 131 F6
Chanderi India 82 D4
Chandigarh India 82 D3
Chandil India 83 F5
Chandler Canada 123 I4
Chandler *AZ* U.S.A. 129 H5
Chandler *IN* U.S.A. 134 B4
Chandler *OK* U.S.A. 131 D5
Chandod India 82 C5
Chandos Lake Canada 135 G1
Chandpur Bangl. 83 G5
Chandpur India 82 D3
Chandragiri India 84 C3
Chandrapur India 84 C2
Chandvad India 84 B1
Chandyr *r.* Turkm. 88 D2
Chandyr Uzbek. 89 G2
Chang, Ko *i.* Thai. 71 C4
Chang'an China 77 F1
Changane *r.* Moz. 101 K3
Changbai China 74 C4

Changbai Shan mts China/N. Korea 74 B4
Chang Cheng research station Antarctica see Great Wall
Changcheng China 77 F5
Changchow Fujian China see Zhangzhou
Changchow Jiangsu China see Changzhou
Changchun China 74 B4
Changchunling China 74 B3
Changde China 77 F2
Changgang China 77 G3
Changge China 77 G1
Changgi-ap pt S. Korea 75 C5
Changgo China 83 F3
Chang Hu l. China 77 G2
Changhua Taiwan 77 I3
Changhŭng S. Korea 75 B6
Changhwa Taiwan see Changhua
Changi Sing. 71 [inset]
Changji China 80 G3
Changjiang China 77 F5
Chang Jiang r. China 77 I2 see Yangtze
Changjiang Kou China see Mouth of the Yangtze
Changjin-ho resr N. Korea 75 B4
Changkiang China see Zhanjiang
Changlang India 83 H4
Changleng China see Xinjian
Changling China 74 A3
Changlung Jammu and Kashmir 87 M3
Changma China 80 I4
Changning Jiangxi China see Xunwu
Changning Sichuan China 76 E2
Changnyŏn N. Korea 75 B5
Ch'ang-pai Shan mts China/N. Korea see Changbai Shan
Changpu China see Suining
Changp'yŏng S. Korea 75 C5
Changsan-got pt N. Korea 75 B5
Changsha China 77 G2
Changshan China 77 H2
Changshi China 76 E3
Changshoujie China 77 G2
Changshu China 77 I2
Changtai China 77 H3
Changteh China see Changde
Changting Fujian China 77 H3
Changting Heilong. China 74 C3
Ch'angwŏn S. Korea 75 C6
Changxing China 77 H2
Changyang China 77 F2
Changyŏn N. Korea 75 B5
Changyuan China 77 G1
Changzhi China 73 K5
Changzhou China 77 H2
Chañi, Nevado de mt. Arg. 144 C2
Chania Greece 59 K7
Chanion, Kolpos b. Greece 59 J7
Chankou China 76 E1
Channahon U.S.A. 134 A3
Channapatna India 84 C3
Channel Islands English Chan. 49 E9
Channel Islands U.S.A. 128 D5
Channel Islands National Park U.S.A. 128 D4
Channel-Port-aux-Basques Canada 123 K5
Channel Rock i. Bahamas 133 E8
Channel Tunnel France/U.K. 49 I7
Channing U.S.A. 131 C5
Chantada Spain 57 C2
Chanthaburi Thai. 71 C4
Chantilly France 52 C5
Chanumla India 71 A5
Chanute U.S.A. 130 E4
Chanuwala Pak. 89 I3
Chany, Ozero salt l. Rus. Fed. 64 I4
Chaohu China 77 H2
Chao Hu l. China 77 H2
Chaor He r. China see Qulin Gol
Chaouèn Morocco 57 D6
Chaowula Shan mt. China 76 C1
Chaoyang Guangdong China 77 H4
Chaoyang Heilong. China see Jiayin
Chaoyang Liaoning China 73 M4
Chaoyangcun China 74 B2
Chaozhong China 74 A2
Chaozhou China 77 H4
Chapada Diamantina, Parque Nacional nat. park Brazil 145 C1
Chapada dos Veadeiros, Parque Nacional da nat. park Brazil 145 B1
Chapais Canada 122 G4
Chapak Guzar Afgh. 89 G2
Chapala, Laguna de l. Mex. 136 D4
Chapayev Kazakh. 78 E1
Chapayevo Kazakh. see Chapayev
Chapayevsk Rus. Fed. 43 K5
Chapecó Brazil 144 F3
Chapecó r. Brazil 144 F3
Chapel-en-le-Frith U.K. 48 F5
Chapelle-lez-Herlaimont Belgium 52 E4
Chapeltown U.K. 48 F5
Chapleau Canada 122 E5
Chaplin Canada 121 J5
Chaplin Lake Canada 121 J5
Chaplygin Rus. Fed. 43 H5
Chapman, Mount Canada 120 G5
Chapmanville U.S.A. 134 D5
Chappell U.S.A. 130 C3
Chappell Islands Australia 111 [inset]
Chapra Bihar India see Chhapra
Chapra Jharkhand India see Chatra
Chapri Pass Afgh. 89 G3
Charagua Bol. 142 F7
Charay Mex. 127 F8
Charcas Mex. 136 D4
Charcot Island Antarctica 152 L2
Chard Canada 121 I4
Chard U.K. 49 E8
Chardara Kazakh. see Shardara
Chardara, Step' plain Kazakh. 80 C3
Chardon U.S.A. 134 E3
Chardzhev Turkm. see Turkmenabat
Chardzhou Turkm. see Turkmenabat
Charef Alg. 57 H6
Charef, Oued watercourse Morocco 54 D5
Charente r. France 56 D4
Chari r. Cameroon/Chad 97 E3
Chārī Iran 88 E4
Chārīkār Afgh. 89 H3
Chariton U.S.A. 130 E3
Chärjew Turkm. see Turkmenabat
Charkayuvom Rus. Fed. 42 L2
Chār Kent Afgh. 89 G2
Charkhlik China see Ruoqiang
Charleroi Belgium 52 E4
Charles, Cape U.S.A. 135 H5
Charlesbourg Canada 123 H5
Charles City IA U.S.A. 130 E3
Charles City VA U.S.A. 135 G5
Charles de Gaulle airport France 52 C5
Charles Hill Botswana 100 E2
Charles Island Galápagos Ecuador see Santa María, Isla
Charles Lake Canada 121 I3
Charles Point Australia 108 E3
Charleston N.Z. 113 C5
Charleston IL U.S.A. 130 F4
Charleston MO U.S.A. 131 F4
Charleston SC U.S.A. 133 E5

▶Charleston WV U.S.A. 134 E4
State capital of West Virginia.

Charleston Peak U.S.A. 129 F3
Charlestown Rep. of Ireland 51 D4
Charlestown IN U.S.A. 134 C4
Charlestown NH U.S.A. 135 I2
Charlestown RI U.S.A. 135 J3
Charles Town U.S.A. 135 G4
Charleville Australia 111 D5
Charleville Rep. of Ireland see Rathluirc
Charleville-Mézières France 52 E5
Charlevoix U.S.A. 134 C1
Charlie Lake Canada 120 F3
Charlotte MI U.S.A. 134 C2
Charlotte NC U.S.A. 133 D5
Charlotte TN U.S.A. 134 B5

▶Charlotte Amalie Virgin Is (U.S.A.) 137 L5
Capital of the U.S. Virgin Islands.

Charlotte Harbor b. U.S.A. 133 D7
Charlotte Lake Canada 120 E4
Charlottesville U.S.A. 135 F4

▶Charlottetown Canada 123 J5
Provincial capital of Prince Edward Island.

Charlton Australia 112 A6
Charlton Island Canada 122 F3
Charron Lake Canada 121 M4
Charsadda Pak. 89 H3
Charshanga Turkm. 89 G2
Charshangngy Turkm. see Charshanga
Charters Towers Australia 110 D4
Chartres France 56 E2
Chas India 83 F5
Chase Canada 120 G5
Chase U.S.A. 134 C2
Chase City U.S.A. 135 F5
Chashmeh Nūrī Iran 88 E3
Chashmeh-ye Ab-e Garm spring Iran 88 E3
Chashmeh-ye Garm Ab spring Iran 88 E3
Chashmeh-ye Magu well Iran 88 E3
Chashmeh-ye Mūkīk spring Iran 88 E3
Chashmeh-ye Palasi Iran 88 D3
Chashmeh-ye Safīd spring Iran 88 E3
Chashmeh-ye Shotoran well Iran 88 D3
Chashniki Belarus 43 F5
Chaska U.S.A. 130 E2
Chaslands Mistake c. N.Z. 113 B8
Chasŏng N. Korea 74 B4
Chasseral mt. Switz. 47 K7
Chassiron, Pointe de pt France 56 D3
Chastab, Kūh-e mts Iran 88 D3
Chāt Iran 88 D2
Chatanika U.S.A. 118 D3
Châteaubriant France 56 D3
Château-du-Loir France 56 E3
Châteaudun France 56 E2
Chateaugay U.S.A. 135 H1
Châteauguay Canada 135 I1
Châteauguay r. Canada 123 H2
Châteauguay, Lac l. Canada 123 H2
Châteaulin France 56 B2
Châteaumeillant France 56 F3
Châteauneuf-en-Thymerais France 52 B6
Châteauneuf-sur-Loire France 56 F3
Chateau Pond l. Canada 123 K3
Châteauroux France 56 E3
Château-Salins France 52 G6
Château-Thierry France 52 D5
Chateh Canada 120 G3
Châtelet Belgium 52 E4
Châtellerault France 56 E3
Chatfield U.S.A. 122 B6
Chatham Canada 134 D2
Chatham U.K. 49 H7
Chatham MA U.S.A. 135 K3
Chatham NY U.S.A. 135 I2
Chatham PA U.S.A. 135 H4
Chatham VA U.S.A. 134 F5
Chatham, Isla i. Chile 144 B8
Chatham Island Galápagos Ecuador see San Cristóbal, Isla
Chatham Island N.Z. 107 I6
Chatham Island Samoa see Savai'i
Chatham Islands N.Z. 107 I6
Chatham Rise sea feature S. Pacific Ocean 150 I8
Chatham Strait U.S.A. 120 C3
Châtillon-sur-Seine France 56 G3
Chatkal Range mts Kyrg./Uzbek. 80 D3
Chatom U.S.A. 131 F6
Chatra India 83 F4
Chatra Nepal 83 F4
Chatsworth Canada 134 E1
Chatsworth U.S.A. 135 H4
Chattagam Bangl. see Chittagong
Chattanooga U.S.A. 133 C5
Chattarpur India see Chhatarpur
Chatteris U.K. 49 H6
Chattisgarh state India see Chhattisgarh
Chatturat Thai. 70 C4
Chatyr-Tash Kyrg. 80 E3
Châu Đôc Vietnam 71 D5
Chauhtan India 82 B4
Chauk Myanmar 70 A2
Chaumont France 56 G2
Chauncey U.S.A. 134 D4
Chaungzon Myanmar 70 B3
Chaunskaya Guba b. Rus. Fed. 65 R3
Chauny France 52 D5
Chau Phu Vietnam see Châu Đôc
Chausy Belarus see Chavusy
Chautauqua, Lake U.S.A. 134 F2
Chauter Pak. 89 G4
Chauvin Canada 121 I4
Chavakachcheri Sri Lanka 84 D4
Chaves Port. 57 C3
Chavigny, Lac l. Canada 122 G2
Chavusy Belarus 43 F5
Chawal r. Pak. 89 G4
Chây r. Vietnam 70 D2
Chayatyn, Khrebet ridge Rus. Fed. 74 E1
Chayevo Rus. Fed. 42 H4
Chaykovskiy Rus. Fed. 41 Q4
Chazhegovo Rus. Fed. 42 L3
Chazy U.S.A. 135 I1
Cheadle U.K. 49 F6
Cheaha Mountain hill U.S.A. 133 C5
Cheat r. U.S.A. 134 F4
Cheatham Lake U.S.A. 134 B5
Cheb Czech Rep. 53 M4
Chebba Tunisia 58 D7
Cheboksarskoye Vodokhranilishche resr Rus. Fed. 42 J5
Cheboksary Rus. Fed. 42 J4
Cheboygan U.S.A. 132 C2
Chechen', Ostrov i. Rus. Fed. 91 G2
Chech'ŏn S. Korea 75 C5
Chedabucto Bay Canada 123 J5
Cheddar U.K. 49 E7
Cheduba Myanmar 70 A3
Cheduba Island Myanmar 70 A3
Chée r. France 52 E6
Cheektowaga U.S.A. 135 F2
Cheepie Australia 112 B1
Cheetham, Cape Antarctica 152 H2
Chefoo China see Yantai
Chefornak U.S.A. 118 B3
Chefu Moz. 101 K2
Chegdomyn Rus. Fed. 74 D2
Chegga Mauritania 96 C2
Chegutu Zimbabwe 99 D5
Chehalis U.S.A. 126 C3
Chehar Burj Iran 88 E2
Chehardeh Iran 88 E3
Chehel Chashmeh, Kūh-e hill Iran 88 B3
Chehel Dokhtarān, Kūh-e mt. Iran 89 F4
Chehell'āyeh Iran 88 E4
Cheju S. Korea 75 B6
Cheju-do i. S. Korea 75 B6
Cheju-haehyŏp sea chan. S. Korea 75 B6
Chek Chue Hong Kong China see Stanley
Chekhov Moskovskaya Oblast' Rus. Fed. 43 H5
Chekhov Sakhalinskaya Oblast' Rus. Fed. 74 F3
Chekiang prov. China see Zhejiang
Chekichler Turkm. see Chekishlyar
Chekishlyar Turkm. 88 D2
Chek Lap Kok reg. Hong Kong China 77 [inset]
Chek Mun Hoi Hap Hong Kong China see Tolo Channel
Chekunda Rus. Fed. 74 D2
Chela, Serra da mts Angola 99 B5
Chelan, Lake U.S.A. 126 C2
Cheleken Turkm. 88 D2
Chélif, Oued r. Alg. 57 G5
Cheline Moz. 101 L2
Chelkar Kazakh. see Shalkar
Chełm Poland 43 D6
Chelmer r. U.K. 49 H7
Chełmno Poland 47 Q4
Chelmsford U.K. 49 H7
Chelsea MI U.S.A. 134 C2
Chelsea VT U.S.A. 135 I2
Cheltenham U.K. 49 E7
Chelva Spain 57 F4
Chelyabinsk Rus. Fed. 64 H4
Chelyuskin Rus. Fed. 153 E1
Chemba Moz. 99 D5
Chêm Co l. China 82 D2
Chemenibit Turkm. 89 F3
Chemnitz Germany 53 M4
Chemulpo S. Korea see Inch'ŏn
Chenab r. India/Pak. 82 B3
Chenachane, Oued watercourse Alg. 96 C2
Chendir r. Turkm. see Chandyr
Cheney U.S.A. 126 D3
Cheney Reservoir U.S.A. 130 D4
Chengalpattu India 84 D3
Chengbu China 77 F3
Chengchow China see Zhengzhou
Chengde China 73 L4
Chengdu China 76 E2
Chengele India 76 C2
Chenggong China 76 D3
Chenghai China 77 H4
Cheng Hai l. China 76 D3
Chengjiang China see Taihe
Chengmai China 77 F5
Chengtu China see Chengdu
Chengwu China 77 G1
Chengxian China 76 E1
Chengxiang Chongqing China see Wuxi
Chengxiang Jiangxi China see Quannan
Chengzhong China see Ningming
Cheniu Shan i. China 77 H1
Chenkaladi Sri Lanka 84 D5
Chennai India 84 D3
Chenqian Shan i. China 77 I2
Chenqing China 74 B2
Chenqingqiao China see Chenqing
Chenstokhov Poland see Częstochowa
Chentejn Nuruu mts Mongolia 73 J3
Chenxi China 77 F3
Chenyang China see Chenxi
Chenying China see Wannian
Chenzhou China 77 G3
Cheo Reo Vietnam 71 E4
Chepén Peru 142 C5
Chepes Arg. 144 C4
Chepo Panama 137 I7
Chepstow U.K. 49 E7
Cheptsa r. Rus. Fed. 42 K4
Chequamegon Bay U.S.A. 130 F2
Cher r. France 56 E3
Chera state India see Kerala
Cheraw U.S.A. 133 E5
Cherbaniani Reef India 84 A3
Cherbourg France 56 D2
Cherchell Alg. 57 H5
Cherchen China see Qiemo
Cherdakly Rus. Fed. 43 K5
Cherdyn' Rus. Fed. 41 R3
Chereapani reef India see Byramgore Reef
Cheremkhovo Rus. Fed. 72 I2
Cheremshany Rus. Fed. 74 D3
Cheremukhovka Rus. Fed. 42 K4
Cherepanovo Rus. Fed. 72 E2
Cherepovets Rus. Fed. 42 H4
Cherevkovo Rus. Fed. 42 J3
Chergui, Chott ech imp. l. Alg. 54 D5
Chéria Alg. 58 B7
Cheriton U.S.A. 135 H5
Cheriyam atoll India 84 B4
Cherkassy Ukr. see Cherkasy
Cherkasy Ukr. 43 G6
Cherkessk Rus. Fed. 91 F1
Cherla India 84 D2
Chernaya Rus. Fed. 42 M1
Chernaya r. Rus. Fed. 42 M1
Chernigov Ukr. see Chernihiv
Chernigovka Rus. Fed. 74 D3
Chernihiv Ukr. 43 F6
Cherninivka Ukr. 43 H7
Chernivtsi Ukr. 43 E6
Chernobyl' Ukr. see Chornobyl'
Chernogorsk Rus. Fed. 72 G2
Chernovtsy Ukr. see Chernivtsi
Chernoye More sea Asia/Europe see Black Sea
Chernushka Rus. Fed. 41 R4
Chernyakhiv Ukr. 43 F6
Chernyakhovsk Rus. Fed. 45 L9
Chernyanka Rus. Fed. 43 H6
Chernyayeve Rus. Fed. 74 B1
Chernyshevsk Rus. Fed. 73 L2
Chernyshevskiy Rus. Fed. 65 M3
Chernyshkovskiy Rus. Fed. 43 I6
Chernyye Zemli reg. Rus. Fed. 43 J7
Chernyy Irtysh r. China/Kazakh. see Ertix He
Chernyy Porog Rus. Fed. 42 G3
Chernyy Yar Rus. Fed. 43 J6
Cherokee U.S.A. 130 E3
Cherokee Sound Bahamas 133 E7

▶Cherrapunji India 83 G4
Highest recorded annual rainfall in the world.

Cherry Creek r. U.S.A. 130 C2
Cherry Creek Mountains U.S.A. 129 F1
Cherry Hill U.S.A. 135 H4
Cherry Island Solomon Is 107 G3
Cherry Lake U.S.A. 128 D2
Cherskiy Rus. Fed. 153 C2
Cherskiy Range mts Rus. Fed. see Cherskogo, Khrebet
Cherskogo, Khrebet mts Rus. Fed. 65 P3
Cherskogo, Khrebet mts Rus. Fed. 73 K2
Chertkov Ukr. see Chortkiv
Chertkovo Rus. Fed. 43 I6
Cherven Bryag Bulg. 59 K3
Chervonoarmeyskoye Ukr. see Vil'nyans'k
Chervonoarmiys'k Donets'ka Oblast' Ukr. see Krasnoarmiys'k
Chervonoarmiys'k Rivnens'ka Oblast' Ukr. see Radyvyliv
Chervonograd Ukr. see Chervonohrad
Chervonohrad Ukr. 43 E6
Chervyen' Belarus 43 F5
Cherwell r. U.K. 49 F7
Cherykaw Belarus 43 F5
Chesapeake U.S.A. 135 G5
Chesapeake Bay U.S.A. 135 G4
Chesham U.K. 49 G7
Cheshire Plain U.K. 48 E5
Cheshme 2-y Turkm. 89 F2
Cheshskaya Guba b. Rus. Fed. 42 J2
Cheshtebe Tajik. 89 I2
Cheshunt U.K. 49 G7
Chesnokovka Rus. Fed. see Novoaltaysk
Chester Canada 123 I5
Chester U.K. 48 E5
Chester CA U.S.A. 128 C1
Chester IL U.S.A. 130 F4
Chester MT U.S.A. 126 F2
Chester OH U.S.A. 134 E4
Chester SC U.S.A. 133 D5
Chester r. U.S.A. 135 G4
Chesterfield U.K. 48 F5
Chesterfield U.S.A. 135 G5
Chesterfield, Îles is New Caledonia 107 F3
Chesterfield Inlet Canada 121 N2
Chesterfield Inlet inlet Canada 121 M2
Chester-le-Street U.K. 48 F4
Chestertown MD U.S.A. 135 G4
Chestertown NY U.S.A. 135 I2
Chesterville Canada 135 H1
Chestnut Ridge U.S.A. 134 F3
Chesuncook Lake U.S.A. 132 G2
Chetaïbi Alg. 58 B6
Chéticamp Canada 123 J5
Chetlat i. India 84 B4
Chetumal Mex. 136 G5
Chetwynd Canada 120 F4
Cheung Chau Hong Kong China 77 [inset]
Chevelon Creek r. U.S.A. 129 H4
Cheviot N.Z. 113 D6
Cheviot Hills U.K. 48 E3
Cheviot Range hills Australia 110 C5
Chevreulx r. Canada 122 G3
Cheyenne OK U.S.A. 131 D5

▶Cheyenne WY U.S.A. 126 G4
State capital of Wyoming.

Cheyenne r. U.S.A. 130 C2
Cheyenne Wells U.S.A. 130 C4
Cheyne Bay Australia 109 B8
Cheyur India 84 D3
Chezacut Canada 120 E4
Chhapra India 83 F4
Chhata India 82 D4
Chhatak Bangl. 83 G4
Chhatarpur Jharkhand India 83 F4
Chhatarpur Madhya Pradesh India 82 D4
Chhatr Pak. 89 H4
Chhatrapur India 84 E2
Chhattisgarh state India 83 E5
Chhay Arêng, Stœng r. Cambodia 71 C5
Chhindwara India 82 D5
Chhitkul India 82 D3
Chhukha Bhutan 83 G4
Chi, Lam r. Thai. 71 C4
Chi, Mae Nam r. Thai. 70 D4
Chiai Taiwan 77 I4
Chiamboni Somalia 98 E4
Chiange Angola 99 B5
Chiang Kham Thai. 70 C3
Chiang Khan Thai. 70 C3
Chiang Mai Thai. 70 B3
Chiang Rai Thai. 70 B3
Chiang Saen Thai. 70 C2
Chiari Italy 58 C2
Chiautla Mex. 136 E5
Chiavenno Italy 58 C1
Chiayi Taiwan see Chiai
Chiba Japan 75 F6
Chibi China 77 G2
Chibia Angola 99 B5
Chibizovka Rus. Fed. see Zherdevka
Chiboma Moz. 99 D6
Chibougamau Canada 122 G4
Chibougamau, Lac l. Canada 122 G4
Chibu-Sangaku National Park Japan 75 E5
Chibuto Moz. 101 K3
Chibuzhang Hu l. China 83 G2
Chicacole India see Srikakulam

▶Chicago U.S.A. 134 B3
4th most populous city in North America.

Chic-Chocs, Monts mts Canada 123 I4
Chichagof U.S.A. 120 B3
Chichagof Island U.S.A. 120 C3
Chichak r. Pak. 89 G5
Chichaoua Morocco 54 C5
Chichatka Rus. Fed. 74 A1
Chicheng China see Pengxi
Chichester U.K. 49 G8
Chichester Range mts Australia 108 B5
Chichgarh India 84 D1
Chichibu Japan 75 E6
Chichibu-Tama National Park Japan 75 E6
Chichijima-rettō is Japan 75 F8
Chickasha U.S.A. 131 D5
Chiclana de la Frontera Spain 57 C5
Chiclayo Peru 142 C5
Chico r. Arg. 144 C6
Chico U.S.A. 128 C2
Chicomo Moz. 101 L3
Chicopee U.S.A. 135 I2
Chicoutimi Canada 123 H4
Chicualacuala Moz. 101 J2
Chidambaram India 84 C4
Chidenguele Moz. 101 L3
Chidley, Cape Canada 119 L3
Chido China see Sêndo
Chido S. Korea 75 B6
Chiducuane Moz. 101 L3
Chiefland U.S.A. 133 D6
Chiêm Hoa Vietnam 70 D2
Chiemsee l. Germany 47 N7
Chiengmai Thai. see Chiang Mai
Chiers r. France 52 F5
Chieti Italy 58 F3
Chifeng China 73 L4
Chifre, Serra do mts Brazil 145 C2
Chiganak Kazakh. 80 D2
Chiginagak Volcano, Mount U.S.A. 118 C4
Chigu China 83 G3
Chigubo Moz. 101 K2
Chigu Co l. China 83 G3
Chihli, Gulf of China see Bo Hai
Chihuahua Mex. 127 G7
Chihuahua state Mex. 127 G7
Chiili Kazakh. 80 C3
Chikalda India 82 D5
Chikan China 77 F4
Chikaskia r. U.S.A. 131 D4
Chikhali Kalan Parasia India 82 D5
Chikhli India 84 C1
Chikishlyar Turkm. see Chekishlyar
Chikmagalur India 84 B3
Chikodi India 84 B2
Chilanko r. Canada 120 F4
Chilas Jammu and Kashmir 82 C2
Chilaw Sri Lanka 84 C5
Chilcotin r. Canada 120 F5
Childers Australia 110 F5
Childress U.S.A. 131 C5

▶Chile country S. America 144 B4
South America 9, 140–141

Chile Basin sea feature S. Pacific Ocean 151 O8
Chile Chico Chile 144 B7
Chile Rise sea feature S. Pacific Ocean 151 O8
Chilgir Rus. Fed. 43 J7
Chilhowie U.S.A. 134 E5
Chilia-Nouă Ukr. see Kiliya
Chilik Kazakh. 80 E3
Chilika Lake India 84 E2
Chililabombwe Zambia 99 C5
Chilko r. Canada 120 F4
Chilko Lake Canada 120 E5
Chilkoot Pass Canada/U.S.A. 120 C3
Chilkoot Trail National Historic Site nat. park Canada 120 C3
Chillán Chile 144 B5
Chillicothe MO U.S.A. 130 E4
Chillicothe OH U.S.A. 134 D4
Chilliwack Canada 120 F5
Chil'mamedkum, Peski des. Turkm. 88 D1
Chilo India 82 C4
Chiloé, Isla de i. Chile 144 B6
Chiloé, Isla Grande de i. Chile see Chiloé, Isla de
Chilpancingo Mex. 136 E5
Chilpancingo de los Bravos Mex. see Chilpancingo
Chilpi Jammu and Kashmir 82 C1
Chiltern Hills U.K. 49 G7
Chilton U.S.A. 134 A1
Chiluage Angola 99 C4
Chilubi Zambia 99 C5
Chilung Taiwan 77 I3
Chilwa, Lake Malawi 99 D5
Chimala Tanz. 99 D4
Chimaltenango Guat. 136 F6
Chi Ma Wan Hong Kong China 77 [inset]
Chimay Belgium 52 E4
Chimbas Arg. 144 C4
Chimbay Uzbek. 80 A3
Chimborazo mt. Ecuador 142 C4
Chimbote Peru 142 C5
Chimboy Uzbek. see Chimbay
Chimian Pak. 89 I4
Chimishliya Moldova see Cimişlia
Chimkent Kazakh. see Shymkent
Chimney Rock U.S.A. 129 J3
Chimoio Moz. 99 D5
Chimtargha, Qullai mt. Tajik. 89 H2
Chimtorga, Gora mt. Tajik. see Chimtargha, Qullai

▶China country Asia 72 H5
Most populous country in the world and in Asia. 2nd largest country in Asia and 4th largest in the world.
Asia 6, 62–63

China Mex. 131 D7
China, Republic of country Asia see Taiwan
China Bakir r. Myanmar see To
China Lake CA U.S.A. 128 E4
China Lake ME U.S.A. 135 K1
Chinandega Nicaragua 136 G6
China Point U.S.A. 128 D5
Chinati Peak U.S.A. 131 B6
Chincha Alta Peru 142 C6
Chinchaga r. Canada 120 G3
Chinchilla Australia 112 E1
Chincholi India 84 C2
Chinchorro, Banco sea feature Mex. 137 G5
Chincoteague Bay U.S.A. 135 H5
Chinde Moz. 99 D5
Chindo S. Korea 75 B6
Chin-do i. S. Korea 75 B6
Chindwin r. Myanmar 70 A2
Chinese Turkestan aut. reg. China see Xinjiang Uygur Zizhiqu
Chinghai prov. China see Qinghai
Chingiz-Tau, Khrebet mts Kazakh. 80 E2
Chingleput India see Chengalpattu
Chingola Zambia 99 C5
Chinguar Angola 99 B5
Chinguețți Mauritania 96 B2
Chinhae S. Korea 75 C6
Chinhoyi Zimbabwe 99 D5
Chini India see Kalpa
Chining China see Jining
Chiniot Pak. 89 I4
Chinipas Mex. 127 F8
Chinit, Stœng r. Cambodia 71 D4
Chinju S. Korea 75 C6
Chinle U.S.A. 129 I3
Chinmen Taiwan 77 H3
Chinmen Tao i. Taiwan 77 H3
Chinnamp'o N. Korea see Namp'o
Chinnur India 84 C2
Chino Creek watercourse U.S.A. 129 G4
Chinon France 56 E3
Chinook U.S.A. 126 F2
Chinook Trough sea feature N. Pacific Ocean 150 I3
Chino Valley U.S.A. 129 G4
Chintamani India 84 C3
Chioggia Italy 58 E2
Chios Greece 59 L5
Chios i. Greece 59 K5
Chipata Zambia 99 D5
Chipchihua, Sierra de mts Arg. 144 C6
Chiphu Cambodia 71 D5
Chipindo Angola 99 B5
Chipinga Zimbabwe see Chipinge
Chipinge Zimbabwe 99 D6
Chipley U.S.A. 133 C6
Chipman Canada 123 I5
Chippenham U.K. 49 E7
Chippewa, Lake U.S.A. 130 F2
Chippewa Falls U.S.A. 130 F2
Chipping Norton U.K. 49 F7
Chipping Sodbury U.K. 49 E7
Chipurupalle Andhra Pradesh India 84 D2
Chipurupalle Andhra Pradesh India 84 D2
Chiquilá Mex. 133 C8
Chiquinquira Col. 142 D2
Chir r. Rus. Fed. 43 I6
Chirada India 84 D3
Chirala India 84 D3
Chiras Afgh. 89 G3
Chirchik Uzbek. 80 C3
Chiredzi Zimbabwe 99 D6
Chirfa Niger 96 E2
Chiricahua National Monument nat. park U.S.A. 129 I5
Chiricahua Peak U.S.A. 129 I6
Chirikof Island U.S.A. 118 C4
Chiriquí, Golfo de b. Panama 137 H7
Chiriquí, Volcán de vol. Panama see Barú, Volcán
Chiri-san mt. S. Korea 75 B6
Chirk U.K. 49 D6
Chirnside U.K. 50 G5
Chirripo mt. Costa Rica 137 H7
Chisamba Zambia 99 C5
Chisana r. U.S.A. 120 A2
Chisasibi Canada 122 F3
Chishima-retto is Rus. Fed. see Kuril Islands
Chisholm Canada 120 H4
Chishtian Mandi Pak. 89 I4
Chishui China 76 E2
Chishuihe China 76 E3
Chisimaio Somalia see Kismaayo

▶Chişinău Moldova 59 M1
Capital of Moldova.

Chistopol' Rus. Fed. 42 K5
Chita Rus. Fed. 73 K2
Chitado Angola 99 B5
Chitaldrug India see Chitradurga
Chitalwana India 82 B4
Chitambo Zambia 99 D5
Chita Oblast admin. div. Rus. Fed. see Chitinskaya Oblast'
Chitato Angola 99 C4
Chitek Lake Canada 121 J4
Chitek Lake l. Canada 121 L4
Chitembo Angola 99 B5
Chitina U.S.A. 118 D3

Colonel Hill Bahamas 133 F8
Colonet, Cabo c. Mex. 127 D7
Colônia r. Brazil 145 D1
Colonia Micronesia 69 J5
Colonia Agrippina Germany see Cologne
Colonia Díaz Mex. 127 F7
Colonia Julia Fenestris Italy see Fano
Colonia Las Heras Arg. 144 C7
Colonial Heights U.S.A. 135 G5
Colonna, Capo c. Italy 58 G5
Colonsay i. U.K. 50 C4
Colorado r. Arg. 144 D5
Colorado r. Mex./U.S.A. 127 E7
Colorado r. U.S.A. 131 D6
Colorado state U.S.A. 126 G5
Colorado City AZ U.S.A. 129 G3
Colorado City TX U.S.A. 131 C5
Colorado Desert U.S.A. 128 E5
Colorado National Monument nat. park U.S.A. 129 I2
Colorado Plateau U.S.A. 129 I3
Colorado River Aqueduct canal U.S.A. 129 F4
Colorado Springs U.S.A. 126 G5
Colossae Turkey see Honaz
Colotlán Mex. 136 D4
Cölpin Germany 53 N1
Colquiri Bol. 142 E7
Colquitt U.S.A. 133 C6
Colson U.S.A. 134 D5
Colsterworth U.K. 49 G6
Colstrip U.S.A. 126 G3
Coltishall U.K. 49 I6
Colton CA U.S.A. 128 E4
Colton NY U.S.A. 135 H1
Colton UT U.S.A. 129 H2
Columbia KY U.S.A. 134 C5
Columbia LA U.S.A. 131 E5
Columbia MD U.S.A. 135 G4
Columbia MO U.S.A. 130 E4
Columbia MS U.S.A. 131 F6
Columbia NC U.S.A. 132 E5
Columbia PA U.S.A. 135 G3
▶Columbia SC U.S.A. 133 D5
State capital of South Carolina.
Columbia TN U.S.A. 132 C5
Columbia r. U.S.A. 126 C3
Columbia, District of admin. dist. U.S.A. 135 G4
Columbia, Mount Canada 120 G4
Columbia, Sierra mts Mex. 123 E7
Columbia City U.S.A. 134 C3
Columbia Lake Canada 120 H5
Columbia Mountains Canada 120 F4
Columbia Plateau U.S.A. 126 D3
Columbine, Cape S. Africa 100 C7
Columbus GA U.S.A. 133 C5
Columbus IN U.S.A. 134 C4
Columbus MS U.S.A. 131 F5
Columbus MT U.S.A. 126 F3
Columbus NC U.S.A. 133 D5
Columbus NE U.S.A. 130 D3
Columbus NM U.S.A. 127 G7
▶Columbus OH U.S.A. 134 D4
State capital of Ohio.
Columbus TX U.S.A. 131 D6
Columbus Grove U.S.A. 134 C3
Columbus Salt Marsh U.S.A. 128 D2
Colusa U.S.A. 128 B2
Colville N.Z. 113 E3
Colville U.S.A. 126 D2
Colville r. U.S.A. 118 C2
Colville Channel N.Z. 113 E3
Colville Lake Canada 118 F3
Colwyn Bay U.K. 48 D5
Comacchio Italy 58 E2
Comacchio, Valli di lag. Italy 58 E2
Comai China 83 G3
Comalcalco Mex. 136 F5
Comanche U.S.A. 131 D6
Comandante Ferraz research station Antarctica 152 A2
Comandante Salas Arg. 144 C4
Comănești Romania 59 L1
Combahee r. U.S.A. 133 D5
Combarbalá Chile 144 B4
Comber U.K. 51 G3
Combermere Bay Myanmar 70 A3
Combles France 52 C4
Combol i. Indon. 71 C7
Combomune Moz. 101 K2
Comboyne Australia 112 F3
Comencho, Lac l. Canada 122 G4
Comendador Dom. Rep. see Elías Piña
Comendador Gomes Brazil 145 A2
Comeragh Mountains hills Rep. of Ireland 51 E5
Comercinho Brazil 145 C2
Cometela Moz. 101 L1
Comfort U.S.A. 131 D6
Comilla Bangl. 83 G5
Comines Belgium 52 C4
Comino, Capo c. Sardinia Italy 58 C4
Comitán de Domínguez Mex. 132 F5
Commack U.S.A. 135 I3
Commentry France 56 F3
Committee Bay Canada 119 J3
Commonwealth Territory admin. div. Australia see Jervis Bay Territory
Como Italy 58 C2
Como, Lago di Italy see Como, Lake
Como, Lake Italy 58 C2
Como Chamling l. China 83 G3
Comodoro Rivadavia Arg. 144 C7
Comores country Africa see Comoros
Comorin, Cape India 84 C4
Comoro Islands country Africa see Comoros
▶Comoros country Africa 99 E5
Africa 7, 94–95
Compiègne France 52 C5
Comprida, Ilha i. Brazil 145 B4
Comrat Moldova 59 M1
Comrie U.K. 50 F4
Comstock U.S.A. 131 C6
Cona China 83 G4
▶Conakry Guinea 96 B4
Capital of Guinea.
Cona Niyeo Arg. 144 C6
Conceição r. Brazil 145 B2
Conceição da Barra Brazil 145 D2
Conceição do Araguaia Brazil 143 I5
Conceição do Mato Dentro Brazil 145 C2
Concepción Chile 144 B5
Concepción Mex. 131 C7
Concepción r. Mex. 127 E7
Concepción Para. 144 E2
Concepción, Punta pt Mex. 127 F8
Concepción de la Vega Dom. Rep. see La Vega
Conception, Point U.S.A. 128 C4
Conception Island Bahamas 129 F8
Conchas U.S.A. 127 G6
Conchas Lake U.S.A. 127 G6
Concho U.S.A. 129 I4
Conchos r. Nuevo León/Tamaulipas Mex. 131 D7
Conchos r. Mex. 131 B6
Concord CA U.S.A. 128 B3
Concord NC U.S.A. 133 D5
▶Concord NH U.S.A. 135 J2
State capital of New Hampshire.
Concord VT U.S.A. 135 J1
Concordia Arg. 144 E4
Concordiá Mex. 131 B8
Concordia Peru 142 D4
Concordia S. Africa 100 C5
Concordia KS U.S.A. 130 D4
Concordia KY U.S.A. 134 B4
Concord Peak Afgh. 89 I2
Con Cuông Vietnam 70 D3
Condamine Australia 112 E1
Condamine r. Australia 112 D1
Côn Đao Vietnam 71 D5
Condeúba Brazil 145 C1
Condobolin Australia 112 C4
Condom France 56 E5
Condon U.S.A. 126 C3
Condor, Cordillera del mts Ecuador/Peru 142 C4
Condroz reg. Belgium 52 E4
Conecuh r. U.S.A. 133 C6
Conegliano Italy 58 E2
Conejos Mex. 131 C7
Conejos U.S.A. 127 G5
Conemaugh r. U.S.A. 134 F3
Conestogo Lake Canada 134 E2
Conesus Lake U.S.A. 135 G2
Conflict Group is P.N.G. 110 E1
Confoederatio Helvetica country Europe see Switzerland
Confusion Range mts U.S.A. 129 G2
Congdü China see Nyalam
Conghua China 77 G4
Congjiang China 77 F3
Congleton U.K. 48 E5
▶Congo country Africa 98 B4
Africa 7, 94–95
▶Congo r. Congo/Dem. Rep. Congo 98 B4
2nd longest river and largest drainage basin in Africa.
Formerly known as Zaïre.
Africa 92–93
Congo (Brazzaville) country Africa see Congo
Congo (Kinshasa) country Africa see Congo, Democratic Republic of
▶Congo, Democratic Republic of country Africa 98 C4
3rd largest and 4th most populous country in Africa.
Africa 7, 94–95
Congo, Republic of country Africa see Congo
Congo Basin Dem. Rep. Congo 98 C4
Congo Cone sea feature S. Atlantic Ocean 148 I6
Congo Free State country Africa see Congo, Democratic Republic of
Congonhas Brazil 145 C3
Congress U.S.A. 129 G4
Conimbla National Park Australia 112 D4
Coningsby U.K. 49 G5
Coniston Canada 122 E5
Coniston U.K. 48 D4
Conjuboy Australia 110 D3
Conklin Canada 121 I4
Conn r. Canada 122 F3
Conn, Lough l. Rep. of Ireland 51 C3
Connacht reg. Rep. of Ireland see Connaught
Connaught reg. Rep. of Ireland 51 C4
Conneaut U.S.A. 134 E3
Connecticut state U.S.A. 135 I3
Connemara reg. Rep. of Ireland 51 C4
Connemara National Park Rep. of Ireland 51 C4
Connersville U.S.A. 134 C4
Connolly, Mount Canada 120 C2
Connors Range hills Australia 110 E4
Conoble Australia 112 B4
Conquista Brazil 145 B2
Conrad U.S.A. 126 F2
Conrad Rise sea feature Southern Ocean 149 K9
Conroe U.S.A. 131 E6
Conselheiro Lafaiete Brazil 145 C3
Consett U.K. 48 F4
Consolación del Sur Cuba 133 D8
Côn Sơn i. Vietnam 71 D5
Consort Canada 121 I4
Constance Germany see Konstanz
Constance, Lake Germany/Switz. 47 L7
Constância dos Baetas Brazil 142 F5
Constanța Romania 59 M2
Constantia tourist site Cyprus see Salamis
Constantia Germany see Konstanz
Constantina Spain 57 D5
Constantine Alg. 54 F4
Constantine, Cape U.S.A. 118 C4
Constantinople Turkey see İstanbul
Constitución de 1857, Parque Nacional nat. park Mex. 129 F5
Consul Canada 121 I5
Contact U.S.A. 126 E4
Contagalo Brazil 145 C3
Contamana Peru 142 C5
Contas r. Brazil 145 D1
Contoy, Isla i. Mex. 133 C8
Contria Brazil 145 B2
Contwoyto Lake Canada 121 I1
Convención Col. 142 D2
Convent U.S.A. 131 F6
Conway U.K. see Conwy
Conway AR U.S.A. 131 E5
Conway ND U.S.A. 130 D1
Conway NH U.S.A. 135 J2
Conway SC U.S.A. 133 E5
Conway, Cape Australia 110 E4
Conway, Lake salt flat Australia 111 A6
Conway National Park Australia 110 E4
Conway Reef Fiji see Ceva-i-Ra
Conwy U.K. 48 D5
Conwy r. U.K. 49 D5
Coober Pedy Australia 109 F7
Cooch Behar India see Koch Bihar
Coochbehar India see Koch Bihar
Cook Australia 109 E7
Cook, Cape Canada 120 E5
Cook, Grand Récif de reef New Caledonia 107 G3
Cook, Mount N.Z. see Aoraki
Cookes Peak U.S.A. 127 G6
Cookeville U.S.A. 132 C4
Cookhouse S. Africa 101 G7
Cook Ice Shelf Antarctica 152 H2
Cook Inlet sea chan. U.S.A. 118 C3
▶Cook Islands terr. S. Pacific Ocean 150 J7
Self-governing New Zealand Territory.
Oceania 8, 104–105
Cooksburg U.S.A. 135 H2
Cooks Passage Australia 110 D2
Cookstown U.K. 51 F3
Cook Strait N.Z. 113 E5
Cooktown Australia 110 D2
Coolabah Australia 112 C3
Cooladdi Australia 112 B1
Coolah Australia 112 D3
Coolamon Australia 112 C5
Coolgardie Australia 109 C7
Coolibah Australia 108 E3
Coolidge U.S.A. 129 H5
Cooloola National Park Australia 111 F5
Coolum Beach Australia 111 F5
Cooma Australia 112 D6
Coombah Australia 111 C7
Coonabarabran Australia 112 D3
Coonamble Australia 112 D3
Coondambo Australia 111 A6
Coondapoor India see Kundapura
Coongoola Australia 112 B1
Coon Rapids U.S.A. 130 E2
Cooper Creek watercourse Australia 111 B6
Cooper Mountain Canada 120 G5
Coopernook Australia 112 F3
Cooper's Town Bahamas 133 E7
Cooperstown ND U.S.A. 130 D2
Cooperstown NY U.S.A. 135 H2
Coopracambra National Park Australia 112 D6
Coorabie Australia 109 F7
Coorong National Park Australia 111 B8
Coorow Australia 109 B7
Coosa r. U.S.A. 133 C5
Coos Bay U.S.A. 126 B4
Coos Bay b. U.S.A. 126 B4
Cootamundra Australia 112 D5
Cootehill Rep. of Ireland 51 E3
Cooyar Australia 112 E1
Copala Mex. 136 E5
Cope U.S.A. 130 C4
Copemish U.S.A. 134 C1
▶Copenhagen Denmark 45 H9
Capital of Denmark.
Copenhagen U.S.A. 135 H2
Copertino Italy 58 H4
Copeton Reservoir Australia 112 E2
Cô Pi, Phou mt. Laos/Vietnam 70 D3
Copiapó Chile 144 B3
Copley Australia 111 B6
Copparo Italy 58 D2
Copper Cliff Canada 122 E5
Copper Harbor U.S.A. 132 C2
Coppermine Canada see Kugluktuk
Coppermine r. Canada 120 H1
Coppermine Point Canada 122 D5
Copperton S. Africa 100 F5
Copp Lake Canada 120 H2
Coqên Xizang China 83 F3
Coqên Xizang China see Maindong
Coquilhatville Dem. Rep. Congo see Mbandaka
Coquille i. Micronesia see Pikelot
Coquille U.S.A. 126 B4
Coquimbo Chile 144 B3
Coquitlam Canada 120 F5
Corabia Romania 59 K3
Coração de Jesus Brazil 145 B2
Coracesium Turkey see Alanya
Coraki Australia 112 F2
Coral Bay Australia 109 A5
Coral Harbour Canada 119 J3
Coral Sea S. Pacific Ocean 106 F3
Coral Sea Basin S. Pacific Ocean 150 G6
▶Coral Sea Islands Territory terr. Australia 106 F3
Australian External Territory.
Corangamite, Lake Australia 112 A7
Corat Azer. 91 H2
Corbeny France 52 D5
Corbett Inlet Canada 121 M2
Corbett National Park India 82 D3
Corbie France 52 C5
Corbin U.S.A. 134 C5
Corby U.K. 49 G6
Corcaigh Rep. of Ireland see Cork
Corcoran U.S.A. 128 D3
Corcovado, Golfo de sea chan. Chile 144 B6
Corcyra i. Greece see Corfu
Cordele U.S.A. 133 D6
Cordelia U.S.A. 128 B2
Cordell U.S.A. 131 D5
Cordilheiras, Serra das hills Brazil 143 I5
Cordillera Azul, Parque Nacional nat. park Peru 142 C5
Cordillera de los Picachos, Parque Nacional nat. park Col. 142 D3
Cordillo Downs Australia 111 C5
Cordisburgo Brazil 145 B2
Córdoba Arg. 144 D4
Córdoba Durango Mex. 131 C7
Córdoba Veracruz Mex. 136 E5
Córdoba Spain 57 D5
Córdoba, Sierras de mts Arg. 144 D4
Cordova Spain see Córdoba
Cordova U.S.A. 118 D3
Corduba Spain see Córdoba
Corfu i. Greece 59 H5
Coria Spain 57 C4
Coribe Brazil 145 B1
Coricudgy mt. Australia 112 E4
Corigliano Calabro Italy 58 G5
Coringa Islands Australia 110 E3
Corinium U.K. see Cirencester
Corinth Greece 59 J6
Corinth KY U.S.A. 134 C4
Corinth MS U.S.A. 131 F5
Corinth NY U.S.A. 135 I2
Corinth, Gulf of sea chan. Greece 59 J5
Corinthus Greece see Corinth
Corinto Brazil 145 B2
Cork Rep. of Ireland 51 D6
Corleone Sicily Italy 58 E6
Çorlu Turkey 59 L4
Cormeilles France 49 H9
Cornelia S. Africa 101 I4
Cornélio Procópio Brazil 145 A3
Cornélios Brazil 145 A5
Cornell U.S.A. 130 F2
Corner Brook Canada 123 K4
Corner Inlet b. Australia 112 C7
Corner Seamounts sea feature N. Atlantic Ocean 148 E3
Corneto Italy see Tarquinia
Cornillet, Mont hill France 52 E5
Corning AR U.S.A. 131 F4
Corning CA U.S.A. 128 B2
Corning NY U.S.A. 135 G2
Cornish watercourse Australia 110 D4
Corn Islands is Nicaragua see Maíz, Islas del
Corno, Monte mt. Italy 58 E3
Corno di Campo mt. Italy/Switz. 56 J3
Cornwall Canada 135 H1
Cornwallis Island Canada 119 I2
Cornwall Island Canada 119 I2
Coro Venez. 142 E1
Coroaci Brazil 145 C2
Coroatá Brazil 143 J4
Corofin Rep. of Ireland 51 C5
Coromandel Brazil 145 B2
Coromandel Coast India 84 D4
Coromandel Peninsula N.Z. 113 E3
Coromandel Range hills N.Z. 113 E3
Corona CA U.S.A. 128 E5
Corona NM U.S.A. 127 G6
Coronado U.S.A. 128 E5
Coronado, Bahiá de b. Costa Rica 137 H7
Coronation Canada 121 I4
Coronation Gulf Canada 118 G3
Coronation Island S. Atlantic Ocean 152 A2
Coronda Arg. 144 D4
Coronel Fabriciano Brazil 145 C2
Coronel Oviedo Para. 144 E3
Coronel Pringles Arg. 144 D5
Coronel Suárez Arg. 144 D5
Çorovodë Albania 59 I4
Corowa Australia 112 C5
Corpus Christi U.S.A. 131 D7
Corque Bol. 142 E7
Corral de Cantos mt. Spain 57 D4
Corrales Mex. 131 B7
Corralilla Cuba 133 D8
Corrandibby Range hills Australia 109 A6
Corrente Brazil 143 I6
Corrente r. Bahia Brazil 145 C1
Corrente r. Minas Gerais Brazil 145 A2
Correntes Brazil 143 H7
Correntina Brazil 145 B1
Correntina r. Brazil see Éguas
Corrib, Lough l. Rep. of Ireland 51 C4
Corrientes Arg. 144 E3
Corrientes, Cabo c. Col. 142 C2
Corrientes, Cabo c. Cuba 133 C8
Corrientes, Cabo c. Mex. 136 C4
Corrigin Australia 109 B8
Corris U.K. 49 D6
Corry U.S.A. 134 F3
Corse i. France see Corsica
Corse, Cap c. Corsica France 56 I5
Corsham U.K. 49 E7
Corsica i. France 56 I5
Corsicana U.S.A. 131 D5
Corte Corsica France 56 I5
Cortegana Spain 57 C5
Cortes, Sea of g. Mex. see California, Gulf of
Cortez U.S.A. 129 I3
Cortina d'Ampezzo Italy 58 E1
Cortland U.S.A. 135 G2
Corton U.K. 49 I6
Cortona Italy 58 D3
Coruche Port. 57 B4
Çoruh Turkey see Artvin
Çoruh r. Turkey 91 F2
Çorum Turkey 90 D2
Corumbá Brazil 143 G7
Corumbá r. Brazil 145 A2
Corumbá de Goiás Brazil 145 A1
Corumbaíba Brazil 145 A2
Corumbaú, Ponta pt Brazil 145 D2
Corunna Spain see A Coruña
Corunna U.S.A. 134 C2
Corvallis U.S.A. 126 C3
Corwen U.K. 49 D6
Corydon IA U.S.A. 130 E3
Corydon IN U.S.A. 134 B4
Coryville U.S.A. 135 F3
Cos i. Greece see Kos
Cosentia Italy see Cosenza
Cosenza Italy 58 G5
Coshocton U.S.A. 134 E3
Cosne-Cours-sur-Loire France 56 F3
Costa Blanca coastal area Spain 57 F4
Costa Brava coastal area Spain 57 H3
Costa de la Luz coastal area Spain 57 C5
Costa del Sol coastal area Spain 57 D5
Costa de Miskitos coastal area Nicaragua see Costa de Mosquitos
Costa de Mosquitos coastal area Nicaragua 137 H6
Costa Marques Brazil 142 F6
Costa Rica Brazil 143 H7
▶Costa Rica country Central America 137 H6
North America 9, 116–117
Costa Rica Mex. 136 C4
Costa Verde coastal area Spain 57 C2
Costermansville Dem. Rep. Congo see Bukavu
Costești Romania 59 K2
Costigan Lake Canada 121 J3
Coswig Germany 53 M3
Cotabato Phil. 69 G5
Cotagaita Bol. 142 E8
Cotahuasi Peru 142 D7
Cote, Mount U.S.A. 120 D3
Coteau des Prairies slope U.S.A. 130 D2
Coteau du Missouri slope ND U.S.A. 130 C1
Coteau du Missouri slope SD U.S.A. 130 C2
Côte d'Azur coastal area France 56 H5
▶Côte d'Ivoire country Africa 96 C4
Africa 7, 94–95
Côte Française de Somalis country Africa see Djibouti
Cotentin pen. France 49 F9
Côtes de Meuse ridge France 52 E5
Cothi r. U.K. 49 C7
Cotiaeum Turkey see Kütahya
Cotiella mt. Spain 57 G2
Cotonou Benin 96 D4
Cotopaxi, Volcán vol. Ecuador 142 C4
Cotswold Hills U.K. 49 E7
Cottage Grove U.S.A. 126 C4
Cottbus Germany 47 O5
Cottenham U.K. 49 H6
Cottian Alps mts France/Italy 56 H4
Cottica Suriname 143 H3
Cottiennes, Alpes mts France/Italy see Cottian Alps
Cottonwood AZ U.S.A. 129 G4
Cottonwood CA U.S.A. 128 B1
Cottonwood r. U.S.A. 130 D4
Cottonwood Falls U.S.A. 130 D4
Cotulla U.S.A. 131 D6
Coudersport U.S.A. 135 F3
Couëdic, Cape de Australia 111 B8
Coulee City U.S.A. 126 D3
Coulee Dam U.S.A. 126 D3
Coulman Island Antarctica 152 H2
Coulogne France 52 B4
Coulommiers France 52 D6
Coulonge r. Canada 122 F5
Coulterville U.S.A. 128 C3
Council U.S.A. 126 D3
Council Bluffs U.S.A. 130 E3
Council Grove U.S.A. 130 D4
Councillor Island Australia 111 [inset]
Counselor U.S.A. 129 J3
Coupeville U.S.A. 126 C2
Courageous Lake Canada 121 I1
Courland Lagoon b. Lith./Rus. Fed. 45 L9
Courtenay Canada 120 E5
Courtland U.S.A. 135 G5
Courtmacsherry Rep. of Ireland 51 D6
Courtmacsherry Bay Rep. of Ireland 51 D6
Courtown Rep. of Ireland 51 F5
Courtrai Belgium see Kortrijk
Coushatta U.S.A. 131 E5
Coutances France 56 D2
Coutts Canada 121 I5
Couture, Lac l. Canada 122 G2
Couvin Belgium 52 E4
Cove Fort U.S.A. 129 G2
Cove Island Canada 134 E1
Cove Mountains hills U.S.A. 135 F4
Coventry U.K. 49 F6
Covered Wells U.S.A. 129 G5
Covesville U.S.A. 135 F5
Covilhã Port. 57 C3
Covington GA U.S.A. 133 D5
Covington IN U.S.A. 134 B3
Covington KY U.S.A. 134 C4
Covington LA U.S.A. 131 F6
Covington MI U.S.A. 130 F2
Covington TN U.S.A. 131 F5
Covington VA U.S.A. 134 E5
Cowal, Lake dry lake Australia 112 C4
Cowan, Lake salt flat Australia 109 C7
Cowansville Canada 135 I1
Cowargarzê China 76 C1
Cowcowing Lakes salt flat Australia 109 B7
Cowdenbeath U.K. 50 F4
Cowell Australia 111 B7
Cowes U.K. 49 F8
Cowichan Lake Canada 120 E5
Cowley Australia 112 B1
Cowper Point Canada 119 G2
Cowra Australia 112 D4
Cox r. Australia 110 A2
Coxá r. Brazil 145 B1
Coxen Hole Hond. see Roatán
Coxilha de Santana hills Brazil/Uruguay 144 E4
Coxilha Grande hills Brazil 144 F3
Coxim Brazil 143 H7
Cox's Bazar Bangl. 83 G5
Coyame Mex. 131 B6
Coyhaique Chile see Coihaique
Coyote Lake U.S.A. 128 E4
Coyote Peak hill U.S.A. 129 F5
Cozhê China 83 F2
Cozie, Alpi mts France/Italy see Cottian Alps
Cozumel Mex. 137 G4
Cozumel, Isla de i. Mex. 137 G4
Craboon Australia 112 D4
Cracovia Poland see Kraków
Cracow Australia 110 E5
Cracow Poland see Kraków
Cradle Mountain Lake St Clair National Park Australia 111 [inset]
Cradock S. Africa 101 G7
Craig U.K. 50 D3
Craig AK U.S.A. 120 C4
Craig CO U.S.A. 129 J1
Craigavon U.K. 51 F3
Craigieburn Australia 112 B6
Craig Island Taiwan see Mienhua Yü
Craignure U.K. 50 D4
Craigsville U.S.A. 134 E4
Crail U.K. 50 G4
Crailsheim Germany 53 K5
Craiova Romania 59 J2
Cramlington U.K. 48 F3
Cranberry Lake U.S.A. 135 H1
Cranberry Portage Canada 121 K4
Cranborne Chase for. U.K. 49 E8
Cranbourne Australia 112 B7
Cranbrook Canada 120 H5
Crandon U.S.A. 130 F2
Crane Lake Canada 121 I5
Cranston KY U.S.A. 134 D4
Cranston RI U.S.A. 135 J3
Cranz Rus. Fed. see Zelenogradsk
Crary Ice Rise Antarctica 152 I1
Crary Mountains Antarctica 152 J1
Crater Lake National Park U.S.A. 126 C4
Crater Peak U.S.A. 128 C1
Craters of the Moon National Monument nat. park U.S.A. 126 E4
Crateús Brazil 143 J5
Crato Brazil 143 K5
Crawford CO U.S.A. 129 J2
Crawford NE U.S.A. 130 C3
Crawfordsville U.S.A. 134 B3
Crawfordville FL U.S.A. 133 C6
Crawfordville GA U.S.A. 133 D5
Crawley U.K. 49 G7
Crazy Mountains U.S.A. 126 F3
Creag Meagaidh mt. U.K. 50 E4
Crécy-en-Ponthieu France 52 B4
Credenhill U.K. 49 E6
Crediton U.K. 49 D8
Cree r. Canada 121 J3
Creel Mex. 127 G8
Cree Lake Canada 121 J3
Creemore Canada 134 E1
Creighton Canada 121 K4
Creil France 52 C5
Creil Neth. 52 F2
Crema Italy 58 C2
Cremlingen Germany 53 K2
Cremona Canada 120 H5
Cremona Italy 58 D2
Crépy-en-Valois France 52 C5
Cres i. Croatia 58 F2
Crescent U.S.A. 126 C4
Crescent City CA U.S.A. 126 B4
Crescent City FL U.S.A. 133 D6
Crescent Group is Paracel Is 68 E3
Crescent Head Australia 112 F3
Crescent Junction U.S.A. 129 I2
Crescent Valley U.S.A. 128 E1
Cressy Australia 112 A7
Crest Hill hill Hong Kong China 77 [inset]
Crestline U.S.A. 134 D3
Creston Canada 120 G5
Creston IA U.S.A. 130 E3
Creston WY U.S.A. 126 G4
Crestview U.S.A. 133 C6
Creswick Australia 112 A6
Creta i. Greece see Crete
Crete i. Greece 59 K7
Crete U.S.A. 130 D3
Creus, Cap de c. Spain 57 H2
Creuse r. France 56 E3
Creußen Germany 53 L5
Creutzwald France 52 G5
Creuzburg Germany 53 K3
Crevasse Valley Glacier Antarctica 152 J1
Crewe U.K. 49 E5
Crewe U.S.A. 135 F5
Crewkerne U.K. 49 E8
Crianlarich U.K. 50 E4
Criccieth U.K. 49 C6
Criciúma Brazil 145 A5
Crieff U.K. 50 F4
Criffel hill U.K. 50 F6
Criffell hill U.K. see Criffel
Crikvenica Croatia 58 F2
Crillon, Mount U.S.A. 120 B3
Crimea pen. Ukr. 90 D1
Crimmitschau Germany 53 M4
Crimond U.K. 50 H3
Crisfield U.S.A. 135 H5
Cristalândia Brazil 143 I6
Cristalina Brazil 145 B2
Cristalino r. Brazil see Mariembero
Cristóbal Colón, Pico mt. Col. 142 D1
Crixás Brazil 145 A1
Crixás Açu r. Brazil 145 A1
Crixás Mirim r. Brazil 145 A1
Crna Gora aut. rep. Serb. and Mont. 58 H3
Crni Vrh mt. Serb. and Mont. 59 J2
Črnomelj Slovenia 58 F2
Croagh Patrick hill Rep. of Ireland 51 C4
Croajingolong National Park Australia 112 D6
▶Croatia country Europe 58 G2
Europe 5, 38–39
Crocker, Banjaran mts Malaysia 68 E6
Crockett U.S.A. 131 E6
Crofton KY U.S.A. 134 B5
Crofton NE U.S.A. 130 D3
Croghan U.S.A. 135 H2
Croisilles France 52 C4
Croker, Cape Canada 134 E1
Croker Island Australia 108 F2
Cromarty U.K. 50 E3
Cromarty Firth est. U.K. 50 E3
Cromer U.K. 49 I6
Crook U.K. 48 F4
Crooked Harbour b. Hong Kong China 77 [inset]
Crooked Island Bahamas 133 F8
Crooked Island Hong Kong China 77 [inset]

Daulatpur Bangl. 83 G5
Daun Germany 52 G4
Daungyu r. Myanmar 70 A2
Dauphin Canada 121 K5
Dauphiné reg. France 56 G4
Dauphiné, Alpes du mts France 56 G4
Dauphin Lake Canada 121 L5
Daurie Creek r. Australia 109 A6
Dausa India 82 D4
Dâu Tiêng, Hô resr Vietnam 71 D5
Dava U.K. 50 F3
Däväçi Azer. 91 H2
Davanagere India see Davangere
Davangere India 84 B3
Davao Phil. 69 H5
Davao Gulf Phil. 69 H5
Dāvarī Iran 88 E5
Dāvarzan Iran 88 E2
Davel S. Africa 101 I4
Davenport IA U.S.A. 130 F3
Davenport WA U.S.A. 126 D3
Davenport Downs Australia 110 C5
Davenport Range hills Australia 108 F5
Daventry U.K. 49 F6
Daveyton S. Africa 101 I4
David Panama 137 H7
David City U.S.A. 130 D3
Davidson Canada 121 J5
Davidson, Mount hill Australia 108 E5
Davis research station Antarctica 152 E2
Davis r. Australia 108 C5
Davis i. Myanmar see Than Kyun
Davis CA U.S.A. 128 C2
Davis WV U.S.A. 134 F4
Davis, Mount hill U.S.A. 134 F4
Davis Bay Antarctica 152 G2
Davis Dam U.S.A. 129 F4
Davis Inlet Canada 123 J3
Davis Sea Antarctica 152 F2
Davis Strait Canada/Greenland 119 M3
Davlekanovo Rus. Fed. 41 Q5
Davos Switz. 56 I3
Davy Lake Canada 121 I3
Dawa Co l. China 83 F3
Dawa Wenz r. Eth. 98 E3
Dawaxung China 83 F3
Dawê China 76 D2
Dawei Myanmar see Tavoy
Dawei r. mouth Myanmar see Tavoy
Dawera i. Indon. 108 E1
Dawna Range mts Myanmar/Thai. 70 B3
Dawna Taungdan mts Myanmar/Thai. see Dawna Range
Dawo China see Maqên
Dawqah Oman 87 H6
Dawson r. Australia 110 E4
Dawson Canada 120 B1
Dawson GA U.S.A. 133 C6
Dawson ND U.S.A. 130 D2
Dawson, Mount Canada 120 G5
Dawson Bay Canada 121 K4
Dawson Creek Canada 120 F4
Dawson Inlet Canada 121 M2
Dawson Range mts Canada 120 A2
Dawsons Landing Canada 120 E5
Dawu Hubei China 77 G2
Dawu Qinghai China see Maqên
Dawu Taiwan see Tawu
Dawukou China see Shizuishan
Dawu Shan hill China 77 G2
Dax France 56 D5
Daxian China see Dazhou
Daxiang Ling mts China 76 D2
Daxin China 76 E4
Daxing Yunnan China see Lüchun
Daxing Yunnan China see Ninglang
Daxing'an Ling mts China see Da Hinggan Ling
Da Xueshan mts China 76 D2
Dayan China see Lijiang
Dayangshu China 74 B2
Dayao China 76 D3
Dayao Shan mts China 77 F4
Daye China 77 G2
Daying China 76 E2
Daying Jiang r. China 76 C3
Dayishan China see Guanyun
Daylesford Australia 112 B6
Daylight Pass U.S.A. 128 E3
Dayong China see Zhangjiajie
Dayr Abū Sa'īd Jordan 85 B3
Dayr az Zawr Syria 91 F4
Dayr Ḥāfir Syria 85 C1
Daysland Canada 121 H4
Dayton OH U.S.A. 134 C4
Dayton TN U.S.A. 132 C5
Dayton VA U.S.A. 135 F4
Dayton WA U.S.A. 126 D3
Daytona Beach U.S.A. 133 D6
Dayu Ling mts China 77 G3
Da Yunhe canal China 77 H1
Dayyīna i. U.A.E. 88 D5
Dazhongji China see Dafeng
Dazhou China 76 E2
Dazhou Dao i. China 77 F5
Dazhu China 76 E2
Dazu China 76 E2
Dazu Rock Carvings tourist site China 76 E2
De Aar S. Africa 100 G6
Dead r. Rep. of Ireland 51 D5
Deadman Lake U.S.A. 128 E4
Deadman's Cay Bahamas 133 F8
Dead Mountains U.S.A. 129 F4

▶Dead Sea salt l. Asia 85 B4
Lowest point in the world and in Asia.
Asia 60–61

Deadwood U.S.A. 130 C2
Deakin Australia 109 E7
Deal U.K. 49 I7
Dealesville S. Africa 101 G5
De'an China 77 G2
Dean, Forest of U.K. 49 E7
Deán Funes Arg. 144 D4
Deanuvuotna inlet Norway see Tanafjorden
Dearborn U.S.A. 134 D2
Dearne r. U.K. 48 F5
Deary U.S.A. 126 D3
Dease r. Canada 120 D3
Dease Lake Canada 120 D3
Dease Lake l. Canada 120 D3
Dease Strait Canada 118 H3

▶Death Valley depr. U.S.A. 128 E3
Lowest point in the Americas.
North America 114–115

Death Valley Junction U.S.A. 128 E3
Death Valley National Park U.S.A. 128 E3
Deauville France 56 E2
Deaver U.S.A. 126 F3
De Baai S. Africa see Port Elizabeth
Debao China 76 E4
Debar Macedonia 59 I4
Debden Canada 121 J4
Debenham U.K. 49 I6
De Beque U.S.A. 129 I2
De Biesbosch, Nationaal Park nat. park Neth. 52 E3
Débo, Lac l. Mali 96 C3
Deborah East, Lake salt flat Australia 109 B7
Deborah West, Lake salt flat Australia 109 B7
Debrecen Hungary 59 I1
Debre Markos Eth. 86 E7
Debre Tabor Eth. 86 E7
Debre Zeyit Eth. 98 D3
Decatur AL U.S.A. 133 C5
Decatur GA U.S.A. 133 C5
Decatur IL U.S.A. 130 F4
Decatur IN U.S.A. 134 C3
Decatur MI U.S.A. 134 C2
Decatur MS U.S.A. 131 F5
Decatur TX U.S.A. 131 D5

▶Deccan plat. India 84 C2
Plateau making up most of southern and central India.

Deception Bay Australia 112 F1
Dechang China 76 D3
Děčín Czech Rep. 47 O5
Decker U.S.A. 126 G3
Decorah U.S.A. 130 F3
Dedap i. Indon. see Penasi, Pulau
Dedaye Myanmar 70 A3
Deddington U.K. 49 F7
Dedegöl Dağları mts Turkey 59 N6
Dedeleben Germany 53 K2
Dedelstorf Germany 53 K2
Dedemsvaart Neth. 52 G2
Dedo de Deus mt. Brazil 145 B4
Dédougou Burkina 96 C3
Dedovichi Rus. Fed. 42 F4
Dedu China see Wudalianchi
Dee r. Rep. of Ireland 51 F4
Dee est. U.K. 48 D5
Dee r. England/Wales U.K. 49 D5
Dee r. Scotland U.K. 50 G3
Deel r. Rep. of Ireland 51 D5
Deel r. Rep. of Ireland 51 F4
Deep Bay Hong Kong China 77 [inset]
Deep Creek Lake U.S.A. 134 F4
Deep Creek Range mts U.S.A. 129 G2
Deep River Canada 122 F5
Deepwater Australia 112 E2
Deeri Somalia 98 E3
Deering U.S.A. 118 B3
Deering, Mount Australia 109 E6
Deer Island U.S.A. 118 B4
Deer Lake Canada 121 M4
Deer Lake l. Canada 121 M4
Deer Lodge U.S.A. 126 E3
Deesa India see Disa
Deeth U.S.A. 126 E4
Defeng China see Liping
Defensores del Chaco, Parque Nacional nat. park Para. 144 D2
Defiance U.S.A. 134 C3
Defiance Plateau U.S.A. 129 I4
Degana India 82 C4
Degeh Bur Eth. 98 E3
Degema Nigeria 96 D4
Deggendorf Germany 53 M6
Degh r. Pak. 89 I4
De Grey r. Australia 108 B5
De Groote Peel, Nationaal Park nat. park Neth. 52 F3
Degtevo Rus. Fed. 43 I6
De Haan Belgium 52 D3
Dehak Iran 89 F4
De Hamert, Nationaal Park nat. park Neth. 52 G3
Deh Bīd Iran 88 D4
Deh-Dasht Iran 88 C4
Dehej India 82 C5
Deheq Iran 88 C3
Dehestān Iran 88 D4
Deh Golān Iran 88 B3
Dehgon Afgh. 89 F3
Dehi Afgh. 89 G3
Dehküyeh Iran 88 D5
Dehlorān Iran 88 B3
De Hoge Veluwe, Nationaal Park nat. park Neth. 52 F2
De Hoop Nature Reserve S. Africa 100 E8
Dehqonobod Uzbek. see Dekhkanabad
Dehra Dun India 82 D3
Dehradun India see Dehra Dun
Dehri India 83 F4
Deh Shū Afgh. 89 F4
Deim Zubeir Sudan 97 F4
Deinze Belgium 52 D4
Deir-ez-Zor Syria see Dayr az Zawr
Dej Romania 59 J1
Deji China see Rinbung
Dejiang China 77 F2
De Jouwer Neth. see Joure
De Kalb IL U.S.A. 130 F3
De Kalb MS U.S.A. 131 F5
De Kalb TX U.S.A. 131 E5
De Kalb Junction U.S.A. 135 H1
De-Kastri Rus. Fed. 74 F2
Dekemhare Eritrea 86 E6
Dekhkanabad Uzbek. 89 G2
Dekina Nigeria 96 D4
Dékoa Cent. Afr. Rep. 98 B3
De Koog Neth. 52 E1
De Kooy Neth. 52 E2
Delaki Indon. 108 D2
Delamar Lake U.S.A. 129 F3
De Land U.S.A. 133 D6
Delano U.S.A. 128 D4
Delano Peak U.S.A. 129 G2

▶Delap-Uliga-Djarrit Marshall Is 150 H5
Capital of the Marshall Islands, on Majuro atoll.

Delārām Afgh. 89 F3
Delareyville S. Africa 101 G4
Delaronde Lake Canada 121 J4
Delavan U.S.A. 122 C6
Delaware U.S.A. 134 D3
Delaware r. U.S.A. 135 H4
Delaware state U.S.A. 135 H4
Delaware, East Branch r. U.S.A. 135 H3
Delaware Bay U.S.A. 135 H4
Delaware Lake U.S.A. 134 D3
Delaware Water Gap National Recreational Area park U.S.A. 135 H3
Delay r. Canada 123 H2
Delbarton U.S.A. 134 D5
Delbrück Germany 53 I3
Delburne Canada 120 H4
Delegate Australia 112 D6
De Lemmer Neth. see Lemmer
Delémont Switz. 56 H3
Delevan CA U.S.A. 128 B2
Delevan NY U.S.A. 135 F2
Delfinópolis Brazil 145 B3
Delft Neth. 52 E2
Delfzijl Neth. 52 G1
Delgada, Point U.S.A. 128 A1
Delgado, Cabo c. Moz. 99 E5
Delhi Canada 134 E2
Delhi China 80 I4
Delhi India 82 D3
Delhi CO U.S.A. 127 G5
Delhi LA U.S.A. 131 F5
Delhi NY U.S.A. 135 H2
Delice Turkey 90 D3
Delice r. Turkey 90 D2
Delījān Iran 88 C3
Déljne Canada 120 F1
Delingha China see Delhi
Delisle Canada 121 J5
Delitzsch Germany 53 M3
Delligsen Germany 53 J3
Dell Rapids U.S.A. 130 D3
Dellys Alg. 57 H5
Del Mar U.S.A. 128 E5
Delmenhorst Germany 53 I1
Delnice Croatia 58 F2
Del Norte U.S.A. 127 G5
Delong China see Ande
De-Longa, Ostrova is Rus. Fed. 65 Q2
De Long Islands Rus. Fed. see De-Longa, Ostrova
De Long Mountains U.S.A. 114 B3
De Long Strait Rus. Fed. see Longa, Proliv
Deloraine Canada 121 K5
Delphi U.S.A. 134 B3
Delphos U.S.A. 134 C3
Delportshoop S. Africa 100 G5
Delray Beach U.S.A. 133 D7
Delrey U.S.A. 134 A3
Del Río Mex. 127 F7
Del Rio U.S.A. 131 C6
Delsbo Sweden 45 J6
Delta CO U.S.A. 129 I2
Delta OH U.S.A. 134 C3
Delta UT U.S.A. 129 G2
Delta Downs Australia 110 C3
Delta Junction U.S.A. 118 D3
Deltona U.S.A. 133 D6
Delungra Australia 112 E2
Delvin Rep. of Ireland 51 E4
Delvinë Albania 59 I5
Delwara India 82 C4
Demavend mt. Iran see Damāvand, Qolleh-ye
Demba Dem. Rep. Congo 99 C4
Dembī Dolo Eth. 86 D8
Demerara Guyana see Georgetown
Demerara Abyssal Plain sea feature S. Atlantic Ocean 148 E5
Demidov Rus. Fed. 43 F5
Deming U.S.A. 127 G6
Demirci Turkey 59 M5
Demirköy Turkey 59 L4
Demirtaş Turkey 85 A1
Demmin Germany 47 N4
Demopolis U.S.A. 133 C5
Demotte U.S.A. 134 B3
Dempo, Gunung vol. Indon. 68 C7
Dêmqog Jammu and Kashmir 82 D2
Demta Indon. 69 K7
Dem'yanovo Rus. Fed. 42 J3
De Naawte S. Africa 100 E6
Denakil reg. Africa 98 E2
Denali mt. U.S.A. see McKinley, Mount
Denali National Park and Preserve U.S.A. 118 C3
Denan Eth. 98 E3
Denau Uzbek. 89 G2
Denbigh Canada 135 G1
Denbigh U.K. 48 D5
Den Bosch Neth. see 's-Hertogenbosch
Den Burg Neth. 52 E1
Den Chai Thai. 70 C3
Dendâra Mauritania 96 C3
Dendermonde Belgium 52 E3
Dendi mt. Eth. 98 D3
Dendre r. Belgium 52 E3
Dendron S. Africa 101 I2
Denezhkin Kamen', Gora mt. Rus. Fed. 41 R3
Dêngka China see Têwo
Dêngkagoin China see Têwo
Dengkou China 72 J4
Dêngqên China 76 B2
Dengta China 77 G4
Dengxian China see Dengzhou
Dengzhou China 77 G1
Den Haag Neth. see The Hague
Denham Australia 109 A6
Denham r. Australia 108 E3
Den Ham Neth. 52 G2
Denham Range mts Australia 110 E4
Den Helder Neth. 52 E2
Denholm Canada 121 I4
Denia Spain 57 G4
Denial Bay Australia 111 A7
Deniliquin Australia 112 B5
Denio U.S.A. 126 D4
Denison IA U.S.A. 130 E3
Denison TX U.S.A. 131 D5
Denison, Cape Antarctica 152 G2
Denison Plains Australia 108 E4
Deniyaya Sri Lanka 84 D5
Denizli Turkey 59 M6
Denman Australia 112 E4
Denman Glacier Antarctica 148 F2
Denmark Australia 106 B5
▶Denmark country Europe 45 G8
Europe 5, 38–39
Denmark U.S.A. 134 B1
Denmark Strait Greenland/Iceland 40 A2
Dennis, Lake salt flat Australia 108 E5
Dennison IL U.S.A. 134 B4
Dennison OH U.S.A. 134 E3
Denny U.K. 50 F4
Denow Uzbek. see Denau
Denpasar Indon. 108 A2
Denton MD U.S.A. 135 H4
Denton TX U.S.A. 131 D5
D'Entrecasteaux, Point Australia 109 A8
D'Entrecasteaux, Récifs reef New Caledonia 107 G3
D'Entrecasteaux Islands P.N.G. 106 F2
D'Entrecasteaux National Park Australia 109 A8

▶Denver CO U.S.A. 126 G5
State capital of Colorado.

Denver PA U.S.A. 135 G3
Denys r. Canada 122 F3
Deo India 83 F4
Deoband India 82 D3
Deogarh Jharkhand India see Deoghar
Deogarh Orissa India 83 F5
Deogarh Rajasthan India 82 C4
Deogarh Uttar Pradesh India 82 D4
Deogarh mt. India 83 E5
Deoghar India 83 F4
Deolali India 84 B2
Deoli India 83 F5
Deori Chhattisgarh India 84 D1
Deori Madhya Pradesh India 82 D5
Deoria India 83 E4
Deosai, Plains of Jammu and Kashmir 82 C2
Deosil India 83 E5
De Panne Belgium 52 C3
De Pere U.S.A. 134 A1
Deposit U.S.A. 135 H2
Depsang Point hill Aksai Chin 78 D2
Deputatskiy Rus. Fed. 65 O3
Dêqên Xizang China 83 G3
Dêqên Xizang China 83 G3
Dêqên Xizang China see Dagzê
De Queen U.S.A. 131 E5
Dera Ghazi Khan Pak. 89 H4
Dera Ismail Khan Pak. 89 H4
Derajat reg. Pak. 89 H4
Derawar Fort Pak. 89 H4
Derbent Rus. Fed. 91 H2
Derbesiye Turkey see Şenyurt
Derbur China 74 A2
Derby Australia 108 C4
Derby U.K. 49 F6
Derby CT U.S.A. 135 I3
Derby KS U.S.A. 131 D4
Derby NY U.S.A. 135 F2
Derg r. Rep. of Ireland/U.K. 51 E3
Derg, Lough l. Rep. of Ireland 51 D5
Dergachi Rus. Fed. 43 K6
Dergachi Ukr. see Derhachi
Derhachi Ukr. 43 H6
De Ridder U.S.A. 131 E6
Derik Turkey 91 F3
Derm Namibia 100 D2
Derna Libya see Darnah
Dernberg, Cape Namibia 100 B4
Dêrong China 76 C2
Derravaragh, Lough l. Rep. of Ireland 51 E4
Derry U.K. see Londonderry
Derry U.S.A. 135 J2
Derryveagh Mts hills Rep. of Ireland 51 D3
Dêrub China see Rutög
Derudeb Sudan 86 E6
De Rust S. Africa 100 F7
Derventa Bos.-Herz. 58 G2
Derwent r. England U.K. 48 F6
Derwent r. England U.K. 48 G5
Derwent Water l. U.K. 48 D4
Derweze Turkm. see Darvaza
Derzhavinsk Kazakh. 80 C1
Derzhavinskiy Kazakh. see Derzhavinsk
Desaguadero r. Arg. 144 C4
Désappointement, Îles du is Fr. Polynesia 151 K6
Desatoya Mountains U.S.A. 128 E2
Deschambault Lake Canada 117 K4
Deschutes r. U.S.A. 126 C3
Desē Eth. 98 D2
Deseado Arg. 144 C7
Deseado r. Arg. 144 C7
Desengaño, Punta pt Arg. 144 C7
Deseret U.S.A. 129 G2
Deseret Peak U.S.A. 129 G1
Deseronto Canada 135 G1
Desert Canal Pak. 89 H4
Desert Center U.S.A. 129 F5
Desert Lake U.S.A. 129 F3
Desert View U.S.A. 129 H3
Deshler U.S.A. 134 D3
De Smet U.S.A. 130 D2

▶Des Moines IA U.S.A. 130 E3
State capital of Iowa.

Des Moines NM U.S.A. 131 C4
Des Moines r. U.S.A. 130 F3
Desna r. Rus. Fed./Ukr. 43 F6
Desnogorsk Rus. Fed. 43 G5
Desolación, Isla i. Chile 144 B8
Des Plaines U.S.A. 134 B2
Dessau Germany 53 M3
Dessye Eth. see Desē
Destelbergen Belgium 52 D3
Destruction Bay Canada 153 A2
Desvres France 52 B4
Detah Canada 120 H2
Dete Zimbabwe 99 C5
Detmold Germany 53 I3
Detrital Wash watercourse U.S.A. 129 F3
Detroit U.S.A. 134 D2
Detroit Lakes U.S.A. 130 E2
Dett Zimbabwe see Dete
Deua National Park Australia 108 D5
Deuben Germany 53 M3
Deurne Neth. 52 F3
Deutschland country Europe see Germany
Deutschlandsberg Austria 47 O7
Deutzen Germany 53 M3
Deva Romania 59 J2
Deva U.K. see Chester
Devana U.K. see Aberdeen
Devangere India see Davangere
Devanhalli India 84 C3
Deve Bair pass Bulg./Macedonia see Velbŭzhdki Prokhod
Develi Turkey 90 D3
Deventer Neth. 52 G2
Deveron r. U.K. 50 G3
Devét Skal hill Czech Rep. 47 P6
Devgarh India 84 B2
Devghar India see Deoghar
Devikot India 82 B4
Devil's Bridge U.K. 49 D6
Devil's Gate pass U.S.A. 128 D2
Devil's Lake U.S.A. 130 D1
Devil's Paw mt. U.S.A. 120 C3
Devil's Peak U.S.A. 128 D3
Devil's Point Bahamas 133 F7
Devine U.S.A. 131 D6
Devizes U.K. 49 F7
Devli India 82 C4
Devnya Bulg. 59 L3
Devon r. U.K. 50 F4
Devon Island Canada 119 I2
Devonport Australia 111 [inset]
Devrek Turkey 59 N4
Devrukh India 84 B2
Dewa, Tanjung pt Indon. 71 A7
Dewangiri Bhutan 83 G4
Dewas India 82 D5
De Weerribben, Nationaal Park nat. park Neth. 52 G2
Dewetsdorp S. Africa 101 H5
De Witt AR U.S.A. 131 F5
De Witt IA U.S.A. 130 F3
Dewsbury U.K. 48 F5
Dexing China 77 H2
Dexter ME U.S.A. 135 K1
Dexter MI U.S.A. 134 D2
Dexter MO U.S.A. 131 F4
Dexter NM U.S.A. 127 G6
Dexter NY U.S.A. 135 G1
Deyang China 76 E2
Dey-Dey Lake salt flat Australia 109 E7
Deyhuk Iran 88 E3
Deyong, Tanjung pt Indon. 69 J8
Dêyü Co l. China 83 F2
Deyyer Iran 88 C5
Dez r. Iran 86 G3
Dezadeash Lake Canada 120 B2
Dezfūl Iran 88 C3

▶Dezhneva, Mys c. Rus. Fed. 65 T3
Most easterly point of Asia.

Dezhou Shandong China 73 L5
Dezhou Sichuan China see Dechang
Dezh Shāhpūr Iran see Marīvān
Dhabarau India 83 E4
Dhahab, Wādī adh r. Syria 85 B3
Dhāhiriya West Bank 85 B4
Dhahran Saudi Arabia 88 C5

▶Dhaka Bangl. 83 G5
Capital of Bangladesh and 5th most populous city in Asia.

Dhalbhum reg. India 83 F5
Dhalgaon India 84 B2
Dhamār Yemen 86 F7
Dhamoni India 82 D4
Dhamtari India 84 D1
Dhana Pak. 89 H5
Dhana Sar Pak. 89 H4
Dhanbad India 83 F5
Dhanera India 82 C4
Dhang Range mts Nepal 83 E3
Dhankuta Nepal 83 F4
Dhansia India 82 C3
Dhar India 82 C5
Dhar Adrar hills Mauritania 96 B3
Dharampur India 84 B1
Dharan Bazar Nepal 83 F4
Dharashiv India see Osmanabad
Dhari India 82 B5
Dharmapuri India 84 C3
Dharmavaram India 84 C3
Dharmsala Himachal Pradesh India see Dharmshala
Dharmsala Orissa India 83 F5
Dharmshala India 82 D2
Dharnaoda India 82 D4
Dhar Oualâta hills Mauritania 96 C3
Dhar Tîchît hills Mauritania 96 C3
Dharug National Park Australia 112 E4
Dharur India 84 C2
Dharwad India 84 B3
Dharwar India see Dharwad
Dharwas India 82 D2
Dhasan r. India 82 D4
Dhāt al Ḥājj Saudi Arabia 90 E5
Dhaulagiri mt. Nepal 83 E3
Dhaulpur India see Dholpur
Dhaura India 82 D4
Dhaurahra India 82 E4
Dhawlagiri mt. Nepal see Dhaulagiri
Dhebar Lake India see Jaisamand Lake
Dhekelia Sovereign Base Area military base Cyprus 85 A2
Dhemaji India 83 H4
Dhenkanal India 84 E1
Dhībān Jordan 85 B4
Dhidhimótikhon Greece see Didymoteicho
Dhing India 83 H4
Dhirwāh, Wādī adh watercourse Jordan 85 C4
Dhodhekánisos is Greece see Dodecanese
Dhola India 82 B5
Dholera India 82 C5
Dholpur India 82 D4
Dhomokós Greece see Domokos
Dhone India 84 C3
Dhoraji India 82 B5
Dhori India 82 B5
Dhrangadhra India 82 B5
Dhubāb Yemen 86 F7
Dhubri India 83 G4
Dhuburi India see Dhubri
Dhudial Pak. 89 I3
Dhule India 84 B1
Dhulia India see Dhule
Dhulian India 83 F4
Dhulian Pak. 89 I3
Dhuma India 82 D5
Dhund r. India 82 D4
Dhurwai India 82 D4
Dhuusa Marreeb Somalia 98 E3
Dia i. Greece 59 K7
Diablo, Mount U.S.A. 128 C3
Diablo, Picacho del mt. Mex. 127 E7
Diablo Range mts U.S.A. 128 C3
Diagbe Dem. Rep. Congo 98 C3
Diamante Arg. 144 D4
Diamantina watercourse Australia 110 B5
Diamantina Brazil 145 C2
Diamantina, Chapada plat. Brazil 145 C1
Diamantina Deep sea feature Indian Ocean 149 O8
Diamantina Gates National Park Australia 110 C4
Diamantino Brazil 143 G6
Diamond Islets Australia 110 E3
Diamond Peak U.S.A. 129 F2
Dianbai China 77 F4
Diancang Shan mt. China 76 D3
Dian Chi l. China 76 D3
Diandioumé Mali 96 C3
Diane Bank sea feature Australia 110 E2
Dianjiang China 76 E2
Dianópolis Brazil 143 I6
Dianyang China see Shidian
Diaobingshan China see Tiefa
Diaoling China 74 C3
Diapaga Burkina 96 D3
Diarizos r. Cyprus 85 A2
Diavolo, Mount hill India 71 A4
Diaz Point Namibia 100 B4
Dibaya Dem. Rep. Congo 99 C4
Dibella well Niger 96 E3
Dibeng S. Africa 100 F4
Dibete Botswana 101 H2
Dibrugarh India 83 H4
Dibse Syria see Dibsī
Dibsī Syria 85 D2
Dickens U.S.A. 131 C5
Dickinson U.S.A. 130 C2
Dicle r. Turkey 91 F3 see Tigris
Dīdēsa Wenz r. Eth. 98 D3
Didiéni Mali 96 C3
Didsbury Canada 120 H5
Didwana India 82 C4
Didymoteicho Greece 59 L4
Die France 56 G4
Dieblich Germany 53 H4
Diébougou Burkina 96 C3
Dieburg Germany 53 I5
Diedenhofen France see Thionville
Diefenbaker, Lake Canada 121 I5
Diego de Almagro, Isla i. Chile 144 A8
Diégo Suarez Madag. see Antsirañana
Diekirch Lux. 52 G5
Diéma Mali 96 C3
Diemel r. Germany 53 J3
Điện Biên Vietnam see Điện Biên Phu
Điện Biên Phu Vietnam 70 C2
Diễn Châu Vietnam 70 D3
Diên Khanh Vietnam 71 E4
Diepholz Germany 53 I2
Dieppe France 52 B5
Dierks U.S.A. 131 E5
Di'er Songhua Jiang r. China 74 B3
Diessen Neth. 52 F3
Diest Belgium 52 F4
Dietikon Switz. 56 I3
Diez Germany 53 I4
Diffa Niger 96 E3
Digby Canada 123 I5
Diggi India 82 C4
Diglur India 84 C2
Digne France see Digne-les-Bains
Digne-les-Bains France 56 H4
Digoin France 56 F3
Digos Phil. 69 H5
Digras India 84 C1
Digri Pak. 89 H5
Digul r. Indon. 69 K8
Digya National Park Ghana 96 C4
Dihang r. India 83 H4 see Brahmaputra
Dihōk Iraq see Dahūk
Dihourse, Lac l. Canada 123 I2
Diinsoor Somalia 98 E3
Dijon France 56 G3
Dik Chad 97 E4
Diken India 82 C4
Dikhil Djibouti 86 F7
Dikili Turkey 59 L5
Diklosmta mt. Rus. Fed. 43 J8
Diksal India 84 B2
Diksmuide Belgium 52 C3
Dikson Rus. Fed. 64 J2
Dīla Eth. 98 D3
Dilaram Iran 88 E4

▶Dili East Timor 108 D2
Capital of East Timor.

Di Linh Vietnam 71 E5
Dillenburg Germany 53 I4
Dilley U.S.A. 131 D6
Dillingen (Saar) Germany 52 G5
Dillingen an der Donau Germany 47 M6
Dillingham U.S.A. 118 C4
Dillon r. Canada 121 I4
Dillon MT U.S.A. 126 E3

Dillon SC U.S.A. 133 E5
Dillwyn U.S.A. 135 F5
Dilolo Dem. Rep. Congo 99 C5
Dilsen Belgium 52 F3
Dimapur India 83 H4
Dimashq Syria see Damascus
Dimbokro Côte d'Ivoire 96 C4
Dimboola Australia 111 C8
Dimitrov Ukr. see Dymytrov
Dimitrovgrad Bulg. 59 K3
Dimitrovgrad Rus. Fed. 43 K5
Dimitrovo Bulg. see Pernik
Dimmitt U.S.A. 131 C5
Dīmona Israel 85 B4
Dimpho Pan salt pan Botswana 100 E3
Dinagat i. Phil. 69 H4
Dinajpur Bangl. 83 G4
Dinan France 56 C2
Dinant Belgium 52 E4
Dinapur India 83 F4
Dinar Turkey 59 N5
Dīnār, Kūh-e mt. Iran 88 C4
Dinara Planina mts Bos.-Herz./Croatia see Dinaric Alps
Dinaric Alps mts Bos.-Herz./Croatia 58 G2
Dinbych U.K. see Denbigh
Dinbych-y-pysgod U.K. see Tenby
Dinder National Park Sudan 97 G3
Dindi r. India 84 C2
Dindigul India 84 C4
Dindima Nigeria 96 E3
Dindiza Moz. 101 K2
Dindori India 82 E5
Dingcheng China see Dingyuan
Dingelstädt Germany 53 K3
Dingla Nepal 83 F4
Dingle Rep. of Ireland 51 B5
Dingle Bay Rep. of Ireland 51 B5
Dingnan China 77 G3
Dingo Australia 110 E4
Dingolfing Germany 53 M6
Dingping China see Linshui
Dingtao China 77 G1
Dinguiraye Guinea 96 B3
Dingwall U.K. 50 E3
Dingxi China 76 E1
Dingyuan China 77 H1
Dinh Lập Vietnam 70 D2
Dinkelsbühl Germany 53 K5
Dinngyê China 83 F3
Dinokwe Botswana 101 H2
Dinosaur U.S.A. 129 I1
Dinosaur National Monument nat. park U.S.A. 129 I1
Dinslaken Germany 52 G3
Dinwiddie U.S.A. 135 G5
Dioïla Mali 96 C3
Dionísio Cerqueira Brazil 144 F3
Diorama Brazil 145 A2
Dioscurias Georgia see Sokhumi
Diouloulou Senegal 96 B3
Diourbel Senegal 96 B3
Diphu India 83 H4
Dipkarpaz Cyprus see Rizokarpason
Diplo Pak. 89 H5
Dipolog Phil. 69 G5
Dipperu National Park Australia 110 E4
Dipu China see Anji
Dir reg. Pak. 89 I3
Dirang India 83 H4
Diré Mali 96 C3
Direction, Cape Australia 110 C2
Dirē Dawa Eth. 98 E3
Dirico Angola 99 C5
Dirk Hartog Island Australia 109 A6
Dirranbandi Australia 112 D2
Dirs Saudi Arabia 98 E2
Dirschau Poland see Tczew
Dirty Devil r. U.S.A. 129 H3
Disa India 82 C4
Disang r. India 83 H4
Disappointment, Cape S. Georgia 144 I8
Disappointment, Cape U.S.A. 126 B3
Disappointment Islands Fr. Polynesia see Désappointement, Îles du
Disappointment, Lake salt flat Australia 109 C5
Disappointment Lake Canada 123 J3
Disaster Bay Australia 112 D6
Discovery Bay Australia 111 C8
Disko i. Greenland see Qeqertarsuaq
Disko Bugt b. Greenland see Qeqertarsuup Tunua
Dispur India 83 G4
Disputanta U.S.A. 135 G5
Disraëli Canada 123 H5
Diss U.K. 49 I6
Distrito Federal admin. dist. Brazil 145 B1
Disūq Egypt 90 C5
Ditloung S. Africa 100 F5
Dittaino r. Sicily Italy 58 F6
Diu India 84 A1
Dīvān Darreh Iran 88 B3
Divehi country Indian Ocean see Maldives
Divi, Point India 84 D3
Divichi Azer. see Däväçi
Divide Mountain U.S.A. 120 A2
Divinópolis Brazil 145 B3
Divnoye Rus. Fed. 43 I7
Divo Côte d'Ivoire 96 C4
Divriği Turkey 90 E3
Diwana Pak. 89 G5
Diwaniyah Iraq see Ad Dīwānīyah
Dixfield U.S.A. 135 J1
Dixon CA U.S.A. 128 C2
Dixon IL U.S.A. 130 F3
Dixon KY U.S.A. 134 B5
Dixon MT U.S.A. 126 E3
Dixon Entrance sea chan. Canada/U.S.A. 120 C4
Dixonville Canada 120 G3
Dixville Canada 135 J1
Diyadin Turkey 91 F3
Diyarbakır Turkey 91 F3
Diz Pak. 89 F5
Diz Chah Iran 88 D3
Dize Turkey see Yüksekova
Dizney U.S.A. 134 D5
Djado Niger 96 E2
Djado, Plateau du Niger 96 E2
Djaja, Puntjak mt. Indon. see Jaya, Puncak
Djakarta Indon. see Jakarta
Djakovica Serb. and Mont. see Đakovica
Djakovo Croatia see Đakovo
Djambala Congo 98 B4
Djanet Alg. 96 D2
Djarrit-Uliga-Dalap Marshall Is see Delap-Uliga-Djarrit
Djelfa Alg. 57 H6
Djéma Cent. Afr. Rep. 98 C3
Djenné Mali 96 C3
Djerdap nat. park Serb. and Mont. 59 J2
Djibo Burkina 96 C3
▶Djibouti country Africa 86 F7
Africa 7, 94–95

▶Djibouti Djibouti 86 F7
Capital of Djibouti.

Djidjelli Alg. see Jijel
Djougou Benin 96 D4
Djoum Cameroon 96 E4
Djourab, Erg du des. Chad 97 E3
Djúpivogur Iceland 44 [inset]
Djurås Sweden 45 I6
Djurdjura National Park Alg. 57 I5
Dmitriya Lapteva, Proliv sea chan. Rus. Fed. 65 P2
Dmitriyev-L'govskiy Rus. Fed. 43 G5
Dmitriyevsk Ukr. see Makiyivka
Dmitrov Rus. Fed. 42 H4
Dmytriyevs'k Ukr. see Makiyivka
Dnepr r. Rus. Fed. 43 F5 see Dnieper
Dneprodzerzhinsk Ukr. see Dniprodzerzhyns'k
Dnepropetrovsk Ukr. see Dnipropetrovs'k

▶Dnieper r. Europe 43 G7
3rd longest river in Europe. Also spelt Dnepr (Rus. Fed.) or Dnipro (Ukraine) or Dnyapro (Belarus).

Dniester r. Ukr. 43 F6
also spelt Dnister (Ukraine) or Nistru (Moldova)
Dnipro r. Ukr. 43 G7 see Dnieper
Dniprodzerzhyns'k Ukr. 43 G6
Dnipropetrovs'k Ukr. 43 G6
Dnister r. Ukr. 43 F6 see Dniester
Dno Rus. Fed. 42 F4
Dnyapro r. Belarus 43 F6 see Dnieper
Doāb Afgh. 89 G3
Doaba Pak. 89 H3
Doba Chad 97 E4
Doba China see Toiba
Dobele Latvia 45 M8
Döbeln Germany 53 N3
Doberai, Jazirah pen. Indon. 69 I7
Doberai Peninsula Indon. see Doberai, Jazirah
Dobo Indon. 69 I8
Doboj Bos.-Herz. 58 H2
Do Borjī Iran 88 D4
Döbraberg hill Germany 53 L4
Dobrich Bulg. 59 L3
Dobrinka Rus. Fed. 43 I5
Dobroye Rus. Fed. 43 H5
Dobrudja reg. Romania see Dobruja
Dobruja reg. Romania 59 L3
Dobrush Belarus 43 F5
Dobryanka Rus. Fed. 41 R4
Dobzha China 83 G3
Doce r. Brazil 145 D2
Dochart r. U.K. 50 E4
Do China Qala Afgh. 89 H4
Docking U.K. 49 H6
Doctor Hicks Range hills Australia 109 D7
Doctor Pedro P. Peña Para. 144 D2
Doda India 82 C2
Doda Betta mt. India 84 C4
Dod Ballapur India 84 C3
Dodecanese is Greece 59 L7
Dodekanisos is Greece see Dodecanese
Dodge City U.S.A. 130 C4
Dodgeville U.S.A. 130 F3
Dodman Point U.K. 49 C8

▶Dodoma Tanz. 99 D4
Capital of Tanzania.

Dodsonville U.S.A. 134 D4
Doetinchem Neth. 52 G3
Dog r. Canada 122 C4
Dogai Coring salt l. China 83 G2
Dogaicoring Qangco salt l. China 83 G2
Doğanşehir Turkey 90 E3
Dogên Co l. Xizang China see Bam Tso
Dogên Co l. Xizang China 83 G3
Doghārūn Iran 89 F3
Dog Island Canada 123 J2
Dog Lake Man. Canada 121 L5
Dog Lake Ont. Canada 122 C4
Dog Lake Ont. Canada 122 D4
Dōgo i. Japan 75 D5
Dogondoutchi Niger 96 D3
Dog Rocks is Bahamas 133 E7
Doğubeyazıt Turkey 91 G3
Doğu Menteşe Dağları mts Turkey 59 M6
Dogxung Zangbo r. China 83 F3
Do'gyaling China 83 G3

▶Doha Qatar 88 C5
Capital of Qatar.

Dohad India see Dahod
Dohazari Bangl. 83 H5
Dohrighat India 83 E4
Doi i. Fiji 107 I4
Doi Inthanon National Park Thai. 70 B3
Doi Luang National Park Thai. 70 B3
Doire U.K. see Londonderry
Doi Saket Thai. 70 B3
Dois Irmãos, Serra dos hills Brazil 143 J5
Dok-dō i. N. Pacific Ocean see Liancourt Rocks
Dokhara, Dunes de des. Alg. 54 F5
Dokka Norway 45 G6
Dokkum Neth. 52 F1
Dokri Pak. 89 H5
Dokshukino Rus. Fed. see Nartkala
Dokshytsy Belarus 45 O9
Dokuchayeva, Mys c. Rus. Fed. 74 G3
Dokuchayevka Kazakh. see Karamendy
Dokuchayevs'k Ukr. 43 H7
Dolak, Pulau i. Indon. 69 J8
Dolbenmaen U.K. 49 C6
Dol-de-Bretagne France 56 D2
Dole France 56 G3
Dolgellau U.K. 49 D6
Dolgen Germany 53 N1
Dolgiy, Ostrov i. Rus. Fed. 42 L1
Dolgorukovo Rus. Fed. 43 H5
Dolina Ukr. see Dolyna
Dolinsk Rus. Fed. 74 F3
Dolisie Congo see Loubomo
Dolleman Island Antarctica 152 L2
Dollnstein Germany 53 L6
Dolomites mts Italy 58 D2
Dolomiti mts Italy see Dolomites
Dolomiti Bellunesi, Parco Nazionale delle nat. park Italy 58 D1
Dolomitiche, Alpi mts Italy see Dolomites
Dolonnur China see Duolun
Dolo Odo Eth. 98 E3
Dolores Arg. 144 E5
Dolores Uruguay 144 E4
Dolores U.S.A. 129 I3
Dolphin and Union Strait Canada 118 G3
Dolphin Head hd Namibia 100 B3
Đô Lương Vietnam 70 D3
Dolyna Ukr. 43 D6
Domaniç Turkey 59 M5
Domar China 80 F5
Domartang China see Banbar
Domažlice Czech Rep. 53 M5
Domba China 76 B1
Dom Bākh Iran 88 B3
Dombås Norway 44 F5
Dombóvár Hungary 58 H1
Dombrau Poland see Dąbrowa Górnicza
Dombrovitsa Ukr. see Dubrovytsya
Dombrowa Poland see Dąbrowa Górnicza
Domda China see Qingshuihe
Dome Argus ice feature Antarctica 152 E1
Dome Charlie ice feature Antarctica 152 F2
Dome Creek Canada 120 F4
Dome Rock Mountains U.S.A. 129 F5
Domeyko Chile 144 B3
Domfront France 56 D2
▶Dominica country West Indies 137 L5
North America 9, 116–117
Dominicana, República country West Indies see Dominican Republic
▶Dominican Republic country West Indies 137 J5
North America 9, 116–117
Dominion, Cape Canada 119 K3
Dominique i. Fr. Polynesia see Hiva Oa
Dömitz Germany 53 L1
Dom Joaquim Brazil 145 C2
Dommel r. Neth. 52 F3
Domo Eth. 98 E3
Domokos Greece 59 J5
Dompu Indon. 108 B2
Domula China see Duomula
Domuyo, Volcán vol. Arg. 144 B5
Domville, Mount hill Australia 112 E2
Don Mex. 127 F8

▶Don r. Rus. Fed. 43 H7
5th longest river in Europe.

Don r. U.K. 50 G3
Don, Xé r. Laos 70 D4
Donaghadee U.K. 51 G3
Donaghmore U.K. 51 F3
Donald Australia 112 A6
Donaldsonville U.S.A. 131 F6
Donalsonville U.S.A. 133 C6
Doñana, Parque Nacional de nat. park Spain 57 C5
Donau r. Austria/Germany 47 P6 see Danube
Donauwörth Germany 53 K6
Don Benito Spain 57 D4
Doncaster U.K. 48 F5
Dondo Angola 99 B4
Dondo Moz. 99 D5
Dondra Head hd Sri Lanka 84 D5
Donegal Rep. of Ireland 51 D3
Donegal Bay Rep. of Ireland 51 D3
Donets'k Ukr. 43 H7
Donetsko-Amrovsiyevka Ukr. see Amvrosiyivka
Donets'kyy Kryazh hills Rus. Fed./Ukr. 43 H6
Donga r. Cameroon/Nigeria 96 D4
Dong'an China 77 F3
Dongane, Lagoa lag. Moz. 101 L3
Dongara Australia 109 A7
Dongbo China see Mêdog
Dongchuan Yunnan China see Yao'an
Dongchuan Yunnan China 76 D3
Dongco China 83 F2
Dong Co l. China 83 F2
Dongfang China 77 F5
Dongfanghong China 74 D3
Donggang China 75 B5
Donggi Conag l. China 76 C1
Donggou China see Donggang
Donggu China 77 G3
Dongguan China 77 G4
Dong Hai sea N. Pacific Ocean see East China Sea
Đông Hôi Vietnam 70 D3
Donghuang China see Xishui
Dongjiang Shuiku resr China 77 G3
Dongjug China 76 B2
Dongkou China 77 F3
Donglan China 76 E3
Dongliao He r. China 74 A4
Dongmen China see Luocheng
Dongminzhutun China 74 A3
Dongning China 74 C3
Dongo Angola 99 B5
Dongo Dem. Rep. Congo 98 B3
Dongola Sudan 86 D6
Dongou Congo 98 B3
Dong Phraya Yen esc. Thai. 70 C4
Dongping Guangdong China 77 G4
Dongping Hunan China see Anhua
Dongpo China see Meishan
Dongqiao China 83 G3
Dongshan Fujian China 77 H4
Dongshan Jiangsu China 77 I2
Dongshan Jiangxi China see Shangyou
Dongshao China 77 G3
Dongsha Qundao is China 68 F2
Dongsheng Nei Mongol China 73 K5
Dongsheng Sichuan China see Shuangliu
Dongshuan China see Tangdan
Dongtai China 77 I1
Dongting Hu l. China 77 G2
Dongtou China 77 I3
Đông Triêu Vietnam 70 D2
Dong Ujimqin Qi China see Uliastai
Đông Văn Vietnam 70 D2
Dongxiang China 77 H2
Dongxi Liandao i. China 77 H1
Dongxing Guangxi China 76 E4
Dongxing Heilong. China 74 B3
Dongyang China 77 I2
Dongying China 73 L5
Dongzhi China 77 H2
Donkerbroek Neth. 52 G1
Donnacona Canada 123 H5
Donnellys Crossing N.Z. 113 D2
Donner Pass U.S.A. 128 C2
Donnersberg hill Germany 53 H5
Donostia - San Sebastián Spain 57 F2
Donoussa i. Greece 59 K6
Donskoye Rus. Fed. 43 I7
Donyztau, Sor dry lake Kazakh. 80 A2
Dooagh Rep. of Ireland 51 B4
Doomadgee Australia 110 B3
Doon r. U.K. 50 E5
Doon, Loch l. U.K. 50 E5
Doonbeg r. Rep. of Ireland 51 C5
Doorn Neth. 52 F2
Door Peninsula U.S.A. 134 B1
Doorwerth Neth. 52 F3
Dooxo Nugaaleed valley Somalia 98 E3
Doqêmo China 76 B2
Do Qu r. China 76 D2
Dor watercourse Afgh. 89 F4
Dora U.S.A. 131 C5
Dora, Lake salt flat Australia 108 C5
Dorado Mex. 131 B7
Dorah Pass Pak. 89 H2
Doran Lake Canada 121 I2
Dorbiljin China see Emin
Dorbod China see Taikang
Dorbod Qi China see Ulan Hua
Dorchester U.K. 49 E8
Dordabis Namibia 100 C2
Dordogne r. France 56 D4
Dordrecht Neth. 52 E3
Dordrecht S. Africa 101 H6
Doreenville Namibia 100 D2
Doré Lake Canada 121 J4
Doré Lake l. Canada 121 J4
Dores do Indaiá Brazil 145 B2
Dori r. Afgh. 89 G4
Dori Burkina 96 C3
Doring r. S. Africa 100 D6
do Rio Manso, Represa resr Brazil 143 G6
Dorisvale Australia 108 E3
Dorking U.K. 49 G7
Dormagen Germany 52 G3
Dormans France 52 D5
Dormidontovka Rus. Fed. 74 D3
Dornoch U.K. 50 E3
Dornoch Firth est. U.K. 50 E3
Dornum Germany 53 H1
Doro Mali 96 C3
Dorogobuzh Rus. Fed. 43 G5
Dorogorskoye Rus. Fed. 42 J2
Dorohoi Romania 43 E7
Döröö Nuur salt l. Mongolia 80 H2
Dorostol Bulg. see Silistra
Dorotea Sweden 44 J4
Dorpat Estonia see Tartu
Dorre Island Australia 109 A6
Dorrigo Australia 112 F3
Dorris U.S.A. 126 C4
Dorsale Camerounaise slope Cameroon/Nigeria 96 E4
Dorset Canada 135 F1
Dorsoidong Co l. China 83 G2
Dortmund Germany 53 H3
Dörtyol Turkey 85 C1
Dorum Germany 53 I1
Doruma Dem. Rep. Congo 98 C3
Dorüneh, Kūh-e mts Iran 88 E3
Dorval airport Canada 122 G5
Dörverden Germany 53 J2
Dorylaeum Turkey see Eskişehir
Dos Bahías, Cabo c. Arg. 144 C6
Dos de Mayo Peru 142 C5
Doshakh, Koh-i- mt. Afgh. see Do Shākh, Kūh-e
Do Shākh, Kūh-e mt. Afgh. 89 F3
Đo Son Vietnam 70 D2
Dos Palos U.S.A. 128 C3
Dosse r. Germany 53 M2
Dosso Niger 96 D3
Dothan U.S.A. 133 C6
Dotsero U.S.A. 129 J2
Douai France 52 D4
Douala Cameroon 96 D4
Douarnenez France 56 B2
Double Headed Shot Cays is Bahamas 133 D8
Double Island Hong Kong China 77 [inset]
Double Island Point Australia 111 F5
Double Mountain Fork r. U.S.A. 131 C5
Double Peak U.S.A. 128 D4
Double Point Australia 110 D3
Double Springs U.S.A. 133 C5
Doubs r. France/Switz. 56 G3
Doubtful Sound inlet N.Z. 113 A7
Doubtless Bay N.Z. 113 D2
Douentza Mali 96 C3
Dougga tourist site Tunisia 58 C6

▶Douglas Isle of Man 48 C4
Capital of the Isle of Man.

Douglas S. Africa 100 F5
Douglas U.K. 50 F5
Douglas AZ U.S.A. 127 F7
Douglas GA U.S.A. 133 D6
Douglas WY U.S.A. 126 G4
Douglas Reef i. Japan see Okino-Tori-shima
Douglasville U.S.A. 133 C5
Douhudi China see Gong'an
Doulatpur Bangl. see Daulatpur
Douliu Taiwan see Touliu
Doullens France 52 C4
Douna Mali 96 C3
Doune U.K. 50 E4
Doupovské Hory mts Czech Rep. 53 N4
Dourada, Serra hills Brazil 145 A2
Dourada, Serra mts Brazil 145 A1
Dourados Brazil 144 F2
Douro r. Port. 57 B3
also known as Duero (Spain)
Doushi China see Gong'an
Doushui Shuiku resr China 77 G3
Douve r. France 49 F9
Douzy France 52 F5
Dove r. U.K. 49 F6
Dove Brook Canada 123 K3
Dove Creek U.S.A. 129 I3
Dover U.K. 49 I7

▶Dover DE U.S.A. 135 H4
State capital of Delaware.

Dover NH U.S.A. 135 J2
Dover NJ U.S.A. 135 H3
Dover OH U.S.A. 134 E3
Dover TN U.S.A. 132 C4
Dover, Strait of France/U.K. 56 E1
Dover-Foxcroft U.S.A. 135 K1
Dovey r. U.K. see Dyfi
Dovrefjell Nasjonalpark nat. park Norway 44 F5
Dowagiac U.S.A. 134 B3
Dowi, Tanjung pt Indon. 71 B7
Dowlaiswaram India 84 D2
Dowlatābād Afgh. 89 F3
Dowlatābād Afgh. 89 G3
Dowlatābād Fārs Iran 88 C4
Dowlatābād Fārs Iran 88 D4
Dowlatābād Khorāsān Iran 88 E2
Dowlatābād Khorāsān Iran 89 F2
Dowl at Yār Afgh. 89 G3
Downieville U.S.A. 128 C2
Downpatrick U.K. 51 G3
Downsville U.S.A. 135 H2
Dow Rūd Iran 88 C3
Doyle U.S.A. 128 C1
Doylestown U.S.A. 135 H3
Dozdān r. Iran 88 E5
Dōzen is Japan 75 D5
Dozois, Réservoir resr Canada 122 F5
Dozulé France 49 G9
Dracena Brazil 145 A3
Drachten Neth. 52 G1
Drăgănești-Olt Romania 59 K2
Drăgășani Romania 59 K2
Dragonera, Isla i. Spain see Sa Dragonera
Dragoon U.S.A. 129 H5
Dragsfjärd Fin. 45 M6
Draguignan France 56 H5
Drahichyn Belarus 45 N10
Drake Australia 112 F2
Drake U.S.A. 130 C2
Drakensberg mts S. Africa 101 I3
Drake Passage S. Atlantic Ocean 148 D9
Drakes Bay U.S.A. 128 B3
Drama Greece 59 K4
Drammen Norway 45 G7
Drang, Prêk r. Cambodia 71 D4
Drangedal Norway 45 F7
Dransfeld Germany 53 J3
Draper, Mount U.S.A. 120 B3
Draperstown U.K. 51 F3
Drapsaca Afgh. see Kunduz
Dras Jammu and Kashmir 82 C2
Drasan Pak. 89 I2
Drau r. Austria see Drava
Drava r. Europe 58 H2
also known as Drau (Austria), Drave or Drava (Slovenia and Croatia), Dráva (Hungary)
Dráva r. Hungary see Drava
Drave r. Slovenia/Croatia see Drava
Drayton Valley Canada 120 H4
Drazinda Pak. 89 H4
Dréan Alg. 58 B6
Dreistelzberge hill Germany 53 J4
Drentse Hoofdvaart canal Neth. 52 G2
Drepano, Akra pt Greece 59 J5
Dresden Canada 134 D2
Dresden Germany 47 N5
Dreux France 52 B6
Drevsjø Norway 45 H6
Drewryville U.S.A. 135 G5
Dri China 76 C2
Driffield U.K. 48 G4
Driftwood U.S.A. 135 F3
Driggs U.S.A. 126 F4
Drillham Australia 112 E1
Drimoleague Rep. of Ireland 51 C6
Drina r. Bos.-Herz./Serb. and Mont. 59 H2
Driscoll Island Antarctica 152 J1
Drissa Belarus see Vyerkhnyadzvinsk
Drniš Croatia 58 G3
Drobeta - Turnu Severin Romania 59 J2
Drochtersen Germany 53 J1
Drogheda Rep. of Ireland 51 F4
Drogichin Belarus see Drahichyn
Drogobych Ukr. see Drohobych
Drohobych Ukr. 43 D6
Droichead Átha Rep. of Ireland see Drogheda
Droichead Nua Rep. of Ireland see Newbridge
Droitwich U.K. see Droitwich Spa
Droitwich Spa U.K. 49 E6
Dromedary, Cape Australia 112 E6
Dromod Rep. of Ireland 51 E4
Dromore Northern Ireland U.K. 51 E3
Dromore Northern Ireland U.K. 51 F3
Dronfield U.K. 48 F5
Dronning Louise Land reg. Greenland 153 I1
Dronning Maud Land reg. Antarctica see Queen Maud Land
Dronten Neth. 52 F2
Druk-Yul country Asia see Bhutan
Drumheller Canada 121 H5
Drummond atoll Kiribati see Tabiteuea
Drummond U.S.A. 126 E3
Drummond, Lake U.S.A. 135 G5
Drummond Island Kiribati see McKean
Drummond Range hills Australia 110 D5
Drummondville Canada 123 G5
Drummore U.K. 50 E6
Drury Lake Canada 120 C2
Druskieniki Lith. see Druskininkai
Druskininkai Lith. 45 N10
Druzhina Rus. Fed. 65 P3
Druzhnaya Gorka Rus. Fed. 45 Q7
Dry r. Australia 108 F3
Dryanovo Bulg. 59 K3
Dryberry Lake Canada 121 M5
Dryden Canada 121 M5
Dryden U.S.A. 135 G2
Dry Fork r. U.S.A. 126 G4
Drygalski Ice Tongue Antarctica 152 H1
Drygalski Island Antarctica 152 F2
Dry Lake U.S.A. 129 F3
Dry Lake l. U.S.A. 130 D1
Drymen U.K. 50 E4
Dry Ridge U.S.A. 134 C4
Drysdale r. Australia 108 D3
Drysdale River National Park Australia 108 D3
Dry Tortugas is U.S.A. 133 D7
Du'an China 77 F4
Duaringa Australia 110 E4
Duarte, Pico mt. Dom. Rep. 137 J5
Duartina Brazil 145 A3
Ḑubā Saudi Arabia 86 E4
Dubai U.A.E. 88 D5
Dubakella Mountain U.S.A. 128 B1
Dubawnt r. Canada 121 L2
Dubawnt Lake Canada 121 K2
Dubayy U.A.E. see Dubai
Dubbo Australia 112 D4

▶Dublin Rep. of Ireland 51 F4
Capital of the Republic of Ireland.

Dublin U.S.A. 133 D5
Dubna Rus. Fed. 42 H4
Dubno Ukr. 43 E6
Dubois ID U.S.A. 126 E3
Dubois IN U.S.A. 134 B4
Du Bois U.S.A. 135 F3
Dubovka Rus. Fed. 43 J6
Dubovskoye Rus. Fed. 43 I7
Dübrar Pass Azer. 91 H2
Dubréka Guinea 96 B4
Dubris U.K. see Dover
Dubrovnik Croatia 58 H3
Dubrovytsya Ukr. 43 E6
Dubuque U.S.A. 130 F3
Dubysa r. Lith. 45 M9
Duc de Gloucester, Îles du is Fr. Polynesia 151 K7
Duchang China 77 H2
Ducheng China see Yunan
Duchesne U.S.A. 129 H1
Duchesne r. U.S.A. 129 I1
Duchess Australia 110 B4
Duchess Canada 121 I5
Ducie Island atoll Pitcairn Is 151 L7
Duck Bay Canada 121 K4
Duck Creek r. Australia 108 B5
Duck Lake Canada 121 J4
Duckwater Peak U.S.A. 129 F2
Đưc Trong Vietnam 71 E5
Dudelange Lux. 52 G5
Duderstadt Germany 53 K3
Dudhi India 83 E4
Dudhwa India 82 E3
Dudinka Rus. Fed. 64 J3
Dudley U.K. 49 E6
Dudleyville U.S.A. 129 H5
Dudna r. India 84 C2
Dudu India 82 C4
Duékoué Côte d'Ivoire 96 C4
Duen, Bukit vol. Indon. 68 C7
Duero r. Spain 57 C3
also known as Douro (Portugal)
Duffel Belgium 52 E3
Dufferin, Cape Canada 122 F2
Duffer Peak U.S.A. 126 D4
Duff Islands Solomon Is 107 G2
Duffreboy, Lac l. Canada 123 H2
Dufftown U.K. 50 F3
Dufourspitze mt. Italy/Switz. 54 B2
Dufrost, Pointe pt Canada 122 F1
Dugi Otok i. Croatia 58 F2
Dugi Rat Croatia 58 G3
Du He r. China 77 F1
Duida-Marahuaca, Parque Nacional nat. park Venez. 142 E3
Duisburg Germany 52 G3
Duiwelskloof S. Africa 101 J2
Dujiangyan China 76 D2
Dukān Dam Iraq 91 G4
Dukathole S. Africa 101 H6
Duke Island U.S.A. 120 D4
Duke of Clarence atoll Tokelau see Nukunono
Duke of Gloucester Islands Fr. Polynesia see Duc de Gloucester, Îles du
Duke of York atoll Tokelau see Atafu
Duk Fadiat Sudan 97 G4
Dukhovnitskoye Rus. Fed. 43 K5
Duki Pak. 89 H4
Duki Rus. Fed. 74 D2
Duki r. Rus. Fed. 74 D2
Dukou China see Panzhihua
Dūkštas Lith. 45 O9
Dulac U.S.A. 131 F6
Dulan China 80 I4
Dulce r. Arg. 144 D4
Dulce U.S.A. 127 G5
Dul'durga Rus. Fed. 73 K2
Dulhunty r. Australia 110 C1
Dulishi Hu salt l. China 83 E2
Duliu Jiang r. China 77 F3
Dullewala Pak. 89 H4
Dullstroom S. Africa 101 J3
Dülmen Germany 53 H3
Dulmera India 82 C3
Dulovo Bulg. 59 L3
Duluth U.S.A. 130 E2
Dulverton U.K. 49 D7
Dūmā Syria 85 C3
Dumaguete Phil. 69 G5
Dumai Indon. 71 C7
Dumaran i. Phil. 68 G4
Dumaresq r. Australia 112 E2
Dumas U.S.A. 131 C5
Ḑumayr Syria 85 C3

Ḑumayr, Jabal *mts* Syria 85 C3
Dumbakh Iran *see* Dom Bākh
Dumbarton U.K. 50 E5
Dumbe S. Africa 101 J4
Ďumbier *mt.* Slovakia 47 Q6
Dumchele Jammu and Kashmir 82 D2
Dumdum *i.* Indon. 71 D7
Dumfries U.K. 50 F5
Dumka India 83 F4
Dumont d'Urville *research station* Antarctica 152 G2
Dumont d'Urville Sea Antarctica 152 G2
Dümpelfeld Germany 52 G4
Dumyāṭ Egypt 90 C5
Dumyâṭ Egypt *see* Dumyāṭ
Duna *r.* Hungary 58 H2 *see* Danube
Dünaburg Latvia *see* Daugavpils
Dunaj *r.* Slovakia *see* Danube
Dunajská Streda Slovakia 47 P7
Dunakeszi Hungary 59 H1
Dunany Point Rep. of Ireland 47 F4
Dunărea *r.* Romania *see* Danube
Dunării, Delta Romania/Ukr. *see* Danube Delta
Dunaújváros Hungary 58 H1
Dunav *r.* Bulg./Croatia/Serb. and Mont. 58 L2 *see* Danube
Dunay *r.* Ukr. *see* Danube
Dunayivtsi Ukr. 43 E6
Dunbar Australia 110 C3
Dunbar U.K. 50 G4
Dunblane U.K. 50 F4
Dunboyne Rep. of Ireland 51 F4
Duncan Canada 120 F5
Duncan *AZ* U.S.A. 129 I5
Duncan *OK* U.S.A. 131 D5
Duncan, Cape Canada 122 E3
Duncan, Lac *l.* Canada 122 F3
Duncan Lake Canada 120 H2
Duncan Passage India 71 A5
Duncansby Head *hd* U.K. 50 F2
Duncan Town Bahamas 133 F8
Duncormick Rep. of Ireland 51 F5
Dundaga Latvia 45 M8
Dundalk Rep. of Ireland 51 F3
Dundalk U.S.A. 135 G4
Dundalk Bay Rep. of Ireland 51 F4
Dundas Canada 134 F2
Dundas Greenland 119 L2
Dundas, Lake *salt flat* Australia 109 C8
Dundas Island Canada 120 D4
Dundas Strait Australia 108 E2
Dún Dealgan Rep. of Ireland *see* Dundalk
Dundee S. Africa 101 J5
Dundee U.K. 50 G4
Dundee *MI* U.S.A. 134 D3
Dundee *NY* U.S.A. 135 G2
Dundonald U.K. 51 G3
Dundoo Australia 112 B1
Dundrennan U.K. 50 F6
Dundrum U.K. 51 G3
Dundrum Bay U.K. 51 G3
Dun Duma India 83 H4
Dundwa Range *mts* India/Nepal 83 E4
Dune, Lac *l.* Canada 122 G2
Dunedin N.Z. 113 C7
Dunedin U.S.A. 133 D6
Dunfermline U.K. 50 F4
Dungannon U.K. 51 F3
Dún Garbhán Rep. of Ireland *see* Dungarvan
Dungarpur India 82 C5
Dungarvan Rep. of Ireland 51 E5
Dung Co *l.* China 83 G3
Dungeness *hd* U.K. 49 H8
Dungeness, Punta *pt* Arg. 144 C8
Düngenheim Germany 53 H4
Dungiven U.K. 51 F3
Dungloe Rep. of Ireland 51 D3
Dungog Australia 112 E4
Dungu Dem. Rep. Congo 98 C3
Dungun Malaysia 71 C6
Dungunab Sudan 86 E5
Dunhua China 74 C4
Dunhuang China 80 H3
Dunkeld Australia 112 D1
Dunkeld U.K. 50 F4
Dunkellin *r.* Rep. of Ireland 51 D4
Dunkerque France *see* Dunkirk
Dunkery Beacon *hill* U.K. 49 D7
Dunkirk France 52 C3
Dunkirk U.S.A. 134 F2
Dún Laoghaire Rep. of Ireland 51 F4
Dunlap *IA* U.S.A. 130 E3
Dunlap *TN* U.S.A. 132 C5
Dunlavin Rep. of Ireland 51 F4
Dunleer Rep. of Ireland 51 F4
Dunloy U.K. 51 F2
Dunmanway Rep. of Ireland 51 C6
Dunmarra Australia 108 F4
Dunmor U.S.A. 134 B5
Dunmore Rep. of Ireland 51 D4
Dunmore U.S.A. 135 H3
Dunmore Town Bahamas 133 E7
Dunmurry U.K. 51 G3
Dunnet Head *hd* U.K. 50 F2
Dunnigan U.S.A. 128 C2
Dunning U.S.A. 130 C3
Dunnville Canada 134 F2
Dunnville U.S.A. 134 C5
Dunolly Australia 112 A6
Dunoon U.K. 50 E5
Dunphy U.S.A. 128 E1
Duns U.K. 50 G5
Dunseith U.S.A. 130 C1
Dunstable U.K. 49 G7
Dunstan Mountains N.Z. 113 B7
Dun-sur-Meuse France 52 F5
Duntroon N.Z. 113 C7
Dunvegan Lake Canada 121 J2
Dunyapur Pak. 89 H4
Duolun China 73 L4
Duomula China 83 E2
Dupang Ling *mts* China 77 F3
Duperré Alg. *see* Aïn Defla
Dupnitsa Bulg. 59 J3
Dupree U.S.A. 130 C2
Duque de Bragança Angola *see* Calandula
Dūrā West Bank 85 B4
Durack *r.* Australia 108 D3
Durack Range *hills* Australia 108 D4
Dura Europos Syria *see* Aş Şālihīyah
Durağan Turkey 90 D2
Durance *r.* France 56 G5
Durand U.S.A. 130 F2
Durango Mex. 131 B7
Durango *state* Mex. 131 B7
Durango Spain 57 E2
Durango U.S.A. 129 J3
Durani *reg.* Afgh. 89 G4
Durant U.S.A. 131 D5
Durazno Uruguay 144 E4
Durazzo Albania *see* Durrës
Durban S. Africa 101 J5
Durban-Corbières France 56 F5
Durbanville S. Africa 100 D7
Durbin U.S.A. 134 F4
Durbun Pak. 89 G4
Durbuy Belgium 52 F4
Düren Germany 52 G4
Düren Iran 88 E3
Duren, Kūh-e *mt.* Iran 88 E3
Durg India 82 E5
Durgapur Bangl. 83 G4
Durgapur India 83 F5
Durham Canada 134 E1
Durham U.K. 48 F4
Durham U.S.A. 132 E5
Durham Downs Australia 111 C5
Duri Indon. 71 C7
Durlas Rep. of Ireland *see* Thurles
Durleşti Moldova 59 M1
Durmersheim Germany 53 I6
Durmitor *mt.* Serb. and Mont. 59 H3
Durmitor *nat. park* Serb. and Mont. 58 H3
Durness U.K. 50 E2
Durocortorum France *see* Reims
Durong South Australia 111 E5
Durostorum Bulg. *see* Silistra
Durour Island P.N.G. *see* Aua Island
Durovernum U.K. *see* Canterbury
Durrës Albania 59 H4
Durrie Australia 110 C5
Durrington U.K. 49 F7
Dursey Island Rep. of Ireland 47 B6
Dursunbey Turkey 59 M5
Duru China *see* Wuchuan
Dūrūḩ Iran 89 F3
Durukhsi Somalia 98 E3
Durusu Gölü *l.* Turkey 59 M4
Durūz, Jabal ad *mt.* Syria 85 C3
D'Urville, Tanjung *pt* Indon. 69 J7
D'Urville Island N.Z. 113 D5
Durzab Afgh. 89 G3
Dushai Pak. 89 G4
Dushak Turkm. 89 E2
Dushan China 76 E3

▶Dushanbe Tajik. 89 H2
Capital of Tajikistan.

Dushet'i Georgia 91 G2
Dushore U.S.A. 135 G3
Dusse-Alin', Khrebet *mts* Rus. Fed. 74 D2
Düsseldorf Germany 52 G3
Dusty *NM* U.S.A. 129 J5
Dusty *WA* U.S.A. 126 D3
Dutch East Indies *country* Asia *see* Indonesia
Dutch Guiana *country* S. America *see* Suriname
Dutch Mountain U.S.A. 129 G1
Dutch West Indies *terr.* West Indies *see* Netherlands Antilles
Dutlwe Botswana 100 F2
Dutse Nigeria 96 D3
Dutsin-Ma Nigeria 96 D3
Dutton *r.* Australia 110 C4
Dutton Canada 134 E2
Dutton U.S.A. 126 F3
Dutton, Lake *salt flat* Australia 111 B6
Dutton, Mount U.S.A. 129 G2
Duval Canada 121 J5
Duvert, Lac *l.* Canada 123 H2
Duvno Bos.-Herz. *see* Tomislavgrad
Duwin Iraq 91 G3
Düxanbibazar China 82 E1
Duyun China 76 E3
Duzab Pak. 89 F5
Düzce Turkey 59 N4
Duzdab Iran *see* Zāhedān
Dvina *r.* Europe *see* Zapadnaya Dvina
Dvina *r.* Rus. Fed. *see* Severnaya Dvina
Dvinsk Latvia *see* Daugavpils
Dvinskaya Guba *g.* Rus. Fed. 42 H2
Dwarka India 82 B5
Dwarsberg S. Africa 101 H3
Dwingelderveld, Nationaal Park *nat. park* Neth. 52 G2
Dworshak Reservoir U.S.A. 126 E3
Dwyka S. Africa 100 E7
Dyat'kovo Rus. Fed. 43 G5
Dyce U.K. 50 G3
Dyer, Cape Canada 119 L3
Dyer Bay Canada 134 E1
Dyersburg U.S.A. 131 F4
Dyffryn U.K. *see* Valley
Dyfi *r.* U.K. 49 D6
Dyfrdwy *r.* U.K. *see* Dee
Dyje *r.* Austria/Czech Rep. 47 P6
Dyke U.K. 50 F3

▶Dykh-Tau, Gora *mt.* Rus. Fed. 91 F2
2nd highest mountain in Europe.

Dyle *r.* Belgium 52 E4
Dyleň *hill* Czech Rep. 53 M5
Dylewska Góra *hill* Poland 47 Q4
Dymytrov Ukr. 43 H6
Dynevor Downs Australia 112 B2
Dyoki S. Africa 101 I6
Dyrrhachium Albania *see* Durrës
Dysart Australia 110 E4
Dysselsdorp S. Africa 100 F7
Dyurtyuli Rus. Fed. 41 Q4
Dzamīn Üüd Mongolia 73 K4
Dzanga-Ndoki, Parc National de *nat. park* Cent. Afr. Rep. 98 B3

▶Dzaoudzi Mayotte 99 E5
Capital of Mayotte.

Dzaudzhikau Rus. Fed. *see* Vladikavkaz
Dzerzhinsk Belarus *see* Dzyarzhynsk
Dzerzhinsk Rus. Fed. 42 I4
Dzhagdy, Khrebet *mts* Rus. Fed. 74 C1
Dzhaki-Unakhta Yakbyyana, Khrebet *mts* Rus. Fed. 74 D2
Dzhalalabad Azer. *see* Cälilabad
Dzhalal-Abad Kyrg. *see* Jalal-Abad
Dzhalil' Rus. Fed. 41 Q4
Dzhalinda Rus. Fed. 74 A1
Dzhaltyr Kazakh. *see* Zhaltyr
Dzhambeyty Kazakh. *see* Zhympity
Dzhambul Kazakh. *see* Taraz
Dzhanga Turkm. 88 D1
Dzhangala Kazakh. 41 Q6
Dzhankoy Ukr. 43 G7
Dzhanybek Kazakh. *see* Zhanibek
Dzharkent Kazakh. *see* Zharkent
Dzharkurgan Uzbek. 89 G2
Dzhava Georgia *see* Java
Dzhetygara Kazakh. *see* Zhitikara
Dzhezkazgan Kazakh. *see* Zhezkazgan
Dzhidinskiy, Khrebet *mts* Mongolia/Rus. Fed. 80 J1
Dzhirgatal' Tajik. *see* Jirgatol
Dzhizak Uzbek. 89 G1
Dzhokhar Ghala Rus. Fed. *see* Groznyy
Dzhubga Rus. Fed. 90 E1
Dzhu-Dzhu-Klu Turkm. 89 F2
Dzhugdzhur, Khrebet *mts* Rus. Fed. 65 O4
Dzhul'fa Azer. *see* Culfa
Dzhuma Uzbek. 89 G2
Dzhungarskiy Alatau, Khrebet *mts* China/Kazakh. 80 E3
Dzhusaly Kazakh. 80 B2
Działdowo Poland 47 R4
Dzūkija *nat. park* Lith. 45 N9
Dzungarian Basin China *see* Junggar Pendi
Dzungarian Gate *pass* China/Kazakh. 80 F2
Dzur Mongolia 80 I2
Dzüünharaa Mongolia 72 J3
Dzuunmod Mongolia 72 J3
Dzyaniskavichy Belarus 45 O10
Dzyarzhynsk Belarus 45 O10
Dzyatlavichy Belarus 45 O10

E

Eabamet Lake Canada 122 D4
Eads U.S.A. 130 C4
Eagar U.S.A. 129 I4
Eagle *r.* Canada 123 K3
Eagle *AK* U.S.A. 118 D3
Eagle *CO* U.S.A. 126 G5
Eagle Cap *mt.* U.S.A. 126 D3
Eagle Crags *mt.* U.S.A. 128 E4
Eagle Creek *r.* Canada 121 J4
Eagle Lake Canada 121 M5
Eagle Lake *CA* U.S.A. 128 C1
Eagle Lake *ME* U.S.A. 132 G2
Eagle Mountain U.S.A. 129 F5
Eagle Mountain *hill* U.S.A. 130 F2
Eagle Pass U.S.A. 131 C6
Eagle Peak U.S.A. 127 G7
Eagle Plain Canada 118 E3
Eagle River U.S.A. 130 F2
Eagle Rock U.S.A. 134 F5
Eaglesham Canada 120 G4
Eap *i.* Micronesia *see* Yap
Ear Falls Canada 121 M5
Earlimart U.S.A. 128 D4
Earl's Seat *hill* U.K. 50 E4
Earlston U.K. 50 G5
Earn *r.* U.K. 50 F4
Earn, Loch *l.* U.K. 50 E4
Earp U.S.A. 129 F4
Earth U.S.A. 131 C5
Easington U.K. 48 H5
Easley U.S.A. 133 D5
East Alligator *r.* Australia 108 F3
East Antarctica *reg.* Antarctica 152 F1
East Ararat U.S.A. 135 H3
East Aurora U.S.A. 135 F2
East Bay *inlet* U.S.A. 133 C6
East Bengal *country* Asia *see* Bangladesh
Eastbourne U.K. 49 H8
East Branch Clarion River Reservoir U.S.A. 135 F3
East Caicos *i.* Turks and Caicos Is 133 G8
East Cape N.Z. 113 G3
East Carbon City U.S.A. 129 H2
East Caroline Basin *sea feature* N. Pacific Ocean 150 F5
East China Sea N. Pacific Ocean 73 N6
East Coast Bays N.Z. 113 E3
East Dereham U.K. 49 H6
Eastend Canada 121 I5

▶Easter Island S. Pacific Ocean 151 M7
Part of Chile.

Eastern Cape *prov.* S. Africa 101 H6
Eastern Desert Egypt 86 D4
Eastern Fields *reef* Australia 110 D1
Eastern Ghats *mts* India 84 C4

▶Eastern Island U.S.A. 150 I4
Most northerly point of Oceania.

Eastern Nara *canal* Pak. 89 H5
Eastern Samoa *terr.* S. Pacific Ocean *see* American Samoa
Eastern Sayan Mountains Rus. Fed. *see* Vostochnyy Sayan
Eastern Taurus *plat.* Turkey *see* Güneydoğu Toroslar
Eastern Transvaal *prov.* S. Africa *see* Mpumalanga
Easterville Canada 121 L4
Easterwâlde Neth. *see* Oosterwolde
East Falkland *i.* Falkland Is 144 E8
East Falmouth U.S.A. 135 J3
East Frisian Islands Germany 47 K4
Eastgate U.S.A. 128 E2
East Greenwich U.S.A. 135 J3
East Grinstead U.K. 49 G7
Easthampton U.S.A. 135 I2
East Hampton U.S.A. 135 I3
East Hartford U.S.A. 135 I3
East Indiaman Ridge *sea feature* Indian Ocean 149 O7
East Jordan U.S.A. 134 C1
East Kilbride U.K. 50 E5
Eastlake U.S.A. 134 E3
East Lamma Channel Hong Kong China 77 [inset]
Eastland U.S.A. 131 D5
East Lansing U.S.A. 134 C2
Eastleigh U.K. 49 F8
East Liverpool U.S.A. 134 E3
East London S. Africa 101 H7
East Lynn Lake U.S.A. 134 D4
Eastmain Canada 122 F3
Eastmain *r.* Canada 122 F3
Eastman U.S.A. 133 D5
East Mariana Basin *sea feature* N. Pacific Ocean 150 G5
Eastmere Australia 110 D4
East Naples U.S.A. 133 D7
Easton *MD* U.S.A. 135 G4
Easton *PA* U.S.A. 135 H3
East Orange U.S.A. 135 H3
East Pacific Rise *sea feature* N. Pacific Ocean 151 M4
East Pakistan *country* Asia *see* Bangladesh
East Palestine U.S.A. 134 E3
East Park Reservoir U.S.A. 128 B2
East Point Canada 123 J5
Eastport U.S.A. 132 H2
East Providence U.S.A. 135 J3
East Range *mts* U.S.A. 128 E1
East Retford U.K. *see* Retford
East Sea N. Pacific Ocean *see* Japan, Sea of
East Shoal Lake Canada 121 L5
East Siberian Sea Rus. Fed. 65 P2
East Side Canal *r.* U.S.A. 128 D4
East St Louis U.S.A. 130 F4
East Stroudsburg U.S.A. 135 H3
East Tavaputs Plateau U.S.A. 129 I2
▶East Timor *country* Asia 108 D2
Asia 6, 62–63
East Toorale Australia 112 B3
East Troy U.S.A. 134 A2
East Verde *r.* U.S.A. 129 H4
Eastville U.S.A. 135 H5
East-Vlylân Neth. *see* Oost-Vlieland
East York Canada 134 F2
Eaton U.S.A. 134 C4
Eatonia Canada 121 I5
Eaton Rapids U.S.A. 134 C2
Eatonton U.S.A. 133 D5
Eau Claire U.S.A. 130 F2
Eauripik *atoll* Micronesia 69 K5
Eauripik Rise - New Guinea Rise *sea feature* N. Pacific Ocean 146 F5
Eaurypyg *atoll* Micronesia *see* Eauripik
Ebbw Vale U.K. 49 D7
Ebebiyin Equat. Guinea 96 E4
Ebenerde Namibia 100 C3
Ebensburg U.S.A. 135 F3
Eber Gölü *l.* Turkey 59 N5
Ebergötzen Germany 53 K3
Eberswalde-Finow Germany 47 N4
Ebetsu Japan 74 F4
Ebian China 76 D2
Ebi Nor *salt l.* China *see* Ebinur Hu
Ebinur Hu *salt l.* China 80 F3
Eboli Italy 58 F4
Ebolowa Cameroon 96 E4
Ebony Namibia 100 B2
Ebre *r.* Spain *see* Ebro
Ebro *r.* Spain 57 G3
Ebstorf Germany 53 K1
Eburacum U.K. *see* York
Ebusus *i.* Spain *see* Ibiza
Ecbatana Iran *see* Hamadān
Eceabat Turkey 59 L4
Ech Chélif Alg. 57 G5
Echegárate, Puerto *pass* Spain 57 E2
Echeng China *see* Ezhou
Echeverria, Pico *mt.* Mex. 127 E7
Echmiadzin Armenia *see* Ejmiatsin
Echo U.S.A. 126 D3
Echo Bay *N.W.T.* Canada 120 G1
Echo Bay *Ont.* Canada 122 D5
Echo Cliffs U.S.A. 129 H3
Echoing *r.* Canada 121 M4
Echt Neth. 52 F3
Echternach Lux. 52 G5
Echuca Australia 112 B6
Echzell Germany 53 I4
Écija Spain 57 D5
Eckental Germany 53 L5
Eckernförde Germany 47 L3
Eclipse Sound *sea chan.* Canada 119 J2
Écrins, Parc National des *nat. park* France 56 H4
▶Ecuador *country* S. America 142 C4
South America 9, 140–141
Écueils, Pointe aux *pt* Canada 122 F2
Ed Eritrea 86 F7
Ed Sweden 45 G7
Edam Neth. 52 F2
Eday *i.* U.K. 50 G1
Ed Da'ein Sudan 97 F3
Ed Dair, Jebel *mt.* Sudan 86 D7
Ed Damazin Sudan 86 D7
Ed Damer Sudan 86 D6
Ed Debba Sudan 86 D6
Eddies Cove Canada 123 K4
Ed Dueim Sudan 86 D7
Eddystone Point Australia 111 [inset]
Eddyville U.S.A. 131 F4
Ede Neth. 52 F2
Edéa Cameroon 96 E4
Edehon Lake Canada 121 L2
Edéia Brazil 145 A2
Eden Australia 112 D6
Eden *r.* U.K. 48 D4
Eden *NC* U.S.A. 134 F5
Eden *TX* U.S.A. 131 D6
Edenburg S. Africa 101 G5
Edendale N.Z. 113 B8
Edenderry Rep. of Ireland 51 E4
Edenton U.S.A. 132 E4
Edenville S. Africa 101 H4
Eder *r.* Germany 53 J3
Eder-Stausee *resr* Germany 53 I3
Edessa Greece 59 J4
Edessa Turkey *see* Şanlıurfa
Edewecht Germany 53 H1
Edfu Egypt *see* Idfū
Edgar Ranges *hills* Australia 108 C4
Edgartown U.S.A. 135 J3
Edgecumbe Island Solomon Is *see* Utupua
Edgefield U.S.A. 133 D5
Edge Island Svalbard *see* Edgeøya
Edgemont U.S.A. 130 C3
Edgeøya *i.* Svalbard 64 D2
Edgerton Canada 121 I4
Edgerton U.S.A. 134 C3
Edgeworthstown Rep. of Ireland 51 E4
Édhessa Greece *see* Edessa
Edina U.S.A. 130 E3
Edinboro U.S.A. 134 E3
Edinburg *TX* U.S.A. 131 D7
Edinburg *VA* U.S.A. 135 F4

▶Edinburgh U.K. 50 F5
Capital of Scotland.

Edirne Turkey 59 L4
Edith, Mount U.S.A. 126 F3
Edith Cavell, Mount Canada 120 G4
Edith Ronne Land *ice feature* Antarctica *see* Ronne Ice Shelf
Edjeleh Libya 96 D2
Edjudina Australia 109 C7
Edku Egypt *see* Idkū
Edmond U.S.A. 131 D5
Edmonds U.S.A. 126 C3

▶Edmonton Canada 120 H4
Provincial capital of Alberta.

Edmonton U.S.A. 134 C5
Edmore *MI* U.S.A. 134 C2
Edmore *ND* U.S.A. 130 D1
Edmund Lake Canada 121 M4
Edmundston Canada 123 H5
Edna U.S.A. 131 D6
Edna Bay U.S.A. 120 C4
Edo Japan *see* Tōkyō
Edom *reg.* Israel/Jordan 85 B4
Édouard, Lac *l.* Dem. Rep. Congo/Uganda *see* Edward, Lake
Edremit Turkey 59 L5
Edremit Körfezi *b.* Turkey 59 L5
Edrengiyn Nuruu *mts* Mongolia 80 I3
Edsbyn Sweden 45 I6
Edson Canada 120 G4
Eduni, Mount Canada 120 D1
Edward *r. N.S.W.* Australia 112 B5
Edward *r. Qld* Australia 110 C2
Edward, Lake Dem. Rep. Congo/ Uganda 98 C4
Edward, Mount Antarctica 152 L1
Edwardesabad Pak. *see* Bannu
Edwards U.S.A. 135 H1
Edward's Creek Australia 111 A6
Edwards Plateau U.S.A. 131 C6
Edwardsville U.S.A. 130 F4
Edward VII Peninsula Antarctica 152 I1
Edziza, Mount Canada 120 D3
Edzo Canada *see* Rae-Edzo
Eeklo Belgium 52 D3
Eel *r.* U.S.A. 128 A1
Eel, South Fork *r.* U.S.A. 128 B1
Eem *r.* Neth. 52 F2
Eemshaven *pt* Neth. 52 G1
Eenrum Neth. 52 G1
Eenzamheid Pan *salt pan* S. Africa 100 E4
Eesti *country* Europe *see* Estonia
Éfaté *i.* Vanuatu 107 G3
Effingham U.S.A. 130 F4
Efsus Turkey *see* Afşin
Egadi, Isole *is Sicily* Italy 58 D5
Egan Range *mts* U.S.A. 129 F2
Eganville Canada 135 G1
Egedesminde Greenland *see* Aasiaat
Eger *r.* Germany 53 M4
Eger Hungary 47 R7
Egersund Norway 45 E7
Egerton, Mount *hill* Australia 109 B6
Eggegebirge *hills* Germany 53 I3
Egg Lake Canada 121 J4
Eggolsheim Germany 53 L5
Eghezée Belgium 52 E4
Egilsstaðir Iceland 44 [inset]
Eğin Turkey *see* Kemaliye
Eğirdir Turkey 59 N6
Eğirdir Gölü *l.* Turkey 59 N6
Eglinton U.K. 51 E2
Egmond aan Zee Neth. 52 E2
Egmont, Cape N.Z. 113 D4
Egmont, Mount *vol.* N.Z. *see* Taranaki, Mount
Egmont National Park N.Z. 113 E4
eGoli S. Africa *see* Johannesburg
Eğrigöz Dağı *mts* Turkey 59 M5
Egton U.K. 48 G4
Éguas *r.* Brazil 145 B1
Egvekinot Rus. Fed. 65 T3

▶Egypt *country* Africa 86 C4
2nd most populous country in Africa.
Africa 7, 94–95

Ehden Lebanon 85 B2
Ehen Hudag China 72 I5
Ehingen (Donau) Germany 47 L6
Ehle *r.* Germany 53 L2
Ehra-Lessien Germany 53 K2
Ehrenberg U.S.A. 129 F5
Ehrenberg Range *hills* Australia 109 E5
Eibelstadt Germany 53 K5
Eibergen Neth. 52 G2
Eichenzell Germany 53 J4
Eichstätt Germany 53 L6
Eidfjord Norway 45 E6
Eidsvold Australia 110 E5
Eidsvoll Norway 45 G6
Eifel *hills* Germany 52 G4
Eigg *i.* U.K. 50 C4
Eight Degree Channel India/Maldives 84 B5
Eights Coast Antarctica 152 K2
Eighty Mile Beach Australia 108 C4
Eilat Israel 85 B5
Eildon Australia 112 B6
Eildon, Lake Australia 112 C6
Eileen Lake Canada 121 J2
Eilenburg Germany 53 M3
Eil Malk *i.* Palau 69 I5
Eimke Germany 53 K2
Einasleigh Australia 110 D3
Einasleigh *r.* Australia 110 C3
Einbeck Germany 53 J3
Eindhoven Neth. 52 F3
Einme Myanmar 70 A3
Einsiedeln Switz. 56 I3
Ein Yahav Israel 85 B4
Éire *country* Europe *see* Ireland, Republic of
Eirik Ridge *sea feature* N. Atlantic Ocean 148 F2
Eiriosgaigh *i.* U.K. *see* Eriskay
Eirunepé Brazil 142 E5
Eisberg *hill* Germany 53 J3
Eiseb *watercourse* Namibia 99 C5
Eisenach Germany 53 K4
Eisenberg Germany 53 L4
Eisenhower, Mount Canada *see* Castle Mountain
Eisenhüttenstadt Germany 47 O4
Eisenstadt Austria 47 P7
Eisfeld Germany 53 K4
Eisleben Lutherstadt Germany 53 L3
Eite, Loch *inlet* U.K. *see* Etive, Loch
Eiterfeld Germany 53 J4
Eivissa Spain *see* Ibiza
Eivissa *i.* Spain *see* Ibiza
Ejea de los Caballeros Spain 57 F2
Ejeda Madag. 99 E6
Ejin Horo Qi China *see* Altan Shiret
Ejin Qi China *see* Dalain Hob
Ejmiadzin Armenia *see* Ejmiatsin
Ejmiatsin Armenia 91 G2
Ekalaka U.S.A. 126 G3
Ekenäs Fin. 45 M7
Ekerem Turkm. *see* Okarem
Ekeren Belgium 52 E3
Eketahuna N.Z. 113 E5
Ekibastuz Kazakh. 80 E1
Ekimchan Rus. Fed. 74 D1
Ekinyazı Turkey 85 D1
Ekonda Rus. Fed. 65 L3
Ekostrovskaya Imandra, Ozero *l.* Rus. Fed. 44 R3
Ekshärad Sweden 45 H6
Eksjö Sweden 45 I8
Eksteenfontein S. Africa 100 C5
Ekström Ice Shelf Antarctica 152 B2
Ekwan *r.* Canada 122 E3
Ekwan Point Canada 122 E3
Ela Myanmar 70 B3
El Aaiún W. Sahara *see* Laâyoune
Elafonisou, Steno *sea chan.* Greece 59 J6
El 'Agrûd *well* Egypt *see* Al 'Ajrūd
Elaia, Cape Cyprus 85 B2
El 'Alamein Egypt *see* Al 'Alamayn
El 'Âmirîya Egypt *see* Al 'Āmirīyah
Elands *r.* S. Africa 101 I3
Elandsdoorn S. Africa 101 I3
El Aouinet Alg. 58 B7
Elar Armenia *see* Abovyan
El Araîche Morocco *see* Larache
El Arco Mex. 127 E7
El Ariana Tunisia *see* L'Ariana
El Aricha Alg. 54 D5
El 'Arîsh Egypt *see* Al 'Arīsh
El Arrouch Alg. 58 B6
El Ashmûnein Egypt *see* Al Ashmūnayn
El Asnam Alg. *see* Ech Chélif
Elassona Greece 59 J5
Elat Israel *see* Eilat
Elato *atoll* Micronesia 69 L5
Elazığ Turkey 91 E3
Elba U.S.A. 133 C6
Elba, Isola d' *i.* Italy 58 D3
El'ban Rus. Fed. 74 E2
El Barco de Valdeorras Spain *see* O Barco
El Barreal *salt l.* Mex. 127 G7
Elbasan Albania 59 I4
El Batroun Lebanon *see* Batroûn
El Baúl Venez. 142 E2
El Bawîti Egypt *see* Al Bawītī
El Bayadh Alg. 54 E5
Elbe *r.* Germany 53 J1
also known as Labe (Czech Republic)
Elbe-Havel-Kanal *canal* Germany 53 L2
El Béqaa *valley* Lebanon 85 C2
Elbert, Mount U.S.A. 126 G5
Elberta U.S.A. 129 H2
Elberton U.S.A. 133 D5
Elbeuf France 56 E2
Elbeyli Turkey 85 C1
Elbing Poland *see* Elbląg
Elbistan Turkey 90 E3
Elbląg Poland 47 Q3
El Boulaïda Alg. *see* Blida
Elbow Canada 121 J5
Elbow Lake U.S.A. 130 D2
El Bozal Mex. 131 C8
El Brasil Mex. 131 C7

▶El'brus *mt.* Rus. Fed. 91 F2
Highest mountain in Europe.
Europe 36–37

Elburg Neth. 52 F2
El Burgo de Osma Spain 57 E3
Elburz Mountains Iran 88 C2
El Cajon U.S.A. 128 E5
El Callao Venez. 142 F2
El Campo U.S.A. 131 D6
El Capitan Mountain U.S.A. 127 G6
El Capulin *r.* Mex. 131 C7
El Casco Mex. 131 B7
El Centro U.S.A. 129 F5
El Cerro Bol. 142 F7
Elche Spain *see* Elche-Elx
Elche-Elx Spain 57 F4
El Chilicote Mex. 131 B6
Elcho Island Australia 110 A1
El Coca Ecuador *see* Puerto Francisco de Orellana
El Cocuy, Parque Nacional *nat. park* Col. 142 D2
El Cuyo Mex. 133 C8
Elda Spain 57 F4

El Dátil Mex. 127 E7
El Desemboque Mex. 127 E7
El Diamante Mex. 131 C6
El'dikan Rus. Fed. 65 O3
El Djezair country Africa see Algeria
El Djezair Alg. see Algiers
El Doctor Mex. 129 F6
Eldon U.S.A. 130 E4
Eldorado Arg. 144 F3
Eldorado Brazil 145 A4
El Dorado Col. 142 D3
El Dorado Mex. 124 F7
El Dorado AR U.S.A. 131 E5
El Dorado KS U.S.A. 130 D4
Eldorado U.S.A. 131 C6
El Dorado Venez. 142 F2
Eldorado Mountains U.S.A. 129 F4
Eldoret Kenya 98 D3
Elea, Cape Cyprus see Elaia, Cape
Eleanor U.S.A. 134 E4
Electric Peak U.S.A. 126 F3
Elefantes r. Moz. see Olifants
El Eglab plat. Alg. 96 C2
El Ejido Spain 57 E5

▶Elemi Triangle terr. Africa 98 D3
Disputed territory (Ethiopia/Kenya/Sudan) administered by Kenya.

El Encanto Col. 142 D4
Elend Germany 53 K3
Elephanta Caves tourist site India 84 B2
Elephant Butte Reservoir U.S.A. 127 G6
Elephant Island Antarctica 152 A2
Elephant Pass Sri Lanka 84 D4
Elephant Point Bangl. 83 H5
Eleşkirt Turkey 91 F3
El Eulma Alg. 54 F4
Eleuthera i. Bahamas 133 E7
Eleven Point r. U.S.A. 131 F4
El Fahs Tunisia 58 C6
El Faiyûm Egypt see Al Fayyūm
El Fasher Sudan 97 F3
El Ferrol Spain see Ferrol
El Ferrol del Caudillo Spain see Ferrol
Elfershausen Germany 53 J4
El Fud Eth. 98 E3
El Fuerte Mex. 127 F8
El Gara Egypt see Qārah
El Geneina Sudan 97 F3
El Geteina Sudan 86 D7
El Ghardaqa Egypt see Al Ghurdaqah
El Ghor plain Jordan/West Bank see Al Ghawr
Elgin U.K. 50 F3
Elgin IL U.S.A. 130 F3
Elgin ND U.S.A. 130 C2
Elgin NV U.S.A. 129 F3
Elgin TX U.S.A. 131 D6
El'ginskiy Rus. Fed. 65 P3
El Gîza Egypt see Giza
El Goléa Alg. 54 E5
El Golfo de Santa Clara Mex. 127 E7
Elgon, Mount Kenya/Uganda 78 C6
El Hadjar Alg. 58 B6
El Ḥammâm Egypt see Al Ḥammām
El Hammâmi reg. Mauritania 96 B2
El Ḥank esc. Mali/Mauritania 96 C2
El Ḥarra Egypt see Al Ḥarrah
El Hazim Jordan see Al Hazīm
El Ḥeiz Egypt see Al Ḥayz
El Hierro i. Canary Is 96 B2
El Homr Alg. 54 E6
El Homra Sudan 86 D7
Eliase Indon. 108 E2
Elías Piña Dom. Rep. 137 J5
Elichpur India see Achalpur
Elida U.S.A. 134 C3
Elie U.K. 50 G4
Elila r. Dem. Rep. Congo 98 C4
Elim U.S.A. 118 B3
Elimberrum France see Auch
Eling China see Yinjiang
Elingampangu Dem. Rep. Congo 98 C4
Eliot, Mount Canada 123 J2
Élisabethville Dem. Rep. Congo see Lubumbashi
Eliseu Martins Brazil 143 J5
El Iskandarîya Egypt see Alexandria
Elista Rus. Fed. 43 J7
Elizabeth NJ U.S.A. 135 H3
Elizabeth WV U.S.A. 134 E4
Elizabeth, Mount hill Australia 108 D4
Elizabeth Bay Namibia 100 B4
Elizabeth City U.S.A. 132 E4
Elizabeth Island Pitcairn Is see Henderson Island
Elizabeth Point Namibia 100 B4
Elizabethton U.S.A. 132 D4
Elizabethtown IL U.S.A. 130 F4
Elizabethtown KY U.S.A. 134 C5
Elizabethtown NC U.S.A. 133 E5
Elizabethtown NY U.S.A. 135 I1
El Jadida Morocco 54 C5
El Jaralito Mex. 131 B7
El Jem Tunisia 58 D7
Elk r. Canada 120 H5
Ełk Poland 47 S4
Elk r. U.S.A. 135 H4
El Kaa Lebanon see Qaa
El Kab Sudan 86 D6
Elkader U.S.A. 130 F3
El Kala Alg. 58 C6
Elk City U.S.A. 131 D5
Elkedra Australia 110 A4
Elkedra watercourse Australia 110 B4
El Kef Tunisia see Le Kef
El Kelaâ des Srarhna Morocco 54 C5
Elkford Canada 120 H5
Elk Grove U.S.A. 128 C2
El Khalil West Bank see Hebron
El Khandaq Sudan 86 D6
El Khârga Egypt see Al Khārijah
El Kharrûba Egypt see Al Kharrūbah
Elkhart IN U.S.A. 134 C3
Elkhart KS U.S.A. 131 C4
El Khartûm Sudan see Khartoum
El Khenachich esc. Mali see El Khnâchîch
El Khnâchîch esc. Mali 96 C2
Elkhorn U.S.A. 130 F3
Elkhorn City U.S.A. 134 D5
Elkhovo Bulg. 59 L3
Elki Turkey see Beytüşşebap
Elkin U.S.A. 132 D4
Elkins U.S.A. 134 F4
Elk Island National Park Canada 121 H4
Elk Lake Canada 122 E5
Elk Lake l. U.S.A. 134 C1
Elkland U.S.A. 135 G3
Elk Mountain U.S.A. 126 G4
Elk Mountains U.S.A. 129 J2
Elko Canada 120 H5
Elko U.S.A. 129 F1
Elk Point Canada 121 I4
Elk Point U.S.A. 130 D3
Elk Springs U.S.A. 129 I1
Elkton MD U.S.A. 135 H4
Elkton VA U.S.A. 135 F4
El Kûbri Egypt see Al Kūbrī
El Kuntilla Egypt see Al Kuntillah
Elkview U.S.A. 134 E4
Ellas country Europe see Greece
Ellaville U.S.A. 133 C5
Ell Bay Canada 121 O1
Ellef Ringnes Island Canada 119 H2
Ellen, Mount U.S.A. 129 H2
Ellenburg Depot U.S.A. 135 I1
Ellendale U.S.A. 130 D2
Ellensburg U.S.A. 126 C3
Ellenville U.S.A. 135 H3
El León, Cerro mt. Mex. 131 B7
Ellesmere, Lake N.Z. 113 D6

▶Ellesmere Island Canada 119 J2
4th largest island in North America.

Ellesmere Island National Park Reserve Canada see Quttinirpaaq National Park
Ellesmere Port U.K. 48 E5
Ellettsville U.S.A. 134 B4
Ellice r. Canada 121 K1
Ellice Island atoll Tuvalu see Funafuti
Ellice Islands country S. Pacific Ocean see Tuvalu
Ellicott City U.S.A. 135 G4
Ellijay U.S.A. 133 C5
Ellingen Germany 53 K5
Elliot Australia 108 F4
Elliot S. Africa 101 H6
Elliot, Mount Australia 110 D3
Elliotdale S. Africa 101 I6
Elliot Knob mt. U.S.A. 134 F4
Elliot Lake Canada 122 E5
Ellisras S. Africa 101 H2
Elliston U.S.A. 134 E5
Ellon U.K. 50 G3
Ellora Caves tourist site India 84 B1
Ellsworth KS U.S.A. 130 D4
Ellsworth ME U.S.A. 132 G2
Ellsworth NE U.S.A. 130 C3
Ellsworth WI U.S.A. 130 E2
Ellsworth Land reg. Antarctica 152 K1
Ellsworth Mountains Antarctica 152 L1
Ellwangen (Jagst) Germany 53 K6
El Maghreb country Africa see Morocco
Elmakuz Dağı mt. Turkey 85 A1
Elmalı Turkey 59 M6
El Malpais National Monument nat. park U.S.A. 129 J4
El Manşûra Egypt see Al Manşūrah
El Maţarîya Egypt see Al Maţarīyah
El Mazâr Egypt see Al Mazār
El Meghaïer Alg. 54 F5
El Milia Alg. 54 F4
El Minya Egypt see Al Minyā
Elmira Ont. Canada 134 E2
Elmira P.E.I. Canada 123 J5
Elmira MI U.S.A. 134 C1
Elmira NY U.S.A. 135 G2
El Mirage U.S.A. 129 G5
El Moral Spain 57 E5
Elmore Australia 112 B6
El Mreyyé reg. Mauritania 96 C3
Elmshorn Germany 53 J1
El Muglad Sudan 86 C7
Elmvale Canada 134 F1
Elnesvågen Norway 44 E5
El Nevado, Cerro mt. Col. 142 D3
El Oasis Mex. 129 F5
El Obeid Sudan 86 D7
El Odaiya Sudan 86 C7
El Oro Mex. 131 C7
Elorza Venez. 142 E2
El Oued Alg. 54 F5
Eloy U.S.A. 129 H5
El Palmito Mex. 131 B7
El Paso IL U.S.A. 130 F3
El Paso KS U.S.A. see Derby
El Paso TX U.S.A. 127 G7
Elphin U.K. 50 D2
Elphinstone i. Myanmar see Thayawthadangyi Kyun
El Portal U.S.A. 128 D3
El Porvenir Mex. 131 B6
El Porvenir Panama 137 I7
El Prat de Llobregat Spain 57 H3
El Progreso Hond. 136 G5
El Puerto de Santa María Spain 57 C5
El Qâhira Egypt see Cairo
El Qasimiye r. Lebanon 85 B3
El Quds Israel/West Bank see Jerusalem
El Quşeima Egypt see Al Quşaymah
El Quşeir Egypt see Al Quşayr
El Qûşîya Egypt see Al Qūşīyah
El Regocijo Mex. 131 B8
El Reno U.S.A. 131 D5
Elrose Canada 121 I5
Elsa Canada 120 C2
El Şaff Egypt see Aş Şaff
El Sahuaro Mex. 127 E7
El Salado Mex. 131 C7
El Salto Mex. 131 B8
▶El Salvador country Central America 136 G6
North America 9, 116–117
El Salvador Chile 144 C3
El Salvador Mex. 131 C7
Elsass reg. France see Alsace
El Sauz Mex. 127 G7
Else r. Germany 53 I2
El Sellûm Egypt see As Sallūm
Elsen Nur l. China 83 H2
Elsey Australia 108 F3
El Shallûfa Egypt see Ash Shallūfah
El Sharana Australia 108 F3
El Shaţţ Egypt see Ash Shaţţ
Elsie U.S.A. 134 C2
Elsinore Denmark see Helsingør
Elsinore CA U.S.A. 128 E5
Elsinore UT U.S.A. 129 G2
Elsinore Lake U.S.A. 128 E5
El Sueco Mex. 127 G7
El Suweis Egypt see Suez
El Suweis governorate Egypt see As Suways
El Tama, Parque Nacional nat. park Venez. 142 D2
El Tarf Alg. 58 C6
El Teleno mt. Spain 57 C2
El Temascal Mex. 131 D7
El Ter r. Spain 57 H2
El Thamad Egypt see Ath Thamad
El Tigre Venez. 142 F2
Eltmann Germany 53 K5
El'ton Rus. Fed. 43 J6
El'ton, Ozero l. Rus. Fed. 43 J6
El Tren Mex. 127 E7
El Tuparro, Parque Nacional nat. park Col. 142 E2
El Ţûr Egypt see Aţ Ţūr
El Turbio Chile 144 B8
El Uqşur Egypt see Luxor
Eluru India 84 D2
Elva Estonia 45 O7
Elvanfoot U.K. 50 F5
Elvas Port. 57 C4
Elverum Norway 45 G6
Elvira Brazil 142 D5
El Wak Kenya 98 E3
El Wâţya well Egypt see Al Wāţiyah
Elwood IN U.S.A. 134 C3
Elwood NE U.S.A. 130 D3
El Wuz Sudan 86 D7
Elx Spain see Elche-Elx
Elxleben Germany 53 K3
Ely U.K. 49 H6
Ely MN U.S.A. 130 F2
Ely NV U.S.A. 129 F2
Elyria U.S.A. 134 D3
Elz Germany 53 I4
El Zagâzîg Egypt see Az Zaqāzīq
Elze Germany 53 J2
Émaé i. Vanuatu 107 G3
Emāmrūd Iran 88 D2
Emām Şaḩēb Afgh. 89 H2
Emām Taqī Iran 88 E2
Emån r. Sweden 45 J8
Emas, Parque Nacional das nat. park Brazil 143 H7
Emba Kazakh. 80 A2
Emba r. Kazakh. 80 A2
Embalenhle S. Africa 101 I4
Embarcación Arg. 144 D2
Embarras Portage Canada 121 I3
Embi Kazakh. see Emba
Embira r. Brazil see Envira
Emborcação, Represa de resr Brazil 145 B2
Embrun Canada 135 H1
Embu Kenya 98 D4
Emden Germany 53 H1
Emden Deep sea feature N. Pacific Ocean see Cape Johnson Depth
Emei China see Emeishan
Emeishan China 76 D2
Emei Shan mt. China 76 D2
Emerald Australia 110 E4
Emeril Canada 123 I3
Emerita Augusta Spain see Mérida
Emerson Canada 121 L5
Emerson U.S.A. 134 D4
Emery U.S.A. 129 H2
Emesa Syria see Homs
Emet Turkey 59 M5
eMgwenya S. Africa 101 J3
Emigrant Pass U.S.A. 128 E1
Emigrant Valley U.S.A. 129 F3
eMijindini S. Africa 101 J3
Emi Koussi mt. Chad 97 E3
Emile r. Canada 120 G2
Emiliano Zapata Mex. 136 F5
Emin China 80 F2
Emine, Nos pt Bulg. 59 L3
Eminence U.S.A. 134 C4
Eminska Planina hills Bulg. 59 L3
Emirdağ Turkey 59 N5
Emir Dağı mt. Turkey 59 N5
Emir Dağları mts Turkey 59 N5
Emmaboda Sweden 45 I8
Emmaste Estonia 45 M7
Emmaville Australia 112 E2
Emmeloord Neth. 52 F2
Emmelshausen Germany 53 H4
Emmen Neth. 52 G2
Emmen Switz. 56 I3
Emmerich Germany 52 G3
Emmet Australia 110 D5
Emmetsburg U.S.A. 130 E3
Emmett U.S.A. 126 D4
Emmiganuru India 84 C3
Emo Canada 121 M5
Emona Slovenia see Ljubljana
Emory Peak U.S.A. 131 C6
Empalme Mex. 127 F8
Empangeni S. Africa 101 J5
Emperor Seamount Chain sea feature N. Pacific Ocean 150 H2
Emperor Trough sea feature N. Pacific Ocean 150 H2
Empingham Reservoir U.K. see Rutland Water
Emplawas Indon. 108 E2
Empoli Italy 58 D3
Emporia KS U.S.A. 130 D4
Emporia VA U.S.A. 135 G5
Emporium U.S.A. 135 F3
Empress Canada 121 I5
Empty Quarter des. Saudi Arabia see Rub' al Khālī
Ems r. Germany 53 H1
Emsdale Canada 134 F1
Emsdetten Germany 53 H2
Ems-Jade-Kanal canal Germany 53 H1
Emzinoni S. Africa 101 I4
Enafors Sweden 44 H5
Encantadas, Serra das hills Brazil 144 F4
Encarnación Para. 144 E3
Enchi Ghana 96 C4
Encinal U.S.A. 131 D6
Encinitas U.S.A. 128 E5
Encino U.S.A. 127 G6
Encruzilhada Brazil 145 C1
Endako Canada 120 E4
Endau-Rompin nat. park Malaysia 71 C7
Ende Indon. 108 C2
Endeavour Strait Australia 110 C1
Endeh Indon. see Ende
Enderby Canada 120 G5
Enderby atoll Micronesia see Puluwat
Enderby Land reg. Antarctica 152 D2
Endicott U.S.A. 135 G2
Endicott Mountains U.S.A. 118 C3
EnenKio terr. N. Pacific Ocean see Wake Island
Energodar Ukr. see Enerhodar
Enerhodar Ukr. 43 G7
Enewetak atoll Marshall Is 150 G5
Enez Turkey 59 L4
Enfe Lebanon 85 B2
Enfião, Ponta do pt Angola 99 B5
Enfidaville Tunisia 58 D6
Enfield U.S.A. 132 E4
Engan Norway 44 F5
Engaru Japan 74 F3
Engcobo S. Africa 101 H6
En Gedi Israel 85 B4
Engelhard U.S.A. 132 F5
Engel's Rus. Fed. 43 J6
Engelschmangat sea chan. Neth. 52 E1
Enggano i. Indon. 68 C8
Enghien Belgium 52 E4
England admin. div. U.K. 49 E6
Englee Canada 123 L4
Englehart Canada 122 F5
Englewood FL U.S.A. 133 D7
Englewood OH U.S.A. 134 C4
English r. Canada 121 M5
English U.S.A. 134 B4
English Bazar India see Ingraj Bazar
English Channel France/U.K. 49 F9
English Coast Antarctica 152 L2
Engozero Rus. Fed. 42 G2
Enhlalakahle S. Africa 101 J5
Enid U.S.A. 131 D4
Eniwa Japan 74 F4
Eniwetok atoll Marshall Is see Enewetak
Enjiang China see Yongfeng
Enkeldoorn Zimbabwe see Chivhu
Enkhuizen Neth. 52 F2
Enköping Sweden 45 J7
Enna Sicily Italy 58 F6
Ennadai Lake Canada 121 K2
En Nahud Sudan 86 C7
Ennedi, Massif mts Chad 97 F3
Ennell, Lough l. Rep. of Ireland 51 E4
Enngonia Australia 112 B2
Enning U.S.A. 130 C2
Ennis Rep. of Ireland 51 D5
Ennis MT U.S.A. 126 F3
Ennis TX U.S.A. 131 D5
Enniscorthy Rep. of Ireland 51 F5
Enniskillen U.K. 51 E3
Ennistymon Rep. of Ireland 51 C5
Enn Nâqoûra Lebanon 85 B3
Enns r. Austria 47 O6
Eno Fin. 44 Q5
Enoch U.S.A. 129 G3
Enontekiö Fin. 44 M2
Enosburg Falls U.S.A. 135 I1
Enosville U.S.A. 134 B4
Enping China 77 G4
Ens Neth. 52 F2
Ensay Australia 112 C6
Enschede Neth. 52 G2
Ense Germany 53 I3
Ensenada Mex. 127 D7
Enshi China 77 F2
Ensley U.S.A. 133 C6
Entebbe Uganda 98 D3
Enterprise Canada 120 G2
Enterprise AL U.S.A. 133 C6
Enterprise OR U.S.A. 126 D3
Enterprise UT U.S.A. 129 G3
Entre Ríos Bol. 142 F8
Entre Rios Brazil 143 H5
Entre Rios de Minas Brazil 145 B3
Entroncamento Port. 57 B4
Enugu Nigeria 96 D4
Enurmino Rus. Fed. 65 T3
Envira Brazil 142 D5
Envira r. Brazil 142 D5
Enyamba Dem. Rep. Congo 98 C4
Eochaill Rep. of Ireland see Youghal
Epe Neth. 52 F2
Epéna Congo 98 B3
Épernay France 52 D5
Ephraim U.S.A. 129 H2
Ephrata U.S.A. 135 G3
Epi i. Vanuatu 107 G3
Epidamnus Albania see Durrës
Épinal France 56 H2
Episkopi Bay Cyprus 85 A2
Episkopis, Kolpos b. Cyprus see Episkopi Bay
ePitoli S. Africa see Pretoria
Epomeo, Monte hill Italy 58 E4
Epping U.K. 49 H7
Epping Forest National Park Australia 110 D4
Eppstein Germany 53 I4
Eppynt, Mynydd hills U.K. 49 D6
Epsom U.K. 49 G7
Epte r. France 52 B5
Eqlīd Iran 88 D4
▶Equatorial Guinea country Africa 96 D4
Africa 7, 94–95
Équerdreville-Hainneville France 49 F9
Erac Creek watercourse Australia 112 B1
Erandol India 84 B1
Erawadi r. Myanmar see Irrawaddy
Erawan National Park Thai. 71 B4
Erbaa Turkey 90 E2
Erbendorf Germany 53 M5
Erbeskopf hill Germany 52 H5
Ercan airport Cyprus 85 A2
Erciş Turkey 91 F3
Erciyes Dağı mt. Turkey 90 D3
Érd Hungary 58 H1
Erdaobaihe China see Baihe
Erdaogou China 76 B1
Erdao Jiang r. China 74 B4
Erdek Turkey 59 L4
Erdemli Turkey 85 B1
Erdenet Mongolia 80 J2
Erdi reg. Chad 97 F3
Erdniyevskiy Rus. Fed. 43 J7
Erebus, Mount vol. Antarctica 152 H1
Erechim Brazil 144 F3
Ereentsav Mongolia 73 L3
Ereğli Konya Turkey 90 D3
Ereğli Zonguldak Turkey 59 N4
Erego Moz. see Errego
Erei, Monti mts Sicily Italy 58 F6
Erementaū Kazakh. see Yereymentau
Erenhot China 73 K4
Erepucu, Lago de l. Brazil 143 G4
Erevan Armenia see Yerevan
Erfurt Germany 53 L4
Erfurt airport Germany 53 K4
Ergani Turkey 91 E3
'Erg Chech des. Alg./Mali 96 C2
Ergel Mongolia 73 J4
Ergene r. Turkey 59 L4
Ērgļi Latvia 45 N8
Ergu China 74 C3
Ergun China 73 M2
Ergun He r. China/Rus. Fed. see Argun'
Ergun Youqi China see Ergun
Ergun Zuoqi China see Genhe
Er Hai l. China 76 D3
Erhulai China 74 B4
Eriboll, Loch inlet U.K. 50 E2
Ericht r. U.K. 50 F4
Ericht, Loch l. U.K. 50 E4
Erickson Canada 121 L5
Erie KS U.S.A. 131 E4
Erie PA U.S.A. 134 E2
Erie, Lake Canada/U.S.A. 134 E2
'Erîgât des. Mali 96 C3
Erik Eriksenstretet sea chan. Svalbard 64 D2
Eriksdale Canada 121 L5
Erimo-misaki c. Japan 74 F4
Erin Canada 134 E2
Erinpura Road India 82 C4
Eriskay i. U.K. 50 B3
▶Eritrea country Africa 86 E6
Africa 7, 94–95
Erlangen Germany 53 L5
Erlangping China 77 F1
Erldunda Australia 109 F6
Erlistoun watercourse Australia 109 C6
Erlong Shan mt. China 74 C4
Erlongshan Shuiku resr China 74 B4
Ermak Kazakh. see Aksu
Ermelo Neth. 52 F2
Ermelo S. Africa 101 I4
Ermenek Turkey 85 A1
Ermenek r. Turkey 85 A1
Ermont Egypt see Armant
Ermoupoli Greece 59 K6
Ernakulam India 84 C4
Erne r. Rep. of Ireland/U.K. 51 D3
Ernest Giles Range hills Australia 109 C6
Erode India 84 C4
Eromanga Australia 111 C5
Erongo admin. reg. Namibia 100 B1
Erp Neth. 52 F3
Erqu China see Zhouzhi
Errabiddy Hills Australia 109 A6
Er Rachidia Morocco 54 D5
Er Raoui des. Alg. 54 D6
Errego Moz. 99 D5
Er Remla Tunisia 58 D7
Er Renk Sudan 86 D7
Errigal hill Rep. of Ireland 51 D2
Errinundra National Park Australia 112 D6
Erris Head hd Rep. of Ireland 51 B3
Errol U.S.A. 135 J1
Erromango i. Vanuatu 107 G3
Erronan i. Vanuatu see Futuna
Erseka Albania see Ersekë
Ersekë Albania 59 I4
Erskine U.S.A. 130 E2
Ersmark Sweden 44 L5
Ertai China 80 H2
Ertil' Rus. Fed. 43 I6
Ertis r. Kazakh./Rus. Fed. see Irtysh
Ertix He r. China/Kazakh. 80 G2
Ērtra country Africa see Eritrea
Eruh Turkey 91 F3
Erwin U.S.A. 132 D4
Erwitte Germany 53 I3
Erxleben Sachsen-Anhalt Germany 53 L2
Erxleben Sachsen-Anhalt Germany 53 L2
Eryuan China 76 C3
Erzerum Turkey see Erzurum
Erzgebirge mts Czech Rep./Germany 53 N4
Erzhan China 74 B2
Erzin Turkey 85 C1
Erzincan Turkey 91 E3
Erzurum Turkey 91 F3
Esa-ala P.N.G. 110 E1
Esan-misaki pt Japan 74 F4
Esashi Japan 74 F3
Esbjerg Denmark 45 F9
Esbo Fin. see Espoo
Escalante U.S.A. 129 H3
Escalante r. U.S.A. 129 H3
Escalante Desert U.S.A. 129 G3
Escalón Mex. 131 B7
Escambia r. U.S.A. 133 C6
Escanaba U.S.A. 132 C2
Escárcega Mex. 136 F5
Escatrón Spain 57 F3
Escaut r. Belgium 52 D4
Esch Neth. 52 F3
Eschede Germany 53 K2
Eschscholtz atoll Marshall Is see Bikini
Esch-sur-Alzette Lux. 52 F5
Eschwege Germany 53 K3
Eschweiler Germany 52 G4
Escondido r. Mex. 131 C6
Escondido U.S.A. 128 E5
Escudilla mt. U.S.A. 129 I5
Escuinapa Mex. 136 C4
Escuintla Guat. 136 F6
Eséka Cameroon 96 E4
Eşen Turkey 59 M6
Esenguly Turkm. 88 D2
Esens Germany 53 H1
Eşfahān Iran 88 C3
Esfarayen, Reshteh-ye mts Iran 88 E2
Esfideh Iran 89 E3
Eshan China 76 D3
Eshāqābād Iran 88 E3
Eshkamesh Afgh. 89 H2
Eshkanān Iran 88 D5
Eshowe S. Africa 101 J5
Esikhawini S. Africa 101 K5
Esil Kazakh. see Yesil'
Esil r. Kazakh./Rus. Fed. see Ishim
Esk Australia 112 F1
Esk r. Australia 111 [inset]
Esk r. U.K. 48 D4
Eskdalemuir U.K. 50 F5
Esker Canada 123 I3
Eskifjörður Iceland 44 [inset]
Eski Gediz Turkey 59 M5
Eskilstuna Sweden 45 J7
Eskimo Lakes Canada 118 E3
Eskimo Point Canada see Arviat
Eski Mosul Iraq 91 F3
Eskipazar Turkey 90 D2
Eskişehir Turkey 59 N5
Eski-Yakkabag Uzbek. 89 G2
Esla r. Spain 57 C3
Eslāmābād-e Gharb Iran 88 B3
Esler Dağı mt. Turkey 59 M6
Eslohe (Sauerland) Germany 53 I3
Eslöv Sweden 45 H9
Esmā'īlī-ye Soflá Iran 88 E4
Eşme Turkey 59 M5
Esmeraldas Ecuador 142 C3
Esmont U.S.A. 135 F5
Esnagami Lake Canada 122 D4
Esnes France 52 D4
Espakeh Iran 89 F5
Espalion France 56 F4
España country Europe see Spain
Espanola Canada 122 E5
Espanola U.S.A. 131 B4
Espelkamp Germany 53 I2
Esperance Australia 109 C8
Esperance Bay Australia 109 C8
Esperanza research station Antarctica 152 A2
Esperanza Arg. 144 B8
Esperanza Mex. 127 F8
Espichel, Cabo c. Port. 57 B4
Espigão, Serra do mts Brazil 141 A4
Espigüete mt. Spain 57 D2
Espinazo Mex. 131 C7
Espinhaço, Serra do mts Brazil 145 C2
Espinosa Brazil 145 C1
Espírito Santo Brazil see Vila Velha
Espírito Santo state Brazil 145 C2
Espíritu Santo i. Vanuatu 107 G3
Espíritu Santo, Isla i. Mex. 124 E7
Espoo Fin. 45 N6
Espuña mt. Spain 57 F5
Esqueda Mex. 127 F7
Esquel Arg. 144 B6
Esquimalt Canada 120 F5
Essaouira Morocco 96 C1
Es Semara W. Sahara 96 B2
Essen Belgium 52 E3

▶Essen Germany 52 H3
5th most populous city in Europe.

Essen (Oldenburg) Germany 53 H2
Essequibo r. Guyana 143 G2
Essex Canada 134 D2
Essex CA U.S.A. 129 F4
Essex MD U.S.A. 135 G4
Essex NY U.S.A. 135 I1
Essexville U.S.A. 134 D2
Esslingen am Neckar Germany 53 J6
Esso Rus. Fed. 65 Q4
Essoyla Rus. Fed. 42 G3
Eşţahbān Iran 88 D4
Estância Brazil 143 K6
Estancia U.S.A. 127 G6
Estand, Kūh-e mt. Iran 89 F4
Estats, Pic d' mt. France/Spain 56 E5
Estcourt S. Africa 101 I5
Este r. Germany 53 J1
Estelí Nicaragua 137 G6
Estella Spain 57 E2
Estepa Spain 57 D5
Estepona Spain 57 D5
Esteras de Medinaceli Spain 57 E3
Esterhazy Canada 121 K5
Estero Bay U.S.A. 128 C4
Esteros Para. 144 D2
Estevan Canada 121 K5
Estevan Group is Canada 120 D4
Estherville U.S.A. 130 E3
Estill U.S.A. 133 D5
Eston Canada 121 I5
▶Estonia country Europe 45 N7
Europe 5, 38–39
Estonskaya S.S.R. country Europe see Estonia
Estrées-St-Denis France 52 C5
Estrela Brazil 145 A5
Estrela, Serra da mts Port. 57 C3
Estrela do Sul Brazil 145 B2
Estrella mt. Spain 57 E4
Estrella, Punta pt Mex. 127 E7
Estremoz Port. 57 C4
Estrondo, Serra hills Brazil 143 I5
Etadunna Australia 111 B6
Etah India 82 D4
Étain France 52 F5
Etamamiou Canada 123 K4
Étampes France 56 F2
Étaples France 52 B4
Etawah Rajasthan India 82 D4
Etawah Uttar Pradesh India 82 D4
eThandakukhanya S. Africa 101 J4
Ethelbert Canada 121 K5
Ethel Creek Australia 109 C5
E'Thembini S. Africa 100 F5

▶Ethiopia country Africa 98 D3
3rd most populous country in Africa.
Africa 7, 94–95

Etimesğut Turkey 90 D3

Etive, Loch inlet U.K. 50 D4
Etna, Mount vol. Sicily Italy 58 F6
Etne Norway 45 D7
Etobicoke Canada 134 F2
Etolin Strait U.S.A. 118 B3
Etorofu-tō i. Rus. Fed. see Iturup, Ostrov
Etosha National Park Namibia 99 B5
Etosha Pan salt pan Namibia 99 B5
Etoumbi Congo 98 B3
Etrek r. Iran/Turkm. see Atrek
Étrépagny France 52 B5
Étretat France 49 H9
Ettelbruck Lux. 52 G5
Etten-Leur Neth. 52 E3
Ettlingen Germany 53 I6
Ettrick Water r. U.K. 50 F5
Euabalong Australia 112 C4
Euboea i. Greece see Evvoia
Eucla Australia 109 E7
Euclid U.S.A. 134 E3
Euclides da Cunha Brazil 143 K6
Eucumbene, Lake Australia 112 D6
Eudistes, Lac des l. Canada 123 I4
Eudora U.S.A. 131 F5
Eudunda Australia 111 B7
Eufaula AL U.S.A. 133 C6
Eufaula OK U.S.A. 131 E5
Eufaula Lake resr U.S.A. 131 E5
Eugene U.S.A. 126 C3
Eugenia, Punta pt Mex. 127 E8
Eugowra Australia 112 D4
Eulo Australia 112 B2
Eumungerie Australia 112 D3
Eungella Australia 110 E4
Eungella National Park Australia 110 E4
Eunice LA U.S.A. 131 E6
Eunice NM U.S.A. 131 C5
Eupen Belgium 52 G4

▶Euphrates r. Asia 91 G5
Longest river in western Asia. Also known as Al Furāt (Iraq/Syria) or Fırat (Turkey).

Eura Fin. 45 M6
Eure r. France 52 B5
Eureka CA U.S.A. 126 B4
Eureka KS U.S.A. 130 D4
Eureka MT U.S.A. 126 E2
Eureka NV U.S.A. 129 F2
Eureka OH U.S.A. 134 D4
Eureka SD U.S.A. 130 D2
Eureka UT U.S.A. 129 G2
Eureka Sound sea chan. Canada 119 J2
Eureka Springs U.S.A. 131 E4
Eureka Valley U.S.A. 128 E3
Euriowie Australia 111 C6
Euroa Australia 112 B6
Eurombah Australia 111 E5
Eurombah Creek r. Australia 111 E5
Europa, Île i. Indian Ocean 99 E6
Europa, Punta de pt Gibraltar see Europa Point
Europa Point Gibraltar 57 D5
Euskirchen Germany 52 G4
Eutaw U.S.A. 133 C5
Eutsuk Lake Canada 120 E4
Eutzsch Germany 53 M3
Eva Downs Australia 108 F4
Evans, Lac l. Canada 122 F4
Evans, Mount U.S.A. 126 G5
Evansburg Canada 120 H4
Evans City U.S.A. 134 E3
Evans Head Australia 112 F2
Evans Head hd Australia 112 F2
Evans Ice Stream Antarctica 152 L1
Evans Strait Canada 121 P2
Evanston IL U.S.A. 134 B2
Evanston WY U.S.A. 126 F4
Evansville Canada 122 E5
Evansville IN U.S.A. 134 B5
Evansville WY U.S.A. 126 G4
Evant U.S.A. 131 D6
Eva Perón Arg. see La Plata
Evart U.S.A. 134 C2
Evaton S. Africa 101 H4
Evaz Iran 88 D5
Evening Shade U.S.A. 131 F4
Evensk Rus. Fed. 65 Q3
Everard, Cape Australia 112 D6
Everard, Lake salt flat Australia 111 A6
Everard, Mount Australia 109 F5
Everard Range hills Australia 109 F6
Everdingen Neth. 52 F3
Everek Turkey see Develi

▶Everest, Mount China/Nepal 83 F4
Highest mountain in the world and in Asia.
Asia 60–61
World 12–13

Everett PA U.S.A. 135 F3
Everett WA U.S.A. 126 C3
Evergem Belgium 52 D3
Everglades swamp U.S.A. 133 D7
Everglades National Park U.S.A. 133 D7
Evergreen U.S.A. 133 C6
Evesham Australia 110 C4
Evesham U.K. 49 F6
Evesham, Vale of valley U.K. 49 F6
Evijärvi Fin. 44 M5
Evje Norway 45 E7
Évora Port. 57 C4
Evoron, Ozero l. Rus. Fed. 74 E2
Évreux France 52 B5
Evros r. Bulgaria see Maritsa
Evros r. Turkey see Meriç
Evrotas r. Greece 59 J6
Évry France 52 C6
Evrychou Cyprus 85 A2
Evrykhou Cyprus see Evrychou
Evvoia i. Greece 59 K5
Ewan Australia 110 D3
Ewaso Ngiro r. Kenya 98 E3
Ewe, Loch b. U.K. 50 D3
Ewing U.S.A. 134 D5
Ewo Congo 98 B4
Exaltación Bol. 142 E6
Excelsior S. Africa 101 H5
Excelsior Mountain U.S.A. 128 D2
Excelsior Mountains U.S.A. 128 D2
Exe r. U.K. 49 D8
Exeter Australia 112 E5
Exeter Canada 134 E2
Exeter U.K. 49 D8
Exeter CA U.S.A. 128 D3
Exeter NH U.S.A. 135 J2
Exeter Lake Canada 121 I1
Exloo Neth. 52 G2
Exminster U.K. 49 D8
Exmoor hills U.K. 49 D7
Exmoor National Park U.K. 49 D7
Exmore U.S.A. 135 H5
Exmouth Australia 108 A5
Exmouth U.K. 49 D8
Exmouth, Mount Australia 112 D3
Exmouth Gulf Australia 108 A5
Exmouth Lake Canada 120 H1
Exmouth Plateau sea feature Indian Ocean 149 P7
Expedition National Park Australia 110 E5
Expedition Range mts Australia 110 E5
Exploits r. Canada 123 L4
Exton U.S.A. 135 H3
Extremadura aut. comm. Spain 57 D4
Exuma Cays is Bahamas 133 E7
Exuma Sound sea chan. Bahamas 133 F7
Eyasi, Lake salt l. Tanz. 98 D4
Eyawadi r. Myanmar see Irrawaddy
Eye U.K. 49 I6
Eyeberry Lake Canada 121 J2
Eyelenoborsk Rus. Fed. 41 S3
Eyemouth U.K. 50 G5
Eyjafjörður inlet Iceland 44 [inset]
Eyl Somalia 98 E3
Eylau Rus. Fed. see Bagrationovsk
Eynsham U.K. 49 F7

▶Eyre, Lake salt lake Australia 111 B6
Largest lake in Oceania and lowest point.
Oceania 102–103

Eyre (North), Lake salt lake Australia 111 B6
Eyre (South), Lake salt lake Australia 111 B6
Eyre Creek watercourse Australia 110 B5
Eyre Mountains N.Z. 113 B7
Eyre Peninsula Australia 111 A7
Eystrup Germany 53 J2
Eysturoy i. Faroe Is 44 [inset]
Ezakheni S. Africa 101 J5
Ezel U.S.A. 134 D5
Ezenzeleni S. Africa 101 I4
Ezequiel Ramos Mexía, Embalse resr Arg. 144 C5
Ezhou China 77 G2
Ezhva Rus. Fed. 42 K3
Ezine Turkey 59 L5
Ezo i. Japan see Hokkaidō
Ezousa r. Cyprus 85 A2

F

Faaborg Denmark see Fåborg
Faadhippolhu Atoll Maldives 84 B5
Faafxadhuun Somalia 98 E3
Fabens U.S.A. 127 G7
Faber, Mount hill Sing. 71 [inset]
Faber Lake Canada 120 G2
Fåborg Denmark 45 G9
Fabriano Italy 58 E3
Faches-Thumesnil France 52 D4
Fachi Niger 96 E3
Fada Chad 97 F3
Fada-N'Gourma Burkina 96 D3
Fadghāmī Syria 91 F4
Fadiffolu Atoll Maldives see Faadhippolhu Atoll
Fadippolu Atoll Maldives see Faadhippolhu Atoll
Faenza Italy 58 D2
Færoerne terr. N. Atlantic Ocean see Faroe Islands
Faeroes terr. N. Atlantic Ocean see Faroe Islands
Făgăraș Romania 59 K2

▶Fagatogo American Samoa 107 I3
Capital of American Samoa.

Fagersta Sweden 45 I7
Fagne reg. Belgium 52 E4
Fagurhólsmýri Iceland 44 [inset]
Fagwir Sudan 86 D8
Fahraj Iran 88 D4
Fā'id Egypt 90 D5
Fairbanks U.S.A. 118 D3
Fairborn U.S.A. 134 C4
Fairbury U.S.A. 130 D3
Fairchance U.S.A. 134 F4
Fairfax U.S.A. 135 G4
Fairfield CA U.S.A. 128 B2
Fairfield IA U.S.A. 130 F3
Fairfield ID U.S.A. 126 E4
Fairfield IL U.S.A. 130 F4
Fairfield OH U.S.A. 134 C4
Fairfield TX U.S.A. 131 D6
Fair Haven U.S.A. 135 I2
Fair Head hd U.K. 51 F2
Fair Isle i. U.K. 50 H1
Fairlee U.S.A. 135 I2
Fairmont MN U.S.A. 130 E3
Fairmont WV U.S.A. 134 E4
Fair Oaks U.S.A. 134 B3
Fairview Australia 110 D2
Fairview Canada 120 G3
Fairview MI U.S.A. 134 C1
Fairview OK U.S.A. 131 D4
Fairview PA U.S.A. 134 E2
Fairview UT U.S.A. 129 H2
Fairview Park Hong Kong China 77 [inset]
Fairweather, Cape U.S.A. 120 B3
Fairweather, Mount Canada/U.S.A. 120 B3
Fais i. Micronesia 69 K5
Faisalabad Pak. 89 I4
Faissault France 52 E5
Faith U.S.A. 130 C2
Faizabad Afgh. see Feyzābād
Faizabad India 83 E4
Fakaofo atoll Tokelau 107 I2
Fakaofu atoll Tokelau see Fakaofo
Fakenham U.K. 49 H6
Fåker Sweden 44 I5
Fakfak Indon. 69 I7
Fakhrabad Iran 88 D4
Fakiragram India 83 G4
Fako vol. Cameroon see Cameroun, Mont
Fal r. U.K. 49 C8
Falaba Sierra Leone 96 B4
Falaise Lake Canada 120 G2
Falam Myanmar 70 A2
Falavarjan Iran 88 C3
Falcon Lake Canada 121 M5
Falcon Lake l. Mex./U.S.A. 131 D7
Falenki Rus. Fed. 42 K4
Falfurrias U.S.A. 131 D7
Falher Canada 120 G4
Falkenberg Germany 53 N3
Falkenberg Sweden 45 H8
Falkenhagen Germany 53 M1
Falkenhain Germany 53 M3
Falkensee Germany 53 N2
Falkenstein Germany 53 M5
Falkirk U.K. 50 F5
Falkland U.K. 50 F4
Falkland Escarpment sea feature S. Atlantic Ocean 148 E9

▶Falkland Islands terr. S. Atlantic Ocean 144 E8
United Kingdom Overseas Territory.
South America 9, 140–141

Falkland Plateau sea feature S. Atlantic Ocean 148 E9
Falkland Sound sea chan. Falkland Is 144 D8
Falköping Sweden 45 H7
Fallbrook U.S.A. 128 E5
Fallieres Coast Antarctica 152 L2
Fallingbostel Germany 53 J2
Fallon U.S.A. 128 D2
Fall River U.S.A. 135 J3
Fall River Pass U.S.A. 126 G4
Falls City U.S.A. 130 E3
Falmouth U.K. 49 B8
Falmouth KY U.S.A. 134 C4
Falmouth VA U.S.A. 135 G4
False r. Canada 123 H2
False Bay S. Africa 100 D8
False Point India 83 F5
Falster i. Denmark 45 G9
Fălticeni Romania 43 E7
Falun Sweden 45 I6
Famagusta Cyprus 85 A2
Famagusta Bay Cyprus see Ammochostos Bay
Fameck France 52 G5
Famenin Iran 88 C3
Fame Range hills Australia 109 C6
Family Lake Canada 121 M5
Family Well Australia 108 D5
Fāmūr, Daryācheh-ye l. Iran 88 C4
Fana Mali 96 C3
Fanad Head hd Rep. of Ireland 47 E2
Fandriana Madag. 99 E6
Fane r. Rep. of Ireland 51 F4
Fang Thai. 70 B3
Fangcheng Guangxi China see Fangchenggang
Fangcheng Henan China 77 G1
Fangchenggang China 77 F4
Fangdou Shan mts China 77 F2
Fangliao Taiwan 77 I4
Fangshan Taiwan 77 I4
Fangxian China 77 F1
Fangzheng China 74 C3
Fankuai China 77 F2
Fankuaidian China see Fankuai
Fanling Hong Kong China 77 [inset]
Fannich, Loch l. U.K. 50 D3
Fannūj Iran 89 E5
Fano Italy 58 E3
Fanshan Anhui China 77 H2
Fanshan Zhejiang China 77 I3
Fan Si Pan mt. Vietnam 70 C2
Fanum Fortunae Italy see Fano
Faqīh Aḥmadān Iran 88 C4
Farab Turkm. see Farap
Faraba Mali 96 B3
Faradofay Madag. see Tôlañaro
Farafangana Madag. 99 E6
Farāfirah, Wāḥāt al oasis Egypt 86 C4
Farafra Oasis oasis Egypt see Farāfirah, Wāḥāt al
Farāh Afgh. 89 F3
Faraḥābād Iran see Khezerābād
Farallon de Medinilla i. N. Mariana Is 69 L3
Farallon de Pajaros vol. N. Mariana Is 69 K2
Farallones de Cali, Parque Nacional nat. park Col. 142 C3
Faranah Guinea 96 B3
Farap Turkm. 89 F2
Fararah Oman 87 I6
Farasān, Jazā'ir is Saudi Arabia 86 F6
Faraulep atoll Micronesia 69 K5
Fareham U.K. 49 F8
Farewell, Cape Greenland 119 N3
Farewell, Cape N.Z. 113 D5
Farewell Spit N.Z. 113 D5
Färgelanda Sweden 45 H7
Farghona Uzbek. see Fergana
Fargo U.S.A. 130 D2
Faribault U.S.A. 130 E2
Faribault, Lac l. Canada 123 H2
Faridabad India 82 D3
Faridkot India 82 C3
Faridpur Bangl. 83 G5
Farīmān Iran 89 E3
Farkhar Afgh. see Farkhato
Farkhato Afgh. 89 H2
Farkhor Tajik. 89 H2
Farmahin Iran 88 C3
Farmer Island Canada 122 E2
Farmerville U.S.A. 131 E5
Farmington Canada 120 F4
Farmington ME U.S.A. 135 J1
Farmington MO U.S.A. 130 F4
Farmington NH U.S.A. 135 J2
Farmington NM U.S.A. 129 I3
Farmington Hills U.S.A. 134 D2
Far Mountain Canada 120 E4
Farmville U.S.A. 135 F5
Farnborough U.K. 49 G7
Farne Islands U.K. 48 F3
Farnham U.K. 49 G7
Farnham, Lake salt flat Australia 109 D6
Farnham, Mount Canada 120 G5
Faro Brazil 143 G4
Faro Canada 120 C2
Faro Port. 57 C5
Fårö i. Sweden 45 K8
Faroe - Iceland Ridge sea feature Arctic Ocean 153 I2

▶Faroe Islands terr. N. Atlantic Ocean 44 [inset]
Self-governing Danish Territory.
Europe 5, 38–39

Fårösund Sweden 45 K8
Farquhar Group is Seychelles 99 F5
Farquharson Tableland hills Australia 109 C6
Farrāshband Iran 88 D4
Farr Bay Antarctica 152 F2
Farristown U.S.A. 134 C5
Farrukhabad India see Fatehgarh
Fārsī Afgh. 89 F3
Farsund Norway 45 E7
Fārūj Iran 88 E2
Farwell MI U.S.A. 134 C2
Farwell TX U.S.A. 131 C5
Fasā Iran 88 D4
Fasano Italy 58 G4
Fașikan Geçidi pass Turkey 85 A1
Faßberg Germany 53 K2
Fastiv Ukr. 43 F6
Fastov Ukr. see Fastiv
Fatehabad India 82 C3
Fatehgarh India 82 D4
Fatehpur Rajasthan India 82 C4
Fatehpur Uttar Pradesh India 82 E4
Fatick Senegal 96 B3
Fattoilep atoll Micronesia see Faraulep
Faughan r. U.K. 51 E2
Faulkton U.S.A. 130 D2
Faulquemont France 52 G5
Fauresmith S. Africa 101 G5
Fauske Norway 44 I3
Faust Canada 120 H4
Fawcett Canada 120 H4
Fawley U.K. 49 F8
Fawn r. Canada 121 N4
Faxaflói b. Iceland 44 [inset]
Faxälven r. Sweden 44 J5
Faya Chad 97 E3
Fayette AL U.S.A. 133 C5
Fayette MO U.S.A. 130 E4
Fayette MS U.S.A. 131 F6
Fayette OH U.S.A. 134 C3
Fayetteville AR U.S.A. 131 E4
Fayetteville NC U.S.A. 133 E5
Fayetteville TN U.S.A. 133 C5
Fayetteville WV U.S.A. 134 E4
Fâyid Egypt see Fā'id
Faylakah i. Kuwait 88 C4
Fazao Malfakassa, Parc National de nat. park Togo 96 D4
Fazilka India 82 C3
Fazrān, Jabal hill Saudi Arabia 88 C5
Fdérik Mauritania 96 B2
Fead Group is P.N.G. see Nuguria Islands
Feale r. Rep. of Ireland 51 C5
Fear, Cape U.S.A. 133 E5
Featherston N.Z. 113 E5
Feathertop, Mount Australia 112 C6
Fécamp France 56 E2
Federal District admin. dist. Brazil see Distrito Federal
Federalsburg U.S.A. 135 H4
Federated Malay States country Asia see Malaysia
Fedusar India 82 C4
Fehet Lake Canada 121 M1
Fehmarn i. Germany 47 M3
Fehrbellin Germany 53 M2
Feia, Lagoa lag. Brazil 145 C3
Feicheng China see Feixian
Feijó Brazil 142 D5
Feilding N.Z. 113 E5
Fei Ngo Shan hill Hong Kong China see Kowloon Peak
Feio r. Brazil see Aguapeí
Feira de Santana Brazil 145 D1
Feixi China 77 H2
Feixian China 77 H1
Fejd-el-Abiod pass Alg. 58 B6
Feke Turkey 90 D3
Felanitx Spain 57 H4
Feldberg Germany 53 N1
Feldberg mt. Germany 47 L7
Feldkirch Austria 47 L7
Feldkirchen in Kärnten Austria 47 O7
Felidhu Atoll Maldives 81 D11
Felidu Atoll Maldives see Felidhu Atoll
Felipe C. Puerto Mex. 136 G5
Felixlândia Brazil 145 B2
Felixstowe U.K. 49 I7
Felixton S. Africa 101 J5
Fellowsville U.S.A. 134 F4
Felsina Italy see Bologna
Felton U.S.A. 135 H4
Feltre Italy 58 D1
Femunden l. Norway 44 G5
Femundsmarka Nasjonalpark nat. park Norway 44 H5
Fenaio, Punta del pt Italy 58 D3
Fence Lake U.S.A. 129 I4
Fener Burnu hd Turkey 85 B1
Fénérive Madag. see Fenoarivo Atsinanana
Fengari mt. Greece 59 K4
Fengcheng Fujian China see Lianjiang
Fengcheng Fujian China see Anxi
Fengcheng Fujian China see Yongding
Fengcheng Guangdong China see Xinfeng
Fengcheng Guangxi China see Fengshan
Fengcheng Guizhou China see Tianzhu
Fengcheng Jiangxi China 77 G2
Fenggang Fujian China see Shaxian
Fenggang Guizhou China 76 E3
Fenggang Jiangxi China see Yihuang
Fengguang China 74 B3
Fenghuang China 77 F3
Fengjiaba China see Wangcang
Fengjie China 77 F2
Fengkai China 77 F4
Fenglin Taiwan 77 I4
Fengming Shaanxi China see Qishan
Fengming Sichuan China see Pengshan
Fengqing China 76 C3
Fengshan Fujian China see Luoyuan
Fengshan Guangxi China 76 E3
Fengshan Hubei China see Luotian
Fengshan Yunnan China see Fengqing
Fengshuba Shuiku resr China 77 G3
Fengshui Shan mt. China 74 A1
Fengtongzai Giant Panda Reserve nature res. China 76 D2
Fengxian China 76 E1
Fengxiang Heilong. China see Luobei
Fengxiang Yunnan China see Lincang
Fengyang China 77 H1
Fengyüan Taiwan 77 I3
Fengzhen China 73 K4
Feni Bangl. 83 G5
Feni Islands P.N.G. 106 F2
Fennville U.S.A. 134 B2
Feno, Capo di c. Corsica France 56 I6
Fenoarivo Atsinanana Madag. 99 E5
Fenshui Guan pass China 77 H3
Fenton U.S.A. 134 D2
Fenua Ura atoll Fr. Polynesia see Manuae
Fenyi China 77 G3
Feodosiya Ukr. 90 D1
Fer, Cap de c. Alg. 58 B6
Férai Greece see Feres
Ferdows Iran 88 E3
Fère-Champenoise France 52 D6
Feres Greece 59 L4
Fergana Uzbek. 87 L1
Fergus Canada 134 E2
Fergus Falls U.S.A. 130 D2
Ferguson Lake Canada 121 L2
Fergusson Island P.N.G. 106 F2
Fériana Tunisia 58 C7
Ferijaz Serb. and Mont. see Uroševac
Ferkessédougou Côte d'Ivoire 96 C4
Fermo Italy 58 E3
Fermont Canada 123 I3
Fermoselle Spain 57 C3
Fermoy Rep. of Ireland 51 D5
Fernandina, Isla i. Galápagos Ecuador 142 [inset]
Fernandina Beach U.S.A. 133 D6
Fernando de Magallanes, Parque Nacional nat. park Chile 144 B8
Fernando de Noronha i. Brazil 148 F6
Fernandópolis Brazil 145 A3
Fernando Poó i. Equat. Guinea see Bioco
Fernão Dias Brazil 145 B2
Ferndale U.S.A. 128 A1
Ferndown U.K. 49 F8
Fernlee Australia 112 C2
Fernley U.S.A. 128 D2
Ferns Rep. of Ireland 51 F5
Ferozepore India see Firozpur
Ferrara Italy 58 D2
Ferreira-Gomes Brazil 143 H3
Ferro, Capo c. Sardinia Italy 58 C4
Ferrol Spain 57 B2
Ferron U.S.A. 129 H2
Ferros Brazil 145 C2
Ferryland Canada 123 L5
Ferryville Tunisia see Menzel Bourguiba
Fertő-tavi nat. park Hungary 58 G1
Ferwerd Neth. 52 F1
Ferwert Neth. see Ferwerd
Fès Morocco 54 D5
Feshi Dem. Rep. Congo 99 B4
Fessenden U.S.A. 130 D2
Festus U.S.A. 130 F4
Fété Bowé Senegal 96 B3
Fethard Rep. of Ireland 51 E5
Fethiye Malatya Turkey see Yazıhan
Fethiye Muğla Turkey 59 M6
Fethiye Körfezi b. Turkey 59 M6
Fetisovo Kazakh. 91 I2
Fetlar i. U.K. 50 [inset]
Fettercairn U.K. 50 G4
Feucht Germany 53 L5
Feuchtwangen Germany 53 K5
Feuilles, Rivière aux r. Canada 123 H2
Fevral'sk Rus. Fed. 74 C1
Fevzipaşa Turkey 90 E3
Feyzābād Afgh. 89 H2
Feyzābād Kermān Iran 88 D4
Feyzābād Khorāsān Iran 88 E3
Fez Morocco see Fès
Ffestiniog U.K. 49 D6
Fianarantsoa Madag. 99 E6
Fichē Eth. 98 D3
Fichtelgebirge hills Germany 53 M4
Field U.S.A. 134 D5
Fier Albania 59 H4
Fiery Creek r. Australia 110 B3
Fife Lake U.S.A. 134 C1
Fife Ness pt U.K. 50 G4
Fifield Australia 112 C4
Fifth Meridian Canada 120 H3
Figeac France 56 F4
Figueira da Foz Port. 57 B3
Figueras Spain see Figueres
Figueres Spain 57 H2
Figuig Morocco 54 D5
Figuil Cameroon 97 E4

▶Fiji country S. Pacific Ocean 107 H3
4th most populous and 5th largest country in Oceania.
Oceania 8, 104–105

Fīk' Eth. 98 E3
Filadelfia Para. 144 D2
Filchner Ice Shelf Antarctica 152 A1
Filey U.K. 48 G4
Filibe Bulg. see Plovdiv
Filingué Niger 96 D3
Filipinas country Asia see Philippines
Filippiada Greece 59 I5
Filipstad Sweden 45 I7
Fillan Norway 44 F5
Fillmore CA U.S.A. 128 D4
Fillmore UT U.S.A. 129 G2
Fils r. Germany 53 J6
Filtu Eth. 98 E3
Fimbull Ice Shelf Antarctica 152 C2
Fin Iran 88 C3
Finch Canada 135 H1
Findhorn r. U.K. 50 F3
Fındık Turkey 88 A2
Findlay U.S.A. 134 D3
Fine U.S.A. 135 H1
Finger Lake Canada 121 M4
Finger Lakes U.S.A. 135 G2
Finike Turkey 59 N6
Finike Körfezi b. Turkey 59 N6
Finisterre Spain see Fisterra
Finisterre, Cabo c. Spain see Finisterre, Cape
Finisterre, Cape Spain 57 B2
Finke watercourse Australia 110 A5
Finke, Mount hill Australia 109 F7
Finke Bay Australia 108 E3
Finke Gorge National Park Australia 109 F6

▶Finland country Europe 44 O5
Europe 5, 38–39

Finland, Gulf of Europe 45 M7
Finlay r. Canada 120 E3
Finlay, Mount Canada 120 E3
Finlay Forks Canada 120 F4
Finley U.S.A. 130 D2
Finn r. Rep. of Ireland 51 E3
Finne ridge Germany 53 L3
Finnigan, Mount Australia 110 D2
Finniss, Cape Australia 109 F8
Finnmarksvidda reg. Norway 44 H2
Finnsnes Norway 44 J2
Fins Oman 88 E6
Finschhafen P.N.G. 69 L8
Finspång Sweden 45 I7
Fintona U.K. 51 E3
Fintown Rep. of Ireland 51 D3
Finucane Range hills Australia 110 C4
Fionn Loch l. U.K. 50 D3
Fionnphort U.K. 50 C4
Fiordland National Park N.Z. 113 A7
Fir reg. Saudi Arabia 88 B4
Fırat r. Turkey 90 E3 see Euphrates
Firebaugh U.S.A. 128 C3
Firedrake Lake Canada 121 J2
Firenze Italy see Florence
Fireside Canada 120 E3
Firk, Sha'īb watercourse Iraq 91 G5
Firmat Arg. 144 D4
Firminy France 56 G4
Firmum Italy see Fermo
Firmum Picenum Italy see Fermo
Firovo Rus. Fed. 42 G4
Firozabad India 82 D4
Firozkoh reg. Afgh. 89 G3
Firozpur India 82 C3
First Three Mile Opening sea chan. Australia 110 D2
Fīrūzābād Iran 88 D4
Fīrūzkūh Iran 88 D3
Firyuza Turkm. 88 E2
Fischbach Germany 53 H5
Fischersbrunn Namibia 100 B3
Fish watercourse Namibia 100 C5
Fisher Australia 109 E7
Fisher Bay Antarctica 152 G2
Fisher Glacier Antarctica 152 E2
Fisher River Canada 121 L5
Fishers U.S.A. 134 B4
Fishers Island U.S.A. 135 J3
Fisher Strait Canada 119 J3
Fishguard U.K. 49 C7
Fishing Creek U.S.A. 135 G4
Fishing Lake Canada 121 M4
Fish Lake Canada 120 F2
Fish Point U.S.A. 134 D2
Fish Ponds Hong Kong China 77 [inset]
Fiske, Cape Antarctica 152 L2
Fiskenæsset Greenland see Qeqertarsuatsiaat
Fismes France 52 D5
Fisterra Spain 57 B2
Fisterra, Cabo c. Spain see Finisterre, Cape
Fitchburg U.S.A. 130 F3
Fitri, Lac l. Chad 97 E3
Fitzgerald Canada 121 I3
Fitzgerald U.S.A. 133 D6
Fitzgerald River National Park Australia 109 B8
Fitz Hugh Sound sea chan. Canada 120 D5
Fitz Roy Arg. 144 C7
Fitzroy r. Australia 108 C4
Fitz Roy, Cerro mt. Arg. 144 B7
Fitzroy Crossing Australia 108 D4
Fitzwilliam Island Canada 134 E1
Fiume Croatia see Rijeka
Fivemiletown U.K. 51 E3
Five Points U.S.A. 128 C3
Fizi Dem. Rep. Congo 99 C4
Fizuli Azer. see Füzuli
Flå Norway 45 F6
Flagstaff S. Africa 101 I6
Flagstaff U.S.A. 129 H4
Flagstaff Lake U.S.A. 132 G2
Flaherty Island Canada 122 F2
Flambeau r. U.S.A. 130 F2
Flamborough Head hd U.K. 48 G4
Fläming hills Germany 53 M2
Flaming Gorge Reservoir U.S.A. 126 F4
Flaminksvlei salt pan S. Africa 100 E6
Flanagan r. Canada 121 M4
Flandre reg. France 52 C4
Flannagan Lake U.S.A. 134 D5
Flannan Isles U.K. 50 B2
Flåsjön l. Sweden 44 I4
Flat r. Canada 120 E2
Flat r. U.S.A. 134 C2
Flat Creek Canada 120 B2
Flathead r. U.S.A. 124 E2
Flathead Lake U.S.A. 126 E3
Flatiron mt. U.S.A. 126 E3
Flat Island S. China Sea 68 F4
Flat Lick U.S.A. 134 D5
Flattery, Cape Australia 110 D2
Flattery, Cape U.S.A. 126 B2
Flat Top mt. Canada 120 B2
Flatwillow Creek r. U.S.A. 126 G3

Ghantila India 82 B5
Ghanwā Saudi Arabia 86 G4
Ghanzi Botswana 99 C6
Ghanzi admin. dist. Botswana 100 F2
Ghap'an Armenia see Kapan
Ghardaïa Alg. 54 E5
Gharghoda India 84 D1
Ghârib, Gebel mt. Egypt see Ghārib, Jabal
Ghārib, Jabal mt. Egypt 90 D5
Gharm Tajik. 89 H2
Gharq Ābād Iran 88 C3
Gharwa India see Garhwa
Gharyān Libya 97 E1
Ghāt Libya 96 E2
Ghatgan India 83 F5
Ghatol India 82 C5
Ghawdex i. Malta see Gozo
Ghazal, Bahr el watercourse Chad 97 E3
Ghazaouet Alg. 57 F6
Ghaziabad India 82 D3
Ghazi Ghat Pak. 89 H4
Ghazipur India 83 E4
Ghazna Afgh. see Ghaznī
Ghaznī Afgh. 89 H3
Ghazni r. Afgh. 89 G3
Ghazoor Afgh. 89 G3
Ghazzah Gaza see Gaza
Ghebar Gumbad Iran 88 E3
Ghent Belgium 52 D3
Gheorghe Gheorghiu-Dej Romania see Onești
Gheorgheni Romania 59 K1
Gherla Romania 59 J1
Ghijduwon Uzbek. see Gizhduvan
Ghilzai reg. Afgh. 89 G4
Ghīnah, Wādī al watercourse Saudi Arabia 85 D4
Ghisonaccia Corsica France 56 I5
Ghorak Afgh. 89 G3
Ghost Lake Canada 120 H2
Ghotaru India 82 B4
Ghotki Pak. 89 H5
Ghuari r. India 83 F4
Ghudamis Libya see Ghadāmis
Ghurayfah hill Saudi Arabia 85 C4
Ghūrī Iran 88 D4
Ghurian Afgh. 89 F3
Ghurrab, Jabal hill Saudi Arabia 88 B5
Ghuzor Uzbek. see Guzar
Ghyvelde France 52 C3
Gia Đinh Vietnam 71 D5
Giaginskaya Rus. Fed. 91 F1
Gialias r. Cyprus 85 A2
Gia Nghia Vietnam 71 D4
Giannitsa Greece 59 J4
Giant's Castle mt. S. Africa 101 I5
Giant's Causeway lava field U.K. 51 F2
Gianysada i. Greece 59 L7
Gia Rai Vietnam 71 D5
Giarre Sicily Italy 58 F6
Gibb r. Australia 108 D3
Gibbonsville U.S.A. 126 E3
Gibeon Namibia 100 C3
Gibraltar terr. Europe 57 D5

▶Gibraltar Gibraltar 148 H3
United Kingdom Overseas Territory.
Europe 5, 38–39

Gibraltar, Strait of Morocco/Spain 57 C6
Gibraltar Range National Park Australia 112 F2
Gibson Australia 109 C8
Gibson City U.S.A. 134 A3
Gibson Desert Australia 109 C6
Gichgeniyn Nuruu mts Mongolia 80 H2
Gidar Pak. 89 G4
Giddalur India 84 C3
Gîddi, Gebel el hill Egypt see Jiddī, Jabal al
Giddings U.S.A. 131 D6
Gīdolē Eth. 97 G4
Gien France 56 F3
Gießen Germany 53 I4
Gīfan Iran 88 E2
Gifford r. Canada 119 J2
Gifhorn Germany 53 K2
Gift Lake Canada 120 H4
Gifu Japan 75 E6
Giganta, Cerro mt. Mex. 127 F8
Gigha i. U.K. 50 D5
Gīgīga Eth. see Jijiga
Gijón Spain see Gijón-Xixón
Gijón-Xixón Spain 57 D2
Gila r. U.S.A. 129 F5
Gila Bend U.S.A. 129 G5
Gila Bend Mountains U.S.A. 129 G5
Gīlān-e Gharb Iran 88 B3
Gilbert r. Australia 110 C3
Gilbert AZ U.S.A. 129 H5
Gilbert WV U.S.A. 134 E5
Gilbert Islands Kiribati 150 H5
Gilbert Islands country Pacific Ocean see Kiribati
Gilbert Peak U.S.A. 129 H1
Gilbert Ridge sea feature Pacific Ocean 150 H6
Gilbert River Australia 110 C3
Gilbués Brazil 143 I5
Gil Chashmeh Iran 88 E3
Gilé Moz. 99 D5
Giles Creek r. Australia 108 E4
Gilford Island Canada 120 E5
Gilgai Australia 112 E2
Gilgandra Australia 112 D3
Gil Gil Creek r. Australia 112 D2
Gilgit Jammu and Kashmir 82 C2
Gilgit r. Jammu and Kashmir 87 L2
Gilgunnia Australia 112 C4
Gılındire Turkey see Aydıncık
Gillam Canada 121 M3
Gillen, Lake salt flat Australia 109 D6
Gilles, Lake salt flat Australia 111 B7
Gillett U.S.A. 135 G3
Gillette U.S.A. 126 G3
Gilliat Australia 110 C4
Gillingham England U.K. 49 E7
Gillingham England U.K. 49 H7
Gilling West U.K. 48 F4
Gilman U.S.A. 134 B3
Gilmer U.S.A. 131 E5
Gilmour Island Canada 122 F2
Gilroy U.S.A. 128 C3
Gīmbī Eth. 98 D3
Gimhae S. Korea see Kimhae
Gimli Canada 121 L5
Gimol'skoye, Ozero l. Rus. Fed. 42 G3
Ginebra, Laguna l. Bol. 142 E6
Gineifa Egypt see Junayfah
Gin Gin Australia 110 E5
Gingin Australia 109 A7
Gīnīr Eth. 98 E3
Ginosa Italy 58 G4
Ginzo de Limia Spain see Xinzo de Limia
Gioia del Colle Italy 58 G4
Gipouloux r. Canada 122 G3
Gippsland reg. Australia 112 B7
Girâ, Wâdi watercourse Egypt see Jirā', Wādī
Gīrān Rīg mt. Iran 88 E4
Girard U.S.A. 134 E2
Girardin, Lac l. Canada 123 I2
Girdab Iran 88 E3
Giresun Turkey 90 E2
Girgenti Sicily Italy see Agrigento
Giridh India see Giridih
Giridih India 83 F4
Girilambone Australia 112 C3
Girna r. India 82 C5
Gir National Park India 82 B5
Girne Cyprus see Kyrenia
Girón Ecuador 142 C4
Giron Sweden see Kiruna
Girona Spain 57 H3
Gironde est. France 56 D4
Girot Pak. 89 I3
Girral Australia 112 C4
Girraween National Park Australia 112 E2
Girvan U.K. 50 E5
Girvas Rus. Fed. 42 G3
Gisborne N.Z. 113 G4
Giscome Canada 120 F4
Gislaved Sweden 45 H8
Gisors France 52 B5
Gissar Tajik. see Hisor
Gissar Range mts Tajik./Uzbek. 89 G2
Gissarskiy Khrebet mts Tajik./Uzbek. see Gissar Range
Gitarama Rwanda 98 C4
Gitega Burundi 98 C4
Giuba r. Somalia see Jubba
Giulianova Italy 58 E3
Giurgiu Romania 59 K3
Giuvala, Pasul pass Romania 59 K2
Givar Iran 88 E2
Givet France 52 E4
Givors France 56 G4
Givry-en-Argonne France 52 E6
Giyani S. Africa 101 J2
Giza Egypt 90 C5
Gizhduvan Uzbek. 89 G1
Gizhiga Rus. Fed. 65 R3
Gjakovë Serb. and Mont. see Đakovica
Gjilan Serb. and Mont. see Gnjilane
Gjirokastër Albania 59 I4
Gjirokastra Albania see Gjirokastër
Gjoa Haven Canada 119 I3
Gjøra Norway 44 F5
Gjøvik Norway 45 G6
Glace Bay Canada 123 K5
Glacier Bay National Park and Preserve U.S.A. 120 B3
Glacier National Park Canada 120 G5
Glacier National Park U.S.A. 126 E2
Glacier Peak vol. U.S.A. 126 C2
Gladstad Norway 44 G4
Gladstone Australia 110 E4
Gladstone Canada 121 L5
Gladwin U.S.A. 134 C2
Gladys U.S.A. 134 F5
Gladys Lake Canada 120 C3
Glamis U.K. 50 F4
Glamis U.S.A. 129 F5
Glamoč Bos.-Herz. 58 G2
Glan r. Germany 53 H5
Glandorf Germany 53 I2
Glanton U.K. 48 F3
Glasgow U.K. 50 E5
Glasgow KY U.S.A. 134 C5
Glasgow MT U.S.A. 126 G2
Glasgow VA U.S.A. 134 F5
Glaslyn Canada 121 I4
Glass, Loch l. U.K. 50 E3
Glass Mountain U.S.A. 128 D3
Glastonbury U.K. 49 E7
Glauchau Germany 53 M4
Glazov Rus. Fed. 42 L4
Gleiwitz Poland see Gliwice
Glen U.S.A. 135 J1
Glen Allen U.S.A. 135 G5
Glen Alpine Dam S. Africa 101 I2
Glenamaddy Rep. of Ireland 51 D4
Glenamoy r. Rep. of Ireland 51 C3
Glen Arbor U.S.A. 134 C1
Glenbawn Reservoir Australia 112 E4
Glenboro Canada 121 L5
Glen Canyon gorge U.S.A. 129 H3
Glen Canyon Dam U.S.A. 129 H3
Glencoe Canada 134 E2
Glencoe S. Africa 101 J5
Glencoe U.S.A. 130 E2
Glendale AZ U.S.A. 129 G5
Glendale CA U.S.A. 128 D4
Glendale UT U.S.A. 129 G3
Glendale Lake U.S.A. 135 F3
Glen Davis Australia 112 E4
Glenden Australia 110 E4
Glendive U.S.A. 126 G3
Glendon Canada 121 I4
Glendo Reservoir U.S.A. 126 G4
Glenfield U.S.A. 135 H2
Glengavlen Rep. of Ireland 51 E3
Glengyle Australia 110 B5
Glen Innes Australia 112 E2
Glenluce U.K. 50 E6
Glen Lyon U.S.A. 135 G3
Glenlyon Peak Canada 120 C2
Glen More valley U.K. 50 E3
Glenmorgan Australia 112 D1
Glenn U.S.A. 128 B2
Glennallen U.S.A. 118 D3
Glennie U.S.A. 134 D1
Glenns Ferry U.S.A. 126 E4
Glenora Canada 120 D3
Glenore Australia 110 C3
Glenormiston Australia 110 B4
Glenreagh Australia 112 F3
Glen Rose U.S.A. 131 D5
Glenrothes U.K. 50 F4
Glens Falls U.S.A. 135 I2
Glen Shee valley U.K. 50 F4
Glenties Rep. of Ireland 51 D3
Glenveagh National Park Rep. of Ireland 51 E2
Glenville U.S.A. 134 E4
Glenwood AR U.S.A. 131 E5
Glenwood IA U.S.A. 130 E3
Glenwood MN U.S.A. 130 E2
Glenwood NM U.S.A. 129 I5
Glenwood Springs U.S.A. 129 J2
Glevum U.K. see Gloucester
Glinde Germany 53 K1
Glittertinden mt. Norway 45 F6
Gliwice Poland 47 Q5
Globe U.S.A. 129 H5
Glogau Poland see Głogów
Głogów Poland 47 P5
Glomfjord Norway 44 H3
Glomma r. Norway 44 G7
Glommersträsk Sweden 44 K4
Glorieuses, Îles is Indian Ocean 99 E5
Glorioso Islands Indian Ocean see Glorieuses, Îles
Gloster U.S.A. 131 F6
Gloucester Australia 112 E3
Gloucester U.K. 49 E7
Gloucester MA U.S.A. 135 J2
Gloucester VA U.S.A. 135 G5
Gloversville U.S.A. 135 H2
Glovertown Canada 123 L4
Glöwen Germany 53 M2
Glubinnoye Rus. Fed. 74 D3
Glubokiy Krasnoyarskiy Kray Rus. Fed. 72 H2
Glubokiy Rostovskaya Oblast' Rus. Fed. 43 I6
Glubokoye Belarus see Hlybokaye
Glubokoye Kazakh. 80 F1
Gluggarnir hill Faroe Is 44 [inset]
Glukhov Ukr. see Hlukhiv
Glusburn U.K. 48 F5
Glynebwy U.K. see Ebbw Vale
Gmelinka Rus. Fed. 43 J6
Gmünd Austria 47 O6
Gmunden Austria 47 N7
Gnarp Sweden 45 J5
Gnarrenburg Germany 53 J1
Gnesen Poland see Gniezno
Gniezno Poland 47 P4
Gnjilane Serb. and Mont. 59 I3
Gnowangerup Australia 109 B8
Gnows Nest Range hills Australia 109 B7
Goa India 84 B3
Goa state India 84 B3
Goageb Namibia 100 C4
Goalen Head hd Australia 112 E6
Goalpara India 83 G4
Goat Fell hill U.K. 50 D5
Goba Eth. 98 E3
Gobabis Namibia 100 D2
Gobannium U.K. see Abergavenny
Gobas Namibia 100 D4
Gobi des. China/Mongolia 72 J4
Gobindpur India 83 F5
Gobles U.S.A. 134 C2
Gobō Japan 75 D6
Goch Germany 52 G3
Gochas Namibia 100 D3
Go Công Vietnam 71 D5
Godalming U.K. 49 G7
Godavari r. India 84 D2
Godavari, Cape India 84 D2
Godda India 83 F4
Godē Eth. 98 E3
Godere Eth. 98 E3
Goderich Canada 134 E2
Goderville France 49 H9
Godhavn Greenland see Qeqertarsuaq
Godhra India 82 C5
Godia Creek b. India 89 H6
Gods r. Canada 121 M3
Gods Lake Canada 121 M4
God's Mercy, Bay of Canada 121 O2
Godthåb Greenland see Nuuk
Godwin-Austen, Mount China/Jammu and Kashmir see K2
Goedereede Neth. 52 D3
Goedgegun Swaziland see Nhlangano
Goegap Nature Reserve S. Africa 100 D5
Goélands, Lac aux l. Canada 123 J3
Goes Neth. 52 D3
Gogama Canada 122 E5
Gogebic Range hills U.S.A. 130 F2
Gogra r. India see Ghaghara
Goiana Brazil 143 L5
Goiandira Brazil 145 A2
Goianésia Brazil 145 A1
Goiânia Brazil 145 A2
Goiás Brazil 145 A1
Goiás state Brazil 145 A2
Goinsargoin China 76 C2
Goio-Erê Brazil 144 F2
Gojra Pak. 89 I4
Gokak India 84 B2
Gokarn India 84 B3
Gök Çay r. Turkey 85 A1
Gökçeada i. Turkey 59 K4
Gökdepe Turkm. see Gekdepe
Gökdere r. Turkey 85 A1
Goklenkuy, Solonchak salt l. Turkm. 88 E1
Gökova Körfezi b. Turkey 59 L6
Gokprosh Hills Pak. 89 F5
Göksun Turkey 90 E3
Goksu Parkı Turkey 85 A1
Gokteik Myanmar 70 B2
Gokwe Zimbabwe 99 C5
Gol Norway 45 F6
Golaghat India 83 H4
Golbāf Iran 88 E4
Gölbaşı Turkey 90 E3
Golconda U.S.A. 128 E1
Gölcük Turkey 59 M4
Gold U.S.A. 135 G3
Goldap Poland 47 S3
Gold Beach U.S.A. 126 B4
Goldberg Germany 53 M1
Gold Coast country Africa see Ghana
Gold Coast Australia 112 F2
Golden U.S.A. 126 G5
Golden Bay N.Z. 113 D5
Goldendale U.S.A. 126 C3
Goldene Aue reg. Germany 53 K3
Golden Gate Highlands National Park S. Africa 101 I5
Golden Hinde mt. Canada 120 E5
Golden Lake Canada 135 G1
Golden Prairie Canada 121 I5
Goldenstedt Germany 53 I2
Goldfield U.S.A. 128 E3
Goldsand Lake Canada 121 K3
Goldsboro U.S.A. 133 E5
Goldstone Lake U.S.A. 128 E4
Goldsworthy Australia 108 B5
Goldthwaite U.S.A. 131 D6
Goldvein U.S.A. 135 G4
Göle Turkey 91 F2
Golestān Afgh. 89 F3
Goleta U.S.A. 128 D4
Golets-Davydov, Gora mt. Rus. Fed. 73 J2
Golfo di Orosei Gennargentu e Asinara, Parco Nazionale del nat. park Sardinia Italy 58 C4
Gölgeli Dağları mts Turkey 59 M6
Goliad U.S.A. 131 D6
Golingka China see Gongbo'gyamda
Gölköy Turkey 90 E2
Gollel Swaziland see Lavumisa
Golm Germany 53 M2
Golmberg hill Germany 53 N2
Golmud China 80 H4
Golovnino Rus. Fed. 74 G4
Golpāyegān Iran 88 C3
Gölpazarı Turkey 59 N4
Golspie U.K. 50 F3
Gol Vardeh Iran 89 F3
Golyama Syutkya mt. Bulg. 59 K4
Golyam Persenk mt. Bulg. 59 K4
Golyshi Rus. Fed. see Vetluzhskiy
Golzow Germany 53 M2
Goma Dem. Rep. Congo 98 C4
Gomang Co salt l. China 83 G3
Gomati r. India 87 N4
Gombak, Bukit hill Sing. 71 [inset]
Gombe Nigeria 96 E3
Gombe r. Tanz. 99 D4
Gombi Nigeria 96 E3
Gombroon Iran see Bandar-e 'Abbās
Gomel' Belarus see Homyel'
Gómez Palacio Mex. 131 C7
Gomīshān Iran 88 D2
Gommern Germany 53 L2
Gomo Co salt l. China 83 F2
Gonābād Iran 88 E2
Gonaïves Haiti 137 J5
Gonarezhou National Park Zimbabwe 99 D6
Gonbad-e Kavus Iran 88 D2
Gonda India 83 E4
Gondal India 82 B5
Gondar Eth. see Gonder
Gonder Eth. 98 D2
Gondia India 82 E5
Gondiya India see Gondia
Gönen Turkey 59 L4
Gonfreville-l'Orcher France 49 H9
Gong'an China 77 G2
Gongbalou China see Gamba
Gongbo'gyamda China 76 B2
Gongchang China see Longxi
Gongcheng China 77 F3
Gongga Shan mt. China 76 D2
Gonghe Qinghai China 80 J4
Gonghe Yunnan China see Mouding
Gongjiang China see Yudu
Gongogi r. Brazil 145 D1
Gongolgon Australia 112 C3
Gongpoquan China 80 I3
Gongquan China see Gongxian
Gongtang China see Damxung
Gongwang Shan mts China 76 D3
Gongxian China 76 E2
Gonjo China 76 C2
Gonjog China see Coqên
Gonzales CA U.S.A. 128 C3
Gonzales TX U.S.A. 131 D6
Gonzha Rus. Fed. 74 B1
Goochland U.S.A. 135 G5
Goodenough, Cape Antarctica 152 G2
Goodenough Island P.N.G. 106 F2
Gooderham Canada 135 F1
Good Hope, Cape of S. Africa 100 D8
Good Hope Mountain Canada 126 B2
Gooding U.S.A. 126 E4
Goodland IN U.S.A. 134 B3
Goodland KS U.S.A. 130 C4
Goodlettsville U.S.A. 134 B5
Goodooga Australia 112 C2
Goodspeed Nunataks Antarctica 152 E2
Goole U.K. 48 G5
Goolgowi Australia 112 B5
Goolma Australia 112 D4
Gooloogong Australia 112 D4
Goomalling Australia 109 B7
Goombalie Australia 112 B2
Goondiwindi Australia 112 E2
Goongarrie, Lake salt flat Australia 109 C7
Goongarrie National Park Australia 109 C7
Goonyella Australia 110 D4
Goorly, Lake salt flat Australia 109 B7
Goose Bay Canada see Happy Valley - Goose Bay
Goose Creek U.S.A. 133 D5
Goose Lake U.S.A. 126 C4
Gooty India 84 C3
Gopalganj Bangl. 83 G5
Gopalganj India 83 F4
Gopeshwar India 82 D3
Göppingen Germany 53 J6
Gorakhpur India 83 E4
Goražde Bos.-Herz. 58 H3
Gorbernador U.S.A. 129 J3
Gorczański Park Narodowy nat. park Poland 47 R6
Gorda, Punta pt U.S.A. 128 A1
Gördes Turkey 59 M5
Gordil Cent. Afr. Rep. 98 C3
Gordon r. Canada 121 O1
Gordon U.K. 50 G5
Gordon U.S.A. 130 C3
Gordon, Lake Australia 111 [inset]
Gordon Downs Australia 108 E4
Gordon Lake Canada 121 I3
Gordon Lake U.S.A. 135 F4
Gordonsville U.S.A. 135 F4
Goré Chad 97 E4
Gorē Eth. 98 D3
Gore N.Z. 113 B8
Gore U.S.A. 135 F4
Gorebridge U.K. 50 F5
Gore Point U.S.A. 118 C4
Gorey Rep. of Ireland 51 F5
Gorg Iran 89 E4
Gorgān Iran 88 D2
Gorgan Bay Iran 88 D2
Gorge Range hills Australia 108 B5
Gorgona, Isla i. Col. 142 C3
Gorham U.S.A. 135 J1
Gori Georgia 86 F1
Gorinchem Neth. 52 E3
Goris Armenia 91 G3
Gorizia Italy 58 E2
Gorki Belarus see Horki
Gor'kiy Rus. Fed. see Nizhniy Novgorod
Gor'kovskoye Vodokhranilishche resr Rus. Fed. 42 I4
Gorlice Poland 43 D6
Görlitz Germany 47 O5
Gorlovka Ukr. see Horlivka
Gorna Dzhumaya Bulg. see Blagoevgrad
Gorna Oryakhovitsa Bulg. 59 K3
Gornji Milanovac Serb. and Mont. 59 I2
Gornji Vakuf Bos.-Herz. 58 G3
Gorno-Altaysk Rus. Fed. 80 G1
Gornotrakiyska Nizina lowland Bulg. 59 K3
Gornozavodsk Permskaya Oblast' Rus. Fed. 41 R4
Gornozavodsk Sakhalinskaya Oblast' Rus. Fed. 74 F3
Gornyak Rus. Fed. 80 F1
Gornye Klyuchi Rus. Fed. 74 D3
Gornyy Rus. Fed. 43 K6
Goro i. Fiji see Koro
Gorodenka Ukr. see Horodenka
Gorodets Rus. Fed. 42 I4
Gorodishche Penzenskaya Oblast' Rus. Fed. 43 J5
Gorodishche Volgogradskaya Oblast' Rus. Fed. 43 J6
Gorodok Belarus see Haradok
Gorodok Rus. Fed. see Zakamensk
Gorodok Khmel'nyts'ka Oblast' Ukr. see Horodok
Gorodok L'vivs'ka Oblast' Ukr. see Horodok
Gorodovikovsk Rus. Fed. 43 I7
Goroka P.N.G. 69 L8
Gorokhovets Rus. Fed. 42 I4
Gorom Gorom Burkina 96 C3
Gorong, Kepulauan is Indon. 69 I7
Gorongosa mt. Moz. 99 D5
Gorongosa, Parque Nacional de nat. park Moz. 99 D5
Gorontalo Indon. 69 G6
Gorshechnoye Rus. Fed. 43 H6
Gort Rep. of Ireland 51 D4
Gortahork Rep. of Ireland 51 D2
Gorutuba r. Brazil 145 C1
Gorveh Iran 88 E4
Goryachiy Klyuch Rus. Fed. 91 E1
Görzke Germany 53 M2
Gorzów Wielkopolski Poland 47 O4
Gosainthan mt. China see Xixabangma Feng
Gosforth U.K. 48 F3
Goshen CA U.S.A. 128 D3
Goshen IN U.S.A. 134 C3
Goshen NH U.S.A. 135 I2
Goshen NY U.S.A. 135 H3
Goshen VA U.S.A. 134 F5
Goshoba Turkm. see Koshoba
Goslar Germany 53 K3
Gospić Croatia 58 F2
Gosport U.K. 49 F8
Gossi Mali 96 C3
Gostivar Macedonia 59 I4
Gosu China 76 C1
Göteborg Sweden see Gothenburg
Götene Sweden 45 H7
Gotenhafen Poland see Gdynia
Gotha Germany 53 K4
Gothenburg Sweden 45 G8
Gothenburg U.S.A. 130 C3
Gotland i. Sweden 45 K8
Gotō-rettō is Japan 75 C6
Gotse Delchev Bulg. 59 J4
Gotska Sandön i. Sweden 45 K7
Gōtsu Japan 75 D6
Göttingen Germany 53 J3
Gott Peak Canada 120 F5
Gottwaldow Czech Rep. see Zlín
Gouda Neth. 52 E2
Goudiri Senegal 96 B3
Goudoumaria Niger 96 E3
Goûgaram Niger 96 D3

▶Gough Island S. Atlantic Ocean 148 H8
Dependency of St Helena.

Gouin, Réservoir resr Canada 122 G4
Goulburn Australia 112 D5
Goulburn r. N.S.W. Australia 112 E4
Goulburn r. Vic. Australia 112 B6
Goulburn Islands Australia 108 F2
Goulburn River National Park Australia 112 E4
Gould Coast Antarctica 152 J1
Goulou atoll Micronesia see Ngulu
Goundam Mali 96 C3
Goundi Chad 97 E4
Goupil, Lac l. Canada 123 H3
Gouraya Alg. 57 G5
Gourcy Burkina 96 C3
Gourdon France 56 E4
Gouré Niger 96 E3
Gouripur Bangl. 83 G4
Gourits r. S. Africa 100 E8
Gourma-Rharous Mali 96 C3
Gournay-en-Bray France 52 B5
Goussainville France 52 C5
Gouverneur U.S.A. 135 H1
Governador Valadares Brazil 145 C2
Governor's Harbour Bahamas 133 E7
Govĭ Altayn Nuruu mts Mongolia 80 I3
Govind Ballash Pant Sagar resr India 83 E4
Gowal Pak. 89 H4
Gowanda U.S.A. 135 F2
Gowan Range hills Australia 110 D5
Gowārān Afgh. 89 G4
Gowd-e Mokh l. Iran 88 D4
Gowd-e Zereh plain Afgh. 89 F4
Gowmal Kalay Afgh. 89 H3
Gowna, Lough l. Rep. of Ireland 51 E4
Goya Arg. 144 E3
Göyçay Azer. 91 G2
Goyder watercourse Australia 109 F6
Goymatdag hills Turkm. see Koymatdag, Gory
Göynük Turkey 59 N4
Goyoum Cameroon 96 E4
Gozareh Afgh. 89 F3
Goz-Beïda Chad 97 F3
Gozha Co salt l. China 82 E2
Gözkaya Turkey 85 C1
Gozo i. Malta 58 F6
Graaf-Reinet S. Africa 100 G7
Grabfeld plain Germany 53 K4
Grabo Côte d'Ivoire 96 C4
Grabouw S. Africa 100 D8
Grabow Germany 53 L1
Gračac Croatia 58 F2
Gracefield Canada 122 F5
Gracey U.S.A. 134 B5
Gradaús, Serra dos hills Brazil 143 H5
Gradiška Bos.-Herz. see Bosanska Gradiška
Grady U.S.A. 131 C5
Gräfenhainichen Germany 53 M3
Grafenwöhr Germany 53 L5
Grafton Australia 112 F2
Grafton ND U.S.A. 130 D1
Grafton WI U.S.A. 134 B2
Grafton WV U.S.A. 134 E4
Grafton, Cape Australia 110 D3
Grafton, Mount U.S.A. 129 F2
Grafton Passage Australia 110 D3
Graham NC U.S.A. 132 E4
Graham TX U.S.A. 131 D5
Graham, Mount U.S.A. 129 I5
Graham Bell Island Rus. Fed. see Greem-Bell, Ostrov
Graham Island B.C. Canada 120 C4
Graham Island Nunavut Canada 119 I2
Graham Land reg. Antarctica 152 L2
Grahamstown S. Africa 101 H7
Grahovo Bos.-Herz. see Bosansko Grahovo
Graigue Rep. of Ireland 51 F5
Grajaú Brazil 143 I5
Grajaú r. Brazil 143 J4
Grammont Belgium see Geraardsbergen
Grammos mt. Greece 59 I4
Grampian Mountains U.K. 50 E4
Grampians National Park Australia 111 C8
Granada Nicaragua 137 G6
Granada Spain 57 E5
Granada U.S.A. 130 C4
Granard Rep. of Ireland 51 E4
Granbury U.S.A. 131 D5
Granby Canada 123 G5
Gran Canaria i. Canary Is 96 B2
Gran Chaco reg. Arg./Para. 144 D3
Grand r. MO U.S.A. 134 B2
Grand r. SD U.S.A. 130 C2
Grand Atlas mts Morocco see Haut Atlas
Grand Bahama i. Bahamas 133 E7
Grand Ballon mt. France 47 K7
Grand Bank Canada 123 L5
Grand Banks of Newfoundland sea feature N. Atlantic Ocean 148 E3
Grand-Bassam Côte d'Ivoire 96 C4
Grand Bay Canada 123 I5
Grand Bend Canada 134 E2
Grand Blanc U.S.A. 134 D2
Grand Canal Rep. of Ireland 51 E4
Grand Canary i. Canary Is see Gran Canaria
Grand Canyon U.S.A. 129 G3
Grand Canyon gorge U.S.A. 129 G3
Grand Canyon National Park U.S.A. 129 G3
Grand Canyon - Parashant National Monument nat. park U.S.A. 129 G3
Grand Cayman i. Cayman Is 137 H5
Grande r. Bahia Brazil 145 B1
Grande r. São Paulo Brazil 145 A3
Grande r. Nicaragua 137 H6
Grande, Bahía b. Arg. 144 C8
Grande, Ilha i. Brazil 145 B3
Grande Cache Canada 120 G4
Grande Comore i. Comoros see Njazidja
Grande Prairie Canada 120 G4
Grand Erg de Bilma des. Niger 96 E3
Grand Erg Occidental des. Alg. 54 D5
Grand Erg Oriental des. Alg. 54 F6
Grande-Rivière Canada 123 I4
Grandes, Salinas salt marsh Arg. 144 C4
Grande-Vallée Canada 123 I4
Grand Falls N.B. Canada 123 I5
Grand Falls Nfld. and Lab. Canada 123 L4
Grand Forks Canada 120 G5
Grand Forks U.S.A. 130 D2
Grand Gorge U.S.A. 135 H2
Grand Haven U.S.A. 134 B2
Grandin, Lac l. Canada 120 G1
Grandioznyy, Pik mt. Rus. Fed. 72 H2
Grand Island U.S.A. 130 D3
Grand Isle U.S.A. 131 F6
Grand Junction U.S.A. 129 I2
Grand Lac Germain l. Canada 123 I4
Grand-Lahou Côte d'Ivoire 96 C4
Grand Lake N.B. Canada 123 I5
Grand Lake Nfld. and Lab. Canada 123 J3
Grand Lake Nfld. and Lab. Canada 123 K4
Grand Lake LA U.S.A. 131 E6
Grand Lake MI U.S.A. 134 D1
Grand Lake St Marys U.S.A. 130 C3
Grand Ledge U.S.A. 134 C2
Grand Manan Island Canada 123 I5
Grand Marais MI U.S.A. 132 C2
Grand Marais MN U.S.A. 130 F2

Grand-Mère Canada 123 G5
Grand Mesa U.S.A. 129 J2
Grândola Port. 57 B4
Grand Passage New Caledonia 107 G3
Grand Rapids Canada 121 L4
Grand Rapids *MI* U.S.A. 134 C2
Grand Rapids *MN* U.S.A. 130 E2
Grand-Sault Canada *see* Grand Falls
Grand St-Bernard, Col du *pass* Italy/Switz. *see* Great St Bernard Pass
Grand Teton *mt.* U.S.A. 126 F4
Grand Teton National Park U.S.A. 126 F4
Grand Traverse Bay U.S.A. 134 C1

▶Grand Turk Turks and Caicos Is 137 J4
Capital of the Turks and Caicos Islands.

Grandville U.S.A. 134 C2
Grandvilliers France 52 B5
Grand Wash Cliffs *mts* U.S.A. 129 F4
Grange Rep. of Ireland 51 E6
Grängesberg Sweden 45 I6
Grangeville U.S.A. 126 D3
Granisle Canada 120 E4
Granite Falls U.S.A. 130 E2
Granite Mountain U.S.A. 128 E1
Granite Mountains *CA* U.S.A. 129 F4
Granite Mountains *CA* U.S.A. 129 F5
Granite Peak *MT* U.S.A. 126 F3
Granite Peak *UT* U.S.A. 129 G1
Granite Range *mts AK* U.S.A. 120 A3
Granite Range *mts NV* U.S.A. 128 D1
Granitola, Capo *c. Sicily* Italy 58 E6
Granja Brazil 143 J4
Gran Laguna Salada *l.* Arg. 144 C6
Gränna Sweden 45 I7
Gran Paradiso *mt.* Italy 58 B2
Gran Paradiso, Parco Nazionale del *nat. park* Italy 58 B2
Gran Pilastro *mt.* Austria/Italy 47 M7
Gran San Bernardo, Colle del *pass* Italy/Switz. *see* Great St Bernard Pass
Gran Sasso e Monti della Laga, Parco Nazionale del *nat. park* Italy 58 E3
Granschütz Germany 53 M3
Gransee Germany 53 N1
Grant U.S.A. 130 C3
Grant, Mount U.S.A. 128 E2
Grantham U.K. 49 G6
Grant Island Antarctica 152 J2
Grant Lake Canada 120 G1
Grantown-on-Spey U.K. 50 F3
Grant Range *mts* U.S.A. 129 F2
Grants U.S.A. 129 J4
Grants Pass U.S.A. 126 C4
Grantsville *UT* U.S.A. 129 G1
Grantsville *WV* U.S.A. 134 E4
Granville Canada 120 B2
Granville France 56 D2
Granville *AZ* U.S.A. 129 I5
Granville *NY* U.S.A. 135 I2
Granville *TN* U.S.A. 134 C5
Granville Lake Canada 121 K3
Grão Mogol Brazil 145 C2
Grapevine Mountains U.S.A. 128 E3
Gras, Lac de *l.* Canada 121 I1
Graskop S. Africa 101 J3
Grasplatz Namibia 100 B4
Grass *r.* Canada 121 L3
Grass *r.* U.S.A. 135 H1
Grasse France 56 H5
Grassflat U.S.A. 135 F3
Grassington U.K. 48 F4
Grasslands National Park Canada 121 J5
Grassrange U.S.A. 126 F3
Grass Valley U.S.A. 128 C2
Grassy Butte U.S.A. 130 C2
Grästorp Sweden 45 H7
Gratz U.S.A. 134 C4
Graudenz Poland *see* Grudziądz
Graus Spain 57 G2
Gravataí Brazil 145 A5
Grave, Pointe de *pt* France 56 D4
Gravelbourg Canada 121 J5
Gravel Hill Lake Canada 121 K2
Gravelines France 52 C4
Gravelotte S. Africa 101 J2
Gravenhurst Canada 134 F1
Grave Peak U.S.A. 126 E3
Gravesend Australia 112 E2
Gravesend U.K. 49 H7
Gravina in Puglia Italy 58 G4
Grawn U.S.A. 134 C1
Gray France 56 G3
Gray *GA* U.S.A. 133 D5
Gray *KY* U.S.A. 134 C5
Gray *ME* U.S.A. 135 J2
Grayback Mountain U.S.A. 126 C4
Gray Lake Canada 121 I2
Grayling *r.* Canada 120 E3
Grayling U.S.A. 134 C1
Grays U.K. 49 H7
Grays Harbor *inlet* U.S.A. 126 B3
Grays Lake U.S.A. 126 F4
Grayson U.S.A. 134 D4
Graz Austria 47 O7
Greasy Lake Canada 120 F2
Great Abaco *i.* Bahamas 133 E7
Great Australian Bight *g.* Australia 109 E8
Great Baddow U.K. 49 H7
Great Bahama Bank *sea feature* Bahamas 133 E7
Great Barrier Island N.Z. 113 E3
Great Barrier Reef Australia 110 D1
Great Barrier Reef Marine Park (Cairns Section) Australia 110 D3
Great Barrier Reef Marine Park (Capricorn Section) Australia 110 E4
Great Barrier Reef Marine Park (Central Section) Australia 110 E3
Great Barrier Reef Marine Park (Far North Section) Australia 110 D2
Great Barrington U.S.A. 135 I2
Great Basalt Wall National Park Australia 110 D3
Great Basin U.S.A. 128 E2
Great Basin National Park U.S.A. 129 F2
Great Bear *r.* Canada 120 E1

▶Great Bear Lake Canada 120 G1
4th largest lake in North America.

Great Belt *sea chan.* Denmark 45 G9
Great Bend U.S.A. 130 D4
Great Bitter Lake Egypt 85 A4
Great Blasket Island Rep. of Ireland 51 B5

▶Great Britain *i.* U.K. 46 G4
Largest island in Europe.
Europe 36–37

Great Clifton U.K. 48 D4
Great Coco Island Cocos Is 68 A4
Great Cumbrae *i.* U.K. 50 E5
Great Dismal Swamp National Wildlife Refuge *nature res.* U.S.A. 135 G5
Great Dividing Range *mts* Australia 112 B6
Great Eastern Erg *des.* Alg. *see* Grand Erg Oriental
Greater Antarctica *reg.* Antarctica *see* East Antarctica
Greater Antilles *is* Caribbean Sea 137 H4
Greater Khingan Mountains China *see* Da Hinggan Ling
Greater St Lucia Wetland Park *nature res.* S. Africa 101 K4
Greater Tunb *i.* The Gulf 88 D5
Great Exuma *i.* Bahamas 133 F8
Great Falls U.S.A. 126 F3
Great Fish *r.* S. Africa 101 H7
Great Fish Point S. Africa 101 H7
Great Fish River Reserve Complex *nature res.* S. Africa 101 H7
Great Gandak *r.* India 83 F4
Great Ganges *atoll* Cook Is *see* Manihiki
Great Guana Cay *i.* Bahamas 133 E7
Great Inagua *i.* Bahamas 137 J4
Great Karoo *plat.* S. Africa 100 F7
Great Kei *r.* S. Africa 101 I7
Great Lake Australia 111 [inset]
Great Malvern U.K. 49 E6
Great Meteor Tablemount *sea feature* N. Atlantic Ocean 148 G4
Great Namaqualand *reg.* Namibia 100 C4
Great Nicobar *i.* India 71 A6
Great Ormes Head *hd* U.K. 48 D5
Great Ouse *r.* U.K. 49 H6
Great Oyster Bay Australia 111 [inset]
Great Palm Islands Australia 106 D3
Great Plain of the Koukdjuak Canada 119 K3
Great Plains U.S.A. 130 C3
Great Point U.S.A. 135 J3
Great Rift Valley Africa 98 D4
Great Ruaha *r.* Tanz. 99 D4
Great Sacandaga Lake U.S.A. 135 H2
Great Salt Lake U.S.A. 129 G1
Great Salt Lake Desert U.S.A. 129 G1
Great Sand Hills Canada 121 I5
Great Sand Sea *des.* Egypt/Libya 90 B5
Great Sandy Desert Australia 108 C5
Great Sandy Island Australia *see* Fraser Island
Great Sea Reef Fiji 107 H3

▶Great Slave Lake Canada 120 H2
Deepest and 5th largest lake in North America.

Great Smoky Mountains U.S.A. 133 C5
Great Smoky Mountains National Park U.S.A. 132 D5
Great Snow Mountain Canada 120 E3
Great St Bernard Pass Italy/Switz. 58 B2
Greatstone-on-Sea U.K. 49 H8
Great Stour *r.* U.K. 49 I7
Great Torrington U.K. 49 C8
Great Victoria Desert Australia 109 E7
Great Wall *research station* Antarctica 152 A2
Great Wall *tourist site* China 73 L4
Great Waltham U.K. 49 H7
Great Western Erg *des.* Alg. *see* Grand Erg Occidental
Great West Torres Islands Myanmar 71 B5
Great Whernside *hill* U.K. 48 F4
Great Yarmouth U.K. 49 I6
Grebenkovskiy Ukr. *see* Hrebinka
Grebyonka Ukr. *see* Hrebinka
Greco, Cape Cyprus *see* Greko, Cape
Gredos, Sierra de *mts* Spain 57 D3
▶Greece *country* Europe 59 I5
Europe 5, 38–39
Greece U.S.A. 135 G2
Greeley U.S.A. 126 G4
Greely Center U.S.A. 130 D3
Greem-Bell, Ostrov *i.* Rus. Fed. 64 H1
Green *r. KY* U.S.A. 134 B5
Green *r. WY* U.S.A. 129 I2
Green Bay U.S.A. 134 A1
Green Bay *b.* U.S.A. 134 B1
Greenbrier U.S.A. 134 B5
Greenbrier *r.* U.S.A. 134 E5
Green Cape Australia 112 E6
Greencastle Bahamas 133 E7
Greencastle U.K. 51 F3
Greencastle U.S.A. 134 B4
Green Cove Springs U.S.A. 133 D6
Greene *ME* U.S.A. 135 J1
Greene *NY* U.S.A. 135 H2
Greeneville U.S.A. 132 D4
Greenfield *CA* U.S.A. 128 C3
Greenfield *IN* U.S.A. 134 C4
Greenfield *MA* U.S.A. 135 I2
Greenfield *OH* U.S.A. 134 D4
Green Head *hd* Australia 109 A7
Greenhill Island Australia 108 F2
Green Island Taiwan *see* Lü Tao
Green Lake Canada 121 J4

▶Greenland *terr.* N. America 119 N3
Self-governing Danish Territory. Largest island in the world and in North America.
North America 9, 114–115, 116–117
World 12–13

Greenland Basin *sea feature* Arctic Ocean 153 I2
Greenland Fracture Zone *sea feature* Arctic Ocean 153 I1
Greenland Sea Greenland/Svalbard 64 A2
Greenlaw U.K. 50 G5
Green Mountains U.S.A. 135 I1
Greenock U.K. 50 E5
Greenore Rep. of Ireland 51 F3
Greenport U.S.A. 135 I3
Green River P.N.G. 69 K7
Green River *UT* U.S.A. 129 H2
Green River *WY* U.S.A. 126 F4
Green River Lake U.S.A. 134 C5
Greensboro U.S.A. 133 D5
Greensburg *IN* U.S.A. 134 C4
Greensburg *KS* U.S.A. 130 D4
Greensburg *KY* U.S.A. 134 C5
Greensburg *LA* U.S.A. 131 F6
Greensburg *PA* U.S.A. 134 F3
Greens Peak U.S.A. 129 I4
Greenstone Point U.K. 50 D3
Green Swamp U.S.A. 133 E5
Greentown U.S.A. 134 C3
Greenup *IL* U.S.A. 130 F4
Greenup *KY* U.S.A. 134 D4
Green Valley Canada 135 H1
Greenville Canada 120 D4
Greenville Liberia 96 C4
Greenville *AL* U.S.A. 133 C6
Greenville *IL* U.S.A. 130 F4
Greenville *KY* U.S.A. 134 B5
Greenville *ME* U.S.A. 132 G2
Greenville *MI* U.S.A. 134 C2
Greenville *MS* U.S.A. 131 F5
Greenville *NC* U.S.A. 132 E5
Greenville *NH* U.S.A. 135 J2
Greenville *OH* U.S.A. 134 C3
Greenville *PA* U.S.A. 134 E3
Greenville *SC* U.S.A. 133 D5
Greenville *TX* U.S.A. 131 D5
Greenwich *atoll* Micronesia *see* Kapingamarangi
Greenwich *CT* U.S.A. 135 I3
Greenwich *OH* U.S.A. 134 D3
Greenwood *AR* U.S.A. 131 E5
Greenwood *IN* U.S.A. 134 B4
Greenwood *MS* U.S.A. 131 F5
Greenwood *SC* U.S.A. 133 D5
Gregory *r.* Australia 110 B3
Gregory, Lake *salt flat S.A.* Australia 111 B6
Gregory, Lake *salt flat W.A.* Australia 108 D5
Gregory, Lake *salt flat W.A.* Australia 109 B6
Gregory Downs Australia 110 B3
Gregory National Park Australia 108 E4
Gregory Range *hills Qld* Australia 110 C3
Gregory Range *hills W.A.* Australia 108 C5
Greifswald Germany 47 N3
Greiz Germany 53 M4
Greko, Cape Cyprus 85 B2
Gremikha Rus. Fed. 153 G2
Gremyachinsk Rus. Fed. 41 R4
Grenå Denmark 45 G8
Grenaa Denmark *see* Grenå
Grenada U.S.A. 131 F5
▶Grenada *country* West Indies 137 L6
North America 9, 116–117
Grenade France 56 E5
Grenen *spit* Denmark 45 G8
Grenfell Australia 112 D4
Grenfell Canada 121 K5
Grenoble France 56 G4
Grense-Jakobselv Norway 44 Q2
Grenville, Cape Australia 110 C1
Grenville Island Fiji *see* Rotuma
Greshak Pak. 89 G5
Gresham U.S.A. 126 C3
Gressåmoen Nasjonalpark *nat. park* Norway 44 H4
Greta *r.* U.K. 48 E4
Gretna U.K. 50 F6
Gretna *LA* U.S.A. 131 F6
Gretna *VA* U.S.A. 134 F5
Greußen Germany 53 K3
Grevelingen *sea chan.* Neth. 52 D3
Greven Germany 53 H2
Grevena Greece 59 I4
Grevenbicht Neth. 52 F3
Grevenbroich Germany 52 G3
Grevenmacher Lux. 52 G5
Grevesmühlen Germany 47 M4
Grey, Cape Australia 110 B2
Greybull U.S.A. 126 F3
Greybull *r.* U.S.A. 126 F3
Grey Hunter Peak Canada 120 C2
Grey Islands Canada 123 L4
Greylock, Mount U.S.A. 135 I2
Greymouth N.Z. 113 C6
Grey Range *hills* Australia 112 A2
Grey's Plains Australia 109 A6
Greytown S. Africa 101 J5
Grez-Doiceau Belgium 52 E4
Gribanovskiy Rus. Fed. 43 I6
Gridley U.S.A. 128 C2
Griffin U.S.A. 133 C5
Griffith Australia 112 C5
Grigan *i.* N. Mariana Is *see* Agrihan
Grik Malaysia *see* Gerik
Grim, Cape Australia 111 [inset]
Grimari Cent. Afr. Rep. 98 C3
Grimma Germany 53 M3
Grimmen Germany 47 N3
Grimnitzsee *l.* Germany 53 N2
Grimsby U.K. 48 G5
Grímsey *i.* Iceland 44 [inset]
Grimshaw Canada 120 G3
Grímsstaðir Iceland 44 [inset]
Grimstad Norway 45 F7
Grindavík Iceland 44 [inset]
Grindsted Denmark 45 F9
Grind Stone City U.S.A. 134 D1
Grindul Chituc *spit* Romania 59 M2
Grinnell Peninsula Canada 119 I2
Griqualand East *reg.* S. Africa 101 I6
Griqualand West *reg.* S. Africa 100 F5
Griquatown S. Africa 100 F5
Grise Fiord Canada 119 J2
Grishino Ukr. *see* Krasnoarmiys'k
Gris Nez, Cap *c.* France 52 B4
Gritley U.K. 50 G2
Grizzly Bear Mountain *hill* Canada 120 F1
Grmeč *mts* Bos.-Herz. 58 G2
Grobbendonk Belgium 52 E3
Groblersdal S. Africa 101 I3
Groblershoop S. Africa 100 F5
Grodekovo Rus. Fed. 74 C3
Grodno Belarus *see* Hrodna
Groen *watercourse* S. Africa 100 F6
Groen *watercourse* S. Africa 100 C6
Groix, Île de *i.* France 56 C3
Grombalia Tunisia 58 D6
Gronau (Westfalen) Germany 52 H2
Grong Norway 44 H4
Groningen Neth. 52 G1
Groninger Wad *tidal flat* Neth. 52 G1
Grønland *terr.* N. America *see* Greenland
Groom Lake U.S.A. 129 F3
Groot-Aar Pan *salt pan* S. Africa 100 E4
Groot Berg *r.* S. Africa 100 D7
Groot Brakrivier S. Africa 100 F8
Grootdraaidam *dam* S. Africa 101 I4
Grootdrink S. Africa 100 E5
Groote Eylandt *i.* Australia 110 B2
Grootfontein Namibia 99 B5
Groot Karas Berg *plat.* Namibia 100 D4
Groot Letaba *r.* S. Africa 101 J2
Groot Marico S. Africa 101 H3
Groot Swartberge *mts* S. Africa 100 E7
Grootvloer *salt pan* S. Africa 100 E5
Groot Winterberg *mt.* S. Africa 101 H7
Gros Morne National Park Canada 123 K4
Gross Barmen Namibia 100 C2
Große Aue *r.* Germany 53 J2
Große Laaber *r.* Germany 53 M6
Großengottern Germany 53 K3
Großenkneten Germany 53 I2
Großenlüder Germany 53 J4
Großer Arber *mt.* Germany 53 N5
Großer Beerberg *hill* Germany 53 K4
Großer Eyberg *hill* Germany 53 H5
Großer Gleichberg *hill* Germany 53 K4
Großer Kornberg *hill* Germany 53 M4
Großer Osser *mt.* Czech Rep./Germany 53 N5
Großer Rachel *mt.* Germany 47 N6
Grosser Speikkogel *mt.* Austria 47 O7
Grosseto Italy 58 D3
Grossevichi Rus. Fed. 74 E3
Groß-Gerau Germany 53 I5
Großglockner *mt.* Austria 47 N7
Groß Oesingen Germany 53 K2
Großrudestedt Germany 53 L3
Groß Schönebeck Germany 53 N2
Gross Ums Namibia 100 D2
Großvenediger *mt.* Austria 47 N7
Gros Ventre Range *mts* U.S.A. 126 F4
Groswater Bay Canada 123 K3
Groton U.S.A. 130 D2
Grottoes U.S.A. 135 F4
Grou Neth. *see* Grouw
Groundhog *r.* Canada 122 E4
Grouw Neth. 52 F1
Grove U.S.A. 131 E4
Grove City U.S.A. 134 D4
Grove Hill U.S.A. 133 C6
Grove Mountains Antarctica 152 E2
Grover Beach U.S.A. 128 C4
Grovertown U.S.A. 134 B3
Groveton *NH* U.S.A. 135 J1
Groveton *TX* U.S.A. 131 E6
Growler Mountains U.S.A. 129 G5
Groznyy Rus. Fed. 91 G2
Grubišno Polje Croatia 58 G2
Grudovo Bulg. *see* Sredets
Grudziądz Poland 47 Q4
Grünau Namibia 100 D4
Grünberg Poland *see* Zielona Góra
Grundarfjörður Iceland 44 [inset]
Grundy U.S.A. 134 D5
Gruñidora Mex. 131 C7
Grünstadt Germany 53 I5
Gruver U.S.A. 131 C4
Gruzinskaya S.S.R. *country* Asia *see* Georgia
Gryazi Rus. Fed. 43 H5
Gryazovets Rus. Fed. 42 I4
Gryfice Poland 47 O4
Gryfino Poland 47 O4
Gryfów Śląski Poland 47 O5
Grylleфjord Norway 44 J2
Grytviken S. Georgia 144 I8
Gua India 83 F5
Guacanayabo, Golfo de *b.* Cuba 137 I4
Guachochi Mex. 127 G8
Guadajoz *r.* Spain 57 D5
Guadalajara Mex. 136 D4
Guadalajara Spain 57 E3
Guadalcanal *i.* Solomon Is 107 G2
Guadalete *r.* Spain 57 C5
Guadalope *r.* Spain 57 F3
Guadalquivir *r.* Spain 57 C5
Guadalupe Mex. 131 C7
Guadalupe *i.* Mex. 127 D7
Guadalupe *watercourse* Mex. 128 E5
Guadalupe U.S.A. 128 C4
Guadalupe, Sierra de *mts* Spain 57 D4
Guadalupe Aguilera Mex. 131 B7
Guadalupe Bravos Mex. 127 G7
Guadalupe Mountains National Park U.S.A. 127 G7
Guadalupe Peak U.S.A. 127 G7
Guadalupe Victoria *Baja California* Mex. 129 F5
Guadalupe Victoria *Durango* Mex. 131 B7
Guadarrama, Sierra de *mts* Spain 57 D3

▶Guadeloupe *terr.* West Indies 137 L5
French Overseas Department.
North America 9, 116–117

Guadeloupe Passage Caribbean Sea 137 L5
Guadiana *r.* Port./Spain 57 C5
Guadix Spain 57 E5
Guafo, Isla *i.* Chile 144 B6
Guaíba Brazil 145 A5
Guaiçuí Brazil 145 B2
Guaíra Brazil 144 F2
Guajaba, Cayo *i.* Cuba 133 E8
Guaje, Llano de *plain* Mex. 131 C7
Gualala U.S.A. 128 B2
Gualeguay Arg. 144 E4
Gualeguaychu Arg. 144 E4
Gualicho, Salina *salt flat* Arg. 144 C6

▶Guam *terr.* N. Pacific Ocean 69 K4
United States Unincorporated Territory.
Oceania 8, 104–105

Guamblin, Isla *i.* Chile 144 A6
Guampí, Sierra de *mts* Venez. 142 E2
Guamúchil Mex. 127 F8
Guanabacoa Cuba 133 D8
Guanacevi Mex. 131 B7
Guanahacabibes, Península de *pen.* Cuba 133 C8
Guanajay Cuba 133 D8
Guanajuato Mex. 136 D4
Guanambi Brazil 145 C1
Guanare Venez. 142 E2
Guandu China 77 G3
Guane Cuba 137 H4
Guang'an China 76 E2
Guangchang China 77 H3
Guangdong *prov.* China 77 [inset]
Guanghai China 77 G4
Guanghan China 76 E2
Guanghua China *see* Laohekou
Guangming China *see* Xide
Guangming Ding *mt.* China 77 H2
Guangnan China 76 E3
Guangshan China 77 G2
Guangxi *aut. reg.* China *see* Guangxi Zhuangzu Zizhiqu
Guangxi Zhuangzu Zizhiqu *aut. reg.* China 76 F4
Guangyuan China 76 E1
Guangze China 77 H3
Guangzhou China 77 G4
Guanhães Brazil 145 C2
Guanhe Kou *r. mouth* China 77 H1
Guanipa *r.* Venez. 142 F2
Guanling China 76 E3
Guanmian Shan *mts* China 77 F2
Guannan China 77 H1
Guanpo China 77 F1
Guanshui China 74 B4
Guansuo China *see* Guanling
Guantánamo Cuba 137 I4
Guanxian China *see* Dujiangyan
Guanyang China 77 F3
Guanyinqiao China 76 D2
Guanyun China 77 H1
Guapé Brazil 145 B3
Guapí Col. 142 C3
Guaporé *r.* Bol./Brazil 142 E6
Guaporé Brazil 145 A5
Guaqui Bol. 142 E7
Guará *r.* Brazil 145 B1
Guarabira Brazil 143 K5
Guaranda Ecuador 142 C4
Guarapari Brazil 145 C3
Guarapuava Brazil 145 A4
Guararapes Brazil 145 A3
Guaratinguetá Brazil 145 B3
Guaratuba Brazil 145 A4
Guaratuba, Baía de *b.* Brazil 145 A4
Guarda Port. 57 C3
Guardafui, Cape Somalia *see* Gwardafuy, Gees
Guardiagrele Italy 58 F3
Guardo Spain 57 D2
Guárico, del Embalse *resr* Venez. 142 E2
Guarujá Brazil 145 B3
Guasave Mex. 127 F8
Guasdualito Venez. 142 D2

▶Guatemala *country* Central America 136 F5
4th most populous country in Central and North America.
North America 9, 116–117

Guatemala Guat. *see* Guatemala City

▶Guatemala City Guat. 136 F6
Capital of Guatemala.

Guaviare *r.* Col. 142 E3
Guaxupé Brazil 145 B3
Guayaquil Ecuador 142 C4
Guayaquil, Golfo de *g.* Ecuador 142 B4
Guaymas Mex. 127 F8
Guba Eth. 98 D2
Gubakha Rus. Fed. 41 R4
Gubbi India 84 C3
Gubio Nigeria 96 E3
Gubkin Rus. Fed. 43 H6
Gucheng China 77 F1
Gudari India 84 D2
Gudbrandsdalen *valley* Norway 45 F6
Gudermes Rus. Fed. 91 G2
Gudivada India 84 D2
Gudiyattam India 84 C3
Gudur *Andhra Pradesh* India 84 C3
Gudur *Andhra Pradesh* India 84 C3
Gudvangen Norway 45 E6
Gudzhal *r.* Rus. Fed. 74 D2
Guè, Rivière du *r.* Canada 123 H2
Guecho Spain *see* Algorta
Guéckédou Guinea 96 B4
Guelma Alg. 58 B6
Guelmine Morocco 96 B2
Guelph Canada 134 E2
Guémez Mex. 131 D8
Guénange France 52 G5
Guerara Alg. 54 E5
Guérard, Lac *l.* Canada 123 I2
Guercif Morocco 54 D5
Guéret France 56 E3

▶Guernsey *terr.* Channel Is 49 E9
United Kingdom Crown Dependency.
Europe 5, 38–39

Guernsey U.S.A. 126 G4
Guérou Mauritania 96 B3
Guerrah Et-Tarf *salt pan* Alg. 58 B7
Guerrero Negro Mex. 127 E8
Guers, Lac *l.* Canada 123 I2
Gueugnon France 56 G3
Gufeng China *see* Pingnan
Gufu China *see* Xingshan
Gugē *mt.* Eth. 98 D3
Gügerd, Küh-e *mts* Iran 88 D3
Guguan *i.* N. Mariana Is 69 L3
Guhakolak, Tanjung *pt* Indon. 68 D8
Guhe China 77 H2
Güh Küh *mt.* Iran 88 E5
Guhuai China *see* Pingyu
Guiana Basin *sea feature* N. Atlantic Ocean 148 E5
Guiana Highlands *mts* S. America 142 E2
Guichi China *see* Chizhou
Guidan-Roumji Niger 96 D3
Guider Cameroon 97 E4
Guiding China 76 E3
Guidong China 77 G3
Guidonia-Montecelio Italy 58 E4
Guigang China 77 F4
Guiglo Côte d'Ivoire 96 C4
Guignicourt France 52 D5
Guija Moz. 101 K3
Guiji Shan *mts* China 77 I2
Guildford U.K. 49 G7
Guilford U.S.A. 132 G2
Guilherme Capelo Angola *see* Cacongo
Guilin China 77 F3
Guillaume-Delisle, Lac *l.* Canada 122 F2
Guimarães Brazil 143 J4
Guimarães Port. 57 B3
Guinan China 76 D1
▶Guinea *country* Africa 96 B3
Africa 7, 94–95
Guinea, Gulf of Africa 96 D4
Guinea Basin *sea feature* N. Atlantic Ocean 148 H5
▶Guinea-Bissau *country* Africa 96 B3
africa 7, 94–95
Guinea-Conakry *country* Africa *see* Guinea
Guinea Ecuatorial *country* Africa *see* Equatorial Guinea
Guiné-Bissau *country* Africa *see* Guinea-Bissau
Guinée *country* Africa *see* Guinea
Güines Cuba 137 H4
Guînes France 52 B4
Guines, Lac *l.* Canada 123 J3
Guingamp France 56 C2
Guipavas France 56 B2
Guiping China 77 F4
Güira de Melena Cuba 133 D8
Guiratinga Brazil 143 H7
Guiscard France 52 D5
Guise France 52 D5
Guishan China *see* Xinping
Guishun China 76 E3
Guixi *Chongqing* China *see* Dianjiang
Guixi *Jiangxi* China 77 H2
Guiyang *Guizhou* China 76 E3
Guiyang *Hunan* China 77 G3
Guizhou *prov.* China 76 E3
Guizi China 77 F4
Gujarat *state* India 82 C5
Gujar Khan Pak. 89 I3
Gujerat *state* India *see* Gujarat
Gujranwala Pak. 89 I3
Gujrat Pak. 89 I3
Gukovo Rus. Fed. 43 H6
Gulabgarh Jammu and Kashmir 82 D2
Gulbarga India 84 C2
Gulbene Latvia 45 O8
Gul'cha Kyrg. *see* Gülchö
Gülchö Kyrg. 80 D3
Gülcihan Turkey 85 B1
Gülek Boğazı *pass* Turkey 90 D3
Gulfport U.S.A. 131 F6
Gulian China 74 A1
Gulin China 76 E3
Gulistan Uzbek. 80 C3
Guliston Uzbek. *see* Gulistan
Gülitz Germany 53 L1
Guliya Shan *mt.* China 74 A2
Gulja China *see* Yining
Gul Kach Pak. 89 H4
Gul'kevichi Rus. Fed. 91 F1
Gull Lake Canada 121 I5
Gullrock Lake Canada 121 M5
Gullträsk Sweden 44 L3
Güllük Körfezi *b.* Turkey 59 L6
Gülnar Turkey 85 A1
Gulü China *see* Xincai
Gulu Uganda 98 D3
Guluwuru Island Australia 110 B1
Gulyayevskiye Koshki, Ostrova *is* Rus. Fed. 42 L1
Guma China *see* Pishan
Gumal *r.* Pak. 89 H4
Gumare Botswana 99 C5
Gumbaz Pak. 89 H4
Gumbinnen Rus. Fed. *see* Gusev
Gumdag Turkm. 88 D2
Gumel Nigeria 96 D3
Gümgüm Turkey *see* Varto
Gumla India 83 F5
Gummersbach Germany 53 H3
Gümüşhacıköy Turkey 90 D2
Gümüşhane Turkey 91 E2
Guna India 82 D4
Gunan China *see* Qijiang
Guna Terara *mt.* Eth. 86 E7
Gunbar Australia 112 B5
Gunbower Australia 112 B5
Güncang China 76 B2
Gund *r.* Tajik. *see* Gunt
Gundagai Australia 112 D5
Gundelsheim Germany 53 J5
Güney Turkey 59 M5
Güneydoğu Toroslar *plat.* Turkey 90 F3
Gunglilap Myanmar 70 B1
Gungu Dem. Rep. Congo 99 B4
Gunib Rus. Fed. 91 G2
Gunisao *r.* Canada 121 L4
Gunisao Lake Canada 121 L4
Gunnaur India 82 D3
Gunnbjørn Fjeld *nunatak* Greenland 119 P3
Gunnedah Australia 112 E3
Gunning Australia 112 D5
Gunnison U.S.A. 127 G5
Gunnison *r.* U.S.A. 129 I2
Güns Hungary *see* Kőszeg
Gunt *r.* Tajik. 89 H2
Guntakal India 84 C3
Güntersberge Germany 53 K3
Guntur India 84 D2
Gunung Gading National Park Malaysia 71 E7
Gunung Leuser National Park Indon. 71 B7
Gunung Lorentz National Park Indon. 69 J7

Gunung Niyut Reserve nature res. Indon. 71 E7
Gunung Palung National Park Indon. 68 E7
Gunungsitoli Indon. 71 B7
Günyüzü Turkey 90 C3
Gunza Angola see Porto Amboim
Günzburg Germany 47 M6
Gunzenhausen Germany 53 K5
Guo He r. China 77 H1
Guovdageaidnu Norway see Kautokeino
Guozhen China see Baoji
Gupis Jammu and Kashmir 82 C1
Gurbantünggüt Shamo des. China 80 G3
Gurdaspur India 82 C2
Gurdon U.S.A. 131 E5
Gurdzhaani Georgia see Gurjaani
Güre Turkey 59 M5
Gurgan Iran see Gorgān
Gurgaon India 82 D3
Gurgei, Jebel mt. Sudan 97 F3
Gurha India 82 B4
Guri, Embalse de resr Venez. 142 F2
Gurig National Park Australia 108 F2
Gurinhatã Brazil 145 A2
Gurjaani Georgia 91 G2
Gur Khar Iran 89 E4
Guro Moz. 99 D5
Guru China 83 G3
Gürün Turkey 90 E3
Gurupá Brazil 143 H4
Gurupi Brazil 143 I6
Gurupi r. Brazil 143 I4
Gurupi, Serra do hills Brazil 143 I4
Guru Sikhar mt. India 82 C4
Guruzala India 84 C2
Gur'yev Kazakh. see Atyrau
Gur'yevsk Rus. Fed. 45 L9
Gur'yevskaya Oblast' admin. div. Kazakh. see Atyrauskaya Oblast'
Gurz Afgh. 89 G3
Gusau Nigeria 96 D3
Güsen Germany 53 L2
Gusev Rus. Fed. 45 M9
Gushan China 75 A5
Gushgy Turkm. 89 F3
Gushi China 77 G1
Gusino Rus. Fed. 43 F5
Gusinoozersk Rus. Fed. 65 L4
Gus'-Khrustal'nyy Rus. Fed. 42 I5
Guspini Sardinia Italy 58 C5
Gustav Holm, Kap c. Greenland see Tasiilap Karra
Gustavo Sotelo Mex. 127 E7
Güsten Germany 53 L3
Gustine U.S.A. 128 C3
Güstrow Germany 47 N4
Güterfelde Germany 53 N2
Gütersloh Germany 53 I3
Guthrie AZ U.S.A. 129 I5
Guthrie KY U.S.A. 134 B5
Guthrie OK U.S.A. 131 D5
Guthrie TX U.S.A. 131 C5
Gutian Fujian China 77 H3
Gutian Fujian China 77 H3
Gutian Shuiku resr China 77 H3
Guting China see Yutai
Gutsuo China 83 F3
Guwahati India 83 G4
Guwēr Iraq 91 F3
Guwlumayak Turkm. see Kuuli-Mayak
Guxhagen Germany 53 J3
Guxian China 77 G3
▶Guyana country S. America 143 G2
South America 9, 140–141
Guyane Française terr. S. America see French Guiana
Guyang Hunan China see Guzhang
Guyang Nei Mongol China 73 K4
Guyenne reg. France 56 D4
Guy Fawkes River National Park Australia 112 F3
Guyi China see Sanjiang
Guymon U.S.A. 131 C4
Guyra Australia 112 E3
Guysborough Canada 123 J5
Guyuan Hebei China 73 L4
Guyuan Ningxia China 72 J5
Guzar Uzbek. 89 G2
Güzeloluk Turkey 85 B1
Güzelyurt Cyprus see Morfou
Guzhang China 77 F2
Guzhen China 77 H1
Guzhou China see Rongjiang
Guzmán Mex. 127 G7
Guzmán, Lago de l. Mex. 127 G7
Gvardeysk Rus. Fed. 45 L9
Gvasyugi Rus. Fed. 74 E3
Gwa Myanmar 70 A3
Gwabegar Australia 112 D3
Gwadar West Bay Pak. 89 F5
Gwaii Haanas National Park Reserve Canada 120 D4
Gwalior India 82 D4
Gwanda Zimbabwe 99 C6
Gwane Dem. Rep. Congo 98 C3
Gwardafuy, Gees c. Somalia 98 F2
Gwash Pak. 89 G4
Gwatar Bay Pak. 89 F5
Gwedaukkon Myanmar 70 A1
Gweebarra Bay Rep. of Ireland 51 D3
Gweedore Rep. of Ireland 51 D2
Gwelo Zimbabwe see Gweru
Gweru Zimbabwe 99 C5
Gweta Botswana 99 C6
Gwinner U.S.A. 130 D2
Gwoza Nigeria 96 E3
Gwydir r. Australia 112 D2
Gyablung China 76 B2
Gyaca China 76 B2
Gyagartang China 76 D1
Gya'gya China see Saga
Gyaijêpozhanggê China see Zhidoi
Gyai Qu r. China 76 B2
Gyairong China 76 C1
Gyaisi China see Jiulong
Gyali i. Greece 59 L6
Gyamotang China see Dêngqên
Gyamug China 82 E2
Gyandzha Azer. see Gäncä
Gyangkar China see Dinngyê
Gyangnyi Caka salt l. China 83 F2
Gyangrang China 83 F3
Gyangtse China see Gyangzê
Gyangzê China 83 G3
Gyaring China 76 C1
Gyaring Co l. China 83 G3
Gyaring Hu l. China 76 C1
Gyarishing India 76 B2
Gyaros i. Greece 59 K6
Gyarubtang China 76 B2
Gydan, Khrebet mts Rus. Fed. see Kolymskiy, Khrebet
Gydan Peninsula Rus. Fed. 64 I2
Gydanskiy Poluostrov pen. Rus. Fed. see Gydan Peninsula
Gyêgu China see Yushu
Gyêmdong China 76 B2
Gyigang China see Zayü
Gyimda China 76 B2
Gyirong Xizang China 83 F3
Gyirong Xizang China 83 F3
Gyiza China 76 B1
Gyldenløve Fjord inlet Greenland see Umiiviip Kangertiva
Gympie Australia 111 F5
Gyobingauk Myanmar 70 A3
Gyöngyös Hungary 47 Q7
Győr Hungary 58 G1
Gypsum Point Canada 120 H2
Gypsumville Canada 121 L5
Gyrfalcon Islands Canada 123 H2
Gytheio Greece 59 J6
Gyula Hungary 59 I1
Gyulafehérvár Romania see Alba Iulia
Gyümai China see Darlag
Gyumri Armenia 91 F2
Gyzylarbat Turkm. 88 E2
Gyzylbaydak Turkm. see Krasnoye Znamya
Gyzyletrek Turkm. 88 D2
Gzhatsk Rus. Fed. see Gagarin

H

Ha Bhutan 83 G4
Haa-Alif Atoll Maldives see Ihavandhippolhu Atoll
Ha'apai Group is Tonga 107 I3
Haapajärvi Fin. 44 N5
Haapavesi Fin. 44 N4
Haapsalu Estonia 45 M7
Ha 'Arava watercourse Israel/Jordan see 'Arabah, Wādī al
Ha'Arava, Naḥal watercourse Israel/Jordan see Jayb, Wādī al
Haarlem Neth. 52 E2
Haarlem S. Africa 100 F7
Haarstrang ridge Germany 53 H3
Hab r. Pak. 89 G5
Habahe China 80 G2
Habana Cuba see Havana
Habarane Sri Lanka 84 D4
Habarōn well Saudi Arabia 88 C6
Habaswein Kenya 98 D3
Habay Canada 120 G3
Habbān Yemen 86 G7
Ḥabbānīyah, Hawr al l. Iraq 91 F4
Hab Chauki Pak. 89 G5
Habiganj Bangl. 83 G5
Habra India 83 G5
Hachijō-jima i. Japan 75 E6
Hachinohe Japan 74 F4
Hachita U.S.A. 129 I6
Hacıköy Turkey see Çekerek
Hack, Mount Australia 111 B6
Hackberry U.S.A. 129 G4
Hackensack U.S.A. 135 H3
Ha Côi Vietnam 70 D2
Hacufera Moz. 99 D6
Hadabat al Budū plain Saudi Arabia 88 C6
Haḍabat al Jilf al Kabīr plat. Egypt see Jilf al Kabīr, Haḍabat al
Hadagalli India 84 B3
Hada Mountains Afgh. 89 G4
Hadapu China 76 E1
Hadayang China 74 B2
Ḥadd, Ra's al pt Oman 89 E6
Haddington U.K. 50 G5
Haddumati Atoll Maldives see Hadhdhunmathi Atoll
Haddunmahti Atoll Maldives see Hadhdhunmathi Atoll
Hadejia Nigeria 96 E3
Ḥadera Israel 85 B3
Ḥadera r. Israel 85 B3
Haderslev Denmark 45 F9
Hadhdhunmathi Atoll Maldives 81 D11
Hadhramaut reg. Yemen see Ḥaḍramawt
Hādī, Jabal al mts Jordan 85 C4
Hadım Turkey 90 D3
Hadleigh U.K. 49 H6
Hadong S. Korea 75 B6
Ḥaḍraj, Wādī watercourse Saudi Arabia 85 C4
Ḥaḍramawt reg. Yemen 98 E2
Hadranum Sicily Italy see Adrano
Hadrian's Wall tourist site U.K. 48 E3
Hadrumetum Tunisia see Sousse
Hadsund Denmark 45 G8
Hadyach Ukr. 43 G6
Haeju N. Korea 75 B5
Haeju-man b. N. Korea 75 B5
Haenam S. Korea 75 B6
Haenertsburg S. Africa 101 I2
Ha'erbin China see Harbin
Ḥafar al 'Atk well Saudi Arabia 88 B5
Ḥafar al Bāṭin Saudi Arabia 86 G4
Hafford Canada 121 J4
Hafik Turkey 90 E3
Ḥafīrah, Qā' al salt pan Jordan 85 C4
Hafirat Nasah Saudi Arabia 88 B5
Hafizabad Pak. 89 I3
Haflong India 83 H4
Hafnarfjörður Iceland 44 [inset]
Hafren r. U.K. see Severn
Haft Gel Iran 88 C4
Hafursfjörður b. Iceland 44 [inset]
Haga Myanmar see Haka
Hagar Nish Plateau Eritrea 86 E6
▶Hagåtña Guam 69 K4
Capital of Guam.
Hagelberg hill Germany 53 M2
Hagen Germany 53 H3
Hagenow Germany 53 L1
Hagerhill U.S.A. 134 D5
Hagerstown U.S.A. 135 G4
Hagfors Sweden 45 H6
Haggin, Mount U.S.A. 126 E3
Hagi Japan 75 C6
Ha Giang Vietnam 70 D2
Ha Giao, Sông r. Vietnam 71 E4
Hagley U.K. 49 E6
Hag's Head hd Rep. of Ireland 51 C5
Hague U.S.A. 135 I2
Haguenau France 53 H6
Hahajima-rettō is Japan 75 F8
Hai Tanz. 97 G5
Hai'an China 77 F4
Haib watercourse Namibia 100 C5
Haibowan China see Wuhai
Haicheng Guangdong China see Haifeng
Haicheng Liaoning China 73 M4
Hai Dương Vietnam 70 D2
Haifa Israel 85 B3
Haifa, Bay of Israel 85 B3
Haifeng China 77 G4
Haig Australia 109 D7
Haiger Germany 53 I4
Haikakan country Asia see Armenia
Haikang China see Leizhou
Haikou China 77 F4
Ḥā'il Saudi Arabia 91 F6
Ḥā'il, Wādī watercourse Saudi Arabia 91 F6
Hailar China 73 L3
Hailey U.S.A. 126 E4
Haileybury Canada 122 F5
Hailin China 74 C3
Hailong China see Meihekou
Hailsham U.K. 49 H8
Hailun China 74 B3
Hailuoto Fin. 44 N4
Hainan i. China 77 F5
Hainan prov. China 77 F5
Hai-nang Myanmar 70 B2
Hainan Strait China 77 F5
Hainaut reg. France 52 D4
Haines U.S.A. 120 C3
Haines Junction Canada 120 B2
Haines Road Canada/U.S.A. 120 B2
Hainichen Germany 53 N4
Hainleite ridge Germany 53 K3
Hai Phong Vietnam 70 D2
Haiphong Vietnam see Hai Phong
Haiqing China 74 D3
Haitan Dao i. China 77 H3
▶Haiti country West Indies 137 J5
North America 9, 116–117
Haitou China 77 F5
Haiwee Reservoir U.S.A. 128 E3
Haiya Sudan 86 E6
Haiyan Qinghai China 72 I5
Haiyan Zhejiang China 77 I2
Haiyang China see Xiuning
Haiyang Dao i. China 75 A5
Haiyou China see Sanmen
Haizhou Wan b. China 77 H1
Hāj Ali Qoli, Kavīr-e salt l. Iran 88 D3
Hajdúböszörmény Hungary 59 I1
Hajeb El Ayoun Tunisia 58 C7
Ḥajhir mt. Yemen 87 H7
Haji Pak. 89 G4
Hajipur India 83 F4
Hajir reg. Saudi Arabia 88 C5
Ḥajjah Yemen 86 F6
Ḥājjīābād Fārs Iran 88 D4
Ḥājjīābād Hormozgan Iran 88 D4
Ḥajjīābād Iran 88 D3
Haka Myanmar 70 A2
Hakha Myanmar see Haka
Hakkârı Turkey 91 F3
Hakkas Sweden 44 L3
Hakken-zan mt. Japan 75 D6
Hako-dake mt. Japan 74 F3
Hakodate Japan 74 F4
Hakos Mountains Namibia 100 C2
Hakseen Pan salt pan S. Africa 100 E4
Hakui Japan 75 E5
Haku-san vol. Japan 75 E5
Hal Belgium see Halle
Hala Pak. 89 H5
Ḥalab Syria see Aleppo
Halabja Iraq 91 G4
Halaç Turkm. see Khalach
Halaha China 74 B3
Halahai China 74 B3
Halaib Sudan 86 E5
▶Halaib Triangle terr. Egypt/Sudan 86 E5
Disputed territory (Egypt/Sudan) administered by Sudan.
Halâl, Gebel hill Egypt see Hilāl, Jabal
Ḥalāniyāt, Juzur al is Oman 87 I6
Halawa HI U.S.A. 127 [inset]
Halba Lebanon 85 C2
Halban Mongolia 80 I2
Halberstadt Germany 53 L3
Halcon, Mount Phil. 69 G4
Halden Norway 45 G7
Haldensleben Germany 53 L2
Haldwani India 82 D3
Hale watercourse Australia 110 A5
Hale U.S.A. 134 D1
Hāleh Iran 88 D5
Haleparki Deresi r. Syria/Turkey see Quwayq, Nahr
Halesowen U.K. 49 E6
Halesworth U.K. 49 I6
Half Assini Ghana 96 C4
Halfmoon Bay N.Z. 113 B8
Halfway r. Canada 120 F3
Halfway Rep. of Ireland 51 D6
Halfweg Neth. 52 E2
Halhgol Mongolia 73 L3
Halia India 83 E4
Ḥalībīyah Syria 91 E4
Haliburton Canada 135 F1
Haliburton Highlands hills Canada 135 F1
Halicarnassus Turkey see Bodrum
▶Halifax Canada 123 J5
Provincial capital of Nova Scotia.
Halifax U.K. 48 F5
Halifax NC U.S.A. 132 E4
Halifax VA U.S.A. 135 F5
Halifax, Mount Australia 110 D3
Ḥalīmah mt. Lebanon/Syria 85 C2
Halkirk U.K. 50 F2
Hall U.S.A. 134 C5
Hälla Sweden 44 J5
Halladale r. U.K. 50 F2
Halla-san National Park S. Korea 75 B6
Hall Beach Canada 119 J3
Halle Belgium 52 E4
Halle Neth. 52 G3
Halle (Saale) Germany 53 L3
Halleck U.S.A. 129 F1
Hällefors Sweden 45 I7
Hallein Austria 47 N7
Halle-Neustadt Germany 53 L3
Hallett, Cape Antarctica 152 H2
Hallettsville U.S.A. 131 D6
Halley research station Antarctica 152 B1
Hallgreen, Mount Antarctica 148 B2
Halliday U.S.A. 130 C2
Halliday Lake Canada 121 I2
Hall Islands Micronesia 150 G5
Hällnäs Sweden 44 K4
Hallock U.S.A. 130 D1
Hall Peninsula Canada 119 L3
Hallsberg Sweden 45 I7
Halls Creek Australia 108 D4
Halls Gap U.S.A. 134 C5
Halls Lake Canada 135 F1
Hallstead U.S.A. 135 H3
Halluin Belgium 52 D4
Hallviken Sweden 44 I5
Halmahera i. Indon. 69 H6
Halmahera, Laut sea Indon. 69 H7
Halmahera Sea Indon. see Halmahera, Laut
Halmstad Sweden 45 H8
Hals Denmark 45 G8
Hälsingborg Sweden see Helsingborg
Halsua Fin. 44 N5
Haltern Germany 53 H3
Haltwhistle U.K. 48 E4
Ḥālūl i. Qatar 88 D5
Ḥalvān Iran 88 E3
Halver Germany 53 H3
Haly, Mount hill Australia 112 E1
Ham France 52 D5
Hamada Japan 75 D6
Ḥamâda El Ḥaricha des. Mali 96 C2
Hamadān Iran 88 C3
Ḥamādat Murzuq plat. Libya 98 B1
Ḥamāh Syria 85 C2
Hamam Turkey 85 C1
Hamamatsu Japan 75 E6
Hamar Norway 45 G6
Hamarøy Norway 44 I2
Ḥamâṭa, Gebel mt. Egypt see Ḥamāṭah, Jabal
Ḥamāṭah, Jabal mt. Egypt 86 D5
Hamatonbetsu Japan 74 F3
Hambantota Sri Lanka 84 D5
Hambergen Germany 53 I1
Hambleton Hills U.K. 48 F4
Hamburg Germany 53 J1
Hamburg land Germany 53 J1
Hamburg S. Africa 101 H7
Hamburg AR U.S.A. 131 F5
Hamburg NY U.S.A. 135 F2
Hamburgisches Wattenmeer, Nationalpark nat. park Germany 47 L4
Ḥamḍ, Wādī al watercourse Saudi Arabia 86 E4
Hamden U.S.A. 135 I3
Hämeenlinna Fin. 45 N6
HaMelaḥ, Yam salt l. Asia see Dead Sea
Hamelin Australia 109 A6
Hameln Germany 53 J2
Hamersley Lakes salt flat Australia 109 B7
Hamersley Range mts Australia 108 B5
Hamhŭng N. Korea 75 B5
Hami China 80 H3
Hamid Sudan 86 D5
Hamilton Qld Australia 110 C4
Hamilton S.A. Australia 111 A5
Hamilton Vic. Australia 111 C8
Hamilton watercourse Qld Australia 110 B4
Hamilton watercourse S.A. Australia 111 A5
▶Hamilton Bermuda 137 L2
Capital of Bermuda.
Hamilton Canada 134 F2
Hamilton r. Canada see Churchill
Hamilton N.Z. 113 E3
Hamilton U.K. 50 E5
Hamilton AL U.S.A. 133 C5
Hamilton CO U.S.A. 129 J1
Hamilton MI U.S.A. 134 B2
Hamilton MT U.S.A. 126 E3
Hamilton NY U.S.A. 135 H2
Hamilton OH U.S.A. 134 C4
Hamilton TX U.S.A. 131 D6
Hamilton, Mount CA U.S.A. 128 C3
Hamilton, Mount NV U.S.A. 129 F2
Hamilton City U.S.A. 128 B2
Hamilton Inlet Canada 123 K3
Hamilton Mountain hill U.S.A. 135 H2
Ḥamīm, Wādī al watercourse Libya 55 I5
Hamina Fin. 45 O6
Hamirpur Himachal Pradesh India 82 D3
Hamirpur Uttar Pradesh India 82 E4
Hamitabat Turkey see Isparta
Hamju N. Korea 75 B5
Hamlet U.S.A. 133 E5
Hamlin TX U.S.A. 131 C5
Hamlin WV U.S.A. 134 D4
Hamm Germany 53 H3
Hammada du Drâa plat. Alg. 54 C6
Ḥammām al 'Alīl Iraq 91 F3
Hammam Boughrara Alg. 57 F6
Hammamet Tunisia 58 D6
Hammamet, Golfe de g. Tunisia 58 D6
Ḥammār, Hawr al imp. l. Iraq 91 G5
Hammarstrand Sweden 44 J5
Hammelburg Germany 53 J4
Hammerdal Sweden 44 I5
Hammerfest Norway 44 M1
Hamminkeln Germany 52 G3
Hammond U.S.A. 134 B3
Hammone, Lac l. Canada 123 K4
Hammonton U.S.A. 135 H4
Ham Ninh Vietnam 71 D5
Hamoir Belgium 52 F4
Hampden Sydney U.S.A. 135 F5
Hampshire Downs hills U.K. 49 F7
Hampton AR U.S.A. 131 E5
Hampton IA U.S.A. 130 E3
Hampton NH U.S.A. 135 J2
Hampton SC U.S.A. 133 D5
Hampton VA U.S.A. 135 G5
Hampton Tableland reg. Australia 109 D8
Ḥamrā, Birkat al well Saudi Arabia 91 F5
Hamra, Vâdii watercourse Syria/Turkey see Ḥimār, Wādī al
Ḥamrā Jūdah plat. Saudi Arabia 88 C5
Hamrat esh Sheikh Sudan 86 C7
Ham Tân Vietnam 71 D5
Hamta Pass India 82 D2
Hāmūn-e Jaz Mūrīān salt marsh Iran 88 E5
Hāmūn-e Lowrah dry lake Afgh./Pak. see Hamun-i-Lora
Hāmūn Helmand salt flat Afgh./Iran 89 F4
Hamun-i-Lora dry lake Afgh./Pak. 89 G4
Hamun-i-Mashkel salt flat Pak. 89 F4
Hāmūn Pu marsh Afgh. 89 F4
Hamunt Kūh hill Iran 89 F5
Hamur Turkey 91 F3
Hamwic U.K. see Southampton
Hana HI U.S.A. 127 [inset]
Hanábana r. Cuba 133 D8
Hanahai watercourse Botswana/Namibia 100 F2
Ḥanak Saudi Arabia 86 E4
Hanakpınar Turkey see Çınar
Hanalei HI U.S.A. 127 [inset]
Hanamaki Japan 75 F5
Hanang mt. Tanz. 99 D4
Hanau Germany 53 I4
Hanbin China see Ankang
Hanchang China see Pingjiang
Hancheng China 77 F1
Hanchuan China 77 G2
Hancock MD U.S.A. 135 F4
Hancock NY U.S.A. 135 H3
Handa Island U.K. 50 D2
Handan China 73 K5
Handeni Tanz. 99 D4
HaNegev des. Israel see Negev
Haneqarot watercourse Israel 85 B4
Hanfeng China see Kaixian
Hanford U.S.A. 128 D3
Hangan Myanmar 70 B4
Hangayn Nuruu mts Mongolia 80 I2
Hangchow China see Hangzhou
Hangchuan China see Guangze
Hangö Fin. see Hanko
Hangu China 73 L5
Hanguang China 77 G3
Hangya China 80 I4
Hangzhou China 77 I2
Hangzhou Wan b. China 77 I2
Hani Turkey 91 F3
Hanish Kabir i. Yemen see Al Ḥanīsh al Kabīr
Hanjia China see Pengshui
Hankensbüttel Germany 53 K2
Hankey S. Africa 100 G7
Hanko Fin. 45 M7
Hanksville U.S.A. 129 H2
Hanle Jammu and Kashmir 82 D2
Hanley Canada 121 J5
Hann, Mount hill Australia 108 D3
Hanna Canada 121 I5
Hannagan Meadow U.S.A. 129 I5
Hannah Bay Canada 122 E4
Hannibal MO U.S.A. 130 F4
Hannibal NY U.S.A. 135 G2
Hannover Germany 53 J2
Hannoversch Münden Germany 53 J3
Hann Range mts Australia 109 F5
Hannut Belgium 52 F4
Hanöbukten b. Sweden 45 I9
▶Ha Nôi Vietnam 70 D2
Capital of Vietnam.
Hanoi Vietnam see Ha Nôi
Hanover Canada 134 E1
Hanover Germany see Hannover
Hanover S. Africa 100 G6
Hanover NH U.S.A. 135 I2
Hanover PA U.S.A. 135 G4
Hanover VA U.S.A. 135 G5
Hansen Mountains Antarctica 152 D2
Hanshou China 77 F2
Han Shui r. China 77 G2
Hansi India 82 D3
Hansnes Norway 44 K2
Hanstholm Denmark 45 F8
Han-sur-Nied France 52 G6
Hantsavichy Belarus 45 O10
Hanumangarh India 82 C3
Hanwwod Australia 112 C5
Hanyang China see Caidian
Hanyang Feng mt. China 77 G2
Hanyin China 77 F1
Hanzhong China 76 E1
Hao atoll Fr. Polynesia 151 K7
Haora India 83 G5
Haparanda Sweden 44 N4
Happy Jack U.S.A. 129 H4
Happy Valley - Goose Bay Canada 123 J3
Ḥaql Saudi Arabia 85 B5
Haqshah well Saudi Arabia 88 C6
Ḥaraḍ well Saudi Arabia 88 C5
Ḥarad, Jabal al mt. Jordan 85 B5
Haraḍh Saudi Arabia 86 G5
Haradok Belarus 43 F5
Haramachi Japan 75 F5
Haramukh mt. Jammu and Kashmir 82 C2
Haran Turkey see Harran
Harappa Road Pak. 89 I4
Harar Eth. see Hārer
▶Harare Zimbabwe 99 D5
Capital of Zimbabwe.
Ḥarāsīs, Jiddat al des. Oman 87 I6
Harāt Iran 88 D4
Har-Ayrag Mongolia 73 J3
Haraze-Mangueigne Chad 97 F3
Harb, Jabal mt. Saudi Arabia 90 D6
Harbin China 74 B3
Harboi Hills Pak. 89 G4
Harbor Beach U.S.A. 134 D2
Harchoka India 83 E5
Harda India 82 D5
Harda Khas India see Harda
Hardangerfjorden sea chan. Norway 45 D7
Hardangervidda plat. Norway 45 E6
Hardangervidda Nasjonalpark nat. park Norway 45 E6
Hardap admin. reg. Namibia 100 C3
Hardap nature res. Namibia 100 C3
Hardap Dam Namibia 100 C3
Hardenberg Neth. 52 G2
Harderwijk Neth. 52 F2
Hardeveld mts S. Africa 100 D6
Hardheim Germany 53 J5
Hardin U.S.A. 126 G3
Harding S. Africa 101 I6
Harding Range hills Australia 109 B6
Hardinsburg IN U.S.A. 134 B4
Hardinsburg KY U.S.A. 134 B5
Hardoi India 82 E4
Hardwar India see Haridwar
Hardwick U.S.A. 135 I1
Hardy U.S.A. 131 F4
Hardy Reservoir U.S.A. 134 C2
Hare Bay Canada 123 L4
Ḥareidīn, Wâdi watercourse Egypt see Ḥuraydīn, Wādī
Harelbeke Belgium 52 D4
Haren Neth. 52 G1
Haren (Ems) Germany 53 H2
Hārer Eth. 98 E3
Harf el Mreffi mt. Lebanon 85 B3
Hargeisa Somalia see Hargeysa
Hargele Eth. 98 E3
Hargeysa Somalia 98 E3
Harghita-Mădăraş, Vârful mt. Romania 59 K1
Harhorin Mongolia 80 J2
Har Hu l. China 80 I4
Haridwar India 82 D3
Harif, Har mt. Israel 85 B4
Harihar India 84 B3
Harihari N.Z. 113 C6
Hariharpur India 84 B3
Ḥārim Syria 85 C1
Harīm, Jabal al mt. Oman 88 E5
Harima-nada b. Japan 75 D6
Haringhat r. Bangl. 83 G5
Haringvliet est. Neth. 52 E3
Harīr, Wādī adh r. Syria 85 C3
Hari Rūd r. Afgh./Iran 89 F2
Harjavalta Fin. 45 M6
Harlan IA U.S.A. 130 E3
Harlan KY U.S.A. 134 D5
Harlan County Lake U.S.A. 130 D3
Harlech U.K. 49 C6
Harleston U.K. 49 I6
Harlingen Neth. 52 F1
Harlingen U.S.A. 131 D7
Harlow U.K. 49 H7
Harlowton U.S.A. 126 F3
Harly France 52 D5
Harman U.S.A. 134 F4
Harmancık Turkey 59 M5
Harmony U.S.A. 135 K1
Harmsdorf Germany 53 K1
Harnai India 84 B2
Harnai Pak. 89 G4
Harnes France 52 C4
Harney Basin U.S.A. 126 D4
Harney Lake U.S.A. 126 D4
Härnösand Sweden 44 J5
Harns Neth. see Harlingen
Har Nuur l. Mongolia 80 H2
Haroldswick U.K. 50 [inset]
Harper Liberia 96 C4
Harper U.S.A. 131 D4
Harper, Mount U.S.A. 118 D3
Harper Creek r. Canada 120 H3
Harper Lake U.S.A. 128 E4
Harp Lake Canada 123 J3
Harpstedt Germany 53 I2
Harquahala Mountains U.S.A. 127 E6
Harrai India 82 D5
Harran Turkey 85 D1
Harrand Pak. 89 H4
Harricanaw r. Canada 122 F4
Harrington Australia 112 F3
Harrington U.S.A. 135 H4
Harris, Lake salt flat Australia 111 A6
Harris, Mount Australia 109 E6
Harris, Sound of sea chan. U.K. 50 B3
Harrisburg AR U.S.A. 131 F5
Harrisburg IL U.S.A. 130 F4
Harrisburg NE U.S.A. 130 C3
▶Harrisburg PA U.S.A. 135 G3
State capital of Pennsylvania.
Harrismith Australia 109 B8
Harrison AR U.S.A. 131 E4
Harrison MI U.S.A. 134 C1
Harrison NE U.S.A. 130 C3
Harrison OH U.S.A. 134 C4
Harrison, Cape Canada 123 K3
Harrison Bay U.S.A. 118 C2
Harrisonburg LA U.S.A. 131 F6
Harrisonburg VA U.S.A. 135 F4
Harrisonville U.S.A. 130 E4
Harriston Canada 134 E2
Harrisville MI U.S.A. 134 D1
Harrisville NY U.S.A. 135 H1
Harrisville PA U.S.A. 134 E3
Harrisville WV U.S.A. 134 E4
Harrodsburg IN U.S.A. 134 B4
Harrodsburg KY U.S.A. 134 C5
Harrodsville N.Z. see Otorohanga
Harrogate U.K. 48 F5
Harrowsmith Canada 135 G1

Harry S. Truman Reservoir U.S.A. 130 E4
Har Sai Shan *mt.* China 76 C1
Harsefeld Germany 53 J1
Harsīn Iran 88 B3
Harşit *r.* Turkey 90 E2
Hârşova Romania 59 L2
Harstad Norway 44 J2
Harsud India 82 D5
Harsum Germany 53 J2
Hart *r.* Canada 118 E3
Hart U.S.A. 134 B2
Hartbees *watercourse* S. Africa 100 E5
Hartberg Austria 47 O7
Harteigan *mt.* Norway 45 E6
Harter Fell *hill* U.K. 48 E4

▶**Hartford** *CT* U.S.A. 135 I3
State capital of Connecticut.

Hartford *KY* U.S.A. 134 B5
Hartford *MI* U.S.A. 134 B2
Hartford City U.S.A. 134 C3
Hartland U.K. 49 C8
Hartland U.S.A. 135 K1
Hartland Point U.K. 49 C7
Hartlepool U.K. 48 F4
Hartley U.S.A. 131 C5
Hartley Zimbabwe *see* **Chegutu**
Hartley Bay Canada 120 D4
Hartola Fin. 45 O6
Harts *r.* S. Africa 101 G5
Härtsfeld *hills* Germany 53 K6
Harts Range *mts* Australia 109 F5
Hartsville U.S.A. 134 B5
Hartswater S. Africa 100 G4
Hartville U.S.A. 131 E4
Hartwell U.S.A. 133 D5
Har Us Nuur *l.* Mongolia 80 H2
Harūz-e Bālā Iran 88 E4
Harvard, Mount U.S.A. 126 G5
Harvey Australia 109 A8
Harvey U.S.A. 130 C2
Harvey Mountain U.S.A. 128 C1
Harwich U.K. 49 I7
Haryana *state* India 82 D3
Harz *hills* Germany 47 M5
Har Zin Israel 85 B4
Ḩaşāh, Wādī al *watercourse* Jordan 85 B4
Ḩaşāh, Wādī al *watercourse* Jordan/Saudi Arabia 85 C4
Hasalbag China 89 J2
Ḩasanah, Wādī *watercourse* Egypt 85 A4
Hasan Dağı *mts* Turkey 90 D3
Hasan Guli Turkm. *see* **Esenguly**
Hasankeyf Turkey 91 F3
Hasan Küleh Afgh. 89 F3
Hasanur India 84 C4
Hasbaïya Lebanon 85 B3
Hasbaya Lebanon *see* **Hasbaïya**
Hase *r.* Germany 53 H2
Haselünne Germany 53 H2
Hashak Iran 89 F5
HaSharon *plain* Israel 85 B3
Hashtgerd Iran 88 C3
Hashtpar Iran 88 C2
Hashtrud Iran 88 B2
Haskell U.S.A. 131 D5
Haslemere U.K. 49 G7
Hăşmaşul Mare *mt.* Romania 55 K1
Ḩaşş, Jabal al *hills* Syria 85 C1
Hassan India 84 C3
Hassayampa *watercourse* U.S.A. 129 G5
Haßberge *hills* Germany 53 K4
Hasselt Belgium 52 F4
Hasselt Neth. 52 G2
Hassi Bel Guebbour Alg. 96 D2
Hassi Messaoud Alg. 54 F5
Hässleholm Sweden 45 H8
Hastings Australia 112 B7
Hastings *r.* Australia 112 F3
Hastings Canada 135 G1
Hastings N.Z. 113 F4
Hastings U.K. 49 H8
Hastings *MI* U.S.A. 134 C2
Hastings *MN* U.S.A. 130 E2
Hastings *NE* U.S.A. 130 D3
Hata India 83 E4
Hatay Turkey *see* **Antakya**
Hatay *prov.* Turkey 85 C1
Hatch U.S.A. 129 G3
Hatches Creek Australia 110 A4
Hatchet Lake Canada 121 K3
Hatfield Australia 112 A4
Hatfield U.K. 48 G5
Hatgal Mongolia 80 J1
Hath India 84 D1
Hat Head National Park Australia 112 F3
Hathras India 82 D4
Ha Tiên Vietnam 71 D5
Ha Tinh Vietnam 70 D3
Hatisar Bhutan *see* **Gelephu**
Hatod India 82 C5
Hato Hud East Timor *see* **Hatudo**
Hatra Iraq 91 F4
Hattah Australia 111 C7
Hatteras, Cape U.S.A. 133 F5
Hatteras Abyssal Plain *sea feature* S. Atlantic Ocean 148 D4
Hattfjelldal Norway 44 H4
Hattiesburg U.S.A. 131 F6
Hattingen Germany 53 H3
Hattras Passage Myanmar 71 B4
Hatudo East Timor 108 D2
Hat Yai Thai. 71 C6
Hau Bon Vietnam *see* **Cheo Reo**
Haubstadt U.S.A. 134 B4
Haud *reg.* Eth. 98 E3
Hauge Norway 45 E7
Haugesund Norway 45 D7
Haukeligrend Norway 45 E7
Haukipudas Fin. 44 N4
Haukivesi *l.* Fin. 44 P5
Haultain *r.* Canada 121 J4
Hauraki Gulf N.Z. 113 E3
Haut Atlas *mts* Morocco 54 C5
Haute-Normandie *admin. reg.* France 52 B5
Haute-Volta *country* Africa *see* **Burkina**
Haut-Folin *hill* France 56 G3
Hauts Plateaux Alg. 54 D5

▶**Havana** Cuba 137 H4
Capital of Cuba.

Havana U.S.A. 130 F3
Havant U.K. 49 G8
Havasu, Lake U.S.A. 129 F4
Havel *r.* Germany 53 L2
Havelange Belgium 52 F4
Havelberg Germany 53 M2
Havelock Canada 135 G1
Havelock N.Z. 113 D5
Havelock Swaziland *see* **Bulembu**
Havelock U.S.A. 133 E5
Havelock Falls Australia 108 F3
Havelock Island India 71 A5
Havelock North N.Z. 113 F4
Haverfordwest U.K. 49 C7
Haverhill U.S.A. 135 J2
Haveri India 84 B3
Haversin Belgium 52 F4
Havixbeck Germany 53 H3
Havlíčkův Brod Czech Rep. 47 O6
Havøysund Norway 44 N1
Havran Turkey 59 L5
Havre U.S.A. 126 F2
Havre Aubert, Île du *i.* Canada 123 J5
Havre Rock *i.* Kermadec Is 107 I5
Havre-St-Pierre Canada 123 J4
Havza Turkey 90 D2
Hawaii *i. HI* U.S.A. 127 [inset]
Hawaiian Islands N. Pacific Ocean 150 I4
Hawaiian Ridge *sea feature* N. Pacific Ocean 150 I4
Hawaii Volcanoes National Park *HI* U.S.A. 127 [inset]
Ḩawallī Kuwait 88 C4
Hawar *i.* Bahrain *see* **Ḩuwār**
Hawarden U.K. 48 D5
Hawea, Lake N.Z. 113 B7
Hawera N.Z. 113 E4
Hawes U.K. 48 E4
Hawesville U.S.A. 134 B5
Hawi *HI* U.S.A. 127 [inset]
Hawick U.K. 50 G5
Ḩawīzah, Hawr al *imp. l.* Iraq 87 G5
Hawkdun Range *mts* N.Z. 113 B7
Hawke Bay N.Z. 113 F4
Hawkes Bay Canada 123 K4
Hawkins Peak U.S.A. 129 G3
Hawlēr Iraq *see* **Arbīl**
Hawley U.S.A. 135 H3
Hawng Luk Myanmar 70 B2
Ḩawrān, Wādī *watercourse* Iraq 91 F4
Ḩawshah, Jibāl al *mts* Saudi Arabia 88 B6
Hawston S. Africa 100 D8
Hawthorne U.S.A. 128 D2
Haxat China 74 B3
Haxby U.K. 48 F4
Hay Australia 112 B5
Hay *watercourse* Australia 110 B5
Hay *r.* Canada 120 H2
Haya China 72 I4
Hayachine-san *mt.* Japan 75 F5
Hayastan *country* Asia *see* **Armenia**
Haydān, Wādī al *r.* Jordan 85 B4
Haydarābad Iran 88 B2
Hayden *AZ* U.S.A. 129 H5
Hayden *CO* U.S.A. 129 J1
Hayden *IN* U.S.A. 134 C4
Hayes *r. Man.* Canada 121 M3
Hayes *r. Nunavut* Canada 119 I3
Hayes Halvø *pen.* Greenland 119 L2
Hayfield Reservoir U.S.A. 129 F5
Hayfork U.S.A. 128 B1
Hayl, Wādī *watercourse* Syria 85 C3
Hayl, Wādī al *watercourse* Syria 85 D2
Hayle U.K. 49 B8
Haymā' Oman 87 I6
Haymana Turkey 90 D3
Haymarket U.S.A. 135 G4
Hay-on-Wye U.K. 49 D6
Hayrabolu Turkey 59 L4
Hay River Canada 118 G3
Hay River Reserve Canada 120 H2
Hays *KS* U.S.A. 130 D4
Hays *MT* U.S.A. 126 F2
Ḩays Yemen 86 F7
Haysville U.S.A. 131 D4
Haysyn Ukr. 43 F6
Ḩaytān, Jabal *hill* Egypt 85 A4
Hayward *CA* U.S.A. 128 B3
Hayward *WI* U.S.A. 130 F2
Haywards Heath U.K. 49 G8
Hazar Turkm. *see* **Cheleken**
Hazarajat *reg.* Afgh. 89 G3
Hazard U.S.A. 134 D5
Hazaribag India *see* **Hazaribagh**
Hazaribagh India 83 F5
Hazaribagh Range *mts* India 83 E5
Hazār Masjed, Kūh-e *mts* Iran 88 E2
Hazebrouck France 52 C4
Hazelton Canada 120 E4
Hazen Strait Canada 119 G2
Hazerswoude-Rijndijk Neth. 52 E2
Hazhdanahr *reg.* Afgh. 89 G2
Hazleton *IN* U.S.A. 134 B4
Hazleton *PA* U.S.A. 135 H3
Hazlett, Lake *salt flat* Australia 108 E5
Hazrat Sultan Afgh. 89 G2
H. Bouchard Arg. 144 D4
Headford Rep. of Ireland 51 C4
Headingly Australia 110 B4
Head of Bight *b.* Australia 109 E7
Healdsburg U.S.A. 128 B2
Healesville Australia 112 B6
Healy U.S.A. 118 D3
Heanor U.K. 49 F5

▶**Heard and McDonald Islands** *terr.* Indian Ocean 149 M9
Australian External Territory.

Heard Island Indian Ocean 149 M9
Hearne U.S.A. 131 D6
Hearne Lake Canada 121 H2
Hearrenfean Neth. *see* **Heerenveen**
Hearst Canada 122 E4
Hearst Island Antarctica 152 L2
Heart *r.* U.S.A. 130 C2
Heart of Neolithic Orkney *tourist site* U.K. 50 F1
Heathcote Australia 112 B6
Heathfield U.K. 49 H8
Heathsville U.S.A. 135 G5
Hebbardsville U.S.A. 134 B5
Hebbronville U.S.A. 131 D7
Hebei *prov.* China 73 L5
Hebel Australia 112 C2
Heber U.S.A. 129 H4
Heber City U.S.A. 129 H1
Heber Springs U.S.A. 131 E5
Hebi China 73 K5
Hebron Canada 123 J2
Hebron U.S.A. 130 D3
Hebron West Bank 85 B4
Hecate Strait Canada 120 D4
Hecheng *Jiangxi* China *see* **Zixi**
Hecheng *Zhejiang* China *see* **Qingtian**
Hechi China 77 F3
Hechuan *Chongqing* China 76 E2
Hechuan *Jiangxi* China *see* **Yongxing**
Hecla Island Canada 121 L5
Hede China *see* **Sheyang**
Hede Sweden 44 H5
Hedemora Sweden 45 I6
He Devil Mountain U.S.A. 126 D3
Hedi Shuiku *resr* China 77 F4
Heech Neth. *see* **Heeg**
Heeg Neth. 52 F2
Heek Germany 52 H2
Heer Belgium 52 E4
Heerde Neth. 52 G2
Heerenveen Neth. 52 F2
Heerhugowaard Neth. 52 E2
Heerlen Neth. 52 F4
Hefa Israel *see* **Haifa**
Hefa, Mifraz Israel *see* **Haifa, Bay of**
Hefei China 77 H2
Hefeng China 77 F2
Heflin U.S.A. 133 C5
Hegang China 74 C3
Heho Myanmar 70 B2
Heidan *r.* Jordan *see* **Haydān, Wādī al**
Heidberg *hill* Germany 53 L3
Heide Germany 47 L3
Heide Namibia 100 C2
Heidelberg Germany 53 I5
Heidelberg S. Africa 101 I4
Heidenheim an der Brenz Germany 53 K6
Heihe China 74 B2
Heilbron S. Africa 101 H4
Heilbronn Germany 53 J5
Heiligenhafen Germany 47 M3
Hei Ling Chau *i.* Hong Kong China 77 [inset]
Heilongjiang *prov.* China 74 C3
Heilong Jiang *r.* China 74 D2
also known as Amur (Rus. Fed.)
Heilong Jiang *r.* Rus. Fed. *see* **Amur**
Heilsbronn Germany 53 K5
Heilungkiang *prov.* China *see* **Heilongjiang**
Heinola Fin. 45 O6
Heinze Islands Myanmar 71 B4
Heirnkut Myanmar 70 A1
Heishi Beihu *l.* China 83 E2
Heishui China 76 D1
Heisker Islands U.K. *see* **Monach Islands**
Heist-op-den-Berg Belgium 52 E3
Heitân, Gebel *hill* Egypt *see* **Ḩaytān, Jabal**
Hejaz *reg.* Saudi Arabia *see* **Hijaz**
Hejiang China 76 E2
He Jiang *r.* China 77 F4
Hejing China 80 G3
Hekimhan Turkey 90 E3
Hekla *vol.* Iceland 44 [inset]
Hekou *Gansu* China 72 I5
Hekou *Hubei* China 77 G2
Hekou *Jiangxi* China *see* **Yanshan**
Hekou *Sichuan* China *see* **Yajiang**
Hekou *Yunnan* China 76 D4
Helagsfjället *mt.* Sweden 44 H5
Helam India 76 B3
Helan Shan *mts* China 72 J5
Helbra Germany 53 L3
Helen *atoll* Palau 69 I6
Helena *AR* U.S.A. 131 F5

▶**Helena** *MT* U.S.A. 126 E3
State capital of Montana.

Helen Reef Palau 69 I6
Helensburgh U.K. 50 E4
Helen Springs Australia 108 F4
Ḩeleẕ Israel 85 B4
Helgoland *i.* Germany 47 K3
Helgoländer Bucht *g.* Germany 47 L3
Heligoland *i.* Germany *see* **Helgoland**
Heligoland Bight *g.* Germany *see* **Helgoländer Bucht**
Heliopolis Lebanon *see* **Ba'albek**
Helixi China *see* **Ningguo**
Hella Iceland 44 [inset]
Helland Norway 44 J2
Hellas *country* Europe *see* **Greece**
Helleh *r.* Iran 88 C4
Hellespont *strait* Turkey *see* **Dardanelles**
Hellevoetsluis Neth. 52 E3
Hellhole Gorge National Park Australia 110 D5
Hellín Spain 57 F4
Hellinikon *tourist site* Greece 86 A3
Hells Canyon *gorge* U.S.A. 126 D3
Hell-Ville Madag. *see* **Andoany**
Helmand *r.* Afgh. 89 F4
Helmantica Spain *see* **Salamanca**
Helmbrechts Germany 53 L4
Helme *r.* Germany 53 L3
Helmeringhausen Namibia 100 C3
Helmond Neth. 52 F3
Helmsdale U.K. 50 F2
Helmsdale *r.* U.K. 50 F2
Helmstedt Germany 53 L2
Helong China 74 C4
Helper U.S.A. 129 H2
Helpter Berge *hills* Germany 53 N1
Helsingborg Sweden 45 H8
Helsingfors Fin. *see* **Helsinki**
Helsingør Denmark 45 H8

▶**Helsinki** Fin. 45 N6
Capital of Finland.

Helston U.K. 49 B8
Helvécia Brazil 145 D2
Helvetic Republic *country* Europe *see* **Switzerland**
Ḩelwân Egypt *see* **Ḩulwān**
Hemel Hempstead U.K. 49 G7
Hemet U.S.A. 128 E5
Hemingford U.S.A. 130 C3
Hemlock Lake U.S.A. 135 G2
Hemmingen Germany 53 J2
Hemmingford Canada 135 I1
Hemmoor Germany 53 J1
Hempstead U.S.A. 131 D6
Hemsby U.K. 49 I6
Hemse Sweden 45 K8
Henan China 76 D1
Henan *prov.* China 77 G1
Henares *r.* Spain 57 E3
Henashi-zaki *pt* Japan 75 E4
Henbury Australia 109 F6
Hendek Turkey 59 N4
Henderson *KY* U.S.A. 134 B5
Henderson *NC* U.S.A. 132 E4
Henderson *NV* U.S.A. 129 F3
Henderson *NY* U.S.A. 135 G2
Henderson *TN* U.S.A. 131 F5
Henderson *TX* U.S.A. 131 E5
Henderson Island Pitcairn Is 151 L7
Hendersonville *NC* U.S.A. 133 D5
Hendersonville *TN* U.S.A. 134 B5
Henderville *atoll* Kiribati *see* **Aranuka**
Hendon U.K. 49 G7
Hendorābī *i.* Iran 88 D5
Hendy-Gwyn U.K. *see* **Whitland**
Hengām Iran 89 E5
Hengduan Shan *mts* China 76 C2
Hengelo Neth. 52 G2
Hengfeng China 77 H2
Hengnan China *see* **Hengyang**
Hengshan China 74 C3
Heng Shan *mt.* China 77 G3
Hengshui *Hebei* China 73 L5
Hengshui *Jiangxi* China *see* **Chongyi**
Hengxian China 77 F4
Hengyang *Hunan* China 77 G3
Hengyang *Hunan* China 77 G3
Hengzhou China *see* **Hengxian**
Heniches'k Ukr. 43 G7
Henley N.Z. 113 C7
Henley-on-Thames U.K. 49 G7
Henlopen, Cape U.S.A. 135 H4
Hennef (Sieg) Germany 53 H4
Hennenman S. Africa 101 H4
Hennepin U.S.A. 130 F3
Hennessey U.S.A. 131 D4
Hennigsdorf Berlin Germany 53 N2
Henniker U.S.A. 135 J2
Henning U.S.A. 134 B3
Henrietta U.S.A. 131 D5
Henrietta Maria, Cape Canada 122 E3
Henrieville U.S.A. 129 H3
Henrique de Carvalho Angola *see* **Saurimo**
Henry, Cape U.S.A. 135 G5
Henry Ice Rise Antarctica 152 A1
Henryk Arctowski *research station* Antarctica *see* **Arctowski**
Henry Kater, Cape Canada 119 L3
Henry Mountains U.S.A. 129 H2
Hensall Canada 134 E2
Henshaw, Lake U.S.A. 128 E5
Hentiesbaai Namibia 100 B2
Henty Australia 112 C5
Henzada Myanmar 70 A3
Heping *Guangdong* China 77 G3
Heping *Guizhou* China *see* **Huishui**
Heping *Guizhou* China *see* **Yanhe**
Hepo China *see* **Jiexi**
Heppner U.S.A. 126 D3
Heptanesus *is* Greece *see* **Ionian Islands**
Hepu China 77 F4
Heqing China 76 D3
Heraclea Turkey *see* **Ereğli**
Heraclea Pontica Turkey *see* **Ereğli**
Heraklion Greece *see* **Iraklion**
Herald Cays *atolls* Australia 110 E3
Herāt Afgh. 89 F3
Hérault *r.* France 56 F5
Herbertabad India 71 A5
Herbert Downs Australia 110 B4
Herbert River Falls National Park Australia 110 D3
Herbert Wash *salt flat* Australia 109 D6
Herborn Germany 53 I4
Herbstein Germany 53 J4
Hercules Dome *ice feature* Antarctica 152 K1
Herdecke Germany 53 H3
Herdorf Germany 53 H4
Hereford U.K. 49 E6
Hereford U.S.A. 131 C5
Héréhérétué *atoll* Fr. Polynesia 151 K7
Herent Belgium 52 E4
Herford Germany 53 I2
Heringen (Werra) Germany 53 K4
Herington U.S.A. 130 D4
Herīs Iran 88 B2
Herisau Switz. 56 I3
Herkimer U.S.A. 135 H2
Herlen Gol *r.* China/Mongolia 73 L3
Herlen He *r.* China/Mongolia *see* **Herlen Gol**
Herleshausen Germany 53 K3
Herlong U.S.A. 128 C1
Herm *i.* Channel Is 49 E9
Hermanas Mex. 131 C7
Herma Ness *hd* U.K. 50 [inset]
Hermann U.S.A. 130 F4
Hermannsburg Germany 53 K2
Hermanus S. Africa 100 D8
Hermel Lebanon 85 C2
Hermes, Cape S. Africa 101 I6
Hermidale Australia 112 C3
Hermiston U.S.A. 126 D3
Hermitage *MO* U.S.A. 130 E4
Hermitage *PA* U.S.A. 134 E3
Hermitage Bay Canada 123 K5
Hermite, Islas *is* Chile 144 C9
Hermit Islands P.N.G. 69 L7
Hermon, Mount Lebanon/Syria 85 B3
Hermonthis Egypt *see* **Armant**
Hermopolis Magna Egypt *see* **Al Ashmūnayn**
Hermosa U.S.A. 129 J3
Hermosillo Mex. 127 F7
Hernandarias Para. 144 F3
Hernando U.S.A. 131 F5
Herndon *CA* U.S.A. 128 D3
Herndon *PA* U.S.A. 135 G3
Herndon *WV* U.S.A. 134 E5
Herne Germany 53 H3
Herne Bay U.K. 49 I7
Herning Denmark 45 F8
Heroica Nogales Mex. *see* **Nogales**
Heroica Puebla de Zaragoza Mex. *see* **Puebla**
Hérouville-St-Clair France 49 G9
Herowābād Iran *see* **Khalkhāl**
Herrera del Duque Spain 57 D4
Herrieden Germany 53 K5
Hershey U.S.A. 135 G3
Hertford U.K. 49 G7
Hertzogville S. Africa 101 G5
Herve Belgium 52 F4
Hervé, Lac *l.* Canada 123 H3
Hervey Islands Cook Is 151 J7
Herzberg *Brandenburg* Germany 53 M2
Herzberg *Brandenburg* Germany 53 N3
Herzlake Germany 53 H2
Herzliyya Israel 85 B3
Herzogenaurach Germany 53 K5
Herzsprung Germany 53 M1
Ḩesār Iran 88 C4
Ḩeşār Iran 88 E5
Hesdin France 52 C4
Hesel Germany 53 H1
Heshan China 77 F4
Heshengqiao China 77 G2
Hesperia U.S.A. 128 E4
Hesperus U.S.A. 129 I3
Hesperus Peak U.S.A. 129 I3
Hesquiat Canada 120 E5
Hess *r.* Canada 120 C2
Heßdorf Germany 53 K5
Hesse *land* Germany *see* **Hessen**
Hesselberg *hill* Germany 53 K5
Hessen *land* Germany 53 J4
Hessisch Lichtenau Germany 53 J3
Hess Mountains Canada 120 C2
Het *r.* Laos 70 D2
Heteren Neth. 52 F3
Hetou China 77 F4
Hettinger U.S.A. 130 C2
Hetton U.K. 48 E4
Hettstedt Germany 53 L3
Heung Kong Tsai Hong Kong China *see* **Aberdeen**
Ḩevron West Bank *see* **Hebron**
Hexham U.K. 48 E4
Hexian *Anhui* China 77 H2
Hexian *Guangxi* China *see* **Hezhou**
Heyang China 77 F1
Ḩeydarābād Iran 89 F4
Heydebreck Poland *see* **Kędzierzyn-Koźle**
Heysham U.K. 48 E4
Heyshope Dam S. Africa 101 J4
Heyuan China 77 G4
Heywood U.K. 48 E5
Heze China 77 G1
Hezhang China 76 E3
Hezheng China 76 D1
Hezhou China 77 F3
Hezuo China 76 D1
Hezuozhen China *see* **Hezuo**
Hialeah U.S.A. 133 D7
Hiawassee U.S.A. 133 D5
Hiawatha U.S.A. 130 E4
Hibbing U.S.A. 130 E2
Hibbs, Point Australia 111 [inset]
Hibernia Reef Australia 108 C3
Hīchān Iran 89 F5
Hicks Bay N.Z. 113 G3
Hicks Lake Canada 121 K2
Hicksville U.S.A. 134 C3
Hico U.S.A. 131 D5
Hidaka-sanmyaku *mts* Japan 74 F4
Hidalgo Mex. 131 D7
Hidalgo del Parral Mex. 131 B7
Hidrolândia Brazil 145 A2
Hierosolyma Israel/West Bank *see* **Jerusalem**
Higashi-suidō *sea chan.* Japan 75 C6
Higgins U.S.A. 131 C4
Higgins Bay U.S.A. 135 H2
Higgins Lake U.S.A. 134 C1
High Atlas *mts* Morocco *see* **Haut Atlas**
High Desert U.S.A. 126 C4
High Island *i.* Hong Kong China 77 [inset]
High Island U.S.A. 131 E6
High Island Reservoir Hong Kong China 77 [inset]
Highland Peak *CA* U.S.A. 128 D2
Highland Peak *NV* U.S.A. 129 F3
Highlands U.S.A. 135 I3
Highland Springs U.S.A. 135 G5
High Level Canada 120 G3
Highmore U.S.A. 130 D2
High Point U.S.A. 132 E5
High Point *hill* U.S.A. 135 H3
High Prairie Canada 120 G4
High River Canada 120 H5
Highrock Lake *Man.* Canada 121 K4
Highrock Lake *Sask.* Canada 121 J3
High Springs U.S.A. 133 D6
High Tatras *mts* Poland/Slovakia *see* **Tatra Mountains**
High Wycombe U.K. 49 G7
Higuera de Zaragoza Mex. 127 F8
Higüey Dom. Rep. 137 K5
Hiiumaa *i.* Estonia 45 M7
Hijānah, Buḩayrat al *imp. l.* Syria 85 C3
Hijaz *reg.* Saudi Arabia 86 E4
Ḩikmah, Ra's al *pt* Egypt 90 B5
Hiko U.S.A. 129 F3
Hikone Japan 75 E6
Hikurangi *mt.* N.Z. 113 G3
Hila Indon. 108 D1
Hilāl, Jabal *hill* Egypt 85 A4
Hilāl, Ra's al *pt* Libya 86 B3
Hilary Coast Antarctica 152 H1
Hildale U.S.A. 129 G3
Hildburghausen Germany 53 K4
Hilders Germany 53 K4
Hildesheim Germany 53 J2
Hillah Iraq 91 G4
Hill City U.S.A. 130 D4
Hillegom Neth. 52 E2
Hill End Australia 112 D4
Hillerød Denmark 45 H9
Hillgrove Australia 110 D3
Hill Island Lake Canada 121 I2
Hillman U.S.A. 134 D1
Hillsboro *ND* U.S.A. 130 D2
Hillsboro *NM* U.S.A. 127 G6
Hillsboro *OH* U.S.A. 134 D4
Hillsboro *OR* U.S.A. 126 C3
Hillsboro *TX* U.S.A. 131 D5
Hillsdale *IN* U.S.A. 134 B4
Hillsdale *MI* U.S.A. 134 C3
Hillside Australia 108 B5
Hillston Australia 112 B4
Hillsville U.S.A. 134 E5
Hilo *HI* U.S.A. 127 [inset]
Hilton Australia 110 B4
Hilton S. Africa 101 J5
Hilton U.S.A. 135 G2
Hilton Head Island U.S.A. 133 D5
Hilvan Turkey 90 E3
Hilversum Neth. 52 F2
Himachal Pradesh *state* India 82 D3
Himalaya *mts* Asia 82 D2
Himalchul *mt.* Nepal 83 F3
Himanka Fin. 44 M4
Ḩimār, Wādī al *watercourse* Syria/Turkey 85 D1
Himarë Albania 59 H4
Himatnagar India 82 C5
Himeji Japan 75 D6
Ḩimş Syria *see* **Homs**
Ḩimş, Baḩrat *resr* Syria *see* **Qaţţīnah, Buḩayrat**
Hinchinbrook Island Australia 110 D3
Hinckley U.K. 49 F6
Hinckley *MN* U.S.A. 130 E2
Hinckley *UT* U.S.A. 129 G2
Hinckley Reservoir U.S.A. 135 H2
Hindaun India 82 D4
Hinderwell U.K. 48 G4
Hindley U.K. 48 E5
Hindman U.S.A. 134 D5
Hindmarsh, Lake *dry lake* Australia 111 C8
Hindu Kush *mts* Afgh./Pak. 89 G3
Hindupur India 84 C3
Hines Creek Canada 120 G3
Hinesville U.S.A. 133 D6
Hinganghat India 84 C1
Hingoli India 84 C2
Hınıs Turkey 91 F3
Hinnøya *i.* Norway 44 I2
Hinojosa del Duque Spain 57 D4
Hinsdale U.S.A. 135 I2
Hinte Germany 53 H1
Hinthada Myanmar *see* **Henzada**
Hinton Canada 120 G4
Hinton U.S.A. 134 E5
Hiort *i.* U.K. *see* **St Kilda**
Hippolytushoef Neth. 52 E2
Hipponium Italy *see* **Vibo Valentia**
Hippo Regius Alg. *see* **Annaba**
Hippo Zarytus Tunisia *see* **Bizerte**
Hirabit Dağ *mt.* Turkey 91 G3
Hirakud Dam India 83 E5
Hirakud Reservoir India 83 E5
Hirapur India 82 D4
Hiriyur India 84 C3
Hirosaki Japan 74 F4
Hiroshima Japan 75 D6
Hirschaid Germany 53 L5
Hirschberg Germany 53 L4
Hirschberg *mt.* Germany 47 M7
Hirschberg Poland *see* **Jelenia Góra**
Hirschenstn *mt.* Germany 53 M6
Hirson France 52 E5
Hîrşova Romania *see* **Hârşova**
Hirta *is* U.K. *see* **St Kilda**
Hirtshals Denmark 45 F8
Hisar India 82 C3
Hisar Iran 88 C2
Hisarköy Turkey *see* **Domaniç**
Hisarönü Turkey 59 O4
Ḩisb, Sha'īb *watercourse* Iraq 91 G5
Ḩisbān Jordan 85 B4
Hisiu P.N.G. 69 L8
Hisor Tajik. 89 H2
Hisor Tizmasi *mts* Tajik./Uzbek. *see* **Gissar Range**
Hispalis Spain *see* **Seville**
Hispania *country* Europe *see* **Spain**

▶**Hispaniola** *i.* Caribbean Sea 137 J4
Consists of the Dominican Republic and Haiti.

Hispur Glacier Jammu and Kashmir 82 C1
Hissar India *see* **Hisar**
Hisua India 83 F4
Ḩisyah Syria 85 C2
Hīt Iraq 91 F4
Hitachi Japan 75 F5
Hitachinaka Japan 75 F5
Hitra *i.* Norway 44 F5
Hitzacker Germany 53 L1
Hiva Oa *i.* Fr. Polynesia 151 K6
Hixon Canada 120 F4
Hixson Cay *reef* Australia 110 F4
Hiyon *watercourse* Israel 85 B4
Hizan Turkey 91 F3
Hjälmaren *l.* Sweden 45 I7
Hjerkinn Norway 44 F5
Hjo Sweden 45 I7
Hjørring Denmark 45 G8
Hkakabo Razi *mt.* China/Myanmar 76 C2
Hlaingdet Myanmar 70 B2
Hlako Kangri *mt.* China *see* **Lhagoi Kangri**
Hlane Royal National Park Swaziland 101 J4
Hlatikulu Swaziland 101 J4
Hlegu Myanmar 70 B3
Hlohlowane S. Africa 101 H5
Hlotse Lesotho 101 I5
Hluhluwe-Umfolozi Park *nature res.* S. Africa 101 J5
Hlukhiv Ukr. 43 G6
Hlung-Tan Myanmar 70 B2
Hlusha Belarus 43 F5
Hlybokaye Belarus 45 O9
Ho Ghana 96 D4

Hoa Binh Vietnam 70 D2
Hoachanas Namibia 100 D2
Hoagland U.S.A. 134 C3
Hoang Liên Son mts Vietnam 70 C2
Hoang Sa is S. China Sea see Paracel Islands

▶Hobart Australia 111 [inset]
State capital of Tasmania.

Hobart U.S.A. 131 D5
Hobbs U.S.A. 131 C5
Hobbs Coast Antarctica 152 J1
Hobe Sound U.S.A. 133 D7
Hobiganj Bangl. see Habiganj
Hobro Denmark 45 F8
Hobyo Somalia 98 E3
Hoceima, Baie d'Al b. Morocco 57 E6
Höchberg Germany 53 J5
Hochfeiler mt. Austria/Italy see Gran Pilastro
Hochfeld Namibia 99 B6
Hochharz nat. park Germany 53 K3
Hô Chi Minh Vietnam see Ho Chi Minh City
Ho Chi Minh City Vietnam 71 D5
Hochschwab mt. Austria 47 O7
Hochschwab mts Austria 47 O7
Hockenheim Germany 53 I5
Ḥôḍ reg. Mauritania 96 C3
Hoddesdon U.K. 49 G7
Hodeidah Yemen 86 F7
Hodgenville U.S.A. 134 C5
Hodgson Downs Australia 108 F3
Hódmezővásárhely Hungary 59 I1
Hodna, Chott el salt l. Alg. 57 I6
Hodo-dan pt N. Korea 75 B5
Hoek van Holland Neth. see Hook of Holland
Hoensbroek Neth. 52 F4
Hoeryŏng N. Korea 74 C4
Hof Germany 53 L4
Hoffman Mountain U.S.A. 135 I2
Hofheim in Unterfranken Germany 53 K4
Hofmeyr S. Africa 101 G6
Höfn Iceland 44 [inset]
Hofors Sweden 45 J6
Hofsjökull ice cap Iceland 44 [inset]
Hofsós Iceland 44 [inset]
Hōfu Japan 75 C6
Hofūf Saudi Arabia see Al Hufūf
Höganäs Sweden 45 H8
Hogan Group is Australia 112 C7
Hogansburg U.S.A. 135 H1
Hogback Mountain U.S.A. 130 C3
Hoge Vaart canal Neth. 52 F2
Hogg, Mount Canada 120 C2
Hoggar plat. Alg. 96 D2
Hog Island U.S.A. 135 H5
Högsby Sweden 45 J8
Hohenloher Ebene plain Germany 53 J5
Hohenmölsen Germany 53 M3
Hohennauen Germany 53 M2
Hohensalza Poland see Inowrocław
Hohenwald U.S.A. 132 C5
Hohenwartetalsperre resr Germany 53 L4
Hoher Dachstein mt. Austria 47 N7
Hohe Rhön mts Germany 53 J4
Hohe Tauern mts Austria 47 N7
Hohe Venn moorland Belgium 52 G4
Hohhot China 73 K4
Hohneck mt. France 56 H2
Hoh Sai Hu l. China 83 H2
Hoh Xil Hu salt l. China 83 G2
Hoh Xil Shan mts China 83 G2
Hôi An Vietnam 70 E4
Hoima Uganda 98 D3
Hôi Xuân Vietnam 70 D2
Hojagala Turkm. see Khodzha-Kala
Hojai India 83 H4
Hojambaz Turkm. see Khodzhambaz
Højryggen mts Greenland 119 M2
Hokitika N.Z. 113 C6
Hokkaidō i. Japan 74 F4
Hokksund Norway 45 F7
Hoktemberyan Armenia 91 G2
Hol Norway 45 F6
Holbæk Denmark 45 G9
Holbeach U.K. 49 H6
Holbrook Australia 112 C5
Holbrook U.S.A. 129 H4
Holden U.S.A. 129 G2
Holdenville U.S.A. 131 D5
Holdrege U.S.A. 130 D3
Holgate U.S.A. 134 C3
Holguín Cuba 137 I4
Höljes Sweden 45 H6
Holland country Europe see Netherlands
Holland MI U.S.A. 134 B2
Holland NY U.S.A. 135 F2
Hollandia Indon. see Jayapura
Hollick-Kenyon Peninsula Antarctica 152 L2
Hollick-Kenyon Plateau Antarctica 152 K1
Hollidaysburg U.S.A. 135 F3
Hollis AK U.S.A. 120 C4
Hollis OK U.S.A. 131 D5
Hollister U.S.A. 128 C3
Holly U.S.A. 134 D2
Hollyhill U.S.A. 134 C5
Holly Springs U.S.A. 131 F5
Hollywood U.S.A. 133 D7
Holm Norway 44 H4
Holman Canada 118 G2
Holmes Reef Australia 110 D3
Holmestrand Norway 45 G7
Holmgard Rus. Fed. see Velikiy Novgorod
Holm Ø i. Greenland see Kiatassuaq
Holmön i. Sweden 44 L5
Holmsund Sweden 44 L5
Ḥolon Israel 85 B3
Holoog Namibia 100 C4
Holothuria Banks reef Australia 108 D3
Holroyd r. Australia 110 C2
Holstebro Denmark 45 F8
Holstein U.S.A. 130 E3
Holsteinsborg Greenland see Sisimiut
Holston r. U.S.A. 132 D4
Holsworthy U.K. 49 C8
Holt U.K. 49 I6
Holt U.S.A. 134 C2
Holton U.S.A. 134 B2
Holwerd Neth. 52 F1
Holwert Neth. see Holwerd
Holycross Rep. of Ireland 51 E5
Holy Cross U.S.A. 118 C3
Holy Cross, Mount of the U.S.A. 126 G5
Holyhead U.K. 48 C5
Holyhead Bay U.K. 48 C5
Holy Island England U.K. 48 F3
Holy Island Wales U.K. 48 C5
Holyoke U.S.A. 130 C3
Holy See Europe see Vatican City
Holywell U.K. 48 D5
Holzhausen Germany 53 M3
Holzkirchen Germany 47 M7
Holzminden Germany 53 J3
Homand Iran 89 E3
Homāyūnshahr Iran see Khomeynīshahr
Homberg (Efze) Germany 53 J3
Hombori Mali 96 C3
Homburg Germany 53 H5
Home Bay Canada 119 L3
Homécourt France 52 F5
Homer GA U.S.A. 133 D5
Homer LA U.S.A. 131 E5
Homer MI U.S.A. 134 C2
Homer NY U.S.A. 135 G2
Homerville U.S.A. 133 D6
Homestead Australia 110 D4
Homnabad India 84 C2
Homoine Moz. 101 L2
Homs Libya see Al Khums
Homs Syria 85 C2
Homyel' Belarus 43 F5
Honan prov. China see Henan
Honavar India 84 B3
Honaz Turkey 59 M6
Hon Chông Vietnam 71 D5
Hondeklipbaai S. Africa 100 C6
Hondo U.S.A. 131 D6
Hondsrug reg. Neth. 52 G1

▶Honduras country Central America 137 G6
5th largest country in Central and North America.
North America 9, 116–117

Hønefoss Norway 45 G6
Honesdale U.S.A. 135 H3
Honey Lake salt l. U.S.A. 128 C1
Honeyoye Lake U.S.A. 135 G2
Honfleur France 56 E2
Hong, Mouths of the Vietnam see Red River, Mouths of the
Hông, Sông r. Vietnam see Red
Hongchuan China see Hongya
Hông Gai Vietnam 70 D2
Hongguo China see Panxian
Honghai Wan b. China 77 G4
Honghe China 76 D4
Hong He r. China 77 G1
Honghu China 77 G2
Hongjiang Hunan China 77 F3
Hongjiang Sichuan China see Wangcang
▶Hong Kong Hong Kong China 77 [inset]
Asia 6, 62–63
Hong Kong aut. reg. China 77 [inset]
Hong Kong Harbour sea chan. Hong Kong China 77 [inset]
Hong Kong Island Hong Kong China 77 [inset]
Hongliuwan China see Aksay
Hongliuyuan China 80 I3
Hongqiao China see Qidong
Hongqizhen China see Tongshi
Hongshi China 74 B4
Hongshui He r. China 76 F4
Honguedo, Détroit d' sea chan. Canada 123 I4
Hongwŏn N. Korea 75 B4
Hongxing China 74 A3
Hongya China 76 D2
Hongyuan China 76 D1
Hongze China 77 H1
Hongze Hu l. China 77 H1

▶Honiara Solomon Is 107 F2
Capital of the Solomon Islands.

Honiton U.K. 49 D8
Honjō Japan 75 F5
Honkajoki Fin. 45 M6
Honningsvåg Norway 44 N1
Honokaa HI U.S.A. 127 [inset]

▶Honolulu HI U.S.A. 127 [inset]
State capital of Hawaii.

▶Honshū i. Japan 75 D6
3rd largest island in Asia.

Honwad India 84 B2
Hood, Mount vol. U.S.A. 126 C3
Hood Point Australia 109 B8
Hood Point P.N.G. 110 D1
Hood River U.S.A. 126 C3
Hoogeveen Neth. 52 G2
Hoogezand-Sappemeer Neth. 48 G1
Hooghly r. mouth India see Hugli
Hooker U.S.A. 131 C4
Hook Head hd Rep. of Ireland 51 F5
Hook of Holland Neth. 52 E3
Hook Reef Australia 110 E3
Hoonah U.S.A. 120 C3
Hooper Bay U.S.A. 153 B2
Hooper Island U.S.A. 135 G4
Hoopeston U.S.A. 134 B3
Hoopstad S. Africa 101 G4
Höör Sweden 45 H9
Hoorn Neth. 52 F2
Hoorn, Îles de is Wallis and Futuna Is 107 I3
Hoosick U.S.A. 135 I2
Hoover Dam U.S.A. 129 F3
Hoover Memorial Reservoir U.S.A. 134 D3
Hopa Turkey 91 F2
Hope Canada 120 F5
Hope r. N.Z. 113 D6
Hope AR U.S.A. 131 E5
Hope IN U.S.A. 134 C4
Hope, Lake salt flat Australia 109 C8
Hope, Point U.S.A. 118 B3
Hopedale Canada 123 J3
Hopefield S. Africa 100 D7
Hopei prov. China see Hebei
Hope Mountains Canada 123 J3
Hope Saddle pass N.Z. 113 D5
Hopes Advance, Baie b. Canada 123 H2
Hopes Advance, Cap c. Canada 119 L3
Hopes Advance Bay Canada see Aupaluk
Hopetoun Australia 111 C7
Hopetown S. Africa 100 G5
Hopewell U.S.A. 135 G5
Hopewell Islands Canada 122 F2
Hopin Myanmar 70 B1
Hopkins r. Australia 111 C8
Hopkins, Lake salt flat Australia 109 E6
Hopkinsville U.S.A. 134 B5
Hopland U.S.A. 128 B2
Hoquiam U.S.A. 126 C3
Hor China 76 D1
Horasan Turkey 91 F2
Hörby Sweden 45 H9
Horgo Mongolia 80 I2

▶Horizon Deep sea feature S. Pacific Ocean 150 I7
2nd deepest point in the world (Tonga Trench).

Horki Belarus 43 F5
Horlick Mountains Antarctica 152 K1
Horlivka Ukr. 43 H6
Hormoz i. Iran 88 E5
Hormoz, Kūh-e mt. Iran 88 D5
Hormuz, Strait of Iran/Oman 88 E5
Horn Austria 47 O6
Horn r. Canada 120 G2
Horn c. Iceland 44 [inset]

▶Horn, Cape Chile 144 C9
Most southerly point of South America.

Hornavan l. Sweden 44 J3
Hornbrook U.S.A. 126 C4
Hornburg Germany 53 K2
Horncastle U.K. 48 G5
Horndal Sweden 45 J6
Horne, Îles de is Wallis and Futuna Is see Hoorn, Îles de
Horneburg Germany 53 J1
Hörnefors Sweden 44 K5
Hornell U.S.A. 135 G2
Hornepayne Canada 122 D4
Hornillos Mex. 127 F8
Hornisgrinde mt. Germany 47 L6
Hornkranz Namibia 100 C2
Horn Mountains Canada 120 F2
Hornos, Cabo de Chile see Horn, Cape
Hornoy-le-Bourg France 52 B5
Horn Peak Canada 120 D2
Hornsby Australia 112 E4
Hornsea U.K. 48 G5
Hornslandet pen. Sweden 45 J6
Horodenka Ukr. 43 E6
Horodnya Ukr. 43 F6
Horodok Khmel'nyts'ka Oblast' Ukr. 43 E6
Horodok L'vivs'ka Oblast' Ukr. 43 D6
Horokanai Japan 74 F3
Horoshiri-dake mt. Japan 74 F4
Horqin Youyi Qianqi China see Ulanhot
Horqin Zuoyi Houqi China see Ganjig
Horqin Zuoyi Zhongqi China see Baokang
Horrabridge U.K. 49 C8
Horrocks Australia 109 A7
Horru China 83 G3
Horse Cave U.S.A. 134 C5
Horsefly Canada 120 F4
Horseheads U.S.A. 135 G2
Horse Islands Canada 123 L4
Horseleap Rep. of Ireland 51 D4
Horsens Denmark 45 F9
Horseshoe Bend Australia 109 F6
Horseshoe Reservoir U.S.A. 129 H4
Horseshoe Seamounts sea feature N. Atlantic Ocean 148 G3
Horsham Australia 111 C8
Horsham U.K. 49 G7
Horšovský Týn Czech Rep. 53 M5
Horst hill Germany 53 J4
Hörstel Germany 53 H2
Horten Norway 45 G7
Hortobágyi nat. park Hungary 59 I1
Horton r. Canada 118 F3
Horwood Lake Canada 122 E4
Hösbach Germany 53 J4
Hose, Pegunungan mts Malaysia 68 E6
Ḥoseynābād Iran 88 B3
Ḥoseynīyeh Iran 88 C4
Hoshab Pak. 89 F5
Hoshangabad India 82 D5
Hoshiarpur India 82 C3
Hospet India 84 C3
Hospital Rep. of Ireland 51 D5
Hosséré Vokre mt. Cameroon 96 E4
Hosta Butte mt. U.S.A. 129 I4
Hotagen r. Sweden 44 I5
Hotahudo East Timor see Hatudo
Hotan China 82 E1
Hotazel S. Africa 100 F4
Hot Creek Range mts U.S.A. 128 E2
Hotgi India 84 C2
Hotham r. Australia 109 B8
Hoting Sweden 44 J4
Hot Springs AR U.S.A. 131 E5
Hot Springs NM U.S.A. see Truth or Consequences
Hot Springs SD U.S.A. 130 C3
Hot Sulphur Springs U.S.A. 126 G4
Hottah Lake Canada 120 G1
Hottentots Bay Namibia 100 B4
Hottentots Point Namibia 100 B4
Houdan France 52 B6
Houffalize Belgium 52 F4
Hougang Sing. 71 [inset]
Houghton MI U.S.A. 130 F2
Houghton NY U.S.A. 135 F2
Houghton Lake U.S.A. 134 C1
Houghton Lake l. U.S.A. 134 C1
Houghton le Spring U.K. 48 F4
Houie Moc, Phou mt. Laos 70 C2
Houlton U.S.A. 132 H2
Houma China 77 F1
Houma U.S.A. 131 F6
Houmen China 77 G4
House Range mts U.S.A. 129 G2
Houston Canada 120 E4
Houston MO U.S.A. 131 F4
Houston MS U.S.A. 131 F5
Houston TX U.S.A. 131 E6
Hout r. S. Africa 101 I2
Houtman Abrolhos is Australia 109 A7
Houton U.K. 50 F2
Houwater S. Africa 100 F6
Hovd Hovd Mongolia 80 H2
Hovd Övörhangay Mongolia 80 J3
Hove U.K. 49 G8
Hoveton U.K. 49 I6
Hovmantorp Sweden 45 I8
Hövsgöl Nuur l. Mongolia 80 J1
Hövüün Mongolia 80 J3
Howar, Wadi watercourse Sudan 86 C6
Howard Australia 110 F5
Howard PA U.S.A. 135 G3
Howard SD U.S.A. 130 D2
Howard WI U.S.A. 134 A1
Howard City U.S.A. 134 C2
Howard Lake Canada 121 J2
Howden U.K. 48 G5
Howe, Cape Australia 112 D6
Howe, Mount Antarctica 152 J1
Howell U.S.A. 134 D2
Howick Canada 135 I1
Howick S. Africa 101 J5
Howland U.S.A. 132 G2

▶Howland Island terr. N. Pacific Ocean 107 I1
United States Unincorporated Territory.

Howlong Australia 112 C5
Howrah India see Haora
Howth Rep. of Ireland 51 F4
Ḥowz well Iran 88 E3
Ḥowz-e Khān well Iran 88 E3
Ḥowz-e Panj Iran 88 E4
Ḥowz-e Panj waterhole Iran 88 D3
Howz i-Mian i-Tak Iran 88 D3
Höxter Germany 53 J3
Hoy i. U.K. 50 F2
Hoya Germany 53 J2
Høyanger Norway 45 E6
Hoyerswerda Germany 47 O5
Høylandet Norway 44 H4
Hoym Germany 53 L3
Höytiäinen l. Fin. 44 P5
Hoyt Peak U.S.A. 129 H1
Hpa-an Myanmar see Pa-an
Hradec Králové Czech Rep. 47 O5
Hradiště hill Czech Rep. 53 N4
Hrasnica Bos.-Herz. 58 H3
Hrazdan Armenia 91 G2
Hrebinka Ukr. 43 G6
Hrodna Belarus 45 M10
Hrvatska country Europe see Croatia
Hrvatsko Grahovo Bos.-Herz. see Bosansko Grahovo
Hsataw Myanmar 70 B3
Hsenwi Myanmar 70 B2
Hsiang Chang i. Hong Kong China see Hong Kong Island
Hsiang Kang Hong Kong China see Hong Kong
Hsi-hseng Myanmar 70 B2
Hsin-chia-p'o country Asia see Singapore
Hsin-chia-p'o Sing. see Singapore
Hsinchu Taiwan 77 I3
Hsinking China see Changchun
Hsinying Taiwan 77 I4
Hsipaw Myanmar 70 B2
Hsi-sha Ch'ün-tao is S. China Sea see Paracel Islands
Hsiyüp'ing Yü i. Taiwan 77 H4
Hsüeh Shan mt. Taiwan 77 I3
Huab watercourse Namibia 99 B6
Huachinera Mex. 127 F7
Huacho Peru 142 C6
Huachuan China 74 C3
Huade China 73 K4
Huadian China 74 B4
Huadu China 77 G4
Hua Hin Thai. 71 B4
Huai'an Jiangsu China 77 H1
Huai'an Jiangsu China see Chuzhou
Huaibei China 77 H1
Huaibin China 77 G1
Huaicheng Guangdong China see Huaiji
Huaicheng Jiangsu China see Chuzhou
Huaidezhen China 74 B4
Huaidian China see Shenqiu
Huai Had National Park Thai. 70 D3
Huaihua China 77 F3
Huaiji China 77 G4
Huai Kha Khaeng Wildlife Reserve nature res. Thai. 70 B4
Huailillas mt. Peru 142 C5
Huainan China 77 H1
Huaining Anhui China 77 H2
Huaining Anhui China see Shipai
Huaiyang China 77 G1
Huaiyin Jiangsu China 77 H1
Huaiyin Jiangsu China see Huai'an
Huaiyuan China 77 H1
Huajialing China 76 E1
Huajuápan de León Mex. 136 E5
Hualapai Peak U.S.A. 129 G4
Hualian Taiwan see Hualien
Hualien Taiwan 77 I3
Huallaga r. Peru 142 C5
Huambo Angola 99 B5
Huanan China 74 C3
Huancane Peru 142 E7
Huancavelica Peru 142 C6
Huancayo Peru 142 C6
Huangbei China 77 G3
Huangcaoba China see Xingyi
Huangchuan China 77 G1
Huanggang China see Huangzhou
Huang Hai sea N. Pacific Ocean see Yellow Sea
Huang He r. China see Yellow River
Huangjiajian China 77 I1
Huangling China 77 F1
Huangliu China 77 F5
Huanglongsi China see Kaifeng
Huangmao Jian mt. China 77 H3
Huangmei China 77 G2
Huangpu China 77 G4
Huangqi China 77 H3
Huangshan China 77 H2
Huangshi China 77 G2
Huangtu Gaoyuan plat. China 73 J5
Huangyan China 77 I2
Huangzhou China 77 G2
Huaning China 76 D3
Huanjiang China 77 F3
Huanren China 74 B4
Huanshan China see Yuhuan
Huánuco Peru 142 C5
Huaping China 76 D3
Huap'ing Yü i. Taiwan 77 I3
Huaqiao China 76 E2
Huaqiaozhen China see Huaqiao
Huaráz Peru 142 C5
Huarmey Peru 142 C6
Huarong China 77 G2
Huascarán, Nevado de mt. Peru 142 C5
Huasco Chile 144 B3
Hua Shan mt. China 77 F1
Huashixia China 76 C1
Huashugou China see Jingtieshan
Huashulinzi China 74 B4
Huatabampo Mex. 127 F8
Huaxian Guangdong China see Huadu
Huaxian Henan China 77 G1
Huayang China see Jixi
Huayin China 77 F1
Huayuan China 77 F2
Huazangsi China see Tianzhu
Hubbard, Mount Canada/U.S.A. 120 B2
Hubbard, Pointe pt Canada 123 I2
Hubbard Lake U.S.A. 134 D1
Hubbart Point Canada 121 M3
Hubei prov. China 77 G2
Hubli India 84 B3
Hückelhoven Germany 52 G3
Hucknall U.K. 49 F5
Huddersfield U.K. 48 F5
Huder China 74 A2
Hudiksvall Sweden 45 J6
Hudson MA U.S.A. 135 J2
Hudson MD U.S.A. 135 G4
Hudson MI U.S.A. 134 C3
Hudson NH U.S.A. 135 J2
Hudson NY U.S.A. 135 I2
Hudson r. U.S.A. 135 I3
Hudson, Baie d' sea Canada see Hudson Bay
Hudson, Détroit d' strait Canada see Hudson Strait
Hudson Bay Canada 121 K4
Hudson Bay sea Canada 119 J4
Hudson Falls U.S.A. 135 I2
Hudson Island Tuvalu see Nanumanga
Hudson Mountains Antarctica 152 K2
Hudson's Hope Canada 120 F3
Hudson Strait Canada 119 K3
Huê Vietnam 70 D3
Huehuetenango Guat. 136 F5
Huehueto, Cerro mt. Mex. 131 B7
Huelva Spain 57 C5
Huentelauquén Chile 144 B4
Huépac Mex. 127 F7
Huércal-Overa Spain 57 F5
Huertecillas Mex. 131 C7
Huesca Spain 57 F2
Huéscar Spain 57 E5
Hughenden Australia 110 D4
Hughes Australia 109 E7
Hughes r. Canada 121 K3
Hughson U.S.A. 128 C3
Hugli r. mouth India 83 F5
Hugo CO U.S.A. 130 C4
Hugo OK U.S.A. 131 E5
Hugo Lake U.S.A. 131 E5
Hugoton U.S.A. 131 C4
Huhehot China see Hohhot
Huhhot China see Hohhot
Huhudi S. Africa 100 G4
Hui'an China 77 H3
Hui'anpu China 72 J5
Huiarau Range mts N.Z. 113 F4
Huib-Hoch Plateau Namibia 100 C4
Huichang China 77 G3
Huicheng Anhui China see Shexian
Huicheng Guangdong China see Huilai
Huidong China 76 D3
Huijbergen Neth. 52 E3
Huila, Nevado de vol. Col. 142 C3
Huilai China 77 H4
Huíla Plateau Angola 99 B5
Huili China 76 D3
Huimanguillo Mex. 136 F5
Huinahuaca Arg. 144 C2
Huinan China see Nanhui
Huining China 76 E1
Huishi China see Huining
Huishui China 76 E3
Huiten Nur l. China 83 G2
Huitong China 77 F3
Huittinen Fin. 45 M6
Huixian Gansu China 76 E1
Huixian Henan China 77 G1
Huiyang China see Huizhou
Huize China 76 D3
Huizhou China 77 G4
Hujirt Mongolia 72 I3
Hujr Saudi Arabia 86 F4
Hukawng Valley Myanmar 70 B1
Hukuntsi Botswana 100 E2
Hulan China 74 B3
Hulan Ergi China 74 A3
Ḥulayfah Saudi Arabia 86 F4
Ḥulayḥilah well Syria 85 D2
Huliao China see Dabu
Hulilan Iran 88 B3
Hulin China 74 D3
Hulin Gol r. China 74 B3
Hull Canada 135 H1
Hull U.K. see Kingston upon Hull
Hull Island atoll Kiribati see Orona
Hultsfred Sweden 45 I8
Hulun China see Hailar
Hulun Nur l. China 73 L3
Ḥulwān Egypt 90 C5
Huma China 74 B2
Humaitá Brazil 142 F5
Humaya r. Mex. 127 G8
Humaym well U.A.E. 88 D6
Humayyān, Jabal hill Saudi Arabia 88 B5
Humber, Mouth of the U.K. 48 H5
Humboldt Canada 121 J4
Humboldt AZ U.S.A. 129 G4
Humboldt NE U.S.A. 130 E3
Humboldt NV U.S.A. 128 D1
Humboldt r. U.S.A. 128 D1
Humboldt Bay U.S.A. 126 B4
Humboldt Range mts U.S.A. 128 D1
Humbolt Salt Marsh U.S.A. 128 E2
Hume r. Canada 120 D1
Humeburn Australia 112 B1
Hu Men sea chan. China 77 G4
Hume Reservoir Australia 112 C5
Humphrey Island atoll Cook Is see Manihiki
Humphreys, Mount U.S.A. 128 D3
Humphreys Peak U.S.A. 129 H4
Hūn Libya 97 E2
Húnaflói b. Iceland 44 [inset]
Hunan prov. China 77 F3
Hundeluft Germany 53 M3
Hunedoara Romania 59 J2
Hünfeld Germany 53 J4
▶Hungary country Europe 55 H2
Europe 5, 38–39
Hungerford Australia 112 B2
Hung Fa Leng hill Hong Kong China see Robin's Nest
Hŭngnam N. Korea 75 B5
Hung Shui Kiu Hong Kong China 77 [inset]
Hưng Yên Vietnam 70 D2
Hunjiang China see Baishan
Huns Mountains Namibia 100 C4
Hunstanton U.K. 49 H6
Hunte r. Germany 53 I1
Hunter r. Australia 112 E4
Hunter Island Australia 111 [inset]
Hunter Island Canada 120 D5
Hunter Island S. Pacific Ocean 107 H4
Hunter Islands Australia 111 [inset]
Huntingburg U.S.A. 134 B4
Huntingdon Canada 135 H1
Huntingdon U.K. 49 G6
Huntingdon PA U.S.A. 135 G3
Huntingdon TN U.S.A. 131 F4
Huntington IN U.S.A. 134 C3
Huntington OR U.S.A. 126 D3
Huntington WV U.S.A. 134 D4
Huntington Beach U.S.A. 128 D5
Huntington Creek r. U.S.A. 129 F1
Huntly N.Z. 113 E3
Huntly U.K. 50 G3
Hunt Mountain U.S.A. 126 G3
Huntsville Canada 134 F1
Huntsville AL U.S.A. 133 C5
Huntsville AR U.S.A. 131 E4
Huntsville TN U.S.A. 134 C5
Huntsville TX U.S.A. 131 E6
Hunza reg. Jammu and Kashmir 82 C1
Huolin He r. China see Hulin Gol
Huolongmen China 74 B2
Hương Khê Vietnam 70 D3
Hương Thuy Vietnam 70 D3
Huonville Australia 111 [inset]
Huoqiu China 77 H1
Huoshan China 77 H2
Huo Shan mt. China see Baima Jian
Huoshao Tao i. Taiwan see Lü Tao
Hupeh prov. China see Hubei
Hupnik r. Turkey 85 C1
Hupu India 76 B2
Ḥūr Iran 88 E4
Hurault, Lac l. Canada 123 H3
Ḥuraydīn, Wādī watercourse Egypt 85 A4
Huraysān reg. Saudi Arabia 88 B6
Hurd, Cape Canada 134 E1
Hurd Island Kiribati see Arorae
Hurghada Egypt see Al Ghurdaqah
Hurler's Cross Rep. of Ireland 51 D5
Hurley NM U.S.A. 129 I5
Hurley WI U.S.A. 130 F2
Hurmagai Pak. 89 G4
Huron CA U.S.A. 128 C3
Huron SD U.S.A. 130 D2

▶Huron, Lake Canada/U.S.A. 134 D1
2nd largest lake in North America and 4th in the world.
World 12–13

Hurricane U.S.A. 129 G3
Hursley U.K. 49 F7
Hurst Green U.K. 49 H7
Husain Nika Pak. 89 H4
Húsavík Norðurland eystra Iceland 44 [inset]
Húsavík Vestfirðir Iceland 44 [inset]
Huseyinabat Turkey see Alaca
Huseyinli Turkey see Kızılırmak
Hushan Zhejiang China 77 H2
Hushan Zhejiang China see Cixi
Hushan Zhejiang China see Wuyi
Huşi Romania 59 M1
Huskvarna Sweden 45 I8
Husn Jordan see Al Ḥiṣn
Ḥusn Āl 'Abr Yemen 86 G6
Husnes Norway 45 D7
Husum Germany 47 L3
Husum Sweden 44 K5
Hutag Mongolia 80 J2
Hutchinson KS U.S.A. 130 D4
Hutchinson MN U.S.A. 130 E2
Hutch Mountain U.S.A. 129 H4
Hutou China 74 D3
Hutsonville U.S.A. 134 B4
Huttah Kulkyne National Park Australia 111 C7
Hutton, Mount hill Australia 111 E5
Hutton Range hills Australia 109 C6
Hưu Đô Vietnam 70 D2
Huvadhu Atoll Maldives 81 D11
Hüvek Turkey see Bozova
Hūvīān, Kūh-e mts Iran 89 E5
Huwār i. Bahrain 88 C5
Huwaytat reg. Saudi Arabia 85 C5
Huxi China 77 G3
Huzhong China 74 A2

Huzhou China 77 I2
Hvannadalshnúkur vol. Iceland 44 [inset]
Hvar i. Croatia 58 G3
Hvide Sande Denmark 45 F8
Hvíta r. Iceland 44 [inset]
Hwange Zimbabwe 99 C5
Hwange National Park Zimbabwe 99 C5
Hwang Ho r. China see Yellow River
Hwedza Zimbabwe 99 D5
Hwlffordd U.K. see Haverfordwest
Hyannis MA U.S.A. 135 J3
Hyannis NE U.S.A. 130 C3
Hyargas Nuur salt l. Mongolia 80 H2
Hyco Lake U.S.A. 134 F5
Hyde N.Z. 113 C7
Hyden Australia 109 B8
Hyden U.S.A. 134 D5
Hyde Park U.S.A. 135 I1
Hyderabad India 84 C2
Hyderabad Pak. 89 H5
Hydra i. Greece see Ydra
Hyères France 56 H5
Hyères, Îles d' is France 56 H5
Hyesan N. Korea 74 C4
Hyland, Mount Australia 112 F3
Hyland Post Canada 120 D3
Hyllestad Norway 45 D6
Hyltebruk Sweden 45 H8
Hyndman Peak U.S.A. 126 E4
Hyōno-sen mt. Japan 75 D6
Hyrcania Iran see Gorgān
Hyrynsalmi Fin. 44 P4
Hysham U.S.A. 126 G3
Hythe Canada 120 G4
Hythe U.K. 49 I7
Hyūga Japan 75 C6
Hyvinkää Fin. 45 N6

I

Iaciara Brazil 145 B1
Iaco r. Brazil 142 E5
Iaçu Brazil 145 C1
Iadera Croatia see Zadar
Iaeger U.S.A. 134 E5
Iakora Madag. 99 E6
Ialomița r. Romania 59 L2
Ianca Romania 59 L2
Iași Romania 59 L1
Iba Phil. 69 F3
Ibadan Nigeria 96 D4
Ibagué Col. 142 C3
Ibaiti Brazil 145 A3
Ibapah U.S.A. 129 G1
Ibarra Ecuador 142 C3
Ibb Yemen 86 F7
Ibbenbüren Germany 53 H2
Iberá, Esteros del marsh Arg. 144 E3
Iberia Peru 142 E6

▶Iberian Peninsula Europe 57
Consists of Portugal, Spain and Gibraltar.

Iberville, Lac d' l. Canada 123 G3
Ibeto Nigeria 96 D3
iBhayi S. Africa see Port Elizabeth
Ibi Indon. 71 B6
Ibi Nigeria 96 D4
Ibiá Brazil 145 B2
Ibiaí Brazil 145 B2
Ibiapaba, Serra da hills Brazil 143 J4
Ibiassucê Brazil 145 C1
Ibicaraí Brazil 145 D1
Ibiquera Brazil 145 C1
Ibirama Brazil 145 A4
Ibiranhém Brazil 145 C2
Ibitinga Brazil 145 A3
Ibiza Spain 57 G4
Ibiza i. Spain 57 G4
Iblei, Monti mts Sicily Italy 58 F6
Ibn Buşayyiş well Saudi Arabia 88 B5
Ibotirama Brazil 143 J6
Iboundji, Mont hill Gabon 98 B4
Ibrā' Oman 88 E6
İbradı Turkey 90 C3
Ibrī Oman 88 E6
Ica Peru 142 C6
Ica r. Peru see Putumayo
Içana Brazil 142 E3
Içana r. Brazil 142 E3
Icaria i. Greece see Ikaria
Icatu Brazil 143 J4
Iceberg Canyon gorge U.S.A. 129 F3
İçel Turkey 85 B1
İçel prov. Turkey 85 A1

▶Iceland country Europe 44 [inset]
2nd largest island in Europe.
Europe 5, 38–39

Iceland Basin sea feature
N. Atlantic Ocean 148 G2
Icelandic Plateau sea feature
N. Atlantic Ocean 153 I2
Ichalkaranji India 84 B2
Ichinomiya Japan 75 E6
Ichinoseki Japan 75 F5
Ichinskiy, Vulkan vol. Rus. Fed. 65 Q4
Ichkeul National Park Tunisia 58 C6
Ichnya Ukr. 43 G6
Ichtegem Belgium 52 D3
Ichtershausen Germany 53 K4
Icó Brazil 143 K5
Iconha Brazil 145 C3
Iconium Turkey see Konya
Icosium Alg. see Algiers
Iculisma France see Angoulême
Icy Cape U.S.A. 118 B2
Id Turkey see Narman
Idabel U.S.A. 131 E5
Ida Grove U.S.A. 130 E3
Idah Nigeria 96 D4
Idaho state U.S.A. 126 E3
Idaho City U.S.A. 126 E4
Idaho Falls U.S.A. 126 E4
Idalia National Park Australia 110 D5
Idar India 82 C5
Idar-Oberstein Germany 53 H5
Ideriyn Gol r. Mongolia 80 J2
Idfū Egypt 86 D5
Idhān Awbārī des. Libya 96 E2
Idhān Murzūq des. Libya 96 E2
Idhra i. Greece see Ydra
Idi Amin Dada, Lake
Dem. Rep. Congo/Uganda see
Edward, Lake
Idiofa Dem. Rep. Congo 99 B4
Idivuoma Sweden 44 M2
Idkū Egypt 90 C5
Idle r. U.K. 48 G5
Idlewild airport U.S.A. see
John F. Kennedy
Idlib Syria 85 C2
Idra i. Greece see Ydra
Idre Sweden 45 H6
Idstein Germany 53 I4
Idutywa S. Africa 101 I7
Idzhevan Armenia see Ijevan
Iecava Latvia 45 N8
Iepê Brazil 145 A3
Ieper Belgium 52 C4
Ierapetra Greece 59 K7
Ierissou, Kolpos b. Greece 59 J4
Ifakara Tanz. 99 D4
Ifalik atoll Micronesia 69 K5
Ifaluk atoll Micronesia see Ifalik
Ifanadiana Madag. 99 E6
Ife Nigeria 96 D4
Ifenat Chad 97 E3
Iferouâne Niger 96 D3
Iffley Australia 110 C3
Ifjord Norway 44 O1
Ifôghas, Adrar des hills Mali 92 D3
Iforas, Adrar des hills Mali see
Ifôghas, Adrar des
Igan Sarawak Malaysia 68 E6
Iganga Uganda 97 G4
Igarapava Brazil 145 B3
Igarka Rus. Fed. 64 J3
Igatpuri India 84 B2
Igbeti Nigeria see Igbetti
Igbetti Nigeria 96 D4
Igdir Iran 88 B2
Iğdır Turkey 91 G3
Iggesund Sweden 45 J6
Igikpak, Mount U.S.A. 118 C3
Igizyar China 89 J2
Iglesias Sardinia Italy 58 C5
Iglesiente reg. Sardinia Italy 58 C5
Igloolik Canada 119 J3
Igluligaarjuk Canada see
Chesterfield Inlet
Ignace Canada 121 N5
Ignacio Zaragosa Mex. 127 G7
Ignacio Zaragoza Mex. 131 C8
Ignalina Lith. 45 O9
İğneada Turkey 59 L4
İğneada Burnu pt Turkey 59 M4
Ignoitijala India 71 A5
iGoli S. Africa see Johannesburg
Igoumenitsa Greece 59 I5
Igra Rus. Fed. 41 Q4
Igrim Rus. Fed. 41 S3
Iguaçu r. Brazil 145 A4
Iguaçu, Saltos do waterfall Arg./Brazil see
Iguaçu Falls
Iguaçu Falls Arg./Brazil 144 F3
Iguaí Brazil 145 C1
Iguala Mex. 136 E5
Igualada Spain 57 G3
Iguape Brazil 145 B4
Iguaraçu Brazil 145 A3
Iguatama Brazil 145 B3
Iguatemi Brazil 144 F2
Iguatu Brazil 143 K5
Iguazú, Cataratas do waterfall Arg./Brazil
see Iguaçu Falls
Iguéla Gabon 98 A4
Iguidi, Erg des. Alg./Mauritania 96 C2
Igunga Tanz. 99 D4
Iharaña Madag. 99 E5
Ihavandhippolhu Atoll Maldives 84 B5
Ihavandiffulu Atoll Maldives see
Ihavandhippolhu Atoll
Ih Bogd Uul mt. Mongolia 80 J3
Ihosy Madag. 99 E6
Iide-san mt. Japan 75 E5
Iijärvi l. Fin. 44 O2
Iijoki r. Fin. 44 N4
Iisalmi Fin. 44 O5
Iizuka Japan 75 C6
Ijebu-Ode Nigeria 96 D4
Ijevan Armenia 91 G2
IJmuiden Neth. 52 E2
IJssel r. Neth. 52 F2
IJsselmeer l. Neth. 52 F2
IJzer r. Belgium see Yser
Ikaahuk Canada see Sachs Harbour
Ikaalinen Fin. 45 M6
Ikageleng S. Africa 101 H3
Ikageng S. Africa 101 H4
iKapa S. Africa see Cape Town
Ikare Nigeria 96 D4
Ikaria i. Greece 59 L6
Ikast Denmark 45 F8
Ikeda Japan 74 F4
Ikela Dem. Rep. Congo 98 C4
Ikhtiman Bulg. 59 J3
Ikhutseng S. Africa 100 G5
Iki-Burul Rus. Fed. 43 J7
Ikom Nigeria 96 D4
Iksan S. Korea 75 B6
Ikungu Tanz. 99 D4
Ilagan Phil. 77 I5
Ilaisamis Kenya 98 D3
Īlām Iran 88 B3
Ilam Nepal 83 F4
Ilan Taiwan 77 I3
Ilave Peru 142 E7
Iława Poland 47 Q4
Ilazārān, Kūh-e mt. Iran 88 E4
Île-à-la-Crosse Canada 121 J4
Île-à-la-Crosse, Lac l. Canada 121 J4
Ilebo Dem. Rep. Congo 99 C4
Île-de-France admin. reg. France 52 C6
Île Europa i. Indian Ocean see Europa, Île
Ilek Kazakh. 41 Q5
Ilen r. Rep. of Ireland 51 C6
Ileret Kenya 98 D3
Ileza Rus. Fed. 42 I3
Ilfeld Germany 53 K3
Ilford Canada 121 M3
Ilford U.K. 49 H7
Ilfracombe Australia 110 D4
Ilfracombe U.K. 49 C7
Ilgaz Turkey 90 D2
Ilgın Turkey 90 C3
Ilha Grande, Represa resr Brazil 144 F2
Ilha Solteíra, Represa resr Brazil 145 A3
Ílhavo Port. 57 B3
Ilhéus Brazil 145 D1
Ili Kazakh. see Kapchagay
Iliamna Lake U.S.A. 118 C4
İliç Turkey 90 E3
Il'ichevsk Azer. see Şärur
Il'ichevsk Ukr. see Illichivs'k
Ilici Spain see Elche-Elx
Iligan Phil. 69 G5
Ilimananngip Nunaa i. Greenland 119 P2
Il'inka Rus. Fed. 43 J7
Il'inskiy Permskaya Oblast' Rus. Fed. 41 R4
Il'inskiy Sakhalinskaya Oblast' Rus. Fed.
74 F3
Il'insko-Podomskoye Rus. Fed. 42 J3
Ilion U.S.A. 135 H2
Ilium tourist site Turkey see Troy
Iliysk Kazakh. see Kapchagay
Ilkal India 84 C3
Ilkeston U.K. 49 F6
Ilkley U.K. 48 F5
Illapel Chile 144 B4
Illéla Niger 96 D3
Iller r. Germany 47 L6
Illichivs'k Ukr. 59 N1
Illimani, Nevado de mt. Bol. 142 E7
Illinois r. U.S.A. 130 F4
Illinois state U.S.A. 134 A3
Illizi Alg. 96 D2
Illogwa watercourse Australia 106 A5
Ilm r. Germany 53 L3
Ilmajoki Fin. 44 M5
Il'men', Ozero l. Rus. Fed. 42 F4
Ilmenau Germany 53 K4
Ilmenau r. Germany 53 K1
Ilminster U.K. 49 E8
Ilo Peru 142 D7
Iloilo Phil. 69 G4
Ilomantsi Fin. 44 Q5
Ilong India 76 B3
Ilorin Nigeria 96 D4
Ilovlya Rus. Fed. 43 I6
Ilsede Germany 53 K2
Iluka Australia 112 F2
Ilulissat Greenland 119 M3
Iluppur India 84 C4
Ilva i. Italy see Elba, Isola d'
Imabari Japan 75 D6
Imaichi Japan 75 E5
Imala Moz. 99 D5
Imam-baba Turkm. 89 F2
İmamoğlu Turkey 90 D3
Iman Rus. Fed. see Dal'nerechensk
Iman r. Rus. Fed. 74 D3
Imari Japan 75 C6
Imaruí Brazil 145 A5
Imataca, Serranía de mts Venez. 142 F2
Imatra Fin. 45 P6
Imbituva Brazil 145 A4
imeni Babushkina Rus. Fed. 38 I4
imeni 26 Bakinskikh Komissarov Azer. see
26 Bakı Komissarı
imeni 26 Bakinskikh Komissarov Turkm.
88 D2
imeni C. A. Niyazova Turkm. 89 F2
imeni Chapayevka Turkm. see
imeni C. A. Niyazova
imeni Kalinina Tajik. see Cheshtebe
imeni Kerbabayeva Turkm. 89 F2
imeni Kirova Kazakh. see Kopbirlik
imeni Petra Stuchki Latvia see Aizkraukle
imeni Poliny Osipenko Rus. Fed. 74 E1
imeni Tel'mana Rus. Fed. 74 D2
Īmī Eth. 98 E3
Imishli Azer. see İmişli
İmişli Azer. 91 H3
Imit Jammu and Kashmir 82 C1
Imja-do i. S. Korea 75 B6
Imlay U.S.A. 128 D1
Imlay City U.S.A. 134 D2
Imola Italy 58 D2
iMonti S. Africa see East London
Impendle S. Africa 101 I5
Imperatriz Brazil 143 I5
Imperia Italy 58 C3
Imperial CA U.S.A. 129 F5
Imperial NE U.S.A. 130 C3
Imperial Beach U.S.A. 128 E5
Imperial Dam U.S.A. 129 F5
Imperial Valley plain U.S.A. 129 F5
Imperieuse Reef Australia 108 B4
Impfondo Congo 98 B3
Imphal India 83 H4
İmralı Adası i. Turkey 59 M4
İmroz Turkey 59 K4
İmroz i. Turkey see Gökçeada
Imtān Syria 85 C3
Imuris Mex. 127 F7
In r. Rus. Fed. 74 D2
Ina Japan 75 E6
Inambari r. Peru 142 E6
Inari Fin. 44 O2
Inarijärvi l. Fin. 44 O2
Inarijoki r. Fin./Norway 44 N2
Inca Spain 57 H4
İnce Burnu pt Turkey 59 L4
İnce Burun pt Turkey 55 L3
Inch Rep. of Ireland 51 F5
Inchard, Loch b. U.K. 50 D2
Incheon S. Korea see Inch'ŏn
Inchicronan Lough l. Rep. of Ireland
51 D5
Inch'ŏn S. Korea 75 B5
Incirli Turkey see Karasu
Indaal, Loch b. U.K. 50 C5
Indalsälven r. Sweden 44 J5
Indalstø Norway 45 D6
Inda Silasē Eth. 98 D2
Indaw Myanmar 70 A2
Indawgyi, Lake Myanmar 76 C3
Indé Mex. 131 B7
Indefatigable Island Galápagos Ecuador
see Santa Cruz, Isla
Independence CA U.S.A. 128 D3
Independence IA U.S.A. 130 F3
Independence KS U.S.A. 131 E4
Independence KY U.S.A. 134 C4
Independence MO U.S.A. 130 E4
Independence VA U.S.A. 134 E5
Independence Mountains U.S.A. 126 D4
Inder China 74 A3
Inderborskiy Kazakh. 78 E2
Indi India 84 C2

▶India country Asia 81 E7
2nd most populous country in the world
and in Asia. 3rd largest country in Asia.
Asia 6, 62–63

Indian r. Canada 120 B2
Indiana U.S.A. 134 F3
Indiana state U.S.A. 134 B3
Indian-Antarctic Ridge sea feature
Southern Ocean 150 D9

▶Indianapolis U.S.A. 134 B4
State capital of Indiana.

Indian Cabins Canada 120 G3
Indian Desert India/Pak. see Thar Desert
Indian Harbour Canada 123 K3
Indian Head Canada 121 K5
Indian Lake U.S.A. 135 H2
Indian Lake l. NY U.S.A. 135 H2
Indian Lake l. OH U.S.A. 134 D3
Indian Lake l. PA U.S.A. 135 F3

▶Indian Ocean 149
3rd largest ocean in the world.

Indianola IA U.S.A. 130 E3
Indianola MS U.S.A. 131 F5
Indian Peak U.S.A. 129 G2
Indian Springs IN U.S.A. 134 B4
Indian Springs NV U.S.A. 129 F3
Indian Wells U.S.A. 129 H4
Indiga Rus. Fed. 42 K2
Indigirka r. Rus. Fed. 65 P2
Indigskaya Guba b. Rus. Fed. 38 K2
Inđija Serb. and Mont. 59 I2
Indin Lake Canada 120 H1
Indio U.S.A. 128 E5
Indira Point India see Pygmalion Point
Indispensable Reefs Solomon Is 107 G3
Indjija Serb. and Mont. see Inđija
Indo-China reg. Asia 70 D3

▶Indonesia country Asia 68 E7
4th most populous country in the world
and 3rd in Asia.
Asia 6, 62–63

Indore India 82 C5
Indrapura, Gunung vol. Indon. see
Kerinci, Gunung
Indravati r. India 84 D2
Indre r. France 56 E3
Indulkana Australia 109 F6
Indur India see Nizamabad
Indus r. China/Pak. 89 G6
also known as Sênggê Zangbo or
Shiquan He
Indus, Mouths of the Pak. 89 G5
Indus Cone sea feature Indian Ocean
149 M4
Indwe S. Africa 101 H6
İnebolu Turkey 90 D2
İnegöl Turkey 59 M4
Inevi Turkey see Cihanbeyli
Inez U.S.A. 134 D5
Infantes Spain see
Villanueva de los Infantes
Infiernillo, Presa resr Mex. 136 D5
Ing, Nam Mae r. Thai. 70 C2
Inga Rus. Fed. 44 S3
Ingalls, Mount U.S.A. 128 C2
Ingelmunster Belgium 52 D4
Ingenika r. Canada 120 E3
Ingersoll Canada 134 E2
Ingham Australia 110 D3
Inglchka Uzbek. 89 G2
Ingleborough hill U.K. 48 E4
Inglefield Land reg. Greenland 119 K2
Ingleton U.K. 48 E4
Inglewood Qld Australia 112 E2
Inglewood Vic. Australia 112 A6
Inglewood U.S.A. 128 D5
Ingoka Pum mt. Myanmar 70 B1
Ingoldmells U.K. 48 H5
Ingolstadt Germany 53 L6
Ingomar Australia 109 F7
Ingomar U.S.A. 126 G3
Ingonish Canada 123 J5
Ingraj Bazar India 83 G4
Ingram U.S.A. 134 F5
Ingray Lake Canada 120 G1
Ingrid Christensen Coast Antarctica
152 E2
Ingwavuma S. Africa 101 K4
Ingwavuma r. S. Africa/Swaziland see
Ngwavuma
Ingwiller France 53 H6
Inhaca Moz. 101 K3
Inhaca, Península pen. Moz. 101 K4
Inhambane Moz. 101 L2
Inhambane prov. Moz. 101 L2
Inhaminga Moz. 99 D5
Inharrime Moz. 101 L3
Inhassoro Moz. 99 D6
Inhaúmas Brazil 145 B1
Inhobim Brazil 145 C1
Inhumas Brazil 145 A2
Inis Rep. of Ireland see Ennis
Inis Córthaidh Rep. of Ireland see
Enniscorthy
Inishark i. Rep. of Ireland 51 B4
Inishbofin i. Rep. of Ireland 51 B4
Inisheer i. Rep. of Ireland 51 C4
Inishkea North i. Rep. of Ireland 51 B3
Inishkea South i. Rep. of Ireland 51 B3
Inishmaan i. Rep. of Ireland 51 C4
Inishmore i. Rep. of Ireland 51 C4
Inishmurray i. Rep. of Ireland 51 D3
Inishowen pen. Rep. of Ireland 51 E2
Inishowen Head hd Rep. of Ireland 51 F2
Inishtrahull i. Rep. of Ireland 51 E2
Inishturk i. Rep. of Ireland 51 B4
Injune Australia 111 E5
Inkerman Australia 110 C3
Inklin Canada 120 C3
Inklin r. Canada 120 C3
Inkylap Turkm. 89 F2
Inland Kaikoura Range mts N.Z. 113 D6
Inland Sea Japan see Seto-naikai
Inlet U.S.A. 135 H2
Inn r. Europe 47 M7
Innaanganeq c. Greenland 119 L2
Innamincka Australia 111 C5
Innamincka Regional Reserve nature res.
Australia 111 C5
Inndyr Norway 44 I3
Inner Sound sea chan. U.K. 50 D3
Innes National Park Australia 111 B7
Innisfail Australia 110 D3
Innisfail Canada 120 H4
Innokent'yevka Rus. Fed. 74 C2
Innoko r. U.S.A. 118 C3
Innsbruck Austria 47 M7
Innuksuak r. Canada 122 F2
Inny r. Rep. of Ireland 51 E4
Inocência Brazil 145 A2
Inongo Dem. Rep. Congo 98 B4
İnönü Turkey 59 N5
Inoucdjouac Canada see Inukjuak
Inowrocław Poland 47 Q4
In Salah Alg. 96 D2
Insch U.K. 50 G3

▶Inscription, Cape Austr. 110 B3
Most westerly point of Oceania.

Insein Myanmar 70 B3
Insterburg Rus. Fed. see Chernyakhovsk
Inta Rus. Fed. 41 S2
Interamna Italy see Teramo
Interlaken Switz. 56 H3
International Falls U.S.A. 130 E1
Interview Island India 71 A4
Intracoastal Waterway canal U.S.A. 131 E6
Intutu Peru 142 D4
Inubō-zaki pt Japan 75 F6
Inukjuak Canada 122 F2
Inuvik Canada 118 E3
Inveraray U.K. 50 D4
Inverbervie U.K. 50 G4
Invercargill N.Z. 113 B8
Inverell Australia 112 E2
Invergordon U.K. 50 E3
Inverkeithing U.K. 50 F4
Inverleigh Australia 110 C3
Invermay Canada 121 K5
Inverness Canada 123 J5
Inverness U.K. 50 E3
Inverness CA U.S.A. 128 B2
Inverness FL U.S.A. 133 D6
Inverurie U.K. 50 G3
Investigator Channel Myanmar 71 B4
Investigator Group is Australia 109 F8
Investigator Ridge sea feature
Indian Ocean 149 O6
Investigator Strait Australia 111 B7
Inwood U.S.A. 135 F4
Inya Rus. Fed. 80 G1
Inyanga Zimbabwe see Nyanga
Inyangani mt. Zimbabwe 99 D5
Inyokern U.S.A. 128 E4
Inyo Mountains U.S.A. 128 D3
Inyonga Tanz. 99 D4
Inza Rus. Fed. 43 J5
Inzhavino Rus. Fed. 43 I5
Ioannina Greece 59 I5
Iokanga r. Rus. Fed. 42 H2
Iola U.S.A. 130 E4
Iolgo, Khrebet mts Rus. Fed. 80 G1
Iolotan' Turkm. see Yeloten
Iona Canada 123 J5
Iona i. U.K. 50 C4
Iona, Parque Nacional do nat. park
Angola 99 B5
Ione U.S.A. 128 E2
Iongo Angola 99 B4
Ionia U.S.A. 134 C2
Ionian Islands Greece 59 H5
Ionian Sea Greece/Italy 58 H5
Ionioi Nisoi is Greece see Ionian Islands
Ios i. Greece 59 K6
Iowa state U.S.A. 130 E3
Iowa City U.S.A. 130 F3
Iowa Falls U.S.A. 130 E3
Ipameri Brazil 145 A2
Ipanema Brazil 145 C2
Iparía Peru 142 D5
Ipatinga Brazil 145 C2
Ipatovo Rus. Fed. 43 I7
Ipelegeng S. Africa 101 G4
Ipiales Col. 142 C3
Ipiaú Brazil 145 D1
Ipirá Brazil 145 D1
Ipiranga Brazil 145 A4
iPitoli S. Africa see Pretoria
Ipixuna r. Brazil 142 F5
Ipoh Malaysia 71 C6
Iporá Brazil 145 A2
Ippy Cent. Afr. Rep. 98 C3
İpsala Turkey 59 L4
Ipswich Australia 112 F1
Ipswich U.K. 49 I6
Ipswich U.S.A. 130 D2
Ipu Brazil 143 J4

▶Iqaluit Canada 119 L3
Territorial capital of Nunavut.

Iquique Chile 144 B2
Iquiri r. Brazil see Ituxi
Iquitos Peru 142 D4
Īrafshān reg. Iran 89 F5
Irai Brazil 144 F3
Irakleio Greece see Iraklion
Iraklion Greece 59 K7
Iramaia Brazil 145 C1
▶Iran country Asia 88 D3
Asia 6, 62–63
Iran, Pegunungan mts Indon. 68 E6
Īrānshahr Iran 89 F5
Irapuato Mex. 136 D4
▶Iraq country Asia 91 F4
Asia 6, 62–63
Irara Brazil 145 D1
Irati Brazil 145 A4
Irayel' Rus. Fed. 42 L2
Irazú, Volcán vol. Costa Rica 133 H7
Irbid Jordan 85 B3
Irbīl Iraq see Arbīl
Irbit Rus. Fed. 64 H4
Irecê Brazil 143 J6

▶Ireland i. Rep. of Ireland/U.K. 51
4th largest island in Europe.

▶Ireland, Republic of country Europe
51 E4
Europe 5, 38–39
Irema Dem. Rep. Congo 98 C4
Irgiz Kazakh. 80 B2
Irgiz r. Kazakh. 80 B2
Iri S. Korea see Iksan
Irian, Teluk b. Indon. see
Cenderawasih, Teluk
Iriba Chad 97 F3
Īrī Dāgh mt. Iran 88 B2
Iriga Phil. 69 G4
Irîgui reg. Mali/Mauritania 96 C3
Iringa Tanz. 99 D4
Iriri r. Brazil 143 H4
Irish Free State country Europe see
Ireland, Republic of
Irish Sea Rep. of Ireland/U.K. 51 G4
Irituia Brazil 143 I4
'Irj well Saudi Arabia 88 C5
Irkutsk Rus. Fed. 72 I2
Irma Canada 121 I4
Irmak Turkey 90 D3
Irminger Basin sea feature
N. Atlantic Ocean 148 F2
Iron Baron Australia 111 B7
Irondequoit U.S.A. 135 G2
Iron Mountain U.S.A. 130 F2
Iron Mountain mt. U.S.A. 129 G3
Iron Range National Park Australia
110 C2
Iron River U.S.A. 130 F2
Ironton MO U.S.A. 130 F4
Ironton OH U.S.A. 134 D4
Ironwood Forest National Monument
nat. park U.S.A. 129 H5
Iroquois r. U.S.A. 134 B3
Iroquois Falls Canada 122 E4
Irosin Phil. 69 G4
Irpen' Ukr. see Irpin'
Irpin' Ukr. 43 F6
'Irq al Ḩarūrī des. Saudi Arabia 88 B5
'Irq al Mazhūr des. Saudi Arabia 88 A5
'Irq Banbān des. Saudi Arabia 88 B5
'Irq Jahām des. Saudi Arabia 88 B5
Irrawaddy r. Myanmar 70 A4
Irrawaddy, Mouths of the Myanmar 70 A4
Irshad Pass Afgh./Jammu and Kashmir
89 I2
Irta Rus. Fed. 42 K3
Irthing r. U.K. 48 E4

▶Irtysh r. Kazakh./Rus. Fed. 80 E1
5th longest river in Asia. Part of the 2nd
longest river in Asia (Ob'-Irtysh).

Irún Spain 57 F2
Iruña Spain see Pamplona
Iruñea Spain see Pamplona
Irvine U.K. 50 E5
Irvine CA U.S.A. 128 E5
Irvine KY U.S.A. 134 D5
Irvine Glacier Antarctica 152 L2
Irving U.S.A. 131 D5
Irvington U.S.A. 134 B5
Irwin r. Australia 109 A7
Irwinton U.S.A. 133 D5
Isa Nigeria 96 D3
Isaac r. Australia 110 E4
Isabel U.S.A. 130 C2
Isabela Phil. 69 G5
Isabela, Isla i. Galápagos Ecuador
142 [inset]
Isabelia, Cordillera mts Nicaragua 137 G6
Isabella Lake U.S.A. 128 D4
Isachsen, Cape Canada 119 H2
Ísafjarðardjúp est. Iceland 44 [inset]
Ísafjörður Iceland 44 [inset]
Isa Khel Pak. 89 H3
Isar r. Germany 53 M6
Isbister U.K. 50 [inset]
Ischia, Isola d' i. Italy 58 E4
Ise Japan 75 E6
Isère r. France 56 G4
Isère, Pointe pt Fr. Guiana 143 H2
Iserlohn Germany 53 H3
Isernhagen Germany 53 J2
Isernia Italy 58 F4
Ise-shima National Park Japan 75 E6
Ise-wan b. Japan 75 E6
Iseyin Nigeria 96 D4
Isfahan Iran see Eşfahān
Isfana Kyrg. 89 H2
Isheyevka Rus. Fed. 43 K5
Ishigaki Japan 73 M8
Ishikari-wan b. Japan 74 F4
Ishim r. Kazakh./Rus. Fed. 80 D1
Ishinomaki Japan 75 F5
Ishinomaki-wan b. Japan 73 Q5
Ishioka Japan 75 F5
Ishkoshim Tajik. 89 H2
Ishpeming U.S.A. 132 C2
Ishtikhon Uzbek. see Ishtykhan
Ishtragh Afgh. 89 H2
Ishtykhan Uzbek. 89 G2
Ishurdi Bangl. 83 G4
Ishwardi Bangl. see Ishurdi
Isiboro Sécure, Parque Nacional nat. park
Bol. 142 E7
Isigny-sur-Mer France 49 F9
Işıklar Dağı mts Turkey 59 L4
Işıklı Turkey 59 M5
Isil'kul' Rus. Fed. 64 I4
Isipingo S. Africa 101 J5
Isiro Dem. Rep. Congo 98 C3
Isisford Australia 110 D5
Iskateley Rus. Fed. 42 L2
İskenderun Turkey 85 C1
İskenderun Körfezi b. Turkey 81 B1
İskilip Turkey 90 D2

Iskitim Rus. Fed. 64 J4
Iskūr r. Bulg. 59 K3
Iskushuban Somalia 98 F2
Isla r. Scotland U.K. 50 F4
Isla r. Scotland U.K. 50 G3
Isla Gorge National Park Australia 110 E5
İslahiye Turkey 90 E3
Islamabad India see Anantnag
▶Islamabad Pak. 89 I3
Capital of Pakistan.
Islamgarh Pak. 89 H5
Islamkot Pak. 89 H5
Island r. Canada 120 F2
Ísland country Europe see Iceland
Island U.S.A. 134 B5
Island Falls U.S.A. 132 G2
Island Lagoon salt flat Australia 111 B6
Island Lake Canada 121 M4
Island Lake l. Canada 121 M4
Island Magee pen. U.K. 51 G3
Island Pond U.S.A. 135 J1
Islands, Bay of N.Z. 113 E2
Islay i. U.K. 50 C5
▶Isle of Man terr. Irish Sea 48 C4
United Kingdom Crown Dependency.
Europe 5
Isle of Wight U.S.A. 135 G5
Isle Royale National Park U.S.A. 130 F2
Ismail Ukr. see Izmayil
Ismâ'ilîya Egypt see Al Ismā'īlīyah
Ismâ'ilîya governorate Egypt see Ismā'īlīyah
Ismā'īlīyah governorate Egypt 85 A4
Ismailly Azer. see İsmayıllı
İsmayıllı Azer. 91 H2
Isojoki Fin. 44 L5
Isoka Zambia 99 D5
Isokylä Fin. 44 O3
Isokyrö Fin. 44 M5
Isola di Capo Rizzuto Italy 58 G5
Ispahan Iran see Eşfahān
Isparta Turkey 59 N6
Isperikh Bulg. 59 L3
Ispikan Pak. 89 F5
İspir Turkey 91 F2
Ispisar Tajik. see Khŭjand
Isplinji Pak. 89 G4
▶Israel country Asia 85 B4
Asia 6, 62–63
Israelite Bay Australia 109 C8
Isra'īl country Asia see Israel
Isselburg Germany 52 G3
Issia Côte d'Ivoire 96 C4
Issoire France 56 F4
Issyk-Kul' Kyrg. see Balykchy
Issyk-Kul', Ozero salt l. Kyrg. see Ysyk-Köl
Istalif Afgh. 89 H3
▶İstanbul Turkey 59 M4
2nd most populous city in Europe.
İstanbul Boğazı strait Turkey see Bosporus
İstgāh-e Eznā Iran 88 C3
Istiaia Greece 59 J5
Istik r. Tajik. 89 I2
Istra pen. Croatia see Istria
Istres France 56 G5
Istria pen. Croatia 58 E2
Iswardi Bangl. see Ishurdi
Itabapoana r. Brazil 145 C3
Itaberá Brazil 145 A3
Itaberaba Brazil 145 C1
Itaberaí Brazil 145 A2
Itabira Brazil 145 C2
Itabirito Brazil 145 C3
Itabuna Brazil 145 D1
Itacajá Brazil 143 I5
Itacarambi Brazil 145 B1
Itacoatiara Brazil 143 G4
Itaetê Brazil 145 C1
Itagmatana Iran see Hamadān
Itaguaçu Brazil 145 C2
Itaí Brazil 145 A3
Itaiópolis Brazil 145 A4
Itäisen Suomenlahden kansallispuisto nat. park Fin. 45 O6
Itaituba Brazil 143 G4
Itajaí Brazil 145 A4
Itajubá Brazil 145 B3
Itajuipe Brazil 145 D1
Italia country Europe see Italy
Italia, Laguna l. Bol. 142 F6
▶Italy country Europe 58 E3
5th most populous country in Europe.
Europe 5, 38–39
Itamarandiba Brazil 145 C2
Itambé Brazil 145 C1
Itambé, Pico de mt. Brazil 145 C2
It Amelân i. Neth. see Ameland
Itampolo Madag. 99 E6
Itanagar India 83 H4
Itanguari r. Brazil 145 B1
Itanhaém Brazil 145 B4
Itanhém Brazil 145 C2
Itanhém r. Brazil 145 D2
Itaobím Brazil 145 C2
Itapaci Brazil 145 A1
Itapajipe Brazil 145 A2
Itapebi Brazil 145 D1
Itapecerica Brazil 145 B3
Itapemirim Brazil 145 C3
Itaperuna Brazil 145 C3
Itapetinga Brazil 145 C1
Itapetininga Brazil 145 A3
Itapeva Brazil 145 A3
Itapeva, Lago l. Brazil 145 A5
Itapicuru Brazil 143 J6
Itapicuru, Serra de hills Brazil 143 I5
Itapicuru Mirim Brazil 143 J4
Itapipoca Brazil 143 K4
Itapira Brazil 145 B3
Itaporanga Brazil 145 A3
Itapuã Brazil 145 A5
Itaqui Brazil 144 E3
Itararé Brazil 145 A4
Itarsi India 82 D5
Itarumã Brazil 145 A2
Itatiba Brazil 145 B3
Itatuba Brazil 142 F5
Itaúna Brazil 145 B3
Itaúnas Brazil 145 D2
Itbayat i. Phil. 69 G2
Itchen Lake Canada 121 H1
Itea Greece 59 J5
Ithaca MI U.S.A. 134 C2
Ithaca NY U.S.A. 135 G2
It Hearrenfean Neth. see Heerenveen
iThekweni S. Africa see Durban
Ith Hils ridge Germany 53 J2
Ithrah Saudi Arabia 85 C4
Itihusa-yama mt. Japan 75 C6
Itilleq Greenland 119 M3
Itimbiri r. Dem. Rep. Congo 98 C3
Itinga Brazil 145 C2
Itiquira Brazil 143 H7
Itiruçu Brazil 145 C1
Itiúba, Serra de hills Brazil 143 K6
Itō Japan 75 E6
iTswane S. Africa see Pretoria
Ittiri Sardinia Italy 58 C4
Ittoqqortoormiit Greenland 119 P2
Itu Brazil 145 B3
Itu Abu Island Spratly Is 68 E4
Ituaçu Brazil 145 C1
Ituberá Brazil 145 D1
Ituí r. Brazil 142 D4
Ituiutaba Brazil 145 A2
Itumbiara Brazil 145 A2
Itumbiara, Barragem resr Brazil 145 A2
Ituni Guyana 143 G2
Itupiranga Brazil 143 I5
Ituporanga Brazil 145 A4
Iturama Brazil 145 A2
Iturbide Mex. 131 D7
Ituri r. Dem. Rep. Congo 98 C3
Iturup, Ostrov i. Rus. Fed. 74 G3
Itutinga Brazil 145 B3
Ituxi r. Brazil 142 F5
Ityop'ia country Africa see Ethiopia
Itz r. Germany 53 K5
Itzehoe Germany 47 L4
Iuka U.S.A. 131 F5
Iul'tin Rus. Fed. 65 T3
Ivalo Fin. 44 O2
Ivalojoki r. Fin. 44 O2
Ivanava Belarus 45 N10
Ivanhoe Australia 112 B4
Ivanhoe U.S.A. 130 D2
Ivanhoe Lake Canada 121 J2
Ivankiv Ukr. 43 F6
Ivankovtsy Rus. Fed. 74 D2
Ivano-Frankivs'k Ukr. 43 E6
Ivano-Frankovsk Ukr. see Ivano-Frankivs'k
Ivanovka Rus. Fed. 74 B2
Ivanovo Belarus see Ivanava
Ivanovo tourist site Bulg. 59 K3
Ivanovo Rus. Fed. 42 I4
Ivanteyevka Rus. Fed. 43 K5
Ivantsevichi Belarus see Ivatsevichy
Ivatsevichy Belarus 45 N10
Ivaylovgrad Bulg. 59 L4
Ivdel' Rus. Fed. 41 S3
Ivittuut Greenland 119 N3
Iviza i. Spain see Ibiza
Ivory Coast country Africa see Côte d'Ivoire
Ivrea Italy 58 B2
İvrindi Turkey 59 L5
Ivris Ugheltekhili pass Georgia 91 G2
Ivry-la-Bataille France 52 B6
Ivugivik Canada see Ivujivik
Ivujivik Canada 119 K3
Ivyanyets Belarus 45 O10
Ivydale U.S.A. 134 E4
Iwaki Japan 75 F5
Iwaki-san vol. Japan 74 F4
Iwakuni Japan 75 D6
Iwamizawa Japan 74 F4
Iwo Nigeria 96 D4
Iwye Belarus 45 N10
Ixelles Belgium 52 E4
Ixiamas Bol. 142 E6
Ixmiquilpán Mex. 136 E4
Ixopo S. Africa 101 J6
Ixtlán Mex. 136 D4
Ixworth U.K. 49 H6
İyirmi Altı Bakı Komissarı Azer. see 26 Bakı Komissarı
Izabal, Lago de l. Guat. 136 G5
Izberbash Rus. Fed. 91 G2
Izegem Belgium 52 D4
Īzeh Iran 88 C4
Izgal Pak. 89 I3
Izhevsk Rus. Fed. 41 Q4
Izhma Respublika Komi Rus. Fed. 42 L2
Izhma Respublika Komi Rus. Fed. see Sosnogorsk
Izhma r. Rus. Fed. 42 L2
Izmail Ukr. see Izmayil
Izmayil Ukr. 59 M2
İzmir Turkey 59 L5
İzmir Körfezi g. Turkey 59 L5
İzmit Turkey see Kocaeli
İzmit Körfezi b. Turkey 59 M4
Izozog Bol. 142 F7
Izra' Syria 85 C3
Iztochni Rodopi mts Bulg. 59 K4
Izu-hantō pen. Japan 75 E6
Izuhara Japan 75 C6
Izumo Japan 75 D6
▶Izu-Ogasawara Trench sea feature N. Pacific Ocean 150 F3
5th deepest trench in the world.
Izu-shotō is Japan 75 E6
Izyaslav Ukr. 43 E6
Iz"yayu Rus. Fed. 42 M2
Izyum Ukr. 43 H6

J

Jabal Dab Saudi Arabia 88 C6
Jabalón r. Spain 57 D4
Jabalpur India 82 D5
Jabbūl, Sabkhat al salt flat Syria 85 C2
Jabir reg. Oman 88 E6
Jabiru Australia 108 F3
Jablah Syria 85 B2
Jablanica Bos.-Herz. 58 G3
Jaboatão Brazil 143 L5
Jaboticabal Brazil 145 A3
Jabung, Tanjung pt Indon. 68 C7
Jacaraci Brazil 145 C1
Jacareacanga Brazil 143 G5
Jacareí Brazil 145 B3
Jacarézinho Brazil 145 A3
Jáchymov Czech Rep. 53 M4
Jacinto Brazil 145 C2
Jack r. Australia 110 D2
Jack Lake Canada 135 F1
Jackman U.S.A. 132 G2
Jacksboro U.S.A. 131 D5
Jackson Australia 112 D1
Jackson AL U.S.A. 133 C6
Jackson CA U.S.A. 128 C2
Jackson GA U.S.A. 133 D5
Jackson KY U.S.A. 134 D5
Jackson MI U.S.A. 134 C2
Jackson MN U.S.A. 130 E3
▶Jackson MS U.S.A. 131 F5
State capital of Mississippi.
Jackson NC U.S.A. 132 E4
Jackson OH U.S.A. 134 D4
Jackson TN U.S.A. 131 F5
Jackson WY U.S.A. 126 F4
Jackson, Mount Antarctica 152 L2
Jackson Head hd N.Z. 113 B6
Jacksonville AR U.S.A. 131 E5
Jacksonville FL U.S.A. 133 D6
Jacksonville IL U.S.A. 130 F4
Jacksonville NC U.S.A. 133 E5
Jacksonville OH U.S.A. 134 D4
Jacksonville TX U.S.A. 131 E6
Jacksonville Beach U.S.A. 133 D6
Jack Wade U.S.A. 118 D3
Jacmel Haiti 137 J5
Jacobabad Pak. 89 H4
Jacobina Brazil 143 J6
Jacob Lake U.S.A. 129 G3
Jacobsdal S. Africa 100 G5
Jacques-Cartier, Détroit de sea chan. Canada 123 I4
Jacques Cartier, Mont mt. Canada 123 I4
Jacques Cartier Passage Canada see Jacques-Cartier, Détroit de
Jacuí Brazil 145 B3
Jacuípe r. Brazil 143 K6
Jacunda Brazil 143 I4
Jaddangi India 84 D2
Jaddi, Ras pt Pak. 89 F5
Jadebusen b. Germany 53 I1
J. A. D. Jensen Nunatakker nunataks Greenland 119 N3
Jadotville Dem. Rep. Congo see Likasi
Jādū Libya 96 E1
Jaén Spain 57 E5
Ja'farābād Iran 88 E2
Jaffa, Cape Australia 111 B8
Jaffna Sri Lanka 84 C4
Jafr, Qa' al imp. l. Jordan 85 C4
Jagadhri India 82 D3
Jagalur India 84 C3
Jagatsinghapur India see Jagatsinghpur
Jagatsinghpur India 83 F5
Jagdalpur India 84 D2
Jagdaqi China 74 B2
Jagersfontein S. Africa 101 G5
Jaggang China 82 D2
Jaggayyapeta India 84 D2
Jaghīn Iran 88 E5
Jagok Tso salt l. China see Urru Co
Jagsamka China see Luding
Jagst r. Germany 53 J5
Jagtial India 84 C2
Jaguariaíva Brazil 145 A4
Jaguaripe Brazil 145 D1
Jagüey Grande Cuba 133 D8
Jahanabad India see Jehanabad
Jahmah well Iraq 91 G5
Jahrom Iran 88 D4
Jaicós Brazil 143 J5
Jaigarh India 84 B2
Jailolo Gilolo i. Indon. see Halmahera
Jaintapur Bangl. see Jaintiapur
Jaintiapur Bangl. 83 H4
Jaipur India 82 C4
Jaipurhat Bangl. see Joypurhat
Jais India 83 E4
Jaisalmer India 82 B4
Jaisamand Lake India 82 C4
Jaitaran India 82 C4
Jaitgarh hill India 84 C1
Jajapur India see Jajpur
Jajarkot Nepal 87 N4
Jajce Bos.-Herz. 58 G2
Jajnagar state India see Orissa
Jajpur India 83 F5
Jakar Bhutan 83 G4
▶Jakarta Indon. 68 D8
Capital of Indonesia.
Jakes Corner Canada 120 C2
Jakhan India 82 B5
Jakin mt. Afgh. 89 G4
Jakkī Kowr Iran 89 F5
Jäkkvik Sweden 44 J3
Jakliat India 82 C3
Jakobshavn Greenland see Ilulissat
Jakobstad Fin. 44 M5
Jal U.S.A. 131 C5
Jalaid China see Inder
Jalājil Saudi Arabia 88 B5
Jalālābād Afgh. 89 H3
Jalal-Abad Kyrg. 80 D3
Jalālah al Baḥrīyah, Jabal plat. Egypt 90 C5
Jalāmid, Ḩazm al ridge Saudi Arabia 91 E5
Jalandhar India 82 C3
Jalapa Mex. 136 E5
Jalapa Enríquez Mex. see Jalapa
Jalapur Pirwala Pak. 89 H4
Jalasjärvi Fin. 44 M5
Jalaun India 82 D4
Jalawlā' Iraq 91 G4
Jaldak Afgh. 89 G4
Jaldrug India 84 C2
Jales Brazil 145 A3
Jalesar India 82 D4
Jalgaon India 82 C5
Jalībah Iraq 91 G5
Jalingo Nigeria 96 E4
Jallābī Iran 88 E5
Jalna India 84 B2
Jālo Iran 89 F5
Jalón r. Spain 57 F3
Jalor India see Jalore
Jalore India 82 C4
Jalpa Mex. 136 D4
Jalpaiguri India 83 G4
Jālū Libya 97 F2
Jalūlā Iraq see Jalawlā'
Jām reg. Iran 89 F3
▶Jamaica country West Indies 137 I5
North America 9, 116–117
Jamaica Channel Haiti/Jamaica 137 I5
Jamalpur Bangl. 83 G4
Jamalpur India 83 F4
Jamanxim r. Brazil 143 G4
Jambi Indon. 68 C7
Jambin Australia 110 E5
Jambo India 82 C4
Jambuair, Tanjung pt Indon. 67 B6
Jamda India 83 F5
Jamekunte India 84 C2
James r. N. Dakota/S. Dakota U.S.A. 130 D3
James r. VA U.S.A. 135 G5
James, Baie b. Canada see James Bay
Jamesabad Pak. 89 H5
James Bay Canada 122 E3
Jamesburg U.S.A. 135 H3
James Island Galápagos Ecuador see San Salvador, Isla
Jameson Land reg. Greenland 119 P2
James Peak N.Z. 113 B7
James Ranges mts Australia 109 F6
James Ross Island Antarctica 152 A2
James Ross Strait Canada 119 I3
Jamestown Australia 111 B7
Jamestown Canada see Wawa
Jamestown S. Africa 101 H6
▶Jamestown St Helena 148 H7
Capital of St Helena and Dependencies.
Jamestown ND U.S.A. 130 D2
Jamestown NY U.S.A. 134 F2
Jamestown TN U.S.A. 134 C5
Jamkhed India 84 B2
Jammu India 82 C2
▶Jammu and Kashmir terr. Asia 82 D2
Disputed territory (India/Pakistan).
Asia 6, 62–63
Jamnagar India 82 B5
Jampur Pak. 89 H4
Jamrud Pak. 89 H3
Jämsä Fin. 45 N6
Jamsah Egypt 90 D6
Jämsänkoski Fin. 44 N6
Jamshedpur India 83 F5
Jamtari Nigeria 96 E4
Jamui India 83 F4
Jamuna r. Bangl. see Raimangal
Jamuna r. India see Yamuna
Janā i. Saudi Arabia 88 C5
Janāb, Wādī al watercourse Jordan 85 C4
Janakpur India 83 E5
Janaúba Brazil 145 C1
Jand Pak. 89 I3
Jandaia Brazil 145 A2
Jandaq Iran 88 D3
Jandola Pak. 89 H3
Jandowae Australia 112 E1
Janesville CA U.S.A. 128 C1
Janesville WI U.S.A. 130 F3
Jangada Brazil 145 A4
Jangal Iran 88 E3
Jangamo Moz. 101 L3
Jangaon India 84 C2
Jangipur India 83 G4
Jangnga Turkm. see Dzhanga
Jangngai Ri mts China 83 F2
Jänickendorf Germany 53 N2
Jani Khel Pak. 89 H3
▶Jan Mayen terr. Arctic Ocean 153 I2
Part of Norway.
Jan Mayen Fracture Zone sea feature Arctic Ocean 153 I2
Janos Mex. 127 F7
Jans Bay Canada 121 I4
Jansenville S. Africa 100 G7
Januária Brazil 145 B1
Janūb Sīnā' governorate Egypt 85 A5
Janūb Sīnā' governorate Egypt see Janūb Sīnā'
Janzar mt. Pak. 89 F5
Jaodar Pak. 89 F5
▶Japan country Asia 75 D5
Asia 6, 62–63
Japan, Sea of N. Pacific Ocean 75 D5
Japan Alps National Park Japan see Chibu-Sangaku National Park
Japan Trench sea feature N. Pacific Ocean 150 F3
Japiim Brazil 142 D5
Japurá r. Brazil 142 F4
Japvo Mount India 83 H4
Jarābulus Syria 85 D1
Jaraguá Brazil 145 A1
Jaraguá, Serra mts Brazil 145 A4
Jaraguá do Sul Brazil 145 A4
Jarash Jordan 85 B3
Jarboesville U.S.A. see Lexington Park
Jardine River National Park Australia 110 C1
Jardinésia Brazil 145 A2
Jardinópolis Brazil 145 B3
Jargalang China 74 A4
Jargalant Bayanhongor Mongolia 80 I2
Jargalant Dornod Mongolia 73 L3
Jargalant Hovd Mongolia see Hovd
Jari r. Brazil 143 H4
Järna Sweden 45 J7
Jarocin Poland 47 P5
Jarosław Poland 43 D6
Järpen Sweden 44 H5
Jarqŭrghon Uzbek. see Dzharkurgan
Jarrettsville U.S.A. 135 G4
Jarú Brazil 142 F6
Jarud China see Lubei
Järvakandi Estonia 45 N7
Järvenpää Fin. 45 N6
▶Jarvis Island terr. S. Pacific Ocean 150 J6
United States Unincorporated Territory.
Jarwa India 83 E4
Jashpurnagar India 83 F5
Jāsk Iran 88 E5
Jāsk-e Kohneh Iran 88 E5
Jasliq Uzbek. see Zhaslyk
Jasło Poland 43 D6
Jasol India 82 C4
Jason Islands Falkland Is 144 D8
Jason Peninsula Antarctica 152 L2
Jasonville U.S.A. 134 B4
Jasper Canada 118 G4
Jasper AL U.S.A. 133 C5
Jasper FL U.S.A. 133 D6
Jasper GA U.S.A. 133 C5
Jasper IN U.S.A. 134 B4
Jasper NY U.S.A. 135 G2
Jasper TN U.S.A. 133 C5
Jasper TX U.S.A. 131 E6
Jasper National Park Canada 120 G4
Jasrasar India 82 C4
Jaşşān Iraq 91 G4
Jassy Romania see Iaşi
Jastrzębie-Zdrój Poland 47 Q6
Jaswantpura India 82 C4
Jászberény Hungary 59 H1
Jataí Brazil 145 A2
Jatapu r. Brazil 143 G4
Jath India 84 B2
Jati Pak. 89 H5
Jatibonico Cuba 133 E8
Játiva Spain see Xátiva
Jatoi Pak. 89 H4
Jat Poti Afgh. 89 G4
Jaú Brazil 145 A3
Jaú r. Brazil 142 F4
Jaú, Parque Nacional do nat. park Brazil 142 F4
Jaua Sarisariñama, Parque Nacional nat. park Venez. 142 F3
Jauja Peru 142 C6
Jaunlutriņi Latvia 45 M8
Jaunpiebalga Latvia 45 O8
Jaunpur India 83 E4
Jauri Iran 89 F4
Java Georgia 91 F2
▶Java i. Indon. 108 A1
5th largest island in Asia.
Javaés r. Brazil see Formoso
Javand Afgh. 89 G3
Javari r. Brazil/Peru see Yavari
Java Ridge sea feature Indian Ocean 149 P6
Javarthushuu Mongolia 73 K3
Java Sea Indon. see Jawa, Laut
▶Java Trench sea feature Indian Ocean 149 O6
Deepest point in the Indian Ocean.
Java Trench sea feature Indian Ocean 149 P6
Jävenitz Germany 53 L2
Jävre Sweden 44 L4
Jawa i. Indon. see Java
Jawa, Laut sea Indon. 68 E7
Jawhar India 84 B2
Jawhar Somalia 98 E3
Jawor Poland 47 P5
Jay U.S.A. 131 E4
▶Jaya, Puncak mt. Indon. 69 J7
Highest mountain in Oceania.
Oceania 102–103
Jayakusumu mt. Indon. see Jaya, Puncak
Jayakwadi Sagar l. India 84 B2
Jayantiapur Bangl. see Jaintiapur
Jayapura Indon. 69 K7
Jayawijaya, Pegunungan mts Indon. 69 J7
Jayb, Wādī al watercourse Israel/Jordan 85 B4
Jayfī, Wādī al watercourse Egypt 85 B4
Jaypur India 84 D2
Jayrūd Syria 85 C3
Jayton U.S.A. 131 C5
Jazīreh-ye Shīf Iran 88 C4
Jazminal Mex. 131 C7
Jbail Lebanon 85 B2
J. C. Murphey Lake U.S.A. 134 B3
Jean U.S.A. 129 F4
Jean Marie River Canada 120 F2
Jeannin, Lac l. Canada 123 I2
Jebāl Bārez, Kūh-e mts Iran 88 E4
Jebel, Bahr el r. Sudan/Uganda see White Nile
Jebel Abyad Plateau Sudan 86 C6
Jech Doab lowland Pak. 89 I4
Jedburgh U.K. 50 G5
Jeddah Saudi Arabia 86 E5
Jedeida Tunisia 58 C6
Jeetze r. Germany 53 L1
Jefferson IA U.S.A. 130 E3
Jefferson NC U.S.A. 132 D4
Jefferson OH U.S.A. 134 E3
Jefferson TX U.S.A. 131 E5
Jefferson, Mount U.S.A. 128 E2
Jefferson, Mount vol. U.S.A. 126 C3
▶Jefferson City U.S.A. 130 E4
State capital of Missouri.
Jeffersonville GA U.S.A. 133 D5
Jeffersonville IN U.S.A. 134 C4
Jeffersonville OH U.S.A. 134 D4
Jeffrey's Bay S. Africa 100 G8
Jehanabad India 83 F4
Jeju S. Korea see Cheju
Jejuí Guazú r. Para. 144 E2
Jēkabpils Latvia 45 N8
Jelbart Ice Shelf Antarctica 152 B2
Jelenia Góra Poland 47 O5
Jelep La pass China/India 83 G4
Jelgava Latvia 45 M8
Jellico U.S.A. 134 C5
Jellicoe Canada 122 D4
Jelloway U.S.A. 134 D3
Jemaja i. Indon. 71 D7
Jember Indon. 68 E8
Jempang, Danau l. Indon. 68 F7
Jena Germany 53 L4
Jena U.S.A. 131 E6
Jendouba Tunisia 58 C6
Jengish Chokusu mt. China/Kyrg. see Pobeda Peak
Jenīn West Bank 85 B3
Jenkins U.S.A. 134 D5
Jenne Mali see Djenné
Jenner Canada 121 I5
Jennings r. Canada 120 C3
Jennings U.S.A. 131 E6
Jenolan Caves Australia 112 E4
Jenpeg Canada 121 L4
Jensen U.S.A. 129 I1
Jens Munk Island Canada 119 K3
Jeparit Australia 111 C8
Jequié Brazil 145 C1
Jequitaí r. Brazil 145 B2
Jequitinhonha Brazil 145 C2
Jequitinhonha r. Brazil 145 D1
Jerba, Île de i. Tunisia 54 G5
Jerbar Sudan 97 G4
Jereh Iran 88 C4
Jérémie Haiti 137 J5
Jerez Mex. 136 D4
Jerez de la Frontera Spain 57 C5
Jerggul Norway 44 N2
Jergucat Albania 59 I5
Jericho Australia 110 D4
Jericho West Bank 85 B4
Jerichow Germany 53 M2
Jerid, Chott el salt l. Tunisia 54 F5
Jerilderie Australia 112 B5
Jerimoth Hill hill U.S.A. 135 J3
Jeroaquara Brazil 145 A1
Jerome U.S.A. 126 E4
Jerruck Pak. 89 H5
▶Jersey terr. Channel Is 49 E9
United Kingdom Crown Dependency.
Europe 5, 38–39
Jersey City U.S.A. 135 H3
Jersey Shore U.S.A. 135 G3
Jerseyville U.S.A. 130 F4
Jerumenha Brazil 143 J5
▶Jerusalem Israel/West Bank 85 B4
Capital of Israel (De facto capital. Disputed).
Jervis Bay Australia 112 E5
Jervis Bay b. Australia 112 E5
Jervis Bay Territory admin. div. Australia 112 E5
Jesenice Slovenia 58 F1
Jesenice, Vodní nádrž resr Czech Rep. 53 M4
Jesi Italy 58 E3
Jesselton Sabah Malaysia see Kota Kinabalu
Jessen Germany 53 M3
Jessheim Norway 45 G6
Jessore Bangl. 83 G5
Jesteburg Germany 53 J1
Jesu Maria Island P.N.G. see Rambutyo Island
Jesup U.S.A. 133 D6
Jesús María, Barra spit Mex. 131 D7
Jetmore U.S.A. 130 D4
Jever Germany 53 H1
Jewell Ridge U.S.A. 134 E5
Jewish Autonomous Oblast admin. div. Rus. Fed. see Yevreyskaya Avtonomnaya Oblast'
Jeypur India see Jaypur
Jezzine Lebanon 85 B3
Jhabua India 82 C5
Jhajhar India see Jhajjar
Jhajjar India 82 D3
Jhal Pak. 89 G4
Jhalawar India 82 D4
Jhal Jhao Pak. 89 G5
Jhang Pak. 89 I4
Jhansi India 82 D4
Jhanzi r. India 70 A1
Jhapa Nepal 83 F4
Jharia India 83 F5
Jharkhand state India 83 F5
Jharsuguda India 83 F5
Jhawani Nepal 83 F4
Jhelum r. India/Pak. 89 I4
Jhelum Pak. 89 I3
Jhenaidah Bangl. 83 G5
Jhenaidaha Bangl. see Jhenaidah
Jhenida Bangl. see Jhenaidah
Jhimpir Pak. 89 H5
Jhudo Pak. 89 H5
Jhumritilaiya India 83 F4
Jhund India 82 B5
Jhunjhunun India 82 C3
Jiachuan China 76 E1
Jiachuanzhen China see Jiachuan
Jiading Jiangxi China see Xinfeng
Jiading Shanghai China 77 I2
Jiahe China 77 G3
Jiajiang China 76 D2
Jiamusi China 74 C3
Ji'an Jiangxi China 77 G3
Ji'an Jilin China 74 B4
Jianchuan China 76 C3
Jiande China 77 H2
Jiangbei China see Yubei
Jiangbiancun China 77 G3
Jiangcheng China 76 D4

Jiangcun China 77 F3
Jiangdu China 77 H1
Jiange China see Pu'an
Jianghong China 77 F4
Jiangjin China 76 E2
Jiangjunmiao China 80 G3
Jiangkou Guangdong China see Fengkai
Jiangkou Guizhou China 77 F3
Jiangkou Shaanxi China 76 E1
Jiangling China see Jingzhou
Jiangluozhen China 76 E1
Jiangmen China 77 G4
Jiangna China see Yanshan
Jiangshan China 77 H2
Jiangsi China see Dejiang
Jiangsu prov. China 77 H1
Jiangxi prov. China 77 G3
Jiangxia China 77 G2
Jiangyan China 77 I1
Jiangyin China 77 I2
Jiangyou China 76 E2
Jiangzhesongrong China 83 F3
Jianjun China see Yongshou
Jiankang China 76 D3
Jianli China 77 G2
Jian'ou China 77 H3
Jianping China see Langxi
Jianpur India 83 E4
Jianshe China see Baiyü
Jianshi China 77 F2
Jianshui China 76 D4
Jianshui Hu l. China 83 E2
Jianxing China 76 E2
Jianyang Fujian China 77 H3
Jianyang Sichuan China 76 E2
Jiaochang China 76 D1
Jiaochangba China see Jiaochang
Jiaocheng China see Jiaoling
Jiaohe China 74 B4
Jiaojiang China see Taizhou
Jiaokui China see Yiliang
Jiaoling China 77 H3
Jiaopingdu China 76 D3
Jiaowei China 77 H3
Jiaozuo China 77 G1
Jiasa China 76 D3
Jiashan China see Mingguang
Jia Tsuo La pass China 83 F3
Jiawang China 77 H1
Jiaxian China 77 G1
Jiaxing China 77 I2
Jiayi Taiwan see Chiai
Jiayin China 74 C2
Jiayuguan China 80 I4
Jiazi China 77 H4
Jibūtī country Africa see Djibouti
Jibuti Djibouti see Djibouti
Jiddah Saudi Arabia see Jeddah
Jiddī, Jabal al hill Egypt 85 A4
Jidong China 74 C3
Jiehkkevarri mt. Norway 44 K2
Jieshi China 77 G4
Jieshipu China 76 E1
Jieshi Wan b. China 77 G4
Ješjávri l. Norway 44 N2
Jiexi China 77 G4
Jiexiu China 73 K5
Jieyang China 77 H4
Jieznas Lith. 45 N9
Jigzhi China 76 D1
Jiḩār, Wādī al watercourse Syria 85 C2
Jihlava Czech Rep. 47 O6
Jija Sarai Afgh. 89 F3
Jijel Alg. 54 F4
Jijiga Eth. 98 E3
Jījirud Iran 88 C3
Jijü China 76 D2
Jil'ād reg. Jordan 85 B3
Jilf al Kabīr, Haḑabat al plat. Egypt 86 C5
Jilh al 'Ishār plain Saudi Arabia 88 B5
Jilib Somalia 98 E3
Jilin China 74 B4
Jilin prov. China 74 B4
Jilin Hada Ling mts China 74 B4
Jiliu He r. China 74 A2
Jilo India 82 C4
Jilong Taiwan see Chilung
Jīma Eth. 98 D3
Jimda China see Zindo
Jiménez Chihuahua Mex. 131 B7
Jiménez Coahuila Mex. 131 C6
Jiménez Tamaulipas Mex. 131 D7
Jimía, Cerro mt. Hond. 136 G5
Jimsar China 80 G3
Jim Thorpe U.S.A. 135 H3
Jinan China 73 L5
Jin'an China see Songpan
Jinbi China see Dayao
Jinchang China 72 I5
Jincheng Shanxi China 77 G1
Jincheng Sichuan China see Yilong
Jincheng Yunnan China see Wuding
Jinchengjiang China see Hechi
Jinchuan Gansu China see Jinchang
Jinchuan Jiangxi China see Xingan
Jind India 82 D3
Jinding China see Lanping
Jindřichův Hradec Czech Rep. 47 O6
Jin'e China see Longchang
Jingbian China 73 J5
Jingchuan China 76 E1
Jingde China 77 H2
Jingdezhen China 77 H2
Jingellic Australia 112 C5
Jinggangshan China 77 G3
Jinggang Shan hill China 77 G3
Jinggongqiao China 77 H2
Jinggu China 76 D4
Jing He r. China 77 F1
Jinghong China 76 D4
Jingle China 73 K5
Jingmen China 77 G2
Jingpo China 74 C4
Jingpo Hu resr China 74 C4
Jingsha China see Jingzhou
Jingtai China 72 I5
Jingtieshan China 80 I4
Jingxi China 76 E4
Jingxian Anhui China 77 H2
Jingxian Hunan China see Jingzhou
Jingyang China see Jingde
Jingyu China 74 B4
Jingyuan China 72 I5
Jingzhou Hubei China 77 G2
Jingzhou Hubei China 77 G2
Jingzhou Hunan China 77 F3
Jinhe Nei Mongol China 74 A2
Jinhe Yunnan China see Jinping
Jinhu China 77 H1
Jinhua Yunnan China see Jianchuan
Jinhua Zhejiang China 77 H2
Jining Nei Mongol China 73 K4
Jining Shandong China 77 H1
Jinja Uganda 98 D3
Jinjiang Hainan China see Chengmai
Jinjiang Yunnan China 76 D3
Jin Jiang r. China 77 G2
Jinka Eth. 98 D3
Jinmen Taiwan see Chinmen
Jinmen Dao i. Taiwan see Chinmen Tao
Jinmu Jiao pt China 77 F5
Jinning China 76 D3
Jinotepe Nicaragua 137 G6
Jinping Guizhou China 77 F3
Jinping Yunnan China 76 D4
Jinping Yunnan China see Qiubei
Jinping Shan mts China 76 D3
Jinsen S. Korea see Inch'ŏn
Jinsha China 76 E3
Jinsha Jiang r. China 76 E2 see Yangtze
Jinshan Nei Mongol China see Guyang
Jinshan Shanghai China 77 I2
Jinshan Yunnan China see Lufeng
Jinshi Hunan China 77 F2
Jinshi Hunan China see Xinning
Jintur India 84 C2
Jinxi Anhui China see Taihu
Jinxi Jiangxi China 77 H3
Jinxi Liaoning China see Lianshan
Jin Xi r. China 77 H3
Jinxian China 77 H2
Jinxiang China 77 H1
Jinyun China 77 I2
Jinz, Qa' al salt flat Jordan 85 C4
Jinzhai China 77 G2
Jinzhong China 73 K5
Jinzhou China 73 M4
Jinzhu China see Daocheng
Ji-Paraná Brazil 142 F6
Jipijapa Ecuador 142 B4
Ji Qu r. China 76 C2
Jiquiriçá Brazil 145 D1
Jiquitaia Brazil 145 D2
Jirā', Wādī watercourse Egypt 85 A5
Jirānīyāt, Shi'bān al watercourse Saudi Arabia 85 D4
Jirgatol Tajik. 89 H2
Jiri r. India 70 A1
Jīroft Iran 88 E4
Jirriiban Somalia 98 E3
Jirwān Saudi Arabia 88 C6
Jirwan well Saudi Arabia 88 C6
Jishou China 77 F2
Jisr ash Shughūr Syria 85 C2
Jitian China see Lianshan
Jitra Malaysia 71 C6
Jiu r. Romania 59 J3
Jiuding Shan mt. China 76 D2
Jiujiang Jiangxi China 77 G2
Jiujiang Jiangxi China 77 H2
Jiulian China see Mojiang
Jiuling Shan mts China 77 G2
Jiulong Hong Kong China see Kowloon
Jiulong Sichuan China 76 D2
Jiuqian China 77 F3
Jiuquan China 80 I4
Jiuxu China 76 E3
Jiuzhou Jiang r. China 77 F4
Jiwani Pak. 89 F5
Jiwen China 74 A2
Jixi Anhui China 77 H2
Jixi Heilong. China 74 C3
Jixian China 74 C3
Jiyuan China 77 G1
Jīzah, Ahrāmāt al tourist site Egypt see Pyramids of Giza
Jīzān Saudi Arabia 86 F6
Jizzakh Uzbek. see Dzhizak
Joaçaba Brazil 145 A4
Joaíma Brazil 145 C2
João Belo Moz. see Xai-Xai
João de Almeida Angola see Chibia
João Pessoa Brazil 143 L5
João Pinheiro Brazil 145 B2
Joaquin V. González Arg. 144 D3
Job Peak U.S.A. 128 D2
Jocketa Germany 53 M4
Joda India 83 F5
Jodhpur India 82 C4
Jodiya India 82 B5
Joensuu Fin. 44 P5
Jōetsu Japan 75 E5
Jofane Moz. 99 D6
Joffre, Mount Canada 120 H5
Jogbura Nepal 82 E3
Jõgeva Estonia 45 O7
Jogjakarta Indon. see Yogyakarta
Jōgua Estonia 45 O7
Johannesburg S. Africa 101 H4
Johannesburg U.S.A. 128 E4
Johan Peninsula Canada 119 K2
Johi Pak. 89 G5
John Day U.S.A. 126 D3
John Day r. U.S.A. 126 C3
John D'Or Prairie Canada 120 H3
John F. Kennedy airport U.S.A. 135 I3
John H. Kerr Reservoir U.S.A. 135 F5
John Jay, Mount Canada/U.S.A. 120 D3
John o'Groats U.K. 50 F2
Johnson U.S.A. 130 C4
Johnsonburg U.S.A. 135 F3
Johnson City NY U.S.A. 135 H2
Johnson City TN U.S.A. 132 D4
Johnson City TX U.S.A. 131 D6
Johnsondale U.S.A. 128 D4
Johnson Draw watercourse U.S.A. 131 C6
Johnson's Crossing Canada 120 C2
Johnston, Lake salt flat Australia 109 C8
Johnston and Sand Islands terr. N. Pacific Ocean see Johnston Atoll
►Johnston Atoll terr. N. Pacific Ocean 150 I4
United States Unincorporated Territory.
Johnstone U.K. 50 E5
Johnstone Lake Canada see Old Wives Lake
Johnston Range hills Australia 109 B7
Johnstown Rep. of Ireland 51 E5
Johnstown NY U.S.A. 135 H2
Johnstown PA U.S.A. 135 F3
Johor, Selat strait Malaysia/Sing. 71 [inset]
Johor, Sungai r. Malaysia 71 [inset]
Johor Bahru Malaysia 71 [inset]
Johore Bahru Malaysia see Johor Bahru
Jõhvi Estonia 45 O7
Joinville Brazil 145 A4
Joinville France 56 G2
Joinville Island Antarctica 152 A2
Jokkmokk Sweden 44 K3
Jökulsá r. Iceland 44 [inset]
Jökulsá á Fjöllum r. Iceland 44 [inset]
Jökulsá í Fljótsdal r. Iceland 44 [inset]
Jolfa Iran 88 B2
Joliet U.S.A. 134 A3
Joliet, Lac l. Canada 122 F4
Joliette Canada 123 G5
Jolly Lake Canada 121 H1
Jolo Phil. 69 G5
Jolo i. Phil. 69 G5
Jomda China 76 C2
Jonancy U.S.A. 134 D5
Jonava Lith. 45 N9
Jonê China 76 D1
Jonesboro AR U.S.A. 131 F5
Jonesboro LA U.S.A. 131 E5
Jones Sound sea chan. Canada 119 J2
Jonesville MI U.S.A. 134 C3
Jonesville VA U.S.A. 134 D5
Jonglei Canal Sudan 86 D8
Jönköping Sweden 45 I8
Jonquière Canada 123 H4
Joplin U.S.A. 131 E4
Joppa Israel see Tel Aviv-Yafo
Jora India 82 D4
►Jordan country Asia 85 C4
Asia 6, 62–63
Jordan r. Asia 85 B4
Jordan U.S.A. 126 G3
Jordan r. U.S.A. 126 D4
Jordânia Brazil 145 C1
Jordet Norway 45 H6
Jorhat India 83 H4
Jork Germany 53 J1
Jorm Afgh. 89 H2
Jörn Sweden 44 L4
Joroinen Fin. 44 O5
Jørpeland Norway 45 E7
Jos Nigeria 96 D4
José de San Martin Arg. 144 B6
Joseph, Lac l. Canada 123 I3
Joseph Bonaparte Gulf Australia 108 E3
Joseph City U.S.A. 129 H4
Joshimath India 82 D3
Joshipur India 84 E1
Joshua Tree National Park U.S.A. 129 F5
Jos Plateau Nigeria 96 D4
Jostedalsbreen Nasjonalpark nat. park Norway 45 E6
Jotunheimen Nasjonalpark nat. park Norway 45 F6
Jouaiya Lebanon 85 B3
Joubertina S. Africa 100 F7
Jouberton S. Africa 101 H4
Joûnié Lebanon 85 B3
Joure Neth. 52 F2
Joutsa Fin. 45 O6
Joutseno Fin. 45 P6
Jouy-aux-Arches France 52 G5
Jovellanos Cuba 133 D8
Jowai India 83 H4
Jowr Deh Iran 88 C2
Jowzak Iran 89 F4
Joy, Mount Canada 120 C2
Joyce's Country reg. Rep. of Ireland 51 C4
Joypurhat Bangl. 83 G4
Juan Aldama Mex. 131 C7
Juancheng China 77 G1
Juan de Fuca Strait Canada/U.S.A. 124 C2
Juan Fernández, Archipiélago is S. Pacific Ocean 151 O8
Juan Fernández Islands S. Pacific Ocean see Juan Fernández, Archipiélago
Juanjuí Peru 142 C5
Juankoski Fin. 44 P5
Juan Mata Ortíz Mex. 127 F7
Juaréz Mex. 131 C7
Juárez, Sierra de mts Mex. 123 D6
Juàzeiro Brazil 143 J5
Juàzeiro do Norte Brazil 143 K5
Juba r. Somalia see Jubba
Juba Sudan 97 G4
Jubany research station Antarctica 152 A2
Jubba r. Somalia 98 E4
Jubbah Saudi Arabia 91 F5
Jubbulpore India see Jabalpur
Jubilee Lake salt flat Australia 109 D7
Juby, Cap c. Morocco 96 B2
Júcar r. Spain 57 F4
Juçara Brazil 145 A1
Juchitán Mex. 136 E5
Jucuruçu Brazil 145 D2
Jucuruçu r. Brazil 145 D2
Judaberg Norway 45 D7
Judaidat al Hamir Iraq 91 F5
Judayyidat 'Ar'ar well Iraq 91 F5
Judenburg Austria 47 O7
Judian China 76 C3
Judith Gap U.S.A. 126 F3
Juegang China see Rudong
Juelsminde Denmark 45 G9
Juerana Brazil 145 D2
Jugar China see Sêrxü
Juigalpa Nicaragua 137 G6
Juillet, Lac l. Canada 123 J3
Juína Brazil 143 G6
Juist i. Germany 52 H1
Juiz de Fora Brazil 145 C3
Julaca Bol. 142 E8
Julesburg U.S.A. 130 C3
Julia Brazil 142 E4
Juliaca Peru 142 D7
Julia Creek Australia 110 C4
Julian U.S.A. 128 E5
Julian, Lac l. Canada 122 F3
Julianadorp Neth. 52 E2
Julian Alps mts Slovenia see Julijske Alpe
Julianatop mt. Indon. see Mandala, Puncak
Juliana Top mt. Suriname 143 G3
Julianehåb Greenland see Qaqortoq
Jülich Germany 52 G4
Julijske Alpe mts Slovenia 58 E1
Julimes Mex. 131 B6
Juliomagus France see Angers
Julius, Lake Australia 110 B4
Jullundur India see Jalandhar
Juma Uzbek. see Dzhuma
Jumbilla Peru 142 C5
Jumilla Spain 57 F4
Jumla Nepal 83 E3
Jümme r. Germany 53 H1
Jumna r. India see Yamuna
Jump r. U.S.A. 130 F2
Junagadh India 82 B5
Junagarh India 84 D2
Junan China 77 H1
Junayfah Egypt 85 A4
Junbuk Iran 88 E3
Junction TX U.S.A. 131 D6
Junction UT U.S.A. 129 G2
Junction City KS U.S.A. 130 D4
Junction City KY U.S.A. 134 C5
Junction City OR U.S.A. 126 C3
Jundiaí Brazil 145 B3
Jundian China 77 F1
►Juneau AK U.S.A. 120 C3
State capital of Alaska.
Juneau WI U.S.A. 130 F3
Juneau Icefield Canada 120 C3
Junee Australia 112 C5
Jûn el Khudr b. Lebanon 85 B3
Jungar Qi China see Shagedu
Jungfrau mt. Switz. 56 H3
Junggar Pendi basin China 80 G2
Juniata r. U.S.A. 135 G3
Junín Arg. 144 D4
Junín Peru 142 C6
Junior U.S.A. 134 F4
Juniper Mountain U.S.A. 129 I1
Juniper Mountains U.S.A. 129 G4
Junipero Serro Peak U.S.A. 124 C3
Junlian China 76 E2
Junmenling China 77 G3
Juno U.S.A. 131 C6
Junsele Sweden 44 J5
Junshan Hu l. China 77 H2
Junxi China see Datian
Junxian China see Danjiangkou
Ju'nyung China 76 C1
Ju'nyunggoin China see Ju'nyung
Juodupė Lith. 45 N8
Jupiá Brazil 145 A3
Jupía, Represa resr Brazil 145 A3
Jupiter U.S.A. 133 D7
Juquiá r. Brazil 145 B4
Jur r. Sudan 86 C8
Jura mts France/Switz. 56 G4
Jura i. U.K. 50 D4
Jura, Sound of sea chan. U.K. 50 D5
Jurací Brazil 145 C1
Jurbarkas Lith. 45 M9
Jurf ad Darāwīsh Jordan 85 B4
Jürgenstorf Germany 53 M1
Jurhen Ul mts China 83 G2
Jūrmala Latvia 45 M8
Jurmu Fin. 44 O4
Jurong Sing. 71 [inset]
Jurong, Sungai r. Sing. 71 [inset]
Jurong Island reg. Sing. 71 [inset]
Juruá r. Brazil 142 E4
Juruena r. Brazil 143 G5
Juruti Brazil 143 G4
Jurva Fin. 44 L5
Jūshqān Iran 88 E2
Jūsīyah Syria 85 C2
Justice U.S.A. 134 E5
Jutaí Brazil 142 E5
Jutaí r. Brazil 142 E4
Jüterbog Germany 53 N3
Jutiapa Guat. 136 G6
Juticalpa Hond. 137 G6
Jutis Sweden 44 J3
Jutland pen. Denmark 45 F8
Juuka Fin. 44 P5
Juva Fin. 44 O6
Juwain Afgh. 89 F4
Juye China 77 H1
Jūyom Iran 88 D4
Južnoukrajinsk Ukr. see Yuzhnoukrayinsk
Jwaneng Botswana 100 G3
Jylland pen. Denmark see Jutland
Jyväskylä Fin. 44 N5

K

►K2 mt. China/Jammu and Kashmir 82 D2
2nd highest mountain in the world and in Asia.
World 12–13
Ka r. Nigeria 96 D3
Kaafu Atoll Maldives see Male Atoll
Kaa-Iya, Parque Nacional nat. park Bol. 142 F7
Kaakhka Turkm. see Kaka
Kaala mt. HI U.S.A. 127 [inset]
Kaapstad S. Africa see Cape Town
Kaarina Fin. 45 M6
Kaarßen Germany 53 L1
Kaarst Germany 52 G3
Kaavi Fin. 44 P5
Kaba China see Habahe
Kabakly Turkm. 89 F2
Kabala Sierra Leone 96 B4
Kabale Uganda 98 C4
Kabalega Falls National Park Uganda see Murchison Falls National Park
Kabalo Dem. Rep. Congo 99 C4
Kabambare Dem. Rep. Congo 99 C4
Kabangu Dem. Rep. Congo 99 C5
Kabanjahe Indon. 71 B7
Kabara i. Fiji 107 I3
Kabarega National Park Uganda see Murchison Falls National Park
Kabaw Valley Myanmar 70 A2
Kabbani r. India 84 C3
Kåbdalis Sweden 44 L3
Kabinakagami r. Canada 122 D4
Kabinakagami Lake Canada 122 D4
Kabinda Dem. Rep. Congo 99 C4
Kabīr r. Syria 85 B2
Kabīrkūh mts Iran 88 B3
Kabo Cent. Afr. Rep. 98 B3
Kābol Afgh. see Kābul
Kabompo r. Zambia 99 C5
Kabongo Dem. Rep. Congo 99 C4
Kabūdeh Iran 89 F3
Kabūd Gonbad Iran 89 E2
Kabūd Rāhang Iran 88 C3
►Kābul Afgh. 89 H3
Capital of Afghanistan.
Kābul r. Afgh. 89 I3
Kabuli P.N.G. 69 L7
Kabunda Dem. Rep. Congo 99 C5
Kabunduk Indon. 108 B2
Kaburuang i. Indon. 69 H6
Kabūtar Khān Iran 88 E4
Kabwe Zambia 99 C5
Kacha Kuh mts Iran/Pak. 89 F4
Kachalinskaya Rus. Fed. 43 J6
Kachchh, Great Rann of marsh India see Kachchh, Rann of
Kachchh, Gulf of India 82 B5
Kachchh, Rann of marsh India 82 B4
Kachia Nigeria 96 D4
Kachiry Kazakh. 72 D2
Kachkanar Rus. Fed. 41 R4
Kachret'i Georgia 91 G2
Kachug Rus. Fed. 72 J2
Kaçkar Dağı mt. Turkey 91 F2
Kadaingti Myanmar 70 B3
Kadaiyanallur India 84 C4
Kadanai r. Afgh./Pak. 89 G4
Kadan Kyun i. Myanmar 71 B4
Kadavu i. Fiji 107 H3
Kadavu Passage Fiji 107 H3
Kaddam l. India 84 C2
Kade Ghana 96 C4
Kādhimain Iraq see Al Kāẓimīyah
Kadi India 82 C5
Kadıköy Turkey 59 M4
Kadınhanı Turkey 90 D3
Kadiolo Mali 96 C3
Kadiri India 84 C3
Kadirli Turkey 90 E3
Kadirpur Pak. 89 I4
Kadiyevka Ukr. see Stakhanov
Kadmat atoll India 84 B4
Ka-do i. N. Korea 75 B5
Kadok Malaysia 71 C6
Kadoka U.S.A. 130 C3
Kadoma Zimbabwe 99 C5
Kadonkani Myanmar 70 A4
Kadu Myanmar 70 B1
Kadugli Sudan 86 C7
Kaduna Nigeria 96 D3
Kaduna r. Nigeria 96 D4
Kadusam mt. China/India 83 I3
Kaduy Rus. Fed. 42 H4
Kadyy Rus. Fed. 42 I4
Kadzherom Rus. Fed. 42 L2
Kaédi Mauritania 96 B3
Kaélé Cameroon 97 E3
Kaeng Krachan National Park Thai. 71 B4
Kaesŏng N. Korea 75 B5
Kāf Saudi Arabia 85 C4
Kafa Ukr. see Feodosiya
Kafakumba Dem. Rep. Congo 99 C4
Kafan Armenia see Kapan
Kafanchan Nigeria 96 D4
Kafireas, Akra pt Greece 59 K5
Kafiristan reg. Pak. 89 H3
Kafr ash Shaykh Egypt 90 C5
Kafr el Sheikh Egypt see Kafr ash Shaykh
Kafue Zambia 99 C5
Kafue r. Zambia 99 C5
Kafue National Park Zambia 99 C5
Kaga Japan 75 E5
Kaga Bandoro Cent. Afr. Rep. 98 B3
Kagan Pak. 89 I3
Kagan Uzbek. 89 G2
Kagang China 76 D1
Kaganovichabad Tajik. see Kolkhozobod
Kaganovichi Pervyye Ukr. see Polis'ke
Kagarlyk Ukr. see Kaharlyk
Kåge Sweden 44 L4
Kağızman Turkey 91 F2
Kagmar Sudan 86 D7
Kagoshima Japan 75 C7
Kagoshima pref. Japan 75 C7
Kagul Moldova see Cahul
Kahama Tanz. 98 D4
Kaharlyk Ukr. 43 F6
Kaherekoau Mountains N.Z. 113 A7
Kahla Germany 53 L4
Kahnūj Iran 88 E4
Kahoka U.S.A. 130 F3
Kahoolawe i. HI U.S.A. 127 [inset]
Kahperusvaarat mts Fin. 44 L2
Kahramanmaraş Turkey 90 E3
Kahror Pak. 89 H4
Kâhta Turkey 90 E3
Kahuku HI U.S.A. 127 [inset]
Kahuku Point HI U.S.A. 127 [inset]
Kahului i. U.S.A. see Kahoolawe
Kahurangi National Park N.Z. 113 D5
Kahurangi Point N.Z. 113 D5
Kahuta Pak. 89 I3
Kahuzi-Biega, Parc National du nat. park Dem. Rep. Congo 98 C4
Kai, Kepulauan is Indon. 69 I8
Kaiapoi N.Z. 113 D6
Kaibab U.S.A. 129 G3
Kaibab Plateau U.S.A. 129 G3
Kai Besar i. Indon. 69 I8
Kaibito Plateau U.S.A. 129 H3
Kaifeng Henan China 77 G1
Kaifeng Henan China 77 G1
Kaihua Yunnan China see Wenshan
Kaihua Zhejiang China 77 H2
Kaiingveld reg. S. Africa 100 E5
Kaijiang China 76 E2
Kai Kecil i. Indon. 69 I8
Kai Keung Leng Hong Kong China 77 [inset]
Kaikoura N.Z. 113 D6
Kailas mt. China see Kangrinboqê Feng
Kailasahar India see Kailashahar
Kailashahar India 83 H4
Kailas Range mts China see Gangdisê Shan
Kaili China 76 E3
Kailu China 73 M4
Kailua HI U.S.A. 127 [inset]
Kailua Kona HI U.S.A. 127 [inset]
Kaimana Indon. 69 I7
Kaimanawa Mountains N.Z. 113 E4
Kaimar China 76 B1
Kaimur Range hills India 82 E4
Käina Estonia 45 M7
Kainan Japan 75 D6
Kainda Kyrg. see Kayyngdy
Kaindy Kyrg. see Kayyngdy
Kainji Lake National Park Nigeria 96 D4
Kaipara Harbour N.Z. 113 E3
Kaiparowits Plateau U.S.A. 129 H3
Kaiping China 77 G4
Kaipokok Bay Canada 123 K3
Kairana India 82 D3
Kairiru Island P.N.G. 69 K7
Kaironi Indon. 69 I7
Kairouan Tunisia 58 D7
Kaiserslautern Germany 53 H5
Kaiser Wilhelm II Land reg. Antarctica 152 E2
Kaitaia N.Z. 113 D2
Kaitangata N.Z. 113 B8
Kaitawa N.Z. 113 F4
Kaithal India 82 D3
Kaitum Sweden 44 L3
Kaiwatu Indon. 108 D2
Kaiwi Channel HI U.S.A. 127 [inset]
Kaixian China 77 F2
Kaiyang China 76 E3
Kaiyuan Liaoning China 74 B4
Kaiyuan Yunnan China 76 D4
Kajaani Fin. 44 O4
Kajabbi Australia 110 C4
Kajaki Afgh. 89 G3
Kajrān Afgh. 89 G3
Kaka Turkm. 89 E2
Kakabeka Falls Canada 122 C4
Kakadu National Park Australia 108 F3
Kakagi Lake Canada 121 M5
Kakamas S. Africa 100 E5
Kakamega Kenya 98 D3
Kakana India 71 A5
Kakar Pak. 89 G5
Kakata Liberia 96 B4
Kake U.S.A. 120 C3
Kakenge Dem. Rep. Congo 99 C4
Kakerbeck Germany 53 L2
Kakhi Azer. see Qax
Kakhovka Ukr. 59 O1
Kakhovs'ke Vodoskhovyshche resr Ukr. 43 G7
Kakhul Moldova see Cahul
Kākī Iran 88 C4
Kakinada India 84 D2
Kakisa Canada 120 G2
Kakisa r. Canada 120 G2
Kakisa Lake Canada 120 G2
Kakogawa Japan 75 D6
Kakori India 82 E4
Kakshaal-Too mts China/Kyrg. 80 E3
Kaktovik U.S.A. 118 D2
Kakul Pak. 89 I3
Kakwa r. Canada 120 G4
Kala Pak. 89 H4
Kala Tanz. 99 D4
Kalaâ Kebira Tunisia 58 D7
Kalaallit Nunaat terr. N. America see Greenland
Kalabahi Indon. 108 D2
Kalabáka Greece see Kalampaka
Kalabgur India 84 C2
Kalabo Zambia 99 C5
Kalach Rus. Fed. 43 I6
Kalacha Dida Kenya 98 D3
Kalach-na-Donu Rus. Fed. 43 I6
Kaladan r. India/Myanmar 70 A2
Kaladar Canada 135 G1
Ka Lae pt HI U.S.A. 127 [inset]
Kalagwe Myanmar 70 B2
Kalahari Desert Africa 100 F2
Kalahari Gemsbok National Park S. Africa 100 E3
Kalaikhum Tajik. see Qal'aikhum
Kalai-Khumb Tajik. see Qal'aikhum
Kala-I-Mor Turkm. 89 F3
Kalajoki Fin. 44 M4
Kalalé Benin 96 D3
Kalam India 84 C1
Kalam Pak. 89 I3
Kalámai Greece see Kalamata
Kalamare Botswana 101 H2
Kalamaria Greece 59 J4
Kalamata Greece 59 J6
Kalamazoo U.S.A. 134 C2
Kalampaka Greece 59 I5
Kalanchak Ukr. 59 O1
Kalandi Pak. 89 F4
Kalandula Angola see Calandula
Kalannie Australia 109 B7
Kalān Zīād Iran 89 E5
Kalapana HI U.S.A. 127 [inset]
Kalār Iraq 91 G4
Kalasin Thai. 70 C3
Kalāt Afgh. 89 G3
Kalāt Khorāsān Iran see Kabūd Gonbad
Kalāt Sīstān va Balūchestān Iran 89 E5
Kalat Balochistan Pak. 89 G4

Kalat *Balochistan* Pak. **89** G5
Kalat, Kūh-e *mt.* Iran **88** E3
Kalaupapa U.S.A. **127** [inset]
Kalaus *r.* Rus. Fed. **43** J7
Kalaw Myanmar **70** B2
Kälbäcär Azer. **91** G2
Kalbarri Australia **109** A6
Kalbarri National Park Australia **109** A6
Kalbe (Milde) Germany **53** L2
Kale Turkey **59** M6
Kalecik Turkey **90** D2
Kalefeld Germany **53** K3
Kaleindaung *inlet* Myanmar **70** A3
Kalemie Dem. Rep. Congo **99** C4
Kalemyo Myanmar **70** A2
Kāl-e Namak Iran **88** D3
Kalevala Rus. Fed. **44** Q4
Kalewa Myanmar **70** A2
Kaleybar Iran **88** B2
Kalgan China *see* **Zhangjiakou**
Kalghatgi India **84** B3
Kalgoorlie Australia **109** C7
Kāl Gūsheh Iran **88** E4
Kali Croatia **58** F2
Kali *r.* India/Nepal **82** E3
Kaliakra, Nos *pt* Bulg. **59** M3
Kali Gandaki *r.* Nepal **83** F4
Kaligiri India **84** C3
Kalikata India *see* **Kolkata**
Kalima Dem. Rep. Congo **98** C4
Kalimantan *reg.* Indon. **68** E7
Kálimnos *i.* Greece *see* **Kalymnos**
Kalinin Rus. Fed. *see* **Tver'**
Kalinin Adyndaky Tajik. *see* **Cheshtebe**
Kaliningrad Rus. Fed. **45** L9
Kalinino Armenia *see* **Tashir**
Kalinino Rus. Fed. **42** I4
Kalininsk Rus. Fed. **43** J6
Kalininskaya Rus. Fed. **43** H7
Kalinjara India **82** C5
Kalinkavichy Belarus **43** F5
Kalinkovichi Belarus *see* **Kalinkavichy**
Kalisch Poland *see* **Kalisz**
Kalispell U.S.A. **126** E2
Kalisz Poland **47** Q5
Kalitva *r.* Rus. Fed. **43** I6
Kaliua Tanz. **99** D4
Kaliujar India **82** E4
Kalix Sweden **44** M4
Kalkalighat India **83** H4
Kalkalpen, Nationalpark *nat. park* Austria **47** O7
Kalkan Turkey **59** M6
Kalkaska U.S.A. **134** C1
Kalkfeld Namibia **99** B6
Kalkfonteindam *dam* S. Africa **97** G5
Kalkudah Sri Lanka **84** D5
Kall Germany **52** G4
Kallang *r.* Sing. **71** [inset]
Kallaste Estonia **45** O7
Kallavesi *l.* Fin. **44** O5
Kallsedet Sweden **44** H5
Kallsjön *l.* Sweden **44** H5
Kallur India **84** C2
Kalmar Sweden **45** J8
Kalmarsund *sea chan.* Sweden **45** J8
Kalmit *hill* Germany **53** I5
Kalmūkh Qal'eh Iran **88** E2
Kalmunai Sri Lanka **84** D5
Kalmykia *aut. rep.* Rus. Fed. *see* **Kalmykiya-Khalm'g-Tangch, Respublika**
Kalmykiya-Khalm'g-Tangch, Respublika *aut. rep.* Rus. Fed. **91** G1
Kalmykovo Kazakh. *see* **Taypak**
Kalmytskaya Avtonomnaya Oblast' *aut. rep.* Rus. Fed. *see* **Kalmykiya-khalm'g-Tangch, Respublika**
Kalnai India **83** E5
Kalodnaye Belarus **45** O11
Kalol India **82** C5
Kalomo Zambia **99** C5
Kalone Peak Canada **120** E4
Kalpa India **82** D3
Kalpeni *atoll* India **84** B4
Kalpetta India **84** C4
Kalpi India **82** D4
Kaltag U.S.A. **118** C3
Kaltensundheim Germany **53** K4
Kaltukatjara Australia **109** E6
Kalu India **89** I4
Kaluga Rus. Fed. **43** H5
Kalukalukuang *i.* Indon. **68** F8
Kalundborg Denmark **45** G9
Kalush Ukr. **43** E6
Kalvakol India **84** C2
Kälviä Fin. **44** M5
Kal'ya Rus. Fed. **41** R3
Kalyan India **84** B2
Kalyandurg India **87** M7
Kalyansingapuram India **84** D2
Kalyazin Rus. Fed. **42** H4
Kalymnos *i.* Greece **59** L6
Kama Dem. Rep. Congo **98** C4
Kama Myanmar **70** A3

▶**Kama** *r.* Rus. Fed. **42** L4
4th longest river in Europe.

Kamaishi Japan **75** F5
Kamalia Pak. **89** I4
Kaman Turkey **90** D3
Kamaniskeg Lake Canada **135** G1
Kamanjab Namibia **99** B5
Kamarān *i.* Yemen **86** F6
Kamaran Island Yemen *see* **Kamarān**
Kamard *reg.* Afgh. **89** G3
Kamarod Pak. **89** F5
Kamaron Sierra Leone **96** B4
Kamashi Uzbek. **89** G2
Kamasin India **82** E4
Kambaiti Myanmar **70** B1
Kambalda Australia **109** C7
Kambam India **84** C4
Kambara *i.* Fiji *see* **Kabara**
Kambia Sierra Leone **96** B4
Kambing, Pulau *i.* East Timor *see* **Ataúro, Ilha de**
Kambo-san *mt.* N. Korea *see* **Kwanmo-bong**
Kambove Dem. Rep. Congo **99** C5
Kambūt Libya **90** B5
Kamchatka, Poluostrov *pen.* Rus. Fed. *see* **Kamchatka Peninsula**
Kamchatka Basin *sea feature* Bering Sea **150** H2
Kamchatka Peninsula Rus. Fed. **65** Q4
Kamchiya *r.* Bulg. **59** L3
Kameia, Parque Nacional de *nat. park* Angola *see* **Cameia, Parque Nacional da**
Kamelik *r.* Rus. Fed. **43** K5
Kamen Germany **53** H3
Kamen', Gory *mt.* Rus. Fed. **64** K3
Kamenets-Podol'skiy Ukr. *see* **Kam"yanets'-Podil's'kyy**
Kamenitsa *mt.* Bulg. **59** J4
Kamenjak, Rt *pt* Croatia **58** E2
Kamenka Kazakh. **41** Q5
Kamenka *Arkhangel'skaya Oblast'* Rus. Fed. **42** J2
Kamenka *Penzenskaya Oblast'* Rus. Fed. **43** J5
Kamenka *Primorskiy Kray* Rus. Fed. **74** E3
Kamenka-Bugskaya Ukr. *see* **Kam"yanka-Buz'ka**
Kamenka-Strumilovskaya Ukr. *see* **Kam"yanka-Buz'ka**
Kamen'-na-Obi Rus. Fed. **72** E2
Kamennogorsk Rus. Fed. **45** P6
Kamennomostskiy Rus. Fed. **91** F1
Kamenolomni Rus. Fed. **43** I7
Kamenongue Angola *see* **Camanongue**
Kamen'-Rybolov Rus. Fed. **74** D3
Kamenskoye Rus. Fed. **65** R3
Kamenskoye Ukr. *see* **Dniprodzerzhyns'k**
Kamensk-Shakhtinskiy Rus. Fed. **43** I6
Kamensk-Ural'skiy Rus. Fed. **64** H4
Kamet *mt.* China **82** D3
Kamiesberge *mts* S. Africa **100** D6
Kamieskroon S. Africa **100** C6
Kamileroi Australia **110** C3
Kamilukuak Lake Canada **121** K2
Kamina Dem. Rep. Congo **99** C4
Kaminak Lake Canada **121** M2
Kaminuriak Lake Canada *see* **Qamanirjuaq Lake**
Kamishihoro Japan **74** F4
Kamloops Canada **120** F5
Kamo Armenia **91** G2
Kamoke Pak. **89** I4
Kamonia Dem. Rep. Congo **99** C4

▶**Kampala** Uganda **98** D3
Capital of Uganda.

Kampar *r.* Indon. **68** C6
Kampar Malaysia **71** C6
Kampara India **84** D1
Kampen Neth. **52** F2
Kampene Dem. Rep. Congo **98** C4
Kamphaeng Phet Thai. **70** B3
Kampinoski Park Narodowy *nat. park* Poland **47** R4
Kâmpóng Cham Cambodia **71** D5
Kâmpóng Chhnăng Cambodia **71** D4
Kâmpóng Khleăng Cambodia **71** D4
Kâmpóng Saôm Cambodia *see* **Sihanoukville**
Kâmpóng Spœ Cambodia **71** D5
Kâmpóng Thum Cambodia **71** D4
Kâmpóng Trâbêk Cambodia **71** D5
Kâmpôt Cambodia **71** D5
Kampuchea *country* Asia *see* **Cambodia**
Kamrau, Teluk *b.* Indon. **69** I7
Kamsack Canada **121** K5
Kamskoye Vodokhranilishche *resr* Rus. Fed. **41** R4
Kamsuuma Somalia **98** E3
Kamuchawie Lake Canada **121** K3
Kamuli Uganda **98** D3
Kam"yanets'-Podil's'kyy Ukr. **43** E6
Kam"yanka-Buz'ka Ukr. **43** E6
Kamyanyets Belarus **45** M10
Kāmyārān Iran **88** B3
Kamyshin Rus. Fed. **43** J6
Kamyslybas, Ozero *l.* Kazakh. **80** B2
Kamyzyak Rus. Fed. **43** K7
Kamzar Oman **88** E5
Kanaaupscow *r.* Canada **122** F3
Kanab U.S.A. **129** G3
Kanab Creek *r.* U.S.A. **129** G3
Kanairiktok *r.* Canada **123** K3
Kanak Pak. **89** G4
Kananga Dem. Rep. Congo **99** C4
Kanangio, Mount *vol.* P.N.G. **69** L7
Kanangra-Boyd National Park Australia **112** E4
Kanarak India *see* **Konarka**
Kanarraville U.S.A. **129** G3
Kanas *watercourse* Namibia **100** C4
Kanash Rus. Fed. **42** J5
Kanauj India *see* **Kannauj**
Kanazawa Japan **75** E5
Kanbalu Myanmar **70** A2
Kanchanaburi Thai. **71** B4
Kanchanjanga *mt.* India/Nepal *see* **Kangchenjunga**
Kanchipuram India **84** C3
Kand *mt.* Pak. **89** G4
Kanda Pak. **89** G4
Kandahār Afgh. **89** G4
Kandalaksha Rus. Fed. **44** R3
Kandalakshskiy Zaliv *g.* Rus. Fed. **44** R3
Kandang Indon. **71** B7
Kandar Indon. **108** E2
Kandavu *i.* Fiji *see* **Kadavu**
Kandavu Passage Fiji *see* **Kadavu Passage**
Kandé Togo **96** D4
Kandhkot Pak. **89** H4
Kandi Benin **96** D3
Kandi India **84** C2
Kandiaro Pak. **89** H5
Kandıra Turkey **59** N4
Kandos Australia **112** D4
Kandreho Madag. **99** E5
Kandrian P.N.G. **69** L8
Kandukur India **84** C3
Kandy Sri Lanka **84** D5
Kandyagash Kazakh. **80** A2
Kane U.S.A. **135** F3
Kane Bassin *b.* Greenland **153** K1
Kaneh *watercourse* Iran **88** D5
Kaneohe *HI* U.S.A. **127** [inset]
Kaneti Pak. **89** G4
Kanevskaya Rus. Fed. **43** H7
Kang Afgh. **89** F4
Kang Botswana **100** F2
Kangaamiut Greenland **119** M3
Kangaarsussuaq *c.* Greenland **119** K2
Kangaba Mali **96** C3
Kangal Turkey **90** E3
Kangān *Būshehr* Iran **88** D5
Kangān *Hormozgan* Iran **88** E5
Kangandala, Parque Nacional de *nat. park* Angola *see* **Cangandala, Parque Nacional de**
Kangar Malaysia **71** C6
Kangaroo Island Australia **111** B7
Kangaroo Point Australia **110** B3
Kangaslampi Fin. **44** P5
Kangasniemi Fin. **44** O6
Kangāvar Iran **88** B3

▶**Kangchenjunga** *mt.* India/Nepal **83** G4
3rd highest mountain in the world and in Asia.
World 12–13

Kangding China **76** D2
Kangean, Kepulauan *is* Indon. **68** F8
Kangen *r.* Sudan **97** G4
Kangerlussuaq Greenland **119** M3
Kangerlussuaq *inlet* Greenland **119** M3
Kangerlussuaq *inlet* Greenland **153** J2
Kangersuatsiaq Greenland **119** M2
Kangertittivaq *sea chan.* Greenland **119** P2
Kanggye N. Korea **74** B4
Kanghwa S. Korea **75** B5
Kangikajik *c.* Greenland **119** P2
Kangiqsualujjuaq Canada **123** I2
Kangirsuk Canada **123** H1
Kang Krung National Park Thai. **71** B5
Kangle *Gansu* China **76** D1
Kangle *Jiangxi* China *see* **Wanzai**
Kanglong China **76** C1
Kangmar China **83** F3
Kangnŭng S. Korea **75** C5
Kango Gabon **98** B3
Kangping China **74** A4
Kangri Karpo Pass China/India **83** I3
Kangrinboqê Feng *mt.* China **82** E3
Kangsangdobdê China *see* **Xainza**
Kangto *mt.* China/India **83** H4
Kangtog China **83** F2
Kangxian China **76** E1
Kanibongan *Sabah* Malaysia **68** F5
Kanifing Gambia **96** B3
Kanigiri India **84** C3
Kanimekh Uzbek. **89** G1
Kanin, Poluostrov *pen.* Rus. Fed. **42** J2
Kanin Nos Rus. Fed. **153** G2
Kanin Nos, Mys *c.* Rus. Fed. **42** I1
Kaninskiy Bereg *coastal area* Rus. Fed. **42** I2
Kanjiroba *mt.* Nepal **83** E3
Kankaanpää Fin. **45** M6
Kankakee U.S.A. **134** B3
Kankan Guinea **96** C3
Kanker India **84** D1
Kankesanturai Sri Lanka **84** D4
Kankossa Mauritania **96** B3
Kanmaw Kyun *i.* Myanmar **71** B5
Kannauj India **82** D4
Kanniya Kumari *c.* India *see* **Comorin, Cape**
Kannonkoski Fin. **44** N5
Kannur India *see* **Cannanore**
Kannus Fin. **44** M5
Kano Nigeria **96** D3
Kanonpunt *pt* S. Africa **100** E8
Kanosh U.S.A. **129** G2
Kanovlei Namibia **99** B5
Kanoya Japan **75** C7
Kanpur *Orissa* India **84** E1
Kanpur *Uttar Pradesh* India **82** E4
Kanpur Pak. **89** H4
Kanrach *reg.* Pak. **89** G5
Kansai *airport* Japan **75** D6
Kansas U.S.A. **134** B4
Kansas *r.* U.S.A. **130** E4
Kansas *state* U.S.A. **130** D4
Kansas City *KS* U.S.A. **130** E4
Kansas City *MO* U.S.A. **130** E4
Kansk Rus. Fed. **65** K4
Kansu *prov.* China *see* **Gansu**
Kantang Thai. **71** B6
Kantara *hill* Cyprus **85** A2
Kantaralak Thai. **71** D4
Kantavu *i.* Fiji *see* **Kadavu**
Kantchari Burkina **96** D3
Kantemirovka Rus. Fed. **43** H6
Kanthi India **83** F5
Kantishna *r.* U.S.A. **118** C3
Kanton *atoll* Kiribati **107** I2
Kantulong Myanmar **70** B3
Kanturk Rep. of Ireland **51** D5
Kanuku Mountains Guyana **143** G3
Kanur India **84** C3
Kanus Namibia **100** D4
Kanyakubja India *see* **Kannauj**
KaNyamazane S. Africa **101** J3
Kanye Botswana **101** G3
Kaôh Pring *i.* Cambodia **71** C5
Kaohsiung Taiwan **77** I4
Kaôh Smăch *i.* Cambodia **71** C5
Kaôh Tang *i.* Cambodia **71** C5
Kaokoveld *plat.* Namibia **99** B5
Kaolack Senegal **96** B3
Kaoma Zambia **99** C5
Kaouadja Cent. Afr. Rep. **98** C3
Kapa S. Africa *see* **Cape Town**
Kapaa *HI* U.S.A. **127** [inset]
Kapaau *HI* U.S.A. **127** [inset]
Kapan Armenia **91** G3
Kapanga Dem. Rep. Congo **99** C4
Kaparhā Iran **88** C4
Kapatu Zambia **99** D4
Kapchagay Kazakh. **80** E3
Kapchagayskoye Vodokhranilishche *resr* Kazakh. **80** E3
Kap Dan Greenland *see* **Kulusuk**
Kapellen Belgium **52** E3
Kapello, Akra *pt* Greece **59** J6
Kapellskär Sweden **45** K7
Kapelskär Sweden *see* **Kapellskär**
Kapili *r.* India **83** G4
Kapingamarangi *atoll* Micronesia **150** G5
Kapingamarangi Rise *sea feature* N. Pacific Ocean **150** G5
Kapıorman Dağları *mts* Turkey **59** N4
Kapip Pak. **89** H4
Kapiri Mposhi Zambia **99** C5
Kapisillit Greenland **119** M3
Kapiskau *r.* Canada **122** E3
Kapit *Sarawak* Malaysia **68** E6
Kapiti Island N.Z. **113** E5
Kaplankyr, Chink *hills* Asia **91** I2
Kaplankyrskiy Gosudarstvennyy Zapovednik *nature res.* Turkm. **88** E1
Kapoeta Sudan **97** G4
Kapondai, Tanjung *pt* Indon. **69** G8
Kaposvár Hungary **58** G1
Kappel Germany **53** H5
Kappeln Germany **47** L3
Kapsukas Lith. *see* **Marijampolė**
Kaptai Bangl. **83** H5
Kapuas *r.* Indon. **68** D7
Kapuriya India **82** C4
Kapurthala India **82** C3
Kapuskasing Canada **122** E4
Kapustin Yar Rus. Fed. **43** J6
Kaputar *mt.* Australia **112** E3
Kaputir Kenya **98** D3
Kapuvár Hungary **58** G1
Kapydzhik, Gora *mt.* Armenia/Azer. *see* **Qazangödağ**
Kapyl' Belarus **45** O10
Kaqung China **89** J2
Kara India **82** E4
Kara Togo **96** D4
Kara *r.* Turkey **91** F3
Kara Art Pass China/Tajik. **89** I2
Kara-Balta Kyrg. **80** D3
Karabalyk Kazakh. **78** F1
Karabekaul' Turkm. *see* **Garabekevyul**
Karabiga Turkey **59** L4
Karabil', Vozvyshennost' *hills* Turkm. **89** F2
Kara-Bogaz-Gol, Proliv *sea chan.* Turkm. **91** I2
Kara-Bogaz-Gol, Zaliv *b.* Turkm. **91** I2
Kara-Bogaz-Gol'skiy Zaliv *b.* Turkm. *see* **Kara-Bogaz-Gol, Zaliv**
Karabük Turkey **90** D2
Karaburun Turkey **59** L5
Karabutak Kazakh. **80** B2
Karacabey Turkey **59** M4
Karacaköy Turkey **59** M4
Karacalı Dağ *mt.* Turkey **91** E3
Karaçal Tepe *mt.* Turkey **85** A1
Karacasu Turkey **59** M6
Karaca Yarımadası *pen.* Turkey **59** N6
Karachayevsk Rus. Fed. **91** F2
Karachev Rus. Fed. **43** G5
Karachi Pak. **89** G5
Karacurun Turkey *see* **Hilvan**
Karad India **84** B2
Kara Dağ *hill* Turkey **85** D1
Kara Dağ *mt.* Turkey **90** D3
Kara-Dar'ya Uzbek. *see* **Payshanba**
Kara Deniz *sea* Asia/Europe *see* **Black Sea**
Karagan Rus. Fed. **74** A1
Karaganda Kazakh. **80** D2
Karagayly Kazakh. **80** E2
Karaginskiy Zaliv *b.* Rus. Fed. **65** R4
Karagiye, Vpadina *depr.* Kazakh. **91** H2
Karagola India **83** F4
Karahallı Turkey **59** M5
Karahasanlı Turkey **90** D3
Karaikal India **84** C4
Karaikkudi India **84** C4
Karaisalı Turkey **90** D3
Karaj Iran **88** C3
Karak Jordan *see* **Al Karak**
Karakalli Turkey *see* **Özalp**
Karakax China *see* **Moyu**
Karakax He *r.* China **82** E1
Karakax Shan *mts* China **82** E2
Karakelong *i.* Indon. **69** H6
Karaki China **82** E1
Karaklis Armenia *see* **Vanadzor**
Karakoçan Turkey **91** F3
Kara-Köl Kyrg. **79** G2
Karakol Kyrg. **80** E3
Karakoram Pass China/Jammu and Kashmir **82** D2
Karakoram Range *mts* Asia **89** I2
Kara K'orē Eth. **98** D2
Karakorum Range *mts* Asia *see* **Karakoram Range**
Karaköse Turkey *see* **Ağrı**
Kara Kul' Kyrg. *see* **Kara-Köl**
Karakul' Uzbek. **89** F2
Karakul', Ozero *l.* Tajik. *see* **Qarokŭl**
Kara Kum *des.* Turkm. *see* **Kara Kumy**
Kara Kum *des.* Turkm. *see* **Karakum Desert**
Karakum, Peski Kazakh. *see* **Karakum Desert**
Karakum Desert Kazakh. **78** E2
Karakum Desert Turkm. *see* **Kara Kumy**
Karakum Desert Turkm. **88** F2
Karakumskiy Kanal *canal* Turkm. **89** F2
Kara Kumy *des.* Turkm. **88** E2
Karakurt Turkey **91** F2
Karakuş Dağı *ridge* Turkey **59** N5
Karal Chad **97** E3
Karala Estonia **45** L7
Karalundi Australia **109** B6
Karama *r.* Indon. **68** F7
Karaman Turkey **90** D3
Karaman *prov.* Turkey **85** A1
Karamanlı Turkey **59** M6
Karamay China **80** F2
Karambar Pass Afgh./Pak. **89** I2
Karamea N.Z. **113** D5
Karamea Bight *b.* N.Z. **113** C5
Karamendy Kazakh. **80** B1
Karamet-Niyaz Turkm. **89** G2
Karamiran China **83** F1
Karamiran Shankou *pass* China **83** F1
Karamürsel Turkey **59** M4
Karamyshevo Rus. Fed. **45** P8
Karān *i.* Saudi Arabia **88** C5
Karangasem Indon. **108** A2
Karanja India **84** C1
Karanjia India **82** E5
Karapınar *Gaziantep* Turkey **85** C1
Karapınar *Konya* Turkey **90** D3
Karas *admin. reg.* Namibia **100** C4
Karasay China **83** E1
Karasburg Namibia **100** D5
Kara Sea Rus. Fed. **64** I2
Kárášjohka Norway **44** N2
Karasjok Norway *see* **Kárášjohka**
Kara Strait Rus. Fed. *see* **Karskiye Vorota, Proliv**
Karasu *r.* Syria/Turkey **85** C1
Karasu *Bitlis* Turkey *see* **Hizan**
Karasu *Sakarya* Turkey **59** N4
Karasu *r.* Turkey **91** F3
Karasubazar Ukr. *see* **Bilohirs'k**
Karasuk Rus. Fed. **64** I4
Karāt Iran **89** F3
Karataş Turkey **85** B1
Karataş Burnu *hd* Turkey *see* **Fener Burnu**
Karatau Kazakh. **80** D3
Karatau, Khrebet *mts* Kazakh. **80** C3
Karatepe Turkey **85** A1
Karathuri Myanmar **71** B5
Karativu *i.* Sri Lanka **84** C4
Karatsu Japan **75** C6
Karaudanawa Guyana **143** G3
Karaulbazar Uzbek. **89** G2
Karauli India **82** D4
Karavan Kyrg. *see* **Kerben**
Karavostasi Cyprus **85** A2
Karawang Indon. **68** D8
Karayılan Turkey **85** C1
Karayulgan China **80** F3
Karazhal Kazakh. **80** D2
Karbalā' Iraq **91** G4
Karben Germany **53** I4
Karcag Hungary **59** I1
Karden Germany **53** H4
Kardhítsa Greece *see* **Karditsa**
Karditsa Greece **59** I5
Kärdla Estonia **45** M7
Karee S. Africa **101** H5
Kareeberge *mts* S. Africa **100** E6
Kareima Sudan **86** D6
Kareli India **82** D5
Karelia *aut. rep.* Rus. Fed. *see* **Kareliya, Respublika**
Kareliya, Respublika *aut. rep.* Rus. Fed. **44** R5
Karel'skaya A.S.S.R. *aut. rep.* Rus. Fed. *see* **Kareliya, Respublika**
Karel'skiy Bereg *coastal area* Rus. Fed. **44** R3
Karema Tanz. **99** D4
Karera India **82** D4
Karesuando Sweden **44** M2
Karevāndar Iran **89** F5
Kargalinskaya Rus. Fed. **91** G2
Kargalinski Rus. Fed. *see* **Kargalinskaya**
Kargapazarı Dağları *mts* Turkey **91** F3
Karghalik China *see* **Yecheng**
Kargı Turkey **90** D2
Kargil India **82** D2
Kargilik China *see* **Yecheng**
Kargıpınarı Turkey **85** B1
Kargopol' Rus. Fed. **42** H3
Karholmsbruk Sweden **45** J6
Kari Nigeria **96** E3
Karīān Iran **88** E5
Kariba Zimbabwe **99** C5
Kariba, Lake *resr* Zambia/Zimbabwe **99** C5
Kariba Dam Zambia/Zimbabwe **99** C5
Kariba-yama *vol.* Japan **74** E4
Karibib Namibia **100** B1
Karigasniemi Fin. **44** N2
Karijini National Park Australia **109** B5
Karijoki Fin. **44** L5
Karikachi-tōge *pass* Japan **74** F4
Karikari, Cape N.Z. **113** D2
Karimata, Pulau-pulau *is* Indon. **68** D7
Karimata, Selat *strait* Indon. **68** D7
Karimganj India **83** H4
Karimnagar India **84** C2
Karimun Besar *i.* Indon. **71** C7
Karimunjawa, Pulau-pulau *is* Indon. **68** E8
Káristos Greece *see* **Karystos**
Karjat *Maharashtra* India **84** B2
Karjat *Maharashtra* India **84** B2
Karkaralinsk Kazakh. **80** E2
Karkar Island P.N.G. **69** L7
Karkh Pak. **89** G5
Karkinits'ka Zatoka *g.* Ukr. **59** O2
Kärkölä Fin. **45** N6
Karkonoski Park Narodowy *nat. park* Czech Rep./Poland *see* **Krkonošský národní park**
Karksi-Nuia Estonia **45** N7
Karkük Iraq *see* **Kirkūk**
Karlachi Pak. **89** H3
Karlik Shan *mt.* China **80** H3
Karlıova Turkey **91** F3
Karlivka Ukr. **43** G6
Karl Marks, Qullai *mt.* Tajik. **89** I2
Karl-Marx-Stadt Germany *see* **Chemnitz**
Karlovac Croatia **58** F2
Karlovka Ukr. *see* **Karlivka**
Karlovo Bulg. **59** K3
Karlovy Vary Czech Rep. **53** M4
Karlsbad Germany **53** I6
Karlsborg Sweden **45** I7
Karlsburg Romania *see* **Alba Iulia**
Karlshamn Sweden **45** I8
Karlskoga Sweden **45** I7
Karlskrona Sweden **45** I8
Karlsruhe Germany **53** I5
Karlstad Sweden **45** H7
Karlstad U.S.A. **130** D1
Karlstadt Germany **53** J5
Karluk U.S.A. **118** C4
Karlyuk Turkm. **89** G2
Karmala India **84** B2
Karmel, Har *hill* Israel *see* **Carmel, Mount**
Karmona Spain *see* **Córdoba**
Karmøy *i.* Norway **45** D7
Karmpur Pak. **89** I4
Karnabchul', Step' *plain* Uzbek. **89** G2
Karnafuli Reservoir Bangl. **83** H5
Karnal India **82** D3
Karnataka *state* India **84** B3
Karnavati India *see* **Ahmadabad**
Karnes City U.S.A. **131** D6
Karnobat Bulg. **59** L3
Karodi Pak. **89** G5
Karoi Zimbabwe **99** C5
Karokpi Myanmar **70** B4
Karo La *pass* China **83** G3
Karong India **83** H4
Karonga Malawi **99** D4
Karonie Australia **109** C7
Karoo National Park S. Africa **100** F7
Karoo Nature Reserve S. Africa **100** G7
Karoonda Australia **111** B7
Karora Eritrea **86** E6
Káros *i.* Greece *see* **Keros**
Karossa Indon. **68** F7
Karossa, Tanjung *pt* Indon. **108** B2
Karow Germany **53** M1
Karpasia *pen.* Cyprus **85** B2
Karpas Peninsula Cyprus *see* **Karpasia**
Karpathos *i.* Greece **59** L7
Karpathou, Steno *sea chan.* Greece **59** L6
Karpaty *mts* Europe *see* **Carpathian Mountains**
Karpenisi Greece **59** I5
Karpilovka Belarus *see* **Aktsyabrski**
Karpinsk Rus. Fed. **41** S4
Karpogory Rus. Fed. **42** J2
Karpuz *r.* Turkey **85** A1
Karratha Australia **108** B5
Karroo *plat.* S. Africa *see* **Great Karoo**
Karrychirla Turkm. *see* **imeni Kerbabayeva**
Kars Turkey **91** F2
Kärsämäki Fin. **44** N5
Kārsava Latvia **45** O8
Karshi Turkm. **91** I2
Karshi Uzbek. **89** G2
Karshinskaya Step' *plain* Uzbek. **89** G2
Karskiye Vorota, Proliv *strait* Rus. Fed. **64** G3
Karskoye More *sea* Rus. Fed. *see* **Kara Sea**
Karstädt Germany **53** L1
Karstula Fin. **44** N5
Karsu Turkey **85** C1
Karsun Rus. Fed. **43** J5
Kartal Turkey **59** M4
Kartaly Rus. Fed. **64** H4
Kartayel' Rus. Fed. **42** L2
Karttula Fin. **44** O5
Karumba Australia **110** C3
Karumbhar Island India **82** B5
Karun, Kūh-e *hill* Iran **88** C4
Kārūn, Rūd-e *r.* Iran **88** C4
Karuni Indon. **108** B2
Karur India **84** C4
Karvia Fin. **44** M5
Karviná Czech Rep. **47** Q6
Karwar India **84** B3
Karyagino Azer. *see* **Füzuli**
Karymskoye Rus. Fed. **73** K2
Karynzharyk, Peski *des.* Kazakh. **91** I2
Karystos Greece **59** K5
Kaş Turkey **59** M6
Kasa India **84** B2
Kasaba Turkey *see* **Turgutlu**
Kasabonika Canada **122** C3
Kasabonika Lake Canada **122** C3
Kasaï *r.* Dem. Rep. Congo **98** B4
also known as Kwa
Kasaï, Plateau du Dem. Rep. Congo **99** C4
Kasaji Dem. Rep. Congo **99** C5
Kasama Zambia **99** D5
Kasan Uzbek. **89** G2
Kasane Botswana **99** C5
Kasaragod India **84** B3
Kasargod India *see* **Kasaragod**
Kasargode India *see* **Kasaragod**
Kasatkino Rus. Fed. **74** C2
Kasba Lake Canada **121** K2
Kasba Tadla Morocco **54** C5
Kasenga Dem. Rep. Congo **99** C5
Kasengu Dem. Rep. Congo **99** C4
Kasese Dem. Rep. Congo **98** C4
Kasese Uganda **98** D3
Kasevo Rus. Fed. *see* **Neftekamsk**
Kasganj India **82** D4
Kasha China *see* **Gonjo**
Kashabowie Canada **122** C4
Kāshān Iran **88** C3
Kashary Rus. Fed. **43** I6
Kashechewan Canada **122** E3
Kashgar China *see* **Kashi**
Kashi China **80** E4
Kashihara Japan **75** D6
Kashima-nada *b.* Japan **75** F5
Kashin Rus. Fed. **42** H4
Kashipur India **82** D3
Kashira Rus. Fed. **43** H5
Kashiwazaki Japan **75** E5
Kashkarantsy Rus. Fed. **42** H2
Kashku'iyeh Iran **88** D4
Kāshmar Iran **88** E3
Kashmir *terr.* Asia *see* **Jammu and Kashmir**
Kashmir, Vale of *reg.* India **82** C2
Kashyukulu Dem. Rep. Congo **99** C4
Kasi India *see* **Varanasi**
Kasigar Afgh. **89** H3
Kasimov Rus. Fed. **43** I5
Kaskattama *r.* Canada **121** N3
Kaskinen Fin. **44** L5
Kas Klong *i.* Cambodia *see* **Kŏng, Kaôh**
Kaskö Fin. *see* **Kaskinen**
Kaslo Canada **120** G5
Kasmere Lake Canada **121** K3
Kasongo Dem. Rep. Congo **99** C4
Kasongo-Lunda Dem. Rep. Congo **99** B4
Kasos *i.* Greece **59** L7
Kaspīy Mangy Oypaty *lowland* Kazakh./Rus. Fed. *see* **Caspian Lowland**
Kaspiysk Rus. Fed. **91** G2
Kaspiyskiy Rus. Fed. *see* **Lagan'**
Kaspiyskoye More *l.* Asia/Europe *see* **Caspian Sea**
Kassa Slovakia *see* **Košice**
Kassala Sudan **86** E6
Kassandras, Akra *pt* Greece **59** J5
Kassandras, Kolpos *b.* Greece **59** J4
Kassel Germany **53** J3
Kasserine Tunisia **58** C7
Kastag Pak. **89** F5
Kastamonu Turkey **90** D2
Kastellaun Germany **53** H4

Kastelli Greece 59 J7
Kastéllion Greece see Kastelli
Kastellorizon i. Greece see Megisti
Kasterlee Belgium 52 E3
Kastoria Greece 59 I4
Kastornoye Rus. Fed. 43 H6
Kastsyukovichy Belarus 43 G5
Kasulu Tanz. 99 D4
Kasumkent Rus. Fed. 91 H2
Kasungu Malawi 99 D5
Kasungu National Park Malawi 99 D5
Kasur Pak. 89 I4
Katâdtlit Nunât terr. N. America see Greenland
Katahdin, Mount U.S.A. 132 G2
Kataklik Jammu and Kashmir 82 D2
Katako-Kombe Dem. Rep. Congo 98 C4
Katakwi Uganda 98 D3
Katana India 82 C5
Katangi India 82 D5
Katanning Australia 109 B8
Katavi National Park Tanz. 99 D4
Katawaz reg. Afgh. 89 G3
Katchall i. India 71 A6
Katea Dem. Rep. Congo 99 C4
Katerini Greece 59 J4
Katesh Tanz. 99 D4
Kate's Needle mt. Canada/U.S.A. 120 C3
Katete Zambia 99 D5
Katherîna, Gebel mt. Egypt see Kātrīnā, Jabal
Katherine Australia 108 F3
Katherine Gorge National Park Australia see Nitmiluk National Park
Kathi India 89 I6
Kathiawar pen. India 82 B5
Kathihar India see Katihar
Kathiraveli Sri Lanka 84 D4
Kathiwara India 82 C5
Kathleen Falls Australia 108 E3
Kathlehong S. Africa 101 I4

▶Kathmandu Nepal 83 F4
Capital of Nepal.

Kathu S. Africa 100 F4
Kathua India 82 C2
Kati Mali 96 C3
Katihar India 83 F4
Kati-Kati S. Africa 101 H7
Katima Mulilo Namibia 99 C5
Katimik Lake Canada 121 L4
Katiola Côte d'Ivoire 96 C4
Kā Tiritiri o te Moana mts N.Z. see Southern Alps
Katkop Hills S. Africa 100 E6
Katmai National Park and Preserve U.S.A. 118 C4
Katmandu Nepal see Kathmandu
Kato Achaïa Greece 59 I5
Kat O Chau Hong Kong China see Crooked Island
Kat O Hoi b. Hong Kong China see Crooked Harbour
Katoomba Australia 112 E4
Katowice Poland 47 Q5
Katoya India 83 G5
Katrancık Dağı mts Turkey 59 M6
Kātrīnā, Jabal mt. Egypt 90 D5
Katrine, Loch l. U.K. 50 E4
Katrineholm Sweden 45 J7
Katse Dam Lesotho 101 I5
Katsina Nigeria 96 D3
Katsina-Ala Nigeria 96 D4
Katsuura Japan 75 F6
Kattaktoc, Cap c. Canada 123 I2
Kattakurgan Uzbek. 89 G2
Kattamudda Well Australia 108 D5
Kattaqŭrghon Uzbek. see Kattakurgan
Kattasang Hills Afgh. 89 G3
Kattegat strait Denmark/Sweden 45 G8
Kattowitz Poland see Katowice
Katumbar India 82 D4
Katunino Rus. Fed. 42 J4
Katuri Pak. 89 H4
Katwa India see Katoya
Katwijk aan Zee Neth. 52 E2
Katzenbuckel hill Germany 53 J5
Kauai i. U.S.A. 127 [inset]
Kauai Channel U.S.A. 127 [inset]
Kaub Germany 53 H4
Kaufungen Germany 53 J3
Kauhajoki Fin. 44 M5
Kauhava Fin. 44 M5
Kaukauna U.S.A. 134 A1
Kaukkwè Hills Myanmar 70 B1
Kaukonen Fin. 44 N3
Kaula i. HI U.S.A. 127 [inset]
Kaulakahi Channel HI U.S.A. 127 [inset]
Kaumajet Mountains Canada 123 J2
Kaunakakai HI U.S.A. 127 [inset]
Kaunas Lith. 45 M9
Kaunata Latvia 45 O8
Kaundy, Vpadina depr. Kazakh. 91 I2
Kaunia Bangl. 83 G4
Kaura-Namoda Nigeria 96 D3
Kau Sai Chau i. Hong Kong China 77 [inset]
Kaustinen Fin. 44 M5
Kautokeino Norway 44 M2
Kau-ye Kyun i. Myanmar 71 B5
Kavadarci Macedonia 59 J4
Kavak Turkey 90 E2
Kavaklıdere Turkey 59 M6
Kavala Greece 59 K4
Kavalas, Kolpos b. Greece 59 K4
Kavalerovo Rus. Fed. 74 D3
Kavali India 84 D3
Kavār Iran 88 D4
Kavaratti India 84 B4
Kavaratti atoll India 84 B4
Kavarna Bulg. 59 M3
Kavendou, Mont mt. Guinea 96 B3
Kaveri r. India 84 C4
Kavīr Iran 88 C3
Kavīr salt flat Iran 88 D3
Kavīr, Dasht-e des. Iran 88 D3
Kavīr Kūshk well Iran 88 E3
Kavkasioni mts Asia/Europe see Caucasus
Kawa Myanmar 70 B3
Kawagama Lake Canada 135 F1
Kawagoe Japan 75 E6
Kawaguchi Japan 75 E6
Kawaihae HI U.S.A. 127 [inset]
Kawaikini, Mount HI U.S.A. 127 [inset]
Kawakawa N.Z. 113 E2
Kawambwa Zambia 99 C4
Kawana Zambia 99 C5
Kawardha India 82 E5
Kawartha Lakes Canada 135 F1
Kawasaki Japan 75 E6
Kawau Island N.Z. 113 E3
Kawawachikamach Canada 123 I3
Kawdut Myanmar 70 B4
Kawerau N.Z. 113 F4
Kawhia N.Z. 113 E4
Kawhia Harbour N.Z. 113 E4
Kawich Peak U.S.A. 128 E3
Kawich Range mts U.S.A. 128 E3
Kawinaw Lake Canada 121 L4
Kaw Lake U.S.A. 131 D4
Kawlin Myanmar 70 A2
Kawm Umbū Egypt 86 D5
Kawngmeum Myanmar 70 B2
Kawthaung Myanmar 71 B5
Kaxgar China see Kashi
Kaxgar He r. China 80 E4
Kax He r. China 80 F3
Kaxtax Shan mts China 83 E1
Kaya Burkina 96 C3
Kayadibi Turkey 90 E3
Kayan r. Indon. 68 F6
Kayankulam India 84 C4
Kayar India 84 C2
Kaycee U.S.A. 126 G4
Kaydak, Sor dry lake Kazakh. 91 I1
Kaydanovo Belarus see Dzyarzhynsk
Kayembe-Mukulu Dem. Rep. Congo 99 C4
Kayenta U.S.A. 129 H3
Kayes Mali 96 B3
Kaymaz Turkey 59 N5
Kaynar Kazakh. 80 E2
Kaynar Turkey 90 E3
Kayseri Turkey 90 D3
Kayuyu Dem. Rep. Congo 98 C4
Kayyngdy Kyrg. 80 D3
Kazach'ye Rus. Fed. 65 O2
Kazakh Azer. see Qazax
Kazakhskaya S.S.R. country Asia see Kazakhstan
Kazakhskiy Melkosopochnik plain Kazakh. 80 D1
Kazakhskiy Zaliv b. Kazakh. 91 I2

▶Kazakhstan country Asia 78 F2
4th largest country in Asia.
Asia 6, 62–63

Kazakhstan Kazakh. see Aksay
Kazakstan country Asia see Kazakhstan
Kazan r. Canada 121 M2
Kazan' Rus. Fed. 42 K5
Kazandzhik Turkm. see Gazandzhyk
Kazanka r. Rus. Fed. 42 K5
Kazanlı Turkey 85 B1
Kazanlŭk Bulg. 59 K3
Kazan-rettō is Japan see Volcano Islands
Kazatin Ukr. see Kozyatyn

▶Kazbek mt. Georgia/Rus. Fed. 43 J8
4th highest mountain in Europe.

Kaz Dağı mts Turkey 59 L5
Kāzerūn Iran 88 C4
Kazhim Rus. Fed. 42 K3
Kazidi Tajik. see Qozideh
Kazi Magomed Azer. see Qazımämmäd
Kazincbarcika Hungary 43 D6
Kaziranga National Park India 83 H4
Kazret'i Georgia 91 G2
Kaztalovka Kazakh. 41 P6
Kazy Turkm. 88 E2
Kazym r. Rus. Fed. 41 T3
Kazymskiy Mys Rus. Fed. 41 T3
Kea i. Greece 59 K6
Keady U.K. 51 F3
Keams Canyon U.S.A. 129 H4
Kéamu i. Vanuatu see Anatom
Kearney U.S.A. 130 D3
Kearny U.S.A. 129 H5
Keban Turkey 90 E3
Keban Barajı resr Turkey 90 E3
Kébémèr Senegal 96 B3
Kebili Tunisia 54 F5
Kebīr, Nahr al r. Lebanon/Syria 85 B2
Kebkabiya Sudan 97 F3
Kebnekaise mt. Sweden 44 K3
Kebock Head hd U.K. 50 C2
K'ebrī Dehar Eth. 98 E3
Kech reg. Pak. 89 F5
Kechika r. Canada 120 E3
Keçiborlu Turkey 59 N6
Kecskemét Hungary 59 H1
K'eda Georgia 91 F2
Kėdainiai Lith. 45 M9
Kedairu Passage Fiji see Kadavu Passage
Kedgwick Canada 123 I5
Kedian China 77 G2
Kedong China 74 B3
Kedva r. Rus. Fed. 42 L2
Kędzierzyn-Koźle Poland 47 Q5
Keele r. Canada 120 E1
Keele Peak Canada 120 D2
Keeler U.S.A. 128 E3
Keeley Lake Canada 121 I4
Keeling Islands terr. Indian Ocean see Cocos Islands
Keen, Mount hill U.K. 50 G4
Keene CA U.S.A. 128 D4
Keene KY U.S.A. 134 C5
Keene NH U.S.A. 135 I2
Keene OH U.S.A. 134 E3
Keepit, Lake resr Australia 112 E3
Keep River National Park Australia 108 E3
Keerbergen Belgium 52 E3
Keer-weer, Cape Australia 110 C2
Keetmanshoop Namibia 100 D4
Keewatin Canada 121 M5
Kefallinía i. Greece see Cephalonia
Kefallonia i. Greece see Cephalonia
Kefamenanu Indon. 108 D2
Kefe Ukr. see Feodosiya
Keffi Nigeria 96 D4
Keflavík Iceland 44 [inset]
Kegalla Sri Lanka 84 D5
Kegen Kazakh. 80 E3
Keglo, Baie de b. Canada 123 I2
Keg River Canada 120 G3
Kegul'ta Rus. Fed. 43 J7
Kehra Estonia 45 N7
Kehsi Mansam Myanmar 70 B2
Keighley U.K. 48 F5
Keila Estonia 45 N7
Keimoes S. Africa 100 E5
Keitele Fin. 44 O5
Keitele l. Fin. 44 O5
Keith Australia 111 C8
Keith U.K. 50 G3
Keith Arm b. Canada 120 F1
Kejimkujik National Park Canada 123 I5
Kekaha HI U.S.A. 127 [inset]
Kékes mt. Hungary 47 R7
Kekri India 82 C4
K'elafo Eth. 98 E3
Kelai i. Maldives 84 B5
Kelang Malaysia 71 C7
Kelberg Germany 52 G4
Kelheim Germany 53 L6
Kelibia Tunisia 58 D6
Kelifskiy Uzboy marsh Turkm. 89 F2
Kelīrī Iran 88 E5
Kelkheim (Taunus) Germany 53 I4
Kelkit Turkey 91 E2
Kelkit r. Turkey 90 E2
Kéllé Congo 98 B4
Keller Lake Canada 120 F2
Kellett, Cape Canada 118 F2
Kelleys Island U.S.A. 134 D3
Kelliher Canada 121 K5
Kelloselkä Fin. 44 P3
Kells Rep. of Ireland 51 F4
Kells r. U.K. 51 F3
Kelly U.S.A. 134 B5
Kelly Lake Canada 120 E1
Kelly Range hills Australia 109 C6
Kelmė Lith. 45 M9
Kelmis Belgium 52 G4
Kelo Chad 97 E4
Kelowna Canada 120 G5
Kelp Head hd Canada 120 E5
Kelseyville U.S.A. 128 B2
Kelso U.K. 50 G5
Kelso CA U.S.A. 129 F4
Kelso WA U.S.A. 126 C3
Keluang Malaysia 71 C7
Kelvington Canada 121 K4
Kem' Rus. Fed. 42 G2
Kem' r. Rus. Fed. 42 G2
Ke Macina Mali see Massina
Kemah Turkey 90 E3
Kemaliye Turkey 90 E3
Kemalpaşa Turkey 59 L5
Kemano Canada 120 E4
Kembé Cent. Afr. Rep. 98 C3
Kemeneshát hills Hungary 58 G1
Kemer Antalya Turkey 59 N6
Kemer Muğla Turkey 59 M6
Kemer Barajı resr Turkey 59 M6
Kemerovo Rus. Fed. 64 J4
Kemi Fin. 44 N4
Kemijärvi Fin. 44 O3
Kemijärvi l. Fin. 44 O3
Kemijoki r. Fin. 44 N4
Kemiö Fin. see Kimito
Kemir Turkm. 88 D2
Kemmerer U.S.A. 126 F4
Kemnath Germany 53 L5
Kemnay U.K. 50 G3
Kemp Coast reg. Antarctica see Kemp Land
Kempele Fin. 44 N4
Kempen Germany 52 G3
Kempisch Kanaal canal Belgium 52 F3
Kemp Land reg. Antarctica 152 D2
Kemp Peninsula Antarctica 152 A2
Kemp's Bay Bahamas 133 E7
Kempsey Australia 112 F3
Kempt, Lac l. Canada 122 G5
Kempten (Allgäu) Germany 47 M7
Kempton U.S.A. 134 B3
Kempton Park S. Africa 101 I4
Kemptville Canada 135 H1
Kemujan i. Indon. 68 E8
Ken r. India 82 E4
Kenai U.S.A. 118 C3
Kenai Fiords National Park U.S.A. 118 C4
Kenai Mountains U.S.A. 118 C4
Kenamu r. Canada 123 K3
Kenansville U.S.A. 133 E5
Kenâyis, Râs el pt Egypt see Ḥikmah, Ra's al
Kenbridge U.S.A. 135 F5
Kendal U.K. 48 E4
Kendall Australia 112 F3
Kendall, Cape Canada 119 J3
Kendallville U.S.A. 134 C3
Kendari Indon. 69 G7
Kendawangan Indon. 68 E7
Kendégué Chad 97 E3
Kendrapara India 83 F5
Kendraparha India see Kendrapara
Kendrick Peak U.S.A. 129 H4
Kendujhar India see Keonjhar
Kendujhargarh India see Keonjhar
Kendyrli-Kayasanskoye, Plato plat. Kazakh. 91 I2
Kendyrlisor, Solonchak salt l. Kazakh. 91 I2
Kenebri Australia 112 D3
Kenedy U.S.A. 131 D6
Kenema Sierra Leone 96 B4
Keneurgench Turkm. 87 I1
Kenge Dem. Rep. Congo 99 B4
Keng Lap Myanmar 70 C2
Kengtung Myanmar 70 B2
Kenhardt S. Africa 100 E5
Kéniéba Mali 96 B3
Kénitra Morocco 54 C5
Kenmare Rep. of Ireland 51 C6
Kenmare U.S.A. 130 C1
Kenmare River inlet Rep. of Ireland 51 B6
Kenmore U.S.A. 135 F2
Kenn Germany 52 G5
Kenna U.S.A. 131 C5
Kennebec U.S.A. 130 D3
Kennebec r. U.S.A. 132 G2
Kennebunkport U.S.A. 135 J2
Kennedy, Cape U.S.A. see Canaveral, Cape
Kennedy Range National Park Australia 109 A6
Kennedy Town Hong Kong China 77 [inset]
Kenner U.S.A. 131 F6
Kennet r. U.K. 49 G7
Kenneth Range hills Australia 109 B5
Kennett U.S.A. 131 F4
Kennewick U.S.A. 126 D3
Kenn Reef Australia 110 F4
Kenogami r. Canada 122 D4
Keno Hill Canada 120 C2
Kenora Canada 121 M5
Kenosha U.S.A. 134 B2
Kenozero, Ozero l. Rus. Fed. 42 H3
Kent r. U.K. 48 E4
Kent OH U.S.A. 134 E3
Kent TX U.S.A. 131 B6
Kent VA U.S.A. 134 E5
Kent WA U.S.A. 126 C3
Kentani S. Africa 101 I7
Kent Group is Australia 111 [inset]
Kentland U.S.A. 134 B3
Kenton U.S.A. 134 D3
Kent Peninsula Canada 118 H3
Kentucky state U.S.A. 134 C5
Kentucky Lake U.S.A. 131 F4
▶Kenya country Africa 98 D3
Africa 7, 94–95

▶Kenya, Mount Kenya 98 D4
2nd highest mountain in Africa.

Kenyir, Tasik resr Malaysia 71 C6
Keokuk U.S.A. 130 F3
Keoladao National Park India 82 D4
Keonjhar India 83 F5
Keonjhargarh India see Keonjhar
Keosauqua U.S.A. 130 F3
Keowee, Lake resr U.S.A. 133 D5
Kepina r. Rus. Fed. 42 I2
Keppel Bay Australia 110 E4
Kepsut Turkey 59 M5
Kera India 83 F5
Kerāh Iran 88 E4
Kerala state India 84 B4
Kerang Australia 112 A5
Kerava Fin. 45 N6
Kerba Alg. 57 G5
Kerbela Iraq see Karbalā'
Kerben Kyrg. 80 D3
Kerbi r. Rus. Fed. 74 E1
Kerbodot, Lac l. Canada 123 I3
Kerch Ukr. 90 E1
Kerchem'ya Rus. Fed. 42 L3
Kerema P.N.G. 69 L8
Keremeos Canada 120 G5
Kerempe Burun pt Turkey 90 D2
Keren Eritrea 86 E6
Kerewan Gambia 96 B3
Kergeli Turkm. 88 E2
Kerguélen, Îles is Indian Ocean 149 M9
Kerguelen Islands Indian Ocean see Kerguélen, Îles
Kerguelen Plateau sea feature Indian Ocean 149 M9
Kericho Kenya 98 D4
Kerikeri N.Z. 113 D2
Kerimäki Fin. 44 P6
Kerinci, Gunung vol. Indon. 68 C7
Kerinci Seblat National Park Indon. 68 C7
Kerintji vol. Indon. see Kerinci, Gunung
Keriya He watercourse China 72 E5
Keriya Shankou pass China 83 E2
Kerken Germany 52 G3
Kerkenah, Îles is Tunisia 58 D7
Kerki Turkm. 89 G2
Kerkichi Turkm. 89 G2
Kerkinitis, Limni l. Greece 59 J4
Kérkira i. Greece see Corfu
Kerkouane tourist site Tunisia 58 D6
Kerkyra Greece 59 H5
Kerkyra i. Greece see Corfu
Kerma Sudan 86 D6
Kermadec Islands S. Pacific Ocean 107 I5

▶Kermadec Trench sea feature S. Pacific Ocean 150 I8
4th deepest trench in the world.

Kermān Iran 88 E4
Kerman U.S.A. 128 C3
Kermān Desert Iran 88 E4
Kermānshāh Iran 88 B3
Kermānshāhān Iran 88 D4
Kermine Uzbek. see Navoi
Kermit U.S.A. 131 C6
Kern r. U.S.A. 128 D4
Kernertut, Cap c. Canada 123 I2
Keros i. Greece 59 K6
Keros Rus. Fed. 42 L3
Kérouané Guinea 96 C4
Kerpen Germany 52 G4
Kerr, Cape Antarctica 152 H1
Kerrobert Canada 121 I5
Kerrville U.S.A. 131 D6
Kerry Head hd Rep. of Ireland 51 C5
Kerteminde Denmark 45 G9
Kerulen r. China/Mongolia see Herlen Gol
Kerur India 84 B2
Keryneia Cyprus see Kyrenia
Kerzaz Alg. 96 C2
Kerzhenets r. Rus. Fed. 42 J4
Kesagami Lake Canada 122 E4
Kesälahti Fin. 44 P6
Keşan Turkey 59 L4
Keşap Turkey 43 H8
Kesariya India 83 F4
Kesennuma Japan 75 F5
Keshan China 74 B2
Keshem Afgh. 89 H2
Keshena U.S.A. 134 A1
Keshendeh-ye Bala Afgh. 89 G2
Keshod India 82 B5
Keshvar Iran 88 C3
Keskin Turkey 90 D3
Keskozero Rus. Fed. 42 G3
Kesova Gora Rus. Fed. 42 H4
Kessel Neth. 52 G3
Kestell S. Africa 101 I5
Kesten'ga Rus. Fed. 44 Q4
Kestilä Fin. 44 O4
Keswick Canada 134 F1
Keswick U.K. 48 D4
Keszthely Hungary 58 G1
Ketapang Indon. 68 E7
Ketchikan U.S.A. 120 D4
Keti Bandar Pak. 89 G5
Ketmen', Khrebet mts China/Kazakh. 80 F3
Kettering U.K. 49 G6
Kettering U.S.A. 134 C4
Kettle r. Canada 120 G5
Kettle Creek r. U.S.A. 135 G3
Kettle Falls U.S.A. 126 D2
Kettleman City U.S.A. 128 D3
Kettle River Range mts U.S.A. 126 D2
Keuka U.S.A. 135 G2
Keuka Lake U.S.A. 135 G2
Keumgang, Mount N. Korea see Kumgang-san
Keumsang, Mount N. Korea see Kumgang-san
Keuruu Fin. 44 N5
Kew Turks and Caicos Is 133 F8
Kewanee U.S.A. 130 F3
Kewaunee U.S.A. 134 B1
Keweenaw Bay U.S.A. 130 F2
Keweenaw Peninsula U.S.A. 130 F2
Keweenaw Point U.S.A. 132 C2
Key, Lough l. Rep. of Ireland 51 D3
Keyala Sudan 97 G4
Keyano Canada 123 G3
Keya Paha r. U.S.A. 130 D3
Key Harbour Canada 122 E5
Keyihe China 74 A2
Key Largo U.S.A. 133 D7
Keymir Turkm. see Kemir
Keynsham U.K. 49 E7
Keyser U.S.A. 135 F4
Keystone Lake U.S.A. 131 D4
Keystone Peak U.S.A. 129 H6
Keysville U.S.A. 135 F5
Keytesville U.S.A. 130 E4
Keyvy, Vozvyshennost' hills Rus. Fed. 42 H2
Key West U.S.A. 133 D7
Kez Rus. Fed. 41 Q4
Kezi Zimbabwe 99 C6
Kgalagadi admin. dist. Botswana 100 E3
Kgalazadi admin. dist. Botswana see Kgalagadi
Kgatlen admin. dist. Botswana see Kgatleng
Kgatleng admin. dist. Botswana 101 H3
Kgomofatshe Pan salt pan Botswana 100 E2
Kgoro Pan salt pan Botswana 100 G3
Kgotsong S. Africa 101 H4
Khabab Syria 85 C3
Khabar Iran 88 D4
Khabarikha Rus. Fed. 42 L2
Khabarovsk Rus. Fed. 74 D2
Khabarovskiy Kray admin. div. Rus. Fed. 74 D2
Khabarovsk Kray admin. div. Rus. Fed. see Khabarovskiy Kray
Khabary Rus. Fed. 72 D2
Khabis Iran see Shahdād
Khabody Pass Afgh. 89 F3
Khachmas Azer. see Xaçmaz
Khadar, Jabal mt. Oman 88 E6
Khadro Pak. 89 H5
Khafs Banbān well Saudi Arabia 88 B5
Khagaria India 83 F4
Khagrachari Bangl. 83 G5
Khagrachhari Bangl. see Khagrachari
Khairgarh Pak. 89 H4
Khairpur Punjab Pak. 89 I4
Khairpur Sindh Pak. 89 H5
Khāīz, Kūh-e mt. Iran 88 C4
Khaja Du Koh hill Afgh. 89 G2
Khajuha India 82 E4
Khāk-e Jabbar Afgh. 89 H3
Khakhea Botswana 100 F3
Khakīr Afgh. 89 G3
Khak-rēz Afgh. 89 G4
Khakriz reg. Afgh. 89 G4
Khalach Turkm. 89 G2
Khalajestan reg. Iran 88 C3
Khalatse Jammu and Kashmir 82 D2
Khalifat mt. Pak. 89 G4
Khalīj Surt g. Libya see Sirte, Gulf of
Khalilabad India 83 E4
Khalīlī Iran 88 D5
Khalkabad Turkm. 89 F1
Khalkhāl Iran 88 C2
Khálki i. Greece see Chalki
Khalkís Greece see Chalkida
Khallikot India 84 E2
Khalturin Rus. Fed. see Orlov
Khamar-Daban, Khrebet mts Rus. Fed. 72 I2
Khamaria India 84 D1
Khambhat India 82 C5
Khambhat, Gulf of India 84 A2
Khamgaon India 84 C1
Khamir Yemen 86 F6
Khamis Mushayṭ Saudi Arabia 86 F6
Khamkkeut Laos 70 D3
Khamma well Saudi Arabia 88 B5
Khammam India 84 D2
Khammouan Laos see Muang Khammouan
Khamra Rus. Fed. 65 M3
Khamseh reg. Iran 88 C3
Khan Afgh. 89 H3
Khan, Nam r. Laos 70 C3
Khānābād Afgh. 89 H2
Khān al Baghdādī Iraq 91 F4
Khān al Mashāhidah Iraq 91 G4
Khān al Muṣallá Iraq 91 G4
Khanapur India 84 B2
Khān ar Raḥbah Iraq 91 G5
Khanasur Pass Iran/Turkey 91 G3
Khanbalik China see Beijing
Khānch Iran 88 B2
Khandu India 89 I6
Khandwa India 82 D5
Khandyga Rus. Fed. 65 O3
Khanewal Pak. 89 H4
Khanh Dương Vietnam 71 E4
Khan Hung Vietnam see Soc Trăng
Khaniá Greece see Chania
Khānī Yek Iran 88 D4
Khanka, Lake China/Rus. Fed. 74 D3
Khanka, Ozero l. China/Rus. Fed. see Khanka, Lake
Khankendi Azer. see Xankändi
Khanna India 82 D3
Khannā, Qā' salt pan Jordan 85 C3
Khanpur Pak. 89 H4
Khān Ruḥābah Iraq see Khān ar Raḥbah
Khansar Pak. 89 H4
Khān Shaykhūn Syria 85 C2
Khantayskoye, Ozero l. Rus. Fed. 64 K3
Khanthabouli Laos see Savannakhét
Khanty-Mansiysk Rus. Fed. 64 H3
Khān Yūnis Gaza 85 B4
Khanzi admin. dist. Botswana see Ghanzi
Khao Ang Rua Nai Wildlife Reserve nature res. Thai. 71 C4
Khao Banthat Wildlife Reserve nature res. Thai. 71 B6
Khao Chum Thong Thai. 71 B5
Khaoen Si Nakarin National Park Thai. 71 B4
Khao Laem National Park Thai. 70 B4
Khao Laem Reservoir Thai. 70 B4
Khao Luang National Park Thai. 71 B5
Khao Pu-Khao Ya National Park Thai. 71 B6
Khao Soi Dao Wildlife Reserve nature res. Thai. 71 C4
Khao Sok National Park Thai. 67 B5
Khao Yai National Park Thai. 71 C4
Khapalu Jammu and Kashmir 80 E4
Khaptad National Park Nepal 82 E3
Kharabali Rus. Fed. 43 J7
Kharagpur Bihar India 83 F4
Kharagpur W. Bengal India 83 F5
Khārān r. Iran 87 I4
Kharari India see Abu Road
Kharda India 84 B2
Khardi India 82 C6
Khardong La pass Jammu and Kashmir see Khardung La
Khardung La pass Jammu and Kashmir 82 D2
Kharez Ilias Afgh. 89 F3
Kharfiyah Iraq 91 G5
Kharga Egypt see Al Khārijah
Kharga r. Rus. Fed. 74 D1
Khârga, El Wâhât el oasis Egypt see Khārijah, Wāḥāt al
Kharga Oasis Egypt see Khārijah, Wāḥāt al
Khārg Islands Iran 88 C4
Khargon India 82 C5
Khari r. Rajasthan India 82 C4
Khari r. Rajasthan India 82 C4
Kharian Pak. 89 I3
Khariar India 84 D1
Khārijah, Wāḥāt al oasis Egypt 86 D5
Kharîm, Gebel hill Egypt see Kharīm, Jabal
Kharīm, Jabal hill Egypt 85 A4
Kharkhara r. India 82 E5
Kharkiv Ukr. 43 H6
Khar'kov Ukr. see Kharkiv
Khār Kūh mt. Iran 88 D4
Kharlovka Rus. Fed. 42 H1
Kharlu Rus. Fed. 44 Q6
Kharmanli Bulg. 59 K4
Kharoti reg. Afgh. 89 H3
Kharovsk Rus. Fed. 42 I4
Kharsia India 83 E5

▶Khartoum Sudan 86 D6
Capital of Sudan.

Kharwar reg. Afgh. 89 H3
Khasardag, Gora mt. Turkm. 88 E2
Khasav'yurt Rus. Fed. 91 G2
Khash Afgh. 89 F4
Khāsh Iran 89 F4
Khash Desert Afgh. 89 F4
Khashgort Rus. Fed. 41 T2
Khashm el Girba Sudan 86 E7
Khashm Ṣana' Saudi Arabia 90 E6
Khash Rūd r. Afgh. 89 F4
Khashuri Georgia 91 F2
Khasi Hills India 83 G4
Khaskovo Bulg. 59 K4
Khatanga Rus. Fed. 65 L2
Khatanga, Gulf of Rus. Fed. see Khatangskiy Zaliv
Khatangskiy Zaliv b. Rus. Fed. 65 L2
Khatayakha Rus. Fed. 42 M2
Khatinza Pass Pak. 89 H2
Khatmat al Malāha Oman 88 E5
Khatyrka Rus. Fed. 65 S3
Khavda India 82 B5
Khawak Pass Afgh. 89 H3
Khayamnandi S. Africa 101 G6
Khaybar Saudi Arabia 86 E4
Khayelitsha S. Africa 100 D8
Khayrān, Ra's al pt Oman 88 E6
Khê Bo Vietnam 70 D3
Khedrī Iran 88 E3
Khefa Israel see Haifa
Khehuene, Ponta pt Moz. 101 L2
Khemis Miliana Alg. 57 H5
Khemmarat Thai. 70 D3
Khenchela Alg. 58 B7
Khenifra Morocco 54 C5
Kherāmeh Iran 88 D4
Kherrata Alg. 57 I5
Kherreh Iran 88 D5
Khersan r. Iran 88 C4
Kherson Ukr. 59 O1
Kheta r. Rus. Fed. 65 L2
Kheyrābād Iran 88 D4
Khezerābād Iran 88 D2
Khiching India 83 F5
Khilok Rus. Fed. 73 K2
Khilok r. Rus. Fed. 73 J2
Khinganskiy Zapovednik nature res. Rus. Fed. 74 C2
Khinsar Pak. 89 H5
Khíos i. Greece see Chios
Khirbat Isrīyah Syria 85 C2

Khitai Pass Aksai Chin 82 D2
Khīyāv Iran 88 B2
Khiytola Rus. Fed. 45 P6
Khlevnoye Rus. Fed. 43 H5
Khlong, Mae r. Thai. 71 C4
Khlong Saeng Wildlife Reserve nature res. Thai. 71 B5
Khlong Wang Chao National Park Thai. 70 B3
Khlung Thai. 71 C4
Khmel'nik Ukr. see Khmil'nyk
Khmel'nitskiy Ukr. see Khmel'nyts'kyy
Khmel'nyts'kyy Ukr. 43 E6
Khmer Republic country Asia see Cambodia
Khmil'nyk Ukr. 43 E6
Khoai, Hon i. Vietnam 71 D5
Khobda Kazakh. 80 A1
Khobi Georgia 91 F2
Khodā Āfarīd spring Iran 88 E3
Khodzha-Kala Turkm. 88 E2
Khodzhambaz Turkm. 89 G2
Khodzhaolen Turkm. 88 E2
Khodzhapir'yakh, Gora mt. Uzbek. 89 G2
Khodzhent Tajik. see Khŭjand
Khodzheyli Uzbek. 80 A3
Khojand Tajik. see Khŭjand
Khokhowe Pan salt pan Botswana 100 E3
Khokhropar Pak. 89 H5
Khoksar India 82 D2
Kholm Afgh. 89 G2
Kholm Poland see Chełm
Kholm Rus. Fed. 42 F4
Kholmsk Rus. Fed. 74 F3
Kholon Israel see Ḥolon
Khomas admin. reg. Namibia 100 C2
Khomas Highland hills Namibia 100 B2
Khomeyn Iran 88 C3
Khomeynīshahr Iran 88 C3
Khong, Mae Nam r. Laos/Thai. 66 D4 see Mekong
Khonj Iran 88 D5
Khonj, Kūh-e mts Iran 88 D5
Khon Kaen Thai. 70 C3
Khon Kriel Cambodia see Phumĭ Kon Kriel
Khonsa India 83 H4
Khonuu Rus. Fed. 65 P3
Khoper r. Rus. Fed. 43 I6
Khor Rus. Fed. 74 D3
Khor r. Rus. Fed. 74 D3
Khorat Plateau Thai. 70 C3
Khorda India see Khurda
Khordha India see Khurda
Khoreyver Rus. Fed. 42 M2
Khorinsk Rus. Fed. 73 J2
Khorixas Namibia 99 B6
Khormūj, Kūh-e mt. Iran 88 C4
Khorog Tajik. see Khorugh
Khorol Rus. Fed. 74 D3
Khorol Ukr. 43 G6
Khoroslū Dāgh hills Iran 88 B2
Khorramābād Iran 88 C3
Khorramshahr Iran 88 C4
Khorugh Tajik. 89 H2
Khosheutovo Rus. Fed. 43 J7
Khosūyeh Iran 88 D4
Khotan China see Hotan
Khouribga Morocco 54 C5
Khovaling Tajik. 89 H2
Khowrjān Iran 88 D4
Khowrnag, Kūh-e mt. Iran 88 D3
Khowst reg. Afgh./Pak. 89 H3
Khreum Myanmar 70 A2
Khroma r. Rus. Fed. 65 P2
Khromtau Kazakh. 80 A1
Khrushchev Ukr. see Svitlovods'k
Khrysokhou Bay Cyprus see Chrysochou Bay
Khrystynivka Ukr. 43 F6
Khuar Pak. 89 I3
Khudumelapye Botswana 100 G2
Khudzhand Tajik. see Khŭjand
Khufaysah, Khashm al hill Saudi Arabia 88 B6
Khugiana Afgh. see Pirzada
Khuis Botswana 100 E4
Khŭjand Tajik. 80 C3
Khŭjayli Uzbek. see Khodzheyli
Khu Khan Thai. 71 D4
Khulays Saudi Arabia 86 E5
Khulkhuta Rus. Fed. 43 J7
Khulm r. Afgh. 89 G2
Khulna Bangl. 83 G5
Khulo Georgia 91 F2
Khuma S. Africa 101 H4
Khŭm Batheay Cambodia 71 D5
Khunayzīr, Jabal al mts Syria 81 C2
Khūnīk Bālā Iran 88 E3
Khūnīnshahr Iran see Khorramshahr
Khunjerab Pass China/Jammu and Kashmir 82 C1
Khunsar Iran 88 C3
Khun Yuam Thai. 70 B3
Khūr Iran 88 E3
Khūran sea chan. Iran 88 D5
Khurays Saudi Arabia 86 G4
Khurd, Koh-i- mt. Afgh. 89 G3
Khurda India 84 E1
Khurdha India see Khurda
Khurja India 82 D3
Khurmalik Afgh. 89 F3
Khurmuli Rus. Fed. 74 E2
Khūrrāb Iran 88 D4
Khurz Iran 88 D3
Khushab Pak. 89 I3
Khushalgarh Pak. 89 H3
Khushshah, Wādī al watercourse Jordan/Saudi Arabia 85 C5
Khust Ukr. 43 D6
Khutse Game Reserve nature res. Botswana 100 G2
Khutsong S. Africa 101 H4
Khutu r. Rus. Fed. 74 E2
Khuzdar Pak. 89 G5
Khvāf Iran 89 F3
Khvāf reg. Iran 89 F3
Khvājeh Iran 88 B2
Khvalynsk Rus. Fed. 43 K5
Khvodrān Iran 88 D4
Khvord Nārvan Iran 88 E3
Khvormūj Iran 88 C4
Khvoy Iran 88 B2
Khvoynaya Rus. Fed. 42 G4
Khwaja Amran mt. Pak. 89 G4
Khwaja Muhammad Range mts Afgh. 89 H2
Khyber Pass Afgh./Pak. 89 H3
Kiama Australia 112 E5
Kiamichi r. U.S.A. 131 E5
Kiangsi prov. China see Jiangxi
Kiangsu prov. China see Jiangsu
Kiantajärvi l. Fin. 44 P4
Kīāseh Iran 88 D2
Kiatassuaq i. Greenland 119 M2
Kibaha Tanz. 99 D4
Kibali r. Dem. Rep. Congo 98 C3
Kibangou Congo 98 B4
Kibaya Tanz. 99 D4
Kiboga Uganda 98 D3
Kibombo Dem. Rep. Congo 98 C4
Kibondo Tanz. 98 D4
Kibre Mengist Eth. 97 G4
Kibris country Asia see Cyprus
Kibungo Rwanda 98 D4
Kičevo Macedonia 59 I4
Kichmengskiy Gorodok Rus. Fed. 42 J4
Kiçik Qafqaz mts Asia see Lesser Caucasus
Kicking Horse Pass Canada 116 G5
Kidal Mali 96 D3
Kidderminster U.K. 49 E6
Kidepo Valley National Park Uganda 98 D3
Kidira Senegal 96 B3
Kidmang Jammu and Kashmir 82 D2
Kidnappers, Cape N.Z. 113 F4
Kidsgrove U.K. 49 E5
Kiel Germany 47 M3
Kiel U.S.A. 134 A2
Kiel Canal Germany 47 L3
Kielce Poland 47 R5
Kielder Water resr U.K. 48 E3
Kieler Bucht b. Germany 47 M3
Kienge Dem. Rep. Congo 99 C5
Kierspe Germany 53 H3

▶Kiev Ukr. 43 F6
Capital of Ukraine.

Kiffa Mauritania 96 B3
Kifisia Greece 59 J5
Kifrī Iraq 91 G4

▶Kigali Rwanda 98 D4
Capital of Rwanda.

Kiğı Turkey 91 F3
Kiglapait Mountains Canada 123 J2
Kigoma Tanz. 99 C4
Kihlanki Fin. 44 M3
Kihniö Fin. 44 M5
Kiholo HI U.S.A. 127 [inset]
Kiiminki Fin. 44 N4
Kii-sanchi mts Japan 75 D6
Kii-suidō sea chan. Japan 75 D6
Kikerino Rus. Fed. 45 P7
Kikinda Serb. and Mont. 59 I2
Kikki Pak. 89 F5
Kikládhes is Greece see Cyclades
Kiknur Rus. Fed. 42 J4
Kikonai Japan 74 F4
Kikori P.N.G. 69 K8
Kikori r. P.N.G. 69 K8
Kikwit Dem. Rep. Congo 99 B4
Kilafors Sweden 45 J6
Kilar India 82 D2
Kilauea HI U.S.A. 127 [inset]
Kilauea Crater HI U.S.A. 127 [inset]
Kilchu N. Korea 74 C4
Kilcoole Rep. of Ireland 51 F4
Kilcormac Rep. of Ireland 51 E4
Kilcoy Australia 112 F1
Kildare Rep. of Ireland 51 F4
Kil'dinstroy Rus. Fed. 44 R2
Kilemary Rus. Fed. 42 J4
Kilembe Dem. Rep. Congo 99 B4
Kilfinan U.K. 50 D5
Kilgore U.S.A. 131 E5
Kilham U.K. 48 E3
Kilia Ukr. see Kiliya
Kılıç Dağı mt. Syria/Turkey see Aqra', Jabal al
Kilifi Kenya 98 D4
Kilik Pass China/Jammu and Kashmir 82 C1

▶Kilimanjaro vol. Tanz. 98 D4
Highest mountain in Africa.
Africa 92–93

Kilimanjaro National Park Tanz. 98 D4
Kilinailau Islands P.N.G. 106 F2
Kilindoni Tanz. 99 D4
Kilingi-Nõmme Estonia 45 N7
Kilis Turkey 85 C1
Kilis prov. Turkey 85 C1
Kiliya Ukr. 59 M2
Kilkee Rep. of Ireland 51 C5
Kilkeel U.K. 51 G3
Kilkenny Rep. of Ireland 51 E5
Kilkhampton U.K. 49 C8
Kilkis Greece 59 J4
Killala Rep. of Ireland 51 C3
Killala Bay Rep. of Ireland 51 C3
Killaloe Rep. of Ireland 51 D5
Killam Canada 121 I4
Killarney N.T. Australia 108 E4
Killarney Qld Australia 112 F2
Killarney Canada 122 E5
Killarney Rep. of Ireland 51 C5
Killarney National Park Rep. of Ireland 51 C6
Killary Harbour b. Rep. of Ireland 51 C4
Killbuck U.S.A. 134 E3
Killeen U.S.A. 131 D6
Killenaule Rep. of Ireland 51 E5
Killimor Rep. of Ireland 51 D4
Killin U.K. 50 E4
Killinchy U.K. 51 G3
Killíni mt. Greece see Kyllini
Killinick Rep. of Ireland 51 F5
Killorglin Rep. of Ireland 51 C5
Killurin Rep. of Ireland 51 F5
Killybegs Rep. of Ireland 51 D3
Kilmacrenan Rep. of Ireland 51 E2
Kilmaine Rep. of Ireland 51 C4
Kilmallock Rep. of Ireland 51 D5
Kilmaluag U.K. 50 C3
Kilmarnock U.K. 50 E5
Kilmelford U.K. 50 D4
Kil'mez' Rus. Fed. 42 K4
Kil'mez' r. Rus. Fed. 42 K4
Kilmona Rep. of Ireland 51 D6
Kilmore Australia 112 B6
Kilmore Quay Rep. of Ireland 51 F5
Kilosa Tanz. 99 D4
Kilpisjärvi Fin. 44 L2
Kilrea U.K. 51 F3
Kilrush Rep. of Ireland 51 C5
Kilsyth U.K. 50 E5
Kiltan atoll India 84 B4
Kiltullagh Rep. of Ireland 51 D4
Kilwa Masoko Tanz. 99 D4
Kilwinning U.K. 50 E5
Kim U.S.A. 131 C4
Kimba Australia 109 G8
Kimba Congo 98 B4
Kimball U.S.A. 130 C3
Kimball, Mount U.S.A. 118 D3
Kimbe P.N.G. 106 F2
Kimberley S. Africa 100 G5
Kimberley Plateau Australia 108 D4
Kimberley Range hills Australia 109 B6
Kimch'aek N. Korea 75 C4
Kimch'ŏn S. Korea 75 C5
Kimhae S. Korea 75 C6
Kimhandu mt. Tanz. 99 D4
Kími Greece see Kymi
Kimito Fin. 45 M6
Kimmirut Canada 119 L3
Kimolos i. Greece 59 K6
Kimovsk Rus. Fed. 43 H5
Kimpese Dem. Rep. Congo 99 B4
Kimpoku-san mt. Japan see Kinpoku-san
Kimry Rus. Fed. 42 H4
Kimsquit Canada 120 E4
Kimvula Dem. Rep. Congo 99 B4
Kinabalu, Gunung mt. Sabah Malaysia 68 F5
Kinango Kenya 99 D4
Kinaskan Lake Canada 120 D3
Kinbasket Lake Canada 120 G4
Kinbrace U.K. 50 F2
Kincaid Canada 121 J5
Kincardine Canada 134 E1
Kincardine U.K. 50 F4
Kinchega National Park Australia 111 C7
Kincolith Canada 120 D4
Kinda Dem. Rep. Congo 99 C4
Kindat Myanmar 70 A2
Kinde U.S.A. 134 D2
Kinder Scout hill U.K. 48 F5
Kindersley Canada 121 I5
Kindia Guinea 96 B3
Kindu Dem. Rep. Congo 98 C4
Kinel' Rus. Fed. 43 K5
Kineshma Rus. Fed. 42 I4
Kingaroy Australia 112 E1
King Christian Island Canada 119 H2
King City U.S.A. 128 C3
King Edward VII Land pen. Antarctica see Edward VII Peninsula
Kingfield U.S.A. 135 J1
Kingfisher U.S.A. 131 D5
King George U.S.A. 135 G4
King George, Mount Canada 126 E2
King George Island Antarctica 152 A2
King George Islands Canada 122 F2
King George Islands Fr. Polynesia see Roi Georges, Îles du
King Hill hill Australia 108 C5
Kingisepp Rus. Fed. 45 P7
King Island Australia 111 [inset]
King Island Canada 120 E4
King Island Myanmar see Kadan Kyun
Kingisseppa Estonia see Kuressaare
Kinglake National Park Australia 112 B6
King Leopold and Queen Astrid Coast Antarctica 152 E2
King Leopold Range National Park Australia 108 D4
King Leopold Ranges hills Australia 108 D4
Kingman U.S.A. 129 F4

▶Kingman Reef terr. N. Pacific Ocean 150 J5
United States Unincorporated Territory.

King Mountain Canada 120 D3
King Mountain hill U.S.A. 131 C6
Kingoonya Australia 111 A6
King Peak Antarctica 152 L1
King Peninsula Antarctica 152 K2
Kingri Pak. 89 H4
Kings r. Rep. of Ireland 51 E5
Kings r. CA U.S.A. 128 C3
Kings r. NV U.S.A. 126 D4
King Salmon U.S.A. 118 C4
Kingsbridge U.K. 49 D8
Kingsburg U.S.A. 128 D3
Kings Canyon National Park U.S.A. 128 D3
Kingscliff Australia 112 F2
Kingscote Australia 111 B7
Kingscourt Rep. of Ireland 51 F4
King Sejong research station Antarctica 152 A2
King's Lynn U.K. 49 H6
Kingsmill Group is Kiribati 107 H2
Kingsnorth U.K. 49 H7
King Sound b. Australia 108 C4
Kings Peak U.S.A. 129 H1
Kingsport U.S.A. 132 D4
Kingston Australia 111 [inset]
Kingston Canada 135 G1

▶Kingston Jamaica 137 I5
Capital of Jamaica.

▶Kingston Norfolk I. 107 G4
Capital of Norfolk Island.

Kingston MO U.S.A. 130 E4
Kingston NY U.S.A. 135 H3
Kingston OH U.S.A. 134 D4
Kingston PA U.S.A. 135 H3
Kingston Peak U.S.A. 129 F4
Kingston South East Australia 111 B8
Kingston upon Hull U.K. 48 G5

▶Kingstown St Vincent 137 L6
Capital of St Vincent.

Kingstree U.S.A. 133 E5
Kingsville U.S.A. 131 D7
Kingswood U.K. 49 E7
Kington U.K. 49 D6
Kingungi Dem. Rep. Congo 99 B4
Kingurutik r. Canada 123 J2
Kingussie U.K. 50 E3
King William U.S.A. 135 G5
King William Island Canada 119 I3
King William's Town S. Africa 101 H7
Kingwood TX U.S.A. 131 E6
Kingwood WV U.S.A. 134 F4
Kinloch N.Z. 113 B7
Kinloss U.K. 50 F3
Kinmen Taiwan see Chinmen
Kinmen i. Taiwan see Chinmen Tao
Kinmount Canada 135 F1
Kinna Sweden 45 H8
Kinnegad Rep. of Ireland 51 E4
Kinneret, Yam l. Israel see Galilee, Sea of
Kinniyai Sri Lanka 84 D4
Kinnula Fin. 44 N5
Kinoje r. Canada 122 E3
Kinoosao Canada 121 K3
Kinpoku-san mt. Japan 75 E5
Kinross U.K. 50 F4
Kinsale Rep. of Ireland 51 D6
Kinsale U.S.A. 135 G4

▶Kinshasa Dem. Rep. Congo 99 B4
Capital of the Democratic Republic of Congo and 3rd most populous city in Africa.

Kinsley U.S.A. 130 D4
Kinsman U.S.A. 134 E3
Kinston U.S.A. 133 E5
Kintore U.K. 50 G3
Kintyre pen. U.K. 50 D5
Kinu Myanmar 70 A2
Kinushseo r. Canada 122 E3
Kinyeti mt. Sudan 97 G4
Kinzig r. Germany 53 I4
Kiowa CO U.S.A. 126 G5
Kiowa KS U.S.A. 131 D4
Kipahigan Lake Canada 121 K4
Kiparissía Greece see Kyparissia
Kipawa, Lac l. Canada 122 F5
Kipling Canada 121 K5
Kipling Station Canada see Kipling
Kipnuk U.S.A. 118 B4
Kiptopeke U.S.A. 135 H5
Kipungo Angola see Quipungo
Kipushi Dem. Rep. Congo 99 C5
Kirakira Solomon Is 107 G3
Kirandul India 84 D2
Kirchdorf Germany 53 I2
Kirchheim-Bolanden Germany 53 I5
Kirchheim unter Teck Germany 53 J6
Kircubbin U.K. 51 G3
Kirdimi Chad 97 E3
Kirenga r. Rus. Fed. 73 J1
Kirensk Rus. Fed. 65 L4
Kireyevsk Rus. Fed. 43 H5
Kirghizia country Asia see Kyrgyzstan
Kirghiz Range mts Kazakh./Kyrg. 80 D3
Kirgizskaya S.S.R. country Asia see Kyrgyzstan
Kirgizskiy Khrebet mts Kazakh./Kyrg. see Kirghiz Range
Kirgizstan country Asia see Kyrgyzstan
Kiri Dem. Rep. Congo 98 B4
Kiribati country Pacific Ocean 150 I6
Kırıkhan Turkey 85 C1
Kırıkkale Turkey 90 D3
Kirillov Rus. Fed. 42 H4
Kirillovo Rus. Fed. 74 F3
Kirin China see Jilin
Kirin prov. China see Jilin
Kirinda Sri Lanka 84 D5
Kirinyaga mt. Kenya see Kenya, Mount
Kirishi Rus. Fed. 42 G4
Kirishima-Yaku National Park Japan 75 C7
Kirishima-yama vol. Japan 75 C7
Kiritimati atoll Kiribati 151 J5
Kiriwina Islands P.N.G. see Trobriand Islands
Kırkağaç Turkey 59 L5
Kirk Bulāg Dāgi mt. Iran 88 B2
Kirkby U.K. 48 E5
Kirkby in Ashfield U.K. 49 F5
Kirkby Lonsdale U.K. 48 E4
Kirkby Stephen U.K. 48 E4
Kirkcaldy U.K. 50 F4
Kirkcolm U.K. 50 D6
Kirkcudbright U.K. 50 E6
Kirkenær Norway 45 H6
Kirkenes Norway 44 Q2
Kirkfield Canada 135 F1
Kirkintilloch U.K. 50 E5
Kirkkonummi Fin. 45 N6
Kirkland U.S.A. 129 G4
Kirkland Lake Canada 122 E4
Kırklareli Turkey 59 L4
Kirklin U.S.A. 134 B3
Kirk Michael Isle of Man 48 C4
Kirkoswald U.K. 48 E4
Kirkpatrick, Mount Antarctica 152 H1
Kirksville U.S.A. 130 E3
Kirkūk Iraq 91 G4
Kirkwall U.K. 50 G2
Kirkwood S. Africa 101 G7
Kirman Iran see Kermān
Kirn Germany 53 H5
Kirov Kaluzhskaya Oblast' Rus. Fed. 43 G5
Kirov Kirovskaya Oblast' Rus. Fed. 42 K4
Kirova, Zaliv b. Azer. see Qızılağac Körfäzi
Kirovabad Azer. see Gäncä
Kirovabad Tajik. see Panj
Kirovakan Armenia see Vanadzor
Kirovo Ukr. see Kirovohrad
Kirovo-Chepetsk Rus. Fed. 42 K4
Kirovo-Chepetskiy Rus. Fed. see Kirovo-Chepetsk
Kirovograd Ukr. see Kirovohrad
Kirovohrad Ukr. 43 G6
Kirovsk Leningradskaya Oblast' Rus. Fed. 42 F4
Kirovsk Murmanskaya Oblast' Rus. Fed. 44 R3
Kirovsk Turkm. see Babadaykhan
Kirovs'ke Ukr. 90 D1
Kirovskiy Rus. Fed. 74 D3
Kirovskoye Ukr. see Kirovs'ke
Kırpaşa pen. Cyprus see Karpasia
Kirpili Turkm. 88 E2
Kirriemuir U.K. 50 F4
Kirs Rus. Fed. 42 L4
Kirsanov Rus. Fed. 43 I5
Kırşehir Turkey 90 D3
Kirthar National Park Pak. 89 G5
Kirthar Range mts Pak. 89 G5
Kirtland U.S.A. 129 I3
Kirtorf Germany 53 J4
Kiruna Sweden 44 L3
Kirundu Dem. Rep. Congo 98 C4
Kirwan Escarpment Antarctica 152 B2
Kiryū Japan 75 E5
Kisa Sweden 45 I8
Kisama, Parque Nacional de nat. park Angola see Quiçama, Parque Nacional do
Kisandji Dem. Rep. Congo 99 B4
Kisangani Dem. Rep. Congo 98 C3
Kisantu Dem. Rep. Congo 99 B4
Kisar i. Indon. 108 D2
Kisaran Indon. 71 B7
Kiselevsk Rus. Fed. 72 F2
Kisel'ovka Rus. Fed. 74 E2
Kishanganj India 83 F4
Kishangarh Madhya Pradesh India 82 D4
Kishangarh Rajasthan India 82 B4
Kishangarh Rajasthan India 82 C4
Kishangarh Rajasthan India 82 D4
Kishi Nigeria 96 D4
Kishinev Moldova see Chişinău
Kishkenekol' Kazakh. 79 G1
Kishoreganj Bangl. 83 G4
Kishorganj Bangl. see Kishoreganj
Kisi Nigeria see Kishi
Kisii Kenya 98 D4
Kiska Island U.S.A. 65 S4
Kiskittogisu Lake Canada 121 L4
Kiskitto Lake Canada 121 L4
Kiskunfélegyháza Hungary 59 H1
Kiskunhalas Hungary 59 H1
Kiskunsági nat. park Hungary 59 H1
Kislovodsk Rus. Fed. 91 F2
Kismaayo Somalia 98 E4
Kismayu Somalia see Kismaayo
Kisoro Uganda 97 F5
Kispiox Canada 120 E4
Kispiox r. Canada 120 E4
Kisseraing Island Myanmar see Kanmaw Kyun
Kissidougou Guinea 96 B4
Kissimmee U.S.A. 133 D6
Kissimmee, Lake U.S.A. 133 D7
Kississing Lake Canada 121 K4
Kistendey Rus. Fed. 43 I5
Kistigan Lake Canada 121 M4
Kistna r. India see Krishna
Kisumu Kenya 98 D4
Kisykkamys Kazakh. see Dzhangala
Kita Mali 96 C3
Kitab Uzbek. 89 G2
Kita-Daitō-jima i. Japan 73 O7
Kitaibaraki Japan 75 F5
Kita-Iō-jima vol. Japan 69 K1
Kitakami Japan 75 F5
Kita-Kyūshū Japan 75 C6
Kitale Kenya 98 D3
Kitami Japan 74 F4
Kit Carson U.S.A. 130 C4
Kitchener Canada 134 E2
Kitchigama r. Canada 122 F4
Kitee Fin. 44 Q5
Kitgum Uganda 98 D3
Kíthira i. Greece see Kythira
Kíthnos i. Greece see Kythnos
Kiti, Cape Cyprus see Kition, Cape
Kitimat Canada 120 D4
Kitinen r. Fin. 44 O3
Kition, Cape Cyprus 85 A2
Kition, Akra c. Cyprus see Kition, Cape
Kitkatla Canada 120 D4
Kitob Uzbek. see Kitab
Kitsault Canada 120 D4
Kittanning U.S.A. 134 F3
Kittatinny Mountains hills U.S.A. 135 H3
Kittery U.S.A. 135 J2
Kittilä Fin. 44 N3
Kittur India 84 B3
Kitty Hawk U.S.A. 132 F4
Kitui Kenya 98 D4
Kitwanga Canada 120 D4
Kitwe Zambia 99 C5
Kitzbüheler Alpen mts Austria 47 N7
Kitzingen Germany 53 K5
Kitzscher Germany 53 M3
Kiu Lom Reservoir Thai. 70 B3
Kiunga P.N.G. 69 K8
Kiuruvesi Fin. 44 O5
Kivalina U.S.A. 118 B3
Kivijärvi Fin. 44 N5
Kiviõli Estonia 45 O7
Kivu, Lake Dem. Rep. Congo/Rwanda 98 C4
Kiwaba N'zogi Angola 99 B4
Kiwai Island P.N.G. 69 K8
Kiyev Ukr. see Kiev
Kiyevskoye Vodokhranilishche resr Ukr. see Kyyivs'ke Vodoskhovyshche
Kıyıköy Turkey 59 M4
Kizel Rus. Fed. 41 R4
Kizema Rus. Fed. 42 J3
Kızılcadağ Turkey 59 M6
Kızılca Dağ mt. Turkey 90 C3
Kızılcahamam Turkey 90 D2
Kızıldağ mt. Turkey 85 A1
Kızıldağ mt. Turkey 85 B1
Kızıl Dağı mt. Turkey 90 E3
Kızılırmak Turkey 90 D2
Kızılırmak r. Turkey 90 D2
Kızıltepe Turkey 91 F3
Kizil"yurt Rus. Fed. 91 G2
Kızkalesi Turkey 85 B1
Kizlyar Rus. Fed. 91 G2
Kizlyarskiy Zaliv b. Rus. Fed. 91 G1
Kizner Rus. Fed. 42 K4
Kizyl-Arbat Turkm. see Gyzylarbat
Kizyl-Atrek Turkm. see Gyzyletrek
Kjøllefjord Norway 44 O1
Kjøpsvik Norway 44 J2
Kladno Czech Rep. 47 O5
Klagenfurt Austria 47 O7
Klagetoh U.S.A. 129 I4
Klaipėda Lith. 45 L9
Klaksvík Faroe Is 44 [inset]
Klamath U.S.A. 126 B4
Klamath r. U.S.A. 118 F5
Klamath Falls U.S.A. 126 C4
Klamath Mountains U.S.A. 126 C4
Klarälven r. Sweden 45 H7
Klatovy Czech Rep. 47 N6
Klawer S. Africa 100 D6
Klazienaveen Neth. 52 G2
Kleides Islands Cyprus 85 B2
Kleinbegin S. Africa 100 E5
Klein Karas Namibia 100 D4
Klein Nama Land reg. S. Africa see Namaqualand
Klein Roggeveldberge mts S. Africa 100 E7
Kleinsee S. Africa 100 C5
Klemtu Canada 120 D4
Klerksdorp S. Africa 101 H4
Kletnya Rus. Fed. 43 G5
Kletsk Belarus see Klyetsk
Kletskaya Rus. Fed. 43 I6
Kletskiy Rus. Fed. see Kletskaya
Kleve Germany 52 G3
Klidhes Islands Cyprus see Kleides Islands
Klimkovka Rus. Fed. 42 K4
Klimovo Rus. Fed. 43 G5
Klin Rus. Fed. 42 H4
Klingenberg am Main Germany 53 J5
Klingenthal Germany 53 M4
Klingkang, Banjaran mts Indon./Malaysia 68 E6
Klink Germany 53 M1
Klínovec mt. Czech Rep. 53 N4
Klintehamn Sweden 45 K8
Klintsy Rus. Fed. 43 G5
Ključ Bos.-Herz. 58 G2
Kłodzko Poland 47 P5
Klondike r. Canada 120 B1
Klondike Gold Rush National Historical Park nat. park U.S.A. 120 C3
Kloosterhaar Neth. 52 G2
Klosterneuburg Austria 47 P6
Klötze (Altmark) Germany 53 L2
Kluane Lake Canada 120 B2
Kluane National Park Canada 120 B2
Kluang Malaysia see Keluang
Kluczbork Poland 47 Q5
Klukhori Rus. Fed. see Karachayevsk
Klukwan U.S.A. 120 C3
Klupro Pak. 89 H5
Klyetsk Belarus 45 O10
Klyuchevskaya, Sopka vol. Rus. Fed. 65 R4
Klyuchi Rus. Fed. 74 B2
Knåda Sweden 45 I6
Knaresborough U.K. 48 F4
Knee Lake Man. Canada 121 M4
Knee Lake Sask. Canada 121 J4
Knetzgau Germany 53 K5
Knife r. U.S.A. 130 C2
Knight Inlet Canada 120 E5
Knighton U.K. 49 D6
Knights Landing U.S.A. 128 C2
Knightstown U.S.A. 134 C4
Knin Croatia 58 G2
Knittelfeld Austria 47 O7
Knjaževac Serb. and Mont. 59 J3
Knob Lake Canada see Schefferville
Knob Lick U.S.A. 134 C5
Knob Peak hill Australia 108 E3
Knock Rep. of Ireland 51 D4
Knockaboy hill Rep. of Ireland 51 C6
Knockalongy hill Rep. of Ireland 51 D3
Knockalough Rep. of Ireland 51 C5
Knockanaffrin hill Rep. of Ireland 51 E5
Knock Hill hill U.K. 50 G3
Knockmealdown Mts hills Rep. of Ireland 51 D5
Knocknaskagh hill Rep. of Ireland 51 D5
Knokke-Heist Belgium 52 D3
Knorrendorf Germany 53 N1
Knowle U.K. 49 F6
Knowlton Canada 135 I1
Knox IN U.S.A. 134 B3
Knox PA U.S.A. 134 F3
Knox, Cape Canada 120 C4
Knox Coast Antarctica 152 F2
Knoxville GA U.S.A. 133 D5
Knoxville TN U.S.A. 132 D5
Knud Rasmussen Land reg. Greenland 119 L2
Knysna S. Africa 100 F8
Ko, Gora mt. Rus. Fed. 74 E3
Koartac Canada see Quaqtaq
Koba Indon. 68 D7
Kobbfoss Norway 44 P2
Kōbe Japan 75 D6
København Denmark see Copenhagen
Kobenni Mauritania 96 C3
Koblenz Germany 53 H4
Koboldo Rus. Fed. 74 D1
Kobrin Belarus see Kobryn
Kobroör i. Indon. 69 I8
Kobryn Belarus 45 N10
Kobuk Valley National Park U.S.A. 118 C3
K'obulet'i Georgia 91 F2
Kocaeli Turkey 59 M4
Kocaeli Yarımadası pen. Turkey 59 M4
Kočani Macedonia 59 J4
Kocasu r. Turkey 59 M4
Kočevje Slovenia 58 F2
Koch Bihar India 83 G4
Kocher r. Germany 53 J5
Kochevo Rus. Fed. 41 Q4
Kochi India see Cochin
Kōchi Japan 75 D6
Koçhisar Turkey see Kızıltepe

Koch Island Canada 119 K3
Kochkor Kyrg. 80 E3
Kochkorka Kyrg. see Kochkor
Kochkurovo Rus. Fed. 43 J5
Kochubeyevskoye Rus. Fed. 91 F1
Kod India 84 B3
Kodala India 84 E2
Kodarma India 83 F4
Koderma India see Kodarma
Kodiak U.S.A. 118 C4
Kodiak Island U.S.A. 118 C4
Kodibeleng Botswana 101 H2
Kodino Rus. Fed. 42 H3
Kodiyakkarai India 84 C4
Kodok Sudan 86 D8
Kodyma Ukr. 43 F6
Kodzhaele mt. Bulg./Greece 59 K4
Koedoesberg mts S. Africa 100 E7
Koegrabie S. Africa 100 E5
Koekenaap S. Africa 100 D6
Koersel Belgium 52 F3
Koës Namibia 100 D3
Kofa Mountains U.S.A. 129 G5
Koffiefontein S. Africa 100 G5
Koforidua Ghana 96 C4
Kōfu Japan 75 E6
Kogaluc r. Canada 122 F2
Kogaluc, Baie de b. Canada 122 F2
Kogaluk r. Canada 123 J2
Kogan Australia 112 E1
Køge Denmark 45 H9
Kogon r. Guinea 96 B3
Kogon Uzbek. see Kagan
Kohan Pak. 89 G5
Kohat Pak. 89 H3
Kohestānāt Afgh. 89 G3
Kohila Estonia 45 N7
Kohima India 83 H4
Kohistan reg. Afgh. 89 H3
Kohistan reg. Pak. 89 I3
Kohler Range mts Antarctica 148 K2
Kohlu Pak. 89 H4
Kohsan Afgh. 89 F3
Kohtla-Järve Estonia 45 O7
Kohŭng S. Korea 75 B6
Koidern Mountain Canada 120 A2
Koidu Sierra Leone see Sefadu
Koihoa India 71 A5
Koilkonda India 84 C2
Koin N. Korea 75 B4
Koin r. Rus. Fed. 42 K3
Koi Sanjaq Iraq 91 G3
Kŏje-do i. S. Korea 75 C6
Kojonup Australia 109 B8
Kokand Uzbek. 80 D3
Kökar Fin. 45 L7
Kokchetav Kazakh. see Kokshetau
Kokemäenjoki r. Fin. 45 L6
Kokerboom Namibia 100 D5
Ko Kha Thai. 70 B3
Kokkilai Sri Lanka 84 D4
Kokkola Fin. 44 M5
Koko Nigeria 96 D3
Kokomo U.S.A. 134 B3
Kokong Botswana 100 F3
Kokos i. Indon. 71 A7
Kokosi S. Africa 101 H4
Kokpekti Kazakh. 80 F2
Koksan N. Korea 75 B5
Kokshaal-Tau, Khrebet mts China/Kyrg. see Kakshaal-Too
Koksharka Rus. Fed. 42 J4
Kokshetau Kazakh. 79 F1
Koksoak r. Canada 123 H2
Kokstad S. Africa 101 I6
Koktal Kazakh. 80 E3
Kokterek Kazakh. 43 K6
Koktokay China see Fuyun
Kola i. Indon. 69 I8
Kola Rus. Fed. 44 R2
Kolachi r. Pak. 89 G5
Kolahoi mt. Jammu and Kashmir 82 C2
Kolaka Indon. 69 G7
Ko Lanta Thai. 71 B6
Kola Peninsula Rus. Fed. 42 H2
Kolar Chhattisgarh India 84 D2
Kolar Karnataka India 84 C3
Kolaras India 82 D4
Kolar Gold Fields India 84 C3
Kolari Fin. 44 M3
Kolarovgrad Bulg. see Shumen
Kolasib India 83 H4
Kolayat India 82 C4
Kolberg Poland see Kołobrzeg
Kol'chugino Rus. Fed. 42 H4
Kolda Senegal 96 B3
Kolding Denmark 45 F9
Kole Kasaï-Oriental Dem. Rep. Congo 98 C4
Kole Orientale Dem. Rep. Congo 98 C3
Koléa Alg. 57 H5
Kolekole mt. HI U.S.A. 127 [inset]
Koler Sweden 44 L4
Kolguyev, Ostrov i. Rus. Fed. 42 K1
Kolhan reg. India 83 F5
Kolhapur India 84 B2
Kolhumadulu Atoll Maldives 81 D11
Kolikata India see Kolkata
Kõljala Estonia 45 M7
Kolkasrags pt Latvia 45 M8

►Kolkata India 83 G5
3rd most populous city in Asia.

Kolkhozabad Khatlon Tajik. see Vose
Kolkhozabad Khatlon Tajik. see Kolkhozobod
Kolkhozobod Tajik. 89 H2
Kollam India see Quilon
Kolleru Lake India 84 D2
Kollum Neth. 52 G1
Kolmanskop Namibia 100 B4
Köln Germany see Cologne
Köln-Bonn airport Germany 53 H4
Kołobrzeg Poland 47 O3
Kologriv Rus. Fed. 42 J4
Kolokani Mali 96 C3
Kolombangara i. Solomon Is 107 F2
Kolomea Ukr. see Kolomyya
Kolomna Rus. Fed. 43 H5
Kołomyja Ukr. see Kolomyya
Kolomyya Ukr. 43 E6
Kolondiéba Mali 96 C3
Kolonedale Indon. 69 G7
Koloni Cyprus 85 A2
Kolonkwane Botswana 100 E4
Kolozsvár Romania see Cluj-Napoca
Kolpashevo Rus. Fed. 64 J4
Kol'skiy Poluostrov pen. Rus. Fed. see Kola Peninsula
Kölük Turkey see Kâhta
Koluli Eritrea 86 F7
Kolumadulu Atoll Maldives see Kolhumadulu Atoll
Kolva r. Rus. Fed. 42 M2
Kolvan India 84 B2
Kolvereid Norway 44 G4
Kolvik Norway 44 N1
Kolvitskoye, Ozero l. Rus. Fed. 44 R3
Kolwa reg. Pak. 89 G5
Kolwezi Dem. Rep. Congo 99 C5
Kolyma r. Rus. Fed. 65 R3
Kolyma Lowland Rus. Fed. see Kolymskaya Nizmennost'
Kolyma Range mts Rus. Fed. see Kolymskiy, Khrebet
Kolymskaya Nizmennost' lowland Rus. Fed. 65 Q3
Kolymskiy, Khrebet mts Rus. Fed. 65 R3
Kolyshley Rus. Fed. 43 J5
Kom mt. Bulg. 59 J3
Komadugu-gana watercourse Nigeria 96 E3
Komaggas S. Africa 100 C5
Komaio P.N.G. 69 K8
Komaki Japan 75 E6
Komandnaya, Gora mt. Rus. Fed. 74 E2
Komandorskiye Ostrova is Rus. Fed. 65 R4
Komárno Slovakia 47 Q7
Komati r. Swaziland 101 J3
Komatipoort S. Africa 101 J3
Komatsu Japan 75 E5
Komba i. Indon. 108 C1
Komga S. Africa 101 H7
Komintern Ukr. see Marhanets'
Kominternivs'ke Ukr. 59 N1
Komiža Croatia 58 G3
Komló Hungary 58 H1
Kommunarsk Ukr. see Alchevs'k
Komodo National Park Indon. 108 B2
Kôm Ombo Egypt see Kawm Umbū
Komono Congo 98 B4
Komoran i. Indon. 69 J8
Komotini Greece 59 K4
Kompong Cham Cambodia see Kâmpóng Cham
Kompong Chhnang Cambodia see Kâmpóng Chhnăng
Kompong Kleang Cambodia see Kâmpóng Khleăng
Kompong Som Cambodia see Sihanoukville
Kompong Speu Cambodia see Kâmpóng Spœ
Kompong Thom Cambodia see Kâmpóng Thum
Komrat Moldova see Comrat
Komsberg mts S. Africa 100 E7
Komsomol Kazakh. see Karabalyk
Komsomolabad Tajik. see Komsomolobod
Komsomolets Kazakh. see Karabalyk
Komsomolets, Ostrov i. Rus. Fed. 64 K1
Komsomolobod Tajik. 89 H2
Komsomol's'k Ukr. 43 G6
Komsomol'skiy Chukotskiy Avtonomnyy Okrug Rus. Fed. 153 C2
Komsomol'skiy Khanty-Mansiyskiy Avtonomnyy Okrug Rus. Fed. see Yugorsk
Komsomol'skiy Respublika Kalmykiya-Khalm'g-Tangch Rus. Fed. 43 J7
Komsomol'sk-na-Amure Rus. Fed. 74 E2
Komsomol'skoye Kazakh. 80 B1
Komsomol'skoye Rus. Fed. 43 J6
Kömürlü Turkey 91 F2
Kon India 83 E4
Konacık Turkey 85 B1
Konada India 84 D2
Konarak India see Konarka
Konarka India 83 F6
Konch India 82 D4
Kondagaon India 84 D2
Kondinin Australia 109 B8
Kondinskoye Rus. Fed. see Oktyabr'skoye
Kondoa Tanz. 99 D4
Kondol' Rus. Fed. 43 J5
Kondopoga Rus. Fed. 42 G3
Kondoz Afgh. see Kunduz
Kondrovo Rus. Fed. 43 G5
Köneürgenç Turkm. see Keneurgench
Kong Cameroon 96 E4
Kŏng, Kaôh i. Cambodia 71 C5
Kông, Tônlé r. Cambodia 71 D4
Kong, Xé r. Laos 70 D4
Kong Christian IX Land reg. Greenland 119 O3
Kong Christian X Land reg. Greenland 119 P2
Kongelab atoll Marshall Is see Rongelap
Kong Frederik IX Land reg. Greenland 119 M3
Kong Frederik VI Kyst coastal area Greenland 119 N3
Kongolo Dem. Rep. Congo 99 C4
Kongor Sudan 97 G4
Kong Oscars Fjord inlet Greenland 119 P2
Kongoussi Burkina 96 C3
Kongsberg Norway 45 F7
Kongsvinger Norway 45 H6
Kongur Shan mt. China 80 E4
Königsberg Rus. Fed. see Kaliningrad
Königsee Germany 53 L4
Königswinter Germany 53 H4
Königs Wusterhausen Germany 53 N2
Konimekh Uzbek. see Kanimekh
Konin Poland 47 Q4
Konjic Bos.-Herz. 58 G3
Konkiep watercourse Namibia 100 C5
Könnern Germany 53 L3
Konnevesi Fin. 44 O5
Konosha Rus. Fed. 42 I3
Konotop Ukr. 43 G6
Konpara India 83 E5
Kon Plong Vietnam 71 E4
Konqi He r. China 80 G3
Konso Eth. 98 D3
Konstantinograd Ukr. see Krasnohrad
Konstantinovka Rus. Fed. 74 B2
Konstantinovka Ukr. see Kostyantynivka
Konstantinovy Lázně Czech Rep. 53 M5
Konstanz Germany 47 L7
Kontha Myanmar 70 B2
Kontiolahti Fin. 44 P5
Konttila Fin. 44 O4
Kon Tum Vietnam 71 D4
Kontum, Plateau du Vietnam 71 E4
Könugard Ukr. see Kiev
Konushin, Mys pt Rus. Fed. 42 I2
Konya Turkey 90 D3
Konz Germany 52 G5
Konzhakovskiy Kamen', Gora mt. Rus. Fed. 41 R4
Koocanusa, Lake resr Canada/U.S.A. 120 H5
Kooch Bihar India see Koch Bihar
Kookynie Australia 109 C7
Koolyanobbing Australia 109 B7
Koondrook Australia 112 B5
Koorawatha Australia 112 D5
Koordarrie Australia 108 A5
Kootenay r. Canada 120 G5
Kootenay Lake Canada 120 G5
Kootenay National Park Canada 120 G5
Kootjieskolk S. Africa 100 E6
Kópasker Iceland 44 [inset]
Kopbirlik Kazakh. 80 E2
Koper Slovenia 58 E2
Kopet Dag mts Iran/Turkm. 88 E2
Kopet-Dag, Khrebet mts Iran/Turkm. see Kopet Dag
Köpetdag Gershi mts Iran/Turkm. see Kopet Dag
Köping Sweden 45 J7
Köpmanholmen Sweden 44 K5
Kopong Botswana 101 G3
Koppal India 84 C3
Koppang Norway 45 G6
Kopparberg Sweden 45 I7
Koppeh Dāgh mts Iran/Turkm. see Kopet Dag
Köppel hill Germany 53 H4
Koppi r. Rus. Fed. 74 F2
Koppies S. Africa 101 H4
Koppieskraal Pan salt pan S. Africa 100 E4
Koprivnica Croatia 58 G1
Köprülü Turkey 85 A1
Köprülü Kanyon Milli Parkı nat. park Turkey 59 N6
Kopyl' Belarus see Kapyl'
Kora India 82 E4
Korablino Rus. Fed. 43 I5
K'orahē Eth. 98 E3
Korak Pak. 89 G5
Koramlik China 83 F1
Korangal India 84 C2
Korangi Pak. 89 G5
Korān va Monjan Afgh. 89 H2
Koraput India 84 D2
Korat Thai. see Nakhon Ratchasima
Koratla India 84 C2
Korba India 83 E5
Korbach Germany 53 I3
Korçë Albania 59 I4
Korčula Croatia 58 G3
Korčula i. Croatia 58 G3
Korčulanski Kanal sea chan. Croatia 58 G3
Korday Kazakh. 80 D3
Kord Kūv Iran 88 D2
Kords reg. Iran 89 F5
►Korea, North country Asia 75 B5 Asia 6, 62–63
►Korea, South country Asia 75 B5 Asia 6, 62–63
Korea Bay g. China/N. Korea 75 B5
Korea Strait Japan/S. Korea 75 C6
Koregaon India 84 B2
Korenovsk Rus. Fed. 91 E1
Korenovskaya Rus. Fed. see Korenovsk
Korepino Rus. Fed. 41 R3
Korets' Ukr. 43 E6
Körfez Turkey 59 M4
Korff Ice Rise Antarctica 152 L1
Korfovskiy Rus. Fed. 74 D2
Korgalzhyn Kazakh. 80 D1
Korgen Norway 44 H3
Korhogo Côte d'Ivoire 96 C4
Koribundu Sierra Leone 96 B4
Kori Creek inlet India 82 B5
Korinthiakos Kolpos sea chan. Greece see Corinth, Gulf of
Korinthos Greece see Corinth
Kőris-hegy hill Hungary 58 G1
Koritnik mt. Albania 59 I3
Koritsa Albania see Korçë
Kōriyama Japan 75 F5
Korkuteli Turkey 59 N6
Korla China 80 G3
Kormakitis, Cape Cyprus 85 A2
Körmend Hungary 58 G1
Kornat nat. park Croatia 58 F3
Korneyevka Rus. Fed. 43 K6
Koro Côte d'Ivoire 96 C4
Koro i. Fiji 107 H3
Koro Mali 96 C3
Koroc r. Canada 123 I2
Köroğlu Dağları mts Turkey 59 O4
Köroğlu Tepesi mt. Turkey 90 D2
Korogwe Tanz. 99 D4
Korong Vale Australia 112 A6
Koronia, Limni l. Greece 59 J4

►Koror Palau 69 I5
Capital of Palau.

Koro Sea b. Fiji 107 H3
Korosten' Ukr. 43 F6
Korostyshiv Ukr. 43 F6
Koro Toro Chad 97 E3
Korpilahti Fin. 44 N5
Korpo Fin. 45 L6
Korppoo Fin. see Korpo
Korsakov Rus. Fed. 74 F3
Korsnäs Fin. 44 L5
Korsør Denmark 45 G9
Korsun'-Shevchenkivs'kyy Ukr. 43 F6
Korsun'-Shevchenkovskiy Ukr. see Korsun'-Shevchenkivs'kyy
Korsze Poland 47 R3
Kortesjärvi Fin. 44 M5
Korti Sudan 86 D6
Kortkeros Rus. Fed. 42 K3
Kortrijk Belgium 52 D4
Korvala Fin. 44 O3
Koryakskaya, Sopka vol. Rus. Fed. 65 Q4
Koryakskiy Khrebet mts Rus. Fed. 65 S3
Koryazhma Rus. Fed. 42 J3
Koryŏng S. Korea 75 C6
Kos i. Greece 59 L6
Kosa Rus. Fed. 41 Q4
Kosam India 82 E4
Kosan N. Korea 75 B5
Kościan Poland 47 P4
Kosciusko, Mount Australia see Kosciuszko, Mount
Kosciuszko, Mount Australia 112 D6
Kosciuszko National Park Australia 112 D6
Köse Turkey 91 E2
Köseçobanlı Turkey 85 A1
Kosgi India 84 C2
Kosh-Agach Rus. Fed. 80 G2
Koshikijima-rettō is Japan 75 C7
Koshk Afgh. 89 F3
Koshk-e Kohneh Afgh. 89 F3
Koshki Rus. Fed. 43 K5
Koshoba Turkm. 91 I2
Koshrabad Uzbek. 89 G1
Kosi Bay S. Africa 101 K4
Košice Slovakia 43 D6
Kosigi India 84 C3
Koskullskulle Sweden 44 L3
Köslin Poland see Koszalin
Kosma r. Rus. Fed. 42 K2
Koson Uzbek. see Kasan
Kosŏng N. Korea 75 C5
Kosova prov. Serb. and Mont. see Kosovo
Kosovo prov. Serb. and Mont. 59 I3
Kosovo-Metohija prov. Serb. and Mont. see Kosovo
Kosovska Mitrovica Serb. and Mont. 59 I3
Kosrae atoll Micronesia 150 G5
Kosrap China 89 J2
Kösseine hill Germany 53 L5
Kosta-Khetagurovo Rus. Fed. see Nazran'
Kostanay Kazakh. 78 F1
Kostenets Bulg. 59 J3
Kosti Sudan 86 D7
Kostinbrod Bulg. 59 J3
Kostino Rus. Fed. 64 J3
Kostomuksha Rus. Fed. 44 Q4
Kostopil' Ukr. 43 E6
Kostopol' Ukr. see Kostopil'
Kostroma Rus. Fed. 42 I4
Kostrzyn Poland 47 O4
Kostyantynivka Ukr. 43 H6
Kostyukovichi Belarus see Kastsyukovichy
Kos'yu Rus. Fed. 41 R2
Koszalin Poland 47 P3
Kőszeg Hungary 58 G1
Kota Andhra Pradesh India 84 D3
Kota Chhattisgarh India 83 E5
Kota Rajasthan India 82 C4
Kota Baharu Malaysia see Kota Bharu
Kotabaru Aceh Indon. 71 B7
Kotabaru Kalimantan Selatan Indon. 68 F7
Kota Bharu Malaysia 71 C6
Kotabumi Indon. 68 C7
Kot Addu Pak. 89 H4
Kota Kinabalu Sabah Malaysia 68 F5
Kotamobagu Indon. 69 G6
Kotaneelee Range mts Canada 120 E2
Kotaparh India 84 D2
Kotapinang Indon. 71 C7
Kotatengah Indon. 71 C7
Kota Tinggi Malaysia 71 C7
Kotcho r. Canada 120 F3
Kotcho Lake Canada 120 F3
Kot Diji Pak. 89 H5
Kotel'nich Rus. Fed. 42 K4
Kotel'nikovo Rus. Fed. 43 I7
Kotel'nyy, Ostrov i. Rus. Fed. 65 O2
Kotgar India 84 D2
Kotgarh India 82 D3
Kothagudem India see Kottagudem
Köthen (Anhalt) Germany 53 L3
Kotido Uganda 97 G4
Kotikovo Rus. Fed. 74 D3
Kot Imamgarh Pak. 89 H5
Kotka Fin. 45 O6
Kot Kapura India 82 C3
Kotkino Rus. Fed. 42 K2
Kotlas Rus. Fed. 42 J3
Kotli Pak. 89 I3
Kotlik U.S.A. 118 B3
Kötlutangi pt Iceland 44 [inset]
Kotly Rus. Fed. 45 P7
Kotorkoshi Nigeria 96 D3
Kotovo Rus. Fed. 43 J6
Kotovsk Rus. Fed. 43 I5
Kotra India 82 C4
Kotra Pak. 89 G4
Kotri r. India 84 D2
Kot Sarae Pak. 89 G6
Kottagudem India 84 D2
Kottarakara India 84 C4
Kottayam India 84 C4
Kotte Sri Lanka see Sri Jayewardenepura Kotte
Kotto r. Cent. Afr. Rep. 98 C3
Kotturu India 84 C3
Kotuy r. Rus. Fed. 65 L2
Kotzebue U.S.A. 118 B3
Kotzebue Sound sea chan. U.S.A. 118 B3
Kötzting Germany 53 M5
Kouango Cent. Afr. Rep. 98 C3
Koubia Guinea 96 B3
Kouchibouguac National Park Canada 123 I5
Koudougou Burkina 96 C3
Kouebokkeveld mts S. Africa 100 D7
Koufey Niger 96 E3
Koufonisi i. Greece 59 L7
Kougaberge mts S. Africa 100 F7
Koukourou r. Cent. Afr. Rep. 98 B3
Koulen Cambodia see Kulen
Koulikoro Mali 96 C3
Koumac New Caledonia 107 G4
Koumpentoum Senegal 96 B3
Koundâra Guinea 96 B3
Kountze U.S.A. 131 E6
Koupéla Burkina 96 C3
Kourou Fr. Guiana 143 H2
Kouroussa Guinea 96 C3
Kousséri Cameroon 97 E3
Koutiala Mali 96 C3
Kouvola Fin. 45 O6
Kovallberget Sweden 44 J4
Kovdor Rus. Fed. 44 Q3
Kovdozero, Ozero l. Rus. Fed. 40 R3
Kovel' Ukr. 43 E6
Kovernino Rus. Fed. 42 I4
Kovilpatti India 84 C4
Kovno Lith. see Kaunas
Kovriga, Gora hill Rus. Fed. 42 K2
Kovrov Rus. Fed. 42 I4
Kovylkino Rus. Fed. 43 I5
Kovzhskoye, Ozero l. Rus. Fed. 42 H3
Kowanyama Australia 110 C2
Kowloon Hong Kong China 77 [inset]
Kowloon Peak hill Hong Kong China 77 [inset]
Kowloon Peninsula Hong Kong China 77 [inset]
Kowŏn N. Korea 75 B5
Kōyama-misaki pt Japan 75 C6
Köyceğiz Turkey 59 M6
Koygorodok Rus. Fed. 42 K3
Koymatdag, Gory hills Turkm. 88 D1
Koyna Reservoir India 84 B2
Köýtendag Turkm. see Charshanga
Koyuk U.S.A. 118 B3
Koyukuk r. U.S.A. 118 C3
Koyulhisar Turkey 90 E2
Kozağacı Turkey see Günyüzü
Kō-zaki pt Japan 75 C6
Kozan Turkey 90 D3
Kozani Greece 59 I4
Kozara mts Bos.-Herz. 58 G2
Kozara nat. park Bos.-Herz. 58 G2
Kozarska Dubica Bos.-Herz. see Bosanska Dubica
Kozelets' Ukr. 43 F6
Kozel'sk Rus. Fed. 43 G5
Kozhikode India see Calicut
Kozhva Rus. Fed. 42 M2
Kozlu Turkey 59 N4
Koz'modem'yansk Rus. Fed. 42 J4
Kožuf mts Greece/Macedonia 59 J4
Kōzu-shima i. Japan 75 E6
Kozyatyn Ukr. 43 F6
Kpalimé Togo 96 D4
Kpandae Ghana 96 C4
Kpungan Pass India/Myanmar 70 B1
Kra, Isthmus of Thai. 71 B5
Krabi Thai. 71 B5
Kra Buri Thai. 71 B5
Krâchéh Cambodia 71 D4
Kraddsele Sweden 44 J4
Kragerø Norway 45 F7
Kraggenburg Neth. 52 F2
Kragujevac Serb. and Mont. 59 I2
Krakatau vol. Indon. 68 D8
Krakau Poland see Kraków
Kraków Poland 47 Q5
Krakower See l. Germany 53 M1
Krâlănh Cambodia 71 C4
Kralendijk Neth. Antilles 137 K6
Kramators'k Ukr. 43 H6
Kramfors Sweden 44 J5
Krammer est. Neth. 52 E3
Kranidi Greece 59 J6
Kranj Slovenia 58 F1
Kranji Reservoir Sing. 71 [inset]
Kranskop S. Africa 101 J5
Krasavino Rus. Fed. 42 J3
Krasilov Ukr. see Krasyliv
Krasino Rus. Fed. 64 G2
Kraskino Rus. Fed. 74 C4
Krāslava Latvia 45 O9
Kraslice Czech Rep. 53 M4
Krasnaya Gorbatka Rus. Fed. 42 I5
Krasnaya Zarya Rus. Fed. 43 H5
Krasnoarmeysk Rus. Fed. 43 J6
Krasnoarmeysk Ukr. see Krasnoarmiys'k
Krasnoarmiys'k Ukr. 43 H6
Krasnoborsk Rus. Fed. 42 J3
Krasnodar Rus. Fed. 90 E1
Krasnodar Kray admin. div. Rus. Fed. see Krasnodarskiy Kray
Krasnodarskiy Kray admin. div. Rus. Fed. 90 E1
Krasnodon Ukr. 43 H6
Krasnogorodskoye Rus. Fed. 45 P8
Krasnogorsk Rus. Fed. 74 F2
Krasnogorskoye Rus. Fed. 42 L4
Krasnograd Ukr. see Krasnohrad
Krasnogvardeysk Uzbek. see Bulungur
Krasnogvardeyskoye Rus. Fed. 43 I7
Krasnohrad Ukr. 43 G6
Krasnohvardiys'ke Ukr. 43 G7
Krasnokamsk Rus. Fed. 41 R4
Krasnoperekops'k Ukr. 43 G7
Krasnopol'ye Rus. Fed. 74 F2
Krasnorechenskiy Rus. Fed. 74 D3
Krasnoslobodsk Rus. Fed. 43 I5
Krasnotur'insk Rus. Fed. 41 S4
Krasnoufimsk Rus. Fed. 41 R4
Krasnovishersk Rus. Fed. 41 R3
Krasnovodsk Turkm. see Turkmenbashi
Krasnovodsk, Mys pt Turkm. 88 D2
Krasnovodskiy Gosudarstvenny Zapovednik nature res. Turkm. 88 D2
Krasnovodskiy Zaliv b. Turkm. 88 D2
Krasnovodskoye Plato plat. Turkm. 91 I2
Krasnowodsk Aylagy b. Turkm. see Krasnovodskiy Zaliv
Krasnoyarovo Rus. Fed. 74 C2
Krasnoyarsk Rus. Fed. 64 K4
Krasnoyarskoye Vodokhranilishche resr Rus. Fed. 72 G2
Krasnoye Lipetskaya Oblast' Rus. Fed. 43 H5
Krasnoye Respublika Kalmykiya - Khalm'g-Tangch Rus. Fed. see Ulan Erge
Krasnoye Znamya Turkm. 89 F2
Krasnoznamenskiy Kazakh. see Yegindykol'
Krasnoznamenskoye Kazakh. see Yegindykol'
Krasnyy Rus. Fed. 43 F5
Krasnyy Chikoy Rus. Fed. 73 J2
Krasnyye Baki Rus. Fed. 42 J4
Krasnyy Kamyshanik Rus. Fed. see Komsomol'skiy
Krasnyy Kholm Rus. Fed. 42 H4
Krasnyy Kut Rus. Fed. 43 J6
Krasnyy Luch Ukr. 43 H6
Krasnyy Lyman Ukr. 43 H6
Krasnyy Yar Rus. Fed. 43 K7
Krasyliv Ukr. 43 E6
Kratie Cambodia see Krâchéh
Kratke Range mts P.N.G. 69 L8
Kraulshavn Greenland see Nuussuaq
Krâvanh, Chuŏr Phnum mts Cambodia/Thai. see Cardamom Range
Kraynovka Rus. Fed. 91 G2
Krefeld Germany 52 G3
Kremenchug Ukr. see Kremenchuk
Kremenchugskoye Vodokhranilishche resr Ukr. see Kremenchuts'ka Vodoskhovyshche
Kremenchuk Ukr. 43 G6
Kremenchuts'ka Vodoskhovyshche resr Ukr. 43 G6
Křemešník hill Czech Rep. 47 O6
Kremges Ukr. see Svitlovods'k
Kremmidi, Akra pt Greece 59 J6
Krems Austria see Krems an der Donau
Krems an der Donau Austria 47 O6
Kresta, Zaliv g. Rus. Fed. 65 T3
Kresttsy Rus. Fed. 42 G4
Kretinga Lith. 45 L9
Kreuzau Germany 52 G4
Kreuztal Germany 53 H4
Kreva Belarus 45 O9
Kribi Cameroon 96 D4
Krichev Belarus see Krychaw
Kriel S. Africa 101 I4
Krikellos Greece 59 I5
Kril'on, Mys c. Rus. Fed. 74 F3
Krishna India 84 C2
Krishna r. India 84 D2
Krishnanagar India 83 G5
Krishnaraja Sagara l. India 84 C3
Kristiania Norway see Oslo
Kristiansand Norway 45 E7
Kristianstad Sweden 45 I8
Kristiansund Norway 44 E5
Kristiinankaupunki Fin. see Kristinestad
Kristinehamn Sweden 45 I7
Kristinestad Fin. 44 L5
Kristinopol' Ukr. see Chervonohrad
Kriti i. Greece see Crete
Krivoy Rog Ukr. see Kryvyy Rih
Križevci Croatia 58 G1
Krk i. Croatia 58 F2
Krkonošský narodní park nat. park Czech Rep./Poland 47 O5
Krokom Sweden 44 I5
Krokstadøra Norway 44 F5
Krokstranda Norway 44 I3
Krolevets' Ukr. 43 G6
Kronach Germany 53 L4
Krŏng Kaôh Kŏng Cambodia 71 C5
Kronoby Fin. 44 M5
Kronprins Christian Land reg. Greenland 153 I1
Kronprins Frederik Bjerge nunataks Greenland 119 O3
Kronshtadt Rus. Fed. 45 P7
Kronstadt Romania see Braşov
Kronstadt Rus. Fed. see Kronshtadt
Kronwa Myanmar 70 B4
Kroonstad S. Africa 101 H4
Kropotkin Rus. Fed. 91 F1
Kropstädt Germany 53 M3
Krosno Poland 43 D6
Krotoszyn Poland 47 P5
Kruger National Park S. Africa 101 J2
Kruglikovo Rus. Fed. 74 D2
Kruglyakov Rus. Fed. see Oktyabr'skiy
Krui Indon. 68 C8
Kruisfontein S. Africa 100 G8
Kruja Albania see Krujë
Krujë Albania 59 H4
Krumovgrad Bulg. 59 K4
Krungkao Thai. see Ayutthaya
Krung Thep Thai. see Bangkok
Krupa Bos.-Herz. see Bosanska Krupa
Krupa na Uni Bos.-Herz. see Bosanska Krupa
Krupki Belarus 43 F5
Krusenstern, Cape U.S.A. 118 B3
Kruševac Serb. and Mont. 59 I3
Krušné Hory mts Czech Rep. 53 M4
Kruzof Island U.S.A. 120 C3
Krychaw Belarus 43 F5
Krylov Seamount sea feature N. Atlantic Ocean 148 G4
Krym' pen. Ukr. see Crimea
Krymsk Rus. Fed. 90 E1
Krymskaya Rus. Fed. see Krymsk
Kryms'kyy Pivostriv pen. Ukr. see Crimea
Krystynopol Ukr. see Chervonohrad
Krytiko Pelagos sea Greece 59 K6
Kryvyy Rih Ukr. 43 G7
Ksabi Alg. 54 D6
Ksar Chellala Alg. 57 H6
Ksar el Boukhari Alg. 57 H6
Ksar el Kebir Morocco 57 D6
Ksar-es-Souk Morocco see Er Rachidia
Ksenofontova Rus. Fed. 41 R3
Kshirpai India 83 F5
Ksour Essaf Tunisia 58 D7
Kstovo Rus. Fed. 42 J4
Kū', Jabal al hill Saudi Arabia 86 G4
Kuah Malaysia 71 B6
Kuaidamao China see Tonghua
Kuala Belait Brunei 68 E6
Kuala Dungun Malaysia see Dungun
Kuala Kangsar Malaysia 71 C6
Kualakapuas Indon. 68 E7
Kuala Kerai Malaysia 71 C6
Kuala Lipis Malaysia 71 C6

►Kuala Lumpur Malaysia 71 C7
Joint capital of Malaysia, with Putrajaya.

Kuala Nerang Malaysia 71 C6
Kuala Pilah Malaysia 71 C7
Kuala Rompin Malaysia 71 C7
Kuala Selangor Malaysia 71 C7

L

Lee Steere Range hills Australia 109 C6
Leesville U.S.A. 131 E6
Leesville Lake OH U.S.A. 134 E3
Leesville Lake VA U.S.A. 134 F5
Leeton Australia 112 C5
Leeu-Gamka S. Africa 100 E7
Leeuwarden Neth. 52 F1
Leeuwin, Cape Australia 109 A8
Leeuwin-Naturaliste National Park Australia 109 A8
Lee Vining U.S.A. 128 D3
Leeward Islands Caribbean Sea 137 L5
Lefka Cyprus 85 A2
Lefkada Greece 59 I5
Lefkada i. Greece 59 I5
Lefkás Greece see Lefkada
Lefke Cyprus see Lefka
Lefkimmi Greece 59 I5
Lefkoniko Cyprus see Lefkonikon
Lefkonikon Cyprus 85 A2
Lefkoşa Cyprus see Nicosia
Lefkosia Cyprus see Nicosia
Lefroy r. Canada 123 H2
Lefroy, Lake salt flat Australia 109 C7
Legarde r. Canada 122 D4
Legaspi Phil. 69 G4
Legden Germany 52 H2
Legges Tor mt. Australia 111 [inset]
Leghorn Italy see Livorno
Legnago Italy 58 D2
Legnica Poland 47 P5
Le Grand U.S.A. 128 C3
Legune Australia 108 E3
Leh India 82 D2
Le Havre France 56 E2
Lehi U.S.A. 129 H1
Lehighton U.S.A. 135 H3
Lehmo Fin. 44 P5
Lehre Germany 53 K2
Lehrte Germany 53 J2
Lehtimäki Fin. 44 M5
Lehututu Botswana 100 E2
Leiah Pak. 89 H4
Leibnitz Austria 47 O7
Leicester U.K. 49 F6
Leichhardt r. Australia 106 B3
Leichhardt Falls Australia 110 B3
Leichhardt Range mts Australia 110 D4
Leiden Neth. 52 E2
Leie r. Belgium 52 D3
Leigh N.Z. 113 E3
Leigh U.K. 48 E5
Leighton Buzzard U.K. 49 G7
Leikthо Myanmar 70 B3
Leimen Germany 53 I5
Leine r. Germany 53 J2
Leinefelde Germany 53 K3
Leinster Australia 109 C6
Leinster reg. Rep. of Ireland 51 F4
Leinster, Mount hill Rep. of Ireland 51 F5
Leipsic U.S.A. 134 D3
Leipsoi i. Greece 59 L6
Leipzig Germany 53 M3
Leipzig-Halle airport Germany 53 M3
Leiranger Norway 44 I3
Leiria Port. 57 B4
Leirvik Norway 45 D7
Leishan China 77 F3
Leisler, Mount hill Australia 109 E5
Leisnig Germany 53 M3
Leitchfield U.S.A. 134 B5
Leith Hill hill U.K. 49 G7
Leiva, Cerro mt. Col. 142 D3
Leixlip Rep. of Ireland 51 F4
Leiyang China 77 G3
Leizhou China 77 F4
Leizhou Bandao pen. China 77 F4
Leizhou Wan b. China 77 F4
Lek r. Neth. 52 E3
Leka Norway 44 G4
Lékana Congo 98 B4
Le Kef Tunisia 58 C6
Lekhainá Greece see Lechaina
Lekitobi Indon. 69 G7
Lekkersing S. Africa 100 C5
Lékoni Gabon 98 B4
Leksand Sweden 45 I6
Leksozero, Ozero l. Rus. Fed. 44 Q5
Lelai, Tanjung pt Indon. 69 H6
Leland U.S.A. 134 C1
Leli China see Tianlin
Lélouma Guinea 96 B3
Lelystad Neth. 52 F2
Le Maire, Estrecho de sea chan. Arg. 144 C9
Léman, Lac l. France/Switz. see Geneva, Lake
Le Mans France 56 E2
Le Mars U.S.A. 130 D3
Lemberg France 53 H5
Lemberg Ukr. see L'viv
Lembruch Germany 53 I2
Lemdiyya Alg. see Médéa
Leme Brazil 145 B3
Lemele Neth. 52 G2
Lemesos Cyprus see Limassol
Lemgo Germany 53 I2
Lemhi Range mts U.S.A. 126 E3
Lemi Fin. 45 O6
Lemieux Islands Canada 119 L3
Lemmenjoen kansallispuisto nat. park Fin. 44 N2
Lemmer Neth. 52 F2
Lemmon U.S.A. 130 C2
Lemmon, Mount U.S.A. 129 H5
Lemnos i. Greece see Limnos
Lemoncove U.S.A. 128 D3
Lemoore U.S.A. 128 D3
Le Moyne, Lac l. Canada 123 H2
Lemro r. Myanmar 70 A2
Lemtybozh Rus. Fed. 41 R3
Le Murge hills Italy 58 G4
Lemvig Denmark 45 F8
Lem'yu r. Rus. Fed. 42 M3
Lena r. Rus. Fed. 72 J1
Lena U.S.A. 134 A1
Lena, Mount U.S.A. 129 I1
Lenadoon Point Rep. of Ireland 51 C3
Lenchung Tso salt l. China 83 E2
Lençóis Brazil 145 C1
Lençóis Maranhenses, Parque Nacional dos nat. park Brazil 143 J4
Lendeh Iran 88 C4
Lendery Rus. Fed. 44 Q5
Le Neubourg France 49 H9
Lengerich Germany 53 H2
Lenglong Ling mts China 72 I5
Lengshuijiang China 77 F3
Lengshuitan China 77 F3
Lenham U.K. 49 H7
Lenhovda Sweden 45 I8
Lenin Tajik. 89 H2
Lenin, Qullai mt. Kyrg./Tajik. see Lenin Peak
Lenina, Pik mt. Kyrg./Tajik. see Lenin Peak
Leninabad Tajik. see Khŭjand
Leninakan Armenia see Gyumri
Lenin Atyndagy Choku mt. Kyrg./Tajik. see Lenin Peak
Lenine Ukr. 90 D1
Leningrad Rus. Fed. see St Petersburg
Leningrad Tajik. 89 H2
Leningrad Oblast admin. div. Rus. Fed. see Leningradskaya Oblast'
Leningradskaya Rus. Fed. 43 H7
Leningradskaya Oblast' admin. div. Rus. Fed. 45 R7
Leningradskiy Rus. Fed. 65 S3
Leningradskiy Tajik. see Leningrad
Lenino Ukr. see Lenine
Leninobod Tajik. see Khŭjand
Lenin Peak Kyrg./Tajik. 89 I2
Leninsk Kazakh. see Baykonyr
Leninsk Rus. Fed. 43 J6
Leninskiy Rus. Fed. 43 H5
Leninsk-Kuznetskiy Rus. Fed. 64 J4
Leninskoye Kazakh. 43 K6
Leninskoye Kirovskaya Oblast' Rus. Fed. 42 J4
Leninskoye Yevreyskaya Avtonomnaya Oblast' Rus. Fed. 74 D3
Lenkoran' Azer. see Länkäran
Lenne r. Germany 53 H3
Lennoxville Canada 135 J1
Lenoir U.S.A. 132 D5
Lenore U.S.A. 134 D5
Lenore Lake Canada 121 J4
Lenox U.S.A. 135 I2
Lens France 52 C4
Lensk Rus. Fed. 65 M3
Lenti Hungary 58 G1
Lentini Sicily Italy 58 F6
Lenya Myanmar 71 B5
Lenzen Germany 53 L1
Léo Burkina 96 C3
Leoben Austria 47 O7
Leodhais, Eilean i. U.K. see Lewis, Isle of
Leominster U.K. 49 E6
Leominster U.S.A. 135 J2
León Mex. 136 D4
León Nicaragua 137 G6
León Spain 57 D2
Leon r. U.S.A. 131 D6
Leonardtown U.S.A. 135 G4
Leonardville Namibia 100 D2
Leongatha Australia 112 B7
Leonidi Greece 59 J6
Leonidovo Rus. Fed. 74 F2
Leonora Australia 109 C7
Leopold U.S.A. 134 E4
Leopold and Astrid Coast Antarctica see King Leopold and Queen Astrid Coast
Léopold II, Lac l. Dem. Rep. Congo see Mai-Ndombe, Lac
Leopoldina Brazil 145 C3
Leopoldo de Bulhões Brazil 145 A2
Léopoldville Dem. Rep. Congo see Kinshasa
Leoti U.S.A. 130 C4
Leoville Canada 121 J4
Lepalale S. Africa see Ellisras
Lepaya Latvia see Liepāja
Lepel' Belarus see Lyepyel'
Lepellé r. Canada 123 H1
Lephalala r. S. Africa 101 H2
Lephepe Botswana 101 G2
Lephoi S. Africa 101 G6
Leping China 77 H2
Lepontine, Alpi mts Italy/Switz. 58 C1
Leppävirta Fin. 44 O5
Lepreau, Point Canada 123 I5
Lepsa Kazakh. see Lepsy
Lepsy Kazakh. 80 E2
Le Puy France see Le Puy-en-Velay
Le Puy-en-Velay France 56 F4
Le Quesnoy France 52 D4
Lerala Botswana 101 H2
Leratswana S. Africa 101 H5
Léré Mali 96 C3
Lereh Indon. 69 J7
Leribe Lesotho see Hlotse
Lérida Col. 142 D4
Lérida Spain see Lleida
Lerik Azer. 91 H3
Lerma Spain 57 E2
Lermontov Rus. Fed. 91 F1
Lermontovka Rus. Fed. 74 D3
Lermontovskiy Rus. Fed. see Lermontov
Leros i. Greece 59 L6
Le Roy U.S.A. 135 G2
Le Roy, Lac l. Canada 122 G2
Lerum Sweden 45 H8
Lerwick U.K. 50 [inset]
Les Amirantes is Seychelles see Amirante Islands
Lesbos i. Greece 59 K5
Les Cayes Haiti 137 J5
Le Seu d'Urgell Spain 57 G2
Leshan China 76 D2
Leshukonskoye Rus. Fed. 42 J2
Lesi watercourse Sudan 97 F4
Leskhimstroy Ukr. see Syeverodonets'k
Leskovac Serb. and Mont. 59 I3
Leslie U.S.A. 134 C2
Lesneven France 56 B2
Lesnoy Kirovskaya Oblast' Rus. Fed. 42 L4
Lesnoy Murmanskaya Oblast' Rus. Fed. see Umba
Lesnoye Rus. Fed. 42 G4
Lesogorsk Rus. Fed. 74 F2
Lesopil'noye Rus. Fed. 74 D3
Lesosibirsk Rus. Fed. 64 K4
▶Lesotho country Africa 101 I5
Africa 7, 94–95
Lesozavodsk Rus. Fed. 74 D3
L'Espérance Rock i. Kermadec Is 107 I5
Les Pieux France 49 F9
Les Sables-d'Olonne France 56 D3
Lesse r. Belgium 52 E4
Lesser Antarctica reg. Antarctica see West Antarctica
Lesser Antilles is Caribbean Sea 137 K6
Lesser Caucasus mts Asia 91 F2
Lesser Himalaya mts India/Nepal 82 D3
Lesser Khingan Mountains China see Xiao Hinggan Ling
Lesser Slave Lake Canada 120 H4
Lesser Tunb i. The Gulf 88 D5
Lessines Belgium 52 D4
L'Est, Canal de France 52 G6
L'Est, Île de i. Canada 123 J5
L'Est, Pointe de pt Canada 123 J4
Lester U.S.A. 134 E5
Lestijärvi Fin. 44 N5
Les Vans France 56 G4
Lesvos i. Greece see Lesbos
Leszno Poland 47 P5
Letaba S. Africa 101 J2
Letchworth U.K. 49 G7
Le Télégraphe hill France 56 G3
Leteri India 82 D4
Letha Range mts Myanmar 70 A2
Lethbridge Alta Canada 121 H5
Lethbridge Nfld. and Lab. Canada 123 L4
Leti i. Indon. 108 D2
Leti, Kepulauan is Indon. 108 D2
Leticia Col. 142 E4
Letlhakeng Botswana 101 G3
Letnerechenskiy Rus. Fed. 42 G2
Letniy Navolok Rus. Fed. 42 H2
Le Touquet-Paris-Plage France 52 B4
Letpadan Myanmar 70 A3
Le Tréport France 52 B4
Letsitele S. Africa 101 J2
Letsopa S. Africa 101 G4
Letterkenny Rep. of Ireland 51 E3
Letung Indon. 71 D7
Lëtzebuerg country Europe see Luxembourg
Letzlingen Germany 53 L2
Léua Angola 99 C5
Leucas Greece see Lefkada
Leucate, Étang de l. France 56 F5
Leuchars U.K. 50 G4
Leukas Greece see Lefkada
Leung Shuen Wan Chau i. Hong Kong China see High Island
Leunovo Rus. Fed. 42 I2
Leupp U.S.A. 129 H4
Leupung Indon. 71 A6
Leura Australia 110 E4
Leusden Neth. 52 F2
Leuser, Gunung mt. Indon. 71 B7
Leutershausen Germany 53 K5
Leuven Belgium 52 E4
Levadeia Greece 59 J5
Levan U.S.A. 129 H2
Levanger Norway 44 G5
Levante, Riviera di coastal area Italy 58 C2
Levanto Italy 58 C2
Levashi Rus. Fed. 91 G2
Levelland U.S.A. 131 C5
Leven England U.K. 48 G5
Leven Scotland U.K. 50 G4
Leven, Loch l. U.K. 50 F4
Lévêque, Cape Australia 108 C4
Leverkusen Germany 52 G3
Lévézou mts France 56 F4
Levice Slovakia 47 Q6
Levin N.Z. 113 E5
Lévis Canada 123 H5
Levitha i. Greece 59 L6
Levittown NY U.S.A. 135 I3
Levittown PA U.S.A. 135 H3
Levkás i. Greece see Lefkada
Levkímmi Greece see Lefkimmi
Levskigrad Bulg. see Karlovo
Lev Tolstoy Rus. Fed. 43 H5
Lévy, Cap c. France 49 F9
Lewe Myanmar 70 B3
Lewerberg mt. S. Africa 100 C5
Lewes U.K. 49 H8
Lewes U.S.A. 135 H4
Lewis CO U.S.A. 129 I3
Lewis IN U.S.A. 134 B4
Lewis KS U.S.A. 130 D4
Lewis, Isle of i. U.K. 50 C2
Lewis, Lake salt flat Australia 104 F5
Lewisburg KY U.S.A. 134 B5
Lewisburg PA U.S.A. 135 G3
Lewisburg WV U.S.A. 134 E5
Lewis Cass, Mount Canada/U.S.A. 120 D3
Lewis Hills hill Canada 123 K4
Lewis Pass N.Z. 113 D6
Lewis Range hills Australia 108 E5
Lewis Range mts U.S.A. 126 E2
Lewis Smith, Lake U.S.A. 133 C5
Lewiston ID U.S.A. 126 D3
Lewiston ME U.S.A. 135 J1
Lewistown IL U.S.A. 130 F3
Lewistown MT U.S.A. 126 F3
Lewistown PA U.S.A. 135 G3
Lewisville U.S.A. 131 E5
Lexington KY U.S.A. 134 C4
Lexington MI U.S.A. 134 D2
Lexington NC U.S.A. 132 D5
Lexington NE U.S.A. 130 D3
Lexington TN U.S.A. 131 F5
Lexington VA U.S.A. 134 F5
Lexington Park U.S.A. 135 G4
Leyden Neth. see Leiden
Leye China 76 E3
Leyla Dāgh mt. Iran 88 B2
Leyte i. Phil. 69 G4
Lezha Albania see Lezhë
Lezhë Albania 59 H4
Lezhi China 76 E2
Lezhu China 77 G4
L'gov Rus. Fed. 43 G6
Lhagoi Kangri mt. China 83 F3
Lhari China 76 B2
Lharigarbo China see Amdo
Lhasa China 83 G3
Lhasoi China 76 B2
Lhatog China 76 C2
Lhaviyani Atoll Maldives see Faadhippolhu Atoll
Lhazê Xizang China 76 B2
Lhazê Xizang China 83 F3
Lhazhong China 83 F3
Lhokkruet Indon. 71 A6
Lhokseumawe Indon. 71 B6
Lhoksukon Indon. 71 B6
Lhomar China 83 G3
Lhorong China 76 B2
▶Lhotse mt. China/Nepal 83 F4
4th highest mountain in the world and in Asia.
World 12–13
Lhozhag China 83 G3
Lhuentse Bhutan 83 G4
Lhünzê China 76 B2
Lhünzhub China 83 G3
Liancheng China see Guangnan
Liancourt France 52 C5
Liancourt Rocks i. N. Pacific Ocean 75 C5
Liandu China see Lishui
Liangdang China 76 E1
Liangdaohe China 83 G3
Lianghe Chongqing China 77 F2
Lianghe Yunnan China 76 C3
Lianghekou Chongqing China see Lianghe
Lianghekou Gansu China 76 E1
Lianghekou Sichuan China 76 D2
Liangping China 76 E2
Liangshan China see Liangping
Liang Shan mt. Myanmar 70 B1
Liangshi China see Shaodong
Liangtian China 77 F4
Liangyuan China see Shangqiu
Liangzhou China see Wuwei
Liangzi Hu l. China 77 G2
Lianhe China see Qianjiang
Lianhua China 77 G3
Lianhua Shan mts China 77 G4
Lianjiang Fujian China 77 H3
Lianjiang Jiangxi China see Xingguo
Liannan China 77 G3
Lianping China 77 G3
Lianran China see Anning
Lianshan Guangdong China 77 G3
Lianshan Liaoning China 73 M4
Lianshui China 77 H1
Liant, Cape i. Thai. see Samae San, Ko
Liantang China see Nanchang
Lianxian China see Lianzhou
Lianyin China 74 A1
Lianyungang China 77 H1
Lianzhou Guangdong China 77 G3
Lianzhou Guangxi China see Hepu
Liaocheng China 73 L5
Liaodong Bandao pen. China 69 M4
Liaodong Wan b. China 73 M4
Liaogao China see Songtao
Liao He r. China 74 A4
Liaoning prov. China 74 A4
Liaoyang China 74 A4
Liaoyuan China 74 B4
Liaozhong China 74 A4
Liapades Greece 59 H5
Liard r. Canada 120 F2
Liard Highway Canada 120 F2
Liard Plateau Canada 120 E2
Liard River Canada 120 E3
Liari Pak. 89 G5
Liathach mt. U.K. 50 D3
Liban country Asia see Lebanon
Liban, Jebel mts Lebanon 85 C2
Libau Latvia see Liepāja
Libby U.S.A. 126 E2
Libenge Dem. Rep. Congo 98 B3
Liberal U.S.A. 131 C4
Liberdade Brazil 145 B3
Liberec Czech Rep. 47 O5
▶Liberia country Africa 96 C4
Africa 7, 94–95
Liberia Costa Rica 137 G6
Liberty IN U.S.A. 134 C4
Liberty KY U.S.A. 134 C5
Liberty ME U.S.A. 135 K1
Liberty MO U.S.A. 130 E4
Liberty MS U.S.A. 131 F6
Liberty NY U.S.A. 135 H3
Liberty TX U.S.A. 131 E6
Liberty Lake U.S.A. 135 G4
Libin Belgium 52 F5
Libni, Gebel hill Egypt see Libnī, Jabal
Libnī, Jabal hill Egypt 85 A4
Libo China 76 E3
Libobo, Tanjung pt Indon. 69 H7
Libode S. Africa 101 I6
Libong, Ko i. Thai. 71 B6
Libourne France 56 D4
Libral Well Australia 108 D5
Libre, Sierra mts Mex. 127 F7
▶Libreville Gabon 98 A3
Capital of Gabon.
▶Libya country Africa 97 E2
4th largest country in Africa.
Africa 7, 94–95
Libyan Desert Egypt/Libya 86 C5
Libyan Plateau Egypt 90 B5
Licantén Chile 144 B4
Licata Sicily Italy 58 E6
Lice Turkey 91 F3
Lich Germany 53 I4
Lichas pen. Greece 59 J5
Licheng Guangxi China see Lipu
Licheng Jiangsu China see Jinhu
Lichfield U.K. 49 F6
Lichinga Moz. 99 D5
Lichte Germany 53 L4
Lichtenau Germany 53 I3
Lichtenburg S. Africa 101 H4
Lichtenfels Germany 53 L4
Lichtenvoorde Neth. 52 G3
Lichuan Hubei China 77 F2
Lichuan Jiangxi China 77 H3
Lida Belarus 45 N10
Liddel Water r. U.K. 50 G5
Lidfontein Namibia 100 D3
Lidköping Sweden 45 H7
Lidsjöberg Sweden 44 I4
Liebenau Germany 53 J2
Liebenburg Germany 53 K2
Liebenwalde Germany 53 N2
Liebig, Mount Australia 109 E5
▶Liechtenstein country Europe 56 I3
Europe 5, 38–39
Liège Belgium 52 F4
Liegnitz Poland see Legnica
Lieksa Fin. 44 Q5
Lielupe r. Latvia 45 N8
Lielvārde Latvia 45 N8
Lienart Dem. Rep. Congo 98 C3
Lienchung i. Taiwan see Matsu Tao
Lienz Austria 47 N7
Liepāja Latvia 45 L8
Liepaya Latvia see Liepāja
Lier Belgium 52 E3
Lierre Belgium see Lier
Lieshout Neth. 52 F3
Lietuva country Europe see Lithuania
Liévin France 52 C4
Lièvre r. Canada 122 G5
Liezen Austria 47 O7
Liffey r. Rep. of Ireland 51 F4
Lifford Rep. of Ireland 51 E3
Lifi Mahuida mt. Arg. 144 C6
Lifou i. New Caledonia 107 G4
Lifu i. New Caledonia see Lifou
Līgatne Latvia 45 N8
Lightning Ridge Australia 112 C2
Ligny-en-Barrois France 52 F6
Ligonha r. Moz. 99 D5
Ligonier U.S.A. 134 C3
Ligui Mex. 127 F8
Ligure, Mar sea France/Italy see Ligurian Sea
Ligurian Sea France/Italy 58 C3
Ligurienne, Mer sea France/Italy see Ligurian Sea
Ligurta U.S.A. 129 F5
Lihir Group is P.N.G. 106 F2
Lihou Reef and Cays Australia 110 E3
Liivi laht b. Estonia/Latvia see Riga, Gulf of
Lijiang Yunnan China 76 D3
Lijiang Yunnan China see Yuanjiang
Lijiazhai China 77 G2
Lika reg. Croatia 58 F2
Likasi Dem. Rep. Congo 99 C5
Likati Dem. Rep. Congo 98 C3
Likely Canada 120 F4
Likhachevo Ukr. see Pervomays'kyy
Likhachyovo Ukr. see Pervomays'kyy
Likhapani India 83 H4
Likhás pen. Greece see Lichas
Likhoslavl' Rus. Fed. 42 G4
Liku Indon. 68 D6
Likurga Rus. Fed. 42 I4
L'Île-Rousse Corsica France 56 I5
Lilienthal Germany 53 I1
Liling China 77 G3
Lilla Pak. 89 I3
Lilla Edet Sweden 45 H7
Lille Belgium 52 E3
Lille France 52 D4
Lille (Lesquin) airport France 52 D4
Lille Bælt sea chan. Denmark see Little Belt
Lillebonne France 49 H9
Lillehammer Norway 45 G6
Lillers France 52 C4
Lillesand Norway 45 F7
Lillestrøm Norway 45 G7
Lilley U.S.A. 134 C2
Lillholmsjö Sweden 44 I5
Lillian, Point hill Australia 109 D6
Lillington U.S.A. 133 E5
Lillooet Canada 120 F5
Lillooet r. Canada 120 F5
Lillooet Range mts Canada 116 F5
▶Lilongwe Malawi 99 D5
Capital of Malawi.
Lilydale Australia 111 B7
▶Lima Peru 142 C6
Capital of Peru and 4th most populous city in South America.
Lima MT U.S.A. 126 E3
Lima NY U.S.A. 135 G2
Lima OH U.S.A. 134 C3
Lima Duarte Brazil 145 C3
Lima Islands China see Wanshan Qundao
Liman Rus. Fed. 43 J7
Limar Indon. 108 D1
Limassol Cyprus 85 A2
Limavady U.K. 51 F2
Limay r. Arg. 144 C5
Limbaži Latvia 45 N8
Limbunya Australia 108 E4
Limburg an der Lahn Germany 53 I4
Lim Chu Kang hill Sing. 71 [inset]
Lime Acres S. Africa 100 F5
Limeira Brazil 145 B3
Limerick Rep. of Ireland 51 D5
Limestone Point Canada 121 L4
Limingen Norway 44 H4
Limingen l. Norway 44 H4
Limington U.S.A. 135 J2
Liminka Fin. 44 N4
Limmen Bight b. Australia 110 B2
Limnos i. Greece 59 K5
Limoeiro Brazil 143 K5
Limoges Canada 135 H1
Limoges France 56 E4
Limón Costa Rica see Puerto Limón
Limon U.S.A. 130 C4
Limonlu Turkey 85 B1
Limonum France see Poitiers
Limousin reg. France 56 E4
Limoux France 56 F5
Limpopo prov. S. Africa 101 I2
Limpopo r. S. Africa/Zimbabwe 101 K3
Limu China 77 F3
Līnah well Saudi Arabia 91 F5
Linakhamari Rus. Fed. 44 Q2
Lin'an China see Jianshui
Linares Chile 144 B5
Linares Mex. 131 D7
Linares Spain 57 E4
Lincang China 76 D4
Lincheng Hainan China see Lingao
Lincheng Hunan China see Huitong
Linchuan China see Fuzhou
Linck Nunataks nunataks Antarctica 152 K1
Lincoln Arg. 144 D4
Lincoln U.K. 48 G5
Lincoln CA U.S.A. 128 C2
Lincoln IL U.S.A. 130 F3
Lincoln MI U.S.A. 134 D1
▶Lincoln NE U.S.A. 130 D3
State capital of Nebraska.
Lincoln City IN U.S.A. 134 B4
Lincoln City OR U.S.A. 126 B3
Lincoln Island Paracel Is 68 E3
Lincoln National Park Australia 111 A7
Lincoln Sea Canada/Greenland 153 J1
Lincolnshire Wolds hills U.K. 48 G5
Lincolnton U.S.A. 133 D5
Linda, Serra hills Brazil 145 C1
Linda Creek watercourse Australia 110 B4
Lindau Germany 53 M2
Lindau (Bodensee) Germany 47 L7
Lindeman Group is Australia 110 E4
Linden Canada 120 H5
Linden Germany 53 I4
Linden Guyana 143 G2
Linden AL U.S.A. 133 C5
Linden MI U.S.A. 134 D2
Linden TN U.S.A. 132 C5
Linden TX U.S.A. 131 E5
Linden Grove U.S.A. 130 E2
Lindern (Oldenburg) Germany 53 H2
Lindesnes c. Norway 45 E7
Líndhos Greece see Lindos
Lindi r. Dem. Rep. Congo 98 C3
Lindi Tanz. 99 D4
Lindian China 74 B3
Lindisfarne i. U.K. see Holy Island
Lindley S. Africa 101 H4
Lindos Greece 55 J4
Lindos, Akra pt Greece 59 M6
Lindsay Canada 135 F1
Lindsay CA U.S.A. 128 D3
Lindsay MT U.S.A. 126 G3
Lindsborg U.S.A. 130 D4
Lindside U.S.A. 134 E5
Lindum U.K. see Lincoln
Line Islands Kiribati 151 J5
Linesville U.S.A. 134 E3
Linfen China 73 K5
Lingampet India 84 C2
Linganamakki Reservoir India 84 B3
Lingao China 77 F5
Lingayen Phil. 69 G3
Lingbi China 77 H1
Lingcheng Anhui China see Lingbi
Lingcheng Guangxi China see Lingshan
Lingcheng Hainan China see Lingshui
Lingchuan Guangxi China 77 F3
Lingchuan Shanxi China 77 G1
Lingelethu S. Africa 101 H7
Lingen (Ems) Germany 53 H2
Lingga, Kepulauan is Indon. 68 D7
Lingle U.S.A. 126 G4
Lingomo Dem. Rep. Congo 98 C3
Lingshan China 77 F4
Lingshui China 77 F5
Lingshui Wan b. China 77 F5
Lingsugur India 84 C2
Lingtai China 76 E1
Linguère Senegal 96 B3
Lingui China 77 F3
Lingxi China see Yongshun
Lingxian China see Yanling
Lingxiang China 77 G2
Lingyang China see Cili
Lingyun China 76 E3
Lingzi Thang Plains reg. Aksai Chin 82 D2
Linhai China 77 I2
Linhares Brazil 145 C2
Linh Cam Vietnam 70 D3
Linhe China 73 J4
Linhpa Myanmar 70 A1
Linjiang China 74 B4
Linjin China 77 F1
Linköping Sweden 45 I7
Linkou China 74 C3
Linli China 77 F2
Linlithgow U.K. 50 F5
Linn MO U.S.A. 130 F4
Linn TX U.S.A. 131 D7
Linn, Mount U.S.A. 128 B1
Linnansaaren kansallispuisto nat. park Fin. 44 P5
Linnhe, Loch inlet U.K. 50 D4
Linnich Germany 52 G4
Linosa, Isola di i. Sicily Italy 58 E7
Linpo Myanmar 70 B2
Linquan China 77 G1
Linru China see Ruzhou
Linruzhen China 77 G1
Lins Brazil 145 A3
Linshu China 77 H1
Linshui China 76 E2
Lintan China 76 D1
Lintao China 76 D1
Linton IN U.S.A. 134 B4
Linton ND U.S.A. 130 C2
Linwu China 77 G3
Linxi China 73 L4
Linxia China 76 D1
Linxiang China 77 G2
Linyi Shandong China 73 L5
Linyi Shandong China 77 H1
Linying China 77 G1
Linz Austria 47 O6
Lion, Golfe du g. France 56 F5
Lions, Gulf of France see Lion, Golfe du
Lions Bay Canada 120 F5
Lioua Chad 97 E3
Lipari Sicily Italy 58 F5
Lipari, Isole is Italy 58 F5
Lipetsk Rus. Fed. 43 H5
Lipin Bor Rus. Fed. 42 H3

Liping China 77 F3
Lipova Romania 59 I1
Lipovtsy Rus. Fed. 74 C3
Lippe r. Germany 53 G3
Lippstadt Germany 53 I3
Lipsoí i. Greece see Leipsoi
Lipti Lekh pass Nepal 82 E3
Liptrap, Cape Australia 112 B7
Lipu China 77 F3
Lira Uganda 98 D3
Liranga Congo 98 B4
Lircay Peru 142 D6
Lisala Dem. Rep. Congo 98 C3
L'Isalo, Massif de mts Madag. 99 E6
L'Isalo, Parc National de nat. park Madag. 99 E6
Lisbellaw U.K. 51 E3
Lisboa Port. see Lisbon

▶Lisbon Port. 57 B4
Capital of Portugal.

Lisbon ME U.S.A. 135 J1
Lisbon NH U.S.A. 135 J1
Lisbon OH U.S.A. 134 E3
Lisburn U.K. 51 F3
Liscannor Bay Rep. of Ireland 47 C5
Lisdoonvarna Rep. of Ireland 51 C4
Lishan Taiwan 77 I3
Lishe Jiang r. China 76 D3
Lishi Jiangxi China see Dingnan
Lishi Shanxi China 73 K5
Lishu China 74 B4
Lishui China 77 H2
Li Shui r. China 77 F2
Lisichansk Ukr. see Lysychans'k
Lisieux France 56 E2
Liskeard U.K. 49 C8
Liski Rus. Fed. 43 H6
Liskot India 82 D3
L'Isle-Adam France 52 C5
Lismore Australia 112 F2
Lismore Rep. of Ireland 51 E5
Lisnarrick U.K. 51 E3
Lisnaskea U.K. 51 E3
Liss mt. Saudi Arabia 85 D4
Lissa Poland see Leszno
Lister, Mount Antarctica 152 H1
Listowel Canada 134 E2
Listowel Rep. of Ireland 51 C5
Lit Sweden 44 I5
Litang Guangxi China 77 F4
Litang Sichuan China 76 D2
Līţānī, Nahr el r. Lebanon 85 B3
Litchfield CA U.S.A. 128 C1
Litchfield CT U.S.A. 135 I3
Litchfield IL U.S.A. 130 F4
Litchfield MI U.S.A. 134 C2
Litchfield MN U.S.A. 130 E2
Lit-et-Mixe France 56 D4
Lithgow Australia 112 E4
Lithino, Akra pt Greece 59 K7
▶Lithuania country Europe 45 M9
Europe 5, 38–39
Lititz U.S.A. 135 G3
Litoměřice Czech Rep. 47 O5
Litovko Rus. Fed. 74 D2
Litovskaya S.S.R. country Europe see Lithuania
Little r. U.S.A. 131 E6
Little Abaco i. Bahamas 133 E7
Little Abitibi r. Canada 122 E4
Little Abitibi Lake Canada 122 E4
Little Andaman i. India 71 A5
Little Bahama Bank sea feature Bahamas 133 E7
Little Barrier i. N.Z. 113 E3
Little Belt sea chan. Denmark 45 F9
Little Belt Mountains U.S.A. 122 F3
Little Bitter Lake Egypt 85 A4
Little Cayman i. Cayman Is 137 H5
Little Churchill r. Canada 121 M3
Little Chute U.S.A. 134 A1
Little Coco Island Cocos Is 71 A4
Little Colorado r. U.S.A. 129 H3
Little Creek Peak U.S.A. 129 G3
Little Current Canada 122 E5
Little Current r. Canada 122 D4
Little Desert National Park Australia 111 C8
Little Egg Harbor inlet U.S.A. 135 H4
Little Exuma i. Bahamas 133 F8
Little Falls U.S.A. 130 E2
Littlefield AZ U.S.A. 129 G3
Littlefield TX U.S.A. 131 C5
Little Fork r. U.S.A. 130 E1
Little Grand Rapids Canada 121 M4
Littlehampton U.K. 49 G8
Little Inagua Island Bahamas 133 F8
Little Karas Berg plat. Namibia 100 D4
Little Karoo plat. S. Africa 100 E7
Little Lake U.S.A. 128 E4
Little Mecatina r. Nfld. and Lab./Que. Canada see Petit Mécatina
Little Mecatina Island Canada see Petit Mécatina, Île du
Little Minch sea chan. U.K. 50 B3
Little Missouri r. U.S.A. 130 C2
Little Namaqualand reg. S. Africa see Namaqualand
Little Nicobar i. India 71 A6
Little Ouse r. U.K. 49 H6
Little Pamir mts Asia 89 I2
Little Rancheria r. Canada 120 D2
Little Rann marsh India 82 B5
Little Red River Canada 120 H3

▶Little Rock U.S.A. 131 E5
State capital of Arkansas.

Littlerock U.S.A. 128 E4
Little Sable Point U.S.A. 134 B2
Little Salmon Lake Canada 116 C2
Little Salt Lake U.S.A. 129 G3
Little Sandy Desert Australia 109 B5
Little San Salvador i. Bahamas 133 F7
Little Smoky Canada 120 G4
Little Tibet reg. Jammu and Kashmir see Ladakh
Littleton U.S.A. 126 G5
Little Valley U.S.A. 135 F2
Little Wind r. U.S.A. 126 F4
Litunde Moz. 99 D5
Liu'an China see Lu'an
Liuba China 76 E1
Liucheng China 77 F3
Liuchiu Yü i. Taiwan 77 I4
Liuchong He r. China 76 E3
Liuchow China see Liuzhou
Liuhe China 74 B4
Liuheng Dao i. China 77 I2
Liujiachang China 77 F2
Liujiaxia Shuiku resr China 76 D1
Liukesong China 74 B3
Liulin China see Jonê
Liupan Shan mts China 76 E1
Liupanshui China see Lupanshui
Liuquan China 77 H1
Liuwa Plain National Park Zambia 99 C5
Liuyang China 77 G2
Liuzhan China 74 B2
Liuzhou China 77 F3
Līvāni Latvia 45 O8
Live Oak U.S.A. 133 D6
Liveringa Australia 106 C3
Livermore CA U.S.A. 128 C3
Livermore KY U.S.A. 134 B5
Livermore, Mount U.S.A. 131 B6
Livermore Falls U.S.A. 135 J1
Liverpool Australia 112 E4
Liverpool Canada 123 I5
Liverpool U.K. 48 E5
Liverpool Bay Canada 118 E3
Liverpool Plains Australia 112 E3
Liverpool Range mts Australia 112 D3
Livia U.S.A. 134 B5
Livingston U.K. 50 F5
Livingston AL U.S.A. 131 F5
Livingston KY U.S.A. 134 C5
Livingston MT U.S.A. 126 F3
Livingston TN U.S.A. 134 C5
Livingston TX U.S.A. 131 E6
Livingston, Lake U.S.A. 131 E6
Livingstone Zambia 99 C5
Livingston Island Antarctica 148 L2
Livingston Manor U.S.A. 135 H3
Livno Bos.-Herz. 58 G3
Livny Rus. Fed. 43 H5
Livojoki r. Fin. 44 O4
Livonia MI U.S.A. 134 D2
Livonia NY U.S.A. 135 G2
Livorno Italy 58 D3
Livramento do Brumado Brazil 145 C1
Liwā Oman 88 E5
Liwā', Wādī al watercourse Syria 85 C3
Liwale Tanz. 99 D4
Lixian Gansu China 76 E1
Lixian Sichuan China 76 D2
Lixus Morocco see Larache
Liyang China see Hexian
Liyuan China see Sangzhi
Lizard U.K. 49 B9
Lizarda Brazil 143 I5
Lizard Point U.K. 49 B9
Lizarra Spain see Estella
Lizemores U.S.A. 134 E4
Liziping China 76 D2
Lizy-sur-Ourcq France 52 D5
Ljouwert Neth. see Leeuwarden

▶Ljubljana Slovenia 58 F1
Capital of Slovenia.

Ljugarn Sweden 45 K8
Ljungan r. Sweden 44 J5
Ljungaverk Sweden 44 J5
Ljungby Sweden 45 H8
Ljusdal Sweden 45 J6
Ljusnan r. Sweden 45 J6
Ljusne Sweden 45 J6
Llaima, Volcán vol. Chile 144 B5
Llanandras U.K. see Presteigne
Llanbadarn Fawr U.K. 49 C6
Llanbedr Pont Steffan U.K. see Lampeter
Llanbister U.K. 49 D6
Llandeilo U.K. 49 D7
Llandissilio U.K. 49 C7
Llandovery U.K. 49 D7
Llandrindod Wells U.K. 49 D6
Llandudno U.K. 48 D5
Llandysul U.K. 49 C6
Llanegwad U.K. 49 C7
Llanelli U.K. 49 C7
Llanfair Caereinion U.K. 49 D6
Llanfair-ym-Muallt U.K. see Builth Wells
Llangefni U.K. 48 C5
Llangollen U.K. 49 D6
Llangurig U.K. 49 D6
Llanllyfni U.K. 49 C5
Llannerch-y-medd U.K. 48 C5
Llannor U.K. 49 C6
Llano Mex. 127 F7
Llano U.S.A. 131 D6
Llano r. U.S.A. 131 D6
Llano Estacado plain U.S.A. 131 C5
Llanos plain Col./Venez. 142 E2
Llanquihue, Lago l. Chile 144 B6
Llanrhystud U.K. 49 C6
Llantrisant U.K. 49 D7
Llanuwchllyn U.K. 49 D6
Llanwnog U.K. 49 D6
Llanymddyfri U.K. see Llandovery
Llay U.K. 49 D5
Lleida Spain 57 G3
Llerena Spain 57 C4
Lliria Spain 57 F4
Llodio Spain 57 E2
Lloyd George, Mount Canada 120 E3
Lloyd Lake Canada 121 I3
Lloydminster Canada 121 I4
Lluchmayor Spain see Llucmajor
Llucmajor Spain 57 H4
Llullaillaco, Volcán vol. Chile 144 C2
Lô r. China/Vietnam 70 D2
Loa r. Chile 144 B2
Loa U.S.A. 129 H2
Loban' r. Rus. Fed. 42 K4
Lobatejo mt. Spain 57 D5
Lobatse Botswana 101 G3
Lobaye r. Cent. Afr. Rep. 98 B3
Löbejün Germany 53 L3
Löbenberg hill Germany 53 M3
Loberia Arg. 144 E5
Lobito Angola 99 B5
Lobos Arg. 144 E5
Lobos, Cabo c. Mex. 127 E7
Lobos, Isla i. Mex. 127 F8
Lobos de Tierra, Isla i. Peru 142 B5
Loburg Germany 53 M2
Lôc Binh Vietnam 70 D2
Lochaline U.K. 50 D4
Lo Chau Hong Kong China see Beaufort Island
Loch Baghasdail U.K. see Lochboisdale
Lochboisdale U.K. 50 B3
Lochcarron U.K. 50 D3
Lochearnhead U.K. 50 E4
Lochem Neth. 52 G2
Lochern National Park Australia 110 C5
Loches France 56 E3
Loch Garman Rep. of Ireland see Wexford
Lochgelly U.K. 50 F4
Lochgilphead U.K. 50 D4
Lochinver U.K. 50 D2
Loch Lomond and The Trossachs National Park U.K. 50 E4
Lochmaddy U.K. 50 B3
Lochnagar mt. U.K. 50 F4
Loch nam Madadh U.K. see Lochmaddy
Loch Raven Reservoir U.S.A. 135 G4
Lochy, Loch l. U.K. 50 E4
Lock Australia 111 A7
Lockerbie U.K. 50 F5
Lockhart Australia 112 C5
Lockhart U.S.A. 131 D6
Lock Haven U.S.A. 135 G3
Löcknitz r. Germany 53 L1
Lockport U.S.A. 135 F2
Lôc Ninh Vietnam 71 D5
Lod Israel 85 B4
Loddon r. Australia 112 A5
Lodève France 56 F5
Lodeynoye Pole Rus. Fed. 42 G3
Lodge, Mount Canada/U.S.A. 120 B3
Lodhikheda India 82 D5
Lodhran Pak. 89 H4
Lodi Italy 58 C2
Lodi CA U.S.A. 128 C2
Lodi OH U.S.A. 134 D3
Lødingen Norway 44 I2
Lodja Dem. Rep. Congo 98 C4
Lodomeria Rus. Fed. see Vladimir
Lodrani India 82 B5
Lodwar Kenya 98 D3
Łódź Poland 47 Q5
Loei Thai. 70 C3
Loeriesfontein S. Africa 100 D6
Lofoten is Norway 44 H2
Lofusa Sudan 97 G4
Log Rus. Fed. 43 I6
Loga Niger 96 D3
Logan IA U.S.A. 130 E3
Logan OH U.S.A. 134 D4
Logan UT U.S.A. 126 F4
Logan WV U.S.A. 134 E5

▶Logan, Mount Canada 120 A2
2nd highest mountain in North America.

Logan, Mount U.S.A. 126 C2
Logan Creek r. Australia 110 D4
Logan Lake Canada 120 F5
Logan Mountains Canada 120 D2
Logansport IN U.S.A. 134 B3
Logansport LA U.S.A. 131 E6
Logatec Slovenia 58 F2
Logpung China 76 D1
Logroño Spain 57 E2
Logtak Lake India 83 H4
Lohardaga India 83 F5
Loharu India 82 C3
Lohatlha S. Africa 100 F5
Lohawat India 82 C4
Lohfelden Germany 53 J3
Lohil r. China/India see Zayü Qu
Lohiniva Fin. 44 N3
Lohjanjärvi l. Fin. 45 M6
Löhne Germany 53 I2
Lohne (Oldenburg) Germany 53 I2
Lohtaja Fin. 44 M4
Loi, Nam r. Myanmar 70 C2
Loikaw Myanmar 70 B3
Loi Lan mt. Myanmar/Thai. 70 B3
Loi-lem Myanmar 70 B2
Loi Lun Myanmar 70 B2
Loimaa Fin. 45 M6
Loipyet Hills Myanmar 70 B1
Loire r. France 56 C3
Loi Sang mt. Myanmar 70 B2
L'Oise à l'Aisne, Canal de France 52 D5
Loi Song mt. Myanmar 70 B2
Loja Ecuador 142 C4
Loja Spain 57 D5
Lokan tekojärvi l. Fin. 44 O3
Lokchim r. Rus. Fed. 42 K3
Lokeren Belgium 52 E3
Lokgwabe Botswana 100 E3
Lokichar Kenya 78 C6
Lokichokio Kenya 98 D3
Lokilalaki, Gunung mt. Indon. 69 G7
Løkken Denmark 45 F8
Løkken Norway 44 F5
Loknya Rus. Fed. 42 F4
Lokoja Nigeria 96 D4
Lokolama Dem. Rep. Congo 98 B4
Lokossa Benin 96 D4
Lokot' Rus. Fed. 43 G5
Lol Sudan 97 F4
Lola Guinea 96 C4
Lola, Mount U.S.A. 128 C2
Loleta U.S.A. 128 A1
Lolland i. Denmark 45 G9
Lollondo Tanz. 98 D4
Lolo U.S.A. 126 E3
Loloda Indon. 69 H6
Lolo Pass U.S.A. 126 E3
Lolowau Indon. 71 B7
Lolwane S. Africa 100 F4
Lom Bulg. 59 J3
Lom Norway 45 F6
Loma U.S.A. 129 I2
Lomami r. Dem. Rep. Congo 98 C3
Lomar Pass Afgh. 89 G3
Lomas, Bahía de b. Chile 144 C8
Lomas de Zamora Arg. 144 E4
Lombarda, Serra hills Brazil 143 H3
Lomblen i. Indon. 108 C2
Lombok Indon. 108 B2
Lombok i. Indon. 108 B2
Lombok, Selat sea chan. Indon. 108 A2

▶Lomé Togo 96 D4
Capital of Togo.

Lomela Dem. Rep. Congo 98 C4
Lomela r. Dem. Rep. Congo 97 F5
Lomira U.S.A. 134 A2
Lomme France 52 C4
Lommel Belgium 52 F3
Lomond Canada 123 K4
Lomond, Loch l. U.K. 50 E4
Lomonosov Rus. Fed. 45 P7
Lomonosov Ridge sea feature Arctic Ocean 153 B1
Lomovoye Rus. Fed. 42 I2
Lomphat Cambodia see Lumphăt
Lompoc U.S.A. 128 C4
Lom Sak Thai. 70 C3
Łomża Poland 47 S4
Lơn, Hon i. Vietnam 71 E4
Lonar India 84 C2
Londa Bangl. 83 G5
Londa India 84 B3
Londinières France 52 B5
Londinium U.K. see London
Londoko Rus. Fed. 74 D2
London Canada 134 E2

▶London U.K. 49 G7
Capital of the United Kingdom and of England. 4th most populous city in Europe.

London KY U.S.A. 134 C5
London OH U.S.A. 134 D4
Londonderry U.K. 51 E3
Londonderry OH U.S.A. 134 D4
Londonderry VT U.S.A. 135 I2
Londonderry, Cape Australia 108 D3
Londrina Brazil 145 A3
Lone Pine U.S.A. 128 D3
Long Thai. 70 B3
Longa Angola 99 B5
Longa, Proliv sea chan. Rus. Fed. 65 S2
Long'an China 76 E4
Long Ashton U.K. 49 E7
Long Bay U.S.A. 133 E5
Longbeach N.Z. 113 C7
Long Beach U.S.A. 128 D5
Longbo China see Shuangpai
Long Branch U.S.A. 135 I3
Longchang China 76 E2
Longcheng Anhui China see Xiaoxian
Longcheng Guangdong China see Longmen
Longcheng Yunnan China see Chenggong
Longchuan China see Nanhua
Longchuan Jiang r. China 76 C4
Long Creek r. Canada 121 K5
Long Creek U.S.A. 126 D3
Long Eaton U.K. 49 F6
Longford Rep. of Ireland 51 E4
Longgang Chongqing China see Dazu
Longgang Guangdong China 77 G4
Longhoughton U.K. 48 F3
Longhui China 77 F3
Longhurst, Mount Antarctica 152 H1
Long Island Bahamas 133 F8
Long Island N.S. Canada 123 I5
Long Island Nunavut Canada 122 F3
Long Island India 71 A4
Long Island P.N.G. 69 L8
Long Island U.S.A. 135 I3
Long Island Sound sea chan. U.S.A. 135 I3
Longjiang China 74 A3
Longjin China see Qingliu
Longju China 76 B2
Longlac Canada 122 D4
Long Lake l. Canada 122 D4
Long Lake U.S.A. 135 H2
Long Lake l. ME U.S.A. 132 G2
Long Lake l. MI U.S.A. 134 D1
Long Lake l. ND U.S.A. 130 C2
Long Lake l. NY U.S.A. 135 H1
Longli China 76 E3
Longlin China 76 E3
Longling China 76 C3
Longmeadow U.S.A. 135 I2
Long Melford U.K. 49 H6
Longmen Guangdong China 77 G4
Longmen Heilong. China 74 B2
Longmen Shan hill China 77 F1
Longmen Shan mts China 76 E1
Longming China 76 E4
Longmont U.S.A. 126 G4
Longnan China 77 G3
Long Phu Vietnam 71 D5
Longping China see Luodian
Long Point Ont. Canada 134 E2
Long Point Man. Canada 121 L4
Long Point Ont. Canada 134 E2
Long Point N.Z. 113 B8
Long Point Bay Canada 134 E2
Long Prairie U.S.A. 130 E2
Long Preston U.K. 48 E4
Longquan Guizhou China see Fenggang
Longquan Guizhou China see Danzhai
Longquan Hunan China see Xintian
Longquan Xi r. China 77 I2
Long Range Mountains Nfld. and Lab. Canada 123 K4
Long Range Mountains Nfld. and Lab. Canada 123 K5
Longreach Australia 110 D4
Longriba China 76 D1
Longshan Guizhou China see Longli
Longshan Hunan China 77 F2
Longshan Yunnan China see Longling
Long Shan mts China 76 E1
Longsheng China 77 F3
Longs Peak U.S.A. 126 G4
Long Stratton U.K. 49 I6
Longtom Lake Canada 120 G1
Longtown U.K. 48 E3
Longue-Pointe Canada 123 I4
Longueuil Canada 122 G5
Longuyon France 52 F5
Longvale U.S.A. 128 B2
Longview TX U.S.A. 131 E5
Longview WA U.S.A. 126 C3
Longwangmiao China 74 D3
Longwei Co l. China 83 G2
Longxi China 76 E1
Longxian Guangdong China see Wengyuan
Longxian Shaanxi China 76 E1
Longxingchang China see Wuyuan
Longxi Shan mt. China 77 H3
Longxu China see Cangwu
Long Xuyên Vietnam 71 D5
Longyan China 77 H3

▶Longyearbyen Svalbard 64 C2
Capital of Svalbard.

Longzhen China 74 B2
Longzhou China 76 E4
Longzhouping China see Changyang
Löningen Germany 53 H2
Lonoke U.S.A. 131 F5
Lönsboda Sweden 45 I8
Lons-le-Saunier France 56 G3
Lonton Myanmar 70 B1
Looc Phil. 69 G4
Loochoo Islands Japan see Ryukyu Islands
Loogootee U.S.A. 134 B4
Lookout, Cape Canada 122 E3
Lookout, Cape U.S.A. 133 E5
Lookout, Point Australia 112 F1
Lookout, Point U.S.A. 134 D1
Lookout Mountain U.S.A. 129 I4
Lookout Point Australia 109 B8
Loolmalasin vol. crater Tanz. 98 D4
Loon Canada 122 C4
Loon r. Canada 120 H3
Loongana Australia 109 D7
Loon Lake Canada 121 I4
Loop Head hd Rep. of Ireland 47 C5
Lop China 82 E1
Lopasnya Rus. Fed. see Chekhov
Lopatina, Gora mt. Rus. Fed. 74 F2
Lop Buri Thai. 70 C4
Lopez Phil. 69 G4
Lopez, Cap c. Gabon 98 A4
Lop Nur salt flat China 80 H3
Lopphavet b. Norway 44 L1
Loptyuga Rus. Fed. 42 K3
Lora Pak. 89 G5
Lora r. Venez. 142 D2
Lora del Río Spain 57 D5
Lorain U.S.A. 134 D3
Loralai Pak. 89 H4
Loralai r. Pak. 89 H4
Loramie, Lake U.S.A. 134 C3
Lorca Spain 57 F5
Lorch Germany 53 H4
Lordegān Iran 88 C4
Lord Howe Atoll Solomon Is see Ontong Java Atoll
Lord Howe Island Australia 107 F5
Lord Howe Rise sea feature S. Pacific Ocean 150 G7
Lord Loughborough Island Myanmar 71 B5
Lordsburg U.S.A. 129 I5
Lore East Timor 108 D2
Lore Lindu National Park Indon. 68 G7
Lorena Brazil 145 B3
Lorengau P.N.G. 69 L7
Loreto Brazil 143 I5
Loreto Mex. 127 F8
Lorient France 56 C3
Lorillard r. Canada 121 N1
Loring U.S.A. 126 G2
Lorn, Firth of est. U.K. 50 D4
Lorne Australia 110 D5
Lorne watercourse Australia 110 B3
Lorrain, Plateau France 53 G6
Lorraine Australia 110 B3
Lorraine admin. reg. France 52 G6
Lorraine reg. France 52 F5
Lorsch Germany 53 I5
Lorup Germany 53 H2
Losal India 82 C4
Los Alamitos, Sierra de mt. Mex. 131 C7
Los Alamos CA U.S.A. 128 C4
Los Alamos NM U.S.A. 127 G6
Los Alerces, Parque Nacional nat. park Arg. 144 B6
Los Ángeles Chile 144 B5

▶Los Angeles U.S.A. 128 D4
3rd most populous city in North America.

Los Angeles Aqueduct canal U.S.A. 128 D4
Los Arabos Cuba 133 D8
Los Banos U.S.A. 128 C3
Los Blancos Arg. 144 D2
Los Caballos Mesteños, Llano de plain Mex. 131 B6
Los Canarreos, Archipiélago de is Cuba 137 H4
Los Cerritos watercourse Mex. 127 F8
Los Chonos, Archipiélago de is Chile 144 A6
Los Coronados, Islas is Mex. 128 E5
Los Desventurados, Islas de is S. Pacific Ocean 151 O7
Los Estados, Isla de i. Arg. 140 D8
Los Gigantes, Llanos de plain Mex. 131 B6
Los Glaciares, Parque Nacional nat. park Arg. 144 B8
Losheim Germany 52 G5
Los Hoyos Mex. 127 F7
Lošinj i. Croatia 58 F2
Los Jardines de la Reina, Archipiélago de is Cuba 137 I4
Los Juríes Arg. 144 D3
Los Katios, Parque Nacional nat. park Col. 137 I7
Loskop Dam S. Africa 101 I3
Los Lunas U.S.A. 127 G6
Los Menucos Arg. 144 C6
Los Mexicanos, Lago de l. Mex. 127 G7
Los Mochis Mex. 127 F8
Los Molinos U.S.A. 128 B1
Los Mosquitos, Golfo de b. Panama 137 H7
Losombo Dem. Rep. Congo 98 B3
Los Palacios Cuba 133 D8
Los Picos de Europa, Parque Nacional de nat. park Spain 57 D2
Los Remedios r. Mex. 131 B7
Los Roques, Islas is Venez. 142 E1
Losser Neth. 52 G2
Lossie r. U.K. 50 F3
Lossiemouth U.K. 50 F3
Lößnitz Germany 53 M4
Lost Creek KY U.S.A. 134 D5
Lost Creek WV U.S.A. 134 E4
Los Teques Venez. 142 E1
Los Testigos is Venez. 142 F1
Lost Hills U.S.A. 128 D4
Lost Trail Pass U.S.A. 126 E3
Lostwithiel U.K. 49 C8
Los Vidrios Mex. 129 G6
Los Vilos Chile 144 B4
Lot r. France 56 E4
Lota Chile 144 B5
Lotfābād Turkm. 88 E2
Lothringen reg. France see Lorraine
Lotikipi Plain Kenya/Sudan 98 D3
Loto Dem. Rep. Congo 98 C4
Lotsane r. Botswana 101 I2
Lot's Wife i. Japan see Sōfu-gan
Lotta r. Fin./Rus. Fed. 44 Q2
also known as Lutto
Lotte Germany 53 H2
Louang Namtha Laos 70 C2
Louangphrabang Laos 70 C3
Loubomo Congo 99 B4
Loudéac France 56 C2
Loudi China 77 F3
L'Ouest, Pointe de pt Canada 123 I4
Louga Senegal 96 B3
Loughborough U.K. 49 F6
Lougheed Island Canada 119 H2
Loughor r. U.K. 49 C7
Loughrea Rep. of Ireland 51 D4
Loughton U.K. 49 H7
Louhans France 56 G3
Louisa KY U.S.A. 134 D4
Louisa VA U.S.A. 135 G4
Louisbourg Canada 123 K5
Louisburg Canada see Louisbourg
Louisburgh Rep. of Ireland 51 C4
Louise Falls Canada 120 G2
Louis-Gentil Morocco see Youssoufia
Louisiade Archipelago is P.N.G. 110 F1
Louisiana U.S.A. 130 F4
Louisiana state U.S.A. 131 F6
Louis Trichardt S. Africa 101 I2
Louisville GA U.S.A. 133 D5
Louisville IL U.S.A. 130 F4
Louisville KY U.S.A. 134 C4
Louisville MS U.S.A. 131 F5
Louisville Ridge sea feature S. Pacific Ocean 150 I8
Louis-XIV, Pointe pt Canada 122 F3
Loukhi Rus. Fed. 44 R3
Loukoléla Congo 98 B4
Loukouo Congo 97 E5
Loulé Port. 57 B5
Loum Cameroon 96 D4
Louny Czech Rep. 47 N5
Loup r. U.S.A. 130 D3
Loups-Marins, Lacs des lakes Canada 122 G2
Loups-Marins, Petit lac des l. Canada 123 G2
L'Our, Vallée de valley Germany/Lux. 52 G5
Lourdes Canada 123 K4
Lourdes France 56 D5
Lourenço Marques Moz. see Maputo
Lousã Port. 57 B3
Loushan China 74 C3
Loushanguan China see Tongzi
Louth Australia 112 B3
Louth U.K. 48 G5
Loutra Aidipsou Greece 59 J5
Louvain Belgium see Leuven
Louviers France 52 B5
Louwater-Suid Namibia 100 C2
Louwsburg S. Africa 101 J4
Lövånger Sweden 44 L4
Lovat' r. Rus. Fed. 42 F4
Lovech Bulg. 59 K3
Lovell U.S.A. 135 J1
Lovelock U.S.A. 128 D1
Lovendegem Belgium 52 D3
Lovers' Leap mt. U.S.A. 134 E5
Loviisa Fin. 45 O6
Lovington U.S.A. 131 C5
Lovozero Rus. Fed. 42 G1
Lóvua Angola 99 C4
Lóvua Angola 99 C5
Low, Cape Canada 119 J3
Lowa Dem. Rep. Congo 98 C4
Lowa r. Dem. Rep. Congo 98 C4
Lowarai Pass Pak. 89 H3
Lowell IN U.S.A. 134 B3
Lowell MA U.S.A. 135 J2
Lower Arrow Lake Canada 120 G5
Lower California pen. Mex. see Baja California
Lower Glenelg National Park Australia 111 C8
Lower Granite Gorge U.S.A. 129 G4
Lower Hutt N.Z. 113 E5
Lower Laberge Canada 120 C2
Lower Lake U.S.A. 128 B2
Lower Lough Erne l. U.K. 51 E3
Lower Post Canada 120 D3
Lower Red Lake U.S.A. 130 E2
Lower Saxony land Germany see Niedersachsen
Lower Tunguska r. Rus. Fed. see Nizhnyaya Tunguska
Lower Zambezi National Park Zambia 99 C5
Lowestoft U.K. 49 I6
Łowicz Poland 47 Q4
Low Island Kiribati see Starbuck Island
Lowkhi Afgh. 89 F4
Lowther Hills U.K. 50 F5
Lowville U.S.A. 135 H2
Loxstedt Germany 53 I1
Loxton Australia 111 C7
Loyal, Loch l. U.K. 50 E2
Loyalsock Creek r. U.S.A. 135 G3
Loyalton U.S.A. 128 C2

Loyalty Islands New Caledonia see Loyauté, Îles
Loyang China see Luoyang
Loyauté, Îles is New Caledonia 107 G4
Loyev Belarus see Loyew
Loyew Belarus 43 F6
Lozère, Mont mt. France 56 F4
Loznica Serb. and Mont. 59 H2
Lozova Ukr. 43 H6
Lozovaya Ukr. see Lozova
Lua r. Dem. Rep. Congo 98 B3
Luacano Angola 99 C5
Lu'an China 77 H2
Luân Châu Vietnam 70 C2
Luanchuan China 77 F1

▶Luanda Angola 99 B4
Capital of Angola.

Luang, Khao mt. Thai. 71 B5
Luang, Thale lag. Thai. 71 C6
Luang Namtha Laos see Louang Namtha
Luang Phrabang, Thiu Khao mts Laos/Thai. 70 C3
Luang Prabang Laos see Louangphrabang
Luanhaizi China 76 B1
Luanshya Zambia 99 C5
Luanza Dem. Rep. Congo 99 C4
Luao Angola see Luau
Luarca Spain 57 C2
Luashi Dem. Rep. Congo 99 C5
Luau Angola 99 C5
Luba Equat. Guinea 96 D4
Lubaczów Poland 43 D6
Lubalo Angola 99 B4
Lubānas ezers l. Latvia 45 O8
Lubang Islands Phil. 68 F4
Lubango Angola 99 B5
Lubao Dem. Rep. Congo 99 C4
Lubartów Poland 43 D6
Lübbecke Germany 53 I2
Lubbeskolk salt pan S. Africa 100 D5
Lubbock U.S.A. 131 C5
Lübbow Germany 53 L2
Lübeck Germany 47 M4
Lubeck U.S.A. 134 E4
Lubefu Dem. Rep. Congo 99 C4
Lubei China 73 M4
Lüben Poland see Lubin
Lubersac France 56 E4
Lubin Poland 47 P5
Lublin Poland 43 D6
Lubnān country Asia see Lebanon
Lubnān, Jabal mts Lebanon see Liban, Jebel
Lubny Ukr. 43 G6
Lubok Antu Sarawak Malaysia 64 E6
Lübtheen Germany 53 L1
Lubudi Dem. Rep. Congo 99 C4
Lubuklinggau Indon. 68 C7
Lubukpakam Indon. 71 B7
Lubuksikaping Indon. 68 C6
Lubumbashi Dem. Rep. Congo 99 C5
Lubutu Dem. Rep. Congo 98 C4
Lübz Germany 53 M1
Lucala Angola 99 B4
Lucan Canada 134 E2
Lucan Rep. of Ireland 51 F4
Lucania, Mount Canada 120 A2
Lucapa Angola 99 C4
Lucas U.S.A. 134 B5
Lucasville U.S.A. 134 D4
Lucca Italy 58 D3
Luce Bay U.K. 50 E6
Lucedale U.S.A. 131 F6
Lucélia Brazil 145 A3
Lucena Phil. 69 G4
Lucena Spain 57 D5
Lučenec Slovakia 47 Q6
Lucera Italy 58 F4
Lucerne Switz. 56 I3
Lucerne Valley U.S.A. 128 E4
Lucero Mex. 127 G7
Luchegorsk Rus. Fed. 74 D3
Lucheng Guangxi China see Luchuan
Lucheng Sichuan China see Kangding
Luchuan China 77 F4
Lüchun China 76 D4
Lucipara, Kepulauan is Indon. 69 H8
Łuck Ukr. see Luts'k
Luckeesarai India see Lakhisarai
Luckenwalde Germany 53 N2
Luckhoff S. Africa 100 G5
Lucknow Canada 134 E2
Lucknow India 82 E4
Lücongpo China 77 F2
Lucrecia, Cabo c. Cuba 137 I4
Lucusse Angola 99 C5
Lucy Creek Australia 110 B4
Lüda China see Dalian
Lüdenscheid Germany 53 H3
Lüderitz Namibia 100 B4
Ludewa Tanz. 99 D5
Ludhiana India 82 C3
Ludian China 76 D3
Luding China 76 D2
Ludington U.S.A. 134 B2
Ludlow U.K. 49 E6
Ludlow U.S.A. 128 E4
Ludogorie reg. Bulg. 59 L3
Ludowici U.S.A. 133 D6
Ludvika Sweden 45 I6
Ludwigsburg Germany 53 J6
Ludwigsfelde Germany 53 N2
Ludwigshafen am Rhein Germany 53 I5
Ludwigslust Germany 53 L1
Ludza Latvia 45 O8
Luebo Dem. Rep. Congo 99 C4
Luena Angola 99 B5
Luena Flats plain Zambia 99 C5
Lüeyang China 76 E1
Lufeng Guangdong China 77 G4
Lufeng Yunnan China 76 D3
Lufkin U.S.A. 131 E6
Lufu China see Shilin
Luga Rus. Fed. 45 P7
Luga r. Rus. Fed. 45 P7
Lugano Switz. 56 I3
Lugansk Ukr. see Luhans'k
Lugau Germany 53 M4
Lügde Germany 53 J3
Lugdunum France see Lyon
Lugg r. U.K. 49 E6
Luggudontsen mt. China 83 G3
Lugo Italy 58 D2
Lugo Spain 57 C2
Lugoj Romania 59 I2
Luhans'k Ukr. 43 H6
Luhe China 77 H1
Luhe r. Germany 53 K1
Luḥfī, Wādī watercourse Jordan 85 C3
Luhit r. China/India see Zayü Qu
Luhit r. India 83 H4
Luhua China see Heishui
Luhuo China 76 D2
Luhyny Ukr. 43 F6
Luia Angola 99 C4
Luiana Angola 99 C5
Luichow Peninsula China see Leizhou Bandao
Luik Belgium see Liège
Luimneach Rep. of Ireland see Limerick
Luiro r. Fin. 44 O3
Luis Echeverría Álvarez Mex. 128 E5
Luitpold Coast Antarctica 152 A1
Luiza Dem. Rep. Congo 99 C4
Lujiang China 77 H2
Lüjing China 76 E1
Lukackek Rus. Fed. 74 D1
Lukapa Angola see Lucapa
Lukavac Bos.-Herz. 58 H2
Lukenga, Lac l. Dem. Rep. Congo 99 C4
Lukenie r. Dem. Rep. Congo 98 B4
Lukh r. Rus. Fed. 42 I4
Lukhovitsy Rus. Fed. 43 H5
Luk Keng Hong Kong China 77 [inset]
Lukou China see Zhuzhou
Lukovit Bulg. 59 K3
Łuków Poland 43 D6
Lukoyanov Rus. Fed. 43 J5
Lukusuzi National Park Zambia 99 D5
Luleå Sweden 44 M4
Luleälven r. Sweden 44 M4
Lüleburgaz Turkey 59 L4
Luliang China 76 D3
Lüliang Shan mts China 73 K5
Lulimba Dem. Rep. Congo 99 C4
Luling U.S.A. 131 D6
Lulonga r. Dem. Rep. Congo 98 B3
Luluabourg Dem. Rep. Congo see Kananga
Lülung China 83 F3
Lumachomo China 83 F3
Lumajang Indon. 68 E8
Lumajangdong Co salt l. China 82 E2
Lumbala Moxico Angola see Lumbala Kaquengue
Lumbala Moxico Angola see Lumbala N'guimbo
Lumbala Kaquengue Angola 99 C5
Lumbala N'guimbo Angola 99 C5
Lumberton U.S.A. 133 E5
Lumbini Nepal 83 E4
Lumbis Indon. 68 F6
Lumbrales Spain 57 C3
Lumezzane Italy 58 D2
Lumi P.N.G. 69 K7
Lumphăt Cambodia 71 D4
Lumpkin U.S.A. 133 C5
Lumsden Canada 121 J5
Lumsden N.Z. 113 B7
Lumut Malaysia 71 C6
Lumut, Tanjung pt Indon. 68 D7
Luna U.S.A. 129 I5
Lunan China see Shilin
Lunan Bay U.K. 50 G4
Lunan Lake Canada 121 M1
Lunan Shan mts China 76 D3
Luna Pier U.S.A. 134 D3
Lund Pak. 89 H5
Lund Sweden 45 H9
Lund NV U.S.A. 129 F2
Lund UT U.S.A. 129 G2
Lundar Canada 121 L5
Lundy Island U.K. 49 C7
Lune r. Germany 53 I1
Lune r. U.K. 48 E4
Lüneburg Germany 53 K1
Lüneburger Heide reg. Germany 53 K1
Lünen Germany 53 H3
Lunenburg U.S.A. 135 F5
Lunéville France 56 H2
Lunga r. Zambia 99 C5
Lungdo China 83 E2
Lunggar China 83 E3
Lung Kwu Chau i. Hong Kong China 77 [inset]
Lungleh India see Lunglei
Lunglei India 83 H5
Lungmari mt. China 83 F3
Lungmu Co salt l. China 82 E2
Lungnaquilla Mountain hill Rep. of Ireland 51 F5
Lungwebungu r. Zambia 99 C5
Lunh Nepal 83 E3
Luni India 82 C4
Luni r. India 82 B4
Luni r. Pak. 89 H4
Luninets Belarus see Luninyets
Luning U.S.A. 128 D2
Luninyets Belarus 45 O10
Lunkaransar India 82 C3
Lunkha India 82 C3
Lünne Germany 53 H2
Lunsar Sierra Leone 96 B4
Lunsklip S. Africa 101 I3
Luntai China 80 F3
Luobei China 74 C3
Luobuzhuang China 80 G4
Luocheng Fujian China see Hui'an
Luocheng Guangxi China 77 F3
Luodian China 76 E3
Luoding China 77 F4
Luodou Sha i. China 77 F4
Luohe China 77 G1
Luo He r. China 77 G1
Luonan China 77 F1
Luoning China 77 F1
Luoping China 76 E3
Luotian China 77 G2
Luoto Fin. 44 M5
Luoxiao Shan mts China 77 G3
Luoxiong China see Luoping
Luoyang Guangdong China see Boluo
Luoyang Henan China 77 G1
Luoyang Zhejiang China see Taishun
Luoyuan China 77 H3
Luozigou China 74 C4
Lupane Zimbabwe 99 C5
Lupanshui China 76 E3
L'Upemba, Parc National de nat. park Dem. Rep. Congo 99 C4
Lupeni Romania 59 J2
Lupilichi Moz. 99 D5
Lupton U.S.A. 129 I4
Luqiao China see Luding
Luqu China 76 D1
Lu Qu r. China see Tao He
Luquan China 70 C1
Luray U.S.A. 135 F4
Luremo Angola 99 B4
Lurgan U.K. 51 F3
Luring China see Oma
Lúrio Moz. 99 E5
Lurio r. Moz. 99 E5

▶Lusaka Zambia 99 C5
Capital of Zambia.

Lusambo Dem. Rep. Congo 99 C4
Lusancay Islands and Reefs P.N.G. 106 F2
Lusangi Dem. Rep. Congo 99 C4
Luseland Canada 121 I4
Lush, Mount hill Australia 108 D4
Lushi China 77 F1
Lushnja Albania see Lushnjë
Lushnjë Albania 59 H4
Lushui China 76 C3
Lushuihe China 74 B4
Lüsi China 77 I1
Lusikisiki S. Africa 101 I6
Lusk U.S.A. 126 G4
Luso Angola see Luena
Lussvale Australia 112 C1
Lut, Bahrat salt l. Asia see Dead Sea
Lut, Dasht-e des. Iran 88 E4
Lü Tao i. Taiwan 77 I4
Lutetia France see Paris
Lüt-e Zangī Aḥmad des. Iran 88 E4
Luther U.S.A. 134 C1
Luther Lake Canada 134 E2
Lutherstadt Wittenberg Germany 53 M3
Luton U.K. 49 G7
Łutselk'e Canada 121 I2
Luts'k Ukr. 43 E6
Luttelgeest Neth. 52 F2
Luttenberg Neth. 52 G2
Lutto r. Fin./Rus. Fed. see Lotta
Lutz U.S.A. 133 D6
Lützelbach Germany 53 J5
Lützow-Holm Bay Antarctica 152 D2
Lutzputs S. Africa 100 E5
Lutzville S. Africa 100 D6
Luumäki Fin. 45 O6
Luuq Somalia 98 E3
Luverne AL U.S.A. 133 C6
Luverne MN U.S.A. 130 D3
Luvuei Angola 99 C5
Luvuvhu r. S. Africa 101 J2
Luwero Uganda 98 D3
Luwingu Zambia 99 C5
Luwuk Indon. 69 G7
▶Luxembourg country Europe 52 G5
Europe 5, 38–39

▶Luxembourg Lux. 52 G5
Capital of Luxembourg.

Luxemburg country Europe see Luxembourg
Luxeuil-les-Bains France 56 H3
Luxi Hunan China 77 F2
Luxi Yunnan China 76 C3
Luxi Yunnan China 76 D3
Luxolweni S. Africa 101 G6
Luxor Egypt 86 D4
Luyi China 77 G1
Luyksgestel Neth. 52 F3
Luza Rus. Fed. 42 J3
Luza r. Rus. Fed. 42 J3
Luza r. Rus. Fed. 42 M2
Luzern Switz. see Lucerne
Luzhai China 77 F3
Luzhang China see Lushui
Luzhi China 76 E3
Luzhou China 76 E2
Luziânia Brazil 145 B2
Luzon i. Phil. 69 G3
Luzon Strait Phil. 69 G2
Luzy France 56 F3
L'viv Ukr. 43 E6
L'vov Ukr. see L'viv
Lwów Ukr. see L'viv
Lyady Rus. Fed. 45 P7
Lyakhavichy Belarus 45 O10
Lyakhovichi Belarus see Lyakhavichy
Lyallpur Pak. see Faisalabad
Lyamtsa Rus. Fed. 42 H2
Lycia reg. Turkey 59 M6
Lyck Poland see Ełk
Lycksele Sweden 44 K4
Lycopolis Egypt see Asyūţ
Lydd U.K. 49 H8
Lydda Israel see Lod
Lyddan Island Antarctica 152 B2
Lydenburg S. Africa 101 J3
Lydia reg. Turkey 59 L5
Lydney U.K. 49 E7
Lyel'chytsy Belarus 43 F6
Lyell, Mount U.S.A. 128 D3
Lyell Brown, Mount hill Australia 109 E5
Lyell Island Canada 120 D4
Lyepyel' Belarus 45 P9
Lykens U.S.A. 135 G3
Lyman U.S.A. 126 F4
Lyme Bay U.K. 49 E8
Lyme Regis U.K. 49 E8
Lymington U.K. 49 F8
Lynchburg OH U.S.A. 134 D4
Lynchburg TN U.S.A. 132 C5
Lynchburg VA U.S.A. 134 F5
Lynchville U.S.A. 135 J1
Lyndhurst N.S.W. Australia 112 D4
Lyndhurst Qld Australia 110 D3
Lyndhurst S.A. Australia 111 B6
Lyndon Australia 109 A5
Lyndon r. Australia 109 A5
Lyndonville U.S.A. 135 I1
Lyne r. U.K. 48 D4
Lyness U.K. 50 F2
Lyngdal Norway 45 E7
Lynn U.K. see King's Lynn
Lynn IN U.S.A. 134 C3
Lynn MA U.S.A. 135 J2
Lynndyl U.S.A. 129 G2
Lynn Lake Canada 121 K3
Lynton U.K. 49 D7
Lynx Lake Canada 121 J2
Lyon France 56 G4
Lyon r. U.K. 50 F4
Lyon Mountain U.S.A. 135 I1
Lyons Australia 109 F7
Lyons France see Lyon
Lyons GA U.S.A. 133 D5
Lyons NY U.S.A. 135 G2
Lyons Falls U.S.A. 135 H2
Lyozna Belarus 43 F5
Lyra Reef P.N.G. 106 F2
Lys r. France 52 D4
Lysekil Sweden 45 G7
Lyskovo Rus. Fed. 42 J4
Lys'va Rus. Fed. 41 R4
Lysychans'k Ukr. 43 H6
Lysyye Gory Rus. Fed. 43 J6
Lytham St Anne's U.K. 48 D5
Lytton Canada 120 F5
Lyuban' Belarus 45 P10
Lyubertsy Rus. Fed. 41 N4
Lyubeshiv Ukr. 43 E6
Lyubim Rus. Fed. 42 I4
Lyubytino Rus. Fed. 42 G4
Lyudinovo Rus. Fed. 43 G5
Lyunda r. Rus. Fed. 42 J4
Lyzha r. Rus. Fed. 42 M2

M

Ma r. Myanmar 70 B2
Ma, Nam r. Laos 70 C2
Ma'agan Israel 85 B3
Maale Maldives see Male
Maale Atholhu atoll Maldives see Male Atoll
Maalhosmadulu Atholhu Uthuruburi atoll Maldives see North Maalhosmadulu Atoll
Maalhosmadulu Atoll Maldives 84 B5
Ma'ān Jordan 85 B4
Maan Turkey see Nusratiye
Maaninka Fin. 44 O5
Maaninkavaara Fin. 44 P3
Ma'anshan China 77 H2
Maardu Estonia 45 N7
Maarianhamina Fin. see Mariehamn
Ma'arrat an Nu'mān Syria 85 C2
Maarssen Neth. 52 F2
Maas r. Neth. 52 E3
also known as Meuse (Belgium/France)
Maaseik Belgium 52 F3
Maasin Phil. 69 G4
Maasmechelen Belgium 52 F4
Maas-Schwalm-Nette nat. park Germany/Neth. 52 F3
Maastricht Neth. 52 F4
Maaza Plateau Egypt 90 C6
Maba Guangdong China see Qujiang
Maba Jiangsu China 77 H1
Mabai China see Maguan
Mabalane Moz. 101 K2
Mabana Dem. Rep. Congo 98 C3
Mabaruma Guyana 142 G2
Mabein Myanmar 70 B2
Mabel Creek Australia 109 F7
Mabel Downs Australia 108 D4
Mabella Canada 122 C4
Mabel Lake Canada 120 G5
Maberly Canada 135 G1
Mabian China 76 D2
Mablethorpe U.K. 48 H5
Mabopane S. Africa 101 I3
Mabote Moz. 101 L2
Mabou Canada 123 J5
Mabrak, Jabal mt. Jordan 85 B4
Mabuasehube Game Reserve nature res. Botswana 100 F3
Mabule Botswana 100 G3
Mabutsane Botswana 100 F3
Macá, Monte mt. Chile 144 B7
Macadam Plains Australia 109 B6
Macaé Brazil 145 C3
Macajuba Brazil 145 C1
Macaloge Moz. 99 D5
MacAlpine Lake Canada 119 H3
Macamic Canada 122 F4
Macandze Moz. 101 K2
Macao China see Macau
Macao aut. reg. China see Macau
Macapá Brazil 143 H3
Macará Ecuador 142 C4
Macarani Brazil 145 C1
Macas Ecuador 142 C4
Macassar Indon. see Makassar
Macau Brazil 143 K5
Macau China 77 G4
Macau aut. reg. China 77 G4
Macaúba Brazil 143 H6
Macauley Island N.Z. 107 I5
Macau Special Administrative Region aut. reg. China see Macau
Maccaretane Moz. 101 K3
Macclenny U.S.A. 133 D6
Macclesfield U.K. 48 E5
Macdiarmid Canada 122 C4
Macdonald, Lake salt flat Australia 109 E5
Macdonald Range hills Australia 108 D3
Macdonnell Ranges mts Australia 109 E5
MacDowell Lake Canada 121 M4
Macduff U.K. 50 G3
Macedo de Cavaleiros Port. 57 C3
Macedon mt. Australia 112 B6
Macedon country Europe see Macedonia
▶Macedonia country Europe 59 I4
Europe 5, 38–39
Maceió Brazil 143 K5
Macenta Guinea 96 C4
Macerata Italy 58 E3
Macfarlane, Lake salt flat Australia 111 B7
Macgillycuddy's Reeks mts Rep. of Ireland 51 C6
Machachi Ecuador 142 C4
Machaila Moz. 101 K2
Machakos Kenya 98 D4
Machala Ecuador 142 C4
Machali China see Madoi
Machanga Moz. 99 D6
Machar Marshes Sudan 86 D8
Machattie, Lake salt flat Australia 110 B5
Machatuine Moz. 101 K3
Machault France 52 E5
Machaze Moz. see Chitobe
Macheng China 77 G2
Macherla India 84 C2
Machhagan India 83 F5
Machias ME U.S.A. 132 H2
Machias NY U.S.A. 135 F2
Machilipatnam India 84 D2
Machiques Venez. 142 D1
Māch Kowr Iran 89 F5
Machrihanish U.K. 50 D5
Machu Picchu tourist site Peru 142 D6
Machynlleth U.K. 49 D6
Macia Moz. 101 K3
Macias Nguema i. Equat. Guinea see Bioco
Măcin Romania 59 M2
Macintyre r. Australia 112 E2
Macintyre Brook r. Australia 112 E2
Mack U.S.A. 129 I2
Maçka Turkey 91 E2
Mackay Australia 110 E4
MacKay r. Canada 121 I3
Mackay U.S.A. 126 E3
Mackay, Lake salt flat Australia 108 E5
MacKay Lake Canada 121 I2
Mackenzie r. Australia 110 E4
Mackenzie Canada 120 F4
Mackenzie r. Canada 120 F2
Mackenzie Guyana see Linden
Mackenzie atoll Micronesia see Ulithi
Mackenzie Bay Antarctica 152 E2
Mackenzie Bay Canada 118 E3
Mackenzie Highway Canada 120 G2
Mackenzie King Island Canada 119 G2
Mackenzie Mountains Canada 120 C1

▶Mackenzie-Peace-Finlay r. Canada 118 E3
2nd longest river in North America.

Mackillop, Lake salt flat Australia see Yamma Yamma, Lake
Mackintosh Range hills Australia 109 D6
Macklin Canada 121 I4
Macksville Australia 112 F3
Maclean Australia 112 F2
Maclear S. Africa 101 I6
MacLeod Canada see Fort Macleod
MacLeod, Lake imp. l. Australia 109 A6
Macmillan r. Canada 120 C2
Macmillan Pass Canada 120 D2
Macomb U.S.A. 130 F3
Macomer Sardinia Italy 58 C4
Mâcon France 56 G3
Macon GA U.S.A. 133 D5
Macon MO U.S.A. 130 E4
Macon MS U.S.A. 131 F5
Macon OH U.S.A. 134 D4
Macondo Angola 99 C5
Macoun Lake Canada 121 K3
Macpherson Robertson Land reg. Antarctica see Mac. Robertson Land
Macpherson's Strait India 71 A5
Macquarie r. Australia 112 C3
Macquarie, Lake b. Australia 112 E4

▶Macquarie Island S. Pacific Ocean 150 G9
Part of Australia. Most southerly point of Oceania.

Macquarie Marshes Australia 112 C3
Macquarie Mountain Australia 112 D4
Macquarie Ridge sea feature S. Pacific Ocean 150 G9
MacRitchie Reservoir Sing. 71 [inset]
Mac. Robertson Land reg. Antarctica 152 E2
Macroom Rep. of Ireland 51 D6
Macumba Australia 111 A5
Macumba watercourse Australia 111 B5
Macuzari, Presa resr Mex. 127 F8
Mādabā Jordan 85 B4
Madadeni S. Africa 101 J4

▶Madagascar country Africa 99 E6
Largest island in Africa and 4th in the world.
Africa 7, 92–93, 94–95
World 12–13

Madagascar Basin sea feature Indian Ocean 149 L7
Madagascar Ridge sea feature Indian Ocean 149 K8
Madagasikara country Africa see Madagascar
Madakasira India 84 C3
Madama Niger 97 E2
Madan Bulg. 59 K4
Madanapalle India 84 C3
Madang P.N.G. 69 L8
Madaoua Niger 96 D3
Madaripur Bangl. 83 G5
Madau Turkm. 88 D2
Madaw Turkm. see Madau
Madawaska Canada 135 G1
Madawaska r. Canada 135 G1
Madaya Myanmar 70 B2
Madded India 84 D2

▶Madeira r. Brazil 142 G4
4th longest river in South America.

▶Madeira terr. N. Atlantic Ocean 96 B1
Autonomous Region of Portugal.
Africa 7, 94–95

Madeira, Arquipélago da terr. N. Atlantic Ocean see Madeira
Maden Turkey 91 E3
Madera Mex. 127 F7
Madera U.S.A. 128 C3
Madgaon India 84 B3
Madha India 84 B2
Madhavpur India 82 B5
Madhepura India 83 F4
Madhipura India see Madhepura
Madhubani India 83 F4
Madhya Pradesh state India 82 D5
Madibogo S. Africa 101 G4
Madidi r. Bol. 142 E6
Madikeri India 84 B3
Madikwe Game Reserve nature res. S. Africa 101 H3
Madill U.S.A. 131 D5
Madīnat ath Thawrah Syria 85 D2
Madingo-Kayes Congo 99 B4
Madingou Congo 99 B4
Madison FL U.S.A. 133 D6
Madison GA U.S.A. 133 D5
Madison IN U.S.A. 134 C4
Madison ME U.S.A. 135 K1
Madison NE U.S.A. 130 D3
Madison SD U.S.A. 130 D2
Madison VA U.S.A. 135 F4

▶Madison WI U.S.A. 130 F3
State capital of Wisconsin.

Madison WV U.S.A. 134 E4
Madison r. U.S.A. 126 F3
Madison Heights U.S.A. 134 F5
Madisonville KY U.S.A. 134 B5
Madisonville TX U.S.A. 131 E6
Madiun Indon. 68 E8
Madley, Mount hill Australia 109 C6
Madoc Canada 135 G1
Mado Gashi Kenya 98 D3
Madoi China 76 C1
Madona Latvia 45 O8
Madpura India 82 B4
Madra Dağı mts Turkey 59 L5
Madrakah Saudi Arabia 86 E5
Madrakah, Ra's c. Oman 87 I6
Madras India see Chennai
Madras state India see Tamil Nadu
Madras U.S.A. 126 C3
Madre, Laguna lag. Mex. 131 D7
Madre, Laguna lag. U.S.A. 131 D7
Madre de Dios r. Peru 142 E6
Madre de Dios, Isla i. Chile 144 A8
Madre del Sur, Sierra mts Mex. 136 D5
Madre Mountain U.S.A. 129 J4
Madre Occidental, Sierra mts Mex. 127 F7
Madre Oriental, Sierra mts Mex. 131 C7

▶Madrid Spain 57 E3
Capital of Spain.

Madridejos Spain 57 E4
Madruga Cuba 133 D8
Madugula India 84 D2
Madura i. Indon. 68 E8
Madura, Selat sea chan. Indon. 68 E8
Madurai India 84 C4
Madurantakam India 84 C3
Madvār, Kūh-e mt. Iran 88 D4
Madvezh'ya vol. Rus. Fed. 74 H3
Madwas India 83 E4
Maé i. Vanuatu see Émaé
Maebashi Japan 75 E5
Mae Hong Son Thai. 70 B3
Mae Ping National Park Thai. 70 B3
Mae Ramat Thai. 70 B3
Mae Sai Thai. 70 B2
Mae Sariang Thai. 70 B3
Mae Sot Thai. 70 B3
Mae Suai Thai. 70 B3
Mae Tuen Wildlife Reserve nature res. Thai. 70 B3
Maevatanana Madag. 99 E5
Maéwo i. Vanuatu 107 G3
Mae Wong National Park Thai. 70 B4
Mae Yom National Park Thai. 70 C3
Mafeking Canada 121 K4
Mafeking S. Africa see Mafikeng
Mafeteng Lesotho 101 H5
Maffra Australia 112 C6
Mafia Island Tanz. 99 D4
Mafikeng S. Africa 101 G3
Mafinga Tanz. 99 D4
Mafra Brazil 145 A4
Mafraq Jordan see Al Mafraq
Magabeni S. Africa 101 J6
Magadan Rus. Fed. 65 Q4
Magadi Kenya 98 D4
Magaiza Moz. 101 K2
Magallanes Chile see Punta Arenas
Magallanes, Estrecho de Chile see Magellan, Strait of
Magangue Col. 142 D2
Mağara Dağı mt. Turkey 85 A1
Magaramkent Rus. Fed. 91 H2
Magaria Niger 96 D3
Magarida P.N.G. 110 E1
Magas Rus. Fed. 91 G2
Magazine Mountain hill U.S.A. 131 E5
Magdagachi Rus. Fed. 74 B1
Magdalena Bol. 142 F6
Magdalena r. Col. 142 D1
Magdalena Baja California Sur Mex. 127 E8
Magdalena Sonora Mex. 127 F7
Magdalena r. Mex. 127 F7
Magdalena, Bahía b. Mex. 136 B4
Magdalena, Isla i. Chile 144 B6
Magdeburg Germany 53 L2
Magdelaine Cays atoll Australia 110 E3

Magellan, Strait of Chile 144 B8
Magellan Seamounts sea feature N. Pacific Ocean 150 F4
Magenta, Lake salt flat Australia 109 B8
Magerøya i. Norway 44 N1
Maggiorasca, Monte mt. Italy 58 C2
Maggiore, Lago Italy see Maggiore, Lake
Maggiore, Lake Italy 58 C2
Maghâgha Egypt see Maghāghah
Maghāghah Egypt 90 C5
Maghama Mauritania 96 B3
Maghâra, Gebel hill Egypt see Maghārah, Jabal
Maghārah, Jabal hill Egypt 85 A4
Maghera U.K. 51 F3
Magherafelt U.K. 51 F3
Maghnia Alg. 57 F6
Maghor Afgh. 89 F3
Maghull U.K. 48 E5
Magilligan Point U.K. 51 F2
Magma U.S.A. 129 H5
Magna Grande mt. Sicily Italy 58 F6
Magnetic Island Australia 110 D3
Magnetic Passage Australia 110 D3
Magnetity Rus. Fed. 44 R2
Magnitogorsk Rus. Fed. 64 G4
Magnolia AR U.S.A. 131 E5
Magnolia MS U.S.A. 131 F6
Magny-en-Vexin France 52 B5
Mago Rus. Fed. 74 F1
Màgoé Moz. 99 D5
Magog Canada 135 I1
Mago National Park Eth. 98 D3
Magosa Cyprus see Famagusta
Magpie r. Canada 123 I4
Magpie, Lac l. Canada 123 I4
Magṭa' Lahjar Mauritania 96 B3
Magu Tanz. 98 D4
Magu, Khrebet mts Rus. Fed. 74 E1
Maguan China 76 E4
Magude Moz. 101 K3
Magueyal Mex. 131 C7
Magura Bangl. 83 G5
Maguse Lake Canada 121 M2
Magway Myanmar see Magwe
Magwe Myanmar 70 A2
Magyar Köztársaság country Europe see Hungary
Magyichaung Myanmar 70 A2
Mahābād Iran 88 B2
Mahabharat Range mts Nepal 83 F4
Mahaboobnagar India see Mahbubnagar
Mahad India 84 B2
Mahadeo Hills India 82 D5
Mahaffey U.S.A. 135 F3
Mahajan India 82 C3
Mahajanga Madag. 99 E5
Mahakam r. Indon. 68 F7
Mahalapye Botswana 101 H2
Mahale Mountains National Park Tanz. 99 C4
Mahalevona Madag. 99 E5
Mahallāt Iran 88 C3
Māhān Iran 88 E4
Mahanadi r. India 84 E1
Mahanoro Madag. 99 E5
Maha Oya Sri Lanka 84 D5
Maharashtra state India 84 B2
Maha Sarakham Thai. 70 C3
Mahasham, Wâdi el watercourse Egypt see Muhashsham, Wādī al
Mahaxai Laos 70 D3
Mahbubabad India 84 D2
Mahbubnagar India 84 C2
Mahd adh Dhahab Saudi Arabia 86 F5
Mahdia Alg. 57 G6
Mahdia Guyana 143 G2
Mahdia Tunisia 58 D7
Mahe China 76 E1
Mahé i. Seychelles 149 L6
Mahendragiri mt. India 84 E2
Mahenge Tanz. 99 D4
Mahesana India 82 C5
Mahi r. India 82 C5
Mahia Peninsula N.Z. 113 F4
Mahilyow Belarus 43 F5
Mahim India 84 B2
Mah Jān Iran 88 D4
Mahlabatini S. Africa 101 J5
Mahlsdorf Germany 53 L2
Mahmudabad Iran 88 D2
Maḥmūd-e 'Erāqī Afgh. see Maḥmūd-e Rāqī
Maḥmūd-e Rāqī Afgh. 89 H3
Mahnomen U.S.A. 130 D2
Maho Sri Lanka 84 D5
Mahoba India 82 D4
Maholi India 82 E4
Mahón Spain 57 I4
Mahony Lake Canada 120 E1
Mahrauni India 82 D4
Mahrès Tunisia 58 D7
Māhrūd Iran 89 F3
Mahsana India see Mahesana
Mahudaung mts Myanmar 70 A2
Mahukona HI U.S.A. 127 [inset]
Mahur India 84 C2
Mahuva India 82 B5
Mahwa India 82 D4
Mahya Dağı mt. Turkey 59 L4
Mai i. Vanuatu see Émaé
Maiaia Moz. see Nacala
Maibang India 70 A1
Maicao Col. 142 D1
Maicasagi r. Canada 122 F4
Maicasagi, Lac l. Canada 122 F4
Maichen China 77 F4
Maidenhead U.K. 49 G7
Maidstone Canada 121 I4
Maidstone U.K. 49 H7
Maiduguri Nigeria 96 E3
Maiella, Parco Nazionale della nat. park Italy 58 F3
Mai Gudo mt. Eth. 98 D3
Maigue r. Rep. of Ireland 51 D5
Maihar India 82 E4
Maiji Shan mt. China 76 E1
Maikala Range hills India 82 E5
Maiko r. Dem. Rep. Congo 98 C3
Mailan Hill mt. India 83 E5
Mailly-le-Camp France 52 E6
Mailsi Pak. 89 I4
Main r. Germany 53 I4
Main r. U.K. 51 F3
Main Brook Canada 123 L4
Mainburg Germany 53 L6
Main Channel lake channel Canada 134 E1
Maindargi India 84 C2
Mai-Ndombe, Lac l. Dem. Rep. Congo 98 B4
Main-Donau-Kanal canal Germany 53 K5
Maindong China 83 F3
Main Duck Island Canada 135 G2
Maine state U.S.A. 135 K1
Maine, Gulf of Canada/U.S.A. 135 K2
Mainé Hanari, Cerro hill Col. 142 D4
Maïné-Soroa Niger 96 E3
Maingkaing Myanmar 70 A1
Maingkwan Myanmar 70 B1
Maingy Island Myanmar 71 B4
Mainhardt Germany 53 J5
Mainkung China 76 C2
Mainland i. Scotland U.K. 50 F1
Mainland i. Scotland U.K. 50 [inset]
Mainleus Germany 53 L4
Mainoru Australia 108 F3
Mainpat reg. India 83 E5
Mainpuri India 82 D4
Main Range National Park Australia 112 F2
Maintenon France 52 B6
Maintirano Madag. 99 E5
Mainz Germany 53 I4
Maio i. Cape Verde 96 [inset]
Maipú Arg. 144 E5
Maiskhal Island Bangl. 83 G5
Maisons-Laffitte France 52 C6
Maitengwe Botswana 99 C6
Maitland N.S.W. Australia 112 E4
Maitland S.A. Australia 111 B7
Maitland r. Australia 108 B5
Maitri research station Antarctica 152 C2
Maiwo i. Vanuatu see Maéwo
Maiyu, Mount hill Australia 108 E4
Maíz, Islas del is Nicaragua 137 H6
Maizar Pak. 89 H3
Maizuru Japan 75 D6
Maja Jezercë mt. Albania 59 H3
Majene Indon. 68 F7
Majestic U.S.A. 134 D5
Majhūd well Saudi Arabia 88 C6
Majī Eth. 98 D3
Majiang Guangxi China 77 F4
Majiang Guizhou China 76 E3
Majiazi China 74 B2
Majōl country N. Pacific Ocean see Marshall Islands
Major, Puig mt. Spain 57 H4
Majorca i. Spain 57 H4
Mājro atoll Marshall Is see Majuro
Majunga Madag. see Mahajanga
Majuro atoll Marshall Is 150 H5
Majwemasweu S. Africa 101 H5
Makabana Congo 98 B4
Makale Indon. 69 F7

▶Makalu mt. China/Nepal 83 F4
5th highest mountain in the world and in Asia.
World 12–13

Makalu Barun National Park Nepal 83 F4
Makanchi Kazakh. 80 F2
Makanpur India 82 E4
Makari Mountain National Park Tanz. see Mahale Mountains National Park
Makarov Rus. Fed. 74 F2
Makarov Basin sea feature Arctic Ocean 153 B1
Makarska Croatia 58 G3
Makarwal Pak. 89 H3
Makar'ye Rus. Fed. 42 K4
Makar'yev Rus. Fed. 42 I4
Makasar, Selat strait Indon. see Makassar, Selat
Makassar Indon. 68 F8
Makassar, Selat strait Indon. 68 F7
Makassar Strait Indon. see Makassar, Selat
Makat Kazakh. 78 E2
Makatini Flats lowland S. Africa 101 K4
Makedonija country Europe see Macedonia
Makeni Sierra Leone 96 B4
Makete Tanz. 99 D4
Makeyevka Ukr. see Makiyivka
Makgadikgadi depr. Botswana 99 C6
Makgadikgadi Pans National Park Botswana 99 C6
Makhachkala Rus. Fed. 91 G2
Makhad Pak. 89 H3
Makhado S. Africa see Louis Trichardt
Makhāzin, Kathīb al des. Egypt 85 A4
Makhâzin, Kathîb el des. Egypt see Makhāzin, Kathīb al
Makhazine, Barrage El dam Morocco 57 D6
Makhmūr Iraq 91 F4
Makhtal India 84 C2
Makin atoll Kiribati see Butaritari
Makindu Kenya 98 D4
Makinsk Kazakh. 79 G1
Makira i. Solomon Is see San Cristobal
Makiyivka Ukr. 43 H6
Makkah Saudi Arabia see Mecca
Makkovik Canada 123 K3
Makkovik, Cape Canada 123 K3
Makkum Neth. 52 F1
Makó Hungary 59 I1
Makokou Gabon 98 B3
Makopong Botswana 100 F3
Makotipoko Congo 97 E5
Makran reg. Iran/Pak. 89 F5
Makrana India 82 C4
Makran Coast Range mts Pak. 89 F5
Makri India 84 D2
Maksatikha Rus. Fed. 42 G4
Maksi India 82 D5
Maksimovka Rus. Fed. 74 E3
Maksotag Iran 89 F4
Maksudangarh India 82 D5
Mākū Iran 88 B2
Makunguwiro Tanz. 99 D5
Makurdi Nigeria 96 D4
Makwassie S. Africa 101 G4
Mal India 83 G4
Mala Rep. of Ireland see Mallow
Mala i. Solomon Is see Malaita
Malå Sweden 44 K4
Mala, Punta pt Panama 137 H7
Malabar Coast India 84 B3

▶Malabo Equat. Guinea 96 D4
Capital of Equatorial Guinea.

Malaca Spain see Málaga
Malacca Malaysia see Melaka
Malacca, Strait of Indon./Malaysia 71 B6
Malad City U.S.A. 126 E4
Maladzyechna Belarus 45 O9
Malá Fatra nat. park Slovakia 47 Q6
Málaga Spain 57 D5
Malaga U.S.A. 131 B5
Malagasy Republic country Africa see Madagascar
Malaita i. Solomon Is 107 G2
Malakal Sudan 86 D8
Malakanagiri India see Malkangiri
Malakheti Nepal 82 E3
Malakula i. Vanuatu 107 G3
Malan, Ras pt Pak. 89 G5
Malang Indon. 68 E8
Malangana Nepal see Malangwa
Malange Angola see Malanje
Malangwa Nepal 83 F4
Malanje Angola 99 B4
Malappuram India 84 C4
Mälaren l. Sweden 45 J7
Malargüe Arg. 144 C5
Malartic Canada 122 F4
Malaspina Glacier U.S.A. 120 A3
Malatya Turkey 90 E3
Malavalli India 84 C3
▶Malawi country Africa 99 D5
Africa 7, 94–95
Malawi, Lake Africa see Nyasa, Lake
Malawi National Park Zambia see Nyika National Park
Malaya pen. Malaysia see Peninsular Malaysia
Malaya Pera Rus. Fed. 42 L2
Malaya Vishera Rus. Fed. 42 G4
Malaybalay Phil. 69 H5
Malāyer Iran 88 C3
Malay Peninsula Asia 71 B4
Malay Reef Australia 110 E3
▶Malaysia country Asia 68 D5
Asia 6, 62–63
Malaysia, Semenanjung pen. Malaysia see Peninsular Malaysia
Malazgirt Turkey 91 F3
Malbon Australia 110 C4
Malbork Poland 47 Q3
Malborn Germany 52 G5
Malchin Germany 47 N4
Malcolm Australia 109 C7
Malcolm, Point Australia 109 C8
Malcolm Island Myanmar 71 B5
Maldegem Belgium 52 D3
Malden U.S.A. 131 F4
Malden Island Kiribati 151 J6
▶Maldives country Indian Ocean 81 D10
Asia 6, 62–63
Maldon Australia 112 B6
Maldon U.K. 49 H7
Maldonado Uruguay 144 F4

▶Male Maldives 81 D11
Capital of the Maldives.

Maleas, Akra pt Greece 59 J6
Male Atoll Maldives 81 D11
Malebogo S. Africa 101 G5
Malegaon Maharashtra India 84 B1
Malegaon Maharashtra India 84 C2
Malé Karpaty hills Slovakia 47 P6
Malek Sīāh, Kūh-e mt. Afgh. 89 F4
Malele Dem. Rep. Congo 99 B4
Maler Kotla India 82 C3
Maleševske Planine mts Bulg./Macedonia 59 J4
Malgobek Rus. Fed. 91 G2
Malgomaj l. Sweden 44 J4
Malḥa, Naqb mt. Egypt see Māliḥah, Naqb
Malhada Brazil 145 C1
Malheur r. U.S.A. 126 D3
Malheur Lake U.S.A. 126 D4
▶Mali country Africa 96 C3
Africa 7, 94–95
Mali Dem. Rep. Congo 98 C4
Mali Guinea 96 B3
Maliana East Timor 108 D2
Malianjing China 80 I3
Māliḥah, Naqb mt. Egypt 85 A5
Malik Naro mt. Pak. 89 F4
Mali Kyun i. Myanmar 71 B4
Malili Indon. 69 G7
Malin Ukr. see Malyn
Malindi Kenya 98 E4
Malines Belgium see Mechelen
Malin Head hd Rep. of Ireland 51 E2
Malin More Rep. of Ireland 51 D3
Malipo China 76 E4
Mali Raginac mt. Croatia 58 F2
Malita Phil. 69 H5
Malka r. Rus. Fed. 91 G2
Malkangiri India 84 D2
Malkapur India 84 B2
Malkara Turkey 59 L4
Mal'kavichy Belarus 45 O10
Malko Tŭrnovo Bulg. 59 L4
Mallacoota Australia 112 D6
Mallacoota Inlet b. Australia 112 D6
Mallaig U.K. 50 D4
Mallani reg. India 89 H5
Mallawī Egypt 90 C6
Mallee Cliffs National Park Australia 111 C7
Mallery Lake Canada 121 L1
Mallét Brazil 145 A4
Mallorca i. Spain see Majorca
Mallow Rep. of Ireland 51 D5
Mallowa Well Australia 108 D5
Mallwyd U.K. 49 D6
Malm Norway 44 G4
Malmberget Sweden 44 L3
Malmédy Belgium 52 G4
Malmesbury S. Africa 100 D7
Malmesbury U.K. 49 E7
Malmö Sweden 45 H9
Malmyzh Rus. Fed. 42 K4
Maloca Brazil 143 G3
Malone U.S.A. 135 H1
Malonje mt. Tanz. 99 D4
Maloshuyka Rus. Fed. 42 H3
Malosmadulu Atoll Maldives see Maalhosmadulu Atoll
Måløy Norway 44 D6
Maloyaroslavets Rus. Fed. 43 H5
Malozemel'skaya Tundra lowland Rus. Fed. 42 K2
Malpelo, Isla de i. N. Pacific Ocean 137 H8
Malprabha r. India 84 C2
▶Malta country Europe 58 F7
Europe 5, 38–39
Malta Latvia 45 O8
Malta ID U.S.A. 126 E4
Malta MT U.S.A. 126 G2
Malta Channel Italy/Malta 58 F6
Maltahöhe Namibia 100 C3
Maltby U.K. 48 F5
Maltby le Marsh U.K. 48 H5
Malton U.K. 48 G4
Malukken is Indon. see Moluccas
Maluku is Indon. see Moluccas
Maluku, Laut sea Indon. 69 H6
Ma'lūlā, Jabal mts Syria 85 C3
Malung Sweden 45 H6
Maluti Mountains Lesotho 101 I5
Malu'u Solomon Is 107 G2
Malvan India 84 B2
Malvasia Greece see Monemvasia
Malvern U.K. see Great Malvern
Malvern U.S.A. 131 E5
Malvérnia Moz. see Chicualacuala
Malvinas, Islas terr. S. Atlantic Ocean see Falkland Islands
Malyn Ukr. 43 F6
Malyy Anyuy r. Rus. Fed. 65 R3
Malyye Derbety Rus. Fed. 43 J7
Malyy Kavkaz mts Asia see Lesser Caucasus
Malyy Lyakhovskiy, Ostrov i. Rus. Fed. 65 P2
Malyy Uzen' r. Kazakh./Rus. Fed. 43 K6
Mama r. Rus. Fed. 65 P3
Mamadysh Rus. Fed. 42 K5
Mamafubedu S. Africa 101 I4
Mamatān Nāvar l. Afgh. 89 G4
Mamba China 76 B2
Mambai Brazil 145 B1
Mambasa Dem. Rep. Congo 98 C3
Mamburao Phil. 69 G4
Mamelodi S. Africa 101 I3
Mamfe Cameroon 96 D4
Mamison Pass Georgia/Rus. Fed. 91 F2
Mamit India 83 H5
Mammoth U.S.A. 129 H5
Mammoth Cave National Park U.S.A. 134 B5
Mammoth Reservoir U.S.A. 128 D3
Mamonas Brazil 145 C1
Mamoré r. Bol./Brazil 142 E6
Mamou Guinea 96 B3
Mampikony Madag. 99 E5
Mampong Ghana 96 C4
Mamuju Indon. 68 F7
Mamuno Botswana 100 E2
Man Côte d'Ivoire 96 C4
Man India 84 B2
Man r. India 84 B2
Man U.S.A. 134 E5

▶Man, Isle of terr. Irish Sea 48 C4
United Kingdom Crown Dependency.
Europe 5

Manacapuru Brazil 142 F4
Manacor Spain 57 H4
Manado Indon. 69 G6

▶Managua Nicaragua 137 G6
Capital of Nicaragua.

Manakara Madag. 99 E6
Manakau mt. N.Z. 113 D6
Manākhah Yemen 86 F6

▶Manama Bahrain 88 C5
Capital of Bahrain.

Manamadurai India 84 C4
Mana Maroka National Park S. Africa 101 H5
Manamelkudi India 84 C4
Manam Island P.N.G. 69 L7
Mananara Avaratra Madag. 99 E5
Manangoora Australia 110 B3
Mananjary Madag. 99 E6
Manantali, Lac de l. Mali 96 B3
Manantenina Madag. 99 E6
Mana Pass China/India 82 D3
Mana Pools National Park Zimbabwe 99 C5

▶Manapouri, Lake N.Z. 113 A7
Deepest lake in Oceania.

Manasa India 82 C4
Manas He r. China 80 G2
Manas Hu l. China 80 G2
Manāṣīr reg. U.A.E. 88 D6
Manaslu mt. Nepal 83 F3
Manassas U.S.A. 135 G4
Manastir Macedonia see Bitola
Manas Wildlife Sanctuary nature res. Bhutan 83 G4
Man-aung Myanmar see Cheduba
Man-aung Kyun i. Myanmar see Cheduba Island
Manaus Brazil 142 F4
Manavgat Turkey 90 C3
Manbazar India 83 F5
Manbij Syria 85 C1
Manby U.K. 48 H5
Mancelona U.S.A. 134 C1
Manchar India 84 B2
Manchester U.K. 48 E5
Manchester CT U.S.A. 135 I3
Manchester IA U.S.A. 130 F3
Manchester KY U.S.A. 134 D5
Manchester MD U.S.A. 135 G4
Manchester MI U.S.A. 134 C2
Manchester NH U.S.A. 135 J2
Manchester OH U.S.A. 134 D4
Manchester TN U.S.A. 132 C5
Manchester VT U.S.A. 135 I2
Mancılık Turkey 90 E3
Mand Pak. 89 F5
Mand, Rūd-e r. Iran 88 C4
Manda Tanz. 99 D4
Manda, Jebel mt. Sudan 97 F4
Manda, Parc National de nat. park Chad 97 E4
Mandabe Madag. 99 E6
Mandai Sing. 71 [inset]
Mandal Afgh. 89 F3
Mandal Norway 45 E7

▶Mandala, Puncak mt. Indon. 69 K7
3rd highest mountain in Oceania.

Mandalay Myanmar 70 B2
Mandale Myanmar see Mandalay
Mandalgovĭ Mongolia 72 J3
Mandalī Iraq 91 G4
Mandalt China 73 K4
Mandan U.S.A. 130 C2
Mandas Sardinia Italy 58 C5
Mandasa India 84 E2
Mandasor India see Mandsaur
Mandav Hills India 82 B5
Mandera Kenya 98 E3
Manderfield U.S.A. 129 G2
Manderscheid Germany 52 G4
Mandeville Jamaica 137 I5
Mandeville N.Z. 113 B7
Mandha India 82 B4
Mandhoúdhíon Greece see Mantoudi
Mandi India 82 D3
Mandiana Guinea 96 C3
Mandi Burewala Pak. 89 I4
Mandié Moz. 99 D5
Mandini S. Africa 101 J5
Mandira Dam India 83 F5
Mandla India 82 E5
Mandleshwar India 82 C5
Mandrael India 82 D4
Mandritsara Madag. 99 E5
Mandsaur India 82 C4
Mandurah Australia 109 A8
Manduria Italy 58 G4
Mandvi India 82 B5
Mandya India 84 C3
Manerbio Italy 58 D2
Manevychi Ukr. 43 E6
Manfalūṭ Egypt 90 C6
Manfredonia Italy 58 F4
Manfredonia, Golfo di g. Italy 58 G4
Manga Brazil 145 C1
Manga Burkina 96 C3
Mangabeiras, Serra das hills Brazil 143 I6
Mangai Dem. Rep. Congo 98 B4
Mangaia i. Cook Is 151 J7
Mangakino N.Z. 113 E4
Mangalagiri India 84 D2
Mangaldai India 70 A1
Mangaldoi India see Mangaldai
Mangalia Romania 59 M3
Mangalmé Chad 97 E3
Mangalore India 84 B3
Mangaon India 84 B2
Mangareva Islands Fr. Polynesia see Gambier, Îles
Mangaung Free State S. Africa 97 H5
Mangaung Free State S. Africa see Bloemfontein
Mangawan India 83 E4
Ma'ngê China see Luqu
Mangea i. Cook Is see Mangaia
Mangghyshlaq Kazakh. see Mangystau
Mangghystaū Kazakh. see Mangystau
Mangghystaū admin. div. Kazakh. see Mangistauskaya Oblast'
Mangghyt Uzbek. see Mangit
Manghit Uzbek. see Mangit
Mangin Range mts Myanmar see Mingin Range
Mangistau Kazakh. see Mangystau
Mangistauskaya Oblast' admin. div. Kazakh. 91 I2
Mangit Uzbek. 80 B3
Mangla Bangl. see Mongla
Mangla China see Guinan
Mangla Pak. 89 I3
Manglaqiongtuo China see Guinan
Mangnai China 80 H4
Mangnai Zhen China 80 H4
Mangochi Malawi 99 D5
Mangoky r. Madag. 99 E6
Mangole i. Indon. 69 H7
Mangoli India 84 B2
Mangotsfield U.K. 49 E7
Mangqystaū Shyghanaghy b. Kazakh. see Mangyshlakskiy Zaliv
Mangra China see Guinan
Mangral India 82 B5
Mangrul India 84 C1
Mangshi China see Luxi
Mangualde Port. 57 C3
Manguéni, Plateau du Niger 96 E2
Mangui China 74 A2
Mangula Zimbabwe see Mhangura
Mangum U.S.A. 131 D5
Mangyshlak Kazakh. see Mangystau
Mangyshlak, Poluostrov pen. Kazakh. 91 H1
Mangyshlak Oblast admin. div. Kazakh. see Mangistauskaya Oblast'
Mangyshlakskaya Oblast' admin. div. Kazakh. see Mangistauskaya Oblast'
Mangyshlakskiy Zaliv b. Kazakh. 91 H1
Mangystau Kazakh. 91 H2
Manhã Brazil 145 B1
Manhattan U.S.A. 130 D4
Manhica Moz. 101 K3
Manhoca Moz. 101 K4
Manhuaçu Brazil 145 C3
Manhuaçu r. Brazil 145 C2
Mani China 83 F2
Mania r. Madag. 99 E5
Maniago Italy 58 E1
Manicouagan Canada 123 H4
Manicouagan r. Canada 123 H4
Manicouagan, Réservoir resr Canada 123 H4
Manic Trois, Réservoir resr Canada 123 H4
Manīfah Saudi Arabia 88 C5
Maniganggo China 76 C2
Manigotagan Canada 121 L5
Manihiki atoll Cook Is 150 J6
Maniitsoq Greenland 119 M3
Manikchhari Bangl. 83 H5
Manikgarh India see Rajura

▶Manila Phil. 69 G4
Capital of the Philippines.

Manila U.S.A. 126 F4
Manildra Australia 112 D4
Manilla Australia 112 E3
Maningrida Australia 108 F3
Manipur India see Imphal
Manipur state India 83 H4
Manisa Turkey 59 L5
Manistee U.S.A. 134 B1
Manistee r. U.S.A. 134 B1
Manistique U.S.A. 132 C2
Manitoba prov. Canada 121 L4
Manitoba, Lake Canada 121 L5
Manito Lake Canada 121 I4
Manitou Canada 121 L5
Manitou, Lake U.S.A. 134 B3
Manitou Beach U.S.A. 135 G2
Manitou Falls Canada 121 M5
Manitou Islands U.S.A. 134 B1
Manitoulin Island Canada 122 E5
Manitouwadge Canada 122 D4
Manitowoc U.S.A. 134 B1
Maniwaki Canada 122 G5
Manizales Col. 142 C2
Manja Madag. 99 E6
Manjarabad India 84 B3
Manjeri India 84 C4
Manjhand Pak. 89 H5
Manjhi India 83 F4
Manjra r. India 84 C2
Man Kabat Myanmar 70 B1
Mankaiana Swaziland see Mankayane
Mankato KS U.S.A. 130 D4
Mankato MN U.S.A. 130 E2
Mankayane Swaziland 101 J4
Mankera Pak. 89 H4
Mankono Côte d'Ivoire 96 C4
Mankota Canada 121 J5
Manley Hot Springs U.S.A. 118 C3
Manmad India 84 B1
Mann r. Australia 108 F3
Mann, Mount Australia 109 E6
Manna Indon. 68 C7
Man Na Myanmar 70 B2
Mannahill Australia 111 B7
Mannar Sri Lanka 84 C4
Mannar, Gulf of India/Sri Lanka 84 C4
Manneru r. India 84 D3
Mannessier, Lac l. Canada 123 H3
Mannheim Germany 53 I5
Mannicolo Islands Solomon Is see Vanikoro Islands
Manning r. Australia 112 F3
Manning Canada 120 G3
Manning U.S.A. 133 D5
Mannington U.S.A. 134 E4
Manningtree U.K. 49 I7
Mann Ranges mts Australia 109 E6
Mannsville KY U.S.A. 134 C5
Mannsville NY U.S.A. 135 G2
Mannu, Capo c. Sardinia Italy 58 C4
Mannville Canada 121 I4
Man-of-War Rocks is U.S.A. see Gardner Pinnacles
Manoharpur India 82 D4
Manohar Thana India 82 D4
Manokotak U.S.A. 118 C4
Manokwari Indon. 69 I7
Manoron Myanmar 71 B5
Manosque France 56 G5
Manouane r. Canada 123 H4
Manouane, Lac l. Canada 123 H4
Man Pan Myanmar 70 B2
Manp'o N. Korea 74 B4
Manra i. Kiribati 107 I2
Manresa Spain 57 G3
Mansa Gujarat India 82 C5
Mansa Punjab India 82 C3
Mansa Zambia 99 C5
Mansa Konko Gambia 96 B3
Man Sam Myanmar 70 B2
Mansehra Pak. 87 L3
Mansel Island Canada 119 K3
Mansfield Australia 112 C6
Mansfield U.K. 49 F5
Mansfield LA U.S.A. 131 E5
Mansfield OH U.S.A. 134 D3
Mansfield PA U.S.A. 135 G3
Mansfield, Mount U.S.A. 135 I1
Man Si Myanmar 70 B1
Mansi Myanmar 70 A1
Manso r. Brazil see Mortes, Rio das
Manta Ecuador 142 B4
Mantaro r. Peru 142 D6
Manteca U.S.A. 128 C3
Mantena Brazil 145 C2
Manteo U.S.A. 132 F5
Mantes-la-Jolie France 52 B6
Mantiqueira, Serra da mts Brazil 145 B3
Manton U.S.A. 134 C1
Mantoudi Greece 59 J5
Mantova Italy see Mantua
Mäntsälä Fin. 45 N6
Mänttä Fin. 44 N5
Mantua Cuba 133 C8
Mantua Italy 58 D2
Mantuan Downs Australia 110 D5
Manturovo Rus. Fed. 42 J4

Mäntyharju Fin. 45 O6
Mäntyjärvi Fin. 44 O3
Manú Peru 142 D6
Manu, Parque Nacional nat. park Peru 142 D6
Manuae atoll Fr. Polynesia 151 J7
Manua Islands American Samoa 107 I3
Manuel Ribas Brazil 145 A4
Manuel Vitorino Brazil 145 C1
Manuelzinho Brazil 143 H5
Manui i. Indon. 69 G7
Manukau N.Z. 113 E3
Manukau Harbour N.Z. 113 E3
Manunda watercourse Australia 111 B7
Manusela National Park Indon. 69 H7
Manus Island P.N.G. 69 L7
Manvi India 84 C3
Many U.S.A. 131 E6
Manyana Botswana 101 G3
Manyas Turkey 59 L4
Manyas Gölü l. Turkey see Kuş Gölü
Manych-Gudilo, Ozero l. Rus. Fed. 43 I7
Many Island Lake Canada 121 I5
Manyoni Tanz. 99 D4
Manzai Pak. 89 H3
Manzanares Spain 57 E4
Manzanillo Cuba 137 I4
Manzanillo Mex. 136 D5
Manzhouli China 73 L3
Manzini Swaziland 101 J4
Mao Chad 97 E3
Maó Spain see Mahón
Maoba Guizhou China 76 E3
Maoba Hubei China 77 F2
Maocifan China 77 G2
Mao'ergai China 76 D1
Maoke, Pegunungan mts Indon. 69 J7
Maokeng S. Africa 101 H4
Maokui Shan mt. China 74 A4
Maolin China 74 A4
Maoming China 77 F4
Ma On Shan hill Hong Kong China 77 [inset]
Maopi T'ou c. Taiwan 77 I4
Maopora i. Indon. 108 D1
Maotou Shan mt. China 76 D3
Mapai Moz. 101 J2
Mapam Yumco l. China 83 E3
Mapanza Zambia 99 C5
Maphodi S. Africa 101 G6
Mapimí Mex. 131 C7
Mapimí, Bolsón de des. Mex. 131 B7
Mapin i. Phil. 68 F5
Mapinhane Moz. 101 L2
Mapiri Bol. 142 E7
Maple r. MI U.S.A. 134 C2
Maple r. ND U.S.A. 130 D2
Maple Creek Canada 121 I5
Maple Heights U.S.A. 134 E3
Maple Peak U.S.A. 129 I5
Mapmakers Seamounts sea feature N. Pacific Ocean 150 H4
Mapoon Australia 110 C1
Mapor i. Indon. 71 D7
Mapoteng Lesotho 101 H5
Maprik P.N.G. 69 K7
Mapuera r. Brazil 143 G4
Mapulanguene Moz. 101 K3

▶Maputo Moz. 101 K3
Capital of Mozambique.

Maputo prov. Moz. 101 K3
Maputo r. Moz./S. Africa 101 K4
Maputo, Baía de b. Moz. 101 K4
Maputsoe Lesotho 101 H5
Maqanshy Kazakh. see Makanchi
Maqar an Na'am well Iraq 91 F5
Maqat Kazakh. see Makat
Maqên China 76 D1
Maqên Kangri mt. China 76 C1
Maqnā Saudi Arabia 90 D5
Maqteïr reg. Mauritania 96 B2
Maqu China 76 D1
Ma Qu r. China see Yellow River
Maquan He r. China 83 F3
Maquela do Zombo Angola 99 B4
Maquinchao Arg. 144 C6
Mar r. Pak. 89 G5
Mar, Serra do mts Rio de Janeiro/São Paulo Brazil 145 B3
Mar, Serra do mts Rio Grande do Sul/Santa Catarina Brazil 145 A5
Mara r. Canada 121 I1
Mara India 83 E5
Mara S. Africa 101 I2
Maraã Brazil 142 E4
Maraba Brazil 143 I5
Maraboon, Lake resr Australia 110 E4
Maracá, Ilha de i. Brazil 143 H3
Maracaibo Venez. 142 D1
Maracaibo, Lago de Venez. see Maracaibo, Lake
Maracaibo, Lake Venez. 142 D2
Maracaju Brazil 144 E2
Maracaju, Serra de hills Brazil 144 E2
Maracanda Uzbek. see Samarkand
Maracás Brazil 145 C1
Maracás, Chapada de hills Brazil 145 C1
Maracay Venez. 142 E1
Marādah Libya 97 E2
Maradi Niger 96 D3
Marāgheh Iran 88 B2
Marahuaca, Cerro mt. Venez. 142 E3
Marajó, Baía de est. Brazil 143 I4
Marajó, Ilha de i. Brazil 143 H4
Marakele National Park S. Africa 101 H3
Maralal Kenya 98 D3
Maralbashi China see Bachu
Maralinga Australia 109 E7
Maralwexi China see Bachu
Maramasike i. Solomon Is 107 G2
Maramba Zambia see Livingstone
Marambio research station Antarctica 152 A2
Maran Malaysia 71 C7
Maran mt. Pak. 89 G4
Marana U.S.A. 129 H5
Marand Iran 88 B2
Marandellas Zimbabwe see Marondera
Marang Malaysia 71 C6
Marang Myanmar 71 B5
Maranhão r. Brazil 145 A1
Maranoa r. Australia 112 D1
Marañón r. Peru 142 D4
Marão Moz. 101 L3
Marão mt. Port. 57 C3
Mara Rosa Brazil 145 A1
Maraş Turkey see Kahramanmaraş
Marathon Canada 122 D4
Marathon FL U.S.A. 133 D7
Marathon NY U.S.A. 135 G2
Marathon TX U.S.A. 131 C6
Maratua i. Indon. 68 F6
Maraú Brazil 145 D1
Maravillas Creek watercourse U.S.A. 131 C6
Mārāzā Azer. 91 H2
Marbella Spain 57 D5
Marble Bar Australia 108 B5
Marble Canyon U.S.A. 129 H3
Marble Canyon gorge U.S.A. 129 H3
Marble Hall S. Africa 101 I3
Marble Hill U.S.A. 131 F4
Marble Island Canada 121 N2
Marbul Pass Jammu and Kashmir 82 C2
Marburg S. Africa 101 J6
Marburg Slovenia see Maribor
Marburg an der Lahn Germany 53 I4
Marca, Ponta do pt Angola 99 B5
Marcali Hungary 58 G1
Marcelino Ramos Brazil 145 A4
March U.K. 49 H6
Marche reg. France 56 E3
Marche-en-Famenne Belgium 52 F4
Marchena Spain 57 D5
Marchinbar Island Australia 110 B1
Mar Chiquita, Lago l. Arg. 144 D4
Marchtrenk Austria 47 O6
Marco U.S.A. 133 D7
Marcoing France 52 D4
Marcona Peru 142 C7
Marcopeet Islands Canada 122 F2
Marcus Baker, Mount U.S.A. 118 D3
Marcy, Mount U.S.A. 135 I1
Mardan Pak. 89 I3
Mar del Plata Arg. 144 E5
Mardīan Afgh. 89 G2
Mardın Turkey 91 F3
Maré i. New Caledonia 107 G4
Maree, Loch l. U.K. 50 D3
Mareh Iran 89 E5
Marengo IA U.S.A. 130 E3
Marengo IN U.S.A. 134 B4
Marevo Rus. Fed. 42 G4
Marfa U.S.A. 131 B6
Marganets Ukr. see Marhanets'
Margao India see Madgaon
Margaret r. Australia 108 D4
Margaret watercourse Australia 111 B6
Margaret, Mount hill Australia 108 B5
Margaret Lake Alta Canada 120 H3
Margaret Lake N.W.T. Canada 120 G1
Margaret River Australia 109 A8
Margaretville U.S.A. 135 H2
Margarita, Isla de i. Venez. 142 F1
Margaritovo Rus. Fed. 74 D4
Margate U.K. 49 I7
Margherita, Lake Eth. see Abaya, Lake

▶Margherita Peak Dem. Rep. Congo/Uganda 98 C3
3rd highest mountain in Africa.

Marghilon Uzbek. see Margilan
Margilan Uzbek. 80 D3
Mārgo, Dasht-i des. Afgh. see Mārgow, Dasht-e
Margog Caka l. China 83 F2
Mārgow, Dasht-e des. Afgh. 89 F4
Margraten Neth. 52 F4
Marguerite Canada 120 F4
Marguerite, Pic mt. Dem. Rep. Congo/Uganda see Margherita Peak
Marguerite Bay Antarctica 152 L2
Margyang China 83 G3
Marhaj Khalīl Iraq 91 G4
Marhanets' Ukr. 43 G7
Marhoum Alg. 54 D5
Mari Myanmar 70 B1
Maria atoll Fr. Polynesia 151 J7
María Elena Chile 144 C2
Maria Island Australia 110 A2
Maria Island Myanmar 71 B5
Maria Island National Park Australia 111 [inset]
Mariala National Park Australia 111 D5
Mariana Brazil 145 C3
Marianao Cuba 133 D8
Mariana Ridge sea feature N. Pacific Ocean 150 F4

▶Mariana Trench sea feature N. Pacific Ocean 150 F5
Deepest trench in the world.

Mariani India 83 H4
Mariánica, Cordillera mts Spain see Morena, Sierra
Marian Lake Canada 120 G2
Marianna AR U.S.A. 131 F5
Marianna FL U.S.A. 133 C6
Mariano Machado Angola see Ganda
Mariánské Lázně Czech Rep. 53 M5
Marias r. U.S.A. 126 F3
Marías, Islas is Mex. 136 C4

▶Mariato, Punta pt Panama 137 H7
Most southerly point of North America.

Maria van Diemen, Cape N.Z. 113 D2
Ma'rib Yemen 86 G6
Maribor Slovenia 58 F1
Marica r. Bulg. see Maritsa
Maricopa AZ U.S.A. 129 G5
Maricopa CA U.S.A. 128 D4
Maricopa Mountains U.S.A. 129 G5
Maridi Sudan 97 F4
Marie Byrd Land reg. Antarctica 152 J1
Marie-Galante i. Guadeloupe 133 L5
Mariehamn Fin. 45 K6
Mariembero r. Brazil 145 A1
Marienbad Czech Rep. see Mariánské Lázně
Marienberg Germany 53 N4
Marienburg Poland see Malbork
Marienhafe Germany 53 H1
Mariental Namibia 100 C3
Marienwerder Poland see Kwidzyn
Mariestad Sweden 45 H7
Mariet r. Canada 122 F2
Marietta GA U.S.A. 133 C5
Marietta OH U.S.A. 134 E4
Marietta OK U.S.A. 131 D5
Marignane France 56 G5
Marii, Mys pt Rus. Fed. 66 G2
Mariinsk Rus. Fed. 64 J4
Mariinskiy Posad Rus. Fed. 42 J4
Marijampolė Lith. 45 M9
Marília Brazil 145 A3
Marillana Australia 108 B5
Marimba Angola 99 B4
Marín Spain 57 B2
Marina U.S.A. 128 C3
Marina di Gioiosa Ionica Italy 58 G5
Mar'ina Gorka Belarus see Mar''ina Horka
Mar''ina Horka Belarus 45 P10
Marinduque i. Phil. 69 G4
Marinette U.S.A. 134 B1
Maringá Brazil 145 A3
Maringa r. Dem. Rep. Congo 98 B3
Maringo U.S.A. 134 D3
Marinha Grande Port. 57 B4
Marion AL U.S.A. 133 C5
Marion AR U.S.A. 131 F5
Marion IL U.S.A. 130 F4
Marion IN U.S.A. 134 C3
Marion KS U.S.A. 130 D4
Marion MI U.S.A. 134 C1
Marion NY U.S.A. 135 G2
Marion OH U.S.A. 134 D3
Marion SC U.S.A. 133 E5
Marion VA U.S.A. 134 E5
Marion, Lake U.S.A. 133 D5
Marion Reef Australia 110 F3
Maripa Venez. 142 E2
Mariposa U.S.A. 128 D3
Marisa Indon. 69 G6
Mariscal Estigarribia Para. 144 D2
Maritime Alps mts France/Italy 56 H4
Maritime Kray admin. div. Rus. Fed. see Primorskiy Kray
Maritimes, Alpes mts France/Italy see Maritime Alps
Maritsa r. Bulg. 59 L4
also known as Evros (Greece), Marica (Bulgaria), Meriç (Turkey)
Marittime, Alpi mts France/Italy see Maritime Alps
Mariupol' Ukr. 43 H7
Mariusa nat. park Venez. 142 F2
Marīvān Iran 88 B3
Marjan Afgh. see Wazi Khwa
Marjayoûn Lebanon 85 B3
Marka Somalia 98 E3
Markala Mali 96 C3
Markam China 76 C2
Markaryd Sweden 45 H8
Markdale Canada 134 E1
Marken S. Africa 101 I2
Markermeer l. Neth. 52 F2
Market Deeping U.K. 49 G6
Market Drayton U.K. 49 E6
Market Harborough U.K. 49 G6
Markethill U.K. 51 F3
Market Weighton U.K. 48 G5
Markha r. Rus. Fed. 65 M3
Markham Canada 134 F2
Markit China 80 E4
Markkleeberg Germany 53 M3
Markleeville U.S.A. 128 D2
Marklohe Germany 53 J2
Markog Qu r. China 76 D1
Markounda Cent. Afr. Rep. 98 B3
Markovo Rus. Fed. 65 S3
Markranstädt Germany 53 M3
Marks Rus. Fed. 43 J6
Marks U.S.A. 131 F5
Marksville U.S.A. 131 E6
Marktheidenfeld Germany 53 J5
Marktredwitz Germany 53 M4
Marl Germany 52 H3
Marla Australia 109 F6
Marlborough Downs hills U.K. 49 F7
Marle France 52 D5
Marlette U.S.A. 134 D2
Marlin U.S.A. 131 D6
Marlinton U.S.A. 134 E4
Marlo Australia 112 D6
Marmagao India 84 B3
Marmande France 56 E4
Marmara, Sea of g. Turkey 59 M4
Marmara Denizi g. Turkey see Marmara, Sea of
Marmara Gölü l. Turkey 59 M5
Marmarica reg. Libya 90 B5
Marmaris Turkey 59 M6
Marmarth U.S.A. 130 C2
Marmet U.S.A. 134 E4
Marmion, Lake salt l. Australia 109 C7
Marmion Lake Canada 121 N5
Marmolada mt. Italy 58 D1
Marne r. France 52 C6
Marne-la-Vallée France 52 C6
Marnitz Germany 53 L1
Maroantsetra Madag. 99 E5
Maroc country Africa see Morocco
Marol Jammu and Kashmir 82 D2
Marol Pak. 89 I4
Maroldsweisach Germany 53 K4
Maromokotro mt. Madag. 99 E5
Marondera Zimbabwe 99 D5
Maroochydore Australia 112 F1
Maroonah Australia 109 A5
Maroon Peak U.S.A. 126 G5
Marosvásárhely Romania see Târgu Mureş
Maroua Cameroon 97 E3
Marovoay Madag. 99 E5
Marqādah Syria 91 F4
Mar Qu r. China see Markog Qu
Marquard S. Africa 101 H5
Marquesas Islands Fr. Polynesia 151 K6
Marquesas Keys is U.S.A. 133 D7
Marquês de Valença Brazil 145 C3
Marquette U.S.A. 132 C2
Marquez U.S.A. 131 D6
Marquion France 52 D4
Marquise France 52 B4
Marquises, Îles is Fr. Polynesia see Marquesas Islands
Marra Australia 112 A3
Marra r. Australia 112 C3
Marra, Jebel mt. Sudan 97 F3
Marracuene Moz. 101 K3
Marrakech Morocco 54 C5
Marrakesh Morocco see Marrakech
Marrangua, Lagoa l. Moz. 101 L3
Marra Plateau Sudan 97 F3
Marrar Australia 112 C5
Marrawah Australia 111 [inset]
Marree Australia 111 B6
Marrowbone U.S.A. 134 C5
Marruecos country Africa see Morocco
Marrupa Moz. 99 D5
Marryat Australia 109 F6
Marsá al 'Alam Egypt 86 D4
Marsa 'Alam Egypt see Marsá al 'Alam
Marsa al Burayqah Libya 97 E1
Marsabit Kenya 98 D3
Marsala Sicily Italy 58 E6
Marsá Maṭrūḥ Egypt 90 B5
Marsberg Germany 53 I3
Marsciano Italy 58 E3
Marsden Australia 112 C4
Marsden Canada 121 I4
Marsdiep sea chan. Neth. 52 E2
Marseille France 56 G5
Marseilles France see Marseille
Marsfjället mt. Sweden 44 I4
Marshall watercourse Australia 110 B4
Marshall AR U.S.A. 131 E5
Marshall IL U.S.A. 134 B4
Marshall MI U.S.A. 134 C2
Marshall MN U.S.A. 130 E2
Marshall MO U.S.A. 130 E4
Marshall TX U.S.A. 131 E5
▶Marshall Islands country N. Pacific Ocean 150 H5
Oceania 8, 104–105
Marshalltown U.S.A. 130 E3
Marshfield MO U.S.A. 131 E4
Marshfield WI U.S.A. 130 F2
Marsh Harbour Bahamas 133 E7
Mars Hill U.S.A. 132 H2
Marsh Island U.S.A. 131 F6
Marsh Peak U.S.A. 129 I1
Marsh Point Canada 121 M3
Marsing U.S.A. 126 D4
Märsta Sweden 45 J7
Marsyaty Rus. Fed. 41 S3
Martaban Myanmar 70 B3
Martaban, Gulf of Myanmar 70 B3
Martapura Indon. 68 E7
Marten River Canada 122 F5
Marte R. Gómez, Presa resr Mex. 131 D7
Martha's Vineyard i. U.S.A. 135 J3
Martigny Switz. 56 H3
Martim Vaz, Ilhas is S. Atlantic Ocean see Martin Vas, Ilhas
Martin r. Canada 120 F2
Martin Slovakia 47 Q6
Martin MI U.S.A. 134 C2
Martin SD U.S.A. 130 C3
Martinez Lake U.S.A. 129 F5
Martinho Campos Brazil 145 B2

▶Martinique terr. West Indies 137 L6
French Overseas Department.
North America 9, 116–117

Martinique Passage Dominica/Martinique 137 L5
Martin Peninsula Antarctica 152 K2
Martinsburg U.S.A. 135 G4
Martins Ferry U.S.A. 134 E3
Martinsville IL U.S.A. 134 B4
Martinsville IN U.S.A. 134 B4
Martinsville VA U.S.A. 134 F5

▶Martin Vas, Ilhas is S. Atlantic Ocean 148 G7
Most easterly point of South America.

Martin Vaz Islands S. Atlantic Ocean see Martin Vas, Ilhas
Martök Kazakh. see Martuk
Marton N.Z. 113 E5
Martorell Spain 57 G3
Martos Spain 57 E5
Martuk Kazakh. 78 E1
Martuni Armenia 91 G2
Maruf Afgh. 89 G4
Maruim Brazil 143 K6
Marukhis Ugheltekhili pass Georgia/Rus. Fed. 91 F2
Marulan Australia 112 D5
Marusthali reg. India 89 H5
Marvast Iran 88 D4
Marv Dasht Iran 88 D4
Marvejols France 56 F4
Marvine, Mount U.S.A. 129 H2
Marwayne Canada 121 I4
Mary r. Australia 108 E3
Mary Turkm. 89 F2
Maryborough Qld Australia 111 F5
Maryborough Vic. Australia 112 A6
Marydale S. Africa 100 F5
Mary Frances Lake Canada 121 J2
Mary Lake Canada 121 K2
Maryland state U.S.A. 135 G4
Maryport U.K. 48 D4
Mary's Harbour Canada 123 L3
Marysvale U.S.A. 129 G2
Marysville CA U.S.A. 128 C2
Marysville KS U.S.A. 130 D4
Marysville OH U.S.A. 134 D3
Maryvale N.T. Australia 109 F6
Maryvale Qld Australia 110 D3
Maryville MO U.S.A. 130 E3
Maryville TN U.S.A. 132 D5
Marzagão Brazil 145 A2
Marzahna Germany 53 M2
Masada tourist site Israel 85 B4
Masāhūn, Kūh-e mt. Iran 88 D4
Masai Steppe plain Tanz. 99 D4
Masaka Uganda 98 D4
Masakhane S. Africa 101 H6
Masalembu Besar i. Indon. 68 E8
Masallı Azer. 91 H3
Masan S. Korea 75 C6
Masasi Tanz. 99 D5
Masavi Bol. 142 F7
Masbate Phil. 69 G4
Masbate i. Phil. 69 G4
Mascara Alg. 57 G6
Mascarene Basin sea feature Indian Ocean 149 L7
Mascarene Plain sea feature Indian Ocean 149 L7
Mascarene Ridge sea feature Indian Ocean 149 L6
Mascote Brazil 145 D1
Masein Myanmar 70 A2
Masela Indon. 108 E2
Masela i. Indon. 108 E2

▶Maseru Lesotho 101 H5
Capital of Lesotho.

Mashai Lesotho 101 I5
Mashan China 77 F4
Masherbrum mt. Jammu and Kashmir 82 D2
Mashhad Iran 89 E2
Mashket r. Pak. 89 F5
Mashki Chah Pak. 89 F4
Masi Norway 44 M2
Masiáca Mex. 127 F8
Masibambane S. Africa 101 H6
Masīlah, Wādī al watercourse Yemen 86 H6
Masilo S. Africa 101 H5
Masi-Manimba Dem. Rep. Congo 99 B4
Masindi Uganda 98 D3
Masinyusane S. Africa 100 F6
Masira, Gulf of Oman see Maṣīrah, Khalīj
Maṣīrah, Jazīrat i. Oman 87 I5
Maṣīrah, Khalīj b. Oman 87 I6
Masira Island Oman see Maṣīrah, Jazīrat
Masjed Soleymān Iran 88 C4
Mask, Lough l. Rep. of Ireland 51 C4
Maskūtān Iran 89 E5
Maslovo Rus. Fed. 41 S3
Masoala, Tanjona c. Madag. 99 F5
Mason MI U.S.A. 134 C2
Mason OH U.S.A. 134 C4
Mason TX U.S.A. 131 D6
Mason, Lake salt flat Australia 109 B6
Mason Bay N.Z. 113 A8
Mason City U.S.A. 130 E3
Masontown U.S.A. 134 F4
Masqaṭ Oman see Muscat
Masqaṭ reg. Oman see Muscat
'Masrūg well Oman 88 D6
Massa Italy 58 D2
Massachusetts state U.S.A. 135 I2
Massachusetts Bay U.S.A. 135 J2
Massadona U.S.A. 129 I1
Massafra Italy 58 G4
Massakory Chad 97 E3
Massa Marittimo Italy 58 D3
Massangena Moz. 99 D6
Massango Angola 99 B4
Massawa Eritrea 86 E6
Massawippi, Lac l. Canada 135 I1
Massena U.S.A. 135 H1
Massenya Chad 97 E3
Masset Canada 120 C4
Massieville U.S.A. 134 D4
Massif Central mts France 56 F4
Massilia France see Marseille
Massillon U.S.A. 134 E3
Massina Mali 96 C3
Massinga Moz. 101 L2
Massingir Moz. 101 K2
Massingir, Barragem de resr Moz. 101 K2
Masson Island Antarctica 152 F2
Mastchoh Tajik. 89 H2
Masterton N.Z. 113 E5
Masticho, Akra pt Greece 59 L5
Mastung Pak. 78 F4
Mastūrah Saudi Arabia 86 E5
Masty Belarus 45 N10
Masuda Japan 75 C6
Masuku Gabon see Franceville
Masulipatam India see Machilipatnam
Masulipatnam India see Machilipatnam
Masuna i. American Samoa see Tutuila
Masvingo Zimbabwe 99 D6
Masvingo prov. Zimbabwe 101 J1
Maswa Tanz. 98 D4
Maswaar i. Indon. 69 I7
Maṣyāf Syria 85 C2
Mat, Hon i. Vietnam 70 D3
Mat, Nam r. Laos 70 D3
Mata Myanmar 70 B1
Matabeleland South prov. Zimbabwe 101 I1
Matachewan Canada 122 E5
Matadi Dem. Rep. Congo 99 B4
Matador U.S.A. 131 C5
Matagalpa Nicaragua 137 G6
Matagami Canada 122 F4
Matagami, Lac l. Canada 122 F4
Matagorda Island U.S.A. 131 D6
Matak i. Indon. 71 D7
Matakana Island N.Z. 113 F3
Matala Angola 99 B5
Maṭāli', Jabal hill Saudi Arabia 91 F6
Matam Senegal 96 B3
Matamey Niger 96 D3
Matamoras U.S.A. 135 H3
Matamoros Coahuila Mex. 131 C7
Matamoros Tamaulipas Mex. 131 D7
Matandu r. Tanz. 99 D4
Matane Canada 123 I4
Matanzas Cuba 137 H4
Matapan, Cape pt Greece see Tainaro, Akra
Matapédia, Lac l. Canada 123 I4
Maṭār well Saudi Arabia 88 B5
Matara Sri Lanka 84 D5
Mataram Indon. 108 B2
Matarani Peru 142 D7
Mataranka Australia 108 F3
Mataripe Brazil 145 D1
Mataró Spain 57 H3
Matasiri i. Indon. 68 F7
Matatiele S. Africa 101 I6
Matatila Dam India 82 D4
Mataura N.Z. 113 B8

▶Matā'utu Wallis and Futuna Is 107 I3
Capital of Wallis and Futuna.

Mata-Utu Wallis and Futuna Is see Matā'utu
Matawai N.Z. 113 F4
Matay Kazakh. 80 E2
Matcha Tajik. see Mastchoh
Mategua Bol. 142 F6
Matehuala Mex. 131 C8
Matemanga Tanz. 99 D5
Matera Italy 58 G4
Mateur Tunisia 58 C6
Mathaji India 82 B4
Matheson Canada 122 E4
Mathews U.S.A. 135 G5
Mathis U.S.A. 131 D6
Mathoura Australia 112 B5
Mathura India 82 D4
Mati Phil. 69 H5
Matiali India 83 G4
Matias Cardoso Brazil 145 C1
Matías Romero Mex. 136 E5
Matimekosh Canada 123 I3
Matin India 83 E5
Matinenda Lake Canada 122 E5
Matizi China 76 D1
Matla r. India 83 G5
Matlabas r. S. Africa 101 H2
Matli Pak. 89 H5
Matlock U.K. 49 F5
Mato, Cerro mt. Venez. 142 E2
Matobo Hills Zimbabwe 99 C6
Mato Grosso Brazil 142 G7
Mato Grosso state Brazil 145 A1
Mato Grosso, Planalto do plat. Brazil 143 H7
Matopo Hills Zimbabwe see Matobo Hills
Matos Costa Brazil 145 A4
Matosinhos Port. 57 B3
Mato Verde Brazil 145 C1
Maṭraḥ Oman 88 E6
Matroosberg mt. S. Africa 100 D7
Matsesta Rus. Fed. 91 E2
Matsue Japan 75 D6
Matsumoto Japan 75 E5
Matsu Tao i. Taiwan 77 I3
Matsuyama Japan 75 D6
Mattagami r. Canada 122 E4
Mattamuskeet, Lake U.S.A. 132 E5
Mattawa Canada 122 F5
Matterhorn mt. Italy/Switz. 58 B2
Matterhorn mt. U.S.A. 126 E4
Matthew Town Bahamas 137 J4
Maṭṭī, Sabkhat salt pan Saudi Arabia 88 D6
Mattoon U.S.A. 130 F4
Matturai Sri Lanka see Matara
Matuku i. Fiji 107 H3
Matumbo Angola 99 B5
Maturín Venez. 142 F2
Matusadona National Park Zimbabwe 99 C5
Matwabeng S. Africa 101 H5
Maty Island P.N.G. see Wuvulu Island
Mau India see Maunath Bhanjan
Maúa Moz. 99 D5
Maubeuge France 52 D4
Maubin Myanmar 70 A3
Ma-ubin Myanmar 70 B1
Maubourguet France 56 E5
Mauchline U.K. 50 E5
Maudaha India 82 E4
Maude Australia 111 D7
Maud Seamount sea feature S. Atlantic Ocean 148 I10
Mau-é-ele Moz. see Marão
Maués Brazil 143 G4
Maughold Head hd Isle of Man 48 C4
Maug Islands N. Mariana Is 69 L2
Maui i. HI U.S.A. 127 [inset]
Maukkadaw Myanmar 70 A2
Maulbronn Germany 53 I6
Maule r. Chile 144 B5
Maulvi Bazar Bangl. see Moulvibazar
Maumee U.S.A. 134 D3
Maumee Bay U.S.A. 134 D3
Maumere Indon. 108 C2
Maumturk Mts hills Rep. of Ireland 51 C4
Maun Botswana 99 C5
Mauna Kea vol. HI U.S.A. 127 [inset]
Mauna Loa vol. HI U.S.A. 127 [inset]
Maunath Bhanjan India 83 E4
Maunatlala Botswana 101 H2
Maungaturoto N.Z. 113 E3
Maungdaw Myanmar 70 A2
Maungmagan Islands Myanmar 71 B4
Maurepas, Lake U.S.A. 131 F6
Maurice France 56 F4
Maurice country Indian Ocean see Mauritius
Maurice, Lake salt flat Australia 109 E7
Maurik Neth. 52 F3
▶Mauritania country Africa 96 B3
Africa 7, 94–95
Mauritanie country Africa see Mauritania
▶Mauritius country Indian Ocean 149 L7
Africa 7, 94–95
Maurs France 56 F4
Mauston U.S.A. 130 F3
Mava Dem. Rep. Congo 98 C3
Mavago Moz. 99 D5
Mavan, Kūh-e hill Iran 88 E3
Mavanza Moz. 101 L2
Mavinga Angola 99 C5
Mavrovo nat. park Macedonia 59 I4
Mavume Moz. 101 L2
Mavuya S. Africa 101 H6
Ma Wan i. Hong Kong China 77 [inset]
Māwān, Khashm hill Saudi Arabia 88 B6
Mawana India 82 D3
Mawanga Dem. Rep. Congo 99 B4
Ma Wang Dui tourist site China 77 G2
Mawei China 77 H3

Mawjib, Wādī al r. Jordan 85 B4
Mawkmai Myanmar 70 B2
Mawlaik Myanmar 70 A2
Mawlamyaing Myanmar see Moulmein
Mawlamyine Myanmar see Moulmein
Mawqaq Saudi Arabia 91 F6
Mawson research station Antarctica 152 E2
Mawson Coast Antarctica 152 E2
Mawson Escarpment Antarctica 152 E2
Mawson Peninsula Antarctica 152 H2
Maw Taung mt. Myanmar 71 B5
Mawza Yemen 86 F7
Maxán Arg. 144 C3
Maxhamish Lake Canada 120 F3
Maxia, Punta mt. Sardinia Italy 58 C5
Maxixe Moz. 101 L2
Maxmo Fin. 44 M5
May, Isle of i. U.K. 50 G4
Maya r. Rus. Fed. 65 O3
Mayaguana i. Bahamas 133 F8
Mayaguana Passage Bahamas 133 F8
Mayagüez Puerto Rico 137 K5
Mayahi Niger 96 D3
Mayakovskiy, Qullai mt. Tajik. 89 H2
Mayakovskogo, Pik mt. Tajik. see Mayakovskiy, Qullai
Mayama Congo 98 B4
Maya Mountains Belize/Guat. 136 G5
Mayan China see Mayanhe
Mayang China 77 F3
Mayanhe China 76 E1
Mayar hill U.K. 50 F4
Maybeury U.S.A. 134 E5
Maybole U.K. 50 E5
Maych'ew Eth. 98 D2
Maydān Shahr Afgh. see Meydān Shahr
Maydh Somalia 86 G7
Maydos Turkey see Eceabat
Mayen Germany 53 H4
Mayenne France 56 D2
Mayenne r. France 56 D3
Mayer U.S.A. 129 G4
Mayêr Kangri mt. China 83 F2
Mayersville U.S.A. 131 F5
Mayerthorpe Canada 120 H4
Mayfield N.Z. 113 C6
Mayi He r. China 74 C3
Maykop Rus. Fed. 91 E1
Maymyo Myanmar 70 B2
Mayna Respublika Khakasiya Rus. Fed. 64 K4
Mayna Ul'yanovskaya Oblast' Rus. Fed. 43 J5
Mayni India 84 B2
Maynooth Canada 135 G1
Mayo Canada 120 C2
Mayo U.S.A. 133 D6
Mayo Alim Cameroon 96 E4
Mayoko Congo 98 B4
Mayo Lake Canada 120 C2
Mayo Landing Canada see Mayo
Mayor, Puig mt. Spain see Major, Puig
Mayor Island N.Z. 113 F3
Mayor Pablo Lagerenza Para. 144 D1

▶Mayotte terr. Africa 99 E5
French Territorial Collectivity.
Africa 7, 94–95

Mayskiy Amurskaya Oblast' Rus. Fed. 74 C1
Mayskiy Kabardino-Balkarskaya Respublika Rus. Fed. 91 G2
Mays Landing U.S.A. 135 H4
Mayson Lake Canada 121 J3
Maysville U.S.A. 134 D4
Mayumba Gabon 98 B4
Mayum La pass China 83 E3
Mayuram India 84 C4
Mayville MI U.S.A. 134 D2
Mayville ND U.S.A. 130 D2
Mayville NY U.S.A. 134 F2
Mayville WI U.S.A. 134 A2
Mazabuka Zambia 99 C5
Mazaca Turkey see Kayseri
Mazagan Morocco see El Jadida
Mazar China 82 D1
Mazar, Koh-i- mt. Afgh. 89 G3
Mazara, Val di valley Sicily Italy 58 E6
Mazara del Vallo Sicily Italy 58 E6
Mazār-e Sharīf Afgh. 89 G2
Mazārī' reg. U.A.E. 88 D6
Mazatán Mex. 127 F7
Mazatlán Mex. 136 C4
Mazatzal Peak U.S.A. 129 H4
Mazdaj Iran 91 H4
Mažeikiai Lith. 45 M8
Mazīm Oman 88 E6
Mazocahui Mex. 127 F7
Mazocruz Peru 142 E7
Mazomora Tanz. 99 D4
Mazu Dao i. Taiwan see Matsu Tao
Mazunga Zimbabwe 99 C6
Mazyr Belarus 43 F5
Mazzouna Tunisia 58 C7

▶Mbabane Swaziland 101 J4
Capital of Swaziland.

Mbahiakro Côte d'Ivoire 96 C4
Mbaïki Cent. Afr. Rep. 98 B3
Mbakaou, Lac de l. Cameroon 96 E4
Mbala Zambia 99 D4
Mbale Uganda 98 D3
Mbalmayo Cameroon 96 E4
Mbam r. Cameroon 96 E4
Mbandaka Dem. Rep. Congo 98 B4
M'banza Congo Angola 99 B4
Mbarara Uganda 97 G5
Mbari r. Cent. Afr. Rep. 98 C3
Mbaswana S. Africa 101 K4
Mbemkuru r. Tanz. 99 D4
Mbeya Tanz. 99 D4
Mbinga Tanz. 99 D5
Mbini Equat. Guinea 96 D4
Mbizi Zimbabwe 99 D6
Mboki Cent. Afr. Rep. 98 C3
Mbomo Congo 98 B3
Mbouda Cameroon 96 E4
Mbour Senegal 96 B3
Mbout Mauritania 96 B3
Mbozi Tanz. 99 D4
Mbrès Cent. Afr. Rep. 98 B3
Mbuji-Mayi Dem. Rep. Congo 99 C4
Mbulu Tanz. 98 D4
Mburucuyá Arg. 144 E3
McAdam Canada 123 I5
McAlester U.S.A. 131 E5
McAlister mt. Australia 112 D5
McAllen U.S.A. 131 D7
McArthur r. Australia 110 B2
McArthur U.S.A. 134 D4
McArthur Mills Canada 135 G1
McBain U.S.A. 134 C1
McBride Canada 120 F4
McCall U.S.A. 126 D3
McCamey U.S.A. 131 C6
McCammon U.S.A. 126 E4
McCauley Island Canada 120 D4
McClintock, Mount Antarctica 152 H1
McClintock Channel Canada 119 H2
McClintock Range hills Australia 108 D4
McClure, Lake U.S.A. 128 C3
McClure Strait Canada 118 G2
McClusky U.S.A. 130 C2
McComb U.S.A. 131 F6
McConaughy, Lake U.S.A. 130 C3
McConnellsburg U.S.A. 135 G4
McConnelsville U.S.A. 134 E4
McCook U.S.A. 130 C3
McCormick U.S.A. 133 D5
McCrea r. Canada 120 H2
McCreary Canada 121 L5
McDame Canada 120 D3
McDermitt U.S.A. 126 D4
McDonald Islands Indian Ocean 149 M9
McDonald Peak U.S.A. 126 E3
McDonough U.S.A. 133 C5
McDougall's Bay S. Africa 100 C5
McDowell Peak U.S.A. 129 H5
McFarland U.S.A. 128 D4
McGill U.S.A. 129 F2
McGivney Canada 123 I5
McGrath AK U.S.A. 118 C3
McGrath MN U.S.A. 130 E2
McGraw U.S.A. 135 G2
McGregor r. Canada 120 F4
McGregor S. Africa 100 D7
McGregor, Lake Canada 120 H5
McGregor Range hills Australia 111 C5
McGuire, Mount U.S.A. 126 E3
Mchinga Tanz. 99 D4
Mchinji Malawi 99 D5
McIlwraith Range hills Australia 110 C2
McInnes Lake Canada 121 M4
McIntosh U.S.A. 130 C2
McKay Range hills Australia 108 C5
McKean i. Kiribati 107 I2
McKee U.S.A. 134 C5
McKenzie r. U.S.A. 126 C3
McKinlay r. Australia 110 C4

▶McKinley, Mount U.S.A. 118 C3
Highest mountain in North America.
North America 114–115

McKinney U.S.A. 131 D5
McKittrick U.S.A. 128 D4
McLaughlin U.S.A. 130 C2
McLeansboro U.S.A. 130 F4
McLennan Canada 120 G4
McLeod r. Canada 120 H4
McLeod Bay Canada 121 I2
McLeod Lake Canada 120 F4
McLoughlin, Mount U.S.A. 126 C4
McMillan, Lake U.S.A. 131 B5
McMinnville OR U.S.A. 126 C3
McMinnville TN U.S.A. 132 C5
McMurdo research station Antarctica 152 H1
McMurdo Sound b. Antarctica 152 H1
McNary U.S.A. 129 I4
McNaughton Lake Canada see Kinbasket Lake
McPherson U.S.A. 130 D4
McQuesten r. Canada 120 B2
McRae U.S.A. 133 D5
McTavish Arm b. Canada 120 G1
McVeytown U.S.A. 135 G3
McVicar Arm b. Canada 120 F1
Mdantsane S. Africa 101 H7
M'Daourouch Alg. 58 B6
Mê, Hon i. Vietnam 70 D3
Mead, Lake resr U.S.A. 129 F3
Meade U.S.A. 131 C4
Meade r. U.S.A. 118 C2
Meadow Australia 109 A6
Meadow SD U.S.A. 130 C2
Meadow UT U.S.A. 129 G2
Meadow Lake Canada 121 I4
Meadville MS U.S.A. 131 F6
Meadville PA U.S.A. 134 E3
Meaford Canada 134 E1
Meaken-dake vol. Japan 74 G4
Mealhada Port. 57 B3
Mealy Mountains Canada 123 K3
Meandarra Australia 112 D1
Meander River Canada 120 G3
Meaux France 52 C6
Mecca Saudi Arabia 86 E5
Mecca CA U.S.A. 128 E5
Mecca OH U.S.A. 134 E3
Mechanic Falls U.S.A. 135 J1
Mechanicsville U.S.A. 135 G5
Mechelen Belgium 52 E3
Mechelen Neth. 52 F4
Mecherchar i. Palau see Eil Malk
Mecheria Alg. 54 D5
Mechernich Germany 52 G4
Mecitözü Turkey 90 D2
Meckenheim Germany 52 H4
Mecklenburger Bucht b. Germany 47 M3
Mecklenburg-Vorpommern land Germany 53 M1
Mecklenburg - West Pomerania land Germany see Mecklenburg-Vorpommern
Meda r. Australia 108 C4
Meda Port. 57 C3
Medak India 84 C2
Medan Indon. 71 B7
Medanosa, Punta pt Arg. 144 C7
Médanos de Coro, Parque Nacional nat. park Venez. 142 E1
Medawachchiya Sri Lanka 84 D4
Médéa Alg. 57 H5
Medebach Germany 53 I3
Medellín Col. 142 C2
Meden r. U.K. 48 G5
Medenine Tunisia 54 G5
Mederdra Mauritania 96 B3
Medford NY U.S.A. 135 I3
Medford OK U.S.A. 131 D4
Medford OR U.S.A. 126 C4
Medford WI U.S.A. 130 F2
Medgidia Romania 59 M2
Media U.S.A. 135 H4
Mediaș Romania 59 K1
Medicine Bow r. U.S.A. 126 G4
Medicine Bow Mountains U.S.A. 126 G4
Medicine Bow Peak U.S.A. 126 G4
Medicine Hat Canada 121 I5
Medicine Lake U.S.A. 126 G2
Medicine Lodge U.S.A. 131 D4
Medina Brazil 145 C2
Medina Saudi Arabia 86 E5
Medina ND U.S.A. 130 D2
Medina NY U.S.A. 135 F2
Medina OH U.S.A. 134 E3
Medinaceli Spain 57 E3
Medina del Campo Spain 57 D3
Medina de Rioseco Spain 57 D3
Medina Lake U.S.A. 131 D6
Medinipur India 83 F5
Mediolanum Italy see Milan
Mediterranean Sea 54 K5
Mednyy, Ostrov i. Rus. Fed. 150 H2
Médoc reg. France 56 D4
Mêdog China 76 B2
Medora U.S.A. 130 C2
Medstead Canada 121 I4
Meduro atoll Marshall Is see Majuro
Medvedevo Rus. Fed. 42 J4
Medveditsa r. Rus. Fed. 43 I6
Medvednica mts Croatia 58 F2
Medvezh'i, Ostrova is Rus. Fed. 65 R2
Medvezh'ya, Gora mt. Rus. Fed. 74 E3
Medvezh'yegorsk Rus. Fed. 42 G3
Medway r. U.K. 49 H7
Meekatharra Australia 109 B6
Meeker CO U.S.A. 129 J1
Meeker OH U.S.A. 134 D3
Meelpaeg Reservoir Canada 123 K4
Meemu Atoll Maldives see Mulaku Atoll
Meerane Germany 53 M4
Meerlo Neth. 52 G3
Meerut India 82 D3
Mega Escarpment Eth./Kenya 98 D3
Megalopoli Greece 59 J6
Megamo Indon. 69 I7
Mégantic, Lac l. Canada 123 H5
Megara Greece 59 J5
Megezez mt. Eth. 98 D3

▶Meghalaya state India 83 G4
Highest mean annual rainfall in the world.

Meghasani mt. India 83 F5
Meghri Armenia 91 G3
Megin Turkm. 88 E2
Megisti i. Greece 59 M6
Megri Armenia see Meghri
Mehamn Norway 44 O1
Mehar Pak. 89 G5
Meharry, Mount Australia 109 B5
Mehbubnagar India see Mahbubnagar
Mehdia Tunisia see Mahdia
Meherpur Bangl. 83 G5
Meherrin U.S.A. 135 F5
Meherrin r. U.S.A. 135 G5
Mehlville U.S.A. 130 F4
Mehrakān salt marsh Iran 88 D5
Mehrān Hormozgan Iran 88 D5
Mehrān Īlām Iran 88 B3
Mehren Germany 52 G4
Mehriz Iran 88 D4
Mehsana India see Mahesana
Mehtar Lām Afgh. 89 H3
Meia Ponte r. Brazil 145 A2
Meicheng China see Minqing
Meiganga Cameroon 97 E4
Meighen Island Canada 119 I2
Meigu China 76 D2
Meihekou China 74 B4
Meikeng China 77 G3
Meikle r. Canada 120 G3
Meikle Says Law hill U.K. 50 G5
Meiktila Myanmar 70 A2
Meilin China see Ganxian
Meilleur r. Canada 120 E2
Meilu China 77 F4
Meine Germany 53 K2
Meinersen Germany 53 K2
Meiningen Germany 53 K4
Meishan Anhui China see Jinzhai
Meishan Sichuan China 76 D2
Meishan Shuiku resr China 77 G2
Meißen Germany 47 N5
Meister r. Canada 120 D2
Meitan China 76 E3
Meixi China 74 C3
Meixian China see Meizhou
Meixing China see Xiaojin
Meizhou China 77 H3
Mej r. India 82 D4
Mejicana mt. Arg. 144 C3
Mejillones Chile 144 B2
Mékambo Gabon 98 B3
Mek'elē Eth. 98 D2
Mekelle Eth. see Mek'elē
Mékhé Senegal 96 B3
Mekhtar Pak. 89 H4
Meknassy Tunisia 58 C7
Meknès Morocco 54 C5
Mekong r. Xizang/Yunnan China 72 C2
Mekong r. Laos/Thai. 70 D4
also known as Mae Nam Khong (Laos/Thailand)
Mekong, Mouths of the Vietnam 71 D5
Mekoryuk U.S.A. 118 B3
Melaka Malaysia 71 C7
Melanau, Gunung hill Indon. 71 E7
Melanesia is Pacific Ocean 150 G6
Melanesian Basin sea feature Pacific Ocean 150 G5

▶Melbourne Australia 112 B6
State capital of Victoria. 2nd most populous city in Oceania.

Melbourne U.S.A. 133 D6
Melby U.K. 50 [inset]
Meldorf Germany 47 L3
Melekess Rus. Fed. see Dimitrovgrad
Melenki Rus. Fed. 43 I5
Melet Turkey see Mesudiye
Mélèzes, Rivière aux r. Canada 123 H2
Melfa U.S.A. 135 H5
Melfi Chad 97 E3
Melfi Italy 58 F4
Melfort Canada 121 J4
Melhus Norway 44 G5
Meliadine Lake Canada 121 M2
Melide Spain 57 C2

▶Melilla N. Africa 57 E6
Spanish Territory.

Melimoyu, Monte mt. Chile 144 B6
Meliskerke Neth. 52 D3
Melita Canada 121 K5
Melitene Turkey see Malatya
Melitopol' Ukr. 43 G7
Melk Austria 47 O6
Melka Guba Eth. 98 D3
Melksham U.K. 49 E7
Mellakoski Fin. 44 N3
Mellansel Sweden 44 K5
Melle Germany 53 I2
Mellerud Sweden 45 H7
Mellette U.S.A. 130 D2
Mellid Spain see Melide
Mellilia N. Africa see Melilla
Mellor Glacier Antarctica 152 E2
Mellrichstadt Germany 53 K4
Mellum i. Germany 53 I1
Melmoth S. Africa 101 J5
Mel'nichoye Rus. Fed. 74 D3
Melo Uruguay 144 F4
Meloco Moz. 99 D5
Melolo Indon. 108 C2
Melozitna r. U.S.A. 118 C3
Melrhir, Chott salt l. Alg. 54 F5
Melrose Australia 109 C6
Melrose U.K. 50 G5
Melrose U.S.A. 130 E2
Melsungen Germany 53 J3
Melton Australia 112 B6
Melton Mowbray U.K. 49 G6
Melun France 56 F2
Melville Canada 121 K5
Melville, Cape Australia 110 D2
Melville, Lake Canada 123 K3
Melville Bugt b. Greenland see Qimusseriarsuaq
Melville Island Australia 108 E2
Melville Island Canada 119 H2
Melville Peninsula Canada 119 J3
Melvin U.S.A. 134 A3
Melvin, Lough l. Rep. of Ireland/U.K. 51 D3
Mêmar Co salt l. China 83 E2
Memba Moz. 99 E5
Memberamo r. Indon. 69 J7
Memel Lith. see Klaipėda
Memel S. Africa 101 I4
Memmelsdorf Germany 53 K5
Memmingen Germany 47 M7
Mempawah Indon. 68 D6
Memphis tourist site Egypt 90 C5
Memphis MI U.S.A. 134 D2
Memphis TN U.S.A. 131 F5
Memphis TX U.S.A. 131 C5
Memphrémagog, Lac l. Canada 135 I1
Mena Ukr. 43 G6
Mena U.S.A. 131 E5
Menado Indon. see Manado
Ménaka Mali 96 D3
Menard U.S.A. 131 D6
Menasha U.S.A. 134 A1
Mendanha Brazil 145 C2
Mendarik i. Indon. 71 D7
Mende France 56 F4
Mendefera Eritrea 86 E7
Mendeleyev Ridge sea feature Arctic Ocean 153 B1
Mendeleyevsk Rus. Fed. 42 L5
Mendenhall U.S.A. 131 F6
Mendenhall, Cape U.S.A. 118 B4
Mendenhall Glacier U.S.A. 120 C3
Méndez Mex. 131 D7
Mendī Eth. 98 D3
Mendi P.N.G. 69 K8
Mendip Hills U.K. 49 E7
Mendocino U.S.A. 128 B2
Mendocino, Cape U.S.A. 128 A1
Mendocino, Lake U.S.A. 128 B2
Mendooran Australia 112 D3
Mendota CA U.S.A. 128 C3
Mendota IL U.S.A. 130 F3
Mendoza Arg. 144 C4
Menemen Turkey 59 L5
Ménerville Alg. see Thenia
Mengban China 76 D4
Mengcheng China 77 H1
Menghai China 76 D4
Mengjin China 77 G1
Mengla China 76 D4
Menglang China see Lancang
Menglie China see Jiangcheng
Mengyang China see Mingshan
Mengzi China 76 D4
Menihek Canada 123 I3
Menihek Lakes Canada 123 I3
Menindee Australia 111 C7
Menindee Lake Australia 111 C7
Ménistouc, Lac l. Canada 123 I3
Menkere Rus. Fed. 65 N3
Mennecy France 52 C6
Menominee U.S.A. 134 B1
Menomonee Falls U.S.A. 134 A2
Menomonie U.S.A. 130 F2
Menongue Angola 99 B5
Menorca i. Spain see Minorca
Mentawai, Kepulauan is Indon. 68 B7
Mentawai, Selat sea chan. Indon. 68 C7
Menteroda Germany 53 K3
Mentmore U.S.A. 129 I4
Menton France 56 H5
Mentone U.S.A. 131 C6
Menuf Egypt see Minūf
Menzel Bourguiba Tunisia 58 C6
Menzelet Barajı resr Turkey 90 E3
Menzelinsk Rus. Fed. 41 Q4
Menzel Temime Tunisia 58 D6
Menzies Australia 109 C7
Menzies, Mount Antarctica 148 E2
Meobbaai b. Namibia 100 B3
Meoqui Mex. 131 B6
Meppel Neth. 52 G2
Meppen Germany 53 H2
Mepuze Moz. 101 K2
Meqheleng S. Africa 101 H5
Mequon U.S.A. 134 B2
Merak Indon. 68 D8
Meråker Norway 44 G5
Merano Italy 58 D1
Meratswe r. Botswana 100 G2
Merauke Indon. 69 K8
Merca Somalia see Marka
Mercantour, Parc National du nat. park France 56 H4
Merced U.S.A. 128 C3
Merced r. U.S.A. 128 C3
Mercedes Arg. 144 E3
Mercedes Uruguay 144 E4
Mercer ME U.S.A. 135 K1
Mercer PA U.S.A. 134 E3
Mercer WI U.S.A. 130 F2
Mercês Brazil 145 C3
Mercury Islands N.Z. 113 E3
Mercy, Cape Canada 119 L3
Merdenik Turkey see Göle
Mere Belgium 52 D4
Mere U.K. 49 E7
Meredith U.S.A. 135 J2
Meredith, Lake U.S.A. 131 C5
Merefa Ukr. 43 H6
Merga Oasis Sudan 86 C6
Mergui Myanmar 71 B4
Mergui Archipelago is Myanmar 71 B5
Meriç r. Turkey 59 L4
also known as Evros (Greece), Marica, Maritsa (Bulgaria)
Mérida Mex. 136 G4
Mérida Spain 57 C4
Mérida Venez. 142 D2
Mérida, Cordillera de mts Venez. 142 D2
Meriden U.S.A. 135 I3
Meridian MS U.S.A. 131 F5
Meridian TX U.S.A. 131 D6
Mérignac France 56 D4
Merijärvi Fin. 44 N4
Merikarvia Fin. 45 L6
Merimbula Australia 112 D6
Merín, Laguna l. Brazil/Uruguay see Mirim, Lagoa
Meringur Australia 111 C7
Merir i. Palau 69 I6
Merjayoun Lebanon see Marjayoûn
Merkel U.S.A. 131 C5
Merluna Australia 110 C2
Mermaid Reef Australia 108 B4
Meron, Har mt. Israel 85 B3
Merowe Sudan 86 D6
Mêrqung Co l. China 83 F3
Merredin Australia 109 B7
Merrick hill U.K. 50 E5
Merrickville Canada 135 H1
Merrill MI U.S.A. 134 C2
Merrill WI U.S.A. 130 F2
Merrill, Mount Canada 120 E2
Merrillville U.S.A. 134 B3
Merriman U.S.A. 130 C3
Merritt Canada 120 F5
Merritt Island U.S.A. 133 D6
Merriwa Australia 112 E4
Merrygoen Australia 112 D3
Mersa Fatma Eritrea 86 F7
Mersa Maṭrûḥ Egypt see Marsá Maṭrūḥ
Mersch Lux. 52 G5
Merseburg (Saale) Germany 53 L3
Mersey est. U.K. 48 E5
Mersin Turkey see İçel
Mersing Malaysia 71 C7
Mērsrags Latvia 45 M8
Merta India 82 C4
Merthyr Tydfil U.K. 49 D7
Mértola Port. 57 C5
Mertz Glacier Antarctica 152 G2
Mertz Glacier Tongue Antarctica 152 G2
Mertzon U.S.A. 131 C6
Méru France 52 C5

▶Meru vol. Tanz. 98 D4
4th highest mountain in Africa.

Merui Pak. 89 F4
Merv Turkm. see Mary
Merweville S. Africa 100 E7
Merzifon Turkey 90 D2
Merzig Germany 52 G5
Merz Peninsula Antarctica 152 L2
Mesa AZ U.S.A. 129 H5
Mesa NM U.S.A. 127 G6
Mesabi Range hills U.S.A. 130 E2
Mesagne Italy 58 G4
Mesa Negra mt. U.S.A. 129 J4
Mesara, Ormos b. Greece 59 K7
Mesa Verde National Park U.S.A. 129 I3
Meschede Germany 53 I3
Mese Myanmar 70 B3
Meselefors Sweden 44 J4
Mesgouez Lake Canada 122 G4
Meshed Iran see Mashhad
Meshkān Iran 88 E2
Meshra'er Req Sudan 86 C8
Mesick U.S.A. 134 C1
Mesimeri Greece 59 J4
Mesolongi Greece 59 I5
Mesolóngion Greece see Mesolongi
Mesopotamia reg. Iraq 91 F4
Mesquita Brazil 145 C2
Mesquite NV U.S.A. 129 F3
Mesquite TX U.S.A. 131 D5
Mesquite Lake U.S.A. 129 F4
Messaad Alg. 54 E5
Messana Sicily Italy see Messina
Messina Sicily Italy 58 F5
Messina S. Africa 101 J2
Messina, Strait of Italy 58 F5
Messina, Stretta di Italy see Messina, Strait of
Messini Greece 59 J6
Messiniakos Kolpos b. Greece 59 J6
Mesta r. Bulg. 59 K4
Mesta r. Greece see Nestos
Mestghanem Alg. see Mostaganem
Mestlin Germany 53 L1
Meston, Akra pt Greece 59 K5
Mestre Italy 58 E2
Mesudiye Turkey 90 E2
Meta r. Col./Venez. 142 E2
Métabetchouan Canada 123 H4
Meta Incognita Peninsula Canada 119 L3
Metairie U.S.A. 131 F6
Metallifere, Colline mts Italy 58 D3
Metán Arg. 144 C3
Meteghan Canada 123 I5
Meteor Depth sea feature S. Atlantic Ocean 148 G9
Methoni Greece 59 I6
Methuen U.S.A. 135 J2
Methven U.K. 50 F4
Metionga Lake Canada 122 C4
Metković Croatia 58 G3
Metlaoui Tunisia 54 F5
Metoro Moz. 99 D5
Metro Indon. 68 D8
Metropolis U.S.A. 131 F4
Metsada tourist site Israel see Masada
Metter U.S.A. 133 D5
Mettet Belgium 52 E4
Mettingen Germany 53 H2
Mettler U.S.A. 128 D4
Mettur India 84 C4
Metu Eth. 98 D3
Metz France 52 G5
Metz U.S.A. 134 C3
Meulaboh Indon. 71 B6
Meureudu Indon. 71 B6
Meuse r. Belgium/France 52 F3
also known as Maas (Netherlands)
Meuselwitz Germany 53 M3
Mevagissey U.K. 49 C8
Mêwa China 76 D1
Mexia U.S.A. 131 D6
Mexiana, Ilha i. Brazil 143 I3
Mexicali Mex. 129 F5
Mexican Hat U.S.A. 129 I3
Mexican Water U.S.A. 129 I3

▶Mexico country Central America 136 D4
2nd most populous and 3rd largest country in Central and North America.
North America 9, 116–117

México Mex. see Mexico City
Mexico ME U.S.A. 135 J1
Mexico MO U.S.A. 130 F4
Mexico NY U.S.A. 135 G2
Mexico, Gulf of Mex./U.S.A. 125 H6

▶Mexico City Mex. 136 E5
Capital of Mexico. Most populous city in North America and 2nd in the world.

Meybod Iran 88 D3
Meydanī, Ra's-e pt Iran 88 E5
Meydān Shahr Afgh. 89 H3
Meyenburg Germany 53 M1
Meyersdale U.S.A. 134 F4
Meymaneh Afgh. 89 G3
Meymeh Iran 88 C3
Meynypil'gyno Rus. Fed. 153 C2
Mezada tourist site Israel see Masada
Mezdra Bulg. 59 J3
Mezen' Rus. Fed. 42 J2
Mezen' r. Rus. Fed. 42 J2
Mézenc, Mont mt. France 56 G4
Mezenskaya Guba b. Rus. Fed. 42 I2
Mezhdurechensk Kemerovskaya Oblast' Rus. Fed. 72 F2
Mezhdurechensk Respublika Komi Rus. Fed. 42 K3
Mezhdurechnye Rus. Fed. see Shali
Mezhdusharskiy, Ostrov i. Rus. Fed. 64 G2
Mezitli Turkey 85 B1
Mezőtúr Hungary 59 I1
Mežvidi Latvia 45 O8
Mhàil, Rubh' a' pt U.K. 50 C5
Mhangura Zimbabwe 99 D5
Mhlume Swaziland 101 J4
Mhow India 82 C5
Mi r. Myanmar 83 H5
Miahuatlán Mex. 136 E5
Miajadas Spain 57 D4
Miaméré Cent. Afr. Rep. 98 B3
Miami AZ U.S.A. 129 H5
Miami FL U.S.A. 133 D7
Miami OK U.S.A. 131 E4
Miami Beach U.S.A. 133 D7
Miancaowan China 76 C1
Miāndehī Iran 88 E3
Miandowāb Iran 88 B2
Miandrivazo Madag. 99 E5
Mīāneh Iran 88 B2
Miang, Phu mt. Thai. 70 C3
Miani India 89 I4
Miani Hor b. Pak. 89 G5
Mianjoi Afgh. 89 G3
Mianning China 76 D2
Mianwali Pak. 89 H3
Mianxian China 76 E1
Mianyang Hubei China see Xiantao
Mianyang Shaanxi China see Mianxian
Mianyang Sichuan China 76 E2
Mianzhu China 76 E2
Miaoli Taiwan 77 I3
Miarinarivo Madag. 99 E5
Miarritze France see Biarritz
Miass Rus. Fed. 64 H4
Mica Creek Canada 120 G4
Mica Mountain U.S.A. 129 H5
Micang Shan mts China 76 E1
Michalovce Slovakia 43 D6

Michel Canada 121 I4
Michelau in Oberfranken Germany 53 L4
Michelson, Mount U.S.A. 118 D3
Michelstadt Germany 53 J5
Michendorf Germany 53 N2
Micheng China see Midu
Michigan state U.S.A. 134 C2

▶Michigan, Lake U.S.A. 134 B2
3rd largest lake in North America and 5th in the world.
World 12–13

Michigan City U.S.A. 134 B3
Michinberi India 84 D2
Michipicoten Bay Canada 122 D5
Michipicoten Island Canada 122 D5
Michipicoten River Canada 122 D5
Michurin Bulg. see Tsarevo
Michurinsk Rus. Fed. 43 I5
Micronesia country N. Pacific Ocean see Micronesia, Federated States of
Micronesia is Pacific Ocean 150 F5
▶Micronesia, Federated States of country N. Pacific Ocean 150 G5
Oceania 8, 104–105
Midai i. Indon. 71 D7
Mid-Atlantic Ridge sea feature Atlantic Ocean 148 E4
Mid-Atlantic Ridge sea feature Atlantic Ocean 148 G8
Middelburg Neth. 52 D3
Middelburg E. Cape S. Africa 101 G6
Middelburg Mpumalanga S. Africa 101 I3
Middelfart Denmark 45 F9
Middelharnis Neth. 52 E3
Middelwit S. Africa 101 H3
Middle Alkali Lake U.S.A. 126 C4
Middle America Trench sea feature N. Pacific Ocean 151 N5
Middle Andaman i. India 71 A4
Middle Atlas mts Morocco see Moyen Atlas
Middle Bay Canada 123 K4
Middlebourne U.S.A. 134 E4
Middleburg U.S.A. 135 G3
Middleburgh U.S.A. 135 H2
Middlebury IN U.S.A. 134 C3
Middlebury VT U.S.A. 135 I1
Middle Caicos i. Turks and Caicos Is 133 G8
Middle Concho r. U.S.A. 131 C6
Middle Congo country Africa see Congo
Middle Island Thai. see Tasai, Ko
Middle Loup r. U.S.A. 130 D3
Middlemarch N.Z. 113 C7
Middlemount Australia 110 E4
Middle River U.S.A. 135 G4
Middlesbrough U.K. 48 F4
Middle Strait India see Andaman Strait
Middleton Australia 110 C4
Middleton Canada 123 I5
Middleton Island atoll American Samoa see Rose Island
Middletown CA U.S.A. 128 B2
Middletown CT U.S.A. 135 I3
Middletown NY U.S.A. 135 H3
Middletown VA U.S.A. 135 F4
Midelt Morocco 54 D5
Midhurst U.K. 49 G8
Midi, Canal du France 56 F5
Mid-Indian Basin sea feature Indian Ocean 149 N6
Mid-Indian Ridge sea feature Indian Ocean 149 M7
Midland Canada 135 F1
Midland CA U.S.A. 129 F5
Midland IN U.S.A. 134 B4
Midland MI U.S.A. 134 C2
Midland SD U.S.A. 130 C2
Midland TX U.S.A. 131 C5
Midleton Rep. of Ireland 51 D6
Midnapore India see Medinipur
Midnapur India see Medinipur
Midongy Atsimo Madag. 99 E6
Mid-Pacific Mountains sea feature N. Pacific Ocean 150 G4
Midu China 76 D3
Miðvágur Faroe Is 44 [inset]
Midway Oman see Thamarīt

▶Midway Islands terr. N. Pacific Ocean 150 I4
United States Unincorporated Territory.

Midway Well Australia 109 C5
Midwest U.S.A. 126 G4
Midwest City U.S.A. 131 D5
Midwoud Neth. 52 F2
Midyat Turkey 91 F3
Midye Turkey see Kıyıköy
Mid Yell U.K. 50 [inset]
Midzhur mt. Bulg./Serb. and Mont. 90 A2
Miehikkälä Fin. 45 O6
Miekojärvi l. Fin. 44 N3
Mielec Poland 43 D6
Mienhua Yü i. Taiwan 77 I3
Mieraslompolo Fin. 44 O2
Mierašluoppal Fin. see Mieraslompolo
Miercurea-Ciuc Romania 59 K1
Mieres Spain 57 D2
Mieres del Camín Spain see Mieres
Mī'ēso Eth. 98 E3
Mieste Germany 53 L2
Mifflinburg U.S.A. 135 G3
Mifflintown U.S.A. 135 G3
Migang Shan mt. China 76 E1
Migdol S. Africa 101 G4
Miging India 76 B2
Miguel Auza Mex. 131 C7
Miguel Hidalgo, Presa resr Mex. 127 F8
Mihalıççık Turkey 59 N5
Mihara Japan 75 D6
Mihintale Sri Lanka 84 D4
Mihmandar Turkey 85 B1
Mijares r. Spain see Millárs
Mijdrecht Neth. 52 E2
Mikhaylov Rus. Fed. 43 H5
Mikhaylovgrad Bulg. see Montana
Mikhaylovka Amurskaya Oblast' Rus. Fed. 74 C2
Mikhaylovka Primorskiy Kray Rus. Fed. 74 D4
Mikhaylovka Tul'skaya Oblast' Rus. Fed. see Kimovsk
Mikhaylovka Volgogradskaya Oblast' Rus. Fed. 43 I6
Mikhaylovskiy Rus. Fed. 80 E1
Mikhaylovskoye Rus. Fed. see Shpakovskoye
Mikhaytov Island Antarctica 152 E2
Mikhrot Timna Israel 85 B5
Mikir Hills India 83 H4
Mikkeli Fin. 45 O6
Mikkelin mlk Fin. 45 O6
Mikkwa r. Canada 120 H3
Míkonos i. Greece see Mykonos
Mikoyan Armenia see Yeghegnadzor
Mikulkin, Mys c. Rus. Fed. 42 J2
Mikumi National Park Tanz. 99 D4
Mikun' Rus. Fed. 42 K3
Mikuni-sanmyaku mts Japan 75 E5
Mikura-jima i. Japan 75 E6
Milaca U.S.A. 130 E2
Miladhunmadulu Atoll Maldives 84 B5
Miladummadulu Atoll Maldives see Miladhunmadulu Atoll
Milan Italy 58 C2
Milan MI U.S.A. 134 D2
Milan MO U.S.A. 130 E3
Milan OH U.S.A. 134 D3
Milange Moz. 99 D5
Milano Italy see Milan
Milas Turkey 59 L6
Milazzo Sicily Italy 58 F5
Milazzo, Capo di c. Sicily Italy 58 F5
Milbank U.S.A. 130 D2
Milbridge U.S.A. 132 H2
Milde r. Germany 53 L2
Mildenhall U.K. 49 H6
Mildura Australia 111 C7
Mile China 76 D3
Mileiz, Wâdi el watercourse Egypt see Mulayz, Wādī al
Miles Australia 112 E1
Miles City U.S.A. 126 G3
Milestone Rep. of Ireland 51 D5
Miletto, Monte mt. Italy 58 F4
Mileura Australia 109 B6
Milford Rep. of Ireland 51 E2
Milford DE U.S.A. 135 H4
Milford IL U.S.A. 134 B3
Milford MA U.S.A. 135 J2
Milford MI U.S.A. 134 D2
Milford NE U.S.A. 130 D3
Milford NH U.S.A. 135 J2
Milford PA U.S.A. 135 H3
Milford UT U.S.A. 129 G2
Milford VA U.S.A. 135 G4
Milford Haven U.K. 49 B7
Milford Sound N.Z. 113 A7
Milford Sound inlet N.Z. 113 A7
Milgarra Australia 110 C3
Milḥ, Baḥr al l. Iraq see Razāzah, Buḥayrat ar
Miliana Alg. 57 H5
Milid Turkey see Malatya
Milikapiti Australia 108 E2
Miling Australia 109 B7
Milk r. U.S.A. 126 G2
Milk, Wadi el watercourse Sudan 86 D6
Mil'kovo Rus. Fed. 65 Q4
Millaa Millaa Australia 110 D3
Millárs r. Spain 57 F4
Millau France 56 F4
Millbrook Canada 135 F1
Mill Creek r. U.S.A. 128 B1
Milledgeville U.S.A. 133 D5
Mille Lacs lakes U.S.A. 130 E2
Mille Lacs, Lac des l. Canada 119 I5
Millen U.S.A. 133 D5
Millennium Island atoll Kiribati see Caroline Island
Miller U.S.A. 130 D2
Miller Lake Canada 134 E1
Millerovo Rus. Fed. 43 I6
Millersburg OH U.S.A. 134 E3
Millersburg PA U.S.A. 135 G3
Millers Creek U.S.A. 134 D5
Millersville U.S.A. 135 G4
Millerton Lake U.S.A. 128 D3
Millet Canada 120 H4
Milleur Point U.K. 50 D5
Mill Hall U.S.A. 135 G3
Millicent Australia 111 C8
Millington MI U.S.A. 134 D2
Millington TN U.S.A. 131 F5
Millinocket U.S.A. 132 G2
Mill Island Canada 119 K3
Millmerran Australia 112 E1
Millom U.K. 48 D4
Millport U.K. 50 E5
Millsboro U.S.A. 135 H4
Mills Creek watercourse Australia 110 C4
Mills Lake Canada 120 G2
Millstone KY U.S.A. 134 D5
Millstone WV U.S.A. 134 E4
Millstream-Chichester National Park Australia 108 B5
Millthorpe Australia 112 D4
Milltown Canada 123 I5
Milltown U.S.A. 126 E3
Milltown Malbay Rep. of Ireland 51 C5
Millungera Australia 110 C3
Millville U.S.A. 135 H4
Millwood U.S.A. 134 B5
Millwood Lake U.S.A. 131 E5
Milly Milly Australia 109 B6
Milne Land i. Greenland see Ilimananngip Nunaa
Milner U.S.A. 129 J1
Milo r. Guinea 96 C3
Milogradovo Rus. Fed. 74 D4
Miloli'i HI U.S.A. 127 [inset]
Milos i. Greece 59 K6
Milparinka Australia 111 C6
Milpitas U.S.A. 128 C3
Milroy U.S.A. 135 G3
Milton N.Z. 113 B8
Milton DE U.S.A. 135 H4
Milton NH U.S.A. 135 J2
Milton WV U.S.A. 134 D4
Milton Keynes U.K. 49 G6
Miluo China 77 G2
Milverton Canada 134 E2
Milwaukee U.S.A. 134 B2

▶Milwaukee Deep sea feature Caribbean Sea 148 D4
Deepest point in the Atlantic Ocean (Puerto Rico Trench).

Mimbres watercourse U.S.A. 129 J5
Mimili Australia 109 F6
Mimisal India 84 C4
Mimizan France 56 D4
Mimongo Gabon 98 B4
Mimosa Rocks National Park Australia 112 E6
Mina Mex. 131 C7
Mina U.S.A. 128 D2
Mīnāb Iran 88 E5
Minaçu Brazil 145 A1
Minahasa, Semenanjung pen. Indon. 69 G6
Minahassa Peninsula Indon. see Minahasa, Semenanjung
Minaker Canada see Prophet River
Mīnakh Syria 85 C1
Minaki Canada 121 M5
Minamia Australia 108 F3
Minami-Daitō-jima i. Japan 73 O7
Minami-Iō-jima vol. Japan 69 K2
Min'an China see Longshan
Minaret of Jam tourist site Afgh. 89 G3
Minas Indon. 71 C7
Minas Uruguay 144 E4
Minas de Matahambre Cuba 133 D8
Minas Gerais state Brazil 145 B2
Minas Novas Brazil 145 C2
Minatitlán Mex. 136 F5
Minbu Myanmar 70 A2
Minbya Myanmar 70 A2
Minchinmávida vol. Chile 144 B6
Mindanao i. Phil. 69 H5
Mindanao Trench sea feature N. Pacific Ocean see Philippine Trench
Mindelo Cape Verde 96 [inset]
Minden Canada 135 F1
Minden Germany 53 I2
Minden LA U.S.A. 131 E5
Minden NE U.S.A. 124 H3
Minden NV U.S.A. 128 D2
Mindon Myanmar 70 A3
Mindoro i. Phil. 69 G4
Mindoro Strait Phil. 69 F4
Mindouli Congo 98 B4
Mine Head hd Rep. of Ireland 51 E6
Minehead U.K. 49 D7
Mineola U.S.A. 135 I3
Mineral U.S.A. 135 G4
Mineral'nyye Vody Rus. Fed. 91 F1
Mineral Wells U.S.A. 131 D5
Mineralwells U.S.A. 134 E4
Minersville PA U.S.A. 135 G3
Minersville UT U.S.A. 129 G2
Minerva U.S.A. 134 E3
Minerva Reefs Fiji 107 I4
Minfeng China 83 E1
Minga Dem. Rep. Congo 99 C5
Mingäçevir Azer. 91 G2
Mingäçevir Su Anbarı resr Azer. 91 G2
Mingala Cent. Afr. Rep. 98 C3
Mingan, Îles de is Canada 123 J4
Mingan Archipelago National Park Reserve Canada see L'Archipélago de Mingan, Réserve du Parc National de
Mingbulak Uzbek. 80 B3
Mingechaur Azer. see Mingäçevir
Mingechaurskoye Vodokhranilishche resr Azer. see Mingäçevir Su Anbarı
Mingenew Australia 109 A7
Mingfeng China see Yuan'an
Minggang China 77 G1
Mingguang China 77 H1
Mingin Range mts Myanmar 70 A2
Minglanilla Spain 57 F4
Mingoyo Tanz. 99 D5
Mingshan China 76 D2
Mingshui Gansu China 80 I3
Mingshui Heilong. China 74 B3
Mingteke China 82 C1
Mingulay i. U.K. 50 B4
Mingxi China 77 H3
Mingzhou China see Suide
Minhe China see Jinxian
Minhla Magwe Myanmar 70 A3
Minhla Pegu Myanmar 70 A3
Minho r. Port./Spain see Miño
Minicoy atoll India 84 B4
Minigwal, Lake salt flat Australia 109 C7
Minilya Australia 109 A5
Minilya r. Australia 109 A5
Minipi Lake Canada 123 J3
Miniss Lake Canada 121 N5
Minitonas Canada 121 K4
Minjian China see Mabian
Min Jiang r. Sichuan China 76 E2
Min Jiang r. China 77 H3
Minna Nigeria 96 D4
Minna Bluff pt Antarctica 152 H1
Minne Sweden 44 I5
Minneapolis KS U.S.A. 130 D4
Minneapolis MN U.S.A. 130 E2
Minnedosa Canada 121 L5
Minnehaha Springs U.S.A. 134 F4
Minneola U.S.A. 131 C4
Minnesota r. U.S.A. 130 E2
Minnesota state U.S.A. 130 E2
Minnewaukan U.S.A. 130 D1
Minnitaki Lake Canada 121 N5
Miño r. Port./Spain 57 B3
also known as Minho
Minorca i. Spain 57 H3
Minot U.S.A. 130 C1
Minqār, Ghadīr imp. l. Syria 85 C3
Minqing China 77 H3
Minquan China 77 G1
Min Shan mts China 76 D1
Minsin Myanmar 70 A1

▶Minsk Belarus 45 O10
Capital of Belarus.

Mińsk Mazowiecki Poland 47 R4
Minsterley U.K. 49 E6
Mintaka Pass China/Jammu and Kashmir 82 C1
Minto, Lac l. Canada 122 G2
Minto, Mount Antarctica 152 H2
Minto Inlet Canada 118 G2
Minton Canada 121 J5
Mīnudasht Iran 88 D2
Minūf Egypt 90 C5
Minusinsk Rus. Fed. 72 G2
Minvoul Gabon 98 B3
Minxian China 76 E1
Minya Konka mt. China see Gongga Shan
Minywa Myanmar 70 A2
Minzong India 83 I4
Mio U.S.A. 134 C1
Miquelon Canada 122 F4
Miquelon i. St Pierre and Miquelon 123 K5
Mirabad Afgh. 89 F4
Mirabel airport Canada 122 G5
Mirabela Brazil 145 B2
Mirador, Parque Nacional de nat. park Brazil 143 I5
Mīrah, Wādī al watercourse Iraq/Saudi Arabia 91 F4
Miraí Brazil 145 C3
Miraj India 84 B2
Miramar Arg. 144 E5
Miramichi Canada 123 I5
Miramichi Bay Canada 123 I5
Mirampelou, Kolpos b. Greece 59 K7
Miranda Brazil 144 E2
Miranda Moz. see Macaloge
Miranda U.S.A. 128 B1
Miranda, Lake salt flat Australia 109 C6
Miranda de Ebro Spain 57 E2
Mirandela Port. 57 C3
Mirandola Italy 58 D2
Mirante Brazil 145 C1
Mirante, Serra do hills Brazil 145 A3
Mirassol Brazil 145 A3
Mir-Bashir Azer. see Tärtär
Mirbāṭ Oman 87 H6
Mirboo North Australia 112 C7
Mirepoix France 56 E5
Mirgarh Pak. 89 I4
Mirgorod Ukr. see Myrhorod
Miri Sarawak Malaysia 68 E6
Miri mt. Pak. 89 F4
Mirialguda India 84 C2
Miri Hills India 83 H4
Mirim, Lagoa l. Brazil/Uruguay 144 F4
Mirim, Lagoa do l. Brazil 145 A5
Mirintu watercourse Australia 112 A2
Mirjan India 84 B3
Mirny research station Antarctica 152 F2
Mirnyy Arkhangel'skaya Oblast' Rus. Fed. 42 I3
Mirnyy Respublika Sakha (Yakutiya) Rus. Fed. 65 M3
Mirond Lake Canada 121 K4
Mironovka Ukr. see Myronivka
Mirow Germany 53 M1
Mirpur Khas Pak. 89 H5
Mirpur Sakro Pak. 89 G5
Mirs Bay Hong Kong China 77 [inset]
Mirtoan Sea Greece see Mirtoö Pelagos
Mirtoö Pelagos sea Greece 59 J6
Miryalaguda India see Mirialguda
Miryang S. Korea 75 C6
Mirzachirla Turkm. see Murzechirla
Mirzachul Uzbek. see Gulistan
Mirzapur India 83 E4
Mirzawal India 82 C3
Misaw Lake Canada 121 K3
Miscou Island Canada 123 I5
Misehkow r. Canada 122 C4
Mīsh, Kūh-e hill Iran 88 E3
Misha India 71 A6
Mishāsh al Ashāwī well Saudi Arabia 88 C5
Mishāsh aẓ Ẓuayyinī well Saudi Arabia 88 C5
Mishawaka U.S.A. 134 B3
Mishicot U.S.A. 134 B1
Mi-shima i. Japan 75 C6
Mishmi Hills India 83 H3
Mishvan' Rus. Fed. 42 L2
Misima Island P.N.G. 110 F1
Misis Dağ hills Turkey 85 B1
Miskin Oman 88 E6
Miskitos, Cayos is Nicaragua 137 H6
Miskolc Hungary 43 D6
Mismā, Tall al hill Jordan 85 C3
Misoöl i. Indon. 69 I7
Misquah Hills U.S.A. 130 F2
Misr country Africa see Egypt
Misraç Turkey see Kurtalan
Miṣrātah Libya 97 E1
Missinaibi r. Canada 122 E4
Mission Beach Australia 110 D3
Mission Viejo U.S.A. 128 E5
Missisa r. Canada 122 D3
Missisa Lake Canada 122 D3
Missisicabi r. Canada 122 F4
Mississauga Canada 134 F2
Mississinewa Lake U.S.A. 134 C3

▶Mississippi r. U.S.A. 131 F6
4th longest river in North America. Part of the longest (Mississippi-Missouri).

Mississippi state U.S.A. 131 F5
Mississippi Delta U.S.A. 131 F6
Mississippi Lake Canada 135 G1

▶Mississippi-Missouri r. U.S.A. 125 I4
Longest river and largest drainage basin in North America and 4th longest river in the world.
North America 114–115
World 12–13

Mississippi Sound sea chan. U.S.A. 131 F6
Missolonghi Greece see Mesolongi
Missoula U.S.A. 126 E3

▶Missouri r. U.S.A. 130 F4
3rd longest river in North America. Part of the longest (Mississippi-Missouri).

Missouri state U.S.A. 130 E4
Mistanipisipou r. Canada 123 J4
Mistassibi r. Canada 119 K5
Mistassini Canada 123 G4
Mistassini r. Canada 123 G4
Mistassini, Lac l. Canada 122 G4
Mistastin Lake Canada 123 J3
Mistelbach Austria 47 P6
Mistinibi, Lac l. Canada 123 J2
Mistissini Canada 122 G4
Misty Fiords National Monument Wilderness nat. park U.S.A. 120 D4
Misumba Dem. Rep. Congo 99 C4
Misuratah Libya see Miṣrātah
Mitchell Australia 111 D5
Mitchell r. N.S.W. Australia 112 F2
Mitchell r. Qld Australia 110 C2
Mitchell r. Vic. Australia 112 C6
Mitchell Canada 134 E2
Mitchell IN U.S.A. 134 B4
Mitchell OR U.S.A. 126 C3
Mitchell SD U.S.A. 130 D3
Mitchell, Lake Australia 110 D3
Mitchell, Mount U.S.A. 132 D5
Mitchell and Alice Rivers National Park Australia 110 C2
Mitchell Island Cook Is see Nassau
Mitchell Island atoll Tuvalu see Nukulaelae
Mitchell Point Australia 108 E2
Mitchelstown Rep. of Ireland 51 D5
Mīt Ghamr Egypt see Mīt Ghamr
Mīt Ghamr Egypt 90 C5
Mithi Pak. 89 H5
Mithrau Pak. 89 H5
Mitilíni Greece see Mytilini
Mitkof Island U.S.A. 120 C3
Mito Japan 75 F5
Mitole Tanz. 99 D4
Mitre mt. N.Z. 113 E5
Mitre Island Solomon Is 107 H3
Mitrofanovka Rus. Fed. 43 H6
Mitrovica Serb. and Mont. see Kosovska Mitrovica
Mitrovicë Serb. and Mont. see Kosovska Mitrovica
Mitsinjo Madag. 99 E5
Mits'iwa Eritrea see Massawa
Mitta Mitta Australia 112 C6
Mittellandkanal canal Germany 53 I2
Mitterteich Germany 53 M5
Mittimatalik Canada see Pond Inlet
Mittweida Germany 53 M4
Mitú Col. 142 D3
Mitumba, Chaîne des mts Dem. Rep. Congo 99 C5
Mitzic Gabon 98 B3
Miughalaigh i. U.K. see Mingulay
Miura Japan 75 E6
Mixian China see Xinmi
Miyake-jima i. Japan 75 E6
Miyako Japan 75 F5
Miyakonojō Japan 75 C7
Miyang China see Mile
Miyani India 82 B5
Miyazaki Japan 75 C7
Miyazu Japan 75 D6
Miyi China 76 D3
Miyoshi Japan 75 D6
Mīzāni Afgh. 89 G3
Mīzan Teferī Eth. 98 D3
Mizdah Libya 97 E1
Mizen Head hd Rep. of Ireland 51 C6
Mizhhir"ya Ukr. 43 D6
Mizo Hills state India see Mizoram
Mizoram state India 83 H5
Mizpe Ramon Israel 85 B4
Mizusawa Japan 75 F5
Mjölby Sweden 45 I7
Mkata Tanz. 99 D4
Mkushi Zambia 99 C5
Mladá Boleslav Czech Rep. 47 O5
Mladenovac Serb. and Mont. 59 I2
Mława Poland 47 R4
Mlilwane Nature Reserve Swaziland 101 J4
Mljet i. Croatia 58 G3
Mlungisi S. Africa 101 H6
Mmabatho S. Africa 101 G3
Mmamabula Botswana 101 H2
Mmathethe Botswana 101 G3
Mo Norway 45 D6
Moa i. Indon. 108 E2
Moab reg. Jordan 85 B4
Moab U.S.A. 129 I2
Moa Island Australia 110 C1
Moala i. Fiji 107 H3
Mo'alla Iran 88 D3
Moamba Moz. 101 K3
Moanda Gabon 98 B4
Moapa U.S.A. 129 F3
Moate Rep. of Ireland 51 E4
Mobārakeh Iran 88 C3
Mobayembongo Dem. Rep. Congo see Mobayi-Mbongo
Mobayi-Mbongo Dem. Rep. Congo 98 C3
Moberly U.S.A. 130 E4
Moberly Lake Canada 120 F4
Mobha India 82 C5
Mobile AL U.S.A. 131 F6
Mobile AZ U.S.A. 129 G5
Mobile Bay U.S.A. 131 F6
Moble watercourse Australia 112 B1
Mobridge U.S.A. 130 C2
Mobutu, Lake Dem. Rep. Congo/Uganda see Albert, Lake
Mobutu Sese Seko, Lake Dem. Rep. Congo/Uganda see Albert, Lake
Moca Geçidi pass Turkey 85 A1
Moçambique country Africa see Mozambique
Moçambique Moz. 99 E5
Moçâmedes Angola see Namibe
Mộc Châu Vietnam 70 D2
Mocha Yemen 86 F7
Mocha, Isla i. Chile 144 B5
Mochirma, Parque Nacional nat. park Venez. 142 F1
Mochudi Botswana 101 H3
Mochudi admin. dist. Botswana see Kgatleng
Mocimboa da Praia Moz. 99 E5
Möckern Germany 53 L2
Möckmühl Germany 53 J5
Mockträsk Sweden 44 L4
Mocoa Col. 142 C3
Mococa Brazil 145 B3
Mocoduene Moz. 101 L2
Mocorito Mex. 127 G8
Moctezuma Chihuahua Mex. 127 G7
Moctezuma San Luis Potosí Mex. 136 D4
Moctezuma Sonora Mex. 127 F7
Mocuba Moz. 99 D5
Mocun China 77 G4
Modan Indon. 69 I7
Modane France 56 H4
Modder r. S. Africa 101 G5
Modena Italy 58 D2
Modena U.S.A. 129 G3
Modesto U.S.A. 128 C3
Modesto Lake U.S.A. 128 C3
Modot Mongolia 73 J3
Modung China 76 C2
Moe Australia 112 C7
Moel Sych hill U.K. 49 D6
Moelv Norway 45 G6
Moen Norway 44 K2
Moenjodaro tourist site Pak. 89 H5
Moenkopi U.S.A. 129 H3
Moenkopi Wash r. U.S.A. 129 H4
Moeraki Point N.Z. 113 C7
Moero, Lake Dem. Rep. Congo/Zambia see Mweru, Lake
Moers Germany 52 G3
Moffat U.K. 50 F5
Moga India 82 C3

▶Mogadishu Somalia 98 E3
Capital of Somalia.

Mogador Morocco see Essaouira
Mogadore Reservoir U.S.A. 134 E3
Moganyaka S. Africa 101 I3
Mogaung Myanmar 70 B1
Mogdy Rus. Fed. 74 D2
Mögelin Germany 53 M2
Mogilev Belarus see Mahilyow
Mogilev Podol'skiy Ukr. see Mohyliv Podil's'kyy
Mogi-Mirim Brazil 145 B3
Mogiquiçaba Brazil 145 D2
Mogocha Rus. Fed. 73 L2
Mogod mts Tunisia 58 C6
Mogoditshane Botswana 101 G3
Mogollon Mountains U.S.A. 125 I5
Mogollon Plateau U.S.A. 129 H4
Mogontiacum Germany see Mainz
Mogroum Chad 97 E3
Moguqi China 74 A3
Mogwadi S. Africa see Dendron
Mogwase S. Africa 101 H3
Mogzon Rus. Fed. 73 K2
Mohács Hungary 58 H2
Mohaka r. N.Z. 113 F4
Mohala India 84 D1
Mohale Dam Lesotho 101 I5
Mohale's Hoek Lesotho 101 H6
Mohall U.S.A. 130 C1
Mohammad Iran 88 E3
Mohammadia Alg. 57 G6
Mohan r. India/Nepal 82 E3
Mohana India 82 D4
Mohave, Lake U.S.A. 129 F4
Mohawk r. U.S.A. 135 I2
Mohawk Mountains U.S.A. 129 G5
Moher, Cliffs of Rep. of Ireland 51 C5
Mohill Rep. of Ireland 51 E4
Möhne r. Germany 53 H3
Möhnetalsperre resr Germany 53 I3
Mohon Peak U.S.A. 129 G4
Mohoro Tanz. 99 D4
Mohyliv Podil's'kyy Ukr. 43 E6
Moi Norway 45 E7
Moijabana Botswana 101 H2
Moincêr China 82 E3
Moinda China 83 G3
Moine Moz. 101 K3
Moinești Romania 59 L1
Mointy Kazakh. see Moyynty
Mo i Rana Norway 44 I3
Moirang India 76 B3
Mõisaküla Estonia 45 N7
Moisie Canada 123 I4
Moisie r. Canada 123 I4
Moissac France 56 E4
Mojave U.S.A. 128 D4
Mojave r. U.S.A. 128 E4
Mojave Desert U.S.A. 128 E4
Mojiang China 76 D4
Moji das Cruzes Brazil 145 B3
Mojos, Llanos de plain Bol. 142 E6
Moju r. Brazil 143 I4
Mokama India 83 F4
Mokau N.Z. 113 E4
Mokau r. N.Z. 113 E4
Mokelumne r. U.S.A. 128 C2
Mokelumne Aqueduct canal U.S.A. 128 C2
Mokhoabong Pass Lesotho 101 I5
Mokhotlong Lesotho 101 I5
Mokhtārān Iran 88 E3
Moknine Tunisia 58 D7
Mokohinau Islands N.Z. 113 E2
Mokokchung India 83 H4
Mokolo Cameroon 97 E3
Mokolo r. S. Africa 101 H2
Mokp'o S. Korea 75 B6
Mokrous Rus. Fed. 43 J6
Moksha r. Rus. Fed. 43 I5
Mokshan Rus. Fed. 43 J5
Möksy Fin. 44 N5
Môktama Myanmar see Martaban
Môktama, Gulf of Myanmar see Martaban, Gulf of
Mokundurra India see Mukandwara
Mokwa Nigeria 96 D4
Molatón mt. Spain 57 F4
Moldavia country Europe see Moldova
Moldavskaya S.S.R. country Europe see Moldova
Molde Norway 44 E5
Moldjord Norway 44 I3
▶Moldova country Europe 43 F7
Europe 5, 38–39

Moldoveanu, Vârful mt. Romania 59 K2
Moldovei de Sud, Cîmpia plain Moldova 59 M1
Molega Lake Canada 123 I5
Molen r. S. Africa 101 I4
Mole National Park Ghana 96 C4
Molepolole Botswana 101 G3
Molėtai Lith. 45 N9
Molfetta Italy 58 G4
Molière Alg. see Bordj Bounaama
Molihong Shan mt. China see Morihong Shan
Molina de Aragón Spain 57 F3
Moline U.S.A. 131 D4
Molkom Sweden 45 H7
Mollagara Turkm. see Mollakara
Mollakara Turkm. 88 D2
Mol Len mt. India 83 H4
Möllenbeck Germany 53 N1
Mollendo Peru 142 D7
Mölln Germany 53 K1
Mölnlycke Sweden 45 H8
Molochnyy Rus. Fed. 44 R2
Molodechno Belarus see Maladzyechna
Molodezhnaya research station Antarctica 152 D2
Molokai i. HI U.S.A. 127 [inset]
Moloma r. Rus. Fed. 42 K4
Molong Australia 112 D4
Molopo watercourse Botswana/S. Africa 100 E5
Molotov Rus. Fed. see Perm'
Molotovsk Kyrg. see Kayyngdy
Molotovsk Arkhangel'skaya Oblast' Rus. Fed. see Severodvinsk
Molotovsk Kirovskaya Oblast' Rus. Fed. see Nolinsk
Moloundou Cameroon 97 E4
Molson Lake Canada 121 L4
Molu i. Indon. 69 I8
Moluccas is Indon. 69 H7
Molucca Sea sea Indon. see Maluku, Laut
Moma Moz. 99 D5
Momba Australia 112 A3
Mombaça Brazil 143 K5
Mombasa Kenya 98 D4
Mombetsu Hokkaidō Japan see Monbetsu
Mombetsu Hokkaidō Japan see Monbetsu
Mombi New India 83 H4
Mombum Indon. 69 J8
Momchilgrad Bulg. 59 K4
Momence U.S.A. 134 B3
Momi, Ra's pt Yemen 87 H7
Mompós Col. 142 D2
Møn i. Denmark 45 H9
Mon India 83 H4
Mona terr. Irish Sea see Isle of Man
Mona U.S.A. 129 H2
Monaca U.S.A. 134 E3
Monach, Sound of sea chan. U.K. 50 B3
Monach Islands U.K. 50 B3
▶Monaco country Europe 56 H5
Europe 5, 38–39
Monaco Basin sea feature N. Atlantic Ocean 148 G4
Monadhliath Mountains U.K. 50 E3
Monaghan Rep. of Ireland 51 F3
Monahans U.S.A. 131 C6
Mona Passage Dom. Rep./Puerto Rico 137 K5
Monapo Moz. 99 E5
Monar, Loch l. U.K. 50 D3
Monarch Mountain Canada 120 E5
Monarch Pass U.S.A. 127 G5
Mona Reservoir U.S.A. 129 H2
Monashee Mountains Canada 120 G5
Monastir Macedonia see Bitola
Monastir Tunisia 58 D7
Monastyrishche Ukr. see Monastyryshche
Monastyryshche Ukr. 43 F6
Monbetsu Hokkaidō Japan 74 F3
Monbetsu Hokkaidō Japan 74 F4
Moncalieri Italy 58 B2
Monchegorsk Rus. Fed. 44 R3
Mönchengladbach Germany 52 G3
Monchique Port. 57 B5
Moncks Corner U.S.A. 133 D5
Monclova Mex. 131 C7
Moncouche, Lac l. Canada 123 H4
Moncton Canada 123 I5
Mondego r. Port. 57 B3
Mondlo S. Africa 101 J4
Mondo Chad 97 E3
Mondovì Italy 58 B2
Mondragone Italy 58 E4
Mondy Rus. Fed. 72 I2
Monemvasia Greece 59 J6
Monessen U.S.A. 134 F3
Moneta U.S.A. 126 G4
Moneygall Rep. of Ireland 51 E5
Moneymore U.K. 51 F3
Monfalcone Italy 58 E2
Monfalut Egypt see Manfalūṭ
Monforte Spain 57 C2
Monga Dem. Rep. Congo 98 C3
Mongala r. Dem. Rep. Congo 98 B3
Mongar Bhutan 83 G4
Mongbwalu Dem. Rep. Congo 98 D3
Mông Cai Vietnam 70 D2
Mongers Lake salt flat Australia 109 B7
Mong Hang Myanmar 70 B2
Mong Hkan Myanmar 70 C2
Mong Hpayak Myanmar 70 B2
Mong Hsat Myanmar 70 B2
Mong Hsawk Myanmar 70 B2
Mong Hsu Myanmar 70 B2
Monghyr India see Munger
Mong Kung Myanmar 70 B2
Mong Kyawt Myanmar 70 B3
Mongla Bangl. 83 G5
Mong Lin Myanmar 70 C2
Mong Loi Myanmar 70 C2
Mong Long Myanmar 70 B2
Mong Nai Myanmar 70 B2
Mong Nawng Myanmar 70 B2
Mongo Chad 97 E3
▶Mongolia country Asia 72 I3
Asia 6, 62–63
Mongol Uls country Asia see Mongolia
Mongonu Nigeria 96 E3
Mongora Pak. 89 I3
Mongour hill U.K. 50 G4
Mong Pan Myanmar 70 B2
Mong Ping Myanmar 70 B2
Mong Pu Myanmar 70 B2
Mong Pu-awn Myanmar 70 B2
Mong Si Myanmar 70 B2
Mongu Zambia 99 C5
Mong Un Myanmar 70 C2
Mong Yai Myanmar 70 B2
Mong Yang Myanmar 70 B2
Mong Yawn Myanmar 70 B2
Mong Yawng Myanmar 70 C2
Mönh Hayrhan Uul mt. Mongolia 80 H2
Moniaive U.K. 50 F5
Monitor Mountain U.S.A. 128 E2
Monitor Range mts U.S.A. 128 E2
Monivea Rep. of Ireland 51 D4
Monkey Bay Malawi 99 D5
Monkira Australia 110 C5
Monkton Canada 134 E2
Monmouth U.K. 49 E7
Monmouth U.S.A. 130 F3
Monmouth Mountain Canada 120 F5
Monnow r. U.K. 49 E7
Mono, Punta del pt Nicaragua 137 H6
Mono Lake U.S.A. 128 D2
Monolithos Greece 59 L6
Monomoy Point U.S.A. 135 J3
Monon U.S.A. 134 B3
Monopoli Italy 58 G4
Monreal del Campo Spain 57 F3
Monreale Sicily Italy 58 E5
Monroe IN U.S.A. 134 C3
Monroe LA U.S.A. 131 E5
Monroe MI U.S.A. 134 D3
Monroe NC U.S.A. 133 D5
Monroe WI U.S.A. 130 F3
Monroe Center U.S.A. 130 F2
Monroe Lake U.S.A. 134 B4
Monroeton U.S.A. 135 G3

▶Monrovia Liberia 96 B4
Capital of Liberia.

Mons Belgium 52 D4
Monschau Germany 52 G4
Monselice Italy 58 D2
Montabaur Germany 53 H4
Montagu S. Africa 100 E7
Montague Canada 123 J5
Montague MI U.S.A. 134 B2
Montague TX U.S.A. 131 D5
Montague Range hills Australia 109 B6
Montalto mt. Italy 58 F5
Montalto Uffugo Italy 58 G5
Montana Bulg. 59 J3
Montana state U.S.A. 126 F3
Montargis France 56 F3
Montauban France 56 E4
Montauk U.S.A. 135 J3
Montauk Point U.S.A. 135 J3
Mont-aux-Sources mt. Lesotho 101 I5
Montbard France 56 G3
Montblanc Spain 57 G3
Montblanch Spain see Montblanc
Montbrison France 56 G4
Montceau-les-Mines France 56 G3
Montcornet France 52 E5
Mont-de-Marsan France 56 D5
Montdidier France 52 C5
Monte Alegre Brazil 143 H4
Monte Alegre de Goiás Brazil 145 B1
Monte Alegre de Minas Brazil 145 A2
Monte Azul Brazil 145 C1
Monte Azul Paulista Brazil 145 A3
Montebello Canada 122 G5
Montebello Islands Australia 104 A5
Montebelluna Italy 58 E2
Monte-Carlo Monaco 56 H5
Monte Christo S. Africa 101 H2
Monte Cristi Dom. Rep. 137 J5
Monte Dourado Brazil 143 H4
Monte Falterona, Campigna e delle Foreste Casentinesi, Parco Nazionale del nat. park Italy 58 D3
Montego Bay Jamaica 137 I5
Montélimar France 56 G4
Monte Lindo r. Para. 144 E2
Montello U.S.A. 130 F3
Montemorelos Mex. 131 D7
Montemor-o-Novo Port. 57 B4
Montenegro aut. rep. Serb. and Mont. see Crna Gora
Montepulciano Italy 58 D3
Monte Quemado Arg. 144 D3
Montereau-faut-Yonne France 56 F2
Monterey Mex. see Monterrey
Monterey CA U.S.A. 128 C3
Monterey VA U.S.A. 134 F4
Monterey Bay U.S.A. 128 B3
Montería Col. 142 C2
Monteros Arg. 144 C3
Monterrey Baja California Mex. 129 F5
Monterrey Nuevo León Mex. 131 C7
Montervary hd Rep. of Ireland 51 C6
Montesano U.S.A. 126 C3
Montesano sulla Marcellana Italy 58 F4
Monte Santo Brazil 143 K6
Monte Santu, Capo di c. Sardinia Italy 58 C4
Montes Claros Brazil 145 C2
Montesilvano Italy 58 F3
Montevarchi Italy 58 D3

▶Montevideo Uruguay 144 E4
Capital of Uruguay.

Montevideo U.S.A. 130 E2
Montezuma U.S.A. 130 E3
Montezuma Creek U.S.A. 129 I3
Montezuma Peak U.S.A. 128 E3
Montfort Neth. 52 F3
Montgomery U.K. 49 D6

▶Montgomery AL U.S.A. 133 C5
State capital of Alabama.

Montgomery WV U.S.A. 134 E4
Montgomery Islands Australia 108 C3
Monthey Switz. 56 H3
Monticello AR U.S.A. 131 F5
Monticello FL U.S.A. 133 D6
Monticello IN U.S.A. 134 B3
Monticello KY U.S.A. 134 C5
Monticello MO U.S.A. 130 F3
Monticello NY U.S.A. 135 H3
Monticello UT U.S.A. 129 I3
Montignac France 56 E4
Montignies-le-Tilleul Belgium 52 E4
Montigny-lès-Metz France 52 G5
Montilla Spain 57 D5
Monti Sibillini, Parco Nazionale dei nat. park Italy 58 E3
Montividiu Brazil 145 A2
Montivilliers France 49 H9
Mont-Joli Canada 123 H4
Mont-Laurier Canada 122 G5
Montluçon France 56 F3
Montmagny Canada 123 H5
Montmédy France 52 F5
Montmirail France 52 D6
Montmorillon France 56 E3
Montmort-Lucy France 52 D6
Monto Australia 110 E5
Montour Falls U.S.A. 135 G2
Montoursville U.S.A. 135 G3
Montpelier ID U.S.A. 126 F4

▶Montpelier VT U.S.A. 135 I1
State capital of Vermont.

Montpellier France 56 F5
Montréal Canada 122 G5
Montreal r. Ont. Canada 122 D5
Montreal r. Ont. Canada 122 F5
Montreal Lake Canada 121 J4
Montreal Lake l. Canada 121 J4
Montreal River Canada 122 D5
Montreuil France 52 B4
Montreux Switz. 56 H3
Montrose well S. Africa 100 E4
Montrose U.K. 50 G4
Montrose CO U.S.A. 129 J2
Montrose PA U.S.A. 135 H3
Montross U.S.A. 135 G4
Monts, Pointe des pt Canada 123 I4

▶Montserrat terr. West Indies 137 L5
United Kingdom Overseas Territory.
North America 9, 116–117

Mont-St-Aignan France 49 I9
Montviel, Lac l. Canada 123 H3
Monument Valley reg. U.S.A. 129 H3
Monywa Myanmar 70 A2
Monza Italy 58 C2
Monze, Cape pt Pak. see Muari, Ras
Monzón Spain 57 G3
Mooi r. S. Africa 101 J5
Mooifontein Namibia 100 C4
Mookane Botswana 101 H2
Mookgopong S. Africa see Naboomspruit
Moolawatana Australia 111 B6
Moomba Australia 111 C6
Moomin Creek r. Australia 112 D2
Moonaree Australia 111 A6
Moonbi Range mts Australia 112 E3
Moonda Lake salt flat Australia 111 C5
Moonie Australia 112 E1
Moonie r. Australia 112 D2
Moora Australia 109 B7
Mooraberree Australia 110 C5
Moorcroft U.S.A. 126 G3
Moore r. Australia 109 A7
Moore U.S.A. 126 F3
Moore, Lake salt flat Australia 109 B7
Moore Embayment b. Antarctica 152 H1
Moorefield U.S.A. 135 F4
Moore Haven U.S.A. 133 D7
Moore Reef Australia 110 E3
Moore Reservoir U.S.A. 135 J1
Moore River National Park Australia 109 A7
Moores Island Bahamas 133 E7
Moorfoot Hills U.K. 50 F5
Moorhead U.S.A. 130 D2
Moorman U.S.A. 134 B5
Moornanyah Lake imp. l. Australia 112 A4
Mooroopna Australia 112 B6
Moorreesburg S. Africa 100 D7
Moorrinya National Park Australia 110 D4
Moose r. Canada 122 E4
Moose Factory Canada 122 E4
Moosehead Lake U.S.A. 132 G2
Moose Jaw Canada 121 J5
Moose Jaw r. Canada 121 J5
Moose Lake U.S.A. 130 E2
Mooselookmeguntic Lake U.S.A. 135 J1
Moose Mountain Creek r. Canada 121 K5
Moosilauke, Mount U.S.A. 135 J1
Moosomin Canada 121 K5
Moosonee Canada 122 E4
Mootwingee National Park Australia 111 C6
Mopane S. Africa 101 I2
Mopeia Moz. 99 D5
Mopipi Botswana 99 C6
Mopti Mali 96 C3
Moqor Afgh. 89 G3
Moquegua Peru 142 D7
Mora Cameroon 97 E3
Mora Spain 57 E4
Mora Sweden 45 I6
Mora MN U.S.A. 130 E2
Mora NM U.S.A. 127 G6
Mora r. U.S.A. 127 G6
Moradabad India 82 D3
Morada Nova Brazil 143 K5
Moraine Lake Canada 121 J1
Moraleda, Canal sea chan. Chile 144 B6
Moram India 84 C2
Moramanga Madag. 99 E5
Moran U.S.A. 126 F4
Moranbah Australia 110 E4
Morang Nepal see Biratnagar
Morar, Loch l. U.K. 50 D4
Morari, Tso l. Jammu and Kashmir 82 D2
Moratuwa Sri Lanka 84 C5
Moravia reg. Czech Rep. 47 P6
Moravia U.S.A. 135 G2
Morawa Australia 109 A7
Moray Firth b. U.K. 50 E3
Moray Range hills Australia 108 E3
Morbach Germany 52 H5
Morbeng S. Africa see Soekmekaar
Morbi India 82 B5
Morcenx France 56 D4
Morcillo Mex. 131 B7
Mordaga China 73 M2
Mor Dağı mt. Turkey 91 G3
Morden Canada 121 L5
Mordovo Rus. Fed. 43 I5
Moreau r. U.S.A. 130 C2
Moreau, South Fork r. U.S.A. 130 C2
Morecambe U.K. 48 E4
Morecambe Bay U.K. 48 D4
Moree Australia 112 D2
Morehead P.N.G. 69 K8
Morehead U.S.A. 134 D4
Morehead City U.S.A. 137 I2
Moreland U.S.A. 134 C5
More Laptevykh sea Rus. Fed. see Laptev Sea
Morelia Mex. 136 D5
Morella Australia 110 C4
Morella Spain 57 F3
Morelos Mex. 127 G8
Morena India 82 D4
Morena, Sierra mts Spain 57 C5
Morenci AZ U.S.A. 129 I5
Morenci MI U.S.A. 134 C3
Moreni Romania 59 K2
Moreno Mex. 127 F7
Moreno Valley U.S.A. 128 E5
Moresby, Mount Canada 120 C4
Moresby Island Canada 120 C4
Moreswe Pan salt pan Botswana 100 G2
Moreton Bay Australia 112 F1
Moreton-in-Marsh U.K. 49 F7
Moreton Island Australia 112 F1
Moreton Island National Park Australia 112 F1
Moreuil France 52 C5
Morez France 56 H3
Morfou Cyprus 85 A2
Morfou Bay Cyprus 85 A2
Morgan U.S.A. 126 F4
Morgan City U.S.A. 131 F6
Morgan Hill U.S.A. 128 C3
Morganton U.S.A. 132 D5
Morgantown KY U.S.A. 134 B5
Morgantown WV U.S.A. 134 F4
Morgenzon S. Africa 101 I4
Morges Switz. 56 H3
Morhar r. India 83 F4
Mori China 80 H3
Mori Japan 74 F4
Moriah, Mount U.S.A. 129 F2
Moriarty's Range hills Australia 112 B2
Morice Lake Canada 120 E4
Morichal Col. 142 D3
Morihong Shan mt. China 74 B4
Morija Lesotho 101 H5
Morin Dawa China see Nirji
Moringen Germany 53 J3
Morioka Japan 75 F5
Moris Mex. 127 F7
Morisset Australia 112 E4
Moriyoshi-zan vol. Japan 75 F5
Morjärv Sweden 44 M3
Morjen r. Pak. 89 F4
Morki Rus. Fed. 42 K4
Morlaix France 56 C2
Morley U.K. 48 F5
Mormam Flat Dam U.S.A. 129 H5
Mormant France 52 C6
Mormon Lake U.S.A. 129 H4
Mormugao India see Marmagao
Morne Diablotins vol. Dominica 137 L5
Morney watercourse Australia 110 C5
Mornington, Isla i. Chile 144 A7
Mornington Abyssal Plain sea feature S. Atlantic Ocean 148 C9
Mornington Island Australia 110 B3
Mornington Peninsula National Park Australia 112 B7
Moro Pak. 89 G5
Moro U.S.A. 126 C3
Morobe P.N.G. 69 L8
▶Morocco country Africa 96 C1
Africa 7, 94–95
Morocco U.S.A. 134 B3
Morococala mt. Bol. 142 E7
Morogoro Tanz. 99 D4
Moro Gulf Phil. 69 G5
Morojaneng S. Africa 101 H5
Morokweng S. Africa 100 F4
Morombe Madag. 99 E6
Morón Cuba 133 E8
Mörön Mongolia 80 J2
Morondava Madag. 99 E6
Morón de la Frontera Spain 57 D5

▶Moroni Comoros 99 E5
Capital of the Comoros.

Moroni U.S.A. 129 H2
Moron Us He r. China see Tongtian He
Morotai i. Indon. 69 H6
Moroto Uganda 98 D3
Morozovsk Rus. Fed. 43 I6
Morpeth Canada 134 E2
Morpeth U.K. 48 F3
Morphou Cyprus see Morfou
Morrill U.S.A. 134 C5
Morrilton U.S.A. 131 E5
Morrin Canada 121 H5
Morrinhos Brazil 145 A2
Morris Canada 121 L5
Morris IL U.S.A. 130 F3
Morris MN U.S.A. 130 E2
Morris PA U.S.A. 135 G3

▶Morris Jesup, Kap c. Greenland 153 I1
Most northerly point of North America.

Morrison U.S.A. 130 F3
Morristown AZ U.S.A. 129 G5
Morristown NJ U.S.A. 135 H3
Morristown NY U.S.A. 135 H1
Morristown TN U.S.A. 132 D4
Morrisville U.S.A. 135 H2
Morro Brazil 145 B2
Morro Bay U.S.A. 128 C4
Morro d'Anta Brazil 145 D2
Morro do Chapéu Brazil 143 J6
Morro Grande hill Brazil 143 H4
Morrosquillo, Golfo de b. Col. 142 C2
Morrumbene Moz. 101 L2
Morschen Germany 53 J3
Morse Canada 121 J5
Morse U.S.A. 131 C4
Morse, Cape Antarctica 152 G2
Morse Reservoir U.S.A. 134 B3
Morshanka Rus. Fed. 43 I5
Morshansk Rus. Fed. see Morshanka
Morsott Alg. 58 C7
Mort watercourse Australia 110 C4
Mortagne-au-Perche France 56 E2
Mortagne-sur-Sèvre France 56 D3
Mortara Italy 58 C2
Mortehoe U.K. 49 C7
Morteros Arg. 144 D4
Mortes, Rio das r. Brazil 145 A1
Mortimer's Bahamas 133 F8
Mortlake Australia 112 A7
Mortlock Islands Micronesia 150 G5
Mortlock Islands P.N.G. see Tauu Islands
Morton U.K. 49 G6
Morton TX U.S.A. 131 C5
Morton WA U.S.A. 126 C3
Morton National Park Australia 112 E5
Morundah Australia 112 C5
Morupule Botswana 101 H2
Moruroa atoll Fr. Polynesia see Mururoa
Moruya Australia 112 E5
Morven Australia 111 D5
Morven hill U.K. 50 F2
Morvern reg. U.K. 50 D4
Morvi India see Morbi
Morwara India 82 B4
Morwell Australia 112 C7
Morzhovets, Ostrov i. Rus. Fed. 42 I2
Mosbach Germany 53 J5
Mosborough U.K. 48 F5
Mosby U.S.A. 126 G3

▶Moscow Rus. Fed. 42 H5
Capital of the Russian Federation and 3rd most populous city in Europe.

Moscow ID U.S.A. 126 D3
Moscow PA U.S.A. 135 H3
Moscow University Ice Shelf Antarctica 152 G2
Mosel r. Germany 53 H4
Moselebe watercourse Botswana 100 F3
Moselle r. France 52 G5
Möser Germany 53 L2
Moses, Mount U.S.A. 128 E1
Moses Lake U.S.A. 126 D3
Mosgiel N.Z. 113 C7
Moshaweng watercourse S. Africa 100 F4
Moshchnyy, Ostrov i. Rus. Fed. 45 O7
Moshi Tanz. 98 D4
Mosh'yuga Rus. Fed. 42 L2
Mosi-oa-Tunya waterfall Zambia/Zimbabwe see Victoria Falls
Mosjøen Norway 44 H4
Moskal'vo Rus. Fed. 74 F1
Moskenesøy i. Norway 44 H3
Moskva Rus. Fed. see Moscow
Moskva Tajik. 89 H2
Mosonmagyaróvár Hungary 47 P7
Mosquera Col. 142 C3
Mosquero U.S.A. 127 G6
Mosquito r. Brazil 145 C1
Mosquito Creek Lake U.S.A. 134 E3
Mosquito Lake Canada 121 K2
Moss Norway 45 G7
Mossâmedes Angola see Namibe
Mossat U.K. 50 G3
Mossburn N.Z. 113 B7
Mosselbaai S. Africa see Mossel Bay
Mossel Bay S. Africa 100 F8
Mossel Bay b. S. Africa 100 F8
Mossgiel Australia 112 B4
Mossman Australia 110 D3
Mossoró Brazil 143 K5
Moss Vale Australia 112 E5
Mossy r. Canada 121 K4
Most Czech Rep. 47 N5
Mostaganem Alg. 57 G6
Mostar Bos.-Herz. 58 G3
Mostoos Hills Canada 121 I4
Mostovskoy Rus. Fed. 91 F1
Mosty Belarus see Masty
Mosul Iraq 91 F3
Møsvatnet l. Norway 45 F7
Motala Sweden 45 I7
Motaze Moz. 101 K3
Motetema S. Africa 101 I3
Moth India 82 D4
Motherwell U.K. 50 F5
Motian Ling hill China 74 A4
Motihari India 83 F4
Motilla del Palancar Spain 57 F4
Motiti Island N.Z. 113 F3
Motokwe Botswana 100 F3
Motril Spain 57 E5
Motru Romania 59 J2
Mott U.S.A. 130 C2
Motu Ihupuku i. N.Z. see Campbell Island
Motul Mex. 136 G4
Mouaskar Alg. see Mascara
Mouding China 76 D3
Moudjéria Mauritania 96 B3
Moudros Greece 59 K5
Mouhijärvi Fin. 45 M6
Mouila Gabon 98 B4
Moulamein Australia 112 B5
Moulamein Creek r. Australia 112 A5
Moulavibazar Bangl. see Moulvibazar
Mould Bay Canada 118 G2
Moulèngui Binza Gabon 98 B4
Moulins France 56 F3
Moulmein Myanmar 70 B3
Moulouya, Oued r. Morocco 54 D4
Moultrie U.S.A. 133 D6
Moultrie, Lake U.S.A. 133 E5
Moulvibazar Bangl. 83 G4
Mound City KS U.S.A. 130 E4
Mound City SD U.S.A. 130 C2
Moundou Chad 97 E4
Moundsville U.S.A. 134 E4
Moŭng Roessei Cambodia 71 C4
Mount Abu India 82 C4
Mountain r. Canada 120 D1
Mountainair U.S.A. 127 G6
Mountain Brook U.S.A. 133 C5
Mountain City U.S.A. 134 E5
Mountain Home AR U.S.A. 131 E4
Mountain Home ID U.S.A. 126 E4
Mountain Home UT U.S.A. 129 H1
Mountain Lake Park U.S.A. 134 F4
Mountain View U.S.A. 131 E5
Mountain Zebra National Park S. Africa 101 G7
Mount Airy U.S.A. 134 E5
Mount Aspiring National Park N.Z. 113 B7
Mount Assiniboine Provincial Park Canada 120 H5
Mount Ayliff S. Africa 101 I6
Mount Ayr U.S.A. 130 E3
Mount Bellew Rep. of Ireland 51 D4
Mount Buffalo National Park Australia 112 C6
Mount Carmel U.S.A. 134 B4
Mount Carmel Junction U.S.A. 129 G3
Mount Cook National Park N.Z. 113 C6
Mount Coolon Australia 110 D4
Mount Darwin Zimbabwe 99 D5
Mount Denison Australia 108 F5
Mount Desert Island U.S.A. 132 G2
Mount Dutton Australia 111 A5
Mount Eba Australia 111 A6
Mount Elgon National Park Uganda 98 D3
Mount Fletcher S. Africa 101 I6
Mount Forest Canada 134 E2
Mount Frankland National Park Australia 109 B8
Mount Frere S. Africa 101 I6
Mount Gambier Australia 111 C8
Mount Gilead U.S.A. 134 D3
Mount Hagen P.N.G. 69 K8
Mount Holly U.S.A. 135 H4
Mount Hope Australia 112 B4
Mount Hope U.S.A. 134 E5
Mount Howitt Australia 111 C5
Mount Isa Australia 110 B4
Mount Jackson U.S.A. 135 F4
Mount Jewett U.S.A. 135 F3
Mount Joy U.S.A. 135 G3
Mount Kaputar National Park Australia 112 E3
Mount Keith Australia 109 C6
Mount Lofty Range mts Australia 111 B7
Mount Magnet Australia 109 B7
Mount Manara Australia 112 A4
Mount McKinley National Park U.S.A. see Denali National Park and Preserve
Mount Meadows Reservoir U.S.A. 128 C1
Mountmellick Rep. of Ireland 51 E4
Mount Moorosi Lesotho 101 H6
Mount Morgan Australia 110 E4
Mount Morris MI U.S.A. 134 D2
Mount Morris NY U.S.A. 135 G2
Mount Murchison Australia 112 A3
Mount Nebo U.S.A. 134 E4
Mount Olivet U.S.A. 134 C4
Mount Pearl Canada 123 L5
Mount Pleasant Canada 123 I5
Mount Pleasant IA U.S.A. 130 F3
Mount Pleasant MI U.S.A. 134 C2
Mount Pleasant TX U.S.A. 131 E5
Mount Pleasant UT U.S.A. 129 H2
Mount Rainier National Park U.S.A. 126 C3
Mount Remarkable National Park Australia 111 B7
Mount Revelstoke National Park Canada 120 G5
Mount Robson Provincial Park Canada 120 G4
Mount Rogers National Recreation Area park U.S.A. 134 E5
Mount Sanford Australia 108 E4
Mount's Bay U.K. 49 B8
Mount Shasta U.S.A. 126 C4
Mountsorrel U.K. 49 F6
Mount Sterling U.S.A. 134 D4
Mount St Helens National Volcanic Monument nat. park U.S.A. 126 C3
Mount Swan Australia 110 A4
Mount Union U.S.A. 135 G3
Mount Vernon Australia 109 B6
Mount Vernon IL U.S.A. 130 F4
Mount Vernon IN U.S.A. 132 C4
Mount Vernon KY U.S.A. 134 C5
Mount Vernon MO U.S.A. 131 E4
Mount Vernon OH U.S.A. 134 D3
Mount Vernon TX U.S.A. 131 E5
Mount Vernon WA U.S.A. 126 C2
Mount William National Park Australia 111 [inset]
Mount Willoughby Australia 109 F6
Moura Australia 110 E5
Moura Brazil 142 F4
Moura Port. 57 C4
Mourdi, Dépression du depr. Chad 97 F3
Mourdiah Mali 96 C3
Mourne r. U.K. 51 E3
Mourne Mountains hills U.K. 51 F3
Mousa i. U.K. 50 [inset]
Mouscron Belgium 52 D4
Mousgougou Chad 98 B2
Moussafoyo Chad 97 E4
Moussoro Chad 97 E3
Moutamba Congo 98 B4
Mouth of the Yangtze China 77 I2
Moutong Indon. 69 G6
Mouy France 52 C5
Mouydir, Monts du plat. Alg. 96 D2
Mouzon France 52 F5
Movas Mex. 127 F7
Mowbullan, Mount Australia 112 E1
Moxey Town Bahamas 133 E7
Moy r. Rep. of Ireland 51 C3
Moyale Eth. 98 D3
Moyen Atlas mts Morocco 54 C5
Moyen Congo country Africa see Congo
Moyeni Lesotho 101 H6
Moynalyk Rus. Fed. 80 I1
Moynaq Uzbek. see Muynak
Moyo i. Indon. 108 B2
Moyobamba Peru 142 C5
Moyock U.S.A. 135 G5

Moyola r. U.K. 51 F3
Moyu China 82 D1
Moyynkum Kazakh. 80 D3
Moyynkum, Peski des. Kazakh. 80 C3
Moyynty Kazakh. 80 D2
▶Mozambique country Africa 99 D6
Africa 7, 94–95
Mozambique Channel Africa 99 E6
Mozambique Ridge sea feature Indian Ocean 149 K7
Mozdok Rus. Fed. 91 G2
Mozdūrān Iran 89 F2
Mozhaysk Rus. Fed. 43 H5
Mozhga Rus. Fed. 42 L4
Mozhnābād Iran 89 F3
Mozo Myanmar 76 B4
Mozyr' Belarus see Mazyr
Mpaathutlwa Pan salt pan Botswana 100 E3
Mpanda Tanz. 99 D4
Mpen India 83 I4
Mpika Zambia 99 D5
Mpolweni S. Africa 101 J5
Mporokoso Zambia 99 D4
Mpulungu Zambia 99 D4
Mpumalanga prov. S. Africa 101 I4
Mpunde mt. Tanz. 99 D4
Mpwapwa Tanz. 99 D4
Mqanduli S. Africa 101 I6
Mqinvartsveri mt. Georgia/Rus. Fed. see Kazbek
Mrewa Zimbabwe see Murehwa
Mrkonjić-Grad Bos.-Herz. 58 G2
M'Saken Tunisia 58 D7
Mshinskaya Rus. Fed. 45 P7
M'Sila Alg. 57 I6
Msta r. Rus. Fed. 42 F4
Mstislavl' Belarus see Mstsislaw
Mstsislaw Belarus 43 F5
Mtelo Kenya 98 D3
Mtoko Zimbabwe see Mutoko
Mtorwi Tanz. 99 D4
Mtsensk Rus. Fed. 43 H5
Mts'ire Kavkasioni Asia see Lesser Caucasus
Mtubatuba S. Africa 101 K5
Mtunzini S. Africa 101 J5
Mtwara Tanz. 99 E5
Mu r. Myanmar 70 A2
Mu'āb, Jibāl reg. Jordan see Moab
Muanda Dem. Rep. Congo 99 B4
Muang Ham Laos 70 D2
Muang Hiam Laos 70 C2
Muang Hinboun Laos 70 D3
Muang Hôngsa Laos 70 C3
Muang Khammouan Laos 70 D3
Muang Khi Laos 70 C3
Muang Không Laos 71 D4
Muang Khoua Laos 70 C2
Muang Lamam Laos see Ban Phon
Muang Mok Laos 70 D3
Muang Ngoy Laos 70 C2
Muang Ou Nua Laos 70 C2
Muang Pakbeng Laos 70 C3
Muang Paktha Laos 70 C2
Muang Pakxan Laos see Muang Xaignabouri
Muang Phalan Laos 68 D3
Muang Phin Laos 70 D3
Muang Phôn-Hông Laos 70 C3
Muang Sam Sip Thai. 70 D4
Muang Sing Laos 70 C2
Muang Soum Laos 70 C3
Muang Souy Laos 70 C3
Muang Thadua Laos 70 C3
Muang Thai country Asia see Thailand
Muang Va Laos 70 C2
Muang Vangviang Laos 70 C3
Muang Xaignabouri Laos 70 C3
Muang Xaignabouri Laos 70 C3
Muang Xay Laos 70 C2
Muang Xon Laos 70 C2
Muar Malaysia 71 C7
Muarabungo Indon. 68 C7
Muarateweh Indon. 68 E7
Muari, Ras pt Pak. 89 G5
Mu'ayqil, Khashm al hill Saudi Arabia 88 C5
Mubarek Uzbek. 89 G2
Mubarraz well Saudi Arabia 91 F5
Mubende Uganda 98 D3
Mubi Nigeria 96 E3
Muborak Uzbek. see Mubarek
Mubur i. Indon. 71 D7
Mucajaí, Serra do mts Brazil 138 F3
Mucalic r. Canada 123 I2
Muccan Australia 108 C5
Much Germany 53 H4
Muchinga Escarpment Zambia 99 D5
Muchuan China 76 D2
Muck i. U.K. 50 C4
Mucojo Moz. 99 E5
Muconda Angola 99 C5
Mucubela Moz. 99 D5
Mucugê Brazil 145 C1
Mucur Turkey 90 D3
Mucuri Brazil 145 D2
Mucuri r. Brazil 145 D2
Mudabidri India 84 B3
Mudan China see Heze
Mudanjiang China 74 C3
Mudan Jiang r. China 74 C3
Mudan Ling mts China 74 B4
Mudanya Turkey 59 M4
Muḍaybī Oman 88 E6
Mudaysīsāt, Jabal al hill Jordan 85 C4
Muddus nationalpark nat. park Sweden 44 K3
Muddy r. U.S.A. 129 F3
Muddy Gap Pass U.S.A. 126 G4
Muddy Peak U.S.A. 129 F3
Mūd-e Dahanāb Iran 88 E3
Mudersbach Germany 53 H4
Mudgal India 84 C3
Mudgee Australia 112 D4
Mudhol India 84 B2
Mudigere India 84 B3
Mudjatik r. Canada 121 J3
Mud Lake U.S.A. 128 E3
Mudraya country Africa see Egypt
Mudurnu Turkey 59 N4
Mud'yuga Rus. Fed. 42 H3
Mueda Moz. 99 D5
Mueller Range hills Australia 108 D4
Muertos Cays is Bahamas 133 D7
Muftyuga Rus. Fed. 42 J2
Mufulira Zambia 99 C5
Mufumbwe Zambia 99 C5
Mufu Shan mts China 77 G2
Muğan Düzü lowland Azer. 91 H3
Mugarripug China 83 F2
Mughalbhin Pak. see Jati
Mughal Kot Pak. 89 H4
Mughal Sarai India 83 E4
Mūghār Iran 88 D3
Mughayrā' Saudi Arabia 85 C5
Mughayrā' well Saudi Arabia 88 B5
Muğla Turkey 59 M6
Mugodzhary, Gory mts Kazakh. 80 A2
Mugxung China 76 B1
Mūḥ, Sabkhat imp. l. Syria 85 D2
Muhammad Ashraf Pak. 89 H5
Muhammad Qol Sudan 86 E5
Muhammarah Iran see Khorramshahr
Muhashsham, Wādī al watercourse Egypt 85 B4
Muḥaysh, Wādī al watercourse Jordan 85 C5
Muhaysin Syria 85 D1
Mühlanger Germany 53 M3
Mühlberg Germany 53 N3
Mühlhausen (Thüringen) Germany 53 K3
Mühlig-Hofmann Mountains Antarctica 152 C2
Muhos Fin. 44 N4
Muḥradah Syria 85 C2
Muhri Pak. 89 G4
Mui Bai Bung c. Vietnam see Mui Ca Mau
Mui Ba Lang An pt Vietnam 70 E4
Mui Ca Mau c. Vietnam 71 D5
Mui Dinh hd Vietnam 71 E5
Mui Độc pt Vietnam 70 D3
Muié Angola 99 C5
Mui Kê pt Vietnam 71 E5
Mui Nây pt Vietnam 71 E4
Muineachán Rep. of Ireland see Monaghan
Muine Bheag Rep. of Ireland 51 F5
Muir U.S.A. 134 C2
Muirkirk U.K. 50 E5
Muir of Ord U.K. 50 E3
Mui Ron hd Vietnam 70 D3
Muite Moz. 99 D5
Muji China 82 D1
Muju S. Korea 75 B5
Mukacheve Ukr. 43 D6
Mukachevo Ukr. see Mukacheve
Mukah Sarawak Malaysia 68 E6
Mukalla Yemen 86 G7
Mukandwara India 82 D4
Mukdahan Thai. 70 D3
Mukden China see Shenyang
Muketei r. Canada 122 D3
Mukhen Rus. Fed. 74 E2
Mukhino Rus. Fed. 74 B1
Mukhtuya Rus. Fed. see Lensk
Mukinbudin Australia 109 B7
Mu Ko Chang Marine National Park Thai. 71 C5
Mukojima-rettō is Japan 75 F8
Mukry Turkm. 89 G2
Muktsar India 82 C3
Mukutawa r. Canada 121 L4
Mukwonago U.S.A. 134 A2
Mula r. India 84 B2
Mulakatholhu atoll Maldives see Mulaku Atoll
Mulaku Atoll Maldives 81 D11
Mulan China 74 C3
Mulanje, Mount Malawi 99 D5
Mulapula, Lake salt flat Australia 111 B6
Mulatos Mex. 127 F7
Mulayḥ Saudi Arabia 88 B5
Mulayḥah, Jabal hill U.A.E. 88 D5
Mulayz, Wādī al watercourse Egypt 85 A4
Mulchatna r. U.S.A. 118 C3
Mulde r. Germany 53 M3
Mule Creek NM U.S.A. 129 I5
Mule Creek WY U.S.A. 126 G4
Mulegé Mex. 127 E8
Mules i. Indon. 108 C2
Muleshoe U.S.A. 131 C5
Mulga Park Australia 109 E6
Mulgathing Australia 109 F7
Mulhacén mt. Spain 57 E5
Mülhausen France see Mulhouse
Mülheim an der Ruhr Germany 52 G3
Mulhouse France 56 H3
Muli China 76 D3
Muli Rus. Fed. see Vysokogorniy
Mulia Indon. 69 J7
Muling Heilong. China 74 C3
Muling Heilong. China 74 C3
Muling He r. China 74 D3
Mull i. U.K. 50 D4
Mull, Sound of sea chan. U.K. 50 C4
Mullaghcleevaun hill Rep. of Ireland 51 F4
Mullaittivu Sri Lanka 84 D4
Mullaley Australia 112 D3
Mullengudgery Australia 112 C3
Mullens U.S.A. 134 E5
Muller watercourse Australia 108 F5
Muller, Pegunungan mts Indon. 68 E6
Mullett Lake U.S.A. 134 C1
Mullewa Australia 109 A7
Mullica r. U.S.A. 135 H4
Mullingar Rep. of Ireland 51 E4
Mullion Creek Australia 112 D4
Mull of Galloway c. U.K. 50 E6
Mull of Kintyre hd U.K. 50 D5
Mull of Oa hd U.K. 50 C5
Mullumbimby Australia 112 F2
Mulobezi Zambia 99 C5
Mulshi Lake India 84 B2
Multai India 82 D5
Multan Pak. 89 H4
Multia Fin. 44 N5
Multien reg. France 52 C6
Mulug India 84 C2
▶Mumbai India 84 B2
2nd most populous city in Asia and 5th in the world.
Mumbil Australia 112 D4
Mumbwa Zambia 99 C5
Muminabad Tajik. see Leningrad
Mŭ'minobod Tajik. see Leningrad
Mun, Mae Nam r. Thai. 70 D4
Muna i. Indon. 69 G8
Muna Mex. 136 G4
Muna r. Rus. Fed. 65 N3
Munabao Pak. 89 H5
Munaðarnes Iceland 44 [inset]
Münchberg Germany 53 L4
München Germany see Munich
München-Gladbach Germany see Mönchengladbach
Münchhausen Germany 53 I4
Muncho Lake Canada 120 E3
Muncie U.S.A. 134 C3
Muncoonie West, Lake salt flat Australia 110 B5
Muncy U.S.A. 135 G3
Munda Pak. 89 H4
Mundel Lake Sri Lanka 84 C5
Mundesley U.K. 49 I6
Mundford U.K. 49 H6
Mundiwindi Australia 109 C5
Mundra India 82 B5
Mundrabilla Australia 106 C5
Munds Park U.S.A. 129 H4
Mundubbera Australia 111 E5
Mundwa India 82 C4
Munfordville U.S.A. 134 C5
Mungallala Australia 111 D5
Mungana Australia 110 D3
Mungári Moz. 99 D5
Mungbere Dem. Rep. Congo 98 C3
Mungeli India 83 E5
Munger India 83 F4
Mu Nggava i. Solomon Is see Rennell
Mungindi Australia 112 D2
Mungla Bangl. see Mongla
Mungo Angola 99 B5
Mungo, Lake Australia 112 A4
Mungo National Park Australia 112 A4
Munich Germany 47 M6
Munising U.S.A. 132 C2
Munjpur India 82 B5
Munkács Ukr. see Mukacheve
Munkedal Sweden 45 G7
Munkelva Norway 44 P2
Munkfors Sweden 45 H7
Munkhafaḍ al Qaṭṭārah depr. Egypt see Qattara Depression
Munku-Sardyk, Gora mt. Mongolia/Rus. Fed. 72 I2
Münnerstadt Germany 53 K4
Munnik S. Africa 101 I2
Munroe Lake Canada 121 L3
Munsan S. Korea 75 B5
Münster Hessen Germany 53 I5
Münster Niedersachsen Germany 53 K2
Münster Nordrhein-Westfalen Germany 53 H3
Munster reg. Rep. of Ireland 51 D5
Münsterland reg. Germany 53 H3
Muntadgin Australia 109 B7
Munyal-Par sea feature India see Bassas de Pedro Padua Bank
Munzur Vadisi Milli Parkı nat. park Turkey 55 L4
Muojärvi l. Fin. 44 P4
Mương Lam Vietnam 70 D3
Mương Nhie Vietnam 70 C2
Muong Sai Laos see Muang Xay
Muonio Fin. 44 M3
Muonioälven r. Fin./Sweden 44 M3
Muonionjoki r. Fin./Sweden see Muonioälven
Mupa, Parque Nacional da nat. park Angola 99 B5
Muping China see Baoxing
Muqaynimah well Saudi Arabia 88 C6
Muqdisho Somalia see Mogadishu
Muquem Brazil 145 A1
Muqui Brazil 145 C3
Mur r. Austria 47 P7
also known as Mura (Croatia/Slovenia)
Mura r. Croatia/Slovenia see Mur
Murai, Tanjong pt Sing. 71 [inset]
Murai Reservoir Sing. 71 [inset]
Murakami Japan 75 E5
Murallón, Cerro mt. Chile 144 B7
Muramvya Burundi 98 C4
Murashi Rus. Fed. 42 K4
Murat r. Turkey 91 E3
Muratlı Turkey 59 L4
Muraysah, Ra's al pt Libya 90 B5
Murchison watercourse Australia 109 A6
Murchison, Mount Antarctica 152 H2
Murchison, Mount hill Australia 109 B6
Murchison Falls National Park Uganda 98 D3
Murcia Spain 57 F5
Murcia aut. comm. Spain 57 F5
Murdo U.S.A. 130 C3
Murehwa Zimbabwe 99 D5
Mureșul r. Romania 59 I1
Muret France 56 E5
Murewa Zimbabwe see Murehwa
Murfreesboro AR U.S.A. 131 E5
Murfreesboro TN U.S.A. 132 C5
Murg r. Germany 53 I6
Murgab Tajik. see Murghob
Murgab Turkm. see Murgap
Murgab r. Turkm. see Murgap
Murgap Turkm. 89 F2
Murgap r. Turkm. 87 J2
Murghab r. Afgh. 89 F3
Murghab reg. Afgh. 89 F3
Murgha Kibzai Pak. 89 H4
Murghob Tajik. 89 I2
Murgh Pass Afgh. 89 H3
Murgon Australia 111 E5
Murgoo Australia 109 B6
Muri India 83 F5
Muriaé Brazil 145 C3
Murid Pak. 89 G4
Muriege Angola 99 C4
Müritz l. Germany 53 M1
Müritz, Nationalpark nat. park Germany 53 N1
Murmansk Rus. Fed. 44 R2
Murmanskaya Oblast' admin. div. Rus. Fed. 44 S2
Murmanskiy Bereg coastal area Rus. Fed. 42 G1
Murmansk Oblast admin. div. Rus. Fed. see Murmanskaya Oblast'
Muro, Capo di c. Corsica France 56 I6
Murom Rus. Fed. 42 I5
Muroran Japan 74 F4
Muros Spain 57 B2
Muroto Japan 75 D6
Muroto-zaki pt Japan 75 D6
Murphy ID U.S.A. 126 D4
Murphy NC U.S.A. 133 D5
Murphysboro U.S.A. 130 F4
Murrah reg. Saudi Arabia 88 C6
Murrah al Kubrá, Al Buḥayrah al l. Egypt see Great Bitter Lake
Murrah aş Şughrá, Al Buḥayrah al l. Egypt see Little Bitter Lake
Murra Murra Australia 112 C2
Murrat el Kubra, Buheirat l. Egypt see Great Bitter Lake
Murrat el Sughra, Buheirat l. Egypt see Little Bitter Lake
▶Murray r. S.A. Australia 111 B7
3rd longest river in Oceania. Part of the longest (Murray-Darling).
Murray r. W.A. Australia 109 A8
Murray KY U.S.A. 131 F4
Murray UT U.S.A. 129 H1
Murray, Lake P.N.G. 69 K8
Murray, Lake U.S.A. 133 D5
Murray, Mount Canada 120 D2
Murray Bridge Australia 111 B7
▶Murray-Darling r. Austr. 106 E5
Longest river and largest drainage basin in Oceania.
Oceania 102–103
Murray Downs Australia 108 F5
Murray Range hills Australia 109 E6
Murraysburg S. Africa 100 F6
Murray Sunset National Park Australia 111 C7
Murrhardt Germany 53 J6
Murrieta U.S.A. 128 E5
Murringo Australia 112 D5
Murrisk reg. Rep. of Ireland 51 C4
Murroogh Rep. of Ireland 51 C4
▶Murrumbidgee r. Australia 112 A5
4th longest river in Oceania.
Murrumburrah Australia 112 D5
Murrurundi Australia 112 E3
Mursan India 82 D4
Murshidabad India 83 G4
Murska Sobota Slovenia 58 G1
Mürt Iran 89 F5
Murtoa Australia 111 C8
Murua i. P.N.G. see Woodlark Island
Murud India 84 B2
Murud, Gunung mt. Indon. 68 F6
Murunkan Sri Lanka 84 D4
Murupara N.Z. 113 F4
Mururoa atoll Fr. Polynesia 151 K7
Murviedro Spain see Sagunto
Murwara India 82 E5
Murwillumbah Australia 112 F2
Murzechirla Turkm. 89 F2
Murzūq Libya 97 E2
Mürzzuschlag Austria 47 O7
Muş Turkey 91 F3
Mūsā, Khowr-e b. Iran 88 C4
Musa Khel Bazar Pak. 89 H4
Musala mt. Bulg. 59 J3
Musala i. Indon. 71 B7
Musan N. Korea 74 C4
Musandam Peninsula Oman/U.A.E. 88 E5
Mūsá Qal'eh, Rūd-e r. Afgh. 89 G3
Musay'īd Qatar see Umm Sa'id
▶Muscat Oman 88 E6
Capital of Oman.
Muscat reg. Oman 88 E5
Muscat and Oman country Asia see Oman
Muscatine U.S.A. 130 F3
Musgrave Australia 110 C2
Musgrave Harbour Canada 123 L4
Musgrave Ranges mts Australia 109 E6
Mushāsh al Kabid well Jordan 85 C5
Mushayyish, Wādī al watercourse Jordan 85 C4
Mushie Dem. Rep. Congo 98 B4
Mushkaf Pak. 89 G4
Music Mountain U.S.A. 129 G4
Musinia Peak U.S.A. 129 H2
Muskeg r. Canada 120 F2
Muskeget Channel U.S.A. 135 J3
Muskegon MI U.S.A. 132 C3
Muskegon MI U.S.A. 134 B2
Muskegon r. U.S.A. 134 B2
Muskegon Heights U.S.A. 134 B2
Muskeg River Canada 120 G4
Muskogee U.S.A. 131 E5
Muskoka, Lake Canada 134 F1
Muskrat Dam Lake Canada 121 N4
Musmar Sudan 86 E6
Musoma Tanz. 98 D4
Musquanousse, Lac l. Canada 123 J4
Musquaro, Lac l. Canada 123 J4
Mussau Island P.N.G. 69 L7
Musselburgh U.K. 50 F5
Musselkanaal Neth. 52 H2
Musselshell r. U.S.A. 126 G3
Mussende Angola 99 B5
Mustafakemalpaşa Turkey 59 M4
Mustjala Estonia 45 M7
Mustvee Estonia 45 O7
Musu-dan pt N. Korea 74 C4
Muswellbrook Australia 112 E4
Mūṭ Egypt 86 C4
Mut Turkey 85 A1
Mutá, Ponta do pt Brazil 145 D1
Mutare Zimbabwe 99 D5
Mutayr reg. Saudi Arabia 88 B5
Mutina Italy see Modena
Muting Indon. 69 K8
Mutis Col. 142 C2
Mutnyy Materik Rus. Fed. 42 L2
Mutoko Zimbabwe 99 D5
Mutsamudu Comoros 99 E5
Mutsu Japan 74 F4
Muttaburra Australia 110 D4
Muttonbird Islands N.Z. 113 A8
Mutton Island Rep. of Ireland 51 C5
Muttukuru India 84 D3
Muttupet India 84 C4
Mutum Brazil 145 C2
Mutunópolis Brazil 145 A1
Mutur Sri Lanka 84 D4
Mutusjärvi r. Fin. 44 O2
Muurola Fin. 44 N3
Mu Us Shamo des. China 73 J5
Muxaluando Angola 99 B4
Muxi China see Muchuan
Muxima Angola 99 B4
Muyezerskiy Rus. Fed. 44 R5
Muyinga Burundi 98 D4
Muynak Uzbek. 80 A3
Mŭynoq Uzbek. see Muynak
Muyumba Dem. Rep. Congo 99 C4
Muyunkum, Peski des. Kazakh. see Moyynkum, Peski
Muyuping China 77 F2
Muzaffarabad Pak. 89 I3
Muzaffargarh Pak. 89 H4
Muzaffarnagar India 82 D3
Muzaffarpur India 83 F4
Muzamane Moz. 101 K2
Muzhi Rus. Fed. 41 S2
Mūzīn Iran 89 F5
Muzon, Cape U.S.A. 120 C4
Múzquiz Mex. 131 C7
Muztag mt. China 82 E2
Muz Tag mt. China 83 F1
Muztagata mt. China 89 I2
Muztor Kyrg. see Toktogul
Mvadi Gabon 98 B3
Mvolo Sudan 97 F4
Mvuma Zimbabwe 99 D5
Mwanza Malawi 99 D5
Mwanza Tanz. 98 D4
Mweelrea hill Rep. of Ireland 51 C4
Mweka Dem. Rep. Congo 99 C4
Mwene-Ditu Dem. Rep. Congo 99 C4
Mwenezi Zimbabwe 99 D6
Mwenga Dem. Rep. Congo 98 C4
Mweru, Lake Dem. Rep. Congo/Zambia 99 C4
Mweru Wantipa National Park Zambia 99 C4
Mwimba Dem. Rep. Congo 99 C4
Mwinilunga Zambia 99 C5
Myadaung Myanmar 70 B2
Myadzyel Belarus 45 O9
Myajlar India 82 B4
Myall Lakes National Park Australia 112 F4
Myanaung Myanmar 70 A3
▶Myanmar country Asia 70 A2
Asia 6, 62–63
Myauk-U Myanmar see Myohaung
Myaungmya Myanmar 70 A3
Myawadi Thai. 70 B3
Mybster U.K. 50 F2
Myebon Myanmar 70 A2
Myede Myanmar 70 A3
Myeik Myanmar see Mergui
Myingyan Myanmar 70 A2
Myinkyado Myanmar 70 B2
Myinmoletkat mt. Myanmar 71 B4
Myitkyina Myanmar 70 B1
Myitson Myanmar 70 B2
Myitta Myanmar 71 B4
Myittha Myanmar 70 B2
Mykolayiv Ukr. 59 O1
Mykonos i. Greece 59 K6
Myla Rus. Fed. 42 K2
Myla r. Rus. Fed. 42 K2
Mylae Sicily Italy see Milazzo
Mylasa Turkey see Milas
Mymensing Bangl. see Mymensingh
Mymensingh Bangl. 83 G4
Mynämäki Fin. 45 M6
Myohaung Myanmar 70 A2
Myŏnggan N. Korea 74 C4
Myory Belarus 45 O9
Mýrdalsjökull ice cap Iceland 44 [inset]
Myre Norway 44 I2
Myrheden Sweden 44 L4
Myrhorod Ukr. 43 G6
Myrnam Canada 121 I4
Myronivka Ukr. 43 F6
Myrtle Beach U.S.A. 133 E5
Myrtleford Australia 112 C6
Myrtle Point U.S.A. 126 B4
Mys Articheskiy c. Rus. Fed. 153 E1
Mysia reg. Turkey 59 L5
Mys Lazareva Rus. Fed. see Lazarev
Myślibórz Poland 47 O4
My Son Sanctuary tourist site Vietnam 70 E4
Mysore India 84 C3
Mysore state India see Karnataka
Mys Shmidta Rus. Fed. 65 T3
Mysy Rus. Fed. 42 L3
My Tho Vietnam 71 D5
Mytilene i. Greece see Lesbos
Mytilini Greece 59 L5
Mytilini Strait Greece/Turkey 59 L5
Mytishchi Rus. Fed. 42 H5
Myton U.S.A. 129 H1
Myyeldino Rus. Fed. 42 L3
Mzamomhle S. Africa 101 H6
Mže r. Czech Rep. 53 M5
Mzimba Malawi 99 D5
Mzuzu Malawi 99 D5
N
Naab r. Germany 53 M5
Naalehu HI U.S.A. 127 [inset]
Naantali Fin. 45 M6
Naas Rep. of Ireland 51 F4
Naba Myanmar 70 B1
Nababeep S. Africa 100 C5
Nababganj Bangl. see Nawabganj
Nabadwip India see Navadwip
Nabarangapur India 84 D2
Nabarangpur India see Nabarangapur
Nabari Japan 75 E6
Nabatîyé et Tahta Lebanon 85 B3
Nabatiyet et Tahta Lebanon see Nabatîyé et Tahta
Nabberu, Lake salt flat Australia 109 C6
Nabburg Germany 53 M5
Naberera Tanz. 99 D4
Naberezhnyye Chelny Rus. Fed. 41 Q4
Nabesna U.S.A. 120 A2
Nabeul Tunisia 58 D6
Nabha India 82 D3
Nabil'skiy Zaliv lag. Rus. Fed. 74 F2
Nabire Indon. 69 J7
Nabi Younés, Ras en pt Lebanon 85 B3
Nāblus West Bank 85 B3
Naboomspruit S. Africa 101 I3
Nabq Reserve nature res. Egypt 90 D5
Nābulus West Bank see Nāblus
Nacala Moz. 99 E5
Nachalovo Rus. Fed. 43 K7
Nachicapau, Lac l. Canada 123 I2
Nachingwea Tanz. 99 D5
Nachna India 82 B4
Nachuge India 71 A5
Nacimiento Reservoir U.S.A. 128 C4
Naco U.S.A. 127 F7
Nacogdoches U.S.A. 131 E6
Nada China see Danzhou
Nadaleen r. Canada 120 C2
Nådendal Fin. see Naantali
Nadezhdinskoye Rus. Fed. 74 D2
Nadiad India 82 C5
Nadol India 82 C4
Nador Morocco 57 E6
Nadqān, Qalamat well Saudi Arabia 88 C6
Nadūshan Iran 88 D3
Nadvirna Ukr. 43 E6
Nadvoitsy Rus. Fed. 42 G3
Nadvornaya Ukr. see Nadvirna
Nadym Rus. Fed. 64 I3
Næstved Denmark 45 G9
Nafarroa aut. comm. Spain see Navarra
Nafas, Ra's an mt. Egypt 85 B5
Nafḥa, Har hill Israel 85 B4
Nafpaktos Greece 59 I5
Nafplio Greece 59 J6
Naftalan Azer. 91 G2
Naft-e Safid Iran 88 C4
Naft-e Shāh Iran see Naft Shahr
Naft Shahr Iran 88 B3
Nafūd ad Daḥl des. Saudi Arabia 88 B6
Nafūd al Ghuwayṭah des. Saudi Arabia 85 D5
Nafūd al Jur'ā des. Saudi Arabia 88 B5
Nafūd as Sirr des. Saudi Arabia 88 B5
Nafūd as Surrah des. Saudi Arabia 88 A6
Nafūd Qunayfidhah des. Saudi Arabia 88 B5
Nafūsah, Jabal hills Libya 96 E1
Nafy Saudi Arabia 86 F4
Nag, Co l. China 83 G2
Naga Phil. 69 G4
Nagagami r. Canada 122 D4
Nagagami Lake Canada 122 D4
Nagahama Japan 75 D6
Naga Hills India 83 H4
Naga Hills state India see Nagaland
Nagaland state India 83 H4
Nagamangala India 84 C3
Nagambie Australia 112 B6
Nagano Japan 75 E5
Nagaoka Japan 75 E5
Nagaon India 83 H4
Nagapatam India see Nagapattinam
Nagapattinam India 84 C4
Nagar Himachal Pradesh India 87 M3
Nagar Karnataka India 84 B3
Nagaram India 84 D2
Nagari Hills India 84 C3
Nagarjuna Sagar Reservoir India 84 C2
Nagar Parkar Pak. 89 H5
Nagasaki Japan 75 C6
Nagato Japan 75 C6
Nagaur India 82 C4
Nagbhir India 84 C1
Nagda India 82 C5
Nageezi U.S.A. 129 J3
Nagercoil India 84 C4
Nagha Kalat Pak. 89 G5
Nag' Ḥammâdî Egypt see Naj' Ḥammādī
Nagina India 82 D3
Nagold r. Germany 53 I6
Nagong Chu r. China see Parlung Zangbo
Nagorno-Karabakh aut. reg. Azer. see Dağlıq Qarabağ
Nagornyy Karabakh aut. reg. Azer. see Dağlıq Qarabağ
Nagorsk Rus. Fed. 42 K4
Nagoya Japan 75 E6
Nagpur India 82 D5
Nagqu China 76 B2
Nag Qu r. China 76 B2
Nagurskoye Rus. Fed. 64 F1
Nagyatád Hungary 58 G1
Nagybecskerek Serb. and Mont. see Zrenjanin
Nagyenyed Romania see Aiud
Nagykanizsa Hungary 58 G1
Nagyvárad Romania see Oradea
Naha Japan 73 N7
Nahan India 82 D3
Nahanni Butte Canada 120 F2
Nahanni National Park Canada 120 E2
Nahanni Range mts Canada 120 F2
Naharāyim Jordan 85 B3
Nahariyya Israel 85 B3
Nahāvand Iran 88 C3
Nahr Dijlah r. Iraq/Syria 91 G5 see Tigris
Nahuel Huapi, Parque Nacional nat. park Arg. 144 B6
Nahunta U.S.A. 133 D6
Naica Mex. 131 B7
Nai Ga Myanmar 76 C3
Naij Tal China 83 H2

Naikliu Indon. 108 C2
Nain Canada 123 J2
Nā'īn Iran 88 D3
Nainital India 82 D3
Naini Tal India see Nainital
Nairn U.K. 50 F3
Nairn r. U.K. 50 F3

▶Nairobi Kenya 98 D4
Capital of Kenya.

Naissus Serb. and Mont. see Niš
Naivasha Kenya 98 D4
Najafābād Iran 88 C3
Na'jān Saudi Arabia 88 B5
Najd *reg.* Saudi Arabia 86 F4
Nájera Spain 57 E2
Naj' Ḥammādī Egypt 86 D4
Naji China 74 A2
Najibabad India 82 D3
Najin N. Korea 74 C4
Najitun China see Naji
Najrān Saudi Arabia 86 F6
Nakadōri-shima *i.* Japan 75 C6
Na Kae Thai. 70 D3
Nakambé *r.* Burkina/Ghana see White Volta
Nakanbe *r.* Burkina/Ghana see White Volta
Nakanno Rus. Fed. 65 L3
Nakano-shima *i.* Japan 75 D5
Nakasongola Uganda 97 G4
Nakatsu Japan 75 C6
Nakatsugawa Japan 75 E6
Nakfa Eritrea 86 E6
Nakhichevan' Azer. see Naxçıvan
Nakhl Egypt 85 A5
Nakhodka Rus. Fed. 74 D4
Nakhola India 83 H4
Nakhon Nayok Thai. 71 C4
Nakhon Pathom Thai. 71 C4
Nakhon Phanom Thai. 70 D3
Nakhon Ratchasima Thai. 70 C4
Nakhon Sawan Thai. 70 C4
Nakhon Si Thammarat Thai. 71 B5
Nakhtarana India 82 B5
Nakina Canada 122 D4
Nakina *r.* Canada 120 C3
Naknek U.S.A. 118 C4
Nakonde Zambia 99 D4
Nakskov Denmark 45 G9
Naktong-gang *r.* S. Korea 75 C6
Nakuru Kenya 98 D4
Nakusp Canada 120 G5
Nal Pak. 89 G5
Nal *r.* Pak. 89 G5
Na-lang Myanmar 70 B2
Nalázi Moz. 101 K3
Nalbari India 83 G4
Nal'chik Rus. Fed. 91 F2
Naldurg India 84 C2
Nalgonda India 84 C2
Naliya India 82 B5
Nallamala Hills India 84 C3
Nallıhan Turkey 59 N4
Nālūt Libya 96 E1
Namaacha Moz. 101 K3
Namacurra Moz. 99 D5
Namadgi National Park Australia 112 D5
Namahadi S. Africa 101 I4
Namak, Daryācheh-ye *salt flat* Iran 88 C3
Namak, Kavīr-e *salt flat* Iran 88 E3
Namakkal India 84 C4
Namakwaland *reg.* Namibia see Great Namaqualand
Namakzar-e Shadad *salt flat* Iran 88 E4
Namaland *reg.* Namibia see Great Namaqualand
Namangan Uzbek. 80 D3
Namaqualand *reg.* Namibia see Great Namaqualand
Namaqualand *reg.* S. Africa 100 C5
Namaqua National Park S. Africa 100 C6
Namas Indon. 69 K8
Namatanai P.N.G. 106 F2
Nambour Australia 112 F1
Nambucca Heads Australia 112 F3
Nambung National Park Australia 109 A7
Năm Căn Vietnam 71 D5
Namcha Barwa *mt.* China see Namjagbarwa Feng
Namche Bazar Nepal 83 F4
Nam Co *salt l.* China 83 G3
Namdalen *valley* Norway 44 H4
Namdalseid Norway 44 G4
Nam Định Vietnam 70 D2
Namen Belgium see Namur
Nam-gang *r.* N. Korea 75 B5
Namhae-do *i.* S. Korea 75 B6
Namhsan Myanmar 70 B2
Namib Desert Namibia 100 B3
Namibe Angola 99 B5
▶Namibia *country* Africa 99 B6
Africa 7, 94–95
Namibia Abyssal Plain *sea feature* N. Atlantic Ocean 148 I8
Namib-Naukluft Game Park *nature res.* Namibia 100 B3
Namie Japan 75 F5
Namīn Iran 91 H3
Namjagbarwa Feng *mt.* China 76 B2
Namlan Myanmar 70 B2
Namlang *r.* Myanmar 70 B2
Nam Loi *r.* Myanmar see Nanlei He
Nam Nao National Park Thai. 70 C3
Nam Ngum Reservoir Laos 70 C3
Namoi *r.* Australia 112 D3
Namonuito *atoll* Micronesia 69 L5
Nampa *mt.* Nepal 82 E3
Nampa U.S.A. 126 D4
Nampala Mali 96 C3
Nam Phong Thai. 70 C3
Namp'o N. Korea 75 B5
Nampula Moz. 99 D5
Namsai Myanmar 70 B1
Namsang Myanmar 70 B2
Namsen *r.* Norway 44 G4
Nam She Tsim *hill* Hong Kong China see Sharp Peak
Namsos Norway 44 G4
Namti Myanmar 70 B1
Namtok Myanmar 70 B3
Namtok Chattakan National Park Thai. 70 C3
Namton Myanmar 70 B2
Namtsy Rus. Fed. 65 N3
Namtu Myanmar 70 B2
Namu Canada 120 E5
Namuli, Monte *mt.* Moz. 99 D5
Namuno Moz. 99 D5
Namur Belgium 52 E4
Namutoni Namibia 99 B5
Namwŏn S. Korea 75 B6
Namya Ra Myanmar 70 B1
Namyit Island S. China Sea 68 E4
Nan Thai. 70 C3
Nana Bakassa Cent. Afr. Rep. 98 B3
Nanaimo Canada 120 F5
Nanam N. Korea 74 C4
Nan'an China 77 H3
Nanango Australia 112 F1
Nananib Plateau Namibia 100 C3
Nanao Japan 75 E5
Nanatsu-shima *i.* Japan 75 E5
Nanbai China see Zunyi
Nanbin China see Shizhu
Nanbu China 76 E2
Nancha China 74 C3
Nanchang *Jiangxi* China 77 G2
Nanchang *Jiangxi* China 77 G2
Nanchong China 76 E2
Nanchuan China 76 E2
Nancowry *i.* India 71 A6
Nancun China 77 G1
Nancy France 52 G6
Nancy (Essey) *airport* France 52 G6
Nanda Devi *mt.* India 82 E3
Nanda Kot *mt.* India 82 E3
Nandan China 76 E3
Nandapur India 84 D2
Nanded India 84 C2
Nander India see Nanded
Nandewar Range *mts* Australia 112 E3
Nandod India 84 B1
Nandurbar India 82 C5
Nandyal India 84 C3
Nanfeng *Guangdong* China 77 F4
Nanfeng *Jiangxi* China 77 H3
Nang China 76 B2
Nanga Eboko Cameroon 96 E4
Nanga Parbat *mt.* Jammu and Kashmir 82 C2
Nangar National Park Australia 112 D4
Nangatayap Indon. 68 E7
Nangin Myanmar 71 B5
Nangnim-sanmaek *mts* N. Korea 75 B4
Nangqên China 76 C1
Nangulangwa Tanz. 99 D4
Nanguneri India 84 C4
Nanhua China 76 D3
Nanhui China 77 I2
Nanjian China 76 D3
Nanjiang China 76 E1
Nanjing China 77 H1
Nanji Shan *i.* China 77 I3
Nanka Jiang *r.* China 76 C4
Nankang China 77 G3
Nanking China see Nanjing
Nankova Angola 99 B5
Nanlei He *r.* China 76 C4
also known as Nam Loi (Myanmar)
Nanling China 77 H2
Nan Ling *mts* China 77 F3
Nanliu Jiang *r.* China 77 F4
Nanlong China see Nanbu
Nannilam India 84 C4
Nannine Australia 109 B6
Nanning China 77 F4
Nannup Australia 109 A8
Na Noi Thai. 70 C3
Nanortalik Greenland 119 N3
Nanouki *atoll* Kiribati see Nonouti
Nanouti *atoll* Kiribati see Nonouti
Nanpan Jiang *r.* China 76 E3
Nanping China 77 H3
Nanpu China see Pucheng
Nanri Dao *i.* China 77 H3
Nansei-shotō *is* Japan see Ryukyu Islands
Nansen Basin *sea feature* Arctic Ocean 153 H1
Nansen Sound *sea chan.* Canada 119 I1
Nan-sha Ch'ün-tao *is* S. China Sea see Spratly Islands
Nanshan Island S. China Sea 68 F4
Nansha Qundao *is* S. China Sea see Spratly Islands
Nansio Tanz. 98 D4
Nantes France 56 D3
Nantes à Brest, Canal de France 56 C3
Nanteuil-le-Haudouin France 52 C5
Nanthi Kadal *lag.* Sri Lanka 84 D4
Nanticoke Canada 134 E2
Nanticoke U.S.A. 135 H4
Nantong China 77 I2
Nantou China 77 [inset]
Nant'ou Taiwan 77 I4
Nantucket U.S.A. 135 J3
Nantucket Island U.S.A. 135 K3
Nantucket Sound *g.* U.S.A. 135 J3
Nantwich U.K. 49 E5
Nanumaga *i.* Tuvalu see Nanumanga
Nanumanga *i.* Tuvalu 107 H2
Nanumea *atoll* Tuvalu 107 H2
Nanuque Brazil 145 C2
Nanusa, Kepulauan *is* Indon. 69 H6
Nanxi China 76 E2
Nanxian China 77 G2
Nanxiong China 77 G3
Nanyang China 77 G1
Nanyuki Kenya 98 D4
Nanzhang China 77 F2
Nanzhao China see Zhao'an
Nanzhou China see Nanxian
Naococane, Lac *l.* Canada 123 H3
Naoero *country* S. Pacific Ocean see Nauru
Naogaon Bangl. 83 G4
Naokot Pak. 89 H5
Naoli He *r.* China 74 D3
Naomid, Dasht-e *des.* Afgh./Iran 89 F3
Naoshera Jammu and Kashmir 82 C2
Napa U.S.A. 128 B2
Napaktulik Lake Canada 121 H1
Napanee Canada 135 G1
Napasoq Greenland 119 M3
Naperville U.S.A. 134 A3
Napier N.Z. 113 F4
Napier Range *hills* Australia 108 D4
Napierville Canada 135 I1
Naples Italy 58 F4
Naples *FL* U.S.A. 133 D7
Naples *ME* U.S.A. 135 J2
Naples *TX* U.S.A. 131 E5
Naples *UT* U.S.A. 129 I1
Napo China 76 E4
Napoleon *IN* U.S.A. 134 C4
Napoleon *ND* U.S.A. 130 D2
Napoleon *OH* U.S.A. 134 C3
Napoli Italy see Naples
Naqadeh Iran 88 B2
Nara India 82 B5
Nara Japan 75 D6
Nara Mali 96 C3
Narach Belarus 45 O9
Naracoorte Australia 111 C8
Naradhan Australia 112 C4
Naraingpur India 84 D2
Naralua India 83 F4
Naranjal Ecuador 142 C4
Naranjo Mex. 127 F8
Narasapur India 84 D2
Narasaraopet India 84 D2
Narasinghapur India 84 E1
Narathiwat Thai. 71 C6
Nara Visa U.S.A. 131 C5
Narayanganj Bangl. 83 G5
Narayanganj India 82 E5
Narayangarh India 82 C4
Narbada *r.* India see Narmada
Narberth U.K. 49 C7
Narbo France see Narbonne
Narbonne France 56 F5
Narborough Island *Galápagos* Ecuador see Fernandina, Isla
Narcea *r.* Spain 57 C2
Narcondam Island India 71 A4
Nardò Italy 58 H4
Narechi *r.* Pak. 89 H4
Narembeen Australia 109 B8
Nares Abyssal Plain *sea feature* S. Atlantic Ocean 148 D4
Nares Deep *sea feature* N. Atlantic Ocean 148 D4
Nares Strait Canada/Greenland 119 K2
Naretha Australia 109 D7
Narew *r.* Poland 47 R4
Narib Namibia 100 C3
Narikel Jinjira *i.* Bangl. see St Martin's Island
Narimanov Rus. Fed. 43 J7
Narimskiy Khrebet *mts* Kazakh. see Narymskiy Khrebet
Narin Afgh. 89 H2
Narin *reg.* Afgh. 89 H2
Narince Turkey 90 E3
Narin Gol *watercourse* China 83 H1
Narizon, Punta *pt* Mex. 127 F8
Narkher India 82 D5
Narmada *r.* India 82 C5
Narman Turkey 91 F2
Narnaul India 82 D3
Narni Italy 58 E3
Narnia Italy see Narni
Narodnaya, Gora *mt.* Rus. Fed. 41 S3
Naro-Fominsk Rus. Fed. 43 H5
Narok Kenya 98 D4
Narooma Australia 112 E6
Narovchat Rus. Fed. 43 I5
Narowlya Belarus 43 F6
Närpes Fin. 44 L5
Narrabri Australia 112 D3
Narragansett Bay U.S.A. 135 J3
Narran *r.* Australia 112 C2
Narrandera Australia 112 C5
Narran Lake Australia 112 C2
Narrogin Australia 109 B8
Narromine Australia 112 D4
Narrows U.S.A. 134 E5
Narrowsburg U.S.A. 135 H3
Narsapur India 84 C2
Narsaq Greenland 119 N3
Narshingdi Bangl. see Narsingdi
Narsimhapur India see Narsinghpur
Narsingdi Bangl. 83 G5
Narsinghpur India 82 D5
Narsipatnam India 84 D2
Nartkala Rus. Fed. 91 F2
Naruto Japan 75 D6
Narva Estonia 45 P7
Narva Bay Estonia/Rus. Fed. 45 O7
Narva laht *b.* Estonia/Rus. Fed. see Narva Bay
Narva Reservoir *resr* Estonia/Rus. Fed. see Narvskoye Vodokhranilishche
Narva veehoidla *resr* Estonia/Rus. Fed. see Narvskoye Vodokhranilishche
Narvik Norway 44 J2
Narvskiy Zaliv *b.* Estonia/Rus. Fed. see Narva Bay
Narvskoye Vodokhranilishche *resr* Estonia/Rus. Fed. 45 P7
Narwana India 82 D3
Nar'yan-Mar Rus. Fed. 42 L2
Narymskiy Khrebet *mts* Kazakh. 80 F2
Naryn Kyrg. 80 E3
Näsåker Sweden 44 J5
Nashik India 84 B1
Nashua U.S.A. 135 J2
Nashville *AR* U.S.A. 131 E5
Nashville *GA* U.S.A. 133 D6
Nashville *IN* U.S.A. 134 B4
Nashville *NC* U.S.A. 132 E5
Nashville *OH* U.S.A. 134 D3

▶Nashville *TN* U.S.A. 132 C4
State capital of Tennessee.

Naşīb Syria 85 C3
Näsijärvi *l.* Fin. 45 M6
Nasik India see Nashik
Nasir Pak. 89 H4
Nasir Sudan 86 D8
Nasirabad Bangl. see Mymensingh
Nasirabad India 82 C4
Naskaupi *r.* Canada 123 J3
Naşr Egypt 90 C5
Nasratabad Iran see Zābol
Naṣrīān-e Pā'īn Iran 88 B3
Nass *r.* Canada 120 D4
Nassau *r.* Australia 110 C2

▶Nassau Bahamas 133 E7
Capital of The Bahamas.

Nassau *i.* Cook Is 107 J3
Nassau U.S.A. 135 I2
Nassawadox U.S.A. 135 H5
Nasser, Lake *resr* Egypt 86 D5
Nässjö Sweden 45 I8
Nassuttooq *inlet* Greenland 119 M3
Nastapoca *r.* Canada 122 F2
Nastapoka Islands Canada 122 F2
Nasugbu Phil. 69 G4
Nasva Rus. Fed. 42 F4
Nata Botswana 99 C6
Natal Brazil 143 K5
Natal Indon. 68 B6
Natal *prov.* S. Africa see Kwazulu-Natal
Natal Basin *sea feature* Indian Ocean 149 K8
Natal Drakensberg Park *nat. park* S. Africa 101 I5
Naṭanz Iran 88 C3
Natashquan Canada 123 J4
Natashquan *r.* Canada 123 J4
Natchez U.S.A. 131 F6
Natchitoches U.S.A. 131 E6
Nathalia Australia 112 B6
Nathia Gali Pak. 89 I3
Nati, Punta *pt* Spain 57 H3
Natillas Mex. 131 C7
National City U.S.A. 128 E5
National West Coast Tourist Recreation Area *park* Namibia 100 B2
Natitingou Benin 96 D3
Natividad, Isla *i.* Mex. 127 E8
Natividade Brazil 143 I6
Natkyizin Myanmar 70 B4
Natla *r.* Canada 120 D2
Natmauk Myanmar 70 A2
Nator Bangl. see Natore
Nátora Mex. 127 F7
Natore Bangl. 83 G4
Natori Japan 75 F5
Natron, Lake *salt l.* Tanz. 98 D4
Nattai National Park Australia 112 E5
Nattalin Myanmar 70 A3
Nattaung *mt.* Myanmar 70 B3
Na'tū Iran 89 F3
Natuna, Kepulauan *is* Indon. 71 D6
Natuna Besar *i.* Indon. 71 E6
Natural Bridges National Monument *nat. park* U.S.A. 129 H3
Naturaliste, Cape Australia 109 A8
Naturaliste Plateau *sea feature* Indian Ocean 149 P8
Naturita U.S.A. 129 I2
Nauchas Namibia 100 C2
Nau Co *l.* China 83 E2
Nauen Germany 53 M2
Naufragados, Ponta dos *pt* Brazil 145 A4
Naujoji Akmenė Lith. 45 M8
Naukh India 82 C4
Naumburg (Hessen) Germany 53 J3
Naumburg (Saale) Germany 53 L3
Naunglon Myanmar 70 B3
Naungpale Myanmar 70 B3
Naupada India 84 E2
Na'ūr Jordan 85 B4
Nauroz Kalat Pak. 89 G4
Naurskaya Rus. Fed. 91 G2
Nauru *i.* Nauru 107 G2
▶Nauru *country* S. Pacific Ocean 107 G2
Oceania 8, 104–105
Naustdal Norway 45 D6
Nauta Peru 142 D4
Nautaca Uzbek. see Karshi
Naute Dam Namibia 100 C4
Nauzad Afgh. 89 G3
Nava Mex. 131 C6
Navadwip India 83 G5
Navahrudak Belarus 45 N10
Navajo Lake U.S.A. 129 J3
Navajo Mountain U.S.A. 129 H3
Navalmoral de la Mata Spain 57 D4
Navalvillar de Pela Spain 57 D4
Navan Rep. of Ireland 51 F4
Navangar India see Jamnagar
Navapolatsk Belarus 45 P9
Nāvar, Dasht-e *depr.* Afgh. 89 G3
Navarin, Mys *c.* Rus. Fed. 65 S3
Navarra *aut. comm.* Spain 57 F2
Navarra, Comunidad Foral de *aut. comm.* Spain see Navarra
Navarre Australia 112 A6
Navarre *aut. comm.* Spain see Navarra
Navarro *r.* U.S.A. 128 B2
Navashino Rus. Fed. 42 I5
Navasota U.S.A. 131 D6

▶Navassa Island *terr.* West Indies 137 I5
United States Unincorporated Territory.

Naver *r.* U.K. 50 E2
Näverede Sweden 44 I5
Navlakhi India 82 B5
Navlya Rus. Fed. 43 G5
Năvodari Romania 59 M2
Navoi Uzbek. 89 G1
Navoiy Uzbek. see Navoi
Navojoa Mex. 127 F8
Navolato Mex. 136 C4
Návpaktos Greece see Nafpaktos
Návplion Greece see Nafplio
Navşar Turkey see Şemdinli
Navsari India 84 B1
Nawá Syria 85 C3
Nawabganj Bangl. 83 G4
Nawabshah Pak. 89 H5
Nawada India 83 F4
Nāwah Afgh. 89 G3
Nawalgarh India 82 C4
Nawanshahr India 82 D3
Nawan Shehar India see Nawanshahr
Nawar, Dasht-i *depr.* Afgh. see Nāvar, Dasht-e
Nawarangpur India see Nabarangapur
Nawngcho Myanmar see Nawnghkio
Nawnghkio Myanmar 70 B2
Nawng Hpa Myanmar 70 B2
Nawngleng Myanmar 70 B2
Nawoiy Uzbek. see Navoi
Naxçıvan Azer. 91 G3
Naxos *i.* Greece 59 K6
Nayagarh India 84 E1
Nayak Afgh. 89 G3
Nayar Mex. 136 D4
Nāy Band, Kūh-e *mt.* Iran 88 E3
Nayong China 76 E3
Nayoro Japan 74 F3
Nazaré Brazil 145 D1
Nazareno Mex. 131 C7
Nazareth Israel 85 B3
Nazário Brazil 145 A2
Nazas Mex. 131 B7
Nazas *r.* Mex. 131 B7
Nazca Peru 142 D6
Nazca Ridge *sea feature* S. Pacific Ocean 151 O7
Nāzīl Iran 89 F4
Nazilli Turkey 59 M6
Nazimabad Pak. 89 G5
Nazımiye Turkey 91 E3
Nazir Hat Bangl. 83 G5
Nazko Canada 120 F4
Nazran' Rus. Fed. 91 G2
Nazrēt Eth. 98 D3
Nazwá Oman 88 E6
Ncojane Botswana 100 E2
N'dalatando Angola 99 B4
Ndélé Cent. Afr. Rep. 98 C3
Ndendé Gabon 98 B4
Ndende *i.* Solomon Is see Ndeni
Ndeni *i.* Solomon Is 107 G3

▶Ndjamena Chad 97 E3
Capital of Chad.

N'Djamena Chad see Ndjamena
Ndjouani *i.* Comoros see Nzwani
Ndoi *i.* Fiji see Doi
Ndola Zambia 99 C5
Nduke *i.* Solomon Is see Kolombangara
Ndwedwe S. Africa 101 J5
Ne, Hon *i.* Vietnam 70 D3
Neabul Creek *r.* Australia 112 C1
Neagh, Lough *l.* U.K. 51 F3
Neah Bay U.S.A. 126 B2
Neale, Lake *salt flat* Australia 109 E6
Nea Liosia Greece 59 J5
Neapoli Greece 59 J6
Neapolis Italy see Naples
Nea Roda Greece 59 J4
Neath U.K. 49 D7
Neath *r.* U.K. 49 D7
Nebbi Uganda 98 D3
Nebine Creek *r.* Australia 112 C2
Nebitdag Turkm. 88 D2
Neblina, Pico da *mt.* Brazil 142 E3
Nebo Australia 110 E4
Nebo, Mount U.S.A. 129 H2
Nebolchi Rus. Fed. 42 G4
Nebraska *state* U.S.A. 130 C3
Nebraska City U.S.A. 130 E3
Nebrodi, Monti *mts Sicily* Italy 58 F6
Neches *r.* U.S.A. 131 E6
Nechisar National Park Eth. 98 D3
Nechranice, Vodní nádrž *resr* Czech Rep. 53 N4
Neckar *r.* Germany 53 I5
Neckarsulm Germany 53 J5
Necker Island U.S.A. 150 J4
Necochea Arg. 144 E5
Nederland *country* Europe see Netherlands
Nederlandse Antillen *terr.* West Indies see Netherlands Antilles
Neder Rijn *r.* Neth. 52 F3
Nedlouc, Lac *l.* Canada 123 G2
Nedluk Lake Canada see Nedlouc, Lac
Nêdong China 83 G3
Nedre Soppero Sweden 44 L2
Nédroma Alg. 57 F6
Needle Mountain U.S.A. 126 F3
Needles U.S.A. 129 F4
Neemach India see Neemuch
Neemuch India 82 C4
Neenah U.S.A. 134 A1
Neepawa Canada 121 L5
Neergaard Lake Canada 119 J2
Neerijnen Neth. 52 F3
Neerpelt Belgium 52 F3
Neftçala Azer. 91 H3
Neftechala Azer. see 26 Bakı Komissarı
Neftechala Azer. see Neftçala
Neftegorsk *Sakhalinskaya Oblast'* Rus. Fed. 74 F1
Neftegorsk *Samarskaya Oblast'* Rus. Fed. 43 K5
Neftekamsk Rus. Fed. 41 Q4
Neftekumsk Rus. Fed. 91 G1
Nefteyugansk Rus. Fed. 64 I3
Neftezavodsk Turkm. see Seydi
Neftezawodsk Turkm. see Seydi
Nefyn U.K. 49 C6
Nefza Tunisia 58 C6
Negage Angola 99 B4
Negār Iran 88 E4
Negara Indon. 108 A2
Negēlē Eth. 98 D3
Negev *des.* Israel 85 B4
Negomane Moz. 99 D5
Negombo Sri Lanka 84 C5
Negotino Macedonia 59 J4
Negra, Cordillera *mts* Peru 142 C5
Negra, Punta *pt* Peru 142 B5
Negra, Serra *mts* Brazil 145 C2
Negrais, Cape Myanmar 70 A4
Négrine Alg. 58 B7
Negro *r.* Arg. 144 D6
Negro *r.* Brazil 143 G7
Negro *r.* Brazil 145 A4
Negro *r.* S. America 142 G4
Negro, Cabo *c.* Morocco 57 D6
Negroponte *i.* Greece see Evvoia
Negros *i.* Phil. 69 G5
Negru Vodă, Podişul *plat.* Romania 59 M3
Nehbandān Iran 89 F4
Nehe China 74 B2
Neijiang China 76 E2
Neilburg Canada 121 I4
Neimenggu *aut. reg.* China see Nei Mongol Zizhiqu
Nei Mongol Zizhiqu *aut. reg.* China 74 A2
Neinstedt Germany 53 L3
Neiva Col. 142 C3
Neixiang China 77 F1
Nejanilini Lake Canada 121 L3
Nejd *reg.* Saudi Arabia see Najd
Neka Iran 88 D2
Nek'emtē Eth. 98 D3
Nekrasovskoye Rus. Fed. 42 I4
Neksø Denmark 45 I9
Nelang India 82 D3
Nelia Australia 110 C4
Nelidovo Rus. Fed. 42 G4
Neligh U.S.A. 130 D3
Nel'kan Rus. Fed. 65 P3
Nellore India 84 C3
Nelluz *watercourse* Turkey 85 D1
Nel'ma Rus. Fed. 74 E3
Nelson Canada 120 G5
Nelson *r.* Canada 121 M3
Nelson N.Z. 113 D5
Nelson U.K. 48 E5
Nelson U.S.A. 129 G4
Nelson, Cape Australia 111 C8
Nelson, Cape P.N.G. 69 L8
Nelson, Estrecho *strait* Chile 144 A8
Nelson Bay Australia 112 F4
Nelson Forks Canada 120 F3
Nelsonia U.S.A. 135 H5
Nelson Lakes National Park N.Z. 113 D6
Nelson Reservoir U.S.A. 126 G2
Nelspruit S. Africa 101 J3
Néma Mauritania 96 C3
Nema Rus. Fed. 42 K4
Neman *r.* Belarus/Lith. see Nyoman
Neman Rus. Fed. 45 M9
Nemausus France see Nîmes
Nemawar India 82 D5
Nemed Rus. Fed. 42 L3
Nementcha, Monts des *mts* Alg. 58 B7
Nemetocenna France see Arras
Nemetskiy, Mys *c.* Rus. Fed. 44 Q2
Nemirov Ukr. see Nemyriv
Némiscau *r.* Canada 122 F4
Nemiscau, Lac *l.* Canada 122 F4
Nemor He *r.* China 74 B2
Nemours Alg. see Ghazaouet
Nemours France 56 F2
Nemrut Dağı *mt.* Turkey 91 F3
Nemunas *r.* Lith. see Nyoman
Nemuro Japan 74 G4
Nemuro-kaikyō *sea chan.* Japan/Rus. Fed. 74 G4
Nemyriv Ukr. 43 F6
Nenagh Rep. of Ireland 51 D5
Nenana U.S.A. 118 D3
Nene *r.* U.K. 49 H6
Nenjiang China 74 B2
Nen Jiang *r.* China 74 B3
Neosho U.S.A. 131 E4
▶Nepal *country* Asia 83 E3
Asia 6, 62–63
Nepalganj Nepal 83 E3
Nepean Canada 135 H1
Nepean, Point Australia 112 B7
Nephi U.S.A. 129 H2
Nephin *hill* Rep. of Ireland 51 C3
Nephin Beg Range *hills* Rep. of Ireland 51 C3
Nepisiguit *r.* Canada 123 I5
Nepoko *r.* Dem. Rep. Congo 98 C3
Nérac France 56 E4
Nerang Australia 112 F1
Nera Tso *l.* China 83 H3
Nerchinsk Rus. Fed. 73 L2
Nerekhta Rus. Fed. 42 I4
Néret, Lac *l.* Canada 123 H3
Neretva *r.* Bos.-Herz./Croatia 58 G3
Nêri Pünco *l.* China 83 G3
Neriquinha Angola 99 C5
Neris *r.* Lith. 45 M9
also known as Viliya (Belarus/Lithuania)
Nerl' *r.* Rus. Fed. 42 H4
Nerópolis Brazil 145 A2
Neryungri Rus. Fed. 65 N4
Nes Neth. 52 F1
Nes Norway 45 F6
Nes' Rus. Fed. 42 J2
Nesbyen Norway 45 F6
Neskaupstaður Iceland 44 [inset]
Nesle France 52 C5
Nesna Norway 44 H3
Nesri India 84 B2
Ness *r.* U.K. 50 E3
Ness, Loch *l.* U.K. 50 E3
Ness City U.S.A. 130 D4
Nesse *r.* Germany 53 K4
Nesselrode, Mount Canada/U.S.A. 120 C3
Nestor Falls Canada 121 M5
Nestos *r.* Greece 59 K4
also known as Mesta
Nesvizh Belarus see Nyasvizh
Netanya Israel 85 B3
▶Netherlands *country* Europe 52 F2
Europe 5, 38–39

▶Netherlands Antilles *terr.* West Indies 137 K6
Self-governing Netherlands Territory.
North America 9, 116–117

Netphen Germany 53 I4
Netrakona Bangl. 83 G4
Netrokona Bangl. see Netrakona
Nettilling Lake Canada 119 K3
Neubrandenburg Germany 53 N1
Neuburg an der Donau Germany 53 L6
Neuchâtel Switz. 56 H3
Neuchâtel, Lac de *l.* Switz. 56 H3
Neuendettelsau Germany 53 K5
Neuenhaus Germany 52 G2
Neuenkirchen Germany 53 J1
Neuenkirchen (Oldenburg) Germany 53 I2
Neufchâteau Belgium 52 F5
Neufchâteau France 56 G2
Neufchâtel-en-Bray France 52 B5
Neufchâtel-Hardelot France 52 B4
Neuharlingersiel Germany 53 H1

Neuhausen Rus. Fed. see Gur'yevsk
Neuhof Germany 53 J4
Neu Kaliß Germany 53 L1
Neukirchen Hessen Germany 53 J4
Neukirchen Sachsen Germany 53 M4
Neukuhren Rus. Fed. see Pionerskiy
Neumarkt in der Oberpfalz Germany 53 L5
Neumayer research station Antarctica 152 B2
Neumünster Germany 47 L3
Neunburg vorm Wald Germany 53 M5
Neunkirchen Austria 47 P7
Neunkirchen Germany 53 H5
Neuquén Arg. 144 C5
Neuruppin Germany 53 M2
Neu Sandez Poland see Nowy Sącz
Neuse r. U.S.A. 133 E5
Neusiedler See l. Austria/Hungary 47 P7
Neusiedler See Seewinkel, Nationalpark nat. park Austria 47 P7
Neuss Germany 52 G3
Neustadt (Wied) Germany 53 H4
Neustadt am Rübenberge Germany 53 J2
Neustadt an der Aisch Germany 53 K5
Neustadt an der Hardt Germany see Neustadt an der Weinstraße
Neustadt an der Waldnaab Germany 53 M5
Neustadt an der Weinstraße Germany 53 I5
Neustadt bei Coburg Germany 53 L4
Neustadt-Glewe Germany 53 L1
Neustrelitz Germany 53 N1
Neutraubling Germany 53 M6
Neuville-lès-Dieppe France 52 B5
Neuwied Germany 53 H4
Neu Wulmstorf Germany 53 J1
Nevada IA U.S.A. 130 E3
Nevada MO U.S.A. 130 E4
Nevada state U.S.A. 126 D5
Nevada, Sierra mts Spain 57 E5
Nevada, Sierra mts U.S.A. 128 C1
Nevada City U.S.A. 128 C2
Nevado, Cerro mt. Arg. 144 C5
Nevado, Sierra del mts Arg. 140 C5
Nevasa India 84 B2
Nevatim Israel 85 B4
Nevdubstroy Rus. Fed. see Kirovsk
Nevel' Rus. Fed. 42 F4
Nevel'sk Rus. Fed. 74 F3
Never Rus. Fed. 74 B1
Nevers France 56 F3
Nevertire Australia 112 C3
Nevesinje Bos.-Herz. 58 H3
Nevinnomyssk Rus. Fed. 91 F1
Nevşehir Turkey 90 D3
Nevskoye Rus. Fed. 74 D3
New r. CA U.S.A. 129 F5
New r. WV U.S.A. 134 E5
Newala Tanz. 99 D5
New Albany IN U.S.A. 134 C4
New Albany MS U.S.A. 131 F5
New Amsterdam Guyana 143 G2
New Amsterdam U.S.A. see New York
New Angledool Australia 112 C2
Newark DE U.S.A. 135 H4
Newark NJ U.S.A. 135 H3
Newark NY U.S.A. 135 G2
Newark OH U.S.A. 134 D3
Newark airport U.S.A. 132 F3
Newark Lake U.S.A. 129 F2
Newark-on-Trent U.K. 49 G5
New Bedford U.S.A. 135 J3
Newberg U.S.A. 126 C3
New Berlin U.S.A. 135 H2
New Bern U.S.A. 133 E5
Newberry IN U.S.A. 134 B4
Newberry MI U.S.A. 132 C2
Newberry SC U.S.A. 133 D5
Newberry National Volcanic Monument nat. park U.S.A. 122 C4
Newberry Springs U.S.A. 128 E4
New Bethlehem U.S.A. 134 F3
Newbiggin-by-the-Sea U.K. 48 F3
New Bight Bahamas 133 F7
New Bloomfield U.S.A. 135 G3
Newboro Canada 135 G1
New Boston OH U.S.A. 134 D4
New Boston TX U.S.A. 131 E5
New Braunfels U.S.A. 131 D6
Newbridge Rep. of Ireland 51 F4
New Britain i. P.N.G. 69 L8
New Britain U.S.A. 135 I3
New Britain Trench sea feature S. Pacific Ocean 150 G6
New Brunswick prov. Canada 123 I5
New Brunswick U.S.A. 135 H3
New Buffalo U.S.A. 134 B3
Newburgh Canada 135 G1
Newburgh U.K. 50 G3
Newburgh U.S.A. 135 H3
Newbury U.K. 49 F7
Newburyport U.S.A. 135 J2
Newby Bridge U.K. 48 E4

▶New Caledonia terr. S. Pacific Ocean 107 G4
French Overseas Territory.
Oceania 8, 104–105

New Caledonia Trough sea feature Tasman Sea 150 G7
New Carlisle Canada 123 I4
Newcastle Australia 112 E4
Newcastle Canada 135 F2
Newcastle Rep. of Ireland 51 F4
Newcastle S. Africa 101 I4
Newcastle U.K. 51 G3
New Castle CO U.S.A. 129 J2
New Castle IN U.S.A. 134 C4
New Castle KY U.S.A. 134 C4
New Castle PA U.S.A. 134 E3
Newcastle UT U.S.A. 129 G3
New Castle VA U.S.A. 134 E5
Newcastle WY U.S.A. 126 G4
Newcastle Emlyn U.K. 49 C6
Newcastle-under-Lyme U.K. 49 E5
Newcastle upon Tyne U.K. 48 F4
Newcastle Waters Australia 108 F4
Newcastle West Rep. of Ireland 51 C5
Newchwang China see Yingkou
New City U.S.A. 135 I3
Newcomb U.S.A. 129 I3
New Concord U.S.A. 134 E4
New Cumberland U.S.A. 134 E3
New Cumnock U.K. 50 E5
New Deer U.K. 50 G3

▶New Delhi India 82 D3
Capital of India.

New Don Pedro Reservoir U.S.A. 128 C3
Newell U.S.A. 130 C2
Newell, Lake salt flat Australia 109 D6
Newell, Lake Canada 121 I5
New England National Park Australia 112 F3
New England Range mts Australia 112 E3
New England Seamounts sea feature N. Atlantic Ocean 148 E3
Newenham, Cape U.S.A. 118 B4
Newent U.K. 49 E7
New Era U.S.A. 134 B2
Newfane NY U.S.A. 135 F2
Newfane VT U.S.A. 135 I2
Newfoundland i. Canada 123 K4
Newfoundland prov. Canada see Newfoundland and Labrador
Newfoundland and Labrador prov. Canada 123 K3
Newfoundland Evaporation Basin salt l. U.S.A. 129 G1
New Galloway U.K. 50 E5
New Georgia i. Solomon Is 107 F2
New Georgia Islands Solomon Is 107 F2
New Georgia Sound sea chan. Solomon Is 107 F2
New Glasgow Canada 123 J5

▶New Guinea i. Indon./P.N.G. 69 K8
Largest island in Oceania and 2nd in the world.
Oceania 102–103
World 12–13

New Halfa Sudan 86 E6
New Hampshire state U.S.A. 135 J1
New Hampton U.S.A. 130 E3
New Hanover i. P.N.G. 106 F2
New Haven CT U.S.A. 135 I3
New Haven IN U.S.A. 134 C3
New Haven WV U.S.A. 134 E4
New Hebrides country S. Pacific Ocean see Vanuatu
New Hebrides Trench sea feature S. Pacific Ocean 150 H7
New Holstein U.S.A. 134 A2
New Iberia U.S.A. 131 F6
Newington S. Africa 101 J3
Newinn Rep. of Ireland 51 E5
New Ireland i. P.N.G. 106 F2
New Jersey state U.S.A. 135 H4
New Kensington U.S.A. 134 F3
New Kent U.S.A. 135 G5
Newkirk U.S.A. 131 D4
New Lanark U.K. 50 F5
Newland Range hills Australia 109 C7
New Lexington U.S.A. 134 D4
New Liskeard Canada 122 F5
New London CT U.S.A. 135 I3
New London MO U.S.A. 130 F4
New Madrid U.S.A. 131 F4
Newman Australia 109 B5
Newman U.S.A. 128 C3
Newmarket Canada 134 F1
Newmarket Rep. of Ireland 51 C5
Newmarket U.K. 49 H6
New Market U.S.A. 135 F4
Newmarket-on-Fergus Rep. of Ireland 51 D5
New Martinsville U.S.A. 134 E4
New Meadows U.S.A. 126 D3
New Mexico state U.S.A. 127 G6
New Miami U.S.A. 134 C4
New Milford U.S.A. 135 H3
Newnan U.S.A. 133 C5
New Orleans U.S.A. 131 F6
New Paris IN U.S.A. 134 C3
New Paris OH U.S.A. 134 C4
New Philadelphia U.S.A. 134 E3
New Pitsligo U.K. 50 G3
New Plymouth N.Z. 113 E4
Newport Mayo Rep. of Ireland 51 C4
Newport Tipperary Rep. of Ireland 51 D5
Newport England U.K. 49 E6
Newport England U.K. 49 F8
Newport Wales U.K. 49 D7
Newport AR U.S.A. 131 F5
Newport IN U.S.A. 134 B4
Newport KY U.S.A. 134 C4
Newport MI U.S.A. 134 D3
Newport NH U.S.A. 135 I2
Newport NJ U.S.A. 135 H4
Newport OR U.S.A. 126 B3
Newport RI U.S.A. 135 J3
Newport VT U.S.A. 135 I1
Newport WA U.S.A. 126 D2
Newport Beach U.S.A. 128 E5
Newport News U.S.A. 135 G5
Newport Pagnell U.K. 49 G6
New Port Richey U.S.A. 133 D6
New Providence i. Bahamas 133 E7
Newquay U.K. 49 B8
New Roads U.S.A. 131 F6
New Rochelle U.S.A. 135 I3
New Rockford U.S.A. 130 D2
New Romney U.K. 49 H8
New Ross Rep. of Ireland 51 F5
Newry Australia 108 E4
Newry U.K. 51 F3
New Siberia Islands Rus. Fed. 65 P2
New Smyrna Beach U.S.A. 133 D6
New South Wales state Australia 112 C4
New Stanton U.S.A. 134 F3
Newton U.K. 48 E5
Newton GA U.S.A. 133 C6
Newton IA U.S.A. 130 E3
Newton IL U.S.A. 130 F4
Newton KS U.S.A. 130 D4
Newton MA U.S.A. 135 J2
Newton MS U.S.A. 131 F5
Newton NC U.S.A. 132 D5
Newton NJ U.S.A. 135 H3
Newton TX U.S.A. 131 E6
Newton Abbot U.K. 49 D8
Newton Mearns U.K. 50 E5
Newton Stewart U.K. 50 E6
Newtown Rep. of Ireland 51 D5
Newtown England U.K. 49 E6
Newtown Wales U.K. 49 D6
Newtown U.S.A. 134 C4
New Town U.S.A. 130 C1
Newtownabbey U.K. 51 G3
Newtownards U.K. 51 G3
Newtownbarry Rep. of Ireland see Bunclody
Newtownbutler U.K. 51 E3
Newtownmountkennedy Rep. of Ireland 51 F4
Newtown St Boswells U.K. 50 G5
Newtownstewart U.K. 51 E3
New Ulm U.S.A. 130 E2
Newville U.S.A. 135 G3
New World Island Canada 123 L4

▶New York U.S.A. 135 I3
2nd most populous city in North America and 4th in the world.

New York state U.S.A. 135 H2

▶New Zealand country Oceania 113 D5
3rd largest and 3rd most populous country in Oceania.
Oceania 8, 104–105

Neya Rus. Fed. 42 I4
Ney Bīd Iran 88 E4
Neyrīz Iran 88 D4
Neyshābūr Iran 88 E2
Nezhin Ukr. see Nizhyn
Nezperce U.S.A. 126 D3
Ngabé Congo 98 B4
Nga Chong, Khao mt. Myanmar/Thai. 70 B4
Ngagahtawng Myanmar 76 C3
Ngagau mt. Tanz. 99 D4
Ngalu Indon. 108 C2
Ngamring China 83 F3
Ngangla Ringco salt l. China 83 E3
Nganglong Kangri mt. China 82 E2
Nganglong Kangri mts China 82 E2
Ngangzê Co salt l. China 83 F3
Ngangzê Shan mts China 83 F3
Ngaoundal Cameroon 96 E4
Ngaoundéré Cameroon 97 E4
Ngape Myanmar 70 A2
Ngaputaw Myanmar 70 A3
Ngarrab China see Gyaca
Ngathainggyaung Myanmar 70 A3
Ngau i. Fiji see Gau
Ngawa China see Aba
Ngeaur i. Palau see Angaur
Ngeruangel i. Palau 69 I5
Ngga Pulu mt. Indon. see Jaya, Puncak
Ngiap r. Laos 70 C3
Ngilmina Indon. 108 D2
Ngiva Angola see Ondjiva
Ngo Congo 98 B4
Ngoako Ramalepe S. Africa see Duiwelskloof
Ngoc Linh mt. Vietnam 70 D4
Ngoin, Co salt l. China 83 G3
Ngoko r. Cameroon/Congo 97 E4
Ngola Shankou pass China 76 C1
Ngom Qu r. China see Ji Qu
Ngong Shuen Chau pen. Hong Kong China see Stonecutters' Island
Ngoqumaima China 83 F2
Ngoring China 76 C1
Ngoring Hu l. China 76 C1
Ngourti Niger 96 E3
Nguigmi Niger 96 E3
Nguiu Australia 108 E2
Ngükang China 76 B2
Ngukurr Australia 108 F3
Ngulu atoll Micronesia 69 J5
Ngunza Angola see Sumbe
Ngunza-Kabolu Angola see Sumbe
Nguru Nigeria 96 E3
Nguyên Binh Vietnam 70 D2
Ngwaketse admin. dist. Botswana see Southern
Ngwane country Africa see Swaziland
Ngwathe S. Africa 101 H4
Ngwavuma r. S. Africa/Swaziland 101 K4
Ngwelezana S. Africa 101 J5
Nhachengue Moz. 101 L2
Nhamalabué Moz. 99 D5
Nha Trang Vietnam 71 E4
Nhecolândia Brazil 143 G7
Nhill Australia 111 C8
Nhlangano Swaziland 101 J4
Nho Quan Vietnam 70 D2
Nhow i. Fiji see Gau
Nhulunbuy Australia 110 B2
Niacam Canada 121 J4
Niafounké Mali 96 C3
Niagara U.S.A. 132 C2
Niagara Falls Canada 134 F2
Niagara Falls U.S.A. 134 F2
Niagara-on-the-Lake Canada 134 F2
Niagzu Aksai Chin 82 D2
Niah Sarawak Malaysia 68 E6
Niakaramandougou Côte d'Ivoire 96 C4

▶Niamey Niger 96 D3
Capital of Niger.

Nīām Kand Iran 88 E5
Niampak Indon. 69 H6
Niangara Dem. Rep. Congo 98 C3
Niangay, Lac l. Mali 96 C3
Nianzishan China 74 A3
Nias i. Indon. 71 B7
Niassa, Lago l. Africa see Nyasa, Lake
Niaur i. Palau see Angaur
Nīāzābād Iran 89 F3
Nibil Well Australia 108 D5
Nīca Latvia 45 L8

▶Nicaragua country Central America 137 G6
4th largest country in Central and North America.
North America 9, 120–121

Nicaragua, Lago de Nicaragua see Nicaragua, Lake
Nicaragua, Lake Nicaragua 137 G6
Nicastro Italy 58 G5
Nice France 56 H5
Nice U.S.A. 128 B2
Nicephorium Syria see Ar Raqqah
Niceville U.S.A. 133 C6
Nichicun, Lac l. Canada 123 H3
Nicholas Channel Bahamas/Cuba 133 D8
Nicholasville U.S.A. 134 C5
Nichols U.S.A. 134 A1
Nicholson r. Australia 110 B3
Nicholson Lake Canada 121 K2
Nicholson Range hills Australia 109 B6
Nicholville U.S.A. 135 H1
Nicobar Islands India 71 A5
Nicolaus U.S.A. 128 C2

▶Nicosia Cyprus 85 A2
Capital of Cyprus.

Nicoya, Península de pen. Costa Rica 137 G7
Nida Lith. 45 L9
Nidagunda India 84 C2
Nidd r. U.K. 48 F4
Nidda Germany 53 J4
Nidder r. Germany 53 I4
Nidzica Poland 47 R4
Niebüll Germany 47 L3
Nied r. France 52 G5
Niederanven Lux. 52 G5
Niederaula Germany 53 J4
Niedere Tauern mts Austria 47 N7
Niedersachsen land Germany 53 I2
Niedersächsisches Wattenmeer, Nationalpark nat. park Germany 52 G1
Niefang Equat. Guinea 96 E4
Niellé Côte d'Ivoire 96 C3
Nienburg (Weser) Germany 53 J2
Niers r. Germany 52 F3
Nierstein Germany 53 I5
Nieuwe-Niedorp Neth. 52 E2
Nieuwerkerk aan de IJssel Neth. 52 E3
Nieuw Nickerie Suriname 143 G2
Nieuwolda Neth. 52 G1
Nieuwoudtville S. Africa 100 D6
Nieuwpoort Belgium 52 C3
Nieuw-Vossemeer Neth. 52 E3
Niğde Turkey 90 D3
▶Niger country Africa 96 D3
Africa 7, 94–95

▶Niger r. Africa 96 D4
3rd longest river in Africa.

Niger, Mouths of the Nigeria 96 D4
Niger Cone sea feature S. Atlantic Ocean 148 I5

▶Nigeria country Africa 96 D4
Most populous country in Africa.
Africa 7, 94–95

Nighthawk Lake Canada 122 E4
Nigrita Greece 59 J4
Nihing Pak. 89 G4
Nihon country Asia see Japan
Niigata Japan 75 E5
Niihama Japan 75 D6
Niihau i. HI U.S.A. 127 [inset]
Nii-jima i. Japan 75 E6
Niimi Japan 75 D6
Niitsu Japan 75 E5
Nijil, Wādī watercourse Jordan 85 B4
Nijkerk Neth. 52 F2
Nijmegen Neth. 52 F3
Nijverdal Neth. 52 G2
Nikel' Rus. Fed. 44 Q2
Nikki Benin 96 D4
Nikkō National Park Japan 75 E5
Nikolayev Ukr. see Mykolayiv
Nikolayevka Rus. Fed. 43 J5
Nikolayevsk Rus. Fed. 43 J6
Nikolayevskiy Rus. Fed. see Nikolayevsk
Nikolayevsk-na-Amure Rus. Fed. 74 F1
Nikol'sk Rus. Fed. 42 J4
Nikol'skiy Kazakh. see Satpayev
Nikol'skoye Kamchatskaya Oblast' Rus. Fed. 65 R4
Nikol'skoye Vologod. Oblast' Rus. Fed. see Sheksna
Nikopol' Ukr. 43 G7
Niksar Turkey 90 E2
Nīkshahr Iran 89 F5
Nikšić Serb. and Mont. 58 H3
Nīkū Jahān Iran 89 F5
Nikumaroro atoll Kiribati 107 I2
Nikunau i. Kiribati 107 H2
Nîl, Bahr el r. Africa see Nile
Nilagiri India 83 F5
Niland U.S.A. 129 F5
Nilande Atoll Maldives see Nilandhoo Atoll
Nilandhe Atoll Maldives see Nilandhoo Atoll
Nilandhoo Atoll Maldives 81 D11
Nilang India see Nelang
Nilanga India 84 C2
Nilaveli Sri Lanka 84 D4

▶Nile r. Africa 90 C5
Longest river in the world and in Africa.
Africa 92–93
World 12–13

Niles MI U.S.A. 134 B3
Niles OH U.S.A. 134 E3
Nilgiri Hills India 84 C4
Nīl Pass Afgh. 89 G3
Nilphamari Bangl. 83 G4
Nilsiä Fin. 44 P5
Nimach India see Neemuch
Niman r. Rus. Fed. 74 D2
Nimba, Monts mts Africa see Nimba Mountains
Nimbal India 84 B2
Nimba Mountains Africa 96 C4
Nimberra Well Australia 109 C5
Nimelen r. Rus. Fed. 74 E1
Nîmes France 56 G5
Nimmitabel Australia 111 E8
Nimrod Glacier Antarctica 152 H1
Nimu Jammu and Kashmir 82 D2
Nimule Sudan 97 G4
Nimwegen Neth. see Nijmegen
Nindigully Australia 112 D2
Nine Degree Channel India 84 B4
Nine Islands P.N.G. see Kilinailau Islands
Ninepin Group is Hong Kong China 77 [inset]
Ninetyeast Ridge sea feature Indian Ocean 149 N8
Ninety Mile Beach Australia 112 C7
Ninety Mile Beach N.Z. 113 D2
Nineveh U.S.A. 135 H2
Ning'an China 74 C3
Ningbo China 77 I2
Ningde China 77 H3
Ning'er China see Pu'er
Ningguo China 77 H2
Ninghai China 77 I2
Ninghsia Hui Autonomous Region aut. reg. China see Ningxia Huizu Zizhiqu
Ninghua China 77 H3
Ninging India 83 H3
Ningjiang China see Songyuan
Ningjing Shan mts China 76 C2
Ninglang China 76 D3
Ningming China 76 E4
Ningnan China 76 D3
Ningqiang China 76 E1
Ningwu China 73 K5
Ningxia aut. reg. China see Ningxia Huizu Zizhiqu
Ningxia Huizu Zizhiqu aut. reg. China 76 E1
Ningxian China 73 J5
Ningxiang China 77 G2
Ningzhou China see Huaning
Ninh Binh Vietnam 70 D2
Ninh Hoa Vietnam 71 E4
Ninigo Group atolls P.N.G. 69 K7
Ninnis Glacier Antarctica 152 G2
Ninnis Glacier Tongue Antarctica 152 H2
Ninohe Japan 75 F4
Niobrara r. U.S.A. 130 D3
Niokolo Koba, Parc National du nat. park Senegal 96 B3
Niono Mali 96 C3
Nioro Mali 96 C3
Niort France 56 D3
Nipani India 84 B2
Nipawin Canada 121 J4
Niphad India 84 B1
Nipigon Canada 119 J5
Nipigon, Lake Canada 119 J5
Nipishish Lake Canada 123 J3
Nipissing, Lake Canada 122 F5
Nippon country Asia see Japan
Nippon Hai sea N. Pacific Ocean see Japan, Sea of
Nipton U.S.A. 129 F4
Niquelândia Brazil 145 A1
Nīr Ardabīl Iran 88 B2
Nīr Yazd Iran 88 D4
Nira r. India 84 B2
Nirji China 74 B2
Nirmal India 84 C2
Nirmali India 83 F4
Nirmal Range hills India 84 C2
Niš Serb. and Mont. 59 I3
Nisa Port. 57 C4
Nisarpur India 84 B1
Niscemi Sicily Italy 58 F6
Nīshāpūr Iran see Neyshābūr
Nishino-shima vol. Japan 75 F8
Nishi-Sonogi-hantō pen. Japan 75 C6
Nisibis Turkey see Nusaybin
Nísiros i. Greece see Nisyros
Niskibi r. Canada 121 N3
Nisling r. Canada 120 B2
Nispen Neth. 52 E3
Nissan r. Sweden 45 H8
Nistru r. Moldova 59 N1 see Dniester
Nisutlin r. Canada 120 C2
Nisyros i. Greece 59 L6
Niţā Saudi Arabia 88 C5
Nitchequon Canada 123 H3
Nitendi i. Solomon Is see Ndeni
Niterói Brazil 145 C3
Nith r. U.K. 50 F5
Nitibe East Timor 108 D2
Niti Pass China/India 82 D3
Niti Shankou pass China/India see Niti Pass
Nitmiluk National Park Australia 108 F3
Nitra Slovakia 47 Q6
Nitro U.S.A. 134 E4
Niuafo'ou i. Tonga 107 I3
Niuatoputopu i. Tonga 107 I3

▶Niue terr. S. Pacific Ocean 107 J3
Self-governing New Zealand Overseas Territory.
Oceania 8, 104–105

Niujing China see Binchuan
Niulakita i. Tuvalu 107 H3
Niutao i. Tuvalu 107 H2
Niutoushan China 77 H2
Nivala Fin. 44 N5
Nive watercourse Australia 110 D5
Nivelles Belgium 52 E4
Niwai India 82 C4
Niwas India 82 E5
Nixia China see Sêrxü
Nixon U.S.A. 128 D2
Niya China see Minfeng
Niya He r. China 83 E1
Nizamabad India 84 C2
Nizam Sagar l. India 84 C2
Nizh Aydere Turkm. 88 E2
Nizhnedevitsk Rus. Fed. 43 H6
Nizhnekamsk Rus. Fed. 42 K5
Nizhnekamskoye Vodokhranilishche resr Rus. Fed. 41 Q4
Nizhnekolymsk Rus. Fed. 65 R3
Nizhnetambovskoye Rus. Fed. 74 E2
Nizhneudinsk Rus. Fed. 72 H2
Nizhnevartovsk Rus. Fed. 64 I3
Nizhnevolzhsk Rus. Fed. see Narimanov
Nizhneyansk Rus. Fed. 65 O2
Nizhniy Baskunchak Rus. Fed. 43 J6
Nizhniye Kresty Rus. Fed. see Cherskiy
Nizhniy Lomov Rus. Fed. 43 I5
Nizhniy Novgorod Rus. Fed. 42 I4
Nizhniy Odes Rus. Fed. 42 L3
Nizhniy Pyandzh Tajik. see Panji Poyon
Nizhniy Tagil Rus. Fed. 41 R4
Nizhnyaya Mola Rus. Fed. 42 J2
Nizhnyaya Omra Rus. Fed. 42 L3
Nizhnyaya Pirenga, Ozero l. Rus. Fed. 44 R3
Nizhnyaya Tunguska r. Rus. Fed. 64 J3
Nizhnyaya Tura Rus. Fed. 41 R4
Nizhyn Ukr. 43 F6
Nizina r. U.S.A. 120 A2
Nizina Mazowiecka reg. Poland 47 R4
Nizip Turkey 85 C1
Nízke Tatry nat. park Slovakia 47 Q6
Nizwá Oman see Nazwá
Nizza France see Nice
Njallavarri mt. Norway 44 L2
Njavve Sweden 44 K3
Njazidja i. Comoros 99 E5
Njombe Tanz. 99 D4
Njurundabommen Sweden 44 J5
Nkambe Cameroon 96 E4
Nkandla S. Africa 101 J5
Nkawkaw Ghana 96 C4
Nkhata Bay Malawi 99 D5
Nkhotakota Malawi 99 D5
Nkondwe Tanz. 99 D4
Nkongsamba Cameroon 96 D4
Nkululeko S. Africa 101 H6
Nkwenkwezi S. Africa 101 H7
Noakhali Bangl. 83 G5
Noatak r. U.S.A. 118 B3
Nobber Rep. of Ireland 51 F4
Nobeoka Japan 75 C6
Noblesville U.S.A. 134 B3
Noboribetsu Japan 74 F4
Noccundra Australia 111 C5
Nockatunga Australia 111 C5
Nocona U.S.A. 131 D5
Noel Kempff Mercado, Parque Nacional nat. park Bol. 142 F6
Noelville Canada 122 E5
Nogales Mex. 127 F7
Nogales U.S.A. 127 F7
Nōgata Japan 75 C6
Nogent-le-Rotrou France 56 E2
Nogent-sur-Oise France 52 C5
Noginsk Rus. Fed. 42 H5
Nogliki Rus. Fed. 74 F2
Nogoa r. Australia 110 E4
Nohar India 82 C3
Noheji Japan 74 F4
Nohfelden Germany 52 H5
Noida India 82 D3
Noirmoutier, Île de i. France 56 C3
Noirmoutier-en-l'Île France 56 C3
Noisseville France 52 G5
Nokhowch, Kūh-e mt. Iran 89 F5
Nōkis Uzbek. see Nukus
Nok Kundi Pak. 89 F4
Nokomis Canada 121 J5
Nokomis Lake Canada 121 K3
Nokou Chad 97 E3
Nokrek Peak India 83 G4
Nola Cent. Afr. Rep. 98 B3
Nolin River Lake U.S.A. 134 B5
Nolinsk Rus. Fed. 42 K4
No Mans Land i. U.S.A. 135 J3
Nome U.S.A. 118 B3
Nomgon Mongolia 72 J4
Nomhon China 80 I4
Nomoi Islands Micronesia see Mortlock Islands
Nomonde S. Africa 101 H6
Nomzha Rus. Fed. 42 I4
Nonacho Lake Canada 121 I2
Nondweni S. Africa 101 J5
Nong'an China 74 B3
Nông Hèt Laos 70 D3
Nonghui China see Guang'an
Nong Khai Thai. 70 C3
Nongoma S. Africa 101 J4
Nongstoin India 83 G4
Nonidas Namibia 100 B2
Nonni r. China see Nen Jiang
Nonning Australia 111 B7
Nonnweiler Germany 52 G5
Nonoava Mex. 127 G8
Nonouti atoll Kiribati 107 H2
Nonthaburi Thai. 71 C4
Nonzwakazi S. Africa 100 G6
Noolyeanna Lake salt flat Australia 111 B5
Noondie, Lake salt flat Australia 109 B7
Noonkanbah Australia 108 D4
Noonthorangee Range hills Australia 111 C6
Noorama Creek watercourse Australia 112 B1
Noordbeveland i. Neth. 52 D3
Noorderhaaks i. Neth. 52 E2
Noordoost Polder Neth. 52 F2
Noordwijk-Binnen Neth. 52 E2
Nootka Island Canada 120 E5
Nora r. Rus. Fed. 74 C2
Norak Tajik. 89 H2
Norak, Obanbori resr Tajik. 89 H2
Norala Phil. 69 G5
Noranda Canada 122 F4
Nor-Bayazet Armenia see Kamo
Norberg Sweden 45 I6
Nord Greenland see Station Nord
Nord, Canal du France 52 D4
Nordaustlandet i. Svalbard 64 D2
Nordegg Canada 120 G4
Norden Germany 53 H1
Nordenshel'da, Arkhipelag is Rus. Fed. 64 K2
Nordenskjold Archipelago is Rus. Fed. see Nordenshel'da, Arkhipelag

Norderney Germany **53** H1
Norderstedt Germany **53** K1
Nordfjordeid Norway **44** D6
Nordfold Norway **44** I3
Nordfriesische Inseln Germany *see* **North Frisian Islands**
Nordhausen Germany **53** K3
Nordholz Germany **53** I1
Nordhorn Germany **52** H2
Nordkapp *c.* Norway *see* **North Cape**
Nordkjosbotn Norway **44** K2
Nordkynhalvøya *i.* Norway **44** O1
Nordli Norway **44** H4
Nördlingen Germany **53** K6
Nordmaling Sweden **44** K5
Nord- og Østgrønland, Nationalparken i *nat. park* Greenland **119** O2

▶**Nordøstrundingen** *c.* Greenland **153** I1
Most easterly point of North America.

Nord-Ostsee-Kanal Germany *see* **Kiel Canal**
Norðoyar *i.* Faroe Is **40** E3
Nord - Pas-de-Calais *admin. reg.* France **52** C4
Nordpfälzer Bergland *reg.* Germany **53** H5
Nordre Strømfjord *inlet* Greenland *see* **Nassuttooq**
Nordrhein-Westfalen *land* Germany **53** H3
Nordvik Rus. Fed. **65** M2
Nore *r.* Rep. of Ireland **51** F5
Nore, Pic de *mt.* France **56** F5
Noreg *country* Europe *see* **Norway**
Norfolk *NE* U.S.A. **130** D3
Norfolk *NY* U.S.A. **135** H1
Norfolk *VA* U.S.A. **135** G5

▶**Norfolk Island** *terr.* S. Pacific Ocean **107** G4
Australian External Territory.
Oceania 8, 104–105

Norfolk Island Ridge *sea feature* Tasman Sea **150** H7
Norfork Lake U.S.A. **131** E4
Norg Neth. **52** G1
Norge *country* Europe *see* **Norway**
Norheimsund Norway **45** E6
Noril'sk Rus. Fed. **64** J3
Norkyung China *see* **Bainang**
Norland Canada **135** F1
Norma Co *l.* China **83** G2
Norman U.S.A. **131** D5
Norman, Lake *resr* U.S.A. **132** D5
Normanby Island P.N.G. **110** E1
Normandes, Îles *is* English Chan. *see* **Channel Islands**
Normandia Brazil **143** G3
Normandie *reg.* France *see* **Normandy**
Normandie, Collines de *hills* France **56** D2
Normandy *reg.* France **56** D2
Normanton Australia **110** C3
Norquay Canada **121** K5
Ñorquinco Arg. **144** B6
Norra Kvarken *strait* Fin./Sweden **44** L5
Norra Storfjället *mts* Sweden **44** I4
Norrent-Fontes France **52** C4
Norris Lake U.S.A. **134** D5
Norristown U.S.A. **135** H3
Norrköping Sweden **45** J7
Norrtälje Sweden **45** K7
Norseman Australia **109** C8
Norsjö Sweden **44** K4
Norsk Rus. Fed. **74** C1
Norsup Vanuatu **107** G3
Norte, Punta *pt* Arg. **144** E5
Norte, Serra do *hills* Brazil **143** G6
Nortelândia Brazil **143** G6
Nörten-Hardenberg Germany **53** J3
North, Cape Antarctica **152** H2
North, Cape Canada **123** J5
Northallerton U.K. **48** F4
Northam Australia **109** B7
Northampton Australia **106** B4
Northampton U.K. **49** G6
Northampton *MA* U.S.A. **135** I2
Northampton *PA* U.S.A. **135** H3
North Andaman *i.* India **71** A4
North Anna *r.* U.S.A. **135** G5
North Arm *b.* Canada **120** H2
North Atlantic Ocean Atlantic Ocean **125** O4
North Augusta U.S.A. **133** D5
North Aulatsivik Island Canada **123** J2
North Australian Basin *sea feature* Indian Ocean **149** P6
North Baltimore U.S.A. **134** D3
North Battleford Canada **121** I4
North Bay Canada **122** F5
North Belcher Islands Canada **122** F2
North Berwick U.K. **50** G4
North Berwick U.S.A. **135** J2
North Bourke Australia **112** B3
North Branch U.S.A. **130** E2
North Caicos *i.* Turks and Caicos Is **133** G8
North Canton U.S.A. **134** E3
North Cape Canada **123** I5
North Cape Norway **44** N1
North Cape N.Z. **113** D2
North Cape U.S.A. **118** A4
North Caribou Lake Canada **117** N4
North Carolina *state* U.S.A. **132** E4
North Cascades National Park U.S.A. **126** C2
North Channel *lake channel* Canada **122** E5
North Channel U.K. **51** G2
North Charleston U.S.A. **133** E5
North Chicago U.S.A. **134** B2
Northcliffe Glacier Antarctica **152** F2
North Collins U.S.A. **135** F2
North Concho *r.* U.S.A. **131** C6
North Conway U.S.A. **135** J1
North Dakota *state* U.S.A. **130** C2
North Downs *hills* U.K. **49** G7
North East U.S.A. **134** F2
Northeast Foreland *c.* Greenland *see* **Nordøstrundingen**
North-East Frontier Agency *state* India *see* **Arunachal Pradesh**
Northeast Pacific Basin *sea feature* N. Pacific Ocean **151** J4
Northeast Point Bahamas **133** F8
Northeast Providence Channel Bahamas **133** E7
North Edwards U.S.A. **128** E4
Northeim Germany **53** J3
Northern *prov.* S. Africa *see* **Limpopo**
Northern Areas *admin. div.* Pak. **89** I2
Northern Cape *prov.* S. Africa **96** D5
Northern Donets *r.* Rus. Fed./Ukr. *see* **Severskiy Donets**
Northern Dvina *r.* Rus. Fed. *see* **Severnaya Dvina**
Northern Indian Lake Canada **121** L3
Northern Ireland *prov.* U.K. **51** F3
Northern Lau Group *is* Fiji **107** I3
Northern Light Lake Canada **122** C4

▶**Northern Mariana Islands** *terr.* N. Pacific Ocean **69** K3
United States Commonwealth.
Oceania 8, 104–105

Northern Rhodesia *country* Africa *see* **Zambia**
Northern Sporades *is* Greece *see* **Voreioi Sporades**
Northern Territory *admin. div.* Australia **106** D3
Northern Transvaal *prov.* S. Africa *see* **Limpopo**
North Esk *r.* U.K. **50** G4
Northfield *MN* U.S.A. **130** E2
Northfield *VT* U.S.A. **135** I1
North Foreland *c.* U.K. **49** I7
North Fork U.S.A. **128** D3
North Fork Pass Canada **118** E3
North French *r.* Canada **122** E4
North Frisian Islands Germany **47** L3
North Geomagnetic Pole (2004) Arctic Ocean **119** K2
North Grimston U.K. **48** G4
North Haven U.S.A. **135** I3
North Head *hd* N.Z. **113** E3
North Henik Lake Canada **121** L2
North Hero U.S.A. **135** I1
North Horr Kenya **98** D3
North Island India **84** B4

▶**North Island** N.Z. **113** D4
3rd largest island in Oceania.

North Jadito Canyon *gorge* U.S.A. **129** H4
North Judson U.S.A. **134** B3
North Kingsville U.S.A. **134** E3
North Knife *r.* Canada **121** M3
North Knife Lake Canada **121** L3
▶**North Korea** *country* Asia **75** B5
Asia 6, 62–63
North Lakhimpur India **83** H4
North Las Vegas U.S.A. **129** F3
North Little Rock U.S.A. **131** E5
North Loup *r.* U.S.A. **130** D3
North Luangwa National Park Zambia **99** D5
North Maalhosmadulu Atoll Maldives **84** B5
North Magnetic Pole (2004) Canada **119** G1
North Malosmadulu Atoll Maldives *see* **North Maalhosmadulu Atoll**
North Mam Peak U.S.A. **129** J2
North Muskegon U.S.A. **134** B2
North Palisade *mt.* U.S.A. **128** D3
North Perry U.S.A. **134** E3
North Platte U.S.A. **130** C3
North Platte *r.* U.S.A. **130** C3
North Pole Arctic Ocean **153** I1
North Port U.S.A. **133** D7
North Reef Island India **71** A4
North Rhine - Westphalia *land* Germany *see* **Nordrhein-Westfalen**
North Rim U.S.A. **129** G3
North Rona *i.* U.K. *see* **Rona**
North Ronaldsay *i.* U.K. **50** G1
North Ronaldsay Firth *sea chan.* U.K. **50** G1
North Saskatchewan *r.* Canada **121** J4
North Schell Peak U.S.A. **129** F2
North Sea Europe **46** H2
North Seal *r.* Canada **121** L3
North Sentinel Island India **71** A5
North Shields U.K. **48** F3
North Shoal Lake Canada **121** L5
North Shoshone Peak U.S.A. **128** E2
North Siberian Lowland Rus. Fed. **64** L2
North Siberian Lowland Rus. Fed. **153** E2
North Simlipal National Park India **83** F5
North Sinai *governorate* Egypt *see* **Shamāl Sīnā'**
North Slope *plain* U.S.A. **118** D3
North Somercotes U.K. **48** H5
North Spirit Lake Canada **121** M4
North Stradbroke Island Australia **112** F1
North Sunderland U.K. **48** F3
North Syracuse U.S.A. **135** G2
North Taranaki Bight *b.* N.Z. **109** E4
North Terre Haute U.S.A. **134** B4
Northton U.K. **50** B3
North Tonawanda U.S.A. **135** F2
North Trap *reef* N.Z. **113** A8
North Troy U.S.A. **135** I1
North Tyne *r.* U.K. **48** E4
North Uist *i.* U.K. **50** B3
Northumberland National Park U.K. **48** E3
Northumberland Strait Canada **123** I5
North Vancouver Canada **120** F5
North Vernon U.S.A. **134** C4
Northville U.S.A. **135** H2
North Wabasca Lake Canada **120** H3
North Walsham U.K. **49** I6
Northway Junction U.S.A. **120** A2
North West *prov.* S. Africa **100** G4
Northwest Atlantic Mid-Ocean Channel N. Atlantic Ocean **148** E1
North West Cape Australia **108** A5
North West Frontier *prov.* Pak. **89** H3
North West Nelson Forest Park *nat. park* N.Z. *see* **Kahurangi National Park**
Northwest Pacific Basin *sea feature* N. Pacific Ocean **150** G3
Northwest Providence Channel Bahamas **133** E7
North West River Canada **119** K3
Northwest Territories *admin. div.* Canada **120** J2
Northwich U.K. **48** E5
North Wildwood U.S.A. **135** H4
North Windham U.S.A. **135** J2
Northwind Ridge *sea feature* Arctic Ocean **153** B1
Northwood U.S.A. **135** J2
North York Canada **134** F2
North York Moors *moorland* U.K. **48** G4
North York Moors National Park U.K. **48** G4
Norton U.K. **48** G4
Norton *KS* U.S.A. **130** D4
Norton *VA* U.S.A. **134** D5
Norton *VT* U.S.A. **135** J1
Norton de Matos Angola *see* **Balombo**
Norton Shores U.S.A. **134** B2
Norton Sound *sea chan.* U.S.A. **118** B3
Nortonville U.S.A. **134** B5
Norvegia, Cape Antarctica **152** B2
Norwalk *CT* U.S.A. **135** I3
Norwalk *OH* U.S.A. **134** D3
▶**Norway** *country* Europe **44** E6
Europe 5, 38–39
Norway U.S.A. **135** J1
Norway House Canada **121** L4
Norwegian Basin *sea feature* N. Atlantic Ocean **148** H1
Norwegian Bay Canada **119** I2
Norwegian Sea N. Atlantic Ocean **153** H2
Norwich Canada **134** E2
Norwich U.K. **49** I6
Norwich *CT* U.S.A. **135** I3
Norwich *NY* U.S.A. **135** H2
Norwood *CO* U.S.A. **129** I2
Norwood *NY* U.S.A. **135** H1
Norwood *OH* U.S.A. **134** C4
Nose Lake Canada **121** I1
Noshiro Japan **75** F4
Nosop *watercourse* Africa **100** D2 *also known as* Nossob
Nosovaya Rus. Fed. **42** L1
Noşratābād Iran **89** E4
Noss, Isle of *i.* U.K. **50** [inset]
Nossebro Sweden **45** H7
Nossen Germany **53** N3
Nossob *watercourse* Africa **100** D2 *also known as* Nosop
Notakwanon *r.* Canada **123** J2
Notch Peak U.S.A. **129** G2
Noteć *r.* Poland **47** O4
Notikewin *r.* Canada **120** G3
Noto, Golfo di *g. Sicily* Italy **58** F6
Notodden Norway **45** F7
Noto-hantō *pen.* Japan **75** E5
Notre Dame, Monts *mts* Canada **123** H5
Notre Dame Bay Canada **123** L4
Notre-Dame-de-Koartac Canada *see* **Quaqtaq**
Nottawasaga Bay Canada **134** E1
Nottaway *r.* Canada **122** F4
Nottingham U.K. **49** F6
Nottingham Island Canada **119** K3
Nottoway *r.* U.S.A. **135** G5
Nottuln Germany **53** H3
Notukeu Creek *r.* Canada **121** J5
Nouabalé-Ndoki, Parc National *nat. park* Congo **98** B3
Nouâdhibou Mauritania **96** B2
Nouâdhibou, Râs *c.* Mauritania **96** B2

▶**Nouakchott** Mauritania **96** B3
Capital of Mauritania.

Nouâmghâr Mauritania **96** B3
Nouei Vietnam **70** D4

▶**Nouméa** New Caledonia **107** G4
Capital of New Caledonia.

Nouna Burkina **96** C3
Noupoort S. Africa **100** G6
Nousu Fin. **44** P3
Nouveau-Brunswick *prov.* Canada *see* **New Brunswick**
Nouveau-Comptoir Canada *see* **Wemindji**
Nouvelle Calédonie *i.* S. Pacific Ocean **107** G4
Nouvelle Calédonie *terr.* S. Pacific Ocean *see* **New Caledonia**
Nouvelle-France, Cap de *c.* Canada **119** K3
Nouvelles Hébrides *country* S. Pacific Ocean *see* **Vanuatu**
Nova América Brazil **145** A1
Nova Chaves Angola *see* **Muconda**
Nova Freixa Moz. *see* **Cuamba**
Nova Friburgo Brazil **145** C3
Nova Gaia Angola *see* **Cambundi-Catembo**
Nova Goa India *see* **Panaji**
Nova Gradiška Croatia **58** G2
Nova Iguaçu Brazil **145** C3
Nova Kakhovka Ukr. **59** O1
Nova Lima Brazil **145** C2
Nova Lisboa Angola *see* **Huambo**
Novalukoml' Belarus **43** F5
Nova Mambone Moz. **99** D6
Nova Nabúri Moz. **99** D5
Nova Odesa Ukr. **43** F7
Nova Paraiso Brazil **142** F3
Nova Pilão Arcado Brazil **143** J5
Nova Ponte Brazil **145** B2
Nova Ponte, Represa *resr* Brazil **145** B2
Novara Italy **58** C2
Nova Roma Brazil **145** B1
Nova Scotia *prov.* Canada **123** I6
Nova Sento Sé Brazil **143** J5
Novato U.S.A. **128** B2
Nova Trento Brazil **145** A4
Nova Venécia Brazil **145** C2
Nova Xavantino Brazil **143** H6
Novaya Kakhovka Ukr. *see* **Nova Kakhovka**
Novaya Kazanka Kazakh. **41** P6
Novaya Ladoga Rus. Fed. **42** G3
Novaya Lyalya Rus. Fed. **41** S4
Novaya Odessa Ukr. *see* **Nova Odesa**
Novaya Sibir', Ostrov *i.* Rus. Fed. **65** P2
Novaya Ussura Rus. Fed. **74** E2

▶**Novaya Zemlya** *is* Rus. Fed. **64** G2
3rd largest island in Europe.

Nova Zagora Bulg. **59** L3
Novelda Spain **57** F4
Nové Zámky Slovakia **47** Q7
Novgorod Rus. Fed. *see* **Velikiy Novgorod**
Novgorod-Severskiy Ukr. *see* **Novhorod-Sivers'kyy**
Novgorod-Volynskiy Ukr. *see* **Novohrad-Volyns'kyy**
Novhorod-Sivers'kyy Ukr. **43** G6
Novi Grad Bos.-Herz. *see* **Bosanski Novi**
Novi Iskŭr Bulg. **59** J3
Novikovo Rus. Fed. **74** F3
Novi Kritsim Bulg. *see* **Stamboliyski**
Novi Ligure Italy **58** C2
Novi Pazar Bulg. **59** L3
Novi Pazar Serb. and Mont. **59** I3
Novi Sad Serb. and Mont. **59** H2
Novo Acre Brazil **145** C1
Novoalekseyevka Kazakh. *see* **Khobda**
Novoaltaysk Rus. Fed. **72** E2
Novoanninskiy Rus. Fed. **43** I6
Novo Aripuanã Brazil **142** F5
Novoazovs'k Ukr. **43** H7
Novocheboksarsk Rus. Fed. **42** J4
Novocherkassk Rus. Fed. **43** I7
Novo Cruzeiro Brazil **145** C2
Novodugino Rus. Fed. **42** G5
Novodvinsk Rus. Fed. **42** I2
Novoekonomicheskoye Ukr. *see* **Dymytrov**
Novogeorgiyevka Rus. Fed. **74** B2
Novogrudok Belarus *see* **Navahrudak**
Novo Hamburgo Brazil **145** A5
Novohradské Hory *mts* Czech Rep. **47** O6
Novohrad-Volyns'kyy Ukr. **43** E6
Novokhopersk Rus. Fed. **43** I6
Novokiyevskiy Uval Rus. Fed. **74** C2
Novokubansk Rus. Fed. **91** F1
Novokubanskiy Rus. Fed. *see* **Novokubansk**
Novokuybyshevsk Rus. Fed. **43** K5
Novokuznetsk Rus. Fed. **72** F2
Novolazarevskaya *research station* Antarctica **152** C2
Novolukoml' Belarus *see* **Novalukoml'**
Novo Mesto Slovenia **58** F2
Novomikhaylovskiy Rus. Fed. **90** E1
Novomoskovsk Rus. Fed. **43** H5
Novomoskovs'k Ukr. **43** G6
Novonikolayevsk Rus. Fed. *see* **Novosibirsk**
Novonikolayevskiy Rus. Fed. **43** I6
Novooleksiyivka Ukr. **43** G7
Novopashiyskiy Rus. Fed. *see* **Gornozavodsk**
Novopokrovka Rus. Fed. **74** D3
Novopokrovskaya Rus. Fed. **43** I7
Novopolotsk Belarus *see* **Navapolatsk**
Novopskov Ukr. **43** H6
Novo Redondo Angola *see* **Sumbe**
Novorossiyka Rus. Fed. **74** C1
Novorossiysk Rus. Fed. **90** E1
Novorybnaya Rus. Fed. **65** L2
Novorzhev Rus. Fed. **42** F4
Novoselovo Rus. Fed. **72** G1
Novoselskoye Rus. Fed. *see* **Achkhoy-Martan**
Novosel'ye Rus. Fed. **45** P7
Novosergiyevka Rus. Fed. **41** Q5
Novoshakhtinsk Rus. Fed. **43** H7
Novosheshminsk Rus. Fed. **42** K5
Novosibirsk Rus. Fed. **64** J4
Novosibirskiye Ostrova *is* Rus. Fed. *see* **New Siberia Islands**
Novosil' Rus. Fed. **43** H5
Novosokol'niki Rus. Fed. **42** F4
Novospasskoye Rus. Fed. **43** J5
Novotroyits'ke Ukr. **43** G7
Novoukrainka Ukr. *see* **Novoukrayinka**
Novoukrayinka Ukr. **43** F6
Novouzensk Rus. Fed. **43** K6
Novovolyns'k Ukr. **43** E6
Novovoronezh Rus. Fed. **43** H6
Novovoronezhskiy Rus. Fed. *see* **Novovoronezh**
Novo-Voskresenovka Rus. Fed. **74** B1
Novozybkov Rus. Fed. **43** F5
Nový Jičín Czech Rep. **47** P6
Novyy Afon Georgia *see* **Akhali Ap'oni**
Novyy Bor Rus. Fed. **42** L2
Novyy Donbass Ukr. *see* **Dymytrov**
Novyye Petushki Rus. Fed. *see* **Petushki**
Novyy Kholmogory Rus. Fed. *see* **Archangel**
Novyy Margelan Uzbek. *see* **Fergana**
Novyy Nekouz Rus. Fed. **42** H4
Novyy Oskol Rus. Fed. **43** H6
Novyy Port Rus. Fed. **64** I3
Novyy Urengoy Rus. Fed. **64** I3
Novyy Urgal Rus. Fed. **74** D2
Novyy Uzen' Kazakh. *see* **Zhanaozen**
Novyy Zay Rus. Fed. **42** L5
Now Iran **88** D4
Nowabganj Bangl. *see* **Nawabganj**
Nowata U.S.A. **131** E4
Nowdī Iran **88** C2
Nowgong India *see* **Nagaon**
Now Kharegan Iran **88** D2
Nowleye Lake Canada **121** K2
Nowogard Poland **47** O4
Noworadomsk Poland *see* **Radomsko**
Nowra Australia **112** E5
Nowrangapur India *see* **Nabarangapur**
Nowshera Pak. **89** I3
Nowyak Lake Canada **121** L2
Nowy Sącz Poland **47** R6
Nowy Targ Poland **47** R6
Noxen U.S.A. **135** G3
Noy, Xé *r.* Laos **70** D3
Noyabr'sk Rus. Fed. **64** I3
Noyes Island U.S.A. **120** C4
Noyon France **52** C5
Nozizwe S. Africa **101** G6
Nqamakwe S. Africa **101** H7
Nqutu S. Africa **101** J5
Nsanje Malawi **99** D5
Nsombo Zambia **99** C5
Nsukka Nigeria **96** D4
Nsumbu National Park Zambia *see* **Sumbu National Park**
Ntambu Zambia **99** C5
Ntha S. Africa **101** H4
Ntoum Gabon **98** A3
Ntungamo Uganda **98** D4
Nuanetsi Zimbabwe *see* **Mwenezi**
Nu'aym *reg.* Oman **88** D6
Nuba Mountains Sudan **86** D7
Nubian Desert Sudan **86** D5
Nudo Coropuna *mt.* Peru **142** D7
Nueces *r.* U.S.A. **131** D7
Nueltin Lake Canada **121** L2
Nueva Ciudad Guerrero Mex. **131** D7
Nueva Gerona Cuba **137** H4
Nueva Harberton Arg. **144** C8
Nueva Imperial Chile **144** B5
Nueva Loja Ecuador **142** C3
Nueva Rosita Mex. **131** C7
Nueva San Salvador El Salvador **136** G6
Nueva Villa de Padilla Mex. **131** D7
Nueve de Julio Arg. *see* **9 de Julio**
Nuevitas Cuba **137** I4
Nuevo, Golfo *g.* Arg. **144** D6
Nuevo Casas Grandes Mex. **127** G7
Nuevo Ideal Mex. **131** B7
Nuevo Laredo Mex. **131** D7
Nuevo León Mex. **129** F5
Nuevo León *state* Mex. **131** D7
Nuevo Rocafuerte Ecuador **142** C4
Nugaal *watercourse* Somalia **98** E3
Nugget Point N.Z. **113** B8
Nugur India **84** D2
Nuguria Islands P.N.G. **106** F2
Nuh, Ras *pt* Pak. **89** F5
Nuhaka N.Z. **113** F4
Nui *atoll* Tuvalu **107** H2
Nui Con Voi *r.* Vietnam *see* **Red River**
Nuiqsut U.S.A. **118** C2
Nui Ti On *mt.* Vietnam **70** D4
Nujiang China **76** C2
Nu Jiang *r.* China/Myanmar *see* **Salween**
Nu Jiang *r.* China/Myanmar *see* **Salween**
Nukey Bluff *hill* Australia **111** A7
Nukha Azer. *see* **Şäki**

▶**Nuku'alofa** Tonga **107** I4
Capital of Tonga.

Nukufetau *atoll* Tuvalu **107** H2
Nukuhiva *i.* Fr. Polynesia *see* **Nuku Hiva**
Nuku Hiva *i.* Fr. Polynesia **151** K6
Nukuhu P.N.G. **69** L8
Nukulaelae *atoll* Tuvalu **107** H2
Nukulailai *atoll* Tuvalu *see* **Nukulaelae**
Nukumanu Islands P.N.G. **107** F2
Nukunau *i.* Kiribati *see* **Nikunau**
Nukunono *atoll* Tokelau **107** I2
Nukunonu *atoll* Tokelau *see* **Nukunono**
Nukus Uzbek. **80** A3
Nulato U.S.A. **118** C3
Nullagine Australia **108** C5
Nullarbor Australia **109** E7
Nullarbor National Park Australia **109** E7
Nullarbor Plain Australia **109** E7
Nullarbor Regional Reserve *park* Australia **109** E7
Nuluarniavik, Lac *l.* Canada **122** F2
Nulu'erhu Shan *mts* China **73** L4
Num *i.* Indon. **69** J7
Numalla, Lake *salt flat* Australia **112** B2
Numan Nigeria **98** B3
Numanuma P.N.G. **110** E1
Numazu Japan **75** E6
Numbulwar Australia **110** A2
Numedal *valley* Norway **45** F6
Numfoor *i.* Indon. **69** I7
Numin He *r.* China **74** B3
Numurkah Australia **112** B6
Nunaksaluk Island Canada **123** J3
Nunakuluut *i.* Greenland **119** N3
Nunap Isua *c.* Greenland *see* **Farewell, Cape**
Nunarsuit *i.* Greenland *see* **Nunakuluut**
Nunavik *reg.* Canada **122** G1
Nunavut *admin. div.* Canada **121** L2
Nunda U.S.A. **135** G2
Nundle Australia **112** E3
Nuneaton U.K. **49** F6
Nungba India **83** H4
Nungesser Lake Canada **121** M5
Nungnain Sum China **73** L3
Nunivak Island U.S.A. **118** B4
Nunkapasi India **84** E1
Nunkun *mt.* Jammu and Kashmir **82** D2
Nunligran Rus. Fed. **65** T3
Nuñomoral Spain **57** C3
Nunspeet Neth. **52** F2
Nuojiang China *see* **Tongjiang**
Nuoro *Sardinia* Italy **58** C4
Nupani *i.* Solomon Is **107** G3
Nuqrah Saudi Arabia **86** F4
Nur *r.* Iran **88** D2
Nūrābād Iran **88** C4
Nurakita *i.* Tuvalu *see* **Niulakita**
Nurata Uzbek. **80** C3
Nur Dağları *mts* Turkey **85** B1
Nurek Tajik. *see* **Norak**
Nurek Reservoir Tajik. *see* **Norak, Obanbori**
Nurekskoye Vodokhranilishche *resr* Tajik. *see* **Norak, Obanbori**
Nuremberg Germany **53** L5
Nuri Mex. **127** F7
Nuristan *reg.* Afgh. **89** H3
Nurla Jammu and Kashmir **82** D2
Nurlat Rus. Fed. **43** K5
Nurmes Fin. **44** P5
Nurmo Fin. **44** M5
Nürnberg Germany *see* **Nuremberg**
Nurota Uzbek. *see* **Nurata**
Nurri, Mount *hill* Australia **112** C3
Nusawulan Indon. **69** I7
Nusaybin Turkey **91** F3
Nu Shan *mts* China **76** C3
Nushki Pak. **89** G4
Nusratiye Turkey **85** D1
Nutak Canada **123** J2
Nutarawit Lake Canada **121** L2
Nutrioso U.S.A. **129** I5
Nuttal Pak. **89** H4
Nutwood Downs Australia **108** F3
Nutzotin Mountains U.S.A. **120** A2

▶**Nuuk** Greenland **119** M3
Capital of Greenland.

Nuupas Fin. **44** O3
Nuussuaq Greenland **119** M2
Nuussuaq *pen.* Greenland **119** M2
Nuwaybi' al Muzayyinah Egypt **90** D5
Nuweiba el Muzeina Egypt *see* **Nuwaybi' al Muzayyinah**
Nuwerus S. Africa **100** D6
Nuweveldberge *mts* S. Africa **100** E7
Nuyts, Point Australia **109** B8
Nuyts Archipelago *is* Australia **109** F8
Nuzvid India **84** D2
Nwanedi Nature Reserve S. Africa **101** J2
Nxai Pan National Park Botswana **99** C5
Nyagan' Rus. Fed. **41** T3
Nyagquka China *see* **Yajiang**
Nyagrong China *see* **Xinlong**
Nyahururu Kenya **98** D3
Nyah West Australia **112** A5
Nyainqêntanglha Feng *mt.* China **83** G3
Nyainqêntanglha Shan *mts* China **83** G3
Nyainrong China **76** B1
Nyainronglung China *see* **Nyainrong**
Nyåker Sweden **44** K5
Nyakh Rus. Fed. *see* **Nyagan'**
Nyaksimvol' Rus. Fed. **41** S3
Nyala Sudan **97** F3
Nyalam China **83** F3
Nyalikungu Tanz. *see* **Maswa**
Nyamandhlovu Zimbabwe **99** C5
Nyamtumbo Tanz. **99** D5
Nyande Zimbabwe *see* **Masvingo**
Nyandoma Rus. Fed. **42** I3
Nyandomskiy Vozvyshennost' *hills* Rus. Fed. **42** H3
Nyanga Congo **98** B4
Nyanga Zimbabwe **99** D5
Nyangbo China **76** B2
Nyarling *r.* Canada **120** H2

▶**Nyasa, Lake** Africa **99** D4
3rd largest lake in Africa.

Nyasaland *country* Africa *see* **Malawi**
Nyashabozh Rus. Fed. **42** L2
Nyasvizh Belarus **45** O10
Nyaungdon Myanmar *see* **Yandoon**
Nyaunglebin Myanmar **70** B3
Nyborg Denmark **45** G9
Nyborg Norway **44** P1
Nybro Sweden **45** I8
Nyeboe Land *reg.* Greenland **119** M1
Nyêmo China **83** G3
Nyenchen Tanglha Range *mts* China *see* **Nyainqêntanglha Shan**
Nyeri Kenya **98** D4
Nyi, Co *l.* China **83** F2
Nyika National Park Zambia **99** D5
Nyima China **83** F3
Nyimba Zambia **99** D5
Nyingchi China **76** B2
Nyinma China *see* **Maqu**
Nyíregyháza Hungary **43** D7
Nyiru, Mount Kenya **98** D3
Nykarleby Fin. **44** M5
Nykøbing Denmark **45** G9
Nykøbing Sjælland Denmark **45** G9
Nyköping Sweden **45** J7
Nyland Sweden **44** J5
Nylstroom S. Africa **101** I3
Nylsvley *nature res.* S. Africa **101** I3
Nymagee Australia **112** C4
Nymboida National Park Australia **112** F2
Nynäshamn Sweden **45** J7
Nyngan Australia **112** C3
Nyogzê China **83** E3
Nyoman *r.* Belarus/Lith. **45** M10 *also known as* Neman *or* Nemunas
Nyon Switz. **56** H3
Nyons France **56** G4
Nýřany Czech Rep. **53** N5
Nyrob Rus. Fed. **41** R3
Nysa Poland **47** P5
Nysh Rus. Fed. **74** F2
Nyssa U.S.A. **126** D4
Nystad Fin. *see* **Uusikaupunki**
Nytva Rus. Fed. **41** R4
Nyuksenitsa Rus. Fed. **42** J3
Nyunzu Dem. Rep. Congo **99** C4
Nyurba Rus. Fed. **65** M3
Nyyskiy Zaliv *lag.* Rus. Fed. **74** F1
Nzambi Congo **98** B4
Nzega Tanz. **99** D4
Nzérékoré Guinea **96** C4
N'zeto Angola **99** B4
Nzwani *i.* Comoros **99** E5

O

Oahe, Lake U.S.A. **130** C2
Oahu *i. HI* U.S.A. **127** [inset]
Oaitupu *i.* Tuvalu *see* **Vaitupu**
Oak Bluffs U.S.A. **135** J3
Oak City U.S.A. **129** G2
Oak Creek U.S.A. **129** J1
Oakdale U.S.A. **131** E6
Oakes U.S.A. **130** D2
Oakey Australia **112** E1
Oak Grove *KY* U.S.A. **134** B5
Oak Grove *LA* U.S.A. **131** F5
Oak Grove *MI* U.S.A. **134** C1
Oakham U.K. **49** G6
Oak Harbor U.S.A. **134** D3
Oak Hill *OH* U.S.A. **134** D4
Oak Hill *WV* U.S.A. **134** E5
Oakhurst U.S.A. **128** D3
Oak Lake Canada **121** K5

Oakland CA U.S.A. 128 B3
Oakland MD U.S.A. 134 F4
Oakland ME U.S.A. 135 K1
Oakland NE U.S.A. 130 D3
Oakland OR U.S.A. 126 C4
Oakland airport U.S.A. 128 B3
Oakland City U.S.A. 134 B4
Oaklands Australia 112 C5
Oak Lawn U.S.A. 134 B3
Oakley U.S.A. 130 C4
Oakover r. Australia 108 C5
Oak Park IL U.S.A. 134 B3
Oak Park MI U.S.A. 134 C2
Oak Park Reservoir U.S.A. 129 I1
Oakridge U.S.A. 126 C4
Oak Ridge U.S.A. 132 C4
Oakvale Australia 111 C7
Oak View U.S.A. 128 D4
Oakville Canada 134 F2
Oakwood OH U.S.A. 134 C3
Oakwood TN U.S.A. 134 B5
Oamaru N.Z. 113 C7
Oaro N.Z. 113 D6
Oasis CA U.S.A. 128 E3
Oasis NV U.S.A. 126 E4
Oates Coast reg. Antarctica see Oates Land
Oates Land reg. Antarctica 152 H2
Oaxaca Mex. 136 E5
Oaxaca de Juárez Mex. see Oaxaca
Ob' r. Rus. Fed. 72 E2
Ob, Gulf of sea chan. Rus. Fed. see Obskaya Guba
Oba Canada 122 D4
Oba i. Vanuatu see Aoba
Obala Cameroon 96 E4
Obama Japan 75 D6
Oban U.K. 50 D4
O Barco Spain 57 C2
Obbia Somalia see Hobyo
Obdorsk Rus. Fed. see Salekhard
Óbecse Serb. and Mont. see Bečej
Obed Canada 120 G4
Oberaula Germany 53 J4
Oberdorla Germany 53 K3
Oberhausen Germany 52 G3
Oberlin KS U.S.A. 130 C4
Oberlin LA U.S.A. 131 E6
Oberlin OH U.S.A. 134 D3
Obermoschel Germany 53 H5
Oberon Australia 112 D4
Oberpfälzer Wald mts Germany 53 M5
Obersinn Germany 53 J4
Oberthulba Germany 53 J4
Obertshausen Germany 53 I4
Oberwälder Land reg. Germany 53 J3
Obi i. Indon. 69 H7
Óbidos Brazil 143 G4
Obihiro Japan 74 F4
Obil'noye Rus. Fed. 43 J7

▶Ob'-Irtysh r. Rus. Fed. 64 H3
2nd longest river and largest drainage basin in Asia and 5th longest river in the world.
Asia 60–61
World 12–13

Obluch'ye Rus. Fed. 74 C2
Obninsk Rus. Fed. 43 H5
Obo Cent. Afr. Rep. 98 C3
Obock Djibouti 86 F7
Ŏbŏk N. Korea 74 C4
Obokote Dem. Rep. Congo 98 C4
Obo Liang China 80 H4
Obouya Congo 98 B4
Oboyan' Rus. Fed. 43 H6
Obozerskiy Rus. Fed. 42 I3
Obregón, Presa resr Mex. 127 F8
Obrenovac Serb. and Mont. 59 I2
Obruk Turkey 90 D3
Observatory Hill hill Australia 109 F7
Obshchiy Syrt hills Rus. Fed. 41 Q5
Obskaya Guba sea chan. Rus. Fed. 64 I3
Obuasi Ghana 96 C4
Ob"yachevo Rus. Fed. 42 K3
Ocala U.S.A. 133 D6
Ocampo Mex. 131 C7
Ocaña Col. 142 D2
Ocaña Spain 57 E4
Occidental, Cordillera mts Chile 142 E7
Occidental, Cordillera mts Col. 142 C3
Occidental, Cordillera mts Peru 142 D7
Oceana U.S.A. 134 E5
Ocean Cay i. Bahamas 133 E7
Ocean City MD U.S.A. 135 H4
Ocean City NJ U.S.A. 135 H4
Ocean Falls Canada 120 E4
Ocean Island Kiribati see Banaba
Ocean Island atoll U.S.A. see Kure Atoll
Oceanside U.S.A. 128 E5
Ocean Springs U.S.A. 131 F6
Ochakiv Ukr. 59 N1
Och'amch'ire Georgia 91 F2
Ocher Rus. Fed. 41 Q4
Ochiishi-misaki pt Japan 74 G4
Ochil Hills U.K. 50 F4
Ochrida, Lake Albania/Macedonia see Ohrid, Lake
Ochsenfurt Germany 53 K5
Ochtrup Germany 53 H2
Ocilla U.S.A. 133 D6
Ockelbo Sweden 45 J6
Ocolaşul Mare, Vârful mt. Romania 59 K1
Oconomowoc U.S.A. 134 A2
Oconto U.S.A. 134 B1
Octeville-sur-Mer France 49 H9
October Revolution Island Rus. Fed. see Oktyabr'skoy Revolyutsii, Ostrov
Ocussi enclave East Timor 108 D2
Ocussi-Ambeno enclave East Timor see Ocussi
Oda, Jebel mt. Sudan 86 E5
Ódáðahraun lava field Iceland 44 [inset]
Ŏdaejin N. Korea 74 C4
Odae-san National Park S. Korea 75 C5
Ōdate Japan 75 F4
Odawara Japan 75 E6
Odda Norway 45 E6
Odei r. Canada 121 L3
Odell U.S.A. 134 B3
Odem U.S.A. 131 D7
Odemira Port. 57 B5
Ödemiş Turkey 59 L5
Ödenburg Hungary see Sopron
Odense Denmark 45 G9
Odenwald reg. Germany 53 I5
Oder r. Germany 53 J3
also known as Odra (Poland)
Oderbucht b. Germany 47 O3
Oder-Havel-Kanal canal Germany 53 N2
Odesa Ukr. 59 N1
Ödeshog Sweden 45 I7
Odessa Ukr. see Odesa
Odessa TX U.S.A. 131 C6
Odessa WA U.S.A. 126 D3
Odessus Bulg. see Varna
Odiel r. Spain 57 C5
Odienné Côte d'Ivoire 96 C4
Odintsovo Rus. Fed. 42 H5
Ôdôngk Cambodia 71 D5
Odra r. Germany/Pol. 47 Q6
also known as Oder (Germany)
Odzala, Parc National d' nat. park Congo 98 B3
Oea Libya see Tripoli
Oé-Cusse enclave East Timor see Ocussi
Oecussi enclave East Timor see Ocussi
Oeiras Brazil 143 J5
Oekussi enclave East Timor see Ocussi
Oelsnitz Germany 53 M4
Oenkerk Neth. 52 F1
Oenpelli Australia 108 F3
Oesel i. Estonia see Hiiumaa
Oeufs, Lac des l. Canada 123 G3
Of Turkey 91 F2
O'Fallon r. U.S.A. 126 G3
Ofanto r. Italy 58 G4
Ofaqim Israel 85 B4
Offa Nigeria 96 D4
Offenbach am Main Germany 53 I4
Offenburg Germany 47 K6
Oga Japan 75 E5
Ogadēn reg. Eth. 98 E3
Oga-hantō pen. Japan 75 E5
Ōgaki Japan 75 E6
Ogallala U.S.A. 130 C3
Ogasawara-shotō is Japan see Bonin Islands
Ogbomosho Nigeria 96 D4
Ogbomoso Nigeria see Ogbomosho
Ogden IA U.S.A. 130 E3
Ogden UT U.S.A. 126 F4
Ogden, Mount Canada 120 C3
Ogdensburg U.S.A. 135 H1
Ogidaki Canada 122 D5
Ogilvie r. Canada 118 E3
Ogilvie Mountains Canada 118 D3
Oglethorpe, Mount U.S.A. 133 C5
Oglio r. Italy 58 D2
Oglongi Rus. Fed. 74 E1
Ogmore Australia 110 E4
Ogoamas, Gunung mt. Indon. 69 G6
Ogodzha Rus. Fed. 74 D1
Ogoja Nigeria 96 D4
Ogoki r. Canada 122 D4
Ogoki Lake Canada 130 G1
Ogoki Reservoir Canada 122 C4
Ogoron Rus. Fed. 74 C1
Ogosta r. Bulg. 59 J3
Ogre Latvia 45 N8
Ogulin Croatia 58 F2
Ogurchinskiy, Ostrov i. Turkm. 88 D2
Ogurjaly Adasy i. Turkm. see Ogurchinskiy, Ostrov
Oğuzeli Turkey 85 C1
Ohai N.Z. 113 A7
Ohakune N.Z. 113 E4
Ohanet Alg. 96 D2
Ōhata Japan 74 F4
Ohcejohka Fin. see Utsjoki
O'Higgins, Lago l. Chile 144 B7
Ohio r. U.S.A. 134 A5
Ohio state U.S.A. 134 D3
Ohm r. Germany 53 I4
Ohrdruf Germany 53 K4
Ohře r. Czech Rep. 53 N4
Ohre r. Germany 53 L2
Ohrid Macedonia 59 I4
Ohrid, Lake Albania/Macedonia 59 I4
Ohridsko Ezero l. Albania/Macedonia see Ohrid, Lake
Ohrigstad S. Africa 101 J3
Öhringen Germany 53 J5
Ohrit, Liqeni i l. Albania/Macedonia see Ohrid, Lake
Ohura N.Z. 113 E4
Oiapoque r. Brazil/Fr. Guiana 143 H3
Oich r. U.K. 50 E3
Oiga China 76 B2
Oignies France 52 C4
Oil City U.S.A. 134 F3
Oise r. France 52 C6
Ōita Japan 75 C6
Oiti mt. Greece 59 J5
Ojai U.S.A. 128 D4
Ojalava i. Samoa see Upolu
Ojinaga Mex. 131 B6
Ojiya Japan 75 E5
Ojo Caliente U.S.A. 127 G5
Ojo de Laguna Mex. 127 G7

▶Ojos del Salado, Nevado mt. Arg./Chile 144 C3
2nd highest mountain in South America.

Oka r. Rus. Fed. 43 I4
Oka r. Rus. Fed. 72 I1
Okahandja Namibia 100 C1
Okahukura N.Z. 113 E4
Okakarara Namibia 99 B6
Okak Islands Canada 123 J2
Okanagan Lake Canada 120 G5
Okanda Sri Lanka 84 D5
Okano r. Gabon 98 B4
Okanogan U.S.A. 126 D2
Okanogan r. U.S.A. 126 D2
Okara Pak. 89 I4
Okarem Turkm. 88 D2
Okataina vol. N.Z. see Tarawera, Mount
Okaukuejo Namibia 99 B5
Okavango r. Africa 99 C5

▶Okavango Delta swamp Botswana 99 C5
Largest oasis in the world.

Okavango Swamps Botswana see Okavango Delta
Okaya Japan 75 E5
Okayama Japan 75 D6
Okazaki Japan 75 E6
Okeechobee U.S.A. 133 D7
Okeechobee, Lake U.S.A. 133 D7
Okeene U.S.A. 131 D4
Okefenokee Swamp U.S.A. 133 D6
Okehampton U.K. 49 C8
Okemah U.S.A. 131 D5
Oker r. Germany 53 K2
Okha India 82 B5
Okha Rus. Fed. 74 F1
Okha Rann marsh India 82 B5
Okhotsk Rus. Fed. 65 P4
Okhotsk, Sea of Japan/Rus. Fed. 74 G3
Okhotskoye More sea Japan/Rus. Fed. see Okhotsk, Sea of
Okhtyrka Ukr. 43 G6
Okinawa i. Japan 75 B8
Okinawa-guntō is Japan see Okinawa-shotō
Okinawa-shotō is Japan 75 B8
Okino-Daitō-jima i. Japan 73 O8
Okino-Tori-shima i. Japan 73 P8
Oki-shotō is Japan 73 O5
Oki-shotō is Japan 75 D5
Okkan Myanmar 70 A3
Oklahoma state U.S.A. 131 D5

▶Oklahoma City U.S.A. 131 D5
State capital of Oklahoma.

Okmulgee U.S.A. 131 D5
Okolona KY U.S.A. 134 C4
Okolona MS U.S.A. 131 F5
Okondja Gabon 98 B4
Okovskiy Les for. Rus. Fed. 42 G5
Okoyo Congo 98 B4
Øksfjord Norway 44 M1
Oktemberyan Armenia see Hoktemberyan
Oktwin Myanmar 70 B3
Oktyabr' Kazakh. see Kandyagash
Oktyabr'sk Kazakh. see Kandyagash
Oktyabr'skiy Belarus see Aktsyabrski
Oktyabr'skiy Amurskaya Oblast' Rus. Fed. 74 C1
Oktyabr'skiy Arkhangel'skaya Oblast' Rus. Fed. 42 I3
Oktyabr'skiy Kamchatskaya Oblast' Rus. Fed. 65 Q4
Oktyabr'skiy Respublika Bashkortostan Rus. Fed. 41 Q5
Oktyabr'skiy Volgogradskaya Oblast' Rus. Fed. 43 I7
Oktyabr'skoye Rus. Fed. 41 T3
Oktyabr'skoy Revolyutsii, Ostrov i. Rus. Fed. 65 K2
Okulovka Rus. Fed. 42 G4
Okushiri-tō i. Japan 74 E4
Okusi enclave East Timor see Ocussi
Okuta Nigeria 96 D4
Okwa watercourse Botswana 100 G1
Ólafsvík Iceland 44 [inset]
Olakkur India 84 C3
Olancha U.S.A. 128 D3
Olancha Peak U.S.A. 128 D3
Öland i. Sweden 45 J8
Olary Australia 111 C7
Olathe CO U.S.A. 129 J2
Olathe KS U.S.A. 130 E4
Olavarría Arg. 144 D5
Oława Poland 47 P5
Olbernhau Germany 53 N4
Olbia Sardinia Italy 58 C4
Old Bahama Channel Bahamas/Cuba 133 E8
Old Bastar India 84 D2
Oldcastle Rep. of Ireland 51 E4
Old Cork Australia 110 C4
Old Crow Canada 118 E3
Oldeboorn Neth. 52 F1
Oldenburg Germany 53 I1
Oldenburg in Holstein Germany 47 M3
Oldenzaal Neth. 52 G2
Olderdalen Norway 44 L2
Old Forge U.S.A. 135 H2
Old Gidgee Australia 109 B6
Oldham U.K. 48 E5
Old Harbor U.S.A. 118 C4
Old Head of Kinsale hd Rep. of Ireland 51 D6
Oldman r. Canada 120 I5
Oldmeldrum U.K. 50 G3
Old Perlican Canada 123 L5
Old River U.S.A. 128 D4
Olds Canada 120 H5
Old Speck Mountain U.S.A. 135 J1
Old Station U.S.A. 128 C1
Old Wives Lake Canada 121 J5
Olean U.S.A. 135 F2
Olecko Poland 47 S3
Olekma r. Rus. Fed. 65 N3
Olekminsk Rus. Fed. 65 N3
Olekminskiy-Stanovik mts Rus. Fed. 73 M2
Oleksandrivs'k Ukr. see Zaporizhzhya
Oleksandriya Ukr. 43 G6
Ølen Norway 45 D7
Olenegorsk Rus. Fed. 44 R2
Olenek Rus. Fed. 65 M3
Olenek r. Rus. Fed. 65 M2
Olenek Bay Rus. Fed. see Olenekskiy Zaliv
Olenekskiy Zaliv b. Rus. Fed. 65 N2
Olenino Rus. Fed. 42 G4
Olenitsa Rus. Fed. 42 G2
Olenivs'ki Kar"yery Ukr. see Dokuchayevs'k
Olenya Rus. Fed. see Olenegorsk
Oleshky Ukr. see Tsyurupyns'k
Olevs'k Ukr. 43 E6
Ol'ga Rus. Fed. 74 D4
Olga, Lac l. Canada 122 F4
Olga, Mount Australia 109 E6
Ol'ginsk Rus. Fed. 74 D1
Olginskoye Rus. Fed. see Kochubeyevskoye
Ölgiy Mongolia 80 G2
Olhão Port. 57 C5
Olia Chain mts Australia 109 E6
Olifants r. Moz./S. Africa 101 J3
also known as Elefantes
Olifants watercourse Namibia 100 D3
Olifants S. Africa 101 J2
Olifants r. W. Cape S. Africa 100 D6
Olifants r. W. Cape S. Africa 100 E7
Olifantshoek S. Africa 100 F4
Olifantsrivierberge mts S. Africa 100 D7
Olimarao atoll Micronesia 69 L5
Olimbos hill Cyprus see Olympos
Olimbos mt. Greece see Olympus, Mount
Olimpos Beydağları Milli Parkı nat. park Turkey 59 N6
Olinda Brazil 143 L5
Olinga Moz. 99 D5
Olio Australia 110 C4
Oliphants Drift S. Africa 101 H3
Olisipo Port. see Lisbon
Oliva Spain 57 F4
Oliva, Cordillera de mts Arg./Chile 144 C3
Olivares, Cerro de mt. Arg./Chile 144 C4
Olive Hill U.S.A. 134 D4
Olivehurst U.S.A. 128 C2
Oliveira dos Brejinhos Brazil 145 C1
Olivença Moz. see Lupilichi
Olivenza Spain 57 C4
Oliver Lake Canada 121 K3
Olivet MI U.S.A. 134 C2
Olivet SD U.S.A. 130 D3
Olivia U.S.A. 130 E2
Ol'khovka Rus. Fed. 43 J6
Ollagüe Chile 144 C2
Ollombo Congo 98 B4
Olmaliq Uzbek. see Almalyk
Olmos Peru 142 C5
Olmütz Czech Rep. see Olomouc
Olney U.K. 49 G6
Olney IL U.S.A. 130 F4
Olney MD U.S.A. 135 G4
Olney TX U.S.A. 131 D5
Olofström Sweden 45 I8
Olomane r. Canada 123 J4
Olomouc Czech Rep. 47 P6
Olonets Rus. Fed. 42 G3
Olongapo Phil. 69 G4
Oloron-Ste-Marie France 56 D5
Olosenga atoll American Samoa see Swains Island
Olot Spain 57 H2
Olot Uzbek. see Alat
Olovyannaya Rus. Fed. 73 L2
Oloy, Qatorkŭhi mts Asia see Alai Range
Olpe Germany 53 H3
Olsztyn Poland 47 R4
Olt r. Romania 59 K3
Olten Switz. 56 H3
Olteniţa Romania 59 L2
Oltu Turkey 91 F2
Oluan Pi c. Taiwan 77 I4
Ol'viopol' Ukr. see Pervomays'k
Olymbos hill Cyprus see Olympos

▶Olympia U.S.A. 126 C3
State capital of Washington.

Olympic National Park U.S.A. 126 C3
Olympos hill Cyprus 85 A2
Olympos Greece see Olympus, Mount
Olympos nat. park Greece 59 J4
Olympus, Mount Greece 59 J4
Olympus, Mount U.S.A. 126 C3
Olyutorskiy Rus. Fed. 65 R3
Olyutorskiy, Mys c. Rus. Fed. 65 S4
Olyutorskiy Zaliv b. Rus. Fed. 65 R4
Olzheras Rus. Fed. see Mezhdurechensk
Oma China 83 E2
Oma r. Rus. Fed. 42 J2
Omagh U.K. 51 E3
Omaha U.S.A. 130 E3
Omaheke admin. reg. Namibia 100 D2
Omal'skiy Khrebet mts Rus. Fed. 74 E1
▶Oman country Asia 87 I6
Asia 6, 62–63
Oman, Gulf of Asia 88 E5
Omarkot Pak. 89 H4
Omaruru Namibia 99 B6
Omate Peru 142 D7
Omaweneno Botswana 100 F3
Omba i. Vanuatu see Aoba
Ombai, Selat sea chan. East Timor/Indon. 108 D2
Ombalantu Namibia see Uutapi
Omboué Gabon 98 A4
Ombu China 83 F3
Omdraaisvlei S. Africa 100 F6
Omdurman Sudan 86 D6
Omeo Australia 112 C6
Omer U.S.A. 134 D1
Ometepec Mex. 136 E5
Omgoy Wildlife Reserve nature res. Thai. 70 B3
Om Hajēr Eritrea 86 E7
Omīdīyeh Iran 88 C4
Omineca Mountains Canada 116 E3
Omitara Namibia 100 C2
Ōmiya Japan 75 E6
Ommaney, Cape U.S.A. 120 C3
Ommen Neth. 52 G2
Omolon Rus. Fed. 65 R3
Omo National Park Eth. 98 D3
Omsk Rus. Fed. 64 I4
Omsukchan Rus. Fed. 65 Q3
Ōmū Japan 74 F3
O-mu Myanmar 70 B2
Omu, Vârful mt. Romania 59 K2
Ōmura Japan 75 C6
Omutninsk Rus. Fed. 42 L4
Onaman Lake Canada 122 D4
Onamia U.S.A. 130 E2
Onancock U.S.A. 135 H5
Onangué, Lac l. Gabon 98 B4
Onaping Lake Canada 122 E5
Onatchiway, Lac l. Canada 123 H4
Onavas Mex. 127 F7
Onawa U.S.A. 130 D3
Onaway U.S.A. 134 C1
Onbingwin Myanmar 71 B4
Oncativo Arg. 144 D4
Onchan Isle of Man 48 C4
Oncócua Angola 99 B5
Öncül Turkey 85 D1
Ondal India see Andal
Ondangwa Namibia 99 B5
Onderstedorings S. Africa 100 E6
Ondjiva Angola 99 B5
Ondo Nigeria 96 D4
Öndörhaan Mongolia 73 K3
Ondozero Rus. Fed. 42 G3
One Botswana 100 E2
One and a Half Degree Channel Maldives 81 D11
Onega Rus. Fed. 42 H3
Onega r. Rus. Fed. 42 H3
Onega, Lake Rus. Fed. 41 N3

▶Onega, Lake Rus. Fed. 42 G3
3rd largest lake in Europe.

Onega Bay g. Rus. Fed. see Onezhskaya Guba
One Hundred and Fifty Mile House Canada see 150 Mile House
One Hundred Mile House Canada see 100 Mile House
Oneida NY U.S.A. 135 H2
Oneida TN U.S.A. 134 C5
Oneida Lake U.S.A. 135 H2
O'Neill U.S.A. 130 D3
Onekama U.S.A. 134 B1
Onekotan, Ostrov i. Rus. Fed. 65 Q5
Oneonta AL U.S.A. 133 C5
Oneonta NY U.S.A. 135 H2
Oneşti Romania 59 L1
Onezhskaya Guba g. Rus. Fed. 42 G2
Onezhskoye Ozero l. Rus. Fed. see Onega, Lake
Onezhskoye Ozero l. Rus. Fed. see Onega, Lake
Ong r. India 84 D1
Onga Gabon 98 B4
Ongers watercourse S. Africa 100 F5
Ongi Mongolia 72 I3
Ongiyn Gol r. Mongolia 80 J3
Ongjin N. Korea 75 B5
Ongole India 84 D3
Onida U.S.A. 130 C2
Onilahy r. Madag. 99 E6
Onistagane, Lac l. Canada 123 H4
Onitsha Nigeria 96 D4
Onjati Mountain Namibia 100 C2
Onjiva Angola see Ondjiva
Ono-i-Lau i. Fiji 107 I4
Onomichi Japan 75 D6
Onon atoll Micronesia see Namonuito
Onor, Gora mt. Rus. Fed. 74 F2
Onotoa atoll Kiribati 107 H2
Onseepkans S. Africa 100 D5
Onslow Australia 108 A5
Onslow Bay U.S.A. 133 E5
Onstwedde Neth. 52 H1
Ontake-san vol. Japan 75 E6
Ontario prov. Canada 134 E1
Ontario U.S.A. 128 E4
Ontario, Lake Canada/U.S.A. 135 G2
Ontong Java Atoll Solomon Is 107 F2
Onutu atoll Kiribati see Onotoa
Onverwacht Suriname 143 G2
Onyx U.S.A. 128 D4
Oodnadatta Australia 111 A5
Oodweyne Somalia 98 E3
Ooldea Australia 109 E7
Ooldea Range hills Australia 109 E7
Oologah Lake resr U.S.A. 131 E4
Ooratippra r. Australia 110 B4
Oos-Londen S. Africa see East London
Oostburg Neth. 52 D3
Oostende Belgium see Ostend
Oostendorp Neth. 52 F2
Oosterhout Neth. 52 E3
Oosterschelde est. Neth. 52 D3
Oosterwolde Neth. 52 G2
Oostvleteren Belgium 52 C4
Oost-Vlieland Neth. 52 F1
Ootacamund India see Udagamandalam
Ootsa Lake Canada 120 E4
Ootsa Lake l. Canada 120 E4
Opal Mex. 131 C7
Opala Dem. Rep. Congo 98 C4
Oparino Rus. Fed. 42 K4
Oparo i. Fr. Polynesia see Rapa
Opasatika r. Canada 122 E4
Opasatika Lake Canada 122 E4
Opasquia Canada 121 M4
Opataca, Lac l. Canada 122 G4
Opava Czech Rep. 47 P6
Opel hill Germany 53 H5
Opelika U.S.A. 133 C5
Opelousas U.S.A. 131 E6
Opeongo Lake Canada 122 F5
Opheim U.S.A. 126 G2
Opienge Dem. Rep. Congo 98 C3
Opinaca r. Canada 122 F3
Opinaca, Réservoir resr Canada 122 F3
Opinnagau r. Canada 122 E3
Opiscotéo, Lac l. Canada 123 H3
Op Luang National Park Thai. 70 B3
Opmeer Neth. 52 E2
Opochka Rus. Fed. 45 P8
Opocopa, Lac l. Canada 123 I3
Opodepe Mex. 136 B3
Opole Poland 47 P5
Oporto Port. 57 B3
Opotiki N.Z. 113 F4
Opp U.S.A. 133 C6
Oppdal Norway 44 F5
Oppeln Poland see Opole
Opportunity U.S.A. 126 D3
Opunake N.Z. 113 D4
Opuwo Namibia 99 B5
Oqsu r. Tajik. 89 I2
Oracle U.S.A. 129 H5
Oradea Romania 59 I1
Orahovac Serb. and Mont. 59 I3
Orai India 82 D4
Oraibi U.S.A. 129 H4
Oraibi Wash watercourse U.S.A. 129 H4
Oral Kazakh. see Ural'sk
Oran Alg. 57 F6
Orán Arg. 144 D2
O Rang Cambodia 71 D4
Orang India 83 H4
Ŏrang N. Korea 74 C4
Orange Australia 112 D4
Orange France 56 G4
Orange r. Namibia/S. Africa 100 C5
Orange CA U.S.A. 128 E5
Orange MA U.S.A. 135 I2
Orange TX U.S.A. 131 E6
Orange VA U.S.A. 135 F4
Orange, Cabo c. Brazil 143 H3
Orangeburg U.S.A. 133 D5
Orange City U.S.A. 130 D3
Orange Cone sea feature S. Atlantic Ocean 148 I8
Orange Free State prov. S. Africa see Free State
Orangeville Canada 134 E2
Orange Walk Belize 136 G5
Oranienburg Germany 53 N2
Oranje r. Namibia/S. Africa see Orange
Oranje Gebergte hills Suriname 143 G3
Oranjemund Namibia 100 C5

▶Oranjestad Aruba 137 J6
Capital of Aruba.

Oranmore Rep. of Ireland 51 D4
Orapa Botswana 99 C6
Orăştie Romania 59 J2
Oraşul Stalin Romania see Braşov
Oravais Fin. 44 M5
Orba Co l. China 82 E2
Orbetello Italy 58 D3
Orbost Australia 112 D6
Orcadas research station S. Atlantic Ocean 152 A2
Orchard City U.S.A. 129 J2
Orchha India 82 D4
Orchila, Isla i. Venez. 142 E1
Orchy r. U.K. 50 D4
Orcutt U.S.A. 128 C4
Ord r. Australia 108 E3
Ord U.S.A. 130 D3
Ord, Mount hill Australia 108 D4
Órdenes Spain see Ordes
Orderville U.S.A. 129 G3
Ordes Spain 57 B2
Ordesa - Monte Perdido, Parque Nacional nat. park Spain 57 G2
Ord Mountain U.S.A. 128 E4
Ord River Dam Australia 108 E4
Ordu Hatay Turkey see Yayladağı
Ordu Ordu Turkey 90 E2
Ordubad Azer. 91 G3
Ordway U.S.A. 130 C4
Ordzhonikidze Rus. Fed. see Vladikavkaz
Ore Nigeria 96 D4
Oreana U.S.A. 128 D1
Örebro Sweden 45 I7
Oregon IL U.S.A. 130 F3
Oregon OH U.S.A. 134 D3
Oregon state U.S.A. 126 C4
Oregon City U.S.A. 126 C3
Orekhov Ukr. see Orikhiv
Orekhovo-Zuyevo Rus. Fed. 42 H5
Orel Rus. Fed. 43 H5
Orel, Gora mt. Rus. Fed. 74 E1
Orel', Ozero l. Rus. Fed. 74 E1
Orem U.S.A. 129 H1
Ore Mountains Czech Rep./Germany see Erzgebirge
Orenburg Rus. Fed. 64 G4
Orense Spain see Ourense
Oreor Palau see Koror
Orepuki N.Z. 113 A8
Öresund strait Denmark/Sweden 45 H9
Oretana, Cordillera mts Spain see Toledo, Montes de
Orewa N.Z. 113 E3
Oreye Belgium 52 F4
Orfanou, Kolpos b. Greece 59 J4
Orford Australia 111 [inset]
Orford U.K. 49 I6
Orford Ness hd U.K. 49 I6
Organabo Fr. Guiana 143 H2
Organ Pipe Cactus National Monument nat. park U.S.A. 129 G5
Orge r. France 52 C6
Orgūn Afgh. 89 H3
Orhaneli Turkey 59 M5
Orhangazi Turkey 59 M4
Orhon Gol r. Mongolia 80 J2
Orichi Rus. Fed. 42 K4
Oriental, Cordillera mts Bol. 142 E7
Oriental, Cordillera mts Col. 142 D2
Oriental, Cordillera mts Peru 142 E6
Orihuela Spain 57 F4
Orikhiv Ukr. 43 G7
Orillia Canada 134 F1
Orimattila Fin. 45 N6
Orin U.S.A. 126 G4
Orinoco r. Col./Venez. 142 F2
Orinoco Delta Venez. 142 F2
Orissa state India 84 E1
Orissaare Estonia 45 M7
Oristano Sardinia Italy 58 C5
Orivesi Fin. 45 N6
Orivesi l. Fin. 44 P5
Oriximiná Brazil 143 G4
Orizaba Mex. 136 E5

▶Orizaba, Pico de vol. Mex. 136 E5
3rd highest mountain in North America.

Orizona Brazil 145 A2
Orkanger Norway 44 F5
Örkelljunga Sweden 45 H8
Orkla r. Norway 44 F5
Orkney S. Africa 101 H4
Orkney is U.K. 50 F1
Orla U.S.A. 131 C6
Orland U.S.A. 128 B2
Orlândia Brazil 145 B3
Orlando U.S.A. 133 D6
Orland Park U.S.A. 134 B3
Orleaes Brazil 145 A5
Orléans France 56 E3
Orleans IN U.S.A. 134 B4
Orleans VT U.S.A. 135 I1
Orléans, Île d' i. Canada 123 H5
Orléansville Alg. see Ech Chélif

Orlik Rus. Fed. 72 H2
Orlov Rus. Fed. 42 K4
Orlov Gay Rus. Fed. 43 K6
Orlovskiy Rus. Fed. 43 I7
Orly airport France 52 C6
Ormara Pak. 89 G5
Ormara, Ras hd Pak. 89 G5
Ormiston Canada 121 J5
Ormoc Phil. 69 G4
Ormskirk U.K. 48 E5
Ormstown Canada 135 I1
Ornach Pak. 89 G5
Ornain r. France 52 E6
Orne r. France 56 D2
Ørnes Norway 44 H3
Örnsköldsvik Sweden 44 K5
Orobie, Alpi mts Italy 58 C1
Orobo, Serra do hills Brazil 145 C1
Orodara Burkina 96 C3
Orofino U.S.A. 126 D3
Oro Grande U.S.A. 128 E4
Orogrande U.S.A. 127 G6
Orol Dengizi salt l. Kazakh./Uzbek. see Aral Sea
Oromocto Canada 123 I5
Oromocto Lake Canada 123 I5
Oron Israel 85 B4
Orona atoll Kiribati 107 I2
Orono U.S.A. 132 G2
Orontes r. Asia 90 E3 see 'Āṣī, Nahr al
Orontes r. Lebanon/Syria 85 C2
Oroqen Zizhiqi China see Alihe
Oroquieta Phil. 69 G5
Orós, Açude resr Brazil 143 K5
Orosei, Golfo di b. Sardinia Italy 58 C4
Orosháza Hungary 59 I1
Oroville U.S.A. 128 C2
Oroville, Lake U.S.A. 128 C2
Orqohan China 74 A2
Orr U.S.A. 130 E1
Orsa Sweden 45 I6
Orsha Belarus 43 F5
Orshanka Rus. Fed. 42 J4
Orsk Rus. Fed. 64 G4
Ørsta Norway 44 E5
Orta Toroslar plat. Turkey 85 A1
Ortegal, Cabo c. Spain 57 C2
Orthez France 56 D5
Ortigueira Spain 57 C2
Ortiz Mex. 127 F7
Ortles mt. Italy 58 D1
Orton U.K. 48 E4
Ortona Italy 58 F3
Ortonville U.S.A. 130 D2
Ortospana Afgh. see Kābul
Orulgan, Khrebet mts Rus. Fed. 65 N3
Orumbo Namibia 100 C2
Orūmīyeh Iran see Urmia
Oruro Bol. 142 E7
Orūzgān Afgh. 89 G3
Orvieto Italy 58 E3
Orville Coast Antarctica 152 L1
Orwell OH U.S.A. 134 E3
Orwell VT U.S.A. 135 I2
Oryol Rus. Fed. see Orel
Os Norway 44 G5
Osa Rus. Fed. 41 R4
Osa, Península de pen. Costa Rica 137 H7
Osage IA U.S.A. 130 E3
Osage WV U.S.A. 134 E4
Osage WY U.S.A. 126 G3
Ōsaka Japan 75 D6
Osakarovka Kazakh. 80 D1
Osawatomie U.S.A. 130 E4
Osborne U.S.A. 130 D4
Osby Sweden 45 H8
Osceola IA U.S.A. 130 E3
Osceola MO U.S.A. 130 E4
Osceola NE U.S.A. 130 D3
Oschatz Germany 53 N3
Oschersleben (Bode) Germany 53 L2
Oschiri Sardinia Italy 58 C4
Ösel i. Estonia see Hiiumaa
Osetr r. Rus. Fed. 43 H5
Ōse-zaki pt Japan 75 C6
Osgoode Canada 135 H1
Osgood Mountains U.S.A. 126 D4
Osh Kyrg. 80 D3
Oshakati Namibia 99 B5
Oshawa Canada 135 F2
Oshika-hantō pen. Japan 75 F5
Ō-shima i. Japan 74 E4
Ō-shima i. Japan 75 E6
Oshkosh NE U.S.A. 130 C3
Oshkosh WI U.S.A. 134 A1
Oshmyany Belarus see Ashmyany
Oshnovīyeh Iran 88 B2
Oshogbo Nigeria 96 D4
Oshtorān Kūh mt. Iran 88 C3
Oshwe Dem. Rep. Congo 98 B4
Osijek Croatia 58 H2
Osilinka r. Canada 120 E3
Osimo Italy 58 E3
Osipenko Ukr. see Berdyans'k
Osipovichi Belarus see Asipovichy
Osiyan India 82 C4
Osizweni S. Africa 101 J4
Osječenica mts Bos.-Herz. 58 G2
Ösjön l. Sweden 44 I5
Oskaloosa U.S.A. 130 E3
Oskarshamn Sweden 45 J8
Öskemen Kazakh. see Ust'-Kamenogorsk

▶**Oslo** Norway 45 G7
Capital of Norway.

Oslofjorden sea chan. Norway 41 G7
Osmanabad India 84 C2
Osmancık Turkey 90 D2
Osmaneli Turkey 59 M4
Osmaniye Turkey 90 E3
Osmannagar India 84 C2
Os'mino Rus. Fed. 45 P7
Osnabrück Germany 53 I2
Osnaburg atoll Fr. Polynesia see Mururoa
Osogbo Nigeria see Oshogbo
Osogovska Planina mts Bulg./Macedonia 59 J3
Osogovske Planine mts Bulg./Macedonia see Osogovska Planina
Osogovski Planini mts Bulg./Macedonia see Osogovska Planina
Osorno Chile 144 B6
Osorno Spain 57 D2
Osoyoos Canada 120 G5
Osøyri Norway 45 D6
Osprey Reef Australia 110 D2
Oss Neth. 52 F3
Ossa, Mount Australia 111 [inset]
Osseo U.S.A. 122 C5
Ossineke U.S.A. 134 D1
Ossining U.S.A. 135 I3
Ossipee U.S.A. 135 J2
Ossipee Lake U.S.A. 135 J2
Oßmannstedt Germany 53 L3
Ossokmanuan Lake Canada 123 I3
Ossora Rus. Fed. 65 R4
Ostashkov Rus. Fed. 42 G4
Ostbevern Germany 53 H2
Oste r. Germany 53 J1
Ostend Belgium 52 C3
Ostende Belgium see Ostend
Osterburg (Altmark) Germany 53 L2
Österbymo Sweden 45 I8
Österdalälven l. Sweden 45 H6
Østerdalen valley Norway 45 G5
Osterfeld Germany 53 L3
Osterholz-Scharmbeck Germany 53 I1
Osterode am Harz Germany 53 K3
Österreich country Europe see Austria
Östersund Sweden 44 I5
Osterwieck Germany 53 K3
Ostfriesische Inseln Germany see East Frisian Islands
Ostfriesland reg. Germany 53 H1
Östhammar Sweden 45 K6
Ostrava Czech Rep. 47 Q6
Ostróda Poland 47 Q4
Ostrogozhsk Rus. Fed. 43 H6
Ostrov Czech Rep. 53 M4
Ostrov Rus. Fed. 45 P8
Ostrovets Poland see Ostrowiec Świętokrzyski
Ostrovskoye Rus. Fed. 42 I4
Ostrov Vrangelya i. Rus. Fed. see Wrangel Island
Ostrów Poland see Ostrów Wielkopolski
Ostrowiec Poland see Ostrowiec Świętokrzyski
Ostrowiec Świętokrzyski Poland 43 D6
Ostrów Mazowiecka Poland 47 R4
Ostrowo Poland see Ostrów Wielkopolski
Ostrów Wielkopolski Poland 47 P5
O'Sullivan Lake Canada 122 D4
Osŭm r. Bulg. 59 K3
Ōsumi-shotō is Japan 75 C7
Osuna Spain 57 D5
Oswego KS U.S.A. 131 E4
Oswego NY U.S.A. 135 G2
Oswestry U.K. 49 D6
Otago Peninsula N.Z. 113 C7
Otahiti i. Fr. Polynesia see Tahiti
Otaki N.Z. 113 E5
Otanmäki Fin. 44 O4
Otaru Japan 74 F4
Otavi Namibia 99 B5
Ōtawara Japan 75 F5
Otdia atoll Marshall Is see Wotje
Otelnuc, Lac l. Canada 123 H2
Otematata N.Z. 113 C7
Otepää Estonia 45 O7
Otgon Tenger Uul mt. Mongolia 80 I2
Otinapa Mex. 131 B7
Otira N.Z. 113 C6
Otis U.S.A. 130 C3
Otish, Monts hills Canada 123 H4
Otjinene Namibia 99 B6
Otjiwarongo Namibia 99 B6
Otjozondjupa admin. reg. Namibia 100 C1
Otley U.K. 48 F5
Otorohanga N.Z. 113 E4
Otoskwin r. Canada 121 N5
Otpan, Gora hill Kazakh. 91 H1
Otpor Rus. Fed. see Zabaykal'sk
Otradnoye Rus. Fed. see Otradnyy
Otradnyy Rus. Fed. 43 K5
Otranto Italy 58 H4
Otranto, Strait of Albania/Italy 58 H4
Otrogovo Rus. Fed. see Stepnoye
Otrozhnyy Rus. Fed. 65 S3
Otsego Lake U.S.A. 135 H2
Ōtsu Japan 75 D6
Otta Norway 45 F6

▶**Ottawa** Canada 135 H1
Capital of Canada.

Ottawa r. Canada 122 G5
also known as Rivière des Outaouais
Ottawa IL U.S.A. 130 F3
Ottawa KS U.S.A. 130 E4
Ottawa OH U.S.A. 134 C3
Ottawa Islands Canada 122 E2
Otter r. U.K. 49 D8
Otterbein U.S.A. 134 B3
Otterburn U.K. 48 E3
Otter Rapids Canada 122 E4
Ottersberg Germany 53 J1
Ottignies Belgium 52 E4
Ottumwa U.S.A. 130 E3
Ottweiler Germany 53 H5
Otukpo Nigeria 96 D4
Oturkpo Nigeria see Otukpo
Otuzco Peru 142 C5
Otway, Cape Australia 112 A7
Otway National Park Australia 112 A7
Ouachita r. U.S.A. 131 F6
Ouachita, Lake U.S.A. 131 E5
Ouachita Mountains Arkansas/Oklahoma U.S.A. 125 I5
Ouachita Mountains Arkansas/Oklahoma U.S.A. 131 E5
Ouadda Cent. Afr. Rep. 98 C3
Ouaddaï reg. Chad 97 F3

▶**Ouagadougou** Burkina 96 C3
Capital of Burkina.

Ouahigouya Burkina 96 C3
Ouahran Alg. see Oran
Ouaka r. Cent. Afr. Rep. 98 B3
Oualâta Mauritania 96 C3
Ouallam Niger 96 D3
Ouanda-Djailé Cent. Afr. Rep. 94 C3
Ouando Cent. Afr. Rep. 98 C3
Ouango Cent. Afr. Rep. 98 C3
Ouara r. Cent. Afr. Rep. 98 C3
Ouarâne reg. Mauritania 96 C2
Ouargaye Burkina 96 D3
Ouargla Alg. 54 F5
Ouarogou Burkina see Ouargaye
Ouarzazate Morocco 54 C5
Oubangui r. Cent. Afr. Rep./Dem. Rep. Congo see Ubangi
Oubergpas pass S. Africa 100 G7
Oudenaarde Belgium 52 D4
Oudtshoorn S. Africa 100 F7
Oud-Turnhout Belgium 52 E3
Oued Tlélat Alg. 57 F6
Oued Zem Morocco 54 C5
Oued Zénati Alg. 58 B6
Ouessant, Île d' i. France 56 B2
Ouesso Congo 98 B3
Ouezzane Morocco 57 D6
Oughter, Lough l. Rep. of Ireland 51 E3
Ouguati Namibia 100 B1
Ouistreham France 49 G9
Oujda Morocco 57 F6
Oujeft Mauritania 96 B3
Oulainen Fin. 44 N4
Oulangan kansallispuisto nat. park Fin. 44 P3
Ouled Djellal Alg. 57 I6
Ouled Farès Alg. 57 G5
Ouled Naïl, Monts des mts Alg. 57 H6
Oulu Fin. 44 N4
Oulujärvi l. Fin. 44 O4
Oulujoki r. Fin. 44 N4
Oulunsalo Fin. 44 N4
Oulx Italy 58 B2
Oum-Chalouba Chad 97 F3
Oum el Bouaghi Alg. 58 B7
Oum-Hadjer Chad 97 E3
Ounasjoki r. Fin. 44 N3
Oundle U.K. 49 G6
Oungre Canada 121 K5
Ounianga Kébir Chad 97 F3
Oupeye Belgium 52 F4
Our r. Lux. 52 G5
Ouray CO U.S.A. 129 J2
Ouray UT U.S.A. 129 I1
Ourcq r. France 52 D5
Ourense Spain 57 C2
Ouricurí Brazil 143 J5
Ourinhos Brazil 145 A3
Ouro r. Brazil 145 A1
Ouro Preto Brazil 145 C3
Ourthe r. Belgium 52 F4
Ous Rus. Fed. 41 S3
Ouse r. England U.K. 48 G5
Ouse r. England U.K. 49 H8
Outaouais, Rivière des r. Canada 122 G5 see Ottawa
Outardes r. Canada 123 H4
Outardes Quatre, Réservoir resr Canada 123 H4
Outer Hebrides is U.K. 50 B3
Outer Mongolia country Asia see Mongolia
Outer Santa Barbara Channel U.S.A. 128 D5
Outjo Namibia 99 B6
Outlook Canada 121 J5
Outokumpu Fin. 44 P5
Out Skerries is U.K. 50 [inset]
Ouvéa atoll New Caledonia 107 G4
Ouyanghai Shuiku resr China 77 G3
Ouyen Australia 111 C7
Ouzel r. U.K. 49 G6
Ovace, Punta d' mt. Corsica France 56 I6
Ovacık Turkey 85 A1
Ovada Italy 58 C2
Ovalle Chile 144 B4
Ovamboland reg. Namibia 99 B5
Ovan Gabon 98 B3
Ovar Port. 57 B3
Overath Germany 53 H4
Överkalix Sweden 44 M3
Overlander Roadhouse Australia 109 A6
Overland Park U.S.A. 130 E4
Overton U.S.A. 129 F3
Övertorneå Sweden 44 M3
Överum Sweden 45 J8
Overveen Neth. 52 E2
Ovid CO U.S.A. 130 C3
Ovid NY U.S.A. 135 G2
Oviedo Spain 57 D2
Ovoot Mongolia 73 K3
Øvre Anarjokka Nasjonalpark nat. park Norway 44 N2
Øvre Dividal Nasjonalpark nat. park Norway 44 K2
Øvre Rendal Norway 45 G6
Ovruch Ukr. 43 F6
Ovsyanka Rus. Fed. 74 B1
Owando Congo 98 B4
Owa Rafa i. Solomon Is see Santa Ana
Owasco Lake U.S.A. 135 G2
Owase Japan 75 E6
Owatonna U.S.A. 130 E2
Owbeh Afgh. 89 F3
Owego U.S.A. 135 G2
Owel, Lough l. Rep. of Ireland 51 E4
Owen Island Myanmar 71 B5
Owenmore r. Rep. of Ireland 51 C3
Owenmore r. Rep. of Ireland 51 D3
Owenreagh r. U.K. 51 E3
Owen River N.Z. 113 D5
Owens r. U.S.A. 128 E3
Owensboro U.S.A. 134 B5
Owen Sound Canada 134 E1
Owen Sound inlet Canada 134 E1
Owen Stanley Range mts P.N.G. 69 L8
Owenton U.S.A. 134 C4
Owerri Nigeria 96 D4
Owikeno Lake Canada 120 E5
Owingsville U.S.A. 134 D4
Owl r. Canada 121 M3
Owl Creek Mountains U.S.A. 126 F4
Owo Nigeria 96 D4
Owosso U.S.A. 134 C2
Owyhee U.S.A. 126 D4
Owyhee r. U.S.A. 126 D4
Owyhee Mountains U.S.A. 126 D4
Öxarfjörður b. Iceland 44 [inset]
Oxbow Canada 121 K5
Ox Creek r. U.S.A. 130 C1
Oxelösund Sweden 45 J7
Oxford N.Z. 113 D6
Oxford U.K. 49 F7
Oxford IN U.S.A. 134 B3
Oxford MA U.S.A. 135 J2
Oxford MD U.S.A. 135 G4
Oxford MS U.S.A. 131 F5
Oxford NC U.S.A. 132 E4
Oxford NY U.S.A. 135 H2
Oxford OH U.S.A. 134 C4
Oxford House Canada 121 M4
Oxford Lake Canada 121 M4
Oxley Australia 112 B5
Oxleys Peak Australia 112 E3
Oxley Wild Rivers National Park Australia 112 F3
Ox Mountains hills Rep. of Ireland see Slieve Gamph
Oxnard U.S.A. 128 D4
Oxtongue Lake Canada 135 F1
Oxus r. Asia see Amudar'ya
Øya Norway 44 H3
Oyama Japan 75 E5
Oyem Gabon 98 B3
Oyen Canada 121 I5
Oygon Mongolia 80 I2
Oykel r. U.K. 50 E3
Oyo Nigeria 96 D4
Oyonnax France 56 G3
Oyster Rocks is India 84 B3
Oyten Germany 53 J1
Oytograk China 83 E1
Oyukludağı mt. Turkey 85 A1
Özalp Turkey 91 G3
Ozamiz Phil. 69 G5
Ozark AL U.S.A. 133 C6
Ozark AR U.S.A. 131 E5
Ozark MO U.S.A. 131 E4
Ozark Plateau U.S.A. 131 E4
Ozarks, Lake of the U.S.A. 130 E4
O'zbekiston country Asia see Uzbekistan
Özen Kazakh. see Kyzylsay
Ozernovskiy Rus. Fed. 65 Q4
Ozernyy Rus. Fed. 43 G5
Ozerpakh Rus. Fed. 74 F1
Ozersk Rus. Fed. 45 M9
Ozerskiy Rus. Fed. 74 F3
Ozery Rus. Fed. 43 H5
Ozeryane Rus. Fed. 74 C2
Ozieri Sardinia Italy 58 C4
Ozinki Rus. Fed. 43 K6
Oznachennoye Rus. Fed. see Sayanogorsk
Ozona U.S.A. 131 C6
Ozuki Japan 75 C6

P

Paamiut Greenland 119 N3
Pa-an Myanmar 70 B3
Paanopa i. Kiribati see Banaba
Paarl S. Africa 100 D7
Paatsjoki r. Europe see Patsoyoki
Paballelo S. Africa 100 E5
P'abal-li N. Korea 74 C4
Pabbay i. U.K. 50 B3
Pabianice Poland 47 Q5
Pabianitz Poland see Pabianice
Pabna Bangl. 83 G4
Pabradė Lith. 45 N9
Pab Range mts Pak. 89 G5
Pacaás Novos, Parque Nacional nat. park Brazil 142 F6
Pacaraimã, Serra mts S. America see Pakaraima Mountains
Pacasmayo Peru 142 C5
Pachagarh Bangl. see Panchagarh
Pacheco Chihuahua Mex. 127 F7
Pacheco Zacatecas Mex. 131 C7
Pachikha Rus. Fed. 42 J3
Pachino Sicily Italy 58 F6
Pachmarhi India 82 D5
Pachor India 82 D5
Pachora India 84 B1
Pachpadra India 82 C4
Pachuca Mex. 136 E4
Pachuca de Soto Mex. see Pachuca
Pacific-Antarctic Ridge sea feature S. Pacific Ocean 151 J9
Pacific Grove U.S.A. 128 C3

▶**Pacific Ocean** 150-147
Largest ocean in the world.

Pacific Rim National Park Canada 120 E5
Pacitan Indon. 68 E8
Packsaddle Australia 111 C6
Pacoval Brazil 143 H4
Pacuí r. Brazil 145 B2
Paczków Poland 47 P5
Padali Rus. Fed. see Amursk
Padampur India 82 C3
Padang Indon. 68 C7
Padang i. Indon. 71 C7
Padang Endau Malaysia 71 C7
Padangpanjang Indon. 68 C7
Padangsidimpuan Indon. 71 B7
Padany Rus. Fed. 42 G3
Padatha, Kūh-e mt. Iran 88 C3
Padaung Myanmar 70 A3
Padcaya Bol. 142 F8
Padderborn-Lippstadt airport Germany 53 I3
Paden City U.S.A. 134 E4
Paderborn Germany 53 I3
Padeşu, Vârful mt. Romania 59 J2
Padibyu Myanmar 70 B2
Padilla Bol. 142 F7
Padjelanta nationalpark nat. park Sweden 44 J3
Padova Italy see Padua
Padrão, Ponta pt Angola 99 B4
Padrauna India 83 F4
Padre Island U.S.A. 131 D7
Padstow U.K. 49 C8
Padsvillye Belarus 45 O9
Padua India 84 D2
Padua Italy 58 D2
Paducah KY U.S.A. 131 F4
Paducah TX U.S.A. 131 C5
Padum Jammu and Kashmir 82 D2
Paegam N. Korea 74 C4
Paektu-san mt. China/N. Korea see Baotou Shan
Paengnyŏng-do i. S. Korea 75 B5
Pafos Cyprus see Paphos
Pafuri Moz. 101 J2
Pag Croatia 58 F2
Pag i. Croatia 58 F2
Paga Indon. 108 C2
Pagadian Phil. 69 G5
Pagai Selatan i. Indon. 68 C7
Pagalu i. Equat. Guinea see Annobón
Pagan i. N. Mariana Is 69 L3
Pagasitikos Kolpos b. Greece 59 J5
Pagatan Indon. 68 F7
Page U.S.A. 129 H3
Paget, Mount S. Georgia 144 I8
Paget Cay reef Australia 110 F3
Pagon i. N. Mariana Is see Pagan
Pagosa Springs U.S.A. 127 G5
Pagqên China see Gadê
Pagwa River Canada 122 D4
Pagwi P.N.G. 69 K7
Pahala HI U.S.A. 127 [inset]
Pahang r. Malaysia 71 C7
Pahlgam Jammu and Kashmir 82 C2
Pahoa HI U.S.A. 127 [inset]
Pahokee U.S.A. 133 D7
Pahra Kariz Afgh. 89 F3
Pahranagat Range mts U.S.A. 129 F3
Pahrump U.S.A. 129 F3
Pahuj r. India 82 D4
Pahute Mesa plat. U.S.A. 128 E3
Pai Thai. 70 B3
Paicines U.S.A. 128 C3
Paide Estonia 45 N7
Paignton U.K. 49 D8
Päijänne l. Fin. 45 N6
Paikü Co l. China 83 F3
Pailin Cambodia 71 C4
Pailolo Channel HI U.S.A. 127 [inset]
Paimio Fin. 45 M6
Painel Brazil 145 A4
Painesville U.S.A. 134 E3
Pains Brazil 145 B3
Painted Desert U.S.A. 129 H3
Painted Rock Dam U.S.A. 129 G5
Paint Hills Canada see Wemindji
Paint Rock U.S.A. 131 D6
Paintsville U.S.A. 134 D5
Paisley U.K. 50 E5
Paita Peru 142 B5
Paitou China 77 I2
Paiva Couceiro Angola see Quipungo
Paizhou China 77 G2
Pajala Sweden 44 M3
Paka Malaysia 71 C6
Pakala India 84 C3
Pakanbaru Indon. see Pekanbaru
Pakangyi Myanmar 70 A2
Pakaraima Mountains Guyana 142 G3
Pakaraima Mountains S. America 142 F3
Pakaur India 83 F4
Pakesley Canada 122 E5
Pakhachi Rus. Fed. 65 R3
Pakhoi China see Beihai
Paki Nigeria 96 D3

▶**Pakistan** country Asia 89 H4
4th most populous country in Asia.
Asia 6, 62–63

Pakkat Indon. 71 B7
Paknampho Thai. see Nakhon Sawan
Pakokku Myanmar 70 A2
Pakowki Lake imp. l. Canada 121 I5
Pakpattan Pak. 89 I4
Pak Phanang Thai. 71 C5
Pak Phayun Thai. 71 C6
Pakruojis Lith. 45 M9
Paks Hungary 58 H1
Pakse Laos see Pakxé
Pak Tam Chung Hong Kong China 77 [inset]
Pak Thong Chai Thai. 70 C4
Pakur India see Pakaur
Pakxé Laos 70 D4
Pakxeng Laos 70 C2
Pala Chad 97 E4
Pala Myanmar 71 B4
Palaestinia reg. Asia see Palestine
Palaiochora Greece 59 J7
Palaiseau France 52 C6
Palakkad India see Palghat
Palakkat India see Palghat
Palamakoloi Botswana 100 F2
Palamau India see Palamu
Palamós Spain 57 H3
Palamu India 83 F5
Palana Rus. Fed. 65 Q4
Palandur India 84 D1
Palangān, Kūh-e mts Iran 89 F4
Palangkaraya Indon. 68 E7
Palani India 84 C4
Palanpur India 82 C4
Palantak Pak. 89 G5
Palapye Botswana 101 H2
Palatka Rus. Fed. 65 Q3
Palatka U.S.A. 133 D6
▶**Palau** country N. Pacific Ocean 69 I5
Asia 6, 62–63
Palau Islands Palau 69 I5
Palauk Myanmar 71 B4
Palaw Myanmar 71 B4
Palawan i. Phil. 68 F5
Palawan Passage strait Phil. 68 F5
Palawan Trough sea feature N. Pacific Ocean 150 D5
Palayankottai India 84 C4
Palchal Lake India 84 D2
Paldiski Estonia 45 N7
Palekh Rus. Fed. 42 I4
Palembang Indon. 68 C7
Palena Chile 144 B6
Palencia Spain 57 D2
Palermo Sicily Italy 58 E5
Palestine reg. Asia 85 B3
Palestine U.S.A. 131 E6
Paletwa Myanmar 70 A2
Palezgir Pak. 89 H4
Palghat India 84 C4
Palgrave, Mount hill Australia 109 A5
Palhoca Brazil 145 A4
Pali Chhattisgarh India 84 D1
Pali Maharashtra India 84 B2
Pali Rajasthan India 82 C4

▶**Palikir** Micronesia 150 G5
Capital of Micronesia.

Palinuro, Capo c. Italy 58 F4
Paliouri, Akra pt Greece 59 J5
Palisade U.S.A. 129 I2
Paliseul Belgium 52 F5
Palitana India 82 B5
Palivere Estonia 45 M7
Palk Bay Sri Lanka 84 C4
Palkino Rus. Fed. 45 P8
Palkonda Range mts India 84 C3
Palk Strait India/Sri Lanka 84 C4
Palla Bianca mt. Austria/Italy see Weißkugel
Pallamallawa Australia 112 E2
Pallas Green Rep. of Ireland 51 D5
Pallas ja Ounastunturin kansallispuisto nat. park Fin. 44 M2
Pallasovka Rus. Fed. 43 J6
Pallavaram India 84 D3
Palliser, Cape N.Z. 113 E5
Palliser, Îles is Fr. Polynesia 151 K7
Palliser Bay N.Z. 113 E5
Pallu India 82 C3
Palma r. Brazil 145 B1
Palma del Río Spain 57 D5
Palma de Mallorca Spain 57 H4
Palmaner India 84 C3
Palmares Brazil 143 K5
Palmares do Sul Brazil 145 A5
Palmas Paraná Brazil 145 A4
Palmas Tocantins Brazil 143 I6
Palmas, Cape Liberia 96 C4
Palm Bay U.S.A. 133 D7
Palmdale U.S.A. 128 D4
Palmeira Brazil 145 A4
Palmeira das Missões Brazil 144 F3
Palmeira dos Índios Brazil 143 K5
Palmeirais Brazil 143 J5
Palmeiras Brazil 145 C1
Palmeirinhas, Ponta das pt Angola 99 B4
Palmer research station Antarctica 152 L2
Palmer r. Australia 110 C3
Palmer watercourse Australia 109 F6
Palmer U.S.A. 118 D3
Palmer Land reg. Antarctica 152 L2
Palmerston N.T. Australia 108 E3
Palmerston N.T. Australia see Darwin
Palmerston Canada 134 E2
Palmerston atoll Cook Is 107 J3
Palmerston N.Z. 113 C7
Palmerston North N.Z. 113 E5
Palmerton U.S.A. 135 H3
Palmerville Australia 110 D2
Palmetto Point Bahamas 133 E7
Palmi Italy 58 F5
Palmira Col. 142 C3
Palmira Cuba 133 D8
Palm Springs U.S.A. 128 E5
Palmyra Syria see Tadmur
Palmyra MO U.S.A. 130 F4
Palmyra PA U.S.A. 135 G3
Palmyra VA U.S.A. 135 F5

▶**Palmyra Atoll** terr. N. Pacific Ocean 150 J5
United States Unincorporated Territory.

Palmyras Point India 83 F5
Palni Hills India 84 C4
Palo Alto U.S.A. 128 B3
Palo Blanco Mex. 131 C7
Palo Chino watercourse Mex. 127 E7
Palo Duro watercourse U.S.A. 131 C5
Paloich Sudan 86 D7
Palojärvi Fin. 44 M2
Palojoensuu Fin. 44 M2
Palomaa Fin. 44 O2
Palomar Mountain U.S.A. 128 E5
Paloncha India 84 D2
Palo Pinto U.S.A. 131 D5
Palopo Indon. 69 G7
Palos, Cabo de c. Spain 57 F5
Palo Verde U.S.A. 129 F5
Paltamo Fin. 44 O4
Palu Indon. 68 F7
Palu i. Indon. 108 C2
Palu Turkey 91 E3
Pal'vart Turkm. 89 G2
Palwal India 82 D3
Palwancha India see Paloncha
Palyeskaya Nizina marsh Belarus/Ukr. see Pripet Marshes
Pambarra Moz. 101 L1
Pambula Australia 112 D6
Pamidi India 84 C3
Pamiers France 56 E5
Pamir mts Asia 89 I2
Pamlico Sound sea chan. U.S.A. 133 E5
Pamouscachiou, Lac l. Canada 123 H4
Pampa U.S.A. 131 C5
Pampa de Infierno Arg. 144 D3
Pampas reg. Arg. 144 D5
Pampeluna Spain see Pamplona
Pamphylia reg. Turkey 59 N6
Pamplin U.S.A. 135 F5
Pamplona Col. 142 D2
Pamplona Spain 57 F2
Pampow Germany 53 L1
Pamukova Turkey 59 N4
Pamzal Jammu and Kashmir 82 D2
Pana U.S.A. 130 F4
Panaca U.S.A. 129 F3
Panache, Lake Canada 122 E5
Panagyurishte Bulg. 59 K3
Panaitan i. Indon. 68 D8
Panaji India 84 B3
▶**Panama** country Central America 137 H7
North America 9, 116–117

▶**Panama** i. Indon. 108 C2
Most southerly point of Asia.

Panamá Panama see Panama City

Pequeña, Punta pt Mex. 127 E8
Pequop Mountains U.S.A. 129 F1
Peradeniya Sri Lanka 84 D5
Pera Head hd Australia 110 C2
Perak i. Malaysia 71 B6
Perales del Alfambra Spain 57 F3
Perambalur India 84 C4
Perämeren kansallispuisto nat. park Fin. 44 N4
Peräseinäjoki Fin. 44 M5
Percé Canada 123 I4
Percival Lakes salt flat Australia 108 D5
Percy U.S.A. 135 J1
Percy Isles Australia 110 E4
Percy Reach l. Canada 135 G1
Perdizes Brazil 145 B2
Perdu, Lac l. Canada 123 H4
Peregrebnoye Rus. Fed. 41 T3
Pereira Col. 142 C3
Pereira Barreto Brazil 145 A3
Pereira de Eça Angola see Ondjiva
Pere Marquette r. U.S.A. 134 B2
Peremul Par reef India 84 B4
Peremyshlyany Ukr. 43 E6
Perenjori Australia 109 B7
Pereslavl'-Zalesskiy Rus. Fed. 42 H4
Pereslavskiy Natsional'nyy Park nat. park Rus. Fed. 42 H4
Pereyaslavka Rus. Fed. 74 D3
Pereval Klukhorskiy pass Rus. Fed. 91 F2
Pereyaslav-Khmel'nitskiy Ukr. see Pereyaslav-Khmel'nyts'kyy
Pereyaslav-Khmel'nyts'kyy Ukr. 43 F6
Perforated Island Thai. see Bon, Ko
Pergamino Arg. 144 D4
Perhentian Besar, Pulau i. Malaysia 71 C6
Perho Fin. 44 N5
Péribonca, Lac l. Canada 123 H4
Perico Arg. 144 C2
Pericos Mex. 127 G8
Peridot U.S.A. 129 H5
Périgueux France 56 E4
Perijá, Parque Nacional nat. park Venez. 142 D2
Perija, Sierra de mts Venez. 138 D2
Periyar India see Erode
Perkasie U.S.A. 135 H3
Perlas, Punta de pt Nicaragua 137 H6
Perleberg Germany 53 L1
Perm' Rus. Fed. 41 R4
Permas Rus. Fed. 42 J4
Pernambuco Brazil see Recife
Pernambuco Abyssal Plain sea feature S. Atlantic Ocean 148 G6
Pernatty Lagoon salt flat Australia 111 B6
Pernem India 84 B3
Pernik Bulg. 59 J3
Pernov Estonia see Pärnu
Perojpur Bangl. see Pirojpur
Peron Islands Australia 108 E3
Péronne France 52 C5
Perpignan France 56 F5
Perranporth U.K. 49 B8
Perrégaux Alg. see Mohammadia
Perris U.S.A. 128 E5
Perros-Guirec France 56 C2
Perrot, Île i. Canada 135 I1
Perry FL U.S.A. 133 D6
Perry GA U.S.A. 133 D5
Perry MI U.S.A. 134 C2
Perry OK U.S.A. 131 D4
Perry Lake U.S.A. 130 E4
Perryton U.S.A. 131 C4
Perryville AK U.S.A. 118 C4
Perryville MO U.S.A. 130 F4
Perseverancia Bol. 142 F6
Pershore U.K. 49 E6
Persia country Asia see Iran
Persian Gulf Asia see The Gulf
Pertek Turkey 91 E3

▶Perth Australia 109 A7
State capital of Western Australia. 4th most populous city in Oceania.

Perth Canada 135 G1
Perth U.K. 50 F4
Perth Amboy U.S.A. 135 H3
Perth-Andover Canada 123 I5
Perth Basin sea feature Indian Ocean 149 P7
Pertominsk Rus. Fed. 42 H2
Pertunmaa Fin. 45 O6
Pertusato, Capo c. Corsica France 56 I6
Peru atoll Kiribati see Beru

▶Peru country S. America 142 D6
3rd largest and 4th most populous country in South America.
South America 9, 140–141

Peru IL U.S.A. 130 F3
Peru IN U.S.A. 134 B3
Peru NY U.S.A. 135 I1
Peru-Chile Trench sea feature S. Pacific Ocean 151 O6
Perugia Italy 58 E3
Peruru India 84 C3
Perusia Italy see Perugia
Péruwelz Belgium 52 D4
Pervomaysk Rus. Fed. 43 I5
Pervomays'k Ukr. 43 F6
Pervomayskiy Kazakh. 80 F1
Pervomayskiy Arkhangel'skaya Oblast' Rus. Fed. see Novodvinsk
Pervomayskiy Tambovskaya Oblast' Rus. Fed. 43 I5
Pervomays'kyy Ukr. 43 H6
Pervorechenskiy Rus. Fed. 65 R3
Pesaro Italy 58 E3
Pescadores is Taiwan see P'enghu Ch'üntao
Pescara Italy 58 F3
Pescara r. Italy 58 F3
Peschanokopskoye Rus. Fed. 39 I7
Peschanoye Rus. Fed. see Yashkul'
Peschanyy, Mys pt Kazakh. 87 H2
Pesha r. Rus. Fed. 42 J2
Peshanjan Afgh. 89 F3
Peshawar Pak. 89 H3
Peshkopi Albania 59 I4
Peshtera Bulg. 59 K3
Peski Turkm. 89 F2
Peski Karakumy des. Turkm. see Karakum Desert
Peskovka Rus. Fed. 42 L4
Pesnica Slovenia 58 F1
Pessac France 56 D4
Pessin Germany 53 M2
Pestovo Rus. Fed. 42 G4
Pestravka Rus. Fed. 43 K5
Petah Tiqwa Israel 85 B3
Petäjävesi Fin. 44 N5
Petaling Jaya Malaysia 71 C7
Petalion, Kolpos sea chan. Greece 59 K5
Petaluma U.S.A. 128 B2
Pétange Lux. 52 F5
Petatlán Mex. 136 D5
Petauke Zambia 99 D5
Petenwell Lake U.S.A. 130 F2
Peterbell Canada 122 E4
Peterborough Australia 111 B7
Peterborough Canada 135 F1
Peterborough U.K. 49 G6
Peterborough U.S.A. 135 J2
Peterculter U.K. 50 G3
Peterhead U.K. 50 H3
Peter I Island Antarctica 152 K2
Peter I Øy i. Antarctica see Peter I Island
Peter Lake Canada 121 M2
Peterlee U.K. 48 F4
Petermann Bjerg nunatak Greenland 119 P2
Petermann Ranges mts Australia 109 E6
Peter Pond Lake Canada 121 I4
Peters, Lac l. Canada 123 H2
Petersberg Germany 53 J4
Petersburg AK U.S.A. 120 C3
Petersburg IL U.S.A. 130 F4
Petersburg IN U.S.A. 134 B4
Petersburg NY U.S.A. 135 I2
Petersburg VA U.S.A. 135 G5
Petersburg WV U.S.A. 134 F4
Petersfield U.K. 49 G7
Petershagen Germany 53 I2
Petersville U.S.A. 118 C3
Peter the Great Bay Rus. Fed. see Petra Velikogo, Zaliv
Peth India 84 B2
Petilia Policastro Italy 58 G5
Petit Atlas mts Morocco see Anti Atlas
Petitcodiac Canada 123 I5
Petitjean Morocco see Sidi Kacem
Petit Lac Manicouagan l. Canada 123 I3
Petit Mécatina r. Nfld. and Lab./Que. Canada 123 K4
Petit Mécatina, Île du i. Canada 123 K4
Petit Morin r. France 52 D6
Petitot r. Canada 120 F2
Petit Saut Dam resr Fr. Guiana 143 H3
Petit St-Bernard, Col du pass France 56 H4
Peto Mex. 136 G4
Petoskey U.S.A. 132 C2
Petra tourist site Jordan 85 B4
Petra Velikogo, Zaliv b. Rus. Fed. 74 C4
Petre, Point Canada 135 G2
Petrich Bulg. 59 J4
Petrified Forest National Park U.S.A. 129 I4
Petrikau Poland see Piotrków Trybunalski
Petrikov Belarus see Pyetrykaw
Petrinja Croatia 58 G2
Petroaleksandrovsk Uzbek. see Turtkul'
Petrograd Rus. Fed. see St Petersburg
Petrokhanski Prokhod pass Bulg. 59 J3
Petrokov Poland see Piotrków Trybunalski
Petrolia Canada 134 D2
Petrolia U.S.A. 128 A1
Petrolina Brazil 143 J5
Petrolina de Goiás Brazil 145 A2
Petropavl Kazakh. see Petropavlovsk
Petropavlovsk Kazakh. 79 F1
Petropavlovsk Rus. Fed. see Petropavlovsk-Kamchatskiy
Petropavlovsk-Kamchatskiy Rus. Fed. 65 Q4
Petrópolis Brazil 145 C3
Petroşani Romania 59 J2
Petrovsk Rus. Fed. 43 J5
Petrovskoye Rus. Fed. see Svetlograd
Petrovsk-Zabaykal'skiy Rus. Fed. 73 J2
Petrozavodsk Rus. Fed. 42 G3
Petrus Steyn S. Africa 101 I4
Petrusville S. Africa 100 G6
Petsamo Rus. Fed. see Pechenga
Pettau Slovenia see Ptuj
Petten Neth. 52 E2
Pettigo U.K. 51 E3
Petukhovo Rus. Fed. 64 H4
Petushki Rus. Fed. 42 H5
Petzeck mt. Austria 47 N7
Peuetsagu, Gunung vol. Indon. 71 B6
Peureula Indon. 71 B6
Pevek Rus. Fed. 65 S3
Pêxung China 76 B1
Pey Ostān Iran 88 E3
Peza r. Rus. Fed. 42 J2
Pezinok Slovakia 47 P6
Pezu Pak. 89 H3
Pfälzer Wald hills Germany 49 H5
Pforzheim Germany 53 I6
Pfungstadt Germany 53 I5
Phagwara India 82 C3
Phahameng Free State S. Africa 101 H5
Phahameng Limpopo S. Africa 101 I3
Phalaborwa S. Africa 101 J2
Phalodi India 82 C4
Phalsund India 82 B4
Phalta India 83 G5
Phaluai, Ko i. Thai. 71 B5
Phalut Peak India/Nepal 83 G4
Phan Thai. 70 B3
Phanat Nikhom Thai. 71 C4
Phangan, Ko i. Thai. 71 C5
Phang Hoei, San Khao mts Thai. 70 C3
Phangnga Thai. 71 B5
Phanom Dong Rak, Thiu Khao mts Cambodia/Thai. 71 D4
Phan Rang Vietnam 71 E5
Phan Thiêt Vietnam 71 E5
Phapon Myanmar see Pyapon
Phat Diêm Vietnam 70 D2
Phatthalung Thai. 71 C6
Phayam, Ko i. Thai. 71 B5
Phayao Thai. 70 B3
Phayuhakhiri Thai. 70 C4
Phek India 83 H4
Phelps Lake Canada 121 K3
Phen Thai. 70 C3
Phenix U.S.A. 135 F5
Phenix City U.S.A. 133 C5
Phet Buri Thai. 71 B4
Phetchabun Thai. 70 C3
Phiafai Laos 70 D4
Phichai Thai. 70 C3
Phichit Thai. 70 C3
Philadelphia Jordan see 'Ammān
Philadelphia Turkey see Alaşehir
Philadelphia MS U.S.A. 131 F5
Philadelphia NY U.S.A. 135 H1
Philadelphia PA U.S.A. 135 H4
Philip U.S.A. 130 C2
Philip Atoll Micronesia see Sorol
Philippeville Alg. see Skikda
Philippeville Belgium 52 E4
Philippi U.S.A. 134 E4
Philippi, Lake salt flat Australia 110 B5
Philippine Neth. 52 D3
Philippine Basin sea feature N. Pacific Ocean 150 E4
▶Philippines country Asia 69 G4
Asia 6, 62–63
Philippine Sea N. Pacific Ocean 69 G3

▶Philippine Trench sea feature N. Pacific Ocean 150 E4
3rd deepest trench in the world.

Philippolis S. Africa 101 G6
Philippopolis Bulg. see Plovdiv
Philippsburg Germany 53 I5
Philipsburg MT U.S.A. 126 E3
Philipsburg PA U.S.A. 135 F3
Philip Smith Mountains U.S.A. 118 D3
Philipstown S. Africa 100 G6
Phillip Island Australia 112 B7
Phillips ME U.S.A. 135 J1
Phillips WI U.S.A. 130 F2
Phillipsburg U.S.A. 130 D4
Phillips Range hills Australia 108 D4
Philmont U.S.A. 135 I2
Philomelium Turkey see Akşehir
Phiritona S. Africa 101 H4
Phitsanulok Thai. 70 C3

▶Phnom Penh Cambodia 71 D5
Capital of Cambodia.

Phnum Pénh Cambodia see Phnom Penh
Pho, Laem pt Thai. 71 C6
Phoenicia U.S.A. 135 H2

▶Phoenix U.S.A. 127 E6
State capital of Arizona.

Phoenix Island Kiribati see Rawaki
Phoenix Islands Kiribati 107 I2
Phon Thai. 70 C4
Phong Nha Vietnam 70 D3
Phôngsali Laos 70 C2
Phong Saly Laos see Phôngsali
Phong Thô Vietnam 70 C2
Phon Phisai Thai. 70 C3
Phon Thong Thai. 70 C3
Phosphate Hill Australia 110 C4
Phrae Thai. 70 C3
Phra Nakhon Si Ayutthaya Thai. see Ayutthaya
Phrao Thai. 70 B3
Phra Saeng Thai. 71 B5
Phrom Phiram Thai. 70 C3
Phsar Ream Cambodia 71 C5
Phuchong-Nayoi National Park Thai. 71 D4
Phu Cuong Vietnam see Thu Dâu Môt
Phu Hôi Vietnam 71 E4
Phuket Thai. 71 B6
Phuket, Ko i. Thai. 71 B6
Phu-khieo Wildlife Reserve nature res. Thai. 70 C3
Phulabani India see Phulbani
Phulbani India 84 E1
Phulchhari Ghat Bangl. see Fulchhari
Phulji Pak. 89 G5
Phu Lôc Vietnam 70 D3
Phu Luang National Park Thai. 70 C3
Phu Ly Vietnam 70 D2
Phumĭ Bŏeng Mealea Cambodia 71 D4
Phumĭ Chhlong Cambodia 71 D4
Phumĭ Kaôh Kŏng Cambodia 71 C5
Phumĭ Kon Kriel Cambodia 71 C4
Phumĭ Mlu Prey Cambodia 71 D4
Phumĭ Moŭng Cambodia 71 C4
Phumĭ Prêk Kak Cambodia 71 D4
Phumĭ Sâmraông Cambodia 71 C4
Phumĭ Trâm Kak Cambodia 71 D5
Phumĭ Veal Renh Cambodia 71 C5
Phu My Vietnam 71 E4
Phung Hiêp Vietnam 71 D5
Phu Phac Mo mt. Vietnam 70 C2
Phu Phan National Park Thai. 70 C3
Phu Quôc, Đao i. Vietnam 71 C5
Phư Tho Vietnam 70 D2
Phu Vinh Vietnam see Tra Vinh
Piaca Brazil 143 I5
Piacenza Italy 58 C2
Piacouadie, Lac l. Canada 123 H4
Piagochioui r. Canada 122 F3
Piai, Tanjung pt Malaysia 71 C7
Pian r. Australia 112 D3
Pianosa, Isola i. Italy 58 D3
Piatra Neamţ Romania 59 L1
Piave r. Italy 58 E2
Pibor Post Sudan 97 G4
Pic r. Canada 122 D4
Picacho U.S.A. 129 H5
Picachos, Cerro dos mt. Mex. 127 E7
Picardie admin. reg. France 52 C5
Picardie reg. France see Picardy
Picardy admin. reg. France see Picardie
Picardy reg. France 52 B5
Picauville France 49 F9
Picayune U.S.A. 131 F6
Piceance Creek r. U.S.A. 129 I1
Pichanal Arg. 144 D2
Pichhor India 82 D4
Pichilemu Chile 144 B4
Pichilingue Mex. 136 B4
Pickens U.S.A. 134 E4
Pickering Canada 134 F2
Pickering U.K. 48 G4
Pickering, Vale of valley U.K. 48 G4
Pickle Lake Canada 119 I4
Pico da Neblina, Parque Nacional do nat. park Brazil 142 E3
Picos Brazil 143 J5
Pico Truncado Arg. 144 C7
Picton Australia 112 E5
Picton Canada 135 G2
Picton N.Z. 113 E5
Pictou Canada 123 J5
Picture Butte Canada 121 H5
Pidarak Pak. 89 F5
Pidurutalagala mt. Sri Lanka 84 D5
Piedade Brazil 145 B3
Piedra de Águila Arg. 144 B6
Piedras, Punta pt Arg. 144 E5
Piedras Blancas Point U.S.A. 128 C4
Piedras Negras Mex. 131 C6
Pie Island Canada 122 C4
Pieksämäki Fin. 44 O5
Pielavesi Fin. 44 O5
Pielinen l. Fin. 44 P5
Pieljekaise nationalpark nat. park Sweden 44 J3
Pienaarsrivier S. Africa 101 I3
Pieniński Park Narodowy nat. park Poland 47 R6
Pieninský nat. park Slovakia 47 R6
Pierce U.S.A. 130 D3
Pierce Lake Canada 121 M4
Pierceland Canada 121 I4
Pierceton U.S.A. 134 C3
Pieria mts Greece 59 J4
Pierowall U.K. 50 G1
Pierpont U.S.A. 134 E3

▶Pierre U.S.A. 130 C2
State capital of South Dakota.

Pierrelatte France 56 G4
Pietermaritzburg S. Africa 101 J5
Pietersaari Fin. see Jakobstad
Pietersburg S. Africa 101 I2
Pie Town U.S.A. 129 I4
Pietra Spada, Passo di pass Italy 58 G5
Piet Retief S. Africa 101 J4
Pietrosa mt. Romania 59 K1
Pigeon U.S.A. 134 D2
Pigeon Bay Canada 134 D3
Pigeon Lake Canada 120 H4
Piggott U.S.A. 131 F4
Pigg's Peak Swaziland 101 J3
Pigs, Bay of Cuba 133 D8
Pihij India 82 C5
Pihkva järv l. Estonia/Rus. Fed. see Pskov, Lake
Pihlajavesi l. Fin. 44 P6
Pihlava Fin. 45 L6
Pihtipudas Fin. 44 N5
Piippola Fin. 44 N4
Piispajärvi Fin. 44 P4
Pikalevo Rus. Fed. 42 G4
Pike U.S.A. 134 E4
Pike Bay Canada 134 E1
Pikelot i. Micronesia 69 L5
Pikes Peak U.S.A. 126 G5
Piketon U.S.A. 134 D4
Pikeville KY U.S.A. 134 D5
Pikeville TN U.S.A. 132 C5
Pikinni atoll Marshall Is see Bikini
Piła Poland 47 P4
Pilanesberg National Park S. Africa 101 H3
Pilar Arg. 144 E4
Pilar Para. 144 E3
Pilar de Goiás Brazil 145 A1
Pilaya r. Bol. 142 F8
Pilcomayo r. Bol./Para. 142 F8
Piler India 84 C3
Pili, Cerro mt. Chile 144 C2
Pilibangan India 82 C3
Pilibhit India 82 D3
Pilipinas country Asia see Philippines
Pillau Rus. Fed. see Baltiysk
Pillcopata Peru 142 D6
Pilliga Australia 112 D3
Pillsbury, Lake U.S.A. 128 B2
Pil'na Rus. Fed. 42 J5
Pil'nya, Ozero l. Rus. Fed. 42 M1
Pilões, Serra dos mts Brazil 145 B2
Pilos Greece see Pylos
Pilot Knob mt. U.S.A. 126 E3
Pilot Peak U.S.A. 128 E2
Pilot Station U.S.A. 118 B3
Pilsen Czech Rep. see Plzeň
Piltene Latvia 45 L8
Pil'tun, Zaliv lag. Rus. Fed. 74 F1
Pilu Pak. 89 H5
Pima U.S.A. 129 I5
Pimenta Bueno Brazil 142 F6
Pimento U.S.A. 134 B4
Pimpalner India 84 B1
Pin r. India 82 D2
Pin r. Myanmar 70 A2
Pinahat India 82 D4
Pinaleno Mountains U.S.A. 129 H5
Pinamar Arg. 144 E5
Pinang Malaysia see George Town
Pinang i. Malaysia 71 C6
Pınarbaşı Turkey 90 E3
Pinar del Río Cuba 137 H4
Pinarhisar Turkey 59 L4
Piñas Ecuador 142 C4
Pincher Creek Canada 120 H5
Pinckneyville U.S.A. 130 F4
Pinconning U.S.A. 134 D2
Pińczów Poland 47 R5
Pindaí Brazil 145 C1
Pindamonhangaba Brazil 145 B3
Pindar Australia 109 A7
Pindaré r. Brazil 143 J4
Píndhos Óros mts Greece see Pindus Mountains
Pindos mts Greece see Pindus Mountains
Pindrei India 82 E5
Pindus Mountains Greece 59 I5
Pine watercourse Australia 111 C7
Pine r. MI U.S.A. 134 C1
Pine r. MI U.S.A. 134 C2
Pine r. WI U.S.A. 131 E5
Pine Bluffs U.S.A. 126 G4
Pine Creek Australia 108 E3
Pine Creek r. U.S.A. 135 G3
Pinecrest U.S.A. 128 C2
Pinedale NM U.S.A. 129 I4
Pinedale WY U.S.A. 126 F4
Pine Dock Canada 121 L5
Pine Falls Canada 121 L5
Pine Flat Lake U.S.A. 128 D3
Pinega Rus. Fed. 42 I2
Pinega r. Rus. Fed. 42 I2
Pinegrove Australia 109 A6
Pine Grove U.S.A. 135 G3
Pine Hills CA U.S.A. 128 E4
Pine Hills FL U.S.A. 133 D6
Pinehouse Lake Canada 121 J4
Pinehouse Lake l. Canada 121 J4
Pineimuta r. Canada 121 N4
Pineios r. Greece 59 J5
Pine Island Bay Antarctica 151 N10
Pine Island Glacier Antarctica 152 K1
Pine Islands FL U.S.A. 133 D7
Pine Islands FL U.S.A. 133 D7
Pine Knot U.S.A. 134 C5
Pineland U.S.A. 131 E6
Pine Mountain U.S.A. 128 C4
Pine Peak U.S.A. 129 G4
Pine Point Canada 120 H2
Pine Point pt Canada 120 H2
Pineridge U.S.A. 128 D3
Pine Ridge U.S.A. 130 C3
Pinerolo Italy 58 B2
Pines, Isle of i. Cuba see La Juventud, Isla de
Pines, Isle of i. New Caledonia see Pins, Île des
Pinetop U.S.A. 129 I4
Pinetown S. Africa 101 J5
Pine Valley U.S.A. 135 G2
Pineville KY U.S.A. 134 D5
Pineville MO U.S.A. 131 E4
Pineville WV U.S.A. 134 E5
Ping, Mae Nam r. Thai. 70 C4
Ping'an China 72 I5
Ping'anyi China see Ping'an
Pingba China 76 E3
Pingbian China 76 D4
Ping Dao i. China 77 H1
Pingdingbu China see Guyuan
Pingdingshan China 77 G1
Pingdong Taiwan see P'ingtung
Pingdu Jiangxi China see Anfu
Pingdu Shandong China 73 L5
Pinggang China 74 B4
Pinghe China 77 H3
Pinghu China see Pingtang
Pingjiang China 77 G2
Pingjinpu China 76 E2
Pingle China 77 F3
Pingli China 77 F1
Pingliang China 76 E1
Pinglu China 77 F1
Pingma China see Tiandong
Pingnan China 77 H3
Pingqiao China 77 G1
Pingshan Sichuan China 76 E2
Pingshan Yunnan China see Luquan
Pingshi China 77 G3
Pingtan China 77 H3
Pingtan Dao i. China see Haitan Dao
Pingtang China 76 E3
P'ingtung Taiwan 77 I4
Pingxi China see Yuping
Pingxiang Guangxi China 76 E4
Pingxiang Jiangxi China 77 G3
Pingyang Heilong. China 74 B2
Pingyang Zhejiang China 77 I3
Pingyi China 77 H1
Pingyu China 77 G1
Pingyuanjie China 76 D4
Pingzhai China 77 F3
Pinhal Brazil 145 B3
Pinheiro Brazil 143 I4
Pinhoe U.K. 49 D8
Pini i. Indon. 68 B6
Piniós r. Greece see Pineios
Pinjin Australia 109 C7
Pink Mountain Canada 120 F3
Pinlaung Myanmar 70 B2
Pinlebu Myanmar 70 A1
Pinnacle hill U.S.A. 135 F4
Pinnacles National Monument nat. park U.S.A. 128 C3
Pinnau r. Germany 53 J1
Pinneberg Germany 53 J1
Pinnes, Akra pt Greece 59 K4
Pinos, Isla de i. Cuba see La Juventud, Isla de
Pinos, Mount U.S.A. 128 D4
Pinotepa Nacional Mex. 136 E5
Pins, Île des i. New Caledonia 107 G4
Pins, Pointe aux pt Canada 134 E2
Pinsk Belarus 45 O10
Pinta, Sierra hill U.S.A. 129 G5
Pintada Creek watercourse U.S.A. 127 G6
Pintados Chile 144 C2
Pintura U.S.A. 129 G3
Pioche U.S.A. 129 F3
Piodi Dem. Rep. Congo 99 C4
Pioneer Mountains U.S.A. 126 E3
Pioner, Ostrov i. Rus. Fed. 64 K2
Pionerskiy Kaliningradskaya Oblast' Rus. Fed. 45 L9
Pionerskiy Khanty-Mansiyskiy Autonomnyy Okrug Rus. Fed. 41 S3
Pionki Poland 47 R5
Piopio N.Z. 113 E4
Piopiotahi inlet N.Z. see Milford Sound
Piorini, Lago l. Brazil 142 F4
Piotrków Trybunalski Poland 47 Q5
Pipa Dingzi mt. China 74 C4
Pipar India 82 C4
Pipar Road India 82 C4
Piperi i. Greece 59 K5
Piper Peak U.S.A. 128 E3
Pipestone Canada 121 K5
Pipestone r. Canada 121 N4
Pipestone U.S.A. 130 D3
Pipli India 82 C3
Pipmuacan, Réservoir resr Canada 123 H4
Piqua U.S.A. 134 C3
Piquiri r. Brazil 145 A4
Pira Benin 96 D4
Piracanjuba Brazil 145 A2
Piracicaba Brazil 145 B3
Piracicaba r. Brazil 145 C2
Piraçununga Brazil 145 B3
Piracuruca Brazil 143 J4
Piraeus Greece 59 J6
Piraí do Sul Brazil 145 A4
Piráievs Greece see Piraeus
Piraju Brazil 145 A3
Pirajuí Brazil 145 A3
Pirallahı Adası Azer. 91 H2
Piranhas Bahia Brazil 145 C1
Piranhas Goiás Brazil 143 H7
Piranhas r. Rio Grande do Norte Brazil 143 K5
Piranhas r. Brazil 145 A2
Pirapora Brazil 145 B2
Piraube, Lac l. Canada 123 H4
Pirawa India 82 D4
Pirenópolis Brazil 145 A1
Pires do Rio Brazil 145 A2
Pírgos Greece see Pyrgos
Pirin nat. park Bulg. 59 J4
Pirineos mts Europe see Pyrenees
Piripiri Brazil 143 J4
Pirlerkondu Turkey see Taşkent
Pirmasens Germany 53 H5
Pirojpur Bangl. 83 G5
Pir Panjal Pass Jammu and Kashmir 82 C2
Pir Panjal Range mts India/Pak. 89 I3
Piryatin Ukr. see Pyryatyn
Pirzada Afgh. 89 G4
Pisa Italy 58 D3
Pisae Italy see Pisa
Pisagua Chile 142 D7
Pisang, Kepulauan is Indon. 69 I7
Pisaurum Italy see Pesaro
Pisco Peru 142 C6
Písek Czech Rep. 47 O6
Pisha China see Ningnan
Pishan China 82 D1
Pīshīn Iran 89 F5
Pishin Pak. 89 G4
Pishin Lora r. Pak. 89 G4
Pishpek Kyrg. see Bishkek
Pisidia reg. Turkey 90 C3

▶Pissis, Cerro Arg. 144 C3
4th highest mountain in South America.

Pisté Mex. 136 G4
Pisticci Italy 58 G4
Pistoia Italy 58 D3
Pistoriae Italy see Pistoia
Pisuerga r. Spain 57 D3
Pita Guinea 96 B3
Pitaga Canada 123 I3
Pitanga Brazil 145 A4
Pitangui Brazil 145 B2
Pitar India 82 B5
Pitarpunga Lake imp. l. Australia 112 A5
Pitcairn, Henderson, Ducie and Oeno Islands terr. S. Pacific Ocean see Pitcairn Islands
Pitcairn Island Pitcairn Is 151 L7

▶Pitcairn Islands terr. S. Pacific Ocean 151 L7
United Kingdom Overseas Territory.
Oceania 8, 104–105

Piteå Sweden 44 L4
Piteälven r. Sweden 44 L4
Pitelino Rus. Fed. 43 I5
Piterka Rus. Fed. 43 J6
Piteşti Romania 59 K2
Pithoragarh India 82 E3
Pitihra India 82 D5
Pitiquito Mex. 127 E7
Pitkyaranta Rus. Fed. 42 F3
Pitlochry U.K. 50 F4
Pitong China see Pixian
Pitsane Siding Botswana 101 G3
Pitti i. India 84 B4
Pitt Island Canada 120 D4
Pitt Island N.Z. 107 I6
Pitt Islands Solomon Is see Vanikoro Islands
Pittsboro U.S.A. 131 F5
Pittsburg KS U.S.A. 131 E4
Pittsburg TX U.S.A. 131 E5
Pittsburgh U.S.A. 134 F3
Pittsfield MA U.S.A. 135 I2
Pittsfield ME U.S.A. 135 K1
Pittsfield VT U.S.A. 135 I2
Pittston U.S.A. 135 H3
Pittsworth Australia 112 E1
Pitz Lake Canada 121 L2
Piumhí Brazil 145 B3
Piura Peru 142 B5
Piute Mountains U.S.A. 129 F4
Piute Peak U.S.A. 128 D4
Piute Reservoir U.S.A. 129 G2
Piuthan Nepal 83 E3
Pivabiska r. Canada 122 E4
Pivka Slovenia 58 F2
Pixariá mt. Greece see Pyxaria
Pixian China 76 D2
Pixley U.S.A. 128 D4
Piz Bernina mt. Italy/Switz. 58 C1
Piz Buin mt. Austria/Switz. 47 M7
Pizhanka Rus. Fed. 42 K4
Pizhi Nigeria 96 D4
Pizhma Rus. Fed. 42 J4
Pizhma r. Rus. Fed. 42 K4
Pizhma r. Rus. Fed. 42 L2
Pizhou China 77 H1
Placentia Canada 123 L5
Placentia Italy see Piacenza
Placentia Bay Canada 123 L5
Placerville CA U.S.A. 128 C2
Placerville CO U.S.A. 129 I2
Placetas Cuba 133 E8
Plácido de Castro Brazil 142 E6
Plain Dealing U.S.A. 131 E5

Plainfield CT U.S.A. 135 J3
Plainfield IN U.S.A. 134 B4
Plainfield VT U.S.A. 135 I1
Plains KS U.S.A. 131 C4
Plains TX U.S.A. 131 C5
Plainview U.S.A. 131 C5
Plainville IN U.S.A. 134 B4
Plainville KS U.S.A. 130 D4
Plainwell U.S.A. 134 C2
Plaka, Akra pt Greece 59 L7
Plakoti, Cape Cyprus 85 B2
Plamondon Canada 121 H4
Planá Czech Rep. 53 M5
Plana Cays is Bahamas 133 F8
Planada U.S.A. 128 C3
Planaltina Brazil 145 B1
Plane r. Germany 53 M2
Plankinton U.S.A. 130 D3
Plano U.S.A. 131 D5
Planura Brazil 145 A3
Plaquemine U.S.A. 131 F6
Plasencia Spain 57 C3
Plaster City U.S.A. 129 F5
Plaster Rock Canada 123 I5
Plastun Rus. Fed. 74 E3
Platani r. Sicily Italy 58 E6
Platberg mt. S. Africa 101 I5

▶Plateau Antarctica
Lowest recorded annual mean temperature in the world.
World 16-17

Plateau of Tibet China 83 F2
Platina U.S.A. 128 B1
Platinum U.S.A. 153 B3
Plato Col. 142 D2
Platte r. U.S.A. 130 E3
Platte City U.S.A. 130 E4
Plattling Germany 53 M6
Plattsburgh U.S.A. 135 I1
Plattsmouth U.S.A. 130 E3
Plau Germany 53 M1
Plauen Germany 53 M4
Plauer See l. Germany 53 M1
Plavsk Rus. Fed. 43 H5
Playa Noriega, Lago l. Mex. 127 F7
Playas Ecuador 142 B4
Playas Lake U.S.A. 129 I6
Plây Cu Vietnam 71 E4
Pleasant, Lake U.S.A. 129 G5
Pleasant Bay U.S.A. 135 K3
Pleasant Grove U.S.A. 129 H1
Pleasant Hill Lake U.S.A. 134 D3
Pleasanton U.S.A. 131 D6
Pleasant Point N.Z. 113 C7
Pleasantville U.S.A. 135 H4
Pleasure Ridge Park U.S.A. 134 C4
Pleaux France 56 F4
Pledger Lake Canada 122 E4
Plei Doch Vietnam 71 D4
Pleinfeld Germany 53 K5
Pleiße r. Germany 53 M3
Plenty watercourse Australia 110 B5
Plenty, Bay of g. N.Z. 113 F3
Plentywood U.S.A. 126 G2
Plesetsk Rus. Fed. 42 I3
Pleshchentsy Belarus see Plyeshchanitsy
Pletipi, Lac l. Canada 123 H4
Plettenberg Germany 53 H3
Plettenberg Bay S. Africa 100 F8
Pleven Bulg. 59 K3
Plevna Bulg. see Pleven
Pljevlja Serb. and Mont. 59 H3
Płock Poland 47 Q4
Pločno mt. Bos.-Herz. 58 G3
Plodovoye Rus. Fed. 42 F3
Ploemeur France 56 C3
Ploești Romania see Ploiești
Ploiești Romania 59 L2
Plomb du Cantal mt. France 56 F4
Ploskoye Rus. Fed. see Stanovoye
Płoty Poland 47 O4
Ploudalmézeau France 56 B2
Plouzané France 56 B2
Plovdiv Bulg. 59 K3
Plover Cove Reservoir Hong Kong China 77 [inset]
Płozk Poland see Płock
Plum U.S.A. 134 F3
Plumridge Lakes salt flat Australia 109 D7
Plungė Lith. 45 L9
Plutarco Elías Calles, Presa resr Mex. 127 F7
Pluto, Lac l. Canada 123 H3
Plyeshchanitsy Belarus 45 O9
Ply Huey Wati, Khao mt. Myanmar/Thai. 70 B3

▶Plymouth Montserrat 137 L5
Capital of Montserrat, largely abandoned in 1997 owing to volcanic activity.

Plymouth U.K. 49 C8
Plymouth CA U.S.A. 128 C2
Plymouth IN U.S.A. 134 B3
Plymouth MA U.S.A. 135 J3
Plymouth NC U.S.A. 132 E5
Plymouth NH U.S.A. 135 J2
Plymouth WI U.S.A. 134 B2
Plymouth Bay U.S.A. 135 J3
Plynlimon hill U.K. 49 D6
Plyussa Rus. Fed. 45 P7
Plzeň Czech Rep. 47 N6
Pô Burkina 96 C3
Po r. Italy 58 E2
Pô, Parc National de nat. park Burkina 96 C3
Pobeda Peak China/Kyrg. 80 F3
Pobedy, Pik mt. China/Kyrg. see Pobeda Peak
Pocahontas U.S.A. 131 F4
Pocatello U.S.A. 126 E4
Pochala Sudan 97 G4
Pochayiv Ukr. 43 E6
Pochep Rus. Fed. 43 G5
Pochinki Rus. Fed. 43 J5
Pochinok Rus. Fed. 43 G5
Pochutla Mex. 136 E5
Pocking Germany 47 N6
Pocklington U.K. 48 G5
Poções Brazil 145 C1
Pocomoke City U.S.A. 135 H4
Pocomoke Sound b. U.S.A. 135 H5
Poconé Brazil 143 G7
Pocono Mountains hills U.S.A. 135 H3
Pocono Summit U.S.A. 135 H3
Poços de Caldas Brazil 145 B3
Podanur India 84 C4
Poddor'ye Rus. Fed. 42 F4
Podgorenskiy Rus. Fed. 43 H6
Podgorica Serb. and Mont. 59 H3
Podgornoye Rus. Fed. 64 J4
Podile India 84 C3
Podișul Transilvaniei plat. Romania see Transylvanian Basin
Podkamennaya Tunguska r. Rus. Fed. 65 K3
Podocarpus, Parque Nacional nat. park Ecuador 142 C4
Podol'sk Rus. Fed. 43 H5
Podporozh'ye Rus. Fed. 42 G3
Podujevë Serb. and Mont. see Podujevo
Podujevo Serb. and Mont. 59 I3
Podz' Rus. Fed. 42 K3
Poelela, Lagoa l. Moz. 101 L3
Poeppel Corner salt flat Australia 111 B5
Poetovio Slovenia see Ptuj
Pofadder S. Africa 100 D5
Pogar Rus. Fed. 43 G5
Poggibonsi Italy 58 D3
Poggio di Montieri mt. Italy 58 D3
Pogradec Albania 59 I4
Pogranichnik Afgh. 89 F3
Po Hai g. China see Bo Hai
P'ohang S. Korea 75 C5
Pohnpei atoll Micronesia 150 G5
Pohri India 82 D4
Poi India 83 H4
Poiana Mare Romania 59 J3
Poinsett, Cape Antarctica 152 F2
Point Arena U.S.A. 128 B2
Point au Fer Island U.S.A. 131 F6
Pointe a la Hache U.S.A. 131 F6
Pointe-à-Pitre Guadeloupe 137 L5
Pointe-Noire Congo 99 B4
Point Hope U.S.A. 118 B3
Point Lake Canada 120 H1
Point of Rocks U.S.A. 126 F4
Point Pelee National Park Canada 134 D3
Point Pleasant NJ U.S.A. 135 H3
Point Pleasant WV U.S.A. 134 D4
Poitiers France 56 E3
Poitou reg. France 56 E3
Poix-de-Picardie France 52 B5
Pojuca r. Brazil 145 D1
Pokaran India 82 B4
Pokataroo Australia 112 D2
Pokcha Rus. Fed. 41 R3
Pokhara Nepal 83 E3
Pokhvistnevo Rus. Fed. 41 Q5
Pok Liu Chau i. Hong Kong China see Lamma Island
Poko Dem. Rep. Congo 98 C3
Pokosnoye Rus. Fed. 72 I1
Pokran Pak. 89 G5
P'ok'r Kovkas mts Asia see Lesser Caucasus
Pokrovka Chitinskaya Oblast' Rus. Fed. 74 A1
Pokrovka Primorskiy Kray Rus. Fed. 74 C4
Pokrovsk Respublika Sakha (Yakutiya) Rus. Fed. 65 N3
Pokrovsk Saratovskaya Oblast' Rus. Fed. see Engel's
Pokrovskoye Rus. Fed. 43 H7
Pokshen'ga r. Rus. Fed. 42 J3
Pol India 82 C5
Pola Croatia see Pula
Polacca Wash watercourse U.S.A. 129 H4
Pola de Lena Spain 57 D2
Pola de Siero Spain 57 D2
▶Poland country Europe 40 J5
Europe 5, 38-39
Poland NY U.S.A. 135 H2
Poland OH U.S.A. 134 E3
Polar Plateau Antarctica 152 A1
Polatlı Turkey 90 D3
Polatsk Belarus 45 P9
Polavaram India 84 D2
Polcirkeln Sweden 44 L3
Pol-e Fāsā Iran 88 D4
Pole-Khatum Iran 89 F2
Pol-e Khomrī Afgh. 89 H3
Pol-e Safīd Iran 88 D2
Polessk Rus. Fed. 45 L9
Poles'ye marsh Belarus/Ukr. see Pripet Marshes
Polgahawela Sri Lanka 84 D5
Poli Cyprus see Polis
Políaigos i. Greece see Polyaigos
Police Poland 47 O4
Policoro Italy 58 G4
Poligny France 56 G3
Políkastron Greece see Polykastro
Polillo Islands Phil. 69 G3
Polis Cyprus 85 A2
Polis'ke Ukr. 43 F6
Polis'kyy Zapovidnyk nature res. Ukr. 43 F6
Politovo Rus. Fed. 42 K2
Políyiros Greece see Polygyros
Polkowice Poland 47 P5
Pollachi India 84 C4
Pollard Islands U.S.A. see Gardner Pinnacles
Polle Germany 53 J3
Pollino, Monte mt. Italy 58 G5
Pollino, Parco Nazionale del nat. park Italy 58 G5
Pollock Pines U.S.A. 128 C2
Pollock Reef Australia 109 C8
Polmak Norway 44 O1
Polnovat Rus. Fed. 41 T3
Polo Fin. 44 P4
Poloat atoll Micronesia see Puluwat
Pologi Ukr. see Polohy
Polohy Ukr. 43 H7
Polonne Ukr. 43 E6
Polonnoye Ukr. see Polonne
Polotsk Belarus see Polatsk
Polperro U.K. 49 C8
Polska country Europe see Poland
Polson U.S.A. 126 E3
Polta r. Rus. Fed. 42 I2
Poltava Ukr. 43 G6
Poltoratsk Turkm. see Ashgabat
Põltsamaa Estonia 45 N7
Polunochnoye Rus. Fed. 41 S3
Põlva Estonia 45 O7
Polvadera U.S.A. 127 G6
Polvijärvi Fin. 44 P5
Polyaigos i. Greece 59 K6
Polyanovgrad Bulg. see Karnobat
Polyarnyy Chukotskiy Avtonomnyy Okrug Rus. Fed. 65 S3
Polyarnyy Murmanskaya Oblast' Rus. Fed. 44 R2
Polyarnyye Zori Rus. Fed. 44 R3
Polyarnyy Ural mts Rus. Fed. 41 S2
Polygyros Greece 59 J4
Polykastro Greece 59 J4
Polynesia is Pacific Ocean 150 I6
Polynésie Française terr. S. Pacific Ocean see French Polynesia
Pom Indon. 69 J7
Pomarkku Fin. 45 M6
Pombal Pará Brazil 143 H4
Pombal Paraíba Brazil 143 K5
Pombal Port. 57 B4
Pomene Moz. 101 L2
Pomeroy S. Africa 101 J5
Pomeroy U.K. 51 F3
Pomeroy OH U.S.A. 134 D4
Pomeroy WA U.S.A. 126 D3
Pomezia Italy 58 E4
Pomfret S. Africa 100 F3
Pomona Namibia 100 B4
Pomona U.S.A. 128 E4
Pomorie Bulg. 59 L3
Pomorska, Zatoka b. Poland 47 O3
Pomorskie, Pojezierze reg. Poland 47 O4
Pomorskiy Bereg coastal area Rus. Fed. 42 G2
Pomorskiy Proliv sea chan. Rus. Fed. 42 K1
Pomos Point Cyprus 85 A2
Pomo Tso l. China see Puma Yumco
Pomou, Akra pt Cyprus see Pomos Point
Pomozdino Rus. Fed. 42 L3
Pompain China 76 B2
Pompano Beach U.S.A. 133 D7
Pompei Italy 58 F4
Pompéia Brazil 145 A3
Pompey France 52 G6
Pompeyevka Rus. Fed. 74 C2
Ponape atoll Micronesia see Pohnpei
Ponask Lake Canada 121 M4
Ponazyrevo Rus. Fed. 42 J4
Ponca City U.S.A. 131 D4
Ponce Puerto Rico 137 K5
Ponce de Leon Bay U.S.A. 133 D7
Poncheville, Lac l. Canada 122 F4
Pondicherry India 84 C4
Pondicherry union terr. India 84 C4
Pondichéry India see Pondicherry
Pond Inlet Canada 153 K2
Ponds Bay Canada see Pond Inlet
Ponente, Riviera di coastal area Italy 58 B3
Poneto U.S.A. 134 C3
Ponferrada Spain 57 C2
Pongara, Pointe pt Gabon 98 A3
Pongaroa N.Z. 113 F5
Pongo watercourse Sudan 97 F4
Pongola r. S. Africa 101 K4
Pongolapoort Dam l. S. Africa 101 J4
Ponnagyun Myanmar 70 A2
Ponnaivar r. India 84 C4
Ponnampet India 84 B3
Ponnani India 84 B4
Ponnyadaung Range mts Myanmar 70 A2
Pono Indon. 69 I8
Ponoka Canada 120 H4
Ponoy r. Rus. Fed. 42 I2
Pons r. Canada 123 H2

▶Ponta Delgada Arquipélago dos Açores 148 G3
Capital of the Azores.

Ponta Grossa Brazil 145 A4
Pontal Brazil 145 A3
Pontalina Brazil 145 A2
Pont-à-Mousson France 52 G6
Ponta Porã Brazil 144 E2
Pontarfynach U.K. see Devil's Bridge
Pont-Audemer France 49 H9
Pontault-Combault France 52 C6
Pontax r. Canada 122 F4
Pontchartrain, Lake U.S.A. 131 F6
Pont-de-Loup Belgium 52 E4
Ponte Alta do Norte Brazil 143 I6
Ponte de Sor Port. 57 B4
Ponte Firme Brazil 145 B2
Pontefract U.K. 48 F5
Ponteix Canada 121 J5
Ponteland U.K. 48 F3
Ponte Nova Brazil 145 C3
Pontes-e-Lacerda Brazil 143 G7
Pontevedra Spain 57 B2
Ponthierville Dem. Rep. Congo see Ubundu
Pontiac IL U.S.A. 130 F3
Pontiac MI U.S.A. 134 D2
Pontiae is Italy see Ponziane, Isole
Pontianak Indon. 68 D7
Pontine Islands is Italy see Ponziane, Isole
Pont-l'Abbé France 56 B3
Pontoise France 52 C5
Ponton watercourse Australia 105 C7
Ponton Canada 121 L4
Pontotoc U.S.A. 131 F5
Pont-Ste-Maxence France 52 C5
Pontypool U.K. 49 D7
Pontypridd U.K. 49 D7
Ponza, Isola di i. Italy 58 E4
Ponziane, Isole is Italy 58 E4
Poochera Australia 109 F8
Poole U.K. 49 F8
Poole U.S.A. 134 B5
Poolowanna Lake salt flat Australia 111 B5
Poona India see Pune
Pooncarie Australia 111 C7
Poonch India see Punch
Poopelloe, Lake salt l. Australia 112 B3
Poopó, Lago de l. Bol. 142 E7
Poor Knights Islands N.Z. 113 E2
Popayán Col. 142 C3
Poperinge Belgium 52 C4
Popigay r. Rus. Fed. 65 L2
Popiltah Australia 111 C7
Popilta Lake imp. l. Australia 111 C7
Poplar r. Canada 121 L4
Poplar U.S.A. 126 G2
Poplar Bluff U.S.A. 131 F4
Poplar Camp U.S.A. 134 E5
Poplarville U.S.A. 131 F6

▶Popocatépetl, Volcán vol. Mex. 136 E5
5th highest mountain in North America.

Popokabaka Dem. Rep. Congo 99 B4
Popondetta P.N.G. 69 L8
Popovichskaya Rus. Fed. see Kalininskaya
Popovo Bulg. 59 L3
Popovo Polje plain Bos.-Herz. 58 G3
Poppberg hill Germany 53 L5
Poppenberg hill Germany 53 K3
Poprad Slovakia 47 R6
Poquoson U.S.A. 135 G5
Porali r. Pak. 89 G5
Porangahau N.Z. 113 F5
Porangatu Brazil 145 A1
Porbandar India 82 B5
Porcher Island Canada 120 D4
Porcos r. Brazil 145 B1
Porcupine, Cape Canada 123 K3
Porcupine Abyssal Plain sea feature N. Atlantic Ocean 148 G2
Porcupine Gorge National Park Australia 110 D4
Porcupine Hills Canada 121 K4
Porcupine Mountains U.S.A. 130 F2
Poreč Croatia 58 E2
Porecatu Brazil 145 A3
Poretskoye Rus. Fed. 43 J5
Pori Fin. 45 L6
Porirua N.Z. 113 E5
Porkhov Rus. Fed. 45 P8
Porlamar Venez. 142 F1
Pormpuraaw Australia 110 C2
Pornic France 56 C3
Poronaysk Rus. Fed. 74 F2
Porong China see Baingoin
Poros Greece 59 J6
Porosozero Rus. Fed. 42 G3
Porpoise Bay Antarctica 152 G2
Porsangen sea chan. Norway 44 N1
Porsangerhalvøya pen. Norway 44 N1
Porsgrunn Norway 45 F7
Porsuk r. Turkey 59 N5
Portadown U.K. 51 F3
Portaferry U.K. 51 G3
Portage MI U.S.A. 134 C2
Portage PA U.S.A. 135 F3
Portage WI U.S.A. 130 F3
Portage Lakes U.S.A. 134 E3
Portage la Prairie Canada 121 L5
Portal U.S.A. 130 C1
Port Alberni Canada 120 E5
Port Albert Australia 112 C7
Portalegre Port. 57 C4
Portales U.S.A. 131 C5
Port-Alfred Canada see La Baie
Port Alfred S. Africa 101 H7
Port Alice Canada 120 E5
Port Allegany U.S.A. 135 F3
Port Allen U.S.A. 131 F6
Port Alma Australia 110 E4
Port Angeles U.S.A. 126 C2
Port Antonio Jamaica 137 I5
Portarlington Rep. of Ireland 51 E4
Port Arthur Australia 111 [inset]
Port Arthur U.S.A. 131 E6
Port Askaig U.K. 50 C5
Port Augusta Australia 111 B7

▶Port-au-Prince Haiti 137 J5
Capital of Haiti.

Port Austin U.S.A. 134 D1
Port aux Choix Canada 123 K4
Portavogie U.K. 51 G3
Port Beaufort S. Africa 100 E8
Port Blair India 71 A5
Port Bolster Canada 134 F1
Portbou Spain 57 H2
Port Burwell Canada 134 E2
Port Campbell Australia 112 A7
Port Campbell National Park Australia 112 A7
Port Carling Canada 134 F1
Port-Cartier Canada 123 I4
Port Chalmers N.Z. 113 C7
Port Charlotte U.S.A. 133 D7
Port Clements Canada 120 C4
Port Clinton U.S.A. 134 D3
Port Credit Canada 134 F2
Port-de-Paix Haiti 137 J5
Port Dickson Malaysia 71 C7
Port Douglas Australia 110 D3
Port Edward Canada 120 D4
Port Edward S. Africa 101 J6
Porteira Brazil 143 G4
Porteirinha Brazil 145 C1
Portel Brazil 143 H4
Port Elgin Canada 134 E1
Port Elizabeth S. Africa 101 G7
Port Ellen U.K. 50 C5
Port Erin Isle of Man 48 C4
Porter Lake N.W.T. Canada 121 J2
Porter Lake Sask. Canada 121 J3
Porter Landing Canada 120 D3
Porterville S. Africa 100 D7
Porterville U.S.A. 128 D3
Port Étienne Mauritania see Nouâdhibou
Port Everglades U.S.A. see Fort Lauderdale
Port Fitzroy N.Z. 113 E3
Port Francqui Dem. Rep. Congo see Ilebo
Port-Gentil Gabon 98 A4
Port Glasgow U.K. 50 E5
Port Harcourt Nigeria 96 D4
Port Harrison Canada see Inukjuak
Porthcawl U.K. 49 D7
Port Hedland Australia 108 B5
Port Henry U.S.A. 135 I1
Port Herald Malawi see Nsanje
Porthleven U.K. 49 B8
Porthmadog U.K. 49 C6
Port Hope Canada 135 F2
Port Hope Simpson Canada 123 L3
Port Hueneme U.S.A. 128 D4
Port Huron U.S.A. 134 D2
Portimão Port. 57 B5
Port Jackson Australia see Sydney
Port Jackson inlet Australia 112 E4
Port Keats Australia see Wadeye
Port Klang Malaysia see Pelabuhan Kelang
Port Láirge Rep. of Ireland see Waterford
Portland N.S.W. Australia 112 D4
Portland Vic. Australia 111 C8
Portland IN U.S.A. 134 C3
Portland ME U.S.A. 135 J2
Portland MI U.S.A. 134 C2
Portland OR U.S.A. 126 C3
Portland TN U.S.A. 134 B5
Portland, Isle of pen. U.K. 49 E8
Portland Bill hd U.K. see Bill of Portland
Portland Creek Pond l. Canada 123 K4
Portland Roads Australia 110 C2
Port-la-Nouvelle France 56 F5
Portlaoise Rep. of Ireland 51 E4
Port Lavaca U.S.A. 131 D6
Portlaw Rep. of Ireland 51 E5
Portlethen U.K. 50 G3
Port Lincoln Australia 111 A7
Port Loko Sierra Leone 96 B4

▶Port Louis Mauritius 149 L7
Capital of Mauritius.

Port-Lyautrey Morocco see Kénitra
Port Macquarie Australia 112 F3
Portmadoc U.K. see Porthmadog
Port McNeill Canada 120 E5
Port-Menier Canada 123 I4

▶Port Moresby P.N.G. 69 L8
Capital of Papua New Guinea.

Portnaguran U.K. 50 C2
Portnahaven U.K. 50 C5
Port nan Giúran U.K. see Portnaguran
Port Neill Australia 111 B7
Port Ness U.K. 50 C2
Portneuf r. Canada 123 H4
Port Nis U.K. see Port Ness
Port Noarlunga Australia 111 B7
Port Nolloth S. Africa 100 C5
Port Norris U.S.A. 135 H4
Port-Nouveau-Québec Canada see Kangiqsualujjuaq
Porto Port. see Oporto
Porto Acre Brazil 142 E5
Porto Alegre Brazil 145 A5
Porto Alexandre Angola see Tombua
Porto Amboim Angola 99 B5
Porto Amélia Moz. see Pemba
Porto Artur Brazil 143 G6
Porto Belo Brazil 145 A4
Porto de Moz Brazil 143 H4
Porto de Santa Cruz Brazil 145 C1
Porto dos Gaúchos Óbidos Brazil 143 G6
Porto Esperança Brazil 143 G7
Porto Esperidião Brazil 143 G7
Portoferraio Italy 58 D3
Porto Franco Brazil 143 I5

▶Port of Spain Trin. and Tob. 137 L6
Capital of Trinidad and Tobago.

Porto Grande Brazil 143 H3
Portogruaro Italy 58 E2
Porto Jofre Brazil 143 G7
Portola U.S.A. 128 C2
Portomaggiore Italy 58 D2
Porto Mendes Brazil 144 F2
Porto Murtinho Brazil 144 E2
Porto Nacional Brazil 143 I6

▶Porto-Novo Benin 96 D4
Capital of Benin.

Porto Novo Cape Verde 96 [inset]
Porto Primavera, Represa resr Brazil 144 F2
Port Orchard U.S.A. 126 C3
Port Orford U.S.A. 126 B4
Porto Rico Angola 99 B4
Porto Santo, Ilha de i. Madeira 96 B1
Porto Seguro Brazil 145 D2
Porto Tolle Italy 58 E2
Porto Torres Sardinia Italy 58 C4
Porto União Brazil 145 A4
Porto-Vecchio Corsica France 56 I6
Porto Velho Brazil 142 F5
Portoviejo Ecuador 142 B4
Porto Wálter Brazil 142 D5
Portpatrick U.K. 50 D6
Port Perry Canada 135 F1
Port Phillip Bay Australia 112 B7
Port Pirie Australia 111 B7
Port Radium Canada see Echo Bay
Portreath U.K. 49 B8
Portree U.K. 50 C3
Port Rexton Canada 123 L4
Port Royal U.S.A. 135 G4
Port Royal Sound inlet U.S.A. 133 D5
Portrush U.K. 51 F2
Port Safaga Egypt see Būr Safājah
Port Said Egypt 85 A4
Portsalon Rep. of Ireland 51 E2
Port Sanilac U.S.A. 134 D2
Port Severn Canada 134 F1
Port Shepstone S. Africa 101 J6
Port Simpson Canada see Lax Kw'alaams
Portsmouth U.K. 49 F8
Portsmouth NH U.S.A. 135 J2
Portsmouth OH U.S.A. 134 D4
Portsmouth VA U.S.A. 135 G5
Portsoy U.K. 50 G3
Port Stanley Falkland Is see Stanley
Port Stephens b. Australia 112 F4
Portstewart U.K. 51 F2
Port St Joe U.S.A. 133 C6
Port St Lucie City U.S.A. 133 D7
Port St Mary Isle of Man 48 C4
Port Sudan Sudan 86 E6
Port Swettenham Malaysia see Pelabuhan Kelang
Port Talbot U.K. 49 D7
Porttipahdan tekojärvi l. Fin. 44 O2
Port Townsend U.S.A. 126 C2
▶Portugal country Europe 57 C4
Europe 5, 38-39
Portugália Angola see Chitato
Portuguese East Africa country Africa see Mozambique
Portuguese Guinea country Africa see Guinea-Bissau
Portuguese Timor country Asia see East Timor
Portuguese West Africa country Africa see Angola
Portumna Rep. of Ireland 51 D4
Portus Herculis Monoeci country Europe see Monaco
Port-Vendres France 56 F5

▶Port Vila Vanuatu 107 G3
Capital of Vanuatu.

Portville U.S.A. 135 F2
Port Vladimir Rus. Fed. 44 R2
Port Waikato N.Z. 113 E3
Port Washington U.S.A. 134 B2
Port William U.K. 50 E6
Porvenir Bol. 142 E6
Porvenir Chile 144 B8
Porvoo Fin. 45 N6
Posada Spain 57 D2
Posada de Llanera Spain see Posada
Posadas Arg. 144 E3
Posen Poland see Poznań
Posen U.S.A. 134 D1
Poseyville U.S.A. 134 B4
Poshekhon'ye Rus. Fed. 42 H4
Poshekhon'ye-Volodarsk Rus. Fed. see Poshekhon'ye
Posht-e Badam Iran 88 D3
Poshteh-ye Chaqvīr hill Iran 88 E4
Posht-e Kūh mts Iran 88 B3
Posht-e Rūd-e Zamindavar reg. Afgh. see Zamīndāvar
Posht Kūh hill Iran 88 C2
Posio Fin. 44 P3
Poso Indon. 69 G7
Posof Turkey 91 F2
Posŏng S. Korea 75 B6
Possession Island Namibia 100 B4
Pößneck Germany 53 L4
Post U.S.A. 131 C5
Postavy Belarus see Pastavy
Poste-de-la-Baleine Canada see Kuujjuarapik
Postmasburg S. Africa 100 F5
Poston U.S.A. 129 F4
Postville Canada 123 K3
Postville U.S.A. 122 C6
Post Weygand Alg. 96 D2
Postysheve Ukr. see Krasnoarmiys'k
Pota Indon. 108 C2
Pótam Mex. 127 F8
Poté Brazil 145 C2
Poteau U.S.A. 131 E5
Potegaon India 84 D2
Potentia Italy see Potenza
Potenza Italy 58 F4
Potgietersrus S. Africa 101 I3
Poth U.S.A. 131 D6
P'ot'i Georgia 91 F2
Potikal India 84 D2
Potiraguá Brazil 145 D1
Potiskum Nigeria 96 E3
Potlatch U.S.A. 126 D3
Pot Mountain U.S.A. 126 E3
Po Toi i. Hong Kong China 77 [inset]
Potomac r. U.S.A. 135 G4
Potosí Bol. 142 E7
Potosi U.S.A. 130 F4
Potosi Mountain U.S.A. 129 F4
Potrerillos Chile 144 C3
Potrero del Llano Mex. 131 B6
Potsdam Germany 53 N2
Potsdam U.S.A. 135 H1
Potter U.S.A. 130 C3
Potterne U.K. 49 E7
Potters Bar U.K. 49 G7
Potter Valley U.S.A. 128 B2
Pottstown U.S.A. 135 H3
Pottsville U.S.A. 135 G3
Pottuvil Sri Lanka 84 D5
Potwar reg. Pak. 89 I3
Pouch Cove Canada 123 L5
Poughkeepsie U.S.A. 135 I3
Poulin de Courval, Lac l. Canada 123 H4
Poulton-le-Fylde U.K. 48 E5
Pouso Alegre Brazil 145 B3
Poŭthĭsăt Cambodia 71 C4
Poŭthĭsăt, Stœng r. Cambodia 71 D4
Považská Bystrica Slovakia 47 Q6
Povenets Rus. Fed. 42 G3
Poverty Bay N.Z. 113 F4
Povlen mt. Serb. and Mont. 59 H2
Póvoa de Varzim Port. 57 B3
Povorino Rus. Fed. 43 I6
Povorotnyy, Mys hd Rus. Fed. 74 D4
Poway U.S.A. 128 E5
Powder r. U.S.A. 126 G3
Powder, South Fork r. U.S.A. 126 G4
Powder River U.S.A. 126 G4
Powell r. U.S.A. 134 D5
Powell, Lake resr U.S.A. 129 H3
Powell Lake Canada 120 E5
Powell Mountain U.S.A. 128 D2
Powell Point Bahamas 133 E7
Powell River Canada 120 E5
Powhatan AR U.S.A. 131 F4
Powhatan VA U.S.A. 135 G5
Powo China 76 C1
Pōwrize Turkm. see Firyuza
Poxoréu Brazil 143 H7
Poyang China see Boyang
Poyang Hu l. China 77 H2
Poyan Reservoir Sing. 71 [inset]
Poyarkovo Rus. Fed. 74 C2
Pozantı Turkey 90 D3

217

Rayes Peak U.S.A. 128 D4
Rayevskiy Rus. Fed. 41 Q5
Rayleigh U.K. 49 H7
Raymond U.S.A. 135 J2
Raymond Terrace Australia 112 E4
Raymondville U.S.A. 131 D7
Raymore Canada 121 J5
Rayner Glacier Antarctica 152 D2
Rayong Thai. 71 C4
Raystown Lake U.S.A. 135 F3
Raz, Pointe du pt France 56 B2
Razan Iran 88 C3
Rāzān Iran 88 C3
Razani Pak. 89 H3
Razāzah, Buḥayrat ar l. Iraq 91 F4
Razdan Armenia see Hrazdan
Razdel'naya Ukr. see Rozdil'na
Razdol'noye Rus. Fed. 74 C4
Razeh Iran 88 C3
Razgrad Bulg. 59 L3
Razim, Lacul lag. Romania 59 M2
Razisi China 76 D1
Razlog Bulg. 59 J4
Razmak Pak. 89 H3
Raz"yezd 3km Rus. Fed. see Novyy Urgal
Ré, Île de i. France 56 D3
Reading U.K. 49 G7
Reading MI U.S.A. 134 C3
Reading OH U.S.A. 134 C4
Reading PA U.S.A. 135 H3
Reagile S. Africa 101 H3
Realicó Arg. 144 D5
Réalmont France 56 F5
Reăng Kesei Cambodia 71 C4
Reate Italy see Rieti
Rebais France 52 D6
Rebecca, Lake salt flat Australia 109 C7
Rebiana Sand Sea des. Libya 97 F2
Reboly Rus. Fed. 44 Q5
Rebrikha Rus. Fed. 72 E2
Rebun-tō i. Japan 74 F3
Recherche, Archipelago of the is Australia 109 C8
Rechitsa Belarus see Rechytsa
Rechna Doab lowland Pak. 89 I4
Rechytsa Belarus 43 F5
Recife Brazil 143 L5
Recife, Cape S. Africa 101 G8
Recklinghausen Germany 53 H3
Reconquista Arg. 144 E3
Recreo Arg. 144 C3
Rectorville U.S.A. 134 D4
Red r. Australia 110 C3
Red r. Canada 120 E3
Red r. Canada/U.S.A. 130 D1
Red r. TN U.S.A. 134 B5
Red r. U.S.A. 131 F6
Red r. Vietnam 70 D2
Redang i. Malaysia 71 C6
Red Bank NJ U.S.A. 135 H3
Red Bank TN U.S.A. 133 C5
Red Basin China see Sichuan Pendi
Red Bay Canada 123 K4
Redberry Lake Canada 121 J4
Red Bluff U.S.A. 128 B1
Red Bluff Lake U.S.A. 131 C6
Red Butte mt. U.S.A. 129 G4
Redcar U.K. 48 F4
Redcliff Canada 126 F2
Redcliffe, Mount hill Australia 109 C7
Red Cliffs Australia 111 C7
Red Cloud U.S.A. 130 D3
Red Deer Canada 120 H4
Red Deer r. Alberta/Saskatchewan Canada 121 I5
Red Deer r. Man./Sask. Canada 121 K4
Red Deer Lake Canada 121 K4
Reddersburg S. Africa 101 H5
Redding U.S.A. 128 B1
Redditch U.K. 49 F6
Rede r. U.K. 48 E3
Redenção Brazil 143 H5
Redeyef Tunisia 58 C7
Redfield U.S.A. 130 D2
Red Granite Mountain Canada 120 B2
Red Hills U.S.A. 131 D4
Red Hook U.S.A. 135 I3
Red Indian Lake Canada 123 K4
Redkey U.S.A. 134 C3
Redkino Rus. Fed. 42 H4
Redknife r. Canada 120 G2
Red Lake Canada 121 M5
Red Lake U.S.A. 129 G4
Red Lake r. U.S.A. 130 D2
Red Lake Falls U.S.A. 121 L6
Red Lakes U.S.A. 130 E1
Redlands U.S.A. 128 E4
Red Lion U.S.A. 135 G4
Red Lodge U.S.A. 126 F3
Redmesa U.S.A. 129 I3
Redmond OR U.S.A. 126 C3
Redmond UT U.S.A. 129 H2
Red Oak U.S.A. 130 E3
Redonda Island Canada 120 E5
Redondo Port. 57 C4
Redondo Beach U.S.A. 128 D5
Red Peak U.S.A. 126 E3
Red River, Mouths of the Vietnam 70 D2
Red Rock Canada 122 C4
Red Rock AZ U.S.A. 129 H5
Redrock U.S.A. 129 I5
Red Rock PA U.S.A. 135 G3
Redrock Lake Canada 120 H1
Red Sea Africa/Asia 86 D4
Redstone r. Canada 120 E1
Red Sucker Lake Canada 121 M4
Reduzum Neth. see Roordahuizum
Redwater Canada 120 H4
Redway U.S.A. 128 B1
Red Wing U.S.A. 130 E2
Redwood City U.S.A. 128 B3
Redwood Falls U.S.A. 130 E2
Redwood National Park U.S.A. 126 B4
Redwood Valley U.S.A. 128 B2
Ree, Lough l. Rep. of Ireland 51 E4
Reed U.S.A. 134 B5
Reed City U.S.A. 134 C2
Reedley U.S.A. 128 D3
Reedsport U.S.A. 126 B4
Reedsville U.S.A. 134 E4
Reedville U.S.A. 135 G5
Reedy U.S.A. 134 E4
Reedy Glacier Antarctica 152 J1
Reefton N.Z. 113 C6
Rees Germany 52 G3
Reese U.S.A. 134 D2
Reese r. U.S.A. 128 E1
Refahiye Turkey 90 E3
Refugio U.S.A. 131 D6
Regen Germany 53 N6
Regen r. Germany 53 M5
Regência Brazil 145 D2
Regensburg Germany 53 M5
Regenstauf Germany 53 M5
Reggane Alg. 96 D2
Reggio Calabria Italy see Reggio di Calabria
Reggio Emilia-Romagna Italy see Reggio nell'Emilia
Reggio di Calabria Italy 58 F5
Reggio Emilia Italy see Reggio nell'Emilia
Reggio nell'Emilia Italy 58 D2
Reghin Romania 59 K1
Regi Afgh. 89 G3

▶Regina Canada 121 J5
Provincial capital of Saskatchewan.

Régina Fr. Guiana 143 H3
Registān reg. Afgh. 89 G4
Registro Brazil 144 G2
Registro do Araguaia Brazil 145 A1
Regium Lepidum Italy see Reggio nell'Emilia
Regozero Rus. Fed. 44 Q4
Rehau Germany 53 M4
Rehburg (Rehburg-Loccum) Germany 53 J2
Rehli India 82 D5
Rehoboth Namibia 100 C2
Rehoboth Bay U.S.A. 135 H4
Rehovot Israel 85 B4
Reibell Alg. see Ksar Chellala
Reibitz Germany 53 M3
Reichenbach Germany 53 M4
Reichshoffen France 53 H6
Reid Australia 109 E7
Reidh, Rubha pt U.K. 50 D3
Reidsville U.S.A. 132 E4
Reigate U.K. 49 G7
Reiley Peak U.S.A. 129 H5
Reims France 52 E5
Reinbek Germany 53 K1
Reindeer r. Canada 121 K4
Reindeer Island Canada 121 L4
Reindeer Lake Canada 121 K3
Reine Norway 44 H3
Reinosa Spain 57 D2
Reinsfeld Germany 52 G5
Reiphólsfjöll hill Iceland 44 [inset]
Reisaelva r. Norway 44 L2
Reisa Nasjonalpark nat. park Norway 44 M2
Reisjärvi Fin. 44 N5
Reitz S. Africa 101 I4
Rekapalle India 84 D2
Reken Germany 52 H3
Reliance Canada 121 I2
Relizane Alg. 57 G6
Rellano Mex. 131 B7
Rellingen Germany 53 J1
Remagen Germany 53 H4
Remarkable, Mount hill Australia 111 B7
Remedios Cuba 133 E8
Remeshk Iran 88 E5
Remhoogte Pass Namibia 100 C2
Remi France see Reims
Remmel Mountain U.S.A. 126 C2
Remscheid Germany 53 H3
Rena Norway 45 G6
Renaix Belgium see Ronse
Renam Myanmar 76 C3
Renapur India 84 C2
Rendsburg Germany 47 L3
René-Levasseur, Île i. Canada 123 H4
Renews Canada 123 L5
Renfrew Canada 135 G1
Renfrew U.K. 50 E5
Rengali Reservoir India 83 F5
Rengat Indon. 68 C7
Rengo Chile 144 B4
Ren He r. China 77 F1
Renheji China 77 G2
Renhua China 77 G3
Reni Ukr. 59 M2
Renick U.S.A. 134 E5
Renland reg. Greenland see Tuttut Nunaat
Rennell i. Solomon Is 107 G3
Rennerod Germany 53 I4
Rennes France 56 D2
Rennick Glacier Antarctica 152 H2
Rennie Canada 121 M5
Reno r. Italy 58 E2
Reno U.S.A. 128 D2
Renovo U.S.A. 135 G3
Rensselaer U.S.A. 134 B3
Renswoude Neth. 52 F2
Renton U.S.A. 126 C3
Réo Burkina 96 C3
Reo Indon. 108 C2
Repalle India 84 D2
Repetek Turkm. 89 F2
Repetekskiy Zapovednik nature res. Turkm. 89 F2
Repolka Rus. Fed. 45 P7
Republic U.S.A. 126 D2
Republican r. U.S.A. 130 D4
▶Republic of Ireland country Europe 51 E4
Europe 5, 38–39

▶Republic of South Africa country Africa 100 F5
5th most populous country in Africa.
Africa 7, 94–95

Repulse Bay b. Australia 110 E4
Repulse Bay Canada 119 J3
Requena Peru 142 D5
Requena Spain 57 F4
Reşadiye Turkey 90 E2
Reserva Brazil 145 A4
Reserve U.S.A. 129 I5
Reshi China 77 F2
Reshteh-ye Alborz mts Iran see Elburz Mountains
Resistencia Arg. 144 E3
Reşiţa Romania 59 I2
Resolute Bay Canada 119 I2
Resolution Island Canada 119 L3
Resolution Island N.Z. 113 A7
Resplendor Brazil 145 C2
Restigouche r. Canada 123 I5
Resülayn Turkey see Ceylanpınar
Retalhuleu Guat. 136 F6
Retezat, Parcul Naţional nat. park Romania 59 J2
Retford U.K. 48 G5
Rethel France 52 E5
Rethem (Aller) Germany 53 J2
Réthimnon Greece see Rethymno
Rethymno Greece 59 K7
Retreat Australia 110 C5
Reuden Germany 53 M2

▶Réunion terr. Indian Ocean 149 L7
French Overseas Department.
Africa 7, 94–95

Reus Spain 57 G3
Reusam, Pulau i. Indon. 71 B7
Reutlingen Germany 47 L6
Reval Estonia see Tallinn
Revda Rus. Fed. 44 S3
Revel Estonia see Tallinn
Revel France 56 F5
Revelstoke Canada 120 G5
Revigny-sur-Ornain France 52 E6
Revillagigedo, Islas is Mex. 136 B5
Revillagigedo Island U.S.A. 120 D4
Revin France 52 E5
Revivim Israel 85 B4
Revolyutsii, Pik mt. Tajik. see Revolyutsiya, Qullai
Revolyutsiya, Qullai mt. Tajik. 89 I2
Rewa India 82 E4
Rewari India 82 D3
Rexburg U.S.A. 126 F4
Rexton Canada 123 I5
Reyes, Point U.S.A. 128 B2
Reyhanlı Turkey 85 C1
Reykir Iceland 44 [inset]
Reykjanes Ridge sea feature N. Atlantic Ocean 148 F2
Reykjanestá pt Iceland 44 [inset]

▶Reykjavík Iceland 44 [inset]
Capital of Iceland.

Reyneke, Ostrov i. Rus. Fed. 74 E1
Reynoldsburg U.S.A. 134 D4
Reynolds Range mts Australia 108 F5
Reynosa Mex. 131 D7
Rezā Iran 88 D3
Reẕā'īyeh Iran see Urmia
Reẕā'īyeh, Daryācheh-ye salt l. Iran see Urmia, Lake
Rēzekne Latvia 45 O8
Rezvān Iran 89 F4
Reẕvāndeh Iran see Reẕvānshahr
Reẕvānshahr Iran 88 C2
Rhaeader Gwy U.K. see Rhayader
Rhayader U.K. 49 D6
Rheda-Wiedenbrück Germany 53 I3
Rhede Germany 52 G3
Rhegium Italy see Reggio di Calabria
Rheims France see Reims
Rhein r. Germany 53 G3 see Rhine
Rheine Germany 53 H2
Rheinland-Pfalz land Germany 53 H5
Rheinsberg Germany 53 M1
Rheinstetten Germany 53 I6
Rhemilès well Alg. 96 C2
Rhin r. France 53 I6 see Rhine
Rhine r. Germany 53 G3
also spelt Rhein (Germany) or Rhin (France)
Rhinebeck U.S.A. 135 I3
Rhinelander U.S.A. 130 F2
Rhineland-Palatinate land Germany see Rheinland-Pfalz
Rhinkanal canal Germany 53 M2
Rhinow Germany 53 M2
Rhiwabon U.K. see Ruabon
Rho Italy 58 C2
Rhode Island state U.S.A. 135 J3
Rhodes Greece 59 M6
Rhodes i. Greece 59 M6
Rhodesia country Africa see Zimbabwe
Rhodes Peak U.S.A. 126 E3
Rhodope Mountains Bulg./Greece 59 J4
Rhodus i. Greece see Rhodes
Rhône r. France/Switz. 56 G5
Rhum i. U.K. see Rum
Rhuthun U.K. see Ruthin
Rhydaman U.K. see Ammanford
Rhyl U.K. 48 D5
Riachão Brazil 143 I5
Riacho Brazil 145 C2
Riacho de Santana Brazil 145 C1
Riacho dos Machados Brazil 145 C1
Rialma Brazil 145 A1
Rialto U.S.A. 128 E4
Riasi Jammu and Kashmir 82 C2
Riau, Kepulauan is Indon. 68 C6
Ribadeo Spain 57 C2
Ribadesella Spain 57 D2
Ribas do Rio Pardo Brazil 144 F2
Ribat Afgh. 89 H2
Ribat-i-Shur waterhole Iran 88 E3
Ribáuè Moz. 99 D5
Ribble r. U.K. 48 E5
Ribblesdale valley U.K. 48 E4
Ribe Denmark 45 F9
Ribécourt-Dreslincourt France 52 C5
Ribeira r. Brazil 145 B4
Ribeirão Preto Brazil 145 B3
Ribemont France 52 D5
Ribérac France 56 E4
Riberalta Bol. 142 E6
Rîbniţa Moldova 43 F7
Ribnitz-Damgarten Germany 47 N3
Říčany Czech Rep. 47 O6
Rice U.S.A. 135 F5
Rice Lake Canada 135 F1
Richards Bay S. Africa 101 K5
Richards Inlet Antarctica 152 H1
Richards Island Canada 118 E3
Richardson r. Canada 121 I3
Richardson U.S.A. 131 D5
Richardson Island Canada 120 G1
Richardson Lakes U.S.A. 135 J1
Richardson Mountains Canada 118 E3
Richardson Mountains N.Z. 113 B7
Richfield U.S.A. 129 G2
Richfield Springs U.S.A. 135 H2
Richford NY U.S.A. 135 G2
Richford VT U.S.A. 135 I1
Richgrove U.S.A. 128 D4
Richland U.S.A. 126 D3
Richland Center U.S.A. 130 F3
Richmond N.S.W. Australia 112 E4
Richmond Qld Australia 110 C4
Richmond Canada 135 H1
Richmond N.Z. 113 D5
Richmond Kwazulu-Natal S. Africa 101 J5
Richmond N. Cape S. Africa 100 F6
Richmond U.K. 48 F4
Richmond CA U.S.A. 128 B3
Richmond IN U.S.A. 134 C4
Richmond KY U.S.A. 134 C5
Richmond MI U.S.A. 134 D2
Richmond MO U.S.A. 130 E4
Richmond TX U.S.A. 131 E6

▶Richmond VA U.S.A. 135 G5
State capital of Virginia.

Richmond Dale U.S.A. 134 D4
Richmond Hill U.S.A. 133 D6
Richmond Range hills Australia 112 F2
Richtersveld National Park S. Africa 100 C5
Richvale U.S.A. 128 C2
Richwood U.S.A. 134 E4
Rico U.S.A. 129 I3
Ricomagus France see Riom
Riddell Nunataks Antarctica 152 E2
Rideau Lakes Canada 135 G1
Ridge r. Canada 122 D4
Ridgecrest U.S.A. 128 E4
Ridge Farm U.S.A. 134 B4
Ridgeland MS U.S.A. 131 F5
Ridgeland SC U.S.A. 133 D5
Ridgetop U.S.A. 134 B5
Ridgetown Canada 134 E2
Ridgeway OH U.S.A. 134 D3
Ridgeway VA U.S.A. 134 F5
Ridgway CO U.S.A. 129 J2
Ridgway PA U.S.A. 135 F3
Riding Mountain National Park Canada 121 K5
Riecito Venez. 142 E1
Riemst Belgium 52 F4
Riesa Germany 53 N3
Riesco, Isla i. Chile 144 B8
Riet watercourse S. Africa 100 E6
Rietavas Lith. 45 L9
Rietfontein S. Africa 100 E4
Rieti Italy 58 E3
Rifā'ī, Tall mt. Jordan/Syria 85 C3
Rifeng China see Lichuan
Rifle U.S.A. 129 J2
Rifstangi pt Iceland 44 [inset]
Rift Valley Lakes National Park Eth. see Abijatta-Shalla National Park

▶Rīga Latvia 45 N8
Capital of Latvia.

Riga, Gulf of Estonia/Latvia 45 M8
Rigain Pünco l. China 83 F2
Rīgān Iran 88 E4
Rīgas jūras līcis b. Estonia/Latvia see Riga, Gulf of
Rigby U.S.A. 126 F4
Rīgestān reg. Afgh. see Registān
Rigolet Canada 123 K3
Rigside U.K. 50 F5
Riia laht b. Estonia/Latvia see Riga, Gulf of
Riihimäki Fin. 45 N6
Riiser-Larsen Ice Shelf Antarctica 152 B2
Riito Mex. 129 F5
Rijau Nigeria 96 D3
Rijeka Croatia 58 F2
Rikā, Wādī ar watercourse Saudi Arabia 88 B6
Rikitgaib Indon. 71 B6
Rikor India 76 B2
Rikuchū-kaigan National Park Japan 75 F5
Rikuzen-takata Japan 75 F5
Rila mts Bulg. 59 J3
Rila China 83 F3
Riley U.S.A. 126 D4
Rileyville U.S.A. 135 F4
Rillieux-la-Pape France 56 G4
Rillito U.S.A. 129 H5
Rimah, Wādī al watercourse Saudi Arabia 86 F4
Rimavská Sobota Slovakia 47 R6
Rimbey Canada 120 H4
Rimini Italy 58 E2
Rîmnicu Sărat Romania see Râmnicu Sărat
Rîmnicu Vîlcea Romania see Râmnicu Vâlcea
Rimouski Canada 123 H4
Rimpar Germany 53 J5
Rimsdale, Loch l. U.K. 50 E2
Rinbung China 83 G3
Rincão Brazil 145 A3
Rindal Norway 44 F5
Ringarooma Bay Australia 111 [inset]
Ringas India 82 C4
Ringe Germany 52 G2
Ringebu Norway 45 G6
Ringhkung Myanmar 70 B1
Ringkøbing Denmark 45 F8
Ringsend U.K. 51 F2
Ringsted Denmark 45 G9
Ringtor China 83 E3
Ringvassøy i. Norway 44 K2
Ringwood Australia 112 B6
Ringwood U.K. 49 F8
Rinjani, Gunung vol. Indon. 68 F8
Rinns Point U.K. 50 C5
Rinqênzê China 83 G3
Rinteln Germany 53 J2
Rio Azul Brazil 145 A4
Riobamba Ecuador 142 C4
Rio Blanco U.S.A. 129 J2
Rio Bonito Brazil 145 C3
Rio Branco Brazil 142 E6
Rio Branco, Parque Nacional do nat. park Brazil 142 F3
Río Bravo, Parque Internacional del nat. park Mex. 131 C6
Rio Brilhante Brazil 144 F2
Rio Casca Brazil 145 C3
Rio Claro Brazil 145 B3
Río Colorado Arg. 144 D5
Río Cuarto Arg. 144 D4
Rio das Pedras Moz. 101 L2
Rio de Contas Brazil 145 C1

▶Rio de Janeiro Brazil 145 C3
3rd most populous city in South America. Former capital of Brazil.

Rio de Janeiro state Brazil 145 C3

▶Río de la Plata-Paraná r. S. America 144 E4
2nd longest river in South America.

Rio Dell U.S.A. 128 A1
Rio do Sul Brazil 145 A4
Río Gallegos Arg. 144 C8
Río Grande Arg. 144 C8
Rio Grande Brazil 144 F4
Río Grande Mex. 131 C8
Rio Grande r. Mex./U.S.A. 127 G5
also known as Río Bravo del Norte
Rio Grande City U.S.A. 131 D7
Rio Grande do Sul state Brazil 145 A5
Rio Grande Rise sea feature S. Atlantic Ocean 148 F8
Ríohacha Col. 142 D1
Río Hondo, Embalse resr Arg. 144 C3
Rioja Peru 142 C5
Río Lagartos Mex. 133 B8
Rio Largo Brazil 143 K5
Riom France 56 F4
Río Mulatos Bol. 142 E7
Río Muni reg. Equat. Guinea 96 E4
Río Negro, Embalse del resr Uruguay 144 E4
Rioni r. Georgia 91 F2
Rio Novo Brazil 145 C3
Rio Pardo de Minas Brazil 145 C1
Rio Preto Brazil 145 C3
Rio Preto, Serra do hills Brazil 145 B2
Rio Rancho U.S.A. 127 G6
Río Tigre Ecuador 142 C4
Riou Lake Canada 121 J3
Rio Verde Brazil 145 A2
Rio Verde de Mato Grosso Brazil 143 H7
Rio Vista U.S.A. 128 C2
Ripky Ukr. 43 F6
Ripley England U.K. 48 F4
Ripley England U.K. 49 F5
Ripley NY U.S.A. 134 F2
Ripley OH U.S.A. 134 D4
Ripley WV U.S.A. 134 E4
Ripoll Spain 57 H2
Ripon U.K. 48 F4
Ripon U.S.A. 128 C3
Ripu India 83 G4
Risca U.K. 49 D7
Rishiri-tō i. Japan 74 F3
Rishon Le Ẕiyyon Israel 85 B4
Rish Pish Iran 89 F5
Rising Sun IN U.S.A. 134 C4
Rising Sun MD U.S.A. 135 G4
Risle r. France 49 H9
Risør Norway 45 F7
Rissa Norway 44 F5
Ristiina Fin. 45 O6
Ristijärvi Fin. 44 P4
Ristikent Rus. Fed. 44 Q2
Risum China 82 D2
Ritchie S. Africa 100 G5
Ritchie's Archipelago is India 71 A4
Ritscher Upland mts Antarctica 152 B2
Ritsem Sweden 44 J3
Ritter, Mount U.S.A. 128 D3
Ritterhude Germany 53 I1
Ritzville U.S.A. 126 D3
Riu, Laem pt Thai. 71 B5
Riva del Garda Italy 58 D2
Rivas Nicaragua 137 G6
Rivera Arg. 144 D5
Rivera Uruguay 144 E4
River Cess Liberia 96 C4
Riverhead U.S.A. 135 I3
Riverhurst Canada 121 J5
Riverina Australia 109 C7
Riverina reg. Australia 112 B5
Riversdale S. Africa 100 E8
Riverside S. Africa 101 I6
Riverside U.S.A. 128 E5
Rivers Inlet Canada 120 E5
Riversleigh Australia 110 B3
Riverton N.Z. 113 B8
Riverton VA U.S.A. 135 F4
Riverton WY U.S.A. 126 F4
Riverview Canada 123 I5
Rivesaltes France 56 F5
Riviera Beach U.S.A. 133 D7
Rivière-du-Loup Canada 123 H5
Rivière-Pentecôte Canada 123 I4
Rivière-Pigou Canada 123 I4
Rivne Ukr. 43 E6
Rivungo Angola 99 C5
Riwaka N.Z. 113 D5
Riwoqê China 76 C2

▶Riyadh Saudi Arabia 86 G5
Capital of Saudi Arabia.

Riyan India 89 I5
Riza well Iran 88 D3
Rize Turkey 91 F2
Rizhao Shandong China 77 H1
Rizhao Shandong China 77 H1
Rizokarpaso Cyprus see Rizokarpason
Rizokarpason Cyprus 85 B2
Rīzū well Iran 88 E3
Rīzū'īyeh Iran 88 E4
Rjukan Norway 45 F7
Rjuvbrokkene mt. Norway 45 E7
Rkîz Mauritania 96 B3
Roa Norway 45 G6
Roachdale U.S.A. 134 B4
Roach Lake U.S.A. 129 F4
Roade U.K. 49 G6
Roads U.S.A. 134 D4

▶Road Town Virgin Is (U.K.) 137 L5
Capital of the British Virgin Islands.

Roan Norway 44 G4
Roan Fell hill U.K. 50 G5
Roan High Knob mt. U.S.A. 132 D4
Roanne France 56 G3
Roanoke IN U.S.A. 134 C3
Roanoke VA U.S.A. 134 F5
Roanoke r. U.S.A. 132 E4
Roanoke Rapids U.S.A. 132 E4
Roan Plateau U.S.A. 129 I2
Roaring Spring U.S.A. 135 F3
Roaringwater Bay Rep. of Ireland 51 C6
Roatán Hond. 137 G5
Röbäck Sweden 44 L5
Robat r. Afgh. 89 F4
Robāţe Tork Iran 88 C3
Robāţ Karīm Iran 88 C3
Robāt-Sang Iran 88 E3
Robb Canada 120 G4
Robbins Island Australia 111 [inset]
Robbinsville U.S.A. 133 D5
Robe Australia 111 B8
Robe r. Australia 108 A5
Robe r. Rep. of Ireland 51 C4
Röbel Germany 53 M1
Robert Glacier Antarctica 152 D2
Robert Lee U.S.A. 131 C6
Roberts U.S.A. 126 E4
Roberts, Mount Australia 112 F2
Robertsburg U.S.A. 134 E4
Roberts Butte mt. Antarctica 152 H2
Roberts Creek Mountain U.S.A. 128 E2
Robertsfors Sweden 44 L4
Robertsganj India 83 E4
Robertson S. Africa 100 D7
Robertson, Lac l. Canada 123 K4
Robertson Bay Antarctica 152 H2
Robertson Island Antarctica 152 A2
Robertson Range hills Australia 109 C5
Robertsport Liberia 96 B4
Roberval Canada 123 G4
Robhanais, Rubha hd U.K. see Butt of Lewis
Robin Hood's Bay U.K. 48 G4
Robin's Nest hill Hong Kong China 77 [inset]
Robinson Canada 120 C2
Robinson U.S.A. 134 B4
Robinson Range hills Australia 109 B6
Robinson River Australia 110 B3
Robles Pass U.S.A. 129 H5
Roblin Canada 121 K5
Robsart Canada 121 I5
Robson, Mount Canada 120 G4
Robstown U.S.A. 131 D7
Roby U.S.A. 131 C5
Roçadas Angola see Xangongo
Rocca Busambra mt. Sicily Italy 58 E6
Rocha Uruguay 144 F4
Rochdale U.K. 48 E5
Rochechouart France 56 E4
Rochefort Belgium 52 F4
Rochefort France 56 D4
Rochefort, Lac l. Canada 123 G2
Rochegda Rus. Fed. 42 I3
Rochester Australia 112 B6
Rochester U.K. 49 H7
Rochester IN U.S.A. 134 B3
Rochester MN U.S.A. 130 E2
Rochester NH U.S.A. 135 J2
Rochester NY U.S.A. 135 G2
Rochford U.K. 49 H7
Rochlitz Germany 53 M3
Roc'h Trévezel hill France 56 C2
Rock r. Canada 120 E2
Rockall i. N. Atlantic Ocean 40 D4
Rockall Bank sea feature N. Atlantic Ocean 148 G2
Rock Creek Canada 120 B1
Rock Creek U.S.A. 134 E3
Rock Creek r. U.S.A. 126 G2
Rockdale U.S.A. 131 D6
Rockefeller Plateau Antarctica 152 J1
Rockford AL U.S.A. 133 C5
Rockford IL U.S.A. 130 F3
Rockford MI U.S.A. 134 C2
Rockglen Canada 121 J5
Rockhampton Australia 110 E4
Rockhampton Downs Australia 108 F4
Rock Hill U.S.A. 133 D5
Rockingham Australia 109 A8
Rockingham U.S.A. 133 E5
Rockingham Bay Australia 110 D3
Rockinghorse Lake Canada 121 H1
Rock Island Canada 135 I1
Rock Island U.S.A. 130 F3
Rocklake U.S.A. 130 D1
Rockland MA U.S.A. 135 J2
Rockland ME U.S.A. 132 G2
Rocknest Lake Canada 120 H1
Rockport IN U.S.A. 134 B5
Rockport TX U.S.A. 131 D7
Rock Rapids U.S.A. 130 D3
Rock River U.S.A. 126 G4
Rock Sound Bahamas 133 E7
Rock Springs MT U.S.A. 126 G3
Rocksprings U.S.A. 131 C6
Rock Springs WY U.S.A. 126 F4
Rockstone Guyana 143 G2
Rockville CT U.S.A. 135 I3
Rockville IN U.S.A. 134 B4
Rockville MD U.S.A. 135 G4
Rockwell City U.S.A. 130 E3
Rockwood MI U.S.A. 134 D2
Rockwood PA U.S.A. 134 F4
Rockyford Canada 120 H5
Rocky Harbour Canada 123 K4
Rocky Hill U.S.A. 134 D4
Rocky Island Lake Canada 122 E5
Rocky Lane Canada 120 G3
Rocky Mount U.S.A. 134 F5

Rocky Mountain House Canada 120 H4
Rocky Mountain National Park U.S.A. 126 G4
Rocky Mountains Canada/U.S.A. 124 F3
Rocourt-St-Martin France 52 D5
Rocroi France 52 E5
Rodberg Norway 45 F6
Rødbyhavn Denmark 45 G9
Roddickton Canada 123 L4
Rodeio Brazil 145 A4
Rodel U.K. 50 C3
Roden Neth. 52 G1
Rödental Germany 53 L4
Rodeo Arg. 144 C4
Rodeo Mex. 131 B7
Rodeo U.S.A. 127 F7
Rodez France 56 F4
Ródhos i. Greece see Rhodes
Rodi i. Greece see Rhodes
Roding Germany 53 M5
Rodney, Cape U.S.A. 118 B3
Rodniki Rus. Fed. 42 I4
Rodolfo Sanchez Toboada Mex. 127 D7
Rodopi Planina mts Bulg./Greece see Rhodope Mountains
Rodos Greece see Rhodes
Rodos i. Greece see Rhodes
Rodosto Turkey see Tekirdağ
Rodrigues Island Mauritius 149 M7
Roe r. U.K. 51 F2
Roebourne Australia 108 B5
Roebuck Bay Australia 108 C4
Roedtan S. Africa 101 I3
Roe Plains Australia 109 D7
Roermond Neth. 52 F3
Roeselare Belgium 52 D4
Roes Welcome Sound sea chan. Canada 119 J3
Rogachev Belarus see Rahachow
Rogätz Germany 53 L2
Rogers U.S.A. 131 E4
Rogers, Mount U.S.A. 134 E5
Rogers City U.S.A. 134 D1
Rogers Lake U.S.A. 128 E4
Rogerson U.S.A. 126 E4
Rogersville U.S.A. 134 D5
Roggan r. Canada 122 F3
Roggan, Lac l. Canada 122 F3
Roggeveen Basin sea feature S. Pacific Ocean 151 O8
Roggeveld plat. S. Africa 100 E7
Roggeveldberge esc. S. Africa 100 E7
Roghadal U.K. see Rodel
Rognan Norway 44 I3
Rögnitz r. Germany 53 K1
Rogue r. U.S.A. 126 B4
Roha India 84 B2
Rohnert Park U.S.A. 128 B2
Rohrbach in Oberösterreich Austria 47 N6
Rohrbach-lès-Bitche France 53 H5
Rohri Pak. 89 H5
Rohtak India 82 D3
Roi Et Thai. 70 C3
Roi Georges, Îles du is Fr. Polynesia 151 K6
Rois-Bheinn hill U.K. 50 D4
Roisel France 52 D5
Roja Latvia 45 M8
Rojas Arg. 144 D4
Rokeby Australia 110 C2
Rokeby National Park Australia 110 C2
Rokiškis Lith. 45 N9
Roknäs Sweden 44 L4
Rokytne Ukr. 43 E6
Rolagang China 83 G2
Rola Kangri mt. China 83 G2
Rolândia Brazil 145 A3
Rolim de Moura Brazil 142 F6
Roll AZ U.S.A. 129 G5
Roll IN U.S.A. 134 C3
Rolla MO U.S.A. 130 F4
Rolla ND U.S.A. 130 D1
Rollag Norway 45 F6
Rolleston Australia 110 E5
Rolleville Bahamas 133 F8
Rolling Fork U.S.A. 131 F5
Rollins U.S.A. 126 E3
Roma Australia 111 E5
Roma i. Indon. 108 D1
Roma Italy see Rome
Roma Lesotho 101 H5
Roma Sweden 45 K8
Romain, Cape U.S.A. 133 E5
Romaine r. Canada 123 J4
Roman Romania 59 L1
Română, Câmpia plain Romania 59 J2
Romanche Gap sea feature S. Atlantic Ocean 148 G6
Romanet, Lac l. Canada 123 I2
▶Romania country Europe 59 K2
Europe 5, 38–39
Roman-Kosh mt. Ukr. 90 D1
Romano, Cape U.S.A. 133 D7
Romanovka Rus. Fed. 73 K2
Romans-sur-Isère France 56 G4
Romanzof, Cape U.S.A. 118 B3
Rombas France 52 G5
Romblon Phil. 69 G4

▶Rome Italy 58 E4
Capital of Italy.

Rome GA U.S.A. 133 C5
Rome ME U.S.A. 135 K1
Rome NY U.S.A. 135 H2
Rome TN U.S.A. 134 B5
Rome City U.S.A. 134 C3
Romeo U.S.A. 134 D2
Romford U.K. 49 H7
Romilly-sur-Seine France 56 F2
Romitan Uzbek. 89 G2
Romney U.S.A. 135 F4
Romney Marsh reg. U.K. 49 H7
Romny Ukr. 43 G6
Rømø i. Denmark 45 F9
Romodanovo Rus. Fed. 43 J5
Romorantin-Lanthenay France 56 E3
Rompin r. Malaysia 71 C7
Romsey U.K. 49 F8
Romulus U.S.A. 134 D2
Ron India 84 B3
Rona i. U.K. 50 D1
Ronas Hill hill U.K. 50 [inset]
Roncador, Serra do hills Brazil 143 H6
Roncador Reef Solomon Is 107 F2
Ronda Spain 57 D5
Ronda, Serranía de mts Spain 57 D5
Rondane Nasjonalpark nat. park Norway 45 F6
Rondon Brazil 144 F2
Rondonópolis Brazil 143 H7
Rondout Reservoir U.S.A. 135 H3
Rongcheng Anhui China see Qingyang
Rongcheng Guangxi China see Rongxian
Rongcheng Hubei China see Jianli
Rong Chu r. China 83 G3
Rongelap atoll Marshall Is 150 H5
Rongjiang Guizhou China 77 F3
Rongjiang Jiangxi China see Nankang
Rongjiawan China see Yueyang
Rongklang Range mts Myanmar 70 A2
Rongmei China see Hefeng
Rongshui China 77 F3
Rongwo China see Tongren
Rongxian China 77 F4
Rongyul China 76 C2
Rongzhag China see Danba
Rönlap atoll Marshall Is see Rongelap
Rønne Denmark 45 I9
Ronneby Sweden 45 I8
Ronne Entrance strait Antarctica 152 L2
Ronne Ice Shelf Antarctica 152 L1
Ronnenberg Germany 53 J2
Ronse Belgium 52 D4
Roodeschool Neth. 52 G1
Rooke Island P.N.G. see Umboi
Roordahuizum Neth. 52 F1
Roorkee India 82 D3
Roosendaal Neth. 52 E3
Roosevelt AZ U.S.A. 129 H5
Roosevelt UT U.S.A. 129 I1
Roosevelt, Mount Canada 120 E3
Roosevelt Island Antarctica 152 I1
Root r. Canada 120 F2
Root r. U.S.A. 130 F3
Ropar India see Rupnagar
Roper r. Australia 110 A2
Roper Bar Australia 108 F3
Roquefort France 56 D4
Roraima, Mount Guyana 142 F2
Rori India 82 C3
Rori Indon. 69 J7
Røros Norway 44 G5
Rørvik Norway 44 G4
Rosa, Punta pt Mex. 127 F8
Rosalia U.S.A. 126 D3
Rosamond U.S.A. 128 D4
Rosamond Lake U.S.A. 128 D4
Rosario Arg. 144 D4
Rosário Brazil 143 J4
Rosario Baja California Mex. 127 E7
Rosario Coahuila Mex. 131 C7
Rosario Sinaloa Mex. 136 C4
Rosario Sonora Mex. 124 F6
Rosario Zacatecas Mex. 131 C7
Rosario Venez. 142 D1
Rosário do Sul Brazil 144 F4
Rosário Oeste Brazil 143 G6
Rosarito Baja California Mex. 127 E7
Rosarito Baja California Mex. 128 E5
Rosarito Baja California Sur Mex. 127 F8
Rosarno Italy 58 F5
Roscoff France 56 C2
Roscommon Rep. of Ireland 51 D4
Roscommon U.S.A. 134 C1
Roscrea Rep. of Ireland 51 E5
Rose r. Australia 110 A2
Rose, Mount U.S.A. 128 D2
Rose Atoll American Samoa see Rose Island

▶Roseau Dominica 137 L5
Capital of Dominica.

Roseau U.S.A. 130 E1
Roseau r. U.S.A. 130 D1
Roseberth Australia 111 B5
Rose Blanche Canada 123 K5
Rosebud r. Canada 120 H5
Rosebud U.S.A. 126 G3
Roseburg U.S.A. 126 C4
Rose City U.S.A. 134 C1
Rosedale U.S.A. 131 F5
Rosedale Abbey U.K. 48 G4
Roseires Reservoir Sudan 86 D7
Rose Island atoll American Samoa 107 J3
Rosenberg U.S.A. 131 E6
Rosendal Norway 45 E7
Rosendal S. Africa 101 H5
Rosenheim Germany 47 N7
Rose Peak U.S.A. 129 I5
Rose Point Canada 120 D4
Roseto degli Abruzzi Italy 58 F3
Rosetown Canada 121 J5
Rosetta Egypt see Rashīd
Rose Valley Canada 121 K4
Roseville CA U.S.A. 128 C2
Roseville MI U.S.A. 134 D2
Roseville OH U.S.A. 134 D4
Rosewood Australia 112 F1
Roshchino Rus. Fed. 45 P6
Rosh Pinah Namibia 100 C4
Roshtkala Tajik. see Roshtqal'a
Roshtqal'a Tajik. 89 H2
Rosignano Marittimo Italy 58 D3
Roșiori de Vede Romania 59 K2
Roskilde Denmark 45 H9
Roskruge Mountains U.S.A. 129 H5
Roslavl' Rus. Fed. 43 G5
Roslyakovo Rus. Fed. 44 R2
Roslyatino Rus. Fed. 42 J4
Ross N.Z. 113 C6
Ross, Mount hill N.Z. 113 E5
Rossano Italy 58 G5
Rossan Point Rep. of Ireland 51 D3
Ross Barnett Reservoir U.S.A. 131 F5
Ross Bay Junction Canada 123 I3
Ross Carbery Rep. of Ireland 51 C6
Ross Dependency reg. Antarctica 152 I2
Rosseau, Lake Canada 134 F1
Rossel Island P.N.G. 110 F1
Ross Ice Shelf Antarctica 152 I1
Rossignol, Lac l. Canada 122 G3
Rössing Namibia 100 B2
Ross Island Antarctica 152 H1
Rossiyskaya Sovetskaya Federativnaya Sotsialisticheskaya Respublika country Asia/Europe see Russian Federation
Rossland Canada 120 G5
Rosslare Rep. of Ireland 51 F5
Rosslare Harbour Rep. of Ireland 51 F5
Roßlau Germany 53 M3
Rosso Mauritania 96 B3
Ross-on-Wye U.K. 49 E7
Rossony Belarus see Rasony
Rossosh' Rus. Fed. 43 H6
Ross River Canada 120 C2
Ross Sea Antarctica 152 H1
Roßtal Germany 53 K5
Røssvatnet l. Norway 44 I4
Rossville U.S.A. 134 B3
Roßwein Germany 53 N3
Rosswood Canada 120 D4
Rostāq Afgh. 89 H2
Rostāq Iran 88 D5
Rosthern Canada 121 J4
Rostock Germany 47 N3
Rostov Rus. Fed. 42 H4
Rostov-na-Donu Rus. Fed. 43 H7
Rostov-on-Don Rus. Fed. see Rostov-na-Donu
Rosvik Sweden 44 L4
Roswell U.S.A. 127 G6
Rota i. N. Mariana Is 69 L4
Rot am See Germany 53 K5
Rotch Island Kiribati see Tamana
Rote i. Indon. 108 C2
Rotenburg (Wümme) Germany 53 J1
Roth Germany 53 L5
Rothaargebirge hills Germany 53 I4
Rothbury U.K. 48 F3
Rothenburg ob der Tauber Germany 53 K5
Rother r. U.K. 49 G8
Rothera research station Antarctica 152 L2
Rotherham U.K. 48 F5
Rothes U.K. 50 F3
Rothesay U.K. 50 D5
Rothwell U.K. 49 G6
Roti Indon. 108 C2
Roti i. Indon. see Rote
Roto Australia 112 B4
Rotomagus France see Rouen
Rotomanu N.Z. 113 C6
Rotondo, Monte mt. Corsica France 56 I5
Rotorua N.Z. 113 F4
Rotorua, Lake N.Z. 113 F4
Röttenbach Germany 53 L5
Rottendorf Germany 53 K5
Rottenmann Austria 47 O7
Rotterdam Neth. 52 E3
Rottleberode Germany 53 K3
Rottnest Island Australia 109 A8
Rottweil Germany 47 L6
Rotuma i. Fiji 107 H3
Rotumeroog i. Neth. 52 G1
Rotung India 76 B2
Rötviken Sweden 44 I5
Rötz Germany 53 M5
Roubaix France 52 D4
Rouen France 52 B5
Rough River Lake U.S.A. 134 B5
Roulers Belgium see Roeselare
Roumania country Europe see Romania
Roundeyed Lake Canada 123 H3
Round Hill hill U.K. 48 F4
Round Mountain Australia 112 F3
Round Rock AZ U.S.A. 129 I3
Round Rock TX U.S.A. 131 D6
Roundup U.S.A. 126 F3
Rousay i. U.K. 50 F1
Rouses Point U.S.A. 135 I1
Rouxville S. Africa 101 H6
Rouyn Canada 122 F4
Rovaniemi Fin. 44 N3
Roven'ki Rus. Fed. 43 H6
Rovereto Italy 58 D2
Rôviĕng Tbong Cambodia 71 D4
Rovigo Italy 58 D2
Rovinj Croatia 58 E2
Rovno Ukr. see Rivne
Rovnoye Rus. Fed. 43 J6
Rovuma r. Moz./Tanz. see Ruvuma
Rowena Australia 112 D2
Rowley Island Canada 119 K3
Rowley Shoals sea feature Australia 108 B4
Równe Ukr. see Rivne
Roxas Mindoro Phil. 69 G4
Roxas Palawan Phil. 68 F4
Roxas Panay Phil. 69 G4
Roxboro U.S.A. 132 E4
Roxburgh N.Z. 113 B7
Roxburgh Island Cook Is see Rarotonga
Roxby Downs Australia 111 B6
Roxo, Cabo c. Senegal 96 B3
Roy MT U.S.A. 126 F3
Roy NM U.S.A. 127 G5
Royal Canal Rep. of Ireland 51 E4
Royal Chitwan National Park Nepal 83 F4
Royale, Île i. Canada see Cape Breton Island
Royale, Isle i. U.S.A. 130 F1
Royal Natal National Park S. Africa 101 I5
Royal National Park Australia 112 E5
Royal Oak U.S.A. 134 D2
Royal Suklaphanta National Park Nepal 82 E3
Royan France 56 D4
Roye France 52 C5
Roy Hill Australia 108 B5
Royston U.K. 49 G6
Rozdil'na Ukr. 59 N1
Rozivka Ukr. 43 H7
Rtishchevo Rus. Fed. 43 I5
Ruabon U.K. 49 D6
Ruaha National Park Tanz. 99 D4
Ruahine Range mts N.Z. 113 F5
Ruanda country Africa see Rwanda
Ruapehu, Mount vol. N.Z. 113 E4
Ruapuke Island N.Z. 113 B8
Ruatoria N.Z. 113 G3
Ruba Belarus 43 F5

▶Rub' al Khālī des. Saudi Arabia 86 G6
Largest uninterrupted stretch of sand in the world.

Rubaydā reg. Saudi Arabia 88 C5
Rubtsovsk Rus. Fed. 80 F1
Ruby U.S.A. 118 C3
Ruby Dome mt. U.S.A. 129 F1
Ruby Mountains U.S.A. 129 F1
Rubys Inn U.S.A. 129 G3
Ruby Valley U.S.A. 129 F1
Rucheng China 77 G3
Ruckersville U.S.A. 135 F4
Rudall River National Park Australia 108 C5
Rudarpur India 83 E4
Ruda Śląska Poland 47 Q5
Rudauli India 83 E4
Rūdbār Iran 88 C2
Rudkøbing Denmark 45 G9
Rudnaya Pristan' Rus. Fed. 74 D3
Rudnichnyy Rus. Fed. 42 L4
Rudnik Ingichka Uzbek. see Ingichka
Rudnya Smolenskaya Oblast' Rus. Fed. 43 F5
Rudnya Volgogradskaya Oblast' Rus. Fed. 43 J6
Rudnyy Kazakh. 78 F1
Rudolf, Lake salt l. Eth./Kenya see Turkana, Lake

▶Rudol'fa, Ostrov i. Rus. Fed. 64 G1
Most northerly point of Europe.

Rudolph Island Rus. Fed. see Rudol'fa, Ostrov
Rudolstadt Germany 53 L4
Rudong China 77 I1
Rūdsar Iran 88 C2
Rue France 52 B4
Rufiji r. Tanz. 99 D4
Rufino Arg. 144 D4
Rufisque Senegal 96 B3
Rufrufua Indon. 69 I7
Rufunsa Zambia 99 C5
Rugao China 77 I1
Rugby U.K. 49 F6
Rugby U.S.A. 130 C1
Rugeley U.K. 49 F6
Rügen i. Germany 47 N3
Rugged Mountain Canada 120 E5
Rügland Germany 53 K5
Ruḥayyat al Ḥamr'ā' waterhole Saudi Arabia 88 B5
Ruhengeri Rwanda 98 C4
Ruhnu i. Estonia 45 M8
Ruhr r. Germany 53 G3
Ruhuna National Park Sri Lanka 84 D5
Rui'an China 77 I3
Rui Barbosa Brazil 145 C1
Ruicheng China 77 F1
Ruijin China 77 G3
Ruili China 76 C3
Ruin Point Canada 121 P2
Ruipa Tanz. 99 D4
Ruiz Mex. 136 C4
Ruiz, Nevado del vol. Col. 142 C3
Rujaylah, Ḥarrat ar lava field Jordan 85 C3
Rūjiena Latvia 45 N8
Ruk is Micronesia see Chuuk
Rukanpur Pak. 89 I4
Rukumkot Nepal 83 E3
Rukwa, Lake Tanz. 99 D4
Rulin China see Chengbu
Rulong China see Xinlong
Rum i. U.K. 50 C4
Rum, Jebel mts Jordan see Ramm, Jabal
Ruma Serb. and Mont. 59 H2
Rumāh Saudi Arabia 86 G4
Rumania country Europe see Romania
Rumbek Sudan 97 F4
Rumberpon i. Indon. 69 I7
Rum Cay i. Bahamas 133 F8
Rum Jungle Australia 108 E3
Rummānā hill Syria 85 D3
Rumphi Malawi 99 D5
Runan China 77 G1
Runaway, Cape N.Z. 113 F3
Runcorn U.K. 48 E5
Rundu Namibia 99 B5
Rundvik Sweden 44 K5
Rŭng, Kaôh i. Cambodia 71 C5
Rungwa Tanz. 99 D4
Rungwa r. Tanz. 99 D4
Runheji China 77 H1
Runing China see Runan
Runton Range hills Australia 109 C5
Ruokolahti Fin. 45 P6
Ruoqiang China 80 G4
Rupa India 83 H4
Rupat i. Indon. 71 C7
Rupert r. Canada 122 F4
Rupert ID U.S.A. 126 E4
Rupert WV U.S.A. 134 E5
Rupert Bay Canada 122 F4
Rupert Coast Antarctica 152 J1
Rupert House Canada see Waskaganish
Rupnagar India 82 D3
Rupshu reg. Jammu and Kashmir 82 D2
Ruqqād, Wādī ar watercourse Israel 85 B3
Rural Retreat U.S.A. 134 E5
Rusaddir N. Africa see Melilla
Rusape Zimbabwe 99 D5
Ruschuk Bulg. see Ruse
Ruse Bulg. 59 K3
Rusera India 83 F4
Rush U.S.A. 134 D4
Rush Creek r. U.S.A. 130 C4
Rushden U.K. 49 G6
Rushinga Zimbabwe 99 D5
Rushville IL U.S.A. 130 F3
Rushville IN U.S.A. 134 C4
Rushville NE U.S.A. 130 C3
Rushworth Australia 112 B6
Rusk U.S.A. 131 E6
Russell Man. Canada 121 K5
Russell Ont. Canada 135 H1
Russell N.Z. 113 E2
Russell KS U.S.A. 130 D4
Russell PA U.S.A. 134 F3
Russell Bay Antarctica 152 J2
Russell Lake Man. Canada 121 K3
Russell Lake N.W.T. Canada 120 H2
Russell Lake Sask. Canada 121 J3
Russell Range hills Australia 109 C8
Russell Springs U.S.A. 134 C5
Russellville AR U.S.A. 131 E5
Russellville KY U.S.A. 134 B5
Rüsselsheim Germany 53 I4
Russia country Asia/Europe see Russian Federation
Russian r. U.S.A. 128 B2

▶Russian Federation country Asia/Europe 64 I3
Largest country in the world, Europe and Asia. Most populous country in Europe and 5th in Asia.
Asia 6, 62–63
Europe 5, 38–39

Russian Soviet Federal Socialist Republic country Asia/Europe see Russian Federation
Russkiy, Ostrov i. Rus. Fed. 74 C4
Russkiy Kameshkir Rus. Fed. 43 J5
Rust'avi Georgia 91 G2
Rustburg U.S.A. 134 F5
Rustenburg S. Africa 101 H3
Ruston U.S.A. 131 E5
Rutanzige, Lake Dem. Rep. Congo/Uganda see Edward, Lake
Ruteng Indon. 108 C2
Ruth U.S.A. 129 F2
Rüthen Germany 53 I3
Rutherglen Australia 112 C6
Ruther Glen U.S.A. 135 G5
Ruthin U.K. 49 D5
Ruthiyai India 82 D4
Ruth Reservoir U.S.A. 128 B1
Rutka r. Rus. Fed. 42 J4
Rutland U.S.A. 135 I2
Rutland Water resr U.K. 49 G6
Rutledge Lake Canada 121 I2
Rutog Xizang China 76 B2
Rutög China 82 D2
Rutog Xizang China 83 F3
Rutul Rus. Fed. 91 G2
Ruukki Fin. 44 N4
Ruvuma r. Moz./Tanz. 99 E5
also known as Rovuma
Ruwayshid, Wādī watercourse Jordan 85 C3
Ruwayṭah, Wādī watercourse Jordan 85 C5
Ruweis U.A.E. 88 D5
Ruwenzori National Park Uganda see Queen Elizabeth National Park
Ruza Rus. Fed. 42 H5
Ruzayevka Kazakh. 78 F1
Ruzayevka Rus. Fed. 43 J5
Ruzhou China 77 G1
Ružomberok Slovakia 47 Q6
▶Rwanda country Africa 98 C4
Africa 7, 94–95
Ryābād Iran 88 D2
Ryan, Loch b. U.K. 50 D5
Ryazan' Rus. Fed. 43 H5
Ryazhsk Rus. Fed. 43 I5
Rybachiy, Poluostrov pen. Rus. Fed. 44 R2
Rybach'ye Kyrg. see Balykchy
Rybinsk Rus. Fed. 42 H4
Rybinskoye Vodokhranilishche resr Rus. Fed. 42 H4
Rybnik Poland 47 Q5
Rybnitsa Moldova see Rîbnița
Rybnoye Rus. Fed. 43 H5
Rybreka Rus. Fed. 42 G3
Ryd Sweden 45 I8
Rydberg Peninsula Antarctica 152 L2
Ryde U.K. 49 F8
Rye U.K. 49 H8
Rye r. U.K. 48 G4
Rye Bay U.K. 49 H8
Ryegate U.S.A. 126 F3
Rye Patch Reservoir U.S.A. 128 D1
Rykovo Ukr. see Yenakiyeve
Ryl'sk Rus. Fed. 43 G6
Rylstone Australia 112 D4
Ryn-Peski des. Kazakh. 41 P6
Ryukyu Islands Japan 75 B8
Ryūkyū-rettō is Japan see Ryukyu Islands
Ryukyu Trench sea feature N. Pacific Ocean 150 E4
Rzeszów Poland 43 D6
Rzhaksa Rus. Fed. 43 I5
Rzhev Rus. Fed. 42 G4

S

Sa'ādah al Barṣā' pass Saudi Arabia 85 C5
Sa'ādatābād Iran 88 D4
Saal an der Donau Germany 53 L6
Saale r. Germany 53 L3
Saalfeld Germany 53 L4
Saanich Canada 120 F5
Saar land Germany see Saarland
Saar r. Germany 52 G5
Saarbrücken Germany 52 G5
Saaremaa i. Estonia 45 M7
Saarenkylä Fin. 44 N3
Saargau reg. Germany 52 G5
Saarijärvi Fin. 44 N5
Saari-Kämä Fin. 44 O3
Saarikoski Fin. 44 L2
Saaristomeren kansallispuisto nat. park Fin. see Skärgårdshavets nationalpark
Saarland land Germany 52 G5
Saarlouis Germany 52 G5
Saatlı Azer. 91 H3
Saatly Azer. see Saatlı
Sab'a Egypt see Saba'ah
Saba'ah Egypt 85 A4
Sab' Ābār Syria 85 C3
Šabac Serb. and Mont. 59 H2
Sabadell Spain 57 H3
Sabae Japan 75 E6
Sabak Malaysia 71 C7
Sabalana i. Indon. 68 F8
Sabalana, Kepulauan is Indon. 68 F8
Sabana, Archipiélago de is Cuba 137 H4
Sabang Indon. 71 A6
Şabanözü Turkey 90 D2
Sabará Brazil 145 C2
Sabastiya West Bank 85 B3
Sab'atayn, Ramlat as des. Yemen 86 G6
Sabaudia Italy 58 E4
Sabaya Bol. 142 E7
Sabdê China 76 D2
Sabelo S. Africa 100 F6
Ṣabḥā Jordan 85 C3
Sabhā Libya 97 E2
Ṣabḥā' Saudi Arabia 88 B6
Sabhrai India 82 B5
Sabi r. India 82 D3
Sabi r. Moz./Zimbabwe see Save
Sabie Moz. 101 K3
Sabie r. Moz./S. Africa 101 K3
Sabie S. Africa 101 J3
Sabina U.S.A. 134 D4
Sabinal Mex. 127 G7
Sabinal, Cayo i. Cuba 133 E8
Sabinas Mex. 131 C7
Sabinas r. Mex. 131 C7
Sabinas Hidalgo Mex. 131 C7
Sabine r. U.S.A. 131 E6
Sabine Lake U.S.A. 131 E6
Sabine Pass U.S.A. 131 E6
Sabini, Monti mts Italy 58 E3
Sabirabad Azer. 91 H2
Sabkhat al Bardawīl Reserve nature res. Egypt see Lake Bardawil Reserve
Sable, Cape Canada 123 I6
Sable, Cape U.S.A. 133 D7
Sable, Lac du l. Canada 123 I3
Sable Island Canada 123 K6
Sabon Kafi Niger 96 D3
Sabrina Coast Antarctica 152 F2
Sabugal Port. 57 C3
Sabzawar Afgh. see Shīndand
Sabzevār Iran 88 E2
Sabzvārān Iran see Jīroft
Sacalinul Mare, Insula i. Romania 59 M2
Sacaton U.S.A. 129 H5
Sac City U.S.A. 130 E3
Săcele Romania 59 K2
Sachigo r. Canada 121 N4
Sachigo Lake Canada 121 M4
Sachin India 82 C5
Sach'on S. Korea 75 C6
Sach Pass India 82 D2
Sachsen land Germany 53 N3
Sachsen-Anhalt land Germany 53 L2
Sachsenheim Germany 53 J6
Sachs Harbour Canada 118 F2
Sacirsuyu r. Syria/Turkey see Sājūr, Nahr
Sackpfeife hill Germany 53 I4
Sackville Canada 123 I5
Saco ME U.S.A. 135 J2
Saco MT U.S.A. 126 G2
Sacramento Brazil 145 B2

▶Sacramento U.S.A. 128 C2
State capital of California.

Sacramento r. U.S.A. 128 C2
Sacramento Mountains U.S.A. 127 G6
Sacramento Valley U.S.A. 128 B1
Sada S. Africa 101 H7
Sádaba Spain 57 F2
Sá da Bandeira Angola see Lubango
Ṣadad Syria 85 C2
Ṣa'dah Yemen 86 F6
Sadao Thai. 71 C6
Saddat al Hindīyah Iraq 91 G4
Saddleback Mesa mt. U.S.A. 131 C5
Saddle Hill hill Australia 110 D2
Saddle Peak hill India 71 A4
Sa Đec Vietnam 71 D5
Sadêng China 76 B2
Sadieville U.S.A. 134 C4
Sadīj watercourse Iran 88 E5
Sadiola Mali 96 B3
Sadiqabad Pak. 89 H4
Sad Istragh mt. Afgh./Pak. 89 I2
Sa'dīyah, Hawr as imp. l. Iraq 91 G4
Sa'diyyat i. U.A.E. 88 D5
Sado r. Port. 57 B4
Sadoga-shima i. Japan 75 E5
Sadot Egypt see Sadūt
Sadovoye Rus. Fed. 43 J7
Sa Dragonera i. Spain 57 H4
Sadras India 84 D3
Sadūt Egypt 85 B4
Sadût Egypt see Sadūt
Sæby Denmark 45 G8
Saena Julia Italy see Siena
Safad Israel see Ẕefat
Safayal Maqūf well Iraq 91 G5
Safed Khirs mts Afgh. 89 H2
Safed Koh mts Afgh. 89 G3
Safed Koh mts Afgh./Pak. 89 H3
Saffānīyah, Ra's as pt Saudi Arabia 88 C4
Säffle Sweden 45 H7
Safford U.S.A. 129 I5
Saffron Walden U.K. 49 H6
Safi Morocco 54 C5
Safīdār, Kūh-e mt. Iran 88 D4
Safid Kūh mts Afgh. see Paropamisus
Safid Sagak Iran 89 F3
Safiras, Serra das mts Brazil 145 C2
Ṣāfītā Syria 85 C2
Safonovo Arkhangel'skaya Oblast' Rus. Fed. 42 K2
Safonovo Smolenskaya Oblast' Rus. Fed. 43 G5
Safrā' al Asyāḥ esc. Saudi Arabia 88 A5
Safrā' as Sark esc. Saudi Arabia 86 F4
Safranbolu Turkey 90 D2
Saga China 83 F3
Saga Japan 75 C6
Saga Kazakh. 80 B1
Sagaing Myanmar 70 A2
Sagami-nada g. Japan 75 E6
Sagamore U.S.A. 134 F3
Saganthit Kyun i. Myanmar 71 B4
Sagar Karnataka India 84 B3
Sagar Karnataka India 84 C2
Sagar Madhya Pradesh India 82 D5
Sagaredzho Georgia see Sagarejo
Sagarejo Georgia 91 G2
Sagar Island India 83 G5

Sagarmatha National Park Nepal 83 F4
Sagastyr Rus. Fed. 65 N2
Sagavanirktok r. U.S.A. 118 D2
Sage U.S.A. 126 F4
Saggi, Har mt. Israel 85 B4
Saghand Iran 88 D3
Saginaw U.S.A. 134 D2
Saginaw Bay U.S.A. 134 D2
Saglek Bay Canada 123 J2
Saglouc Canada see Salluit
Sagone, Golfe de b. Corsica France 56 I5
Sagres Port. 57 B5
Sagthale India 82 C5
Saguache U.S.A. 127 G5
Sagua la Grande Cuba 137 H4
Saguaro Lake U.S.A. 129 H5
Saguaro National Park U.S.A. 129 H5
Saguenay r. Canada 123 H4
Sagunt Spain see Sagunto
Sagunto Spain 57 F4
Saguntum Spain see Sagunto
Sahagún Spain 57 D2
Sahand, Kūh-e mt. Iran 88 B2

▶Sahara des. Africa 96 D3
Largest desert in the world.

Şahara el Gharbîya des. Egypt see Western Desert
Şahara el Sharqîya des. Egypt see Eastern Desert
Saharan Atlas mts Alg. see Atlas Saharien
Saharanpur India 82 D3
Sahara Well Australia 108 C5
Saharsa India 83 F4
Sahaswan India 82 D3
Sahat, Kūh-e hill Iran 88 D3
Sahatwar India 83 F4
Şahbuz Azer. 91 G3
Şahdol India see Shahdol
Sahebganj India see Sahibganj
Sahebgunj India see Sahibganj
Saheira, Wâdi el watercourse Egypt see Suhaymī, Wādī as
Sahel reg. Africa 96 C3
Sahibganj India 83 F4
Sahiwal Pak. 89 I4
Sahlābād Iran 89 E3
Şaḩm Oman 88 E5
Şaḩneh Iran 88 B3
Şaḩrā al Ḩijārah reg. Iraq 91 G5
Sahuaripa Mex. 127 F7
Sahuayo Mex. 136 D4
Sahuteng China see Zadoi
Sa Huynh Vietnam 71 E4
Sahyadri mts India see Western Ghats
Sahyadriparvat Range hills India 84 B1
Sai r. India 83 E4
Sai Buri Thai. 71 C6
Saïda Alg. 57 G6
Saïda Lebanon see Sidon
Sai Dao Tai, Khao mt. Thai. 71 C4
Saïdia Morocco 57 E6
Sa'īdīyeh Iran see Solţānīyeh
Saidpur Bangl. 83 G4
Saiha India 83 H5
Saihan Tal China 73 K4
Saijō Japan 75 D6
Saikai National Park Japan 75 C6
Saiki Japan 75 C6
Sai Kung Hong Kong China 77 [inset]
Sailana India 82 C5
Saimaa l. Fin. 45 P6
Saimbeyli Turkey 90 E3
Saindak Pak. 89 F4
Sa'īndezh Iran 88 B2
Sa'īn Qal'eh Iran see Sa'īndezh
St Abb's Head hd U.K. 50 G5
St Agnes U.K. 49 B8
St Agnes i. U.K. 49 A9
St Alban's Canada 123 L5
St Albans U.K. 49 G7
St Albans VT U.S.A. 135 I1
St Albans WV U.S.A. 134 E4
St Alban's Head hd U.K. 49 E8
St Albert Canada 120 H4
St Aldhelm's Head hd U.K. see St Alban's Head
St-Amand-les-Eaux France 52 D4
St-Amand-Montrond France 56 F3
St-Amour France 56 G3
St-André, Cap pt Madag. see Vilanandro, Tanjona
St Andrews U.K. 50 G4
St Andrew Sound inlet U.S.A. 133 D6
St Anne U.S.A. 134 B3
St Ann's Bay Jamaica 137 I5
St Anthony Canada 123 L4
St Anthony U.S.A. 126 F4
St-Arnaud Alg. see El Eulma
St Arnaud Australia 112 A6
St Arnaud Range mts N.Z. 113 D6
St-Arnoult-en-Yvelines France 52 B6
St-Augustin Canada 123 K4
St Augustin r. Canada 123 K4
St Augustine U.S.A. 133 D6
St Austell U.K. 49 C8
St-Avertin France 56 E3
St-Avold France 52 G5
St Barbe Canada 123 K4
St-Barthélemy i. West Indies 137 L5
St Bees U.K. 48 D4
St Bees Head hd U.K. 48 D4
St Bride's Bay U.K. 49 B7
St-Brieuc France 56 C2
St Catharines Canada 134 F2
St Catherines Island U.S.A. 133 D6
St Catherine's Point U.K. 49 F8
St-Céré France 56 E4
St-Chamond France 56 G4
St Charles ID U.S.A. 126 F4
St Charles MD U.S.A. 135 G4
St Charles MI U.S.A. 134 C2
St Charles MO U.S.A. 130 F4
St-Chély-d'Apcher France 56 F4
St Christopher and Nevis country West Indies see St Kitts and Nevis
St Clair r. Canada/U.S.A. 134 D2
St Clair, Lake Canada/U.S.A. 134 D2
St-Claude France 56 G3
St Clears U.K. 49 C7
St Cloud U.S.A. 130 E2
St Croix r. U.S.A. 122 B5
St Croix Falls U.S.A. 130 E2
St David U.S.A. 129 H6
St David's Head hd U.K. 49 B7
St-Denis France 52 C6

▶St-Denis Réunion 149 L7
Capital of Réunion.

St-Denis-du-Sig Alg. see Sig
St-Dié France 56 H2
St-Dizier France 52 E6
St-Domingue country West Indies see Haiti
Sainte Anne Canada 121 L5
Ste-Anne, Lac l. Canada 123 I4
St Elias, Cape U.S.A. 118 D4

▶St Elias, Mount U.S.A. 120 A2
4th highest mountain in North America.

St Elias Mountains Canada 120 A2
Ste-Marguerite r. Canada 123 I4
Ste-Marie, Cap c. Madag. see Vohimena, Tanjona
Sainte-Marie, Île i. Madag. see Boraha, Nosy
Ste-Maxime France 56 H5
Sainte Rose du Lac Canada 121 L5
Saintes France 56 D4
Sainte Thérèse, Lac l. Canada 120 F1
St-Étienne France 56 G4
St-Étienne-du-Rouvray France 52 B5
St-Fabien Canada 123 H4
St-Félicien Canada 123 G4
Saintfield U.K. 51 G3
St-Florent Corsica France 56 I5
St-Florent-sur-Cher France 56 F3
St Floris, Parc National nat. park Cent. Afr. Rep. 98 C3
St-Flour France 56 F4
St Francesville U.S.A. 131 F6
St Francis U.S.A. 130 C4
St Francis r. U.S.A. 131 F5
St Francis Isles Australia 109 F8
St-François r. Canada 123 G5
St-François, Lac l. Canada 123 H5
St-Gaudens France 56 E5
St George Australia 112 D2
St George r. Australia 110 D3
St George AK U.S.A. 118 B4
St George SC U.S.A. 133 D5
St George UT U.S.A. 129 G3
St George, Point U.S.A. 126 B4
St George Head hd Australia 112 E5
St George Island U.S.A. 118 B4
St George Ranges hills Australia 108 D4
St-Georges Canada 123 H5

▶St George's Grenada 137 L6
Capital of Grenada.

St George's Bay Nfld. and Lab. Canada 123 K4
St George's Bay N.S. Canada 123 J5
St George's Channel P. N.G. 106 F2
St George's Channel Rep. of Ireland/U.K. 51 F6
St Gotthard Hungary see Szentgotthárd
St Gotthard Pass Switz. 56 I3
St Govan's Head hd U.K. 49 C7
St Helen U.S.A. 134 C1
St Helena U.S.A. 128 B2
St Helena i. S. Atlantic Ocean 148 H7

▶St Helena and Dependencies terr. S. Atlantic Ocean 148 H7
United Kingdom Overseas territory. Consists of St Helena, Ascension, Tristan da Cunha and Gough Island.
Africa 7

St Helena Bay S. Africa 100 D7
St Helens Australia 111 [inset]
St Helens U.K. 48 E5
St Helens U.S.A. 126 C3
St Helens, Mount vol. U.S.A. 126 C3
St Helens Point Australia 111 [inset]

▶St Helier Channel Is 49 E9
Capital of Jersey.

Sainthiya India 83 F5
St-Hubert Belgium 52 F4
St-Hyacinthe Canada 123 G5
St Ignace U.S.A. 132 C2
St Ignace Island Canada 122 D4
St Ishmael U.K. 49 C7
St Ives England U.K. 49 B8
St Ives England U.K. 49 G6
St-Jacques, Cap Vietnam see Vung Tau
St-Jacques-de-Dupuy Canada 122 F4
St James MN U.S.A. 130 E3
St James MO U.S.A. 130 F4
St James, Cape Canada 120 D5
St-Jean r. Canada 123 I4
St-Jean, Lac l. Canada 123 G4
St-Jean-d'Acre Israel see 'Akko
St-Jean-d'Angély France 56 D4
St-Jean-de-Monts France 56 C3
St-Jean-sur-Richelieu Canada 135 I1
St-Jérôme Canada 122 G5
St Joe r. U.S.A. 126 D3
Saint John Canada 123 I5
St John U.S.A. 130 D4
St John r. U.S.A. 132 H2
St John, Cape Canada 123 L4
St John Bay Canada 123 K4
St John Island Canada 123 K4

▶St John's Antigua and Barbuda 137 L5
Capital of Antigua and Barbuda.

▶St John's Canada 123 L5
Provincial capital of Newfoundland and Labrador.

St Johns AZ U.S.A. 129 I4
St Johns MI U.S.A. 134 C2
St Johns OH U.S.A. 134 C3
St Johns r. U.S.A. 133 D6
St Johnsbury U.S.A. 135 I1
St John's Chapel U.K. 48 E4
St Joseph IL U.S.A. 134 A3
St Joseph LA U.S.A. 131 F6
St Joseph MI U.S.A. 134 B2
St Joseph MO U.S.A. 130 E4
St Joseph r. U.S.A. 134 C3
St Joseph, Lake Canada 121 N5
St-Joseph-d'Alma Canada see Alma
St Joseph Island Canada 122 E5
St-Junien France 56 E4
St Just U.K. 49 B8
St-Just-en-Chaussée France 52 C5
St Keverne U.K. 49 B8
St Kilda i. U.K. 40 E4
St Kilda is U.K. 46 C2
▶St Kitts and Nevis country West Indies 137 L5
North America 9, 116–117
St-Laurent inlet Canada see St Lawrence
St-Laurent, Golfe du g. Canada see St Lawrence, Gulf of
St-Laurent-du-Maroni Fr. Guiana 143 H2
St Lawrence Canada 123 L5
St Lawrence inlet Canada 123 H4
St Lawrence, Cape Canada 123 J5
St Lawrence, Gulf of Canada 123 J4
St Lawrence Island U.S.A. 118 B3
St Lawrence Islands National Park Canada 135 H1
St Lawrence Seaway sea chan. Canada/U.S.A. 135 H1
St-Léonard Canada 123 G5
St Leonard U.S.A. 135 G4
St Lewis r. Canada 123 K3
St-Lô France 56 D2
St-Louis Senegal 96 B3
St Louis MI U.S.A. 134 C2
St Louis MO U.S.A. 130 F4
St Louis r. U.S.A. 122 B5
▶St Lucia country West Indies 137 L6
North America 9, 116–117
St Lucia, Lake S. Africa 101 K5
St Lucia Estuary S. Africa 101 K5
St Luke's Island Myanmar see Zadetkale Kyun
St Magnus Bay U.K. 50 [inset]
St-Maixent-l'École France 56 D3
St-Malo France 56 C2
St-Malo, Golfe de g. France 56 C2
St-Marc Haiti 137 J5
St Maries U.S.A. 126 D3
St Marks S. Africa 101 H7
St Mark's S. Africa see Cofimvaba

▶St-Martin i. West Indies 137 L5
Dependency of Guadeloupe (France). The southern part of the island is the Dutch territory of Sint Maarten.

St Martin, Cape S. Africa 100 C7
St Martin, Lake Canada 121 L5
St Martin's i. U.K. 49 A9
St Martin's Island Bangl. 70 A2
St Mary Peak Australia 111 B6
St Mary Reservoir Canada 120 H5
St Mary's Canada 134 E2
St Mary's U.K. 50 G2
St Mary's i. U.K. 49 A9
St Marys PA U.S.A. 135 F3
St Marys WV U.S.A. 134 E4
St Marys r. U.S.A. 134 C3
St Mary's, Cape Canada 123 L5
St Mary's Bay Canada 123 L5
St Marys City U.S.A. 135 G4
St Matthew Island U.S.A. 118 A3
St Matthews U.S.A. 134 C4
St Matthew's Island Myanmar see Zadetkyi Kyun
St Matthias Group is P. N.G. 69 L7
St Maurice r. Canada 123 G5
St Mawes U.K. 49 B8
St-Médard-en-Jalles France 56 D4
St Meinrad U.S.A. 134 B4
St Michaels U.S.A. 135 G4
St Michael's Bay Canada 123 L3
St-Mihiel France 52 F6
St-Nazaire France 56 C3
St Neots U.K. 49 G6
St-Nicolas Belgium see Sint-Niklaas
St-Nicolas, Mont hill Lux. 52 G5
St-Nicolas-de-Port France 56 H2
St-Omer France 52 C4
Saintonge reg. France 56 D4
St-Pacôme Canada 123 H5
St-Palais France 56 D5
St Paris U.S.A. 134 D3
St Pascal Canada 123 H5
St Paul r. Canada 123 K4
St-Paul atoll Fr. Polynesia see Hérèhérétué
St Paul AK U.S.A. 118 A4

▶St Paul MN U.S.A. 130 E2
State capital of Minnesota.

St Paul NE U.S.A. 130 D3
St-Paul, Île i. Indian Ocean 149 N8
St Paul Island U.S.A. 118 A4
St Peter and St Paul Rocks is N. Atlantic Ocean see São Pedro e São Paulo

▶St Peter Port Channel Is 49 E9
Capital of Guernsey.

St Peter's Nova Scotia Canada 123 J5
St Peters P.E.I. Canada 123 J5
St Petersburg Rus. Fed. 45 Q7
St Petersburg U.S.A. 133 D7
St-Pierre mt. France 56 G5

▶St-Pierre St Pierre and Miquelon 123 L5
Capital of St Pierre and Miquelon.

▶St Pierre and Miquelon terr. N. America 123 K5
French Territorial Collectivity.
North America 9, 116–117

St-Pierre-d'Oléron France 56 D4
St-Pierre-le-Moûtier France 56 F3
St-Pol-sur-Ternoise France 52 C4
St-Pourçain-sur-Sioule France 56 F3
St-Quentin France 52 D5
St Regis U.S.A. 126 E3
St Regis Falls U.S.A. 135 H1
St-Rémi Canada 135 I1
St-Saëns France 52 B5
St Sebastian Bay S. Africa 100 E8
St Siméon Canada 123 H5
St Simons Island U.S.A. 133 D6
St Theresa Point Canada 121 M4
St Thomas Canada 134 E2
St-Trond Belgium see Sint-Truiden
St-Tropez France 56 H5
St-Tropez, Cap de c. France 56 H5
St-Vaast-la-Hougue France 49 F9
St-Valery-en-Caux France 49 H9
St-Véran France 56 H4
St Vincent U.S.A. 130 D1
St Vincent country West Indies see St Vincent and the Grenadines
St Vincent, Cape Australia 111 [inset]
St Vincent, Cape Port. see São Vicente, Cabo de
St Vincent, Gulf Australia 111 B7
▶St Vincent and the Grenadines country West Indies 137 L6
North America 9, 116–117
St Vincent Passage St Lucia/St Vincent 137 L6
St-Vith Belgium 52 G4
St Walburg Canada 121 I4
St Williams Canada 134 E2
St-Yrieix-la-Perche France 56 E4
Sain Us China 72 J4
Saioa mt. Spain 57 F2
Saipal mt. Nepal 82 E3
Saipan i. N. Mariana Is 69 L3
Sai Pok Liu Hoi Hap Hong Kong China see West Lamma Channel
Saiteli Turkey see Kadınhanı
Saitlai Myanmar 70 A2
Saittanulkki hill Fin. 44 N3
Sai Yok National Park Thai. 71 B4
Sajam Indon. 69 I7
Sajama, Nevado mt. Bol. 142 E7
Sājir Saudi Arabia 88 B5
Sājūr, Nahr r. Syria/Turkey 85 D1
Sajzī Iran 88 D3
Sak watercourse S. Africa 100 E5
Sakaide Japan 75 D6
Sakākah Saudi Arabia 91 F5
Sakakawea, Lake U.S.A. 130 C2
Sakami Canada 122 G3
Sakami r. Canada 122 F3
Sakami Lake Canada 122 F3
Sakar mts Bulg. 59 L4
Sakaraha Madag. 99 E6
Sak'art'velo country Asia see Georgia
Sakarya Turkey 59 N4
Sakarya r. Turkey 59 N4
Sakassou Côte d'Ivoire 96 C4
Sakata Japan 75 E5
Sakchu N. Korea 75 B4
Sakesar Pak. 89 I3
Sakhalin i. Rus. Fed. 74 F2
Sakhalin Oblast admin. div. Rus. Fed. see Sakhalinskaya Oblast'
Sakhalinskaya Oblast' admin. div. Rus. Fed. 74 F2
Sakhalinskiy Zaliv b. Rus. Fed. 74 F1
Sakhi India 82 C3
Sakhile S. Africa 101 I4
Sakht-Sar Iran 88 C2
Şäki Azer. 91 G2
Şaki Nigeria see Shaki
Saki Ukr. see Saky
Šakiai Lith. 45 M9
Sakir mt. Pak. 89 G4
Sakishima-shotō is Japan 73 M8
Sakoli India 82 D5
Sakon Nakhon Thai. 70 D3
Sakrivier S. Africa 100 E6
Sakura Japan 75 F6
Saky Ukr. 90 D1
Säkylä Fin. 45 M6
Sal i. Cape Verde 96 [inset]
Sal r. Rus. Fed. 43 I7
Sala Sweden 45 J7
Salaberry-de-Valleyfield Canada 135 H1
Salacgrīva Latvia 45 N8
Sala Consilina Italy 58 F4
Salada, Laguna salt l. Mex. 129 F5
Saladas Arg. 144 E3
Salado r. Buenos Aires Arg. 144 E5
Salado r. Santa Fé Arg. 144 D4
Salado r. Mex. 131 D7
Salaga Ghana 96 C4
Salairskiy Kryazh ridge Rus. Fed. 72 E2
Salajwe Botswana 100 G2
Şalālah Oman 87 H6
Salamanca Mex. 136 D4
Salamanca Spain 57 D3
Salamanca U.S.A. 135 F2
Salamanga Moz. 101 K4
Salamantica Spain see Salamanca
Salamat, Bahr r. Chad 97 E4
Salāmī Iran 89 E3
Salamina i. Greece 59 J6
Salamis tourist site Cyprus 85 A2
Salamís i. Greece see Salamina
Salamīyah Syria 85 C2
Salamonie r. U.S.A. 134 C3
Salamonie Lake U.S.A. 134 C3
Salang Tunnel Afgh. 89 H3
Salantai Lith. 45 L8
Salar de Pocitos Arg. 144 C2
Salari Pak. 89 G5
Salas Spain 57 C2
Salaspils Latvia 45 N8
Salawati i. Indon. 69 I7
Salawin, Mae Nam r. China/Myanmar see Salween
Salaya India 82 B5
Salayar i. Indon. 69 G8

▶Sala y Gómez, Isla i. S. Pacific Ocean 151 M7
Most easterly point of Oceania

Salazar Angola see N'dalatando
Salbris France 56 F3
Šalčininkai Lith. 45 N9
Salcombe U.K. 49 D8
Saldae Alg. see Bejaïa
Saldaña Spain 57 D2
Saldanha S. Africa 100 C7
Saldanha Bay S. Africa 100 C7
Saldus Latvia 45 M8
Sale Australia 112 C7
Saleh, Teluk b. Indon. 68 F8
Şāleḩābād Iran 88 C3
Salekhard Rus. Fed. 64 H3
Salem India 84 C4
Salem AR U.S.A. 131 F4
Salem IL U.S.A. 130 F4
Salem IN U.S.A. 134 B4
Salem MA U.S.A. 135 J2
Salem MO U.S.A. 130 F4
Salem NJ U.S.A. 135 H4
Salem NY U.S.A. 135 I2
Salem OH U.S.A. 134 E3

▶Salem OR U.S.A. 126 C3
State capital of Oregon.

Salem SD U.S.A. 130 D3
Salem VA U.S.A. 134 E5
Salen Scotland U.K. 50 D4
Salen Scotland U.K. 50 D4
Salerno Italy 58 F4
Salerno, Golfo di g. Italy 58 F4
Salernum Italy see Salerno
Salford U.K. 48 E5
Salgótarján Hungary 47 Q6
Salgueiro Brazil 143 K5
Salian Afgh. 89 F4
Salibabu i. Indon. 69 H6
Salida U.S.A. 127 G5
Salies-de-Béarn France 56 D5
Salihli Turkey 59 M5
Salihorsk Belarus 45 O10
Salima Malawi 99 D5
Salina KS U.S.A. 130 D4
Salina UT U.S.A. 129 H2
Salina, Isola i. Italy 58 F5
Salina Cruz Mex. 136 E5
Salinas Brazil 145 C2
Salinas Ecuador 142 B4
Salinas Mex. 136 D4
Salinas r. Mex. 131 D7
Salinas U.S.A. 128 C3
Salinas r. U.S.A. 128 C3
Salinas, Cabo de c. Spain see Ses Salines, Cap de
Salinas, Ponta das pt Angola 99 B5
Salinas Peak U.S.A. 127 G6
Saline U.S.A. 134 D2
Saline r. U.S.A. 130 D4
Saline Valley depr. U.S.A. 128 E3
Salinópolis Brazil 143 I4
Salinosó Lachay, Punta pt Peru 142 C6
Salisbury U.K. 49 F7
Salisbury MD U.S.A. 135 H4
Salisbury NC U.S.A. 132 D5
Salisbury Zimbabwe see Harare
Salisbury Plain U.K. 49 E7
Şalkhad Syria 85 C3
Salla Fin. 44 P3
Sallisaw U.S.A. 131 E5
Salluit Canada 153 K2
Sallum, Khalīj as b. Egypt 90 B5
Sallyana Nepal 83 E3
Salmās Iran 88 B2
Salmi Rus. Fed. 42 F3
Salmo Canada 120 G5
Salmon U.S.A. 126 E3
Salmon r. U.S.A. 126 D3
Salmon Arm Canada 120 G5
Salmon Falls Creek r. U.S.A. 126 E4
Salmon Gums Australia 109 C8
Salmon Reservoir U.S.A. 135 H2
Salmon River Mountains U.S.A. 126 E3
Salmtal Germany 52 G5
Salo Fin. 45 M6
Salome U.S.A. 129 G5
Salon India 82 E4
Salon-de-Provence France 56 G5
Salonica Greece see Thessaloniki
Salonika Greece see Thessaloniki
Salpausselkä reg. Fin. 45 N6
Salqīn Syria 85 C1
Salses, Étang de l. France see Leucate, Étang de
Sal'sk Rus. Fed. 43 I7
Salsomaggiore Terme Italy 58 C2
Salt Jordan see As Salt
Salt watercourse S. Africa 100 F7
Salt r. U.S.A. 129 G5
Salta Arg. 144 C2
Saltaire U.K. 48 F5
Saltash U.K. 49 C8
Saltcoats U.K. 50 E5
Saltee Islands Rep. of Ireland 51 F5
Saltfjellet Svartisen Nasjonalpark nat. park Norway 44 I3
Saltfjorden sea chan. Norway 44 H3
Salt Fork Arkansas r. U.S.A. 131 D4
Salt Fork Lake U.S.A. 134 E3
Saltillo Mex. 131 C7
Salt Lake India 89 I5

▶Salt Lake City U.S.A. 129 H1
State capital of Utah.

Salt Lick U.S.A. 134 D4
Salto Brazil 145 B3
Salto Uruguay 144 E4
Salto da Divisa Brazil 145 D2
Salto Grande Brazil 145 A3
Salton Sea salt l. U.S.A. 129 F5
Salto Santiago, Represa de resr Brazil 144 F3
Salt Range hills Pak. 89 I3
Salt River Canada 121 H2
Saluda U.S.A. 135 G5
Salûm Egypt see As Sallūm
Salûm, Khalîg el b. Egypt see Sallum, Khalīj as
Saluq, Kūh-e mt. Iran 88 E2
Salur India 84 D2
Saluzzo Italy 58 B2
Salvador Brazil 145 D1
Salvador country Central America see El Salvador
Salvador, Lake U.S.A. 131 F6
Salvaleón de Higüey Dom. Rep. see Higüey
Salvation Creek r. U.S.A. 129 H2
Salwah Saudi Arabia 98 F1
Salwah, Dawḩat b. Qatar/Saudi Arabia 88 C5
Salween r. China/Myanmar 76 C5
also known as Mae Nam Khong or Mae Nam Salawin or Nu Jiang (China) or Thanlwin (Myanmar)
Salyan Azer. 91 H3
Salyan Nepal see Sallyana
Sal'yany Azer. see Salyan
Salyersville U.S.A. 134 D5
Salzbrunn Namibia 100 C3
Salzburg Austria 47 N7
Salzgitter Germany 53 K2
Salzhausen Germany 53 K1
Salzkotten Germany 53 I3
Salzmünde Germany 53 L3
Salzwedel Germany 53 L2
Sam India 82 B4
Samae San, Ko i. Thai. 71 C4
Samagaltay Rus. Fed. 80 H1
Samāh well Saudi Arabia 88 B4
Samaida Iran see Someydeh
Samaixung China 83 E2
Samakhixai Laos see Attapu
Samalanga Indon. 71 B6
Samalayuca Mex. 127 G7
Samalkot India 84 D2
Samālūţ Egypt 90 C5
Samâlût Egypt see Samālūţ
Samana Cay i. Bahamas 133 F8
Samanala mt. Sri Lanka see Adam's Peak
Samandağı Turkey 85 B1
Samangān Afgh. see Āybak
Samangān Iran 89 F3
Samani Japan 74 F4
Samanlı Dağları mts Turkey 59 M4
Samar Kazakh. see Samarskoye
Samar i. Phil. 69 H4
Samara Rus. Fed. 43 K5
Samara r. Rus. Fed. 41 Q5
Samarga Rus. Fed. 74 E3
Samarinda Indon. 68 F7
Samarka Rus. Fed. 74 D3
Samarkand Uzbek. 89 G2
Samarkand, Pik mt. Tajik. see Samarqand, Qullai
Samarobriva France see Amiens
Samarqand Uzbek. see Samarkand
Samarqand, Qullai mt. Tajik. 89 H2
Sāmarrā' Iraq 91 F4
Samarskoye Kazakh. 80 F2
Samasata Pak. 89 H4
Samastipur India 83 F4
Şamaxı Azer. 91 H2
Samba Jammu and Kashmir 82 C2
Sambaliung mts Indon. 68 F6
Sambalpur India 83 E5
Sambar, Tanjung pt Indon. 68 E7
Sambas Indon. 71 E7
Sambat Ukr. see Kiev
Sambava Madag. 99 F5
Sambha India 83 G4
Sambhajinagar India see Aurangabad
Sambhal India 82 D3
Sambhar Lake India 82 C4
Sambir Ukr. 43 D6
Sambito r. Brazil 143 J5
Sâmbor Cambodia 71 D4
Sambor Ukr. see Sambir
Samborombón, Bahía b. Arg. 144 E5
Sambre r. Belgium/France 52 E4
Samch'ŏk S. Korea 75 C5
Samch'ŏnp'o S. Korea see Sach'on
Same Tanz. 98 D4
Samer France 52 B4
Sami India 82 B5
Samīrah Saudi Arabia 86 F4
Samirum Iran see Yazd-e Khvāst
Samjiyŏn N. Korea 74 C4
Şämkir Azer. 91 G2
Samnan va Damghan reg. Iran 88 D3
Sam Neua Laos see Xam Nua
▶Samoa country S. Pacific Ocean 107 I3
Oceania 8, 104–105
Samoa Basin sea feature S. Pacific Ocean 150 I7
Samoa i Sisifo country S. Pacific Ocean see Samoa
Samobor Croatia 58 F2
Samoded Rus. Fed. 42 I3
Samokov Bulg. 59 J3
Šamorín Slovakia 47 P6
Samos i. Greece 59 L6
Samosir i. Indon. 71 B7
Samothrace i. Greece see Samothraki
Samothraki i. Greece 59 K4
Samoylovka Rus. Fed. 43 I6
Sampê China see Xiangcheng
Sampit Indon. 68 E7
Sampit, Teluk b. Indon. 68 E7
Sam Rayburn Reservoir U.S.A. 131 E6
Samrong Cambodia see Phumĭ Sâmraông
Samsang China 83 E3
Sam Sao, Phou mts Laos/Vietnam 70 C2
Samson U.S.A. 133 C6
Sâm Sơn Vietnam 70 D3
Samsun Turkey 90 E2
Samti Afgh. 89 H2
Samui, Ko i. Thai. 71 C5
Samut Prakan Thai. 71 C4
Samut Sakhon Thai. 71 C4
Samut Songkhram Thai. 71 C4
Samyai China 83 G3
San Mali 96 C3
San, Phou mt. Laos 70 C3
San, Tônlé r. Cambodia 71 D4

▶Şan'ā' Yemen 86 F6
Capital of Yemen.

Sanaa Yemen see Şan'ā'
Sanae research station Antarctica 152 B2
San Agostín U.S.A. see St Augustine
San Agustin, Cape Phil. 69 H5
San Agustin, Plains of U.S.A. 129 I5

Sanak Island U.S.A. 118 B4
Sanandaj Iran 88 B3
San Andreas U.S.A. 128 C2
San Andrés, Isla de i. Caribbean Sea 137 H6
San Andres Mountains U.S.A. 127 G6
San Angelo U.S.A. 131 C6
San Antonio Chile 144 B4
San Antonio NM U.S.A. 127 G6
San Antonio TX U.S.A. 131 D6
San Antonio r. U.S.A. 131 D6
San Antonio, Cabo c. Cuba 137 H4
San Antonio Abad Spain 57 G4
San Antonio del Mar Mex. 127 D7
San Antonio Oeste Arg. 144 D6
San Antonio Reservoir U.S.A. 128 C4
San Augustín de Valle Fértil Arg. 144 C4
San Augustine U.S.A. 131 E6
San Benedetto del Tronto Italy 58 E3
San Benedicto, Isla i. Mex. 136 B5
San Benito U.S.A. 131 D7
San Benito r. U.S.A. 128 C3
San Benito Mountain U.S.A. 128 C3
San Bernardino U.S.A. 128 E4
San Bernardino Mountains U.S.A. 128 E4
San Bernardo Chile 144 B4
San Blas Mex. 127 F8
San Blas, Cape U.S.A. 133 C6
San Borja Bol. 142 E6
Sanbornville U.S.A. 135 J2
Sanbu China see Kaiping
San Buenaventura Mex. 131 C7
San Carlos Chile 144 B5
San Carlos Equat. Guinea see Luba
San Carlos Coahuila Mex. 131 C6
San Carlos Tamaulipas Mex. 131 D7
San Carlos U.S.A. 129 H5
San Carlos Venez. 142 E2
San Carlos de Bariloche Arg. 144 B6
San Carlos de Bolívar Arg. 144 D5
San Carlos Lake U.S.A. 129 H5
Sancha China 76 E1
Sanchahe China see Fuyu
Sancha He r. China 76 E3
Sanchi India 82 D5
San Chien Pau mt. Laos 70 C2
Sanchor India 82 B4
San Clemente U.S.A. 128 E5
San Clemente Island U.S.A. 128 D5
Sanclêr U.K. see St Clears
San Cristóbal Arg. 144 D4
San Cristobal i. Solomon Is 107 G3
San Cristóbal Venez. 142 D2
San Cristóbal, Isla i. Galápagos Ecuador 142 [inset]
San Cristóbal de las Casas Mex. 136 F5
Sancti Spíritus Cuba 137 I4
Sand r. S. Africa 101 J2
Sandagou Rus. Fed. 74 D4
Sanda Island U.K. 50 D5
Sandakan Sabah Malaysia 68 F5
Sândân Cambodia 71 D4
Sandane Norway 44 E6
Sandanski Bulg. 59 J4
Sandaré Mali 96 B3
Sandau Germany 53 M2
Sanday i. U.K. 50 G1
Sandbach U.K. 49 E5
Sandborn U.S.A. 134 B4
Sand Cay reef India 84 B4
Sandefjord Norway 45 G7
Sandercock Nunataks Antarctica 152 D2
Sanders U.S.A. 129 I4
Sandersleben Germany 53 L3
Sanderson U.S.A. 131 C6
Sandfire Roadhouse Australia 108 C4
Sand Fork U.S.A. 134 E4
Sandgate Australia 112 F1
Sandhead U.K. 50 E6
Sand Hill r. U.S.A. 130 D2
Sand Hills U.S.A. 130 C3
Sandia Peru 142 E6
San Diego Mex. 131 B6
San Diego CA U.S.A. 128 E5
San Diego TX U.S.A. 131 D7
San Diego, Sierra mts Mex. 127 F7
Sandıklı Turkey 59 N5
Sandila India 82 E4
Sand Lake Canada 122 D5
Sand Lake l. Canada 121 M5
Sandnes Norway 45 D7
Sandnessjøen Norway 44 H3
Sandoa Dem. Rep. Congo 99 C4
Sandomierz Poland 43 D6
San Donà di Piave Italy 58 E2
Sandover watercourse Australia 110 B4
Sandovo Rus. Fed. 42 H4
Sandoway Myanmar 70 A3
Sandown U.K. 49 F8
Sandoy i. Faroe Is 44 [inset]
Sand Point U.S.A. 118 B4
Sandpoint U.S.A. 126 D2
Sandray i. U.K. 50 B4
Sandringham Australia 110 B5
Şandrul Mare, Vârful mt. Romania 59 L1
Sandsjö Sweden 45 I6
Sandspit Canada 120 D4
Sand Springs U.S.A. 131 D4
Sand Springs Salt Flat U.S.A. 128 D2
Sandstone Australia 109 B6
Sandstone U.S.A. 130 E2
Sandu Guizhou China 76 E3
Sandu Hunan China 77 G3
Sandur Faroe Is 44 [inset]
Sandusky MI U.S.A. 134 D2
Sandusky OH U.S.A. 134 D3
Sandveld mts S. Africa 100 D6
Sandverhaar Namibia 100 C4
Sandvika Akershus Norway 45 G7
Sandvika Nord-Trøndelag Norway 44 H5
Sandviken Sweden 45 J6
Sandwich Bay Canada 123 K3
Sandwich Island Vanuatu see Éfaté
Sandwich Islands N. Pacific Ocean see Hawaiian Islands
Sandwick U.K. 50 [inset]
Sandwip Bangl. 83 G5
Sandy U.S.A. 129 H1
Sandy r. U.S.A. 135 K1
Sandy Bay Canada 121 K4
Sandy Cape Qld Australia 110 F5
Sandy Cape Tas. Australia 111 [inset]
Sandy Hook U.S.A. 134 D4
Sandy Hook pt U.S.A. 135 H3
Sandy Island Australia 108 C3
Sandykachi Turkm. 89 F2
Sandykgachy Turkm. see Sandykachi
Sandykly Gumy des. Turkm. see Sundukli, Peski
Sandy Lake Alta Canada 120 H4
Sandy Lake Ont. Canada 121 M4
Sandy Lake l. Canada 121 M4
Sandy Springs U.S.A. 133 C5
San Estanislao Para. 144 E2
San Esteban, Isla i. Mex. 127 E7
San Felipe Chile 144 B4
San Felipe Baja California Mex. 127 E7
San Felipe Chihuahua Mex. 127 G8
San Felipe Venez. 142 E1
San Felipe, Cayos de is Cuba 133 D8
San Felipe de Puerto Plata Dom. Rep. see Puerto Plata
San Fernando Chile 144 B4
San Fernando Mex. 131 D7
San Fernando watercourse Mex. 127 E7
San Fernando Phil. 69 G3
San Fernando Spain 57 C5
San Fernando Trin. and Tob. 137 L6
San Fernando U.S.A. 128 D4
San Fernando de Apure Venez. 142 E2
San Fernando de Atabapo Venez. 142 E3
San Fernando de Monte Cristi Dom. Rep. see Monte Cristi
Sanford FL U.S.A. 133 D6
Sanford ME U.S.A. 135 J2
Sanford MI U.S.A. 134 C2
Sanford NC U.S.A. 132 E5
Sanford, Mount U.S.A. 118 D3
Sanford Lake U.S.A. 134 C2
San Francisco Arg. 144 D4
San Francisco U.S.A. 128 B3
San Francisco, Cabo de c. Ecuador 142 B3
San Francisco, Passo de pass Arg./Chile 144 C3
San Francisco Bay inlet U.S.A. 128 B3
San Francisco del Oro Mex. 131 B7
San Francisco de Paula, Cabo c. Arg. 144 C7
San Francisco Javier Spain 57 G4
San Gabriel, Punta pt Mex. 127 E7
San Gabriel Mountains U.S.A. 128 D4
Sangachaly Azer. see Sanqaçal
Sangameshwar India 84 B2
Sangamon r. U.S.A. 130 F3
Sangan, Koh-i- mt. Afgh. see Sangān, Kūh-e
Sangān, Kūh-e mt. Afgh. 89 G3
Sangar Rus. Fed. 65 N3
Sangareddi India 84 C2
Sangareddy India see Sangareddi
San Gavino Monreale Sardinia Italy 58 C5
Sangay, Parque Nacional nat. park Ecuador 142 C4
Sangbur Afgh. 89 F3
Sangeang i. Indon. 108 B2
Sanger U.S.A. 128 D3
Sangerfield U.S.A. 135 H2
Sangerhausen Germany 53 L3
Sang-e Surakh Iran 88 E2
Sanggarmai China 76 D1
Sanggau Indon. 68 E6
Sangilen, Nagor'ye mts Rus. Fed. 80 I1
San Giovanni in Fiore Italy 58 G5
Sangir India 82 C5
Sangir i. Indon. 69 H6
Sangir, Kepulauan is Indon. 69 G6
Sangiyn Dalay Mongolia 72 I3
Sangkapura Indon. 68 E8
Sangkulirang Indon. 68 F6
Sangli India 84 B2
Sangmai China see Dêrong
Sangmélima Cameroon 96 E4
Sangngagqoiling China 76 B2
Sango Zimbabwe 99 D6
Sangole India 84 B2
San Gorgonio Mountain U.S.A. 128 E4
Sangpi China see Xiangcheng
Sangre de Cristo Range mts U.S.A. 127 G5
Sangrur India 82 C3
Sangu r. Bangl. 83 G5
Sanguem India 84 B3
Sangutane r. Moz. 101 K3
Sangzhi China 77 F2
Sanhe China see Sandu
San Hipólito, Punta pt Mex. 127 E8
Sanhûr Egypt 90 C5
Sanhûr Egypt see Sanhūr
San Ignacio Beni Bol. 142 E6
San Ignacio Santa Cruz Bol. 142 F7
San Ignacio Santa Cruz Bol. 142 F7
San Ignacio Baja California Mex. 127 E7
San Ignacio Durango Mex. 131 C7
San Ignacio Sonora Mex. 127 F7
San Ignacio Para. 144 E3
San Ignacio, Laguna l. Mex. 127 E8
Sanikiluaq Canada 122 F2
Sanin-kaigan National Park Japan 75 D6
San Jacinto U.S.A. 128 E5
San Jacinto Peak U.S.A. 128 E5
San Javier Bol. 142 F7
Sanjeli India 82 C5
Sanjiang Guangdong China see Liannan
Sanjiang Guangxi China 77 F3
Sanjiang Guizhou China see Jinping
Sanjiangkou China 74 A4
Sanjiaocheng China see Haiyan
Sanjiaoping China 77 F2
Sanjō Japan 75 E5
San Joaquin r. U.S.A. 128 C2
San Joaquin Valley U.S.A. 128 C3
San Jon U.S.A. 131 C5
San Jorge, Golfo de g. Arg. 144 C7
San Jorge, Golfo de g. Spain see Sant Jordi, Golf de
▶San José Costa Rica 137 H7
Capital of Costa Rica.
San Jose Phil. 69 G3
San Jose CA U.S.A. 128 C3
San Jose NM U.S.A. 127 G6
San Jose watercourse U.S.A. 129 J4
San José, Isla i. Mex. 136 B4
San José de Amacuro Venez. 142 F2
San José de Bavicora Mex. 127 G7
San Jose de Buenavista Phil. 69 G4
San José de Chiquitos Bol. 142 F7
San José de Comondú Mex. 127 F8
San José de Gracia Mex. 127 E8
San Josée la Brecha Mex. 127 F8
San José del Cabo Mex. 136 C4
San José del Guaviare Col. 142 D3
San José de Mayo Uruguay 144 E4
San José de Raíces Mex. 131 C7
San Juan Arg. 144 C4
San Juan r. Costa Rica/Nicaragua 137 H6
San Juan mt. Cuba 133 D8
San Juan Mex. 127 G8
San Juan r. Mex. 131 D7
▶San Juan Puerto Rico 137 K5
Capital of Puerto Rico.
San Juan U.S.A. 129 J5
San Juan r. U.S.A. 129 H3
San Juan, Cabo c. Arg. 144 D8
San Juan, Cabo c. Equat. Guinea 96 D4
San Juan Bautista Para. 144 E3
San Juan Bautista de las Misiones Para. see San Juan Bautista
San Juan de Guadalupe Mex. 131 C7
San Juan de los Morros Venez. 142 E2
San Juan Mountains U.S.A. 129 J3
San Juan y Martínez Cuba 129 D8
San Julián Arg. 144 C7
San Justo Arg. 144 D4
Sankari Drug India 84 C4
Sankh r. India 81 F7
Sankhu India 82 C3
Sankra Chhattisgarh India 84 D1
Sankra Rajasthan India 82 B4
Sankt Augustin Germany 53 H4
Sankt Gallen Switz. 56 I3
Sankt-Peterburg Rus. Fed. see St Petersburg
Sankt Pölten Austria 47 O6
Sankt Veit an der Glan Austria 47 O7
Sankt Vith Belgium see St-Vith
Sankt Wendel Germany 53 H5
Sanku Jammu and Kashmir 82 D2
Şanlıurfa Turkey 90 E3
Şanlıurfa prov. Turkey 85 D1
San Lorenzo Arg. 144 D4
San Lorenzo Beni Bol. 142 E7
San Lorenzo Tarija Bol. 142 F8
San Lorenzo Ecuador 142 C3
San Lorenzo mt. Spain 57 E2
San Lorenzo, Cerro mt. Arg./Chile 144 B7
San Lorenzo, Isla i. Mex. 127 E7
Sanlúcar de Barrameda Spain 57 C5
San Lucas Baja California Sur Mex. 127 E8
San Lucas Baja California Sur Mex. 136 C4
San Lucas, Serranía de mts Col. 142 D2
San Luis Arg. 144 C4
San Luis AZ U.S.A. 129 F5
San Luis AZ U.S.A. 129 H5
San Luis CO U.S.A. 131 B4
San Luís, Isla i. Mex. 127 E7
San Luisito Mex. 127 E7
San Luis Obispo U.S.A. 128 C4
San Luis Obispo Bay U.S.A. 128 C4
San Luis Potosí Mex. 136 D4
San Luis Reservoir U.S.A. 128 C3
San Luis Río Colorado Mex. 129 F5
San Manuel U.S.A. 129 H5
San Marcial, Punta pt Mex. 127 F8
San Marcos U.S.A. 131 D6
San Marcos, Isla i. Mex. 127 E8
▶San Marino country Europe 58 E3
Europe 5, 38–39
▶San Marino San Marino 58 E3
Capital of San Marino.
San Martín research station Antarctica 152 L2
San Martín Catamarca Arg. 144 C3
San Martín Mendoza Arg. 144 C4
San Martín, Lago l. Arg./Chile 144 B7
San Martín de los Andes Arg. 144 B6
San Mateo U.S.A. 128 B3
San Mateo Mountains U.S.A. 129 J4
San Matías Bol. 143 G7
San Matías, Golfo g. Arg. 144 D6
Sanmen China 77 I2
Sanmen Wan b. China 77 I2
Sanmenxia China 77 F1
San Miguel El Salvador 136 G6
San Miguel U.S.A. 128 C4
San Miguel r. U.S.A. 129 I2
San Miguel de Huachi Bol. 142 E7
San Miguel de Tucumán Arg. 144 C3
San Miguel do Araguaia Brazil 145 A1
San Miguel Island U.S.A. 128 C4
Sanming China 77 H3
Sanndatti India 84 B3
Sanndraigh i. U.K. see Sandray
Sannicandro Garganico Italy 58 F4
San Nicolás Durango Mex. 131 B7
San Nicolás Tamaulipas Mex. 131 D7
San Nicolas Island U.S.A. 128 D5
Sannieshof S. Africa 101 G4
Sanniquellie Liberia 96 C4
Sanok Poland 43 D6
San Pablo Bol. 142 E8
San Pablo Phil. 69 G4
San Pablo de Manta Ecuador see Manta
San Pedro Arg. 144 D2
San Pedro Bol. 142 F7
San Pedro Chile 144 C2
San-Pédro Côte d'Ivoire 96 C4
San Pedro Baja California Sur Mex. 124 E7
San Pedro Chihuahua Mex. 127 G7
San Pedro Para. see San Pedro de Ycuamandyyú
San Pedro watercourse U.S.A. 129 H5
San Pedro, Sierra de mts Spain 57 C4
San Pedro Channel U.S.A. 128 D5
San Pedro de Arimena Col. 142 D3
San Pedro de Atacama Chile 144 C2
San Pedro de las Colonias Mex. 131 C7
San Pedro de Macorís Dom. Rep. 137 K5
San Pedro de Ycuamandyyú Para. 144 E2
San Pedro Martir, Parque Nacional nat. park Mex. 127 E7
San Pedro Sula Hond. 136 G5
San Pierre U.S.A. 134 B3
San Pietro, Isola di i. Sardinia Italy 58 C5
San Pitch r. U.S.A. 129 H2
Sanqaçal Azer. 91 H2
Sanquhar U.K. 50 F5
Sanquianga, Parque Nacional nat. park Col. 142 C3
San Quintín, Cabo c. Mex. 127 D7
San Rafael Arg. 144 C4
San Rafael CA U.S.A. 128 B3
San Rafael NM U.S.A. 129 J4
San Rafael r. U.S.A. 129 H2
San Rafael Knob mt. U.S.A. 125 H2
San Rafael Mountains U.S.A. 128 C4
San Ramón Bol. 142 F6
Sanrao China 77 H3
San Remo Italy 58 B3
San Roque Spain 57 B2
San Roque, Punta pt Mex. 127 E8
San Saba U.S.A. 131 D6
San Salvador i. Bahamas 133 F7
▶San Salvador El Salvador 136 G6
Capital of El Salvador.
San Salvador, Isla i. Galápagos Ecuador 142 [inset]
San Salvador de Jujuy Arg. 144 C2
Sansanné-Mango Togo 96 D3
San Sebastián Arg. 144 C8
San Sebastián Spain see Donostia - San Sebastián
San Sebastián de los Reyes Spain 57 E3
Sansepolcro Italy 58 E3
San Severo Italy 58 F4
San Simon U.S.A. 129 I5
Sanski Most Bos.-Herz. 58 G2
Sansoral Islands Palau see Sonsorol Islands
Sansui China 77 F3
Santa r. Peru 142 C5
Santa Ana Bol. 142 E7
Santa Ana El Salvador 136 G6
Santa Ana Mex. 127 F7
Santa Ana i. Solomon Is 107 G3
Santa Ana U.S.A. 128 E5
Santa Ana de Yacuma Bol. 142 E6
Santa Anna U.S.A. 131 D6
Santa Bárbara Brazil 145 C2
Santa Bárbara Cuba see La Demajagua
Santa Bárbara Mex. 131 B7
Santa Barbara U.S.A. 128 D4
Santa Bárbara, Ilha i. Brazil 145 D2
Santa Barbara Channel U.S.A. 128 C4
Santa Bárbara d'Oeste Brazil 145 B3
Santa Barbara Island U.S.A. 128 D5
Santa Catalina, Gulf of U.S.A. 128 E5
Santa Catalina, Isla i. Mex. 127 F8
Santa Catalina de Armada Spain 57 B2
Santa Catalina Island U.S.A. 124 D5
Santa Catarina state Brazil 145 A4
Santa Catarina Baja California Mex. 127 E7
Santa Catarina Nuevo León Mex. 131 C7
Santa Catarina, Ilha de i. Brazil 145 A4
Santa Clara Col. 142 E4
Santa Clara Cuba 137 I4
Santa Clara Mex. 131 B6
Santa Clara CA U.S.A. 128 C3
Santa Clara UT U.S.A. 129 G3
Santa Clarita U.S.A. 128 D4
Santa Clotilde Peru 142 D4
Santa Comba Angola see Waku-Kungo
Santa Croce, Capo c. Sicily Italy 58 F6
Santa Cruz Bol. 142 F7
Santa Cruz Brazil 143 K5
Santa Cruz Costa Rica 142 A1
Santa Cruz U.S.A. 128 B3
Santa Cruz watercourse U.S.A. 129 G5
Santa Cruz, Isla i. Galápagos Ecuador 142 [inset]
Santa Cruz, Isla i. Mex. 127 F8
Santa Cruz Cabrália Brazil 145 D2
Santa Cruz de Goiás Brazil 145 A2
Santa Cruz de la Palma Canary Is 96 B2
Santa Cruz del Sur Cuba 137 I4
Santa Cruz de Moya Spain 57 F4
▶Santa Cruz de Tenerife Canary Is 96 B2
Joint capital of the Canary Islands.
Santa Cruz do Sul Brazil 144 F3
Santa Cruz Island U.S.A. 128 D4
Santa Cruz Islands Solomon Is 107 G3
Santa Elena, Bahía de b. Ecuador 142 B4
Santa Elena, Cabo c. Costa Rica 137 G6
Santa Elena, Punta pt Ecuador 142 B4
Santa Eudóxia Brazil 145 B3
Santa Eufemia, Golfo di g. Italy 58 G5
Santa Fé Arg. 144 D4
Santa Fé Cuba 133 D8
▶Santa Fe U.S.A. 127 G6
State capital of New Mexico.
Santa Fé de Bogotá Col. see Bogotá
Santa Fé de Minas Brazil 145 B2
Santa Fé do Sul Brazil 145 A3
Santa Helena Brazil 143 I4
Santa Helena de Goiás Brazil 145 A2
Santai Sichuan China 76 E2
Santai Yunnan China 76 D3
Santa Inês Brazil 143 I4
Santa Inés, Isla i. Chile 152 L3
Santa Isabel Arg. 144 C5
Santa Isabel Equat. Guinea see Malabo
Santa Isabel i. Solomon Is 107 F2
Santa Juliana Brazil 145 B2
Santalpur India 82 B5
Santa Lucia Range mts U.S.A. 128 C3
Santa Margarita U.S.A. 128 C4
Santa Margarita, Isla i. Mex. 136 B4
Santa María Arg. 144 C3
Santa Maria Amazonas Brazil 143 G4
Santa Maria Rio Grande do Sul Brazil 144 F3
Santa Maria Cape Verde 96 [inset]
Santa María r. Mex. 127 G7
Santa María Peru 142 D4
Santa Maria U.S.A. 128 C4
Santa Maria r. U.S.A. 129 G4
Santa Maria, Cabo de c. Moz. 101 K4
Santa Maria, Cabo de c. Port. 57 C5
Santa Maria, Chapadão de hills Brazil 145 B1
Santa María, Isla i. Galápagos Ecuador 142 [inset]
Santa Maria, Serra de hills Brazil 145 B1
Santa Maria da Vitória Brazil 145 B1
Santa María de Cuevas Mex. 131 B7
Santa Maria do Suaçuí Brazil 145 C2
Santa María Island Vanuatu 107 G3
Santa Maria Madalena Brazil 145 C3
Santa Maria Mountains U.S.A. 129 G4
Santa Marta Col. 142 D1
Santa Marta, Cabo de c. Angola 99 B5
Santa Marta Grande, Cabo de c. Brazil 145 A5
Santa Maura i. Greece see Lefkada
Santa Monica U.S.A. 128 D4
Santa Monica, Pico mt. Mex. 127 E8
Santa Monica Bay U.S.A. 128 D5
Santan Indon. 68 F7
Santana Brazil 145 C1
Santana r. Brazil 145 A2
Santana do Araguaia Brazil 143 H5
Santander Spain 57 E2
Santa Nella U.S.A. 128 C3
Santanilla, Islas is Caribbean Sea see Swan Islands
Santan Mountain hill U.S.A. 129 H5
Sant'Antioco Sardinia Italy 58 C5
Sant'Antioco, Isola di i. Sardinia Italy 58 C5
Santapilly India 84 D2
Santaquin U.S.A. 129 H2
Santa Quitéria Brazil 143 J4
Santarém Brazil 143 H4
Santarém Port. 57 B4
Santa Rita Mex. 131 C7
Santa Rosa Arg. 144 D5
Santa Rosa Acre Brazil 142 D5
Santa Rosa Rio Grande do Sul Brazil 144 F3
Santa Rosa Mex. 131 C7
Santa Rosa CA U.S.A. 128 B2
Santa Rosa NM U.S.A. 127 G6
Santa Rosa de Copán Hond. 136 G6
Santa Rosa de la Roca Bol. 142 F7
Santa Rosa Island U.S.A. 128 C5
Santa Rosalía Mex. 127 E8
Santa Rosa Range mts U.S.A. 126 D4
Santa Rosa Wash watercourse U.S.A. 129 G5
Santa Sylvina Arg. 144 D3
Santa Teresa Australia 109 F6
Santa Teresa r. Brazil 145 A1
Santa Teresa Mex. 131 D7
Santa Vitória Brazil 145 A2
Santa Ynez r. U.S.A. 128 C4
Santa Ysabel i. Solomon Is see Santa Isabel
Santee U.S.A. 128 E5
Santee r. U.S.A. 133 E5
Santiago Brazil 144 F3
Santiago i. Cape Verde 96 [inset]
▶Santiago Chile 144 B4
Capital of Chile.
Santiago Dom. Rep. 137 J5
Santiago Panama 137 H7
Santiago Phil. 69 G3
Santiago de Compostela Spain 57 B2
Santiago de Cuba Cuba 137 I4
Santiago del Estero Arg. 144 D3
Santiago de los Caballeros Dom. Rep. see Santiago
Santiago de Veraguas Panama see Santiago
Santiaguillo, Laguna de l. Mex. 131 B7
Santianna Point Canada 121 P2
Santipur India see Shantipur
Sant Jordi, Golf de g. Spain 57 G3
Santo Amaro Brazil 145 D1
Santo Amaro de Campos Brazil 145 C3
Santo Anastácio Brazil 145 A3
Santo André Brazil 145 B3
Santo Angelo Brazil 144 F3
▶Santo Antão i. Cape Verde 96 [inset]
Most westerly point of Africa.
Santo Antônio Brazil 142 F4
Santo Antônio r. Brazil 145 C2
Santo António São Tomé and Príncipe 96 D4
Santo Antônio, Cabo c. Brazil 145 D1
Santo Antônio da Platina Brazil 145 A3
Santo Antônio de Jesus Brazil 145 D1
Santo Antônio do Içá Brazil 142 E4
Santo Corazón Bol. 143 G7
Santo Domingo Cuba 133 D8
▶Santo Domingo Dom. Rep. 137 K5
Capital of the Dominican Republic.
Santo Domingo Baja California Mex. 127 E7
Santo Domingo Baja California Sur Mex. 127 F8
Santo Domingo country West Indies see Dominican Republic
Santo Domingo de Guzmán Dom. Rep. see Santo Domingo
Santo Hipólito Brazil 145 B2
Santorini i. Greece see Thira
Santos Brazil 145 B3
Santos Dumont Brazil 145 C3
Santos Plateau sea feature S. Atlantic Ocean 148 E7
Santo Tomás Mex. 127 E7
Santo Tomás Peru 142 D6
Santo Tomé Arg. 144 E3
Sanup Plateau U.S.A. 129 G3
San Valentín, Cerro mt. Chile 144 B7
San Vicente El Salvador 136 G6
San Vicente Mex. 127 D7
San Vicente de Baracaldo Spain see Barakaldo
San Vicente de Cañete Peru 142 C6
San Vincenzo Italy 58 D3
San Vito, Capo c. Sicily Italy 58 E5
Sanwer India 82 C5
Sanya China 77 F5
Sanyuan China 77 F1
Sanza Pombo Angola 99 B4
Sao, Phou mt. Laos 70 C3
São Bernardo do Campo Brazil 145 B3
São Borja Brazil 144 E3
São Carlos Brazil 145 B3
São Domingos Brazil 145 B1
São Felipe, Serra de hills Brazil 145 B1
São Félix Bahia Brazil 145 D1
São Félix Mato Grosso Brazil 143 H6
São Félix Pará Brazil 143 H5
São Fidélis Brazil 145 C3
São Francisco Brazil 145 B1
▶São Francisco r. Brazil 145 C1
5th longest river in South America.
São Francisco, Ilha de i. Brazil 145 A4
São Francisco de Paula Brazil 145 A5
São Francisco de Sales Brazil 145 A2
São Francisco do Sul Brazil 145 A4
São Gabriel Brazil 144 F4
São Gonçalo Brazil 145 C3
São Gonçalo do Abaeté Brazil 145 B2
São Gonçalo do Sapucaí Brazil 145 B3
São Gotardo Brazil 145 B2
São João, Ilhas de is Brazil 143 J4
São João da Barra Brazil 145 C3
São João da Boa Vista Brazil 145 B3
São João da Madeira Port. 57 B3
São João da Ponte Brazil 145 B1
São João del Rei Brazil 145 B3
São João do Paraíso Brazil 145 C1
São Joaquim Brazil 145 A5
São Joaquim da Barra Brazil 145 B3
São José Amazonas Brazil 142 E4
São José Santa Catarina Brazil 145 A4
São José do Rio Preto Brazil 145 A3
São José dos Campos Brazil 145 B3
São José dos Pinhais Brazil 145 A4
São Leopoldo Brazil 145 A5
São Lourenço Brazil 145 B3
São Lourenço r. Brazil 143 G7
São Luís Brazil 143 J4
São Luís Brazil 143 G4
São Luís de Montes Belos Brazil 145 A2
São Manuel Brazil 145 A3
São Marcos r. Brazil 145 B2
São Mateus Brazil 145 D2
São Mateus do Sul Brazil 145 A4
São Miguel i. Arquipélago dos Açores 148 G3
São Miguel r. Brazil 145 B2
São Miguel do Tapuio Brazil 143 J5
Saône r. France 56 G4
Saoner India 82 D5
São Nicolau i. Cape Verde 96 [inset]
▶São Paulo Brazil 145 B3
Most populous city in South America and 3rd in the world.
São Paulo state Brazil 145 A3
São Paulo de Olivença Brazil 142 E4
São Pedro da Aldeia Brazil 145 C3
São Pedro e São Paulo is N. Atlantic Ocean 148 G5
São Pires r. Brazil see Teles Pires
São Raimundo Nonato Brazil 143 J5
São Romão Amazonas Brazil 142 E5
São Romão Minas Gerais Brazil 145 B2
São Roque Brazil 145 B3
São Roque, Cabo de c. Brazil 143 K5
São Salvador Angola see M'banza Congo
São Salvador do Congo Angola see M'banza Congo
São Sebastião Brazil 145 B3
São Sebastião, Ilha do i. Brazil 145 B3
São Sebastião do Paraíso Brazil 145 B3
São Sebastião dos Poções Brazil 145 B1
São Simão Minas Gerais Brazil 143 H7
São Simão São Paulo Brazil 145 B3
São Simão, Barragem de resr Brazil 145 A2
São Tiago i. Cape Verde see Santiago
▶São Tomé São Tomé and Príncipe 96 D4
Capital of São Tomé and Príncipe.
São Tomé i. São Tomé and Príncipe 96 D4
São Tomé, Cabo de c. Brazil 145 C3
São Tomé, Pico de mt. São Tomé and Príncipe 96 D4
▶São Tomé and Príncipe country Africa 96 D4
Africa 7, 94–95
Saoura, Oued watercourse Alg. 54 D6
São Vicente Brazil 145 B3
São Vicente i. Cape Verde 96 [inset]
São Vicente, Cabo de c. Port. 57 B5
Sapanca Turkey 59 N4
Sapaul India see Supaul
Şaphane Dağı mt. Turkey 59 N5
Sapo National Park Liberia 96 C4
Sapouy Burkina 96 C3
Sapozhok Rus. Fed. 43 I5
Sappa Creek r. U.S.A. 130 D3
Sapporo Japan 74 F4
Sapulpa U.S.A. 131 D4
Sapulut Sabah Malaysia 68 F6
Saputang China see Zadoi
Sāqī Iran 88 E3
Saqqez Iran 88 B2
Sarā Iran 88 B2
Sarāb Iran 88 B2
Sara Buri Thai. 71 C4
Saradiya India 82 B5
Saragossa Spain see Zaragoza
Saragt Akhal'skaya Oblast' Turkm. 89 F2
Saragt Akhal'skaya Oblast' Turkm. see Sarakhs
Saraguro Ecuador 142 C4
Sarahs Turkm. see Sarakhs
Sarai Afgh. 89 G3
Sarai Sidhu Pak. 89 I4

▶Sarajevo Bos.-Herz. 58 H3
Capital of Bosnia-Herzegovina.
Sarakhs Turkm. 89 F2
Saraktash Rus. Fed. 64 G4
Saraland U.S.A. 131 F6
Saramati *mt.* India/Myanmar 70 A1
Saran' Kazakh. 80 D2
Saranac U.S.A. 134 C2
Saranac *r.* U.S.A. 135 I1
Saranac Lake U.S.A. 135 H1
Saranda Albania *see* Sarandë
Sarandë Albania 59 I5
Sarandib *country* Asia *see* Sri Lanka
Sarangani Islands Phil. 69 H5
Sarangpur India 82 D5
Saransk Rus. Fed. 43 J5
Sara Peak Nigeria 96 D4
Saraphi Thai. 70 B3
Sarapul Rus. Fed. 41 Q4
Sarapul'skoye Rus. Fed. 74 E2
Sarāqib Syria 85 C2
Sarasota U.S.A. 133 D7
Saraswati *r.* India 89 H6
Sarata Ukr. 59 M1
Saratoga *CA* U.S.A. 128 B3
Saratoga *WY* U.S.A. 126 G4
Saratoga Springs U.S.A. 132 F3
Saratok *Sarawak* Malaysia 68 E6
Saratov Rus. Fed. 43 J6
Saratovskoye Vodokhranilishche *resr* Rus. Fed. 43 J5
Saravan Iran 89 F5
Saravan Laos 70 D4
Saray Turkey 59 L4
Sarayköy Turkey 59 M6
Sarayönü Turkey 90 D3
Sarbāz Iran 87 J4
Sarbāz *reg.* Iran 89 F5
Sarbhang Bhutan 83 G4
Sarbīsheh Iran 87 I3
Sarda *r.* Nepal 83 E3
Sardab Pass Afgh. 89 H2
Sardarshahr India 82 C3
Sar Dasht Iran 88 B2
Sardegna *i. Sardinia* Italy *see* Sardinia
Sardica Bulg. *see* Sofia
Sardinia *i. Sardinia* Italy 58 C4
Sardis *MS* U.S.A. 131 F5
Sardis *WV* U.S.A. 134 E4
Sardis Lake *resr* U.S.A. 131 F5
Sar-e Būm Afgh. 89 G3
Sareks nationalpark *nat. park* Sweden 44 J3
Sarektjåkkå *mt.* Sweden 44 J3
Sar-e Pol Afgh. 89 G2
Sar-e Pol-e Zahāb Iran 88 B3
Sar Eskandar Iran *see* Hashtrud
Sare Yazd Iran 88 D4
Sargasso Sea N. Atlantic Ocean 151 P4
Sargodha Pak. 89 I3
Sarh Chad 97 E4
Sarhad *reg.* Iran 89 F4
Sārī Iran 88 D2
Saria *i.* Greece 59 L7
Sar-i-Bum Afgh. *see* Sar-e Būm
Sáric Mex. 127 F7
Sarigan *i.* N. Mariana Is 69 L3
Sarigh Jilganang Kol *salt l.* Aksai Chin 82 D2
Sarıgöl Turkey 59 M5
Sarıkamış Turkey 91 F2
Sarikei *Sarawak* Malaysia 68 E6
Sarikŭl, Qatorkŭhi *mts* China/Tajik. *see* Sarykol Range
Sarila India 82 D4
Sarina Australia 110 E4
Sarıoğlan *Kayseri* Turkey 90 D3
Sarıoğlan *Konya* Turkey *see* Belören
Sariqamish Kuli *salt l.* Turkm./Uzbek. *see* Sarykamyshskoye Ozero
Sarīr Tibesti *des.* Libya 97 E2
Sarita U.S.A. 131 D7
Sarıveliler Turkey 85 A1
Sariwŏn N. Korea 75 B5
Sarıyar Barajı *resr* Turkey 59 N5
Sarıyer Turkey 59 M4
Sarız Turkey 90 E3
Sark *i.* Channel Is 49 E9
Sarkand Kazakh. 80 E2
Şarkikaraağaç Turkey 59 N5
Şarkışla Turkey 90 E3
Şarköy Turkey 59 L4
Sarlath Range *mts* Afgh./Pak. 89 G4
Sarmi Indon. 69 J7
Särna Sweden 45 H6
Sarneh Iran 88 B3
Sarnen Switz. 56 I3
Sarni India *see* Amla
Sarnia Canada 134 D2
Sarny Ukr. 43 E6
Sarolangun Indon. 68 C7
Saroma-ko *l.* Japan 74 F3
Saronikos Kolpos *g.* Greece 59 J6
Saros Körfezi *b.* Turkey 59 L4
Sarova Rus. Fed. 43 I5
Sarowbī Afgh. 89 H3
Sarpa, Ozero *l.* Rus. Fed. 43 J6
Sarpan *i.* N. Mariana Is *see* Rota
Sarpsborg Norway 45 G7
Sarqant Kazakh. *see* Sarkand
Sarre *r.* France 52 H5
Sarrebourg France 52 H6
Sarreguemines France 52 H5
Sarria Spain 57 C2
Sarry France 52 E6
Sartana Ukr. 43 H7
Sartanahu Pak. 89 H5
Sartène *Corsica* France 56 I6
Sarthe *r.* France 56 D3
Sartu China *see* Daqing
Saruna Pak. 89 G5
Sarupsar India 82 C3
Şärur Azer. 91 G3
Saru Tara *tourist site* Afgh. 89 F4
Sarv Iran 88 D3
Sarvābād Iran 88 B3
Sárvár Hungary 58 G1
Sarwar India 82 C4
Sarygamysh Köli *salt l.* Turkm./Uzbek. *see* Sarykamyshskoye Ozero
Sary-Ishikotrau, Peski *des.* Kazakh. *see* Saryyesik-Atyrau, Peski
Sarykamyshskoye Ozero *salt l.* Turkm./Uzbek. 91 J2
Sarykol Range *mts* China/Tajik. 89 I2
Saryozek Kazakh. 80 E3
Saryshagan Kazakh. 80 D2
Sarysu *watercourse* Kazakh. 80 C2
Sarytash Kazakh. 91 H1
Sary-Tash Kyrg. 89 I2
Sary Yazikskoye Vodokhranilishche *resr* Turkm. 89 F2
Saryyesik-Atyrau, Peski *des.* Kazakh. 80 E2
Sarzha Kazakh. 91 H2
Sasar, Tanjung *pt* Indon. 108 B2
Sasaram India 83 F4
Sasebo Japan 75 C6
Saskatchewan *prov.* Canada 121 J4
Saskatchewan *r.* Canada 121 K4
Saskatoon Canada 121 J4
Saskylakh Rus. Fed. 65 M2
Saslaya *mt.* Nicaragua 137 H6
Sasoi *r.* India 82 B5
Sasolburg S. Africa 101 H4
Sasovo Rus. Fed. 43 I5
Sass *r.* Canada 120 H2
Sassandra Côte d'Ivoire 96 C4
Sassari *Sardinia* Italy 58 C4
Sassenberg Germany 53 I3
Sassnitz Germany 47 N3
Sass Town Liberia 96 C4
Sasykkol', Ozero *l.* Kazakh. 80 F2
Sasykoli Rus. Fed. 43 J7
Sasyqköl *l.* Kazakh. *see* Sasykkol', Ozero
Satahual *i.* Micronesia *see* Satawal
Sata-misaki *c.* Japan 75 C7
Satana India 84 B1
Satan Pass U.S.A. 129 I4
Satara India 84 B2
Satara S. Africa 101 J3
Satawal *i.* Micronesia 69 L5
Sätbaev Kazakh. *see* Satpayev
Satevó Mex. 131 B7
Satevo *r.* Mex. 127 G8
Satırlar Turkey *see* Yeşilova
Satkania Bangl. 83 H5
Satkhira Bangl. 83 G5
Satluj *r.* India/Pak. *see* Sutlej
Satmala Range *hills* India 84 C2
Satna India 82 E4
Satpayev Kazakh. 80 C2
Satpura Range *mts* India 82 C5
Satsuma-hantō *pen.* Japan 75 C7
Sattahip Thai. 71 C4
Satteldorf Germany 53 K5
Satthwa Myanmar 70 A3
Satu Mare Romania 43 D7
Satun Thai. 71 C6
Satwas India 82 D5
Sauceda Mountains U.S.A. 129 G5
Saucillo Mex. 131 B6
Sauda Norway 45 E7
Sauðárkrókur Iceland 44 [inset]
▶Saudi Arabia *country* Asia 86 F4
Asia 6, 62–63
Sauer *r.* France 53 I6
Saugatuck U.S.A. 134 B2
Saugeen *r.* Canada 134 E1
Sāūjbolāgh Iran *see* Mahābād
Sauk Center U.S.A. 130 E2
Saulieu France 56 G3
Saulnois *reg.* France 52 G6
Sault Sainte Marie Canada 122 D5
Sault Sainte Marie U.S.A. 132 C2
Saumalkol' Kazakh. 78 F1
Saumarez Reef Australia 110 F4
Saumlakki Indon. 108 E2
Saumur France 56 D3
Saunders, Mount *hill* Australia 108 E3
Saunders Coast Antarctica 152 J1
Saurimo Angola 99 C4
Sautar Angola 99 B5
Sauvolles, Lac *l.* Canada 123 G3
Sava *r.* Europe 58 I2
Savage River Australia 111 [inset]
Savai'i *i.* Samoa 107 I3
Savala *r.* Rus. Fed. 43 I6
Savalou Benin 96 D4
Savanat Iran *see* Eştahbān
Savane *r.* Canada 123 H4
Savanna U.S.A. 130 F3
Savannah *GA* U.S.A. 133 D5
Savannah *OH* U.S.A. 134 D3
Savannah *TN* U.S.A. 131 F5
Savannah *r.* U.S.A. 133 D5
Savannah Sound Bahamas 133 E7
Savannakhét Laos 70 D3
Savanna-la-Mar Jamaica 137 I5
Savant Lake Canada 122 C4
Savant Lake *l.* Canada 122 C4
Savanur India 84 B3
Sävar Sweden 44 L5
Savaştepe Turkey 59 L5
Savè Benin 96 D4
Save *r.* Moz./Zimbabwe 99 D6
Sāveh Iran 88 C3
Saverne France 53 H6
Saverne, Col de *pass* France 53 H6
Saviaho Fin. 44 P5
Savinskiy Rus. Fed. 42 I3
Savitri *r.* India 84 B2
Savli India 82 C5
Savoie *reg.* France *see* Savoy
Savona Italy 58 C2
Savonlinna Fin. 44 P6
Savonranta Fin. 44 P5
Savoy *reg.* France 56 H3
Şavşat Turkey 91 F2
Sävsjö Sweden 45 I8
Savu *i.* Indon. 108 C2
Savukoski Fin. 44 P3
Savur Turkey 91 F3
Savu Sea Indon. *see* Sawu, Laut
Saw Myanmar 70 A2
Sawai Madhopur India 82 D4
Sawan Myanmar 70 B1
Sawar India 82 C4
Sawatch Range *mts* U.S.A. 126 G5
Sawel Mountain *hill* U.K. 51 E3
Sawhāj Egypt 86 D4
Sawi, Ao *b.* Thai. 71 B5
Sawn Myanmar 70 B2
Sawtell Australia 112 F3
Sawtooth Range *mts* U.S.A. 126 C2
Sawu Indon. 108 C2
Sawu *i.* Indon. *see* Savu
Sawu, Laut *sea* Indon. 108 C2
Sawye Myanmar 70 B2
Sawyer U.S.A. 134 B3
Saxilby U.K. 48 G5
Saxmundham U.K. 49 I6
Saxnäs Sweden 44 I4
Saxony *land* Germany *see* Sachsen
Saxony-Anhalt *land* Germany *see* Sachsen-Anhalt
Saxton U.S.A. 135 F3
Say Niger 96 D3
Sayabouri Laos *see* Muang Xaignabouri
Sayak Kazakh. 80 E2
Sayanogorsk Rus. Fed. 72 G2
Sayano-Shushenskoye Vodokhranilishche *resr* Rus. Fed. 72 G2
Sayansk Rus. Fed. 72 I2
Sayaq Kazakh. *see* Sayak
Saýat Turkm. *see* Sayat
Sayat Turkm. 89 F2
Şaydā Lebanon *see* Sidon
Sāyen Iran 88 D4
Sayer Island Thai. *see* Similan, Ko
Sayghān Afgh. 89 G3
Sayḥūt Yemen 86 H6
Sayingpan China 76 D3
Saykhin Kazakh. 41 P6
Sāylac Somalia 97 H3
Saylan *country* Asia *see* Sri Lanka
Saynshand Mongolia 73 K4
Sayn-Ust Mongolia 80 H2
Sayoa *mt.* Spain *see* Saioa
Sayot Turkm. *see* Sayat
Şayqal, Baḥr *imp. l.* Syria 85 C3
Sayqyn Kazakh. *see* Saykhin
Sayre *OK* U.S.A. 131 D5
Sayre *PA* U.S.A. 135 G3
Sayreville U.S.A. 135 H3
Sayula Mex. 136 F5
Sayyod Turkm. *see* Sayat
Sazdy Kazakh. 43 K7
Sazin Pak. 89 I3
Sbaa Alg. 54 D6
Sbeitla Tunisia 58 C7
Scaddan Australia 109 C8
Scafell Pike *hill* U.K. 48 D4
Scalasaig U.K. 50 C4
Scalea Italy 58 F5
Scalloway U.K. 50 [inset]
Scalpaigh, Eilean *i.* U.K. *see* Scalpay
Scalpay *i.* U.K. 50 C3
Scapa Flow *inlet* U.K. 50 F2
Scarba *i.* U.K. 50 D4
Scarborough Canada 134 F2
Scarborough Trin. and Tob. 137 L6
Scarborough U.K. 48 G4
Scarborough Shoal *sea feature* S. China Sea 68 F3
Scariff Island Rep. of Ireland 51 B6
Scarp *i.* U.K. 50 B2
Scarpanto *i.* Greece *see* Karpathos
Schaale *r.* Germany 53 K1
Schaalsee *l.* Germany 53 K1
Schaerbeek Belgium 52 E4
Schaffhausen Switz. 56 I3
Schafstädt Germany 53 L3
Schagen Neth. 52 E2
Schagerbrug Neth. 52 E2
Schakalskuppe Namibia 100 C4
Schärding Austria 47 N6
Scharendijke Neth. 52 D3
Scharteberg *hill* Germany 52 G4
Schaumburg U.S.A. 134 A2
Schebheim Germany 53 K5
Scheeßel Germany 53 J1
Schefferville Canada 123 I3
Scheibbs Austria 47 O6
Schelde *r.* Belgium *see* Scheldt
Scheldt *r.* Belgium 52 D3
Schell Creek Range *mts* U.S.A. 129 F2
Schellerten Germany 53 K2
Schellville U.S.A. 128 B2
Schenectady U.S.A. 135 I2
Schenefeld Germany 53 J1
Schermerhorn Neth. 52 E2
Schertz U.S.A. 131 D6
Schierling Germany 53 M6
Schiermonnikoog Neth. 52 G1
Schiermonnikoog *i.* Neth. 52 G1
Schiermonnikoog Nationaal Park *nat. park* Neth. 52 G1
Schiffdorf Germany 53 I1
Schinnen Neth. 52 F4
Schio Italy 58 D2
Schkeuditz Germany 53 M3
Schleiden Germany 52 G4
Schleiz Germany 53 L4
Schleswig Germany 47 L3
Schleswig-Holstein *land* Germany 53 K1
Schleswig-Holsteinisches Wattenmeer, Nationalpark *nat. park* Germany 47 L3
Schleusingen Germany 53 K4
Schlitz Germany 53 J4
Schloss Holte-Stukenbrock Germany 53 I3
Schloss Wartburg *tourist site* Germany 53 K3
Schlüchtern Germany 53 J4
Schlüsselfeld Germany 53 K5
Schmallenberg Germany 53 I3
Schmidt Island Rus. Fed. *see* Shmidta, Ostrov
Schmidt Peninsula Rus. Fed. *see* Shmidta, Poluostrov
Schneeberg Germany 53 M4
Schneidemühl Poland *see* Piła
Schneidlingen Germany 53 L3
Schneverdingen Germany 53 J1
Schoharie U.S.A. 135 H2
Schönebeck Germany 53 M1
Schönebeck (Elbe) Germany 53 L2
Schönefeld *airport* Germany 53 N2
Schöningen Germany 53 K2
Schöntal Germany 53 J5
Schoolcraft U.S.A. 134 C2
Schoonhoven Neth. 52 E3
Schopfloch Germany 53 K5
Schöppenstedt Germany 53 K2
Schortens Germany 53 H1
Schouten Island Australia 111 [inset]
Schouten Islands P.N.G. 69 K7
Schrankogel *mt.* Austria 47 M7
Schreiber Canada 122 D4
Schroon Lake U.S.A. 135 I2
Schröttersburg Poland *see* Płock
Schulenburg U.S.A. 131 D6
Schuler Canada 121 I5
Schull Rep. of Ireland 51 C6
Schultz Lake Canada 121 L1
Schüttorf Germany 53 H2
Schuyler U.S.A. 130 D3
Schuyler Lake U.S.A. 135 H2
Schuylkill Haven U.S.A. 135 G3
Schwabach Germany 53 L5
Schwäbische Alb *mts* Germany 47 L7
Schwäbisch Gmünd Germany 53 J6
Schwäbisch Hall Germany 53 J5
Schwaförden Germany 53 I2
Schwalm *r.* Germany 53 J3
Schwalmstadt-Ziegenhain Germany 53 J4
Schwandorf Germany 53 M5
Schwaner, Pegunungan *mts* Indon. 68 E7
Schwanewede Germany 53 I1
Schwarmstedt Germany 53 J2
Schwarze Elster *r.* Germany 53 M3
Schwarzenbek Germany 53 K1
Schwarzenberg Germany 53 M4
Schwarzer Mann *hill* Germany 52 G4
Schwarzrand *mts* Namibia 100 C3
Schwarzwald *mts* Germany *see* Black Forest
Schwatka Mountains U.S.A. 118 C3
Schwaz Austria 47 M7
Schwedt an der Oder Germany 47 O4
Schwegenheim Germany 53 I5
Schweich Germany 52 G5
Schweinfurt Germany 53 K4
Schweinitz Germany 53 N3
Schweinrich Germany 53 M1
Schweiz *country* Europe *see* Switzerland
Schweizer-Reneke S. Africa 101 G4
Schwelm Germany 53 H3
Schwerin Germany 53 L1
Schweriner See *l.* Germany 53 L1
Schwetzingen Germany 53 I5
Schwyz Switz. 56 I3
Sciacca *Sicily* Italy 58 E6
Scicli *Sicily* Italy 58 F6
Science Hill U.S.A. 134 C5
Scilly, Île *atoll* Fr. Polynesia *see* Manuae
Scilly, Isles of U.K. 49 A9
Scioto *r.* U.S.A. 134 D4
Scipio U.S.A. 129 G2
Scobey U.S.A. 126 G2
Scodra Albania *see* Shkodër
Scofield Reservoir U.S.A. 129 H2
Scole U.K. 49 I6
Scone Australia 112 E4
Scone U.K. 50 F4
Scoresby Land *reg.* Greenland 119 P2
Scoresbysund Greenland *see* Ittoqqortoormiit
Scoresby Sund *sea chan.* Greenland *see* Kangertittivaq
Scorno, Punta dello *pt Sardinia* Italy *see* Caprara, Punta
Scorpion Bight *b.* Australia 109 D8
Scotia Ridge *sea feature* S. Atlantic Ocean 148 E9
Scotia Sea S. Atlantic Ocean 148 F9
Scotland Canada 134 E2
Scotland *admin. div.* U.K. 50 F3
Scotland U.S.A. 135 G4
Scotstown Canada 123 H5
Scott U.S.A. 134 C3
Scott, Cape Australia 108 E3
Scott, Cape Canada 120 D5
Scott, Mount *hill* U.S.A. 131 D5
Scott Base *research station* Antarctica 152 H1
Scottburgh S. Africa 101 J6
Scott City U.S.A. 130 C4
Scott Coast Antarctica 152 H1
Scott Glacier Antarctica 152 I1
Scott Island Antarctica 152 H2
Scott Islands Canada 120 D5
Scott Lake Canada 121 J3
Scott Mountains Antarctica 152 D2
Scott Reef Australia 108 C3
Scottsbluff U.S.A. 130 C3
Scottsboro U.S.A. 133 C5
Scottsburg U.S.A. 134 C4
Scottsville *KY* U.S.A. 134 B5
Scottsville *VA* U.S.A. 135 F5
Scourie U.K. 50 D2
Scousburgh U.K. 50 [inset]
Scrabster U.K. 50 F2
Scranton U.S.A. 135 H3
Scunthorpe U.K. 48 G5
Scuol Switz. 56 J3
Scupi Macedonia *see* Skopje
Scutari Albania *see* Shkodër
Scutari, Lake Albania/Serb. and Mont. 59 H3
Seaboard U.S.A. 135 G5
Seabrook, Lake *salt flat* Australia 109 B7
Seaford U.K. 49 H8
Seaforth Canada 134 E2
Seal *r.* Canada 121 M3
Seal, Cape S. Africa 100 F8
Sea Lake Australia 111 C7
Seal Lake Canada 123 J3
Sealy U.S.A. 131 D6
Seaman U.S.A. 134 D4
Seaman Range *mts* U.S.A. 129 F3
Seamer U.K. 48 G4
Searchlight U.S.A. 129 F4
Searcy U.S.A. 131 F5
Searles Lake U.S.A. 128 E4
Seaside *CA* U.S.A. 127 C5
Seaside *OR* U.S.A. 126 C3
Seaside Park U.S.A. 135 H4
Seattle U.S.A. 126 C3
Seaview Range *mts* Australia 106 D3
Seba Indon. 108 C2
Sebago Lake U.S.A. 135 J2
Sebastea Turkey *see* Sivas
Sebastian U.S.A. 133 D7
Sebastián Vizcaíno, Bahía *b.* Mex. 127 E7
Sebasticook *r.* U.S.A. 135 K1
Sebasticook Lake U.S.A. 135 K1
Sebastopol Ukr. *see* Sevastopol'
Sebastopol U.S.A. 128 B2
Sebatik *i.* Indon. 68 F6
Sebba Burkina 96 D3
Seben Turkey 59 N4
Sebenico Croatia *see* Šibenik
Sebeş Romania 59 J2
Sebewaing U.S.A. 134 D2
Sebezh Rus. Fed. 45 P8
Şebinkarahisar Turkey 90 E2
Sebree U.S.A. 134 B5
Sebring U.S.A. 133 D7
Sebrovo Rus. Fed. 43 I6
Sebta N. Africa *see* Ceuta
Sebuku *i.* Indon. 68 F7
Sechelt Canada 120 F5
Sechenovo Rus. Fed. 43 J5
Sechura Peru 142 B5
Sechura, Bahía de *b.* Peru 142 B5
Seckach Germany 53 J5
Second Mesa U.S.A. 129 H4
Second Three Mile Opening *sea chan.* Australia 110 C2
Secretary Island N.Z. 113 A7
Secunda S. Africa 101 I4
Secunderabad India 84 C2
Sedalia U.S.A. 130 E4
Sedam India 84 C2
Sedan France 52 E5
Sedan U.S.A. 131 D4
Sedan Dip Australia 110 C3
Seddon N.Z. 113 E5
Seddonville N.Z. 113 C5
Sedeh Iran 88 E3
Sederot Israel 85 B4
Sedlčany Czech Rep. 47 O6
Sedlets Poland *see* Siedlce
Sedom Israel 85 B4
Sedona U.S.A. 129 H4
Sédrata Alg. 58 B6
Šeduva Lith. 45 M9
Seedorf Germany 53 K1
Seehausen Germany 53 L2
Seehausen (Altmark) Germany 53 L2
Seeheim Namibia 100 C4
Seeheim-Jugenheim Germany 53 I5
Seelig, Mount Antarctica 152 K1
Seelze Germany 53 J2
Seenu Atoll Maldives *see* Addu Atoll
Sées France 56 E2
Seesen Germany 53 K3
Seevetal Germany 53 K1
Sefadu Sierra Leone 96 B4
Sefare Botswana 101 H2
Seferihisar Turkey 59 L5
Sefīd, Kūh-e *mt.* Iran 88 C3
Sefophe Botswana 101 H2
Segalstad Norway 45 G6
Segamat Malaysia 71 C7
Ségbana Benin 96 D3
Segeletz Germany 53 M2
Segezha Rus. Fed. 42 G3
Seghnān Afgh. 89 H2
Segontia U.K. *see* Caernarfon
Segontium U.K. *see* Caernarfon
Segorbe Spain 57 F4
Ségou Mali 96 C3
Segovia *r.* Hond./Nicaragua *see* Coco
Segovia Spain 57 D3
Segozerskoye, Ozero *resr* Rus. Fed. 42 G3
Seguam Island U.S.A. 118 A4
Séguédine Niger 96 E2
Séguéla Côte d'Ivoire 96 C4
Seguin U.S.A. 131 D6
Segura *r.* Spain 57 F4
Segura, Sierra de *mts* Spain 57 E5
Sehithwa Botswana 99 C6
Sehlabathebe National Park Lesotho 101 I5
Sehore India 82 D5
Sehwan Pak. 89 G5
Seibert U.S.A. 130 C4
Seignelay *r.* Canada 123 H4
Seikpyu Myanmar 70 A2
Seiland *i.* Norway 44 M1
Seille *r.* France 52 G5
Seinäjoki Fin. 44 M5
Seine *r.* Canada 121 N5
Seine *r.* France 52 A5
Seine, Baie de *b.* France 56 D2
Seine, Val de *valley* France 56 F2
Seistan *reg.* Iran *see* Sīstān
Sejny Poland 45 M9
Sekayu Indon. 68 C7
Seke China *see* Sêrtar
Sekoma Botswana 100 F3
Sekondi Ghana 96 C4
Sek'ot'a Eth. 98 D2
Sekura Indon. 71 E7
Šela Rus. Fed. *see* Shali
Selama Malaysia 71 C6
Selaru *i.* Indon. 108 E2
Selassi Indon. 69 I7
Selatan, Tanjung *pt* Indon. 68 E7
Selatpanjang Indon. 71 C7
Selawik U.S.A. 118 B3
Selb Germany 53 M4
Selbekken Norway 44 F5
Selbu Norway 44 G5
Selby U.K. 48 F5
Selby U.S.A. 130 C2
Selbyville U.S.A. 135 H4
Selden U.S.A. 130 C4
Selebi-Phikwe Botswana 99 C6
Selebi-Pikwe Botswana *see* Selebi-Phikwe
Selemdzha *r.* Rus. Fed. 74 C1
Selemdzhinsk Rus. Fed. 74 C1
Selemdzhinskiy Khrebet *mts* Rus. Fed. 74 D1
Selendi Turkey 59 M5
▶Selenga *r.* Mongolia/Rus. Fed. 72 J2
Part of the Yenisey-Angara-Selenga, 3rd longest river in Asia. Also known as Selenga Mörön.
Selenga Mörön *r.* Mongolia *see* Selenga
Seletar Sing. 71 [inset]
Seletar Reservoir Sing. 71 [inset]
Selety *r.* Kazakh. *see* Sileti
Seletyteniz, Ozero *salt l.* Kazakh. *see* Siletiteniz, Ozero
Seleucia Turkey *see* Silifke
Seleucia Pieria Turkey *see* Samandağı
Selfridge U.S.A. 130 C2
Sel'gon Stantsiya Rus. Fed. 74 D2
Selib Rus. Fed. 42 K3
Sélibabi Mauritania 96 B3
Selibe-Phikwe Botswana *see* Selebi-Phikwe
Seligenstadt Germany 53 I4
Seliger, Ozero *l.* Rus. Fed. 42 G4
Seligman U.S.A. 129 G4
Selikhino Rus. Fed. 74 E2
Selima Oasis Sudan 86 C5
Selimiye Turkey 59 L6
Selinsgrove U.S.A. 135 G3
Selizharovo Rus. Fed. 42 G4
Seljord Norway 45 F7
Selkirk Canada 121 L5
Selkirk U.K. 50 G5
Selkirk Mountains Canada 120 G4
Sellafield U.K. 48 D4
Sellersburg U.S.A. 134 C4
Sellore Island Myanmar *see* Saganthit Kyun
Sells U.S.A. 129 H6
Selm Germany 53 H3
Selma *AL* U.S.A. 133 C5
Selma *CA* U.S.A. 128 D3
Selmer U.S.A. 131 F5
Selous, Mount Canada 120 C2
Selseleh-ye Pīr Shūrān *mts* Iran 89 F4
Selsey Bill *hd* U.K. 49 G8
Sel'tso Rus. Fed. 43 G5
Selty Rus. Fed. 42 L4
Selu *i.* Indon. 108 E1
Seluan *i.* Indon. 71 D6
Selvas *reg.* Brazil 142 D5
Selvin U.S.A. 134 B4
Selway *r.* U.S.A. 126 E3
Selwyn Lake Canada 121 J2
Selwyn Mountains Canada 120 D1
Selwyn Range *hills* Australia 110 B4
Selz *r.* Germany 53 I5
Semarang Indon. 68 E8
Semau *i.* Indon. 108 C2
Sembawang Sing. 71 [inset]
Sembé Congo 98 B3
Şemdinli Turkey 91 G3
Semendire Serb. and Mont. *see* Smederevo
Semenivka Ukr. 43 G5
Semenov Rus. Fed. 42 J4
Semenovka Ukr. *see* Semenivka
Semey Kazakh. *see* Semipalatinsk
Semidi Islands U.S.A. 118 C4
Semikarakorsk Rus. Fed. 43 I7
Semiluki Rus. Fed. 43 H6
Seminoe Reservoir U.S.A. 126 G4
Seminole U.S.A. 131 C5
Semipalatinsk Kazakh. 80 F1
Semirara Islands Phil. 69 G4
Semīrom Iran 88 C4
Sem Kolodezey Ukr. *see* Lenine
Semnān Iran 88 D3
Semois *r.* Belgium/France 52 E5
Semyonovskoye *Arkhangel'skaya Oblast'* Rus. Fed. *see* Bereznik
Semyonovskoye *Kostromskaya Oblast'* Rus. Fed. *see* Ostrovskoye
Sena Bol. 142 E6
Sena Madureira Brazil 142 E5
Senanga Zambia 99 C5
Sendai *Kagoshima* Japan 75 C7
Sendai *Miyagi* Japan 75 F5
Sêndo China 76 B2
Senebui, Tanjung *pt* Indon. 71 C7
Seneca *KS* U.S.A. 130 D4
Seneca *OR* U.S.A. 126 D3
Seneca Lake U.S.A. 135 G2
Seneca Rocks U.S.A. 134 F4
Senecaville Lake U.S.A. 134 E4
▶Senegal *country* Africa 96 B3
Africa 7, 94–95
Sénégal *r.* Mauritania/Senegal 96 B3
Seney U.S.A. 130 G2
Senftenberg Germany 47 O5
Senga Hill Zambia 99 D4
Sengerema Tanz. 98 D4
Sengeyskiy, Ostrov *i.* Rus. Fed. 42 K1
Sênggê Zangbo *r.* China 82 D2 *see* Indus
Sengiley Rus. Fed. 43 K5
Sengirli, Mys *pt* Kazakh. *see* Syngyrli, Mys
Senhor do Bonfim Brazil 143 J6
Senigallia Italy 58 E3
Senj Croatia 58 F2
Senja *i.* Norway 44 J2
Sen'kina Rus. Fed. 42 K2
Şenköy Turkey 85 C1
Senlac S. Africa 100 F3
Senlin Shan *mt.* China 74 C4
Senlis France 52 C5
Senmonorom Cambodia 71 D4
Sennar Sudan 86 D7
Sennen U.K. 49 B8
Senneterre Canada 122 F4
Senqu *r.* Lesotho 101 H6
Sens France 56 F2
Sensuntepeque El Salvador 136 G6
Senta Serb. and Mont. 59 I2
Senthal India 82 D3
Sentinel U.S.A. 129 G5
Sentinel Peak Canada 120 F4
Sentosa *i.* Sing. 71 [inset]
Senwabarwana S. Africa *see* Bochum
Şenyurt Turkey 91 F3
Seo de Urgell Spain *see* Le Seu d'Urgell
Seonath *r.* India 84 D1
Seoni India 82 D5
Seorinarayan India 83 E5
▶Seoul S. Korea 75 B5
Capital of South Korea.
Separation Well Australia 108 C5
Sepik *r.* P.N.G. 69 K7
Sep'o N. Korea 75 B5
Sepon India 83 H4
Seppa India 83 H4
Sept-Îles Canada 123 I4
Sequoia National Park U.S.A. 128 D3

Serachis r. Cyprus 85 A2
Serafimovich Rus. Fed. 43 I6
Sêraitang China see Baima
Serakhs Akhal'skaya Oblast' Turkm. see Sarakhs
Serakhs Akhal'skaya Oblast' Turkm. see Saragt
Seram i. Indon. 69 H7
Seram, Laut sea Indon. 69 I7
Serang Indon. 68 D8
Serangoon Harbour b. Sing. 71 [inset]
Serapi, Gunung hill Indon. 71 E7
Serapong, Mount hill Sing. 71 [inset]
Serasan i. Indon. 71 E7
Serasan, Selat sea chan. Indon. 71 E7
Seraya i. Indon. 71 E7
Serbâl, Gebel mt. Egypt see Sirbāl, Jabal
Serbia aut. rep. Serb. and Mont. see Srbija

▶Serbia and Montenegro country Europe 59 I2
Formerly known as Yugoslavia. Up to 1993 included Bosnia-Herzegovina, Croatia, Macedonia and Slovenia.
Europe 5, 38–39

Sêrbug Co l. China 83 G2
Sêrca China 76 B2
Serchhip India 83 H5
Serdar Turkm. see Gyzylarbat
Serder Turkm. see Gyzylarbat
Serdica Bulg. see Sofia
Serdo Eth. 98 E2
Serdoba r. Rus. Fed. 43 J5
Serdobsk Rus. Fed. 43 J5
Serebryansk Kazakh. 80 F2
Seredka Rus. Fed. 45 P7
Şereflikoçhisar Turkey 90 D3
Seremban Malaysia 71 C7
Serengeti National Park Tanz. 98 D4
Serenje Zambia 99 D5
Serezha r. Rus. Fed. 42 I5
Sergach Rus. Fed. 42 J5
Sergeyevka Rus. Fed. 74 B2
Sergiyev Posad Rus. Fed. 42 H4
Sergo Ukr. see Stakhanov
Serh China 80 I4
Serhetabat Turkm. see Gushgy
Serifos i. Greece 59 K6
Sérigny r. Canada 123 H3
Sérigny, Lac l. Canada 123 H3
Serik Turkey 90 C3
Seringapatam Reef Australia 104 C3
Sêrkang China see Nyainrong
Sermata i. Indon. 69 H8
Sermata, Kepulauan is Indon. 108 E2
Sermersuaq glacier Greenland 115 M2
Sermilik inlet Greenland 119 O3
Sernovodsk Rus. Fed. 43 K5
Sernur Rus. Fed. 42 K4
Sernyy Zavod Turkm. see Kukurtli
Seronga Botswana 99 C5
Serov Rus. Fed. 41 S4
Serowe Botswana 101 H2
Serpa Port. 57 C5
Serpa Pinto Angola see Menongue
Serpentine Lakes salt flat Australia 109 E7
Serpukhov Rus. Fed. 43 H5
Serra Brazil 145 C3
Serra Alta Brazil 145 A4
Serra da Bocaina, Parque Nacional da nat. park Brazil 145 B3
Serra da Canastra, Parque Nacional da nat. park Brazil 145 B3
Serra da Mesa, Represa resr Brazil 145 A1
Serra das Araras Brazil 145 B1
Serra do Divisor, Parque Nacional da nat. park Brazil 142 D5
Sérrai Greece see Serres
Serranía de la Neblina, Parque Nacional nat. park Venez. 142 E3
Serraria, Ilha i. Brazil see Queimada, Ilha
Serra Talhada Brazil 143 K5
Serre r. France 52 D5
Serres Greece 59 J4
Serrinha Brazil 143 K6
Sêrro Brazil 145 C2
Sers Tunisia 58 C6
Sertanópolis Brazil 145 A3
Sertãozinho Brazil 145 B3
Sêrtar China 76 D1
Sertavul Geçidi pass Turkey 85 A1
Sertolovo Rus. Fed. 45 Q6
Seruai Indon. 71 B6
Serui Indon. 69 J7
Serule Botswana 99 C6
Seruna India 82 C3
Sêrwolungwa China 76 B1
Sêrxü China 76 C1
Seseganaga Lake Canada 122 C4
Sese Islands Uganda 98 D4
Sesel country Indian Ocean see Seychelles
Sesfontein Namibia 99 B5
Seshachalam Hills India 84 C3
Sesheke Zambia 99 C5
Sesostris Bank sea feature India 84 A3
Ses Salines, Cap de c. Spain 57 H4
Sestri Levante Italy 58 C2
Sestroretsk Rus. Fed. 45 P6
Set, Phou mt. Laos 70 D4
Sète France 56 F5
Sete Lagoas Brazil 145 B2
Setermoen Norway 44 K2
Setesdal valley Norway 45 E7
Seti r. Nepal 82 E3
Sétif Alg. 54 F4
Seto Japan 75 E6
Seto-naikai sea Japan 73 O6
Seto-naikai National Park Japan 75 D6
Setsan Myanmar 70 A3
Settat Morocco 54 C5
Settepani, Monte mt. Italy 58 C2
Settle U.K. 48 E4
Setúbal Port. 57 B4
Setúbal, Baía de b. Port. 57 B4
Seul, Lac l. Canada 121 M5
Sevan Armenia 91 G2
Sevan, Lake Armenia 91 G2
Sevan, Ozero l. Armenia see Sevan, Lake
Sevana Lich l. Armenia see Sevan, Lake
Sevastopol' Ukr. 90 D1
Seven Islands Canada see Sept-Îles
Seven Islands Bay Canada 123 J2
Sevenoaks U.K. 49 H7
Seventy Mile House Canada see 70 Mile House
Sévérac-le-Château France 56 F4
Severn r. Australia 112 E2
Severn r. Canada 122 D3
Severn S. Africa 100 F4
Severn r. U.K. 49 E7
also known as Hafren
Severnaya Dvina r. Rus. Fed. 42 I2
Severnaya Sos'va r. Rus. Fed. 41 T3
Severnaya Zemlya is Rus. Fed. 65 L1
Severn Lake Canada 121 N4
Severnoye Rus. Fed. 41 Q5
Severnyy Nenetskiy Avtonomnyy Okrug Rus. Fed. 42 K1
Severnyy Respublika Komi Rus. Fed. 64 H3
Severobaykal'sk Rus. Fed. 73 J1
Severo-Baykal'skoye Nagor'ye mts Rus. Fed. 65 M4
Severodonetsk Ukr. see Syeverodonets'k
Severodvinsk Rus. Fed. 42 H2
Severo-Kuril'sk Rus. Fed. 65 Q4
Severomorsk Rus. Fed. 44 R2
Severoonezhsk Rus. Fed. 42 H3
Severo-Sibirskaya Nizmennost' lowland Rus. Fed. see North Siberian Lowland
Severoural'sk Rus. Fed. 41 R3
Severo-Yeniseyskiy Rus. Fed. 64 K3
Severskaya Rus. Fed. 90 E1
Severskiy Donets r. Rus. Fed./Ukr. 43 I7
also known as Northern Donets, Sivers'kyy Donets'
Sevier U.S.A. 129 G2
Sevier r. U.S.A. 129 G2
Sevier Desert U.S.A. 129 G2
Sevier Lake U.S.A. 129 G2
Sevierville U.S.A. 132 D5
Sevilla Col. 142 C3
Sevilla Spain see Seville
Seville Spain 57 D5
Sevlyush Ukr. see Vynohradiv
Sewani India 82 C3
Seward AK U.S.A. 118 D3
Seward NE U.S.A. 130 D3
Seward Mountains Antarctica 152 L2
Seward Peninsula U.S.A. 118 B3
Sexi Spain see Almuñécar
Sexsmith Canada 120 G4
Sextín Mex. 131 B7
Seyah Band Koh mts Afgh. 89 F3
Seyakha Rus. Fed. 153 F2
▶Seychelles country Indian Ocean 149 L6
Africa 7, 94–95
Seydi Turkm. 89 F2
Seydişehir Turkey 90 C3
Seyðisfjörður Iceland 44 [inset]
Seyhan Turkey see Adana
Seyhan r. Turkey 85 B1
Seyitgazi Turkey 59 N5
Seym r. Rus. Fed./Ukr. 43 G6
Seymchan Rus. Fed. 65 Q3
Seymour Australia 112 B6
Seymour S. Africa 101 H7
Seymour IN U.S.A. 134 C4
Seymour TX U.S.A. 131 D5
Seymour Inlet Canada 120 E5
Seymour Range mts Australia 109 F6
Seypan i. N. Mariana Is see Saipan
Seyyedābād Afgh. 89 H3
Sézanne France 52 D6
Sfakia Greece 59 K7
Sfântu Gheorghe Romania 59 K2
Sfax Tunisia 58 D7
Sfikia, Limni resr Greece 59 J4
Sfîntu Gheorghe Romania see Sfântu Gheorghe
Sgiersch Poland see Zgierz
's-Graveland Neth. 52 F2
's-Gravenhage Neth. see The Hague
Sgurr Alasdair hill U.K. 50 C3
Sgurr Dhomhnuill hill U.K. 50 D4
Sgurr Mòr mt. U.K. 50 D3
Sgurr na Ciche mt. U.K. 50 D3
Shaanxi prov. China 76 F1
Shaartuz Tajik. see Shahrtuz
Shaban Pak. 89 G4
Shabani Zimbabwe see Zvishavane
Shabestar Iran 88 B2
Shabībī, Jabal ash mt. Jordan 85 B5
Shabla, Nos pt Bulg. 59 M3
Shabogamo Lake Canada 123 I3
Shabunda Dem. Rep. Congo 98 C4
Shache China 80 E4
Shackleton Coast Antarctica 152 H1
Shackleton Glacier Antarctica 148 I1
Shackleton Ice Shelf Antarctica 152 F2
Shackleton Range mts Antarctica 152 A1
Shadaogou China 77 F2
Shādegān Iran 88 C4
Shadihar Pak. 89 G4
Shady Grove U.S.A. 126 C4
Shady Spring U.S.A. 134 E5
Shafer, Lake U.S.A. 134 B3
Shafer Peak Antarctica 152 H2
Shafter U.S.A. 128 D4
Shaftesbury U.K. 49 E7
Shagamu r. Canada 122 D3
Shagedu China 73 K5
Shageluk U.S.A. 118 C3
Shaghyray Üstirti plat. Kazakh. see Shagyray, Plato
Shagonar Rus. Fed. 80 H1
Shag Point N.Z. 113 C7
Shag Rocks is S. Georgia 144 H8
Shagyray, Plato plat. Kazakh. 80 A2
Shahabad Karnataka India 84 C2
Shahabad Rajasthan India 82 D4
Shahabad Uttar Pradesh India 82 E4
Shāhābād Iran see Eslāmābād-e Gharb
Shah Alam Malaysia 71 C7
Shahbandar Pak. 89 G5
Shahdād Iran 88 E4
Shahdol India 82 E5
Shahe China 77 F2
Shahejie China see Jiujiang
Shahezhen China see Jiujiang
Shah Fuladi mt. Afgh. 89 G3
Shahid, Ras pt Pak. 89 F5
Shāhīn Dezh Iran see Sa'īndezh
Shah Ismail Afgh. 89 G4
Shahjahanpur India 82 D4
Shāh Jehān, Kūh-e mts Iran 88 E2
Shāh Jūy Afgh. 89 G3
Shāh Kūh mt. Iran 88 E4
Shāhpūr Iran see Salmās
Shahrak Afgh. 89 G3
Shāhrakht Iran 89 F3
Shahr-e Bābak Iran 88 D4
Shahr-e Kord Iran 88 C3
Shahr-e Şafā Afgh. 89 G4
Shahrezā Iran 88 C3
Shahrig Pak. 89 G4
Shahrisabz Uzbek. see Shakhrisabz
Shahriston Tajik. 89 H2
Shahr Rey Iran 88 C3
Shahr Sultan Pak. 89 H4
Shahrtuz Tajik. 89 H2
Shāhrūd Iran see Emāmrūd
Shāhrūd, Rūdkhāneh-ye r. Iran 88 C2
Shahrud Bustam reg. Iran 88 D3
Shāh Savārān, Kūh-e mts Iran 88 E4
Shāh Taqī Iran see Emām Taqī
Shaighalu Pak. 89 H4
Shaikh Husain mt. Pak. 89 G4
Shaikhpura India see Sheikhpura
Sha'īr, Jabal mts Syria 85 C2
Sha'īra, Gebel mt. Egypt see Sha'īrah, Jabal
Sha'īrah, Jabal mt. Egypt 85 B5
Shaj'ah, Jabal hill Saudi Arabia 88 C5
Shajapur India 82 D5
Shajianzi China 74 B4
Shakaville S. Africa 101 J5
Shakh Tajik. see Shoh
Shakhbuz Azer. see Şahbuz
Shākhen Iran 89 E3
Shakhovskaya Rus. Fed. 42 G4
Shakhrisabz Uzbek. 89 G2
Shakhriston Tajik. see Shahriston
Shakhtinsk Kazakh. 80 D2
Shakhty Respublika Buryatiya Rus. Fed. see Gusinoozersk
Shakhty Rostovskaya Oblast' Rus. Fed. 43 I7
Shakhun'ya Rus. Fed. 42 J4
Shaki Nigeria 96 D4
Shakotan-hantō pen. Japan 74 F4
Shalakusha Rus. Fed. 42 I3
Shalang China 77 F4
Shali Rus. Fed. 91 G2
Shaliuhe China see Gangca
Shalkar India 82 D3
Shalkar Kazakh. 80 A2
Shalqar Kazakh. see Shalkar
Shaluli Shan mts China 76 C2
Shaluni mt. India 83 I3
Shama r. Tanz. 99 D4
Shamāl Sīnā' governorate Egypt 85 A4
Shamâl Sînâ' governorate Egypt see Shamāl Sīnā'
Shamalzā'ī Afgh. 89 G4
Shāmat al Akbād des. Saudi Arabia 91 F5
Shamattawa Canada 121 N4
Shamattawa r. Canada 122 D3
Shambār Iran 88 C3
Shamgong Bhutan see Zhemgang
Shamīl Iran 88 E5
Shāmīyah des. Iraq/Syria 85 D2
Shamkhor Azer. see Şämkir
Shamrock U.S.A. 131 C5
Shanacrane Rep. of Ireland 51 C6
Shancheng Fujian China see Taining
Shancheng Shandong China see Shanxian
Shand Afgh. 89 F4
Shandan China 80 J4
Shandong prov. China 77 H1
Shandong Bandao pen. China 73 M5
Shandur Pass Pak. 89 I2
Shangchao China 77 F3
Shangcheng China 77 G2
Shangchuan Dao i. China 77 G4
Shangdu China 73 K4
Shangganling China 74 C3

▶Shanghai China 77 I2
4th most populous city in Asia.

Shanghai municipality China 77 I2
Shangji China see Xichuan
Shangjie China see Yangbi
Shangjin China 77 F1
Shangmei China see Xinhua
Shangnan China 77 F1
Shangpa China see Fugong
Shangpai China see Feixi
Shangpaihe China see Feixi
Shangqiu Henan China see Suiyang
Shangqiu Henan China 77 G1
Shangrao China 77 H2
Shangshui China 77 G1
Shangyou China 77 G3
Shangyou Shuiku resr China 80 F3
Shangyu China 77 I2
Shangzhi China 74 B3
Shangzhou China 77 F1
Shanhe China see Zhengning
Shanhetun China 74 B3
Shankou China 77 F4
Shannon airport Rep. of Ireland 51 D5
Shannon est. Rep. of Ireland 51 D5
Shannon r. Rep. of Ireland 51 D5
Shannon, Mouth of the Rep. of Ireland 51 C5
Shannon National Park Australia 109 B8
Shannon Ø i. Greenland 153 I1
Shan Plateau Myanmar 70 B2
Shansi prov. China see Shanxi
Shan Teng hill Hong Kong China see Victoria Peak
Shantipur India 83 G5
Shantou China 77 H4
Shantung prov. China see Shandong
Shanwei China 77 G4
Shanxi prov. China 77 F1
Shanxian China 77 H1
Shanyang China 77 F1
Shaodong China 77 F3
Shaoguan China 77 G3
Shaowu China 77 H3
Shaoxing China 77 I2
Shaoyang China 77 F3
Shap U.K. 48 E4
Shapa China 77 F4
Shaping China see Ebian
Shapinsay i. U.K. 50 G1
Shapkina r. Rus. Fed. 42 L2
Shapshal'skiy Khrebet mts Rus. Fed. 80 G1
Shaqrā' Saudi Arabia 86 G4
Shār, Jabal mt. Saudi Arabia 90 D6
Sharaf well Iraq 91 F5
Sharāh, Jibāl ash mts Jordan 85 B4
Sharan Jogizai Pak. 89 H4
Shārb Māh Iran 88 E4
Sharbulag Mongolia 80 H2
Shardara Kazakh. 80 C3
Shardara, Step' plain Kazakh. see Chardara, Step'
Sharga Mongolia 80 I2
Sharhulsan Mongolia 72 I4
Shari r. Cameroon/Chad see Chari
Shārī, Buḩayrat imp. l. Iraq 91 G4
Shari-dake vol. Japan 74 G4
Sharīfah Syria 85 C2
Sharjah U.A.E. 88 D5
Sharka-leb La pass China 83 G3
Sharkawshchyna Belarus 45 O9
Shark Bay Australia 109 A6
Shark Reef Australia 110 D2
Sharlyk Rus. Fed. 41 Q5
Sharm ash Shaykh Egypt 90 D6
Sharm el Sheikh Egypt see Sharm ash Shaykh
Sharon U.S.A. 134 E3
Sharon Springs U.S.A. 130 C4
Sharpe Lake Canada 121 M4
Sharp Peak hill Hong Kong China 77 [inset]
Sharqat Iraq see Ash Sharqāţ
Sharqī, Jabal ash mts Lebanon/Syria 85 B3
Sharur Azer. see Şărur
Shar'ya Rus. Fed. 42 J4
Shashe r. Botswana/Zimbabwe 99 C6
Shashemenē Eth. 98 D3
Shashi China see Jingzhou
Shasta U.S.A. 128 B1
Shasta, Mount vol. U.S.A. 126 C4
Shasta Lake U.S.A. 128 B1
Shatilki Belarus see Svyetlahorsk
Sha Tin Hong Kong China 77 [inset]
Shatki Rus. Fed. 43 J5
Shaţnat as Salmās, Wādī watercourse Syria 85 D2
Sha Tong Hau Shan Hong Kong China see Bluff Island
Shatoy Rus. Fed. 91 G2
Shatsk Rus. Fed. 43 I5
Shaţţ al 'Arab r. Iran/Iraq 91 H5
Shatura Rus. Fed. 43 H5
Shaubak Jordan see Ash Shawbak
Shaunavon Canada 121 I5
Shaver Lake U.S.A. 128 D3
Shaw r. Australia 108 B5
Shawangunk Mountains hills U.S.A. 135 H3
Shawano U.S.A. 134 A1
Shawano Lake U.S.A. 134 A1
Shawinigan Canada 123 G5
Shawnee OK U.S.A. 131 D5
Shawnee WY U.S.A. 126 G4
Shawneetown U.S.A. 130 F4
Shaxian China 77 H3
Shay Gap Australia 108 C5
Shaykh, Jabal ash mt. Lebanon/Syria see Hermon, Mount
Shaykh Miskīn Syria 85 C3
Shayţūr Iran 88 D4
Shāzand Iran 88 C3
Shaẕāẕ, Jabal mt. Saudi Arabia 91 F6
Shazud Tajik. 89 I2
Shchekino Rus. Fed. 43 H5
Shchel'yayur Rus. Fed. 42 L2
Shcherbakov Rus. Fed. see Rybinsk
Shchigry Rus. Fed. 43 H6
Shchors Ukr. 43 F6
Shchuchin Belarus see Shchuchyn
Shchuchyn Belarus 45 N10
Shebalino Rus. Fed. 80 G1
Shebekino Rus. Fed. 43 H6
Sheberghān Afgh. 89 G2
Sheboygan U.S.A. 134 B2
Shebshi Mountains Nigeria 96 E4
Shebunino Rus. Fed. 74 F3
Shediac Canada 123 I5
Shedin Peak Canada 120 E4
Shedok Rus. Fed. 91 F1
Sheelin, Lough l. Rep. of Ireland 51 E4
Sheep Haven b. Rep. of Ireland 51 E2
Sheepmoor S. Africa 101 J4
Sheep Mountain U.S.A. 129 J2
Sheep Peak U.S.A. 129 F3
Sheep's Head hd Rep. of Ireland see Muntervary
Sheerness U.K. 49 H7
Sheet Harbour Canada 123 J5
Shefar'am Israel 85 B3
Sheffield N.Z. 113 D6
Sheffield U.K. 48 F5
Sheffield AL U.S.A. 133 C5
Sheffield PA U.S.A. 134 F3
Sheffield TX U.S.A. 131 C6
Sheffield Lake Canada 123 K4
Shegah Afgh. 89 G4
Shegmas Rus. Fed. 42 K2
Shehong China 76 E2
Sheikh, Jebel esh mt. Lebanon/Syria see Hermon, Mount
Sheikhpura India 83 F4
Shekak r. Canada 122 D4
Shekār Āb Iran 88 D3
Shekhawati reg. India 89 I5
Shekhem West Bank see Nāblus
Shekhpura India see Sheikhpura
Shekhupura Pak. 89 I4
Sheki Azer. see Şăki
Shekka Ch'ün-Tao Hong Kong China see Soko Islands
Shek Kwu Chau i. Hong Kong China 77 [inset]
Shekou China 77 [inset]
Sheksna Rus. Fed. 42 H4
Sheksninskoye Vodokhranilishche resr Rus. Fed. 42 H4
Shek Uk Shan mt. Hong Kong China 77 [inset]
Shela China 76 B2
Shelagskiy, Mys pt Rus. Fed. 65 S2
Shelbina U.S.A. 130 E4
Shelburn U.S.A. 134 B4
Shelburne N.S. Canada 123 I6
Shelburne Ont. Canada 134 E1
Shelburne Bay Australia 110 C1
Shelby MI U.S.A. 134 B2
Shelby MS U.S.A. 131 F5
Shelby MT U.S.A. 126 F2
Shelby NC U.S.A. 133 D5
Shelbyville IL U.S.A. 130 F4
Shelbyville IN U.S.A. 134 C4
Shelbyville KY U.S.A. 134 C4
Shelbyville TN U.S.A. 132 C5
Sheldon IA U.S.A. 130 E3
Sheldon IL U.S.A. 134 B3
Sheldrake Canada 123 I4
Shelek Kazakh. see Chilik
Shelikhova, Zaliv g. Rus. Fed. 61 Q3
Shelikof Strait U.S.A. 118 C4
Shell U.S.A. 130 B2
Shellbrook Canada 121 J4
Shelley U.S.A. 126 E4
Shellharbour Australia 112 E5
Shell Lake Canada 121 J4
Shell Lake U.S.A. 130 F2
Shell Mountain U.S.A. 128 B1
Shelter Bay Canada see Port-Cartier
Shelter Island U.S.A. 135 I3
Shelter Point N.Z. 113 B8
Shelton U.S.A. 126 C3
Shemakha Azer. see Şamaxı
Shemordan Rus. Fed. 42 K4
Shenandoah IA U.S.A. 130 E3
Shenandoah PA U.S.A. 135 G3
Shenandoah Mountains U.S.A. 134 F4
Shenandoah National Park U.S.A. 135 F4
Shendam Nigeria 96 D4
Shending Shan hill China 74 D3
Shengena mt. Tanz. 99 D4
Shengli China 77 G2
Shengli Feng mt. China/Kyrg. see Pobeda Peak
Shengping China 74 B3
Shengrenjian China see Pinglu
Shengsi China 77 I2
Shengsi Liedao is China 77 I2
Shenjiamen China 77 I2
Shen Khan Bandar Afgh. 89 H2
Shenkursk Rus. Fed. 42 I3
Shenmu China 73 K5
Shennong Ding mt. China 77 F2
Shennongjia China 77 F2
Shenqiu China 77 G1
Shenshu China 74 C3
Shensi prov. China see Shaanxi
Shentala Rus. Fed. 43 K5
Shenton, Mount hill Australia 109 C7
Shenyang China 74 A4
Shenzhen China 77 G4
Shenzhen Wan b. Hong Kong China see Deep Bay
Sheopur India 82 D4
Shepetivka Ukr. 43 E6
Shepetovka Ukr. see Shepetivka
Shepherd Islands Vanuatu 107 G3
Shepherdsville U.S.A. 134 C5
Shepparton Australia 112 B6
Sheppey, Isle of i. U.K. 49 H7
Sheqi China 77 G1
Sherabad Uzbek. 89 G2
Sherborne U.K. 49 E8
Sherbro Island Sierra Leone 96 B4
Sherbrooke Canada 123 H5
Sherburne U.S.A. 135 H2
Shercock Rep. of Ireland 51 F4
Shereiq Sudan 86 D6
Shergaon India 83 H4
Shergarh India 82 C4
Sheridan AR U.S.A. 131 E5
Sheridan WY U.S.A. 126 G3
Sheringham U.K. 49 I6
Sherman U.S.A. 131 D5
Sherman Mountain U.S.A. 129 F1
Sherobod Uzbek. see Sherabad
Sherpur Dhaka Bangl. 83 G4
Sherpur Rajshahi Bangl. 83 G4
Sherridon Canada 121 K4
's-Hertogenbosch Neth. 52 F3
Sherwood Forest reg. U.K. 49 F5
Sherwood Lake Canada 121 K2
Sheryshevo Rus. Fed. 74 C2
Sheslay Canada 120 D3
Sheslay r. Canada 120 C3
Shethanei Lake Canada 121 L3
Shetland is U.K. 50 [inset]
Shetpe Kazakh. 78 E2
Sheung Shui Hong Kong China 77 [inset]
Sheung Sze Mun sea chan. Hong Kong China 77 [inset]
Shevchenko Kazakh. see Aktau
Shevli r. Rus. Fed. 74 D1
Shexian China 77 H2
Sheyang China 77 I1
Sheyenne r. U.S.A. 130 D2
Sheykh Sho'eyb i. Iran 88 D5
Shey Phoksundo National Park Nepal 83 E3
Shiant Islands U.K. 50 C3
Shiashkotan, Ostrov i. Rus. Fed. 65 Q5
Shibām Yemen 86 G6
Shibar Pass Afgh. 89 H3
Shibata Japan 75 E5
Shibazhan China 74 B1
Shibh Jazīrat Sīnā' pen. Egypt see Sinai
Shibīn al Kawm Egypt 90 C5
Shibîn el Kôm Egypt see Shibīn al Kawm
Shibogama Lake Canada 122 C3
Shibotsu-jima i. Rus. Fed. see Zelenyy, Ostrov
Shicheng Fujian China see Zhouning
Shicheng Jiangxi China 77 H3
Shidād al Mismā' hill Saudi Arabia 85 D4
Shidao China 73 M5
Shidian China 76 C3
Shiel, Loch l. U.K. 50 D4
Shield, Cape Australia 110 B2
Shieli Kazakh. see Chiili
Shifa, Jabal ash mts Saudi Arabia 90 D5
Shifang China 76 E2
Shigatse China see Xigazê
Shiḩān mt. Jordan 85 B4
Shihezi China 80 G3
Shihkiachwang China see Shijiazhuang
Shijiao China see Fogang
Shijiazhuang China 73 K5
Shijiu Hu l. China 77 H2
Shijiusuo China see Rizhao
Shikag Lake Canada 122 C4
Shikar r. Pak. 89 F4
Shikarpur Pak. 89 H5
Shikengkong mt. China 77 G3
Shikhany Rus. Fed. 43 J5
Shikohabad India 82 D4
Shikoku i. Japan 75 D6
Shikoku-sanchi mts Japan 75 D6
Shikotan, Ostrov i. Rus. Fed. 74 G4
Shikotan-tō i. Rus. Fed. see Shikotan, Ostrov
Shikotsu-Tōya National Park Japan 74 F4
Shildon U.K. 48 F4
Shilega Rus. Fed. 42 J2
Shiliguri India 83 G4
Shilin China 76 D3
Shilipu China 77 G2
Shiliu China see Changjiang
Shilla mt. Jammu and Kashmir 78 D2
Shillelagh Rep. of Ireland 51 F5
Shillo r. Israel 85 B3
Shillong India 83 G4
Shilovo Rus. Fed. 43 I5
Shimada Japan 75 E6
Shimanovsk Rus. Fed. 74 B1
Shimbiris mt. Somalia 98 E2
Shimen Gansu China 76 D1
Shimen Hunan China 77 F2
Shimen Yunnan China see Yunlong
Shimla India 82 D3
Shimoga India 84 B3
Shimokita-hantō pen. Japan 74 F4
Shimoni Kenya 99 D4
Shimonoseki Japan 75 C6
Shimsk Rus. Fed. 42 F4
Shin, Loch l. U.K. 50 E2
Shināfīyah Iraq see Ash Shanāfīyah
Shinan China see Xingye
Shīndand Afgh. 89 F3
Shingbwiyang Myanmar 70 B1
Shing-gai Myanmar 70 B1
Shinghshal Pass Pak. 89 I2
Shingletown U.S.A. 128 C1
Shingū Japan 75 E6
Shingwedzi S. Africa 101 J2
Shingwedzi r. S. Africa 101 J2
Shinkai Hills Afgh. 89 H3
Shīnkāy Afgh. 89 G4
Shinnston U.S.A. 134 E4
Shinshār Syria 85 C2
Shinyanga Tanz. 98 D4
Shiocton U.S.A. 134 A1
Shiogama Japan 75 F5
Shiono-misaki c. Japan 75 D6
Shipai China 77 H2
Shiping China 76 D4
Shipki Pass China/India 82 D3
Shipman U.S.A. 135 F5
Shippegan Island Canada 123 I5
Shippensburg U.S.A. 135 G3
Shiprock U.S.A. 129 I3
Shiprock Peak U.S.A. 129 I3
Shipu China 77 I2
Shipunovo Rus. Fed. 72 E2
Shiqian China 77 F3
Shiqiao China see Panyu
Shiqizhen China see Zhongshan
Shiquan China 77 F1
Shiquanhe Xizang China see Ali
Shiquanhe Xizang China see Gar
Shiquan He r. China see Indus
Shiquan Shuiku resr China 77 F1
Shira Rus. Fed. 72 F2
Shīrābād Iran 88 C2
Shirakawa-go and Gokayama tourist site Japan 75 E5
Shirane-san vol. Japan 75 E5
Shirase Coast Antarctica 152 J1
Shirase Glacier Antarctica 152 D2
Shīrāz Iran 88 D4
Shire r. Malawi 99 D5
Shireza Pak. 89 G5
Shirīn Tagāb Afgh. 89 G2
Shiriya-zaki c. Japan 74 F4
Shirkala reg. Kazakh. 80 A2
Shīr Kūh mt. Iran 88 D4
Shiroro Reservoir Nigeria 96 D3
Shirpur India 82 C5
Shirten Holoy Gobi des. China 76 I3
Shīrvān Iran 88 E2
Shisanzhan China 74 B2
Shishaldin Volcano U.S.A. 118 B4
Shisha Pangma mt. China see Xixabangma Feng
Shishou China 77 G2
Shitan China 77 G3
Shitang China 77 I2
Shithāthah Iraq 91 F4
Shiv India 82 B4
Shiveluch, Sopka vol. Rus. Fed. 65 R4
Shivpuri India 82 D4
Shivwits U.S.A. 129 G3
Shivwits Plateau U.S.A. 129 G3
Shiwan Dashan mts China 76 E4
Shiwa Ngandu Zambia 99 D5
Shixing China 77 G3
Shiyan China 77 F1
Shizhu China 77 F2
Shizilu China see Junan
Shizipu China 77 H2
Shizong China 76 D3
Shizuishan China 72 J5
Shizuoka Japan 75 E6

▶Shkhara mt. Georgia/Rus. Fed. 91 F2
3rd highest mountain in Europe.

Shklov Belarus see Shklow
Shklow Belarus 43 F5
Shkodër Albania 59 H3
Shkodra Albania see Shkodër
Shkodrës, Liqeni i l. Albania/Serb. and Mont. see Scutari, Lake

Shmidta, Ostrov i. Rus. Fed. 64 K1
Shmidta, Poluostrov pen. Rus. Fed. 74 F1
Shoal Lake Canada 121 K5
Shoals U.S.A. 134 B4
Shōbara Japan 75 D6
Shoh Tajik. 89 H2
Shohi Pass Pak. see Tal Pass
Shokanbetsu-dake mt. Japan 74 F4
Sholakkorgan Kazakh. 80 C3
Sholapur India see Solapur
Sholaqorghan Kazakh. see Sholakkorgan
Shomba r. Rus. Fed. 44 R4
Shomvukva Rus. Fed. 42 K3
Shona Ridge sea feature S. Atlantic Ocean 148 I9
Shonzha Kazakh. see Chundzha
Shor India 82 D2
Shorap Pak. 89 G5
Shorapur India 84 C2
Shorawak reg. Afgh. 89 G4
Shorewood IL U.S.A. 134 A3
Shorewood WI U.S.A. 134 B2
Shorkot Pak. 89 I4
Shorkozakhly, Solonchak salt flat Turkm. 91 J2
Shoshone CA U.S.A. 128 E4
Shoshone ID U.S.A. 126 E4
Shoshone r. U.S.A. 126 F3
Shoshone Mountains U.S.A. 128 E2
Shoshone Peak U.S.A. 128 E3
Shoshong Botswana 101 H2
Shoshoni U.S.A. 126 F4
Shostka Ukr. 43 G6
Shouyang Shan mt. China 77 F1
Showak Sudan 86 E7
Show Low U.S.A. 129 H4
Shoyna Rus. Fed. 42 J2
Shpakovskoye Rus. Fed. 91 F1
Shpola Ukr. 43 F6
Shqipëria country Europe see Albania
Shreve U.S.A. 134 D3
Shreveport U.S.A. 131 E5
Shrewsbury U.K. 49 E6
Shri Lanka country Asia see Sri Lanka
Shri Mohangarh India 82 B4
Shrirampur India 83 G5
Shu Kazakh. 80 D3
Shū r. Kazakh./Kyrg. see Chu
Shu'ab, Ra's pt Yemen 87 H7
Shuajingsi China 76 D1
Shuangbai China 76 D3
Shuangcheng Fujian China see Zherong
Shuangcheng Heilong. China 74 B3
Shuanghe China 77 G2
Shuanghechang China 76 E2
Shuanghedagang China 74 C2
Shuangjiang Guizhou China see Jiangkou
Shuangjiang Hunan China see Tongdao
Shuangjiang Yunnan China see Eshan
Shuangliao China 74 A4
Shuangliu China 76 D2
Shuangpai China 77 F3
Shuangshipu China see Fengxian
Shuangxi China see Shunchang
Shuangyang China 74 B4
Shuangyashan China 74 C3
Shubarkuduk Kazakh. 80 A2
Shubayh well Saudi Arabia 85 D4
Shugozero Rus. Fed. 42 G4
Shuicheng China see Lupanshui
Shuidong China see Dianbai
Shuijing China 76 E1
Shuikou China 77 F3
Shuikouguan China 76 E4
Shuikoushan China 77 G3
Shuiluocheng China see Zhuanglang
Shuizhai China see Wuhua
Shulan China 74 B3
Shumagin Islands U.S.A. 118 B4
Shumba Zimbabwe 99 C5
Shumen Bulg. 59 L3
Shumerlya Rus. Fed. 42 J5
Shumilina Belarus 43 F5
Shumyachi Rus. Fed. 43 G5
Shunchang China 77 H3
Shuncheng China 74 A4
Shunde China 77 G4
Shuoxian China see Shuozhou
Shuozhou China 73 K5
Shuqrah Yemen 86 G7
Shūr r. Iran 88 D4
Shūr r. Iran 89 F3
Shūr watercourse Iran 88 D5
Shur watercourse Iran 88 E3
Shūr, Rūd-e watercourse Iran 88 E4
Shūr Āb watercourse Iran 88 D4
Shurchi Uzbek. 89 G2
Shūrjestān Iran 88 D4
Shūrū Iran 89 F4
Shuryshkarskiy Sor, Ozero l. Rus. Fed. 41 T2
Shūsh Iran 88 C3
Shusha Azer. see Şuşa
Shushtar Iran 88 C3
Shutar Khun Pass Afgh. 89 G3
Shutfah, Qalamat well Saudi Arabia 88 D6
Shuwaysh, Tall ash hill Jordan 85 C4
Shuya Ivanovskaya Oblast' Rus. Fed. 42 I4
Shuya Respublika Kareliya Rus. Fed. 42 G3
Shuyskoye Rus. Fed. 42 I4
Shwebo Myanmar 70 A2
Shwedwin Myanmar 70 A1
Shwegun Myanmar 70 B3
Shwegyin Myanmar 70 B3
Shweudaung mt. Myanmar 70 B2
Shyghanaq Kazakh. see Chiganak
Shymkent Kazakh. 80 C3
Shyok Jammu and Kashmir 82 D2
Shypuvate Ukr. 43 H6
Shyroke Ukr. 43 G7
Sia Indon. 69 I8
Siabu Indon. 71 B7
Siahan Range mts Pak. 89 F5
Sīah Chashmeh Iran 88 B2
Siahgird Afgh. 89 G2
Siah Koh mts Afgh. 89 G3
Sialkot Pak. 89 I3
Siam country Asia see Thailand
Sian China see Xi'an
Sian Rus. Fed. 74 B1
Siang r. India see Brahmaputra
Siantan i. Indon. 71 D7
Siargao i. Phil. 69 H5
Siau i. Indon. 69 H6
Šiauliai Lith. 45 M9
Siazan' Azer. see Siyäzän
Si Bai, Lam r. Thai. 70 D4
Sibasa S. Africa 101 J2
Sibayi, Lake S. Africa 101 K4
Sibda China 76 C2
Šibenik Croatia 58 F3
Siberia reg. Rus. Fed. 65 M3
Siberut i. Indon. 68 B7
Siberut, Selat sea chan. Indon. 68 B7
Sibi Pak. 89 G4
Sibidiri P.N.G. 69 K8
Sibigo Indon. 71 A7
Sibiloi National Park Kenya 98 D3
Sibir' reg. Rus. Fed. see Siberia
Sibiti Congo 98 B4
Sibiu Romania 59 K2
Sibley U.S.A. 130 E3
Siboa Indon. 69 G6
Sibolga Indon. 71 B7
Siborongborong Indon. 71 B7
Sibsagar India 83 H4
Sibu Sarawak Malaysia 68 E6
Sibut Cent. Afr. Rep. 98 B3
Sibuyan i. Phil. 69 G4
Sibuyan Sea Phil. 69 G4
Sicamous Canada 120 G5
Sicca Veneria Tunisia see Le Kef
Siccus watercourse Australia 111 B6
Sicheng Anhui China see Sixian
Sicheng Guangxi China see Lingyun
Sichon Thai. 71 B5
Sichuan prov. China 76 D2
Sichuan Pendi basin China 76 E2
Sicié, Cap c. France 56 G5
Sicilia i. Italy see Sicily
Sicilian Channel Italy/Tunisia 58 E6
Sicily i. Italy 58 F5
Sicuani Peru 142 D6
Siddhapur India 82 C5
Siddipet India 84 C2
Sideros, Akra pt Greece 59 L7
Sidesaviwa S. Africa 100 F7
Sidhauli India 82 E4
Sidhi India 83 E4
Sidhpur India see Siddhapur
Sidi Aïssa Alg. 57 H6
Sidi Ali Alg. 57 G5
Sīdī Barrānī Egypt 90 B5
Sidi Bel Abbès Alg. 57 F6
Sidi Bennour Morocco 54 C5
Sidi Bou Sa'id Tunisia see Sidi Bouzid
Sidi Bouzid Tunisia 58 C7
Sidi el Barráni Egypt see Sīdī Barrānī
Sidi El Hani, Sebkhet de salt pan Tunisia 58 D7
Sidi Ifni Morocco 96 B2
Sidi Kacem Morocco 54 C5
Sidikalang Indon. 71 B7
Sidi Khaled Alg. 54 E5
Sid Lake Canada 121 J2
Sidlaw Hills U.K. 50 F4
Sidley, Mount Antarctica 152 J1
Sidli India 83 G4
Sidmouth U.K. 49 D8
Sidney IA U.S.A. 130 E3
Sidney MT U.S.A. 126 G3
Sidney NE U.S.A. 130 C3
Sidney OH U.S.A. 134 C3
Sidney Lanier, Lake U.S.A. 133 D5
Sidoktaya Myanmar 70 A2
Sidon Lebanon 85 B3
Sidr Egypt see Sudr
Siedlce Poland 43 D5
Sieg r. Germany 53 H4
Siegen Germany 53 I4
Siĕmréab Cambodia 71 C4
Siem Reap Cambodia see Siĕmréab
Si'en China see Huanjiang
Siena Italy 58 D3
Sieradz Poland 47 Q5
Sierra Blanca U.S.A. 127 G7
Sierra Colorada Arg. 144 C6
Sierra Grande Arg. 144 C6
▶Sierra Leone country Africa 96 B4
Africa 7, 94–95
Sierra Leone Basin sea feature N. Atlantic Ocean 148 G5
Sierra Leone Rise sea feature N. Atlantic Ocean 148 G5
Sierra Madre Mountains U.S.A. 128 C4
Sierra Mojada Mex. 131 C7
Sierra Nevada, Parque Nacional nat. park Venez. 142 D2
Sierra Nevada de Santa Marta, Parque Nacional nat. park Col. 142 D1
Sierraville U.S.A. 128 C2
Sierra Vista U.S.A. 127 F7
Sierre Switz. 56 H3
Sievi Fin. 44 N5
Sifang Ling mts China 76 E4
Sifangtai China 74 B3
Sīfenī Eth. 98 E2
Sifnos i. Greece 59 K6
Sig Alg. 57 F6
Sigguup Nunaa pen. Greenland 119 M2
Sighetu Marmației Romania 43 D7
Sighișoara Romania 59 K1
Siglap Sing. 71 [inset]
Sigli Indon. 71 A6
Siglufjörður Iceland 44 [inset]
Signal de Botrange hill Belgium 52 G4
Signal de la Ste-Baume mt. France 56 G5
Signal Peak U.S.A. 129 F5
Signy-l'Abbaye France 52 E5
Sigourney U.S.A. 130 E3
Sigri, Akra pt Greece 59 K5
Sigsbee Deep sea feature G. of Mexico 151 N4
Sigüenza Spain 57 E3
Siguiri Guinea 96 C3
Sigulda Latvia 45 N8
Sigurd U.S.A. 129 H2
Sihanoukville Cambodia 71 C5
Sihaung Myauk Myanmar 70 A2
Sihawa India 84 D1
Sihong China 77 H1
Sihora India 82 E5
Sihui China 77 G4
Siikajoki Fin. 44 N4
Siilinjärvi Fin. 44 O5
Siirt Turkey 91 F3
Sijawal Pak. 82 B4
Sika India 82 B5
Sikaka Saudi Arabia see Sakākah
Sikandra Rao India 82 D4
Sikanni Chief Canada 120 F3
Sikanni Chief r. Canada 120 F3
Sikar India 82 C4
Sikaram mt. Afgh. 89 H3
Sikasso Mali 96 C3
Sikaw Myanmar 70 B2
Sikeston U.S.A. 131 F4
Sikhote-Alin' mts Rus. Fed. 74 D4
Sikhote-Alinskiy Zapovednik nature res. Rus. Fed. 74 E3
Sikinos i. Greece 59 K6
Sikkim state India 83 G4
Siksjö Sweden 44 J4
Sil r. Spain 57 C2
Şila' i. Saudi Arabia 90 D6
Šilalė Lith. 45 M9
Si Lanna National Park Thai. 70 B3
Silas U.S.A. 131 F6
Silavatturai Sri Lanka 84 C4
Silawaih Agam vol. Indon. 71 A6
Silberberg hill Germany 53 J1
Silchar India 83 H4
Şile Turkey 59 M4
Sileru r. India 84 D2
Silesia reg. Czech Rep./Poland 47 P5
Sileti r. Kazakh. 72 C2
Siletiteniz, Ozero salt l. Kazakh. 79 G1
Silgadi Nepal see Silgarhi
Silgarhi Nepal 82 E3
Silghat India 83 H4
Siliana Tunisia 58 C6
Silifke Turkey 85 A1
Siliguri India see Shiliguri
Siling Co salt l. China 83 G3
Silipur India 82 D4
Silistra Bulg. 59 L2
Silistria Bulg. see Silistra
Silivri Turkey 59 M4
Siljan l. Sweden 45 I6
Silkeborg Denmark 45 F8
Sillajhuay mt. Chile 142 E7
Sillamäe Estonia 45 O7
Sille Turkey 90 D3
Silli India 83 F5
Sillod India 84 B1
Silobela S. Africa 101 J4
Silsby Lake Canada 121 M4
Silt U.S.A. 129 J2
Siltaharju Fin. 44 O3
Sīlūp r. Iran 89 F5
Šilutė Lith. 45 L9
Silvan Turkey 91 F3
Silvânia Brazil 145 A2
Silvassa India 84 B1
Silver Bank Passage Turks and Caicos Is 137 J4
Silver Bay U.S.A. 130 F2
Silver City Canada 120 B2
Silver City NM U.S.A. 129 I5
Silver City NV U.S.A. 128 D2
Silver Creek r. U.S.A. 129 H4
Silver Lake U.S.A. 126 C4
Silver Lake l. U.S.A. 128 E4
Silvermine Mts hills Rep. of Ireland 51 D5
Silver Peak Range mts U.S.A. 128 E3
Silver Spring U.S.A. 135 G4
Silver Springs U.S.A. 128 D2
Silverthrone Mountain Canada 120 E5
Silvertip Mountain Canada 120 F5
Silverton U.K. 49 D8
Silverton CO U.S.A. 129 J3
Silverton TX U.S.A. 131 C5
Sima China 83 G3
Simanggang Sarawak Malaysia see Sri Aman
Simao China 76 D4
Simàrd, Lac l. Canada 122 F5
Simaria India 83 F4
Simav Turkey 59 M5
Simav Dağları mts Turkey 59 M5
Simba Dem. Rep. Congo 98 C3
Simbirsk Rus. Fed. see Ul'yanovsk
Simcoe Canada 134 E2
Simcoe, Lake Canada 134 F1
Simdega India 84 E1
Simēn mts Eth. 98 D2
Simēn Mountains Eth. see Simēn
Simeulue i. Indon. 71 B7
Simeulue Reserve nature res. Indon. 71 A7
Simferopol' Ukr. 90 D1
Simi i. Greece see Symi
Simikot Nepal 83 E3
Similan, Ko i. Thai. 71 B5
Simi Valley U.S.A. 128 D4
Simla India see Shimla
Simla U.S.A. 126 G5
Şimleu Silvaniei Romania 59 J1
Simmerath Germany 52 G4
Simmern (Hunsrück) Germany 53 H5
Simmesport U.S.A. 131 F6
Simms U.S.A. 126 F3
Simojärvi l. Fin. 44 O3
Simon Mex. 131 C7
Simonette r. Canada 120 G4
Simon Wash watercourse U.S.A. 129 I5
Simoom Sound Canada 120 E5
Simoon Sound Canada see Simoom Sound
Simpang Indon. 68 C7
Simpang Mangayau, Tanjung pt Malaysia 68 F5
Simplício Mendes Brazil 143 J5
Simplon Pass Switz. 56 I3
Simpson Canada 121 J5
Simpson U.S.A. 126 F2
Simpson Desert Australia 110 B5
Simpson Desert National Park Australia 110 B5
Simpson Desert Regional Reserve nature res. Australia 111 B5
Simpson Islands Canada 121 H2
Simpson Park Mountains U.S.A. 128 E2
Simpson Peninsula Canada 119 J3
Simrishamn Sweden 45 I9
Simushir, Ostrov i. Rus. Fed. 73 S3
Sina r. India 84 B2
Sinabang Indon. 71 B7
Sinabung vol. Indon. 71 B7
Sinai pen. Egypt 85 A5
Sinai, Mont hill France 52 E5
Sinai al Janūbîya governorate Egypt see Janūb Sīnā'
Sinai ash Shamâlîya governorate Egypt see Shamāl Sīnā'
Si Nakarin Reservoir Thai. 70 B4
Sinaloa state Mex. 127 F8
Sinalunga Italy 58 D3
Sinan China 77 F3
Sinancha Rus. Fed. see Cheremshany
Sinbo Myanmar 70 B1
Sinbyubyin Myanmar 71 B4
Sinbyugyun Myanmar 70 A2
Sincan Turkey 90 E3
Sincelejo Col. 142 C2
Sinchu Taiwan see T'aoyüan
Sinclair Mills Canada 120 F4
Sincora, Serra do hills Brazil 145 C1
Sind r. India 82 D4
Sind Pak. see Thul
Sind prov. Pak. see Sindh
Sinda Rus. Fed. 74 E2
Sindari India 82 B4
Sindelfingen Germany 53 I6
Sindh prov. Pak. 89 H5
Sindhuli Garhi Nepal 83 F4
Sindhulimadi Nepal see Sindhuli Garhi
Sındırgı Turkey 59 M5
Sindor Rus. Fed. 42 K3
Sindou Burkina 96 C3
Sindri India 83 F5
Sind Sagar Doab lowland Pak. 89 H4
Sinel'nikovo Ukr. see Synel'nykove
Sines Port. 57 B5
Sines, Cabo de c. Port. 57 B5
Sinettä Fin. 44 N3
Sinfra Côte d'Ivoire 96 C4
Sing Myanmar 70 B2
Singa Sudan 86 D7
Singanallur India 84 C4
▶Singapore country Asia 71 [inset]
Asia 6, 62–63

▶Singapore Sing. 71 [inset]
Capital of Singapore.

Singapore r. Sing. 71 [inset]
Singapore, Strait of Indon./Sing. 71 [inset]
Singapura country Asia see Singapore
Singapura Sing. see Singapore
Singapuru India 84 D2
Singaraja Indon. 108 A2
Sing Buri Thai. 70 C4
Singhampton Canada 134 E1
Singhana India 82 C3
Singida Tanz. 99 D4
Singidunum Serb. and Mont. see Belgrade
Singkaling Hkamti Myanmar 70 A1
Singkawang Indon. 68 D6
Singkep i. Indon. 68 C7
Singkil Indon. 71 B7
Singkuang Indon. 71 B7
Singleton Australia 112 E4
Singleton, Mount hill N.T. Australia 108 E5
Singleton, Mount hill W.A. Australia 109 B7
Singora Thai. see Songkhla
Sin'gosan N. Korea see Kosan
Singra India 83 G4
Singri India 83 H4
Singu Myanmar 76 B4
Singwara India 84 D1
Sin'gye N. Korea 75 B5
Sinhala country Asia see Sri Lanka
Sinhkung Myanmar 70 B1
Sining China see Xining
Siniscola Sardinia Italy 58 C4
Sinj Croatia 58 G3
Sinjai Indon. 69 G8
Sinjār, Jabal mt. Iraq 91 F3
Sinkat Sudan 86 E6
Sinkiang aut. reg. China see Xinjiang Uygur Zizhiqu
Sinkiang Uighur Autonomous Region aut. reg. China see Xinjiang Uygur Zizhiqu
Sinmi-do i. N. Korea 75 B5
Sinn Germany 53 I4
Sinnamary Fr. Guiana 143 H2
Sinn Bishr, Gebel hill Egypt see Sinn Bishr, Jabal
Sinn Bishr, Jabal hill Egypt 85 A5
Sinneh Iran see Sanandaj
Sinoia Zimbabwe see Chinhoyi
Sinop Brazil 143 G6
Sinop Turkey 90 D2
Sinope Turkey see Sinop
Sinp'a N. Korea 74 B4
Sinp'o N. Korea 75 C4
Sinsang N. Korea 75 B5
Sinsheim Germany 53 I5
Sintang Indon. 68 E6
Sint Eustatius i. Neth. Antilles 137 L5
Sint-Laureins Belgium 52 D3

▶Sint Maarten i. Neth. Antilles 137 L5
Part of the Netherlands Antilles. The northern part of the island is the French territory of St Martin.

Sint-Niklaas Belgium 52 E3
Sinton U.S.A. 131 D6
Sintra Port. 57 B4
Sint-Truiden Belgium 52 F4
Sinŭiju N. Korea 75 B4
Sinzig Germany 53 H4
Siófok Hungary 58 H1
Sioma Ngwezi National Park Zambia 99 C5
Sion Switz. 56 H3
Sion Mills U.K. 51 E3
Siorapaluk Greenland 119 K2
Sioux Center U.S.A. 125 H3
Sioux City U.S.A. 130 D3
Sioux Falls U.S.A. 130 D3
Sioux Lookout Canada 121 N5
Siphaqeni S. Africa see Flagstaff
Siping China 74 B4
Sipiwesk Canada 121 L4
Sipiwesk Lake Canada 121 L4
Siple, Mount Antarctica 152 J2
Siple Coast Antarctica 152 I1
Siple Island Antarctica 152 J2
Siponj Tajik. see Bartang
Sipsey r. U.S.A. 131 F5
Sipura i. Indon. 68 B7
Sīq, Wādī as watercourse Egypt 85 A5
Sir r. Pak. 89 H6
Sir, Dar"yoi r. Asia see Syrdar'ya
Sira India 84 C3
Sira r. Norway 45 E7
Şīr Abū Nu'āyr i. U.A.E. 88 D5
Siracusa Sicily Italy see Syracuse
Siraha Nepal see Sirha
Sirajganj Bangl. 83 G4
Sir Alexander, Mount Canada 120 F4
Şiran Turkey 91 E2
Sirbāl, Jabal mt. Egypt 90 D5
Şīr Banī Yās i. U.A.E. 88 D5
Sircilla India see Sirsilla
Sirdaryo r. Asia see Syrdar'ya
Sirdaryo Uzbek. see Syrdar'ya
Sirdingka China see Lhari
Sir Edward Pellew Group is Australia 110 B2
Sirha Nepal 83 F4
Sirhān, Wādī as watercourse Jordan/Saudi Arabia 85 C4
Sirik, Tanjung pt Malaysia 68 E6
Siri Kit Dam Thai. 70 C3
Sirína i. Greece see Syrna
Sīrjā Iran 89 F5
Sir James MacBrien, Mount Canada 120 E2
Sīrjān Iran 88 D4
Sīrjān salt flat Iran 88 D4
Sirkazhi India 84 C4
Sirmilik National Park Canada 119 K2
Şırnak Turkey 91 F3
Sirohi India 82 C4
Sirombu Indon. 71 B7
Sironj India 82 D4
Síros i. Greece see Syros
Sirpur India 84 C2
Sirretta Peak U.S.A. 128 D4
Sīrrī, Jazīreh-ye i. Iran 88 D5
Sirsa India 82 C3
Sir Sandford, Mount Canada 120 G5
Sirsi Karnataka India 84 B3
Sirsi Madhya Pradesh India 82 D4
Sirsi Uttar Pradesh India 82 D3
Sirsilla India 84 C2
Sirte Libya 97 E1
Sirte, Gulf of Libya 97 E1
Sir Thomas, Mount hill Australia 109 E6
Siruguppa India 84 C3
Sirur India 84 B2
Şirvan Turkey 91 F3
Sirvel India 84 C3
Širvintai Lith. see Širvintos
Širvintos Lith. 45 N9
Sīrwān r. Iraq 91 G4
Sir Wilfrid Laurier, Mount Canada 120 G4
Sis Turkey see Kozan
Sisak Croatia 58 G2
Sisaket Thai. 70 D4
Siscia Croatia see Sisak
Sishen S. Africa 100 F4
Sishilipu China 76 E1
Sishuang Liedao is China 77 I3
Sisian Armenia 91 G3
Sisimiut Greenland 119 M3
Sisipuk Lake Canada 121 K4
Sisŏphŏn Cambodia 71 C4
Sissano P.N.G. 69 K7
Sisseton U.S.A. 130 D2
Sīstān reg. Iran 89 F4
Sīstan, Daryācheh-ye marsh Afgh./Iran 89 F4
Sisteron France 56 G4
Sisters is India 71 A5
Sīt Iran 88 E5
Sitamarhi India 83 F4
Sitang China see Sinan
Sitapur India 82 E4
Siteia Greece 59 L7
Siteki Swaziland 101 J4
Sithonia pen. Greece 59 J4
Sitía Greece see Siteia
Sitidgi Lake Canada 118 E3
Sitila Moz. 101 L2
Siting China 76 E3
Sítio do Mato Brazil 145 C1
Sitka U.S.A. 120 C3
Sitka National Historical Park nat. park U.S.A. 120 C3
Sitra oasis Egypt see Sitrah
Sitrah oasis Egypt 90 B5
Sittang r. Myanmar 70 B3
Sittard Neth. 52 F4
Sittaung Myanmar 70 A1
Sittaung r. Myanmar see Sittang
Sittensen Germany 53 J1
Sittingbourne U.K. 49 H7
Sittoung r. Myanmar see Sittang
Sittwe Myanmar 70 A2
Situbondo Indon. 68 E8
Siumpu i. Indon. 69 G8
Siuri India 83 F5
Sivaganga India 84 C4
Sivakasi India 84 C4
Sivaki Rus. Fed. 74 B1
Sivan India see Siwan
Sivas Turkey 90 E3
Sivaslı Turkey 59 M5
Siverek Turkey 91 E3
Siverskiy Rus. Fed. 45 Q7
Sivers'kyy Donets' r. Rus. Fed./Ukr. see Severskiy Donets
Sivomaskinskiy Rus. Fed. 41 S2
Sivrice Turkey 91 E3
Sivrihisar Turkey 59 N5
Sivukile S. Africa 101 I4
Sīwa Egypt see Sīwah
Sīwah Egypt 90 B5
Sīwah, Wāḥāt oasis Egypt 90 B5
Siwalik Range mts India/Nepal 82 D3
Siwan India 83 F4
Siwana India 82 C4
Siwa Oasis oasis Egypt see Sīwah, Wāḥāt
Sixian China 77 H1
Sixmilecross U.K. 51 E3
Siyabuswa S. Africa 101 I3
Siyäzän Azer. 91 H2
Sīyunī Iran 88 D3
Sizhan China 74 B2
Siziwang Qi China see Ulan Hua
Sjælland i. Denmark see Zealand
Sjenica Serb. and Mont. 59 I3
Sjöbo Sweden 45 H9
Sjøvegan Norway 44 J2
Skadarsko Jezero nat. park Serb. and Mont. 59 H3
Skadovs'k Ukr. 59 O1
Skaftafell nat. park Iceland 40 [inset]
Skaftárós r. mouth Iceland 44 [inset]
Skagafjörður inlet Iceland 44 [inset]
Skagen Denmark 45 G8
Skagerrak strait Denmark/Norway 45 F8
Skagit r. U.S.A. 126 C2
Skagway U.S.A. 153 A3
Skaidi Norway 44 N1
Skaland Norway 44 J2
Skalmodal Sweden 44 I4
Skanderborg Denmark 45 F8
Skaneateles Lake U.S.A. 135 G2
Skara Sweden 45 H7
Skardarsko Jezero l. Albania/Serb. and Mont. see Scutari, Lake
Skardu Jammu and Kashmir 82 C2
Skärgårdshavets nationalpark nat. park Fin. 45 L7
Skarnes Norway 45 G6
Skarżysko-Kamienna Poland 47 R5
Skaulo Sweden 44 L3
Skawina Poland 47 Q6
Skeena r. Canada 120 D4
Skeena Mountains Canada 120 D3
Skegness U.K. 48 H5
Skellefteå Sweden 44 L4
Skellefteälven r. Sweden 44 L4
Skelleftehamn Sweden 44 L4
Skellig Rocks is Rep. of Ireland 51 B6
Skelmersdale U.K. 48 E5
Skerries Rep. of Ireland 51 F4
Ski Norway 45 G7
Skiathos i. Greece 59 J5
Skibbereen Rep. of Ireland 51 C6
Skibotn Norway 44 L2
Skiddaw hill U.K. 48 D4
Skien Norway 45 F7
Skiermûntseach Neth. see Schiermonnikoog
Skiermûntseach i. Neth. see Schiermonnikoog
Skierniewice Poland 47 R5
Skikda Alg. 58 B6
Skipsea U.K. 48 G5
Skipton Australia 112 A6
Skipton U.K. 48 E5
Skirlaugh U.K. 48 G5
Skíros i. Greece see Skyros
Skive Denmark 45 F8
Skjern Denmark 45 F9
Skjolden Norway 45 E6
Skobelev Uzbek. see Fergana
Skobeleva, Pik mt. Kyrg. 89 I2
Skodje Norway 44 E5
Skoganvarre Norway 44 N2
Skokie U.S.A. 134 B2
Skomer Island U.K. 49 B7
Skopelos i. Greece 59 J5
Skopin Rus. Fed. 43 H5

▶Skopje Macedonia 59 I4
Capital of Macedonia.

Skoplje Macedonia see Skopje
Skövde Sweden 45 H7
Skovorodino Rus. Fed. 74 A1
Skowhegan U.S.A. 135 K1
Skrunda Latvia 45 M8
Skukum, Mount Canada 120 C2
Skukuza S. Africa 101 J3
Skull Valley U.S.A. 129 G4
Skuodas Lith. 45 L8
Skurup Sweden 45 H9
Skutskär Sweden 45 J6
Skvyra Ukr. 43 F6
Skye i. U.K. 50 C3
Skylge i. Neth. see Terschelling
Skyring, Seno b. Chile 144 B8
Skyros Greece 59 K5
Skyros i. Greece 59 K5
Skytrain Ice Rise Antarctica 152 L1
Slættaratindur hill Faroe Is 44 [inset]
Slagelse Denmark 45 G9
Slagnäs Sweden 44 K4
Slane Rep. of Ireland 51 F4
Slaney r. Rep. of Ireland 51 F5
Slantsy Rus. Fed. 45 P7
Slapovi Krke nat. park Croatia 58 F3
Slashers Reefs Australia 110 D3
Slatina Croatia 58 G2
Slatina Romania 59 K2
Slaty Fork U.S.A. 134 E4
Slava Rus. Fed. 74 C1
Slave r. Canada 121 H2
Slave Coast Africa 96 D4
Slave Lake Canada 120 H4
Slave Point Canada 120 H2
Slavgorod Belarus see Slawharad
Slavgorod Rus. Fed. 72 D2
Slavkovichi Rus. Fed. 45 P8
Slavonska Požega Croatia see Požega
Slavonski Brod Croatia 58 H2
Slavuta Ukr. 43 E6
Slavutych Ukr. 43 F6
Slavyanka Rus. Fed. 74 C4
Slavyansk Ukr. see Slov"yans'k
Slavyanskaya Rus. Fed. see Slavyansk-na-Kubani
Slavyansk-na-Kubani Rus. Fed. 90 E1
Slawharad Belarus 43 F5
Sławno Poland 47 P3
Slayton U.S.A. 130 E3
Sleaford U.K. 49 G5
Slea Head hd Rep. of Ireland 51 B5
Sleat Neth. see Sloten
Sleat, Sound of sea chan. U.K. 50 D3
Sled Lake Canada 121 J4

Split Lake l. Canada 121 L3
Spokane U.S.A. 126 D3
Spoletium Italy see Spoleto
Spoleto Italy 58 E3
Spóng Cambodia 71 D4
Spoon r. U.S.A. 130 F3
Spooner U.S.A. 130 F2
Spornitz Germany 53 L1
Spotsylvania U.S.A. 135 G4
Spotted Horse U.S.A. 126 G3
Spranger, Mount Canada 120 F4
Spratly Islands S. China Sea 68 E4
Spray U.S.A. 126 D3
Spree r. Germany 47 N4
Sprimont Belgium 52 F4
Springbok S. Africa 100 C5
Springdale Canada 123 L4
Springdale U.S.A. 134 C4
Springe Germany 53 J2
Springer U.S.A. 127 G5
Springerville U.S.A. 129 I4
Springfield CO U.S.A. 130 C4

▶Springfield IL U.S.A. 130 F4
State capital of Illinois.

Springfield KY U.S.A. 134 C5
Springfield MA U.S.A. 135 I2
Springfield MO U.S.A. 131 E4
Springfield OH U.S.A. 134 D4
Springfield OR U.S.A. 126 C3
Springfield TN U.S.A. 134 B5
Springfield VT U.S.A. 135 I2
Springfield WV U.S.A. 135 F4
Springfontein S. Africa 101 G6
Spring Glen U.S.A. 129 H2
Spring Grove U.S.A. 134 A2
Springhill Canada 123 I5
Spring Hill U.S.A. 133 D6
Springhouse Canada 120 F5
Spring Mountains U.S.A. 129 F3
Springs Junction N.Z. 113 D6
Springsure Australia 110 E5
Spring Valley MN U.S.A. 130 E3
Spring Valley NY U.S.A. 135 H3
Springview U.S.A. 130 D3
Springville CA U.S.A. 128 D3
Springville NY U.S.A. 135 F2
Springville PA U.S.A. 135 H3
Springville UT U.S.A. 129 H1
Sprowston U.K. 49 I6
Spruce Grove Canada 120 H4
Spruce Knob mt. U.S.A. 132 E4
Spruce Mountain CO U.S.A. 129 I2
Spruce Mountain NV U.S.A. 129 F1
Spurn Head hd U.K. 48 H5
Spuzzum Canada 120 F5
Squam Lake U.S.A. 135 J2
Square Lake U.S.A. 123 H5
Squillace, Golfo di g. Italy 58 G5
Squires, Mount hill Australia 109 D6
Srbija aut. rep. Serb. and Mont. 59 I3
Srbinje Bos.-Herz. see Foča
Srê Âmběl Cambodia 71 C5
Srebrenica Bos.-Herz. 58 H2
Sredets Burgas Bulg. 59 L3
Sredets Sofiya-Grad Bulg. see Sofia
Sredinnyy Khrebet mts Rus. Fed. 65 Q4
Sredna Gora mts Bulg. 59 J3
Srednekolymsk Rus. Fed. 65 Q3
Sredne-Russkaya Vozvyshennost' hills Rus. Fed. see Central Russian Upland
Sredne-Sibirskoye Ploskogor'ye plat. Rus. Fed. see Central Siberian Plateau
Sredneye Kuyto, Ozero l. Rus. Fed. 44 Q4
Sredniy Ural mts Rus. Fed. 41 R4
Srednogorie Bulg. 59 K3
Srednyaya Akhtuba Rus. Fed. 43 J6
Sreepur Bangl. see Sripur
Sre Khtum Cambodia 71 D4
Srê Noy Cambodia 71 D4
Sretensk Rus. Fed. 73 L2
Sri Aman Sarawak Malaysia 68 E6
Sriharikota Island India 84 D3

▶Sri Jayewardenepura Kotte Sri Lanka 84 C5
Capital of Sri Lanka.

Srikakulam India 84 E2
Sri Kalahasti India 84 C3
▶Sri Lanka country Asia 84 D5
Asia 6, 62–63
Srinagar India 82 C2
Sri Pada mt. Sri Lanka see Adam's Peak
Sripur Bangl. 83 G4
Srirangam India 84 C4
Sri Thep tourist site Thai. 70 C3
Srivardhan India 84 B2
Staaten r. Australia 110 C3
Staaten River National Park Australia 110 C3
Stabroek Guyana see Georgetown
Stade Germany 53 J1
Staden Belgium 52 D4
Stadskanaal Neth. 52 G2
Stadtallendorf Germany 53 J4
Stadthagen Germany 53 J2
Stadtilm Germany 53 L4
Stadtlohn Germany 52 G3
Stadtoldendorf Germany 53 J3
Stadtroda Germany 53 L4
Staffa i. U.K. 50 C4
Staffelberg hill Germany 53 L4
Staffelstein Germany 53 K4
Stafford U.K. 49 E6
Stafford U.S.A. 135 G4
Stafford Creek Bahamas 133 E7
Stafford Springs U.S.A. 135 I3
Stagg Lake Canada 120 H2
Staicele Latvia 45 N8
Staines U.K. 49 G7
Stakhanov Ukr. 43 H6
Stakhanovo Rus. Fed. see Zhukovskiy
Stalbridge U.K. 49 E8
Stalham U.K. 49 I6
Stalin Bulg. see Varna
Stalinabad Tajik. see Dushanbe
Stalingrad Rus. Fed. see Volgograd
Staliniri Georgia see Ts'khinvali
Stalino Ukr. see Donets'k
Stalinogorsk Rus. Fed. see Novomoskovsk
Stalinogród Poland see Katowice
Stalinsk Rus. Fed. see Novokuznetsk
Stalowa Wola Poland 43 D6
Stamboliyski Bulg. 59 K3
Stamford Australia 110 C4
Stamford U.K. 49 G6
Stamford CT U.S.A. 135 I3
Stamford NY U.S.A. 135 H2
Stampalia i. Greece see Astypalaia
Stampriet Namibia 100 D3
Stamsund Norway 44 H2
Stanardsville U.S.A. 135 F4
Stanberry U.S.A. 130 E3
Stancomb-Wills Glacier Antarctica 152 B1
Standard Canada 120 H5
Standdaarbuiten Neth. 52 E3
Standerton S. Africa 101 I4
Standish U.S.A. 134 D2
Stanfield U.S.A. 129 H5
Stanford KY U.S.A. 134 C5
Stanford MT U.S.A. 126 F3
Stanger S. Africa 101 J5
Stanislaus r. U.S.A. 128 C3
Stanislav Ukr. see Ivano-Frankivs'k
Stanke Dimitrov Bulg. see Dupnitsa
Staňkov Czech Rep. 53 N5
Stanley Australia 111 [inset]
Stanley Hong Kong China 77 [inset]

▶Stanley Falkland Is 144 E8
Capital of the Falkland Islands.

Stanley U.K. 48 F4
Stanley ID U.S.A. 126 E3
Stanley KY U.S.A. 134 B5
Stanley ND U.S.A. 130 C1
Stanley VA U.S.A. 135 F4
Stanley, Mount hill N.T. Australia 108 E5
Stanley, Mount hill Tas. Australia 111 [inset]
Stanley, Mount Dem. Rep. Congo/Uganda see Margherita Peak
Stanleyville Dem. Rep. Congo see Kisangani
Stann Creek Belize see Dangriga
Stannington U.K. 48 F3
Stanovoye Rus. Fed. 43 H5
Stanovoye Nagor'ye mts Rus. Fed. 73 L1
Stanovoy Khrebet mts Rus. Fed. 65 N4
Stansmore Range hills Australia 108 E5
Stanthorpe Australia 112 E2
Stanton U.K. 49 H6
Stanton KY U.S.A. 134 D5
Stanton MI U.S.A. 134 C2
Stanton ND U.S.A. 130 C2
Stanton TX U.S.A. 131 C5
Stapleton U.S.A. 130 C3
Starachowice Poland 47 R5
Stara Planina mts Bulg./Serb. and Mont. see Balkan Mountains
Staraya Russa Rus. Fed. 42 F4
Stara Zagora Bulg. 59 K3
Starbuck Island Kiribati 151 J6
Star City U.S.A. 134 B3
Starcke National Park Australia 110 D2
Stargard in Pommern Poland see Stargard Szczeciński
Stargard Szczeciński Poland 47 O4
Staritsa Rus. Fed. 42 G4
Starke U.S.A. 133 D6
Starkville U.S.A. 131 F5
Star Lake U.S.A. 135 H1
Starnberger See l. Germany 47 M7
Starobel'sk Ukr. see Starobil's'k
Starobil's'k Ukr. 43 H6
Starogard Gdański Poland 47 Q4
Starokonstantinov Ukr. see Starokostyantyniv
Starokostyantyniv Ukr. 43 E6
Starominskaya Rus. Fed. 43 H7
Staroshcherbinovskaya Rus. Fed. 43 H7
Star Peak U.S.A. 128 D1
Start Point U.K. 49 D8
Starve Island Kiribati see Starbuck Island
Staryya Darohi Belarus 43 F5
Staryye Dorogi Belarus see Staryya Darohi
Staryy Kayak Rus. Fed. 65 L2
Staryy Oskol Rus. Fed. 43 H6
Staßfurt Germany 53 L3
State College U.S.A. 135 G3
State Line U.S.A. 131 F6
Staten Island Arg. see Los Estados, Isla de
Statenville U.S.A. 133 D6
Statesboro U.S.A. 133 D5
Statesville U.S.A. 132 D5
Statia i. Neth. Antilles see Sint Eustatius
Station U.S.A. 134 C4
Station Nord Greenland 153 I1
Stauchitz Germany 53 N3
Staufenberg Germany 53 I4
Staunton U.S.A. 134 F4
Stavanger Norway 45 D7
Staveley U.K. 48 F5
Stavropol' Rus. Fed. 91 F1
Stavropol Kray admin. div. Rus. Fed. see Stavropol'skiy Kray
Stavropol'-na-Volge Rus. Fed. see Tol'yatti
Stavropol'skaya Vozvyshennost' hills Rus. Fed. 91 F1
Stavropol'skiy Kray admin. div. Rus. Fed. 91 F1
Stayner Canada 134 E1
Stayton U.S.A. 126 C3
Steadville S. Africa 101 I5
Steamboat Springs U.S.A. 126 G4
Stearns U.S.A. 134 C5
Stebbins U.S.A. 118 B3
Steele Island Antarctica 152 L2
Steelville U.S.A. 130 F4
Steen r. Canada 120 G3
Steenderen Neth. 52 G2
Steenkampsberge mts S. Africa 101 J3
Steen River Canada 120 G3
Steens Mountain U.S.A. 126 D4
Steenstrup Gletscher glacier Greenland see Sermersuaq
Steenvoorde France 52 C4
Steenwijk Neth. 52 G2
Stefansson Island Canada 119 H2
Stegi Swaziland see Siteki
Steigerwald mts Germany 53 K5
Stein Germany 53 L5
Steinach Germany 53 L4
Steinaker Reservoir U.S.A. 129 I1
Steinbach Canada 121 L5
Steinfeld (Oldenburg) Germany 53 I2
Steinfurt Germany 53 H2
Steinhausen Namibia 99 B6
Steinheim Germany 53 J3
Steinkjer Norway 44 G4
Steinkopf S. Africa 100 C5
Steinsdalen Norway 44 G4
Stella S. Africa 100 G4
Stella Maris Bahamas 133 F8
Stellenbosch S. Africa 100 D7
Stello, Monte mt. Corsica France 56 I5
Stelvio, Parco Nazionale dello nat. park Italy 58 D1
Stenay France 52 F5
Stendal Germany 53 L2
Stenhousemuir U.K. 50 F4
Stenungsund Sweden 45 G7
Steornabhagh U.K. see Stornoway
Stepanakert Azer. see Xankändi
Stephens, Cape N.Z. 113 D5
Stephens City U.S.A. 135 F4
Stephens Lake Canada 121 M3
Stephenville U.S.A. 131 D5
Stepnoy Rus. Fed. see Elista
Stepnoye Rus. Fed. 43 J6
Sterkfontein Dam resr S. Africa 101 I5
Sterkstroom S. Africa 101 H6
Sterlet Lake Canada 121 I1
Sterlibashevo Rus. Fed. 41 R5
Sterling S. Africa 100 E6
Sterling CO U.S.A. 130 C3
Sterling IL U.S.A. 130 F3
Sterling MI U.S.A. 134 C1
Sterling UT U.S.A. 129 H2
Sterling City U.S.A. 131 C6
Sterling Heights U.S.A. 134 D2
Sterlitamak Rus. Fed. 64 G4
Stettin Poland see Szczecin
Stettler Canada 121 H4
Steubenville KY U.S.A. 134 C5
Steubenville OH U.S.A. 134 E3
Stevenage U.K. 49 G7
Stevenson U.S.A. 126 C3
Stevenson Lake Canada 121 L4
Stevens Point U.S.A. 130 F2
Stevens Village U.S.A. 118 D3
Stevensville MI U.S.A. 134 B2
Stevensville PA U.S.A. 135 G3
Stewart Canada 120 D4
Stewart r. Canada 120 B2
Stewart, Isla i. Chile 144 B8
Stewart Crossing Canada 120 B2
Stewart Island N.Z. 113 A8
Stewart Islands Solomon Is 107 G2
Stewart Lake Canada 119 J3
Stewarton U.K. 50 E5
Stewarts Point U.S.A. 128 B2
Stewiacke Canada 123 J5
Steynsburg S. Africa 101 G6
Steyr Austria 47 O6
Steytlerville S. Africa 100 G7
Stiens Neth. 52 F1
Stif Alg. see Sétif
Stigler U.S.A. 131 E5
Stikine r. Canada 120 C3
Stikine Plateau Canada 120 D3
Stikine Strait U.S.A. 120 C3
Stilbaai S. Africa 100 E8
Stiles U.S.A. 134 A1
Stillwater MN U.S.A. 130 E2
Stillwater OK U.S.A. 131 D4
Stillwater Range mts U.S.A. 128 D2
Stillwell U.S.A. 134 B3
Stilton U.K. 49 G6
Stilwell U.S.A. 131 E5
Stinnett U.S.A. 131 C5
Štip Macedonia 59 J4
Stirling Australia 108 F5
Stirling Canada 135 G1
Stirling U.K. 50 F4
Stirling Creek r. Australia 108 E4
Stirling Range National Park Australia 109 B8
Stittsville Canada 135 H1
Stjørdalshalsen Norway 44 G5
Stockbridge U.S.A. 134 C2
Stockerau Austria 47 P6
Stockheim Germany 53 L4

▶Stockholm Sweden 45 K7
Capital of Sweden.

Stockinbingal Australia 112 C5
Stockport U.K. 48 E5
Stockton CA U.S.A. 128 C3
Stockton KS U.S.A. 130 D4
Stockton MO U.S.A. 130 E4
Stockton UT U.S.A. 129 G1
Stockton Lake U.S.A. 130 E4
Stockton-on-Tees U.K. 48 F4
Stockville U.S.A. 130 C3
Stod Czech Rep. 53 N5
Stœng Trêng Cambodia 71 D4
Stoer, Point of U.K. 50 D2
Stoke-on-Trent U.K. 49 E5
Stokesley U.K. 48 F4
Stokes Point Australia 111 [inset]
Stokes Range hills Australia 108 E4
Stokkseyri Iceland 44 [inset]
Stokkvågen Norway 44 H3
Stokmarknes Norway 44 I2
Stolac Bos.-Herz. 58 G3
Stolberg (Rheinland) Germany 52 G4
Stolbovoy Rus. Fed. 153 G2
Stolbtsy Belarus see Stowbtsy
Stolin Belarus 45 O11
Stollberg Germany 53 M4
Stolp Poland see Słupsk
Stolzenau Germany 53 J2
Stone U.K. 49 E6
Stoneboro U.S.A. 134 E3
Stonecliffe Canada 122 F5
Stonecutters' Island pen. Hong Kong China 77 [inset]
Stonehaven U.K. 50 G4
Stonehenge Australia 110 C5
Stonehenge tourist site U.K. 49 F7
Stoner U.S.A. 129 I3
Stonewall Canada 121 L5
Stonewall Jackson Lake U.S.A. 134 E4
Stony Creek U.S.A. 135 G5
Stony Lake Canada 121 L3
Stony Point U.S.A. 135 G2
Stony Rapids Canada 121 J3
Stony River U.S.A. 118 C3
Stooping r. Canada 122 E3
Stora Lulevatten l. Sweden 44 K3
Stora Sjöfallets nationalpark nat. park Sweden 44 J3
Storavan l. Sweden 44 K4
Store Bælt sea chan. Denmark see Great Belt
Støren Norway 44 G5
Storfjordbotn Norway 44 O1
Storforshei Norway 44 I3
Storjord Norway 44 I3
Storkerson Peninsula Canada 119 H2
Storm Bay Australia 111 [inset]
Stormberg S. Africa 101 H6
Storm Lake U.S.A. 130 E3
Stornosa mt. Norway 44 E6
Stornoway U.K. 50 C2
Storozhevsk Rus. Fed. 42 L3
Storozhynets' Ukr. 43 E6
Storrs U.S.A. 135 I3
Storseleby Sweden 44 J4
Storsjön l. Sweden 44 H5
Storskrymten mt. Norway 44 F5
Storslett Norway 44 L2
Stortemelk sea chan. Neth. 52 F1
Storuman Sweden 44 J4
Storuman l. Sweden 44 J4
Storvik Sweden 45 J6
Storvorde Denmark 45 G8
Storvreta Sweden 45 J7
Story U.S.A. 126 G3
Stotfold U.K. 49 G6
Stoughton Canada 121 K5
Stour r. England U.K. 49 F6
Stour r. England U.K. 49 F8
Stour r. England U.K. 49 I7
Stour r. England U.K. 49 I7
Stourbridge U.K. 49 E6
Stourport-on-Severn U.K. 49 E6
Stout Lake Canada 121 M4
Stowbtsy Belarus 45 O10
Stowe U.S.A. 135 I1
Stowmarket U.K. 49 H6
Stoyba Rus. Fed. 74 C1
Strabane U.K. 51 E3
Stradbally Rep. of Ireland 51 E4
Stradbroke U.K. 49 I6
Stradella Italy 58 C2
Strakonice Czech Rep. 47 N6
Stralsund Germany 47 N3
Strand S. Africa 100 D8
Stranda Norway 44 E5
Strangford U.K. 51 G3
Strangford Lough inlet U.K. 51 G3
Strangways r. Australia 108 F3
Stranraer U.K. 50 D6
Strasbourg France 56 H2
Strasburg Germany 53 N1
Strasburg U.S.A. 135 F4
Strassburg France see Strasbourg
Stratford Australia 112 C6
Stratford Canada 134 E2
Stratford CA U.S.A. 128 D3
Stratford TX U.S.A. 131 C4
Stratford-upon-Avon U.K. 49 F6
Strathaven U.K. 50 E5
Strathmore Canada 120 H5
Strathmore r. U.K. 50 E2
Strathnaver Canada 120 F4
Strathroy Canada 134 E2
Strathspey valley U.K. 50 F3
Strathy U.K. 50 F2
Stratton U.K. 49 C8
Stratton U.S.A. 135 J1
Stratton Mountain U.S.A. 135 I2
Straubing Germany 53 M6
Straumnes pt Iceland 44 [inset]
Strawberry U.S.A. 129 H4
Strawberry Mountain U.S.A. 126 D3
Strawberry Reservoir U.S.A. 129 H1
Streaky Bay Australia 109 F8
Streaky Bay b. Australia 109 F8
Streator U.S.A. 130 F3
Street U.K. 49 E7
Streetsboro U.S.A. 134 E3
Strehaia Romania 59 J2
Strehla Germany 53 N3
Streich Mound hill Australia 109 C7
Strelka Rus. Fed. 65 Q3
Strel'na r. Rus. Fed. 42 H2
Strenči Latvia 45 N8
Streymoy i. Faroe Is 44 [inset]
Stříbro Czech Rep. 53 M5
Strichen U.K. 50 G3
Strimonas r. Greece 59 J4
also known as Struma (Bulgaria)
Stroeder Arg. 144 D6
Strokestown Rep. of Ireland 51 D4
Stroma, Island of U.K. 50 F2
Stromboli, Isola i. Italy 58 F5
Stromness S. Georgia 144 I8
Stromness U.K. 50 F2
Strömstad Sweden 45 G7
Strömsund Sweden 44 I5
Strongsville U.S.A. 134 E3
Stronsay i. U.K. 50 G1
Stroud Australia 112 E4
Stroud U.K. 49 E7
Stroud Road Australia 112 E4
Stroudsburg U.S.A. 135 H3
Struer Denmark 45 F8
Struga Macedonia 59 I4
Strugi-Krasnyye Rus. Fed. 45 P7
Struis Bay S. Africa 100 E8
Strullendorf Germany 53 K5
Struma r. Bulg. 59 J4
also known as Strimonas (Greece)
Strumble Head hd U.K. 49 B6
Strumica Macedonia 59 J4
Struthers U.S.A. 134 E3
Stryama r. Bulg. 59 K3
Strydenburg S. Africa 100 F5
Stryn Norway 44 E6
Stryy Ukr. 43 D6
Strzelecki, Mount hill Australia 108 F5
Strzelecki Regional Reserve nature res. Australia 111 B6
Stuart FL U.S.A. 133 D7
Stuart NE U.S.A. 130 D3
Stuart VA U.S.A. 134 E5
Stuart Lake Canada 120 E4
Stuart Range hills Australia 111 A6
Stuarts Draft U.S.A. 134 F4
Stuart Town Australia 112 D4
Stuchka Latvia see Aizkraukle
Stučka Latvia see Aizkraukle
Studholme Junction N.Z. 113 C7
Studsviken Sweden 44 K5
Stukley, Lac l. Canada 135 I1
Stung Treng Cambodia see Stœng Trêng
Stupart r. Canada 121 M4
Stupino Rus. Fed. 43 H5
Sturge Island Antarctica 152 H2
Sturgeon r. Ont. Canada 122 F5
Sturgeon r. Sask. Canada 121 J4
Sturgeon Bay b. Canada 121 L4
Sturgeon Bay U.S.A. 134 B1
Sturgeon Bay Canal lake channel U.S.A. 134 B1
Sturgeon Falls Canada 122 F5
Sturgeon Lake Ont. Canada 121 N5
Sturgeon Lake Ont. Canada 135 F1
Sturgis MI U.S.A. 134 C3
Sturgis SD U.S.A. 130 C2
Sturt, Mount hill Australia 111 C6
Sturt Creek watercourse Australia 108 D4
Sturt National Park Australia 111 C6
Sturt Stony Desert Australia 111 C6
Stutterheim S. Africa 101 H7
Stuttgart Germany 53 J6
Stuttgart U.S.A. 131 F5
Stykkishólmur Iceland 44 [inset]
Styr r. Belarus/Ukr. 43 E5
Suaçuí Grande r. Brazil 145 C2
Suai East Timor 108 D2
Suakin Sudan 86 E6
Suao Taiwan 77 I3
Suaqui Grande Mex. 127 F7
Suau P.N.G. 110 E1
Subačius Lith. 45 N9
Subankhata India 83 G4
Subarnapur India see Sonapur
Sūbāshī Iran 88 C3
Subay reg. Saudi Arabia 88 B5
Şubayḩah Saudi Arabia 85 D4
Subei China 80 H4
Subi Besar i. Indon. 71 E7
Subi Kecil i. Indon. 71 E7
Sublette U.S.A. 131 C4
Subotica Serb. and Mont. 59 H1
Success, Lake U.S.A. 128 D3
Succiso, Alpi di mts Italy 58 D2
Suceava Romania 43 E7
Suchan Rus. Fed. see Partizansk
Suck r. Rep. of Ireland 51 D4
Suckling, Mount P.N.G. 110 E1
Suckow Germany 53 L1

▶Sucre Bol. 142 E7
Legislative capital of Bolivia.

Suczawa Romania see Suceava
Sud, Grand Récif du reef New Caledonia 107 G4
Suda Rus. Fed. 42 H4
Sudak Ukr. 90 D1

▶Sudan country Africa 97 F3
Largest country in Africa.
Africa 7, 94–95

Suday Rus. Fed. 42 I4
Sudayr reg. Saudi Arabia 88 B5
Sudbury Canada 122 E5
Sudbury U.K. 49 H6
Sudd swamp Sudan 86 C8
Sude r. Germany 53 K1
Sudest Island P.N.G. see Tagula Island
Sudetenland mts Czech Rep./Poland see Sudety
Sudety mts Czech Rep./Poland 47 O5
Sudislavl' Rus. Fed. 42 I4
Sudlersville U.S.A. 135 H4
Süd-Nord-Kanal canal Germany 52 H2
Sudogda Rus. Fed. 42 I5
Sudr Egypt 85 A5
Suðuroy i. Faroe Is 44 [inset]
Sue watercourse Sudan 97 F4
Sueca Spain 57 F4
Suez Egypt 85 A5
Suez, Gulf of Egypt 85 A5
Suez Bay Egypt 85 A5
Suez Canal Egypt 85 A4
Suffolk U.S.A. 135 G5
Sugarbush Hill hill U.S.A. 130 F2
Sugarloaf Mountain U.S.A. 135 J1
Sugarloaf Point Australia 112 F4
Sugun China 80 E4
Sūhāj Egypt see Sawhāj
Şuḩār Oman 88 E5
Suhaymī, Wādī as watercourse Egypt 85 A4
Sühbaatar Mongolia 72 J2
Suheli Par i. India 84 B4
Suhl Germany 53 K4
Suhlendorf Germany 53 K2
Suhul reg. Saudi Arabia 88 B6
Suhūl al Kidan plain Saudi Arabia 88 D6
Şuhut Turkey 59 N5
Sui Pak. 89 H4
Sui, Laem pt Thai. 71 B5
Suibin China 74 C3
Suid-Afrika country Africa see Republic of South Africa
Suide China 73 K5
Suidzhikurmsy Turkm. see Madau
Suifenhe China 74 C3
Suihua China 74 B3
Suileng China 74 B3
Suining Hunan China 77 F3
Suining Jiangsu China 77 H1
Suining Sichuan China 76 E2
Suippes France 52 E5
Suir r. Rep. of Ireland 51 E5
Suisse country Europe see Switzerland
Sui Vehar Pak. 89 H4
Suixi China 77 H1
Suixian Henan China 77 G1
Suixian Hubei China see Suizhou
Suiyang Guizhou China 76 E3
Suiyang Henan China 77 G1
Suiza country Europe see Switzerland
Suizhong China 73 M4
Suizhou China 77 G2
Sujangarh India 82 C4
Sujawal Pak. 89 H5
Suk atoll Micronesia see Pulusuk
Sukabumi Indon. 68 D8
Sukagawa Japan 75 F5
Sukarnapura Indon. see Jayapura
Sukarno, Puncak mt. Indon. see Jaya, Puncak
Sukchŏn N. Korea 75 B5
Sukhinichi Rus. Fed. 43 G5
Sukhona r. Rus. Fed. 42 J3
Sukhothai Thai. 70 B3
Sukhumi Georgia see Sokhumi
Sukhum-Kale Georgia see Sokhumi
Sukkertoppen Greenland see Maniitsoq
Sukkozero Rus. Fed. 42 G3
Sukkur Pak. 89 H5
Sukma India 84 D2
Sukpay Rus. Fed. 74 E3
Sukpay r. Rus. Fed. 74 E3
Sukri r. India 82 C4
Sukri r. India 82 C4
Suktel r. India 84 D1
Sukun i. Indon. 108 C2
Sula i. Norway 45 D6
Sula r. Rus. Fed. 42 K2
Sula, Kepulauan is Indon. 69 H7
Sulaiman Range mts Pak. 89 H4
Sulak Rus. Fed. 91 G2
Sūlār Iran 88 C4
Sula Sgeir i. U.K. 50 C1
Sulawesi i. Indon. see Celebes
Sulaymān Beg Iraq 91 G4
Sulayyimah Saudi Arabia 88 B6
Sulci Sardinia Italy see Sant'Antioco
Sulcis Sardinia Italy see Sant'Antioco
Suledeh Iran 88 C2
Sule Skerry i. U.K. 50 E1
Sule Stack i. U.K. 50 E1
Sulingen Germany 53 I2
Sulitjelma Norway 44 J3
Sulkava Fin. 44 P6
Sullana Peru 142 B4
Sullivan IL U.S.A. 130 F4
Sullivan IN U.S.A. 134 B4
Sullivan Bay Canada 120 E5
Sullivan Island Myanmar see Lanbi Kyun
Sullivan Lake Canada 121 I5
Sulmo Italy see Sulmona
Sulmona Italy 58 E3
Sulphur LA U.S.A. 131 E6
Sulphur OK U.S.A. 131 D5
Sulphur r. U.S.A. 131 E5
Sulphur Springs U.S.A. 131 E5
Sultan Canada 122 E5
Sultan, Koh-i- mts Pak. 89 F4
Sultanabad India see Osmannagar
Sultanabad Iran see Arāk
Sultan Dağları mts Turkey 59 N5
Sultanıye Turkey see Karapınar
Sultanpur India 83 E4
Sulu Archipelago is Phil. 69 G5
Sulu Basin sea feature N. Pacific Ocean 150 E5
Sülüklü Turkey 90 D3
Sülüktü Kyrg. 89 H2
Sulusaray Turkey 90 E3
Sulu Sea N. Pacific Ocean 68 F5
Suluvvaulik, Lac l. Canada 123 G2
Sulyukta Kyrg. see Sülüktü
Sulzbach-Rosenberg Germany 53 L5
Sulzberger Bay Antarctica 152 I1
Sumāil Oman 88 E6
Sumampa Arg. 144 D3
Sumapaz, Parque Nacional nat. park Col. 142 D3
Sūmār Iran 88 B3
Sumatera i. Indon. see Sumatra

▶Sumatra i. Indon. 71 B7
2nd largest island in Asia.

Šumava nat. park Czech Rep. 47 N6
Sumba i. Indon. 108 C2
Sumba, Selat sea chan. Indon. 108 B2
Sumbar r. Turkm. 88 D2
Sumbawa i. Indon. 108 B2
Sumbawabesar Indon. 108 B2
Sumbawanga Tanz. 99 D4
Sumbe Angola 99 B5
Sumbu National Park Zambia 99 D4
Sumburgh U.K. 50 [inset]
Sumburgh Head hd U.K. 50 [inset]
Sumdo China 76 D2
Sumdum, Mount U.S.A. 120 C3
Sume'eh Sara Iran 88 C2
Sumeih Sudan 86 C8
Sumenep Indon. 68 E8
Sumgait Azer. see Sumqayıt
Sumisu-jima i. Japan 73 Q6
Summēl Iraq 91 F3
Summer Beaver Canada 122 C3
Summerford Canada 123 L4
Summer Island U.S.A. 132 C2
Summer Isles U.K. 50 D2
Summerland Canada 120 G5
Summersville U.S.A. 134 E4
Summit Lake Canada 120 F4
Summit Mountain U.S.A. 128 E2
Summit Peak U.S.A. 127 G5
Sumnal Aksai Chin 82 D2
Sumner N.Z. 113 D6
Sumner, Lake N.Z. 113 D6
Sumon-dake mt. Japan 75 E5
Šumperk Czech Rep. 47 P6
Sumpu Japan see Shizuoka
Sumqayıt Azer. 91 H2
Sumskiy Posad Rus. Fed. 42 G2
Sumter U.S.A. 133 D5
Sumur Jammu and Kashmir 82 D2
Sumy Ukr. 43 G6
Sumzom China 76 C2
Suna Rus. Fed. 42 K4
Sunaj India 82 D4

Sunam India 82 C3
Sunamganj Bangl. 83 G4
Sunart, Loch *inlet* U.K. 50 D4
Şunaynah Oman 88 D6
Sunburst U.S.A. 126 F2
Sunbury Australia 112 B6
Sunbury *OH* U.S.A. 134 D3
Sunbury *PA* U.S.A. 135 G3
Sunch'ŏn S. Korea 75 B6
Sun City S. Africa 101 H3
Sun City *AZ* U.S.A. 129 G5
Sun City *CA* U.S.A. 128 E5
Sunda, Selat *strait* Indon. 68 C8
Sunda Kalapa Indon. *see* Jakarta
Sundance U.S.A. 126 G3
Sundarbans *coastal area* Bangl./India 83 G5
Sundarbans National Park Bangl./India 83 G5
Sundargarh India 83 F5
Sunda Shelf *sea feature* Indian Ocean 149 P5
Sunda Strait Indon. *see* Sunda, Selat
Sunda Trench *sea feature* Indian Ocean *see* Java Trench
Sunda Trench *sea feature* Indian Ocean *see* Java Trench
Sunderland U.K. 48 F4
Sundern (Sauerland) Germany 53 I3
Sündiken Dağları *mts* Turkey 59 N5
Sundown National Park Australia 112 E2
Sundre Canada 120 H5
Sundridge Canada 122 F5
Sundsvall Sweden 44 J5
Sundukli, Peski *des.* Turkm. 89 F2
Sundumbili S. Africa 101 J5
Sungaipenuh Indon. 68 C7
Sungari *r.* China *see* Songhua Jiang
Sungei Petani Malaysia 71 C6
Sungei Seletar Reservoir Sing. 71 [inset]
Sungkiang China *see* Songjiang
Sung Kong *i. Hong Kong* China 77 [inset]
Sungqu China *see* Songpan
Sungsang Indon. 68 C7
Sungurlu Turkey 90 D2
Sun Kosi *r.* Nepal 83 F4
Sunman U.S.A. 134 C4
Sunndal Norway 45 E6
Sunndalsøra Norway 44 F5
Sunne Sweden 45 H7
Sunnyside U.S.A. 126 D3
Sunnyvale U.S.A. 128 B3
Sun Prairie U.S.A. 130 F3
Sunset House Canada 120 G4
Sunset Peak *hill Hong Kong* China 77 [inset]
Suntar Rus. Fed. 65 M3
Suntsar Pak. 89 F5
Sunwi-do *i.* N. Korea 75 B5
Sunwu China 74 B2
Sunyani Ghana 96 C4
Suolijärvet *l.* Fin. 44 P3
Suomi *country* Europe *see* Finland
Suomussalmi Fin. 44 P4
Suō-nada *b.* Japan 75 C6
Suonenjoki Fin. 44 O5
Suong *r.* Laos 70 C3
Suoyarvi Rus. Fed. 42 G3
Supa India 84 B3
Supaul India 83 F4
Superior *AZ* U.S.A. 129 H5
Superior *MT* U.S.A. 126 E3
Superior *NE* U.S.A. 130 D3
Superior *WI* U.S.A. 130 E2

▶Superior, Lake Canada/U.S.A. 125 J2
Largest lake in North America and 2nd in the world.
North America 114–115
World 12–13

Suphan Buri Thai. 71 C4
Süphan Dağı *mt.* Turkey 91 F3
Supiori *i.* Indon. 69 J7
Suponevo Rus. Fed. 43 G5
Support Force Glacier Antarctica 152 A1
Sūq ash Shuyūkh Iraq 91 G5
Suqian China 77 H1
Suquṭrá *i.* Yemen *see* Socotra
Şūr Oman 89 E6
Sur, Point U.S.A. 128 C3
Sur, Punta *pt* Arg. 144 E5
Sura *r.* Rus. Fed. 43 J4
Şuraabad Azer. 91 H2
Surabaya Indon. 68 E8
Sūrak Iran 88 E5
Surakarta Indon. 68 E8
Sūran Iran 89 F5
Şūrān Syria 85 C2
Surat Australia 112 D1
Surat India 82 C5
Suratgarh India 82 C3
Surat Thani Thai. 71 B5
Surazh Rus. Fed. 43 G5
Surbiton Australia 110 D4
Surdulica Serb. and Mont. 59 J3
Sûre *r.* Lux. 52 G5
Surendranagar India 82 B5
Surf U.S.A. 128 C4
Surgut Rus. Fed. 64 I3
Suri India *see* Siuri
Suriapet India 84 C2
Surigao Phil. 69 H5
Surin Thai. 70 C4
Surinam *country* S. America *see* Suriname
▶Suriname *country* S. America 143 G3
South America 9, 140–141
Surin Nua, Ko *i.* Thai. 71 B5
Suriyān Iran 88 D4
Surkhan Uzbek. 89 G2
Surkhduz Afgh. 89 G4
Surkhet Nepal 83 E3
Surkhon Uzbek. *see* Surkhan
Sürmene Turkey 91 F2
Surovikino Rus. Fed. 43 I6
Surpura India 82 C4
Surrey Canada 120 F5
Surry U.S.A. 135 G5
Surskoye Rus. Fed. 43 J5
Surt Libya *see* Sirte
Surtsey *i.* Iceland 44 [inset]
Sūrū *Hormozgan* Iran 88 E5
Sūrū *Sīstān va Balūchestān* Iran 88 E5
Suruç Turkey 85 D1
Surud, Raas *pt* Somalia 98 E2
Surud Ad *mt.* Somalia *see* Shimbiris
Suruga-wan *b.* Japan 75 E6
Surulangun Indon. 68 C7
Surwold Germany 53 H2
Suryapet India *see* Suriapet
Şuşa Azer. 91 G3
Susah Tunisia *see* Sousse
Susaki Japan 75 D6
Susan U.S.A. 135 G5
Süsangerd Iran 88 C4
Susanino Rus. Fed. 74 F1
Susanville U.S.A. 128 C1
Suşehri Turkey 90 E2
Suso Thai. 71 B6
Susong China 77 H2
Susquehanna U.S.A. 135 H3
Susquehanna *r.* U.S.A. 135 G4
Susquehanna, West Branch *r.* U.S.A. 135 G3
Susques Arg. 144 C2
Sussex U.S.A. 135 H3
Susuman Rus. Fed. 65 P3
Susupu Indon. 69 H6
Susurluk Turkey 59 M5
Sutak Jammu and Kashmir 82 D2
Sutherland Australia 112 E5
Sutherland S. Africa 100 E7
Sutherland U.S.A. 130 C3
Sutherland Range *hills* Australia 109 D6
Sutjeska *nat. park* Bos.-Herz. 58 H3
Sutlej *r.* India/Pak. 82 B3
Sütlüce Turkey 85 A1
Sutter U.S.A. 128 C2
Sutterton U.K. 49 G6
Sutton Canada 135 I1
Sutton *r.* Canada 122 E3
Sutton U.K. 49 H6
Sutton *NE* U.S.A. 130 D3
Sutton *WV* U.S.A. 134 E4
Sutton Coldfield U.K. 49 F6
Sutton in Ashfield U.K. 49 F5
Sutton Lake Canada 122 D3
Sutton Lake U.S.A. 134 E4
Suttor *r.* Australia 110 D4
Suttsu Japan 74 F4
Sutwik Island U.S.A. 118 C4
Sutyr' *r.* Rus. Fed. 74 D2

▶Suva Fiji 107 H3
Capital of Fiji.

Suvadiva Atoll Maldives *see* Huvadhu Atoll
Suvalki Poland *see* Suwałki
Suvorov *atoll* Cook Is *see* Suwarrow
Suvorov Rus. Fed. 43 H5
Suwa Japan 75 E5
Suwałki Poland 43 D5
Suwannaphum Thai. 70 C4
Suwannee *r.* U.S.A. 133 D6
Suwanose-jima *i.* Japan 75 C7
Suwarrow *atoll* Cook Is 107 J3
Suwaylih Jordan 85 B3
Suwayr *well* Saudi Arabia 91 F5
Suways, Khalīj as *g.* Egypt *see* Suez, Gulf of
Suweilih Jordan *see* Suwaylih
Suweis, Khalîg el *g.* Egypt *see* Suez, Gulf of
Suweis, Qanâ el *canal* Egypt *see* Suez Canal
Suwŏn S. Korea 75 B5
Suz, Mys *pt* Kazakh. 91 I2
Suzaka Japan 75 E5
Suzdal' Rus. Fed. 42 I4
Suzhou *Anhui* China 77 H1
Suzhou *Gansu* China *see* Jiuquan
Suzhou *Jiangsu* China 77 I2
Suzi He *r.* China 74 B4
Suzuka Japan 75 E6
Suzu-misaki *pt* Japan 75 E5
Sværholthalvøya *pen.* Norway 44 O1

▶Svalbard *terr.* Arctic Ocean 64 C2
Part of Norway.

Svappavaara Sweden 44 L3
Svartenhuk Halvø *pen.* Greenland *see* Sigguup Nunaa
Svatove Ukr. 43 H6
Svay Chék Cambodia 71 C4
Svay Riĕng Cambodia 71 D5
Svecha Rus. Fed. 42 J4
Sveg Sweden 45 I5
Sveķi Latvia 45 O8
Svelgen Norway 44 D6
Svellingen Norway 44 F5
Švenčionėliai Lith. 45 N9
Švenčionys Lith. 45 O9
Svendborg Denmark 45 G9
Svensby Norway 44 K2
Svenstavik Sweden 44 I5
Sverdlovsk Rus. Fed. *see* Yekaterinburg
Sverdlovs'k Ukr. 43 H6
Sverdrup Islands Canada 119 I2
Sverige *country* Europe *see* Sweden
Sveti Nikole Macedonia 59 I4
Svetlaya Rus. Fed. 74 E3
Svetlogorsk Belarus *see* Svyetlahorsk
Svetlogorsk *Kaliningradskaya Oblast'* Rus. Fed. 45 L9
Svetlogorsk *Krasnoyarskiy Kray* Rus. Fed. 64 J3
Svetlograd Rus. Fed. 91 F1
Svetlovodsk Ukr. *see* Svitlovods'k
Svetlyy *Kaliningradskaya Oblast'* Rus. Fed. 45 L9
Svetlyy *Orenburgskaya Oblast'* Rus. Fed. 80 B1
Svetlyy Yar Rus. Fed. 43 J6
Svetogorsk Rus. Fed. 45 P6
Svíahnúkar *vol.* Iceland 44 [inset]
Svilaja *mts* Croatia 58 G3
Svilengrad Bulg. 59 L4
Svinecea Mare, Vârful *mt.* Romania 59 J2
Svintsovyy Rudnik Turkm. 89 G2
Svir Belarus 45 O9
Svir' *r.* Rus. Fed. 42 G3
Svishtov Bulg. 59 K3
Svitava *r.* Czech Rep. 47 P6
Svitavy Czech Rep. 47 P6
Svitlovods'k Ukr. 43 G6
Sviyaga *r.* Rus. Fed. 42 K5
Svizzera *country* Europe *see* Switzerland
Svobodnyy Rus. Fed. 74 C2
Svolvær Norway 44 I2
Svrljiške Planine *mts* Serb. and Mont. 59 J3
Svyatoy Nos, Mys *c.* Rus. Fed. 42 K2
Svyetlahorsk Belarus 43 F5
Swadlincote U.K. 49 F6
Swaffham U.K. 49 H6
Swain Reefs Australia 110 F4
Swainsboro U.S.A. 133 D5
Swains Island *atoll* American Samoa 107 I3
Swakop *watercourse* Namibia 100 B2
Swakopmund Namibia 100 B2
Swale *r.* U.K. 48 F4
Swallow Islands Solomon Is 107 G3
Swamihalli India 84 C3
Swampy *r.* Canada 123 H2
Swan *r.* Australia 109 A7
Swan *r. Man./Sask.* Canada 121 K4
Swan *r. Ont.* Canada 122 E3
Swanage U.K. 49 F8
Swandale U.S.A. 134 E4
Swan Hill Australia 112 A5
Swan Hills Canada 120 H4
Swan Islands *is* Caribbean Sea 137 H5
Swan Lake *B.C.* Canada 120 D4
Swan Lake *Man.* Canada 121 K4
Swanley U.K. 49 H7
Swanquarter U.S.A. 133 E5
Swan Reach Australia 111 B7
Swan River Canada 121 K4
Swansea U.K. 49 D7
Swansea Bay U.K. 49 D7
Swanton *CA* U.S.A. 128 B3
Swanton *VT* U.S.A. 135 I1
Swartbergpas *pass* S. Africa 100 F7
Swart Nossob *watercourse* Namibia *see* Black Nossob
Swartruggens S. Africa 101 H3
Swartz Creek U.S.A. 134 D2
Swasey Peak U.S.A. 129 G2
Swat Kohistan *reg.* Pak. 89 I3
Swatow China *see* Shantou
Swayzee U.S.A. 134 C3
▶Swaziland *country* Africa 101 J4
Africa 7, 94–95

▶Sweden *country* Europe 44 I5
5th largest country in Europe.
Europe 5, 38–39

Sweet Home U.S.A. 126 C3
Sweet Springs U.S.A. 134 E5
Sweetwater U.S.A. 131 C5
Sweetwater *r.* U.S.A. 126 G4
Swellendam S. Africa 100 E8
Świdnica Poland 47 P5
Świdwin Poland 47 O4
Świebodzin Poland 47 O4
Świecie Poland 47 Q4
Swift Current Canada 121 J5
Swiftcurrent Creek *r.* Canada 121 J5
Swilly *r.* Rep. of Ireland 51 E3
Swilly, Lough *inlet* Rep. of Ireland 51 E2
Swindon U.K. 49 F7
Swinford Rep. of Ireland 51 D4
Świnoujście Poland 47 O4
Swinton U.K. 50 G5
Swiss Confederation *country* Europe *see* Switzerland
Swiss National Park Switz. 58 D1
▶Switzerland *country* Europe 56 I3
Europe 5, 38–39
Swords Rep. of Ireland 51 F4
Swords Range *hills* Australia 110 C4
Syamozero, Ozero *l.* Rus. Fed. 42 G3
Syamzha Rus. Fed. 42 I3
Syang Nepal 83 E3
Syas'troy Rus. Fed. 42 G3
Sychevka Rus. Fed. 42 G5
Sydenham *atoll* Kiribati *see* Nonouti

▶Sydney Australia 112 E4
State capital of New South Wales. Most populous city in Oceania.

Sydney Canada 123 J5
Sydney Island Kiribati *see* Manra
Sydney Lake Canada 121 M5
Sydney Mines Canada 123 J5
Syedra *tourist site* Turkey 85 A1
Syeverodonets'k Ukr. 43 H6
Syke Germany 53 I2
Sykesville U.S.A. 135 F3
Syktyvkar Rus. Fed. 42 K3
Sylarna *mt.* Norway/Sweden 44 H5
Sylhet Bangl. 83 G4
Syloga Rus. Fed. 42 I3
Sylt *i.* Germany 47 L3
Sylva U.S.A. 133 D5
Sylvania *GA* U.S.A. 133 D5
Sylvania *OH* U.S.A. 134 D3
Sylvan Lake Canada 120 H4
Sylvester U.S.A. 133 D6
Sylvester, Lake *salt flat* Australia 110 A3
Sylvia, Mount Canada 120 E3
Symerton U.S.A. 134 A3
Symi *i.* Greece 59 L6
Synel'nykove Ukr. 43 G6
Syngyrli, Mys *pt* Kazakh. 91 I2
Synya Rus. Fed. 41 R2
Syowa *research station* Antarctica 152 D2
Syracusae *Sicily* Italy *see* Syracuse
Syracuse *Sicily* Italy 58 F6
Syracuse *KS* U.S.A. 130 C4
Syracuse *NY* U.S.A. 135 G2
Syrdar'ya *r.* Asia 80 C3
Syrdar'ya Uzbek. 80 C3
Syrdaryinskiy Uzbek. *see* Syrdar'ya
▶Syria *country* Asia 90 E4
Asia 6, 62–63
Syriam Myanmar 70 B3
Syrian Desert Asia 90 E4
Syrna *i.* Greece 59 L6
Syros *i.* Greece 59 K6
Syrskiy Rus. Fed. 43 H5
Sysmä Fin. 45 N6
Sysola *r.* Rus. Fed. 42 K3
Syumsi Rus. Fed. 42 K4
Syurkum Rus. Fed. 74 F2
Syurkum, Mys *pt* Rus. Fed. 74 F2
Syzran' Rus. Fed. 43 K5
Szabadka Serb. and Mont. *see* Subotica
Szczecin Poland 47 O4
Szczecinek Poland 47 P4
Szczytno Poland 47 R4
Szechwan *prov.* China *see* Sichuan
Szeged Hungary 59 I1
Székesfehérvár Hungary 58 H1
Szekszárd Hungary 58 H1
Szentes Hungary 59 I1
Szentgotthárd Hungary 58 G1
Szigetvár Hungary 58 G1
Szolnok Hungary 59 I1
Szombathely Hungary 58 G1
Sztálinváros Hungary *see* Dunaújváros

T

Taagga Duudka *reg.* Somalia 98 E3
Tābah Saudi Arabia 86 F4
Tabajara Brazil 142 F5
Tabakhmela Georgia *see* Kazret'i
Tabalo P.N.G. 69 L7
Tabanan Indon. 108 A2
Tabankulu S. Africa 101 I6
Ṭabaqah *Ar Raqqah* Syria *see* Madīnat ath Thawrah
Ṭabaqah *Ar Raqqah* Syria 85 D2
Tabar Islands P.N.G. 106 F2
Tabarka Tunisia 58 C6
Ṭabas Iran 89 F3
Tābāsin Iran 88 E4
Tābask, Kūh-e *mt.* Iran 88 C4
Tabatinga *Amazonas* Brazil 142 E4
Tabatinga *São Paulo* Brazil 145 A3
Tabatinga, Serra da *hills* Brazil 143 J6
Tabatsquri, Tba *l.* Georgia 91 F2
Tabayin Myanmar 70 A2
Tabbita Australia 112 B5
Tabelbala Alg. 54 D6
Taber Canada 121 H5
Tabet, Nam *r.* Myanmar 70 B1
Tabia Tsaka *salt l.* China 83 F3
Tabiteuea *atoll* Kiribati 107 H2
Tabivere Estonia 45 O7
Table Cape N.Z. 113 F4
Tabligbo Togo 96 D4
Tábor Czech Rep. 47 O6
Tabora Tanz. 99 D4
Tabou Côte d'Ivoire 96 C4
Tabrīz Iran 88 B2
Tabuaeran *atoll* Kiribati 151 J5
Tabūk Saudi Arabia 90 E5
Tabulam Australia 112 F2
Tabuyung Indon. 71 B7
Tabwémasana, Mount Vanuatu 107 G3
Täby Sweden 45 K7
Tacalé Brazil 143 H3
Tacheng China 80 F2
Tachie Canada 120 E4
Tachov Czech Rep. 53 M5
Tacloban Phil. 69 H4
Tacna Peru 142 D7
Tacoma U.S.A. 126 C3
Taco Pozo Arg. 144 D3
Tacuarembó Uruguay 144 E4
Tacupeto Mex. 127 F7
Tadcaster U.K. 48 F5
Tademaït, Plateau du Alg. 54 E6
Tadin New Caledonia 107 G4
Tadjikistan *country* Asia *see* Tajikistan
Tadjoura Djibouti 86 F7
Tadmur Syria 85 D2
Tadohae Haesang National Park S. Korea 75 B6
Tadoule Lake Canada 121 L3
Tadoussac Canada 123 H4
Tadpatri India 84 C3
Tadwale India 84 C2
Tadzhikskaya S.S.R. *country* Asia *see* Tajikistan
T'aean Haean National Park S. Korea 75 B5
Taech'ŏng-do *i.* S. Korea 75 B5
Taedasa-do N. Korea 75 B5
Taedong-man *b.* N. Korea 75 B5
Taegu S. Korea 75 C6
Taehan-min'guk *country* Asia *see* South Korea
Taehŭksan-kundo *is* S. Korea 75 B6
Taejŏn S. Korea 75 B5
Taejŏng S. Korea 75 B6
T'aepaek S. Korea 75 C5
Ta'erqi China 73 M3
Taf *r.* U.K. 49 C7
Tafahi *i.* Tonga 107 I3
Tafalla Spain 57 F2
Tafeng China *see* Lanshan
Tafila Jordan *see* Aṭ Ṭafilah
Tafí Viejo Arg. 144 C3
Tafresh Iran 88 C3
Taft Iran 88 D4
Taft U.S.A. 128 D4
Taftān, Kūh-e *mt.* Iran 89 F4
Taftanäz Syria 85 C2
Tafwap India 71 A6
Taganrog Rus. Fed. 43 H7
Taganrog, Gulf of Rus. Fed./Ukr. 43 H7
Taganrogskiy Zaliv *b.* Rus. Fed./Ukr. *see* Taganrog, Gulf of
Tagarev, Gora *mt.* Iran/Turkm. 88 E2
Tagarkaty, Pereval *pass* Tajik. 89 I2
Tagaung Myanmar 70 B2
Tagchagpu Ri *mt.* China 83 E2
Tagdempt Alg. *see* Tiaret
Taghmon Rep. of Ireland 51 F5
Tagish Canada 120 C2
Tagtabazar Turkm. 89 F3
Tagula P.N.G. 110 F1
Tagula Island P.N.G. 110 F1
Tagus *r.* Port. 57 B4
also known as Tajo (Portugal) *or* Tejo (Spain)
Taha China 74 B3
Tahaetkun Mountain Canada 120 G5
Tahan, Gunung *mt.* Malaysia 71 C6
Tahanroz'ka Zatoka *b.* Rus. Fed./Ukr. *see* Taganrog, Gulf of
Tahat, Mont *mt.* Alg. 96 D2
Tahaurawe *i.* U.S.A. *see* Kahoolawe
Tahe China 74 B1
Taheke N.Z. 113 D2
Tahiti *i.* Fr. Polynesia 151 K7
Tahlab *r.* Iran/Pak. 89 F4
Tahlab, Dasht-i- *plain* Pak. 89 F4
Tahlequah U.S.A. 131 E5
Tahltan Canada 120 D3
Tahoe, Lake U.S.A. 128 C2
Tahoe Lake Canada 119 H3
Tahoe Vista U.S.A. 128 C2
Tahoka U.S.A. 131 C5
Tahoua Niger 96 D3
Tahrūd Iran 88 E4
Tahrūd *r.* Iran 88 E4
Tahtsa Peak Canada 120 E4
Tahulandang *i.* Indon. 69 H6
Tahuna Indon. 69 H6
Taï, Parc National de *nat. park* Côte d'Ivoire 96 C4
Tai'an China 73 L5
Taibai China 76 E1
Taibai Shan *mt.* China 76 E1
Taibei Taiwan *see* T'aipei
Taibus Qi China *see* Baochang
T'aichung Taiwan 77 I3
Taidong Taiwan *see* T'aitung
Taigong China *see* Taijiang
Taihang Shan *mts Hebei* China 73 K5
Taihang Shan *mts* China 73 K5
Taihape N.Z. 113 E4
Taihe *Jiangxi* China 77 G3
Taihe *Sichuan* China *see* Shehong
Taihezhen China *see* Shehong
Tai Ho Wan *Hong Kong* China 77 [inset]
Taihu China 77 H2
Tai Hu *l.* China 77 I2
Taijiang China 77 F3
Taikang China 74 B3
Tailai China 74 A3
Tai Lam Chung Shui Tong *resr Hong Kong* China 77 [inset]
Tailem Bend Australia 111 B7
Tai Long Wan *b. Hong Kong* China 77 [inset]
Taimani *reg.* Afgh. 89 F3
Tai Mo Shan *hill Hong Kong* China 77 [inset]
Tain U.K. 50 F2
T'ainan Taiwan *see* Hsinying
T'ainan Taiwan 77 I4
Tainaro, Akra *pt* Greece 59 J6
Taining China 77 H3
Tai O *Hong Kong* China 77 [inset]
Taiobeiras Brazil 145 C1
Tai Pang Wan *b. Hong Kong* China *see* Mirs Bay

▶T'aipei Taiwan 77 I3
Capital of Taiwan.

Taiping *Guangdong* China *see* Shixing
Taiping *Guangxi* China *see* Chongzuo
Taiping *Guangxi* China 77 F4
Taiping Malaysia 71 C6
Taipingchuan China 74 A3
Tai Po *Hong Kong* China 77 [inset]
Tai Po Hoi *b. Hong Kong* China *see* Tolo Harbour
Tai Poutini National Park N.Z. *see* Westland National Park
Tairbeart U.K. *see* Tarbert
Tai Rom Yen National Park Thai. 71 B5
Tairuq Iran 88 B3
Tais P.N.G. 69 K8
Taishan China 77 G4
Taishun China 77 H3
Tai Siu Mo To *is Hong Kong* China *see* The Brothers
Taissy France 52 E5
Taitanu N.Z. 113 D6
Taitao, Península de *pen.* Chile 144 B7
Tai To Yan *mt. Hong Kong* China 77 [inset]
T'aitung Taiwan 77 I4
Tai Tung Shan *hill Hong Kong* China *see* Sunset Peak
Taivalkoski Fin. 44 P4
Taivaskero *hill* Fin. 44 N2
▶Taiwan *country* Asia 77 I4
Asia 6, 62–63
T'aiwan Haihsia *strait* China/Taiwan *see* Taiwan Strait
Taiwan Haixia *strait* China/Taiwan *see* Taiwan Strait
Taiwan Shan *mts* Taiwan *see* Chungyang Shanmo
Taiwan Strait China/Taiwan 77 H4
Taixian China *see* Jiangyan
Taixing China 77 I1
Taiyuan China 73 K5
Tai Yue Shan *i. Hong Kong* China *see* Lantau Island
Taizhao China 76 B2
Taizhong Taiwan *see* T'aichung
Taizhong Taiwan *see* Fengyüan
Taizhou *Jiangsu* China 77 H1
Taizhou *Zhejiang* China 77 I2
Taizhou Liedao *i.* China 77 I2
Taizhou Wan *b.* China 77 I2
Taizi He *r.* China 74 B4
Ta'izz Yemen 86 F7
Tājābād Iran 88 E4
Tajal Pak. 89 H5
Tajamulco, Volcán de *vol.* Guat. 136 F5
Tajerouine Tunisia 58 C7
▶Tajikistan *country* Asia 89 H2
Asia 6, 62–63
Tajitos Mex. 127 E7
Tajo *r.* Spain 57 C4 *see* Tagus
Tajrīsh Iran 88 C3
Tak Thai. 70 B3
Takāb Iran 88 B2
Takabba Kenya 98 E3
Takahashi Japan 75 D6
Takamatsu Japan 75 D6
Takaoka Japan 75 E5
Takapuna N.Z. 113 E3
Ta karpo China 83 G4
Takatokwane Botswana 100 G3
Takatshwaane Botswana 100 E2
Takatsuki-yama *mt.* Japan 75 D6
Takayama Japan 75 E5
Tak Bai Thai. 71 C6
Takefu Japan 75 E6
Takengon Indon. 71 B6
Takeo Cambodia *see* Takêv
Take-shima *i.* N. Pacific Ocean *see* Liancourt Rocks
Takestān Iran 88 C2
Takêv Cambodia 71 D5
Takhemaret Alg. 57 G6
Takhini Hotspring Canada 120 C2
Ta Khli Thai. 70 C4
Ta Khmau Cambodia 71 D5
Takhta-Bazar Turkm. *see* Tagtabazar
Takht Apān, Kūh-e *mt.* Iran 88 C3
Takhta Pul Post Afgh. 89 G4
Takhteh Iran 88 D4
Takht-e Soleymān *mt.* Iran 88 C2
Takht-i-Bakhti *tourist site* Pak. 89 H3
Takht-i-Sulaiman *mt.* Pak. 89 H4
Takijuq Lake Canada *see* Napaktulik Lake
Takingeun Indon. *see* Takengon
Takinoue Japan 74 F3
Takla Lake Canada 120 E4
Takla Landing Canada 120 E4
Takla Makan *des.* China *see* Taklimakan Desert
Taklimakan Desert China 82 E1
Taklimakan Shamo *des.* China *see* Taklimakan Desert
Takpa Shiri *mt.* China 76 B2
Taku Canada 120 C3
Takum Nigeria 96 D4
Talachyn Belarus 43 F5
Talaja India 82 C5
Talakan *Amurskaya Oblast'* Rus. Fed. 74 C2
Talakan *Khabarovskiy Kray* Rus. Fed. 74 D2
Talandzha Rus. Fed. 74 C2
Talangbatu Indon. 68 D7
Talara Peru 142 B4
Talar-i-Band *mts* Pak. *see* Makran Coast Range
Talas Kyrg. 80 D3
Talas Ala-Too *mts* Kyrg. 80 D3
Talas Range *mts* Kyrg. *see* Talas Ala-Too
Talasskiy Alatau, Khrebet *mts* Kyrg. *see* Talas Ala-Too
Ṭal'at Mūsá *mt.* Lebanon/Syria 85 C2
Talaud, Kepulauan *is* Indon. 69 H6
Talavera de la Reina Spain 57 D4
Talawgyi Myanmar 70 B1
Talaya Rus. Fed. 65 Q3
Talbehat India 82 D4
Talbīsah Syria 85 C2
Talbot, Mount *hill* Australia 109 D6
Talbotton U.S.A. 133 C5
Talbragar *r.* Australia 112 D4
Talca Chile 144 B5
Talcahuano Chile 144 B5
Taldan Rus. Fed. 74 B1
Taldom Rus. Fed. 42 H4
Taldykorgan Kazakh. 80 E3
Taldy-Kurgan Kazakh. *see* Taldykorgan
Taldyqorghan Kazakh. *see* Taldykorgan
Tālesh Iran *see* Hashtpar
Talgarth U.K. 49 D7
Talguppa India 84 B3
Talia Australia 111 A7
Taliabu *i.* Indon. 69 G7
Talikota India 84 C2
Talimardzhan Uzbek. 89 G2
Talin Hiag China 74 B3
Taliparamba India 84 B3
Talisay Phil. 69 G4
Talış Dağları *mts* Azer./Iran 88 C2
Talitsa Rus. Fed. 42 J4
Taliwang Indon. 108 B2
Talkeetna U.S.A. 118 C3
Talkeetna Mountains U.S.A. 118 D3
Talkh Āb Iran 88 E3
Tallacootra, Lake *salt flat* Australia 109 F7
Talladega U.S.A. 133 C5

▶Tallahassee U.S.A. 133 C6
State capital of Florida.

Tall al Aḥmar Syria 85 D1
Tall Baydar Syria 91 F3
Tall-e Ḥalāl Iran 88 D4

▶Tallinn Estonia 45 N7
Capital of Estonia.

Tall Kalakh Syria 85 C2
Tall Kayf Iraq 91 F3
Tall Kūjik Syria 91 F3
Tallow Rep. of Ireland 51 D5
Tallulah U.S.A. 131 F5
Tall 'Uwaynāt Iraq 91 F3
Tallymerjen Uzbek. *see* Talimardzhan
Talmont-St-Hilaire France 56 D3
Tal'ne Ukr. 43 F6
Tal'noye Ukr. *see* Tal'ne
Taloda India 82 C5
Talodi Sudan 86 D7
Taloga U.S.A. 131 D4
Talon, Lac *l.* Canada 123 I3
Ta-long Myanmar 70 B2
Tāloqān Afgh. 89 H2
Talos Dome *ice feature* Antarctica 152 H2
Ta Loung San *mt.* Laos 70 C2
Talovaya Rus. Fed. 43 I6
Taloyoak Canada 119 I3
Tal Pass Pak. 89 I3
Talsi Latvia 45 M8
Tal Sīyāh Iran 89 F4
Taltal Chile 144 B3
Taltson *r.* Canada 121 H2
Talu China 76 B2
Talvik Norway 44 M1
Talwood Australia 112 D2
Talyshskiye Gory *mts* Azer./Iran *see* Talış Dağları
Talyy Rus. Fed. 42 L2
Tamala Australia 109 A6
Tamala Rus. Fed. 43 I5
Tamale Ghana 96 C4
Tamana *i.* Kiribati 107 H2

Taman Negara National Park Malaysia 71 C6
Tamano Japan 75 D6
Tamanrasset Alg. 96 D2
Tamanthi Myanmar 70 A1
Tamaqua U.S.A. 135 H3
Tamar India 83 F5
Tamar Syria see Tadmur
Tamar r. U.K. 49 C8
Tamarugal, Pampa de plain Chile 142 E7
Tamasane Botswana 101 H2
Tamatave Madag. see Toamasina
Tamaulipas state Mex. 131 D7
Tambacounda Senegal 96 B3
Tambaqui Brazil 142 F5
Tambar Springs Australia 112 D3
Tambelan, Kepulauan is Indon. 71 D7
Tambelan Besar i. Indon. 71 D7
Tambo r. Australia 112 C6
Tambohorano Madag. 99 E5
Tambora, Gunung vol. Indon. 108 B2
Tamboritha mt. Australia 112 C6
Tambov Rus. Fed. 43 I5
Tambovka Rus. Fed. 74 C2
Tambura Sudan 97 F4
Tamburi Brazil 145 C1
Tâmchekket Mauritania 96 B3
Tamdybulak Uzbek. 80 B3
Tâmega r. Port. 57 B3
Tamenghest Alg. see Tamanrasset
Tamenglong India 83 H4
Tamerza Tunisia 58 B7
Tamgak, Adrar mt. Niger 96 D3
Tamgué, Massif du mt. Guinea 96 B3
Tamiahua, Laguna de lag. Mex. 136 E4
Tamiang, Ujung pt Indon. 71 B6
Tamil Nadu state India 84 C4
Tamitsa Rus. Fed. 42 H2
Ţâmîya Egypt see Ţāmīyah
Ţāmīyah Egypt 90 C5
Tam Ky Vietnam 70 E4
Tammarvi r. Canada 121 K1
Tammerfors Fin. see Tampere
Tammisaari Fin. see Ekenäs
Tampa U.S.A. 133 D7
Tampa Bay U.S.A. 133 D7
Tampere Fin. 45 M6
Tampico Mex. 136 E4
Tampin Malaysia 71 C7
Tampines Sing. 71 [inset]
Tamsagbulag Mongolia 73 L3
Tamsweg Austria 47 N7
Tamu Myanmar 70 A1
Tamworth Australia 112 E3
Tamworth U.K. 49 F6
Tana r. Fin./Norway see Tenojoki
Tana r. Kenya 98 E4
Tana Madag. see Antananarivo
Tana i. Vanuatu see Tanna
Tana, Lake Eth. 98 D2
Tanabe Japan 75 D6
Tanabi Brazil 145 A3
Tana Bru Norway 44 P1
Tanada Lake U.S.A. 120 A2
Tanafjorden inlet Norway 44 P1
Tanah, Tanjung pt Indon. 68 D8
T'ana Hāyk' l. Eth. see Tana, Lake
Tanahgrogot Indon. 68 F7
Tanah Merah Malaysia 71 C6
Tanahputih Indon. 71 C7
Tanakeke i. Indon. 68 F8
Tanami Australia 108 E4
Tanami Desert Australia 108 E4
Tân An Vietnam 71 D5
Tanana r. U.S.A. 120 A2
Tananarive Madag. see Antananarivo
Tanandava Madag. 99 E6
Tancheng China see Pingtan
Tanch'ŏn N. Korea 75 C4
Tanda Côte d'Ivoire 96 C4
Tanda Uttar Pradesh India 82 D3
Tanda Uttar Pradesh India 83 E4
Tandag Phil. 69 H5
Ţăndărei Romania 59 L2
Tandaué Angola 99 B5
Tandi India 82 D2
Tandil Arg. 144 E5
Tando Adam Pak. 89 H5
Tando Alahyar Pak. 89 H5
Tando Bago Pak. 89 H5
Tandou Lake imp. l. Australia 111 C7
Tandragee U.K. 51 F3
Tandur India 84 C2
Tanduri Pak. 89 G4
Tanega-shima i. Japan 75 C7
Tanen Taunggyi mts Thai. 70 B3
Tanezrouft reg. Alg./Mali 96 C2
Ţanf, Jabal aţ hill Syria 85 D3
Tang, Ra's-e pt Iran 89 E5
Tanga Tanz. 99 D4
Tangail Bangl. 83 G4
Tanga Islands P.N.G. 106 F2
Tanganyika country Africa see Tanzania

▶Tanganyika, Lake Africa 99 C4
Deepest and 2nd largest lake in Africa.

Tangará Brazil 145 A4
Tangasseri India 84 C4
Tangdan China 76 D3
Tangeli Iran 88 D2
Tanger Morocco see Tangier
Tangerhütte Germany 53 L2
Tangermünde Germany 53 L2
Tang-e Sarkheh Iran 89 E5
Tanggor China 76 D1
Tanggulashan China 76 B1
Tanggula Shan mt. China 83 G2
Tanggula Shan mts China 83 G2
Tanggula Shankou pass China 83 G2
Tangguo China 83 F3
Tanghe China 77 G1
Tangier Morocco 57 D6
Tangiers Morocco see Tangier
Tang La pass China 83 G4
Tangla India 83 G4
Tanglag China 76 C1
Tanglin Sing. 71 [inset]
Tangmai China 76 B2
Tangnag China 76 D1
Tangorin Australia 110 D4
Tangra Yumco salt l. China 83 F3
Tangse Indon. 71 A6
Tangshan Guizhou China see Shiqian
Tangshan Hebei China 73 L5
Tangte mt. Myanmar 70 B2
Tangtse Jammu and Kashmir see Tanktse
Tangwan China 77 F3
Tangwanghe China 74 C2
Tangyuan China 74 C3
Tangyung Tso salt l. China 83 F3
Tanhaçu Brazil 145 C1
Tanhua Fin. 44 O3
Tani Cambodia 71 D5
Taniantaweng Shan mts China 76 B2
Tanimbar, Kepulauan is Indon. 108 E1
Taninthari Myanmar see Tenasserim
Tanintharyi Myanmar see Tenasserim
Taninthayi Myanmar see Tenasserim
Tanjah Morocco see Tangier
Tanjay Phil. 69 G5
Tanjore India see Thanjavur
Tanjung Indon. 68 F7
Tanjungbalai Indon. 71 B7
Tanjungkarang-Telukbetung Indon. see Bandar Lampung
Tanjungpandan Indon. 68 D7
Tanjungpinang Indon. 71 D7
Tanjungpura Indon. 71 B7
Tanjung Puting National Park Indon. 68 E7
Tanjungredeb Indon. 68 F6
Tanjungselor Indon. 68 F6
Tankse Jammu and Kashmir see Tanktse
Tanktse Jammu and Kashmir 82 D2
Tankuhi India 83 F4
Tankwa-Karoo National Park S. Africa 100 D7
Tanna i. Vanuatu 107 G3
Tannadice U.K. 50 G4
Tännäs Sweden 44 H5
Tanner, Mount Canada 120 G5
Tannu-Ola, Khrebet mts Rus. Fed. 80 H1
Tanot India 82 B4
Tanout Niger 96 D3
Tansen Nepal 83 E4
Tanshui Taiwan 77 I3
Ţanţā Egypt 90 C5
Ţanta Egypt see Ţanţā
Tan-Tan Morocco 96 B2
Tantu China 74 A3
Tantura Israel 85 B3
Tanuku India 84 D2
Tanumbirini Australia 108 F4
Tanumshede Sweden 45 G7
▶Tanzania country Africa 99 D4
Africa 7, 94–95
Tanzilla r. Canada 120 D3
Tao, Ko i. Thai. 71 B5
Tao'an China see Taonan
Taobh Tuath U.K. see Northton
Taocheng China see Daxin
Tao He r. China 76 D1
Taohong China see Longhui
Taohuajiang China see Taojiang
Taohuaping China see Longhui
Taojiang China 77 G2
Taolanaro Madag. see Tôlañaro
Taonan China 74 A3
Taongi atoll Marshall Is 150 H5
Taos U.S.A. 127 G5
Taounate Morocco 54 D5
Taourirt Morocco 54 D5
Taoxi China 77 H3
Taoyang China see Lintao
Taoyuan China 77 F2
T'aoyüan Taiwan 77 I3
Tapa Estonia 45 N7
Tapachula Mex. 136 F6
Tapah Malaysia 71 C6
Tapajós r. Brazil 143 H4
Tapaktuan Indon. 71 B7
Tapauá Brazil 142 F5
Tapauá r. Brazil 142 F5
Taperoá Brazil 145 D1
Tapi r. India 82 C5
Tapiau Rus. Fed. see Gvardeysk
Tapis, Gunung mt. Malaysia 71 C6
Tapisuelas Mex. 127 F8
Taplejung Nepal 83 F4
Tap Mun Chau i. Hong Kong China 77 [inset]
Ta-pom Myanmar 70 B2
Tappahannock U.S.A. 135 G5
Tappeh, Kūh-e hill Iran 88 C3
Taprobane country Asia see Sri Lanka
Tapuaenuku mt. N.Z. 113 D5
Tapulonanjing mt. Indon. 71 B7
Tapurucuara Brazil 142 E4
Taputeouea atoll Kiribati see Tabiteuea
Ţaqţaq Iraq 91 G4
Taquara Brazil 145 A5
Taquarí Mato Grosso Brazil 143 H7
Taquarí Rio Grande do Sul Brazil 145 A5
Taquarí r. Brazil 143 G7
Taquarituba Brazil 145 A3
Tar r. Rep. of Ireland 51 E5
Tara Australia 112 E1
Ţarābulus Lebanon see Tripoli
Ţarābulus Libya see Tripoli
Tarahuwan India 82 E4
Tarai reg. India 83 G4
Tarakan Indon. 68 F6
Tarakan i. Indon. 68 F6
Tarakki reg. Afgh. 89 G3
Taraklı Turkey 59 N4
Taran, Mys pt Rus. Fed. 45 K9
Taranagar India 82 C3
Taranaki, Mount vol. N.Z. 113 E4
Tarancón Spain 57 E3
Tarangambadi India 84 C4
Tarangire National Park Tanz. 98 D4
Taranto Italy 58 G4
Taranto, Golfo di g. Italy 58 G4
Taranto, Gulf of Italy see Taranto, Golfo di
Tarapoto Peru 142 C5
Tarapur India 84 B2
Tararua Range mts N.Z. 113 E5
Tarascon-sur-Ariège France 56 E5
Tarasovskiy Rus. Fed. 43 I6
Tarauacá Brazil 142 D5
Tarauacá r. Brazil 142 E5
Tarawera N.Z. 113 F4
Tarawera, Mount vol. N.Z. 113 F4
Taraz Kazakh. 80 D3
Tarazona Spain 57 F3
Tarazona de la Mancha Spain 57 F4
Tarbagatay, Khrebet mts Kazakh. 80 F2
Tarbat Ness pt U.K. 50 F3
Tarbert Rep. of Ireland 51 C5
Tarbert Scotland U.K. 50 C3
Tarbert Scotland U.K. 50 D5
Tarbes France 56 E5
Tarboro U.S.A. 132 E5
Tarcoola Australia 109 F7
Tarcoon Australia 112 C3
Tarcoonyinna watercourse Australia 109 F6
Tarcutta Australia 112 C5
Tardoki-Yani, Gora mt. Rus. Fed. 74 E2
Taree Australia 112 F3
Tarella Australia 111 C6
Tarentum Italy see Taranto
Ţarfā', Baţn aţ depr. Saudi Arabia 88 C6
Tarfaya Morocco 96 B2
Targa well Niger 96 D3
Targan China see Talin Hiag
Targhee Pass U.S.A. 126 F3
Târgovişte Romania 59 K2
Targuist Morocco 57 D6
Târgu Jiu Romania 59 J2
Târgu Mureş Romania 59 K1
Târgu Neamţ Romania 59 L1
Târgu Secuiesc Romania 59 L1
Targyailing China 83 F3
Tari P.N.G. 69 K8
Tarif U.A.E. 88 D5
Tarifa Spain 57 D5
Tarifa, Punta de pt Spain 57 D5
Tarija Bol. 142 F8
Tarikere India 84 B3
Tariku r. Indon. 69 J7
Tarīm Yemen 86 G6
Tarim Basin China 80 F4
Tarime Tanz. 98 D4
Tarim He r. China 80 G3
Tarim Pendi basin China see Tarim Basin
Tarīn Kowt Afgh. 89 G3
Taritatu r. Indon. 69 J7
Tarka r. S. Africa 101 G7
Tarkastad S. Africa 101 H7
Tarkio U.S.A. 130 E3
Tarko-Sale Rus. Fed. 64 I3
Tarkwa Ghana 96 C4
Tarlac Phil. 69 G3
Tarlo River National Park Australia 112 D5
Tarma Peru 142 C6
Tarmstedt Germany 53 J1
Tarn r. France 56 E4
Tärnaby Sweden 44 I4
Tarnak r. Afgh. 89 G4
Târnăveni Romania 59 K1
Tarnobrzeg Poland 43 D6
Tarnogskiy Gorodok Rus. Fed. 42 I3
Tarnopol Ukr. see Ternopil'
Tarnów Poland 43 D6
Tarnowitz Poland see Tarnowskie Góry
Tarnowskie Góry Poland 47 Q5
Taro Co salt l. China 83 E3
Ţārom Iran 88 D4
Taroom Australia 111 E5
Taroudannt Morocco 54 C5
Tarpaulin Swamp Australia 110 B3
Tarq Iran 88 C3
Tarquinia Italy 58 D3
Tarquinii Italy see Tarquinia
Tarrabool Lake salt flat Australia 110 A3
Tarraco Spain see Tarragona
Tarrafal Cape Verde 96 [inset]
Tarragona Spain 57 G3
Tårrajaur Sweden 44 K3
Tarran Hills hill Australia 112 C4
Tarrant Point Australia 110 B3
Tàrrega Spain 57 G3
Tarrong China see Nyêmo
Tarso Emissi mt. Chad 97 E2
Tarsus Turkey 85 B1
Tart China 83 H1
Tärtär Azer. 91 G2
Tartu Estonia 45 O7
Ţarţūs Syria 85 B2
Tarumovka Rus. Fed. 91 G1
Tarung Hka r. Myanmar 70 B1
Tarutao, Ko i. Thai. 71 B6
Tarutung Indon. 71 B7
Tarvisium Italy see Treviso
Tarz Iran 88 E4
Tasai, Ko i. Thai. 71 B5
Taschereau Canada 122 F4
Taseko Mountain Canada 120 F5
Tashauz Turkm. see Dashoguz
Tashi Chho Bhutan see Thimphu
Tashigang Bhutan see Trashigang
Tashino Rus. Fed. see Pervomaysk
Tashir Armenia 91 G2
Tashk, Daryācheh-ye l. Iran 88 D4

▶Tashkent Uzbek. 80 C3
Capital of Uzbekistan.

Tashkepri Turkm. 89 F2
Tāshqurghān Afgh. see Kholm
Tashtagol Rus. Fed. 72 F2
Tashtyp Rus. Fed. 72 F2
Tasialujjuaq, Lac l. Canada 123 G2
Tasiat, Lac l. Canada 122 G2
Tasiilap Karra c. Greenland 119 O3
Tasiilaq Greenland see Ammassalik
Tasīl Syria 85 B3
Tasiujaq Canada 123 H2
Tasiusaq Greenland 119 M2
Taşkent Turkey 85 A1
Tasker Niger 96 E3
Taskesken Kazakh. 80 F2
Taşköprü Turkey 90 D2
Tasman Abyssal Plain sea feature Tasman Sea 150 G8
Tasman Basin sea feature Tasman Sea 150 G8
Tasman Bay N.Z. 113 D5

▶Tasmania state Australia 111 [inset]
4th largest island in Oceania.

Tasman Islands P.N.G. see Nukumanu Islands
Tasman Mountains N.Z. 113 D5
Tasman Peninsula Australia 111 [inset]
Tasman Sea S. Pacific Ocean 106 H6
Taşova Turkey 90 E2
Tassara Niger 96 D3
Tassialouc, Lac l. Canada 122 G2
Tassili du Hoggar plat. Alg. 96 D2
Tassili n'Ajjer plat. Alg. 96 D2
Tasty Kazakh. 80 C3
Taşucu Turkey 85 A1
Tas-Yuryakh Rus. Fed. 65 M3
Tata Morocco 54 C6
Tatabánya Hungary 58 H1
Tata Mailau, Gunung mt. East Timor 108 D2
Tataouine Tunisia 54 G5
Tatarbunary Ukr. 59 M2
Tatarsk Rus. Fed. 64 I4
Tatarskiy Proliv strait Rus. Fed. 74 F2
Tatar Strait Rus. Fed. see Tatarskiy Proliv
Tate r. Australia 110 C3
Tateyama Japan 75 E6
Tathlina Lake Canada 120 G2
Tathlīth Saudi Arabia 86 F6
Tathlīth, Wādī watercourse Saudi Arabia 86 F5
Tathra Australia 112 D6
Tatinnai Lake Canada 121 L2
Tatishchevo Rus. Fed. 43 J6
Tatkon Myanmar 70 B2
Tatla Lake Canada 120 E5
Tatla Lake l. Canada 120 E5
Tatlayoko Lake Canada 120 E5
Tatnam, Cape Canada 121 N3
Tatra Mountains Poland/Slovakia 47 Q6
Tatry mts Poland/Slovakia see Tatra Mountains
Tatrzański Park Narodowy nat. park Poland 47 Q6
Tatshenshini-Alsek Provincial Wilderness Park Canada 120 B3
Tatsinskiy Rus. Fed. 43 I6
Tatta Pak. 89 G5
Tatuí Brazil 145 B3
Tatuk Mountain Canada 120 E4
Tatum U.S.A. 131 C5
Tatvan Turkey 91 F3
Tau Norway 45 D7
Taua Brazil 143 J5
Tauapeçaçu Brazil 142 F4
Taubaté Brazil 145 B3
Tauber r. Germany 53 J5
Tauberbischofsheim Germany 53 J5
Taucha Germany 53 M3
Taufstein hill Germany 53 J4
Taukum, Peski des. Kazakh. 80 D3
Taumarunui N.Z. 113 E4
Taumaturgo Brazil 142 D5
Taung S. Africa 100 G4
Taungdwingyi Myanmar 70 A2
Taunggyi Myanmar 70 B2
Taunglau Myanmar 70 B2
Taungnyo Range mts Myanmar 70 B3
Taungtha Myanmar 70 A2
Taungup Myanmar 76 B5
Taunton U.K. 49 D7
Taunton U.S.A. 135 J3
Taunus hills Germany 53 H4
Taupo N.Z. 113 F4
Taupo, Lake N.Z. 113 E4
Tauragė Lith. 45 M9
Tauranga N.Z. 113 F3
Taurasia Italy see Turin
Taureau, Réservoir resr Canada 122 G5
Taurianova Italy 58 G5
Tauroa Point N.Z. 113 D2
Taurus Mountains Turkey 85 A1
Taute r. France 49 F9
Tauu Islands P.N.G. 107 F2
Tauz Azer. see Tovuz
Tavas Turkey 59 M6
Tavastehus Fin. see Hämeenlinna
Taverham U.K. 49 I6
Taveuni i. Fiji 107 I3
Tavildara Tajik. 89 H2
Tavira Port. 57 C5
Tavistock Canada 134 E2
Tavistock U.K. 49 C8
Tavoy Myanmar 71 B4
Tavoy r. mouth Myanmar 71 B4
Tavoy Island Myanmar see Mali Kyun
Tavoy Point Myanmar 71 B4
Tavşanlı Turkey 59 M5
Taw r. U.K. 49 C7
Tawang India 83 G4
Tawas City U.S.A. 134 D1
Tawau Sabah Malaysia 68 F6
Tawè Myanmar see Tavoy
Tawe r. U.K. 49 D7
Ţawī Ḩafīr well U.A.E. 88 D5
Ţawī Murra well U.A.E. 88 D5
Tawmaw Myanmar 70 B1
Tawu Taiwan 77 I4
Taxkorgan China 80 E4
Tay r. Canada 120 C2
Tay r. U.K. 50 F4
Tay, Firth of est. U.K. 50 F4
Tay, Lake salt flat Australia 109 C8
Tay, Loch l. U.K. 50 E4
Tayandu, Kepulauan is Indon. 69 I8
Taybola Rus. Fed. 44 R2
Taycheedah U.S.A. 134 A2
Tayinloan U.K. 50 D5
Taylor Canada 120 F3
Taylor AK U.S.A. 118 B3
Taylor MI U.S.A. 134 D2
Taylor NE U.S.A. 130 D3
Taylor TX U.S.A. 131 D6
Taylor, Mount U.S.A. 129 J4
Taylorsville U.S.A. 134 C4
Taylorville U.S.A. 130 F4
Taymā' Saudi Arabia 90 E6
Taymura r. Rus. Fed. 65 K3
Taymyr, Ozero l. Rus. Fed. 65 L2
Taymyr, Poluostrov pen. Rus. Fed. see Taymyr Peninsula
Taymyr Peninsula Rus. Fed. 64 J2
Tây Ninh Vietnam 71 D5
Taypak Kazakh. 41 Q6
Taypaq Kazakh. see Taypak
Tayshet Rus. Fed. 72 H1
Taytay Phil. 68 F4
Tayuan China 74 B2
Tayyebād Iran 89 F3
Taz r. Rus. Fed. 64 I3
Taza Morocco 54 D5
Tāza Khurmātū Iraq 91 G4
Taze Myanmar 70 A2
Tazewell TN U.S.A. 134 D5
Tazewell VA U.S.A. 134 E5
Tazin r. Canada 121 I2
Tazin Lake Canada 121 I3
Tāzirbū Libya 97 F2
Tazmalt Alg. 57 I5
Tazovskaya Guba sea chan. Rus. Fed. 64 I3
Tbessa Alg. see Tébessa

▶T'bilisi Georgia 91 G2
Capital of Georgia.

Tbilisskaya Rus. Fed. 43 I7
Tchabal Mbabo mt. Cameroon 96 E4
Tchad country Africa see Chad
Tchamba Togo 96 D4
Tchibanga Gabon 98 B4
Tchigaï, Plateau du Niger 97 E2
Tchin-Tabaradene Niger 96 D3
Tcholliré Cameroon 97 E4
Tchula U.S.A. 131 F5
Tczew Poland 47 Q3
Te, Prêk r. Cambodia 71 D4
Teague, Lake salt flat Australia 109 C6
Te Anau N.Z. 113 A7
Te Anau, Lake N.Z. 113 A7
Teapa Mex. 136 F5
Te Araroa N.Z. 113 G3
Teate Italy see Chieti
Te Awamutu N.Z. 113 E4
Teba Indon. 69 J7
Tébarat Niger 96 D3
Tebas Indon. 71 E7
Tebay U.K. 48 E4
Tebesjuak Lake Canada 121 L2
Tébessa Alg. 58 C7
Tébessa, Monts de mts Alg. 58 C7
Tebingtinggi Indon. 71 B7
Tébourba Tunisia 58 C6
Téboursouk Tunisia 58 C6
Tebulos Mt'a Georgia/Rus. Fed. 91 G2
Tecate Mex. 128 E5
Tece Turkey 85 B1
Techiman Ghana 96 C4
Tecka Arg. 144 B6
Tecklenburger Land reg. Germany 53 H2
Tecoripa Mex. 127 F7
Técpan Mex. 136 D5
Tecuala Mex. 136 C4
Tecuci Romania 59 L2
Tecumseh MI U.S.A. 134 D3
Tecumseh NE U.S.A. 130 D3
Tedzhen Turkm. 89 F2
Teec Nos Pos U.S.A. 129 I3
Tees r. U.K. 48 F4
Teeswater Canada 134 E1
Tefé r. Brazil 142 F4
Tefenni Turkey 59 M6
Tegal Indon. 68 D8
Tegel airport Germany 53 N2
Tegid, Llyn l. U.K. 49 D6

▶Tegucigalpa Hond. 137 G6
Capital of Honduras.

Teguidda-n-Tessoumt Niger 96 D3
Tehachapi U.S.A. 128 D4
Tehachapi Mountains U.S.A. 128 D4
Tehachapi Pass U.S.A. 128 D4
Tehek Lake Canada 121 M1
Teheran Iran see Tehrān
Tehery Lake Canada 121 M1
Téhini Côte d'Ivoire 96 C4

▶Tehrān Iran 88 C3
Capital of Iran.

Tehri India see Tikamgarh
Tehuacán Mex. 136 E5
Tehuantepec, Golfo de Mex. see Tehuantepec, Gulf of
Tehuantepec, Gulf of Mex. 136 F5
Tehuantepec, Istmo de isthmus Mex. 136 F5
Teide, Pico del vol. Canary Is 96 B2
Teifi r. U.K. 49 C6
Teignmouth U.K. 49 D8
Teixeira de Sousa Angola see Luau
Teixeiras Brazil 145 C3
Teixeira Soares Brazil 145 A4
Tejakula Indon. 108 A2
Tejen Turkm. see Tedzhen
Tejo r. Port. 57 B4 see Tagus
Tejon Pass U.S.A. 128 D4
Tekapo, Lake N.Z. 113 C6
Tekax Mex. 136 G4
Tekeli Kazakh. 80 E3
Tekes China 80 F3
Tekiliktag mt. China 82 E1
Tekin Rus. Fed. 74 D2
Tekirdağ Turkey 59 L4
Tekka India 84 D2
Tekkali India 84 E2
Teknaf Bangl. 83 H5
Tekong Kechil, Pulau i. Sing. 71 [inset]
Te Kuiti N.Z. 113 E4
Tel r. India 84 D1
Télagh Alg. 57 F6
Telanaipura Indon. see Jambi
Tel Ashqelon tourist site Israel 81 B4
Télataï Mali 96 D3
Tel Aviv-Yafo Israel 85 B3
Telč Czech Rep. 47 O6
Telchac Puerto Mex. 136 G4
Telekhany Belarus see Tsyelyakhany
Telêmaco Borba Brazil 145 A4
Teleorman r. Romania 59 K3
Telerhteba, Djebel mt. Alg. 96 D2
Telescope Peak U.S.A. 128 E3
Teles Pires r. Brazil 143 G5
Telford U.K. 49 E6
Telgte Germany 53 H3
Télimélé Guinea 96 B3
Teljo, Jebel mt. Sudan 86 C7
Telkwa Canada 120 E4
Tell Atlas mts Alg. see Atlas Tellien
Tell City U.S.A. 134 B5
Teller U.S.A. 118 B3
Tell es Sultan West Bank see Jericho
Tellicherry India 84 B4
Tellin Belgium 52 F4
Telloh Iraq 91 G5
Telluride U.S.A. 129 J3
Tel'novskiy Rus. Fed. 74 F2
Telok Anson Malaysia see Teluk Intan
Telo Martius France see Toulon
Tel'pos-Iz, Gora mt. Rus. Fed. 41 R3
Telsen Arg. 144 C6
Telšiai Lith. 45 M9
Teltow Germany 53 N2
Teluk Anson Malaysia see Teluk Intan
Telukbetung Indon. see Bandar Lampung
Teluk Cenderawasih Marine National Park Indon. 69 I7
Teluk Intan Malaysia 71 C6
Temagami Lake Canada 122 F5
Temanggung Indon. 68 E8
Têmarxung China 83 G2
Temba S. Africa 101 I3
Tembagapura Indon. 69 J7
Tembenchi r. Rus. Fed. 65 K3
Tembilahan Indon. 68 C7
Tembisa S. Africa 101 I4
Tembo Aluma Angola 99 B4
Teme r. U.K. 49 E6
Temecula U.S.A. 128 E5
Temerloh Malaysia see Temerluh
Temerluh Malaysia 71 C7
Teminabuan Indon. 69 I7
Temirtau Kazakh. 80 D1
Témiscamie r. Canada 123 G4
Témiscamie, Lac l. Canada 123 G4
Temiscaming Canada 122 F5
Témiscamingue, Lac l. Canada 122 F5
Témiscouata, Lac l. Canada 123 H5
Temmes Fin. 44 N4
Temnikov Rus. Fed. 43 I5
Temora Australia 112 C5
Temósachic Mex. 127 G7
Tempe U.S.A. 129 H5
Tempe Downs Australia 109 F6
Tempelhof airport Germany 53 N2
Temple MI U.S.A. 134 C1
Temple TX U.S.A. 131 D6
Temple Bar U.K. 49 C6
Temple Dera Pak. 89 H4
Templemore Rep. of Ireland 51 E5
Temple Sowerby U.K. 48 E4
Templeton watercourse Australia 110 B4
Templin Germany 53 N1
Tempué Angola 99 B5
Temryuk Rus. Fed. 90 E1
Temryukskiy Zaliv b. Rus. Fed. 43 H7
Temuco Chile 144 B5
Temuka N.Z. 113 C7
Temuli China see Butuo
Tena Ecuador 142 C4
Tenabo Mex. 136 F4
Tenabo, Mount U.S.A. 128 E1
Tenali India 84 D2
Tenasserim Myanmar 71 B4
Tenasserim r. Myanmar 71 B4
Tenbury Wells U.K. 49 E6
Tenby U.K. 49 C7
Tendaho Eth. 98 E2
Tende, Col de pass France/Italy 56 H4
Ten Degree Channel India 71 A5
Tendō Japan 75 F5
Tenedos i. Turkey see Bozcaada
Ténenkou Mali 96 C3
Ténéré reg. Niger 96 D2
Ténéré du Tafassâsset des. Niger 96 E2
Tenerife i. Canary Is 96 B2
Ténès Alg. 57 G5
Teng, Nam r. Myanmar 70 B3
Tengah, Kepulauan is Indon. 68 F8
Tengah, Sungai r. Sing. 71 [inset]
Tengcheng China see Tengxian
Tengchong China 76 C3
Tengeh Reservoir Sing. 71 [inset]
Tengger Shamo des. China 72 I5
Tenggul i. Malaysia 71 C6
Tengiz, Ozero salt l. Kazakh. 80 C1
Tengqiao China 77 F5
Tengréla Côte d'Ivoire 96 C3
Ten'gushevo Rus. Fed. 43 I5
Tengxian China 77 F4
Teni India see Theni
Teniente Jubany research station Antarctica see Jubany
Tenille U.S.A. 133 D6
Tenke Dem. Rep. Congo 99 C5
Tenkeli Rus. Fed. 65 P2
Tenkodogo Burkina 96 C3
Ten Mile Lake salt flat Australia 109 C6
Ten Mile Lake Canada 123 K4
Tennant Creek Australia 108 F4
Tennessee r. U.S.A. 131 F4
Tennessee state U.S.A. 134 C5
Tennessee Pass U.S.A. 126 G5
Tennevoll Norway 44 J2
Tenojoki r. Fin./Norway 44 P1
Tenosique Mex. 136 F5
Tenteno Indon. 69 G7
Tenterden U.K. 49 H7
Tenterfield Australia 112 F2
Ten Thousand Islands U.S.A. 133 D7
Tentudia mt. Spain 57 C4
Tentulia Bangl. see Tetulia
Teodoro Sampaio Brazil 144 F2
Teófilo Otôni Brazil 145 C2
Tepa Indon. 108 E1
Tepache Mex. 127 F7
Te Paki N.Z. 113 D2
Tepatitlán Mex. 136 D4
Tepehuanes Mex. 131 B7
Tepeköy Turkey see Karakoçan
Tepelenë Albania 59 I4
Tepelská Vrchovina hills Czech Rep. 53 M5
Tepequem, Serra mts Brazil 137 L8
Tepic Mex. 136 D4
Te Pirita N.Z. 113 C6
Teplá r. Czech Rep. 53 M4
Teplice Czech Rep. 47 N5
Teplogorka Rus. Fed. 42 L3
Teploozersk Rus. Fed. 74 C2

To r. Myanmar 70 B3
Toad r. Canada 120 E3
Toad River Canada 120 E3
Toamasina Madag. 99 E5
Toana mts U.S.A. 129 F1
Toano U.S.A. 135 G5
Toa Payoh Sing. 71 [inset]
Toba China 76 C2
Toba, Danau l. Indon. 71 B7
Toba, Lake Indon. see Toba, Danau
Toba and Kakar Ranges mts Pak. 89 G4
Toba Gargaji Pak. 89 I4
Tobago i. Trin. and Tob. 137 L6
Tobelo Indon. 69 H6
Tobermorey Australia 110 B4
Tobermory Australia 112 A1
Tobermory Canada 134 E1
Tobermory U.K. 50 C4
Tobi i. Palau 69 I6
Tobin, Lake salt flat Australia 108 D5
Tobin, Mount U.S.A. 128 E1
Tobin Lake Canada 121 K4
Tobin Lake l. Canada 121 K4
Tobi-shima i. Japan 75 E5
Tobol r. Kazakh./Rus. Fed. 78 F1
Tobol'sk Rus. Fed. 64 H4
Tô Bong Vietnam 71 E4
Tobruk Libya see Tubruq
Tobseda Rus. Fed. 42 L1
Tobyl r. Kazakh./Rus. Fed. see Tobol
Tobysh r. Rus. Fed. 42 K2
Tocache Nuevo Peru 142 C5
Tocantinópolis Brazil 143 I5
Tocantins r. Brazil 145 A1
Tocantins state Brazil 145 A1
Tocantinzinha r. Brazil 145 A1
Toccoa U.S.A. 133 D5
Tochi r. Pak. 89 H3
Töcksfors Sweden 45 G7
Tocopilla Chile 144 B2
Tocumwal Australia 112 B5
Tod, Mount Canada 120 G5
Todd watercourse Australia 110 A5
Todi Italy 58 E3
Todoga-saki pt Japan 75 F5
Todos Santos Mex. 136 B4
Toe Head hd U.K. 50 B3
Tofino Canada 120 E5
Toft U.K. 50 [inset]
Tofua i. Tonga 107 I3
Togatax China 82 E2
Togian i. Indon. 69 G7
Togian, Kepulauan is Indon. 69 G7
Togliatti Rus. Fed. see Tol'yatti
▶Togo country Africa 96 D4
Africa 7, 94–95
Togtoh China 73 K4
Togton He r. China 83 H2
Togton Heyan China see Tanggulashan
Tohatchi U.S.A. 129 I4
Toholampi Fin. 44 N5
Toiba China 83 G3
Toibalewe India 71 A5
Toijala Fin. 45 M6
Toili Indon. 69 G7
Toi-misaki pt Japan 75 C7
Toivakka Fin. 44 O5
Toiyabe Range mts U.S.A. 128 E2
Tojikiston country Asia see Tajikistan
Tok U.S.A. 120 A2
Tokar Sudan 86 E6
Tokara-rettō is Japan 75 C7
Tokarevka Rus. Fed. 43 I6
Tokat Turkey 90 E2
Tŏkchok-to i. S. Korea 75 B5
Tokdo i. N. Pacific Ocean see Liancourt Rocks

▶Tokelau terr. S. Pacific Ocean 107 I2
New Zealand Overseas Territory.
Oceania 8, 104–105

Tokmak Kyrg. see Tokmok
Tokmak Ukr. 43 G7
Tokmok Kyrg. 80 E3
Tokomaru Bay N.Z. 113 G4
Tokoroa N.Z. 113 E4
Tokoza S. Africa 101 I4
Toksun China 80 G3
Tok-tō i. N. Pacific Ocean see Liancourt Rocks
Toktogul Kyrg. 80 D3
Tokto-ri i. N. Pacific Ocean see Liancourt Rocks
Tokur Rus. Fed. 74 D1
Tokushima Japan 75 D6
Tokuyama Japan 75 C6

▶Tōkyō Japan 75 E6
Capital of Japan. Most populous city in the world and in Asia.

Tokzār Afgh. 89 G3
Tolaga Bay N.Z. 113 G4
Tôlañaro Madag. 99 E6
Tolbo Mongolia 80 H2
Tolbukhin Bulg. see Dobrich
Tolbuzino Rus. Fed. 74 B1
Toledo Brazil 144 F2
Toledo Spain 57 D4
Toledo IA U.S.A. 130 E3
Toledo OH U.S.A. 134 D3
Toledo OR U.S.A. 126 C3
Toledo, Montes de mts Spain 57 D4
Toledo Bend Reservoir U.S.A. 131 E6
Toletum Spain see Toledo
Toliara Madag. 99 E6
Tolitoli Indon. 69 G6
Tol'ka Rus. Fed. 64 J3
Tolleson U.S.A. 129 G5
Tollimarjon Uzbek. see Talimardzhan
Tolmachevo Rus. Fed. 45 P7
Tolo Dem. Rep. Congo 98 B4
Tolo Channel Hong Kong China 77 [inset]
Tolochin Belarus see Talachyn
Tolo Harbour b. Hong Kong China 77 [inset]
Tolosa France see Toulouse
Tolosa Spain 57 E2
Toluca Mex. 136 E5
Toluca de Lerdo Mex. see Toluca
Tol'yatti Rus. Fed. 43 K5
Tom' r. Rus. Fed. 74 B2
Tomah U.S.A. 130 F3
Tomakomai Japan 74 F4
Tomales U.S.A. 128 B2
Tomali Indon. 69 G7
Tomamae Japan 74 F3
Tomanivi mt. Fiji 107 H3
Tomar Brazil 142 F4
Tomar Port. 57 B4
Tomari Rus. Fed. 74 F3
Tomarza Turkey 90 D3
Tomaszów Lubelski Poland 43 D6
Tomaszów Mazowiecki Poland 47 R5
Tomatin U.K. 50 F3
Tomatlán Mex. 136 C5
Tomazina Brazil 145 A3
Tombador, Serra do hills Brazil 143 G6
Tombigbee r. U.S.A. 133 C6
Tomboco Angola 99 B4
Tombouctou Mali see Timbuktu
Tombstone U.S.A. 127 F7
Tombua Angola 99 B5
Tom Burke S. Africa 101 H2
Tomdibuloq Uzbek. see Tamdybulak
Tome Moz. 101 L2
Tomelilla Sweden 45 H9
Tomelloso Spain 57 E4
Tomi Romania see Constanța
Tomingley Australia 112 D4
Tomini, Teluk g. Indon. 69 G7
Tominian Mali 96 C3
Tomintoul U.K. 50 F3
Tomislavgrad Bos.-Herz. 58 G3
Tomkinson Ranges mts Australia 109 E6
Tømmerneset Norway 44 I3
Tommot Rus. Fed. 65 N4
Tomo r. Col. 142 E2
Tomóchic Mex. 127 G7
Tomortei China 73 K4
Tompkinsville U.S.A. 134 C5
Tom Price Australia 108 B5
Tomra China 83 F3
Tomsk Rus. Fed. 64 J4
Toms River U.S.A. 135 H4
Tomtabacken hill Sweden 45 I8
Tomtor Rus. Fed. 65 P3
Tomur Feng mt. China/Kyrg. see Pobeda Peak
Tomuzlovka r. Rus. Fed. 43 J7
Tom White, Mount U.S.A. 118 D3
Tonalá Mex. 136 F5
Tonantins Brazil 142 E4
Tonb-e Bozorg, Jazīreh-ye i. The Gulf see Greater Tunb
Tonb-e Kūchek, Jazīreh-ye i. The Gulf see Lesser Tunb
Tonbridge U.K. 49 H7
Tondano Indon. 69 G6
Tønder Denmark 45 F9
Tondi India 84 C4
Tone r. U.K. 49 E7
Toney Mountain Antarctica 152 K1
▶Tonga country S. Pacific Ocean 107 I4
Oceania 8, 104–105
Tongaat S. Africa 101 J5
Tongariro National Park N.Z. 113 E4
Tongatapu Group is Tonga 107 I4

▶Tonga Trench sea feature S. Pacific Ocean 150 I7
2nd deepest trench in the world.

Tongbai Shan mts China 77 G1
Tongcheng China 77 H2
T'ongch'ŏn N. Korea 75 B5
Tongchuan Shaanxi China 77 F1
Tongchuan Sichuan China see Santai
Tongdao China 77 F3
Tongde China 76 D1
Tongduch'ŏn S. Korea 75 B5
Tongeren Belgium 52 F4
Tonggu China 77 G2
Tonggu Zui pt China 77 F5
Tonghae S. Korea 75 C5
Tonghai China 76 D3
Tonghe China 74 C3
Tonghua Jilin China 74 B4
Tonghua Jilin China 74 B4
Tongi Bangl. see Tungi
Tongjiang Heilong. China 74 D3
Tongjiang Sichuan China 76 E2
Tongking, Gulf of China/Vietnam 70 E2
Tongle China see Leye
Tongliang China 76 E2
Tongliao China 73 M4
Tongling China 77 H2
Tonglu China 77 H2
Tongo Australia 112 A3
Tongo Lake salt flat Australia 112 A3
Tongren Guizhou China 77 F3
Tongren Qinghai China 76 D1
Tongres Belgium see Tongeren
Tongsa Bhutan see Trongsa
Tongshan China 77 H1
Tongshi China 77 F5
Tongta Myanmar 70 B2
Tongtian He r. Qinghai China 76 B1
Tongtian He r. Qinghai China 76 C1 see Yangtze
Tongue U.K. 50 E2
Tongue r. U.S.A. 126 G3
Tongue of the Ocean sea chan. Bahamas 133 E7
Tongxin China 72 J5
T'ongyŏng S. Korea 75 C6
Tongzi China 76 E2
Tónichi Mex. 127 F7
Tonk India 82 C4
Tonkābon Iran 88 C2
Tonkin reg. Vietnam 70 D2
Tônle Repou r. Laos 71 D4
Tônlé Sab l. Cambodia see Tonle Sap

▶Tonle Sap l. Cambodia 71 C4
Largest lake in Southeast Asia.

Tonopah AZ U.S.A. 129 G5
Tonopah NV U.S.A. 128 E2
Tønsberg Norway 45 G7
Tonstad Norway 45 E7
Tonto Creek watercourse U.S.A. 129 H5
Tonvarjeh Iran 88 E3
Tonzang Myanmar 70 A2
Tonzi Myanmar 70 A1
Toobeah Australia 112 D2
Toobli Liberia 96 C4
Tooele U.S.A. 129 G1
Toogoolawah Australia 112 F1
Tooma r. Australia 112 D6
Toompine Australia 112 B1
Toora Australia 112 C7
Tooraweenah Australia 112 D3
Toorberg mt. S. Africa 100 G7
Toowoomba Australia 112 E1
Tooxin Somalia 98 F2
Top Afgh. 89 H3
Top Boğazı Geçidi pass Turkey 85 C1

▶Topeka U.S.A. 130 E4
State capital of Kansas.

Topia Mex. 127 G8
Töplitz Germany 53 M2
Topoľčany Slovakia 47 Q6
Topolobampo Mex. 127 F8
Topolovgrad Bulg. 59 L3
Topozero, Ozero l. Rus. Fed. 44 R4
Topsfield U.S.A. 132 H2
Tor Eth. 97 G4
Tor Baldak mt. Afgh. 89 G4
Torbalı Turkey 59 L5
Torbat-e Heydarīyeh Iran 88 E3
Torbat-e Jām Iran 89 F3
Torbay Bay Australia 109 B8
Torbert, Mount U.S.A. 118 C3
Torbeyevo Rus. Fed. 43 I5
Torch r. Canada 121 K4
Tordesillas Spain 57 D3
Tordesilos Spain 57 F3
Töre Sweden 44 M4
Torelló Spain 57 H2
Torenberg hill Neth. 52 F2
Toretam Kazakh. see Baykonyr
Torgau Germany 53 M3
Torghay Kazakh. see Turgay
Torgun r. Rus. Fed. 43 J6
Torhout Belgium 52 D3
Torino Italy see Turin
Tori-shima i. Japan 75 F7
Torit Sudan 97 G4
Torkamān Iran 88 B2
Torkovichi Rus. Fed. 42 F4
Tornado Mountain Canada 120 H5
Torneå Fin. see Tornio
Torneälven r. Sweden 44 N4
Torneträsk l. Sweden 44 K2
Torngat, Monts mts Canada see Torngat Mountains
Torngat Mountains Canada 123 I2
Tornio Fin. 44 N4
Toro Spain 57 D3
Toro, Pico del mt. Mex. 131 C7
Torom Rus. Fed. 74 D1

▶Toronto Canada 134 F2
Provincial capital of Ontario and 5th most populous city in North America.

Toro Peak U.S.A. 128 E5
Toropets Rus. Fed. 42 F4
Tororo Uganda 98 D3
Toros Dağları mts Turkey see Taurus Mountains
Torphins U.K. 50 G3
Torquay Australia 112 B7
Torquay U.K. 49 D8
Torrance U.S.A. 128 D5
Torrão Port. 57 B4
Torre mt. Port. 57 C3
Torreblanca Spain 57 G3
Torre Blanco, Cerro mt. Mex. 127 E6
Torrecerredo mt. Spain 57 D2
Torre del Greco Italy 58 F4
Torre de Moncorvo Port. 57 C3
Torrelavega Spain 57 D2
Torremolinos Spain 57 D5

▶Torrens, Lake imp. l. Australia 111 B6
2nd largest lake in Oceania.

Torrens Creek Australia 110 D4
Torrent Spain 57 F4
Torrente Spain see Torrent
Torreón Mex. 131 C7
Torres Brazil 145 A5
Torres Mex. 127 F7
Torres del Paine, Parque Nacional nat. park Chile 144 B8
Torres Islands Vanuatu 107 G3
Torres Novas Port. 57 B4
Torres Strait Australia 106 E2
Torres Vedras Port. 57 B4
Torreta, Sierra hill Spain 57 G4
Torrevieja Spain 57 F5
Torrey U.S.A. 129 H2
Torridge r. U.K. 49 C8
Torridon, Loch b. U.K. 50 D3
Torrijos Spain 57 D4
Torrington Australia 112 E2
Torrington CT U.S.A. 132 F3
Torrington WY U.S.A. 126 G4
Torsby Sweden 45 H6

▶Tórshavn Faroe Is 44 [inset]
Capital of the Faroe Islands.

Tortilla Flat U.S.A. 129 H5
Törtköl Uzbek. see Turtkul'
Tortolì Sardinia Italy 58 C5
Tortona Italy 58 C2
Tortosa Spain 57 G3
Tortum Turkey 91 F2
Torūd Iran 88 D3
Torugart, Pereval pass China/Kyrg. see Turugart Pass
Torul Turkey 91 E2
Toruń Poland 47 Q4
Tory Island Rep. of Ireland 51 D2
Tory Sound sea chan. Rep. of Ireland 51 D2
Torzhok Rus. Fed. 42 G4
Tosa Japan 75 D6
Tosbotn Norway 44 H4
Tosca S. Africa 100 F3
Toscano, Arcipelago is Italy 58 C3
Tosham India 82 C3
Tōshima-yama mt. Japan 75 F4
Toshkent Uzbek. see Tashkent
Tosno Rus. Fed. 42 F4
Toson Hu l. China 83 I1
Tostado Arg. 144 D3
Tostedt Germany 53 J1
Tosya Turkey 90 D2
Totapola mt. Sri Lanka 84 D5
Tôtes France 52 B5
Tot'ma Rus. Fed. 42 I4
Totness Suriname 143 G2
Tottenham Australia 112 C4
Totton U.K. 49 F8
Tottori Japan 75 D6
Touba Côte d'Ivoire 96 C4
Touba Senegal 96 B3
Toubkal, Jbel mt. Morocco 54 C5
Toubkal, Parc National nat. park Morocco 54 C5
Touboro Cameroon 97 E4
Tougan Burkina 96 C3
Touggourt Alg. 54 F5
Tougué Guinea 96 B3
Touil Mauritania 96 B3
Toul France 52 F6
Touliu Taiwan 77 I4
Toulon France 56 G5
Toulon U.S.A. 130 F3
Toulouse France 56 E5
Toumodi Côte d'Ivoire 96 C4
Toungoo Myanmar 70 B3
Toupai China 77 F3
Tourane Vietnam see Đa Nẵng
Tourcoing France 52 D4
Tourgis Lake Canada 121 J1
Tourlaville France 49 F9
Tournai Belgium 52 D4
Tournon-sur-Rhône France 56 G4
Tournus France 58 A1
Touros Brazil 143 K5
Tours France 56 E3
Tousside, Pic mt. Chad 97 E2
Toussoro, Mont mt. Cent. Afr. Rep. 98 C3
Toutai China 74 B3
Touwsrivier S. Africa 100 E7
Toužim Czech Rep. 53 M4
Tovarkovo Rus. Fed. 43 G5
Tovil'-Dora Tajik. see Tavildara
Tovuz Azer. 91 G2
Towada Japan 74 F4
Towak Mountain hill U.S.A. 118 B3
Towanda U.S.A. 135 G3
Towaoc U.S.A. 129 I3
Towcester U.K. 49 G6
Tower Rep. of Ireland 51 D6
Towner U.S.A. 130 C1
Townes Pass U.S.A. 128 E3
Townsend U.S.A. 126 F3
Townsend, Mount Australia 112 D6
Townshend Island Australia 110 E4
Townsville Australia 110 D3
Towot Sudan 97 G4
Towr Kham Afgh. 89 H3
Towson U.S.A. 135 G4
Towyn U.K. see Tywyn
Toy U.S.A. 128 D1
Toyah U.S.A. 131 C6
Toyama Japan 75 E5
Toyama-wan b. Japan 75 E5
Toyohashi Japan 75 E6
Toyokawa Japan 75 E6
Toyonaka Japan 75 D6
Toyooka Japan 75 D6
Toyota Japan 75 E6
Tozanlı Turkey see Almus
Tozê Kangri mt. China 83 E2
Tozeur Tunisia 54 F5
Tozi, Mount U.S.A. 118 C3
Tqibuli Georgia 91 F2
Traben Germany 52 H5
Trâblous Lebanon see Tripoli
Trabotivište Macedonia 59 J4
Trabzon Turkey 91 E2
Tracy CA U.S.A. 128 C3
Tracy MN U.S.A. 130 E2
Trading r. Canada 122 C4
Traer U.S.A. 130 E3
Trafalgar U.S.A. 134 B4
Trafalgar, Cabo c. Spain 57 C5
Traffic Mountain Canada 120 D2
Trail Canada 120 G5
Tràille, Rubha na pt U.K. 50 D5
Traill Island Greenland see Traill Ø
Traill Ø i. Greenland 119 P2
Trainor Lake Canada 120 F2
Trajectum Neth. see Utrecht
Trakai Lith. 45 N9
Tra Khuc, Sông r. Vietnam 70 E4
Trakiya reg. Europe see Thrace
Trakt Rus. Fed. 42 K3
Trakya reg. Europe see Thrace
Tralee Rep. of Ireland 51 C5
Tralee Bay Rep. of Ireland 51 C5
Trá Li Rep. of Ireland see Tralee
Tramandaí Brazil 145 A5
Tramán Tepuí mt. Venez. 142 F2
Trá Mhór Rep. of Ireland see Tramore
Tramore Rep. of Ireland 51 E5
Tranås Sweden 45 I7
Trancas Arg. 144 C3
Trancoso Brazil 145 D2
Tranemo Sweden 45 H8
Tranent U.K. 50 G5
Trang Thai. 71 B6
Trangan i. Indon. 108 F1
Trangie Australia 112 C4
Transantarctic Mountains Antarctica 152 H2
Trans Canada Highway Canada 121 H5
Transylvanian Alps mts Romania 59 J2
Transylvanian Basin plat. Romania 59 K1
Trapani Sicily Italy 58 E5
Trapezus Turkey see Trabzon
Trapper Peak U.S.A. 126 E3
Trappes France 52 C6
Traralgon Australia 112 C7
Trashigang Bhutan 83 G4
Trasimeno, Lago l. Italy 58 E3
Trasvase, Canal de Spain 57 E4
Trat Thai. 71 C4
Traunsee l. Austria 47 N7
Traunstein Germany 47 N7
Travellers Lake imp. l. Australia 111 C7
Travers, Mount N.Z. 113 D6
Traverse City U.S.A. 134 C1
Tra Vinh Vietnam 71 D5
Travnik Bos.-Herz. 58 G2
Trbovlje Slovenia 58 F1
Tre, Hon i. Vietnam 71 E4
Treasury Islands Solomon Is 106 F2
Trebbin Germany 53 N2
Trebević nat. park Bos.-Herz. 58 H3
Třebíč Czech Rep. 47 O6
Trebinje Bos.-Herz. 58 H3
Trebišov Slovakia 43 D6
Trebizond Turkey see Trabzon
Trebnje Slovenia 58 F2
Trebur Germany 53 I5
Tree Island India 84 B4
Trefaldwyn U.K. see Montgomery
Treffurt Germany 53 K3
Treffynnon U.K. see Holywell
Trefyclawdd U.K. see Knighton
Trefynwy U.K. see Monmouth
Tregosse Islets and Reefs Australia 110 E3
Treinta y Tres Uruguay 144 F4
Trelew Arg. 144 C6
Trelleborg Sweden 45 H9
Trélon France 52 E4
Tremblant, Mont hill Canada 122 G5
Trembleur Lake Canada 120 E4
Tremiti, Isole is Italy 58 F3
Tremont U.S.A. 135 G3
Tremonton U.S.A. 126 E4
Tremp Spain 57 G2
Trenance U.K. 49 B8
Trenary U.S.A. 132 C2
Trenche r. Canada 123 G5
Trenčín Slovakia 47 Q6
Trendelburg Germany 53 J3
Trêng Cambodia 71 C4
Trenque Lauquén Arg. 144 D5
Trent Italy see Trento
Trent r. U.K. 49 G5
Trento Italy 58 D1
Trenton Canada 135 G1
Trenton FL U.S.A. 133 D6
Trenton GA U.S.A. 133 C5
Trenton KY U.S.A. 134 B5
Trenton MO U.S.A. 130 E3
Trenton NC U.S.A. 133 E5
Trenton NE U.S.A. 130 C3

▶Trenton NJ U.S.A. 135 H3
State capital of New Jersey.

Treorchy U.K. 49 D7
Trepassey Canada 123 L5
Tres Arroyos Arg. 144 D5
Tresco i. U.K. 49 A9
Três Corações Brazil 145 B3
Tres Esquinas Col. 142 C3
Tres Forcas, Cabo c. Morocco see Trois Fourches, Cap des
Três Lagoas Brazil 145 A3
Três Marias, Represa resr Brazil 145 B2
Tres Picachos, Sierra mts Mex. 127 G7
Tres Picos, Cerro mt. Arg. 144 D5
Três Pontas Brazil 145 B3
Tres Puntas, Cabo c. Arg. 144 C7
Três Rios Brazil 145 C3
Tretten Norway 45 G6
Tretyy Severnyy Rus. Fed. see 3-y Severnyy
Treuchtlingen Germany 53 K6
Treuenbrietzen Germany 53 M2
Treungen Norway 45 F7
Treves Germany see Trier
Treviglio Italy 58 C2
Treviso Italy 58 E2
Trevose Head hd U.K. 49 B8
Tri An, Hô resr Vietnam 71 D5
Triánda Greece see Trianta
Triangle U.S.A. 135 G4
Trianta Greece 59 M6
Tribal Areas admin. div. Pak. 89 H3
Tri Brata, Gora hill Rus. Fed. 74 F1
Tribune U.S.A. 130 C4
Tricase Italy 58 H5
Trichinopoly India see Tiruchchirappalli
Trichur India 84 C4
Tricot France 52 C5
Trida Australia 112 B4
Tridentum Italy see Trento
Trier Germany 52 G5
Trieste Italy 58 E2
Trieste, Golfo di g. Europe see Trieste, Gulf of
Trieste, Gulf of Europe 58 E2
Triglav mt. Slovenia 58 E1
Triglavski Narodni Park nat. park Slovenia 58 E1
Trikala Greece 59 I5
Tríkkala Greece see Trikala

▶Trikora, Puncak mt. Indon. 69 J7
2nd highest mountain in Oceania.

Trim Rep. of Ireland 51 F4
Trincomalee Sri Lanka 84 D4
Trindade Brazil 145 A2
Trindade, Ilha da i. S. Atlantic Ocean 148 G7
Trinidad Bol. 142 F6
Trinidad Cuba 137 I4
Trinidad i. Trin. and Tob. 137 L6
Trinidad Uruguay 144 E4
Trinidad U.S.A. 127 G5
Trinidad country West Indies see Trinidad and Tobago
▶Trinidad and Tobago country West Indies 137 L6
North America 9, 116–117
Trinity U.S.A. 131 E6
Trinity r. CA U.S.A. 128 B1
Trinity r. TX U.S.A. 131 E6
Trinity Bay Canada 123 L5
Trinity Islands U.S.A. 118 C4
Trinity Range mts U.S.A. 128 D1
Trinkat Island India 71 A5
Trionto, Capo c. Italy 58 G5
Tripa r. Indon. 71 B7
Tripkau Germany 53 L1
Tripoli Greece 59 J6
Tripoli Lebanon 85 B2

▶Tripoli Libya 97 E1
Capital of Libya.

Trípolis Greece see Tripoli
Tripolis Lebanon see Tripoli
Tripunittura India 84 C4
Tripura state India 83 G5

▶Tristan da Cunha i. S. Atlantic Ocean 148 H8
Dependency of St Helena.

Trisul mt. India 82 D3
Triton Canada 123 L4
Triton Island atoll Paracel Is 68 E3
Trittau Germany 53 K1
Trittenheim Germany 52 G5
Trivandrum India 84 C4
Trivento Italy 58 F4
Trnava Slovakia 47 P6
Trobriand Islands P.N.G. 106 F2
Trochu Canada 120 H5
Trofors Norway 44 H4
Trogir Croatia 58 G3
Troia Italy 58 F4
Troisdorf Germany 53 H4
Trois Fourches, Cap des c. Morocco 57 E6
Trois-Ponts Belgium 52 F4
Trois-Rivières Canada 123 G5
Troitsko-Pechorsk Rus. Fed. 41 R3
Troitskoye Altayskiy Kray Rus. Fed. 72 E2
Troitskoye Khabarovskiy Kray Rus. Fed. 74 E2
Troitskoye Respublika Kalmykiya - Khalm'g-Tangch Rus. Fed. 43 J7
Trollhättan Sweden 45 H7
Trombetas r. Brazil 143 G4
Tromelin, Île i. Indian Ocean 149 L7
Tromelin Island Micronesia see Fais
Tromen, Volcán vol. Arg. 144 B5
Tromie r. U.K. 50 E3
Trompsburg S. Africa 101 G6
Tromsø Norway 44 K2
Trona U.S.A. 128 E4
Tronador, Monte mt. Arg. 144 B6
Trondheim Norway 44 G5
Trondheimsfjorden sea chan. Norway 44 F5
Trongsa Bhutan 83 G4
Troödos, Mount Cyprus 85 A2
Troödos Mountains Cyprus 85 A2
Troon U.K. 50 E5
Tropeiros, Serra dos hills Brazil 145 B1
Tropic U.S.A. 129 G3
Tropic of Cancer 131 B8
Tropic of Capricorn 110 G4
Trosh Rus. Fed. 42 L2
Trostan hill U.K. 51 F2
Trout r. B.C. Canada 120 E3
Trout r. N.W.T. Canada 120 G2
Trout Lake Alta Canada 120 H3
Trout Lake N.W.T. Canada 120 F2
Trout Lake l. N.W.T. Canada 120 F2
Trout Lake l. Ont. Canada 121 M5
Trout Peak U.S.A. 126 F3
Trout Run U.S.A. 135 G3
Trouville-sur-Mer France 49 H9
Trowbridge U.K. 49 E7
Troy tourist site Turkey 59 L5
Troy AL U.S.A. 133 C6
Troy KS U.S.A. 130 E4
Troy MI U.S.A. 134 D2
Troy MO U.S.A. 130 F4
Troy MT U.S.A. 126 E2
Troy NH U.S.A. 135 I2
Troy NY U.S.A. 135 I2
Troy OH U.S.A. 134 C3
Troy PA U.S.A. 135 G3
Troyan Bulg. 59 K3
Troyes France 56 G2
Troy Lake U.S.A. 128 E4
Troy Peak U.S.A. 129 F2
Trstenik Serb. and Mont. 59 I3
Truc Giang Vietnam see Bên Tre
Trucial Coast country Asia see United Arab Emirates
Trucial States country Asia see United Arab Emirates
Trud Rus. Fed. 42 G4
Trufanovo Rus. Fed. 42 J2
Trujillo Hond. 137 G5
Trujillo Peru 142 C5
Trujillo Spain 57 D4
Trujillo Venez. 142 D2
Trujillo, Monte mt. Dom. Rep. see Duarte, Pico
Truk is Micronesia see Chuuk
Trulben Germany 53 H5
Trumbull, Mount U.S.A. 129 G3
Trumon Indon. 71 B7
Trundle Australia 112 C4
Trưng Hiệp Vietnam 70 D4
Trung Khanh Vietnam 70 D2
Truong Sa is S. China Sea see Spratly Islands
Truro Canada 123 J5
Truro U.K. 49 B8
Truskmore hill Rep. of Ireland 51 D3
Trutch Canada 120 F3
Truth or Consequences U.S.A. 127 G6
Trutnov Czech Rep. 47 O5
Truuli Peak U.S.A. 118 C4
Truva tourist site Turkey see Troy
Trypiti, Akra pt Greece 59 K7
Trysil Norway 45 H6
Trzebiatów Poland 47 O3
Tsagaannuur Mongolia 80 G2
Tsagaan-Uul Mongolia see Sharga
Tsagan Aman Rus. Fed. 43 J7
Tsagan-Nur Rus. Fed. 43 J7
Tsaidam Basin China see Qaidam Pendi
Tsaka La pass China/Jammu and Kashmir 82 D2
Tsalenjikha Georgia 91 F2
Tsangbo r. China see Brahmaputra
Tsangpo r. China see Brahmaputra
Tsaratanana, Massif du mts Madag. 99 E5

Tsarevo Bulg. 59 L3
Tsaris Mountains Namibia 100 C3
Tsaritsyn Rus. Fed. see **Volgograd**
Tsaukaib Namibia 100 B4
Tsavo East National Park Kenya 98 D4
Tsavo West National Park Africa 98 D3
Tsefat Israel see **Ẕefat**
Tselinograd Kazakh. see **Astana**
Tsenogora Rus. Fed. 42 J2
Tses Namibia 100 D3
Tsetsegnuur Mongolia 80 H2
Tsetseng Botswana 100 F2
Tsetserleg *Arhangay* Mongolia 80 J2
Tsetserleg *Hövsgöl* Mongolia see **Halban**
Tshabong Botswana 100 F4
Tshad *country* Africa see **Chad**
Tshane Botswana 100 E3
Tshela Dem. Rep. Congo 99 B4
Tshibala Dem. Rep. Congo 99 C4
Tshikapa Dem. Rep. Congo 99 C4
Tshing S. Africa 101 H4
Tshipise S. Africa 101 J2
Tshitanzu Dem. Rep. Congo 99 C4
Tshofa Dem. Rep. Congo 99 C4
Tshokwane S. Africa 101 J3
Tsholotsho Zimbabwe 99 C5
Tshootsha Botswana 100 E2
Tshuapa *r.* Dem. Rep. Congo 97 F5
Tshwane S. Africa see **Pretoria**
Tsil'ma *r.* Rus. Fed. 42 K2
Tsimlyansk Rus. Fed. 43 I7
Tsimlyanskoye Vodokhranilishche *resr* Rus. Fed. 43 I7
Tsimmermanovka Rus. Fed. 74 E2
Tsinan China see **Jinan**
Tsineng S. Africa 100 F4
Tsinghai *prov.* China see **Qinghai**
Tsing Shan Wan *Hong Kong* China see **Castle Peak Bay**
Tsingtao China see **Qingdao**
Tsing Yi *i. Hong Kong* China 77 [inset]
Tsining China see **Jining**
Tsiombe Madag. 99 E6
Tsiroanomandidy Madag. 99 E5
Tsitsihar China see **Qiqihar**
Tsitsikamma Forest and Coastal National Park S. Africa 100 F8
Tsitsutl Peak Canada 120 E4
Tsivil'sk Rus. Fed. 42 J5
Tskhaltubo Georgia see **Tsqaltubo**
Ts'khinvali Georgia 91 F2
Tsna *r.* Rus. Fed. 43 I5
Tsnori Georgia 91 G2
Tsokar Chumo *l.* Jammu and Kashmir 82 D2
Tsolo S. Africa 101 I6
Tsomo S. Africa 101 H7
Tsona China see **Cona**
Tsqaltubo Georgia 91 F2
Tsu Japan 75 E6
Tsuchiura Japan 75 F5
Tsuen Wan *Hong Kong* China 77 [inset]
Tsugarū-kaikyō *strait* Japan 74 F4
Tsugaru Strait Japan see **Tsugarū-kaikyō**
Tsumeb Namibia 99 B5
Tsumis Park Namibia 100 C2
Tsumkwe Namibia 99 C5
Tsuruga Japan 75 E6
Tsurugi-san *mt.* Japan 75 D6
Tsurukhaytuy Rus. Fed. see **Priargunsk**
Tsuruoka Japan 75 E5
Tsushima *is* Japan 75 C6
Tsushima-kaikyō *strait* Japan/S. Korea see **Korea Strait**
Tsuyama Japan 75 D6
Tswaane Botswana 100 E2
Tswaraganang S. Africa 101 G5
Tswelelang S. Africa 101 G4
Tsyelyakhany Belarus 45 N10
Tsyp-Navolok Rus. Fed. 44 R2
Tsyurupyns'k Ukr. 59 O1
Tthenaagoo Canada see **Nahanni Butte**
Tua Dem. Rep. Congo 98 B4
Tual Indon. 69 I8
Tuam Rep. of Ireland 51 D4
Tuamotu, Archipel des *is* Fr. Polynesia see **Tuamotu Islands**
Tuamotu Islands Fr. Polynesia 151 K6
Tuân Giao Vietnam 70 C2
Tuangku *i.* Indon. 71 B7
Tuapse Rus. Fed. 90 E1
Tuas Sing. 71 [inset]
Tuath, Loch a' *b.* U.K. 50 C2
Tuba City U.S.A. 129 H3
Tubarão Brazil 145 A5
Tubarjal Saudi Arabia 85 D4
Tubbercurry Rep. of Ireland 51 D3
Tübingen Germany 47 L6
Tubmanburg Liberia 96 B4
Tubruq Libya 90 A4
Tubuai *i.* Fr. Polynesia 151 K7
Tubuai Islands Fr. Polynesia 151 J7
Tucano Brazil 143 K6
Tucavaca Bol. 143 G7
Tüchen Germany 53 M1
Tuchheim Germany 53 M2
Tuchitua Canada 120 D2
Tuchodi *r.* Canada 120 F3
Tuckerton U.S.A. 135 H4
Tucopia *i.* Solomon Is see **Tikopia**
Tucson U.S.A. 129 H5
Tucson Mountains U.S.A. 129 H5
Tuctuc *r.* Canada 123 I2
Tucumán Arg. see **San Miguel de Tucumán**
Tucumcari U.S.A. 131 C5
Tucupita Venez. 142 F2
Tucuruí Brazil 143 I4
Tucuruí, Represa *resr* Brazil 143 I4
Tudela Spain 57 F2
Tuder Italy see **Todi**
Tuela *r.* Port. 57 C3
Tuen Mun *Hong Kong* China 77 [inset]
Tuensang India 83 H4
Tufts Abyssal Plain *sea feature* N. Pacific Ocean 151 K2
Tugela *r.* S. Africa 101 J5
Tuglung China 76 B2
Tuguegarao Phil. 69 G3
Tugur Rus. Fed. 74 E1
Tuhemberua Indon. 71 B7
Tujiabu China see **Yongxiu**
Tukangbesi, Kepulauan *is* Indon. 69 G8
Tukarak Island Canada 122 F2
Ṭukhmān, Banī *reg.* Saudi Arabia 88 C6
Tukituki *r.* N.Z. 113 F4
Tuktoyaktuk Canada 118 E3
Tuktut Nogait National Park Canada 118 F3
Tukums Latvia 45 M8
Tukuringra, Khrebet *mts* Rus. Fed. 74 B1
Tukuyu Tanz. 99 D4
Tula Rus. Fed. 43 H5
Tulach Mhór Rep. of Ireland see **Tullamore**
Tulagt Ar Gol *r.* China 83 H1
Tulak Afgh. 89 F3
Tulameen Canada 120 F5
Tula Mountains Antarctica 152 D2
Tulancingo Mex. 136 E4
Tulare U.S.A. 128 D3
Tulare Lake Bed U.S.A. 128 D4
Tularosa Mountains U.S.A. 129 I5
Tulasi *mt.* India 84 D2
Tulbagh S. Africa 100 D7
Tulcán Ecuador 142 C3
Tulcea Romania 59 M2
Tule *r.* U.S.A. 131 C5
Tuléar Madag. see **Toliara**
Tulemalu Lake Canada 121 L2
Tulia U.S.A. 131 C5
Tulihe China 74 A2
Tulita Canada 120 E1
Tulkarem West Bank see **Ṭūlkarm**
Ṭūlkarm West Bank 85 B3
Tulla Rep. of Ireland 51 D5
Tullahoma U.S.A. 132 C5
Tullamore Australia 112 C4
Tullamore Rep. of Ireland 51 E4
Tulle France 56 E4
Tulleråsen Sweden 44 I5
Tullibigeal Australia 112 C4
Tullow Rep. of Ireland 51 F5
Tully Australia 110 D3
Tully *r.* Australia 110 D3
Tully U.K. 51 E3
Tulos Rus. Fed. 44 Q5
Tulqarem West Bank see **Ṭūlkarm**
Tulsa U.S.A. 131 E4
Tulsipur Nepal 83 E3
Tuluá Col. 142 C3
Tuluksak U.S.A. 153 B2
Tulūl al Ashāqif *hills* Jordan 85 C3
Tulun Rus. Fed. 72 I2
Tulu-Tuloi, Serra *hills* Brazil 142 F3
Tulu Welel *mt.* Eth. 98 D3
Tuma Rus. Fed. 43 I5
Tumaco Col. 142 C3
Tumahole S. Africa 101 H4
Tumain China 83 G2
Tumannyy Rus. Fed. 44 S2
Tumasik Sing. see **Singapore**
Tumba Dem. Rep. Congo 98 C4
Tumba Sweden 45 J7
Tumba, Lac *l.* Dem. Rep. Congo 98 B4
Tumbarumba Australia 112 D5
Tumbes Peru 142 B4
Tumbler Ridge Canada 120 F4
Tumby Bay Australia 111 B7
Tumcha *r.* Fin./Rus. Fed. 44 Q3
also known as Tuntsajoki
Tumen *Jilin* China 74 C4
Tumen *Shaanxi* China 77 F1
Tumereng Guyana 142 F2
Tumindao *i.* Phil. 68 F6
Tumiritinga Brazil 145 C2
Tumkur India 84 C3
Tummel *r.* U.K. 50 F4
Tummel, Loch *l.* U.K. 50 F4
Tumnin *r.* Rus. Fed. 74 F2
Tump Pak. 89 F5
Tumpat Malaysia 71 C6
Tumpôr, Phnum *mt.* Cambodia 71 C4
Tumshuk Uzbek. 89 G2
Tumu Ghana 96 C3
Tumucumaque, Serra *hills* Brazil 143 G3
Tumudibandh India 84 D2
Tumut Australia 112 D5
Tuna India 82 B5
Ṭunb al Kubrá *i.* The Gulf see **Greater Tunb**
Ṭunb aş Şughrá *i.* The Gulf see **Lesser Tunb**
Tunbridge Wells, Royal U.K. 49 H7
Tunceli Turkey 91 E3
Tunchang China 77 F5
Tuncurry Australia 112 F4
Tundun-Wada Nigeria 96 D3
Tunduru Tanz. 99 D5
Tunes Tunisia see **Tunis**
Tunga Nigeria 96 D4
Tungabhadra Reservoir India 80 C3
Tungi Bangl. 83 G5
Tung Lung Island *Hong Kong* China 77 [inset]
Tungnaá *r.* Iceland 44 [inset]
Tungor Rus. Fed. 74 F1
Tung Pok Liu Hoi Hap *Hong Kong* China see **East Lamma Channel**
Tungsten Canada 120 D2
Tung Wan *b. Hong Kong* China 77 [inset]
Tuni India 84 D2
Tunica U.S.A. 131 F5
Tūnis *country* Africa see **Tunisia**

▶**Tunis** Tunisia 58 D6
Capital of Tunisia.

Tunis, Golfe de *g.* Tunisia 58 D6
▶**Tunisia** *country* Africa 54 F5
Africa 7, 94–95
Tunja Col. 142 D2
Tunkhannock U.S.A. 135 H3
Tunnsjøen *l.* Norway 44 H4
Tunstall U.K. 49 I6
Tuntsa Fin. 44 P3
Tuntsajoki *r.* Fin./Rus. Fed. see **Tumcha**
Tunulic *r.* Canada 123 I2
Tununak U.S.A. 118 B3
Tunungayualok Island Canada 123 J2
Tunxi China see **Huangshan**
Tuodian China see **Shuangbai**
Tuojiang China see **Fenghuang**
Tuŏl Khpos Cambodia 71 D5
Tuoniang Jiang *r.* China 76 E3
Tuotuo He *r.* China see **Togton He**
Tuotuoheyan China see **Tanggulashan**
Tüp Kyrg. 80 E3
Tupã Brazil 145 A3
Tupelo U.S.A. 131 F5
Tupik Rus. Fed. 73 L2
Tupinambarama, Ilha *i.* Brazil 143 G4
Tupiraçaba Brazil 145 A1
Tupiza Bol. 142 E8
Tupper Canada 120 F4
Tupper Lake U.S.A. 135 H1
Tupper Lake *l.* U.S.A. 135 H1
Tüpqaraghan Tübegi *pen.* Kazakh. see **Mangyshlak, Poluostrov**

▶**Tupungato, Cerro** *mt.* Arg./Chile 144 C4
5th highest mountain in South America.

Tuqayyid *well* Iraq 88 B4
Tuquan China 73 M3
Tuqu Wan *b.* China see **Lingshui Wan**
Tura China 83 F1
Tura India 83 G4
Tura Rus. Fed. 65 L3
Turabah Saudi Arabia 86 F5
Turakina N.Z. 113 E5
Turan Rus. Fed. 72 G2
Turana, Khrebet *mts* Rus. Fed. 74 C2
Turan Lowland Asia 80 A4
Turan Oypaty *lowland* Asia see **Turan Lowland**
Turan Pasttekisligi *lowland* Asia see **Turan Lowland**
Turan Pesligi *lowland* Asia see **Turan Lowland**
Turanskaya Nizmennost' *lowland* Asia see **Turan Lowland**
Ṭurāq al 'Ilab *hills* Syria 85 D3
Turar Ryskulov Kazakh. 80 D3
Tura-Ryskulova Kazakh. see **Turar Ryskulov**
Turayf Saudi Arabia 85 D4
Turba Estonia 45 N7
Turbat Pak. 89 F5
Turbo Col. 142 C2
Turda Romania 59 J1
Türeh Iran 88 C3
Turfan China see **Turpan**
Turfan Basin *depr.* China see **Turpan Pendi**
Turfan Depression China see **Turpan Pendi**
Turgay Kazakh. 80 B2
Turgayskaya Dolina *valley* Kazakh. 80 B2
Tŭrgovishte Bulg. 59 L3
Turgutlu Turkey 59 L5
Turhal Turkey 90 E2
Türi Estonia 45 N7
Turia *r.* Spain 57 F4
Turin Canada 121 H5
Turin Italy 58 B2
Turiy Rog Rus. Fed. 74 C3
Turkana, Lake *salt l.* Eth./Kenya 98 D3
Turkestan Kazakh. 80 C3
Turkestan Range *mts* Asia 89 G2
▶**Turkey** *country* Asia/Europe 90 D3
Asia 6, 62–63
Turkey U.S.A. 134 D5
Turkey *r.* U.S.A. 130 F3
Turki Rus. Fed. 43 I6
Türkistan Kazakh. see **Turkestan**
Türkiye *country* Asia/Europe see **Turkey**
Turkmenabat Turkm. 89 F2
Türkmen Adasy *i.* Turkm. see **Ogurchinskiy, Ostrov**
Türkmen Aylagy *b.* Turkm. see **Turkmenskiy Zaliv**
Turkmenbashi Turkm. 88 D1
Türkmenbaşy Turkm. see **Turkmenbashi**
Türkmenbaşy Aylagy *b.* Turkm. see **Krasnovodskiy Zaliv**
Türkmen Dağı *mt.* Turkey 59 N5
▶**Turkmenistan** *country* Asia 87 I2
Asia 6, 62–63
Turkmeniya *country* Asia see **Turkmenistan**
Türkmenostan *country* Asia see **Turkmenistan**
Turkmenskaya S.S.R. *country* Asia see **Turkmenistan**
Turkmenskiy Zaliv *b.* Turkm. 88 D2
Türkoğlu Turkey 90 E3

▶**Turks and Caicos Islands** *terr.* West Indies 137 J4
United Kingdom Overseas Territory.
North America 9, 116–117

Turks Island Passage Turks and Caicos Is 133 G8
Turks Islands Turks and Caicos Is 137 J4
Turku Fin. 45 M6
Turkwel *watercourse* Kenya 98 D3
Turlock U.S.A. 128 C3
Turlock Lake U.S.A. 128 C3
Turmalina Brazil 145 C2
Turnagain *r.* Canada 120 E3
Turnagain, Cape N.Z. 113 F5
Turnberry U.K. 50 E5
Turnbull, Mount U.S.A. 129 H5
Turneffe Islands *atoll* Belize 136 G5
Turner U.S.A. 134 D1
Turner Valley Canada 120 H5
Turnhout Belgium 52 E3
Turnor Lake Canada 121 I3
Tŭrnovo Bulg. see **Veliko Tŭrnovo**
Turnu Măgurele Romania 59 K3
Turnu Severin Romania see **Drobeta - Turnu Severin**
Turon *r.* Australia 112 D4
Turones France see **Tours**
Turovets Rus. Fed. 42 I4
Turpan China 80 G3

▶**Turpan Pendi** *depr.* China 80 G3
Lowest point in northern Asia.

Turquino, Pico *mt.* Cuba 137 I4
Turriff U.K. 50 G3
Turris Libisonis *Sardinia* Italy see **Porto Torres**
Tursāq Iraq 91 G4
Turtkul' Uzbek. 80 B3
Turtle Island Fiji see **Vatoa**
Turtle Lake Canada 121 I4
Turugart Pass China/Kyrg. 80 E3
Turugart Shankou *pass* China/Kyrg. see **Turugart Pass**
Turuvanur India 84 C3
Turvo *r.* Brazil 145 A2
Turvo *r.* Brazil 145 A2
Tusayan U.S.A. 129 G4
Tuscaloosa U.S.A. 133 C5
Tuscarawas *r.* U.S.A. 134 E3
Tuscarora Mountains *hills* U.S.A. 135 G3
Tuscola *IL* U.S.A. 130 F4
Tuscola *TX* U.S.A. 131 D5
Tuscumbia U.S.A. 133 C5
Tuskegee U.S.A. 133 C5
Tussey Mountains *hills* U.S.A. 135 F3
Tustin U.S.A. 134 C1
Tutak Turkey 91 F3
Tutayev Rus. Fed. 42 H4
Tutera Spain see **Tudela**
Tuticorin India 84 C4
Tutong Brunei 68 E6
Tuttle Creek Reservoir U.S.A. 130 D4
Tuttlingen Germany 47 L7
Tuttut Nunaat *reg.* Greenland 119 P2
Tutuala East Timor 108 D2
Tutubu P.N.G. 110 E1
Tutubu Tanz. 99 D4
Tutuila *i.* American Samoa 107 I3
Tutume Botswana 99 C6
Tutwiler U.S.A. 131 F5
Tuun-bong *mt.* N. Korea 74 B4
Tuupovaara Fin. 44 Q5
Tuusniemi Fin. 44 P5
▶**Tuvalu** *country* S. Pacific Ocean 107 H2
Oceania 8, 104–105
Tuwayq, Jabal *hills* Saudi Arabia 86 G4
Tuwayq, Jabal *mts* Saudi Arabia 86 G5
Ṭuwayyil ash Shiḥāq *mt.* Jordan 85 C4
Tuwwal Saudi Arabia 86 E5
Tuxpan Mex. 136 E4
Tuxtla Gutiérrez Mex. 136 F5
Tuya Lake Canada 120 D3
Tuyên Quang Vietnam 70 D2
Tuy Hoa Vietnam 71 E4
Tuz, Lake *salt l.* Turkey 90 D3
Tuz Gölü *salt l.* Turkey see **Tuz, Lake**
Tuzha Rus. Fed. 42 J4
Tuz Khurmātū Iraq 91 G4
Tuzla Bos.-Herz. 58 H2
Tuzla Turkey 85 B1
Tuzla Gölü *lag.* Turkey 59 L4
Tuzlov *r.* Rus. Fed. 43 I7
Tuzu *r.* Myanmar 70 A1
Tvedestrand Norway 45 F7
Tver' Rus. Fed. 42 G4
Twain Harte U.S.A. 128 C2
Tweed Canada 135 G1
Tweed *r.* U.K. 50 G5
Tweed Heads Australia 112 F2
Tweedie Canada 121 I4
Tweefontein S. Africa 100 D7
Twee Rivier Namibia 100 D3
Twentekanaal *canal* Neth. 52 G2
Twentynine Palms U.S.A. 128 E4
Twin Bridges *CA* U.S.A. 128 C2
Twin Bridges *MT* U.S.A. 126 E3
Twin Buttes Reservoir U.S.A. 131 C6
Twin Falls Canada 123 I3
Twin Falls U.S.A. 126 E4
Twin Heads *hill* Australia 108 D5
Twin Peak U.S.A. 128 C2
Twistringen Germany 53 I2
Twitchen Reservoir U.S.A. 128 C4
Twitya *r.* Canada 120 D1
Twofold Bay Australia 112 D6
Two Harbors U.S.A. 130 F2
Two Hills Canada 121 I4
Two Rivers U.S.A. 134 B1
Tyan' Shan' *mts* China/Kyrg. see **Tien Shan**
Tyao *r.* India/Myanmar 76 B4
Tyatya, Vulkan *vol.* Rus. Fed. 74 G3
Tydal Norway 44 G5
Tygart Valley U.S.A. 134 F4
Tygda Rus. Fed. 74 B1
Tygda *r.* Rus. Fed. 74 B1
Tyler U.S.A. 131 E5
Tylertown U.S.A. 131 F6
Tym' *r.* Rus. Fed. 74 F2
Tymovskoye Rus. Fed. 74 F2
Tynda Rus. Fed. 73 M1
Tyndall U.S.A. 130 D3
Tyndinskiy Rus. Fed. see **Tynda**
Tyne *r.* U.K. 50 G4
Tynemouth U.K. 48 F3
Tynset Norway 44 G5
Tyoploozyorsk Rus. Fed. see **Teploozersk**
Tyoploye Ozero Rus. Fed. see **Teploozersk**
Tyr Lebanon see **Tyre**
Tyras Ukr. see **Bilhorod-Dnistrovs'kyy**
Tyre Lebanon 85 B3
Tyree, Mount Antarctica 152 L1
Tyrma Rus. Fed. 74 D2
Tyrma *r.* Rus. Fed. 74 C2
Tyrnävä Fin. 44 N4
Tyrnavos Greece 59 J5
Tyrnyauz Rus. Fed. 91 F2
Tyrone U.S.A. 135 F3
Tyrrell *r.* Australia 112 A5
Tyrrell, Lake *dry lake* Australia 111 C7
Tyrrell Lake Canada 121 J2
Tyrrhenian Sea France/Italy 58 D4
Tyrus Lebanon see **Tyre**
Tysa *r.* Ukr. see **Tisa**
Tyukalinsk Rus. Fed. 64 I4
Tyulen'i Ostrova *is* Kazakh. 91 H1
Tyumen' Rus. Fed. 64 H4
Tyup Kyrg. see **Tüp**
Tyuratam Kazakh. see **Baykonyr**
Tywi *r.* U.K. 49 C7
Tywyn U.K. 49 C6
Tzaneen S. Africa 101 J2

U

Uaco Congo Angola see **Waku-Kungo**
Ualan *atoll* Micronesia see **Kosrae**
Uamanda Angola 99 C5
Uarc, Ras *c.* Morocco see **Trois Fourches, Cap des**
Uaroo Australia 109 A5
Uatumã *r.* Brazil 143 G4
Uauá Brazil 143 K5
Uaupés *r.* Brazil 142 E3
U'aylī, Wādī al *watercourse* Saudi Arabia 85 D4
U'aywij *well* Saudi Arabia 88 B4
U'aywij, Wādī al *watercourse* Saudi Arabia 91 F5
Ubá Brazil 145 C3
Ubaí Brazil 145 B2
Ubaitaba Brazil 145 D1
Ubangi *r.* Cent. Afr. Rep./Dem. Rep. Congo 98 B4
Ubangi-Shari *country* Africa see **Central African Republic**
Ubauro Pak. 89 H4
Ubayyiḍ, Wādī al *watercourse* Iraq/Saudi Arabia 91 F4
Ube Japan 75 C6
Úbeda Spain 57 E4
Uberaba Brazil 145 B2
Uberlândia Brazil 145 A2
Ubin, Pulau *i.* Sing. 71 [inset]
Ubly U.S.A. 134 D2
Ubolratna Reservoir Thai. 70 C3
Ubombo S. Africa 101 K4
Ubon Ratchathani Thai. 70 D4
Ubstadt-Weiher Germany 53 I5
Ubundu Dem. Rep. Congo 97 F5
Ucar Azer. 91 G2
Uçarı Turkey 85 A1
Ucayali *r.* Peru 142 D4
Uch Pak. 89 H4
Uch-Adzhi Turkm. 89 F2
Üchajy Turkm. see **Uch-Adzhi**
Üchān Iran 88 C2
Ucharal Kazakh. 80 F2
Uchiura-wan *b.* Japan 74 F4
Uchkeken Rus. Fed. 91 F2
Uchkuduk Uzbek. 80 B3
Uchquduq Uzbek. see **Uchkuduk**
Uchte Germany 53 I2
Uchte *r.* Germany 53 L2
Uchto *r.* Pak. 89 G5
Uchur *r.* Rus. Fed. 65 O4
Uckermark *reg.* Germany 53 N1
Uckfield U.K. 49 H8
Ucluelet Canada 120 E5
Ucross U.S.A. 126 G3
Uda *r.* Rus. Fed. 73 J2
Uda *r.* Rus. Fed. 74 D1
Udachnoye Rus. Fed. 43 J7
Udachnyy Rus. Fed. 153 E2
Udagamandalam India 84 C4
Udaipur *Orissa* India 83 F5
Udaipur *Rajasthan* India 82 C4
Udaipur *Tripura* India 83 G5
Udanti *r.* India/Myanmar 83 E5
Uday *r.* Ukr. 43 G6
'Udaynān *well* Saudi Arabia 88 C6
Uddevalla Sweden 45 G7
Uddingston U.K. 50 E5
Uddjaure *l.* Sweden 44 J4
'Udeid, Khōr al *inlet* Qatar 88 C5
Uden Neth. 52 F3
Udgir India 84 C2
Udhagamandalam India see **Udagamandalam**
Udhampur India 82 C2
Udia-Milai *atoll* Marshall Is see **Bikini**
Udimskiy Rus. Fed. 42 J3
Udine Italy 58 E1
Udit India 89 I5
Udjuktok Bay Canada 123 J3
Udmalaippettai India see **Udumalaippettai**
Udomlya Rus. Fed. 42 G4
Udon Thani Thai. 70 C3
Udskaya Guba *b.* Rus. Fed. 65 O4
Udskoye Rus. Fed. 74 D1
Udumalaippettai India 84 C4
Udupi India 84 B3
Udyl', Ozero *l.* Rus. Fed. 74 E1
Udzhary Azer. see **Ucar**
Udzungwa Mountains National Park Tanz. 99 D4
Uéa *atoll* New Caledonia see **Ouvéa**
Ueckermünde Germany 47 O4
Ueda Japan 75 E5
Uele *r.* Dem. Rep. Congo 98 C3
Uelen Rus. Fed. 65 U3
Uelzen Germany 53 K2
Uetersen Germany 53 J1
Uettingen Germany 53 J5
Uetze Germany 53 K2
Ufa Rus. Fed. 41 R5
Ufa *r.* Rus. Fed. 41 R5
Uffenheim Germany 53 K5
Uftyuga *r.* Rus. Fed. 42 J3
Ugab *watercourse* Namibia 99 B6
Ugalla *r.* Tanz. 99 D4
▶**Uganda** *country* Africa 98 D3
Africa 7, 94–95
Ugie S. Africa 101 I6
Uğīnak Iran 89 F5
Uglegorsk Rus. Fed. 74 F2
Uglich Rus. Fed. 42 H4
Ugljan *i.* Croatia 58 F2
Uglovoye Rus. Fed. 74 C2
Ugol'noye Rus. Fed. 65 P3
Ugolnyy Rus. Fed. see **Beringovskiy**
Ugol'nyye Kopi Rus. Fed. 65 S3
Ugra Rus. Fed. 43 G5
Uherské Hradiště Czech Rep. 43 P6
Úhlava *r.* Czech Rep. 53 N5
Uhrichsville U.S.A. 134 E3
Uibhist a' Deas *i.* U.K. see **South Uist**
Uibhist a' Tuath *i.* U.K. see **North Uist**
Uig U.K. 50 C3
Uíge Angola 99 B4
Ŭijŏngbu S. Korea 75 B5
Ŭiju N. Korea 75 B4
Uimaharju Fin. 44 Q5
Uinta Mountains U.S.A. 129 H1
Uis Mine Namibia 99 B6
Uitenhage S. Africa 101 G7
Uithoorn Neth. 52 E2
Uithuizen Neth. 52 G1
Uivak, Cape Canada 123 J2
Ujhani India 82 D4
Uji Japan 75 D6
Uji-guntō *is* Japan 75 C7
Ujiyamada Japan see **Ise**
Ujjain India 82 C5
Ujung Pandang Indon. see **Makassar**
Újvidék Serb. and Mont. see **Novi Sad**
Ukal Sagar *l.* India 82 C5
Ukata Nigeria 96 D3
'Ukayrishah *well* Saudi Arabia 88 B5
Ukholovo Rus. Fed. 43 I5
Ukhrul India 83 H4
Ukhta *Respublika Kareliya* Rus. Fed. see **Kalevala**
Ukhta *Respublika Komi* Rus. Fed. 42 L3
Ukiah *CA* U.S.A. 128 B2
Ukiah *OR* U.S.A. 126 D3
Ukkusissat Greenland 119 M2
Ukmergė Lith. 45 N9

▶**Ukraine** *country* Europe 43 F6
2nd largest country in Europe.
Europe 5, 38–39

Ukrainskaya S.S.R. *country* Europe see **Ukraine**
Ukrayina *country* Europe see **Ukraine**
Uku-jima *i.* Japan 75 C6
Ukwi Botswana 100 E2
Ukwi Pan *salt pan* Botswana 100 E2
Ulaanbaatar Mongolia see **Ulan Bator**
Ulaangom Mongolia 80 H2
Ulan Australia 112 D4

▶**Ulan Bator** Mongolia 72 J3
Capital of Mongolia.

Ulanbel' Kazakh. 80 D3
Ulan Erge Rus. Fed. 43 J7
Ulanhad China see **Chifeng**
Ulanhot China 74 A3
Ulan Hua China 73 K4
Ulan-Khol Rus. Fed. 43 J7
Ulan-Ude Rus. Fed. 73 J2
Ulan Ul Hu *l.* China 83 G2
Ulaş Turkey 90 E3
Ulawa Island Solomon Is 107 G2
Ulayyah *reg.* Saudi Arabia 88 B6
Ul'banskiy Zaliv *b.* Rus. Fed. 74 E1
Ulchin S. Korea 75 C5
Uldz *r.* Mongolia 73 L3
Uleåborg Fin. see **Oulu**
Ulefoss Norway 45 F7
Ülenurme Estonia 45 O7
Ulety Rus. Fed. 73 K2
Ulhasnagar India 84 B2
Uliastai China 73 L3
Uliastay Mongolia 80 I2
Uliatea *i.* Fr. Polynesia see **Raiatea**
Ulicoten Neth. 52 E3
Ulie *atoll* Micronesia see **Woleai**
Ulita *r.* Rus. Fed. 44 R2
Ulithi *atoll* Micronesia 69 J4
Ulladulla Australia 112 E5
Ullapool U.K. 50 D3
Ulla Ulla, Parque Nacional *nat. park* Bol. 142 E6
Ullava Fin. 44 M5
Ullersuaq *c.* Greenland 119 K2
Ullswater *l.* U.K. 48 E4
Ullŭng-do *i.* S. Korea 75 C5
Ulm Germany 47 L6
Ulmarra Australia 112 F2
Ulmen Germany 52 G4
Uloowaranie, Lake *salt flat* Australia 111 B5
Ulricehamn Sweden 45 H8
Ulrum Neth. 52 G1
Ulsan S. Korea 75 C6
Ulsberg Norway 44 F5
Ulster *reg.* Rep. of Ireland/U.K. 51 E3
Ulster U.S.A. 135 G3
Ulster Canal Rep. of Ireland/U.K. 51 E3
Ultima Australia 112 A5
Ulubat Gölü *l.* Turkey 59 M4
Ulubey Turkey 59 M5
Uluborlu Turkey 59 N5
Uludağ *mt.* Turkey 59 M4
Uludağ Milli Parkı *nat. park* Turkey 59 M4
Ulugqat China see **Wuqia**
Ulu Kali, Gunung *mt.* Malaysia 71 C7
Ulukışla Turkey 90 D3
Ulundi S. Africa 101 J5
Ulungur Hu *l.* China 80 G2
Ulunkhan Rus. Fed. 73 K2
Uluqsaqtuuq Canada see **Holman**
Uluru *hill* Australia 109 E6
Uluṟu - Kata Tjuṯa National Park Australia 109 E6
Uluru National Park Australia see **Uluṟu - Kata Tjuṯa National Park**
Ulutau Kazakh. see **Ulytau**
Ulutau, Gory *mts* Kazakh. see **Ulytau, Gory**
Uluyatır Turkey 85 C1
Ulva *i.* U.K. 50 C4
Ulvenhout Neth. 52 E3
Ulverston U.K. 48 D4
Ulvsjön Sweden 45 I6
Ül'yanov Kazakh. see **Ul'yanovskiy**
Ul'yanovsk Rus. Fed. 43 K5
Ul'yanovskiy Kazakh. 80 D1
Ul'yanovskoye Kazakh. see **Ul'yanovskiy**
Ulysses *KS* U.S.A. 130 C4
Ulysses *KY* U.S.A. 134 D5
Ulytau Kazakh. 80 C2
Ulytau, Gory *mts* Kazakh. 80 C2
Uma Rus. Fed. 74 A1
Umaltinskiy Rus. Fed. 74 D2
'Umān *country* Asia see **Oman**
Uman' Ukr. 43 F6
Umarao Pak. 89 G4
'Umarī, Qa' al *salt pan* Jordan 85 C4
Umaria India 82 E5
Umarkhed India 84 C2
Umarkot India 84 D2
Umarkot Pak. 89 H5
Umaroona, Lake *salt flat* Australia 111 B5
Umarpada India 82 C5
Umatilla U.S.A. 126 D3
Umba Rus. Fed. 42 G2
Umbagog Lake U.S.A. 135 J1

Umbeara Australia 109 F6
Umboi i. P.N.G. 69 L8
Umeå Sweden 44 L5
Umeälven r. Sweden 44 L5
Umfolozi r. S. Africa 101 K5
Umfreville Lake Canada 121 M5
Umhlanga Rocks S. Africa 101 J5
Umiiviip Kangertiva inlet Greenland 119 N3
Umingmaktok Canada 153 L2
Umirzak Kazakh. 91 H2
Umiujaq Canada 122 F2
Umkomaas S. Africa 101 J6
Umlaiteng India 83 H4
Umlazi S. Africa 101 J5
Umm ad Daraj, Jabal mt. Jordan 85 B3
Umm al 'Amad Syria 85 C2
Umm al Jamājim well Saudi Arabia 88 B5
Umm al Qaiwain U.A.E. see Umm al Qaywayn
Umm al Qaywayn U.A.E. 88 D5
Umm ar Raqabah, Khabrat imp. l. Saudi Arabia 85 C5
Umm at Qalbān Saudi Arabia 91 F6
Umm az Zumūl well Oman 88 D6
Umm Bāb Qatar 88 C5
Umm Bel Sudan 86 C7
Umm Keddada Sudan 86 C7
Umm Lajj Saudi Arabia 86 E4
Umm Nukhaylah hill Saudi Arabia 85 D5
Umm Qaşr Iraq 91 G5
Umm Quşur i. Saudi Arabia 90 D6
Umm Ruwaba Sudan 86 D7
Umm Sa'ad Libya 90 B5
Umm Sa'id Qatar 88 C5
Umm Shugeira Sudan 86 C7
Umm Wa'āl hill Saudi Arabia 85 D4
Umm Wazīr well Saudi Arabia 88 B6
Umnak Island U.S.A. 118 B4
Um Phang Wildlife Reserve nature res. Thai. 70 B4
Umpqua r. U.S.A. 126 B4
Umpulo Angola 99 B5
Umraniye Turkey 59 N5
Umred India 84 C1
Umri India 82 D4
Umtali Zimbabwe see Mutare
Umtata S. Africa 101 I6
Umtentweni S. Africa 101 J6
Umuahia Nigeria 96 D4
Umuarama Brazil 144 F2
Umvuma Zimbabwe see Mvuma
Umzimkulu S. Africa 101 I6
Una r. Bos.-Herz./Croatia 58 G2
Una Brazil 145 D1
Una India 82 D3
'Unāb, Jabal al hill Jordan 85 C5
'Unāb, Wādī al watercourse Jordan 85 C4
Unaí Brazil 145 B2
Unai Pass Afgh. 89 H3
Unalaska Island U.S.A. 118 B4
Unapool U.K. 50 D2
'Unayzah Saudi Arabia 86 F4
'Unayzah, Jabal hill Iraq 91 E4
Uncia Bol. 142 E7
Uncompahgre Peak U.S.A. 129 J2
Uncompahgre Plateau U.S.A. 129 I2
Undara National Park Australia 110 D3
Underberg S. Africa 101 I5
Underbool Australia 111 C7
Underwood U.S.A. 134 C4
Undur Indon. 69 I7
Unecha Rus. Fed. 43 G5
Ungama Bay Kenya see Ungwana Bay
Ungarie Australia 112 C4
Ungava, Baie d' b. Canada see Ungava Bay
Ungava, Péninsule d' pen. Canada 122 G1
Ungava Bay Canada 123 I2
Ungava Peninsula Canada see Ungava, Péninsule d'
Ungeny Moldova see Ungheni
Unggi N. Korea 74 C4
Ungheni Moldova 59 L1
Unguana Moz. 101 L2
Unguja i. Tanz. see Zanzibar Island
Unguz, Solonchakovyye Vpadiny salt flat Turkm. 88 E2
Üngüz Angyrsyndaky Garagum des. Turkm. see Zaunguzskiye Karakumy
Ungvár Ukr. see Uzhhorod
Ungwana Bay Kenya 98 E4
Uni Rus. Fed. 42 K4
União Brazil 143 J4
União da Vitória Brazil 145 A4
União dos Palmares Brazil 143 K5
Unimak Island U.S.A. 118 B4
Unini r. Brazil 142 F4
Union MO U.S.A. 130 F4
Union WV U.S.A. 134 E5
Union, Mount U.S.A. 129 G4
Union City OH U.S.A. 134 C3
Union City PA U.S.A. 134 F3
Union City TN U.S.A. 131 F4
Uniondale S. Africa 100 F7
Unión de Reyes Cuba 133 D8

►Union of Soviet Socialist Republics
Divided in 1991 into 15 independent nations: Armenia, Azerbaijan, Belarus, Estonia, Georgia, Kazakhstan, Kyrgyzstan, Latvia, Lithuania, Moldova, the Russian Federation, Tajikistan, Turkmenistan, Ukraine and Uzbekistan.

Union Springs U.S.A. 133 C5
Uniontown U.S.A. 134 F4
Unionville U.S.A. 135 G3
►United Arab Emirates country Asia 88 D6
Asia 6, 62–63
United Arab Republic country Africa see Egypt

►United Kingdom country Europe 46 G3
3rd most populous country in Europe.
Europe 5, 38–39

United Provinces state India see Uttar Pradesh

►United States of America country N. America 124 F3
Most populous country in North America and 3rd in the world. 3rd largest country in the world and 2nd in North America.
North America 9, 116–117

United States Range mts Canada 119 L1
Unity Canada 121 I4
Unjha India 82 C5
Unna Germany 53 H3
Unnao India 82 E4
Ŭnp'a N. Korea 75 B5
Unsan N. Korea 75 B4
Ŭnsan N. Korea 75 B5
Unst i. U.K. 50 [inset]
Unstrut r. Germany 53 L3
Untari India 83 E4
Untor, Ozero l. Rus. Fed. 41 T3
Unuk r. Canada/U.S.A. 120 D3
Unuli Horog China 83 G2
Unzen-dake vol. Japan 75 C6
Unzha Rus. Fed. 42 J4
Upalco U.S.A. 129 H1
Upar Ghat reg. India 83 F5
Upemba, Lac l. Dem. Rep. Congo 99 C4
Uperbada India 83 F5
Upernavik Greenland 119 M2
Upington S. Africa 100 E5
Upland U.S.A. 128 E4
Upleta India 82 B5
Upoloksha Rus. Fed. 44 Q3
Upolu i. Samoa 107 I3
Upper Arlington U.S.A. 134 D3
Upper Arrow Lake Canada 120 G5
Upper Chindwin Myanmar see Mawlaik
Upper Fraser Canada 120 F4
Upper Garry Lake Canada 121 K1
Upper Hutt N.Z. 113 E5
Upper Klamath Lake U.S.A. 126 C4
Upper Lough Erne l. U.K. 51 E3
Upper Marlboro U.S.A. 135 G4
Upper Mazinaw Lake Canada 135 G1
Upper Missouri Breaks National Monument nat. park U.S.A. 130 A2
Upper Peirce Reservoir Sing. 71 [inset]
Upper Red Lake U.S.A. 130 E1
Upper Sandusky U.S.A. 134 D3
Upper Saranac Lake U.S.A. 135 H1
Upper Seal Lake Canada see Iberville, Lac d'
Upper Tunguska r. Rus. Fed. see Angara
Upper Volta country Africa see Burkina
Upper Yarra Reservoir Australia 112 B6
Uppinangadi India 84 B3
Uppsala Sweden 45 J7
Upsala Canada 122 C4
Upshi Jammu and Kashmir 82 D2
Upton U.S.A. 135 J2
'Uqayqah, Wādī watercourse Jordan 85 B4
'Uqayribāt Syria 85 C2
Uqlat al 'Udhaybah well Iraq 91 G5
Uqturpan China see Wushi
Uracas vol. N. Mariana Is see Farallon de Pajaros
Urad Houqi China see Sain Us
Ūrāf Iran 88 E4
Urakawa Japan 74 F4
Ural hill Australia 112 C4
Ural r. Kazakh./Rus. Fed. 78 E2
Uralla Australia 112 E3
Ural Mountains Rus. Fed. 41 S2
Ural'sk Kazakh. 78 E1
Ural'skaya Oblast' admin. div. Kazakh. see Zapadnyy Kazakhstan
Ural'skiye Gory mts Rus. Fed. see Ural Mountains
Ural'skiy Khrebet mts Rus. Fed. see Ural Mountains
Urambo Tanz. 99 D4
Uran India 84 B2
Urana Australia 112 C5
Urana, Lake Australia 112 C5
Urandangi Australia 110 B4
Urandi Brazil 145 C1
Uranium City Canada 121 I3
Uranquity Australia 112 C5
Uraricoera r. Brazil 142 F3
Urartu country Asia see Armenia
Ura-Tyube Tajik. see Üroteppa
Uravakonda India 84 C3
Uravan U.S.A. 129 I2
Urawa Japan 75 E6
'Urayf an Nāqah, Jabal hill Egypt 85 B4
Uray'irah Saudi Arabia 88 C5
'Urayq ad Duḩūl des. Saudi Arabia 88 B5
'Urayq Sāqān des. Saudi Arabia 88 B5
Urbana IL U.S.A. 130 F3
Urbana OH U.S.A. 134 D3
Urbino Italy 58 E3
Urbinum Italy see Urbino
Urbs Vetus Italy see Orvieto
Urdoma Rus. Fed. 42 K3
Urdyuzhskoye, Ozero l. Rus. Fed. 42 K2
Urdzhar Kazakh. 80 F2
Ure r. U.K. 48 F4
Ureki Georgia 91 F2
Uren' Rus. Fed. 42 J4
Urengoy Rus. Fed. 64 I3
Uréparapara i. Vanuatu 107 G3
Urewera National Park N.Z. 113 F4
Urfa Turkey see Şanlıurfa
Urfa prov. Turkey see Şanlıurfa
Urga Mongolia see Ulan Bator
Urgal r. Rus. Fed. 74 D2
Urganch Uzbek. see Urgench
Urgench Uzbek. 80 B3
Ürgüp Turkey 90 D3
Urgut Uzbek. 89 G2
Urho China 80 G2
Urho Kekkosen kansallispuisto nat. park Fin. 44 O2
Urie r. U.K. 50 G3
Uril Rus. Fed. 74 C2
Urisino Australia 112 A2
Urjala Fin. 45 M6
Urk Neth. 52 F2
Urkan Rus. Fed. 74 B1
Urkan r. Rus. Fed. 74 B1
Urla Turkey 59 L5
Urlingford Rep. of Ireland 51 E5
Urluk Rus. Fed. 73 J2
Urmā aş Şughrá Syria 85 C1
Urmai China 83 F3
Urmia Iran 88 B2
Urmia, Lake salt l. Iran 88 B2
Urmston Road sea chan. Hong Kong China 77 [inset]
Uromi Nigeria 96 D4
Uroševac Serb. and Mont. 59 I3
Urosozero Rus. Fed. 42 G3
Üroteppa Tajik. 89 H2
Urru Co salt l. China 83 F3
Urt Moron China 80 H4
Uruáchic Mex. 124 F6
Uruaçu Brazil 145 A1
Uruana Brazil 145 A1
Uruapan Baja California Mex. 127 D7
Uruapan Michoacán Mex. 136 D5
Urubamba r. Peru 142 D6
Urucara Brazil 143 G4
Urucu r. Brazil 142 F4
Uruçuca Brazil 145 D1
Uruçuí Brazil 143 J5
Uruçuí, Serra do hills Brazil 143 I5
Urucuia Brazil 145 B2
Urucurituba Brazil 143 G4
Uruguai r. Arg./Uruguay see Uruguay
Uruguaiana Brazil 144 E3
Uruguay r. Arg./Uruguay 144 E4
also known as Uruguai
►Uruguay country S. America 144 E4
South America 9, 140–141
Uruhe China 74 B2
Urumchi China see Ürümqi
Ürümqi China 80 G3
Urundi country Africa see Burundi
Urup, Ostrov i. Rus. Fed. 73 S3
Urusha Rus. Fed. 74 A1
Urutaí Brazil 145 A2
Uryl' Kazakh. 80 G2
Uryupino Rus. Fed. 73 M2
Uryupinsk Rus. Fed. 43 I6
Ürzhar Kazakh. see Urdzhar
Urzhum Rus. Fed. 42 K4
Urziceni Romania 59 L2
Usa Japan 75 C6
Usa r. Rus. Fed. 42 M2
Uşak Turkey 59 M5
Usakos Namibia 100 B1
Usarp Mountains Antarctica 152 H2
Usborne, Mount hill Falkland Is 144 E8
Ushakova, Ostrov i. Rus. Fed. 64 I1
Ushant i. France see Ouessant, Île d'
Ūsharal Kazakh. see Ucharal
Ush-Bel'dyr Rus. Fed. 72 H2
Ushtobe Kazakh. 80 E2
Ush-Tyube Kazakh. see Ushtobe
Ushuaia Arg. 144 C8
Ushumun Rus. Fed. 74 B1
Usingen Germany 53 I4
Usinsk Rus. Fed. 41 R2
Usk U.K. 49 E7
Usk r. U.K. 49 E7
Uskhodni Belarus 45 O10
Uskoplje Bos.-Herz. see Gornji Vakuf
Üsküdar Turkey 59 M4
Uslar Germany 53 J3
Usman' Rus. Fed. 43 H5
Usmanabad India see Osmanabad
Usmas ezers l. Latvia 45 M8
Usogorsk Rus. Fed. 42 K3
Usol'ye-Sibirskoye Rus. Fed. 72 I2
Uspenovka Rus. Fed. 74 B1
Ussel France 56 F4
Ussuri r. China/Rus. Fed. 74 D2
Ussuriysk Rus. Fed. 74 C4
Ust'-Abakanskoye Rus. Fed. see Abakan
Usta Muhammad Pak. 89 H4
Ust'-Balyk Rus. Fed. see Nefteyugansk
Ust'-Donetskiy Rus. Fed. 43 I7
Ust'-Dzheguta Rus. Fed. 91 F1
Ust'-Dzhegutinskaya Rus. Fed. see Ust'-Dzheguta
Ustica, Isola di i. Sicily Italy 58 E5
Ust'-Ilimsk Rus. Fed. 65 L4
Ust'-Ilimskiy Vodokhranilishche resr Rus. Fed. 65 L4
Ust'-Ilych Rus. Fed. 41 R3
Ústí nad Labem Czech Rep. 47 O5
Ustinov Rus. Fed. see Izhevsk
Üstirt plat. Kazakh./Uzbek. see Ustyurt Plateau
Ustka Poland 47 P3
Ust'-Kamchatsk Rus. Fed. 65 R4
Ust'-Kamenogorsk Kazakh. 80 F2
Ust'-Kan Rus. Fed. 80 F1
Ust'-Koksa Rus. Fed. 80 G1
Ust'-Kulom Rus. Fed. 42 L3
Ust'-Kut Rus. Fed. 65 L4
Ust'-Kuyga Rus. Fed. 65 O2
Ust'-Labinsk Rus. Fed. 91 E1
Ust'-Labinskaya Rus. Fed. see Ust'-Labinsk
Ust'-Lyzha Rus. Fed. 42 M2
Ust'-Maya Rus. Fed. 65 O3
Ust'-Nera Rus. Fed. 65 P3
Ust'-Ocheya Rus. Fed. 42 K3
Ust'-Olenek Rus. Fed. 65 M2
Ust'-Omchug Rus. Fed. 65 P3
Ust'-Ordynskiy Rus. Fed. 72 I2
Ust'-Penzhino Rus. Fed. see Kamenskoye
Ust'-Port Rus. Fed. 64 J3
Ustrem Rus. Fed. 41 T3
Ust'-Tsil'ma Rus. Fed. 42 L2
Ust'-Uda Rus. Fed. 72 I2
Ust'-Umalta Rus. Fed. 74 D2
Ust'-Undurga Rus. Fed. 73 L2
Ust'-Ura Rus. Fed. 42 J3
Ust'-Urgal Rus. Fed. 74 D2
Ust'-Usa Rus. Fed. 42 M2
Ust'-Vayen'ga Rus. Fed. 42 I3
Ust'-Voya Rus. Fed. 41 R3
Ust'-Vyyskaya Rus. Fed. 42 J3
Ust'ya r. Rus. Fed. 42 I3
Ust'ye Rus. Fed. 42 H4
Ustyurt, Plato plat. Kazakh./Uzbek. see Ustyurt Plateau
Ustyurt Plateau Kazakh./Uzbek. 78 E2
Ustyurt Platosi plat. Kazakh./Uzbek. see Ustyurt Plateau
Ustyuzhna Rus. Fed. 42 H4
Usulután El Salvador 136 G6
Usumbura Burundi see Bujumbura
Usvyaty Rus. Fed. 42 F5
Utah state U.S.A. 126 F5
Utah Lake U.S.A. 129 H1
Utajärvi Fin. 44 O4
Utashinai Rus. Fed. see Yuzhno-Kuril'sk
'Utaybah, Buḩayrat al imp. l. Syria 85 C3
Utena Lith. 45 N9
Uterlai India 82 B4
Uthai Thani Thai. 70 C4
Uthal Pak. 89 G5
'Uthmānīyah Syria 85 C2
Utiariti Brazil 143 G6
Utica NY U.S.A. 135 H2
Utica OH U.S.A. 134 D3
Utiel Spain 57 F4
Utikuma Lake Canada 120 H4
Utlwanang S. Africa 101 G4
Utrecht Neth. 52 F2
Utrecht S. Africa 101 J4
Utrera Spain 57 D5
Utsjoki Fin. 44 O2
Utsunomiya Japan 75 E5
Utta Rus. Fed. 43 J7
Uttaradit Thai. 70 C3
Uttarakhand state India see Uttaranchal
Uttaranchal state India 82 D3
Uttar Kashi India see Uttarkashi
Uttarkashi India 82 D3
Uttar Pradesh state India 82 D4
Uttoxeter U.K. 49 F6
Uttranchal state India see Uttaranchal
Utubulak China 80 G2
Utupua i. Solomon Is 107 G3
Uummannaq Greenland see Dundas
Uummannaq Fjord inlet Greenland 153 J2
Uummannarsuaq c. Greenland see Farewell, Cape
Uurainen Fin. 44 N5
Uusikaarlepyy Fin. see Nykarleby
Uusikaupunki Fin. 45 L6
Uutapi Namibia 99 B5
Uva Rus. Fed. 42 L4
Uvalde U.S.A. 131 D6
Uval Karabaur hills Kazakh./Uzbek. 91 I2
Uval Muzbel' hills Kazakh. 91 I2
Uvarovo Rus. Fed. 43 I6
Uvéa atoll New Caledonia see Ouvéa
Uvinza Tanz. 99 D4
Uvs Nuur salt l. Mongolia 80 H1
Uwajima Japan 75 D6
'Uwayriḍ, Ḩarrat al lava field Saudi Arabia 86 E4
Uwaysiţ well Saudi Arabia 85 D4
Uweinat, Jebel mt. Sudan 86 C5
Uwi i. Indon. 71 D7
Uxbridge Canada 134 F1
Uxbridge U.K. 49 G7
Uxin Qi China see Dabqig
Uyaly Kazakh. 80 B3
Uyar Rus. Fed. 72 G1
Üydzin Mongolia 72 J4
Uyo Nigeria 96 D4
Uyu Chaung r. Myanmar 70 A1
Uyuni Bol. 142 E8
Uyuni, Salar de salt flat Bol. 138 E8
Uza r. Rus. Fed. 43 J5
►Uzbekistan country Asia 80 B3
Asia 6, 62–63
Ŭzbekiston country Asia see Uzbekistan
Uzbekskaya S.S.R. country Asia see Uzbekistan
Uzbek S.S.R. country Asia see Uzbekistan
Uzen' Kazakh. see Kyzylsay
Uzhgorod Ukr. see Uzhhorod
Uzhhorod Ukr. 43 D6
Užhorod Ukr. see Uzhhorod
Užice Serb. and Mont. 59 H3
Uzlovaya Rus. Fed. 43 H5
Üzümlü Turkey 59 M6
Uzun Uzbek. 89 H2
Uzunköprü Turkey 59 L4
Uzynkair Kazakh. 80 B3

V

Vaaf Atoll Maldives see Felidhu Atoll
Vaajakoski Fin. 44 N5
Vaal r. S. Africa 101 F5
Vaala Fin. 44 O4
Vaalbos National Park S. Africa 100 G5
Vaal Dam S. Africa 101 I4
Vaalwater S. Africa 101 I3
Vaasa Fin. 44 L5
Vaavu Atoll Maldives see Felidhu Atoll
Vabkent Uzbek. 89 G1
Vác Hungary 47 Q7
Vacaria Brazil 145 A5
Vacaria, Campo da plain Brazil 145 A5
Vacaville U.S.A. 128 C2
Vachon r. Canada 123 H1
Vad Rus. Fed. 42 J5
Vad r. Rus. Fed. 43 I5
Vada India 84 B2
Vadla Norway 45 E7
Vadodara India 82 C5
Vadsø Norway 44 P1

►Vaduz Liechtenstein 56 I3
Capital of Liechtenstein.

Værøy i. Norway 44 H3
Vaga r. Rus. Fed. 42 I3
Vågåmo Norway 45 F6
Vaganski Vrh mt. Croatia 58 F2
Vágar i. Faroe Is 44 [inset]
Vägsele Sweden 44 K4
Vágur Faroe Is 44 [inset]
Váh r. Slovakia 47 Q7
Vähäkyrö Fin. 44 M5

►Vaiaku Tuvalu 107 H2
Capital of Tuvalu, on Funafuti atoll.

Vaida Estonia 45 N7
Vaiden U.S.A. 131 F5
Vail U.S.A. 124 F4
Vailly-sur-Aisne France 52 D5
Vaitupu i. Tuvalu 107 H2
Vajrakarur India see Kanur
Vakhsh Tajik. 89 H2
Vakhsh r. Tajik. 89 H2
Vakhstroy Tajik. see Vakhsh
Vakīlābād Iran 88 E4
Valbo Sweden 45 J6
Valcheta Arg. 144 C6
Valdai Hills Rus. Fed. see Valdayskaya Vozvyshennost'
Valday Rus. Fed. 42 G4
Valdayskaya Vozvyshennost' hills Rus. Fed. 42 G4
Valdecañas, Embalse de resr Spain 57 D4
Valdemārpils Latvia 45 M8
Valdemarsvik Sweden 45 J7
Valdepeñas Spain 57 E4
Val-de-Reuil France 52 B5

►Valdés, Península pen. Arg. 144 D6
Lowest point in South America.
South America 138–139

Valdez U.S.A. 118 D3
Valdivia Chile 144 B5
Val-d'Or Canada 122 F4
Valdosta U.S.A. 133 D6
Valdres valley Norway 45 F6
Vale Georgia 91 F2
Vale U.S.A. 126 D3
Valemount Canada 120 G4
Valença Brazil 145 D1
Valence France 56 G4
Valencia Spain 57 F4
València Spain see Valencia
Valencia reg. Spain 57 F4
Valencia Venez. 142 E1
Valencia, Golfo de g. Spain 57 G4
Valencia de Don Juan Spain 57 D2
Valencia Island Rep. of Ireland 51 B6
Valenciennes France 52 D4
Valensole, Plateau de France 56 H5
Valentia Spain see Valencia
Valentin Rus. Fed. 74 D4
Valentine U.S.A. 130 C3
Våler Norway 45 G6
Valera Venez. 142 D2
Vale Verde Brazil 145 D2
Val Grande, Parco Nazionale della nat. park Italy 58 C1
Valjevo Serb. and Mont. 59 H2
Valka Latvia 45 O8
Valkeakoski Fin. 45 N6
Valkenswaard Neth. 52 F3
Valky Ukr. 43 G6
Valkyrie Dome ice feature Antarctica 152 D1
Valladolid Mex. 136 G4
Valladolid Spain 57 D3
Vallard, Lac l. Canada 123 H3
Vall de Uxó Spain 57 F4
Valle Norway 45 E7
Vallecillos Mex. 131 D7
Vallecito Reservoir U.S.A. 129 J3
Valle de la Pascua Venez. 142 E2
Valledupar Col. 142 D1
Vallée-Jonction Canada 123 H5
Valle Fértil, Sierra de mts Arg. 144 C4
Valle Grande Bol. 142 F7
Valle Hermoso Mex. 131 D7
Vallejo U.S.A. 128 B2
Vallenar Chile 144 B3

►Valletta Malta 58 F7
Capital of Malta.

Valley r. Canada 121 L5
Valley U.K. 48 C5
Valley City U.S.A. 130 D2
Valleyview Canada 120 G4
Valls Spain 57 G3
Val Marie Canada 121 J5
Valmiera Latvia 45 N8
Valmy U.S.A. 128 E1
Valnera mt. Spain 57 E2
Valognes France 49 F9
Valona Albania see Vlorë
Valozhyn Belarus 45 O9
Val-Paradis Canada 122 F4
Valparai India 84 C4
Valparaíso Chile 144 B4
Valparaiso U.S.A. 134 B3
Valpoi India 84 B3
Valréas France 56 G4
Vals, Tanjung c. Indon. 69 J8
Valsad India 84 B1
Valspan S. Africa 100 G4
Val'tevo Rus. Fed. 42 J2
Valtimo Fin. 44 P5
Valuyevka Rus. Fed. 43 I7
Valuyki Rus. Fed. 43 H6
Vammala Fin. 45 M6
Van Turkey 91 F3
Van, Lake salt l. Turkey 91 F3
Vanadzor Armenia 91 G2
Van Buren AR U.S.A. 131 E5
Van Buren MO U.S.A. 131 F4
Van Buren OH U.S.A. see Kettering
Vanceburg U.S.A. 134 D4
Vanch Tajik. see Vanj
Vancleve U.S.A. 134 D5
Vancouver Canada 120 F5
Vancouver U.S.A. 126 C3
Vancouver, Mount Canada/U.S.A. 120 B2
Vancouver Island Canada 120 E5
Vanda Fin. see Vantaa
Vandalia IL U.S.A. 130 F4
Vandalia OH U.S.A. 134 C4
Vandekerckhove Lake Canada 121 K3
Vanderbijlpark S. Africa 101 H4
Vanderbilt U.S.A. 134 C1
Vandergrift U.S.A. 134 F3
Vanderhoof Canada 120 E4
Vanderkloof Dam resr S. Africa 100 G6
Vanderlin Island Australia 110 B2
Vanderwagen U.S.A. 129 I4
Van Diemen, Cape N.T. Australia 108 E2
Van Diemen, Cape Qld Australia 110 B3
Van Diemen Gulf Australia 108 F2
Van Diemen's Land state Australia see Tasmania
Vändra Estonia 45 N7
Väner, Lake Sweden see Vänern

►Vänern l. Sweden 45 H7
4th largest lake in Europe.

Vänersborg Sweden 45 H7
Vangaindrano Madag. 99 E6
Van Gölü salt l. Turkey see Van, Lake
Van Horn U.S.A. 127 G7
Vanikoro Islands Solomon Is 107 G3
Vanimo P.N.G. 69 K7
Vanino Rus. Fed. 74 F2
Vanivilasa Sagara resr India 84 C3
Vaniyambadi India 84 C3
Vanj Tajik. 89 H2
Vanna i. Norway 44 K1
Vännäs Sweden 44 K5
Vannes France 56 C3
Vannes, Lac l. Canada 123 I3
Vannovka Kazakh. see Turar Ryskulov
Van Rees, Pegunungan mts Indon. 69 J7
Vanrhynsdorp S. Africa 100 D6
Vansant U.S.A. 134 D5
Vansbro Sweden 45 I6
Vansittart Island Canada 119 J3
Van Starkenborgh Kanaal canal Neth. 52 G1
Vantaa Fin. 45 N6
Van Truer Tableland reg. Australia 109 C6
Vanua Lava i. Vanuatu 107 G3
Vanua Levu i. Fiji 107 H3
►Vanuatu country S. Pacific Ocean 107 G3
Oceania 8, 104–105
Van Wert U.S.A. 134 C3
Vanwyksvlei S. Africa 100 E6
Vanwyksvlei l. S. Africa 100 E6
Văn Yên Vietnam 70 D2
Van Zylsrus S. Africa 100 F4
Varadero Cuba 133 D8
Varahi India 82 B5
Varakļāni Latvia 45 O8
Varalé Côte d'Ivoire 96 C4
Varāmīn Iran 88 C3
Varanasi India 83 E4
Varandey Rus. Fed. 42 M1
Varangerfjorden sea chan. Norway 44 P1
Varanger Halvøya pen. Norway 41 L1
Varangerhalvøya pen. Norway 44 P1
Varaždin Croatia 58 G1
Varberg Sweden 45 H8
Vardar r. Macedonia 59 J4
Varde Denmark 45 F9
Vardenis Armenia 91 G2
Vardø Norway 44 Q1
Varel Germany 53 I1
Varėna Lith. 45 N9
Varese Italy 58 C2
Varfolomeyevka Rus. Fed. 74 D3
Vårgårda Sweden 45 H7
Varginha Brazil 145 B3
Varik Neth. 52 F3
Varillas Chile 144 B2
Varkana Iran see Gorgān
Varkaus Fin. 44 O5
Varna Bulg. 59 L3
Värnamo Sweden 45 I8
Värnäs Sweden 45 H6
Varnavino Rus. Fed. 42 J4
Várnjárg pen. Norway see Varangerhalvøya
Varpaisjärvi Fin. 44 O5
Várpalota Hungary 58 H1
Varsaj Afgh. 89 H2
Varsh, Ozero l. Rus. Fed. 42 J2
Varto Turkey 91 F3
Várzea da Palma Brazil 145 B2
Vasa Fin. see Vaasa
Vasai India 84 B2
Vashka r. Rus. Fed. 42 J2
Vasht Iran see Khāsh
Vasilkov Ukr. see Vasyl'kiv
Vasknarva Estonia 45 O7
Vaslui Romania 59 L1
Vassar U.S.A. 134 D2
Vas-Soproni-síkság hills Hungary 58 G1
Vastan Turkey see Gevaş
Västerås Sweden 45 J7
Västerdalälven r. Sweden 45 I6
Västerfjäll Sweden 44 J3
Västerhaninge Sweden 45 K7
Västervik Sweden 45 J8
Vasto Italy 58 F3
Vasyl'kiv Ukr. 43 F6
Vatan France 56 E3
Vaté i. Vanuatu see Éfaté
Vatersay i. U.K. 50 B4
Vathar India 84 B2
Vathí Greece see Vathy
Vathy Greece 59 L6

►Vatican City Europe 58 E4
Independent papal state, the smallest country in the world.
Europe 5, 38–39

Vaticano, Città del Europe see Vatican City
Vatnajökull ice cap Iceland 40 [inset]
Vatoa i. Fiji 107 I3
Vatra Dornei Romania 59 K1
Vätter, Lake Sweden see Vättern
Vättern l. Sweden 45 I7
Vaughn U.S.A. 127 G6
Vaupés r. Col. 142 E3
Vauquelin r. Canada 122 F3
Vauvert France 56 G5
Vauxhall Canada 121 H5
Vavatenina Madag. 99 E5
Vava'u Group is Tonga 107 I3
Vavitao i. Fr. Polynesia see Raivavae
Vavoua Côte d'Ivoire 96 C4
Vavozh Rus. Fed. 42 K4
Vavuniya Sri Lanka 84 D4
Vawkavysk Belarus 45 N10
Växjö Sweden 45 I8
Vây, Đao i. Vietnam 71 C5
Vayenga Rus. Fed. see Severomorsk
Vazante Brazil 145 B2
Vazáš Sweden see Vittangi
Veaikevárri Sweden see Svappavaara
Veal Vêng Cambodia 71 C4

Vecht r. Neth. 52 G2
also known as Vechte (Germany)
Vechta Germany 53 I2
Vechte r. Germany 53 G2
also known as Vecht (Netherlands)
Veckerhagen (Reinhardshagen) Germany 53 J3
Vedaranniyam India 84 C4
Vedasandur India 84 C4
Veddige Sweden 45 H8
Vedea r. Romania 59 K3
Veedersburg U.S.A. 134 B3
Veendam Neth. 52 G1
Veenendaal Neth. 52 F2
Vega i. Norway 44 G4
Vega U.S.A. 131 C5
Vegreville Canada 121 H4
Vehkalahti Fin. 45 O6
Vehoa Pak. 89 H4
Veinticinco de Mayo Buenos Aires Arg. see 25 de Mayo
Veinticinco de Mayo La Pampa Arg. see 25 de Mayo
Veirwaro Pak. 89 H5
Veitshöchheim Germany 53 J5
Vejle Denmark 45 F9
Vekil'bazar Turkm. 89 F2
Velbert Germany 52 H3
Velbŭzhdki Prokhod pass Bulg./Macedonia 59 J3
Velddrif S. Africa 100 D7
Velebit mts Croatia 58 F2
Velen Germany 52 G3
Velenje Slovenia 58 F1
Veles Macedonia 59 I4
Vélez-Málaga Spain 57 D5
Vélez-Rubio Spain 57 E5
Velhas r. Brazil 145 B2
Velibaba Turkey see Aras
Velika Gorica Croatia 58 G2
Velika Plana Serb. and Mont. 59 I2
Velikaya r. Rus. Fed. 42 K4
Velikaya r. Rus. Fed. 45 P8
Velikaya r. Rus. Fed. 65 S3
Velikaya Kema Rus. Fed. 74 E3
Veliki Preslav Bulg. 59 L3
Velikiye Luki Rus. Fed. 42 F4
Velikiy Novgorod Rus. Fed. 42 F4
Velikiy Ustyug Rus. Fed. 42 J3
Velikonda Range hills India 84 C3
Veliko Tŭrnovo Bulg. 59 K3
Velikoye Rus. Fed. 42 H4
Velikoye, Ozero l. Rus. Fed. 43 I5
Veli Lošinj Croatia 58 F2
Velizh Rus. Fed. 42 F5
Vella Lavella i. Solomon Is 107 F2
Vellar r. India 84 C4
Vellberg Germany 53 J5
Vellmar Germany 53 J3
Vellore India 84 C3
Velpke Germany 53 K2
Vel'sk Rus. Fed. 42 I3
Velsuna Italy see Orvieto
Velten Germany 53 N2
Veluwezoom, Nationaal Park nat. park Neth. 52 F2
Velykyy Tokmak Ukr. see Tokmak
Vel'yu r. Rus. Fed. 42 L3
Vemalwada India 84 C2
Vema Seamount sea feature S. Atlantic Ocean 148 I8
Vema Trench sea feature Indian Ocean 149 M6
Vembe Nature Reserve S. Africa 101 I2
Vempalle India 84 C3
Venado Tuerto Arg. 144 D4
Venafro Italy 58 F4
Venceslau Bráz Brazil 145 A3
Vendinga Rus. Fed. 42 J3
Vendôme France 56 E3
Venegas Mex. 131 C8
Venetia Italy see Venice
Venetie Landing U.S.A. 118 D3
Venev Rus. Fed. 43 H5
Venezia Italy see Venice
Venezia, Golfo di g. Europe see Venice, Gulf of

▶Venezuela country S. America 142 E2
5th most populous country in South America.
South America 9, 140–141

Venezuela, Golfo de g. Venez. 142 D1
Venezuelan Basin sea feature S. Atlantic Ocean 148 D4
Vengurla India 84 B3
Veniaminof Volcano U.S.A. 118 C4
Venice Italy 58 E2
Venice U.S.A. 133 D7
Venice, Gulf of Europe 58 E2
Vénissieux France 56 G4
Venkatapalem India 84 D2
Venkatapuram India 84 D2
Venlo Neth. 52 G3
Vennesla Norway 45 E7
Venray Neth. 52 F3
Venta r. Latvia/Lith. 45 M8
Venta Lith. 45 M8
Ventersburg S. Africa 101 H5
Ventersdorp S. Africa 101 H4
Venterstad S. Africa 101 G6
Ventnor U.K. 49 F8
Ventotene, Isola i. Italy 58 E4
Ventoux, Mont mt. France 56 G4
Ventspils Latvia 45 L8
Ventura U.S.A. 128 D4
Venus Bay Australia 112 B7
Venustiano Carranza Mex. 131 C7
Venustiano Carranza, Presa resr Mex. 131 C7
Vera Arg. 144 D3
Vera Spain 57 F5
Vera Cruz Brazil 145 A3
Vera Cruz Mex. see Veracruz
Veracruz Mex. 136 E5
Veraval India 82 B5
Verbania Italy 58 C2
Vercelli Italy 58 C2
Vercors reg. France 56 G4
Verdalsøra Norway 44 G5
Verde r. Goiás Brazil 145 A2
Verde r. Goiás Brazil 145 A2
Verde r. Goiás Brazil 145 B2
Verde r. Minas Gerais Brazil 145 A2
Verde r. Mex. 127 G8
Verde r. U.S.A. 129 H5
Verden (Aller) Germany 53 J2
Verde Pequeno r. Brazil 145 C1
Verdi U.S.A. 128 D2
Verdon r. France 56 G5
Verdun France 52 F5
Vereeniging S. Africa 101 H4
Vereshchagino Rus. Fed. 41 Q4
Vergennes U.S.A. 135 I1
Véria Greece see Veroia
Verín Spain 57 C3
Veríssimo Brazil 145 A2
Verkhneimbatsk Rus. Fed. 64 J3
Verkhnekolvinsk Rus. Fed. 42 M2
Verkhnespasskoye Rus. Fed. 42 J4
Verkhnetulomskiy Rus. Fed. 44 Q2
Verkhnetulomskoye Vdkhr. res. Rus. Fed. 44 Q2
Verkhnevilyuysk Rus. Fed. 65 N3
Verkhneye Kuyto, Ozero l. Rus. Fed. 44 Q4
Verkhnezeysk Rus. Fed. 73 N2
Verkhniy Vyalozerskiy Rus. Fed. 42 G2
Verkhnyaya Khava Rus. Fed. 43 H6
Verkhnyaya Salda Rus. Fed. 41 S4
Verkhnyaya Tunguska r. Rus. Fed. see Angara
Verkhnyaya Tura Rus. Fed. 41 R4
Verkhoshizhem'ye Rus. Fed. 42 K4
Verkhovazh'ye Rus. Fed. 42 I3
Verkhov'ye Rus. Fed. 43 H5
Verkhoyansk Rus. Fed. 65 O3
Verkhoyanskiy Khrebet mts Rus. Fed. 65 N2
Vermand France 52 D5
Vermelho r. Brazil 145 A1
Vermilion Canada 121 I4
Vermilion Bay U.S.A. 131 F6
Vermilion Cliffs AZ U.S.A. 129 G3
Vermilion Cliffs UT U.S.A. 129 G3
Vermilion Cliffs National Monument nat. park U.S.A. 129 H3
Vermilion Lake U.S.A. 130 E2
Vermillion U.S.A. 130 D3
Vermillion Bay Canada 121 M5
Vermont state U.S.A. 135 I1
Vernadsky research station Antarctica 152 L2
Vernal U.S.A. 129 I1
Verner Canada 122 E5
Verneuk Pan salt pan S. Africa 100 E5
Vernon Canada 120 G5
Vernon France 52 B5
Vernon AL U.S.A. 131 F5
Vernon IN U.S.A. 134 C4
Vernon TX U.S.A. 131 D5
Vernon UT U.S.A. 129 G1
Vernon Islands Australia 108 E3
Vernoye Rus. Fed. 74 C2
Vernyy Kazakh. see Almaty
Vero Beach U.S.A. 133 D7
Veroia Greece 59 J4
Verona Italy 58 D2
Verona U.S.A. 134 F4
Versailles France 52 C6
Versailles IN U.S.A. 134 C4
Versailles KY U.S.A. 134 C4
Versailles OH U.S.A. 134 C3
Versec Serb. and Mont. see Vršac
Versmold Germany 53 I2
Vert, Île i. Canada 123 H4
Vertou France 56 D3
Verulam S. Africa 101 J5
Verulamium U.K. see St Albans
Verviers Belgium 52 F4
Vervins France 52 D5
Verwood Canada 121 J5
Verzy France 52 E5
Vescovato Corsica France 56 I5
Vesele Ukr. 43 G7
Veselyy Rus. Fed. 43 I7
Veshenskaya Rus. Fed. 43 I6
Vesle r. France 52 D5
Veslyana r. Rus. Fed. 42 L3
Vesontio France see Besançon
Vesoul France 56 H3
Vesselyy Yar Rus. Fed. 74 D4
Vessem Neth. 52 F3
Vesterålen is Norway 44 H2
Vesterålsfjorden sea chan. Norway 44 H2
Vestertana Norway 44 O1
Vestfjorddalen valley Norway 45 F7
Vestfjorden sea chan. Norway 44 H3
Véstia Brazil 145 A3
Vestmanna Faroe Is 44 [inset]
Vestmannaeyjar Iceland 44 [inset]
Vestmannaeyjar is Iceland 44 [inset]
Vestnes Norway 44 E5
Vesturhorn hd Iceland 44 [inset]
Vesuvio vol. Italy see Vesuvius
Vesuvius vol. Italy 58 F4
Ves'yegonsk Rus. Fed. 42 H4
Veszprém Hungary 58 G1
Veteli Fin. 44 M5
Veteran Canada 121 I4
Vetlanda Sweden 45 I8
Vetluga Rus. Fed. 42 J4
Vetluga r. Rus. Fed. 42 J4
Vetluzhskiy Kostromskaya Oblast' Rus. Fed. 42 J4
Vetluzhskiy Nizhegorodskaya Oblast' Rus. Fed. 42 J4
Vettore, Monte mt. Italy 58 E3
Veurne Belgium 52 C3
Vevay U.S.A. 134 C4
Vevey Switz. 56 H3
Vexin Normand reg. France 52 B5
Veyo U.S.A. 129 G3
Vézère r. France 56 E4
Vezirköprü Turkey 90 D2
Vialar Alg. see Tissemsilt
Viamao Brazil 145 A5
Viana Espírito Santo Brazil 145 C3
Viana Maranhão Brazil 143 J4
Viana do Castelo Port. 57 B3
Vianen Neth. 52 F3
Viangchan Laos see Vientiane
Viangphoukha Laos 70 C2
Vianópolis Brazil 145 A2
Viareggio Italy 58 D3
Viborg Denmark 45 F8
Viborg Rus. Fed. see Vyborg
Vibo Valentia Italy 58 G5
Vic Spain 57 H3
Vicam Mex. 127 F8
Vicecomodoro Marambio research station Antarctica see Marambio
Vicente, Point U.S.A. 128 D5
Vicente Guerrero Mex. 127 D7
Vicenza Italy 58 D2
Vich Spain see Vic
Vichada r. Col. 142 E3
Vichadero Uruguay 144 F4
Vichy France 56 F3
Vicksburg AZ U.S.A. 129 G5
Vicksburg MS U.S.A. 131 F5
Viçosa Brazil 145 C3
Victor, Mount Antarctica 152 D2
Victor Harbor Australia 111 B7
Victoria Arg. 144 D4
Victoria r. Australia 108 E3
Victoria state Australia 112 B6

▶Victoria Canada 120 F5
Provincial capital of British Columbia.

Victoria Chile 144 B5
Victoria Malaysia see Labuan
Victoria Malta 58 F6

▶Victoria Seychelles 149 L6
Capital of the Seychelles.

Victoria TX U.S.A. 131 D6
Victoria VA U.S.A. 135 F5
Victoria prov. Zimbabwe see Masvingo

▶Victoria, Lake Africa 98 D4
Largest lake in Africa and 3rd in the world.
Africa 92–93
World 12–13

Victoria, Lake Australia 111 C7
Victoria, Mount Fiji see Tomanivi
Victoria, Mount Myanmar 70 A2
Victoria, Mount P. N.G. 69 L8
Victoria and Albert Mountains Canada 119 K2
Victoria Falls Zambia/Zimbabwe 99 C5
Victoria Harbour sea chan. Hong Kong China see Hong Kong Harbour

▶Victoria Island Canada 118 H2
3rd largest island in North America.

Victoria Land coastal area Antarctica 152 H2
Victoria Peak Belize 136 G5
Victoria Peak hill Hong Kong China 77 [inset]
Victoria Range mts N.Z. 113 D6
Victoria River Downs Australia 108 E4
Victoriaville Canada 123 H5
Victoria West S. Africa 100 F6
Victorica Arg. 144 C5
Victorville U.S.A. 128 E4
Victory Downs Australia 109 F6
Vidalia U.S.A. 131 F6
Vidal Junction U.S.A. 129 F4
Videle Romania 59 K2
Vidisha India 82 D5
Vidlin U.K. 50 [inset]
Vidlitsa Rus. Fed. 42 G3
Viechtach Germany 53 M5
Viedma Arg. 144 D6
Viedma, Lago l. Arg. 144 B7
Viejo, Cerro mt. Mex. 127 E7
Vielank Germany 53 L1
Vielsalm Belgium 52 F4
Vienenburg Germany 53 K3

▶Vienna Austria 47 P6
Capital of Austria.

Vienna MO U.S.A. 130 F4
Vienna WV U.S.A. 134 E4
Vienne France 56 G4
Vienne r. France 56 E3

▶Vientiane Laos 70 C3
Capital of Laos.

Vieques i. Puerto Rico 137 K5
Vieremä Fin. 44 O5
Viersen Germany 52 G3
Vierzon France 56 F3
Viesca Mex. 131 C7
Viesīte Latvia 45 N8
Vieste Italy 58 G4
Vietas Sweden 44 K3
Việt Nam country Asia see Vietnam
▶Vietnam country Asia 70 D3
Asia 6, 62–63
Việt Tri Vietnam 70 D2
Vieux Comptoir, Lac du l. Canada 122 F3
Vieux-Fort Canada 123 K4
Vieux Poste, Pointe du pt Canada 123 J4
Vigan Phil. 69 G3
Vigevano Italy 58 C2
Vigia Brazil 143 I4
Vignacourt France 52 C4
Vignemale mt. France 54 D3
Vignola Italy 58 D2
Vigo Spain 57 B2
Vihanti Fin. 44 N4
Vihari Pak. 89 I4
Vihti Fin. 45 N6
Viipuri Rus. Fed. see Vyborg
Viitasaari Fin. 44 N5
Vijayadurg India 84 B2
Vijayanagaram India see Vizianagaram
Vijayapati India 84 C4
Vijayawada India 84 D2
Vík Iceland 44 [inset]
Vikajärvi Fin. 44 O3
Vikeke East Timor see Viqueque
Viking Canada 121 I4
Vikna i. Norway 44 G4
Vikøyri Norway 45 E6
Vila Vanuatu see Port Vila
Vila Alferes Chamusca Moz. see Guija
Vila Bittencourt Brazil 142 E4
Vila Bugaço Angola see Camanongue
Vila Cabral Moz. see Lichinga
Vila da Ponte Angola see Kuvango
Vila de Aljustrel Angola see Cangamba
Vila de Almoster Angola see Chiange
Vila de João Belo Moz. see Xai-Xai
Vila de María Arg. 144 D3
Vila de Trego Morais Moz. see Chókwé
Vila Fontes Moz. see Caia
Vila Franca de Xira Port. 57 B4
Vilagarcía de Arousa Spain 57 B2
Vila Gomes da Costa Moz. 101 K3
Vilalba Spain 57 C2
Vila Luísa Moz. see Marracuene
Vila Marechal Carmona Angola see Uíge
Vila Miranda Moz. see Macaloge
Vilanandro, Tanjona pt Madag. 99 E5
Vilanculos Moz. 101 L1
Vila Nova de Gaia Port. 57 B3
Vilanova i la Geltrú Spain 57 G3
Vila Pery Moz. see Chimoio
Vila Real Port. 57 C3
Vilar Formoso Port. 57 C3
Vila Salazar Angola see N'dalatando
Vila Salazar Zimbabwe see Sango
Vila Teixeira de Sousa Angola see Luau
Vila Velha Brazil 145 C3
Vilcabamba, Cordillera mts Peru 142 D6
Vil'cheka, Zemlya i. Rus. Fed. 64 H1
Viled' r. Rus. Fed. 42 J3
Vileyka Belarus see Vilyeyka
Vil'gort Rus. Fed. 42 K3
Vilhelmina Sweden 44 J4
Vilhena Brazil 142 F6
Viliya r. Belarus/Lith. see Neris
Viljandi Estonia 45 N7
Viljoenskroon S. Africa 101 H4
Vilkaviškis Lith. 45 M9
Vilkija Lith. 45 M9
Vil'kitskogo, Proliv strait Rus. Fed. 65 K2
Vilkovo Ukr. see Vylkove
Villa Abecia Bol. 142 E8
Villa Ahumada Mex. 127 G7
Villa Ángela Arg. 144 D3
Villa Bella Bol. 142 E6
Villa Bens Morocco see Tarfaya
Villablino Spain 57 C2
Villacañas Spain 57 E4
Villach Austria 47 N7
Villacidro Sardinia Italy 58 C5
Villa Cisneros W. Sahara see Ad Dakhla
Villa Constitución Mex. see Ciudad Constitución
Villa Dolores Arg. 144 C4
Villagarcía de Arosa Spain see Vilagarcía de Arousa
Villagrán Mex. 131 D7
Villaguay Arg. 144 E4
Villahermosa Mex. 136 F5
Villa Insurgentes Mex. 127 F8
Villajoyosa Spain see Villajoyosa - La Vila Joíosa
Villajoyosa - La Vila Joíosa Spain 57 F4
Villaldama Mex. 131 C7
Villa Mainero Mex. 131 D7
Villa María Arg. 144 D4
Villa Montes Bol. 142 F8
Villa Nora S. Africa 101 I2
Villanueva de la Serena Spain 57 D4
Villanueva de los Infantes Spain 57 E4
Villanueva-y-Geltrú Spain see Vilanova i la Geltrú
Villa Ocampo Arg. 144 E3
Villa Ocampo Mex. 131 B7
Villa Ojo de Agua Arg. 144 D3
Villaputzu Sardinia Italy 58 C5
Villa Regina Arg. 144 C5
Villarrica Para. 144 E3
Villarrica, Lago l. Chile 144 B5
Villarrica, Parque Nacional nat. park Chile 144 B5
Villarrobledo Spain 57 E4
Villas U.S.A. 135 H4
Villasalazar Zimbabwe see Sango
Villa San Giovanni Italy 58 F5
Villa Sanjurjo Morocco see Al Hoceima
Villa San Martín Arg. 144 D3
Villa Unión Arg. 144 C3
Villa Unión Coahuila Mex. 131 C6
Villa Unión Durango Mex. 131 B8
Villa Unión Sinaloa Mex. 136 C4
Villa Valeria Arg. 144 D4
Villavicencio Col. 142 D3
Villazon Bol. 142 E8
Villefranche-sur-Saône France 56 G4
Ville-Marie Canada see Montréal
Villena Spain 57 F4
Villeneuve-sur-Lot France 56 E4
Villeneuve-sur-Yonne France 56 F2
Villers-Cotterêts France 52 D5
Villers-sur-Mer France 49 G9
Villerupt France 52 F5
Villeurbanne France 56 G4
Villiers S. Africa 101 I4
Villingen Germany 47 L6
Villuppuram India see Villupuram
Villupuram India 84 C4
Vilna Canada 121 I4
Vilna Lith. see Vilnius

▶Vilnius Lith. 45 N9
Capital of Lithuania.

Vil'nyans'k Ukr. 43 G7
Vilppula Fin. 44 N5
Vils r. Germany 53 L5
Vils r. Germany 53 N6
Vilvoorde Belgium 52 E4
Vilyeyka Belarus 45 O9
Vilyuy r. Rus. Fed. 65 N3
Vilyuyskoye Vodokhranilishche resr Rus. Fed. 65 M3
Vimmerby Sweden 45 I8
Vimy France 52 C4
Vina r. Cameroon 97 E4
Vina U.S.A. 128 B2
Viña del Mar Chile 144 B4
Vinalhaven Island U.S.A. 132 G2
Vinaròs Spain 57 G3
Vinaroz Spain see Vinaròs
Vincelotte, Lac l. Canada 123 G3
Vincennes U.S.A. 134 B4
Vincennes Bay Antarctica 152 F2
Vinchina Arg. 144 C3
Vindelälven r. Sweden 44 K5
Vindeln Sweden 44 K4
Vindhya Range hills India 82 C5
Vindobona Austria see Vienna
Vine Grove U.S.A. 134 C5
Vineland U.S.A. 135 H4
Vinh Vietnam 70 D3
Vinh Linh Vietnam 70 D3
Vinh Long Vietnam 71 D5
Vinh Thuc, Đao i. Vietnam 70 D2
Vinita U.S.A. 131 E4
Vinjhan India 82 B5
Vinland i. Canada see Newfoundland
Vinnitsa Ukr. see Vinnytsya
Vinnytsya Ukr. 43 F6
Vinogradov Ukr. see Vynohradiv

▶Vinson Massif mt. Antarctica 152 L1
Highest mountain in Antarctica.

Vinstra Norway 45 F6
Vinton U.S.A. 130 E3
Vinukonda India 84 C2
Violeta Cuba see Primero de Enero
Vipperow Germany 53 M1
Viqueque East Timor 108 D2
Virac Phil. 69 G4
Viramgam India 82 C5
Viranşehir Turkey 91 E3
Virawah Pak. 89 H5
Virchow, Mount hill Australia 108 B5
Virdel India 82 C5
Virden Canada 121 K5
Virden U.S.A. 129 I5
Vire France 56 D2
Virei Angola 99 B5
Virgem da Lapa Brazil 145 C2
Virgilina U.S.A. 135 F5
Virgin r. U.S.A. 129 F3
Virginia Rep. of Ireland 51 E4
Virginia S. Africa 101 H5
Virginia U.S.A. 130 F4
Virginia state U.S.A. 134 F5
Virginia Beach U.S.A. 135 H5
Virginia City MT U.S.A. 126 F3
Virginia City NV U.S.A. 128 D2
Virginia Falls Canada 120 E2

▶Virgin Islands (U.K.) terr. West Indies 137 L5
United Kingdom Overseas Territory.
North America 9, 116–117

▶Virgin Islands (U.S.A.) terr. West Indies 137 L5
United States Unincorporated Territory.
North America 9, 116–117

Virgin Mountains U.S.A. 129 F3
Virginópolis Brazil 145 C2
Virkkala Fin. 45 N6
Virôchey Cambodia 71 D4
Viroqua U.S.A. 130 F3
Virovitica Croatia 58 G2
Virrat Fin. 44 M5
Virton Belgium 52 F5
Virtsu Estonia 45 M7
Virudhunagar India 84 C4
Virudunagar India see Virudhunagar
Virunga, Parc National des nat. park Dem. Rep. Congo 98 C4
Vis i. Croatia 58 G3
Visaginas Lith. 45 O9
Visakhapatnam India see Vishakhapatnam
Visalia U.S.A. 128 D3
Visapur India 84 B2
Visayan Sea Phil. 69 G4
Visbek Germany 53 I2
Visby Sweden 45 K8
Viscount Melville Sound sea chan. Canada 119 G2
Visé Belgium 52 F4
Vise, Ostrov i. Rus. Fed. 64 I2
Viseu Brazil 143 I4
Viseu Port. 57 C3
Vishakhapatnam India 84 D2
Vishera r. Rus. Fed. 41 R4
Vishera r. Rus. Fed. 42 L3
Višķi Latvia 45 O8
Visnagar India 82 C5
Viso, Monte mt. Italy 58 B2
Visoko Bos.-Herz. 58 H3
Visp Switz. 56 H3
Visselhövede Germany 53 J2
Vista U.S.A. 128 E5
Vista Lake U.S.A. 128 D4
Vistonida, Limni lag. Greece 59 K4
Vistula r. Poland 47 Q3
Vitebsk Belarus see Vitsyebsk
Viterbo Italy 58 E3
Vitichi Bol. 142 E8
Vitigudino Spain 57 C3
Viti Levu i. Fiji 107 H3
Vitimskoye Ploskogor'ye plat. Rus. Fed. 73 K2
Vitória Brazil 145 C3
Vitória da Conquista Brazil 145 C1
Vitoria-Gasteiz Spain 57 E2
Vitória Seamount sea feature S. Atlantic Ocean 148 F7
Vitré France 56 D2
Vitry-en-Artois France 52 C4
Vitry-le-François France 52 E6
Vitsyebsk Belarus 43 F5
Vittangi Sweden 44 L3
Vittel France 56 G2
Vittoria Sicily Italy 58 F6
Vittorio Veneto Italy 58 E2
Viveiro Spain 57 C2
Vivero Spain see Viveiro
Vivo S. Africa 101 I2
Vizagapatam India see Vishakhapatnam
Vizcaíno, Desierto de des. Mex. 127 E8
Vizcaíno, Sierra mts Mex. 127 E8
Vize Turkey 59 L4
Vizhas r. Rus. Fed. 42 J2
Vizianagaram India 84 D2
Vizinga Rus. Fed. 42 K3
Vlaardingen Neth. 52 E3
Vlădeasa, Vârful mt. Romania 59 J1
Vladikavkaz Rus. Fed. 91 G2
Vladimir Primorskiy Kray Rus. Fed. 74 D4
Vladimir Vladimirskaya Oblast' Rus. Fed. 42 I4
Vladimiro-Aleksandrovskoye Rus. Fed. 74 D4
Vladimir-Volynskiy Ukr. see Volodymyr-Volyns'kyy
Vladivostok Rus. Fed. 74 C4
Vlakte S. Africa 101 I3
Vlasotince Serb. and Mont. 59 J3
Vlas'yevo Rus. Fed. 74 F1
Vlieland i. Neth. 52 E1
Vlissingen Neth. 52 D3
Vlora Albania see Vlorë
Vlorë Albania 59 H4
Vlotho Germany 53 I2
Vlotslavsk Poland see Włocławek
Vltava r. Czech Rep. 47 O5
Vöcklabruck Austria 47 N6
Vodlozero, Ozero l. Rus. Fed. 42 H3
Voe U.K. 50 [inset]
Voerendaal Neth. 52 F4
Vogelkop Peninsula Indon. see Doberai, Jazirah
Vogelsberg hills Germany 53 I4
Voghera Italy 58 C2
Vohburg an der Donau Germany 53 L6
Vohémar Madag. see Iharaña
Vohenstrauß Germany 53 M5
Vohibinany Madag. see Ampasimanolotra
Vohimarina Madag. see Iharaña
Vohimena, Tanjona c. Madag. 99 E6
Vohipeno Madag. 99 E6
Vöhl Germany 53 I3
Võhma Estonia 45 N7
Voinjama Liberia 96 C4
Vojens Denmark 45 F9
Vojvodina prov. Serb. and Mont. 59 H2
Vokhma Rus. Fed. 42 J4
Voknavolok Rus. Fed. 44 Q4
Vol' r. Rus. Fed. 42 L3
Volcano Bay Japan see Uchiura-wan

▶Volcano Islands Japan 69 K2
Part of Japan.

Volda Norway 44 E5
Vol'dino Rus. Fed. 42 L3
Volendam Neth. 52 F2
Volga Rus. Fed. 42 H4

▶Volga r. Rus. Fed. 43 J7
Longest river and largest drainage basin in Europe.
Europe 36–37

Volga Upland hills Rus. Fed. see Privolzhskaya Vozvyshennost'
Volgodonsk Rus. Fed. 43 I7
Volgograd Rus. Fed. 43 J6
Volgogradskoye Vodokhranilishche resr Rus. Fed. 43 J6
Völkermarkt Austria 47 O7
Volkhov Rus. Fed. 42 G4
Volkhov r. Rus. Fed. 42 G3
Völklingen Germany 52 G5
Volkovysk Belarus see Vawkavysk
Volksrust S. Africa 101 I4
Vol'no-Nadezhdinskoye Rus. Fed. 74 C4
Volnovakha Ukr. 43 H7
Vol'nyansk Ukr. see Vil'nyans'k
Volochanka Rus. Fed. 64 K2
Volochisk Ukr. see Volochys'k
Volochys'k Ukr. 43 E6
Volodars'ke Ukr. 43 H7
Volodarskoye Kazakh. see Saumalkol'
Volodymyr-Volyns'kyy Ukr. 43 E6
Vologda Rus. Fed. 42 H4
Volokolamsk Rus. Fed. 42 G4
Volokovaya Rus. Fed. 42 K2
Volos Greece 59 J5
Volosovo Rus. Fed. 45 P7
Volot Rus. Fed. 42 F4
Volovo Rus. Fed. 43 H5
Volozhin Belarus see Valozhyn
Volsinii Italy see Orvieto
Vol'sk Rus. Fed. 43 J5

▶Volta, Lake resr Ghana 96 D4
5th largest lake in Africa.

Volta Blanche r. Burkina/Ghana see White Volta
Voltaire, Cape Australia 108 D3
Volta Redonda Brazil 145 B3
Volturno r. Italy 58 E4
Volubilis tourist site Morocco 54 C5
Volvi, Limni l. Greece 59 J4
Volzhsk Rus. Fed. 42 K5
Volzhskiy Samarskaya Oblast' Rus. Fed. 43 K5
Volzhskiy Volgogradskaya Oblast' Rus. Fed. 43 J6
Vondanka Rus. Fed. 42 J4
Vontimitta India 84 C3
Vopnafjörður Iceland 44 [inset]
Vopnafjörður b. Iceland 44 [inset]
Vörå Fin. 44 M5
Voranava Belarus 45 N9
Voreioi Sporades is Greece 59 J5
Voríai Sporádhes is Greece see Voreioi Sporades
Voring Plateau sea feature N. Atlantic Ocean 148 I1
Vorjing mt. India 83 H3
Vorkuta Rus. Fed. 64 H3
Vormsi i. Estonia 45 M7
Vorona r. Rus. Fed. 43 I6
Voronezh Rus. Fed. 43 H6

Voronezh r. Rus. Fed. 43 H6
Voronov, Mys pt Rus. Fed. 42 I2
Vorontsovo-Aleksandrovskoye Rus. Fed. see Zelenokumsk
Voroshilov Rus. Fed. see Ussuriysk
Voroshilovgrad Ukr. see Luhans'k
Voroshilovsk Rus. Fed. see Stavropol'
Voroshilovsk Ukr. see Alchevs'k
Vorotynets Rus. Fed. 42 J4
Vorozhba Ukr. 43 G6
Vorpommersche Boddenlandschaft, Nationalpark nat. park Germany 47 N3
Vorskla r. Rus. Fed. 43 G6
Võrtsjärv l. Estonia 45 N7
Võru Estonia 45 O8
Vorukh Tajik. 89 H2
Vosburg S. Africa 100 F6
Vose Tajik. 89 H2
Vosges mts France 56 H3
Voskresensk Rus. Fed. 43 H5
Voskresenskoye Rus. Fed. 42 H4
Voss Norway 45 E6
Vostochno-Sakhalinskiy Gory mts Rus. Fed. 74 F2
Vostochno-Sibirskoye More sea Rus. Fed. see East Siberian Sea
Vostochnyy Kirovskaya Oblast' Rus. Fed. 42 L4
Vostochnyy Sakhalinskaya Oblast' Rus. Fed. 74 F2
Vostochnyy Chink Ustyurta esc. Uzbek. 80 A3
Vostochnyy Sayan mts Rus. Fed. 72 G2

▶Vostok research station Antarctica 152 F1
Lowest recorded screen temperature in the world.

Vostok Primorskiy Kray Rus. Fed. 74 D3
Vostok Sakhalinskaya Oblast' Rus. Fed. see Neftegorsk
Vostok Island Kiribati 151 J6
Vostroye Rus. Fed. 42 J3
Votkinsk Rus. Fed. 41 Q4
Votkinskoye Vodokhranilishche resr Rus. Fed. 41 R4
Votuporanga Brazil 145 A3
Vouziers France 52 E5
Voves France 56 E2
Voyageurs National Park U.S.A. 130 E1
Voynitsa Rus. Fed. 44 Q4
Vöyri Fin. see Vörå
Voyvozh Rus. Fed. 42 L3
Vozhayel' Rus. Fed. 42 K3
Vozhe, Ozero l. Rus. Fed. 42 H3
Vozhega Rus. Fed. 42 I3
Vozhgaly Rus. Fed. 42 K4
Voznesens'k Ukr. 43 F7
Vozonin Trough sea feature Arctic Ocean 153 F1
Vozrozhdeniya, Ostrov i. Uzbek. 80 A3
Vozzhayevka Rus. Fed. 74 C2
Vrangel' Rus. Fed. 74 D4
Vrangelya, Mys pt Rus. Fed. 74 E1
Vranje Serb. and Mont. 59 I3
Vratnik pass Bulg. 59 L3
Vratsa Bulg. 59 J3
Vrbas Serb. and Mont. 59 H2
Vrede S. Africa 101 I4
Vredefort S. Africa 101 H4
Vredenburg S. Africa 100 C7
Vredendal S. Africa 100 D6
Vresse Belgium 52 E5
Vriddhachalam India 84 C4
Vries Neth. 52 G1
Vrigstad Sweden 45 I8
Vršac Serb. and Mont. 59 I2
Vryburg S. Africa 100 G4
Vryheid S. Africa 101 J4
Vsevidof, Mount vol. U.S.A. 118 B4
Vsevolozhsk Rus. Fed. 42 F3
Vu Ban Vietnam 70 D2
Vučitrn Serb. and Mont. 59 I3
Vukovar Croatia 59 H2
Vuktyl' Rus. Fed. 41 R3
Vukuzakhe S. Africa 101 I4
Vulcan Canada 120 H5
Vulcan Island P. N.G. see Manam Island
Vulcano, Isola i. Italy 58 F5
Vu Liêt Vietnam 70 D3
Vulture Mountains U.S.A. 129 G5
Vung Tau Vietnam 71 D5
Vuohijärvi Fin. 45 O6
Vuolijoki Fin. 44 O4
Vuollerim Sweden 44 L3
Vuostimo Fin. 44 O3
Vurnary Rus. Fed. 42 J5
Vushtri Serb. and Mont. see Vučitrn
Vvedenovka Rus. Fed. 74 C2
Vyara India 82 C5
Vyarkhowye Belarus see Ruba
Vyatka Rus. Fed. see Kirov
Vyatka r. Rus. Fed. 42 K5
Vyatskiye Polyany Rus. Fed. 42 K4
Vyazemskiy Rus. Fed. 74 D3
Vyaz'ma Rus. Fed. 43 G5
Vyazniki Rus. Fed. 42 I4
Vyazovka Rus. Fed. 43 J5
Vyborg Rus. Fed. 45 P6
Vychegda r. Rus. Fed. 42 J3
Vychegodskiy Rus. Fed. 42 J3
Vyerkhnyadzvinsk Belarus 45 O9
Vyetryna Belarus 45 P9
Vygozero, Ozero l. Rus. Fed. 42 G3
Vyksa Rus. Fed. 43 I5
Vylkove Ukr. 59 M2
Vym' r. Rus. Fed. 42 K3
Vynohradiv Ukr. 43 D6
Vypin Island India 84 C4
Vypolzovo Rus. Fed. 42 G4
Vyritsa Rus. Fed. 45 Q7
Vyrnwy, Lake U.K. 49 D6
Vyselki Rus. Fed. 43 H7
Vysha Rus. Fed. 43 I5
Vyshhorod Ukr. 43 F6
Vyshnevolotskaya Gryada ridge Rus. Fed. 42 G4
Vyshniy-Volochek Rus. Fed. 42 G4
Vyškov Czech Rep. 47 P6
Vysokaya Gora Rus. Fed. 42 K5
Vysokogorniy Rus. Fed. 74 E2
Vystupovychi Ukr. 43 F6
Vytegra Rus. Fed. 42 H3
Vyya r. Rus. Fed. 42 J3
Vyžuona r. Lith. 45 N9

W

Wa Ghana 96 C3
Waal r. Neth. 52 E3
Waalwijk Neth. 52 F3
Waat Sudan 86 D8
Wabag P.N.G. 69 K8
Wabakimi Lake Canada 122 C4
Wabasca r. Canada 120 H3
Wabasca-Desmarais Canada 120 H4
Wabash U.S.A. 134 C3
Wabash r. U.S.A. 134 A5
Wabasha U.S.A. 130 E2
Wabassi r. Canada 122 D4
Wabatongushi Lake Canada 122 D4
Wabē Gestro r. Eth. 78 D6
Wabē Shebelē Wenz r. Eth. 98 E3
Wabigoon Lake Canada 121 M5
Wabowden Canada 121 L4
Wabrah well Saudi Arabia 88 B5
Wabu China 77 H1
Wabuk Point Canada 122 D3
Wabush Canada 123 I3
Waccasassa Bay U.S.A. 133 D6
Wächtersbach Germany 53 J4
Waco Canada 123 I4
Waco U.S.A. 131 D6
Waconda Lake U.S.A. 130 D4
Wad Pak. 89 G5
Wadbilliga National Park Australia 112 D6
Waddān Libya 55 H6
Waddell Dam U.S.A. 129 G5
Waddeneilanden Neth. see West Frisian Islands
Waddenzee sea chan. Neth. 52 E2
Waddington, Mount Canada 120 E5
Waddinxveen Neth. 52 E2
Wadebridge U.K. 49 C8
Wadena Canada 121 K5
Wadena U.S.A. 130 E2
Wadern Germany 52 G5
Wadesville U.S.A. 134 B4
Wadeye Australia 108 E3
Wadgassen Germany 52 G5
Wadhwan India see Surendranagar
Wadi India 84 C2
Wādī as Sīr Jordan 85 B4
Wadi Halfa Sudan 86 D5
Wad Medani Sudan 86 D7
Wad Rawa Sudan 86 D6
Wadsworth U.S.A. 128 D2
Waenhuiskrans S. Africa 100 E8
Wafangdian China 73 M5
Wafra Kuwait see Al Wafrah
Wagenfeld Germany 53 I2
Wagenhoff Germany 53 K2
Wagga Wagga Australia 112 C5
Wagner U.S.A. 130 D3
Wagoner U.S.A. 131 E4
Wagon Mound U.S.A. 127 G5
Wah Pak. 89 I3
Wahai Indon. 69 H7
Wāhāt Jālū Libya 97 F2
Wahemen, Lac l. Canada 123 H3
Wahiawa HI U.S.A. 127 [inset]
Wahlhausen Germany 53 J3
Wahpeton U.S.A. 130 D2
Wahran Alg. see Oran
Wah Wah Mountains U.S.A. 125 G2
Wai India 84 B2
Waialua HI U.S.A. 127 [inset]
Waiau N.Z. see Franz Josef Glacier
Waiau r. N.Z. 113 D6
Waiblingen Germany 53 J6
Waidhofen an der Ybbs Austria 47 O7
Waigeo i. Indon. 69 I7
Waiheke Island N.Z. 113 E3
Waikabubak Indon. 108 B2
Waikaia r. N.Z. 113 B7
Waikari N.Z. 113 D6
Waikerie Australia 111 B7
Waikouaiti N.Z. 113 C7
Wailuku HI U.S.A. 127 [inset]
Waimangaroa N.Z. 113 C5
Waimarama N.Z. 113 F4
Waimate N.Z. 113 C7
Waimea HI U.S.A. 127 [inset]
Wainganga r. India 84 C2
Waingapu Indon. 108 C2
Wainhouse Corner U.K. 49 C8
Waini Point Guyana 143 G2
Wainwright Canada 121 I4
Wainwright U.S.A. 118 C2
Waiouru N.Z. 113 E4
Waipahi N.Z. 113 B8
Waipaoa r. N.Z. 113 F4
Waipara N.Z. 113 D6
Waipawa N.Z. 113 F4
Waipukurau N.Z. 113 F4
Wairarapa, Lake N.Z. 113 E5
Wairau r. N.Z. 113 E5
Wairoa N.Z. 113 F4
Wairoa r. N.Z. 113 F4
Waitahanui N.Z. 113 F4
Waitahuna N.Z. 113 B7
Waitakaruru N.Z. 113 E3
Waitaki r. N.Z. 113 C7
Waitangi N.Z. 107 I6
Waite River Australia 108 F5
Waiuku N.Z. 113 E3
Waiwera South N.Z. 113 B8
Waiyang China 77 H3
Wajima Japan 75 E5
Wajir Kenya 98 E3
Waka Indon. 108 C2
Wakasa-wan b. Japan 75 D6
Wakatipu, Lake N.Z. 113 B7
Wakaw Canada 121 J4
Wakayama Japan 75 D6
Wake Atoll terr. N. Pacific Ocean see Wake Island
WaKeeney U.S.A. 130 D4
Wakefield N.Z. 113 D5
Wakefield U.K. 48 F5
Wakefield MI U.S.A. 130 F2
Wakefield RI U.S.A. 135 J3
Wakefield VA U.S.A. 135 G5

▶Wake Island terr. N. Pacific Ocean 150 H4
United States Unincorporated Territory.

Wakema Myanmar 70 A3
Wakhan reg. Afgh. 89 I2
Wakkanai Japan 74 F3
Wakkerstroom S. Africa 101 J4
Wakool Australia 112 B5
Wakool r. Australia 112 A5
Wakuach, Lac l. Canada 123 I3
Waku-Kungo Angola 99 B5
Wałbrzych Poland 47 P5
Walcha Australia 112 E3
Walcott U.S.A. 126 G4
Walcourt Belgium 52 E4
Wałcz Poland 47 P4
Waldburg Range mts Australia 109 B6
Walden U.S.A. 135 H3
Waldenbuch Germany 53 J6
Waldenburg Poland see Wałbrzych
Waldkraiburg Germany 47 N6
Waldo U.S.A. 134 D3
Waldoboro U.S.A. 135 K1
Waldorf U.S.A. 135 G4
Waldport U.S.A. 126 B3
Waldron U.S.A. 131 E5
Waldron, Cape Antarctica 152 F2
Walebing Australia 109 B7
Walêg China 76 D2
Wales admin. div. U.K. 49 D6
Walgaon India 82 D5
Walgett Australia 112 D3
Walgreen Coast Antarctica 152 K1
Walhalla MI U.S.A. 134 B2
Walhalla ND U.S.A. 130 D1
Walikale Dem. Rep. Congo 97 F5
Walingai P.N.G. 69 L8
Walker r. Australia 110 A2
Walker watercourse Australia 109 F6
Walker MI U.S.A. 134 C2
Walker MN U.S.A. 130 E2
Walker r. U.S.A. 128 D2
Walker Bay S. Africa 100 D8
Walker Creek r. Australia 110 C3
Walker Lake Canada 121 L4
Walker Lake U.S.A. 128 D2
Walker Pass U.S.A. 128 D4
Walkersville U.S.A. 135 G4
Walkerton Canada 134 E1
Walkerton U.S.A. 134 B3
Wall, Mount hill Australia 108 B5
Wallaby Island Australia 110 C2
Wallace ID U.S.A. 126 D3
Wallace NC U.S.A. 133 E5
Wallace VA U.S.A. 134 D5
Wallaceburg Canada 134 D2
Wallal Downs Australia 108 C4
Wallangarra Australia 112 E2
Wallaroo Australia 111 B7
Wallasey U.K. 48 D5
Walla Walla Australia 112 C5
Walla Walla U.S.A. 126 D3
Walldürn Germany 53 J5
Wallekraal S. Africa 100 C6
Wallendbeen Australia 112 D5
Wallingford U.K. 49 F7
Wallis, Îles is Wallis and Futuna Is 107 I3

▶Wallis and Futuna Islands terr. S. Pacific Ocean 107 I3
French Overseas Territory.
Oceania 8, 104–105

Wallis et Futuna, Îles terr. S. Pacific Ocean see Wallis and Futuna Islands
Wallis Islands Wallis and Futuna Is see Wallis, Îles
Wallis Lake inlet Australia 112 F4
Wallops Island U.S.A. 135 H5
Wallowa Mountains U.S.A. 126 D3
Walls U.K. 50 [inset]
Walls of Jerusalem National Park Australia 111 [inset]
Wallumbilla Australia 111 E5
Walmsley Lake Canada 121 I2
Walney, Isle of i. U.K. 48 D4
Walnut Creek U.S.A. 128 B3
Walnut Grove U.S.A. 128 C2
Walnut Ridge U.S.A. 131 F4
Walong India 83 I3
Walpole U.S.A. 135 I2
Walsall U.K. 49 F6
Walsenburg U.S.A. 127 G5
Walsh U.S.A. 131 C4
Walsrode Germany 53 J2
Waltair India 84 D2
Walterboro U.S.A. 133 D5
Walters U.S.A. 131 D5
Walter's Range hills Australia 112 B2
Walthall U.S.A. 131 F5
Waltham U.S.A. 135 J2
Walton IN U.S.A. 134 B3
Walton KY U.S.A. 134 C4
Walton NY U.S.A. 135 H2
Walton WV U.S.A. 134 E4
Walvisbaai Namibia see Walvis Bay
Walvisbaai b. Namibia see Walvis Bay
Walvis Bay Namibia 100 B2
Walvis Bay b. Namibia 100 B2
Walvis Ridge sea feature S. Atlantic Ocean 148 H8
Wama Afgh. 89 H3
Wamba Équateur Dem. Rep. Congo 97 F5
Wamba Orientale Dem. Rep. Congo 98 C3
Wamba Nigeria 96 D4
Wampum U.S.A. 134 E3
Wampusirpi Hond. 137 H5
Wamsutter U.S.A. 126 G4
Wana Pak. 89 H3
Wanaaring Australia 112 B2
Wanaka N.Z. 113 B7
Wanaka, Lake N.Z. 113 B7
Wan'an China 77 G3
Wanapitei Lake Canada 122 E5
Wanbi Australia 111 C7
Wanbrow, Cape N.Z. 113 C7
Wanda Shan mts China 74 D3
Wandering River Canada 121 H4
Wandersleben Germany 53 K4
Wandlitz Germany 53 N2
Wando S. Korea 75 B6
Wandoan Australia 111 E5
Wanganui N.Z. 113 E4
Wanganui r. N.Z. 113 E4
Wangaratta Australia 112 C6
Wangcang China 76 E1
Wangda China see Zogang
Wangdain China 83 G3
Wangdue Phodrang Bhutan 83 G4
Wanggamet, Gunung mt. Indon. 108 C2
Wanggao China 77 F3
Wang Gaxun China 83 I1
Wangiwangi i. Indon. 69 G8
Wangkui China 74 B3
Wangmo China 76 E3
Wangqing China 74 C4
Wangwu Shan mts China 77 F1
Wangying China see Huaiyin
Wangziguan China 76 E1
Wanham Canada 120 G4
Wan Hsa-la Myanmar 70 B2
Wanie-Rukula Dem. Rep. Congo 98 C3
Wankaner India 82 B5
Wankie Zimbabwe see Hwange
Wanlaweyn Somalia 98 E3
Wanna Germany 53 I1
Wanna Lakes salt flat Australia 109 E7
Wannian China 77 H2
Wanning China 77 F5
Wanroij Neth. 52 F3
Wanshan China 77 F3
Wanshan Qundao is China 77 G4
Wansheng China 76 E2
Wanshengchang China see Wansheng
Wantage U.K. 49 F7
Wanxian Chongqing China see Shahe
Wanxian Chongqing China 77 F2
Wanyuan China 77 F1
Wanzai China 77 G2
Wanze Belgium 52 F4
Wapakoneta U.S.A. 134 C3
Wapawekka Lake Canada 121 J4
Wapello U.S.A. 130 F3
Wapikaimaski Lake Canada 122 C4
Wapikopa Lake Canada 122 C3
Wapiti r. Canada 120 G4
Wapusk National Park Canada 121 M3
Waqên China 76 D1
Waqf aş Şawwān, Jibāl hills Jordan 85 C4
War U.S.A. 134 E5
Warab Sudan 86 C8
Warangal India 84 C2
Waranga Reservoir Australia 112 B6
Waratah Bay Australia 112 B7
Warbreccan Australia 110 C5
Warburg Germany 53 J3
Warburton Australia 109 D6
Warburton watercourse Australia 111 B5
Warburton Bay Canada 121 I2
Warche r. Belgium 52 F4
Ward, Mount N.Z. 113 B6
Warden S. Africa 101 I4
Wardenburg Germany 53 I1
Wardha India 84 C1
Wardha r. India 84 C2
Ward Hill hill U.K. 50 F2
Ward Hunt, Cape P.N.G. 69 L8
Ware Canada 120 E3
Ware U.S.A. 135 I2
Wareham U.K. 49 E8
Waremme Belgium 52 F4
Waren Germany 53 M1
Warendorf Germany 53 H3
Warginburra Peninsula Australia 110 E4
Wargla Alg. see Ouargla
Warialda Australia 112 E2
Warin Chamrap Thai. 70 D4
Warkum Neth. see Workum
Warkworth U.K. 48 F3
Warli China see Walêg
Warloy-Baillon France 52 C4
Warman Canada 121 J4
Warmbad Namibia 100 D5
Warmbad S. Africa 101 I3
Warmbaths S. Africa see Warmbad
Warminster U.K. 49 E7
Warminster U.S.A. 135 H3
Warmond Neth. 52 E2
Warm Springs NV U.S.A. 128 E2
Warm Springs VA U.S.A. 134 F4
Warmwaterberg mts S. Africa 96 E7
Warner Canada 121 H5
Warner Lakes U.S.A. 126 D4
Warner Mountains U.S.A. 126 C4
Warnes Bol. 142 F7
Warning, Mount Australia 112 F2
Waronda India 84 C2
Warora India 84 C1
Warra Australia 112 E1
Warragamba Reservoir Australia 112 E5
Warragul Australia 112 B7
Warrambool r. Australia 112 C3
Warrandirinna, Lake salt flat Australia 111 B5
Warrandyte Australia 112 B6
Warrawagine Australia 108 C5
Warrego r. Australia 112 B3
Warrego Range hills Australia 110 D5
Warren Australia 112 C3
Warren AR U.S.A. 131 E5
Warren MI U.S.A. 134 D2
Warren MN U.S.A. 130 D1
Warren OH U.S.A. 134 E3
Warren PA U.S.A. 134 F3
Warren Hastings Island Palau see Merir
Warren Island U.S.A. 120 C4
Warrenpoint U.K. 51 F3
Warrensburg MO U.S.A. 130 E4
Warrensburg NY U.S.A. 135 I2
Warrenton S. Africa 100 G5
Warrenton GA U.S.A. 133 D5
Warrenton MO U.S.A. 130 F4
Warrenton VA U.S.A. 135 G4
Warri Nigeria 96 D4
Warriners Creek watercourse Australia 111 B6
Warrington N.Z. 113 C7
Warrington U.K. 48 E5
Warrington U.S.A. 133 C6
Warrnambool Australia 111 C8
Warroad U.S.A. 130 E1
Warrumbungle National Park Australia 112 D3

▶Warsaw Poland 47 R4
Capital of Poland.

Warsaw IN U.S.A. 134 C3
Warsaw KY U.S.A. 134 C4
Warsaw MO U.S.A. 130 E4
Warsaw NY U.S.A. 135 F2
Warsaw VA U.S.A. 135 G5
Warshiikh Somalia 98 E3
Warstein Germany 53 I3
Warszawa Poland see Warsaw
Warta r. Poland 47 O4
Warwick Australia 112 F2
Warwick U.K. 49 F6
Warwick U.S.A. 135 J3
Warzhong China 76 D2
Wasaga Beach Canada 134 E1
Wasatch Range mts U.S.A. 126 F5
Wasbank S. Africa 101 J5
Wasco U.S.A. 128 D4
Washburn ND U.S.A. 130 C2
Washburn WI U.S.A. 130 F2
Washim India 84 C1
Washimeska r. Canada 123 G4

▶Washington DC U.S.A. 135 G4
Capital of the United States of America.

Washington GA U.S.A. 133 D5
Washington IA U.S.A. 130 F3
Washington IN U.S.A. 134 B4
Washington MO U.S.A. 130 F4
Washington NC U.S.A. 132 E5
Washington NJ U.S.A. 135 H3
Washington PA U.S.A. 134 E3
Washington UT U.S.A. 129 G3
Washington state U.S.A. 126 C3
Washington, Cape Antarctica 152 H2
Washington, Mount U.S.A. 135 J1
Washington Court House U.S.A. 134 D4
Washington Island U.S.A. 132 C2
Washington Land reg. Greenland 119 L2
Washir Afgh. 89 F3
Washita r. U.S.A. 131 D5
Washpool National Park Australia 112 F2
Washtucna U.S.A. 126 D3
Washuk Pak. 89 G5
Wasi India 84 B2
Wāsiʻ Saudi Arabia 88 B5
Wāsiʻ well Saudi Arabia 88 C6
Waskaganish Canada 122 F4
Waskagheganish Canada see Waskaganish
Waskaiowaka Lake Canada 121 L3
Waskey, Mount U.S.A. 118 C4
Wassenaar Neth. 52 E2
Wasser Namibia 100 D4
Wasserkuppe hill Germany 53 J4
Wassertrüdingen Germany 53 K5
Wassuk Range mts U.S.A. 128 D2
Wasua P.N.G. 69 K8
Wasum P.N.G. 69 L8
Waswanipi r. Canada 122 F4
Waswanipi, Lac l. Canada 122 F4
Watam P.N.G. 69 K7
Watampone Indon. 69 G7
Watapi Lake Canada 121 I4
Watarrka National Park Australia 109 E6
Watenstadt-Salzgitter Germany see Salzgitter
Waterbury CT U.S.A. 135 I3
Waterbury VT U.S.A. 135 I1
Waterbury Lake Canada 121 J3
Water Cays i. Bahamas 133 E8
Waterdown Canada 134 F2
Wateree r. U.S.A. 133 D5
Waterfall U.S.A. 120 C4
Waterford Rep. of Ireland 51 E5
Waterford PA U.S.A. 134 F3
Waterford WI U.S.A. 134 A2
Waterford Harbour Rep. of Ireland 51 F5
Watergrasshill Rep. of Ireland 51 D5
Waterhen Lake Canada 121 L4
Waterloo Australia 108 E4
Waterloo Belgium 52 E4
Waterloo Ont. Canada 134 E2
Waterloo Que. Canada 135 I1
Waterloo IA U.S.A. 130 E3
Waterloo IL U.S.A. 130 F4
Waterloo NY U.S.A. 135 G2
Waterlooville U.K. 49 F8
Waterton Lakes National Park Canada 120 H5
Watertown NY U.S.A. 135 H2
Watertown SD U.S.A. 130 D2
Watertown WI U.S.A. 130 F3
Waterval-Boven S. Africa 101 J3
Water Valley U.S.A. 131 F5
Waterville ME U.S.A. 135 K1
Waterville WA U.S.A. 126 C3
Watford Canada 134 E2
Watford U.K. 49 G7
Watford City U.S.A. 130 C2
Wathaman r. Canada 121 K3
Wathaman Lake Canada 121 K3
Watheroo National Park Australia 109 A7
Wathlingen Germany 53 K2
Watino Canada 120 G4
Watīr, Wādī watercourse Egypt 85 B5
Watkins Glen U.S.A. 135 G2
Watling Island Bahamas see San Salvador
Watmuri Indon. 108 E1
Watonga U.S.A. 131 D5
Watrous Canada 121 J5
Watrous U.S.A. 127 G6
Watseka U.S.A. 134 B3
Watsi Kengo Dem. Rep. Congo 97 F5
Watson r. Australia 110 C2
Watson Canada 121 J4
Watson Lake Canada 120 D2
Watsontown U.S.A. 135 G3
Watsonville U.S.A. 128 C3
Watten U.K. 50 F2
Watterson Lake Canada 121 L2
Watton U.K. 49 H6
Watts Bar Lake resr U.S.A. 132 C5
Wattsburg U.S.A. 134 F2
Watubela, Kepulauan is Indon. 69 I7
Wau P.N.G. 69 L8
Wau Sudan 86 C8
Waubay Lake U.S.A. 130 D2
Wauchope N.S.W. Australia 108 F3
Wauchope N.T. Australia 108 F5
Waukaringa Australia 111 B7
Waukarlycarly, Lake salt flat Australia 108 C5
Waukegan U.S.A. 134 B2
Waukesha U.S.A. 134 A2
Waupaca U.S.A. 130 F2
Waupun U.S.A. 130 F3
Waurika U.S.A. 131 D5
Wausau U.S.A. 130 F2
Wausaukee U.S.A. 132 C2
Wauseon U.S.A. 134 C3
Wautoma U.S.A. 130 F2
Wave Hill Australia 108 E4
Waveney r. U.K. 49 I6
Waverly IA U.S.A. 130 E3
Waverly NY U.S.A. 135 G2
Waverly OH U.S.A. 134 D4
Waverly TN U.S.A. 132 C4
Waverly VA U.S.A. 135 G5
Wavre Belgium 52 E4
Waw Myanmar 70 B3
Wawa Canada 122 D5
Wawalalindu Indon. 69 G7
Wāw al Kabīr Libya 97 E2
Wawasee, Lake U.S.A. 134 C3
Wawo Indon. 69 G7
Waxahachie U.S.A. 131 D5
Waxü China 76 D1
Waxxari China 80 G4
Way, Lake salt flat Australia 109 C6
Waycross U.S.A. 133 D6
Wayland KY U.S.A. 134 D5
Wayland MI U.S.A. 134 C2
Wayne NE U.S.A. 130 D3
Wayne WV U.S.A. 134 D4
Waynesboro GA U.S.A. 133 D5
Waynesboro MS U.S.A. 131 F6
Waynesboro TN U.S.A. 132 C5
Waynesboro VA U.S.A. 135 F4
Waynesburg U.S.A. 134 E4
Waynesville MO U.S.A. 130 E4
Waynesville NC U.S.A. 132 D5
Waynoka U.S.A. 131 D4
Waza, Parc National de nat. park Cameroon 97 E3
Wāzah Khwāh Afgh. see Wazi Khwa
Wazi Khwa Afgh. 89 H3
Wazirabad Pak. 89 I3
W du Niger, Parcs Nationaux du nat. park Niger 96 D3
We, Pulau i. Indon. 71 A6
Weagamow Lake Canada 121 N4
Weam P.N.G. 69 K8
Wear r. U.K. 48 F4
Weare U.S.A. 135 J2
Weatherford U.S.A. 131 D5
Weaver Lake Canada 121 L4
Weaverville U.S.A. 126 C4
Webb, Mount hill Australia 108 E5
Webequie Canada 122 D3
Weber, Mount Canada 120 D4
Weber Basin sea feature Laut Banda 150 E6

▶Webi Shabeelle r. Somalia 98 E3
5th longest river in Africa.

Webster IN U.S.A. 134 C4
Webster MA U.S.A. 135 J2
Webster SD U.S.A. 130 D2
Webster City U.S.A. 130 E3
Webster Springs U.S.A. 134 E4
Wecho Lake Canada 120 H2
Wedau P.N.G. 110 E1
Weddell Abyssal Plain sea feature Southern Ocean 152 A2
Weddell Island Falkland Is 140 D8
Weddell Sea Antarctica 152 A2
Wedderburn Australia 112 A6
Weddin Mountains National Park Australia 112 D4
Wedel (Holstein) Germany 53 J1
Wedge Mountain Canada 120 F5
Wedowee U.S.A. 133 C5
Weedville U.S.A. 135 F3
Weenen S. Africa 101 J5
Weener Germany 53 H1
Weert Neth. 52 F3
Weethalle Australia 112 C4
Wee Waa Australia 112 D3
Wegberg Germany 52 G3
Węgorzewo Poland 47 R3
Weichang China 73 L4
Weida Germany 53 M4
Weidenberg Germany 53 L5
Weiden in der Oberpfalz Germany 53 M5
Weidongmen China see Qianjin
Weifang China 73 L5
Weihai China 73 M5
Wei He r. Shaanxi China 76 F1
Wei He r. China 77 G1
Weilburg Germany 53 I4
Weilmoringle Australia 112 C2
Weimar Germany 53 L4
Weinan China 77 F1
Weinheim Germany 53 I5
Weining China 76 E3
Weinsberg Germany 53 J5
Weipa Australia 110 C2
Weiqu China see Chang'an
Weir r. Australia 112 D2
Weir River Canada 121 M3
Weirton U.S.A. 134 E3
Weiser U.S.A. 126 D3
Weishan China 76 D3
Weishan Hu l. China 77 H1
Weishi China 77 G1
Weiße Elster r. Germany 53 L3
Weißenburg in Bayern Germany 53 K5

Weißenfels Germany 53 L3
Weißkugel mt. Austria/Italy 47 M7
Weissrand Mountains Namibia 100 D3
Weiterstadt Germany 53 I5
Weitzel Lake Canada 121 J3
Weixi China 76 C3
Weixin China 76 E3
Weiya China 80 H3
Weiyuan Gansu China 76 E1
Weiyuan Sichuan China 76 E2
Weiyuan Yunnan China see Jinggu
Weiyuan Jiang r. China 76 D4
Weiz Austria 47 O7
Weizhou China see Wenchuan
Weizhou Dao i. China 77 F4
Wejherowo Poland 47 Q3
Wekilbazar Turkm. see Vekil'bazar
Wekusko Canada 121 L4
Wekusko Lake Canada 121 L4
Wekweti Canada 120 H1
Welatam Myanmar 70 B1
Welbourn Hill Australia 109 F6
Welch U.S.A. 134 E5
Weld U.S.A. 135 J1
Weldiya Eth. 98 D2
Welford National Park Australia 110 C5
Welk'ït'ē Eth. 98 D3
Welkom S. Africa 101 H4
Welland Canada 134 F2
Welland r. U.K. 49 G6
Welland Canal Canada 134 F2
Wellesley Canada 134 E2
Wellesley Islands Australia 110 B3
Wellesley Lake Canada 120 B2
Wellfleet U.S.A. 135 J3
Wellin Belgium 52 F4
Wellingborough U.K. 49 G6
Wellington Australia 112 D4
Wellington Canada 135 G2

▶Wellington N.Z. 113 E5
Capital of New Zealand.

Wellington S. Africa 100 D7
Wellington England U.K. 49 D8
Wellington England U.K. 49 E6
Wellington CO U.S.A. 126 G4
Wellington IL U.S.A. 134 B3
Wellington KS U.S.A. 131 D4
Wellington NV U.S.A. 128 D2
Wellington OH U.S.A. 134 D3
Wellington TX U.S.A. 131 C5
Wellington UT U.S.A. 129 H2
Wellington, Isla i. Chile 144 B7
Wellington Range hills N.T. Australia 108 F3
Wellington Range hills W.A. Australia 109 C6
Wells Canada 120 F4
Wells U.K. 49 E7
Wells U.S.A. 126 E4
Wells, Lake salt flat Australia 109 C6
Wellsboro U.S.A. 135 G3
Wellsburg U.S.A. 134 E3
Wellsford N.Z. 113 E3
Wells-next-the-Sea U.K. 49 H6
Wellston U.S.A. 134 C1
Wellsville U.S.A. 135 G2
Wellton U.S.A. 129 F5
Wels Austria 47 O6
Welshpool U.K. 49 D6
Welsickendorf Germany 53 N3
Welwitschia Namibia see Khorixas
Welwyn Garden City U.K. 49 G7
Welzheim Germany 53 J6
Wem U.K. 49 E6
Wembesi S. Africa 101 I5
Wembley Canada 120 G4
Wemindji Canada 122 F3
Wenatchee U.S.A. 126 C3
Wenatchee Mountains U.S.A. 126 C3
Wenbu China see Nyima
Wenchang Hainan China 77 F5
Wenchang Sichuan China see Zitong
Wenchow China see Wenzhou
Wenchuan China 76 D2
Wendelstein Germany 53 L5
Wenden Germany 53 H4
Wenden Latvia see Cēsis
Wenden U.S.A. 129 G5
Wendover U.S.A. 129 F1
Weng'an China 76 E3
Wengshui China 76 C2
Wengyuan China 77 G3
Wenhua China see Weishan
Wenlan China see Mengzi
Wenling China 77 I2
Wenlock r. Australia 110 C2
Wenping China see Ludian
Wenquan Guizhou China 76 E2
Wenquan Henan China see Wenxian
Wenquan Hubei China see Yingshan

▶Wenquan Qinghai China 83 G2
Highest settlement in the world.

Wenquan Xinjiang China 80 F3
Wenshan China 76 E4
Wenshui China 76 E2
Wensum r. U.K. 49 I6
Wentorf bei Hamburg Germany 53 K1
Wentworth Australia 111 C7
Wenxi China 77 F1
Wenxian Gansu China 76 E1
Wenxian Henan China 77 G1
Wenxing China see Xiangyin
Wenzhou China 77 I3
Wenzlow Germany 53 M2
Wepener S. Africa 101 H5
Wer India 82 D4
Werben (Elbe) Germany 53 L2
Werda Botswana 100 F3
Werdau Germany 53 M4
Werdēr Eth. 98 E3
Werder Germany 53 M2
Werdohl Germany 53 H3
Werl Germany 53 H3
Wernberg-Köblitz Germany 53 M5
Werne Germany 53 H3
Wernecke Mountains Canada 120 B1
Wernigerode Germany 53 K3
Werra r. Germany 53 J3
Werris Creek Australia 112 E3
Wertheim Germany 53 J5
Wervik Belgium 52 D4
Wesel Germany 52 G3
Wesel-Datteln-Kanal canal Germany 52 G3
Wesenberg Germany 53 M1
Wesendorf Germany 53 K2
Weser r. Germany 53 I1
Weser sea chan. Germany 53 I1
Wesergebirge hills Germany 53 I2
Weslaco U.S.A. 131 D7
Weslemkoon Lake Canada 135 G1
Wesleyville Canada 123 L4
Wessel, Cape Australia 110 B1
Wessel Islands Australia 110 B1
Wesselsbron S. Africa 101 H4
Wesselton S. Africa 101 I4
Wessington Springs U.S.A. 130 D2
Westall, Point Australia 109 F8
West Allis U.S.A. 134 A2
West Antarctica reg. Antarctica 152 J1
West Australian Basin sea feature Indian Ocean 149 O7

▶West Bank terr. Asia 85 B3
Territory occupied by Israel.
Asia 6

West Bay Canada 123 K3
West Bay inlet U.S.A. 133 C6
West Bend U.S.A. 134 A2
West Bengal state India 83 F5
West Branch U.S.A. 134 C1
West Bromwich U.K. 49 F6
Westbrook U.S.A. 135 J2
West Burke U.S.A. 135 J1
West Burra i. U.K. 50 [inset]
Westbury U.K. 49 E7
West Caicos i. Turks and Caicos Is 133 F8
West Cape Howe Australia 109 B8
West Caroline Basin sea feature N. Pacific Ocean 150 F5
West Chester U.S.A. 135 H4
Westcliffe U.S.A. 127 G5
West Coast National Park S. Africa 100 D7
West End Bahamas 133 E7
Westerburg Germany 53 H4
Westerholt Germany 53 H1
Westerland Germany 47 L3
Westerlo Belgium 52 E3
Westerly U.S.A. 135 J3
Western r. Canada 121 J1
Western Australia state Australia 109 C6
Western Cape prov. S. Africa 100 E7
Western Desert Egypt 90 C6
Western Dvina r. Europe see Zapadnaya Dvina
Western Ghats mts India 84 B3
Western Port b. Australia 112 B7

▶Western Sahara terr. Africa 96 B2
Disputed territory (Morocco).
Africa 7, 94–95

Western Samoa country S. Pacific Ocean see Samoa
Western Sayan Mountains reg. Rus. Fed. see Zapadnyy Sayan
Westerschelde est. Neth. 52 D3
Westerstede Germany 53 H1
Westerville U.S.A. 134 D3
Westerwald hills Germany 53 H4
West Falkland i. Falkland Is 144 D8
West Fargo U.S.A. 130 D2
West Fayu atoll Micronesia 69 L5
Westfield IN U.S.A. 134 B3
Westfield MA U.S.A. 135 I2
Westfield NY U.S.A. 134 F2
Westfield PA U.S.A. 135 G3
West Frisian Islands Neth. 52 E1
Westgat sea chan. Neth. 52 G1
Westgate Australia 112 C1
West Glacier U.S.A. 126 E2
West Grand Lake U.S.A. 132 H2
West Hartford U.S.A. 135 I3
Westhausen Germany 53 K6
West Haven U.S.A. 135 I3
Westhill U.K. 50 G3
Westhope U.S.A. 130 C1
West Ice Shelf Antarctica 152 E2
West Indies is Caribbean Sea 137 J4
West Island India 71 A4
Westkapelle Neth. 52 D3
West Kazakhstan Oblast admin. div. Kazakh. see Zapadnyy Kazakhstan
West Kingston U.S.A. 135 J3
West Lafayette U.S.A. 134 B3
West Lamma Channel Hong Kong China 77 [inset]
Westland Australia 110 C4
Westland National Park N.Z. 113 C6
Westleigh S. Africa 101 H4
Westleton U.K. 49 I6
West Liberty U.S.A. 134 D5
West Linton U.K. 50 F5
West Loch Roag b. U.K. 50 C2
Westlock Canada 120 H4
West Lorne Canada 134 E2
West Lunga National Park Zambia 99 C5
West MacDonnell National Park Australia 109 F5
West Malaysia pen. Malaysia see Peninsular Malaysia
Westmalle Belgium 52 E3
Westmar Australia 112 D1
West Mariana Basin sea feature N. Pacific Ocean 150 F4
West Memphis U.S.A. 131 F5
Westminster U.S.A. 135 G4
Westmoreland Australia 110 B3
Westmoreland U.S.A. 134 B5
Westmorland U.S.A. 129 F5
Weston OH U.S.A. 134 D3
Weston WV U.S.A. 134 E4
Weston-super-Mare U.K. 49 E7
West Palm Beach U.S.A. 133 D7
West Plains U.S.A. 131 F4
West Point pt Australia 111 [inset]
West Point CA U.S.A. 128 C2
West Point KY U.S.A. 134 C5
West Point MS U.S.A. 131 F5
West Point NE U.S.A. 130 D3
West Point VA U.S.A. 135 G5
West Point Lake resr U.S.A. 133 C5
Westport Canada 135 G1
Westport N.Z. 113 C5
Westport Rep. of Ireland 51 C4
Westport CA U.S.A. 128 B2
Westport KY U.S.A. 134 C4
Westport NY U.S.A. 135 I1
Westray Canada 121 K4
Westray i. U.K. 50 F1
Westray Firth sea chan. U.K. 50 F1
Westree Canada 122 E5
West Rutland U.S.A. 135 I2
West Salem U.S.A. 134 D3
West Siberian Plain Rus. Fed. 64 J3
West-Skylge Neth. see West-Terschelling
West Stewartstown U.S.A. 135 J1
West-Terschelling Neth. 52 F1
West Topsham U.S.A. 135 I1
West Union IA U.S.A. 130 F3
West Union IL U.S.A. 134 B4
West Union OH U.S.A. 134 D4
West Union WV U.S.A. 134 E4
West Valley City U.S.A. 129 H1
Westville U.S.A. 134 B3
West Virginia state U.S.A. 134 E4
Westwood U.S.A. 128 C1
West Wyalong Australia 112 C4
West York U.S.A. 135 G4
Westzaan Neth. 52 E2
Wetar i. Indon. 108 D1
Wetar, Selat sea chan. East Timor/Indon. 108 D2
Wetaskiwin Canada 120 H4
Wete Tanz. 99 D4
Wetter r. Germany 53 I4
Wettin Germany 53 L3
Wetumpka U.S.A. 133 C5
Wetwun Myanmar 70 B2
Wetzlar Germany 53 I4
Wewahitchka U.S.A. 133 C6
Wewak P.N.G. 69 K7
Wewoka U.S.A. 131 D5
Wexford Rep. of Ireland 51 F5
Wexford Harbour b. Rep. of Ireland 51 F5
Weyakwin Canada 121 J4
Weybridge U.K. 49 G7
Weyburn Canada 121 K5
Weyhe Germany 53 I2
Weymouth U.K. 49 E8
Weymouth U.S.A. 135 J2
Wezep Neth. 52 G2
Whakaari i. N.Z. 113 F3
Whakatane N.Z. 113 F3
Whalan Creek r. Australia 112 D2
Whale r. Canada see La Baleine, Rivière à
Whalsay i. U.K. 50 [inset]
Whampoa China see Huangpu
Whangamata N.Z. 113 E3
Whanganui National Park N.Z. 113 E4
Whangarei N.Z. 113 E2
Whapmagoostui Canada 122 F3
Wharfe r. U.K. 48 F5
Wharfedale valley U.K. 48 F4
Wharton U.S.A. 131 D6
Wharton Lake Canada 121 L1
Wha Ti Canada 120 G2
Wheatland IN U.S.A. 134 B4
Wheatland WY U.S.A. 126 G4
Wheaton IL U.S.A. 134 A3
Wheaton MN U.S.A. 130 D2
Wheaton-Glenmont U.S.A. 135 G4
Wheeler U.S.A. 131 C5
Wheeler Lake Canada 120 H2
Wheeler Lake resr U.S.A. 133 C5
Wheeler Peak NM U.S.A. 127 G5
Wheeler Peak NV U.S.A. 129 F2
Wheelersburg U.S.A. 134 D4
Wheeling U.S.A. 134 E3
Whernside hill U.K. 48 E4
Whinham, Mount Australia 109 E6
Whiskey Jack Lake Canada 121 K3
Whitburn U.K. 50 F5
Whitby Canada 135 F2
Whitby U.K. 48 G4
Whitchurch U.K. 49 E6
Whitchurch-Stouffville Canada 134 F2
White r. Canada 122 D4
White r. Canada/U.S.A. 120 B2
White r. AR U.S.A. 125 I5
White r. AR U.S.A. 131 F5
White r. CO U.S.A. 129 I1
White r. IN U.S.A. 134 B4
White r. MI U.S.A. 134 B2
White r. NV U.S.A. 129 F3
White r. SD U.S.A. 130 D3
White r. VT U.S.A. 135 I2
White watercourse U.S.A. 129 H5
White, Lake salt flat Australia 108 E5
White Bay Canada 123 K4
White Butte mt. U.S.A. 130 C2
White Canyon U.S.A. 129 H3
White Cloud U.S.A. 134 C2
Whitecourt Canada 120 H4
Whiteface Mountain U.S.A. 135 I1
Whitefield U.S.A. 135 J1
Whitefish r. Canada 120 E1
Whitefish U.S.A. 126 E2
Whitefish Bay U.S.A. 134 B1
Whitefish Lake Canada 121 J2
Whitefish Point U.S.A. 132 C2
Whitehall Rep. of Ireland 51 E5
Whitehall U.K. 50 G1
Whitehall NY U.S.A. 135 I2
Whitehall WI U.S.A. 130 F2
Whitehaven U.K. 48 D4
Whitehead U.K. 51 G3
White Hill hill Canada 123 J5
Whitehill U.K. 49 G7

▶Whitehorse Canada 120 C2
Territorial capital of Yukon.

White Horse U.S.A. 129 J4
White Horse, Vale of valley U.K. 49 F7
White Horse Pass U.S.A. 129 F1
White House U.S.A. 134 B5
White Island Antarctica 152 D2
White Island N.Z. see Whakaari
White Lake Ont. Canada 122 D4
White Lake Ont. Canada 135 G1
White Lake LA U.S.A. 131 E6
White Lake MI U.S.A. 134 B2
Whitemark Australia 111 [inset]
White Mountain Peak U.S.A. 128 D3
White Mountains U.S.A. 135 J1
White Mountains National Park Australia 110 D4
Whitemouth Lake Canada 121 M5
Whitemud r. Canada 120 G3
White Nile r. Sudan/Uganda 86 D6
also known as Bahr el Abiad or Bahr el Jebel
White Nossob watercourse Namibia 100 D2
White Oak U.S.A. 134 D5
White Otter Lake Canada 121 N5
White Pass Canada/U.S.A. 120 C3
White Pine Range mts U.S.A. 129 F2
White Plains U.S.A. 135 I3
White River Canada 122 D4
Whiteriver U.S.A. 129 I5
White River U.S.A. 130 C3
White River Valley U.S.A. 129 F2
White Rock Peak U.S.A. 129 F2
White Russia country Europe see Belarus
Whitesail Lake Canada 120 E4
White Salmon U.S.A. 126 C3
Whitesand r. Canada 120 H2
White Sands National Monument nat. park U.S.A. 127 G6
Whitesburg U.S.A. 134 D5
White Sea Rus. Fed. 42 H2
White Stone U.S.A. 135 G5
White Sulphur Springs MT U.S.A. 126 F3
White Sulphur Springs WV U.S.A. 134 E5
Whitesville U.S.A. 134 E5
Whiteville U.S.A. 133 E5
White Volta r. Burkina/Ghana 96 C4
also known as Nakambé or Nakanbe or Volta Blanche
Whitewater U.S.A. 129 I2
Whitewater Baldy mt. U.S.A. 129 I5
Whitewater Lake Canada 122 C4
Whitewood Australia 110 C4
Whitewood Canada 121 K5
Whitfield U.K. 49 I7
Whithorn U.K. 50 E6
Whitianga N.Z. 113 E3
Whitland U.K. 49 C7
Whitley Bay U.K. 48 F3
Whitmore Mountains Antarctica 152 K1
Whitney Canada 135 F1
Whitney, Mount U.S.A. 128 D3
Whitney Point U.S.A. 135 H2
Whitstable U.K. 49 I7
Whitsunday Group is Australia 110 E4
Whitsunday Island National Park Australia 110 E4
Whitsun Island Vanuatu see Pentecost Island
Whittemore U.S.A. 134 D1
Whittlesea Australia 112 B6
Whittlesey U.K. 49 G6
Whitton Australia 112 C5
Wholdaia Lake Canada 121 J2
Why U.S.A. 129 G5
Whyalla Australia 111 B7
Wiang Sa Thai. 70 C3
Wiarton Canada 134 E1
Wibaux U.S.A. 126 G3
Wichelen Belgium 52 D3
Wichita U.S.A. 130 D4
Wichita r. U.S.A. 131 D5
Wichita Falls U.S.A. 131 D5
Wichita Mountains U.S.A. 131 D5
Wick U.K. 50 F2
Wick r. U.K. 50 F2
Wickenburg U.S.A. 129 G5
Wickes U.S.A. 131 E5
Wickford U.K. 49 H7
Wickham r. Australia 108 E4
Wickham, Cape Australia 107 [inset]
Wickham, Mount hill Australia 108 E4
Wickliffe U.S.A. 131 F4
Wicklow Rep. of Ireland 51 F5
Wicklow Head hd Rep. of Ireland 51 G5
Wicklow Mountains Rep. of Ireland 51 F5
Wicklow Mountains National Park Rep. of Ireland 51 F4
Widerøe, Mount Antarctica 148 C2
Widerøefjellet mt. Antarctica see Widerøe, Mount
Widgeegoara watercourse Australia 112 B1
Widgiemooltha Australia 109 C7
Widnes U.K. 48 E5
Wi-do i. S. Korea 75 B6
Wied r. Germany 53 H4
Wiehengebirge hills Germany 53 I2
Wiehl Germany 53 H4
Wielkopolskie, Pojezierze reg. Poland 47 O4
Wielkopolski Park Narodowy nat. park Poland 47 P4
Wieluń Poland 47 Q5
Wien Austria see Vienna
Wiener Neustadt Austria 47 P7
Wierden Neth. 52 G2
Wieren Germany 53 K2
Wieringerwerf Neth. 52 F2
Wiesbaden Germany 53 I4
Wiesenfelden Germany 53 M5
Wiesentheid Germany 53 K5
Wiesloch Germany 53 I5
Wiesmoor Germany 53 H1
Wietze Germany 53 J2
Wietzendorf Germany 53 J2
Wieżyca hill Poland 47 Q3
Wigan U.K. 48 E5
Wiggins U.S.A. 131 F6
Wight, Isle of i. England U.K. 49 F8
Wignes Lake Canada 121 J2
Wigston U.K. 49 F6
Wigton U.K. 48 D4
Wigtown U.K. 50 E6
Wigtown Bay U.K. 50 E6
Wijchen Neth. 52 F3
Wijhe Neth. 52 G2
Wilberforce, Cape Australia 110 B1
Wilbur U.S.A. 126 D3
Wilburton U.S.A. 131 E5
Wilcannia Australia 112 A3
Wilcox U.S.A. 135 F3
Wilczek Land i. Rus. Fed. see Vil'cheka, Zemlya
Wildberg Germany 53 M2
Wildcat Peak U.S.A. 128 E2
Wild Coast S. Africa 101 I6
Wilderness National Park S. Africa 100 F8
Wildeshausen Germany 53 I2
Wild Horse Hill mt. U.S.A. 130 C3
Wildspitze mt. Austria 47 M7
Wildwood FL U.S.A. 133 D6
Wildwood NJ U.S.A. 135 H4
Wilge r. S. Africa 101 I4
Wilge r. S. Africa 101 I3
Wilgena Australia 109 F7

▶Wilhelm, Mount P.N.G. 69 L8
5th highest mountain in Oceania.

Wilhelm II Land reg. Antarctica see Kaiser Wilhelm II Land
Wilhelmina Gebergte mts Suriname 143 G3
Wilhelmina Kanaal canal Neth. 52 F3
Wilhelmshaven Germany 53 I1
Wilhelmstal Namibia 100 C1
Wilkes-Barre U.S.A. 135 H3
Wilkesboro U.S.A. 132 D4
Wilkes Coast Antarctica 152 G2
Wilkes Land reg. Antarctica 152 G2
Wilkie Canada 121 I4
Wilkins Coast Antarctica 152 L2
Wilkins Ice Shelf Antarctica 152 L2
Wilkinson Lakes salt flat Australia 109 F7
Will, Mount Canada 120 D3
Willand U.K. 49 D8
Willandra Billabong watercourse Australia 112 B4
Willandra National Park Australia 112 B4
Willapa Bay U.S.A. 126 B3
Willard Mex. 127 F7
Willard NM U.S.A. 127 G6
Willard OH U.S.A. 134 D3
Willcox U.S.A. 129 I5
Willcox Playa salt flat U.S.A. 129 I5
Willebadessen Germany 53 J3
Willebroek Belgium 52 E3

▶Willemstad Neth. Antilles 137 K6
Capital of the Netherlands Antilles.

Willeroo Australia 108 E3
Willette U.S.A. 134 C5
William, Mount Australia 111 C8
William Creek Australia 111 B6
William Lake Canada 121 L4
Williams AZ U.S.A. 129 G4
Williams CA U.S.A. 128 B2
Williamsburg KY U.S.A. 134 C5
Williamsburg OH U.S.A. 134 C4
Williamsburg VA U.S.A. 135 G5
Williams Lake Canada 120 F4
William Smith, Cap c. Canada 123 I1
Williamson NY U.S.A. 135 G2
Williamson WV U.S.A. 134 D5
Williamsport IN U.S.A. 134 B3
Williamsport PA U.S.A. 135 G3
Williamston U.S.A. 132 E5
Williamstown KY U.S.A. 134 C4
Williamstown NJ U.S.A. 135 H4
Willimantic U.S.A. 135 I3
Willis Group atolls Australia 110 E3
Williston S. Africa 100 E6
Williston ND U.S.A. 130 C1
Williston SC U.S.A. 133 D5
Williston Lake Canada 120 F4
Williton U.K. 49 D7
Willits U.S.A. 128 B2
Willmar U.S.A. 130 E2
Willoughby, Lake U.S.A. 135 I1
Willow Beach U.S.A. 129 F4
Willow Bunch Canada 121 J5
Willow Hill U.S.A. 135 G3
Willow Lake Canada 120 G2
Willowlake r. Canada 120 F2
Willowmore S. Africa 100 F7
Willowra Australia 108 F5
Willows U.S.A. 128 B2
Willow Springs U.S.A. 131 F4
Willowvale S. Africa 101 I7
Wills, Lake salt flat Australia 108 E5
Wilma U.S.A. 133 C6
Wilmington DE U.S.A. 135 H4
Wilmington NC U.S.A. 133 E5
Wilmington OH U.S.A. 134 D4
Wilmore U.S.A. 134 C5
Wilmslow U.K. 48 E5
Wilno Lith. see Vilnius
Wilnsdorf Germany 53 I4
Wilpattu National Park Sri Lanka 84 D4
Wilseder Berg hill Germany 53 J1
Wilson watercourse Australia 107 C5
Wilson atoll Micronesia see Ifalik
Wilson KS U.S.A. 130 D4
Wilson NC U.S.A. 132 E5
Wilson NY U.S.A. 135 F2
Wilson, Mount CO U.S.A. 129 J3
Wilson, Mount NV U.S.A. 129 F2
Wilson, Mount OR U.S.A. 126 C3
Wilsonia U.S.A. 128 D3
Wilson's Promontory pen. Australia 112 C7
Wilson's Promontory National Park Australia 112 C7
Wilsum Germany 52 G2
Wilton r. Australia 108 F3
Wilton U.S.A. 135 J1
Wiltz Lux. 52 F5
Wiluna Australia 109 C6
Wimereux France 52 B4
Wina r. Cameroon see Vina
Winamac U.S.A. 134 B3
Winbin watercourse Australia 111 D5
Winburg S. Africa 101 H5
Wincanton U.K. 49 E7
Winchester Canada 135 H1
Winchester U.K. 49 F7
Winchester IN U.S.A. 134 C3
Winchester KY U.S.A. 134 C5
Winchester NH U.S.A. 135 I2
Winchester TN U.S.A. 133 C5
Winchester VA U.S.A. 135 F4
Wind r. Canada 120 C1
Wind r. U.S.A. 126 F4
Windau Latvia see Ventspils
Windber U.S.A. 135 F3
Wind Cave National Park U.S.A. 130 C3
Windermere U.K. 48 E4
Windermere l. U.K. 48 E4
Windham U.S.A. 120 C3

▶Windhoek Namibia 100 C2
Capital of Namibia.

Windigo Lake Canada 121 N4
Windlestraw Law hill U.K. 50 G5
Wind Mountain U.S.A. 127 G6
Windom U.S.A. 130 E3
Windom Peak U.S.A. 129 J3
Windorah Australia 110 C5
Window Rock U.S.A. 129 I4
Wind Point U.S.A. 134 B2
Wind River Range mts U.S.A. 126 F4
Windrush r. U.K. 49 F7
Windsbach Germany 53 K5
Windsor Australia 112 E4
Windsor N.S. Canada 123 I5
Windsor Ont. Canada 134 D2
Windsor U.K. 49 G7
Windsor NC U.S.A. 132 E4
Windsor NY U.S.A. 135 H2
Windsor VA U.S.A. 135 G5
Windsor VT U.S.A. 135 I2
Windsor Locks U.S.A. 135 I3
Windward Islands Caribbean Sea 137 L5
Windward Passage Cuba/Haiti 137 J5
Windy U.S.A. 118 D3
Winefred Lake Canada 121 I4
Winfield KS U.S.A. 131 D4
Winfield WV U.S.A. 134 E4
Wingate U.K. 48 F4
Wingen Australia 112 E3
Wingene Belgium 52 D3
Wingen-sur-Moder France 53 H6
Wingham Australia 112 F3
Wingham Canada 134 E2
Winisk Canada 122 D3
Winisk r. Canada 122 D3
Winisk Lake Canada 122 D3
Winkana Myanmar 70 B4
Winkelman U.S.A. 129 H5
Winkler Canada 121 L5
Winlock U.S.A. 126 C3
Winneba Ghana 96 C4
Winnebago, Lake U.S.A. 134 A1
Winnecke Creek watercourse Australia 108 E4
Winnemucca U.S.A. 128 E1
Winnemucca Lake U.S.A. 128 D1
Winner U.S.A. 130 C3
Winnett U.S.A. 126 F3
Winnfield U.S.A. 131 E6
Winnibigoshish, Lake U.S.A. 130 E2
Winnie U.S.A. 131 E6
Winning Australia 109 A5

▶Winnipeg Canada 121 L5
Provincial capital of Manitoba.

Winnipeg r. Canada 121 L5
Winnipeg, Lake Canada 121 L5
Winnipegosis Canada 121 L5
Winnipegosis, Lake Canada 121 K4
Winnipesaukee, Lake U.S.A. 135 J2
Winona AZ U.S.A. 129 H4
Winona MN U.S.A. 130 F2
Winona MO U.S.A. 131 F4
Winona MS U.S.A. 131 F5
Winschoten Neth. 52 H1
Winsen (Aller) Germany 53 J2
Winsen (Luhe) Germany 53 K1
Winsford U.K. 48 E5
Winslow AZ U.S.A. 129 H4
Winslow ME U.S.A. 135 K1
Winsop, Tanjung pt Indon. 69 I7
Winsted U.S.A. 135 I3
Winston-Salem U.S.A. 132 D4
Winterberg Germany 53 I3
Winter Haven U.S.A. 133 D6
Winters CA U.S.A. 128 C2
Winters TX U.S.A. 131 D6
Wintersville U.S.A. 134 E3
Winterswijk Neth. 52 G3
Winterthur Switz. 56 I3
Winterton S. Africa 101 I5
Winthrop U.S.A. 135 K1
Winton Australia 110 C4
Winton N.Z. 113 B8
Winton U.S.A. 132 E4
Winwick U.K. 49 G6
Wirral pen. U.K. 48 D5
Wirrulla Australia 111 A7
Wisbech U.K. 49 H6
Wiscasset U.S.A. 135 K1
Wisconsin r. U.S.A. 130 F3
Wisconsin state U.S.A. 134 A1
Wisconsin Rapids U.S.A. 130 F2
Wise U.S.A. 134 D5
Wiseman U.S.A. 118 C3
Wishaw U.K. 50 F5
Wisher U.S.A. 130 D2
Wisil Dabarow Somalia 98 E3
Wisła r. Poland see Vistula
Wismar Germany 47 M4
Wistaria Canada 120 E4
Witbank S. Africa 101 I3
Witbooisvlei Namibia 100 D3
Witham U.K. 49 H7
Witham r. U.K. 49 H6
Witherbee U.S.A. 135 I1
Withernsea U.K. 48 H5
Witjira National Park Australia 111 A5
Witmarsum Neth. 52 F1
Witney U.K. 49 F7
Witrivier S. Africa 101 J3
Witry-lès-Reims France 52 E5
Witteberg mts S. Africa 101 H6
Wittenberg Germany see Lutherstadt Wittenberg
Wittenberge Germany 53 L2
Wittenburg Germany 53 L1
Wittingen Germany 53 K2

Wittlich Germany 52 G5
Wittmund Germany 53 H1
Wittstock Germany 53 M1
Witu Islands P.N.G. 69 L7
Witvlei Namibia 100 D2
Witzenhausen Germany 53 J3
Wivenhoe, Lake Australia 112 F1
Władysławowo Poland 47 Q3
Włocławek Poland 47 Q4
Wobkent Uzbek. *see* **Vabkent**
Wodonga Australia 112 C6
Wœrth France 53 H6
Wohlthat Mountains Antarctica 152 C2
Woippy France 52 G5
Wōjjā *atoll* Marshall Is *see* **Wotje**
Wokam *i.* Indon. 69 I8
Woken He *r.* China 74 C3
Wokha India 83 H4
Woking U.K. 49 G7
Wokingham *watercourse* Australia 110 C4
Wokingham U.K. 49 G7
Woko National Park Australia 112 E3
Wolcott *IN* U.S.A. 134 B3
Wolcott *NY* U.S.A. 135 G2
Woldegk Germany 53 N1
Wolea *atoll* Micronesia *see* **Woleai**
Woleai *atoll* Micronesia 69 K5
Wolf *r.* Canada 120 C2
Wolf *r. TN* U.S.A. 131 F5
Wolf *r. WI* U.S.A. 130 F2
Wolf Creek *MT* U.S.A. 126 E3
Wolf Creek *OR* U.S.A. 126 C4
Wolf Creek Pass U.S.A. 127 G5
Wolfen Germany 53 M3
Wolfenbüttel Germany 53 K2
Wolfhagen Germany 53 J3
Wolf Lake Canada 120 D2
Wolf Point U.S.A. 126 G2
Wolfsberg Austria 47 O7
Wolfsburg Germany 53 K2
Wolfstein Germany 53 H5
Wolfville Canada 123 I5
Wolgast Germany 47 N3
Wolin Poland 47 O4
Wollaston Lake Canada 121 K3
Wollaston Lake *l.* Canada 121 K3
Wollaston Peninsula Canada 118 G3
Wollemi National Park Australia 112 E4
Wollongong Australia 112 E5
Wolmaransstad S. Africa 101 G4
Wolmirstedt Germany 53 L2
Wolong Reserve *nature res.* China 76 D2
Wolseley Australia 111 C8
Wolseley S. Africa 100 D7
Wolsey U.S.A. 130 D2
Wolsingham U.K. 48 F4
Wolvega Neth. 52 G2
Wolvegea Neth. *see* **Wolvega**
Wolverhampton U.K. 49 E6
Wolverine U.S.A. 134 C1
Wommelgem Belgium 52 E3
Womrather Höhe *hill* Germany 53 H5
Wonarah Australia 110 B3
Wondai Australia 111 E5
Wongalarroo Lake *salt l.* Australia 112 B3
Wongarbon Australia 112 D4
Wong Chuk Hang *Hong Kong* China 77 [inset]
Wong Leng *hill Hong Kong* China 77 [inset]
Wong Wan Chau *Hong Kong* China *see* **Double Island**
Wŏnju S. Korea 75 B5
Wonowon Canada 120 F3
Wŏnsan N. Korea 75 B5
Wonthaggi Australia 112 B7
Wonyulgunna, Mount *hill* Australia 109 B6
Woocalla Australia 111 B6
Wood, Mount Canada 120 A2
Woodbine *GA* U.S.A. 133 D6
Woodbine *NJ* U.S.A. 135 H4
Woodbridge U.K. 49 I6
Woodbridge U.S.A. 135 G4
Wood Buffalo National Park Canada 120 H3
Woodburn U.S.A. 126 C3
Woodbury *NJ* U.S.A. 135 H4
Woodbury *TN* U.S.A. 131 G5
Wooded Bluff *hd* Australia 112 F2
Wood Lake Canada 121 K4
Woodlake U.S.A. 128 D3
Woodland *CA* U.S.A. 128 C2
Woodland *PA* U.S.A. 135 F3
Woodland *WA* U.S.A. 126 C3
Woodlands Sing. 71 [inset]
Woodlark Island P.N.G. 106 F2
Woodridge Canada 121 L5
Woodroffe *watercourse* Australia 110 B4
Woodroffe, Mount Australia 109 E6
Woodruff *UT* U.S.A. 126 F4
Woodruff *WI* U.S.A. 130 F2
Woods, Lake *salt flat* Australia 108 F4
Woods, Lake of the Canada/U.S.A. 125 I2
Woodsfield U.S.A. 134 E4
Woodside Australia 112 C7
Woodstock *N.B.* Canada 123 I5
Woodstock *Ont.* Canada 134 E2
Woodstock *IL* U.S.A. 130 F3
Woodstock *VA* U.S.A. 135 F4
Woodstock *VT* U.S.A. 135 I2
Woodsville U.S.A. 135 I1
Woodville Canada 135 F1
Woodville *MS* U.S.A. 131 F6
Woodville *OH* U.S.A. 134 D3
Woodville *TX* U.S.A. 131 E6
Woodward U.S.A. 131 D4
Woody U.S.A. 128 D4
Wooler U.K. 48 E3
Woolgoolga Australia 112 F3
Wooli Australia 112 F2
Woollard, Mount Antarctica 152 K1
Woollett, Lac *l.* Canada 122 G4
Woolyeenyer Hill *hill* Australia 109 C8
Woomera Australia 111 B6
Woomera Prohibited Area Australia 109 F7
Woonsocket *RI* U.S.A. 135 J2
Woonsocket *SD* U.S.A. 130 D2
Woorabinda Australia 110 E5
Wooramel *r.* Australia 109 A6
Wooster U.S.A. 134 E3
Worbis Germany 53 K3
Worbody Point Australia 110 C2
Worcester S. Africa 100 D7
Worcester U.K. 49 E6
Worcester *MA* U.S.A. 135 J2
Worcester *NY* U.S.A. 135 H2
Wörgl Austria 47 N7
Workai *i.* Indon. 69 I8
Workington U.K. 48 D4
Worksop U.K. 48 F5
Workum Neth. 52 F2
Worland U.S.A. 126 G3
Wörlitz Germany 53 M3
Wormerveer Neth. 52 E2
Worms Germany 53 I5
Worms Head *hd* U.K. 49 C7
Wortel Namibia 100 C2
Wörth am Rhein Germany 53 I5
Worthing U.K. 49 G8
Worthington *IN* U.S.A. 134 B4
Worthington *MN* U.S.A. 130 E3
Wotje *atoll* Marshall Is 150 H5
Wotu Indon. 69 G7
Woudrichem Neth. 52 E3
Woustviller France 52 H5
Wowoni *i.* Indon. 69 G7
Wozrojdeniye Oroli *i.* Uzbek. *see* **Vozrozhdeniya, Ostrov**
Wrangel Island Rus. Fed. 65 T2
Wrangell Island U.S.A. 120 C3
Wrangell Mountains U.S.A. 153 B3
Wrangell-St Elias National Park and Preserve U.S.A. 120 A2
Wrath, Cape U.K. 50 D2
Wray U.S.A. 130 C3
Wreake *r.* U.K. 49 F6
Wreck Point S. Africa 100 C5
Wreck Reef Australia 110 F4
Wrecsam U.K. *see* **Wrexham**
Wrestedt Germany 53 K2
Wrexham U.K. 49 E5
Wrightmyo India 71 A5
Wrightson, Mount U.S.A. 127 F7
Wrightwood U.S.A. 128 E4
Wrigley Canada 120 F2
Wrigley U.S.A. 134 D4
Wrigley Gulf Antarctica 152 J2
Wrocław Poland 47 P5
Września Poland 47 P4
Wu'an China *see* **Changtai**
Wubin Australia 109 B7
Wuchang *Heilong.* China 74 B3
Wuchang *Hubei* China *see* **Jiangxia**
Wuchow China *see* **Wuzhou**
Wuchuan *Guangdong* China *see* **Meilu**
Wuchuan *Guizhou* China 76 E2
Wudalianchi China 74 B2
Wudām 'Alwā Oman 88 E6
Wudang Shan *mt.* China 77 F1
Wudaoliang China 76 B1
Wuding China 76 D3
Wudinna Australia 109 F8
Wudu China 76 E1
Wufeng *Hubei* China 77 F2
Wufeng *Yunnan* China *see* **Zhenxiong**
Wugang China 77 F3
Wuhai China 72 J5
Wuhan China 77 G2
Wuhe China 77 H1
Wuhu China 77 H2
Wuhua China 77 G4
Wuhubei China 77 H2
Wūjang China 82 D2
Wu Jiang *r.* China 76 E2
Wujin *Jiangsu* China *see* **Changzhou**
Wujin *Sichuan* China *see* **Xinjin**
Wukari Nigeria 96 D4
Wulang China 76 B2
Wuli China 76 B1
Wulian Feng *mts* China 76 D2
Wuliang Shan *mts* China 76 D3
Wuliaru *i.* Indon. 108 E1
Wuli Jiang *r.* China 77 F4
Wuling Shan *mts* China 77 F2
Wulong China 76 E2
Wulongji China *see* **Huaibin**
Wulur Indon. 108 E1
Wumeng Shan *mts* China 76 D3
Wuming China 77 F4
Wümme *r.* Germany 53 I1
Wundwin Myanmar 70 B2
Wungda China 76 D2
Wuning China 77 G2
Wünnenberg Germany 53 I3
Wunnummin Lake Canada 119 J4
Wunsiedel Germany 53 M4
Wunstorf Germany 53 J2
Wupatki National Monument *nat. park* U.S.A. 129 H4
Wuping China 77 H3
Wuppertal Germany 53 H3
Wuppertal S. Africa 100 D7
Wuqi China 73 J5
Wuqia China 80 D4
Wuquan China *see* **Wuyang**
Wuranga Australia 109 B7
Wurno Nigeria 96 D3
Würzburg Germany 53 J5
Wurzen Germany 53 M3
Wushan *Chongqing* China 77 F2
Wushan *Gansu* China 76 E1
Wu Shan *mts* China 77 F2
Wushi *Guangdong* China 77 F4
Wushi *Xinjiang* China 80 E3
Wüstegarten *hill* Germany 53 J3
Wusuli Jiang *r.* China/Rus. Fed. *see* **Ussuri**
Wuvulu Island P.N.G. 69 K7
Wuwei China 72 I5
Wuxi *Chongqing* China 77 F2
Wuxi *Hunan* China *see* **Luxi**
Wuxi *Hunan* China *see* **Qiyang**
Wuxi *Jiangsu* China 77 I2
Wuxia China *see* **Wushan**
Wuxian China *see* **Suzhou**
Wuxing China *see* **Huzhou**
Wuxu China 77 F4
Wuxuan China 77 F4
Wuxue China 77 G2
Wuyang *Guizhou* China *see* **Zhenyuan**
Wuyang *Henan* China 77 G1
Wuyang *Zhejiang* China *see* **Wuyi**
Wuyi China 77 H2
Wuyiling China 74 C2
Wuyi Shan *mts* China 77 H3
Wuyuan *Jiangxi* China 77 H2
Wuyuan *Nei Mongol* China 73 J4
Wuyuan *Zhejiang* China *see* **Haiyan**
Wuyun China *see* **Jinyun**
Wuzhi Shan *mts* China 77 F5
Wuzhong China 72 J5
Wuzhou China 77 F4
Wyalkatchem Australia 109 B7
Wyalong Australia 112 C4
Wyandra Australia 112 B1
Wyangala Reservoir Australia 112 D4
Wyara, Lake *salt flat* Australia 112 B2
Wycheproof Australia 112 A6
Wylliesburg U.S.A. 135 F5
Wyloo Australia 108 B5
Wylye *r.* U.K. 49 F7
Wymondham U.K. 49 I6
Wymore U.S.A. 130 D3
Wynbring Australia 109 F7
Wyndham Australia 108 E3
Wyndham-Werribee Australia 112 B6
Wynne U.S.A. 131 F5
Wynyard Canada 121 J5
Wyola Lake *salt flat* Australia 109 E7
Wyoming U.S.A. 134 C2
Wyoming *state* U.S.A. 126 G4
Wyoming Peak U.S.A. 126 F4
Wyoming Range *mts* U.S.A. 126 F4
Wyong Australia 112 E4
Wyperfeld National Park Australia 111 C7
Wysox U.S.A. 135 G3
Wyszków Poland 47 R4
Wythall U.K. 49 F6
Wytheville U.S.A. 134 E5
Wytmarsum Neth. *see* **Witmarsum**

X

Xaafuun Somalia 98 F2

▶**Xaafuun, Raas** *pt* Somalia 86 H7
Most easterly point of Africa.

Xabyaisamba China 76 C2
Xaçmaz Azer. 91 H2
Xago China 83 G3
Xagquka China 76 B2
Xaidulla China 82 D1
Xaignabouri Laos *see* **Muang Xaignabouri**
Xainza China 83 G3
Xai-Xai Moz. 101 K3
Xalapa Mex. *see* **Jalapa**
Xambioa Brazil 143 I5
Xam Nua Laos 70 D2
Xá-Muteba Angola 99 B4
Xan *r.* Laos 70 C3
Xanagas Botswana 100 E2
Xangda China *see* **Nangqên**
Xangdin Hural China 73 K4
Xangdoring China 83 E2
Xangongo Angola 99 B5
Xankändi Azer. 91 G3
Xanlar Azer. 91 G2
Xanthi Greece 59 K4
Xarag China 83 I1
Xarardheere Somalia 98 E3
Xátiva Spain 57 F4
Xavantes, Serra dos *hills* Brazil 143 I6
Xaxa China 83 E2
Xayar China 80 F3
Xela Guat. *see* **Quetzaltenango**
Xelva Spain *see* **Chelva**
Xenia U.S.A. 134 D4
Xero Potamos *r.* Cyprus *see* **Xeros**
Xeros *r.* Cyprus 85 A2
Xhora S. Africa *see* **Elliotdale**
Xiabole Shan *mt.* China 74 B2
Xiachuan Dao *i.* China 77 G4
Xiaguan China *see* **Dali**
Xiahe China 76 D1
Xiamen China 77 H3
Xi'an China 77 F1
Xianfeng China 77 F2
Xiangcheng *Sichuan* China 76 C2
Xiangcheng *Yunnan* China *see* **Xiangyun**
Xiangfan China 77 G1
Xiangfeng China *see* **Laifeng**
Xianggang *Hong Kong* China *see* **Hong Kong**
Xianggang Tebie Xingzhengqu *aut. reg.* China *see* **Hong Kong**
Xiangjiang China *see* **Huichang**
Xiangkhoang Laos 70 C3
Xiangkhoang Plateau Laos 70 C3
Xiangkou China *see* **Wulong**
Xiangning China 73 K5
Xiangquan He *r.* China *see* **Langqên Zangbo**
Xiangride China 83 I2
Xiangshan China *see* **Menghai**
Xiangshui China 77 H1
Xiangshuiba China 77 F3
Xiangtan China 77 G3
Xiangxiang China 77 G3
Xiangyang China *see* **Xiangfan**
Xiangyang Hu *l.* China 83 G2
Xiangyin China 77 G2
Xiangyun China 76 D3
Xianju China 77 I2
Xianning China 77 G2
Xiannümiao China *see* **Jiangdu**
Xianshui He *r.* China 76 D2
Xiantao China 77 G2
Xianxia Ling *mts* China 77 H3
Xianyang China 77 F1
Xiaocaohu China 80 G3
Xiaodong China 77 F4
Xiaodongliang China 76 C1
Xiao'ergou China 74 A2
Xiaogan China 77 G2
Xiaogang China *see* **Dongxiang**
Xiao Hinggan Ling *mts* China 74 B2
Xiaojin China 76 D2
Xiaonanchuan China 83 H2
Xiaosanjiang China 77 G3
Xiaoshan China 77 I2
Xiao Shan *mts* China 77 F1
Xiaoshi China *see* **Benxi**
Xiao Surmang China 76 C1
Xiaotao China 77 H3
Xiaoxi China *see* **Pinghe**
Xiaoxian China 77 H1
Xiaoxiang Ling *mts* China 76 D2
Xiaoxita China *see* **Yichang**
Xiapu China 77 I3
Xiaqiong China *see* **Batang**
Xiashan China *see* **Zhanjiang**
Xiayang China *see* **Yanling**
Xiayanjing China *see* **Yanjing**
Xiayingpan *Guizhou* China *see* **Luzhi**
Xiayingpan *Guizhou* China *see* **Lupanshui**
Xiayukou China 77 F1
Xiazhuang China *see* **Linshu**
Xibdê China 76 C2
Xibing China 77 H3
Xibu China *see* **Dongshan**
Xichang China 76 D3
Xichou China 76 E4
Xichuan China 77 F1
Xide China 76 D2
Xidu China *see* **Hengyang**
Xiemahe' China 77 F2
Xieng Khouang Laos *see* **Xiangkhoang**
Xieyang Dao *i.* China 77 F4
Xifeng *Gansu* China 76 E1
Xifeng *Guizhou* China 76 E3
Xifeng *Liaoning* China 74 B4
Xifengzhen China *see* **Xifeng**
Xigazê China 83 G3
Xihan Shui *r.* China 76 E1
Xi He *r.* China 76 E2
Xi Jiang *r.* China 77 G4
Xijir China 83 G2
Xijir Ulan Hu *salt l.* China 83 G2
Xiliao He *r.* China 74 A4
Xilin China 76 E3
Xilinhot China 73 L4
Ximiao China 80 J3
Xin'an *Anhui* China *see* **Lai'an**
Xin'an *Guizhou* China *see* **Anlong**
Xin'an *Henan* China 77 G1
Xin'anjiang China 77 H2
Xin'anjiang Shuiku *resr* China 77 H2
Xinavane Moz. 101 K3
Xin Barag Zuoqi China *see* **Amgalang**
Xincai China 77 G1
Xinchang *Jiangxi* China *see* **Yifeng**
Xinchang *Zhejiang* China 77 I2
Xincheng *Fujian* China *see* **Gutian**
Xincheng *Guangdong* China *see* **Xinxing**
Xincheng *Guangxi* China 77 F3
Xincheng *Sichuan* China *see* **Zhaojue**
Xincun China *see* **Dongchuan**
Xindi *Guangxi* China 77 F4
Xindi *Hubei* China *see* **Honghu**
Xindian China 74 B3
Xindu *Guangxi* China 77 F4
Xindu *Sichuan* China *see* **Luhuo**
Xindu *Sichuan* China 76 E2
Xinduqiao China 76 D2
Xinfeng *Guangdong* China 77 G3
Xinfeng *Jiangxi* China 77 G3
Xinfengjiang Shuiku *resr* China 77 G4
Xing'an *Guangxi* China 77 F3
Xingan China 77 G3
Xing'an *Shaanxi* China *see* **Ankang**
Xingba China *see* **Lhünzê**
Xingguo *Gansu* China *see* **Qin'an**
Xingguo *Hubei* China *see* **Yangxin**
Xingguo *Jiangxi* China 77 G3
Xinghai China 80 I4
Xinghua China 77 H1
Xinghua Wan *b.* China 77 H3
Xingkai China 74 D3
Xingkai Hu *l.* China/Rus. Fed. *see* **Khanka, Lake**
Xinglong China 74 B2
Xinglongzhen *Gansu* China 76 E1
Xinglongzhen *Heilong.* China 74 B3
Xingning *Guangdong* China 77 G3
Xingning *Hunan* China 77 G3
Xingou China 77 G2
Xingping China 77 F1
Xingqêngoin China 76 D2
Xingren China 76 E3
Xingsagoinba China 76 D1
Xingshan *Guizhou* China *see* **Majiang**
Xingshan *Hubei* China 77 F2
Xingtai China 73 K5
Xingu *r.* Brazil 143 H4
Xingu, Parque Indígena do *res.* Brazil 143 H6
Xinguara Brazil 143 H5
Xingye China 77 F4
Xingyi China 76 E3
Xinhua *Guangdong* China *see* **Huadu**
Xinhua *Hunan* China 77 F3
Xinhua *Yunnan* China *see* **Qiaojia**
Xinhua *Yunnan* China *see* **Funing**
Xinhuang China 77 F3
Xinhui China 77 G4
Xining China 72 I5
Xinjian China 77 G2
Xinjiang China 77 F1
Xinjiang *aut. reg.* China *see* **Xinjiang Uygur Zizhiqu**
Xinjiangkou China *see* **Songzi**
Xinjiang Uygur Zizhiqu *aut. reg.* China 82 E1
Xinjie *Qinghai* China 76 D1
Xinjie *Yunnan* China 76 C3
Xinjie *Yunnan* China 76 D4
Xinjin China 76 D2
Xinjing China *see* **Jingxi**
Xinkai He *r.* China 74 A4
Xinling China *see* **Badong**
Xinlitun China 74 B2
Xinlong China 76 D2
Xinmi China 77 G1
Xinning *Gansu* China *see* **Ningxian**
Xinning *Hunan* China 77 F3
Xinning *Jiangxi* China *see* **Wuning**
Xinning *Sichuan* China *see* **Kaijiang**
Xinping China 76 D3
Xinqiao China 77 G1
Xinqing China 74 C2
Xinquan China 77 H3
Xinshan China *see* **Anyuan**
Xinshiba China *see* **Ganluo**
Xinsi China 76 E1
Xintai China 73 L5
Xintanpu China 77 G2
Xintian China 77 G3
Xinxiang China 77 G1
Xinxing China 77 G4
Xinyang *Henan* China 77 G1
Xinyang *Henan* China *see* **Pingqiao**
Xinye China 77 G1
Xinyi *Guangdong* China 77 F4
Xinyi *Jiangsu* China 77 H1
Xinying China 77 F5
Xinying Taiwan *see* **Hsinying**
Xinyu China 77 G3
Xinyuan *Qinghai* China *see* **Tianjun**
Xinyuan *Xinjiang* China 80 F3
Xinzhangfang China 74 A2
Xinzhou *Guangxi* China *see* **Longlin**
Xinzhou *Hubei* China 77 G2
Xinzhou *Shanxi* China 73 K5
Xinzhu Taiwan *see* **Hsinchu**
Xinzo de Limia Spain 57 C2
Xiongshan China *see* **Zhenghe**
Xiongshi China *see* **Guixi**
Xiongzhou China *see* **Nanxiong**
Xiping *Henan* China 77 F1
Xiping *Henan* China 77 G1
Xiqing Shan *mts* China 76 D1
Xique Xique Brazil 143 J6
Xisa China *see* **Xichou**
Xisha Qundao *is* S. China Sea *see* **Paracel Islands**
Xishuangbanna *reg.* China 76 D4
Xishui *Guizhou* China 76 E2
Xishui *Hubei* China 77 G2
Xitianmu Shan *mt.* China 77 H2
Xiugu China *see* **Jinxi**
Xi Ujimqin Qi China *see* **Bayan Ul Hot**
Xiuning China 77 H2
Xiushan *Chongqing* China 77 F2
Xiushan *Yunnan* China *see* **Tonghai**
Xiushui China 77 G2
Xiuwen China 76 E3
Xiuwu China 77 G1
Xiuying China 77 F4
Xiwu China 76 C1
Xixabangma Feng *mt.* China 83 F3
Xixia China 77 F1
Xixiang China 76 E1
Xixiu China *see* **Anshun**
Xixón Spain *see* **Gijón-Xixón**
Xiyang Dao *i.* China 77 I3
Xiyang Jiang *r.* China 76 E3
Xizang *aut. reg.* China *see* **Xizang Zizhiqu**
Xizang Gaoyuan *plat.* China *see* **Plateau of Tibet**
Xizang Zizhiqu *aut. reg.* China 83 G3
Xom An Lôc Vietnam 71 D5
Xom Dưc Hanh Vietnam 71 D5
Xorkol China 80 H4
Xuancheng China 77 H2
Xuan'en China 77 F2
Xuanhua China 73 L4
Xuân Lôc Vietnam 71 D5
Xuanwei China 76 E3
Xuanzhou China *see* **Xuancheng**
Xuchang China 77 G1
Xucheng China *see* **Xuwen**
Xuddur Somalia 98 E3
Xuefeng China *see* **Mingxi**
Xuefeng Shan *mts* China 77 F3
Xue Shan *mts* China 76 C3
Xugui China 80 I4
Xuguit Qi China *see* **Yakeshi**
Xujiang China *see* **Guangchang**
Xümatang China 76 C1
Xunde Qundao *is* Paracel Is *see* **Amphitrite Group**
Xungba China *see* **Xangdoring**
Xungmai China 83 G3
Xunhe China 74 B2
Xun He *r.* China 74 C2
Xun Jiang *r.* China 77 F4
Xunwu China 77 G3
Xunyi China 77 F1
Xuru Co *salt l.* China 83 F3
Xuwen China 68 E2
Xuyên Môc Vietnam 71 D5
Xuyi China 77 H1
Xuyong China 76 E2
Xuzhou China *see* **Tongshan**

Y

Ya'an China 76 D2
Yabanabat Turkey *see* **Kızılcahamam**
Yabēlo Eth. 98 D3
Yablonovyy Khrebet *mts* Rus. Fed. 73 J2
Yabrīn *reg.* Saudi Arabia 88 C6
Yabuli China 74 C3
Yacha China *see* **Baisha**
Yacheng China 77 F5
Yachi He *r.* China 76 E3
Yacuma *r.* Bol. 142 E6
Yadgir India 84 C2
Yadrin Rus. Fed. 42 J5
Yaeyama-rettō *is* Japan 73 M8
Yafa Israel *see* **Tel Aviv-Yafo**
Yagaba Ghana 96 C3
Yağda Turkey *see* **Erdemli**
Yaghan Basin *sea feature* S. Atlantic Ocean 148 D9
Yagman Turkm. 88 D2
Yagmo China 83 F3
Yagodnoye Rus. Fed. 65 P3
Yagodnyy Rus. Fed. 74 E2
Yagoua Cameroon 97 E3
Yagra China 83 E3
Yagradagzê Shan *mt.* China 76 B1
Yaguajay Cuba 133 E8
Yaha Thai. 71 C6
Yahk Canada 120 G5
Yahualica Mex. 136 D4
Yahyalı Turkey 55 L4
Yai Myanmar *see* **Ye**
Yai, Khao *mt.* Thai. 71 B4
Yaizu Japan 75 E6
Yajiang China 76 D2
Yakacık Turkey 85 C1
Yakeshi China 73 M3
Yakhab *waterhole* Iran 88 E3
Yakhehal Afgh. 89 G4
Yakima U.S.A. 126 C3
Yakima *r.* U.S.A. 126 D3
Yakmach Pak. 89 F4
Yako Burkina 96 C3
Yakovlevka Rus. Fed. 74 D3
Yaku-shima *i.* Japan 75 C7
Yakutat U.S.A. 120 B3
Yakutat Bay U.S.A. 120 A3
Yakutsk Rus. Fed. 65 N3
Yakymivka Ukr. 43 G7
Yala Thai. 71 C6
Yalai China 83 F3
Yala National Park Sri Lanka *see* **Ruhuna National Park**
Yalan Dünya Mağarası *tourist site* Turkey 85 A1
Yale Canada 120 F5
Yale U.S.A. 134 D2
Yalgoo Australia 109 B7
Yalleroi Australia 110 D5
Yaloké Cent. Afr. Rep. 98 B3
Yalova Turkey 59 M4
Yalta Ukr. 90 D1
Yalu Jiang *r.* China/N. Korea 74 B4
Yalujiang Kou *r. mouth* China/N. Korea 75 B5
Yalvaç Turkey 59 N5
Yamagata Japan 75 F5
Yamaguchi Japan 75 C6
Yamal, Poluostrov *pen.* Rus. Fed. *see* **Yamal Peninsula**
Yam Alin', Khrebet *mts* Rus. Fed. 74 D1
Yamal Peninsula Rus. Fed. 64 H2
Yamanie Falls National Park Australia 110 D3
Yamba Australia 112 F2
Yamba Lake Canada 121 I1
Yambarran Range *hills* Australia 108 E3
Yambi, Mesa de *hills* Col. 142 D3
Yambio Sudan 97 F4
Yambol Bulg. 59 L3
Yamdena *i.* Indon. 108 E1
Yamethin Myanmar 70 B2

▶**Yamin, Puncak** *mt.* Indon. 69 J7
4th highest mountain in Oceania.

Yamkanmardi India 84 B2
Yamkhad Syria *see* **Aleppo**
Yamm Rus. Fed. 45 P7
Yamma Yamma, Lake *salt flat* Australia 111 C5

▶**Yamoussoukro** Côte d'Ivoire 96 C4
Capital of Côte d'Ivoire.

Yampa *r.* U.S.A. 129 I1
Yampil' Ukr. 43 F6
Yampol' Ukr. *see* **Yampil'**
Yamuna *r.* India 82 E4
Yamunanagar India 82 D3
Yamzho Yumco *l.* China 83 G3
Yana *r.* Rus. Fed. 65 O2
Yanam India 84 D2
Yan'an China 73 J5
Yanaoca Peru 142 D6
Yanaon India *see* **Yanam**
Yanaul Rus. Fed. 41 Q4
Yanbu' al Baḩr Saudi Arabia 86 E5
Yanceyville U.S.A. 132 E4
Yancheng *Henan* China 77 G1
Yancheng *Jiangsu* China 77 I1
Yanchep Australia 109 A7
Yanco Australia 112 C5
Yanco Creek *r.* Australia 112 B5
Yanco Glen Australia 111 C6
Yanda *watercourse* Australia 112 B3
Yandama Creek *watercourse* Australia 111 C6
Yandao China *see* **Yingjing**
Yandoon Myanmar 70 A3
Yandun China 80 H3
Yanfolila Mali 96 C3
Ya'ngamdo China 76 B2
Yangbi China 76 C3
Yangcheng *Guangdong* China *see* **Yangshan**
Yangcheng *Shanxi* China 77 G1
Yangchuan China *see* **Suiyang**
Yangchun China 77 F4
Yangcun China 77 G4
Yangdok N. Korea 75 B5
Yang Hu *l.* China 83 F2
Yangikishlak Uzbek. 80 C3
Yangi-Nishan Uzbek. 89 G2
Yangi Qal'eh Afgh. 89 H2
Yangirabad Uzbek. 89 G1
Yangiyul' Uzbek. 80 C3
Yangjiajiang China 77 G2
Yangjiang China 77 F4
Yangming China *see* **Heping**
Yangôn Myanmar *see* **Rangoon**
Yangping China 77 F2
Yangquan China 73 K5
Yangshan China 77 G3
Yang Talat Thai. 70 C3
Yangtouyan China 76 D3

▶**Yangtze** *r.* China 76 E2
Longest river in Asia and 3rd in the world. Also known as Chang Jiang or Jinsha Jiang or Tongtian He or Yangtze Kiang or Zhi Qu.
Asia 60–61
World 12–13

Yangtze Kiang *r.* China *see* **Yangtze**
Yangudi Rassa National Park Eth. 98 E2
Yangweigang China 77 H1
Yangxi China 77 F4
Yangxian China 76 E1
Yangxin China 77 G2
Yangyang S. Korea 75 C5
Yangzhou *Jiangsu* China 77 H1
Yangzhou *Shaanxi* China *see* **Yangxian**
Yanhe China 77 F2
Yanhuqu China 83 E2
Yanishpole Rus. Fed. 42 G3
Yanis"yarvi, Ozero *l.* Rus. Fed. 44 Q5
Yanji China 74 C4
Yanjiang China *see* **Ziyang**
Yanjin *Henan* China 77 G1
Yanjin *Yunnan* China 76 E2
Yanjing *Sichuan* China *see* **Yanyuan**
Yanjing *Xizang* China 76 C2
Yanjing *Yunnan* China *see* **Yanjin**
Yankara National Park Nigeria 96 E4

Zanaga Congo 98 B4
Zancle Sicily Italy see Messina
Zandamela Moz. 101 L3
Zandvliet Belgium 52 E3
Zanesville U.S.A. 134 D4
Zangguy China 82 D1
Zangsêr Kangri mt. China 83 F2
Zangskar reg. Jammu and Kashmir see Zanskar
Zangskar Mountains India see Zanskar Mountains
Zanjān Iran 88 C2
Zanjān Rūd r. Iran 88 B2
Ẓannah, Jabal aẓ hill U.A.E. 88 D5
Zanskar reg. Jammu and Kashmir 82 D2
Zanskar Mountains India 82 D2
Zante i. Greece see Zakynthos
Zanthus Australia 109 C7
Zanughān Iran 88 E3
Zanzibar Tanz. 99 D4
Zanzibar Island Tanz. 99 D4
Zaoshi Hubei China 77 G2
Zaoshi Hunan China 77 G3
Zaouatallaz Alg. 96 D2
Zaouet el Kahla Alg. see Bordj Omer Driss
Zaoyang China 77 G1
Zaoyangzhan China 77 G1
Zaozernyy Rus. Fed. 65 K4
Zaozhuang China 77 H1
Zapadnaya Dvina r. Europe 42 F5 also known as Dvina or Zakhodnyaya Dzvina. English form Western Dvina
Zapadnaya Dvina Rus. Fed. 42 G4
Zapadni Rodopi mts Bulg. 59 J4
Zapadno-Kazakhstanskaya Oblast' admin. div. Kazakh. see Zapadnyy Kazakhstan
Zapadno-Sakhalinskiy Khrebet mts Rus. Fed. 74 F2
Zapadno-Sibirskaya Nizmennost' plain Rus. Fed. see West Siberian Plain
Zapadno-Sibirskaya Ravnina plain Rus. Fed. see West Siberian Plain
Zapadnyy Chink Ustyurta esc. Kazakh. 91 I2
Zapadnyy Chink Ustyurta esc. Kazakh. 91 I2
Zapadnyy Kazakhstan admin. div. Kazakh. 41 Q6
Zapadnyy Kil'din Rus. Fed. 44 S2
Zapadnyy Sayan reg. Rus. Fed. 72 F2
Zapata U.S.A. 131 D7
Zapata, Península de pen. Cuba 133 D8
Zapiga Chile 142 E7
Zapolyarnyy Rus. Fed. 44 Q2
Zapol'ye Rus. Fed. 42 H4
Zaporizhzhya Ukr. 43 G7
Zaporozh'ye Ukr. see Zaporizhzhya
Zapug China 82 E2
Zaqatala Azer. 91 G2
Zaqên China 76 B1
Za Qu r. China 76 C2
Zaqungngomar mt. China 83 G2
Zara China see Moinda
Zara Croatia see Zadar
Zara Turkey 90 E3
Zarafshan Uzbek. 80 B3
Zarafshon Uzbek. see Zarafshan
Zarafshon, Qatorkŭhi mts Tajik. 89 G2
Zaragoza Spain 57 F3
Zarand Iran 88 E4
Zarang China 82 D3
Zaranikh Reserve nature res. Egypt 85 B4
Zaranj Afgh. 89 F4
Zarasai Lith. 45 O9
Zárate Arg. 144 E4
Zaraysk Rus. Fed. 43 H5
Zaraza Venez. 142 E2
Zarbdar Uzbek. 89 H1
Zārdab Azer. 43 J8
Zarechensk Rus. Fed. 44 Q3
Zāreh Iran 88 C3
Zarembo Island U.S.A. 120 C3
Zargun mt. Pak. 89 G4
Zari Afgh. 89 G3
Zaria Nigeria 96 D3
Zarichne Ukr. 43 E6
Zarifête, Col des pass Alg. 57 F6
Zaring China see Liangdaohe
Zarinsk Rus. Fed. 72 E2
Zarmardan Afgh. 89 F3
Zarneh Iran 88 B3
Zărneşti Romania 59 K2
Zarqā' Jordan see Az Zarqā'
Zarqā', Nahr az r. Jordan 85 B3
Zarubino Rus. Fed. 74 C4
Żary Poland 47 O5
Zarzis Tunisia 54 G5
Zasheyek Rus. Fed. 44 Q3
Zaskar reg. Jammu and Kashmir see Zanskar
Zaskar Range mts India see Zanskar Mountains
Zaslawye Belarus 45 O9
Zastron S. Africa 101 H6
Za'tarī, Wādī az watercourse Jordan 85 C3
Zaterechnyy Rus. Fed. 43 J7
Zauche reg. Germany 53 M2
Zaunguzskiye Karakumy des. Turkm. 88 E1
Zavalla U.S.A. 131 E6
Zavetnoye Rus. Fed. 43 I7
Zavety Il'icha Rus. Fed. 74 F2
Zavidoviči Bos.-Herz. 58 H2
Zavitaya Rus. Fed. see Zavitinsk
Zavitinsk Rus. Fed. 74 C2
Zavolzhsk Rus. Fed. 42 I4
Zavolzh'ye Rus. Fed. see Zavolzhsk
Závora, Ponta pt Moz. 101 L3
Zawiercie Poland 47 Q5
Zawīlah Libya 97 E2
Zāwīyah, Jabal az hills Syria 85 C2
Zawr, Ra's az pt Saudi Arabia 88 C5
Zaydī, Wādī az watercourse Syria 85 C3
Zaysan Kazakh. 80 F2
Zaysan, Lake Kazakh. 80 F2
Zaysan, Ozero l. Kazakh. see Zaysan, Lake
Zayü China 76 C2
Zayü Qu r. China/India 83 I3
Žďar nad Sázavou Czech Rep. 47 O6
Zdolbuniv Ukr. 43 E6
Zdolbunov Ukr. see Zdolbuniv
Zealand i. Denmark 45 G9
Zēbāk Afgh. 82 B1
Zebulon U.S.A. 134 D5
Zedelgem Belgium 52 D3
Zeebrugge Belgium 52 D3
Zeeland U.S.A. 134 B2
Zeerust S. Africa 101 H3
Ẕefat Israel 85 B3
Zehdenick Germany 53 N2
Zeil, Mount Australia 109 F5
Zeil am Main Germany 53 K4
Zeist Neth. 52 F2
Zeitz Germany 53 M3
Zêkog China 76 D1
Zela Turkey see Zile
Zelennik Rus. Fed. 42 J3
Zelenoborsk Rus. Fed. 41 S3
Zelenoborskiy Rus. Fed. 44 R3
Zelenodol'sk Rus. Fed. 42 K5
Zelenogorsk Rus. Fed. 45 P6
Zelenograd Rus. Fed. 42 H4
Zelenogradsk Rus. Fed. 45 L9
Zelenokumsk Rus. Fed. 91 F1
Zelentsovo Rus. Fed. 42 J4
Zelenyy, Ostrov i. Rus. Fed. 74 G4
Zell am See Austria 47 N7
Zellingen Germany 53 J5
Zelzate Belgium 52 D3
Žemaitijos nacionalinis parkas nat. park Lith. 45 L8
Zêmdasam China 76 D1
Zemetchino Rus. Fed. 43 I5
Zémio Cent. Afr. Rep. 98 C3
Zemmora Alg. 57 G6
Zempoaltépetl, Nudo de mt. Mex. 136 E5
Zengcheng China 77 G4
Zenica Bos.-Herz. 58 G2
Ẕenifim watercourse Israel 85 B4
Zennor U.K. 49 B8
Zenta Serb. and Mont. see Senta
Zenzach Alg. 57 H6
Zeravshanskiy Khrebet mts Tajik. see Zarafshon, Qatorkŭhi
Zerbst Germany 53 M3
Zerenike Reserve nature res. Egypt see Zaranikh Reserve
Zerf Germany 52 G5
Zernien Germany 53 K1
Zernitz Germany 53 M2
Zernograd Rus. Fed. 43 I7
Zernovoy Rus. Fed. see Zernograd
Zêtang China see Nêdong
Zetel Germany 53 H1
Zeulenroda Germany 53 L4
Zeven Germany 53 J1
Zevenaar Neth. 52 G3
Zevgari, Cape Cyprus 85 A2
Zeya Rus. Fed. 74 B1
Zeya r. Rus. Fed. 74 B2
Zeydar Iran 88 E2
Zeydī Iran 89 F5
Zeyskiy Zapovednik nature res. Rus. Fed. 74 B1
Zeysko-Bureinskaya Vpadina depr. Rus. Fed. 74 C2
Zeyskoye Vodokhranilishche resr Rus. Fed. 74 B1
Zeytin Burnu c. Cyprus see Elaia, Cape
Zêzere r. Port. 57 B4
Zgharta Lebanon 85 B2
Zghorta Lebanon see Zgharta
Zgierz Poland 47 Q5
Zhabdün China see Zhongba
Zhabinka Belarus 45 N10
Zhaggo China see Luhuo
Zhaglag China 76 C1
Zhag'yab China 76 C2
Zhaksy Sarysu watercourse Kazakh. see Sarysu
Zhalanash Kazakh. see Damdy
Zhalpaktal Kazakh. 41 P6
Zhalpaqtal Kazakh. see Zhalpaktal
Zhaltyr Kazakh. 80 C1
Zhambyl Karagandinskaya Oblast' Kazakh. 80 D2
Zhambyl Zhambylskaya Oblast' Kazakh. see Taraz
Zhamo China see Bomi
Zhanakorgan Kazakh. 80 C3
Zhanaozen Kazakh. 78 E2
Zhanatas Kazakh. 80 C3
Zhanbei China 74 B2
Zhangaözen Kazakh. see Zhanaozen
Zhanga Qazan Kazakh. see Novaya Kazanka
Zhangaqorghan Kazakh. see Zhanakorgan
Zhangatas Kazakh. see Zhanatas
Zhangbei China 73 K4
Zhangcheng China see Yongtai
Zhangcunpu China 77 H1
Zhangde China see Anyang
Zhangdian China see Zibo
Zhanggu China see Danba
Zhangguangcai Ling mts China 74 C3
Zhanghua Taiwan see Changhua
Zhangjiabang China 77 G2
Zhangjiajie China 77 F2
Zhangjiakou China 73 K4
Zhangjiang China see Taoyuan
Zhangjiapan China see Jingbian
Zhangla China 76 D1
Zhangling China 74 A1
Zhanglou China 77 H1
Zhangping China 77 H3
Zhangqiangzhen China 74 A4
Zhangqiao China 77 H1
Zhangshu China 77 G2
Zhangxian China 76 E1
Zhangye China 80 J4
Zhangzhou China 77 H3
Zhanhe China see Zhanbei
Zhanibek Kazakh. 41 P6
Zhanjiang China 77 F4
Zhanjiang Bei China see Chikan
Zhao'an China 77 H4
Zhaodong China 74 B3
Zhaojue China 76 D2
Zhaoliqiao China 77 G2
Zhaoping China 77 F3
Zhaoqing China 77 G4
Zhaotong China 76 D3
Zhaoyuan China 74 B3
Zhaozhou China 74 B3
Zhari Namco salt l. China 83 F3
Zharkamys Kazakh. 80 A2
Zharkent Kazakh. 80 F3
Zharkovskiy Rus. Fed. 42 G5
Zharma Kazakh. 80 F2
Zhashkiv Ukr. 43 F6
Zhashkov Ukr. see Zhashkiv
Zhaslyk Uzbek. 91 J2
Zhaxi China see Weixin
Zhaxi Co salt l. China 83 F2
Zhaxigang China 82 D2
Zhaxizê China 76 C2
Zhaxizong China 83 F3
Zhayü China 76 C2
Zhayyq r. Kazakh./Rus. Fed. see Ural
Zhdanov Ukr. see Mariupol'
Zhdanovsk Azer. see Beyläqan
Zhedao China see Lianghe
Zhêhor China 76 D2
Zhejiang prov. China 77 I2
Zhelaniya, Mys c. Rus. Fed. 64 H2
Zheleznodorozhnyy Rus. Fed. see Yemva
Zheleznodorozhnyy Uzbek. see Kungrad
Zheleznogorsk Rus. Fed. 43 G5
Zhelou China see Ceheng
Zheltyye Vody Ukr. see Zhovti Vody
Zhem Kazakh. see Emba
Zhemgang Bhutan 83 G4
Zhen'an China 77 F1
Zhenba China 76 E1
Zhenghe China 77 H3
Zhengjiatun China see Shuangliao
Zhengning China 77 F1
Zhengyang China 77 G1
Zhengyangguan China 77 H1
Zhengzhou China 77 G1
Zhenhai China 77 I2
Zhenjiang China see Dantu
Zhenjiangguan China 76 D1
Zhenlai China 74 A3
Zhenning China 76 E3
Zhenping China 77 F2
Zhenxi China 74 A3
Zhenxiong China 76 E3
Zhenyang China see Zhengyang
Zhenyuan China 77 F3
Zherdevka Rus. Fed. 43 I6
Zherong China 77 H3
Zheshart Rus. Fed. 42 K3
Zhetikara Kazakh. see Zhitikara
Zhêxam China 83 F3
Zhexi Shuiku resr China 77 F2
Zhezkazgan Kazakh. 80 C2
Zhezqazghan Kazakh. see Zhezkazgan
Zhicheng Hubei China 77 F2
Zhicheng Zhejiang China see Changxing
Zhidoi China 76 B1
Zhifang China see Jiangxia
Zhigalovo Rus. Fed. 72 J2
Zhigansk Rus. Fed. 65 N3
Zhigung China 83 G3
Zhijiang Hubei China 77 F2
Zhijiang Hunan China 70 E1
Zhijin China 76 E3
Zhilong China see Yangxi
Zhi Qu r. China see Yangtze
Zhitikara Kazakh. 78 F1
Zhitkovichi Belarus see Zhytkavichy
Zhitkur Rus. Fed. 43 J6
Zhitomir Ukr. see Zhytomyr
Zhīvār Iran 88 B3
Zhiziluo China 76 C3
Zhlobin Belarus 43 F5
Zhmerinka Ukr. see Zhmerynka
Zhmerynka Ukr. 43 F6
Zhob Pak. 89 H4
Zhob r. Pak. 89 H3
Zhong'an China see Fuyuan
Zhongba Guangdong China 77 G4
Zhongba Sichuan China see Jiangyou
Zhongba Xizang China 83 F3
Zhongdian China 76 C3
Zhongduo China see Youyang
Zhongguo country Asia see China
Zhongguo Renmin Gongheguo country Asia see China
Zhonghe China see Xiushan
Zhongping China see Huize
Zhongshan research station Antarctica 152 E2
Zhongshan Guangdong China 77 G4
Zhongshan Guangxi China 77 F3
Zhongshan Guizhou China see Lupanshui
Zhongshu Yunnan China see Luliang
Zhongshu Yunnan China see Luxi
Zhongtai China see Lingtai
Zhongtiao Shan mts China 77 F1
Zhongwei China 72 J5
Zhongxin Guangdong China 77 G3
Zhongxin Yunnan China see Zhongdian
Zhongxin Yunnan China see Huaping
Zhongxingji China 77 H2
Zhongyaozhan China 74 B2
Zhongyicun China 76 D3
Zhongyuan China 77 F5
Zhongzhai China 76 E1
Zhosaly Kazakh. see Dzhusaly
Zhoujiajing China 72 I5
Zhoukou Henan China 77 G1
Zhoukou Sichuan China see Peng'an
Zhouning China 77 H3
Zhoushan China 77 I2
Zhoushan Dao i. China 77 I2
Zhoushan Qundao is China 77 I2
Zhouzhi China 77 F1
Zhovti Vody Ukr. 43 G6
Zhuanghe China 75 A5
Zhuanglang China 76 E1
Zhubgyügoin China 76 C1
Zhudong Taiwan see Chutung
Zhugla China 76 B2
Zhugqu China 76 E1
Zhuhai China 77 G4
Zhuji Henan China see Shangqiu
Zhuji Zhejiang China 77 I2
Zhujing China see Jinshan
Zhukeng China 77 G4
Zhukovka Rus. Fed. 43 G5
Zhukovskiy Rus. Fed. 43 H5
Zhumadian China 77 G1
Zhuokeji China 76 D2
Zhushan Hubei China 77 F1
Zhushan Hubei China see Xuan'en
Zhuxi China 77 F1
Zhuxiang China 77 H1
Zhuyang China see Dazhu
Zhuzhou Hunan China 77 G3
Zhuzhou Hunan China 77 G3
Zhydachiv Ukr. 43 E6
Zhympity Kazakh. 41 Q5
Zhytkavichy Belarus 45 O10
Zhytomyr Ukr. 43 F6
Zīā'ābād Iran 88 C3
Žiar nad Hronom Slovakia 47 Q6
Zibā salt pan Saudi Arabia 85 D4
Zibo China 73 L5
Zicheng China see Zijin
Zidi Pak. 89 G5
Ziel, Mount Australia see Zeil, Mount
Zielona Góra Poland 47 O5
Ziemelkursas augstiene hills Latvia 45 M8
Zierenberg Germany 53 J3
Ziesar Germany 53 M2
Ziftá Egypt 90 C5
Zīghan Libya 97 F2
Zigong China 76 E2
Ziguey Chad 97 E3
Ziguinchor Senegal 96 B3
Žīguri Latvia 45 O8
Zihuatanejo Mex. 136 D5
Zijin China 77 G4
Zijpenberg hill Neth. 52 G2
Ziketan China see Xinghai
Zile Turkey 90 D2
Žilina Slovakia 47 Q6
Zillah Libya 97 E2
Zima Rus. Fed. 72 I2
Zimba Zambia 99 C5
▶Zimbabwe country Africa 99 C5 Africa 7, 94–95
Zimi Sierra Leone see Zimmi
Zimmerbude Rus. Fed. see Svetlyy
Zimmi Sierra Leone 96 B4
Zimnicea Romania 59 K3
Zimniy Bereg coastal area Rus. Fed. 42 H2
Zimovniki Rus. Fed. 43 I7
Zimrīn Syria 85 B2
Ẕin watercourse Israel 85 B4
Zin Pak. 89 H4
Zinave, Parque Nacional de nat. park Moz. 99 D6
Zinder Niger 96 D3
Zindo China 76 D2
Ziniaré Burkina 96 C3
Zinjibār Yemen 86 G7
Zinoyevsk Ukr. see Kirovohrad
Zion U.S.A. 134 B2
Zion National Park U.S.A. 129 G3
Zionz Lake Canada 121 N5
Zippori Israel 85 B3
Ziqudukou China 76 B1
Zirc Hungary 58 G1
Zirkel, Mount U.S.A. 126 G4
Zirkūh i. U.A.E. 88 D5
Zirndorf Germany 53 K5
Ziro India 83 H4
Zirreh Afgh. 89 F4
Zīr Rūd Iran 88 C4
Zi Shui r. China 73 K7
Zistersdorf Austria 47 P6
Zitácuaro Mex. 136 D5
Zito China see Lhorong
Zitong China 76 E2
Zittau Germany 47 O5
Zixi China 77 H3
Zixing China see Xingning
Ziyang Jiangxi China see Wuyuan
Ziyang Shaanxi China 77 F1
Ziyang Sichuan China 76 E2
Ziyaret Dağı hill Turkey 85 B1
Ziyuan China 77 F3
Ziyun China 76 E3
Ziz, Oued watercourse Morocco 54 D5
Zizhong China 76 E2
Zlatoustovsk Rus. Fed. 74 D1
Zlín Czech Rep. 47 P6
Zmeinogorsk Rus. Fed. 80 F1
Zmiyevka Rus. Fed. 43 H5
Znamenka Rus. Fed. 43 I5
Znamenka Ukr. see Znam"yanka
Znam"yanka Ukr. 43 G6
Znojmo Czech Rep. 47 P6
Zoar S. Africa 100 E7
Zoetermeer Neth. 52 E2
Zogainrawar China see Huashixia
Zogang China 76 C2
Zogqên China 76 C1
Zoigê China 76 D1
Zoji La pass Jammu and Kashmir 82 C2
Zola S. Africa 101 H7
Zolder Belgium 52 F3
Zolochev Kharkivs'ka Oblast' Ukr. see Zolochiv
Zolochev L'vivs'ka Oblast' Ukr. see Zolochiv
Zolochiv Kharkivs'ka Oblast' Ukr. 43 G6
Zolochiv L'vivs'ka Oblast' Ukr. 43 E6
Zolotonosha Ukr. 43 G6
Zolotoye Rus. Fed. 43 J6
Zolotukhino Rus. Fed. 43 H5
▶Zomba Malawi 99 D5 Former capital of Malawi.
Zombor Serb. and Mont. see Sombor
Zomin Uzbek. see Zaamin
Zongga China see Gyirong
Zongo Dem. Rep. Congo 98 B3
Zonguldak Turkey 59 N4
Zongxoi China 83 G3
Zörbig Germany 53 M3
Zorgho Burkina 96 C3
Zorgo Burkina see Zorgho
Zorn r. France 53 I6
Żory Poland 47 Q5
Zossen Germany 53 N2
Zottegem Belgium 52 D4
Zouar Chad 97 E2
Zoucheng China 77 H1
Zouérat Mauritania 96 B2
Zousfana, Oued watercourse Alg. 54 D5
Zoushi China 77 F2
Zouxian China see Zoucheng
Zrenjanin Serb. and Mont. 59 I2
Zschopau Germany 53 N4
Zschopau r. Germany 53 N3
Zschornewitz Germany 53 M3
Zubālah, Birkat waterhole Saudi Arabia 91 F5
Zubillaga Arg. 144 D5
Zubova Polyana Rus. Fed. 43 I5
Zubtsov Rus. Fed. 42 G4
Zuénoula Côte d'Ivoire 96 C4
Zug Switz. 56 I3
Zugdidi Georgia 91 F2
Zugspitze mt. Austria/Germany 47 M7
Zugu Nigeria 96 D3
Zuider Zee l. Neth. see IJsselmeer
Zuidhorn Neth. 52 G1
Zuid-Kennemerland Nationaal Park nat. park Neth. 52 E2
Zuitai China see Kangxian
Zuitaizi China see Kangxian
Zuitou China see Taibai
Zújar r. Spain 57 D4
Zülpich Germany 52 G4
Zumba Ecuador 142 C4
Zunheboto India 83 H4
Zuni U.S.A. 129 I4
Zuni watercourse U.S.A. 129 I4
Zuni Mountains U.S.A. 129 I4
Zunyi Guizhou China 76 E3
Zunyi Guizhou China 76 E3
Zuo Jiang r. China/Vietnam 70 E2
Županja Croatia 58 H2
Zūrābād Āzarbāyjān-e Gharbī Iran 88 B2
Zūrābād Khorāsān Iran 89 F3
Zürich Switz. 56 I3
Zurmat reg. Afgh. 89 H3
Zuru Nigeria 96 D3
Zurzuna Turkey see Çıldır
Zutphen Neth. 52 G2
Zuwārah Libya 96 E1
Zuyevka Rus. Fed. 42 K4
Zūzan Iran 89 E3
Zvishavane Zimbabwe 99 D6
Zvolen Slovakia 47 Q6
Zvornik Bos.-Herz. 59 H2
Zwedru Liberia 96 C4
Zweeloo Neth. 52 G2
Zweibrücken Germany 53 H5
Zweletemba S. Africa 100 D7
Zwelitsha S. Africa 101 H7
Zwethau Germany 53 N3
Zwettl Austria 47 O6
Zwickau Germany 53 M4
Zwochau Germany 53 M3
Zwolle Neth. 52 G2
Zwönitz Germany 53 M4
Zyablovo Rus. Fed. 42 L4
Zygi Cyprus 85 A2
Zyryan Kazakh. see Zyryanovsk
Zyryanka Rus. Fed. 65 Q3
Zyryanovsk Kazakh. 80 F2
Zyyi Cyprus see Zygi

Acknowledgements

Maps and data

General

Maps designed and created by HarperCollins Reference, Glasgow, UK, www.bartholomewmaps.com
Cross-sections (pp36–37, 60–61, 92–93, 102–103, 114–115, 138–139) and globes (pp14–15, 146–147): Geo-Innovations, Llandudno, UK, www.geoinnovations.co.uk

The publishers would like to thank all national survey departments, road, rail and national park authorities, statistical offices and national place name committees throughout the world for their valuable assistance, and in particular the following:
British Antarctic Survey, Cambridge, UK
Tony Champion, Professor of Population Geography, University of Newcastle upon Tyne, UK
Mr P J M Geelan, London, UK

International Boundary Research Unit, University of Durham, UK
The Meteorological Office, Bracknell, Berkshire, UK
Permanent Committee on Geographical Names for British Official Use, London, UK

Data

Bathymetric data: The GEBCO Digital Atlas published by the British Oceanographic Data Centre on behalf of IOC and IHO, 1994
Earthquakes data (pp14–15): United States Geological Survey (USGS) National Earthquakes Information Center, Denver, USA
Coral reefs data (p18): UNEP World Conservation Monitoring Centre, Cambridge, UK and World Resources Institute (WRI), Washington DC, USA
Desertification data (p18): U.S. Department of Agriculture Natural Resources Conservation Service

Population data (pp20–21): Center for International Earth Science Information Network (CIESIN), Columbia University; International Food Policy Research Institute (IFPRI); and World Resources Institute (WRI). 2000. Gridded Population of the World (GPW), Version 2. Palisades, NY: CIESIN, Columbia University. http://sedac.ciesin.columbia.edu/plue/gpw
Company sales figures (p29): Reprinted by permission of Forbes Magazine © 2004 Forbes Inc.
Terrorism data (p31): Rand-MIPT Terrorist Incident Database (Rand Corporation, Santa Monica, Ca and Oklahoma City National Memorial Institute for the Prevention of Terrorism, 2003) db.mipt.org/mipt_rand.cfm
Antarctica (p152): Antarctic Digital Database (versions 1 and 2), © Scientific Committee on Antarctic Research (SCAR), Cambridge, UK (1993, 1998)

Photographs and images

Page	Image	Satellite/Sensor	Credit	Page	Image	Satellite/Sensor	Credit	Page	Image	Satellite/Sensor	Credit
5	The Alps	MODIS	MODIS/NASA		Tōkyō		Cities Revealed aerial photography © The GeoInformation Group, 1998		Gaza/Egypt/Israel border	Shuttle	Digital image ©1996 CORBIS; Original image courtesy of NASA/CORBIS
	Amsterdam	IKONOS	Space Imaging Europe/Science Photo Library	24–25	International telecommunications traffic map		© PriMetrica, Inc. www.telegeography.com and www.primetrica.com	92–93	Congo	Shuttle	NASA
	Italy	AVHRR	Earth Satellite Corporation/Science Photo Library						Lake Victoria	MODIS	MODIS/NASA
6	Ganges Delta	SPOT	CNES, 1987 Distribution Spot Image/Science Photo Library		Internet topology		CAIDA/Science Photo Library		Kilimanjaro	Landsat	USGS/NASA
	Cyprus	MODIS	MODIS/NASA	26–27	Health care facilities		John Cole/Science Photo Library	94–95	Cape Verde	MODIS	MODIS/NASA
	Indian subcontinent	AVHRR	Earth Satellite Corporation/Science Photo Library		Education		Moacyr Lopes Junior/UNEP/Still Pictures		Cairo	IKONOS	IKONOS satellite imagery provided by Space Imaging, Thornton, Colorado, www.spaceimaging.com
7	Victoria Falls		Roger De La Harpe, Gallo Images/CORBIS	28–29	Sudan Village		Mark Edwards/Still Pictures		Cape Town	IKONOS	IKONOS satellite imagery provided by Space Imaging, Thornton, Colorado, www.spaceimaging.com
	Sinai Peninsula	Shuttle	NASA		The City		London Aerial Photo Library/CORBIS				
8	Mt Cook		Mike Schroder/Still Pictures	30–31	Egypt/Gaza border		Marc Schlossman/Panos Pictures	102–103	Lake Eyre	Shuttle	NASA
	Bora Bora	SPOT	CNES, Distribution Spot Image/Science Photo Library		Spratly Islands	IKONOS	IKONOS satellite imagery provided by Space Imaging, Thornton, Colorado, www.spaceimaging.com		New Caledonia and Vanuatu	SeaWiFS	Image provided by ORBIMAGE © Orbital Imaging Corporation and processing by NASA Goddard Space Flight Center.
	Ayers Rock		ImageState		İstanbul		Getty Images				
	Sydney	IKONOS	IKONOS satellite imagery provided by Space Imaging, Thornton, Colorado, www.spaceimaging.com	32–33	Water		Harmut Schwarzbach/Still Pictures		Banks Peninsula		Institute of Geological and Nuclear Sciences, New Zealand
9	The Pentagon	IKONOS	IKONOS satellite imagery provided by Space Imaging, Thornton, Colorado, www.spaceimaging.com		Drugs		Getty Images	104–105	Wellington		NZ Aerial Mapping Ltd www.nzam.com
					Aids		Friedrich Stark/Still Pictures		Tasmania	SeaWiFS	Image provided by ORBIMAGE © Orbital Imaging Corporation and processing by NASA Goddard Space Flight Center.
	Panama Canal	Landsat	Clifton-Campbell Imaging Inc. www.tmarchive.com	34–35	Aral Sea	Landsat	Data available from the U.S. Geological Survey, EROS Data Center, Sioux Falls, SD				
	Cuba	MODIS	MODIS/NASA		Abu Dhabi 1972	Landsat	Science Photo Library				
10–11	Dili	SPOT	CNES, Distribution Spot Image/Science Photo Library		Abu Dhabi 2000	IKONOS	IKONOS satellite imagery provided by Space Imaging, Thornton, Colorado, www.spaceimaging.com		Tahiti and Moorea	SPOT	CNES, Distribution Spot Image/Science Photo Library
	Vatican City	IKONOS	IKONOS satellite imagery provided by Space Imaging, Thornton, Colorado, www.spaceimaging.com		3 Gorges Dam Before		Wolfgang Kaehler/CORBIS	114–115	Mississippi	ASTER	ASTER/NASA
12–13	Greenland	MODIS	MODIS/NASA		3 Gorges Dam Construction		Reuters/CORBIS		Grand Canyon	SPOT	CNES, 1996 Distribution Spot Image/Science Photo Library
	Nile Valley	MODIS	MODIS/NASA		Mesopotamian marshlands		NASA/EROS Data Center		Yucatan	MODIS	MODIS/NASA
14–15	Bam		Fatih Saribas/Reuters/CORBIS	36–37	Iceland	MODIS	MODIS/NASA	116–117	The Bahamas	MODIS	MODIS/NASA
	Mt Etna		Bernhard Edmaier/Science Photo Library		Danube delta	MODIS	MODIS/NASA		El Paso	Shuttle	NASA
16–17	Tropical Cyclone Dina	MODIS	MODIS/NASA/GSFC		Caucasus	MODIS	MODIS/NASA		Washington DC		US Geological Society/Science Photo Library
	Annual precipitation map	Microwave infrared	NASA/Goddard Space Flight Centre	38–39	Paris	IKONOS	Space Imaging Europe/Science Photo Library	138–139	Lake Titicaca	Shuttle	NASA
	Climate change maps		Met. Office, Hadley Centre for Climate Prediction and Research		Bosporus	SPOT	CNES, 1991 Distribution Spot Image/Science Photo Library		Tierra del Fuego	MODIS	MODIS/NASA
18–19	Snow and ice		Klaus Andrews/Still Pictures		Belgrade	SIR-C/X-SAR	NASA JPL		Amazon/Rio Negro	Terra/MISR	NASA
	Urban		Ron Giling/Still Pictures	60–61	Kamchatka Peninsula	MODIS	MODIS/NASA	140–141	Galapagos Islands	SPOT	CNES, 1988 Distribution Spot Image/Science Photo Library
	Forest		Wolfgang Kaehler/CORBIS		Caspian Sea	MODIS	MODIS/NASA		Falkland Islands	MODIS	MODIS/NASA
	Barren/Shrubland		Simon Fraser/Science Photo Library		Yangtze	MODIS	MODIS/NASA		Rio de Janeiro	SPOT	Earth Satellite Corporation/Science Photo Library
20–21	Kuna Indians		Royalty-Free/CORBIS	62–63	Timor	MODIS	MODIS/NASA	146–147	Antarctica	AVHRR	NRSC Ltd/Science Photo Library
	Masai Village		Yann Arthus-Bertrand/CORBIS		Beijing	IKONOS	IKONOS satellite imagery provided by Space Imaging, Thornton, Colorado, www.spaceimaging.com		Novaya Zemlya	Landsat ETM	NASA
22–23	Los Angeles	SRTM/Landsat 5	NASA								

240